Summary of Financial Statement Ratios
(Exhibit 6.14, p. 273)

Ratio	Numerator	Denominator
Profitability Ratios		
Rate of Return on Assets (ROA)	Net Income + Interest Expense (net of tax effects)[a]	Average Total Assets during the Period
Profit Margin for ROA Ratio (before interest effects)	Net Income + Interest Expense (net of tax effects)[a]	Sales
Various Expense Ratios	Various Expenses	Sales
Total Assets Ratio Turnover	Sales	Average Total Assets during the Period
Accounts Receivable Turnover Ratio	Sales	Average Accounts Receivable during the Period
Inventory Turnover Ratio	Cost of Goods Sold	Average Inventory during the Period
Fixed Asset Turnover Ratio	Sales	Average Fixed Assets during the Period
Rate of Return on Common Shareholders' Equity (ROCE)	Net Income − Preferred Stock Dividends	Average Common Shareholders' Equity during the Period
Profit Margin for ROCE Ratio (after interest expense and preferred dividends)	Net Income − Preferred Stock Dividends	Sales
Capital Structure Leverage Ratio	Average Total Assets during the Period	Average Common Shareholders' Equity during the Period
Earnings per Share of Common Stock[b]	Net Income − Preferred Stock Dividends	Weighted Average Number of Common Shares Outstanding
Short-Term Liquidity Risk Ratios		
Current Ratio	Current Assets	Current Liabilities
Quick or Acid Test Ratio	Highly Liquid Assets (cash, marketable securities, and accounts receivable)[c]	Current Liabilities
Cash Flow from Operations to Current Liabilities Ratio	Cash Flow from Operations	Average Current Liabilities during the Period
Accounts Payable Turnover Ratio	Purchases[d]	Average Accounts Payable during the Period
Days Accounts Receivable Outstanding	365 days	Accounts Receivable Turnover Ratio
Days Inventories Held	365 days	Inventory Turnover Ratio
Days Accounts Payable Outstanding	365 days	Accounts Payable Turnover Ratio
Long-Term Liquidity Ratios		
Liabilities to Assets Ratio	Liabilities	Assets
Long-Term Debt Ratio	Long-Term Debt	Assets
Debt-Equity Ratio	Long-Term Debt	Shareholders' Equity
Cash Flow from Operations to Total Liabilities Ratio	Cash Flow from Operations	Average Total Liabilities during the Period
Interest Coverage Ratio	Income before Interest and Income Taxes	Interest Expense

[a]If a parent company does not own all of a consolidated subsidiary, the calculation also adds back to net income the noncontrolling interest share of net income. See **Chapter 13** for discussion of noncontrolling interest.

[b]This calculation is more complicated when there are convertible securities, options, or warrants outstanding.

[c]The calculation could conceivably exclude receivables for some firms and include inventories for others.

[d]Purchases = Cost of Goods Sold + Ending Inventories − Beginning Inventories.

FINANCIAL ACCOUNTING

AN INTRODUCTION TO CONCEPTS, METHODS, AND USES

     **13E**

Clyde P. Stickney

Dartmouth College

Roman L. Weil

University of Chicago

Katherine Schipper

Duke University

Jennifer Francis

Duke University

SOUTH-WESTERN
CENGAGE Learning™

Australia • Brazil • Japan • Korea • Mexico • Singapore • Spain • United Kingdom • United States

SOUTH-WESTERN
CENGAGE Learning™

Financial Accounting, An Introduction
to Concepts, Methods, and Uses, 13e
Clyde P. Stickney, Roman L. Weil, Katherine Schipper,
Jennifer Francis

Vice President of Editorial, Business: Jack W. Calhoun

Editor-in-Chief: Rob Dewey

Senior Acquisitions Editor: Matthew Filimonov

Senior Developmental Editor: Craig Avery

Marketing Manager: Steven Joos

Marketing Coordinator: Heather McAuliffe

Senior Content Project Manager: Tim Bailey

Director of Program Management: John Barans

Senior Frontlist Buyer, Manufacturing: Doug Wilke

Production Service: Lachina Publishing Services, Inc.

Senior Art Director: Stacy Jenkins Shirley

Cover and Internal Designer: Joe DeVine, Red Hangar
   Design

Cover Image: © Getty Images/Photographer's Choice

For product information and technology assistance, contact us at
Cengage Learning Customer & Sales Support, 1-800-354-9706

For permission to use material from this text or product,
submit all requests online at **www.cengage.com/permissions**
Further permissions questions can be emailed to
permissionrequest@cengage.com

Exam*View*® is a registered trademark of eInstruction Corp. Windows is a registered
trademark of the Microsoft Corporation used herein under license.

Library of Congress Control Number: 2008943209

ISBN-13: 978-0-324-65114-0
ISBN-10: 0-324-65114-7

South-Western Cengage Learning
5191 Natorp Boulevard
Mason, OH 45040
USA

Cengage Learning products are represented in Canada by Nelson Education, Ltd.

For your course and learning solutions, visit **www.cengage.com**

Purchase any of our products at your local college store or at our preferred
online store **www.ichapters.com**

Printed in Canada
3 4 5 6 7 12 11 10

For Our Students

*W*hatever be the detail with which you cram your students, the chance of their meeting in after-life exactly that detail is infinitesimal; and if they do meet it, they will probably have forgotten what you taught them about it. The really useful training yields a comprehension of a few general principles with a thorough grounding in the way they apply to a variety of concrete details. In subsequent practice the students will have forgotten your particular details; but they will remember by an unconscious common sense how to apply principles to immediate circumstances.

Alfred North Whitehead
The Aims of Education and Other Essays

> WARNING: Study of this book is known to cause thinking, occasionally deep thinking. Typical side effects include mild temporary anxiety followed by profound long-term understanding and satisfaction.

PREFACE

Our perspective in this textbook derives from our belief that effective financial reporting, starting with financial statement preparation and ending with financial statement analysis and use, requires ruthless objectivity and extreme expertise. For the financial reporting process to have its intended effects, preparers of financial statements must make unbiased and informed measurements—in particular, fair value measurements—and users of financial statements must comprehend and analyze those measurements with skill and objectivity.

Over the years, we have come to refer to our book's title by the acronym FACMU—*Financial Accounting: An Introduction to Concepts, Methods, and Uses*. We take *concepts, methods,* and *uses* to be the central elements in learning and teaching about financial accounting. The 13th Edition of *FACMU* has the same objectives as the previous editions:

- ■ To help students develop a sufficient understanding of the basic concepts underlying financial reports so that they can apply the concepts to new and different situations.
- ■ To train students in accounting terminology and methods so that they can interpret, analyze, and evaluate financial statements and notes currently published in corporate annual reports.

Most introductory financial accounting textbooks state these, or similar, objectives. Textbooks differ in their relative emphases on concepts, methods, and uses.

1. **Concepts**   This book emphasizes the rationale for, and implications of, accounting concepts. To learn accounting, students must develop the ability to conceptualize the transactions that accounting summarizes and the process of summarization. *Without such concepts, students will have difficulty focusing on the relevant issues in new and different situations.*

   Accordingly, each chapter identifies important accounting concepts, and includes numerical examples illustrating their application. The end-of-chapter material includes numerous short exercises and longer problems to check students' ability to apply the concepts to different situations.

2. **Methods**   We place enough emphasis on accounting procedures to enable students to interpret, analyze, and evaluate published financial statements. The text does not emphasize procedures to such an extent that students bog down in detail. All writers of accounting textbooks must decide just how much accounting procedure to include. We believe students learn most effectively by working exercises and problems. Too much emphasis on accounting procedures, however, lulls students into the security of thinking they understand accounting concepts when they do not. We have for many years used the mixture of concepts and procedures in this book and have found it effective in the classroom.

   Understanding the accounting implications of an event requires that students construct the journal entry for that event. Throughout this book we use journal entries in describing the nature of accounting events. Moreover, most chapters contain exercises and problems that require the analysis of transactions with debits and credits. *Do not conclude by a glance at this text, however, that it is primarily procedural. We want students to learn concepts; the procedures enhance the learning of concepts.*

3. **Uses**   *This book attempts to bridge the gap between the preparation of financial reports and their use in various decision situations.* The chapters consider the effects of alternative accounting principles on the measurement of earnings and financial position and the appropriate interpretations of them. Numerous problems based on financial statement data of actual companies appear at the end of most chapters.

OVERVIEW OF CHANGES IN THE 13TH EDITION

New authors. We have added **Jennifer Francis** and **Katherine Schipper** to the team. They bring teaching excellence and the experience of a standard setter to the collaboration. That they have had outstanding careers as accounting scholars enables them to contribute beyond their roles as outstanding teachers.

We four authors have made the following changes in the 13th Edition:

1. **Integration of International Financial Reporting Standards (IFRS).** As this book goes to press, the SEC has announced a decision process that, within seven years, may result in IFRS replacing U.S. GAAP as the body of accounting principles that U.S. companies must follow. We have integrated IFRS into the text. We start from the premise that U.S. GAAP and IFRS use the same concepts, but sometimes require or permit different methods. At the FACMU level, for MBA students and upperclass undergraduates, the methods are often identical or similar; where they are not, we describe and illustrate the differences. You can easily see the scope of the U.S. GAAP/IFRS details in this book by examining the chart in the front endpapers, inside the front cover. That chart shows you the chapters and topics where the discussion includes IFRS as well as U.S. GAAP.

2. **New emphasis on fair values and components of other comprehensive income.** As U.S. GAAP and IFRS incorporate more required or permitted fair value measurements, we have broadened our coverage. The fair value option in U.S. GAAP and IFRS affects accounting for some debt securities and some investments. We discuss these in **Chapters 10**, **12**, and **13**, both concepts and methods. Insofar as changes in fair values affect other comprehensive income, we've expanded that discussion as well. We refer to the December 2008 report by the SEC on its "Study on Mark-to-Market Accounting" at the several places where this report affects the material we discuss.

3. **Codification of U.S. GAAP.** In its Accounting Standards Codification™ system, the Financial Accounting Standards Board (FASB) has issued a compilation of U.S. GAAP, including *Statements of Financial Accounting Standards*, *Accounting Principles Board Opinions*, *Accounting Research Bulletins*, *Staff Accounting Bulletins*, *EITF Consensuses*, *FASB Interpretations*, and several other sorts of pronouncements. This compilation, which organizes the material by topic, brings together into one place the various accounting methods and procedures that treat that topic. If you see *SFAS No. 2*, you likely think about research and development costs, not Codification Topic 730. In the future, however, students will need to think in terms of topic numbers, not pronouncement names and numbers, in order to participate in accounting conversations during their professional careers. We provide both conventional citations and Codification Topic numbers in all citations to U.S. GAAP (except for Statements of Financial Accounting Concepts, which are not part of the Codification). The Codification topic numbers within citations will look like this: **(Codification Topic 730)**.

4. **Increased use of actual financial statements.** We have increased the use of actual financial statement excerpts in the chapters and in end-of-chapter assignment materials. You will see that **Chapter 1**, for example, reprints the actual financial statements of both Nordstrom and Scania, while **Chapter 6** uses most of the financial statements of Wal-Mart.

The preceding changes affect more than one chapter of the book. The following affect individual chapters.

5. **Addition of an early chapter treating the record-keeping cycle.** Given the success our new Duke University authors have had with the record-keeping material they give to their MBA students before the financial accounting course begins, we have reorganized the balance sheet and income statement record-keeping material into a single chapter. **Chapter 2** introduces assets, liabilities, shareholders' equity, journal entries, T-accounts, recording of operating transactions, elementary adjusting entries, closing entries, and preparation of financial statements. **Chapter 2** accomplishes all this without overwhelming the student with advanced accounting and economic concepts. The problem material includes the "working backward" problems that have distinguished this text from many of its competitors. The basic record-keeping cycle gives students transactions, then asks for recording entries and adjusting entries, then asks for preparation of the income state-

ment, then closing entries, and finally the ending balance sheet and statement of cash flows. In the working backward problems, we give students some of the later items and ask them to derive earlier items. We say one doesn't understand accounting until one can work through the record-keeping cycle backward as well as forward. The typical accounting problem gives facts and asks the students to derive the financial statements. The working backward problems start with some subset of the financial statements and ask the students to derive the underlying transaction.

6. **Enhanced focus on balance sheet and income statement measurements, formats, and conventions.** Chapter 3 (balance sheet) introduces the asset and liability recognition criteria and measurement bases, including fair value measurement. **Chapter 4** (income statement) continues by describing basic revenue and expense recognition criteria and measurement and timing issues; **Chapter 7** contains a more detailed discussion of revenue recognition. Both chapters highlight classification and display differences that exist across firms, as well as between firms that follow U.S. GAAP and IFRS.

7. **Increased emphasis on the direct method of computing cash flow from operations.** Both the FASB and the IASB have expressed a preference for the direct method of computing cash flow from operations. Students are likely to increasingly encounter the direct method during their professional careers. Thus, we place increased emphasis on the direct method in the 13th Edition. Our students encounter difficulty with the indirect method of computing cash flow from operations when they initially study the statement of cash flows in **Chapter 5**. We have found that introducing the direct method initially helps them to understand the adjustments required to convert net income to cash flow from operations under the indirect method. **Chapter 5** therefore places increased emphasis on the direct method, without deleting material on the indirect method commonly found in practice. **Chapter 15** revisits the statement of cash flows, integrating material on more advanced topics into discussions of both the direct and indirect methods for presenting cash flow from operations. For example, we now include transactions for, and income tax effects of, stock option compensation expense, impairment loss, and employees' exercise of their stock options.

8. **Reorganization of topics involving revenue recognition and working capital.** Chapter 7 treats revenue recognition, receivables, and advances from customers. **Chapter 8** treats other current assets and current liabilities, including inventories, payables, and restructuring liabilities, whose treatment is new in this edition. The decision to bring all the working capital account issues together results from our view that the accounting for current liabilities has more in common with the accounting for current assets than with the accounting for noncurrent liabilities. Think, for example, about the allowance method applied both to uncollectibles and to warranty costs.

9. **IFRS differences from U.S. GAAP for noncurrent assets.** Chapter 9 contrasts the U.S. GAAP and IFRS treatments of noncurrent assets. At the elementary level of this book, the major differences between U.S. GAAP and IFRS in the accounting for noncurrent assets occur in the accounting for development costs and impairments.

10. **Reorganization of noncurrent liability topics.** Chapter 10 treats mortgages, bonds, installment notes, and lease liabilities, this last moved here from the following chapter. **Chapter 11** treats income taxes with the same coverage as in preceding editions and adds additional material on off-balance sheet financing and defined benefit pension arrangements. Leases are so common in business that we now treat them as a basic, not an advanced, topic in liabilities. We have structured the presentation of the advanced topics in liabilities so that the instructor can omit any of the three without loss of continuity to the others. For example, you can easily skip the pension material and assign the material on income taxes. We do. We don't expect students to master all this material during their first term in accounting, but many will not take more accounting and find later in their careers that they need to understand the basics of accounting for these more advanced topics. We have included this material, in the FACMU style of concepts, methods, and uses, so that this book can serve as a reference on these topics for our alumni.

11. **Separation of investments in marketable securities and derivatives from treatment of the equity method and consolidated statements.** Chapter 12 expands our coverage of accounting for derivatives, while **Chapter 13** adds material on joint ventures and variable interest entities (U.S. GAAP) and special purpose entities (IFRS). We have expanded this material into two chapters so that we can provide more coverage on derivatives without

having a single enormous chapter. As in **Chapter 11**, we have provided a significant amount of advanced materials to support instructor choice as to which advanced topics to cover and to ensure that our alumni will have this material at the ready when they encounter these issues on the job or in more advanced courses in the MBA curriculum.

12. **Summary of the FASB's and IASB's joint projects on the conceptual framework and financial statement presentation.** Chapter 16 discusses the current status of the joint FASB-IASB conceptual framework project and the likely changes under consideration. It also describes and illustrates the tentative conclusions of these standard setting bodies on the format of the financial statements.

13. **More complex topics appear on the Web site.** We have placed complex material on deferred taxes, foreign currency translation, and general price-level-adjusted accounting on the text's Web site.

ORGANIZATION

This book comprises four major parts:

- Part One: "Overview of Financial Statements," consisting of Chapters 1 and 2.
- Part Two: "Accounting Concepts and Methods," Chapters 3 through 6.
- Part Three: "Measuring and Reporting Assets and Equities Using U.S. GAAP and IFRS," Chapters 7 through 14.
- Part Four: "Synthesis," Chapters 15 and 16.

In our view, the four parts are tiers, or steps, in the learning process. **Part One** presents a general overview of the principal financial statements and basic transactions recording and financial statement preparation. **Part Two** discusses the basic accounting model accountants use to generate the principal financial statements. **Part Three** considers the specific accounting principles or methods used in preparing the financial statements. **Part Four** summarizes and integrates the material from the first three parts. This organization reflects the view that learning takes place most effectively when students begin with a broad picture, then break up that broad picture into smaller pieces until achieving the desired depth, and finally synthesize so that the relation between the parts and the whole retains its perspective.

Chapter 1 presents a brief description of the principal activities of a business firm (goal setting and strategy formulation, investing, financing, and operating) and shows how the principal financial statements—the balance sheet, the income statement, and the statement of cash flows—report the results of these activities. We use the business activities and the financial statements of Nordstrom and Scania to illustrate the important concepts. **Chapter 1** also provides an overview of the financial reporting environment. Many students feel deluged with the multitude of new terms and concepts after reading **Chapter 1**. However, most of these same students admit later that the broad overview helped piece material together as they later explored individual topics at greater length and in greater depth. The new **Chapter 2** focuses on record-keeping vocabulary and processes. **Chapter 2** uses T-accounts and journal entries as tools for recording transactions. The appendix to **Chapter 2** describes and illustrates the use of a Microsoft Excel® spreadsheet for recording transactions for instructors who prefer this approach. **Chapter 2**, unlike treatments in other texts, integrates the accounting entries for transactions during a period with the related adjusting entries at the end of the period. When textbooks discuss these two types of entries in separate chapters, students often lose sight of the fact that measurement of net income and financial position requires both kinds of entries.

Chapters 3 through **5** present the basic accounting model that generates the financial statements.

Chapters 3 and **4** discuss the elements of financial statements: assets, liabilities, shareholders' equity, revenue, and expenses. The conceptual frameworks of the FASB and the IASB provide the basis for these discussions, which include fair value measurements for assets and liabilities.

Chapter 5 discusses cash flows. We continue to put coverage of the statement of cash flows early in the text. This placement serves two purposes. First, it elevates the statement to its rightful place among the principal financial statements. Students can thereby integrate the concepts of profitability and cash flow more effectively and begin to understand that one does not necessarily accompany the other. Covering this statement at the end of the course can lead students to think the cash flow statement less important. Placing this chapter early in the book forces the student to cement understanding of the basic accounting model from **Chapters 2**, **3**, and **4**. Preparing the statement of cash flows requires the student to work backward from the balance sheet and income statement to reconstruct the transactions that took place. As the previous section discussed, we place increased emphasis on the direct method of computing cash flow from operations, without detracting from the importance of understanding the indirect method. The FASB, for more than a decade, and the IASB have expressed a preference for the direct method. Few U.S. companies currently use it, but we think this will change during the careers of your students.

Chapters 2 to **5** use the balance sheet equation or changes in the balance sheet equation to motivate understanding. Each of these chapters includes one or more simple problems that students can work using the balance sheet approach to prepare the principal financial statements. Although these chapters emphasize debit/credit procedures, instructors can use the balance sheet equation approach to communicate the basics of statement preparation.

Chapters 3, **4**, and **5** each contain a section on analyzing and interpreting the financial statement introduced in the chapter. This presages the integrated analysis of profitability and risk in **Chapter 6**.

Chapter 6 describes and illustrates tools for analyzing the financial statements, using the financial statements of Wal-Mart. The discussion structures the various financial statement ratios in a multi-level format that, students have found, reduces the need to memorize formulas. Instructors who incorporate annual reports of actual companies throughout their course, as we do with Nordstrom and Scania, will find that analysis of the financial statements of such companies provides an effective synthesis at this point. An appendix to **Chapter 6** illustrates procedures for preparing pro forma financial statements. This topic helps cement understanding of the relations among the principal financial statements.

Chapters 7 through **14** discuss the guidance in U.S. GAAP and IFRS for generating the financial statements. Each chapter not only describes and illustrates the application of the guidance, but also considers how accounting principles affect the financial statements. This approach reflects the view that students should be able to interpret and analyze published financial statements and to understand the effect of alternative accounting methods on such assessments.

Chapter 15 deepens the exploration of the statement of cash flows by presenting a comprehensive illustration using the transactions in **Chapters 7** to **14**. **Chapter 16** reviews the accounting principles discussed in **Chapters 7** to **14** and discusses reporting issues that standard-setting bodies are currently addressing, particularly those where U.S. GAAP and IFRS diverge. Problems 3 and 4 at the end of **Chapter 16** provide a review for the entire book.

An **appendix** to the book describes compound interest and present value computations for students not previously exposed to this topic.

The end of the book includes a comprehensive **glossary** of accounting terms. It serves as a reference tool for accounting and other business terms and provides additional descriptions of a few topics, such as *accounting changes* and *inventory profit*, considered only briefly in the text.

RELATED MATERIALS ACCOMPANYING THE TEXTBOOK

Contact the publisher to receive the following supplementary materials that augment the textbook:

Instructor's Resource CD-ROM (ISBN 0-324-78801-0) The Instructor's Resource CD-ROM includes the following supplements:

- **Solutions Manual** The Solutions Manual, written by the authors, provides full solutions for all end-of-chapter assignment items, including questions, exercises, and problems. We give computations, allowing the instructor to show how to reach a particular answer. The Solutions Manual also appears as a printed item.
- **Solutions Transparency Masters** Transparency masters, available to adopting instructors, accompany all numerical end-of-chapter exercises and problems.

- **Test Bank**   Prepared by Peter Ben Ezra (George Washington University), the Test Bank includes multiple-choice items, matching questions, short essay questions, and problems.
- **ExamView Computerized Testing Software**   All items in the Test Bank are available in ExamView computerized testing software format for Microsoft Windows. This supplement allows instructors to add or edit questions, instructions, and answers by previewing them onscreen. They can also create and administer quizzes online—whether over the internet, a local area network (LAN), or wide area network (WAN).
- **Lecture Presentations in PowerPoint**   These sample lectures aid in class preparation by those using this text. The PowerPoint slides are also available by download to instructors on the book's Web site.

Printed Solutions Manual (ISBN 0-324-78901-7)
The Solutions Manual, written by the authors, provides full solutions for all end-of-chapter assignment items, including questions, exercises, and problems.. We give computations, allowing the instructor to show how to reach a particular answer.

Spreadsheet Template Software
To reduce tedium in solving problems and increase student awareness of basic software applications, at least three problems per chapter have a corresponding template where basic problem data appear on a Microsoft Excel® spreadsheet. Additional spreadsheet templates are a pedagogical tool in learning selected topics such as for the statement of cash flows. The templates, both student and instructor versions, are available by download on the book's Web site.

Student Solutions Manual (ISBN 0-324-78900-9)
The Student Solutions Manual, written by the authors, provides full solutions for the odd end-of-chapter assignment items, including questions, exercises, and problems.

Web Resources.
Many helpful Web resources, including topical discussions, advanced topics, regulatory updates, editorial and marketing contacts, and more are available for students to access. These items help reinforce and shed light on text topics. We invite you to discover this wealth of student and instructor resources by logging into the text Web site. (www.cengage.com/accounting/stickney)

Community Web Site.
For those who do not have a physical copy of the book, this Web site contains information about the revision: www.cengage.com.community/facmu

We encourage instructors to contact their South-Western Cengage Learning sales representative for information and samples of these items.

Instructors may also contact the publisher directly with questions, comments, or concerns:

Matt Filimonov, Senior Acquisitions Editor – matt.filimonov@cengage.com
Steve Joos, Marketing Manager – steven.joos@cengage.com
Craig Avery, Senior Developmental Editor – craig.avery@cengage.com

ACKNOWLEDGMENTS

The following individuals provided invaluable and insightful comments during the development of the 13th Edition:

Robert Bowen University of Washington
Douglas DeJong University of Iowa
Elizabeth Demers INSEAD
Ellen Engel University of Chicago
Rick Johnston The Ohio State University
Peggy Bishop Lane University of Pennsylvania
Mark Lang University of North Carolina
Danny S. Litt University of California, Los Angeles
Sarah E. Nutter George Mason University
Allen Schiff Fordham University
John Shon Baruch College
Suraj Srinivasan Harvard University
Phillip C. Stocken Dartmouth College
Stephen A. Zeff Rice University

The last-mentioned Steve Zeff has given us so many helpful comments and materials over the years that we have lost count, including half a dozen definitions about international accounting standard setting for the glossary. Most of these appear in the **Glossary**. He deserves and gets our special thanks.

Thomas Horton and Daughters, Inc. permits us to reproduce material from *Accounting: The Language of Business*. Problems 42, 43, and 44 in **Chapter 2** derive from ones prepared by George H. Sorter. These problems involve working backward from one financial statement to another, and we have found them useful in cementing understanding.

We thank Mark Sears for his work on the solutions, Katherine Xenophon-Rybowiak for helping us to prepare the manuscript for this edition, and Cherie Weil for preparing the index.

We are grateful to Michael Sandretto (University of Illinois, Chicago) for his careful reading of and helpful suggestions for chapters in the text and solutions manual. We've had many such helpers over the years and Mike has been, by far, the best.

We thank the following at Cengage Learning: Matt Filimonov and Craig Avery for providing general guidance for the direction and scope of the revision and coordinating the revision process, Steve Joos for his marketing effort, and Tim Bailey for coordinating the production.

We thank the employees of Lachina Publishing Services, Inc. for their copyediting and compositing expertise and for their excellent work on page makeup.

Thanks to Michael Behnke for inspiring the WARNING on the dedication page.

Finally, Sidney Davidson. What can we say? For over thirty-five years he taught us and guided us and wrote with us. All four of us. We're all the intellectual grandchildren of William Paton. Thank you.

CPS
RLW
KS
JF

BRIEF CONTENTS

CONTENTS

PART 1

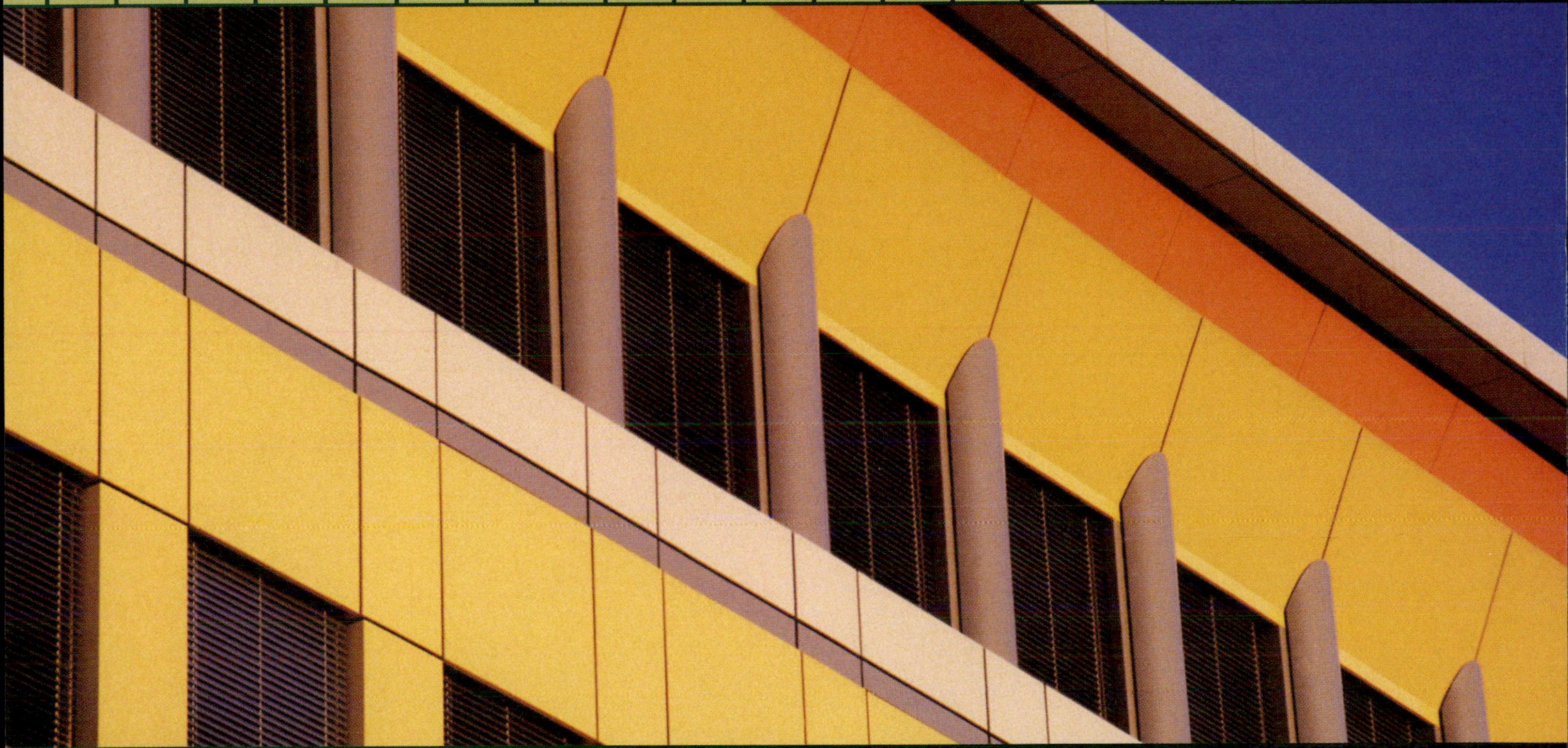

FACMU13

Overview of Financial Statements

Introduction to Business Activities and Overview of Financial Statements and the Reporting Process

1. Understand four principal activities of business entities: (a) establish goals and strategies, (b) obtain financing, (c) make investments, and (d) conduct operations.
2. Understand the purpose and content of the principal financial statements: (a) balance sheet, (b) income statement, (c) statement of cash flows, and (d) statement of shareholders' equity.
3. Understand the roles of participants in the financial reporting process, including managers and governing boards, accounting standard setters and regulators, independent external auditors, and financial statement users.

4. Gain an awareness of financial reporting as part of a global system for providing information for resource allocation decisions, including the existence of two financial reporting systems (U.S. GAAP and International Financial Reporting Standards).
5. Understand the difference between the cash basis and the accrual basis of accounting, and why the latter provides a more informative measure of performance.

Resource allocation decisions of investors and creditors depend on reliable and relevant information about firms' financial positions, profitability, and risk. Financial reports prepared by firms are a key source of this information. The process of preparing those reports is *financial accounting*, or, more broadly, *financial reporting*. Understanding the basics of the financial reporting process is fundamental to understanding how to use financial reports for resource allocation decisions, such as making investments.

You are about to embark on the study of financial accounting. You will learn the concepts underlying the accounting principles firms use to measure the results of their business activities, the accounting principles themselves, some of the judgments and estimates managers must make to apply accounting principles, and tools for analyzing financial statements. You will learn about two similar—but not identical—financial accounting systems: U.S. GAAP[1] and International Financial Reporting Standards (IFRS). Accounting systems specify the financial accounting principles and procedures that firms must use, and the kinds of estimates and judgments that managers must make in applying those principles. We introduce these two systems in this chapter, illustrate them with a firm that uses U.S. GAAP (Nordstrom, Inc.) and a firm that uses IFRS (Scania Group), and continue to present both systems throughout the book.

Our aim is to equip you with sufficient understanding of the concepts, methods, and uses of financial statements to enable you to use financial accounting information effectively. As a financial statement user, you will encounter financial reports that use a variety of formats

---

[1]GAAP refers to Generally Accepted Accounting Principles. These are the authoritative guidance for financial accounting in the United States. We discuss U.S. GAAP and IFRS in more detail later in this chapter and throughout the book.

and presentations. We attempt to show a few of those variations, with the understanding that you will encounter many more.

This chapter overviews the book, beginning with a description of Nordstrom's and Scania's business activities. We next see how firms measure the results of their business activities and report those results in their financial statements. Finally, we describe several components of the financial reporting process and introduce U.S. GAAP and IFRS. This chapter introduces material that later chapters will cover in greater depth. At this point, you will not fully understand all the concepts and terms discussed in this chapter. As the chapter title suggests, this chapter introduces the concepts, methods, and uses that later chapters discuss in detail.

 # OVERVIEW OF BUSINESS ACTIVITIES

The managers of a business[2] prepare financial statements to present meaningful information about that business's activities to external users, including owners, lenders, regulators, and employees. Understanding those financial statements, therefore, requires an understanding of the activities of the business:

1. Establishing goals and strategies
2. Obtaining financing
3. Making investments
4. Conducting operations.

We illustrate these four principal business activities using two firms, Nordstrom, Inc. and Scania Group.

Example 1 Per their 2006 annual report, Nordstrom, Inc. operates 155 specialty retail stores in the United States. It prepares its financial statements using U.S. GAAP. Its business has three principal components:

- Retail stores selling high-quality clothing, shoes, cosmetics, and accessories.
- Catalog and Internet sales selling the same products as the retail stores.
- Private-label debit and credit cards, plus Nordstrom-branded ® credit cards, generating finance charges.

Example 2 Scania Group, based in Sweden, prepares its financial statements using IFRS. Scania produces high-quality heavyweight vehicles and engines and provides a range of transport-related services. It operates in approximately 100 countries; Europe is its largest market. Its business has three principal components:

- Manufacturing: trucks, buses and coaches, and industrial and marine engines.
- Support services: parts, maintenance agreements, repairs, driver training, and information technology support for transport planning.
- Customer finance.

Although Nordstrom and Scania differ markedly in terms of their business size, and geographical scope, their managers must carry out similar kinds of business activities, discussed next. Differences in the two firms' business models affect the content of each of the activities.

ESTABLISH CORPORATE GOALS AND STRATEGIES

Goals are the end results toward which the firm directs its energies, and **strategies** are the means for achieving those results. Examples of corporate goals include maximizing the return to the firm's owners, providing a good working environment for employees, and improving

---

[2]We use "managers" and "management" to refer to employees who make operating, investing, and financing decisions and apply applicable accounting standards to prepare financial statements, subject to the oversight of the firm's governing board (or boards). We also use "firms" to refer to these same decision makers.

the environmental performance of both the firm's products and the processes that generate those products. Management, under the oversight of the firm's governing board (or boards),[3] sets the firm's strategies—for example, determining the firm's lines of business and its geographic locations, the strategies for each business unit or product, and the degree to which a given business unit will engage in new product development. We discuss the roles of management and governing boards in financial reporting later in this chapter.

Examples of factors from the operating environment that would affect a firm's goals and strategies include the following:

1. Goals and strategies of the firm's competitors.
2. Barriers to entry of the firm's industry, such as patents or large investments in buildings and equipment.
3. Nature of the demand for the firm's products and services. For example, demand might be increasing rapidly, such as for certain pharmaceutical products, or demand might be relatively stable, such as for groceries.
4. Existence and nature of government regulation.

Firms provide extensive information about their corporate goals and strategies. For example, Scania's 2006 annual financial report states that one corporate goal is to grow by 10% annually, with margins of 12–15%.[4] One strategy for achieving this goal is to adapt its production processes so as to reduce labor costs below 15% of total production costs. Scania's 2006 annual report also announced plans to increase its production capacity from 70,000 vehicles to 100,000 vehicles annually, by 2010. Similarly, Nordstrom's 2006 annual report announced a plan to open 26 new or relocated stores and to remodel 69 existing stores.

Establishing corporate goals and strategies does not directly affect the firm's cash flows. The other three business activities—obtaining financing, making investments, and carrying out operations—either generate cash or use cash. The statement of cash flows, introduced later in the chapter, separates cash inflows and outflows into those related to operations, those related to investing, and those related to financing.

OBTAIN FINANCING

To carry out their plans, firms such as Scania and Nordstrom require **financing**, that is, funds from owners and creditors. Owners provide funds to a firm and in return receive ownership interests. For a corporation, the ownership interests are shares of common stock and the owners are **shareholders** or **stockholders**.[5] In some cases the common shares trade in active markets such as the New York Stock Exchange and the London Stock Exchange. Firms whose shares trade in active markets are **publicly traded** and subject to special regulations, which this chapter discusses later. When the firm raises funds from owners, it has no obligataion to repay these funds. Sometimes, a firm's governing board may decide to distribute **dividends** to that firm's shareholders. Dividends are a distribution of the firm's assets to owners; the assets are often cash (dividends paid in cash) but could take other forms as well (including dividends paid with other assets, such as shares in other companies).

Creditors provide funds that the firm must repay, usually with interest, in specific amounts at specific dates. *Long-term* creditors require repayment from the borrower over a period of time that exceeds one year. One common form of long-term financing is *bonds*. A bond agreement specifies the amount borrowed and the terms of repayment, including the interest rate and the timing and amounts of cash the borrower agrees to pay to the creditors. Banks usually lend for periods between several months and several years. A *note*, in which the borrowing company promises to repay the amount borrowed plus interest at some future date, provides evidence of bank borrowings. Finally, suppliers of raw materials or merchandise that do not require payment for 30 days also provide *short-term* funds—the firm gets raw

---

[3]By law, some countries require firms to have two governing boards; other countries require one.

[4]"Margin" in this context means the difference between what Scania charges customers for its products and services and Scania's costs to create those goods and services.

[5]If the business is organized as a partnership, the owners are partners. If the business is organized as a proprietorship, the owner is the proprietor. This book considers corporations, in which the owners are shareholders or stockholders.

materials or merchandise now but need not pay cash until later. Likewise, employees paid weekly or monthly, and governmental units requiring quarterly tax payments, provide funds by not demanding payment on a more frequent basis (such as daily).

Each firm makes financing decisions about the proportion of funds to obtain from owners, long-term creditors, and short-term creditors. Corporate finance courses cover the techniques that firms use to make financing decisions.

MAKE INVESTMENTS

A firm makes investments to obtain productive capacity to carry out its business activities. **Investing activities** involve acquiring some of the following:

1. **Land, buildings, and equipment.** These long-term investments provide the capacity to manufacture and sell products. They are usually long term, in the sense that they provide productive capacity for a number of years.

2. **Patents, licenses, and other contractual rights.** These long-term investments provide rights to use ideas and processes. They are intangible, in the sense that the rights have a legal existence but not a physical existence.

3. **Common shares or bonds of other firms.** These investments make a firm an owner or creditor of another firm. Short-term investments in equity interests typically involve partial ownership, involving temporarily excess cash, while long-term investments in equity interests involve partial or complete ownership of another business. An example of the latter would be a situation where one firm wishes to secure a source for critical raw materials and purchases a long-term equity stake in a supplier.

4. **Inventories.** Firms maintain an inventory of products to sell to customers. For example, Nordstrom maintains inventories of apparel, shoes, accessories, and cosmetics.

5. **Accounts receivable from customers.** In many businesses, customers do not pay for goods and services immediately. The firm uses the term *accounts receivable* to describe the amounts owed to it by customers for short periods, such as 30 days. In extending credit to customers, the firm forgoes collecting its cash right away, but if it did not extend the credit, it might not make the sale in the first place. The firm delays the collection of needed cash from its customers, so it must obtain funds elsewhere.

6. **Cash.** Most firms maintain cash balances (like a corporate checking account) to pay their current bills. Firms use cash management systems to keep these amounts small.

Managerial accounting courses and corporate finance courses cover the techniques that firms use to make investment decisions.

CARRY OUT OPERATIONS

Management operates the productive capacity of the firm to generate earnings. **Operating activities** include the following:

1. **Purchasing.** The purchasing department of a retailer, such as Nordstrom, acquires items to sell to customers. The purchasing department of a manufacturing firm, such as Scania, acquires raw materials needed for production.

2. **Production.** The production department in a manufacturing firm combines raw materials, labor services, and other manufacturing inputs to produce goods for sale; a service firm combines labor inputs and other inputs to provide services to customers. Scania is both a manufacturing firm and a service firm.

3. **Marketing.** The marketing department oversees selling and distributing products and services to customers.

4. **Administration.** Administrative activities include data processing, human resource management, legal services, and other support services.

5. **Research and development.** A firm undertakes research and development in the hope (and expectation) of discovering new knowledge that it can use to create new products, new processes, or new services.

Managerial accounting, marketing, and operations management courses cover the techniques that firms use to make operating decisions.

PRINCIPAL FINANCIAL STATEMENTS

Firms communicate the results of their business activities in the **annual report to shareholders**.[6] The annual report may contain letters from the firm's management describing the firm's goals, strategies, and accomplishments, as well as descriptions and pictures of the firm's products, facilities, and employees. If the firm's shares trade publicly, it will also file an annual report with a regulator, typically a government agency.[7] The applicable laws and regulations of the country where the shares trade specify the form and content of the annual report. In the United States, regulatory requirements applicable to publicly traded firms also require the inclusion of a **Management's Discussion and Analysis (MD&A)**, in which management discusses operating results, liquidity (sources and uses of cash), capital resources, and reasons for changes in profitability and risk during the past year.

We focus on the firm's four financial statements and the supplementary information, including the following:

1. *Balance sheet* or *statement of financial position* at a specified time.
2. *Income statement* or *statement of profit and loss* for a specified time period.
3. *Statement of cash flows*.
4. *Statement of shareholders' equity*.
5. *Notes* to the financial statements, including various supporting schedules.

The following sections of this chapter briefly discuss each of these five items. In describing these items here and throughout the book, we refer to the financial statements of Nordstrom and Scania. Nordstrom's financial statements appear in **Exhibits 1.1–1.4**, and Scania's financial statements appear in **Exhibits 1.5–1.8**. We begin by making several observations about certain conventions and concepts that apply to financial statements in general.

FINANCIAL REPORTING CONVENTIONS

As you read financial statements, you will see both commonalities and differences. In this section we describe some conventions commonly used in financial statement preparation. These conventions govern the length of time covered by the financial statements (the accounting period), the number of reporting periods included in a given financial statement presentation, the monetary amounts, and the terminology and level of detail in the financial statements.

Length of Reporting (Accounting) Period
Financial statement presentations can span intervals of any length. The most common reporting interval for external reporting is one year, called the **fiscal year**. While many firms use the calendar year as their fiscal year (that is, the fiscal year ends on December 31), some firms select other fiscal year-ends. For example, retailers like Nordstrom often use a fiscal year ending on or close to January 31, after the end of the holiday shopping season. When the fiscal year ends in June–December of calendar year T, convention describes the financial reports as pertaining to fiscal year T. For example, Scania's financial report for the year ended December 31, 2006, reports Scania's performance for fiscal 2006. When the fiscal year ends in January–May of year T, convention describes the financial reports as pertaining to fiscal year T − 1. For example, Nordstrom's financial report for the year ended February 3, 2007, reports Nordstrom's performance for fiscal 2006.[8] We discuss reporting periods in more detail later in this chapter.

Number of Reporting Periods
To assist users of financial reports in making over-time comparisons, both U.S. GAAP and IFRS require firms to include results for multiple reporting periods in each report. Firms must include two balance sheets describing the beginning

---

[6]Many firms provide these annual reports on their Web sites. Nordstrom's and Scania's annual reports appear at the investor relations sections of *www.nordstrom.com* and *www.scania.com*, respectively.

[7]The regulator may also require *interim reports*, for example, on a quarterly basis. In the United States, firms whose shares trade publicly file quarterly reports that contain a subset of the information that is in the annual report. The reports filed with the U.S. regulator appear on the regulator's Web site (*www.sec.gov*). The U.S. regulator is the Securities and Exchange Commission (SEC).

[8]Not all firms follow this convention in describing their financial results, so use caution in comparing results of two or more firms.

EXHIBIT 1.1	Nordstrom, Inc. Consolidated Balance Sheets (amounts in thousands)

	February 3, 2007	January 28, 2006
Assets		
Current assets:		
Cash and cash equivalents	$402,559	$462,656
Short-term investments	–	54,000
Accounts receivable, net	684,376	639,558
Investment in asset backed securities	428,175	561,136
Merchandise inventories	997,289	955,978
Current deferred tax assets, net	169,320	145,470
Prepaid expenses and other	60,474	55,359
Total current assets	2,742,193	2,874,157
Land, buildings and equipment, net	1,757,215	1,773,871
Goodwill	51,714	51,714
Acquired tradename	84,000	84,000
Other assets	186,456	137,607
Total assets	**$4,821,578**	**$4,921,349**
Liabilities and Shareholders' Equity		
Current liabilities:		
Accounts payable	$576,796	$540,019
Accrued salaries, wages and related benefits	339,965	285,982
Other current liabilities	433,487	409,076
Income taxes payable	76,095	81,617
Current portion of long-term debt	6,800	306,618
Total current liabilities	1,433,143	1,623,312
Long-term debt, net	623,652	627,776
Deferred property incentives, net	356,062	364,382
Other liabilities	240,200	213,198
Shareholders' equity:		
Common stock, no par value: 1,000,000 shares authorized;		
257,313 and 269,549 shares issued and outstanding	826,421	685,934
Unearned stock compensation	–	(327)
Retained earnings	1,350,680	1,404,366
Accumulated other comprehensive (loss) earnings	(8,580)	2,708
Total shareholders' equity	2,168,521	2,092,681
Total liabilities and shareholders' equity	**$4,821,578**	**$4,921,349**

and ending balances of the accounts for the current fiscal year. Refer to **Exhibit 1.1**, which shows that Nordstrom includes in its fiscal 2006 annual report to shareholders a balance sheet as of February 3, 2007, and a balance sheet as of January 28, 2006, showing the beginning balances for fiscal year 2006 (which are also the ending balances for fiscal 2005). Some firms may include more comparative balance sheets. Refer to **Exhibit 1.5**, which shows that Scania provides balance sheet information for December 31, 2004, 2005, and 2006. For the income statement, statement of cash flows, and statement of shareholders' equity, SEC rules require statements for the current year and the two prior years; IFRS requires statements for the current year and the prior year. Both Nordstrom and Scania provide these three financial statements for fiscal 2004, 2005, and 2006.

Monetary Amounts The financial statements report numerical amounts for each listed item on the financial statements. The numerical amount reported is a **monetary amount**. The financial statements indicate the measuring units, both the numerical expression such as in

EXHIBIT 1.2

Nordstrom, Inc.
Consolidated Statements of Earnings

Fiscal year	2006	2005	2004
Net sales	$8,560,698	$7,722,860	$7,131,388
Cost of sales and related buying and occupancy costs	(5,353,949)	(4,888,023)	(4,559,388)
Gross profit	3,206,749	2,834,837	2,572,000
Selling, general and administrative expenses	(2,296,863)	(2,100,666)	(2,020,233)
Operating income	909,886	734,171	551,767
Interest expense, net	(42,758)	(45,300)	(77,428)
Other income including finance charges, net	238,525	196,354	172,942
Earnings before income tax expense	1,105,653	885,225	647,281
Income tax expense	(427,654)	(333,886)	(253,831)
Net earnings	**$677,999**	$551,339	$393,450
Earnings per basic share	$2.60	$2.03	$1.41
Earnings per diluted share	$2.55	$1.98	$1.38
Basic shares	260,689	271,958	278,993
Diluted shares	265,712	277,776	284,533
Cash dividends paid per share of common stock outstanding	$0.42	$0.32	$0.24

thousands, in millions, or in billions, and the currency, such as dollars ($), euros (€), or Swedish kronor (SEK). A firm typically reports in the currency of the country where it is headquartered or where it conducts most of its business. For example, a firm with headquarters and most of its business activities in England would report its results in pounds sterling (£). However, a firm need not report in the currency of its home country.

Terminology and Level of Detail U.S. GAAP and IFRS contain broad guidance on what the financial statements must contain, but neither system completely specifies the level of detail or the names of accounts. IFRS contains relatively more prescriptive guidance, listing, for example, the line items that the balance sheet must display and listing items that the firm must separately disclose.[9] U.S. GAAP contains no analog to this IFRS guidance.[10] *You should therefore expect to encounter variation in the ways financial statements display information and variation in the level of detail provided.* In addition, the rules do not always require firms to use specific names for accounts and line items on the financial statements. While practice tends to converge on certain descriptive names, such as cash, accounts receivable, and inventories, *you should expect to encounter variation in account titles as well as variation in format and display.*

With these conventions in mind, we turn to a discussion of the principal financial statements.

BALANCE SHEET

The **balance sheet,** also called the **statement of financial position,** provides information, at a point in time, on the firm's productive resources and the financing used to pay for those resources. **Exhibit 1.1** presents Nordstrom's balance sheet as of January 28, 2006, and February 3, 2007. **Exhibit 1.5** presents Scania's balance sheet as of December 31, 2004, December 31, 2005, and December 31, 2006. The balance sheet presents information at a point in time, in this case, the end of the firm's fiscal year. Nordstrom's annual report states that its fiscal

---

[9]International Accounting Standards Board, *International Accounting Standard 1*, "Presentation of Financial Statements," revised 2003.

[10]As this book goes to press, a project is underway to improve and converge the U.S. GAAP and IFRS guidance for financial statement presentation. **Chapter 16** discusses this project more fully.

EXHIBIT 1.3

Nordstrom, Inc.
Consolidated Statements of Cash Flows
(amounts in thousands)

Fiscal year	2006	2005	2004
Operating Activities			
Net earnings	$677,999	$551,339	$393,450
Adjustments to reconcile net earnings to net cash provided by operating activities:			
Depreciation and amortization of buildings and equipment	284,520	276,328	264,769
Amortization of deferred property incentives and other, net	(36,293)	(33,350)	(31,378)
Stock-based compensation expense	37,362	13,285	8,051
Deferred income taxes, net	(58,274)	(11,238)	(8,040)
Tax benefit from stock-based payments	43,552	41,092	25,442
Excess tax benefit from stock-based payments	(38,293)	–	–
Provision for bad debt expense	17,064	20,918	24,639
Change in operating assets and liabilities:			
Accounts receivable	(61,301)	(15,140)	(2,950)
Investment in asset backed securities	127,984	(135,790)	(149,970)
Merchandise inventories	(38,649)	(20,804)	(11,771)
Prepaid expenses	(4,723)	(1,035)	(3,163)
Other assets	(7,661)	(3,473)	(8,143)
Accounts payable	84,291	31,721	23,930
Accrued salaries, wages and related benefits	48,719	(11,284)	15,055
Other current liabilities	23,533	38,755	58,471
Income taxes payable	(5,522)	(33,877)	(18,999)
Deferred property incentives	30,723	49,480	19,837
Other liabilities	17,334	19,305	7,116
Net cash provided by operating activities	1,142,365	776,232	606,346
Investing Activities			
Capital expenditures	(264,437)	(271,659)	(246,851)
Proceeds from sale of assets	224	107	5,473
Purchases of short-term investments	(109,550)	(542,925)	(3,232,250)
Sales of short-term investments	163,550	530,750	3,366,425
Other, net	(8,067)	(8,366)	(2,830)
Net cash used in investing activities	(218,280)	(292,093)	(110,033)
Financing Activities			
Principal payments on long-term debt	(307,559)	(101,047)	(205,252)
(Decrease) increase in cash book overdrafts	(50,853)	4,946	(2,680)
Proceeds from exercise of stock options	50,900	73,023	87,061
Proceeds from employee stock purchase plan	16,300	15,600	12,892
Excess tax benefit from stock-based payments	38,293	–	–
Cash dividends paid	(110,158)	(87,196)	(67,240)
Repurchase of common stock	(621,527)	(287,080)	(300,000)
Other, net	422	(352)	(752)
Net cash used in financing activities	(984,182)	(382,106)	(475,971)
Net (decrease) increase in cash and cash equivalents	(60,097)	102,033	20,342
Cash and cash equivalents at beginning of year	462,656	360,623	340,281
Cash and cash equivalents at end of year	$402,559	$462,656	$360,623

year ends on the Saturday closest to January 31; Scania states that its fiscal year ends on December 31. The financial position of the firm at other times during the year can differ substantially from that depicted on the end-of-year balance sheet.

Concepts of Assets, Liabilities, and Shareholders' Equity
The balance sheet lists the firm's assets, liabilities, and shareholders' equity and provides totals and subtotals. Each line item on the balance sheet has a descriptive title that indicates the nature of the item and a numerical amount reported in units of currency. For example, the first item on Nordstrom's balance sheet is Cash and Cash Equivalents in the amount of $402,559; the upper left corner of the balance sheet indicates the measuring unit is thousands of U.S dollars. The first item on Scania's balance sheet is Intangible Noncurrent Assets, measured in millions (m.) of Swedish kronor (SEK) in the amount of SEK2,464.

Assets are economic resources with the potential to provide future economic benefits to a firm. The firm's investments in items to provide productive capacity are examples of assets.

EXHIBIT 1.4

Nordstrom, Inc.
Consolidated Statements of Shareholders' Equity
(amounts in thousands except per share amounts)

	Common Stock Shares	Common Stock Amount	Unearned Stock Compensation	Retained Earnings	Accumulated Other Comprehensive Earnings (Loss)	Total
Balance at January 31, 2004	276,753	$424,645	$(597)	$1,201,093	$8,868	$1,634,009
Net earnings	–	–	–	393,450	–	393,450
Other comprehensive earnings:						
Foreign currency translation adjustment	–	–	–	–	493	493
Unrecognized loss on SERP, net of tax of $76	–	–	–	–	(119)	(119)
Fair value adjustment to investment in asset backed securities, net of tax of $(59)	–	–	–	–	93	93
Comprehensive net earnings	–	–	–	–	–	393,917
Cash dividends paid ($0.24 per share)	–	–	–	(67,240)	–	(67,240)
Issuance of common stock for:						
Stock option plans	7,238	111,315	–	–	–	111,315
Employee stock purchase plan	977	14,081	–	–	–	14,081
Other	178	2,614	298	–	–	2,912
Repurchase of common stock	(13,815)	–	–	(300,000)	–	(300,000)
Balance at January 29, 2005	271,331	552,655	(299)	1,227,303	9,335	1,788,994
Net earnings	–	–	–	551,339	–	551,339
Other comprehensive earnings:						
Foreign currency translation adjustment	–	–	–	–	(1,815)	(1,815)
Unrecognized loss on SERP, net of tax of $4,950	–	–	–	–	(7,742)	(7,742)
Fair value adjustment to investment in asset backed securities, net of tax of $(1,875)	–	–	–	–	2,930	2,930
Comprehensive net earnings	–	–	–	–	–	544,712
Cash dividends paid ($0.32 per share)	–	–	–	(87,196)	–	(87,196)
Issuance of common stock for:						
Stock option plans	5,820	112,948	–	–	–	112,948
Employee stock purchase plan	757	16,767	–	–	–	16,767
Other	136	3,564	(28)	–	–	3,536
Repurchase of common stock	(8,495)	–	–	(287,080)	–	(287,080)
Balance at January 28, 2006	269,549	685,934	(327)	1,404,366	2,708	2,092,681
Net earnings	–	–	–	677,999	–	677,999
Other comprehensive earnings:						
Foreign currency translation adjustment	–	–	–	–	1,309	1,309
Unrecognized gain on SERP, net of tax of $(1,938), prior to adoption of SFAS 158	–	–	–	–	3,032	3,032
Fair value adjustment to investment in asset backed securities, net of tax of $2,173	–	–	–	–	(2,805)	(2,805)
Comprehensive net earnings	–	–	–	–	–	679,535
Adjustment to initially apply SFAS 158, net of tax of $8,199	–	–	–	–	(12,824)	(12,824)
Cash dividends paid ($0.42 per share)	–	–	–	(110,158)	–	(110,158)
Issuance of common stock for:						
Stock option plans	3,838	94,099	–	–	–	94,099
Employee stock purchase plan	446	16,652	–	–	–	16,652
Other	27	721	327	–	–	1,048
Stock-based compensation	–	29,015	–	–	–	29,015
Repurchase of common stock	(16,547)	–	–	(621,527)	–	(621,527)
Balance at February 3, 2007	257,313	$826,421	–	$1,350,680	$(8,580)	$2,168,521

For example, both Nordstrom and Scania list buildings and equipment (Scania calls these "tangible non-current assets") among the assets on their balance sheets. Note that the order in which the assets appear differs between Nordstrom's and Scania's balance sheets; we discuss this ordering in **Chapter 2**.

    Liabilities are creditors' claims for funds, usually because they have provided funds, or goods and services, to the firm. We describe two examples of liabilities that result from a

EXHIBIT 1.5 Scania Group
Consolidated Balance Sheets

31 December, SEK m.	Note	2006	2005	2004
ASSETS				
Non-current assets				
Intangible non-current assets	11	**2,464**	2,698	2,626
Tangible non-current assets	12	**17,130**	16,715	14,766
Lease assets	12	**9,666**	9,883	9,144
Financial non-current assets				
Holdings in associated companies and joint ventures	13	**173**	96	92
Long-term interest-bearing receivables		**16,599**	15,543	12,756
Other long-term receivables [1]	15, 17	**1,023**	1,393	503
Total financial non-current assets		**17,795**	17,032	13,351
Deferred tax assets	8	**649**	565	383
Tax assets		**34**	0	0
Total non-current assets		**47,738**	46,893	40,270
Current assets				
Inventories	14	**10,100**	9,949	9,487
Current receivables				
Tax assets		**370**	206	733
Interest-bearing trade receivables		**8,600**	7,847	7,875
Non-interest-bearing trade receivables		**7,379**	8,008	7,641
Other current receivables [1]	15	**3,046**	2,522	2,199
Total current receivables		**19,395**	18,583	18,448
Short-term investments		**911**	1,194	909
Cash and cash equivalents				
Short-term investments comprising cash and cash equivalents		**8,808**	493	470
Cash and bank balances		**1,126**	1,106	1,119
Total cash and cash equivalents		**9,934**	1,599	1,589
Total current assets		**40,340**	31,325	30,433
Total assets		**88,078**	78,218	70,703

firm's having previously received benefits (inventories, labor services) for which it must pay a specified amount on a specified date.:

■ First, both Nordstrom and Scania have made purchases but have not yet paid the entire amount owed. Nordstrom includes the amount owed to its suppliers in Accounts Payable; Scania calls this account Trade Payables.[11]

■ Second, employees have provided labor services for which Nordstrom and Scania have not made full payment as of the balance sheet date. Nordstrom includes the amounts owed to employees in Accrued Salaries, Wages and Related Benefits; Scania includes them in Accrued Expenses and Deferred Income.

Shareholders' equity shows the amounts of funds owners have provided and, in parallel, their claims on the assets of a firm. The owners have a residual interest in the firm's assets; that is, owners have a claim on all assets in excess of those required to meet creditors' claims. Shareholders' equity lists both the amounts invested by shareholders for their ownership interests and retained earnings. Scania uses the word *Equity* to describe its sharehold-

---

[11]Here and elsewhere, we note that many account titles are not standardized. Firms use a variety of descriptive titles to refer to the same account.

EXHIBIT 1.5   Scania Group
Consolidated Balance Sheets (Continued)

31 December, SEK m.	Note	2006	2005	2004
EQUITY AND LIABILITIES				
Equity				
Share capital		2,000	2,263	2,000
Contributed capital		1,120	1,120	1,120
Hedge reserve		87	-83	–
Accumulated exchange rate difference		243	903	-400
Retained earnings		22,679	19,524	18,708
Equity attributable to Scania shareholders		26,129	23,727	21,428
Minority interest		5	9	5
Total equity	16	26,134	23,736	21,433
Non-current liabilities				
Non-current interest-bearing liabilities		17,918	19,323	19,809
Provisions for pensions	17	3,605	3,458	2,499
Other non-current provisions	18	1,473	1,310	1,236
Accrued expenses and deferred income	19	1,861	2,126	2,369
Deferred tax liabilities	8	2,278	2,140	2,305
Other tax liabilities		170	195	187
Other non-current liabilities [1]		536	621	394
Total non-current liabilities		27,841	29,173	28,799
Current liabilities				
Current interest-bearing liabilities		16,350	9,351	5,804
Current provisions	18	1,125	962	1,366
Accrued expenses and deferred income	19	7,283	6,836	5,543
Advance payments from customers		449	593	611
Trade payables		6,011	4,901	4,167
Tax liabilities		946	645	1,377
Other current liabilities [1]		1,939	2,021	1,603
Total current liabilities		34,103	25,309	20,471
Total equity and liabilities		88,078	78,218	70,703

ers' equity and lists both share capital and contributed capital; the sum of these amounts (SEK3,120 million at December 31, 2006) is the amount invested by Scania's shareholders for their ownership interests. Nordstrom uses the phrase *Shareholders' Equity*; as of February 3, 2007, there were 257,313 thousand shares issued to shareholders, who had provided funds to Nordstrom equal to $826,421 thousand in exchange for those shares.

Retained earnings represent the *net assets* (= total assets − total liabilities) a firm derives from its earnings that exceed the dividends it has distributed to shareholders since its formation. Earnings generate additional assets or reduce liabilities. To the extent the firm does not distribute those additional assets to shareholders, it has retained earnings. The Retained Earnings designation in the Shareholders' Equity section shows the source of the funding for assets reinvested by management for the benefit of shareholders and the shareholders' claims on those assets. Management operates the firm's assets with the intent of generating earnings; that is, the firm expects to receive more assets than it consumes in operations. The increase in assets, after claims of creditors, belongs to the firm's owners. As of February 3, 2007, Nordstrom's retained earnings is $1,350,680 thousand; that is, its cumulative earnings exceed its cumulative dividends by approximately $1.35 billion. As of December 31, 2006, Scania's retained earnings is SEK22,679 million.

An amount of assets equal to retained earnings does not appear on any single line on the balance sheet. Instead, a firm such as Nordstrom has used the assets generated by the retention of earnings to acquire various assets including inventories, new stores, new equipment,

EXHIBIT 1.6

Scania Group
Consolidated Income Statements

January – December, SEK m.	Note	2006	2005	2004
Vehicles and Service				
Net sales	4	**70,738**	63,328	56,788
Cost of goods sold	5	**-52,255**	-47,835	-42,528
Gross income		**18,483**	15,493	14,260
Research and development expenses [1]	5, 11	**-3,023**	-2,484	-1,987
Selling expenses	5	**-6,016**	-5,829	-5,343
Administrative expenses	5	**-1,189**	-858	-789
Share of income in associated companies and joint ventures [2]	13	**5**	8	8
Operating income, Vehicles and Service		**8,260**	6,330	6,149
Customer Finance	6			
Interest and lease income		**3,527**	3,518	3,427
Interest and depreciation expenses		**-2,608**	-2,575	-2,572
Interest surplus		**919**	943	855
Other income		**232**	178	134
Other expenses		**-179**	-138	-132
Gross income		**972**	983	857
Selling and administrative expenses	5	**-416**	-374	-318
Bad debt expenses		**-63**	-80	-89
Operating income, Customer Finance		**493**	529	450
Operating income		**8,753**	6,859	6,599
Interest income		**632**	679	346
Interest expenses		**-863**	-866	-638
Other financial income		**142**	299	96
Other financial expenses		**-81**	-206	-127
Total financial items	7	**-170**	-94	-323
Income after financial items		**8,583**	6,765	6,276
Taxes	8	**-2,644**	-2,100	-1,960
Net income		**5,939**	4,665	4,316
Attributable to:				
Scania shareholders		**5,939**	4,665	4,314
Minority interest		**0**	0	2

and other assets. Almost all successful firms use a large percentage of the assets they generate by earnings to replace assets and to grow, rather than to pay dividends.

Equality of Assets and Liabilities Plus Shareholders' Equity As the balance sheets for Nordstrom and Scania show, the total of all assets equals the total of all liabilities and all shareholders' equity amounts:

$$\text{Assets} \quad = \text{Liabilities}^{12} + \text{Shareholder's Equity}$$

Nordstrom: $\$4,821,578 = \$2,653,057 + \$2,168,521$

Scania: $\text{SEK}88,078 = \text{SEK}61,944 + \text{SEK}26,134$

A firm invests the resources it obtains from financing. The balance sheet views the same resources from two angles: as the assets the firm currently holds, having acquired them with its funds, and as the claims of creditors and owners who provided the funds. Thus,

---

[12]Neither Nordstrom nor Scania reports a subtotal for liabilities. To obtain total liabilities, sum the liability accounts.

EXHIBIT 1.7

Scania Group
Consolidated Statements of Cash Flows

January – December, SEK m.	Note	**2006**	2005	2004
Operating activities				
Income after financial items	24 a	**8,583**	6,765	6,276
Items not affecting cash flow	24 b	**3,236**	2,953	2,386
Taxes paid		**-2,552**	-2,450	-1,784
Cash flow from operating activities before change in working capital		**9,267**	7,268	6,878
Cash flow from change in working capital				
Inventories		**-627**	284	-959
Receivables		**8**	439	-1,664
Provisions for pensions		**96**	124	250
Trade payables		**1,276**	646	864
Other liabilities and provisions		**1,126**	-731	356
Total change in working capital		**1,879**	762	-1,153
Cash flow from operating activities		**11,146**	8,030	5,725
Investing activities				
Net investments through acquisitions/ divestments of businesses	24 c	**–**	-205	-49
Net investments in non-current assets	24 d	**-3,810**	-3,597	-2,798
Net investments in credit portfolio etc., Customer Finance	24 d	**-3,514**	-1,410	-478
Cash flow from investing activities		**-7,324**	-5,212	-3,325
Cash flow before financing activities		**3,822**	2,818	2,400
Financing activities				
Change in net debt from financing activities	24 e	**7,591**	62	-1,264
Dividend to shareholders		**-3,000**	-3,000	-1,200
Cash flow from financing activities		**4,591**	-2,938	-2,464
Cash flow for the year		**8,413**	-120	-64
Cash and cash equivalents, 1 January		**1,599**	1,589	1,663
Exchange rate differences in cash and cash equivalents		**-78**	130	-10
Cash and cash equivalents, 31 December	24 f	**9,934**	1,599	1,589

$$\text{Assets} = \text{Liabilities} + \text{Shareholder's Equity}$$

or

$$\text{Investing} = \text{Financing}$$

$$\text{Resources} = \text{Sources of Resources}$$

$$\text{Resources} = \text{Claims on Resources}$$

The amounts of individual assets that make up total assets, represented by accounts receivable, inventories, equipment, and other assets, reflect a firm's investment decisions, and the mix of liabilities plus shareholders' equity reflects a firm's financing decisions, each measured at the balance sheet date.

Balance Sheet Classification and Aggregation Both U.S. GAAP and IFRS require that balance sheets separate current items from noncurrent items.[13]

---

[13]Nordstrom displays its current assets and current liabilities first, and Scania displays its noncurrent assets and noncurrent liabilities first. IFRS, but not U.S. GAAP, permits the display used by Scania.

| EXHIBIT 1.8 | Scania Group
Consolidated Total Recognised Income
and Expenses as Well as Changes in Equity | | |

January – December, SEK m.	2006	2005	2004
Exchange rate difference for the year	-661	1,304	-103
Hedge reserve			
Fair value changes on cash flow hedging recognised directly in equity	340	-607	–
Cash flow reserve transferred to sales revenue in income statement	-103	415	–
Actuarial gains/losses related to pension liabilities recognised directly in equity	-68	-770	-72
Taxes attributable to items recognised directly in equity	-46	271	21
Total income and expenses recognised directly in equity	**-538**	613	-154
Net income for the year	5,939	4,665	4,316
Total recognised income and expenses for the year	**5,401**	5,278	4,162
Of which, attributable to:			
Scania AB shareholders	5,402	5,277	4,162
Minority interest	-1	1	0

January – December, SEK m.	2006	2005	2004
Equity, 1 January	**23,736**	21,433	18,471
Change in accounting principles	–	22	–
Adjusted opening balance	**23,736**	21,455	18,471
Total recognised income and expenses for the year	5,401	5,278	4,162
Change in minority share related to Ainax	-3	3	0
Dividend to shareholders	-3,000	-3,000	-1,200
Equity, 31 December	**26,134**	23,736	21,433
Of which, attributable to:			
Scania AB shareholders	26,129	23,727	21,428
Minority interest	5	9	5

- *Current assets* include cash and assets that a firm expects to turn into cash, or sell, or consume within approximately one year from the date of the balance sheet. Examples are accounts receivable and inventory.

- *Current liabilities* represent obligations a firm expects to pay within one year. Examples are accounts payable to suppliers and salaries payable to employees.

- *Noncurrent assets*, typically held and used for several years, include land, buildings, equipment; patents; and long-term investments in securities.

- *Noncurrent liabilities* and *shareholders' equity* are sources of funds where the supplier of funds does not expect to receive them all back within the next year.

The line items on the balance sheet represent *aggregated* amounts. For example, the amount shown for the line item Merchandise Inventories on Nordstrom's balance sheet represents all Nordstrom's inventories, and the amount shown for the line item Land, Buildings, and Equipment, Net, contains the aggregated amounts of these resources.

Balance Sheet Measurement Both U.S. GAAP and IFRS use two conceptual bases to measure the monetary amounts at which assets, liabilities, and shareholders' equity appear on the balance sheet:

1. The **historical amount**, which reflects the acquisition cost of assets or the amount of funds originally obtained from creditors or owners, or

2. The **current amount**, which reflects some measure of current value as of the balance sheet date. The notion of a current amount, or current value, can be applied to assets, to liabilities, or to shareholders' equity.

Some accounting information is reported at *historical cost* and some at *current cost* (or *fair value*), depending on the requirements of U.S. GAAP and IFRS. Later chapters discuss and illustrate both of these measurement bases.

Analysis of the Balance Sheet

Analysis of the Balance Sheet Firms typically finance current assets with current liabilities and finance noncurrent assets with noncurrent liabilities and shareholders' equity. Current assets such as accounts receivable generally convert into cash within one year. Firms can use this near-term cash flow to pay current liabilities, which require payment within one year. Long-term liabilities require payment over some number of future years. Noncurrent assets, such as buildings and equipment, generate cash flows over longer periods. Firms can use these more extended cash inflows to repay noncurrent liabilities as they come due. A recurring theme in analyzing troubled businesses is the problem a business faces when it tries to finance noncurrent assets with current liabilities.

Scania's balance sheet as of December 31, 2006, reveals the following about the current versus noncurrent structure of its resources (assets, in SEK millions) and its financing (liabilities and equity, in SEK millions):

Current Assets	SEK 40,340	Current Liabilities	SEK 34,103
		Noncurrent Liabilities	
Noncurrent Assets	47,738	and Shareholders' Equity	53,975
Total	SEK 88,078	Total	SEK 88,078

Similar information reported in Nordstrom's balance sheet as of February 3, 2007, shows the following (in thousands of $):

Current Assets	$2,742,193	Current Liabilities	$1,433,143
		Noncurrent Liabilities	
Noncurrent Assets	2,079,385	and Shareholders' Equity	3,388,435
Total	$4,821,578	Total	$4,821,578

These data show that both Scania and Nordstrom have raised funds from noncurrent sources in amounts approximately equal to, or slightly greater than, the amount of noncurrent assets.

INCOME STATEMENT

The second principal financial statement, the **income statement** (sometimes called the **statement of profit and loss** by firms applying IFRS), provides information on profitability. The terms **net income**, **earnings**, and **profit** are interchangeable. **Exhibit 1.2** shows Nordstrom's income statement for fiscal years 2004, 2005, and 2006, and **Exhibit 1.6** shows Scania's income statement for the same three fiscal years. Whereas the balance sheet reports amounts at a specific date, the income statement reports amounts for a period of time, the reporting period.[14]

The income statement reports a firm's success in achieving the goal of generating *earnings* (or *profit*, or *net income*) during a given reporting period. Net income is equal to revenues (and gains) minus expenses (and losses). (We ignore gains and losses in this introduction.) The income statement reports the sources and amounts of a firm's revenues and the nature and amounts of its expenses. A firm strives to generate asset inflows from revenues that exceed asset outflows from expenses. Net income indicates a firm's accomplishments (revenues) relative to the efforts required (expenses) in pursuing its operating activities. When expenses for a period exceed revenues, the result is a **net loss**.

---

[14]An income statement can report for a period of any length: a year, a quarter, or a month, for example. In all cases, the reporting period is the amount of time between two successive balance sheets, and the time period over which the firm measures net income.

Revenues (also **sales** or **sales revenue**; or **turnover**, a term used by some firms reporting under IFRS) measure the inflows of assets (or reductions in liabilities) from selling goods and providing services to customers. In exchange for providing goods and services, firms receive assets (either cash or promises to pay cash, Accounts Receivable). A firm cannot generate revenues without simultaneously generating net assets. Nordstrom reports net sales of $8,560,698 thousand in fiscal 2006. Scania reports net sales of vehicles and services in fiscal 2006 of SEK70,738 million.

Expenses measure the outflow of assets (or increases in liabilities) used in generating revenues. *Cost of goods sold* or *cost of sales* (an expense) measures the cost of inventories sold to customers, or, for service firms, the cost of providing those services. S*elling and administrative expenses* measure the cash paid or the liabilities incurred in exchange for selling and administrative services received during the period. An *expense* means that an asset decreases or a liability increases.

Classification of Revenues and Expenses

Firms classify revenues and expenses in different ways and apply different levels of aggregation. For example, Scania reports expenses for research and development of SEK3,023 million in 2006; some firms might include this expense in another income statement line item. Scania's income statement classifies some expenses by the department that carried out the activities (selling expenses and administrative expenses) and some expenses by their nature (interest expense, income taxes).

Relation Between the Income Statement and the Balance Sheet

The income statement links the balance sheet at the beginning of the period with the balance sheet at the end of the period. The balance sheet amount for retained earnings represents the sum of all prior earnings of a firm in excess of dividends.[15] Net income for the current period helps explain the change in retained earnings between the beginning and the end of the period. For example, Nordstrom's income for fiscal 2006 was $677,999 thousand, and it paid cash dividends of $110,158 thousand to shareholders. Retained earnings declined by $621,527 thousand, reflecting cash Nordstrom paid to repurchase its common shares from shareholders. (**Chapter 14** discusses share repurchases). We can use this information, along with the information in **Exhibit 1.4**, to analyze the change in Nordstrom's retained earnings (dollar amounts in thousands):

Retained Earnings, January 28, 2006	$1,404,366
Add Net Income for 2006	677,999
Subtract Dividends Declared and Paid During 2006	(110,158)
Subtract Other Changes Affecting Retained Earnings	(621,527)
Retained Earnings, February 3, 2007	$1,350,680

STATEMENT OF CASH FLOWS

The third principal financial statement, the **statement of cash flows** (also called the **cash flow statement**) reports information about cash generated from (or used by) operating, investing, and financing activities during specified time periods. The statement of cash flows shows where the firm obtains or generates cash and where it spends or uses cash. If a firm is to continue operating successfully, it must generate more cash than it spends. A firm generates cash from operations when it collects more cash from customers than it spends on operating activities. While firms can borrow cash from creditors, future operations must generate cash to repay these loans. Often a growing business cannot collect cash from customers fast enough to pay its own bills even though the customers owe the firm more cash than the firm owes to its suppliers. For example, a firm may agree to pay its suppliers within 20 days, but it has agreed with its customers that they need not pay for 60 days.

Exhibits **1.3** and **1.7** present the statements of cash flows for Nordstrom and Scania, respectively, for the fiscal years 2004, 2005, and 2006. These statements have three sections, describing operating, investing, and financing activities that generate or use cash. This three-way classification captures the categories of business activities described earlier in this chapter.

---

[15]Other items can also affect retained earnings. Later chapters discuss some of these (for example, some share repurchases) and others are beyond the scope of this book.

Operating Activities Most firms expect to collect more cash from customers than they pay to suppliers, employees, and others in carrying out operating activities. For many firms and most successful firms, operating activities provide the largest source of cash. Both Nordstrom and Scania generated significant cash flows from operating activities in all three years presented; for example, Scania's net cash provided by operating activities in 2006 was SEK11,146 million and Nordstrom's was $1,142,365 thousand. Both of these statements begin with net income and make adjustments to convert net income to cash flow from operations; **Chapter 5** discusses these adjustments.

Investing Activities Firms acquire buildings, equipment, and other noncurrent assets to maintain or expand their productive capacity. These acquisitions, sometimes referred to as **capital expenditures**, use cash. A firm can obtain the cash needed for capital expenditures from selling existing assets, from operating activities, and from financing activities. Nordstrom's cash paid for capital expenditures was $264,437 thousand in fiscal 2006. Scania uses the line item "Net investments in non-current assets" to describe its cash outflows for the acquisition of property, plant, and equipment; in 2006 its cash outflow for such investments was SEK3,810 million.

Financing Activities Firms obtain financing to support operating and investing activities by issuing bonds or common shares. The firm uses cash to pay dividends and to retire old financing, such as repaying long-term debt. For example, Nordstrom's statement of cash flows shows that it paid cash to make principal payments on long-term debt equal to $307,559 thousand, it paid $110,158 thousand in cash dividends, and it used $621,527 of cash to repurchase shares of its common stock. In contrast, Scania was a net borrower, as indicated by the SEK7,591 million increase in net debt from financing activities, and it paid cash dividends of SEK3,000 million.

Relation of the Statement of Cash Flows to the Balance Sheet and Income Statement The statement of cash flows explains the change in cash between the beginning and the end of the period, and separately displays the changes in cash from operating, investing, and financing activities. The panel of data below analyzes the changes in cash for Nordstrom (for the year ending February 3, 2007) and for Scania (for the year ending December 31, 2006).[16] Results for Nordstrom are in thousands of U.S. dollars and for Scania in millions of Swedish kronor (SEK millions).

Changes in Cash for Nordstrom and Scania During Fiscal 2006

	Nordstrom	Scania
Cash at the Start of Fiscal 2006	$ 462,656	SEK 1,599
Cash Flow from Operations During 2006	1,142,365	11,146
Cash Flow from Investing During 2006	(218,280)	(7,324)
Cash Flow from Financing During 2006	(984,182)	4,591
Adjustment for Exchange Rate Differences	—	(78)
Cash at the End of Fiscal 2006	$ 402,559	SEK 9,934

In addition to sources and uses of cash, the statement of cash flows shows the relation between net income and cash flow from operations. Cash flow from operations exceeds net income for each of the three years shown for both Nordstrom and Scania. **Chapter 5** discusses the reasons for this excess.

STATEMENT OF SHAREHOLDERS' EQUITY

The fourth principal financial statement presents changes in shareholders' equity. Firms use various titles for this statement; for example, Nordstrom's statement, in **Exhibit 1.4**, is called

---

[16]Scania operates in approximately 100 countries, implying that its activities involve many different currencies. Scania reports the effects of exchange rate changes on cash flows, measured in millions of SEK, as (78) and includes that amount in this table. (The parentheses around the number indicated it is subtracted in the calculation.) This book does not consider the accounting effects of different currencies or of changes in exchange rates among currencies.

the **statement of shareholders' equity**, while Scania's statement, in **Exhibit 1.8**, is called Consolidated Total Recognised Income and Expenses as Well as Changes in Equity. This statement displays components of shareholders' equity, including common shares and retained earnings, and changes in those components. For example, Nordstrom's retained earnings changed between January 28, 2006, and February 3, 2007, because Nordstrom earned net income (an increase of $677,999 thousand), because it paid cash dividends (a decrease of $110,158 thousand), and because it repurchased shares (a decrease of $621,527). Both Nordstrom and Scania also present other changes in shareholders' equity that later chapters discuss.

SUPPORTING SCHEDULES AND NOTES

The financial statements present aggregated information, for example, the total amount of land, buildings, and equipment. Financial reports provide more detail for some of the items reported in the financial statements, and they provide additional explanatory material to help the user to understand the information in the financial statements. This information appears in **schedules** and **notes** that are an integral part of the financial reports.

A firm applies authoritative accounting guidance to prepare its financial reports. This book considers two accounting systems, U.S. GAAP and IFRS, both of which provide authoritative guidance. The notes to a firm's financial statements describe the accounting guidance, including specific methods and policies that the firm uses to prepare those financial statements. The notes also provide information that elaborates on, or disaggregates, items presented in the financial statements. Understanding a firm's balance sheet, income statement, statement of cash flows, and statement of changes in shareholders' equity requires understanding the notes. For example, Nordstrom uses a note to explain that its annual reporting period (fiscal year) ends on the Saturday closest to January 31. As **Exhibit 1.9** illustrates, Scania uses a schedule in its Note 4 to report disaggregated data on the net vehicle and service sales of SEK70,738 reported on its income statement. This note shows that sales of trucks and sales of service-related products are the largest components of Scania's total sales.

SUMMARY: PRINCIPAL FINANCIAL STATEMENTS

The financial statements provide information about a firm's financial position (balance sheet), its profitability (income statement), its cash-generating activity (statement of cash flows), and its changes in shareholders' equity. The balance sheet reports the results of investing and financing activities as at the balance sheet date. The income statement reports the outcome of using assets to generate earnings during a reporting period (for example, a year) and helps explain the change in retained earnings on the balance sheet between the beginning and end of the period. The statement of cash flows reports the cash inflows and outflows from operating, investing, and financing activities for the same period and explains the change in cash

EXHIBIT 1.9   Scania Group
Note 4 to the Financial Statements

NOTE 4 Net sales			
Vehicles and Service	2006	2005	2004
Trucks	43,021	37,778	33,407
Buses	6,766	6,256	5,504
Engines	1,024	803	658
Service related producs	13,595	12,591	11,418
Used vehicles	5,189	4,897	4,470
Other products	3,032	2,773	2,322
Total delivery value	72,627	65,098	57,779
Adjustment for lease income [1]	-1,889	-1,770	-991
Net sales	70,738	63,328	56,788

on the balance sheet between the beginning and end of the period. The statement of changes in shareholders' equity reports the reasons why the components of shareholders' equity increased or decreased during the reporting period. Users should read all of the financial statements in conjunction with the supporting notes and schedules, which provide explanations and disaggregations of the reported numbers.

PROBLEM 1.1 for Self-Study

Preparing a balance sheet and an income statement. The following information is based on the annual report of Siemens AG, a German multinational, for the fiscal years ending September 30, 2007, and September 30, 2006. Amounts are reported in millions of euros (€).

	September 30	
	2007	**2006**
Balance Sheet Items		
Accounts Payable	€ 8,382	€ 8,443
Property and Equipment (net of accumulated depreciation)	10,555	12,072
Cash and Cash Equivalents	4,005	10,214
Common Stock	8,823	8,335
Intangible Assets	17,120	13,074
Other Noncurrent Assets	3,371	4,370
Long-Term Investment Securities	12,577	7,998
Inventories	12,930	12,790
Long-Term Debt	9,860	13,122
Other Noncurrent Liabilities	8,174	9,547
Other Shareholders' Equity Items	351	858
Accounts Receivable	14,620	15,148
Other Current Assets	16,377	11,862
Other Current Liabilities	33,098	28,939
Retained Earnings	20,453	16,702
Current Income Taxes Payable	2,414	1,582
Income Statement Items		
Cost of Sales	51,572	
Income Tax Expense	1,192	
Other (Nonoperating) Expense	144	
Sales	72,448	
Research & Development Expenses	3,399	
Selling, General, and Administrative Expenses	12,103	

a. Prepare a comparative balance sheet for Siemens as of September 30, 2007 (fiscal 2007), and September 30, 2006 (fiscal 2006) in the format used in **Exhibit 1.1**. Classify the balance sheet items into the following categories: current assets, noncurrent assets, current liabilities, noncurrent liabilities, and shareholders' equity. Refer to the **Glossary** at the back of the book if you have difficulty with any of the accounts. For each year, verify that assets equal liabilities plus shareholders' equity on your balance sheet.

b. Prepare an income statement for Siemens for the year ending September 30, 2007. Classify income statement items into revenues and expenses.

c. Based only on the information given here, did Siemens pay cash dividends to its shareholders during the year ending September 30, 2007? If yes, what is the amount?

Solutions to self-study problems appear at the end of each chapter.

FINANCIAL REPORTING PROCESS

The **financial reporting process** involves four principal types of participants:

1. Managers and governing boards of reporting entities.
2. Accounting standard setters and regulatory bodies.
3. Independent external auditors.
4. Users of financial statements.

This section discusses the role of each of these participants. In addition, this section discusses three concepts and conventions that underpin the financial reporting process:

1. The distinction between recognition and realization.
2. Materiality.
3. The accounting period convention.

MANAGERS AND GOVERNING BOARDS OF REPORTING ENTITIES

Firms receive funds from owners with the expectation that managers will use the funds to increase the market value of the firm. From a legal perspective, **managers** are agents of the shareholders and have responsibility for safeguarding and properly using the firm's resources. Managers establish internal control procedures to ensure the proper recording of transactions and the appropriate measurement and reporting of the results of those transactions. Shareholders elect a **governing board**, sometimes called a *board of directors*, which is responsible for selecting, compensating, and overseeing managers; for setting the firm's dividend policy; and for making decisions on major issues such as acquisitions of other firms and divestitures of lines of business. Some governing boards, including all boards of publicly traded U.S. firms, have a special committee charged with oversight of financial reporting.

Under the oversight of governing boards, managers have responsibility for preparing the firm's financial reports. If the firm's shares trade publicly, laws and regulations may specify the accounting system the firm must follow (for example, U.S. GAAP or IFRS). Management has responsibility for understanding the transactions, events, and arrangements that it reports in the firm's financial statements and for properly applying accounting requirements.

ACCOUNTING STANDARD SETTERS AND REGULATORY BODIES

Firms apply accounting standards (or rules) to prepare their financial reports. The two systems of accounting standards considered in this book are U.S. GAAP and IFRS. This section discusses these two sets of standards and the related regulatory regimes.

U.S. GAAP In the United States the **Securities and Exchange Commission (SEC)**, an agency of the federal government, has the legal authority to set acceptable accounting methods, or standards. The SEC is also the enforcement agency for U.S. securities laws that apply to firms that access the public debt and equity markets of the United States. For example, the SEC enforces the proper application of required accounting standards for **U.S. SEC registrants** as well as **non-U.S. SEC registrants** (also called **foreign private issuers**). A U.S. SEC registrant is a firm incorporated in the United States that lists and trades its securities in the United States; a non-U.S. SEC registrant is a firm incorporated under non-U.S. laws that has filed the necessary documents with the SEC to list and trade its securities in the United States.

Although it occasionally issues accounting guidance, the SEC has largely delegated the task of setting U.S. financial accounting standards to the **Financial Accounting Standards Board (FASB)**, a private-sector body comprising five voting members. FASB Board members work full time for the FASB and sever all relations with their previous employers. As the FASB contemplates a reporting issue, its due-process procedures ensure that it receives input from all interested constituencies, including preparers, auditors, and financial statement users.

Common terminology includes the pronouncements of the FASB (and its predecessors) in the compilation of accounting rules, procedures, and practices known as **generally accepted accounting principles (GAAP)**. The applicable accounting guidance for preparing financial reports of U.S. firms is U.S. GAAP (a singular noun). The applicable guidance includes, as well, writings of the SEC, consensuses of the Emerging Issues Task Force (a committee that operates under the oversight of the FASB), and some pronouncements of the American Institute of Certified Public Accountants (AICPA), a professional association. The FASB issues its major pronouncements in the form of *Statements of Financial Accounting Standards* (SFAS) that are available on the FASB's Web site (*www.fasb.org*). These standards have both a number (for example, *SFAS 95*) and a title (for example, "Statement of Cash Flows").

As this book goes to press, the FASB is in the midst of a **codification project** that will organize all of U.S. GAAP by topic (for example, revenues), eliminate duplications, and correct inconsistencies. The FASB intends this project to change how U.S. GAAP is organized and accessed by those who wish to read and apply. The project will not change the actual content of the guidance. This textbook uses both the current style of reference (by SFAS number and title) and the codification reference in parentheses. You can access the test version of codified U.S. GAAP on the FASB's Web site.

FASB board members make standard-setting decisions guided by a **conceptual framework** that addresses the following issues:[17]

1. **Objectives of financial reporting.** The conceptual framework establishes the objective of providing information to current and potential investors, creditors, and others to assist them in making resource allocation decisions.[18]

2. **Qualitative characteristics of accounting information.** The conceptual framework establishes the features of financial information that enable the information to meet the objectives of financial reporting. For example, the information should possess the following qualitative characteristics:

   ■ **Relevance.** The information should be pertinent to the decisions made by users of financial statements, in the sense of having the capacity to affect their resource allocation decisions.

   ■ **Reliability.** The information should represent what it is supposed to represent, in the sense that the information should correspond to the phenomenon being reported, and it should be verifiable and free from bias.

   ■ **Comparability.** The information should facilitate comparisons across firms and over time. Accounting information is comparable if firms account for similar events and transactions the same way.

3. **Elements of financial statements.** The conceptual framework defines assets, liabilities, revenues, expenses, and other items that the financial statements contain. An item can appear in the financial statements only if it meets these definitions. Items that do not meet these definitions might be disclosed in the notes, which follow immediately after the four principal financial statements.

4. **Recognition and measurement principles.** The conceptual framework defines **recognition** as depiction in words and numbers in the financial statements with the amount included in the totals. Other items in financial reports, such as the notes and schedules, are **disclosures**, not recognized items. The conceptual framework specifies criteria that an item must meet in order for it to be recognized as a financial statement element. The framework also describes various ways to measure recognized items.

The conceptual framework guides the FASB in setting accounting standards. However, the conceptual framework is not a rigorous, analytical structure from which the FASB can logically deduce acceptable accounting methods. **Chapter 16** discusses the FASB's conceptual framework more fully.

---

[17]The FASB reports the components of its conceptual framework in *Statements of Financial Accounting Concepts*. These are available on the FASB's Web site.

[18]We distinguish this objective from some other possible objectives, such as calculating income for the purpose of imposing an income tax. With the exception of one method of accounting for inventories and cost of goods sold, the accounting methods permitted or required by U.S. GAAP differ from the methods required for calculating taxable income in the United States. With the exception of inventories, you should assume that there will be significant differences between tax accounting methods and financial accounting methods. See **LIFO conformity rule** in the **Glossary**.

Concerns over the quality of financial reporting have led, and continue to lead, to government initiatives in the United States. For example, the **Sarbanes-Oxley Act** of 2002, among other things, established the **Public Company Accounting Oversight Board (PCAOB)**, which is responsible for monitoring the quality of audits of SEC registrants. This Act requires the PCAOB to register firms conducting independent audits of SEC registrants; establish or adopt acceptable auditing, quality control, and independence standards; and provide for periodic inspections of the registered auditors.

International Financial Reporting Standards (IFRS)

At one time, accounting was a largely jurisdiction-specific activity, in that each country with a developed capital market had accounting requirements different from others'. The result was that firms in the same industry but based in different countries reported different amounts in financial statements, impeding comparisons of firms by investors and creditors. The globalization of capital markets has increased the need for comparable and understandable financial statements across countries.

The **International Accounting Standards Board (IASB)** is an independent accounting standard-setting entity with 14 voting members from a number of countries. Standards set by the IASB are **International Financial Reporting Standards (IFRS)**. The IASB also has a conceptual framework that is similar to the FASB's conceptual framework and that is used for similar purposes. The IASB began operating in 2001; the standards set by its predecessor body, the International Accounting Standards Committee (IASC) are called *International Accounting Standards (IAS)*, and IFRS includes them. Over 100 countries require or permit firms incorporated under the laws of those countries to use IFRS, or standards based on IFRS, to prepare their financial reports or have announced plans to do so. Each of these countries has its own regulatory arrangements for enforcing the proper application of IFRS in that jurisdiction; these arrangements differ considerably across countries. As a result, different firms subject to IFRS do not necessarily account for the same transaction using the same set of rules.

In 2007 the U.S. SEC adopted new rules that permit non-U.S. firms that list and trade their securities in the United States (non-U.S. SEC registrants) to apply IFRS in their financial reports filed with the SEC without any reconciliation to U.S. GAAP. Prior to this rule change, non-U.S. SEC registrants could apply any financial reporting system to prepare their financial reports, but they had to reconcile those reported numbers to the numbers that they would have reported had they prepared the financial statements using U.S. GAAP.[19] The main effect of this 2007 rule change is to create *two* sets of acceptable financial reporting systems in the United States, specifically, U.S. GAAP for U.S. SEC registrants and IFRS for non-U.S. SEC registrants.[20]

In 2008 the SEC issued a proposed rule that would allow certain large, multinational U.S. firms that meet certain qualifying criteria to select between U.S. GAAP and IFRS for preparing their financial reports filed with the SEC, starting in 2009.[21] A second proposal would require U.S. SEC registrants to report using IFRS, on a staggered basis, beginning in 2014, provided that certain conditions have been met by 2011. As this book goes to press, the proposed rule is open to comment.

The FASB and IASB have committed to work toward converging their standards, based on an agreement reached in 2002 and updated since then. The boards intend the **convergence** process to eliminate differences between U.S. GAAP and IFRS and to improve the resulting standards. The boards intend to arrive at a single set of high-quality financial reporting standards for use in all countries. In addition, the boards have undertaken a separate project to converge, complete, and improve their conceptual frameworks. Specific information about convergence activities appears on the FASB's Web site (*www.fasb.org*) and on the IASB's Web site (*www.iasb.org.uk*). **Chapter 16** summarizes some of the important differences between U.S. GAAP and IFRS.

---

[19]SEC Form 20-F was the required filing for the reconciliation.

[20]Non-U.S. SEC registrants could also choose to apply U.S. GAAP or apply some other accounting standards and reconcile the resulting numbers to U.S. GAAP.

[21]One estimate is that approximately 110 large U.S. SEC registrants would be eligible for the 2010 voluntary choice to report using IFRS.

INDEPENDENT AUDITORS

Regulatory bodies generally require firms whose securities trade publicly (for example, common shares) to obtain an audit of their financial reports by an independent external auditor.[22] Even if the securities do not trade publicly, financing sources such as banks may require that the firm obtain an independent audit of its financial statements.

An audit involves:

1. An assessment of the capability of a firm's accounting system to accumulate, measure, and synthesize transactional data properly.

2. An assessment of the operational effectiveness of this accounting system.

3. A determination of whether the financial report complies with the requirements of the applicable authoritative guidance.

The auditor obtains evidence for the first assessment by studying the procedures and internal controls built into the accounting system. The auditor obtains evidence for the second assessment by examining a sample of actual transactions. The auditor obtains evidence for the third determination through a combination of audit procedures. The auditor's conclusions appear in the **audit opinion**, part of the financial report. In addition, for most firms whose shares trade in the United States, the Sarbanes-Oxley Act requires that the audit involve an assessment, by the independent auditor, of the effectiveness of a firm's internal control system for financial reporting. The auditor provides a separate report on internal control effectiveness.

USERS OF FINANCIAL STATEMENTS

Standard setters and securities regulators intend that financial reports provide information to investors, creditors, and others that helps decision makers allocate resources and evaluate the results of their decisions. Financial reporting does not intend to measure firm value or to provide *all* the information that decision makers might need to make resource allocation decisions. As later chapters discuss, financial reporting, under either U.S. GAAP or IFRS, intends to provide information that is useful in helping decision makers assess the amount, timing, and uncertainty of future cash flows of firms.

In order to make sense of financial reports, users of financial statements must have a reasonable knowledge of firms' businesses and of the kinds of events, transactions, and arrangements that firms engage in. They must also have a reasonable knowledge of the financial accounting principles and procedures that firms follow to prepare financial reports, and a reasonable understanding of the judgments and estimates required by those principles.

BASIC ACCOUNTING CONVENTIONS AND CONCEPTS

Recognition and **realization** are two fundamental accounting concepts. Recognized items are depicted in words and numbers on the face of the financial statements, with amounts included in the totals. As discussed later in this chapter and elsewhere in this book, items must meet certain conditions (recognition criteria) in order for the financial statements to include them. Realization refers to converting a noncash item to cash, for example, collecting an account receivable. Accounting conventions recognize many accounting items (that is, include them in the financial statements) before the firm realizes them (that is, converts them to cash). To illustrate, suppose a firm ships an item for $1,000 on account, payable in 30 days, to a creditworthy customer. The firm *recognizes* revenue when it ships the goods but *realizes* revenue when it collects the cash.

Materiality captures the qualitative notion that financial reports need not include items that are so small as to be meaningless to users of the reports. No precise quantitative materiality threshold exists, so preparers and auditors must apply judgment to decide whether a

---

[22]Employees of a firm might also conduct audits (called *internal audits*). The employees' knowledge and familiarity with the activities of their firm probably enhance the quality of the audit work and increase the likelihood that the audit will generate suggestions for improving operations.

given item would be immaterial, meaning not relevant to a user of the financial reports, and therefore need not appear in the financial reports.

The **accounting period convention** refers to the uniform length of accounting reporting periods. Most business activities do not divide into distinguishable projects. For example, a firm acquires a plant and uses it in manufacturing products for a period of 20 years or more. A firm purchases delivery equipment and uses it to transport merchandise to customers for four or more years. There is no natural stopping point in business activities, so financial statements are, by convention, prepared for periods of uniform length. This approach facilitates timely comparisons and analyses among firms.

An accounting period (also called a **reporting period**) is the time between two successive balance sheet dates. Balance sheets prepared at the end of the day on December 31 of one year and at the end of the day on December 31 of the next year bound a calendar-year accounting period; the December 31 balance sheet is also the beginning balance sheet for the next year. Balance sheets prepared at the end of the day on November 30 and at the end of the day on December 31 bound a one-month accounting period—the month of December.

Although many firms use the calendar year as the accounting period, some use a **natural business year** that coincides with changes in the level of operating activities, for example, when inventories are at their lowest level during the year. The ending date of a natural business year is therefore associated with the activities of the particular firm's business. Many retailers, including Nordstrom, use a year ending close to the end of January, the natural end of the holiday sales season. Winnebago Industries, a U.S. manufacturer of recreational vehicles, uses a year ending in late August, the end of its model year.

Firms may prepare *interim reports* for periods shorter than a year. Preparing interim reports does not eliminate the need to prepare an annual report. Firms with publicly traded securities in the United States must prepare and file (with the Securities and Exchange Commission) quarterly reports as well as annual reports. Firms file quarterly reports on SEC form 10-Q (the 10-Q report) and file annual reports using SEC form 10-K (the 10-K report). Some firms use the 10-K report as their annual report to shareholders; some incorporate the 10-K report into their annual report; and some prepare a separate annual report to shareholders in addition to the 10-K report.

ACCOUNTING METHODS FOR MEASURING PERFORMANCE

Many operating activities start in one accounting period and finish in another. For example, a firm may acquire a building in one period and use it for 30 years; that operating process extends over 30 years. Firms may purchase merchandise in one accounting period, pay for it in a second, sell it during a third, and collect cash from customers in a fourth. Cash collection can precede the sale of merchandise, as occurs when customers make advance payments, or follow it, as occurs with sales on account. To measure performance for a specific accounting period requires measuring the amount of revenues and expenses from operating activities that span more than that one accounting period (the activities have begun but are not yet complete at the end of the period). Two approaches to measuring operating performance are

1. The cash basis of accounting.
2. The accrual basis of accounting.

CASH BASIS OF ACCOUNTING

Under the **cash basis of accounting**, a firm measures performance from selling goods and providing services as it receives cash from customers and makes cash expenditures to providers of goods and services. The performance measurement does not include cash receipts from financing activities. To understand the measurement of performance under the cash basis of accounting, consider the following information.

Example 3 Joan Adam opens an art supply store (Adam-Art Supply) on January 1, 2008. The financing of the store consists of €150,000 in cash, provided by Joan Adam in exchange for all of the common stock of the firm. The firm rents space on January 1 and pays two months' rent of €14,000 in advance. During January it acquires merchandise costing €140,000, of which it purchases €86,000 for cash and €54,000 on account for payment in February. Sales to customers during January total €140,000, of which €114,000 is for cash and €26,000 is on account for collection in February and March. The cost of the merchandise sold during January was €42,000. The firm paid €25,000 in salaries.

Using the cash basis of accounting, the firm records sales as it receives cash. Income is cash receipts less cash disbursements for goods and services. Although Adam-Art Supply made €140,000 in sales during January, it records performance equal to cash receipts of €114,000. It will record the remaining €26,000 as performance when customers pay the amounts owed. The firm acquires merchandise costing €140,000 during January but pays only €86,000 cash to suppliers. Under cash-basis accounting, the performance measure subtracts only the cash paid from cash receipts. The firm also subtracts the cash expenditures made during January for salaries (€25,000) and rent (€14,000), even though it paid the rent for both January and February. Cash expenditures for merchandise and services (a total of €125,000 = €86,000 + €25,000 + €14,000) exceeded cash receipts from customers (a total of €114,000) during January by €11,000:

Cash Inflows

Cash Receipts from Customers	€ 114,000
Total Cash Inflows	€ 114,000

Cash Outflows

Cash Paid for Rent	(14,000)
Cash Paid for Merchandise	(86,000)
Cash Paid for Salaries	(25,000)
Total Cash Outflows	€(125,000)
Net Cash Flow	€ (11,000)

As a basis for measuring performance for a particular accounting period, the cash basis of accounting has three weaknesses.

First, the cash basis does not adequately match the cost of the efforts required to generate inflows with the inflows themselves. Cash outflows of one period can relate to operating activities whose cash inflows occur in preceding or succeeding periods. The store rental payment of €14,000 provides rental services for both January and February; the cash basis subtracts the full amount in measuring performance during January and none for February. As a result, February's performance will look better than January's for no reason other than the early timing of cash payments for rent.

For performance measurement over long intervals, the cash basis will do a better job of matching the cost of the efforts required in generating inflows with the inflows themselves than it does for a shorter period. For example, if Adam-Art Supply calculates cash-basis performance over *two* months, January and February, the €14,000 cost of rental services exactly matches the period over which the firm receives the benefits. However, delaying performance measurement is not a good solution because users of financial statements want timely information and because of the reasons given in the description of the accounting period convention—business activities do not divide neatly into discrete projects and discrete periods.

Second, the cash basis of accounting separates the recognition of revenue from the process of earning those revenues. A firm should recognize revenue when it has earned those revenues by delivering goods and services to customers, which often occurs before it collects cash from those customers. In these cases, recognizing revenues when the firm collects cash often results in reporting the effects of operating activities one or more periods after the critical revenue-generating activity—the customer's purchase of goods and service—has occurred. For example, sales to customers during January by Adam-Art Supply were €140,000. Under the cash basis of accounting, the firm will not recognize €26,000 of this amount until it collects the cash during February or later. If the firm checks the creditworthiness of customers before making the sales on account, it will probably collect the cash when it is due, or at least a predictable fraction of the cash, and therefore need not postpone recognition of the revenue until the time it actually collects the cash.

Third, performance measured using the cash basis is sensitive to the timing of cash expenditures. For example, the cash-basis measure reduces the performance for Adam-Art Supply in January by the entire €14,000 cash payment for rent, even though the firm will benefit from the results of those expenditures by consuming those rental services for two months. A delay of even a few days in cash expenditures near the end of the accounting period will increase earnings for that period, while decreasing earnings in one or more subsequent periods.

Most individuals use the cash basis of accounting for computing personal income and personal income taxes. So do firms with no medium-term assets (such as inventories, which have a several-month shelf life) and with no long-term assets (such as property, plant, and equipment). Lawyers, accountants, and other professionals, who have few or no investments in inventories and multi-period assets, and who collect cash from clients soon after they render services, frequently use the cash basis. Even these service firms use a modified cash basis of accounting, under which they treat the costs of buildings, equipment, and similar items as assets when purchased, and recognize a portion of the acquisition cost as an expense when they consume services of these assets. Except for the treatment of these long-lived assets, such firms measure and record business activity at the times they receive and disburse cash.

ACCRUAL BASIS OF ACCOUNTING

The **accrual basis of accounting** typically recognizes revenue when a firm sells goods (manufacturing and retailing firms) or renders services (service firms), and recognizes expenses in the period when the firm recognizes the revenues that the costs helped produce. Thus accrual accounting attempts to match expenses with associated revenues. When the usage of an asset's future benefits does not match with particular revenues, the firm recognizes those costs as expenses of the period during which the firm uses the benefits provided by the assets.

Example 4 Under the accrual basis of accounting Adam-Art Supply recognizes, for January 2008, the entire €140,000 of sales during January as revenue, even though it has received only €114,000 in cash by the end of January. The firm reasonably expects to collect the remaining accounts receivable of €26,000 in February or soon thereafter. The sale of the goods, rather than the collection of cash from customers, triggers the recognition of revenue. The merchandise sold during January cost €42,000. Recognizing this amount as an expense (cost of goods sold) matches the cost of the merchandise sold with revenue from sales of those goods. Of the advance rental payment of €14,000, only €7,000 applies to the cost of benefits consumed during January. The remaining rental of €7,000 purchases benefits for the month of February and will therefore appear on the balance sheet on January 31 as an asset. The salaries and rent expenses, unlike the cost of merchandise sold, do not directly match sales revenues recognized during the period. These costs therefore become expenses of January to the extent that the firm consumed the services during the month. Using the accrual basis of accounting, Adam-Art would report net income of €66,000 for the month of January:

Sales Revenue	€140,000
Cost of Goods Sold	(42,000)
Rent Expense	(7,000)
Salaries Expense	(25,000)
Net Income	€ 66,000

The accrual basis of accounting illustrates the **matching convention**: it matches expenses with their related revenues by subtracting their amount in measuring performance. Accrual accounting and matching separate performance measurement from cash receipts and disbursements. The accrual basis focuses on inflows of net assets from operations (revenues) and the use of net assets in operations (expenses), independent of whether the firm has collected cash for those inflows and spent cash for the outflows of net assets.

The accrual basis of accounting provides a better measure of operating performance for Adam-Art Supply for the month of January than does the cash basis, because revenues more accurately reflect the results of sales activity during January than does cash received from customers during that period, and expenses more closely match reported revenues than expenditures match receipts. Likewise, the accrual basis provides a superior measure of performance for future periods because activities of those periods will bear their share of the costs of rental services and other services the firm will consume.

Most firms, particularly those involved in merchandising and manufacturing activities, use the accrual basis of accounting. From this point on in the book, all discussions assume use of the accrual basis of accounting. We introduced the cash basis of accounting to demonstrate its deficiencies and the related rationale for the accrual basis.

PROBLEM **1.2** for Self-Study

Cash versus accrual basis of accounting. Thompson Hardware Store commences operations on January 1, 2008, when Jacob Thompson invests $30,000 for all of the common stock of the firm. The firm rents a building on January 1 and pays two months' rent in advance in the amount of $2,000. On January 1 it also pays the $1,200 premium for property and liability insurance coverage for the year ending December 31, 2008. The firm purchases $28,000 of merchandise inventory on account on January 2 and pays $10,000 of this amount on January 25. On January 31 the cost of unsold merchandise is $15,000. During January the firm makes cash sales to customers totaling $20,000 and sales on account totaling $9,000. The firm collects $2,000 from these credit sales by the end of January. The firm pays other costs during January as follows: utilities, $400; salaries, $650; and taxes, $350. What are Thompson Hardware Store's revenues, expenses, and income for January, assuming (1) the accrual basis of accounting, and (2) the cash basis of accounting?

SUMMARY

This chapter shows how business activities relate to the principal financial statements included in financial reports to shareholders. The chapter raises questions that it does not fully answer. It provides you with a broad overview of the four basic financial statements before you examine the concepts and procedures underlying each statement in later chapters. The Web site for this book contains additional information on particular topics not covered fully in this book (go to: *www.cengage.com/accounting/stickney*).

This chapter also describes the financial reporting process and introduces the two accounting systems addressed in this book: U.S. GAAP and IFRS. Now we turn to the study of financial accounting. To comprehend the concepts and procedures in the book, you should study the numerical examples presented in each chapter and prepare solutions to several problems, including the self-study problems. You may find the **Glossary** of terms at the back of the book useful.

SOLUTIONS TO SELF-STUDY PROBLEMS

SUGGESTED SOLUTION TO PROBLEM 1.1 FOR SELF-STUDY

(Siemens AG: preparing a balance sheet and an income statement)

a. Balance sheet for years ended September 30, 2007, and September 30, 2006.

	September 30	
	2007	2006
Assets		
Cash and Cash Equivalents	€ 4,005	€10,214
Accounts Receivable	14,620	15,148
Inventories	12,930	12,790
Other Current Assets	16,377	11,862
Total Current Assets	€47,932	€50,014
Property and Equipment (net of accumulated depreciation)	€10,555	€12,072
Intangible Assets	17,120	13,074
Long-Term Investment Securities	12,577	7,998
Other Noncurrent Assets	3,371	4,370
Total Noncurrent Assets	€43,623	€37,514
Total Assets	€91,555	€87,528

(continued)

	September 30	
	2007	2006
Liabilities and Shareholders' Equity		
Accounts Payable	€ 8,382	€ 8,443
Current Income Taxes Payable	2,414	1,582
Other Current Liabilities	33,098	28,939
Total Current Liabilities	€43,894	€38,964
Long-Term Debt	€ 9,860	€13,122
Other Noncurrent Liabilities	8,174	9,547
Total Noncurrent Liabilities	€18,034	€22,669
Total Liabilities	€61,928	€61,633
Common Stock	€ 8,823	€ 8,335
Retained Earnings	20,453	16,702
Other Shareholders' Equity Items.	351	858
Total Shareholders' Equity	€29,627	€25,895
Total Liabilities and Shareholders' Equity	€91,555	€87,528

Assets = Liabilities + Shareholders' Equity

Fiscal 2007: €91,555 million = €61,928 million + €29,627 million

Fiscal 2006: €87,528 million = €61,633 million + €25,895 million

b. Income statement for year ended September 30, 2007:

Sales	€ 72,448
Cost of Sales	(51,572)
Research & Development Expenses	(3,399)
Selling, General, and Administrative Expenses	(12,103)
Operating Profit	€ 5,374
Other (Nonoperating) Expense	(144)
Earnings Before Income Taxes	€ 5,230
Income Tax Expense	(1,192)
Net Income	€ 4,038

c. Yes. The change in Retained Earnings is €3,751 million, and Net Income is €4,038 million. Based on this information only, Siemens must have paid dividends of €287 million (= €4,038 − €3,751).

SUGGESTED SOLUTION TO PROBLEM 1.2 FOR SELF-STUDY

(Thompson Hardware Store: cash versus accrual basis of accounting)
Calculation of revenues, expenses, and income for January 2008 under the cash and accrual basis of accounting:

	Cash Basis	Accrual Basis
Revenues	$22,000	$29,000
Expenses:		
Rent	$ 2,000	$ 1,000
Insurance	1,200	100
Costs of Inventory	10,000	13,000
Utilities	400	400
Salaries	650	650
Taxes	350	350
Total Expenses	$14,600	$15,500
Net Income	$ 7,400	$13,500

Cash basis accounting defines revenues as cash receipts from customers for goods and services. Accrual accounting defines revenues to include net assets (cash or promises to pay cash) from customers in exchange for goods and services. Similar distinctions apply to expenses.

KEY TERMS AND CONCEPTS

Goals contrasted with strategies
Financing
Shareholders, stockholders
Publicly traded
Dividends
Creditors
Investing activities
Operating activities
Annual report to shareholders
Management's Discussion and Analysis (MD&A)
Fiscal year
Monetary amount
Balance sheet or statement of financial position
Assets
Liabilities
Shareholders' equity
Retained earnings
Historical amount
Current amount
Income statement or statement of profit and loss
Net income, earnings, profit
Net loss
Revenues, sales, sales revenue, turnover
Expenses
Statement of cash flows or cash flow statement
Capital expenditures
Statement of shareholders' equity
Schedules and notes
Financial reporting process
Managers
Governing board

Securities and Exchange Commission (SEC)
U.S. SEC registrant
Non-U.S. SEC registrant, foreign private issuer
Financial Accounting Standards Board (FASB)
U.S. GAAP (generally accepted accounting principles)
Statements of Financial Accounting Standards
Codification project
Conceptual framework
Relevance
Reliability
Comparability
Recognition
Disclosure
Sarbanes-Oxley Act
Public Company Accounting Oversight Board (PCAOB)
International Accounting Standards Board (IASB)
International Financial Reporting Standards (IFRS)
Convergence
Audit opinion
Realization
Materiality
Accounting period convention, reporting period
Natural business year
Cash basis of accounting
Accrual basis of accounting
Matching convention

QUESTIONS, EXERCISES, AND PROBLEMS

QUESTIONS

1. Review the meaning of the terms and concepts listed in Key Terms and Concepts.

2. The chapter describes four activities common to all entities: setting goals and strategies, financing activities, investing activities, and operating activities. How would these four activities likely differ for a charitable organization versus a business firm?

3. "The photographic analogy for a balance sheet is a snapshot, and for the income statement and the statement of cash flows it is a motion picture." Explain.

4. What is involved in an audit by an independent external auditor?

5. Who prepares a firm's financial statements?

6. In what sense can suppliers of raw materials, merchandise, or labor services (employees) also be sources of financing for firms?

7. In what sense are a firm's accounts receivable a source of financing for that firm's customers?

8. Investing activities pertain to the acquisition of productive capacity to enable the firm to carry out its activities. Examples of this capacity include (1) land, buildings, and equipment, and (2) patents and licenses. How are these two kinds of capacity the same, and how are they different?

9. When will a firm's fiscal year differ from a calendar year?

10. Financial statements include amounts in units of currency. What is the most common determinant of the firm's choice of currency for financial reporting?

11. Assets and liabilities appear on balance sheets as either current or noncurrent. What is the difference between a current item and a noncurrent item? Why would users of financial statements likely be interested in this distinction?

12. The measurement basis for reporting items on a firm's balance sheet can be either historical amounts or current amounts. What is the difference between these two measurement bases?

13. How does an income statement connect two successive balance sheets? How does a statement of cash flows connect two successive balance sheets?

14. What is the role of the following participants in the financial reporting process: the U.S. Securities and Exchange Commission (SEC); the Financial Accounting Standards Board (FASB); the International Accounting Standards Board (IASB)?

15. This chapter introduces both U.S. GAAP and International Financial Reporting Standards (IFRS). Which of these systems may U.S. firms use, and which may non-U.S. firms that list and trade their securities in the United States use?

16. What is the purpose of the conceptual frameworks developed by the Financial Accounting Standards Board (FASB) and by the International Accounting Standards Board (IASB)?

17. What is the advantage of the accrual basis of accounting, relative to the cash basis of accounting, for measuring performance?

EXERCISES

18. **Understanding the balance sheet.** The balance sheet as of December 31, 2007, of Colgate Palmolive Company (Colgate), a U.S. consumer products manufacturer, appears in **Exhibit 1.10**. Colgate reports all amounts in millions of U.S. dollars ($). Answer the following questions that pertain to the information in this exhibit.

    a. What is Colgate's largest asset, and what is the asset's carrying value on the balance sheet?

    b. What is the total amount of Colgate's noncurrent assets?

    c. What is Colgate's largest liability, and what is the liability's carrying value on the balance sheet?

    d. By how much do Colgate's current assets differ from its current liabilities?

    e. Has Colgate been profitable since its inception? How do you know?

    f. What fraction of its assets does Colgate finance with liabilities?

    g. Verify that Colgate's assets equal the sum of liabilities plus shareholders' equity.

19. **Understanding the income statement.** The income statement for the year ended December 31, 2007, for Mayr Melnhof Karton, an Austrian paper and packaging manufacturer, appears in **Exhibit 1.11**. Mayr Melnhof reports all amounts in thousands of euros (€). Answer the following questions that pertain to the information in this exhibit.

    a. What is Mayr Melnhof's largest expense on its income statement, and what is the amount?

    b. What is Mayr Melnhof's second largest expense on its income statement, and what is the amount?

EXHIBIT 1.10	Colgate Palmolive Company Consolidated Balance Sheet

As of December 31,	2007
Assets	
Current Assets	
Cash and cash equivalents	$ 428.7
Receivables (net of allowances of $50.6 and $46.4, respectively)	1,680.7
Inventories	1,171.0
Other current assets	338.1
Total current assets	3,618.5
Property, plant and equipment, net	3,015.2
Goodwill, net	2,272.0
Other intangible assets, net	844.8
Other assets	361.5
Total assets	$10,112.0
Liabilities and Shareholders' Equity	
Current Liabilities	
Notes and loans payable	$ 155.9
Current portion of long-term debt	138.1
Accounts payable	1,066.8
Accrued income taxes	262.7
Other accruals	1,539.2
Total current liabilities	3,162.7
Long-term debt	3,221.9
Deferred income taxes	264.1
Other liabilities	1,177.1
Total liabilities	7,825.8
Commitments and contingent liabilities	—
Shareholders' Equity	
Preference stock	197.5
Common stock, $1 par value (1,000,000,000 shares authorized, 732,853,180 shares issued)	732.9
Additional paid-in capital	1,517.7
Retained earnings	10,627.5
Accumulated other comprehensive income	(1,666.8)
	11,408.8
Unearned compensation	(218.9)
Treasury stock, at cost	(8,903.7)
Total shareholders' equity	2,286.2
Total liabilities and shareholders' equity	$10,112.0

c. What is the ratio of Mayr Melnhof's gross margin to sales (called the gross margin percentage)?

d. What amount does Mayr Melnhof report as operating profit for 2007? What amount does it report as profit before tax? What explains the difference between the two?

EXHIBIT 1.11   Mayr Melnhof Karton
Consolidated Income Statement

(all amounts in thousands of EUR except share and per share data)	Notes	Year ended Dec. 31, 2007
Sales		1,736,959.2
Cost of sales		(1,331,292.1)
Gross margin		**405,667.1**
Other operating income	5	10,746.7
Selling and distribution expenses		(172,033.4)
Administrative expenses		(74,204.0)
Other operating expenses	6	(758.2)
Operating profit		**169,418.2**
Financial expenses		(9,082.9)
Financial income		14,534.1
Share of profit (loss) of associated companies		377.9
Other income (expenses) – net	7	(4,383.4)
Profit before tax		**170,863.9**
Income tax expense	8	(54,289.9)
Profit for the year		**116,574.0**

e. What is Mayr Melnhof's effective tax rate for the year? (The effective tax rate is the ratio of income tax expense to profit before tax.)

f. Did Mayr Melnhof generate profit for the year, or incur a loss? How much?

20. **Understanding the statement of cash flows.** The statement of cash flows for the year ended March 1, 2008 (fiscal 2007), of Bed, Bath and Beyond, Inc. (BBB), a U.S. home products retailer, appears in **Exhibit 1.12**. BBB reports all amounts in thousands of U.S. dollars ($). Answer the following questions that pertain to the information in this exhibit.

a. Did BBB generate cash inflows or outflows from operating activities in fiscal 2007, and in what amount?

b. Did BBB generate cash inflows or outflows from investing activities in fiscal 2007, and in what amount?

c. Did BBB generate cash inflows or outflows from financing activities in fiscal 2007, and in what amount?

d. What was BBB's net cash flow for fiscal 2007?

e. What was the change in the cash balance between the beginning and end of fiscal 2007? What caused this change?

21. **Balance sheet relations.** The balance sheet of Alcatel-Lucent, a French communications firm, for the year ended December 31, 2007, showed current assets of €20,000 million, current liabilities of €15,849 million, shareholders' equity of €17,154 million, and non-current assets of €29,402 million. Alcatel-Lucent reports all amounts in millions of euros (€). Compute the amount of noncurrent liabilities on Alcatel-Lucent's balance sheet at the end of 2007.

22. **Balance sheet relations.** The balance sheet of Gold Fields Limited, a South African gold mining company, for the year ended June 30, 2007, showed current assets of R6,085.1, noncurrent assets of R49,329.8, noncurrent liabilities of R13,948.4, and current liabilities of R4,360.1. Gold Fields reports all amounts in millions of South African Rand (R). Compute the amount of shareholders' equity on Gold Fields' balance sheet at the end of 2007.

23. **Income statement relations.** The income statement of Rolls Royce Group Plc., a U.K. automotive manufacturer, for the year ended December 31, 2007, reported revenues of

EXHIBIT 1.12   Bed, Bath and Beyond, Inc.
Consolidated Statement of Cash Flows

(in thousands)	March 1, 2008
Cash Flows from Operating Activities:	
Net earnings	$ 562,808
Adjustments to reconcile net earnings to net cash provided by operating activities:	
Depreciation	157,770
Amortization of bond premium	1,538
Stock-based compensation	43,755
Tax benefit from stock-based compensation	2,719
Deferred income taxes	2,315
(Increase) decrease in assets, net of effect of acquisition:	
Merchandise inventories	(96,673)
Trading investment securities	(3,020)
Other current assets	(16,217)
Other assets	529
(Decrease) increase in liabilities, net of effect of acquisition:	
Accounts payable	(31,764)
Accrued expenses and other current liabilities	15,774
Merchandise credit and gift card liabilities	24,430
Income taxes payable	(74,530)
Deferred rent and other liabilities	25,102
Net cash provided by operating activities	614,536
Cash Flows from Investing Activities:	
Purchase of held-to-maturity investment securities	—
Redemption of held-to-maturity investment securities	494,526
Purchase of available-for-sale investment securities	(1,495,155)
Redemption of available-for-sale investment securities	1,546,430
Capital expenditures	(358,210)
Payment for acquisition, net of cash acquired	(85,893)
Net cash provided by (used in) investing activities	101,698
Cash Flows from Financing Activities:	
Proceeds from exercise of stock options	22,672
Excess tax benefit from stock-based compensation	5,990
Repurchase of common stock, including fees	(734,193)
Payment of deferred purchase price for acquisition	—
Net cash used in financing activities	(705,531)
Net increase (decrease) in cash and cash equivalents	10,703
Cash and cash equivalents:	
Beginning of period	213,381
End of period	$ 224,084

£7,435 and cost of sales of £6,003. In addition, it reported other operating expenses of £918, a loss of £2 on the sale of a business, and net financing income of £221. Tax expense for the year was £133. Rolls Royce reports all amounts in millions of pounds sterling (£). Compute the amount of net income or loss that Rolls Royce reported for 2007.

24. **Income statement relations.** The income statement of General Motors Corporation, a U.S. automotive manufacturer, for the year ended December 31, 2007, reported revenues of $207,349, cost of sales of $164,682, other operating expenses, including income taxes, of $50,335, and net financing income, after taxes, of $5,690. General Motors reports all amounts in millions of U.S. dollars ($). Compute the amount of net income or loss that General Motors reported for 2007.

25. **Retained earnings relations.** The balance sheet of Gold Fields Limited (see **Problem 1.22**), for the year ended June 30, 2007, showed a balance in retained earnings of R5,872.4 at

the end of 2007 and R4,640.9 at the end of 2006. Net income for 2007 was R2,362.5 million. Gold Fields reports all amounts in millions of South African Rand (R). Compute the amount of dividends Gold Fields declared during 2007.

26. **Retained earnings relations.** The balance sheet of Sterlite Industries, an Indian producer of copper, showed retained earnings of Rs26,575 at March 31, 2006. At March 31, 2007, the balance in retained earnings was Rs70,463. Sterlite declared dividends during the year ended March 31, 2007, of Rs3,544. Sterlite reports all amounts in millions of Indian Rupees (Rs). Compute Sterlite's net income for the year ended March 31, 2007 (fiscal 2006).

27. **Cash flow relations.** The statement of cash flows for Target Corporation, a U.S. retailer, for the year ended February 2, 2008 (fiscal 2007), showed a net cash inflow from operations of $4,125, a net cash outflow for investing of $6,195, and a net cash inflow for financing of $3,707. The balance sheet at February 3, 2007, showed a balance in cash of $813. Target reports all amounts in millions of U.S. dollars ($). Compute the amount of cash on the balance sheet at February 2, 2008.

28. **Cash flow relations.** The statement of cash flows for Edenor S.A., a leading electric utility in Argentina, for the year ended December 31, 2007, showed a net cash inflow from operations of Ps427,182 and a net cash outflow for financing of Ps21,806. The comparative balance sheets showed a balance in cash of Ps32,673 at December 31, 2006, and Ps101,198 at December 31, 2007. Edenor reports all amounts in millions of pesos (Ps). Compute the net amount of cash provided or used by Edenor's investing activities for 2007.

29. **Preparation of simple balance sheet; current and noncurrent classifications.** Kenton Limited began retail operations on January 1, 2008. On that date it issued 10,000 shares of common stock for £50,000. On January 31, Kenton used £48,000 of the proceeds to rent a store, paying in advance for the next two years. Kenton also purchased £12,000 of merchandise on credit, agreeing to pay the supplier within 30 days. Kenton applies IFRS. Prepare, in good format, Kenton's balance sheet as of January 31, 2008.

30. **Preparation of simple balance sheet; current and noncurrent classifications.** Heckle Group began operations as an engineering consulting firm, on June 1, 2008. On that date it issued 100,000 shares of common stock for €920,000. During June, Heckle used €600,000 of the proceeds to purchase office space and office equipment. It acquired a patent for €120,000, agreeing to pay the seller within 30 days. On June 30 Heckle signed a bank loan for €400,000, bearing interest at 8% per year and payable in full on June 30, 2011. Prepare, in good format, Heckle's balance sheet as of June 30, 2008.

31. **Accrual versus cash basis of accounting.** The following information is based on the financial statements of Boeing Company for the year ended December 31, 2007. During 2007 Boeing reported revenues of $66,387 million and net expenses (including income taxes) of $62,313 million. Assume that during 2007, Boeing collected $65,995 million in cash from customers and had cash outflows associated with payments to suppliers and vendors of $56,411 million.

   a. Calculate Boeing's net income for 2007 and its net cash flow for 2007.

   b. How can Boeing's cash collected from customers in 2007 be less than its revenues in 2007?

   c. How can Boeing's cash payments to suppliers and vendors be less than its expenses for 2007?

32. **Accrual versus cash basis of accounting.** Consider the following information reported by Fonterra Cooperative Group Limited for the year ended May 31, 2007; all figures are in millions of New Zealand dollars ($). Fonterra is the largest dairy cooperative in New Zealand. Fonterra reported revenues of $13,882, cost of goods sold of $11,671, interest and other expenses of $2,113, and tax expense of $67. It also reported $13,894 in cash receipts from customers, $102 in miscellaneous cash receipts, $5,947 in cash payments to employees and creditors, $6,261 in cash payments for milk, $402 in cash payments for interest, and $64 in cash payments for taxes. Calculate Fonterra's net income for 2007 and its net cash flow for 2007.

PROBLEMS

33. **Balance sheet relations.** Selected balance sheet amounts for Dragon Group International Limited, a diversified electronics firm in Singapore, appears next, as of December 31,

2007, and December 31, 2006. Dragon Group International reports all amounts in millions of Singapore dollars ($). Compute the missing amounts for the two years.

	2007	2006
Total Assets	$199,824	?
Noncurrent Liabilities	7,010	?
Noncurrent Assets	?	$ 17,368
Total Liabilities and Shareholders' Equity	?	?
Current Liabilities	139,941	126,853
Shareholders' Equity	?	53,721
Total Liabilities	?	?
Current Assets	170,879	170,234

34. **Balance sheet relations.** Selected balance sheet amounts for Lenovo Group Inc., a Chinese computer manufacturer, appear next, for the years ended March 31, 2008, and March 31, 2007. Lenovo reports all amounts in thousands of U.S. dollars ($). Compute the missing amounts for the two years.

	2008	2007
Total Assets	?	$5,450,838
Current Liabilities	$4,488,461	3,527,504
Current Assets	?	3,062,449
Total Liabilities and Shareholders' Equity	7,199,847	?
Noncurrent Liabilities	1,098,123	?
Shareholders' Equity	?	1,134,276
Noncurrent Assets	2,494,481	?
Total Liabilities	?	?

35. **Income statement relations.** Selected income statement information for Colgate Palmolive Company, a U.S. consumer products manufacturer, appears below for the years ended December 31, 2007, 2006, and 2005. Colgate reports all amounts in millions of U.S. dollars ($). Compute the missing amounts for the three years.

	2007	2006	2005
Sales	$13,790	?	$11,397
Cost of Goods Sold	?	$5,536	5,192
Selling and Administrative Expenses	4,973	4,355	3,921
Other (Income) Expense	121	186	69
Interest Expense, net	157	159	136
Income Tax Expense	759	648	728
Net Income	1,738	1,354	?

36. **Income statement relations.** Selected income statement information for Polo Ralph Lauren, a U.S. clothing manufacturer and distributor, appears next for the years ended March 31, 2007; April 1, 2006; and April 2, 2005. Polo Ralph Lauren reports all amounts in millions of U.S. dollars ($). Compute the missing amounts for the three years.

	2007	2006	2005
Net Revenues	$4,295.4	$3,746.3	$3,305.4
Cost of Goods Sold	1,959.2	1,723.9	1,620.9
Selling and Administrative Expenses	1,663.4	1,476.9	1,377.6
Other (Income) Expense	34.0	?	2.7
Interest (Income) Expense, net	?	(1.2)	6.4
Income Tax Expense	242.4	194.9	107.4
Net Income	400.9	308.0	?

37. **Statement of cash flows relations.** The following information is based on data reported in the statement of cash flows for Ericsson, a Swedish telecommunications firm, for the years ended December 31, 2007, 2006, and 2005. Ericsson reports all amounts in millions of Swedish kronor (SEK).

	2007	2006	2005
Inflows of Cash			
Proceeds from Borrowings	SEK 15,587	SEK 1,290	SEK 657
Sale of Common Stock	94	124	174
Revenues, Net of Expenses, from Operations	19,210	18,489	16,669
Sale of Property and Equipment	152	185	362
Sale of Short-Term Investments	3,499	6,180	6,375
Other Financing Activities	406	58	—
Other Investing Activities	—	663	—
Outflows of Cash			
Acquisition of Property and Equipment	4,319	3,827	3,365
Acquisition of Businesses	26,292	18,078	1,210
Repayment of Borrowings	1,291	9,510	2,784
Dividends Paid	8,132	7,343	4,133
Other Financing Activities	—	—	288
Other Investing Activities	573	—	1,131

Prepare a statement of cash flows for Ericsson for the three years using the format in **Exhibit 1.3**. Set cash flow from operations equal to revenues, net of expenses, from operations. The balance in cash at the beginning of 2005 was SEK30,412. Ericsson classifies changes in short-term investments as investing activities.

38. **Statement of cash flows relations.** Selected data from the statement of cash flows for Jackson Corporation for the years ended October 31, 2008, 2007, and 2006 appear as follows (amounts in millions):

	2008	2007	2006
Inflows of Cash			
Proceeds from Long-Term Borrowings	$ 836	$ 5,096	$ 3,190
Revenues from Operations Increasing Cash	19,536	19,083	17,233
Issue of Common Stock	67	37	3
Sale of Property, Plant, and Equipment	332	401	220
Other Investing Transactions	71	0	268
Total Inflows	$20,842	$24,617	$20,914
Outflows of Cash			
Acquisition of Property, Plant, and Equipment	$ 3,678	$ 3,640	$ 1,881
Expenses for Operations Decreasing Cash	16,394	18,541	18,344
Repayments of Long-Term Debt	766	922	687
Other Investing Activities	0	1,501	0
Total Outflows	$20,838	$24,604	$20,912

Prepare a statement of cash flows for Jackson Corporation for each of the three years 2008, 2007, and 2006 using the format in **Exhibit 1.3**. Set cash flow from operations equal to revenues providing cash minus expenses using cash. The balance in cash at October 31, 2005, was $102 million.

39. **Preparing a balance sheet and income statement.** The accounting records of JetAway Airlines reveal the following for the year ended September 30, 2008 (amounts in thousands):

Balance Sheet Items	September 30	
	2008	2007
Accounts Payable	$ 157,415	$ 156,755
Accounts Receivable	88,799	73,448
Cash	378,511	418,819
Common Stock	352,943	449,934
Current Maturities of Long-Term Debt	11,996	7,873
Inventories	50,035	65,152
Long-Term Debt	623,309	871,717
Other Current Assets	56,810	73,586
Other Current Liabilities	681,242	795,838
Other Noncurrent Assets	4,231	12,942
Other Noncurrent Liabilities	844,116	984,142
Property, Plant, and Equipment (net)	4,137,610	5,008,166
Retained Earnings	2,044,975	2,385,854

Income Statement Items	For the Year Ended September 30, 2008
Fuel Expense	$ 892,415
Interest Expense	22,883
Interest Income	14,918
Maintenance Expense	767,606
Other Operating Expenses	1,938,753
Sales Revenue	4,735,587
Salaries and Benefits Expense	1,455,237

a. Prepare a comparative balance sheet for JetAway Airlines as of September 30, 2008, and September 30, 2007 in the format used in **Exhibit 1.1**. Classify each balance sheet item into one of the following categories: current assets, noncurrent assets, current liabilities, noncurrent liabilities, and shareholders' equity.

b. Prepare an income statement for JetAway Airlines for the year ended September 30, 2008. Separate income items into revenues and expenses.

c. Prepare a schedule explaining the change in retained earnings between September 30, 2007, and September 30, 2008.

40. **Cash versus accrual accounting.** Jack Block opens a tax and bookkeeping services business, Block's Tax and Bookkeeping Services, on July 1, 2008. He invests $40,000 for all the common stock of the business, and the firm borrows $20,000 from the local bank, promising to repay the loan on December 31, 2008, along with interest at 8% per year, or approximately $133 per month (=[.08 × $20,000] / 12 months). The firm rents space on July 1 and pays $6,000 for three months rent in advance, and leases office equipment for the year, prepaying $12,000 for six months rent. The firm hires an office assistant whom it will pay $72,000 per year with payments every two months, issuing the first paycheck on August 31. Finally, the firm pays cash for office supplies during July costing $370; a physical count at the end of July shows that $280 of office supplies are on hand. During July, Block's Tax and Bookkeeping Services performs services and bills customers for $44,000. On July 31, 2008, customers had paid $13,000 of the amount owed.

a. What is income for Block's Tax and Bookkeeping Services for July, 2008:
   (1) Applying cash-basis accounting.
   (2) Applying accrual accounting.

b. How much cash on hand does Block's Tax and Bookkeeping Services have as of July 31, 2008? Why is the amount of cash on hand not a good representation of the firm's performance during July?

41. **Cash versus accrual accounting.** Dina Richards opens a high-end stationery store, Stationery Plus, on November 1, 2008. She finances the store by investing $80,000 in cash in exchange for all the common stock of the firm. She also obtains a bank loan for $100,000,

which she promises to repay in four equal installments of $25,000 at the end of each of the next four months, beginning December 31. The interest rate on the loan's outstanding amount owed is 12% per year (or 1% per month); interest is to be paid along with each principal repayment. The store rents space, paying $9,000 for six months rent, and acquires goods costing $40,000. The supplier agrees to allow Stationery Plus to pay half ($20,000) immediately and half on December 15. To attract customers, the firm allows customers 40 days to pay for their purchases. Stationery Plus's other monthly costs are $10,000 in salaries and $480 in utilities and insurance, all paid in cash at the end of every month. During November total sales to customers were $56,000; Stationary Plus had collected $23,000 by the end of November; it collected the remainder by December 15. During December total sales to customers were $62,000; the firm had collected $34,000 by the end of December. So far, no customers have failed to pay the amount owed within 40 days. During December Stationery Plus acquired more merchandise costing $55,000, paying half immediately and agreeing to pay half in January. During November, Stationery Plus sold goods for which it had paid $29,000 and during December, Stationery Plus sold goods for which it had paid $33,600.

a. What is income for Stationery Plus for November 2008:

    (1) Applying cash-basis accounting.

    (2) Applying accrual accounting.

b. What is income for Stationery Plus for December 2008:

    (1) Applying cash-basis accounting.

    (2) Applying accrual accounting.

42. **Relations between net income and cash flows.** The ABC Company starts the year in fine shape. The firm makes widgets—just what the customer wants. It makes them for $0.75 each and sells them for $1.00. The ABC Company keeps an inventory equal to shipments of the past 30 days, pays its bills promptly, and collects cash from customers within 30 days after the sale. The sales manager predicts a steady increase in sales of 500 widgets each month beginning in February. It looks like a great year, and it begins that way.

January 1	Cash, $875; receivables, $1,000; inventory, $750
January	In January the firm sells, on account for $1,000, 1,000 widgets costing $750. Net income for the month is $250. The firm collects receivables outstanding at the beginning of the month. Production equals 1,000 units at a total cost of $750. The books at the end of January show the following:
February 1	Cash, $1,125; receivables, $1,000; inventory, $750
February	This month's sales jump, as predicted, to 1,500 units. With a corresponding step-up in production to maintain the 30-day inventory, ABC Company makes 2,000 units at a cost of $1,500. It collects all receivables from January sales. Net income so far is $625. Now the books look like this:
March 1	Cash, $625; receivables, $1,500; inventory, $1,125
March	March sales are even better, increasing to 2,000 units. Collections are on time. Production, to adhere to the inventory policy, is 2,500 units. Operating results for the month show net income of $500. Net income to date is $1,125. The books show the following:
April 1	Cash, $250; receivables, $2,000; inventory, $1,500
April	In April, sales jump another 500 units to 2,500, and the manager of ABC Company shakes the sales manager's hand. Customers are paying right on time. Production increases to 3,000 units, and the month's business nets $625 for a net income to date of $1,750. The manager of ABC Company takes off for Miami before the accountant issues a report. Suddenly a phone call comes from the treasurer: "Come home! We need cash!"
May 1	Cash, $0; receivables, $2,500; inventory, $1,875

a. Prepare an analysis that explains what happened to ABC Company. (*Hint:* Compute the amount of cash receipts and cash disbursements for each month during the period January 1 to May 1.)

b. How can a firm show increasing net income but a decreasing amount of cash?

    c. What insights does this problem provide about the need for all three financial statements—balance sheet, income statement, and statement of cash flows?

    d. What actions would you suggest that ABC Company take to deal with its cash flow problem?

43. Balance sheet and income statement relations. (Prepared by Professor Wesley T. Andrews Jr. and reproduced, with adaptation, by permission.)

Once upon a time many, many years ago, a feudal landlord lived in a small province of central Europe. The landlord, called the Red-Bearded Baron, lived in a castle high on a hill. This benevolent fellow took responsibility for the well-being of many peasants who occupied the lands surrounding his castle. Each spring as the snow began to melt, the Baron would decide how to provide for all his serf dependents during the coming year.

    One spring the Baron was thinking about the wheat crop of the coming growing season. "I believe that 30 acres of my land, being worth five bushels of wheat per acre, will produce enough wheat for next winter," he mused, "but who should do the farming? I believe I'll give Ivan the Indefatigable and Igor the Immutable the task of growing the wheat." Whereupon he summoned Ivan and Igor, two gentry noted for their hard work and not overly active minds, for an audience.

    "Ivan, you will farm on the 20-acre plot of ground, and Igor will farm the 10-acre plot," the Baron began. "I will give Ivan 20 bushels of wheat for seed and 20 pounds of fertilizer. (Twenty pounds of fertilizer are worth two bushels of wheat.) Igor will get 10 bushels of wheat for seed and 10 pounds of fertilizer. I will give each of you an ox to pull a plow, but you will have to make arrangements with Feyador, the Plowmaker, for two plows. The oxen, incidentally, are only three years old and have never been used for farming, so they should have a good 10 years of farming ahead of them. Take good care of them, because an ox is worth 40 bushels of wheat. Come back next fall and return the oxen and the plows along with your harvest." Ivan and Igor bowed and withdrew from the Great Hall, taking with them the things provided by the Baron.

    The summer came and went. After the harvest Ivan and Igor returned to the Great Hall to account to their master for the things given them in the spring. Ivan, pouring 223 bushels of wheat onto the floor, said, "My Lord, I present you with a slightly used ox, a plow broken beyond repair, and 223 bushels of wheat. I, unfortunately, owe Feyador, the Plowmaker, three bushels of wheat for the plow I got from him last spring. And, as you might expect, I used all the fertilizer and seed you gave me last spring. You will also remember, my Lord, that you took 20 bushels of my harvest for your own personal use."

    Igor, who had been given 10 acres of land, 10 bushels of wheat, and 10 pounds of fertilizer, spoke next. "Here, my Lord, is a partially used-up ox, the plow for which I gave Feyador, the Plowmaker, three bushels of wheat from my harvest, and 105 bushels of wheat. I, too, used all my seed and fertilizer last spring. Also, my Lord, you took 30 bushels of wheat several days ago for your own table. I believe the plow is good for two more seasons."

    "Knaves, you did well," said the Red-Bearded Baron. Blessed with this benediction, the two serfs departed. After the servants had taken their leave, the Red-Bearded Baron, watching the two hungry oxen slowly eating the wheat piled on the floor, began to contemplate what had happened. "Yes," he thought, "they did well, but I wonder which one did better?"

    a. What measuring unit should the Red-Bearded Baron use to measure financial position and operating performance?

    b. Prepare a balance sheet for Ivan and for Igor at both the beginning and the end of the period.

    c. Prepare an income statement for Ivan and for Igor for the period.

    d. Prepare a schedule reconciling the change in owner's equity between the beginning and the end of the period.

    e. Did Ivan or Igor perform better during the period? Explain.

The Basics of Record Keeping and Financial Statement Preparation

1. Learn the conventions of recording transactions, including the dual nature of transactions, T-accounts, and journal entries.

2. Understand how the recording of transactions forms the foundation for financial statement preparation.

3. Understand how the balance sheet and the income statement articulate.

Businesses engage in transactions with customers, suppliers, employees, governmental entities, and others. This chapter demonstrates how the accountant records transactions and then combines transaction records to prepare financial statements. This chapter focuses, therefore, on bookkeeping and record-keeping procedures, not on accounting principles and judgments. The latter—accounting principles and judgments—form the core of financial accounting. The former—bookkeeping—organizes and presents transactions in a standardized manner so that the reader can readily discern the effects of a transaction on the financial statements from its initial recording. A standardized record-keeping system, which users understand and accept, facilitates communications.

You need to understand both the recording of transactions and the combining of those transaction records to form financial statements to develop two skills: (1) your ability to communicate the results of transactions to others, and (2) your understanding of how transactions affect the financial statements and how the financial statements reflect the transactions. We adopt a user perspective throughout this text, which means we focus on how you, as a user of financial statements, can best understand and analyze financial reports. *You will limit your ability to analyze financial statements if you do not understand how the statements reflect both the record-keeping process and management's choices of accounting principles and its professional judgments.*

Although the rest of this book concerns the accounting principles and professional judgments that form the core of financial reporting, this chapter focuses on the assembly, or bookkeeping, process without further reference to either accounting principles or judgments. Therefore, we examine only transactions that require no judgment, so that no ambiguity arises as to whether and how the procedures recognize and measure the transaction. At this point, we do not explain the judgments that the accounting for many business transactions requires.

This chapter considers four bookkeeping concepts:

1. The dual nature (duality) of transactions and events.
2. The use of T-accounts and journal entries for recording the duality of a transaction or event.
3. The preparation of a simple balance sheet, income statement, and statement of cash flows.
4. The link, or *articulation*, between the balance sheet and the income statement.

Because each of these concepts relies on common record-keeping terminology, we begin with an overview of key terms and their definitions. Subsequent chapters describe the terms in more detail.

ACCOUNTS

COMMON TERMINOLOGY

Accounting relies on a system of accounts, with the name or title of each account intended to capture the nature of the items in the account. An **account** represents an amount on a line of a balance sheet or income statement. A common account is Cash. A detailed system of accounts allows the preparer of financial statements to decompose, or *disaggregate*, each transaction to convey more information about the effects of the transaction than would result from a system that combined the effects of all transactions in a smaller number of more inclusive accounts. To take an example, consider that separate information on Cash, Accounts Receivable, and Inventories conveys more information than a single sum of those three items in an account for Current Assets. The accounts also group the effects of similar transactions that occur during the reporting period. For example, if a firm sells one million copies of a piece of software during a year, little benefit would result from showing in the financial reports the individual effect of *each* of the one million transactions. The accounting process combines, or *aggregates*, the effects of similar transactions for financial reporting.[1]

Nowhere do accounting procedures define a list of accounts that management must use, nor do we know of any exhaustive list of such accounts. Authoritative accounting guidance sometimes prescribes account names, but most often provides financial statements preparers with flexibility to choose both the number of accounts that appear on the financial statements and the account names. Those choices result from the complexity and heterogeneity of the reporting entity's business, proprietary information considerations,[2] the sheer amount of space that a long list of accounts would require, and reporting conventions. With regard to conventions, selecting nonstandard names for accounts will undermine the communication benefits from adopting account names that other firms use. Following conventional naming practices increases the understandability of financial statements to knowledgeable users who apply their common understanding of the account title. We believe that you will increase your effectiveness as a user of financial statements if you also follow conventions—by choosing

---

[1]Consider a corporation with numerous subsidiaries, each of which maintains one Travel Expense account for each of 10 departments. Each department manager and the subsidiary controller might review that department's Travel Expense account; the subsidiary president might review total expenses for that department, as well as other departments. The firm's income statement would likely include the travel expenses for all departments in a general account, such as Selling, General, and Administrative Expenses. Each account would be assigned an account number that would let internal users summarize expenses in various ways; for example, all Travel Expenses for a department, for a subsidiary, or for the entire corporation.

[2]All else equal, a user of financial statements would prefer to have more disaggregated data, since a user can always aggregate data (but cannot do the reverse). Readers of a firm's financial statements include, however, competitors, so accounting guidance provides some amount of flexibility to combine information in ways that mask competitively sensitive (that is, proprietary) information. Authoritative guidance nevertheless requires disaggregated information in some instances. For example, both U.S. GAAP and IFRS require the disclosure of segment information, which details resources (assets) and results of operations (income or loss) by segment. (The **Glossary** defines both *segment* and *segment reporting*.) Users of financial reports value this information because different segments have different risks and rewards. A multiple-segment firm that did not report on its segments would not provide as much information about its resources and operations as would an otherwise similar firm that provided segment reports. **Chapter 6** discusses segment reporting.

account titles that are descriptive and unambiguous, by using identical (or similar) account titles for identical (or similar) items, and as your accounting vocabulary grows, by selecting titles that others commonly use to describe the item.

The word *accounts* refers to both balance sheet accounts and income statement accounts. As we describe later in this chapter, balance sheet accounts are **permanent accounts** in the sense that they remain open, with nonzero balances, at the end of the reporting period. In contrast, income statement accounts are **temporary accounts** in the sense that they start a period with a zero balance, accumulate information during the reporting period, and have a zero balance at the end of the reporting period. As a result, a balance sheet is for a point in time and an income statement is for a period of time, such as a month, quarter, or year. The closing process (discussed later) ensures each income statement account has a zero balance at the end of the reporting period. The recording of transactions during a period causes amounts in accounts to increase and decrease. For balance sheet accounts, the total additions during the period increase the (beginning) balance carried forward from the previous balance sheet date, and the total subtractions decrease this balance; the result is the new (ending) balance.

Recall from **Chapter 1** that one of the principal financial statements is the balance sheet. The balance sheet shows the assets of a firm and the liabilities and shareholders' equity that financed those assets and that therefore have a claim on them at a particular date. The next section describes several typical balance sheet accounts.

THE BALANCE SHEET

COMMON TERMINOLOGY

Typical Asset Accounts This section discusses several typical asset accounts, as well as certain items, such as organization costs and research and development costs, that would seem to meet the definition of an asset even though authoritative accounting guidance does not recognize them as accounting assets.

Cash: coins and currency and items such as bank checks and money orders, bank deposits against which the firm can draw checks, and time deposits, usually savings accounts and certificates of deposit. Although money orders are claims against individuals or institutions, custom calls them *cash.*

Marketable Securities: government bonds or corporate stocks and bonds that the firm will hold for a relatively short time. The word *marketable* implies that the firm can readily buy and sell them, perhaps through an exchange such as the New York Stock Exchange or the London Stock Exchange.

Accounts Receivable: amounts due from customers from the sale of goods or services on account. The firm collects cash from the customer sometime after the sale. Accounts Receivable describes the figure representing the total amount of cash owed by (that is, receivable from) customers. The reporting entity maintains a separate record for each customer and follows up with customers who have not paid within the agreed-upon period of time.

Notes Receivable: amounts due from customers or from others to whom a firm has made loans or extended credit. The customer or other borrower puts the claim into writing in a formal note, which distinguishes the claim from an account receivable.

Interest Receivable: interest, on assets such as promissory notes or bonds, that the borrower owes to the reporting entity because of the passage of time, but that the reporting entity has not collected as of the date of the balance sheet.

Inventory: goods available for sale, partially completed goods, and materials used in the manufacture of products. (Outside the United States, common usage refers to inventories as *stocks*. Do not confuse the use of *stocks* to describe inventory with the phrase "common stock," which refers to a component of shareholders' equity.) Inventory includes several types. *Merchandise Inventory* reflects goods on hand purchased for resale, such as canned goods on grocery store shelves or suits on the racks of a clothing store. *Raw Materials Inventory* includes materials as yet unused for manufacturing products. *Work-in-Process Inventory* includes partially completed manufactured products. *Finished Goods Inventory* is completed but unsold manufactured products.

Advances to Suppliers: payments the firm has made in advance to a supplier for goods (such as raw materials) or services (such as for Web advertising that has not yet run) that it will receive at a later date.

Prepaid Rent: rent paid in advance for the future use of land, buildings, equipment, and other resources.

Prepaid Insurance: insurance premiums paid for future coverage.

Investments in Securities: bonds or shares of common or preferred stock that the firm plans to hold for more than one year.

Land: land used in operations or occupied by buildings used in operations.

Buildings: factory buildings, store buildings, garages, warehouses, and other buildings.

Equipment: lathes, ovens, machine tools, boilers, computers, bins, cranes, conveyors, automobiles, and so forth.

Furniture and Fixtures: desks, tables, chairs, counters, showcases, scales, and other selling and office equipment.

Accumulated Depreciation: the cumulative amount of the acquisition cost of long-term assets (such as buildings and equipment) that the firm has allocated to the costs of production or to current and prior period expenses in measuring net income. The amount in this account is subtracted from the acquisition cost of the long-term asset to which it relates, to measure the *carrying value* (sometimes called the *book value*, or *net book value*) of the asset shown on the balance sheet.

Organization Costs: legal and incorporation fees, costs of printing the certificates for shares of stock, and other costs incurred in organizing a business. Both U.S. GAAP and IFRS require firms to expense such organization costs in the period the costs are incurred.[3] Therefore, although we discuss this account in the context of balance sheet accounts, Organization Costs would not appear on a balance sheet under current authoritative guidance.

Patents: rights granted for varying numbers of years (depending on the country that issues the patent) by a government to exclude others from manufacturing, using, or selling certain processes or devices. The accounting treatment of a cost to acquire a patent depends on whether the firm applies U.S. GAAP or IFRS. Both U.S. GAAP and IFRS require that the firm recognize as an asset the cost to purchase a patent from an external third party. Under U.S. GAAP, firms expense, in the period incurred, the research and development costs incurred to develop a patentable process or device. IFRS requires firms to expense research costs as incurred but, under some circumstances, to recognize development costs as an asset. **Chapter 9** discusses the treatment of internally developed and externally purchased patents in more detail.

Goodwill: When one firm acquires another firm, it measures the individual identifiable assets acquired and liabilities assumed at their current fair values. If the purchase price exceeds the sum of the fair values of the identifiable assets less the identifiable liabilities, the excess is *goodwill,* an accounting asset that includes intangibles that the acquiring firm cannot separately identify, for example, customer loyalty. These desirable attributes cause the amount paid for the acquired firm to exceed the sum of the fair values of all the other assets, less liabilities, identified in the acquisition. **Chapter 3** describes fair values in detail.

Typical Liability Accounts   This section describes typical liability accounts.

Accounts Payable: amounts owed for goods or services acquired under an informal credit agreement. The firm typically pays these liabilities within one or two months after the balance sheet date. (The same items appear as Accounts Receivable on the creditor's balance sheet.)

Notes Payable: the face amount of promissory notes given in connection with loans from a bank or with the purchase of goods or services. (The same items appear as Notes Receivable on the creditor's [lender's] balance sheet.) Most Accounts Payable, Accounts Receivable, Notes Payable, and Notes Receivable are current items, due within a year of the balance sheet date. Similar items due more than one year after the balance sheet date could have the same account titles, but would appear in the noncurrent assets or noncurrent liabilities sections of the balance sheet.

Interest Payable: interest on obligations that has accrued or accumulated with the passage of time but that the firm has not yet paid as of the balance sheet. (The same item appears as Interest Receivable on the creditor's balance sheet.)

---

[3]The U.S. GAAP guidance is in American Institute of Certified Public Accountants, *Statement of Position 98-5,* "Reporting the Cost of Start-up Activities," 1998. *International Accounting Standard 38,* "Intangible Assets," 1998, applies to start-up activities. The criteria for recognizing internally developed intangible assets are such that firms treat start-up costs the same as expenditures on internally developed goodwill; they are expensed as incurred.

Income Taxes Payable: the estimated liability for income taxes, accumulated and unpaid, based on the taxable income of the business.

Advances from Customers: the general name used to indicate the obligation incurred when a firm receives payments in advance for goods or services it will furnish to customers in the future. This is a nonmonetary liability, because the firm has an obligation to deliver goods or services, not to return the cash. Even so, the firm records this liability as the amount of cash received. There is no standardized terminology for this account. **Chapter 7** discusses this account in more detail.

Advances from Tenants, or Rent Received in Advance: another example of a nonmonetary liability that is an advance from a customer. For example, a tenant may prepay for its rented office space for several months in advance. The owner of the office space cannot include the amount applicable to future months in income until it provides rental services as time passes. Meanwhile the advance payment results in a liability payable in services—the use of the building. (On the balance sheet of the tenant, the same amount appears as an asset, Advances to Landlord or Prepaid Rent.[4])

Mortgage Payable: a form of long-term promissory note, or loan, where the borrower has pledged specific pieces of property as security for payment. If the borrower does not pay the loan or interest according to the agreement, the lender can require the sale of the property to generate cash to repay the loan.

Bonds Payable: a form of long-term loan. The borrower has signed a formal written contract called an *indenture*. The borrower usually raises the funds from a number of lenders, each of whom receives written evidence of its share of the loan.

Deferred Income Taxes: income tax amounts that are delayed beyond the current accounting period. **Chapter 11** discusses this item, which appears on the balance sheets of most corporations.

Typical Shareholders' Equity Accounts

This section describes typical shareholders' equity accounts.

Common Stock (at par): the amount of cash or other assets received equal to the par or stated value of a firm's principal class of voting stock.

Additional Paid-In Capital: the amount of cash or other assets received in the issuance of common or preferred stock in excess of par value or stated value. Some firms use the alternative title, Capital Contributed in Excess of Par (or Stated) Value. Accountants and analysts often refer to the sum of the amounts in this account and the common stock at par account as *contributed capital*, because the sum of these two items represents the cash and other assets directly provided by shareholders to a firm.

Preferred Stock: the amount of cash or other assets received for shares of a class of a firm's stock that has some preference relative to common stock. Common forms of preference include a higher dividend or a higher priority in terms of asset distribution in the event the firm liquidates. Preferred stock, if a company has it, is part of contributed capital.

Retained Earnings: net assets (defined as all assets minus all liabilities) increase as a firm generates earnings in excess of cash (or other assets) distributed as dividends. Retained Earnings is the balance sheet account that accumulates amounts that measure the net assets a firm generates from undistributed earnings of the business.

Accumulated Other Comprehensive Income: an account that accumulates changes in net assets that are not included in net income. An example is the remeasurement of certain financial assets. **Chapters 4** and **14** discuss this account further.

A TYPICAL BALANCE SHEET

The balance sheet groups individual accounts by type (asset, liability, or shareholders' equity) and lists these accounts with their balances as of the balance sheet date. The date of the balance sheet appears at the top of the balance sheet. The asset and liability categories further group individual accounts by the expected timing of cash receipts (for assets) or cash payments (for liabilities). Common terminology describes items whose cash receipts or payments the firm expects will occur within one year as *current assets* or *current liabilities*, respectively.

---

[4]Prepaid Rent is the more commonly used account title. This title is confusing, however, because the user of the financial statements cannot tell, without context, whether this account is the asset of the tenant or the liability of the landlord.

If the firm expects to collect or pay more than one year after the balance sheet date, the balance sheet classifies these as *noncurrent assets* and *noncurrent liabilities*, respectively. **Chapter 3** describes the balance sheet classifications in more detail.

The balance sheet begins with a list of assets and then lists liabilities and shareholders' equity. **Exhibit 2.1** shows the balance sheet for Colgate Palmolive Company ("Colgate") for the fiscal year ended December 31, 2007. Colgate is a leading consumer products company that operates in two principal segments: (1) oral, personal, and home care (including products such as toothpaste, soaps, and shampoo), and (2) pet nutrition.

Both U.S. GAAP and IFRS require firms to report balance sheet accounts for the prior year in addition to the current year. Colgate reports the results for the prior year in the rightmost column (the column labeled 2006), and the results for the current year in the column to

EXHIBIT 2.1

Colgate Palmolive Company
Balance Sheet

As of December 31,	2007	2006
Assets		
Current Assets		
Cash and cash equivalents	$ 428.7	$ 489.5
Receivables (net of allowances of $50.6 and $46.4, respectively)	1,680.7	1,523.2
Inventories	1,171.0	1,008.4
Other current assets	338.1	279.9
Total current assets	3,618.5	3,301.0
Property, plant and equipment, net	3,015.2	2,696.1
Goodwill, net	2,272.0	2,081.8
Other intangible assets, net	844.8	831.1
Other assets	361.5	228.0
Total assets	$10,112.0	$ 9,138.0
Liabilities and Shareholders' Equity		
Current Liabilities		
Notes and loans payable	$ 155.9	$ 174.1
Current portion of long-term debt	138.1	776.7
Accounts payable	1,066.8	1,039.7
Accrued income taxes	262.7	161.5
Other accruals	1,539.2	1,317.1
Total current liabilities	3,162.7	3,469.1
Long-term debt	3,221.9	2,720.4
Deferred income taxes	264.1	309.9
Other liabilities	1,177.1	1,227.7
Total liabilities	7,825.8	7,727.1
Commitments and contingent liabilities	—	—
Shareholders' Equity		
Preference stock	197.5	222.7
Common stock, $1 par value (1,000,000,000 shares authorized,		
732,853,180 shares issued)	732.9	732.9
Additional paid-in capital	1,517.7	1,218.1
Retained earnings	10,627.5	9,643.7
Accumulated other comprehensive income	(1,666.8)	(2,081.2)
	11,408.8	9,736.2
Unearned compensation	(218.9)	(251.4)
Treasury stock, at cost	(8,903.7)	(8,073.9)
Total shareholders' equity	2,286.2	1,410.9
Total liabilities and shareholders' equity	$10,112.0	$ 9,138.0

the left of this one (the column labeled 2007).[5] The lists of asset, liability, and shareholders' equity accounts include many of the accounts described earlier, as well as a few (such as treasury stock) described in later chapters. Under U.S. GAAP, assets and liabilities appear in order of decreasing closeness-to-cash; many firms that report under IFRS reverse this ordering.

DUAL EFFECTS OF TRANSACTIONS

Firms engage in transactions, or exchanges, with other entities and individuals during a period. For example, firms acquire merchandise from suppliers, pay employees for labor services, sell merchandise to customers, pay taxes to governments, and so on. In addition, other events not involving exchanges occur during the period. For example, firms consume the services of buildings and equipment as they use them in operations and, as time passes, incur an obligation to pay interest on outstanding loans. Accountants record the effects of *each* of these transactions and events as they occur, and then *accumulate* the effects of all transactions and events for presentation in the financial statements. Thus,

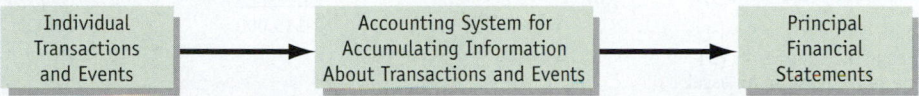

The **balance sheet equation** provides the analytical framework that we use throughout this book to understand the effects of transactions and events on the financial statements. As this and subsequent chapters illustrate, the balance sheet equation underlies the recording of transactions and events. It captures the financial statement effects of operating, investing, and financing transactions—three key activities of business firms. We apply the analytical framework provided by the balance sheet to successively more complex transactions in later chapters.

The balance sheet equation shows the equality of assets with liabilities plus shareholders' equity:

$$\text{Assets} = \text{Liabilities} + \text{Shareholders' Equity}$$

This equation requires that an entity's assets exactly balance, or offset, an equal amount of financing provided by creditors and owners of the corporation. Total liabilities plus shareholders' equity shows the sources of all the firm's financing, and the assets show how the firm holds or has invested those funds. The balance sheet equation maintains this equality by reporting the financial statement effects of each event and transaction in a dual manner, or what we term the **dual effects of transactions**. Any single event or transaction will have one of the following four effects or some combination of these effects:

1. It increases an asset and increases either a liability or shareholders' equity.

2. It decreases an asset and decreases either a liability or shareholders' equity.

3. It increases one asset and decreases another asset.

4. It increases one liability or shareholders' equity and decreases another liability or shareholders' equity.

To understand the dual effects of various transactions on the balance sheet equation, consider the following transactions for Miller Corporation (Miller) during January as it prepares to open for business on February 1:

(1) On January 1, Miller issues 10,000 shares of $10 par value common stock for $100,000 cash.

(2) On January 5, Miller pays $12,000 cash to rent equipment for one year. In this transaction, Miller's asset is prepaid rent, not the equipment itself.

(3) On January 15, Miller purchases merchandise inventory costing $15,000 from a supplier, agreeing to pay later.

(4) On January 21, it pays the supplier in **(3)** $8,000 of the amount due.

---

[5]Firms do not use the same ordering for showing the current year's results and the prior year's results. Some firms order the columns oldest to most recent, while others order most recent to oldest. You must read the column headings to identify the column.

EXHIBIT 2.2	Miller Corporation Illustration of Dual Effects of Transactions on Balance Sheet Equation

Transaction		Assets	=	Liabilities	+	Shareholders' Equity
(1)	On January 1, Miller Corporation issues 10,000 shares of $10 par value common stock for $100,000 cash (an increase in an asset and shareholders' equity).	+$100,000		$ 0		+$100,000
	Subtotal	$100,000	=	$ 0	+	$100,000
(2)	On January 5, the firm pays $12,000 cash to rent some equipment (an increase in one asset and a decrease in another asset).	+ 12,000 − 12,000				
	Subtotal	$100,000	=	$ 0	+	$100,000
(3)	On January 15, the firm purchases merchandise inventory costing $15,000 from a supplier on account (an increase in an asset and a liability).	+ 15,000		+ 15,000		
	Subtotal	$115,000	=	$15,000	+	$100,000
(4)	On January 21, the firm pays the supplier in (3) $8,000 of the amount due (a decrease in an asset and a liability).	− 8,000		− 8,000		
	Subtotal	$107,000	=	$ 7,000	+	$100,000
(5)	On January 25, the supplier in (3) accepts 700 shares of Miller common stock in settlement of the $7,000 still owed (an increase in shareholders' equity and a decrease in a liability).			− 7,000		+ 7,000
	Subtotal	$107,000	=	$ 0	+	$107,000
(6)	On January 31, the firm pays $600 cash for a one-year insurance premium for coverage beginning February 1 (an increase in one asset and a decrease in another asset).	+ 600 − 600				
	Subtotal	$107,000	=	$ 0	+	$107,000
(7)	On January 31, the firm receives $3,000 from a customer for merchandise Miller will deliver during February (an increase in an asset and a liability).	+ 3,000		+ 3,000		
	Subtotal—January 31	$110,000	=	$ 3,000	+	$107,000
(8)	On January 31, the firm purchases a building for $40,000, financed by a note payable with a local bank (an increase in an asset and a liability).	+ 40,000		+ 40,000		
	Total—January 31	$150,000	=	$43,000	+	$107,000

(5) On January 25, the supplier in (3) accepts 700 shares of Miller common stock at par value in settlement of the $7,000 amount still owed.

(6) On January 31, Miller pays $600 cash for a one-year insurance premium for coverage beginning February 1.

(7) On January 31, Miller receives $3,000 from a customer for merchandise Miller will deliver during February.

(8) On January 31, Miller purchases a building for $40,000 and finances this purchase by signing a note payable with a local bank. Miller promises to repay the note in full in three years and to pay interest at 10% per year.

Exhibit 2.2 illustrates the dual effects of these transactions on the balance sheet equation. Note that after each transaction, assets equal liabilities plus shareholders' equity.

Each transaction has two effects.[6] For example, in transaction (1) Miller issues common stock to shareholders and receives cash. In transaction (2) Miller makes a cash expenditure and receives the right to use equipment. In transaction (3) Miller promises to make a future cash payment to a supplier and receives merchandise inventory. These and other transac-

---

[6]In general, each transaction will have at least two effects. All the transactions illustrated here have only two.

tions recorded in the accounting system result from exchanges. The accounting records reflect effects on assets, liabilities, and shareholders equity arising from these exchanges.

The recording of each transaction maintains the balance sheet equality. Transactions **(1)**, **(3)**, **(7)**, and **(8)** increase assets and increase either a liability or shareholders' equity. Transaction **(4)** decreases assets and a liability. Transactions **(2)** and **(6)** increase one asset and decrease another asset. Transaction **(5)** increases shareholders' equity and decreases a liability.

PROBLEM 2.1 for Self-Study

Dual effects of transactions on balance sheet equation. Using the format in **Exhibit 2.2**, indicate the effects of each of the following transactions of Gaines Corporation on the balance sheet equation.

1. The firm issues 20,000 shares of £10 par value common stock for £12 cash per share.

2. The firm issues £100,000 principal amount of bonds for £100,000 cash.

3. The firm acquires, with £220,000 in cash, land costing £40,000 and a building costing £180,000.

4. The firm acquires, on account, equipment costing £25,000 and merchandise inventory costing £12,000. ("On account" means that the firm agrees to pay later for the equipment and inventory.)

5. The firm signs an agreement to rent equipment from its owner and pays £1,500 rental in advance.

6. The firm pays £28,000 to the suppliers in **4**.

T-ACCOUNTS

Although **Exhibit 2.2** illustrates the dual effects of individual transactions, it does not provide a framework for preparing a balance sheet. Specifically, the exhibit does not describe how much of the total assets of $150,000 represents cash, how much represents inventory, how much represents equipment, and so on. A disaggregated display of balance sheet items would provide users of financial statements with information about the sources of a firm's financing and how management has invested the cash and other assets received from shareholders and creditors in specific assets. For example, **Exhibit 2.1** shows that as of December 31, 2007, Colgate has invested over $1 billion in inventories. To move to a disaggregated reporting format, we introduce the use of T-accounts for accumulating information about how transactions and events during a period affect specific asset, liability, and shareholders' equity accounts.

A **T-account** is a device or convention for organizing and accumulating the accounting entries of transactions that affect an *individual* account, such as cash, accounts receivable, bonds payable, or additional paid-in capital. As the name implies, the T-account looks like the letter T, with a horizontal line bisected by a vertical line. Conventionally, the name of the specific individual account title appears on the horizontal line.

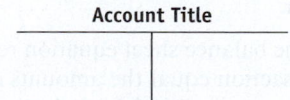

Account Title

Increases and Decreases to the T-Account One side of the space formed by the vertical line records increases in the account, and the other side records decreases. Which side records increases and which side records decreases differs depending on whether the T-account represents an asset account or represents a liability or shareholders' equity account. Long-standing custom follows three rules:

1. Increases in assets appear on the left side, and decreases in assets appear on the right side of T-accounts.

2. Increases in liabilities appear on the right side, and decreases in liabilities appear on the left side of T-accounts.

3. Increases in shareholders' equity appear on the right side, and decreases in shareholders' equity appear on the left side of T-accounts.

This custom reflects the fact that in the balance sheet equation, assets appear to the left of the equal sign, while liabilities and shareholders' equity appear to the right. Following this format, asset balances appear on the left side of T-accounts; liability and shareholders' equity balances appear on the right. Asset balances will appear on the left only if the left side of the accounts records increases in the asset.[7] Similarly, liability and shareholders' equity balances appear on the right only if accounting records liability and shareholders' equity increases on the right side of accounts.

The net amount or balance in an account results from summing the amounts recorded on the left side and right side of the account and netting the two sums. As we noted previously, the net amount, or balance, in an asset account typically appears as an amount on the left side, whereas liability and shareholders' equity accounts typically have net right side balances. The balance in an account at the end of one reporting period is that account's opening balance at the start of the next reporting period. By convention, the first line in the T-account reports the beginning or opening balance, and the last line reports the ending or closing balance. Thus, the following equation describes a typical asset account with a left side balance:

> Beginning Balance in Asset Account (left side)
> + Sum of the transactions affecting the left side of the Asset Account
> − Sum of the transactions affecting the right side of the Asset Account
> = Ending Balance in Asset Account (left side)

For a typical liability or equity account, the T-account equation is:

> Beginning Balance in Liability or Shareholders' Equity Account (right side)
> + Sum of the transactions affecting the right side of the Liability or Shareholders' Equity Account
> − Sum of the transactions affecting the left side of the Liability or Shareholders' Equity Account
> = Ending Balance in Liability or Shareholders' Equity Account (right side)

Proper analysis and recording of the dual effects of a transaction results in recording equal amounts on the left-hand side and the right-hand side of the various accounts; this result is consistent with the balance sheet equation described earlier. The equality of the amounts recorded on the left and right for any transaction provides a powerful check for the accuracy of record keeping. *If you analyze a transaction and get unequal amounts for left and right amounts, you will know you have erred.*

Debit and Credit   Accountants use two abbreviations: debit (Dr.) and credit (Cr.). **Debit**, used as a verb, means "record an entry on the left side of an account" and, used as a noun or an adjective, means "an entry on the left side of an account." **Credit**, used as a verb, means "record an entry on the right side of an account" and, used as a noun or an adjective, means "an entry on the right side of an account." Combining these terms with the three rules for T-accounts, we see the following:

- A debit indicates (1) an increase in an asset, (2) a decrease in a liability, or (3) a decrease in a shareholders' equity item.
- A credit indicates (1) a decrease in an asset, (2) an increase in a liability, or (3) an increase in a shareholders' equity item.

Maintaining the equality of the balance sheet equation requires that the amounts debited to various accounts for each transaction equal the amounts credited to various accounts. As a result, the sum of balances in accounts with debit balances at the end of each period must equal the sum of balances in accounts with credit balances. Debits equal credits: this applies to each individual transaction and to the balance sheet as a whole.

Summary of Account Terminology and Procedure   The following T-accounts summarize the conventional use of the account form and the terms debit and credit.

---

[7]As we describe in a subsequent section of this chapter, some accounts that appear in the asset section of the balance sheet accumulate subtractions from the asset, so they act like a liability or shareholders' equity account in that increases in the account appear on the right side, not the left side. We refer to these accounts, which accumulate subtractions from another account, as *contra-asset* accounts. A contra-asset account appears on the asset side of the balance sheet as a subtraction from an asset, not among the liability or shareholders' equity accounts. Contra-liability and contra-equity accounts also exist; in subsequent chapters, we discuss each of these accounts as they arise.

Any Asset Account		Any Liability Account		Any Shareholders' Equity Account	
Beginning Balance			Beginning Balance		Beginning Balance
Increases	Decreases	Decreases	Increases	Decreases	Increases
+	−	−	+	−	+
Dr.	Cr.	Dr.	Cr.	Dr.	Cr.
Ending Balance			Ending Balance		Ending Balance

REFLECTING THE DUAL EFFECTS OF TRANSACTIONS IN T-ACCOUNTS

To show how the dual effects of transactions change the T-accounts, **Exhibit 2.3** records the transactions of Miller Corporation for January using separate T-accounts for each balance sheet item. The numbers in parentheses refer to the eight January transactions. The data in **Exhibit 2.3** show that Miller Corporation's total assets of $150,000 as of January 31 consist of $82,400 in cash, $15,000 in merchandise inventory, $600 in prepaid insurance (advances *to* the insurance provider), $12,000 in prepaid rent, and $40,000 in building. Total liabilities plus shareholders' equity of $150,000 consists of $3,000 of advances from customers, $40,000 in notes payable, and $107,000 of common stock.

EXHIBIT 2.3 Miller Corporation
Individual T-Accounts Showing Transactions

Cash (Asset)

	Increases (Dr.)	Decreases (Cr.)	
(1)	100,000	12,000	(2)
(7)	3,000	8,000	(4)
		600	(6)
Balance	82,400		

Accounts Payable (Liability)

	Decreases (Dr.)	Increases (Cr.)	
(4)	8,000	15,000	(3)
(5)	7,000		
		0	Balance

Merchandise Inventory (Asset)

	Increases (Dr.)	Decreases (Cr.)	
(3)	15,000		
Balance	15,000		

Advances from Customer (Liability)

	Decreases (Dr.)	Increases (Cr.)	
		3,000	(7)
		3,000	Balance

Prepaid Insurance (Asset)

	Increases (Dr.)	Decreases (Cr.)	
(6)	600		
Balance	600		

Note Payable (Liability)

	Decreases (Dr.)	Increases (Cr.)	
		40,000	(8)
		40,000	Balance

Prepaid Rent (Asset)

	Increases (Dr.)	Decreases (Cr.)	
(2)	12,000		
Balance	12,000		

Common Stock (Shareholders' Equity)

	Decreases (Dr.)	Increases (Cr.)	
		100,000	(1)
		7,000	(5)
		107,000	Balance

Buildings (Asset)

	Increases (Dr.)	Decreases (Cr.)	
(8)	40,000		
Balance	40,000		

Retained Earnings (Shareholders' Equity)

	Decreases (Dr.)	Increases (Cr.)	
		0	Balance

EXHIBIT 2.4

**Miller Corporation
Balance Sheet
January 31**

ASSETS

Current Assets

Cash	$ 82,400
Merchandise Inventory	15,000
Prepaid Insurance	600
Prepaid Rent	12,000
Total Current Assets	$110,000

Property, Plant, and Equipment

Buildings	$ 40,000
Total Assets	$150,000

LIABILITIES AND SHAREHOLDERS' EQUITY

Current Liabilities

Advances from Customer	$ 3,000

Noncurrent Liabilities

Note Payable	40,000
Total Liabilities	$ 43,000

Shareholders' Equity

Common Stock	$107,000
Retained Earnings	—
Total Liabilities and Shareholders' Equity	$150,000

One can prepare the balance sheet using the amounts shown as balances in the T-accounts. The balance sheet of Miller Corporation after the eight transactions of January appears in **Exhibit 2.4**.

PROBLEM 2.2 for Self-Study

> **T-accounts for various transactions.** Set up T-accounts for the following accounts:
>
> | | |
> |---|---|
> | Cash | Bonds Payable |
> | Merchandise Inventory | Land |
> | Prepaid Rent | Buildings |
> | Equipment | Common Stock—Par Value |
> | Accounts Payable | Additional Paid-In Capital |
>
> Indicate whether each account is an asset, a liability, or a shareholders' equity item. Enter in the T-accounts the transactions of Gaines Corporation in **Problem 2.1 for Self-Study**.

JOURNAL ENTRIES

The preceding section illustrated the use of T-accounts to

1. Record the effects of transactions on individual balance sheet accounts, and
2. Sum the effects of all transactions affecting a particular account during a period, obtain an ending balance in that account, and then prepare a balance sheet.

T-accounts are a useful pedagogical device to understand how individual transactions flow to and accumulate within various accounts, and they provide the needed information for a balance sheet. However, if the resulting balance sheet does not balance, then it becomes necessary to retrace the recording of every transaction to find the error. Tracking down the error using T-accounts can be awkward and time consuming because the effects of each transaction spread across two or more T-accounts.

To address this problem, we introduce a step that precedes the recording of individual transactions in T-accounts: the preparation of a journal entry. A **journal entry** uses a standardized format to indicate the accounts and amounts affected by each transaction. Assuming that the journal entry reflects equal debits and credits to various accounts, the accountant would then transfer the amounts from the journal entry to the appropriate T-accounts. Assuming proper recording in the T-accounts and summing of all entries in the T-accounts, the resulting balance sheet should be in balance. Journal entries simply formalize the reasoning that supports entering the results of transactions directly in the T-accounts.

We sometimes use T-accounts, sometimes use journal entries, and sometimes use both to illustrate the effects of transactions in this book. They are both pedagogical devices to assist your understanding of the effects of transactions.[8]

The standard format of a journal entry is:

Account Title	Amount
Account Title	Amount

The journal entry indicates the dual effects of a transaction on both the accounts and the balances in accounts. By convention, the first line of the journal entry is the debit line, and the second (indented) line of the journal entry is the credit line. Thus,

Account Debited	Amount Debited
Account Credited	Amount Credited

Sometimes you will see the following additional (and redundant) notation for debits and credits added to the journal entry:

Dr.	Account Debited	Amount Debited
	Cr. Account Credited	Amount Credited

The recording of journal entries follows the same rules for increases and decreases in asset, liability, and shareholders' equity accounts as illustrated earlier for entries in T-accounts:

1. Debits increase an asset account, or decrease a liability or shareholders' equity account.

2. Credits decrease an asset account, or increase a liability or shareholders' equity account.

Journal entries may have multiple debit lines or multiple credit lines, or both. The dual effects rule requires that the sum of the amounts debited equal the sum of the amounts credited so that the journal entry balances. Ensuring that all individual journal entries balance simultaneously guarantees that all debit balances equal all credit balances in the T-accounts and that total assets equal the sum of total liabilities plus total shareholders' equity, as the balance sheet equation requires.

Journal entries generally include the date of the transaction and an explanation for the transaction(s) journalized; often they include an identifying number, as well. In this book we show you how journal entries affect the balance sheet equation. This equation is not part of

---

[8]Firms initially record individual transactions in journal entries in a *general journal* and then periodically post the journal entries to particular accounts in the *general ledger*. The use of T-accounts, which we use for pedagogical purposes, mimics the use of posting to the general ledger.

the journal entries made in the accounting records, but we find it helps students to understand the transaction better.[9] Thus, the standard format for journal entries in this book is:

(#) Date

Account Debited . . . . Amount

     Account Credited . . . . Amount

Assets	=	Liabilities	+	Shareholders' Equity	(Class.)

Journal entry explanation.

We use the column labeled (Class.) to indicate the classification of the particular shareholders' equity account that the transaction affects.

The journal entries for the eight transactions of Miller Corporation appear next.

(1) January 1

Cash 100,000

     Common Stock 100,000

Assets	=	Liabilities	+	Shareholders' Equity	(Class.)
+100,000				+100,000	ContriCap

Issue 10,000 shares of $10 par value common stock for cash. The issuance of common stock increases the contributed capital portion of shareholders' equity, specifically, common stock.

(2) January 5

Prepaid Rent 12,000

     Cash 12,000

Assets	=	Liabilities	+	Shareholders' Equity	(Class.)
+12,000					
−12,000					

Pay annual rent of $12,000 for use of equipment.

(3) January 15

Merchandise Inventory 15,000

     Accounts Payable 15,000

Assets	=	Liabilities	+	Shareholders' Equity	(Class.)
+15,000		+15,000			

Purchase merchandise inventory costing $15,000 on account.

---

[9]Another approach that is sometimes used, for pedagogical purposes, is to include abbreviations for assets (A), liabilities (L) and shareholders' equity (SE) to describe the type of account affected by each portion of the journal entry. For example, the acquisition of equipment in exchange for a promise to pay the equipment supplier in the future would be journalized (recorded) as follows:

Equipment (A) . . . . Amount Debited

     Notes Payable (L) . . . . Amount Credited

(4) January 21

Accounts Payable   8,000

    Cash   8,000

Assets	=	Liabilities	+	Shareholders' Equity	(Class.)
−8,000		−8,000			

Pay liabilities of $8,000 with cash.

(5) January 25

Accounts Payable   7,000

    Common Stock   7,000

Assets	=	Liabilities	+	Shareholders' Equity	(Class.)
		−7,000		+7,000	ContriCap

Issue 700 shares of $10 par value common stock in settlement of $7,000 accounts payable.

(6) January 31

Prepaid Insurance (or Advances to Insurance Company)   600

    Cash   600

Assets	=	Liabilities	+	Shareholders' Equity	(Class.)
+600					
−600					

Pay one-year insurance premium of $600 in advance.

(7) January 31

Cash   3,000

    Advances from Customers   3,000

Assets	=	Liabilities	+	Shareholders' Equity	(Class.)
+3,000		+3,000			

Receive $3,000 from customer for merchandise to be delivered in February.

(8) January 31

Buildings   40,000

    Note Payable   40,000

Assets	=	Liabilities	+	Shareholders' Equity	(Class.)
+40,000		+40,000			

Purchase building costing $40,000, financed by note payable from local bank.

PROBLEM 2.3 for Self-Study

> **Journal entries for various transactions.** Prepare journal entries for each of the six transactions of Gaines Corporation in **Problem 2.1 for Self-Study**.

PROBLEM **2.4** for Self-Study

Journal entries, T-accounts, and balance sheet preparation. Electronics Appliance Corporation begins operations on September 1 and engages in the following transactions during September:

(1) September 1: Issues 4,000 shares of $10 par value common stock for $12 cash per share.

(2) September 2: Gives 600 shares of $10 par value common stock to acquire a patent from another firm. The two entities agree on a price of $7,200 for the patent.

(3) September 5: Pays $10,000 as two months' rent in advance on a factory building that it leases for the three years beginning October 1. Monthly rental payments are $5,000.

(4) September 12: Purchases raw materials on account for $6,100.

(5) September 15: Receives a check for $900 from a customer as a deposit on a special order for equipment that Electronics plans to manufacture. The contract price is $4,800.

(6) September 20: Acquires office equipment with a list price of $950. After deducting a discount of $25 for prompt payment, it issues a check in full payment.

(7) September 28: Issues a cash advance totaling $200 to three new employees who will begin work on October 1.

(8) September 30: Purchases factory equipment costing $27,500. It issues a check for $5,000 and assumes a long-term note payable for the balance.

(9) September 30: Pays $450 for the labor costs of installing the new equipment in **(8)**.

   a. Prepare journal entries for each of the nine transactions.

   b. Set up T-accounts and enter each of the nine transactions. Note that all account balances are zero at the beginning of September.

   c. Prepare a balance sheet for Electronics Appliance Corporation as of September 30.

THE INCOME STATEMENT

COMMON TERMINOLOGY

The preceding sections described the application of three bookkeeping conventions (dual effects of transactions, T-accounts, and journal entries) to transactions affecting the balance sheet, and emphasized the usefulness of the balance sheet equation. We now consider transactions that affect the income statement, a second principal financial statement that firms prepare to report on their business activities. We begin by describing some account titles used in income statements to provide a sense of typical names (sometimes called "rows" or "line items") used in published income statements.

   Revenues or Sales: assets received (for example, cash) in exchange for goods sold and services rendered. Outside the U.S., sales or revenues are sometimes called *turnover*.

   Cost of Goods Sold: the cost of products sold. *Cost of services* is a similar concept and refers to the cost of services sold.

   Selling, General and Administrative (SG&A): costs incurred to sell products and services (such as salaries of the sales force) as well as costs of administration (such as the salaries of top executives, and rent and insurance on corporate headquarters buildings and furnishings).

   Research and Development (R&D) Expense: costs incurred to create and develop new products, processes, and services.

   Advertising Expense: costs incurred with the goal of increasing sales by attracting more customers or inducing existing customers to increase their purchases. No rule requires that the income statement separately show these items, which can be part of SG&A.

   Interest Expense: the cost of using borrowed funds.

EXHIBIT 2.5   **Colgate Palmolive Company**
Income Statement

For the years ended December 31,	2007	2006	2005
Net sales	$13,789.7	$12,237.7	$11,396.9
Cost of sales	6,042.3	5,536.1	5,191.9
Gross profit	7,747.4	6,701.6	6,205.0
Selling, general and administrative expenses	4,973.0	4,355.2	3,920.8
Other (income) expense, net	121.3	185.9	69.2
Operating profit	2,653.1	2,160.5	2,215.0
Interest expense, net	156.6	158.7	136.0
Income before income taxes	2,496.5	2,001.8	2,079.0
Provision for income taxes	759.1	648.4	727.6
Net income	$ 1,737.4	$ 1,353.4	$ 1,351.4
Earnings per common share, basic	$ 3.35	$ 2.57	$ 2.54
Earnings per common share, diluted	$ 3.20	$ 2.46	$ 2.43

Interest Income: income earned on amounts lent to others or from investments in interest-yielding securities.

Income Tax Expense: federal, state, and local taxes levied on income.

A TYPICAL INCOME STATEMENT

Just as the balance sheet lists accounts, grouped by type, so too does the income statement. The income statement displays, for a given period, revenues (net asset inflows) and expenses (net asset outflows); the difference is net income (also called *earnings* or *profit*). If the expenses exceed the revenues of a period, the result is a *loss* or a *net loss*.

The income statement begins with revenues (sometimes called the "top line") and then subtracts expenses associated with operating the business (for example, cost of goods sold, SG&A, R&D, and advertising). The next line items display other sources of income (such as interest income) and other expenses (such as interest expense) to arrive at income before taxes. Income tax expense is then subtracted to arrive at net income (sometimes called the "bottom line"). Some firms declare, then pay, dividends to their shareholders. A dividend is a distribution of net assets generated by earnings—not a cost incurred in generating earnings—so it never appears as an expense on the income statement.

The income statement of Colgate Palmolive Company for the fiscal year ended December 31, 2007, is shown in **Exhibit 2.5**. Both U.S. GAAP and IFRS require the display of income statements for the current year as well as the two prior years. Colgate reports the results for the current year, 2007, in the first (leftmost) column of numbers, with the results for 2006 and 2005 reported in the remaining two columns. Colgate's income statement reflects a relatively sparse listing of accounts. Most firms' income statements contain more detail, that is, more line items or rows.

Firms have considerable flexibility in the way they present income items. Colgate, for example, reports subtotals for Gross Profit, Operating Profit, and Income Before Income Taxes. A later section of this chapter and subsequent chapters discuss these terms more fully.

RELATION BETWEEN THE BALANCE SHEET AND THE INCOME STATEMENT

The income statement links the beginning and ending balance sheets. The beginning balance of the shareholders' equity account Retained Earnings plus net income from the income statement less dividends equals the ending balance of Retained Earnings. The equation that describes the relation between the balance sheet and the income statement through the Retained Earnings account is as follows:

$$\text{Retained Earnings (beginning)} + \text{Net Income} - \text{Dividends} = \text{Retained Earnings (ending)}$$

In this sense, common terminology often says that the income statement "articulates" with the balance sheet. Retained earnings measures the cumulative excess of net income over dividends for the life of a firm. *Cumulative* means that retained earnings aggregates *all* undistributed earnings.

Inspection of Colgate's balance sheet, shown in **Exhibit 2.1**, reveals that Colgate's Retained Earnings balance increased from $9,643.7 million on December 31, 2006, to $10,627.5 million on December 31, 2007. From **Exhibit 2.5** we see that Colgate's net income for 2007 was $1,737.4 million. Elsewhere in its annual report, Colgate reported 2007 dividends of $721.6 million for common shareholders and $28.0 million for preferred shareholders, or a total of $749.6 million in dividends. Using this information, we can calculate whether Colgate's balance sheet and income statement articulate by examining whether the retained earnings relation holds:

$$\text{Retained Earnings (beginning)} + \text{Net Income} - \text{Dividends} = \text{Retained Earnings (ending)}$$

$$= \$9,643.7 + \$1,737.4 - \$749.6$$

$$= \$10,631.5$$

The calculated amount, $10,631.5, is $4.0 million higher than Colgate's reported balance in Retained Earnings at the end of 2007, $10,627.5 million. The difference of $4.0 million results from an adjustment for the application of a new accounting standard, which Colgate charged to Retained Earnings.

In summary, the retained earnings relation does not hold for Colgate for 2007 because of other transactions that affected its Retained Earnings during the year. We ignore these kinds of items here and revisit them in **Chapter 14**.

The following disaggregation of the balance sheet equation shows the relation of revenues, expenses, and dividends to the components of the balance sheet.

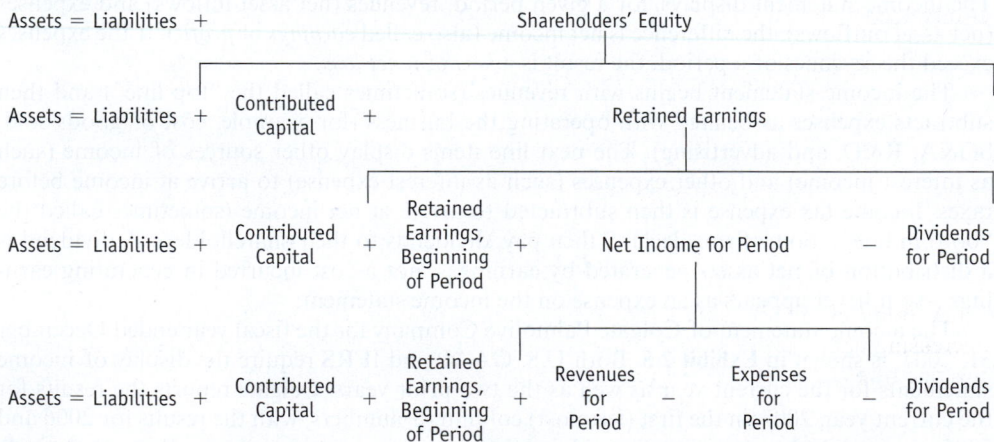

The preceding diagram shows that items that affect net income (revenues and expenses) also affect shareholders' equity. It is, therefore, possible to record revenue and expense amounts directly in the Retained Earnings account. Measuring net income would then involve solving the retained earnings relation for net income, as follows:

$$\text{Net Income} = \frac{\text{Retained Earnings}}{\text{at End of Period}} - \frac{\text{Retained Earnings at}}{\text{Beginning of Period}} + \text{Dividends}$$

The purpose of the income statement is not the calculation of net income, per se, because the reader can do this by analyzing the retained earnings relation. However, recording revenues and expenses directly in the Retained Earnings account suppresses information about the causes of net income. The line items or rows on the income statement display the sources and amounts of revenues as well as the nature and amounts of expenses that net to earnings for the period. Knowing these income components helps the user both to understand the causes of past performance and to forecast future performance. Knowing the purpose of the income statement—to display the line items for components of net income—will help you understand the procedures for preparing it.

Accountants maintain individual revenue and expense accounts during an accounting period to permit preparation of an income statement. Recall from our earlier discussion that income statement accounts are temporary accounts, as opposed to the permanent accounts that appear on the balance sheet. All temporary accounts begin with a zero balance and accumulate information for the period. After preparing the income statement at the end of the period, the accountant transfers the balance in each temporary revenue and expense account to the Retained Earnings account. This procedure is called *closing* the revenue and expense accounts, because after closing (that is, the transfer to Retained Earnings), each revenue and expense account has a zero balance. Retained Earnings increases by the amount of net income (or decreases by the amount of net loss) for the period.

Maintaining separate revenue and expense accounts during the period and transferring their balances to the Retained Earnings account at the end of the period has the same effect on the balance sheet equation as initially recording revenues and expenses directly in the Retained Earnings account. The separate revenue and expense accounts collect the information needed to display the specific types of revenues and expenses in the income statement, which otherwise could show the total amount of net income but not its components. Once revenue and expense accounts serve their purpose of accumulating specific revenue and expense items for an accounting period, they have no further purpose for that period. The accountant closes these accounts so that they begin the following accounting period with a zero balance, ready for the revenue and expense entries of the new period.

ACCOUNTING PROCESS FOR REVENUES, EXPENSES, AND DIVIDENDS

Revenues, expenses, and dividends increase or decrease retained earnings, so the recording procedures for these items are the same as for any other transaction affecting shareholders' equity accounts.

Shareholders' Equity	
Decreases (Debit)	Increases (Credit)
Expenses	Revenues
Dividends	Issues of Capital Stock

A transaction generating revenue increases net assets (either by increasing assets or decreasing liabilities) and increases shareholders' equity. The usual journal entry to record a revenue transaction is therefore as follows:

Asset Increase or Liability Decrease (or both) . . . .   Amount
    Revenue . . . .   Amount

Assets	=	Liabilities	+	Shareholders' Equity	(Class.)
+	or	−		+	IncSt → RE

Typical entry to recognize revenue.

We use the designation IncSt → RE in the "Class." column to indicate an income statement account that is closed to retained earnings at the end of the period.

A transaction generating an expense decreases net assets (either by decreasing assets or increasing liabilities) and decreases shareholders' equity. The usual journal entry to record an expense transaction is therefore as follows:

| Expense . . . . | Amount |
| Asset Decrease or Liability Increase (or both) . . . . | Amount |

Assets	=	Liabilities	+	Shareholders' Equity	(Class.)
−	or	+		−	IncSt → RE

Typical journal entry to recognize expense.

Dividends, which a firm may pay in cash or in other assets, decrease net assets and decrease shareholders' equity. We assume that firms pay dividends in cash unless we have contrary information. The following journal entry records the declaration of a dividend by the board of directors:

| Retained Earnings. . . . . | Amount |
| Dividend Payable . . . . | Amount |

Assets	=	Liabilities	+	Shareholders' Equity	(Class.)
		+		−	RE

Typical entry to record dividend declaration.

The following journal entry records the payment of the dividend:

| Dividend Payable . . . . | Amount |
| Cash. . . . . | Amount |

Assets	=	Liabilities	+	Shareholders' Equity	(Class.)
−		−			

Typical entry to record dividend payment.

Although the journal entries for dividends resemble those for expenses, dividends are not expenses. They are not costs incurred in generating revenues. Rather, dividends represent distributions, to owners, of assets that the firm obtained from its operations. Because dividends are not expenses, they do not affect the measurement of net income and, therefore, are not included in the calculation of net income. Note that Colgate's income statement in **Exhibit 2.5** shows no deduction for the $749.6 million dividends paid in 2007.

ILLUSTRATION OF DUAL EFFECTS AND JOURNAL ENTRIES FOR INCOME TRANSACTIONS

Earlier in this chapter, we illustrated the transactions of Miller Corporation for January. None of those transactions involved income statement accounts, as **Exhibit 2.4** reflects because it shows a zero balance in the Retained Earnings account. The account has a zero balance at the end of January because during January Miller did not generate revenues, incur expenses, or declare a dividend.

In this section, we consider transactions that affect both the income statement and the balance sheet. We consider seven transactions that Miller engages in during February.

Transaction 1: On February 5 Miller purchases an additional $25,000 of merchandise on account.

(1) Merchandise Inventory	25,000
Accounts Payable	25,000
	(continued)

Assets	=	Liabilities	+	Shareholders' Equity	(Class.)
+25,000		+25,000			

Purchase of inventory costing $25,000 on account.

Transaction 2: During February, Miller sells merchandise to customers for $50,000. Of this amount, $3,000 represents sales to customers who paid $3,000 to Miller on January 31. We recorded this amount as Advances from Customer (transaction **(7)** that occurred during January). Miller makes the remaining $47,000 of sales on account. Retail firms such as Miller typically recognize revenue at the time they deliver merchandise to customers, regardless of whether the customers have paid cash. The journal entry to record these sales is:

---

(2) Advances from Customer	. . . .	3,000	
Accounts Receivable	. . . .	47,000	
Sales Revenue	. . . .		50,000

Assets	=	Liabilities	+	Shareholders' Equity	(Class.)
+47,000		−3,000		+50,000	IncSt → RE

Sales of merchandise for $50,000, $3,000 of which Miller had received during January, and $47,000 of which is on account.

Sales Revenue is a temporary income statement account that Miller will close to Retained Earnings at the end of February.

Transaction 3: The acquisition cost of the merchandise sold to customers in transaction **(2)** is $30,000. Because Miller has sold and delivered this merchandise to customers, it is no longer Miller's asset. The following journal entry reduces the balance in Miller's inventory account and recognizes the cost of the inventory sold as an expense.

---

(3) Cost of Goods Sold	. . . .	30,000	
Merchandise Inventory	. . . .		30,000

Assets	=	Liabilities	+	Shareholders' Equity	(Class.)
−30,000				−30,000	IncSt → RE

The cost of merchandise sold to customers during February is $30,000.

Cost of Goods Sold is a temporary income statement account that Miller will close to the Retained Earnings account at the end of February. The minus sign under the Shareholders' Equity column shows the effect on shareholders' equity, not on Cost of Goods Sold.

Transaction 4: Miller Corporation incurs and pays $14,500 of selling and administrative costs during February. The journal entry to record this transaction is:

---

(4) Selling and Administrative Expenses	. . . .	14,500	
Cash	. . . .		14,500

Assets	=	Liabilities	+	Shareholders' Equity	(Class.)
−14,500				−14,500	IncSt → RE

Selling and administrative expenses paid in cash during February total $14,500.

We assume that Miller Corporation received all the benefits of these selling and administrative services during February, so the full amount of cost is an expense for the month. None of the expenditure results in an asset that would appear on the balance sheet at the end of February.

Transaction 5: Miller Corporation collects $35,000 from customers for sales previously made on account. Miller recognized revenue from these sales at the time of sale (see transaction (2) for February); it will not record those revenues again. Collecting cash from customers increases the balance in the cash account and decreases accounts receivable.

| (5) Cash . . . . | 35,000 | |
| Accounts Receivable . . . . | | 35,000 |

Assets	=	Liabilities	+	Shareholders' Equity	(Class.)
+35,000					
−35,000					

Cash collections of $35,000 from sales previously made on account.

Transaction 6: Miller pays $20,000 to suppliers for merchandise previously purchased on account. The journal entry to record this payment is:

| (6) Accounts Payable . . . . | 20,000 | |
| Cash . . . . | | 20,000 |

Assets	=	Liabilities	+	Shareholders' Equity	(Class.)
−20,000		−20,000			

Cash payments of $20,000 for purchases previously made on account.

Transaction 7: Miller Corporation declares and pays a dividend to shareholders of $1,000. The entry to record the dividend is:

| (7) Retained Earnings. . . . . | 1,000 | |
| Cash . . . . | | 1,000 |

Assets	=	Liabilities	+	Shareholders' Equity	(Class.)
−1,000				−1,000	RE

Dividends declared and paid during February total $1,000.

These seven journal entries summarize Miller Corporation's activities during February. Each entry records an exchange between Miller and its suppliers, or its customers, or its shareholders. A typical firm would record entries such as these as the events occur. We have simplified the journal entries by aggregating the month's transactions into a single summary number.

An accounting system would transfer the information in these journal entries to the balance sheet and income statement accounts affected; this activity is the **posting process**. We use T-accounts to show the account balances at the beginning of February and the posting of these seven transactions during February for Miller Corporation. **Exhibit 2.6** shows the T-accounts, with the seven entries recorded in blue. We discuss the entries recorded in red and gold next. The balance sheet accounts have beginning-of-February balances equal to their ending balances at the end of January. The income statement accounts have zero balances at the beginning of February (by design, because they are temporary accounts). Both the balance sheet accounts and the income statement accounts reflect the effects of the seven February transactions.

ADJUSTING ENTRIES

Transactions (1) to (7) involve exchanges between Miller Corporation and other entities or individuals during February. Each of the seven transactions involves a transaction or exchange that triggers accounting recognition in the form of a journal entry. For example, the events in transactions (1) and (2) are a purchase of inventory and the sale of merchandise to a customer, respectively. In addition to accounting entries that result from transactions or exchanges, some entries result from the passage of time. For example, interest expense on borrowing accrues as time passes. The costs of rent and insurance accrue as the firm uses these services.

Most firms record journal entries that result from the passage of time at the end of the accounting period. These entries are called **adjusting entries** because they adjust the accounting records for changes in balance sheet and income statement accounts that continually occur and reflect changes in the firm's resources (assets) and claims on those assets (liabilities and shareholder's equity). The adjusting entries are part of the measurement of net income for the period and financial position at the end of the period.

Miller Corporation will make five adjusting entries at the end of February (shown in red in **Exhibit 2.6**).

Transaction 8: Miller records the cost of insurance, which is the portion of prepaid insurance attributable to insurance services received during February. Miller paid the $600 one-year insurance premium on January 31 for coverage from February 1 of this year through January 31 of next year. Assuming the allocation of an equal amount of this insurance premium to each month of the year, the cost of insurance during February is $50 (= $600/12 months). Miller includes the cost of insurance in selling and administrative expenses. The entry is:

(8) Selling and Administrative Expenses   50
    Prepaid Insurance.   50

Assets	=	Liabilities	+	Shareholders' Equity	(Class.)
−50				−50	IncSt → RE

The cost of insurance services received during February is $50.

The remaining $550 of prepaid insurance becomes an expense during the next 11 months. In the meantime, it remains an asset on the balance sheet.

Transaction 9: Miller Corporation records the cost of rent, which is the portion of prepaid rent that is attributable to rent services consumed during February. Miller paid $12,000 on January 31 to prepay its rent for February 1 of this year through January 31 of next year. Assuming the allocation of an equal amount of rental cost to each month, February's rent expense is $1,000 (= $12,000/12 months). Miller Corporation includes rent expense in selling and administrative expenses. The entry is:

(9) Selling and Administrative Expenses   1,000
    Prepaid Rent   1,000

Assets	=	Liabilities	+	Shareholders' Equity	(Class.)
−1,000				−1,000	IncSt → RE

The cost of rental services received during February is $1,000.

The remaining $11,000 of prepaid rent becomes an expense during the next 11 months.

Transaction 10: Accumulated Depreciation shows the cumulative amount of the acquisition cost of long-lived assets that the firm has allocated to the cost of production or to expenses. On February 1, Miller Corporation begins consuming the services of the building that it purchased on January 31 for $40,000 and recorded as an asset on that date.[10] Miller records depreciation on the building starting from February 1 (the date that it began using the building) to reflect the consumption over time of building services. Assume that Miller expects the building to last for 20 years and that Miller believes the building will have no value at that time (that is, the salvage value at the end of 20 years is zero). Miller will depreciate the cost of the building over its useful life by recording an expense proportional to the amount of the asset's life that has elapsed during the period. The depreciation charge each month is thus $167 [= $40,000/(20 years × 12 months per year)]. Miller includes depreciation on the building in selling and administrative expenses.

---

[10]**Chapter 9** describes the judgments and estimates involved in measuring depreciation on long-lived assets; Transaction **(10)** illustrates only the mechanics and the accounts affected.

EXHIBIT 2.6	Miller Corporation Individual T-Accounts Showing Transactions During February

Cash (A)

✓	82,400		
(5)	35,000	14,500	(4)
		20,000	(6)
		1,000	(7)
✓	81,900		

Accounts Receivable (A)

✓	0		
(2)	47,000	35,000	(5)
✓	12,000		

Merchandise Inventory (A)

✓	15,000		
(1)	25,000	30,000	(3)
✓	10,000		

Prepaid Insurance (A)

✓	600		
		50	(8)
✓	550		

Prepaid Rent (A)

✓	12,000		
		1,000	(9)
✓	11,000		

Buildings (A)

✓	40,000	
✓	40,000	

Accumulated Depreciation (A)

		0	✓
		167	(10)
		167	✓

Accounts Payable (L)

		0	✓
(6)	20,000	25,000	(1)
		5,000	✓

Advances from Customer (L)

		3,000	✓
(2)	3,000		
		0	✓

Note Payable (L)

	40,000	✓
	40,000	✓

Accrued Interest Payable (L)

	0	✓
	333	(11)
	333	✓

(continued)

One way to record depreciation is to reduce the amount in the Buildings account by $167 and recognize an expense of $167. However, instead of reducing the amount in the Buildings account directly, firms use the balance sheet contra account Accumulated Depreciation to accumulate the subtractions for depreciation charges. That is, each accounting period Miller will add to the balance in Accumulated Depreciation the cost of the building services used during the period. The Accumulated Depreciation account appears on the balance sheet as a subtraction from the acquisition cost of the building. An account, such as Accumulated Depreciation, that accumulates subtractions from another account is a **contra account**. Thus, Miller will record depreciation for February as follows:

(10) Selling and Administrative Expenses (Depreciation Expense) 167
      Accumulated Depreciation 167

Assets	=	Liabilities	+	Shareholders' Equity	(Class.)
−167				−167	IncSt → RE

Depreciation of building for February of $167.

	Miller Corporation (Continued)		
EXHIBIT 2.6	**Individual T-Accounts Showing Transactions During February**		

Income Tax Payable (L)			**Income Tax Expense (SE)**	
	0 ✓	✓	0	
	1,382 **(12)**	**(12)** 1,382	1,382	**(13)**
	1,382 ✓	✓	0	

Common Stock (SE)			**Retained Earnings (SE)**	
	107,000 ✓		0	✓
		(7) 1,000	2,568	**(13)**
	107,000 ✓		1,568	✓

Sales Revenue (SE)			**Cost of Goods Sold (SE)**	
	0 ✓	✓ 0		
(13) 50,000	50,000 **(2)**	**(3)** 30,000	30,000	**(13)**
	0 ✓	✓ 0		

Interest Expense (SE)			**Selling and Administrative Expenses (SE)**	
✓ 0		✓ 0		
(11) 333	333 **(13)**	**(4)** 14,500		
✓ 0		**(8)** 50		
		(9) 1,000		
		(10) 167	15,717	**(13)**
		✓ 0		

Black = Balances
Blue = Transaction Entries

Red = Adjusting Entries
Gold = Closing Entries

The minus sign under Assets in the balance sheet equation indicates the effect on assets, not on Accumulated Depreciation. Likewise, the minus sign under Shareholders' Equity indicates the effect on shareholders' equity, not on Selling and Administrative Expense.

Transaction 11: Miller Corporation records interest expense on the note payable for the month of February. On January 31, Miller signed a note payable promising to repay the bank the $40,000 of principal borrowed in three years' time and to make yearly interest payments at the rate of 10% per annum, or $4,000 (= 10% × $40,000) per year. Whenever Miller prepares financial statements, it will compute the amount of interest that has accumulated or accrued since the previous financial statement date. At the end of February, Miller will recognize (accrue) $333 (= $4,000/12) of interest, which is one-twelfth of the total yearly interest amount, by making an adjusting entry:

(11) Interest Expense 333
    Interest Payable 333

Assets	=	Liabilities	+	Shareholders' Equity	(Class.)
		+333		−333	IncSt → RE

The cost of interest on the note payable for the month of February is $333.

Transaction 12: Miller Corporation recognizes income tax expense on February's income before income taxes. Assume an income tax rate of 35%. Net income before income taxes for February is $3,950 (= $50,000 − $30,000 − $14,500 − $50 − $1,000 − $167 − $333). Income tax expense is therefore $1,382 (= 0.35 × $3,950). Firms pay income taxes quarterly, so Miller's income taxes remain unpaid at the end of February. Income taxes are an expense of the accounting period, regardless of when the firm pays them. The adjusting entry to record income tax expense is:

(12) Income Tax Expense.	1,382	
Income Tax Payable		1,382

Assets	=	Liabilities	+	Shareholders' Equity	(Class.)
		+1,382		−1,382	IncSt → RE

Income tax expense for February is $1,382.

In addition to recording effects that arise with the passage of time, adjusting entries also correct recording errors that the firm detects at the end of the period. These entries are sometimes called *correcting entries*. For example, property taxes on the headquarters buildings may appear as a debit to Cost of Goods Sold instead of Selling and Administrative Expenses, or a payment to a supplier for purchases on account may appear as a debit to Accounts Receivable instead of Accounts Payable. There were no such errors for Miller Corporation during February so it need not make adjusting entries to correct errors. After all the adjusting entries are complete, the accountant posts those entries to the accounts affected. Adjusting entries appear in red in **Exhibit 2.6**.

FINANCIAL STATEMENT PREPARATION

PREPARATION OF THE INCOME STATEMENT

The revenue and expense accounts show the effects of income transactions during February and adjusting entries at the end of February. We can use these amounts to prepare an income statement for the month. **Exhibit 2.7** shows Miller Corporation's income statement for February.

This income statement uses the convention that parentheses indicate numbers to be subtracted. Numbers without parentheses are revenues, income subtotals, or net income. **Exhibit 2.7** shows a measure of income before financing charges (that is, interest expense) and before taxes. This measure is called *operating income* in **Exhibit 2.7**; in **Exhibit 2.5** Colgate uses the term *operating profit*. Operating income (or profit) is usually sales revenues less expenses associated with core operations, where *core* refers to transactions that are central to a firm's business. Miller Corporation operates a *retailing* business model: it buys and resells merchandise. Its operating income calculation includes the revenues associated with sales of merchandise and the expenses associated with operating this business. These expenses include, for example, the cost of merchandise sold and selling and administrative expenses. Neither U.S. GAAP nor IFRS defines operating income and profit, although both often appear on income statements. Managers can exercise judgment in determining whether to report this number and, if reported, managers can use judgment in how to calculate it. In addition, IFRS requires separate presentation of financing costs, as shown in **Exhibit 1.6** for Scania. In particular, Scania reports net financial expenses of SEK170 million for 2006.

EXHIBIT 2.7	Miller Corporation Income Statement For the Month of February

Sales Revenue	$50,000
Cost of Goods Sold	(30,000)
Selling and Administrative Expenses	(15,717)
Operating Income	$ 4,283
Interest Expense	(333)
Income Before Income Taxes	$ 3,950
Income Tax Expense	(1,382)
Net Income	$ 2,568

CLOSING ENTRIES

The revenue and expense accounts have now served their purpose in accumulating the amounts to be included as line items on the income statement. That is, each revenue account contains a total of that revenue, and each expense account contains a total for that expense. Income statement accounts are temporary accounts and, as such, will have beginning and ending balances of zero. The next step is to transfer the amounts in the revenue and expense accounts to the Retained Earnings account—that is, to close each revenue and expense account for the period. The **closing process** involves reducing to zero the balance in each income statement account by debiting the revenue accounts and crediting the expense accounts, and transferring to Retained Earnings the differences between total revenues and total expenses. Closing entries are shown in gold in **Exhibit 2.6**.

An income statement account with a debit balance requires a closing entry that credits that account, because a credit closing entry will result in a zero ending balance in the account. Miller's Cost of Goods Sold account has a debit balance of $30,000. The closing entry for this account is:

| Retained Earnings. | 30,000 | |
| Cost of Goods Sold | | 30,000 |

Assets	=	Liabilities	+	Shareholders' Equity	(Class.)
				−30,000	IncSt →RE
				+30,000	IncSt →RE

To close the Cost of Goods Sold account to Retained Earnings at the end of February.

An income statement account with a credit balance requires a closing entry that debits that account, because a debit closing entry will result in a zero ending balance in the account. For example, Miller's Sales Revenue account has a credit balance of $50,000. The closing entry for this account is:

| Sales Revenues. | 50,000 | |
| Retained Earnings. | | 50,000 |

Assets	=	Liabilities	+	Shareholders' Equity	(Class.)
				−50,000	IncSt →RE
				+50,000	IncSt →RE

To close the Sales Revenue account to Retained Earnings at the end of February.

Exhibit 2.6 shows, in gold, the closing entry for the revenue and expense accounts; the entry nets all of the income statement accounts in a single journal entry:

(13) Sales Revenue.	50,000	
Cost of Goods Sold		30,000
Selling and Administrative Expenses		15,717
Interest Expense		333
Income Tax Expense		1,382
Retained Earnings		2,568

To close the income statement accounts to Retained Earnings at the end of February.

The net effect of journal entry **(13)** changes the balance in the Retained Earnings account to reflect the net income of the period. In the case of Miller Corporation, the net effect credits Retained Earnings for February net income of $2,568 (as reported in the income statement shown in **Exhibit 2.7**).

EXHIBIT 2.8	Miller Corporation Comparative Balance Sheets		

		February 28	January 31
ASSETS			
Cash		$ 81,900	$ 82,400
Accounts Receivable		12,000	—
Merchandise Inventory		10,000	15,000
Prepaid Insurance		550	600
Prepaid Rent		11,000	12,000
Total Current Assets		$115,450	$110,000
Buildings		$ 40,000	$ 40,000
Accumulated Depreciation		(167)	0
Buildings, Net of Depreciation		$ 39,833	$ 40,000
Total Assets		$155,283	$150,000
LIABILITIES AND SHAREHOLDERS' EQUITY			
Accounts Payable		$ 5,000	$ —
Advances from Customer		—	3,000
Accrued Interest Payable		333	—
Income Tax Payable		1,382	—
Total Current Liabilities		$ 6,715	$ 3,000
Note Payable		$ 40,000	$ 40,000
Total Liabilities		$ 46,715	$ 43,000
Common Stock		$107,000	$107,000
Retained Earnings		1,568	—
Total Shareholders' Equity		$108,568	$107,000
Total Liabilities and Shareholders' Equity		$155,283	$150,000

PREPARATION OF THE BALANCE SHEET

After the closing process is completed, the accounts with nonzero balances are all balance sheet accounts. We can use these accounts to prepare the balance sheet as at the end of the period. **Exhibit 2.8** presents the comparative balance sheets for Miller Corporation on January 31 and February 28.

The balance in Retained Earnings has increased from zero at the end of January to $1,568 at the end of February. The change in Retained Earnings equals net income of $2,568 minus dividends of $1,000. Retained Earnings will begin March with a balance of $1,568. Net income less dividends (if any) for March will be added to $1,568 to yield the balance in Retained Earnings at the end of March. The balance in the Retained Earnings account, like all other balance sheet accounts, reflects the *cumulative* effect of transactions affecting that account.

PREPARATION OF A STATEMENT OF CASH FLOWS

The statement of cash flows describes the sources and uses of cash during a period and classifies them into operating, investing, and financing activities. It provides a detailed explanation for the change in the balance of the cash account during that period. For example, a statement of cash flows for Miller Corporation explains why the cash balance decreased from $82,400 on February 1 to $81,900 on February 28. **Chapter 5** and **Chapter 15** focus on the statement of cash flows and describe two approaches used to compute cash flow from operations. The first approach, called the *direct method*, involves a relatively straightforward listing of the sources and uses of cash from operating activities, as one would understand from identify-

EXHIBIT 2.9	Miller Corporation Statement of Cash Flows—Direct Method For the Month of February

Sources of Cash	
Cash Received from Customers.	$35,000
Uses of Cash	
Cash Paid for Selling and Administrative Items.	(14,500)
Cash Paid to Suppliers	(20,000)
Dividends Paid	(1,000)
Change in Cash.	$ (500)
Cash, Beginning of Month	82,400
Cash, End of Month.	$81,900

ing and understanding the transactions that affect the Cash account. The second approach, called the *indirect method*, reconciles net income to cash flows from operations by adjusting net income for noncash income statement components. Although the indirect method dominates in practice, it is not intuitive at this point because many of the necessary adjustments to net income involve items that we have not yet covered. For this reason, we illustrate the direct method in this chapter and defer the discussion of the indirect method to **Chapter 5**.

As noted previously, Miller's cash balance declined by $500 during February. A simplified statement of cash flows for February, shown in **Exhibit 2.9**, explains this change.

The rows reported in **Exhibit 2.9** correspond to all transactions that generated cash and all transactions that consumed cash during February. One way to identify these transactions is to look at the T-account for the cash account (shown in **Exhibit 2.6** and reproduced below):

	Cash (A)		
	82,400		
(5)	35,000	14,500	(4)
		20,000	(6)
		1,000	(7)
	81,900		

Recall from transaction **(2)** that the $50,000 in February sales revenues consists of $3,000 in the form of a cash advance received in January (so it is a cash inflow on the January statement of cash flows) and $47,000 in the form of customers' promise to pay in the future (so this amount will be a cash inflow in the accounting period when the cash is collected). For the latter, transaction **(5)** tells us that Miller collected $35,000 in cash from customers in February for goods that customers purchased on credit in February. Therefore, Miller has a $35,000 cash *inflow* for February associated with collections of cash from customers on sales made in February.

Cash outflows in February consist of $14,500 for selling, general, and administrative expenses and $20,000 for items purchased on account in February; Miller also paid a cash dividend of $1,000. Total cash outflows ($35,500) exceed cash inflows ($35,000), meaning that Miller used some cash on hand to cover the shortfall of $500. As shown in **Exhibit 2.9**, the shortfall explains the decrease in the cash balance from $82,400 at the beginning of February to $81,900 at the end of February.

The statement of cash flows in **Exhibit 2.9** is a simplified presentation based on a statement of cash flows prepared using the direct method. Under both U.S. GAAP and IFRS, the statement of cash flows displays sources and uses of cash by activity. That is, the statement contains separate sections for operating cash flows, investing cash flows, and financing cash flows. We leave the discussion of these three sections, as well as more complex issues relating to this statement, to **Chapter 5** and **Chapter 15**.

SUMMARY

Recording the effects of each transaction in a dual manner in the accounts maintains the balance sheet equation: total assets = total liabilities + shareholders' equity. The format of a journal entry to record a transaction is:

Debit Account (Asset Increases and Liability and Shareholders' Equity Decreases)	Debit Amount
Credit Account (Asset Decreases and Liability and Shareholders' Equity Increases)	Credit Amount

T-accounts provide an alternative way of organizing the recording of transactions; they are also convenient devices for collecting the records of a series of transactions or journal entries that affect a single account during a period. Like journal entries, T-accounts reflect the dual effects of transactions as shown by the following T-account format:

Asset Accounts		Liability (or Shareholders' Equity) Accounts	
Beg. Bal.			Beg. Bal.
Increases	Decreases	Decreases	Increases
Dr.	Cr.	Dr.	Cr.
End. Bal.			End. Bal.

Journal entries and T-accounts also record the effects of transactions that affect the income statement. All income statement accounts are temporary: they begin and end with zero balances. The closing process ensures that the ending balance in an income statement account is zero, by debiting or crediting each account with exactly the amount necessary to ensure that debits equal credits, so that the ending account balance is zero. The offsetting credit or debit to each of these closing transactions is generally Retained Earnings. Thus, the closing process reflects the articulation between the income statement and the balance sheet, as expressed in the retained earnings relation:

Retained Earnings (beginning) + Net Income − Dividends = Retained Earnings (ending)

In this equation, net income is a summary measure of the individual revenue and expense amounts.

The dual nature of transactions and the reporting consequences of that dual nature extend to items for which no event triggers a journal entry. Some items give rise to a journal entry and recognition in the financial statements because of the passage of time, such as wages earned but not yet paid to employees, consumption of a portion of a prepaid asset (for example, prepaid rent and prepaid insurance), and interest accrued on loans but not yet paid. These and similar items are recorded using adjusting entries at the end of the reporting period. Adjusting entries may increase or decrease balances in balance sheet accounts and income statement accounts.

OVERVIEW OF THE ACCOUNTING PROCESS

The record-keeping process generally involves the following steps:

1. Recording each transaction in a file or other record in the form of a journal entry.

2. Posting the amounts from the journal entries to individual balance sheet and income statement accounts in a general ledger. In computerized systems, posting occurs instantly and automatically after journalizing. T-accounts are useful devices for textbook illustrations and end-of-chapter problems to accumulate the effects of transactions on balance sheet and income statement accounts.

These first two steps occur daily (and perhaps many times during a day). The remaining steps typically occur at the end of the accounting period:

3. Making adjusting journal entries to the accounts to correct errors and to reflect the financial statement impacts of items that occur because of usage or the passage of time.

FIGURE 2.1

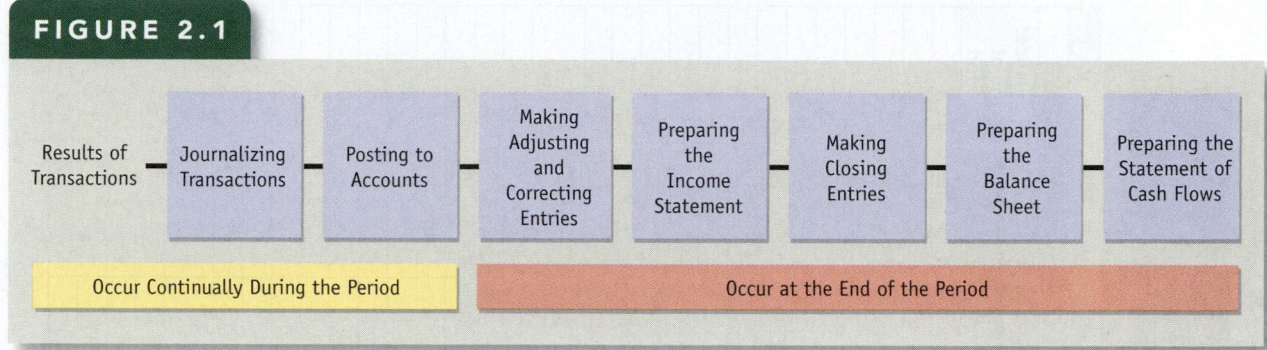

4. Preparing the income statement for the period from amounts in the income statement accounts.
5. Closing the temporary income statement accounts to retained earnings.
6. Preparing the balance sheet from amounts in the balance sheet accounts.
7. Preparing the statement of cash flows from balance sheet amounts and from details of transactions affecting the cash account.

Figure 2.1 shows these operations, which the previous section illustrated using the transactions of Miller Corporation during February.

APPENDIX 2.1: USING A SPREADSHEET TO RECORD BUSINESS TRANSACTIONS

This chapter illustrated the use of journal entries and T-accounts. Some instructors and students might prefer to use a computer spreadsheet to accomplish the same objectives. This appendix illustrates the use of a spreadsheet using the transactions of Miller Corporation discussed in the chapter and summarized in **Exhibit 2.2**.

Exhibit 2.2 presents the balance sheet equation horizontally. That is,

$$\text{Assets} = \text{Liabilities} + \text{Shareholders' Equity}$$

Picture now the balance sheet equation presented vertically at both the beginning and the end of a period. Thus,

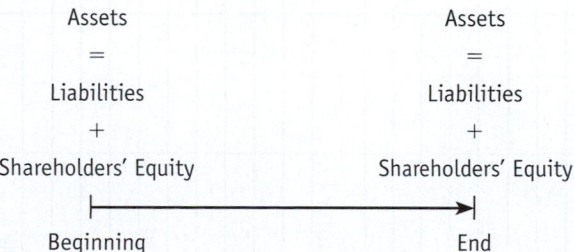

This vertical arrangement of the balance sheet equation corresponds to the actual presentation of balance sheets; see, for example, Colgate's balance sheet in **Exhibit 2.1**. We use this vertical arrangement to design a spreadsheet for recording the dual effects of transactions on the balance sheet equation.

Exhibit 2.10 presents the spreadsheet template, which you can download from the Web site for this book at *www.cengage.com/accounting/stickney*. The column titled Balance: Beginning of Period reports amounts on the balance sheet at the beginning of a period, and the column titled Balance: End of Period reports amounts on the balance sheet at the end of the period. The rows of the spreadsheet show assets (current and noncurrent), liabilities (current and noncurrent), and shareholders' equity. We leave spaces to add individual accounts, such as

EXHIBIT 2.10   Transactions Spreadsheet Template

	A	B	C	D	E	F	G	H	I	J	K
							Transactions, by Number and Description				
1	Balance Sheet Accounts										
2		Balance: Beginning of Period		Describe Transaction here							Balance: End of Period
3				1	2	3	4	5	6	7	8
4	ASSETS										
5	Current Assets:										
6											
7											
8											
9	Total Current Assets										
10	Noncurrent Assets:										
11											
12											
13											
14	Total Noncurrent Assets										
15	Total Assets										
16	LIABILITIES AND SHAREHOLDERS' EQUITY										
17	Current Liabilities:										
18											
19	Total Current Liabilities										
20	Noncurrent Liabilities:										
21											
22	Total Noncurrent Liabilities										
23	Total Liabilities										
24	Shareholders' Equity:										
25											
26											
27	Total Shareholders' Equity										
28	Total Liabilities and Shareholders' Equity										
29											
30	Imbalance, If Any										
31											
32	Income Statement Accounts										

cash, accounts payable, and common stock. The columns labeled Transactions, by Number and Description refer to transactions whose recording transforms the balance sheet at the beginning of the period to the balance sheet at the end of the period. We use this spreadsheet to show the dual effects of transactions, entering the appropriate account titles in the rows in the first column. The next-to-last row of the spreadsheet, labeled Imbalance, If Any, serves as an arithmetical check to ensure that we have recorded each transaction to maintain the balance sheet equation.[11]

We illustrate the use of this spreadsheet template using the eight transactions for Miller Corporation during January as it prepares to open for business on February 1. We indicate whether each account is an asset (A), a liability (L), or a shareholders' equity (SE) account. **Exhibit 2.11** shows the completed spreadsheet incorporating the eight transactions.

Transaction 1: On January 1, Miller issues 10,000 shares of $10 par value common stock for $100,000 cash. This transaction increases cash by $100,000 and common stock, a shareholders' equity account, by an equal amount. Thus,

(A) Cash	+ 100,000
(SE) Common Stock	+ 100,000

We enter the account title, Cash, on the first row under Current Assets and the account title, Common Stock, on the first row under Shareholders' Equity and place 100,000 in each of these accounts under the Transaction 1 column. A nonzero amount in the Imbalance, If Any row would indicate an incorrect recording of the transaction, which we must correct before moving to the next transaction.

Transaction 2: On January 5, Miller pays $12,000 for the use of equipment during the next 12 months. This transaction decreases cash by $12,000 and increases Prepaid Rent, a current asset, by $12,000. Thus,

(A) Cash	− 12,000
(A) Prepaid Rent	+ 12,000

Transaction 3: On January 15, Miller purchases merchandise costing $15,000 from a supplier on account, agreeing to pay later. This transaction increases inventory by $15,000 and accounts payable, a current liability, by $15,000. Thus,

(A) Merchandise Inventory	+ 15,000
(L) Accounts Payable	+ 15,000

Transaction 4: On January 21, Miller pays the supplier in transaction **(3)** $8,000 of the amount due. This transaction reduces cash and accounts payable by $8,000. Thus,

(A) Cash	− 8,000
(L) Accounts Payable	− 8,000

Transaction 5: On January 25, the supplier in transaction **(3)** accepts 700 shares of common stock in settlement of the $7,000 still owed. This transaction reduces accounts payable and increases common stock by $7,000. Thus,

(L) Accounts Payable	− 7,000
(SE) Common Stock	+ 7,000

Transaction 6: On January 31, Miller pays $600 cash for a one-year insurance policy for coverage beginning February 1. This transaction reduces cash by $600 and increases Prepaid Insurance, a current asset, for the future benefits of insurance coverage. Thus,

(A) Cash	− 600
(A) Prepaid Insurance	+ 600

---

[11]The transactions template follows the usual procedures for the use of an Excel spreadsheet. If a particular problem has more than eight transactions, the Insert Column command allows for additional columns. The Insert Row command allows for additional rows for more accounts. Insert columns and rows as indicated on the transactions template to ensure that summation formulas include the effects of additional rows and columns. The Edit Delete Row and Edit Delete Column commands allow for the deletion of unneeded rows and columns.

EXHIBIT 2.11

Miller Corporation
Transactions Spreadsheet

	A	B	C	D	E	F	G	H	I	J	K
						Transactions, by Number and Description					
		Balance: Beginning of Period	Issue Common Stock for Cash	Prepay Rent Equipment for Cash	Purchase Inv. on Account	Pay Cash to Supplier	Give Common Stock to Supplier	Prepay Insurance	Receive Advance from Customer	Purchase Building Using Note Payable	Balance: End of Period
2			1	2	3	4	5	6	7	8	
1	**Balance Sheet Accounts**										
3											
4	**ASSETS**										
5	**Current Assets:**										
6	Cash		100,000	−12,000		−8,000		−600	3,000		82,400
7	Inventory				15,000						15,000
8	Prepaid Insurance							600			600
9	Prepaid Rent			12,000							12,000
10	Total Current Assets										110,000
11	**Noncurrent Assets:**										
12	Buildings									40,000	40,000
13	Total Noncurrent Assets										40,000
14	Total Assets										150,000
15	**LIABILITIES AND SHAREHOLDERS' EQUITY**										
16	**Current Liabilities:**										
17	Accounts Payable				15,000	−8,000	−7,000				3,000
18	Advance from Customer								3,000		3,000
19	Total Current Liabilities										3,000
20	**Noncurrent Liabilities:**										
21	Note Payable									40,000	40,000
22	Total Noncurrent Liabilities										40,000
23	Total Liabilities										43,000
24	**Shareholders' Equity:**										
25	Common Stock		100,000				7,000				107,000
26											
27	Total Shareholders' Equity										107,000
28	Total Liabilities and Shareholders' Equity										150,000
29											
30	**Imbalance, If Any**										
31											
32	**Income Statement Accounts**										

Transaction 7: On January 31, Miller receives $3,000 from a customer for merchandise to be delivered during February. This transaction increases cash and increases Advances from Customers, a current liability, by $3,000. Thus,

(A) Cash	+ 3,000
(L) Advances from Customers	+ 3,000

Transaction 8: On January 31, Miller purchases a building for $40,000 by signing a note payable with its local bank. This transaction increases Buildings by $40,000 (a noncurrent asset) and increases Notes Payable (a noncurrent liability) by the same amount. Thus,

(A) Buildings	+ 40,000
(L) Note Payable....................	+ 40,000

The last column on the right shows the amounts for the balance sheet on January 31. The amounts result from summing the amounts from the balance sheet at the beginning of the period (zero in this case) and the amounts for each transaction during the period. We can then use the amounts in the spreadsheet to prepare a balance sheet. **Exhibit 2.4** in the chapter presents the balance sheet for Miller Corporation on January 31.

PROBLEM 2.5 for Self-Study

Spreadsheet analysis of business transactions. Design a spreadsheet similar to that in **Exhibit 2.10** or use the transactions spreadsheet template available with this text at *www.cengage.com/accounting/stickney.* Enter each of the transactions of Gaines Corporation in **Problem 2.1 for Self-Study** and derive the amounts for the balance sheet after the six transactions.

SOLUTIONS TO SELF-STUDY PROBLEMS

SUGGESTED SOLUTION TO PROBLEM 2.1 FOR SELF-STUDY

(Gaines Corporation; dual effects of transactions on balance sheet equation)

Transaction	Assets	=	Liabilities	+	Shareholders' Equity
1. The firm issues 20,000 shares of £10 par value common stock for £12 cash per share	+£240,000	=	0	+	+£240,000
2. The firm issues £100,000 principal amount of bonds for £100,000 cash...........	+100,000	=	+100,000	+	0
3. The firm acquires, with £220,000 cash, land costing £40,000 and a building costing £180,000	+220,000				
....	−220,000	=	0	+	0
4. The firm acquires, on account, equipment costing £25,000 and merchandise inventory costing £12,000	+37,000	=	+37,000	+	0
5. The firm signs an agreement to rent equipment from its owner and pays £1,500 rental in advance	+1,500				
....	−1,500	=	0	+	0
6. The firm pays £28,000 to the suppliers in 4	−28,000	=	−28,000		
Totals	£349,000	=	£109,000	+	£240,000

SUGGESTED SOLUTION TO PROBLEM 2.2 FOR SELF-STUDY

(Gaines Corporation; T-accounts for various transactions)

Cash (Asset)			
(1) 240,000	220,000	(3)	
(2) 100,000	1,500	(5)	
	28,000	(6)	

Merchandise Inventory (Asset)	
(4) 12,000	

Prepaid Rent (Asset)	
(5) 1,500	

Land (Asset)	
(3) 40,000	

Buildings (Asset)	
(3) 180,000	

Equipment (Asset)	
(4) 25,000	

Accounts Payable (Liability)			
(6) 28,000	37,000	(4)	

Bonds Payable (Liability)		
	100,000	(2)

Common Value (Shareholders' Equity)		
	200,000	(1)

Additional Paid-In Capital (Shareholders' Equity)		
	40,000	(1)

SUGGESTED SOLUTION TO PROBLEM 2.3 FOR SELF-STUDY

(Gaines Corporation; journal entries for various transactions)

(1) Cash.. 240,000

    Common Stock...................................... 200,000

    Additional Paid-In Capital 40,000

Assets	=	Liabilities	+	Shareholders' Equity	(Class.)
+240,000				+200,000	ContriCap
				+40,000	ContriCap

Issue 20,000 shares of £10 par value common stock for £12 cash per share.

(2) Cash.. 100,000

    Bonds Payable 100,000

Assets	=	Liabilities	+	Shareholders' Equity	(Class.)
+100,000		+100,000			

Issue £100,000 principal amount of bonds for £100,000 cash.

(3) Land 40,000

Building 180,000

    Cash... 220,000

Assets	=	Liabilities	+	Shareholders' Equity	(Class.)
+40,000					
+180,000					
−220,000					

Acquire for £220,000 land costing £40,000 and a building costing £180,000.

(4) Equipment... 25,000

Merchandise Inventory 12,000

    Accounts Payable 37,000

Assets	=	Liabilities	+	Shareholders' Equity	(Class.)
+25,000		+37,000			
+12,000					

(continued)

Purchase equipment costing £25,000 and merchandise inventory costing £12,000 on account.

(5) Prepaid Rent   1,500

       Cash.   1,500

Assets	=	Liabilities	+	Shareholders' Equity	(Class.)
+1,500					
−1,500					

Pay £1,500 as advance rental on equipment.

(6) Accounts Payable   28,000

       Cash.   28,000

Assets	=	Liabilities	+	Shareholders' Equity	(Class.)
−28,000		−28,000			

Pay £28,000 to the supplier in **(4)**.

SUGGESTED SOLUTION TO PROBLEM 2.4 FOR SELF-STUDY

(Electronics Appliance Corporation; journal entries, T-accounts, and balance sheet preparation)

a. Journal entries for the nine transactions follow:

(1) Sept. 1

Cash.   48,000

       Common Stock.   40,000

       Additional Paid-In Capital   8,000

Assets	=	Liabilities	+	Shareholders' Equity	(Class.)
+48,000				+40,000	ContriCap
				+8,000	ContriCap

Issue 4,000 shares of $10 par value common stock for $12 cash per share.

(2) Sept. 2

Patent   7,200

       Common Stock.   6,000

       Additional Paid-in Capital   1,200

Assets	=	Liabilities	+	Shareholders' Equity	(Class.)
+7,200				+6,000	ContriCap
				+1,200	ContriCap

Issue 600 shares of $10 par value common stock in the acquisition of a patent.

(3) Sept. 5

Prepaid Rent or Advances to Landlord   10,000

       Cash.   10,000

Assets	=	Liabilities	+	Shareholders' Equity	(Class.)
−10,000					
+10,000					

Prepay rent for October and November on factory building.

(4) Sept. 12

Raw Materials Inventory   6,100

    Accounts Payable   6,100

Assets	=	Liabilities	+	Shareholders' Equity	(Class.)
+6,100		+6,100			

Purchase raw materials costing $6,100 on account.

(5) Sept. 15

Cash.   900

    Advances from Customers   900

Assets	=	Liabilities	+	Shareholders' Equity	(Class.)
+900		+900			

Receive an advance of $900 from a customer as a deposit on equipment to be manufactured in the future.

(6) Sept. 20

Equipment   925

    Cash.   925

Assets	=	Liabilities	+	Shareholders' Equity	(Class.)
+925					
−925					

Acquire equipment with a list price of $950 for $925 after taking a discount for prompt payment.

(7) Sept. 28

Advances to Employees   200

    Cash.   200

Assets	=	Liabilities	+	Shareholders' Equity	(Class.)
+200					
−200					

Give cash advances of $200 to employees beginning work on Oct. 1.

(8) Sept. 30

Equipment   27,500

    Cash.   5,000

    Note Payable   22,500

Assets	=	Liabilities	+	Shareholders' Equity	(Class.)
+27,500		+22,500			
−5,000					

Acquire equipment for $5,000 cash and assume a $22,500 note payable for the balance of the purchase price.

(9) Sept. 30

Equipment   450

    Cash.   450

Assets	=	Liabilities	+	Shareholders' Equity	(Class.)
+450					
−450					

Pay installation cost of $450 on equipment acquired in **(8)**.

EXHIBIT 2.12

Electronics Appliance Corporation
T-Accounts and Transactions During September
(Problem 2.4 for Self-Study)

	Cash (A)		
(1)	48,000	10,000	(3)
(5)	900	925	(6)
		200	(7)
		5,000	(8)
		450	(9)
✓	32,325		

	Advances to Employees (A)	
(7)	200	
✓	200	

	Raw Materials Inventory (A)	
(4)	6,100	
✓	6,100	

	Prepaid Rent (A)	
(3)	10,000	
✓	10,000	

	Equipment (A)	
(6)	925	
(8)	27,500	
(9)	450	
✓	28,875	

	Patent (A)	
(2)	7,200	
✓	7,200	

Accounts Payable (L)		
	6,100	(4)
	6,100	✓

Advances from Customers (L)		
	900	(5)
	900	✓

Note Payable (L)		
	22,500	(8)
	22,500	✓

Common Stock (SE)		
	40,000	(1)
	6,000	(2)
	46,000	✓

Additional Paid-In Capital (SE)		
	8,000	(1)
	1,200	(2)
	9,200	✓

EXHIBIT 2.13

Electronics Appliance Corporation
Balance Sheet
September 30
(Problem 2.4 for Self-Study)

ASSETS		LIABILITIES AND SHAREHOLDERS' EQUITY	
Current Assets		**Current Liabilities**	
Cash	$32,325	Accounts Payable	$ 6,100
Advances to Employees	200	Advances from Customers	900
Raw Materials Inventory	6,100	Total Current Liabilities	$ 7,000
Prepaid Rent	10,000		
Total Current Assets	$48,625	**Long-Term Debt**	
		Note Payable	$22,500
Property, Plant, and Equipment		Total Liabilities	$29,500
Equipment	$28,875		
		Shareholders' Equity	
Intangibles		Common Stock, $10 Par Value	$46,000
Patent	7,200	Additional Paid-In Capital	9,200
		Total Shareholders' Equity	$55,200
		Total Liabilities	
Total Assets	$84,700	and Shareholders' Equity	$84,700

b. **Exhibit 2.12** presents T-accounts for Electronics Appliance Corporation and shows the recording of the nine entries in the accounts. The letters *A, L,* and *SE* after the account titles indicate the balance sheet category of the accounts.

c. **Exhibit 2.13** presents a balance sheet as of September 30.

SUGGESTED SOLUTION TO PROBLEM 2.5 FOR SELF-STUDY

(Gaines Corporation; spreadsheet analysis of business transactions) See **Exhibit 2.14**.

EXHIBIT 2.14

Gaines Corporation
Transactions Spreadsheet
(Problem 2.5 for Self-Study)

	A	B	C	D	E	F	G	H	I
					Transactions, by Number and Description				
	Balance Sheet Accounts	**Balance: Beginning of Period**	**Issue Common Stock for Cash**	**Issue Bond for Cash**	**Acquire Land and Building for Cash**	**Acquire Equip. and Inventory on Account**	**Pay Rental in Advance**	**Pay Supplier**	**Balance: End of Period**
3			1	2	3	4	5	6	
4	**ASSETS**								
5	**Current Assets:**								
6	Cash	0	240,000	100,000	–220,000		–1,500	–28,000	90,500
7	Merchandise Inventory	0				12,000			12,000
8	Prepaid Rent	0					1,500		1,500
9	Total Current Assets	0							104,000
10	**Noncurrent Assets:**								
11	Land	0			40,000				40,000
12	Buildings	0			180,000				180,000
13	Equipment	0				25,000			25,000
14	Total Noncurrent Assets	0							245,000
15	Total Assets	0							349,000
16	**LIABILITIES AND SHAREHOLDERS' EQUITY**								
17	**Current Liabilities:**								
18	Accounts Payable	0				37,000		–28,000	9,000
19	Total Current Liabilities	0							9,000
20	**Noncurrent Liabilities:**								
21	Bonds Payable	0		100,000					100,000
22	Total Noncurrent Liabilities	0							100,000
23	Total Liabilities	0							109,000
24	**Shareholders' Equity:**								
25	Common Stock	0	200,000						200,000
26	Additional Paid-in Capital	0	40,000						40,000
27	Total Shareholders' Equity	0							240,000
28	Total Liabilities and Shareholders' Equity	0							349,000
29									
30	**Imbalance, If Any**								
31									
32	**Income Statement Accounts**								

KEY TERMS AND CONCEPTS

Account	Credit
Permanent accounts	Journal entry
Temporary accounts	Posting process
Balance sheet equation	Adjusting entries
Dual effects of transactions	Contra account
T-account	Closing process
Debit	

QUESTIONS, EXERCISES, AND PROBLEMS

QUESTIONS

1. Review the meaning of the terms and concepts listed above in Key Terms and Concepts.
2. Why does every accounting transaction have two effects?
3. What is the relation between a T-account and a journal entry?
4. What is the purpose of temporary accounts?
5. What distinguishes noncurrent assets from current assets?
6. What does "articulation of the balance sheet with the income statement" refer to?
7. What is the purpose of the income statement?
8. What is the key difference between an adjusting entry and a correcting entry?
9. What is the purpose of using contra accounts? What is the alternative to using them?
10. What is the key difference between the direct method and the indirect method for presenting a statement of cash flows?

EXERCISES

11. **Dual effects on balance sheet equation.** Fresh Foods Group, a European food retailer that operates supermarkets in seven countries, engaged in the following three transactions during 2008: (1) purchased and received inventory costing €678 million on account from various suppliers; (2) returned inventory costing €45 million because of damage that occurred during shipment; (3) paid the various suppliers the total amount due. Indicate the effects of each of these three transactions on the balance sheet equation. Fresh Foods Group applies IFRS, and reports its results in millions of euros.

12. **Dual effects on balance sheet equation.** Cement Plus, a firm specializing in building materials, engaged in the following four transactions during 2008: (1) purchased and received inventory costing $14,300 million, of which $12,000 million was on account with the rest paid in cash; (2) purchased a machine for $3,000 million with cash; (3) issued 2,000 shares of common stock for $6,500 million in cash; (4) issued shares of common stock to its suppliers for the remaining amount due on purchases of inventory. Indicate the effects of each of these four transactions on the balance sheet equation. Cement Plus applies U.S. GAAP financial reporting standards, and reports its results in millions of dollars.

13. **Analyzing changes in accounts receivable.** Braskem S.A., a large Brazilian petrochemical company, reported a balance of R$1,594.9 million in Accounts Receivable at the beginning of 2007 and R$1,497.0 million at the end of 2007. Its income statement reported total Sales Revenue of R$12,134.5 million for 2007. Assuming that Braskem makes all sales on account, compute the amount of cash collected from customers during 2007. Braskem applies Brazilian accounting standards, and reports its results in thousands of reais (R$), the Brazilian currency. In answering this question, assume that Braskem uses either U.S. GAAP or IFRS; for purposes of this problem, this choice will not matter.

14. **Analyzing changes in inventory.** Boeing Company, a U.S. airplane manufacturer, reported a balance of $8,105 million in Inventory at the beginning of 2007 and $9,563 million at the end of 2007. Its income statement reported Cost of Products Sold of $45,375 million

for 2007. Compute the cost of inventory either purchased or manufactured during 2007. Boeing Company applies U.S. GAAP, and reports its results in millions of U.S. dollars.

15. **Analyzing changes in inventory and accounts payable.** Ericsson, a Swedish firm specializing in communication networks, reported a balance in Inventories of SEK21,470 million at the beginning of 2007 and SEK22,475 million at the end of 2007. It also reported a balance in Trade (Accounts) Payable of SEK18,183 million at the beginning of 2007 and SEK17,427 million at the end of 2007. During 2007, Ericsson reported SEK114,059 million in Cost of Sales. Compute the amount of cash paid to suppliers of inventory during 2007 for purchases made on account. Assume that all of Ericsson's inventory purchases are made on account. Ericsson applies IFRS, and reports its results in millions of Swedish kronor (SEK).

16. **Analyzing changes in income taxes payable.** Kajima Corporation, a Japanese construction firm, reported a balance in Income Taxes Payable of ¥3,736 million at the beginning of 2007 and ¥14,310 million at the end of 2007. Net income before income taxes for 2007 totaled ¥73,051 million. Assume that the firm is subject to an income tax rate of 43%. Compute the amount of cash payments made for income taxes during 2007. Kajima Corporation applies Japanese accounting standards, and reports its results in millions of yen (¥). In answering this question, assume that Kajima Corporation uses either U.S. GAAP or IFRS; for purposes of this problem, this choice will not matter.

17. **Analyzing changes in retained earnings.** Eaton Corporation, a U.S. diversified power management company, reported a balance in Retained Earnings of $2,796 million at the beginning of 2007 and $3,257 million at the end of 2007. Based on Eaton Corporation's financial reports for fiscal 2007, it reported dividends declared and paid of $251 million for 2007. Compute the amount of net income for 2007. Eaton Corporation applies U.S. GAAP, and reports its results in millions of U.S. dollars.

18. **Relations between financial statements.** The following selected information is based on the 2007 financial statements of the German healthcare firm, Bayer Group. Bayer Group applies IFRS, and reports its results in millions of euros. Compute the missing information in each of the following four independent cases. The letters in parentheses refer to the following:

BS—Balance sheet

IS—Income statement

SCF—Statement of cash flows

a. Accounts Receivable, January 1, 2007 (BS)	€ 5,868
Sales on Account for 2007 (IS)	32,385
Collections from Customers on Account during 2007 (SCF)	?
Accounts Receivable, December 31, 2007 (BS)	5,830
b. Income Taxes Payable, January 1, 2007 (BS)	€ 109
Income Tax Expense for 2007 (IS)	?
Payments to Governments during 2007 (SCF)	763
Income Taxes Payable, December 31, 2007 (BS)	56
c. Noncurrent financial liabilities, January 1, 2007 (BS)	€14,723
Principal payments of debt during 2007 (SCF)	?
Issuance of new debt during 2007 (SCF)	2,155
Noncurrent financial liabilities, December 31, 2007 (BS)	12,911
d. Retained Earnings, January 1, 2007 (BS)	€ 6,782
Net Income for 2007 (IS)	4,711
Dividends Declared and Paid during 2007 (SCF)	?
Retained Earnings, December 31, 2007 (BS)	10,749

19. **Relations between financial statements.** The following selected information is based on the 2007 financial statements of Beyond Petroleum (BP). BP applies IFRS, and reports its results in millions of U.S. dollars. Compute the missing information in each of the following four independent cases. The letters in parentheses refer to the following:

BS—Balance sheet

IS—Income statement

SCF—Statement of cash flows

a. Accounts Receivable, January 1, 2007 (BS) . . . . $?

Sales on Account for 2007 (IS) 288,951

Collections from Customers on Account during 2007 (SCF) 289,623

Accounts Receivable, December 31, 2007 (BS) 38,020

b. Income Taxes Payable, January 1, 2007 (BS) . . . . $ 2,635

Income Tax Expense for 2007 (IS) 10,442

Payments to Governments during 2007 (SCF) . . . . ?

Income Taxes Payable, December 31, 2007 (BS) 3,282

c. Trade Payables, January 1, 2007 (BS) . . . . $ 42,236

Purchases of Supplies during 2007 (SCF) 15,162

Payments to Suppliers during 2007 (SCF) . . . . ?

Trade Payables, December 31, 2007 (BS) 43,152

d. Retained Earnings, January 1, 2007 (BS) . . . . $ 88,453

Net Income for 2007 (IS) 21,169

Dividends Declared and Paid during 2007 (SCF) 8,106

Retained Earnings, December 31, 2007 (BS) . . . . ?

20. **Journal entries for inventories and accounts payable.** On December 31, 2006, the Merchandise Inventories account of the Japanese electronics firm Fujitsu Limited (Fujitsu) had a balance of ¥408,710 million, based on Fujitsu's financial reports for fiscal 2007. Assume that during 2007, Fujitsu purchased merchandise inventories on account for ¥1,456,412 million. On December 31, 2007, it finds that merchandise inventory on hand is ¥412,387 million. The Accounts Payable account had a balance of ¥757,006 million on December 31, 2006, and ¥824,825 million on December 31, 2007. Present journal entries to account for all changes in the Inventories and Accounts Payable accounts during 2007. Fujitsu applies Japanese accounting standards, and reports its results in millions of yen (¥). In answering this question, assume that Fujitsu uses either U.S. GAAP or IFRS; for purposes of this problem, this choice will not matter.

21. **Journal entries for insurance.** Monana Company, a U.S. clothing designer, manufacturer, and retailer, reported a balance in prepaid insurance of $90.7 million, based on its financial reports dated March 31, 2008, the end of its fiscal year. Assume that of this balance, $24 million relates to an insurance policy with two remaining months of coverage. Assume also that on June 1, 2008, the firm paid $156 million for a one-year renewal of this policy. Give the journal entries that Monana would make on April 30, 2008; May 31, 2008; June 30, 2008; and July 31, 2008; assuming that the firm closes its books monthly. Monana applies U.S. GAAP, and reports its results in millions of U.S. dollars.

22. **Journal entries for prepaid rent.** ABB Group (ABB), headquartered in Switzerland, is one of the world's largest engineering companies. ABB applies U.S. GAAP, and reports its results in millions of U.S. dollars. Based on ABB's financial reports for fiscal 2007, at January 1, 2007, ABB reported a balance in its Prepaid Rent account of $247 million; assume that this amount reflects its prepayments of rent on factory and office space for the next month. Assume also that on January 31, 2007, ABB paid $3,200 million as the annual rent for the period from February 1, 2007, to January 31, 2008. ABB has a calendar year reporting period.

a. Provide the journal entries that ABB Group would make during January 2007 that affect the Prepaid Rent account.

b. Provide the journal entry that ABB Group would make at the end of 2007 that affects the Prepaid Rent account.

23. **Journal entries for borrowing.** Sappi Limited, a South African paper company, reports noncurrent Interest-Bearing Borrowings of $1,634 million at September 30, 2006. Sappi Limited applies IFRS, and reports its results in millions of U.S. dollars. At September 30, 2007, this balance had increased to $1,828 million. Assume that on March 30, 2007,

Sappi Limited borrowed $1,200 million from a local bank. The loan bears interest at an annual rate of 7.5% and is due on March 31, 2009. Assume also that Sappi Limited makes its interest payments once per year on the last day of March. Sappi Limited's fiscal year begins October 1 and ends on September 30. The firm closes its books on September 30 of each year.

a. What journal entry did Sappi Limited record for the repayment of debt during the fiscal year ending September 30, 2007?

b. Present the journal entries that Sappi Limited made in fiscal years ending September 30, 2007, 2008, and 2009, related to the bank loan obtained on March 30, 2007.

24. **Journal entries related to the income statement.** Toyota Motor Company (Toyota), the Japanese car manufacturer, reported Sales of Products of ¥22,670 billion for the year ended March 31, 2007. The Cost of Products Sold was ¥18,356 billion. Assume that Toyota made all sales on credit. By March 31, 2007, Toyota had collected cash for all the sales made on account during the fiscal year ended March 31, 2007. Provide the journal entries that Toyota made during the fiscal year ended March 31, 2007, related to these transactions. Toyota applies U.S. GAAP, and reports its results in millions of yen (¥).

25. **Journal entries related to the income statement.** Teva Pharmaceutical, an Israeli drug company, reported Net Sales of $9,408 million for the year ended December 31, 2007. Based on Teva Pharmaceutical's financial reports for fiscal 2007, the cost of these sales was $6,531 million. Assume that Teva made all sales on credit, and that it collected $2,659 million cash during 2007. Provide the journal entries that Teva Pharmaceutical made in 2007 related to these transactions. Teva Pharmaceutical applies U.S. GAAP, and reports its results in millions of U.S. dollars.

26. **Journal entry to correct recording error.** In the fiscal year ended December 31, 2008, Bostick Enterprises paid $120,000 for equipment, which it had purchased on January 1, 2008. The equipment has an expected useful life of 10 years and zero salvage value. The firm recorded the acquisition by debiting Equipment Expense and crediting Cash for $120,000. Give the journal entries that Bostick Enterprises would make to correct its initial recording error and any related effects (ignore income tax effects). Bostick Enterprises applies U.S. GAAP, and reports its results in millions of U.S. dollars.

PROBLEMS

27. **Dual effects of transactions on balance sheet equation and journal entries.** Assume that during 2008, Bullseye Corporation, a U.S. retailer, engages in the following six transactions. Bullseye Corporation applies U.S. GAAP, and reports its results in millions of U.S. dollars.

(1) The firm issues 20 million shares of $0.0833 par value common stock for a total of $960 million cash.

(2) It purchases merchandise costing $1,500 million on account.

(3) The firm acquires a new store location, consisting of a building costing $3,200 million and land costing $930 million. It pays cash to the owner of the property.

(4) The firm purchases fixtures for the new store costing $860 million, on account.

(5) The firm pays the merchandise supplier in transaction (2) the amount due.

(6) The firm pays the supplier of the fixtures in transaction (4) half of the amount due in cash. The firm pays the other half by issuing 8.6 million common shares to the supplier. At the time of this transaction, Bullseye Corporation's shares traded at $50 per share in the market.

a. Indicate the effects of these six transactions on the balance sheet equation using this format:

Transaction Number	Assets	=	Liabilities	+	Shareholders' Equity
(1)	+$960		$0		+$960
Subtotal	$960	=	$0	+	$960

b. Give the journal entries for each of the six transactions.

28. **Dual effects of transactions on balance sheet equation and journal entries.** Assume that during 2008, Inheritance Brands, a U.S. manufacturer and distributor, engaged in the following five transactions. Inheritance Brands applies U.S. GAAP, and reports its results in millions of U.S. dollars.

    (1) The firm issues 10 million shares of $3.125 par value common stock for $55 cash per share.

    (2) At the end of 2008, the firm acquires land costing $250 million and a building costing $900 million. It pays for the purchase by giving $400 million in cash and promising to pay the remainder in 2009.

    (3) The firm pays $30 million cash for a one-year insurance policy on the land and building. The policy period begins at the start of 2009.

    (4) The firm acquires merchandise inventory costing $400 million on account from various suppliers.

    (5) The firm pays cash to the suppliers in transaction (4) for its purchases on account.

    a. Indicate the effects of these five transactions on the balance sheet equation using this format:

Transaction Number	Assets	=	Liabilities	+	Shareholders' Equity
(1)	+$550		$0		+$550
Subtotal	$550	=	$0	+	$550

    b. Give the journal entries for each of the five transactions.

29. **Preparing a balance sheet and an income statement.** The accounting records of Callen Incorporated reveal the following for 2007 and 2008. Callen applies U.S. GAAP, and reports its results in thousands of euros.

	December 31	
Balance Sheet Items	**2008**	**2007**
Accounts Payable	€ 16,402	€ 14,063
Cash	30,536	2,559
Property, Plant, and Equipment (net)	98,130	149,990
Common Stock	72,325	72,325
Merchandise Inventory	114,249	151,894
Notes Payable to Banks (due within one year)	15,241	43,598
Long-Term Debt	31,566	38,315
Other Current Assets	109,992	134,916
Other Current Liabilities	84,334	109,335
Other Noncurrent Assets	56,459	88,955
Other Noncurrent Liabilities	19,859	27,947
Retained Earnings	169,639	222,731

	For the Year Ended
Income Statement Items	**December 31, 2008**
Administrative Expenses	€141,183
Cost of Goods Sold	382,349
Income Tax Expense	24,324
Interest Expense	2,744
Sales Revenue	695,623
Selling Expenses	72,453

    a. Prepare a comparative balance sheet for Callen Incorporated as of December 31, 2007, and December 31, 2008. Classify each balance sheet item into one of the following categories: current assets, noncurrent assets, current liabilities, noncurrent liabilities, and shareholders' equity. Use the U.S. GAAP convention to order the accounts on the balance sheet.

b. Prepare an income statement for Callen Incorporated for the year ended December 31, 2008. Separate income items into revenues and expenses.

c. Prepare a schedule explaining the change in retained earnings between December 31, 2007, and December 31, 2008.

30. **Preparing a balance sheet and an income statement.** The following information is based on accounting data for 2007 and 2008 for ChemAsia Limited (ChemAsia), a large petrochemicals company in China. ChemAsia applies IFRS, and reports its results in millions of U.S. dollars.

	December 31	
Balance Sheet Items	**2008**	**2007**
Cash	$ 88,589	$ 54,070
Accounts Receivable	18,419	8,488
Advances to Suppliers	20,386	12,664
Inventories	88,467	76,038
Other Current Assets	20,367	13,457
Property, Plant, and Equipment (net)	247,803	231,590
Oil and Gas Properties	326,328	270,496
Intangible Assets	20,022	16,127
Other Noncurrent Assets	163,711	132,214
Accounts Payable to Suppliers	104,460	77,936
Advances from Customers	12,433	11,590
Other Current Liabilities	84,761	90,939
Long-Term Debt	35,305	30,401
Other Noncurrent Liabilities	42,062	36,683
Common Stock	444,527	354,340
Retained Earnings	270,544	213,255

Income Statement Items	**2008**
Net Operating Revenues	$835,037
Interest and Other Revenues	3,098
Cost of Sales	487,112
Selling Expenses	41,345
General & Administrative Expenses	49,324
Other Operating Expenses	64,660
Interest Expense	2,869
Income Taxes	49,331

a. Prepare an income statement for ChemAsia for the year ending December 31, 2008.

b. Prepare a comparative balance sheet for ChemAsia on December 31, 2007, and December 31, 2008. Use the IFRS convention to order the accounts on the balance sheet.

c. Prepare an analysis of the change in Retained Earnings during the year ending December 31, 2008.

31. **Miscellaneous transactions and adjusting entries.** Assume that LJB Group (LJB), a Swiss engineering firm, engaged in the following six transactions during the year ended December 31, 2008. LJB applies U.S. GAAP, and reports its results in millions of U.S. dollars. Give the journal entries to record (1) each of the six transactions, and (2) any necessary adjusting entries on December 31, 2008. You may omit explanations for the journal entries.

a. On November 1, 2008, LJB gives a 90-day note to a supplier in exchange for inventory purchased costing $180,000. The note bears interest at 8% per year and is due on January 31, 2009.

b. On December 5, 2008, LJB receives $842,000 in cash from a customer for products and services that LJB will deliver in January 2009.

c. LJB acquires a machine on October 1, 2008, for $1,400,000 cash. It expects the machine to have a $160,000 salvage value and a 10-year life.

d. On September 30, 2008, LJB sells merchandise to a customer, on credit, for $565,000. The merchandise has a cost to LJB of $422,000.

e. LJB purchases insurance on its headquarters building on September 1, 2008, for the next 12 months beginning on that date. It pays the $360,000 insurance premium in cash.

f. On November 16, 2008, LJB issues 40,000 shares of common stock with a par value of $1 for $26 per share. LJB uses the cash proceeds to repay accounts payable.

32. **Miscellaneous transactions and adjusting entries.** Platinum Fields Limited (Platinum Fields) is a South African platinum producer. Platinum Fields applies IFRS, and reports its results in millions of South African rand (R). For the year ended June 30, 2008, Platinum Fields engaged in the following transactions. Give the journal entries to record (1) each of the following transactions as well as (2) any necessary adjusting entries on June 30, 2008. You may omit explanations for the journal entries.

a. Platinum Fields rented excess office space on March 1, 2008, to a local jeweler. On that date, the jeweler paid Platinum Fields R57,000 in cash for one year's rent.

b. On June 23, 2008, Platinum Fields paid its salaried workers R42,000 for the two weeks ending on this date. Salaried workers are paid biweekly, and salary expense does not vary greatly week to week.

c. On November 1, 2007, Platinum Fields renewed its insurance policy for two more years, by paying the insurance premium of R960,000.

d. On June 15, 2008, Platinum Fields purchased inventory from a supplier on credit for R235,000. As of June 30, 2008, Platinum Fields had not yet paid the supplier.

e. Platinum Fields purchased equipment on January 1, 2008, for R728,000 in cash. The equipment has zero salvage value and an expected five-year life.

f. Platinum Fields declared a dividend of R1,143,000 on March 1, 2008, and paid it in cash on June 15, 2008.

33. **Preparing the income statement and balance sheet using the accrual basis.** Bob Hansen opens a retail store on January 1, 2008. Hansen invests $50,000 for all of the common stock of the firm. The store borrows $40,000 from a local bank. The store must repay the loan with interest for both 2008 and 2009 on December 31, 2009. The interest rate is 10% per year. The store purchases a building for $60,000 cash. The building has a 30-year life, zero estimated salvage value, and is to be depreciated using the straight-line method. The store purchases $125,000 of merchandise on account during 2008 and pays $97,400 of the amount by the end of 2008. A physical inventory taken on December 31, 2008, indicates $15,400 of merchandise is still on hand.

During 2008, the store makes cash sales to customers totaling $52,900 and sales on account totaling $116,100. Of the sales on account, the store collects $54,800 by December 31, 2008. The store incurs and pays other costs as follows: salaries, $34,200; utilities, $2,600. It has unpaid bills at the end of 2008 as follows: salaries, $2,400; utilities, $180. The firm is subject to an income tax rate of 40%. Income taxes for 2008 are payable on March 15, 2009. Assume that Hansen applies U.S. GAAP, and reports in U.S. dollars.

a. Prepare an income statement for Hansen Retail Store for 2008, assuming the accrual basis of accounting and revenue recognition at the time of sale. Show supporting computations for each revenue and expense.

b. Prepare a balance sheet for Hansen Retail Store as of December 31, 2008. Show supporting computations for each balance sheet item.

34. **Recording transactions in T-accounts and preparing a balance sheet.** Veronica Regaldo creates a new business in Mexico on January 1, 2008, to operate a retail store. Transactions of Regaldo Department Stores during January 2008 in preparation for opening its first retail store in February 2008 appear below. Regaldo applies IFRS, and reports its results in thousands of Mexican pesos ($).

(1) January 1, 2008: Receives $500,000 from Veronica Regaldo for all of the common stock of Regaldo Department Stores. The stock has no par or stated value.

(2) January 5, 2008: Pays another firm $20,000 for a patent, and pays the Mexican government $4,000 to register the patent.

(3) January 10, 2008: Orders merchandise from various suppliers at a cost of $200,000. See transactions (5), (6), and (7) below for later information regarding these merchandise orders.

(4) January 15, 2008: Signs a lease to rent land and a building for $30,000 a month. The rental period begins February 1, 2008. Regaldo pays $60,000 for the first two months' rent in advance.

(5) January 20, 2008: Receives the merchandise ordered on January 10, 2008. Regaldo delays payment for the merchandise until it receives an invoice from the supplier—see transaction (7) below.

(6) January 21, 2008: Discovers that merchandise costing $8,000 is defective and returns the items to the supplier.

(7) January 25, 2008: Receives invoices for $160,000 for the merchandise received on January 20, 2008. After subtracting an allowed discount of 2% of the invoice for paying promptly, Regaldo pays the suppliers the amount due of $156,800 (0.98 × $160,000). The firm treats cash discounts taken as a reduction in the acquisition cost of the merchandise.

(8) January 30, 2008: Obtains fire and liability insurance coverage from Windwards Islands Insurance Company for the period beginning February 1, 2008. It pays the one-year insurance premium of $12,000.

a. Record these eight transactions either in T-accounts or a transactions spreadsheet.

b. Prepare a balance sheet for Regaldo Department Stores on January 31, 2008.

Note: **Problem 35** *extends this problem to income transactions for February 2008.*

35. **Analysis of transactions and preparation of the income statement and balance sheet.** Refer to the information for Regaldo Department Stores as of January 31, 2008, in **Problem 34**. Regaldo Department Stores opened for business on February 1, 2008. Transactions and events during February 2008 were as follows.

(1) February 1: Purchased display counters and computer equipment for $90,000. The firm borrowed $90,000 from a local bank to finance the purchases. The bank loan bears interest at a rate of 12% each year and is repayable with interest on February 1, 2009.

(2) During February: Purchased merchandise on account totaling $217,900.

(3) During February: Sold merchandise costing $162,400 to various customers for $62,900 cash and $194,600 on account.

(4) During February: Paid to employees compensation totaling $32,400 for services rendered during the month.

(5) During February: Paid utility (electric, water, gas) bills totaling $2,700 for services received during February 2008.

(6) During February: Collected $84,600 from customers for sales on account (see transaction (3) above).

(7) During February: Paid invoices from suppliers of merchandise (see transaction (2) above) with an original purchase price of $210,000 in time to receive a 2% discount for prompt payment and $29,000 to other suppliers after the discount period had elapsed. The firm treats discounts taken as a reduction in the acquisition cost of merchandise.

(8) February 28: Compensation that employees earned during the last several days in February and that the firm will pay early in March 2008 totaled $6,700.

(9) February 28: Utility services that the firm used during February and that the firm will not pay until March 2008 totaled $800.

(10) February 28: The display counters and computer equipment purchased in transaction (1) have an expected useful life of five years and zero salvage value at the end of the five years. The firm depreciates such equipment on a straight-line basis over the expected life and uses an Accumulated Depreciation account.

(11) February 28: The firm recognizes an appropriate portion of the prepaid rent as of January 31, 2008.

(12) February 28: The firm recognizes an appropriate portion of the prepaid insurance as of January 31, 2008.

(13) February 28: The firm amortizes (that is, recognizes as an expense) the patent over 60 months. The firm does not use a separate Accumulated Amortization account for the patent.

(14) February 28: The firm recognizes an appropriate amount of interest expense on the loan in transaction **(1)** above.

(15) February 28: The firm is subject to an income tax rate of 30% of net income before income taxes. The income tax law requires firms to pay income taxes on the 15th day of the month after the end of each quarter (that is, April 15, 2008, June 15, October 15, and January 15).

a. Using T-accounts, enter the balances in balance sheet accounts on February 1, 2008, from **Problem 34** and the effects of the 15 transactions above.

b. Prepare an income statement for the month of February 2008.

c. Prepare a comparative balance sheet as of January 31, 2008, and February 28, 2008.

36. Analysis of transactions and preparation of the income statement and balance sheet. Zealock Bookstore opened a bookstore near a college campus on July 1, 2008. Transactions and events of Zealock Bookstore during 2008 follow. The firm uses the calendar year as its reporting period.

(1) July 1, 2008: Receives $25,000 from Quinn Zealock for 25,000 shares of the bookstore's $1 par value common stock.

(2) July 1, 2008: Obtains a $30,000 loan from a local bank for working capital needs. The loan bears interest at 6% per year. The loan is repayable with interest on June 30, 2009.

(3) July 1, 2008: Signs a rental agreement for three years at an annual rental of $20,000. Pays the first year's rent in advance.

(4) July 1, 2008: Acquires bookshelves for $4,000 cash. The bookshelves have an estimated useful life of five years and zero salvage value.

(5) July 1, 2008: Acquires computers for $10,000 cash. The computers have an estimated useful life of three years and $1,000 salvage value.

(6) July 1, 2008: Makes security deposits with various book distributors totaling $8,000. The deposits are refundable on June 30, 2009, if the bookstore pays on time all amounts due for books purchased from the distributors between July 1, 2008, and June 30, 2009.

(7) During 2008: Purchases books on account from various distributors costing $160,000.

(8) During 2008: Sells books costing $140,000 for $172,800. Of the total sales, $24,600 is for cash, and $148,200 is on account.

(9) During 2008: Returns unsold books and books ordered in error costing $14,600. The firm had not yet paid for these books.

(10) During 2008: Collects $142,400 from sales on account.

(11) During 2008: Pays employees compensation of $16,700.

(12) During 2008: Pays book distributors $139,800 of the amounts due for purchases on account.

(13) December 28, 2008: Receives advances from customers of $850 for special-order books that the bookstore will order and expects to receive during 2009.

(14) December 31, 2008: Records an appropriate amount of interest expense on the loan in **(2)** for 2008.

(15) December 31, 2008: Records an appropriate amount of rent expense for 2008.

(16) December 31, 2008: Records an appropriate amount of depreciation expense on the bookshelves in **(4)**.

(17) December 31, 2008: Records an appropriate amount of depreciation expense on the computers in **(5)**.

(18) December 31, 2008: Records an appropriate amount of income tax expense for 2008. The income tax rate is 40%. The taxes are payable on March 15, 2009.

a. Using T-accounts, enter the 18 transactions and events above.

b. Prepare an income statement for the six months ending December 31, 2008.

c. Prepare a balance sheet on December 31, 2008.

Note: **Problem 37** *extends this problem to income transactions for 2009.*

37. **Analysis of transactions and preparation of comparative income statements and balance sheets.** Refer to the information for Zealock Bookstore in **Problem 36**. The following transactions relate to 2009.

(1) March 15, 2009: Pays income taxes for 2008.

(2) June 30, 2009: Repays the bank loan with interest.

(3) July 1, 2009: Obtains a new bank loan for $75,000. The loan is repayable on June 30, 2010, with interest due at maturity of 8%.

(4) July 1, 2009: Receives the security deposit back from the book distributors.

(5) July 1, 2009: Pays the rent due for the period July 1, 2009, to June 30, 2010.

(6) During 2009: Purchases books on account costing $310,000.

(7) During 2009: Sells books costing $286,400 for $353,700. Of the total sales, $24,900 is for cash, $850 is from special orders received during December 2008, and $327,950 is on account.

(8) During 2009: Returns unsold books costing $22,700. The firm had not yet paid for these books.

(9) During 2009: Collects $320,600 from sales on account.

(10) During 2009: Pays employees compensation of $29,400.

(11) During 2009: Pays book distributors $281,100 for purchases of books on account.

(12) December 31, 2009: Declares and pays a dividend of $4,000.

a. Using T-accounts, enter the amounts for the balance sheet on December 31, 2008, from **Problem 36**, the effects of the 12 transactions above, and any required entries on December 31, 2009, to properly measure net income for 2009 and financial position on December 31, 2009.

b. Prepare a comparative income statement for 2008 and 2009.

c. Prepare a comparative balance sheet for December 31, 2008, and December 31, 2009.

38. **Reconstructing the income statement and balance sheet.** (Adapted from a problem by Stephen A. Zeff.) Portobello Co., a retailer, is in its 10th year of operation. On December 28, 2008, three days before the close of its fiscal year, a flash flood devastated the company's administrative office and destroyed almost all of its accounting records. The company saved the balance sheet on December 31, 2007 (see **Exhibit 2.15**), the checkbook, the bank statements, and some soggy remains of the specific accounts receivable and accounts payable balances. Based on a review of the surviving documents and a series of interviews with company employees, you obtain the following information.

(1) The company's insurance agency advises that a four-year insurance policy has six months to run as of December 31, 2008. The policy cost $12,000 when the company paid the four-year premium during 2005.

(2) During 2008, the company's board of directors declared $6,000 of dividends, of which the firm paid $3,000 in cash to shareholders during 2008 and will pay the remainder during 2009. Early in 2008, the company also paid dividends of $1,800 cash that the board of directors had declared during 2007.

(3) On April 1, 2008, the company received from Appleton Co. $10,900 cash, which included principal of $10,000 and interest, in full settlement of Appleton's nine-month note dated July 1, 2007. According to the terms of the note, Appleton paid all interest at maturity on April 1, 2008.

(4) The amount owed by the company to merchandise suppliers on December 31, 2008, was $20,000 less than the amount owed on December 31, 2007. During 2008, the company paid $115,000 to merchandise suppliers. The cost of merchandise inventory on December 31, 2008, based on a physical count, was $18,000 larger than the

EXHIBIT 2.15

Portobello Co.
Balance Sheet
December 31, 2007
(Problem 38)

ASSETS	
Cash	$ 18,600
Accounts Receivable	33,000
Notes Receivable	10,000
Interest Receivable	600
Merchandise Inventories	22,000
Prepaid Insurance	4,500
Total Current Assets	$ 88,700
Computer System:	
At Cost	$ 78,000
Less Accumulated Depreciation	(26,000)
Net.	$ 52,000
Total Assets	$140,700
LIABILITIES AND SHAREHOLDERS' EQUITY	
Accounts Payable for Merchandise	$ 36,000
Dividend Payable	1,800
Salaries Payable	6,500
Taxes Payable.	10,000
Advances from Customers.	600
Total Liabilities.	$ 54,900
Common Stock	$ 40,000
Retained Earnings.	45,800
Total Shareholders' Equity.	$ 85,800
Total Liabilities and Shareholders' Equity.	$140,700

balance in the Merchandise Inventory account on the December 31, 2007, balance sheet. On December 8, 2008, the company exchanged shares of its common stock for merchandise inventory costing $11,000. The company's policy is to purchase all merchandise on account.

(5) The company purchased delivery trucks on March 1, 2008, for $60,000. To finance the acquisition, it gave the seller a $60,000 four-year note that bears interest at 10% per year. The company must pay interest on the note each six months, beginning September 1, 2008. The company made the required payment on this date. The delivery trucks have an expected useful life of 10 years and an estimated salvage value of $6,000. The company uses the straight-line depreciation method.

(6) The company's computer system has a six-year total expected life and zero expected salvage value.

(7) The company makes all sales on account and recognizes revenue at the time of shipment to customers. During 2008, the company received $210,000 cash from its customers. The company's accountant reconstructed the Accounts Receivable subsidiary ledger, the detailed record of the amount owed to the company by each customer. It showed that customers owed the company $51,000 on December 31, 2008. A close examination revealed that $1,400 of the cash received from customers during 2008 applies to merchandise that the company will not ship until 2009. Also, $600 of the cash received from customers during 2007 applies to merchandise not shipped to customers until 2008.

(8) The company paid $85,000 in cash to employees during 2008. Of this amount, $6,500 relates to services that employees performed during 2007, and $4,000 relates to services that employees will perform during 2009. Employees performed the

remainder of the services during 2008. On December 31, 2008, the company owes employees $1,300 for services performed during the last several days of 2008.

(9)   The company paid $27,000 in cash for property and income taxes during 2008. Of this amount, $10,000 relates to income taxes applicable to 2007, and $3,000 relates to property taxes applicable to 2009. The company owes $4,000 in income taxes on December 31, 2008.

(10)   The company entered into a contract with a management consulting firm for consulting services. The total contract price is $48,000. The contract requires the company to pay the first installment of $12,000 cash on January 1, 2009, and the company intends to do so. The consulting firm had performed 10% of the estimated total consulting services under the contract by December 31, 2008.

Prepare an income statement for 2008 and a balance sheet on December 31, 2008.

39.   **Reconstructing the income statement and balance sheet.** Computer Needs, Inc., operates a retail store that sells computer hardware and software. It began operations on January 2, 2007, and operated successfully during its first year, generating net income of $8,712 and ending the year with $15,600 in its bank account. **Exhibit 2.16** presents an income statement for 2007, and **Exhibit 2.17** presents a balance sheet as of the end of 2007.

As 2008 progressed, the owners and managers of Computer Needs, Inc., felt that they were doing even better. Sales seemed to be running ahead of 2007, and customers were always in the store. Unfortunately, a freak lightning storm hit the store on December 31, 2008, and completely destroyed the computer on which Computer Needs, Inc., kept its records. It now faces the dilemma of calculating 2008 income in order to assess its operating performance and to calculate income taxes for the year.

You are asked to prepare an income statement for 2008 and a balance sheet at the end of 2008. To assist in this effort, you obtain the following information.

(1)   The bank at which Computer Needs, Inc., maintains its account provided a summary of the transactions during 2008, as shown in **Exhibit 2.18**.

(2)   Cash received during January 2009, from third-party credit card companies and from customers for sales made during 2008 totaled $40,300. This is your best estimate of accounts receivable outstanding on December 31, 2008.

(3)   Clerks took a physical inventory of merchandise on January 1, 2009. Using current catalogs from suppliers, you estimate that the merchandise has a total cost of $60,700.

(4)   Computer Needs, Inc., had paid its annual insurance premium on October 1, 2008 (included in the amounts in **Exhibit 2.18**). You learn that $1,800 of the insurance premium applies to coverage during 2009.

(5)   Based on depreciation claimed during 2007 and new equipment purchased during 2008, you estimate 2008 depreciation expense of $3,300.

(6)   Bills received from merchandise suppliers during January 2009 totaled $45,300. This is your best estimate of accounts payable outstanding to these suppliers on December 31, 2008.

EXHIBIT 2.16	**Computer Needs, Inc.** **Income Statement** **For the Year Ended December 31, 2007** **(Problem 39)**

Sales.	$ 152,700
Cost of Goods Sold	(116,400)
Selling and Administrative Expenses	(17,400)
Depreciation	(2,800)
Interest.	(4,000)
Income Taxes	(3,388)
Net Income	$ 8,712

(7) Other Current Liabilities represent amounts payable to employees and other providers of selling and administrative services. Other Current Liabilities as of December 31, 2008, total $1,200.

Prepare an income statement for Computer Needs, Inc., for 2008 and a balance sheet on December 31, 2008. The income tax rate is 28%.

EXHIBIT 2.17

Computer Needs, Inc.
Balance Sheet
December 31, 2007
(Problem 39)

ASSETS	
Cash	$ 15,600
Accounts Receivable	32,100
Inventories	46,700
Prepayments	1,500
Total Current Assets	$ 95,900
Property, Plant, and Equipment:	
At Cost	$ 59,700
Less Accumulated Depreciation	(2,800)
Net	$ 56,900
Total Assets	$152,800
LIABILITIES AND SHAREHOLDERS' EQUITY	
Accounts Payable—Merchandise Suppliers	$ 37,800
Income Tax Payable	3,388
Other Current Liabilities	2,900
Total Current Liabilities	$ 44,088
Mortgage Payable	50,000
Total Liabilities	$ 94,088
Common Stock	$ 50,000
Retained Earnings	8,712
Total Shareholders' Equity	$ 58,712
Total Liabilities and Shareholders' Equity	$152,800

EXHIBIT 2.18

Computer Needs, Inc.
Analysis of Changes in Bank Accounts
For the Year Ended December 31, 2008
(Problem 39)

Balance, January 1, 2008	$ 15,600
Receipts:	
Cash from Cash Sales	37,500
Checks Received from Third-Party Credit Cards and Customers	151,500
Disbursements:	
To Merchandise Suppliers	(164,600)
To Employees and Other Providers of Selling and Administrative Activities	(21,000)
To U.S. Government for Income Taxes for 2008	(3,388)
To Bank for Interest ($4,000) and Principal on Mortgage ($800)	(4,800)
To Supplier of Equipment	(6,000)
Balance, December 31, 2008	$ 4,812

40. **Effect of errors on financial statements.** Consider the following hypothetical information pertaining to Embotelladora Andina S.A. (Embotelladora), the producer and distributor of Coca-Cola products in Chile. Embotelladora applies Chilean accounting standards, and reports its results in thousands of Chilean pesos ($). Using the notations O/S (overstated), U/S (understated), and NO (no effect), indicate the effects (direction and amount) on assets, liabilities, and shareholders' equity as of December 31, 2008, of the following independent errors or omissions. Ignore income tax implications.

   a. On December 1, 2008, Embotelladora paid $120,000 for rental of a building for December 2008 and January 2009. The firm debited Rent Expense and credited Cash for $120,000 on December 1, and made no further entries with respect to this rental during December or January.

   b. On December 15, 2008, Embotelladora received $82,000 from a customer as a deposit on merchandise that Embotelladora expects to deliver to the customer in January 2009. The firm debited Cash and credited Sales Revenue on December 15, and made no further entries with respect to this deposit during December or January.

   c. On December 1, 2008, Embotelladora acquired a truck to be used to transport beverages from the central warehouse to retailers. The truck cost $98,000, has zero salvage value, and is expected to last four years. The firm recorded the transaction by debiting Truck Expense and crediting Cash for $98,000 and made no further entries during December with respect to the acquisition.

   d. On December 15, 2008, Embotelladora purchased office supplies costing $86,800. It recorded the purchase by debiting Office Supplies Expense and crediting Cash. The Office Supplies Inventory account on December 1 had a balance of $27,700. Based on a physical inventory on December 31, office supplies costing $24,600 were on hand. The firm made no entries in its accounts with respect to office supplies on December 31, 2008.

   e. Embotelladora incurred interest expense of $34,500 for the month of December on a 60-day loan obtained on December 1, 2008. The firm properly recorded the loan on its books on December 1, but made no entry to record interest on December 31, 2008. The loan is payable with interest on January 31, 2009.

   f. Embotelladora purchased merchandise on account costing $17,900 on December 23, 2008, debiting Merchandise Inventory and crediting Accounts Payable. The firm paid for this purchase on December 28, 2008, debiting Cost of Goods Sold and crediting Cash, but had not sold the merchandise by December 31, 2008.

41. **Effect of recording errors on financial statements.** Forgetful Corporation (Forgetful) neglected to make various adjusting entries on December 31, 2008, the end of its accounting period. Forgetful applies U.S. GAAP, and reports in U.S. dollars. Indicate the effects on assets, liabilities, and shareholders' equity on December 31, 2008, of failing to adjust for the following independent items as appropriate, using the notations O/S (overstated), U/S (understated), and NO (no effect). Also, give the amount of the effect. Ignore income tax implications.

   a. On December 15, 2008, Forgetful Corporation received a $1,400 advance from a customer for products to be manufactured and delivered in January, 2009. The firm recorded the advance by debiting Cash and crediting Sales Revenue and made no adjusting entry as of December 31, 2008.

   b. On July 1, 2008, Forgetful Corporation acquired a machine for $5,000 and recorded the acquisition by debiting Cost of Goods Sold and crediting Cash. The machine has a five-year useful life and zero estimated salvage value.

   c. On November 1, 2008, Forgetful Corporation received a $2,000 note receivable from a customer in settlement of an account receivable. It debited Notes Receivable and credited Accounts Receivable on receipt of the note. The note is a six-month note due April 30, 2009, and bears interest at an annual rate of 12%. Forgetful Corporation made no other entries related to this note during 2008.

   d. Forgetful Corporation paid its annual insurance premium of $1,200 on October 1, 2008, the first day of the year of coverage. It debited Prepaid Insurance $900, debited Insurance Expense $300, and credited Cash for $1,200. It made no other entries related to this insurance during 2008.

e. The Board of Directors of Forgetful Corporation declared a dividend of $1,500 on December 31, 2008. The dividend will be paid on January 15, 2009. Forgetful Corporation neglected to record the dividend declaration.

f. On December 1, 2008, Forgetful Corporation purchased a machine on account for $50,000, debiting Machinery and crediting Accounts Payable for $50,000. Ten days later the company paid the account and took the allowed 2% discount. It credited Cash $49,000 and Miscellaneous Revenue $1,000. It debited Accounts Payable $50,000. Forgetful Corporation normally records cash discounts taken as a reduction in the cost of assets. On December 28, 2008, the firm paid $4,000 cash to employees to install the machine; it debited Maintenance Expense and credited Cash for $4,000. The machine started operation on January 1, 2009. Since the firm did not place the machine into operation until January 1, 2009, it correctly recorded no depreciation for 2008.

42. **Working backward to the balance sheet at the beginning of the period.** (Problems 42 through 44 derive from problems by George H. Sorter.) The following data relate to the Prima Company.

   (1) **Exhibit 2.19**: Balance sheet at December 31, 2008.

   (2) **Exhibit 2.20**: Statement of net income and retained earnings for 2008.

   (3) **Exhibit 2.21**: Statement of cash receipts and disbursements for 2008.

   Purchases of merchandise during the period, all on account, were $127,000. All Other Operating Expenses were credited to Prepayments.

   Prepare a balance sheet for December 31, 2007. (*Hint:* Using either T-accounts or a transactions spreadsheet, depending on the preference of your instructor, enter the December 31, 2008, amounts from the balance sheet. Using the information in the income statement and statement of cash receipts and disbursements, reconstruct the transactions that took place during the year and enter the amounts in the appropriate places in the

EXHIBIT 2.19

Prima Company
Balance Sheet
December 31, 2008
(Problem 42)

ASSETS

Cash	$ 10,000
Marketable Securities	20,000
Accounts Receivable	25,000
Merchandise Inventory	30,000
Prepayments for Miscellaneous Services	3,000
Total Current Assets	$ 88,000
Land, Buildings, and Equipment (at cost)	$ 40,000
Less Accumulated Depreciation	(16,000)
Land, Buildings, and Equipment (net)	$ 24,000
Total Assets	$112,000

LIABILITIES AND SHAREHOLDERS' EQUITY

Accounts Payable (for merchandise)	$ 25,000
Interest Payable	300
Taxes Payable	4,000
Total Current Liabilities	$ 29,300
Note Payable (6%, long-term)	20,000
Total Liabilities	$ 49,300
Common Stock	$ 50,000
Retained Earnings	12,700
Total Shareholders' Equity	$ 62,700
Total Liabilities and Shareholders' Equity	$112,000

EXHIBIT 2.20	Prima Company Statement of Net Income and Retained Earnings For Year Ended December 31, 2008 (Problem 42)

Sales	$200,000
Less Expenses:	
Cost of Goods Sold	$130,000
Depreciation Expense	4,000
Taxes Expense	8,000
Other Operating Expenses	47,700
Interest Expense	1,200
Total Expenses	$190,900
Net Income	$ 9,100
Less Dividends	5,000
Increase in Retained Earnings	$ 4,100

EXHIBIT 2.21	Prima Company Statement of Cash Receipts and Disbursements For Year Ended December 31, 2008 (Problem 42)

Cash Receipts	
Cash Sales	$ 47,000
Collection from Credit Customers	150,000
Total Receipts	$197,000
Cash Disbursements	
Payment to Suppliers of Merchandise	$128,000
Payment to Suppliers of Miscellaneous Services	49,000
Payment of Taxes	7,500
Payment of Interest	1,200
Payment of Dividends	5,000
Purchase of Marketable Securities	8,000
Total Disbursements	$198,700
Excess of Disbursements over Receipts	$ 1,700

T-accounts or transactions template. Finally, compute the amounts on the December 31, 2007, balance sheet.)

43. **Working backward to cash receipts and disbursements. Exhibit 2.22** presents the comparative balance sheet of The Secunda Company as of the beginning and end of 2008. **Exhibit 2.23** presents the income statement for 2008. The company makes all sales on account and purchases all goods and services on account. The Other Operating Expenses account includes depreciation charges and expirations of prepayments. The company debits Dividends Declared during the year to Retained Earnings.

Prepare a schedule showing all cash transactions for 2008. (*Hint:* Using either T-accounts or a transactions spreadsheet, depending on the preference of your instructor, enter the amounts shown as of December 31, 2007, and December 31, 2008. Starting with the revenue and expense accounts, reconstruct the transactions that took place during the year, and enter the amounts in the appropriate places in the T-accounts or transactions spreadsheet. Note that the Retained Earnings account in the balance sheet on December 31, 2008, reflects the effects of earnings activities and dividends during 2008.)

EXHIBIT 2.22

The Secunda Company
Balance Sheet
December 31, 2008 and December 31, 2007
(Problem 43)

	December 31,	
	2008	2007
ASSETS		
Cash	$ 9,000	$ 20,000
Accounts Receivable	51,000	36,000
Merchandise Inventory	60,000	45,000
Prepayments	1,000	2,000
Total Current Assets	$121,000	$103,000
Land, Buildings, and Equipment (at cost)	$ 40,000	$ 40,000
Less Accumulated Depreciation	(18,000)	(16,000)
Land, Buildings, and Equipment (net)	$ 22,000	$ 24,000
Total Assets	$143,000	$127,000
LIABILITIES AND SHAREHOLDERS' EQUITY		
Interest Payable	$ 2,000	$ 1,000
Accounts Payable	40,000	30,000
Total Current Liabilities	$ 42,000	$ 31,000
Mortgage Payable	17,000	20,000
Total Liabilities	$ 59,000	$ 51,000
Common Stock	$ 50,000	$ 50,000
Retained Earnings	34,000	26,000
Total Shareholders' Equity	$ 84,000	$ 76,000
Total Liabilities and Shareholders' Equity	$143,000	$127,000

EXHIBIT 2.23

The Secunda Company
Income Statement
For Year ended December 31, 2008
(Problem 43)

Sales Revenue	$100,000
Less Expenses:	
Cost of Goods Sold	$ 50,000
Interest Expense.	3,000
Other Operating Expenses	29,000
Total Expenses	$ 82,000
Net Income	$ 18,000

44. **Working backward to the income statement.** Tertia Company presents balance sheets at the beginning and end of 2008 (**Exhibit 2.24**), as well as a statement of cash receipts and disbursements (**Exhibit 2.25**). Prepare a combined statement of income and retained earnings for 2008. (*Hint:* Using either T-accounts or a transactions spreadsheet, depending on the preference of your instructor, enter the amounts shown as of December 31, 2007, and December 31, 2008. Starting with the cash receipts and disbursements for the year, reconstruct the transactions that took place during the year, and enter them in the appropriate places in the T-accounts or transactions spreadsheet. The Retained Earnings account reflects the effect of earnings activities and dividends for 2008.)

EXHIBIT 2.24

Tertia Company
Balance Sheets
December 31, 2008 and December 31, 2007
(Problem 44)

	December 31,	
	2008	**2007**
ASSETS		
Cash	$ 67,800	$ 40,000
Accounts and Notes Receivable	41,000	36,000
Merchandise Inventory	49,500	55,000
Interest Receivable	700	1,000
Prepaid Miscellaneous Services	5,200	4,000
Building, Machinery, and Equipment	47,000	47,000
Accumulated Depreciation	(12,000)	(10,000)
Total Assets	$199,200	$173,000
LIABILITIES AND SHAREHOLDERS' EQUITY		
Accounts Payable (miscellaneous services)	$ 2,500	$ 2,000
Accounts Payable (merchandise purchases)	41,000	34,000
Property Taxes Payable	1,500	1,000
Mortgage Payable	30,000	35,000
Total Liabilities	$ 75,000	$ 72,000
Common Stock	$ 25,000	$ 25,000
Retained Earnings	99,200	76,000
Total Shareholders' Equity	$124,200	$101,000
Total Liabilities and Shareholders' Equity	$199,200	$173,000

EXHIBIT 2.25

Tertia Company
Statement of Cash Receipts and Disbursements
For Year Ended December 31, 2008
(Problem 44)

	2008
Cash Receipts	
1. Collection from Credit Customers	$144,000
2. Cash Sales	63,000
3. Collection of Interest	1,000
Total Cash Receipts	$208,000
Less Cash Disbursements	
4. Payment to Suppliers of Merchandise	$114,000
5. Repayment on Mortgage	5,000
6. Payment of Interest	500
7. Prepayment to Suppliers of Miscellaneous Services	57,500
8. Payment of Property Taxes	1,200
9. Payment of Dividends	2,000
Total Cash Disbursements	$180,200
Increase in Cash Balance for 2008	$ 27,800

45. Preparing adjusting entries. Assume that a firm closes its books once per year, on December 31. The firm employs a full-time bookkeeper and a part-time professional accountant who makes all necessary adjusting entries to prepare the financial statements on December 31. During the year, the firm uses the following simplified bookkeeping and transactions recording convention: When it receives cash, the firm debits cash and credits a revenue account; when it pays cash, the firm debits an expense account and credits cash. The purposes of using this simplified transaction recording convention are (1) to achieve efficient recording of cash receipts and disbursements so that the firm always has an up-to-date balance in its cash account and (2) to avoid involving the professional accountant until the end of the year. On December 31, the professional accountant makes the adjusting entries necessary to properly record revenues and expenses of the period and calculate the correct balances in balance sheet accounts. Construct the adjusting entry required for each of the following scenarios.

a. On September 1, 2006, a tenant paid $24,000 rent for the one-year period starting at that time. The tenant debited the entire amount to Rent Expense and credited Cash. The tenant made no adjusting entries for rent between September 1 and December 31. Construct the adjusting entry to be made on December 31, 2006, to recognize the proper balances in the Prepaid Rent and Rent Expense accounts. What is the amount of Rent Expense for 2006?

b. Refer to part **a**. The tenant's books for December 31, 2006, after adjusting entries, show a balance in the Prepaid Rent account of $16,000. This amount represents rent for the period January 1 through August 31, 2007. On September 1, 2007, the tenant paid $30,000 for rent for the one-year period starting September 1, 2007. The tenant debited this amount to Rent Expense and credited Cash but made no adjusting entries for rent during 2007. Construct the adjusting entry required on December 31, 2007. What is Rent Expense for 2007?

c. Refer to part **b**. The tenant's books for December 31, 2007, after adjusting entries, show a balance in the Prepaid Rent account of $20,000. This amount represents rent for the period January 1 through August 31, 2008. On September 1, 2008, the tenant paid $18,000 for rent for the six-month period starting September 1, 2008. The tenant debited this amount to Rent Expense and credited Cash but made no adjusting entries during 2008. Construct the adjusting entry required on December 31, 2008. What is Rent Expense for 2008?

d. Whenever the firm makes payments for wages, it debits Wage Expense and credits Cash. At the start of April, the Wages Payable account had a balance of $5,000, representing wages earned but not paid during the last few days of March. During April, the firm paid $30,000 in wages, debiting the entire amount to Wage Expense. At the end of April, analysis of amounts earned since the last payday indicates that employees have earned wages of $4,000 that they have not received. These are the only unpaid wages at the end of April. Construct the required adjusting entry. What is Wage Expense for April?

e. The firm purchased an insurance policy providing one year's coverage from May 1, 2005, and debited the entire amount to Insurance Expense. After the firm made adjusting entries, the balance sheet on December 31, 2005, correctly showed Prepaid Insurance of $3,000. Construct the adjusting entry that the firm must make on January 31, 2006, if the firm closes its books monthly and prepares a balance sheet for January 31, 2006.

f. For receipts a landlord collects related to an apartment building, the bookkeeper always credits Rent Revenue for cash received from tenants. At the beginning of 2007, the liability account Advances from Tenants had a credit balance of $25,000, representing collections from tenants for rental services the landlord will render during 2007. During 2007, the firm collected $250,000 from tenants; it debited Cash and credited Rent Revenue. It made no adjusting entries during 2007. At the end of 2007, analysis of the individual accounts indicates that of the amounts already collected, $30,000 represents collections for rental services the landlord will provide to tenants during 2008. Present the required adjusting entry. What is Rent Revenue for 2007?

g. When the firm acquired new equipment costing $10,000 on January 1, 2005, the bookkeeper debited Depreciation Expense and credited Cash for $10,000 but made no further entries for this equipment during 2005. The equipment has an expected service life of five years and an estimated salvage value of zero. Construct the adjusting entry required before the accountant can prepare a balance sheet for December 31, 2005.

PART 2

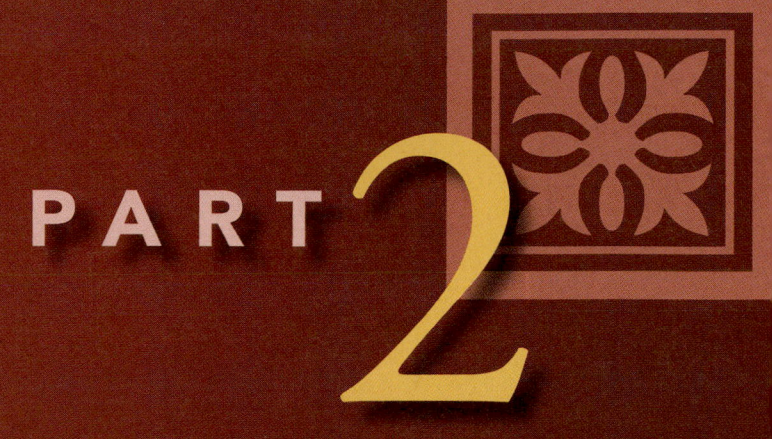

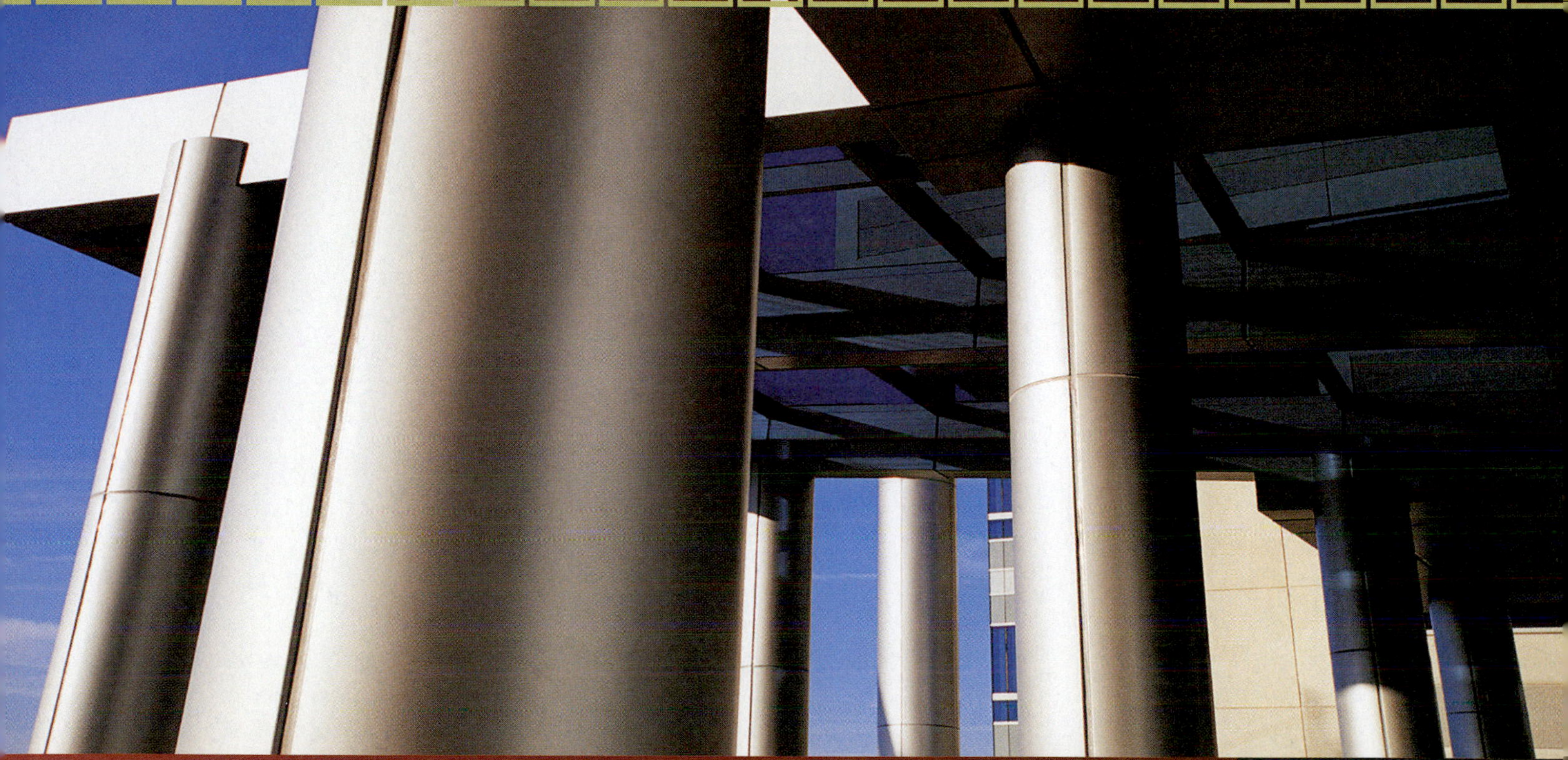

FACMU13

Accounting Concepts and Methods

Balance Sheet: Presenting and Analyzing Resources and Financing

1. Understand the accounting concepts of assets, liabilities, and shareholders' equity, including the criteria for recognizing (recording) these items on the balance sheet, determining their amounts (measurement), and identifying where these items appear on the balance sheet (classification).

2. Understand why and how the recognition and measurement guidance in U.S. GAAP and IFRS affects the information reported on balance sheets, and develop skills for adjusting the reported amounts.

3. Develop skills to analyze the relations among assets, liabilities, and shareholders' equity.

A user of financial statements might raise questions such as the following with respect to a firm's balance sheet:

1. Does the balance sheet show all of the firm's economic resources as assets and all of the claims on those resources as liabilities and shareholders' equity? If not, what kinds of resources and claims are not recognized on the balance sheet and why?

2. How do the asset amounts reported on the balance sheet relate to prices observed in the marketplace? For example, how does the amount reported for a given asset relate to the amount the firm would receive if it sold that asset? Is the amount reported for a liability equal to the amount that the firm would have to pay to settle the obligation? How does the amount shown for shareholders' equity relate to the market value of the firm's equity?

3. What does the balance sheet reveal about how the firm has financed its assets? Why do financing arrangements differ across firms?

Understanding the balance sheet permits the user to answer these and other questions about a firm's financial position. This chapter discusses the following concepts underlying the balance sheet, emphasizing asset and liability:

- Definition
- Recognition
- Measurement

We also highlight relations the user should look for when analyzing the balance sheets of healthy firms in different industries.

This chapter and this book take the perspective of a financial statement user. You must understand the concepts underlying the balance sheet to analyze and interpret balance sheets. Mastery of these concepts also requires understanding the procedures used to prepare the balance sheet, described in **Chapter 2**.

UNDERLYING CONCEPTS

BALANCE SHEET EQUALITY

Chapter 1 introduces the balance sheet, one of the three principal financial statements. The balance sheet is also called the *statement of financial position*. The balance sheet displays resources (assets) and the financing of those resources (liabilities and shareholders' equity) as of a point in time.[1] The balance sheet reflects the following equality, called the **balance sheet equation**:

$$\text{Assets} = \text{Liabilities} + \text{Shareholders' Equity}$$

This equation requires that assets exactly balance with the financing provided by creditors and owners of the firm. Stated differently, management uses the funds provided by creditors (in the form of liabilities) and owners (in the form of shareholders' equity) to acquire resources (in the form of assets). The nature and mix of liabilities and equity comprise the **financing structure**, a topic we return to later in this chapter.

BALANCE SHEET CLASSIFICATION

Balance sheets present lists of items, grouped by category. The lists are additive. For example, the sum of all the listed assets is total assets. Two categories used to group assets, and separately liabilities, result from the timing of cash receipts (for assets) and the timing of cash payments (for liabilities). Assets that management expects to convert to cash, or to sell, or to consume during the normal **operating cycle** of the business are **current assets**. All other assets are **noncurrent assets**. Similarly, obligations that management expects to discharge with a cash payment or otherwise settle during the operating cycle are **current liabilities**, whereas all other obligations are **noncurrent liabilities**.

The operating cycle is the period of time required to convert cash into salable goods and services, sell those goods and services to customers, and receive cash from customers in payment. A firm's business model determines its operating cycle. The operating cycle can be as short as one to three months, although some industries, such as building construction or wine making, have operating cycles that span several years. Unless the operating cycle exceeds one year, accounting convention uses one year to distinguish current items from noncurrent items. Thus, the phrase *current assets* (*current liabilities*) is typically understood to imply assets (liabilities) that will convert to (be paid for with) cash within one year.

Current assets include cash; marketable securities held for the short term; accounts and notes receivable; inventories of merchandise, raw materials, supplies, work in process, and finished goods; and certain prepayments, such as insurance and rent paid for in advance of receiving the insurance or rental services. Noncurrent assets include property, plant, and equipment, long-term investments in securities, and acquired intangible assets (such as patents, trademarks, and goodwill). Noncurrent assets can also include certain internally developed intangible assets, depending on authoritative guidance. **Chapter 9** discusses intangible assets in more detail.

Current liabilities include amounts owed to suppliers (accounts payable), to employees (accrued salaries and wages), and to governmental units (income taxes payable). They also

---

[1]The financial reporting requirements of the jurisdiction in which the firm is domiciled determine how often it must prepare a balance sheet, file it with the appropriate regulatory body, and make it publicly available. For example, in the United States, all firms with publicly traded debt or equity securities must prepare and file financial reports quarterly. Elsewhere, semiannual reporting is more common. Nothing precludes more frequent financial statement preparation, for example, to support internal decision making. In fact, most firms prepare monthly financial statements to support internal decision making. Public dissemination of financial reports, however, follows the financial reporting cycle dictated by the jurisdiction.

include the current portion of long-term debt—that is, the portion of notes and bonds payable that will require the use of current assets within the next year. Noncurrent liabilities include interest-bearing obligations with maturities beyond one year (such as bonds, mortgages, and similar debts), some obligations under long-term leases, some retirement obligations, and certain noninterest-bearing obligations such as deferred income taxes.

BALANCE SHEET FORMAT: U.S. GAAP

The typical balance sheet lists assets first, followed by liabilities and shareholders' equity. In U.S. GAAP, the balance sheet lists assets from most liquid to least liquid, where *liquid* refers to the ease of converting the asset into cash. A balance sheet prepared according to U.S. GAAP begins with the most liquid of the current assets—cash and cash equivalents—and then moves to other current assets (such as marketable securities, accounts receivable, inventory, and prepayments), followed by noncurrent assets (such as long-term receivables, property, plant, and equipment, intangible assets, and goodwill). Similarly, the balance sheet lists liabilities starting with those that the firm will discharge soonest (the most current or closest to maturity liabilities) and ending with those that it will pay latest (the most noncurrent or distant to maturity liabilities).

Exhibit 1.1 (in Chapter 1) shows the balance sheet of Nordstrom Inc., which illustrates the U.S. GAAP format. Nordstrom is a national retailer, with 155 stores located in 27 states. Nordstrom's balance sheet, prepared under U.S GAAP as of February 3, 2007, begins with cash and cash equivalent assets of $402.6 million. The balance sheet then lists, in order, the remaining current assets in decreasing order of liquidity, with prepaid expenses and other (of $60.5 million) being the least liquid of the current assets. The list of noncurrent assets follows:

- Land, buildings, and equipment, net . . . . $1,757.2 million
- Goodwill . . . . $ 51.7 million
- Acquired trade name . . . . $ 84.0 million
- Other noncurrent assets . . . . $ 186.5 million

In the liability section, Nordstrom shows the liability that it must discharge soonest is accounts payable (amounts owed to suppliers and vendors) of $576.8 million. Next in line for payment are amounts accrued but not yet paid to employees (accrued salaries, wages, and related benefits) of $340.0 million. Moving further down the balance sheet, Nordstrom reports long-term debt of $623.7 million. This amount excludes payments of long-term debt due in the coming year; the current portion of long-term debt ($6.8 million) appears among the current liabilities. Within the shareholders' equity section, Nordstrom reports capital provided by shareholders of $826.4 million; this amount reflects what shareholders paid when Nordstrom originally issued those shares. The shareholders' equity section also includes $1,350.7 million of retained earnings, the source for net assets that Nordstrom has generated through its earnings process over time (its cumulative earnings) and has not distributed to shareholders.

Using Nordstrom's balance sheet, we can verify the balance sheet equation: assets ($4,821.6 million) equal liabilities (the sum of $1,433.1, $623.7, $356.1, and $240.2, or $2,653.1 million) plus shareholders' equity ($2,168.5 million).

BALANCE SHEET FORMAT: IFRS

Firms that use International Financial Reporting Standards (IFRS) may, but need not, reverse the ordering of balance sheets and list their assets from least liquid to most liquid, with the same ordering used to list liabilities. This reporting format appears in Exhibit 1.5 (in Chapter 1) which contains the balance sheet for Scania, a Swedish-domiciled multinational firm that is one of the world's largest manufacturers of trucks, buses, and engines. Scania's balance sheet dated December 31, 2006, begins with its least liquid assets—its intangible assets—which were SEK2,464 million. Scania's intangible assets are primarily capitalized development costs and goodwill (topics covered in Chapter 9). Scania's tangible noncurrent assets (SEK17,130 million) consist of land, buildings, and equipment. Moving down the list, Scania's most liquid assets are its cash and cash equivalents, SEK9,934 million at the end of 2006.

We can use Scania's balance sheet and the balance sheet equation to verify that assets equal the sum of liabilities plus shareholders' equity. In Scania's case, total assets (SEK88,078 million) equal the sum of liabilities (SEK61,944 million) and shareholders' equity (SEK26,134 million).

Although Nordstrom uses U.S. GAAP and Scania uses IFRS, their balance sheets appear to present similar information, albeit in differing orders. However, many questions remain unanswered, including:

1. Which resources does a firm recognize as assets, and which obligations does it recognize as liabilities? That is, what conditions must an item meet to be an asset or a liability on a balance sheet? Do these conditions differ between U.S. GAAP and IFRS?

2. How do firms measure assets and liabilities? That is, for an item that meets the conditions to be an asset or a liability, what number appears next to the item on the balance sheet? Do measurements differ between U.S. GAAP and IFRS?

3. How do firms measure shareholders' equity? What are the components of shareholders' equity, and how do they appear on the balance sheet? Are those components, their measurement, and their disclosure the same under U.S. GAAP and IFRS?

The rest of this chapter addresses these questions. We distinguish, where necessary, between the requirements of U.S. GAAP and IFRS; we refer to pronouncements from either the FASB or the IASB as *authoritative guidance*.

 # ASSET RECOGNITION AND MEASUREMENT

ASSET DEFINITION AND RECOGNITION

Asset recognition means that the item is an accounting asset on the balance sheet. For an item to be an asset, it must meet both (1) the definition of an asset, and (2) the asset recognition criteria.[2]

- **Asset Definition** An asset is a probable[3] future economic benefit that a firm controls because of a past event or transaction. The definition of an asset is similar in U.S. GAAP and IFRS.

- **Asset Recognition** The three criteria for asset recognition are:

  1. The firm owns or controls the right to use the item.

  2. The right to use the item arises as a result of a past transaction or exchange.

  3. The future benefit has a relevant measurement attribute that can be quantified with sufficient reliability.

Not all future benefits qualify as assets; that is, although all assets provide future benefits, not all future benefits are assets. This is because a future benefit that qualifies as an accounting asset must meet the three recognition criteria, the first two of which are part of the definition of an asset. The third criterion pertains to recognition, not definition: an item that meets the definition of an asset must be measurable with sufficient reliability. *Reliability* of a reported amount means that the amount corresponds to what it purports to represent and is reasonably free from error and bias, in the sense that multiple independent measurers would agree on the amount.[4] For example, if a reported amount on a balance sheet purports to represent the acquisition cost of inventory, a reliable measure would be the price paid. That price can be confirmed by independent measurers as the amount quoted in the invoice for the

---

[2]The FASB's asset definition is in Financial Accounting Standards Board, *Statement of Financial Accounting Concepts No. 6*, "Elements of Financial Statements," 1985, par. 26; and its asset recognition criteria are in Financial Accounting Standards Board, *Statement of Financial Accounting Concepts No. 5*, "Recognition and Measurement in Financial Statements of Business Enterprises," 1984, par. 63–65. The IASB's asset definition is in the *Framework for the Preparation and Presentation of Financial Statements*, 1989, par. 53–59. The **Glossary** provides more details on the asset definitions.

[3]The word *probable* refers to that which can be reasonably expected or believed on the basis of available evidence. The inclusion of *probable* in the definition acknowledges that commercial activities occur in an uncertain environment.

[4]Broadly similar discussions of reliability appear in the FASB's conceptual framework (*Statement of Financial Concepts No. 2*, "Qualitative Characteristics of Accounting Information," 1980) and in the IASB's *Framework for the Preparation and Presentation of Financial Statements*, 1989, adopted by the IASB in 2001.

inventories. Neither U.S. GAAP nor IFRS specifies what amount of reliability is "sufficient," suggesting that this judgment is context-specific and subjective, not quantifiable.

To understand how these conditions influence asset recognition, we consider several examples of transactions that result in future economic benefits but which may not result in the recognition of an asset. Except where noted, both U.S. GAAP and IFRS require the same accounting treatment for these examples.

Example 1 Nordstrom sold a pair of shoes for $100 to a customer who purchased the shoes using a Nordstrom credit card. Although Nordstrom has not received any cash, it has received a future economic benefit, in the form of a promise of cash payment. Nordstrom would recognize this benefit as an asset (an account receivable) because it has a right to receive a definite amount of cash ($100) as a result of the sale of the shoes.

Example 2 Scania purchased new equipment it will use in producing engines. The new equipment substitutes a robotically controlled machining process for a labor-intensive process. Scania agreed to give the equipment vendor 200,000 shares of its common stock in payment for the equipment. At the time of the transaction, Scania's stock price was SEK175 per share. Scania will recognize the new equipment as an asset because it controls the equipment and it expects to receive future benefits in the form of reduced labor costs. (We discuss the amount Scania will report on its balance sheet for this equipment in a later section; this is the asset *measurement* question.)

Example 3 Scania sold 16 trucks to a customer for a total of SEK80 million. The customer agreed to pay Scania SEK20 million at the time Scania delivered the trucks and the rest in four equal installments at the end of each of the next four years. At the time of the final payment, Scania will transfer the legal title of the trucks to the customer. Although Scania has legal title to the trucks during the next four years, it has no rights to use them. Provided the customer makes the required payments, the future benefits of the trucks reside with, and will stay with, the customer. Thus, the trucks are the customer's assets, not Scania's. Scania will recognize as assets the SEK20 million cash received at the time of delivery and a receivable for the remaining payments.

Example 4 The Nordstrom name has become synonymous with a quality shopping experience. The company has a reputation for the helpfulness and friendliness of its employees in satisfying customer needs, even at the potential cost of losing a Nordstrom sale if the customer will be more satisfied purchasing merchandise at a competitor's store. Nordstrom management invests in this reputation by hiring talented staff, by investing in training, and by forgoing a sale now in order to achieve higher levels of customer satisfaction in the long term. Nordstrom management believes that satisfied customers are more loyal and therefore will spend more at Nordstrom in the future. Thus, satisfied customers provide future benefits in the form of increased future sales. Neither the expected future sales nor the satisfied customers are assets on Nordstrom's balance sheet because Nordstrom cannot control customers' future purchasing decisions.

Example 5 Like many companies, Nordstrom has developed and maintains a list of its customers and their characteristics, which it uses for mailing catalogs and other promotional purposes. Creating and maintaining a customer list takes time and resources, so a decision to have one entails certain investments and continuing expenditures. The expected benefits of a customer list are the future cash inflows associated with purchases made by listed customers after they receive their promotional materials. The larger and more detailed the customer list, and the more high-purchasing customers it includes, the greater are the expected future benefits of the customer list. However, an internally developed customer list is not an accounting asset. Although the item meets the *definition* of an asset, it does not meet the third *recognition* criterion, because the firm cannot measure the future economic benefits of the list with sufficient reliability. However, the firm would recognize an *externally purchased* customer list as an asset at an amount equal to the purchase price. **Chapter 9** discusses the distinction between internally developed and acquired intangible assets in more detail and introduces certain differences between U.S. GAAP and IFRS.

Example 6 Scania plans to open a manufacturing facility in the United States next year. It has identified an existing facility that could be purchased for SEK500 million. Scania believes it could modify this facility for its use at an additional cost of SEK200 million. Scania plans to use a combination of cash on hand and cash recently raised from issuing common shares to finance the transaction. Although Scania has firm plans to buy and modify the facility, it does not have an accounting asset. Until Scania has obtained control of the facility as a result of a transaction with the current owner, it would not recognize the facility as an accounting asset.

Example 7 Continuing with the transaction proposed in **Example 6**, both the owner of the facility and Scania sign a contract in which they *promise* to transact—to sell and purchase the facility—one year later. Such an exchange of promises is an **executory contract**, an exchange of promises for mutual performance in the future that neither party has yet begun to perform. In the executory contract described in this example, Scania has acquired the rights to the future benefits arising from the facility, but the contract is unexecuted by both the facility owner (who must relinquish control of the facility) and Scania (who must pay the agreed purchase price). Executory contracts are typically not assets or liabilities until one or both of the contracting parties begin to complete their contractual obligations.

Example 8 Continuing with the transaction described in **Examples 6** and **7**, Scania pays the owner of the facility SEK100 million toward the purchase of the facility. Scania has now partially performed under the contract and will recognize an accounting asset to the extent of its partial performance. In this example, Scania would recognize an asset called Purchase Deposit, for SEK100 million.

ASSET MEASUREMENT

Each asset on a balance sheet has an associated monetary amount (the amount is the measurement of that asset). Authoritative guidance specifies measurement attributes or bases for measuring those monetary amounts. In this section, we describe several measurement bases that U.S. GAAP and IFRS use.

Acquisition Cost or Historical Cost

Acquisition (historical) cost is the amount of cash paid (or the cash equivalent value of other forms of payment) to acquire an asset. Most assets are initially measured using acquisition cost, which the firm can generally document by reference to contracts, invoices, and canceled checks. The foundation for initially measuring an asset at its acquisition cost is that the buyer believes the asset will generate future benefits (that is, increased cash inflows or reduced cash outflows) that are at least as large as the purchase price. Otherwise, the buyer would have an immediate economic loss and would have no incentive to acquire the asset. This reasoning implies that, at the time of acquisition, acquisition cost sets the lower bound on the asset's expected future benefits.

In the case of a nonfinancial asset, the acquisition cost includes the invoice price and all expenditures made or obligations incurred to prepare that asset for its intended use. For example, transportation costs, installation costs, handling charges, and brokerage fees are among the costs incurred to place the asset into service; acquisition cost includes all of these, as shown in the following illustration:

Invoice Price of Equipment	$120,000
Less: 2% Discount for Prompt Cash Payment	(2,400)
Net Invoice Price	$117,600
Transportation Cost	3,260
Installation Cost	7,350
Total Cost	$128,210

The firm may acquire assets by paying cash or exchanging other items of value. For example, a firm may exchange its own shares to acquire an asset. If the consideration exchanged for an asset is not cash, the acquisition cost is the fair value of the consideration given or the fair value of the asset received, whichever the firm can more reliably measure.

Example 9 Return to **Example 2** where Scania purchased new equipment in exchange for 200,000 shares of its common stock. At the time of the transaction, Scania's stock price was SEK175 per share. Scania would record the equipment on its balance sheet at SEK35 million

(= 200,000 × SEK175), the fair value of the shares exchanged, plus any additional costs incurred to prepare the equipment for its intended use.

Current Replacement Cost

The **current replacement cost** of an asset is the amount a firm would have to pay to obtain another asset with identical service potential; it is therefore an **entry value** that reflects economic conditions at the measurement date. This measurement attribute is used in U.S. GAAP to measure inventories whose usefulness (typically, in terms of salability) to the firm has declined below the cost of the inventories.[5] Because inventories are purchased or produced frequently, measuring their current replacement cost may be as simple as consulting suppliers' catalogs or price lists.

Net Realizable Value

Net realizable value is the net cash (selling price less selling costs) that the firm would receive if it sold the asset today, in orderly fashion in an arm's-length transaction. Net realizable value is an example of an **exit value**, because it reflects a price that the firm would receive in a transaction in which an asset leaves the firm. Net realizable value is similar, but not identical, to fair value, discussed next.

Fair Value

U.S. GAAP explicitly defines the **fair value** of an asset as "the price that would be received to sell an asset [or paid to transfer a liability] in an orderly transaction between market participants at the measurement date."[6] Thus, U.S. GAAP defines fair value as an exit value, namely, the amount the firm would receive if it sold an asset in an orderly, arm's-length transaction at the measurement date. Fair value does not include selling costs or other transaction costs in the measurement, which net realizable value (discussed above) includes. The notion of fair value as an *exit* value applies to both assets and liabilities in U.S. GAAP. IFRS, however, defines fair value more generally as a current *exchange* value, which can mean either a current entry price—that is, replacement cost—or a current exit price.

The fair value of an asset as defined in U.S. GAAP is an **opportunity cost** in the sense that fair value reflects an amount that the firm could receive if it sold the asset today. Fair value is the amount the firm forgoes by not selling the asset. In U.S. GAAP, fair value reflects a *market participant* perspective, so that the intentions of managers regarding how they plan to use the asset do not determine the fair value measurement. Instead, the firm measures fair value based on how market participants would use the asset. In addition, fair value captures current economic conditions, as opposed to acquisition cost, which captures the economic conditions that existed when the firm acquired the asset. As a result, fair value can (and does) change, with the frequency, direction, and magnitude of changes determined by economic conditions.

Fair value is also a hypothetical amount (that is, the price at which the firm *could* sell the asset), so it does not require data from actual transactions for the asset's measurement. In contrast, acquisition costs of assets are typically readily observable from records of actual transactions, such as invoices, contracts, and canceled checks. Fair value measurements need not be based on transactions. The objective is to measure an asset the firm still owns using a *hypothetical* price.[7] Some assets are traded in well-organized and active markets, so the firm can observe fair values. For example, many commodities and securities trade on exchanges that produce daily and even hourly prices. Because many assets do not trade in active markets, the firm must estimate the fair value for such assets. U.S. GAAP requires that a fair value measurement use measurement techniques, inputs, and assumptions that market participants would use if they were arriving at a transaction price.[8] We discuss next an example

---

[5]Chapter 4 of *Accounting Research Bulletin (ARB) No. 43*, "Restatement and Revision of Accounting Research Bulletins," 1953, requires that firms measure inventories at the lower of [acquisition] cost or market (**Codification Topic 330**). In this context, market means the current replacement cost, not to exceed net realizable value or to be less than net realizable value reduced by a normal profit margin. IASB, *International Accounting Standard 2*, "Inventories," 1993, requires that firms measure inventories at the lower of cost or net realizable value.

[6]*Statement of Financial Accounting Standards No. 157*, "Fair Value Measurement," 2006, par. 5 (**Codification Topic 820**).

[7]Many of these comments apply to net realizable value as well.

[8]U.S. GAAP provides this and other guidance for fair value measurements in *SFAS No. 157*, "Fair Value Measurement," 2006 (**Codification Topic 820**). IFRS contains no analogous guidance. As of the writing of this textbook the IASB has undertaken a project that will analyze all the IFRS guidance that requires a fair value measurement to determine whether those measurements were intended to be exit values (similar to the definition of fair value in U.S. GAAP). The IASB will also consider how fair value should be defined in IFRS and will create a single source of measurement guidance. The planned completion date for this project is 2010. The IASB's Discussion Paper, "Fair Value Measurements," issued in November 2006 and available on the IASB's Web site (*iasb.org.uk*), discusses the differences between U.S. GAAP and IFRS notions of fair value.

of a technique that firms can use to arrive at a fair value measurement when active markets for the asset do not exist.

Present Value of Future Net Cash Flows   Present value is the amount that results from using an appropriate interest rate to discount one or more future cash flows to the present. (The **Appendix** discusses the technique.) The **present value of a stream of future cash flows** is the sum of the present values of the individual future cash inflows and outflows associated with an asset. Present value is not, in and of itself, a measurement attribute. Rather, it is a means of arriving at a measurement attribute. The FASB's *Statement of Financial Accounting Concepts No. 7*, "Using Cash Flow Information and Present Value in Accounting Measurements," paragraph 25 states that "[t]he only objective of present value, when used in accounting measurements . . . is to estimate fair value. Stated differently, present value should attempt to capture the elements that taken together would comprise a market price if one existed, that is, fair value."

If the inputs to a present value calculation—the discount rate and the future cash inflows and outflows—are amounts that market participants would use, the firm can use this technique to arrive at a fair value estimate. The present value of an asset is always less than the sum of the undiscounted future cash inflows and outflows associated with that asset, because some amount of implied interest, or capital cost, is always associated with the use of cash and other resources. The following example presents the general approach.

Example 10   Nordstrom lends $1 million to Worldwide Retailers Inc. (Worldwide). The terms of the loan call for Worldwide to pay Nordstrom $130,000 at the end of each of the next five years and an additional $655,000 at the end of the fifth year. The total amount of cash that Worldwide will pay Nordstrom is $1.305 million [= ($130,000 × 5) + $655,000]. The present value of the future cash inflows to Nordstrom associated with this loan differs as the discount rate changes. If the discount rate is the rate that a market participant would demand in an arm's-length lending arrangement, the present value is an estimate of the fair value of the loan. For example, if that rate is 7%, the present value, which is also the fair value, is calculated as follows (with each cash flow occurring at the end of the year indicated, amounts in millions):

First Year:	$130 \div (1.07)^1 = \$121.50$
Second Year:	$130 \div (1.07)^2 = \$113.55$
Third Year:	$130 \div (1.07)^3 = \$106.12$
Fourth Year:	$130 \div (1.07)^4 = \$99.18$
Fifth Year:	$130 \div (1.07)^5 = \$92.69$
Fifth Year:	$655 \div (1.07)^5 = \$467.01$

The sum of these discounted future cash flows is $1 million (after rounding). From a business perspective, Nordstrom is lending $1 million with the expectation that it will receive both the principal of $1 million and an annual return of 7%. Nordstrom expects to receive a total *undiscounted* cash inflow from Worldwide of $1.305 million (= [$130 × 5] + $655); these undiscounted cash inflows include both principal and interest at 7%.

Other techniques for estimating the fair value of assets go beyond the scope of this textbook. We can use the discounted cash flow technique to illustrate the problems that the firm must solve to estimate a fair value in the absence of an observable market price.

First, the firm identifies the amounts of future cash flows. In the loan example, there is no uncertainty about the cash flows, but as a practical matter, the future cash flows associated with an asset may depend on numerous factors, including technological innovation, product introductions by competitors, and inflation rates to name but a few. Even in the example of the loan with contractually specified cash flows, there is some possibility that Worldwide will default (that is, not make the promised payments). In a fair value measurement, Nordstrom would use a market participant perspective to estimate the probability of default.

Second, the firm selects the appropriate rate to discount the future cash flows to the present. To provide an estimate of the asset's fair value, the discount rate should be the rate that market participants would use, reflecting current economic conditions including, for example, expectations of inflation and any uncertainty about the cash flows of the asset.

We discuss fair value measurement more fully in **Chapter 10**.

ASSET MEASUREMENT APPROACHES FOR SPECIFIC ASSETS

The same asset can have different measurements for tax purposes, for financial reporting purposes, and for internal managerial decision-making purposes. In addition, certain specialized business situations call for specific measurements; for example, an insurance policy on a warehouse might specify that the insured amount of the warehouse is the cost to replace the warehouse. In this textbook we focus on measurement for financial reporting, understanding that other purposes and other measurement bases also exist.

Both U.S. GAAP and IFRS specify the asset measurement basis for financial reporting. To repeat, acquisition cost is the initial measurement attribute for most assets. Subsequent measurement depends on the type of asset. We discuss several broad categories of assets and their measurements next; subsequent chapters return to this question in greater detail.

Financial assets include cash and claims to cash that a firm will receive in the near future, such as accounts receivable. The most liquid financial asset, cash, appears as the amount of cash on hand or in the bank. Accounts receivable from customers appears as the amount of cash the firm expects to collect. If the time until collection extends beyond one year, by convention the firm discounts the expected future cash inflow to a present value; otherwise, the process ignores implied interest. Because the firm collects most accounts receivable within one to three months, the convention to ignore discounting for these assets rests on the basis of a lack of materiality. **Chapter 1** discusses the concept of materiality.

In addition to cash and receivables, many firms also have financial assets in the form of investments in marketable securities, typically bonds and stocks issued by other firms. The firm initially measures these assets at acquisition cost, but the subsequent measurement depends on the nature of the investment. **Chapter 12** discusses marketable security investments.

Nonfinancial assets are tangible and intangible resources that firms use in operations to generate future cash flows of uncertain amount. Common examples include inventory, land, buildings, machinery, licenses, and patents. Firms initially measure nonfinancial assets at acquisition cost; they subsequently reduce this amount to reflect the consumption over time of the asset's economic benefits as well as to recognize declines in the fair value of the asset. We introduce these two adjustments here and defer details to subsequent chapters.

The first reduction in the carrying value results from the *depreciation* process, which allocates the asset's acquisition cost less estimated salvage value to the periods during which the asset provides future benefits. Depreciation therefore allocates the asset's cost to the periods of benefit in some systematic and rational way, and it does not attempt to track changes in the asset's fair value. Over the life of the asset, the carrying value changes from acquisition cost to salvage value, which might be zero. The changes in an asset's fair value from period to period need not be downward, but the depreciation process always results in reducing the asset's carrying value. So over the life of an asset, the depreciation process reduces the carrying value from initial acquisition cost to salvage value. The purpose of depreciation is to allocate costs to periods of benefit, not to track changes in fair value.

The second reduction in carrying value results from *impairment*, which occurs in general when an asset's fair value falls below its carrying value. Both U.S. GAAP and IFRS require that firms test assets for impairment and have specific rules for measuring the amount of an impairment loss. **Chapter 9** discusses these requirements more fully.

KEY CONVENTIONS UNDERLYING ASSET MEASUREMENT

GOING CONCERN

The presumption is that a firm will remain in operation long enough to carry out its current plans. A firm that is a **going concern** will, in the normal course of its operations, realize changes in the fair values of its assets either by using those assets or selling them. We use the word **realized** in its accounting sense, meaning, converted to cash. An item is **recognized**, for accounting purposes, when it is displayed in the financial statements.[9] For most assets, U.S. GAAP and IFRS require the following recognition rules:

---

[9]The distinction between recognition and realization is essential to accrual accounting, hence the importance accorded to recognition criteria. Firms recognize items that qualify for inclusion in the financial statements when they enter the financial statements, regardless of when those items are realized by conversion to cash.

■ In the case of value decreases, the firm recognizes the decreases as impairment expenses when the decreases occur before it realizes the collection of the reduced cash flows.

■ In the case of value increases, U.S. GAAP precludes the recognition of unrealized gains from increases in the fair value of some nonfinancial assets. The firm can realize the fair value increase by selling the appreciated asset. IFRS permits, but does not require, firms to recognize unrealized increases in the fair values of some nonfinancial asset on their balance sheets; that is, IFRS permits firms to *revalue* certain nonfinancial assets to fair values that exceed carrying values.[10]

RELEVANCE AND RELIABILITY

Recall the third criterion for asset recognition: the future benefit has a relevant measurement attribute that the firm can measure with sufficient reliability.[11] **Relevance** means that the information is pertinent to the decisions of users of financial reports, in the sense that the information can make a difference in those decisions. Relevant financial accounting information helps users form predictions or correct their expectations. Often, more than one measurement attribute exists for an asset, and standard setters must choose which of those attributes provides the most relevant measurement, subject to reliability considerations.

Reliability means that the information presented is reasonably free from error and bias and faithfully represents what it purports to represent. Standard setters view acquisition cost measurements as providing reliable information, in the sense of faithfully representing the economic value sacrificed to acquire an asset. Reliability also encompasses the ability to verify the measured amount. Acquisition cost is reliable in the sense that different accountants will likely agree on the same amount because each of them can verify the acquisition cost by reference to contracts and invoices. As previously discussed, fair value measurements can be reliable, for example, if the asset being measured trades in an active market. Because many assets do not trade in active markets, some accountants view acquisition costs as more reliable than fair values.

CONSERVATISM

Historically, **conservatism** has described a preference for financial reporting such "that possible errors in measurement be in the direction of understatement rather than overstatement of net income and net assets."[12] Conservatism is the basis for the practice of reporting certain assets at the lower of acquisition cost or fair value.[13] The requirement to test assets for impairment and to record impairment charges rests on the notion that balance sheet carrying values of assets should not exceed the amount of cash that the firm expects to receive by using or selling the asset. Acquisition cost measurement combined with impairment testing thus provides conservative (that is, lower) asset balance sheet values, because possible measurement errors of assets will be in the direction of understatements. Conservatism interacts with reliability, because the firm measures impaired assets at fair value, which it often bases on an estimate that it cannot verify with an invoice or a contract.

The general acceptance of these three conventions does not justify them. Some managers appear to prefer acquisition cost measures to fair value measures because the latter usually cause more volatility in reported income. The increased volatility results from fair values reflecting changes in economic conditions as they occur. Fair values fluctuate more than do acquisition

---

[10]IASB, *International Accounting Standard 16*, "Property, Plant and Equipment," 1993, amended in 1998 and 2000, permits firms to choose a revaluation model to account for property, plant, and equipment (par. 31). Under the revaluation model, the firm records at fair value on its balance sheet an item of property, plant, and equipment whose fair value it can measure reliably. At the date of revaluation, the amount is fair value less any subsequent accumulated depreciation and subsequent impairment losses. The revaluation model thus permits the recognition of unrealized increases in fair value.

[11]Relevance and reliability are discussed in FASB *Statement of Financial Accounting Concepts No. 2*, "Qualitative Characteristics of Accounting Information," 1980, par. 46–57 and par. 58–97, respectively.

[12]Accounting Principles Board, *Statement 4*, par. 171, as discussed in FASB *Statement of Financial Accounting Concepts No. 2*, "Qualitative Characteristics of Accounting Information," 1980. See **Glossary**; however, a conservative reporting of net income in an early period means a later period's income will be higher than if the firm had used an unconservative method in the earlier period.

[13]As previously discussed, IFRS but not U.S. GAAP permits, but does not require, certain assets to be measured at fair value even when fair value exceeds acquisition cost. In this sense, IFRS is less conservative than U.S. GAAP.

costs, which do not fluctuate. For the most part, U.S. GAAP and IFRS specify the measurement basis; we will note the cases in which management has a choice of measurement basis.

PROBLEM **3.1** for Self-Study

Asset recognition and measurement. The transactions listed below relate to Polo Ralph Lauren ("Polo"). For each, indicate whether the transaction immediately gives rise to an asset for Polo and, if so, state the account title and amount Polo will record.

a. Polo spends $16 million to advertise a new line of perfume in the expectation that the advertisements will attract new customers.

b. Polo signs a contract with Nordstrom for the distribution of its fall line of clothes. Polo promises to distribute certain jeans exclusively through Nordstrom, and Nordstrom promises to display and market the jeans in a manner designed to increase sales. Polo estimates the fair value of the contract to be $4 million.

c. Polo invests $24 million in research and development related to its paint line of business.

d. Polo spends $800,000 on tuition-assistance programs for its middle-level managers to obtain MBAs. Historically, 80% of the managers who seek MBAs receive them and remain with the company five years or more.

e. Polo acquires and occupies a warehouse outside of Seattle by signing a mortgage payable for $75 million. Legal title for the warehouse remains with the bank (the holder of the mortgage) because Polo has not completed all required payments under the mortgage.

Solutions to self-study problems appear at the end of the chapter.

LIABILITY RECOGNITION AND MEASUREMENT

LIABILITY DEFINITION AND RECOGNITION

An accounting liability arises when a firm incurs an obligation to make a future sacrifice that, because of a past event or transaction, it has little or no discretion to avoid. For example, a liability arises when a firm receives goods or services and, in exchange, promises to pay the provider of those goods or services a reasonably definite amount at a reasonably definite future time.[14] All accounting liabilities are obligations, but not all obligations are accounting liabilities. To be an accounting liability, an item must meet both (1) the definition of a liability, and (2) recognition criteria:

■ **Liability Definition** Liabilities are probable[15] future sacrifices of economic benefits arising from present obligations of a particular entity to transfer assets or provide services to other entities in the future as a result of a past event or transaction.

■ **Liability Recognition** The criteria for liability recognition are:

1. The item represents a *present* obligation, not a potential future commitment or intent.

2. The obligation must exist as a result of a past transaction or exchange, called the *obligating event*.

---

[14]The FASB's liability definition is in Financial Accounting Standards Board, *Statement of Financial Accounting Concepts No. 6*, "Elements of Financial Statements," 1985, par. 35, and its recognition criteria are in *Statement of Financial Accounting Concepts No.5*, "Recognition and Measurement in Financial Statements of Business Enterprises," 1984, par. 63–65. The IASB's definition is in International Accounting Standards Board, *Framework for the Preparation and Presentation of Financial Statements*, 1989, par. 60–64. The **Glossary** discusses the FASB's and IASB's definitions of a liability.

[15]As was the case with the asset definition, the word *probable* as used in the liability definition refers to that which can be reasonably expected or believed on the basis of available evidence. The inclusion of *probable* in the definition acknowledges that commercial activities occur in an uncertain environment.

3. The obligation must require a probable future economic resource that the firm has little or no discretion to avoid.

4. The obligation must have a relevant measurement attribute that the firm can quantify with sufficient reliability.

To help you better understand liability recognition, we consider several examples of transactions that result in obligations but which need not result in recognition of an accounting liability.

Example 11 Nordstrom purchased merchandise inventory and agreed to pay its supplier $8,000 within 30 days. This obligation is a liability on Nordstrom's balance sheet because Nordstrom received the goods and must pay a definite amount, $8,000, at a reasonably definite future time, within 30 days. Because Nordstrom has promised to pay the amount within one year, it is a current liability (accounts payable).

Example 12 Nordstrom borrowed $4 million by issuing long-term bonds whose terms require that on December 31 of each year, Nordstrom make a payment of 10% of the amount borrowed. In addition, Nordstrom must repay the $4 million initial amount borrowed in 20 years. The $4 million obligation is a liability because Nordstrom received the cash and must repay the debt. Nordstrom reports the borrowed amount as a noncurrent liability on its balance sheet (included in Long-Term Debt) until the last year. At the end of the 19th year, Nordstrom will reclassify the $4 million as a current liability (included in Current Portion of Long-Term Debt). In contrast, the annual 10% interest becomes a liability as time passes. By the end of each year, Nordstrom will record (accrue) $400,000 (= .10 × $4 million) as Interest Payable, a current liability. The obligating event is the passage of time.

Example 13 Scania received an advance of SEK60 million from a customer for trucks that Scania will deliver next year. The cash advance creates a liability for Scania of SEK60 million. The obligating event is Scania's receipt of the cash. Scania has incurred an obligation to deliver the trucks next year, or it must return the cash advance.[16] Because it expects to discharge this obligation within 12 months by delivering the trucks, Scania classifies the SEK60 million as a current liability on its balance sheet, included in Advance Payments from Customers. Advances from customers are a type of *deferred performance obligation* (a liability) that we discuss in **Chapter 7**.

Example 14 Scania signs an agreement with its employees' labor union, promising to increase wages by 6% and to increase medical benefits. Although this agreement creates an obligation, it does not immediately create an accounting liability because the obligating event has not yet occurred. That event occurs when employees provide labor services that require Scania to pay wages and provide medical benefits. As employees work, Scania recognizes a liability on its balance sheet.

The agreement in **Example 14** is, at the time of signing, a **mutually unexecuted contract** (also called an **executory contract**) because neither Scania nor its employees have performed under the contract. Other examples include most purchase orders and some leases. Firms usually do not recognize the obligations created by mutually unexecuted contracts as accounting liabilities, nor do they recognize the benefits of such contracts as assets, as illustrated previously in **Example 7**. **Chapter 11** discusses the accounting treatment of some of these arrangements.

Example 15 Scania provides a five-year warranty on the engines it builds and sells. The promise to stand ready to provide repair services under the warranty agreement creates an obligation, resulting from the sale of the engines under warranty. The selling price for a Scania engine includes payment for future warranty services even if the invoice does not explicitly show the portion of the total purchase price that is associated with the warranty. At the time of sale, Scania receives a benefit (the cash collected from the customer), but it has not fulfilled its obligations with respect to the warranty period. It will fulfill those obligations over the five-year warranty period. Based on past experience, Scania estimates both the proportion of customers who will seek services under the warranty agreement and the expected cost of

---

[16]In some transactions of this sort, the manufacturer does not have the option to return the cash. If the manufacturer does not provide the goods as promised, it may be liable for court-awarded damages based on the economic harm the customer suffered from not getting the promised items.

providing the warranty services. These estimates form the basis for measuring the warranty liability. Scania reports the portion of the liability that it expects to discharge in the next 12 months as a current liability (included in Current Provisions). It reports the portion that relates to warranty obligations it will discharge beyond the next 12 months as a noncurrent liability (included in Other Noncurrent Provisions). **Chapter 8** discusses warranty liabilities.

Example 16 A customer files a suit claiming damages of SEK 10 million from faulty engines that Scania manufactured. The case has not yet gone to trial, so no court has yet rendered a decision or verdict. Firms do not recognize unsettled lawsuits as liabilities unless the firm judges that it will probably lose, and the loss estimate satisfies some other conditions. If the firm judges the eventual loss to be less than probable or if it judges the loss to be probable but it cannot estimate the amount of any payment within a range, it will not recognize a liability. That is, unless it is *probable* that Scania will have to pay and Scania can estimate the amount of payment, then it will not record a liability for the lawsuit. Scania will disclose in notes to its financial statements the existence of the lawsuit (if it is material) and the potential for future payments.

Example 17 To facilitate a sale, Scania guaranteed a customer's bank loan, which the customer had undertaken to raise funds to finance the payments for Scania's product. Scania promises that it will make the specified loan payments if the customer defaults. This arrangement is an example of a *financial guarantee contract*, in which the issuer (Scania) must make payments to the holder of the contract (the bank) for a loss incurred if a specified debtor (the customer) fails to make payments when due. These contracts give rise to accounting liabilities in the form of obligations to stand ready to make payments under circumstances specified in the contract. Both U.S. GAAP and IFRS require initial recognition of the liability at its fair value.[17]

The warranty in **Example 15** illustrates a liability that is of uncertain timing or amount or both. U.S. GAAP refers to these liabilities as **loss contingencies**, and IFRS refers to them as **provisions**.[18] Recall that the word *probable* was also used in the asset and liability definitions, and in that context, it captures the notion of what can be reasonably expected or believed based on the available evidence, acknowledging that the environment of business is inherently uncertain. In contrast, *probable* as a recognition criterion for liabilities with uncertain amount, uncertain timing, or both, has a different meaning. The IFRS guidance for recognizing these liabilities defines *probable* as more likely than not, which implies more than 50%. Applying this criterion to **Example 15,** we can see that Scania would determine whether the likelihood that customers will require warranty services exceeds 50%. U.S. GAAP does not ascribe a precise threshold to *probable*; we believe that in practice the rule of thumb is approximately 80%. That is, a liability with uncertain amount or timing or both must be at least 80% likely in order for a firm to recognize it. U.S. GAAP and IFRS require similar (but not identical) measurements for these liabilities; both specify that the firm will recognize the liability (that is, measure the liability) at the most likely amount.[19]

The lawsuit (**Example 16**) illustrates an obligation that a firm would not recognize under either U.S. GAAP or IFRS, although the firm would disclose it in the notes if it judged the lawsuit to be material. The description of **Example 16** illustrates the applicability of the recognition criteria for uncertain obligations to a lawsuit. In this example, the firm does not judge the obligation arising from the lawsuit as probable and it cannot reasonably estimate

---

[17]Financial Accounting Standards Board, *Interpretation No. 45*, "Guarantor's Accounting and Disclosure Requirements for Guarantees, Including Indirect Guarantees of the Indebtedness of Others," 2002, (**Codification Topic 460**) and IASB, *International Accounting Standard 39*, "Financial Instruments: Recognition and Measurement," revised 2003. U.S. GAAP does not specify how the firm will measure the financial guarantee after initial recognition. IFRS provides for two alternatives for subsequent measurement: (1) remeasurement at fair value (if certain conditions are met); or (2) the higher of the amount that is probable of being paid, or the amount initially recognized less any cumulative amortization.

[18]*Statement of Accounting Standards No. 5*, "Accounting for Contingencies," 1975 (**Codification Topic 450**); and *International Accounting Standard 37*, "Provisions, Contingent Liabilities and Contingent Assets," 1998.

[19]In U.S. GAAP, if there is a range of possible outcomes and no amount in this range is more likely than any other amount, the firm will recognize the minimum of the range. Under IFRS, if the firm's arrangement involves a large number of items, for example, a warranty, the firm will recognize the expected value, which is the probability-weighted sum over all possible outcomes (the product of each possible outcome multiplied by its associated probability). If there is a most likely outcome but other possible outcomes are mostly higher or lower than this amount, the firm should take account of this by adjusting the measurement up or down.

the amount, so the firm does not recognize the potential obligation arising from the lawsuit as an accounting liability. IFRS refers to such items as **contingent liabilities**. (If the arrangement embodies a possible gain—that is, an asset—the IFRS term is **contingent asset**). U.S. GAAP does not have special terms for these items; descriptively, they are unrecognized loss contingencies and unrecognized gain contingencies.

The financial guarantee contract (**Example 17**) illustrates an arrangement that contains both a stand-ready obligation and an obligation that is uncertain as to timing and amount. As described in the example, both U.S. GAAP and IFRS require initial recognition of the fair value of the obligation to stand ready to pay the bank if the customer defaults. In addition, both U.S. GAAP and IFRS would require the recognition of a loss contingency (U.S. GAAP) or a provision (IFRS) if the obligation becomes probable and the amount to be paid is reasonably estimable.

Arrangements of the sort illustrated in **Examples 15, 16,** and **17** are common; for example, most firms that sell products include some kind of warranty (**Example 15**). Arrangements like the lawsuit in **Example 16** are often disclosed, not recognized, because they do not meet the criteria specified for the accounting recognition of obligations as liabilities. For example, Polo Ralph Lauren (whose balance sheet for the year ending March 31, 2007, appears in **Exhibit 3.1**) displays a commitment and contingencies line on the balance sheet, to direct the user of the financial reports to the notes, specifically, note 15. Scania's balance sheet (**Exhibit 1.5**) displays both current and noncurrent provisions, with a reference to note 18. Scania's provision accounts contain, among other items, its warranty liabilities.

SUMMARY OF LIABILITY RECOGNITION

Examples 11–17 illustrate obligations with varying amounts of uncertainty with respect to amount and timing, as well as measurement. **Figure 3.1** classifies obligations into six categories based on these characteristics. As the examples and the figure illustrate, obligations vary considerably in the extent to which they embody uncertainties. In many cases, authoritative guidance precludes the recognition of uncertain obligations that do not meet a probability threshold. However, if the guidance requires fair value measurement, as in **Example 17,** the firm must recognize an obligation that does not meet the probability threshold and record it at its fair value. The reason is that the fair value measurement attribute is based on the amount that a firm would have to pay to transfer the obligation to another party, and that other party would require compensation to assume the stand-ready obligation of the financial guarantee contract even if a payment is not probable.

LIABILITY MEASUREMENT

Most liabilities are financial, requiring settlement with cash or other assets. The firm reports those due within one year or less at the amount required to discharge the obligation. If the payment dates extend more than one year into the future (for example, the case of the Nordstrom bonds in **Example 12**), the firm records the liability on the balance sheet as a noncur-

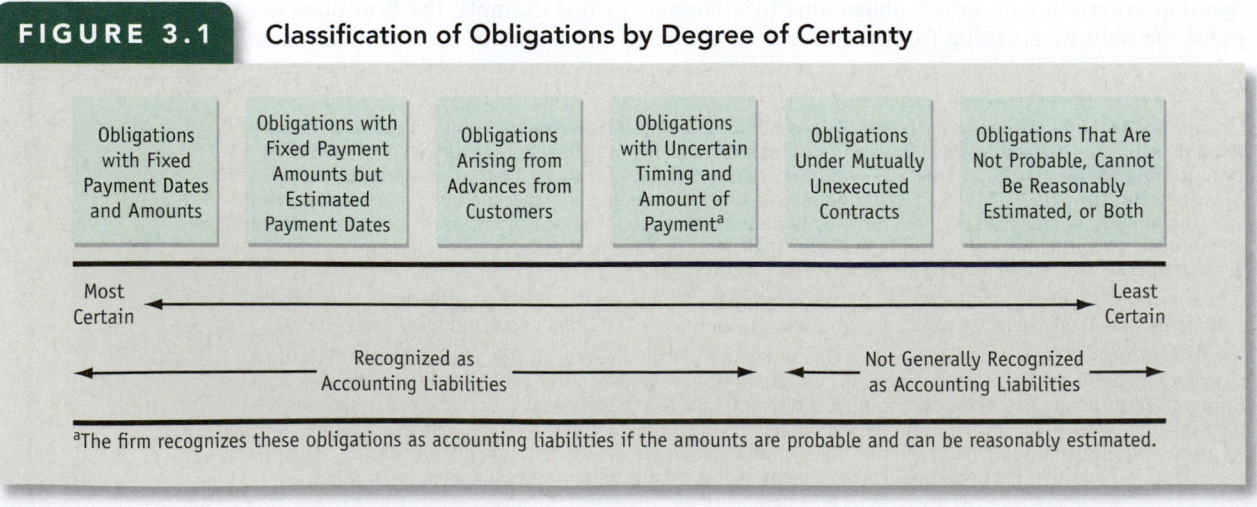

FIGURE 3.1   **Classification of Obligations by Degree of Certainty**

| Obligations with Fixed Payment Dates and Amounts | Obligations with Fixed Payment Amounts but Estimated Payment Dates | Obligations Arising from Advances from Customers | Obligations with Uncertain Timing and Amount of Payment[a] | Obligations Under Mutually Unexecuted Contracts | Obligations That Are Not Probable, Cannot Be Reasonably Estimated, or Both |

Most Certain ←————————————————————————→ Least Certain

←—— Recognized as Accounting Liabilities ——→   ←—— Not Generally Recognized as Accounting Liabilities ——→

[a]The firm recognizes these obligations as accounting liabilities if the amounts are probable and can be reasonably estimated.

EXHIBIT 3.1	Polo Ralph Lauren Consolidated Balance Sheets

(millions)	MARCH 31, 2007	APRIL 1, 2006
ASSETS		
CURRENT ASSETS:		
Cash and cash equivalents	$ 563.9	$ 285.7
Accounts receivable, net of allowances of $138.1 and $115.0 million	467.5	484.2
Inventories	526.9	485.5
Deferred tax assets	44.4	32.4
Prepaid expenses and other	83.2	90.7
TOTAL CURRENT ASSETS	1,685.9	1,378.5
PROPERTY AND EQUIPMENT, NET	629.8	548.8
DEFERRED TAX ASSETS	56.9	–
GOODWILL	790.5	699.7
INTANGIBLE ASSETS, NET	297.7	258.5
OTHER ASSETS	297.2	203.2
TOTAL ASSETS	$ 3,758.0	$ 3,088.7
LIABILITIES AND STOCKHOLDERS' EQUITY		
CURRENT LIABILITIES:		
Accounts payable	$ 174.7	$ 202.2
Income tax payable	74.6	46.6
Accrued expenses and other	391.0	314.3
Current maturities of debt	–	280.4
TOTAL CURRENT LIABILITIES	640.3	843.5
LONG-TERM DEBT	398.8	–
DEFERRED TAX LIABILITIES	–	20.8
OTHER NON-CURRENT LIABILITIES	384.0	174.8
COMMITMENTS AND CONTINGENCIES (NOTE 15)		
TOTAL LIABILITIES	1,423.1	1,039.1
STOCKHOLDERS' EQUITY:		
Class A common stock, par value $.01 per share; 68.6 million and 66.4 million shares issued;		
60.7 million and 62.1 million shares outstanding	0.7	0.7
Class B common stock, par value $.01 per share; 43.3 million shares issued and outstanding	0.4	0.4
Additional paid-in-capital	872.5	783.6
Retained earnings	1,742.3	1,379.2
Treasury stock, Class A, at cost (7.9 million and 4.3 million shares)	(321.5)	(87.1)
Accumulated other comprehensive income	40.5	15.5
Unearned compensation	–	(42.7)
TOTAL STOCKHOLDERS' EQUITY	2,334.9	2,049.6
TOTAL LIABILITIES AND STOCKHOLDERS' EQUITY	$ 3,758.0	$ 3,088.7

rent liability, measured at the present value of the future cash outflows. **Chapter 10** describes the measurement of debt obligations.

A liability that requires delivering goods or rendering services, rather than paying cash, is nonfinancial. The warranty liability in **Example 15** is nonfinancial because Scania has agreed to provide services—engine repairs. The cash advance in **Example 13** is also nonfinancial, because Scania will settle the liability by delivering trucks. Other examples of nonfinancial liabilities arising from cash payments from customers include amounts received by magazine publishers for future magazine deliveries, by theatrical and sports teams for future performances or games, by landlords for future rental services, and by airlines for tickets purchased in advance. Account titles used for liabilities of this type vary and include Advances from Customers, Deferred Revenues, Unearned Revenues, Deferred Income, and (in the case of airlines) Air Traffic Liability.[20]

---

[20]Although these account titles are common in practice, we do not use all of them in this book. The word *revenue* in the account titles might lead the reader to infer that the firm has recognized items in income, when, in fact, this is not the case.

Nonfinancial obligations can be either current or noncurrent, depending on the period over which the firm will discharge them. A firm measures warranties that it includes with the sale of a product at the estimated cost of the warranty services it will provide. In general, firms measure cash payments from customers for goods and services they will deliver later at the amount of cash received. **Chapter 7** explores these issues in more detail.

PROBLEM 3.2 for Self-Study

Liability recognition and measurement. The transactions listed below relate to Polo Ralph Lauren ("Polo"). For each, indicate whether the transaction immediately gives rise to a liability and, if so, state the account title and amount that Polo would recognize.

a. Polo's boutique stores sell gift cards for $100 per card. Assume that gift cards expire 3 years from the date of issuance.

b. Refer to **Problem 3.1 for Self-Study**, part **a**. Polo receives an invoice for $16 million in advertising services from the supplier, an agency that specializes in television advertisements.

c. Attorneys have notified Polo that the firm is a defendant in a lawsuit claiming $12 million in lost profits and damages, based on allegations that Polo unlawfully used fashion designs belonging to the plaintiff. Polo's lawyers predict that the court will probably find Polo liable in the lawsuit, and Polo's management estimates that the range of damages is $2 million to $10 million, with all amounts in this range equally likely.

d. A two-week strike by employees closed down one of Polo's clothing manufacturing facilities. As a result, Polo could not deliver merchandise totaling $20 million, for which it has already received payment.

 # SHAREHOLDERS' EQUITY MEASUREMENT AND DISCLOSURE

Shareholders' equity is a residual interest or claim—that is, the owners (shareholders) of a firm have a claim on assets not required to meet the claims of creditors.[21] The measurement of the assets and liabilities on the balance sheet therefore determines the measurement of total shareholders' equity. The accounting process also provides an independent derivation of the amount of shareholders' equity. You can be sure that the process has gone wrong if the amount does not equal the amount of assets minus liabilities.

Corporate laws within many jurisdictions require that, within shareholders' equity, firms distinguish between amounts received from owners and amounts generated by operations which the firm has not distributed to owners. The amounts that firms report as received from owners are equal to the amounts the firm received when it originally issued those shares. Many firms further disaggregate the initial amounts they received from shareholders for common shares into the **par** or **nominal** or **stated value** of the shares and the amounts received in excess of this value, called **additional paid-in capital (APIC), share premium,** or **capital contributed in excess of par value**.[22] We use *additional paid-in capital,* or *APIC,* to refer to this account. The firm assigns the par value of a share of stock at an amount it chooses. Par values are typically small, often $1 or less per share, and rarely equal the amounts the firm receives when it issues the shares. The sum of the par value amount and the additional paid-in capital amount is the total amount received from shareholders for the shares when the firm first issued them. This total amount is also called **contributed capital** or **paid-in capital**.

---

[21]Financial Accounting Standards Board, *Statement of Financial Accounting Concepts No. 6,* "Elements of Financial Statements," 1985, par. 49.

[22]The distinction between par value and additional paid-in capital has legal significance but not economic significance. For this reason, some firms report a single account, often called common stock, equal to the sum of par value and additional paid-in capital.

Any subsequent sale of common shares from one investor to another (such as occurs on public stock exchanges) has no effect on the recorded amounts of shareholders' equity. The issuing firm does *not* take part in those transactions. As a result, in a rising stock market, the total paid-in capital amount reported on a balance sheet will usually be less than the current market value of the common shares. The balance sheet amount of shareholders' equity does not, and is not intended to, provide the user of the financial reports with a measure of the market value of common equity. The user can, however, easily ascertain market value of common equity for a given publicly traded firm by looking up the most recent share price (as reported in various online services) and then multiplying this share price times the number of common shares outstanding, as reported on the balance sheet.

Retained earnings measures the net assets generated by a firm from operations exceeding dividends declared. The Retained Earnings account accumulates the amounts of these undistributed earnings over time. When the firm has accumulated losses, rather than profits, the account is typically called **Accumulated Deficit** rather than Retained Earnings.

Retained earnings are a source of financing for assets. Retained earnings are not cash or other assets. Retained earnings represent the source of net assets generated by the earnings process that exceed the firm's dividend declarations. In contrast to liabilities and contributed capital, which common practice refers to as *external financing*, common practice refers to the process of curtailing dividends to accumulate assets, represented by retained earnings, as *internal financing*.

Example 18 Hoskins Limited legally incorporated on January 1, 2008. In its initial public offering (IPO), the firm issued 15,000 shares of €0.10 par value common stock for €10 cash per share. During 2008, Hoskins generated net income of €30,000 and paid dividends of €10,000. The shareholders' equity section of the balance sheet of Hoskins on December 31, 2008, is as follows:

Common Stock (at par value of €0.10 per share, 15,000 shares issued and outstanding)	€ 1,500
Additional Paid-in Capital	148,500
Retained Earnings	20,000
Total Shareholders' Equity	€170,000

The €1,500 amount reported as the total par value of the shares is the par value per share times the total number of shares issued, or €0.10 per share × 15,000 shares. The €148,500 amount reported as additional paid-in capital (APIC) is the difference between the proceeds from the sale of stock of €150,000 (= 15,000 × €10) and the par value of €1,500. The €20,000 amount of retained earnings reported by Hoskins for its first year of operations is the amount of undistributed earnings, €30,000 of income minus €10,000 dividends.

Example 19 Continuing **Example 18**, assume another year has passed, and it is now December 31, 2009. During 2009, Hoskins issued another 5,000 shares of stock at €12 per share, earned net income of €5,000, and paid dividends of €10,000. The shareholders' equity section of the balance sheet of Hoskins on December 31, 2009, is as follows:

Common Stock (at par value of €0.10 per share, 20,000 shares issued and outstanding)	€ 2,000
Additional Paid-in Capital	208,000
Retained Earnings	15,000
Total Shareholders' Equity	€225,000

The €2,000 amount reported as total par value is the par value per share times the total number of shares issued, or €0.10 per share × 20,000 shares. This €2,000 amount is the sum of the par value of 1,500 shares issued in 2008 plus the par value of 5,000 shares issued in 2009. The €208,000 amount reported as additional paid-in capital (APIC) is the sum of the €148,500 of APIC from 2008 plus the €59,500 of APIC from the issuance of 5,000 shares in 2009 (= €12 per share × 5,000 shares minus €500 par value, or €60,000 − €500). The increase in Hoskins' share price, from €10 per share in 2008 to €12 per share in 2009, does not change the amount reported on the balance sheet for the 15,000 shares issued in 2008. The firm does not change the amounts reported for total paid-in capital (par value and APIC) to reflect changes in share price; rather, those amounts reflect the share price at the time the firm originally issued the shares.[23]

Hoskins' retained earnings at the end of 2009 of €15,000 is the cumulative undistributed earnings through its second year of operations, equal to the beginning-of-2009 retained earnings of €20,000, plus 2009 earnings of €5,000, minus 2009 dividends of €10,000. Because dividends reduce retained earnings, not current earnings, a firm can declare and pay a dividend that exceeds its net income for the year. A firm could even pay dividends in a year that it generated a loss.

ANALYSIS OF THE BALANCE SHEET

The balance sheet provides information about the nature and mix of assets, as well as the nature and mix of financing for those assets. Although one cannot analyze the financial health of a business from a single financial statement considered in isolation, some simple analyses involving the balance sheet can provide useful signals.

COMMON-SIZE BALANCE SHEET

Many analysts use a **common-size balance sheet**, which expresses each balance sheet item as a percentage of total assets. **Exhibit 3.2** presents a common-size balance sheet for Nordstrom. Common-size balance sheets assist in comparing firms of different sizes. For example, **Exhibit 3.2** reveals that Nordstrom's accounts receivable as a percentage of total assets is 14.2% for the year ended February 3, 2007. Is 14.2% high or low relative to other firms whose business models are similar to Nordstrom's? Comparing the items in Nordstrom's common-size balance sheet to those of other firms in the same industry can provide insight into areas where Nordstrom is performing better than or worse than its competition.

Comparing firms using a common-size balance sheet rests on the assumption that the size or scale of a business does not affect the relation between a given balance sheet item and total assets. This assumption need not hold. Large firms often achieve economies of scale that affect the proportionality of the components of their business, thus reducing the comparability of their common-size ratios with those of smaller-scale competitors. For example, a large purchaser of goods and services has negotiating power over its suppliers, relative to the negotiating power of a smaller purchaser, such as a single local clothing store. The large purchaser can negotiate better terms, including lower per-unit prices (which, holding quantity constant, implies a lower per-unit recorded amount for inventory), more frequent but proportionately smaller quantities purchased (which reduces the quantity of inventory held by the purchaser), and better payment terms (which increases the time the purchaser retains cash as opposed to paying it to the supplier). More negotiating power would appear on the large purchaser's balance sheet as proportionately smaller amounts reported for inventory and proportionately larger amounts reported for accounts payable, relative to the amounts reported by a smaller purchaser with less negotiating power. Typically, users would not compare the common-size balance sheets of two firms that differed significantly in size. For example, an informed user would not compare Nordstrom's common-size balance sheet with the common-size balance sheet of a single boutique shop.

BALANCE SHEET FINANCIAL RATIOS

Many analysts and investors also use ratio analysis to analyze balance sheets (and other financial statements). Common balance sheet ratios include the market-to-book-value ratio and debt ratios. The market-to-book-value ratio compares the market value of common shares with the book value of shareholders' equity as reported on the balance sheet. Recall from our earlier discussion that you can compute the market value of a firm's common shares by multiplying the current share price times the number of common shares outstanding. The market price of a share of Nordstrom's common stock was $56.68 on February 3, 2007, the balance sheet date. On this same date, Nordstrom's balance sheet showed 257,313,000 shares

---

[23]**Chapter 14** describes more complex transactions that affect the additional paid-in capital account.

EXHIBIT 3.2

Nordstrom Inc.
Common-Size Balance Sheet
(amounts in thousands)

	February 3, 2007		January 28, 2006	
ASSETS				
Current assets				
Cash and Cash Equivalents	$ 402,559	8.3%	$ 462,656	9.4%
Short-Term Investments	—	—	54,000	1.1
Accounts Receivable, net	684,376	14.2	639,558	13.0
Investments in Asset-Backed Securities	428,175	8.9	561,136	11.4
Merchandise Inventories	997,289	20.7	955,978	19.4
Current Deferred Tax Assets, net	169,320	3.5	145,470	3.0
Prepaid Expenses and Other	60,474	1.3	55,359	1.1
Total Current Assets	$2,742,193	56.9%	$2,874,157	58.4%
Land, Buildings and Equipment, net	$1,757,215	36.4%	$1,773,871	36.0%
Goodwill	51,714	1.1	51,714	1.1
Acquired Trade Name	84,000	1.7	84,000	1.7
Other Assets	186,456	3.9	137,607	2.8
Total Assets	$4,821,578	100.0%	$4,921,349	100.0%
LIABILITIES AND SHAREHOLDERS' EQUITY				
Current liabilities				
Accounts Payable	$ 576,796	12.0%	$ 540,019	11.0%
Accrued Salaries, Wages, and Related Benefits	339,965	7.1	285,982	5.8
Other Current Liabilities	433,487	9.0	409,076	8.3
Income Taxes Payable	76,095	1.6	81,617	1.7
Current Portion of Long-Term Debt	6,800	0.1	306,618	6.2
Total Current Liabilities	$1,433,143	29.7%	$1,623,312	33.0%
Long-Term Debt, net	$ 623,652	12.9%	$ 627,776	12.8%
Deferred Property Incentives, net	356,062	7.4	364,382	7.4
Other Liabilities	240,200	5.0	213,198	4.3
Shareholders equity				
Common Stock, No Par Value, 1,000,000 Shares Authorized 257,313 and 269,549 Shares Issued and Outstanding	826,421	17.1	685,934	13.9
Unearned Stock Compensation	—	—	(327)	0.0
Retained Earnings	1,350,680	28.0	1,404,366	28.5
Accumulated Other Comprehensive (Loss) Earnings	(8,580)	−0.2	2,708	0.1
Total Shareholders' Equity	$2,168,521	45.0%	$2,092,681	42.5%
Total Liabilities and Shareholders' Equity	$4,821,578	100.0%	$4,921,349	100.0%

outstanding. The market value of Nordstrom's equity, also called its *market capitalization*, on February 3, 2007, is, therefore, $14.584 billion (= $56.68 per share × 257,313,000 shares). Nordstrom's market-to-book-value ratio on this same date is 6.7 (= $14.584 billion/$2.168 billion).

Debt ratios capture the portion of total financing that is debt. Common debt ratios include the ratio of total liabilities to total assets and the ratio of long-term debt to shareholders' equity. The amounts of these two ratios for Nordstrom on February 3, 2007, are as follows:

Total Liabilities to Total Assets ($2,653,057/$4,821,521) 55.0%
Long-Term Debt to Total Shareholders' Equity ($623,652/$2,168,521) 28.8%

The first ratio tells us that Nordstrom finances approximately 55% of its assets with debt (the ratio of total liabilities to total assets), implying that it finances the remainder (45%) with equity. Finally, Nordstrom uses 0.288 dollars in debt financing for each dollar of shareholders' equity capital (the ratio of long-term debt to shareholders' equity). The larger these ratios, the greater is the risk that the firm will experience financial difficulties.

BALANCE SHEET RELATIONS

The balance sheet portrays the effects of a firm's investing and financing decisions. In analyzing these decisions, consider two principles that guide financing decisions:

1. **Matching the duration of the financing with the duration of the asset.** Firms use short-term financing for assets they expect to convert to cash in the short run, such as accounts receivable and inventories, and they use long-term financing (debt or shareholders' equity) for assets to be used over long periods, such as property, plant, and equipment.

2. **Linking the mix of long-term financing (debt versus equity) to the nature of long-term assets and the amount of operating risk.** Firms with tangible long-term assets and predictable cash flows, such as electric utilities, tend to have balance sheets with a high proportion of long-term debt (80% or more). The property, plant, and equipment are collateral for the borrowing (that is, the lender can repossess the assets if the firm fails to make debt payments on time). Thus, physical collateral reduces the cost of borrowing. Predictable cash flows reduce the risk that the firm will not have sufficient cash to make interest and principal payments when due; this predictability also reduces borrowing costs. Firms with tangible long-term assets and less predictable cash flows, such as auto manufacturers and steel companies, whose sales vary with changes in economic conditions, tend to use a more nearly equal mix of long-term debt and shareholders' equity financing. The property, plant, and equipment serve as collateral for the borrowing, but the more uncertain cash flows suggest a lower proportion of long-term debt in the capital structure. Firms with high proportions of intangibles, whether recognized as assets on the balance sheet or not, tend to rely more on equity financing than on long-term debt. Lacking collateral, lenders must rely on cash flows from operations to service the debt. The less predictable these cash flows, the smaller is the proportion of long-term debt.

The reasoning behind these generalizations about financial structure derives from lenders' and investors' assessments of business risk. Operating risk arises from the asset side of the business, and financing risk arises from debt. Operating risks include variability in sales from changing economic conditions (cyclicality risk) or from short product life cycles (because of technological change or changes in consumer taste). Operating risks also include the variability of earnings that arises when the firm has a high proportion of fixed costs that do not change as sales change, such as depreciation on capital-intensive manufacturing facilities. Firms with substantial operating risk tend not to increase their risk by financing with long-term debt. Long-term debt imposes financing risk because it requires principal and interest payments. The more variable are the firm's cash flows from operating activities, the more risk that the firm will not have sufficient cash to meet the required payments. Failure to meet these obligations can result in default, creditor or regulatory intervention in the management of the firm, or bankruptcy.

ASSESSING THE IMPACT OF ASSET AND LIABILITY RECOGNITION AND MEASUREMENT ISSUES

The balance sheet does not provide all the information an analyst wants or needs about a firm's resources and the claims on those resources. Authoritative accounting guidance precludes the recognition of some resources as assets and some obligations as liabilities. In addition, measurement requirements mean that the amounts reported on the balance sheet for assets, liabilities, and shareholders' equity do not necessarily reflect current market conditions.

In assessing the financial condition of a firm, an astute analyst recognizes these features of the balance sheet and adjusts the reported numbers. Although subsequent chapters provide examples of such adjustments, you can now get a sense of why you might need to make the adjustments and how to make them. To illustrate, we revisit the market-to-book-value ratio and the debt ratios discussed in the previous section.

The current price of a share of common stock reflects current economic conditions, not the requirements of authoritative guidance. Suppose Scania discloses that its research and development efforts have resulted in the invention of a more efficient and environmentally safe gasoline engine. The market price of Scania shares will increase regardless of whether Scania records the invention as an asset.[24] This example demonstrates why market-to-book-value ratios tend to be large for firms that make substantial expenditures on internally developed assets, including research and development, advertising, and employee development. (Other factors, such as a firm's competitive position and its growth potential, also influence the market-to-book-value ratio.)

The previous example considers an *unrecognized asset* (an internally developed new product); the next example considers an *unrecognized liability* (also called an off-balance-sheet liability) in the form of an agreement between two parties. Firm B agrees to use an asset, such as a store building, in exchange for periodic and prespecified payments to Firm S, which owns the land and the building. Firm B has the right to return the asset to Firm S at any time. Even if Firm B intends to use the asset and make the periodic payments for the life of the agreement, this arrangement does not give rise to an accounting liability, because the terms of the agreement violate one of the conditions for liability recognition. Specifically, Firm B can avoid paying Firm S in the future by returning the asset, so Firm B has discretion to avoid an economic sacrifice. However, an analyst, knowing about the agreement and Firm B's intention to use the asset and make the periodic payments, might wish to know how Firm B's debt ratios would change if Firm B were to recognize a liability for the future payments and the related asset associated with this arrangement.

To facilitate our calculations, assume that Firm B is Nordstrom and that the measurement of the unrecognized obligation under the agreement is $1 billion. How would Nordstrom's debt ratios change if the arrangement were accorded accounting recognition? From our earlier calculations, we know that Nordstrom's debt ratios on February 3, 2007, are:

Total Liabilities to Total Assets ($2,653,057/$4,821,578)	55.0%
Long-Term Debt to Shareholders' Equity ($623,652/$2,168,578)	28.8%

If a $1 billion asset and liability were recognized on Nordstrom's balance sheet, the debt ratios would be:

Total Liabilities to Total Assets ([$2,653,057 + $1,000,000]/ [$4,821,521 + $1,000,000])	62.8%
Long-Term Debt to Shareholders' Equity ([$623,652 + $1,000,000]/ $2,168,521)	74.9%

Both of the adjusted (or "as-if") debt ratios are higher than their unadjusted counterparts, so nonrecognition of the arrangement as an asset and a liability on the balance sheet reduces these two measures of financial risk. Arrangements that result in unrecognized (that is, off-balance-sheet) items typically have the effect of reducing debt ratios from their amounts if the same transaction required balance sheet recognition. An example that we examine in **Chapter 10** involves the structure of leases; operating leases result in unrecognized (off-balance sheet) assets and liabilities, whereas capital leases result in balance sheet recognition of assets and liabilities.

In summary, the balance sheet imperfectly describes both resources and financing (claims on those resources). Applying asset and liability definitions and recognition criteria under U.S. GAAP and IFRS does not result in the balance sheet including all economic benefits (resources) and obligations. In this text, when we use the terms assets and liabilities, we mean resources and obligations that appear on the balance sheet. Further, measurement rules do not

---

[24]IFRS does not permit a firm to recognize *research* expenditures as an asset. IFRS requires the firm to recognize *development* expenditures as assets when certain conditions are met, including technological feasibility. With the exception of internally developed software costs, U.S. GAAP requires that the firm expense both research and development expenditures as incurred. **Chapter 9** describes this guidance.

always ensure that the balance sheet shows amounts for assets, liabilities, and shareholders' equity that reflect current economic conditions, even though presumptively an investor would view measurements that reflect current conditions as the most relevant for making investment decisions. Although analysts should keep these limitations in mind, they should not ignore the balance sheet. U.S. GAAP and IFRS require that balance sheets recognize most resources and claims (sources of financing), and measurement guidance has increasingly focused on fair values, at least for financial assets and financial liabilities. In addition, even if authoritative guidance introduces biases into the reported amounts, these biases usually affect firms consistently, so the financial statements are reasonably comparable. By adjusting for known biases, users can accommodate many of the deficiencies in the balance sheet caused by the application of U.S. GAAP and IFRS.

SUMMARY

The balance sheet displays three classes of items: assets, liabilities, and shareholders' equity. These items depict a firm's financial position at a point in time. Broadly speaking, assets represent future economic benefits in the form of resources available to carry out operations; liabilities and shareholders' equity show the sources of funds the firm used to acquire the resources and show the claims on them. Two key factors in preparing a balance sheet are:

1. Deciding whether items meet the definitions and recognition criteria for assets and liabilities and, if so,

2. Deciding how to measure the items.

For a firm to recognize an asset, a resource must represent a future economic benefit that the firm controls as a result of a past transaction or exchange, and the firm must be able to measure the resource with sufficient reliability. For a firm to recognize an obligation as a liability, the obligation must impose a future economic sacrifice because of a past event or transaction that the firm has little or no discretion to avoid, and the firm must be able to measure the obligation with sufficient reliability. Shareholders' equity reports the amounts of funding attributable to owners' contributions and resulting from the retention of net assets generated by earnings. Shareholders' equity equals the difference between total assets and total liabilities and typically comprises contributed (paid-in) capital and retained earnings.

Most asset and liability definitions and recognition criteria—particularly for items that we focus on in this book—are similar under U.S. GAAP and IFRS. One difference, probed further in **Chapter 9**, pertains to internally developed intangibles. U.S. GAAP generally does not permit firms to recognize research or development expenditures as assets on the balance sheet. IFRS requires, under specified conditions, the recognition as an asset of *development* expenditures. Under both sets of standards, the firm must expense expenditures on *research*, so these do not result in an asset.

Once an item has met the appropriate recognition criteria, the firm must measure the amount it will report on the balance sheet. Measurement depends on the item being considered. U.S. GAAP and IFRS specify how a firm should measure each asset and liability. Firms generally measure financial assets other than investments in marketable securities at their cash equivalent amounts on the balance sheet, while they generally report nonfinancial assets at acquisition cost, reduced for use and impairment. Asset and liability measurement approaches and rules (particularly for the assets and liabilities that we focus on in this book) are generally similar under U.S. GAAP and IFRS, although there are exceptions; for example, the specifics of impairment testing and the IFRS option to revalue certain nonfinancial assets upward to amounts that exceed acquisition costs.

The balance sheet does not present a complete portrayal of all resources and obligations, nor does it report the details of operating activities. In addition to intentionally not capturing information included in other financial statements, balance sheets based on U.S. GAAP and IFRS omit some items and measure others with bias, relative to measurements based on current economic conditions. These omissions and biases involve the nonrecognition of certain resources and obligations as assets and liabilities and the measurement of recognized assets and liabilities at amounts that do not reflect current economic conditions.

SOLUTIONS TO SELF-STUDY PROBLEMS

SUGGESTED SOLUTION TO PROBLEM 3.1 FOR SELF-STUDY

(Polo Ralph Lauren; asset recognition and measurement)

a. Polo does not recognize an asset. U.S. GAAP and IFRS do not allow firms to capitalize most advertising expenditures as assets (the exception is direct-response marketing costs) because of the uncertainty of future benefits and measurement uncertainty.[25]

b. Polo does not recognize an asset. U.S. GAAP and IFRS do not allow firms to record exchanges of promises as assets.

c. U.S. GAAP and IFRS do not permit the recognition of research expenditures as assets because of the uncertainty of future benefits and measurement uncertainty. IFRS requires a firm to recognize an asset for development expenditures that meet certain criteria; U.S. GAAP precludes asset recognition except in the case of software (discussed more fully in **Chapter 9**).

d. Polo does not recognize an asset because of the uncertainty of future benefits and measurement uncertainty, as given in part **a** above.

e. Polo will recognize an asset, Land and Building, and measure it at $75 million. Polo must allocate the purchase price between the land and the building because the building is depreciable and the land is not. Polo will likely base the allocation on appraisals for the land and building evaluated separately. Legal passage of title is not necessary to justify asset recognition. Polo has acquired the rights to use the land and building and can sustain those rights as long as it makes the required payments on the mortgage obligation.

SUGGESTED SOLUTION TO PROBLEM 3.2 FOR SELF-STUDY

(Polo Ralph Lauren; liability recognition and measurement)

a. Polo would record a liability, Advances from Customers, measured as the amount received on the sale of the gift cards.

b. Polo would record a liability, Accounts Payable, measured as $16 million.

c. Polo will recognize a liability, measured at the minimum point of the range, applying U.S. GAAP.

d. At the time it received the payment, Polo recorded a liability for $20 million, Advances from Customers. Because the firm has already recognized a liability, and assuming the customers are willing to wait for the delayed delivery, the firm need recognize no additional liability.

KEY TERMS AND CONCEPTS

Balance sheet equation	Asset recognition
Financing structure	Executory contract
Operating cycle	Acquisition (historical) cost
Current assets	Current replacement cost
Noncurrent assets	Entry value
Current liabilities	Net realizable value
Noncurrent liabilities	Exit value
Asset definition	Fair value

---

[25]Direct-response marketing costs consist primarily of advertisements, including coupons for a firm's products or services. U.S. GAAP concluded that firms can measure the probable future economic benefits of these costs with a sufficient degree of reliability, so the firm should recognize the costs as assets on the balance sheet. The firm then amortizes the asset over its expected period of future benefits; in the case of coupons, this service life is three months. (American Institute of Certified Public Accounting, Accounting Standards Executive Committee, Statement of Position 937, *Reporting on Advertising Costs*, 1994.)

Opportunity cost	Loss contingencies
Present value of future net cash flows	Provisions
Financial assets	Contingent liabilities
Nonfinancial assets	Contingent asset
Going concern	Shareholders' equity
Realized	Par, nominal, or stated value
Recognized	Additional paid-in capital (APIC), share
Relevance	premium, capital contributed in excess
Reliability	of par value
Conservatism	Contributed capital, paid-in capital
Liability definition	Retained earnings
Liability recognition	Accumulated deficit
Mutually unexecuted contract, executory contract	Common-size balance sheet

QUESTIONS, EXERCISES, AND PROBLEMS

QUESTIONS

1. Review the meaning of the terms and concepts listed in Key Terms and Concepts.

2. Whom might the accounting convention of conservatism hurt?

3. One of the criteria for the recognition of an asset or a liability is that there be an exchange. What justification can you see for this requirement?

4. Identify the underlying accounting principle that guides the measurement of the acquisition cost of inventories, equipment, buildings, and other similar assets. What is the rationale for this accounting principle?

5. Accounting typically does not recognize either assets or liabilities for mutually unexecuted contracts. What justification can you see for this treatment?

6. Accounting treats cash discounts taken on the purchase of merchandise or equipment as a reduction in the amount recorded for the assets acquired. What justification can you see for this treatment?

7. A group of investors owns an office building that it rents unfurnished to tenants. It purchased the building five years previously from a construction company. At that time, it expected the building to have a useful life of 40 years. Indicate the procedures you might follow to ascertain the measurement amount for this building under each of the following measurement approaches:

   a. Acquisition cost.

   b. Adjusted acquisition cost (reduced for services already consumed).

   c. Current replacement cost.

   d. Net realizable value.

   e. Fair value.

8. Some of the assets of one firm correspond to the liabilities of another firm. For example, an account receivable on the seller's balance sheet is an account payable on the buyer's balance sheet. For each of the following items, indicate whether it is an asset or a liability and give the corresponding account title on the balance sheet of the other party to the transaction:

   a. Advances from Customers.

   b. Bonds Payable.

   c. Interest Receivable.

   d. Prepaid Insurance.

   e. Rental Fees Received in Advance.

9. For each of the following items, indicate whether the item meets all of the criteria in the definition of a liability. If so, how does the firm value it?

a. Interest accrued but not paid on a note.

b. Advances from customers for goods and services to be delivered later.

c. Confirmed orders from customers for goods and services to be delivered later.

d. Bonds payable.

e. Product warranties.

f. Damages the company must pay if it loses a pending lawsuit.

g. Future costs of restoring strip-mining sites after completing mining operations.

h. Contractual promises to purchase specific quantities of natural gas for each of the next 10 years.

i. Promises by an airline to provide flights in the future in exchange for miles flown, if customers accumulate a certain number of miles at regular fares.

10. What is the amount of the liability that the company recognizes in each of the following independent cases?

a. A plaintiff files a lawsuit against the company. The probability is 90% that the company will lose. If it loses, the amount of the loss will most likely be $100,000.

b. A cereal company issues coupons that can be exchanged for boxes of cereal. It issues 1 million coupons that promise the retailer who redeems the coupons $1 per coupon. The probability of redemption of any one coupon is 9%.

11. The word *probable* appears in the definitions of assets and liabilities and in the recognition criteria for liabilities with uncertain amount and/or timing.

a. What is the meaning (or the interpretation) of *probable* as used in the definitions of assets and liabilities?

b. How does the meaning (or the interpretation) of *probable* as used in the recognition criteria for liabilities with uncertain amount and/or timing differ between U.S. GAAP and IFRS?

EXERCISES

12. **Balance sheet formats.** The following information is based on the balance sheet of Aracruz Celulose, a Brazilian manufacturer of bleached pulp used to make paper, for the year ended December 31, 2006. Aracruz Celulose applies U.S. GAAP and reports its results in thousands of U.S. dollars:

Inventories	$ 202,704
Other Current Assets	132,782
Other Long-Term Liabilities	350,761
Property, Plant, and Equipment, net	2,151,212
Retained Earnings	1,293,301
Cash and Short-Term Investments	579,643
Goodwill	192,035
Common Stock (no par)	295,501
Preferred Stock	614,496
Other Noncurrent Assets	451,757
Current Liabilities	286,819
Long-Term Debt	1,155,050
Accounts Receivable	285,795

a. Prepare a balance sheet for Aracruz Celulose assuming the firm follows U.S. GAAP.

b. Prepare a balance sheet for Aracruz Celulose assuming the firm follows IFRS.

13. **Balance sheet formats.** The following information is based on the balance sheet of Delhaize Group (Delhaize), the Belgian food distributor, for 2007 (in € million). Delhaize applies IFRS and reports its results in millions of euros. Prepare a balance sheet for Delhaize that uses a format common to firms reporting under U.S. GAAP.

Assets	
Goodwill	€ 2,445.7
Intangible Assets	552.1
Property, Plant, and Equipment	3,383.1
Other Noncurrent Assets	244.0
	€ 6,624.9
Inventories	€ 1,262.0
Receivables	564.6
Other Current Assets	121.5
Cash and Cash Equivalents	248.9
	€ 2,197.0
Total Assets	€ 8,821.9
Liabilities and Equity	
Share Capital	€ 50.1
Share Premium	2,698.9
Retained Earnings	2,355.3
Other Reserves and Adjustments	(1,428.3)
Total Shareholders' Equity	€ 3,676.0
Long-Term Debt	€ 1,911.7
Obligations Under Finance Leases	595.9
Provisions	207.2
Other Noncurrent Liabilities	210.4
Total Noncurrent Liabilities	€ 2,925.2
Short-Term Borrowings	€ 41.5
Long-Term Debt, Current Portion	108.9
Obligations Under Finance Lease, Current Portion	39.0
Provisions	41.8
Income Tax Payable	58.7
Accounts Payable	1,435.8
Accrued Expenses	375.7
Other Current Liabilities	119.3
Total Current Liabilities	€ 2,220.7
Total Liabilities	€ 5,145.9
Total Liabilities and Equity	€ 8,821.9

14. **Classifying financial statement accounts.** The balance sheet or income statement classifies various items in one of the following ways:

> CA—Current assets
>
> NA—Noncurrent assets
>
> CL—Current liabilities
>
> NL—Noncurrent liabilities
>
> CC—Contributed capital
>
> RE—Retained earnings
>
> NI—Income statement item (revenue or expense)
>
> X—Item generally does not appear on a balance sheet or an income statement

Using the abbreviations in the previous list, indicate the classification of each of the following items under U.S. GAAP and IFRS. If the classifications differ between U.S. GAAP and IFRS, indicate what that difference would be.

a. Factory.

b. Interest revenue.

c. Treasury shares repurchased by a corporation.

d. Research and development expenditures.

    e. Automobiles used by sales staff.

    f. Cash on hand.

    g. Promise to a vendor to buy inventory from it next period.

    h. Commissions earned by sales staff.

    i. Supplies inventory.

    j. Note payable, due in three months.

    k. Increase in fair value of land held.

    l. Dividends declared.

    m. Income taxes owed to state or city government.

    n. Note payable, due in six years.

    o. The portion of the note payable in part **n** that is due next year.

15. Balance sheet relations. Genting Group, a Malaysian investment management company, reported the following data for four recent years. Genting Group applies Malaysian accounting standards and reports its results in millions of ringgit (RM). Compute the missing balance sheet amounts for each of the four years. In answering this question, assume that Genting Group uses U.S. GAAP.

	2007	2006	2005	2004
Noncurrent Assets	?	RM 18,717.4	RM 11,289.1	RM 9,713.9
Shareholders' Equity	RM 21,537.3	16,666.9	9,002.0	?
Total Assets	?	28,224.7	?	?
Current Liabilities	?	4,351.3	1,494.2	1,755.2
Current Assets	10,999.2	?	?	6,882.6
Noncurrent Liabilities	5,721.7	?	?	3,540.7
Total Liabilities and Shareholders' Equity	30,178.9	?	18,491.3	?

16. Balance sheet relations. Selected balance sheet amounts for Kajima Corporation, a Japanese construction firm, are shown in the following table for four recent years. Kajima applies Japanese accounting standards and reports its results in billions of yen (¥). Compute the missing balance sheet amounts for each of the four years. In answering this question, assume that Kajima uses IFRS.

	2007	2006	2005	2004
Total Assets	¥2,107	?	?	¥1,870
Noncurrent Liabilities	437	?	¥ 411	467
Noncurrent Assets	?	¥ 773	703	?
Total Liabilities	?	?	1,583	?
Current Liabilities	1,318	1,148	?	1,172
Shareholders' Equity	?	298	220	?
Current Assets	1,323	1,133	?	1,110
Total Liabilities and Shareholders' Equity	?	?	?	?

17. Balance sheet relations. Selected data based on the balance sheet amounts for Metso Corporation, a Finnish paper company, for four recent years appear in the following table. Metso applies IFRS and reports its results in millions of euros (€). Compute the missing balance sheet amounts for each of the four years.

	2007	2006	2005	2004
Current Assets	€3,357	€2,995	?[a]	€2,097
Noncurrent Assets	?	1,973	?	?
Total Liabilities	?	?	?	?
Total Assets	?	?	€3,904	?
Current Liabilities	?[c]	2,610	1,802	1,466
Noncurrent Liabilities	957	?	?	1,109

(continued)

	2007	2006	2005	2004
Total Shareholders' Equity.	?	?	1,292	?
Contributed Capital	?	711	?	634
Retained Earnings	910	? b	553	361
Total Liabilities and Shareholders' Equity.	5,254	?	?	?

[a]Current Assets − Current Liabilities = €675.

[b]Net income for 2006 is €252 and dividends are €66.

[c]Current Assets − Current Liabilities = €651.

18. **Asset and liability recognition and measurement.** After winning "America's Next Top Model" in 2006, Danielle Evans signed a contract with Ford Models, was named a spokesmodel for CoverGirl, and signed a contract for a photo spread in *Elle* magazine. Although Ford did not disclose the details of the contract, typical terms would provide for payments of $500,000 for each of the next three years. Assume that the present value of these payments is $1.2 million. At the time that Danielle signs the contract, Ford Models also provides her with a BMW M3 convertible sports car, valued at $70,000. How should Ford Models treat this contract at the time of signing?

19. **Asset recognition and measurement.** Duke University, a U.S. university, provides tuition support for up to eight semesters of undergraduate education for up to two children of faculty and staff of the university. To qualify for this tuition benefit, the faculty or staff member must have at least seven contiguous years of full-time service and be a full-time employee when the benefits are received. Duke estimates that this tuition benefit helps retain and attract employees. How should Duke treat its expenditures on tuition benefits each year?

20. **Asset measurement.** Assume that Trader Joe's, an organic food retailer in the United States, recently purchased a new refrigeration system for its Chapel Hill, North Carolina, store. Trader Joe's paid $1.3 million for the refrigeration unit and paid an additional $120,000 to modify the unit to meet its specific needs. Trader Joe's paid $55,000 for the transportation and installation of the unit, plus $48,000 for an annual insurance premium for the first year, which begins next month. Finally, assume that Trader Joe's hired a refrigeration technician, who is charged with the maintenance of the unit; that technician's annual salary is $80,000. How much should Trader Joe's record as the acquisition cost of the refrigeration unit? Describe the treatment of any of the above amounts that you did not include in the acquisition cost of the unit.

21. **Recognition of a loss contingency.** Consider the following hypothetical series of events. While shopping in a Nordstrom store on July 5, 2007, a customer slips on the escalator and falls, sustaining back and neck injuries. On January 15, 2008, the customer sues Nordstrom for $1 million. The case comes to trial on April 30, 2008. The jury renders its verdict on June 15, 2008, and finds Nordstrom liable for negligence. The jury grants a damage award of $400,000 to the customer. Nordstrom, on June 25, 2008, appeals the decision to a higher court, which rules on November 1, 2008, that the trial court should retry the case. The trial court retries the case beginning March 21, 2009. Another jury, on April 20, 2009, again finds Nordstrom liable for negligence and awards $500,000. On May 15, 2009, the store pays the $500,000 judgment. Nordstrom applies U.S. GAAP.

    a. When, if at all, should Nordstrom recognize a liability from these events? If Nordstrom recognizes a liability, what is the amount? Explain your reasoning.

    b. How would your response change if Nordstrom were applying IFRS?

22. **Asset recognition and measurement.** The following hypothetical transactions relate to Nestlé S.A., the Swiss chocolate manufacturer. Indicate whether each transaction immediately gives rise to an asset of the company under U.S. GAAP and separately, under IFRS. If Nestlé recognizes an asset, state the account title, the amount, and the classification of the asset on the balance sheet as either a current asset or a noncurrent asset. Nestlé reports its results in millions of Swiss Francs (CHF).

    a. Nestlé invests CHF800 million in a government bond. The bond has a maturity value of CHF1,000 million in five years, and Nestlé intends to hold the bond to maturity.

    b. Two months prior to its year-end, Nestle pays its insurer CHF240 million to cover annual premiums on its European plants.

c. Nestlé pays a developer in the Czech Republic CHF6 million for an option to purchase a tract of land on which it intends to build a warehouse to serve the eastern European markets. The price of the land is CHF450 million.

d. Nestlé signs a four-year employment agreement with its chief executive officer for a package valued at CHF17.4 million per year. Of this amount, CHF3.1 million is base salary; the rest is expected bonus and deferred compensation arrangements. The contract period begins next month.

e. Nestlé spends CHF80 million on research and development related to a new, low-calorie chocolate; 60% of the total amount was spent on pure research, the rest on development. The R&D is successful, and the firm is able to acquire a patent on the new formula. The cost of filing the paperwork and other procedures to obtain the patent is CHF0.5 million.

f. Nestlé received notice that a cocoa supplier had shipped by freight cocoa beans invoiced at CHF700 million with payment due in 30 days. The supplier retains title to the cocoa beans until received by Nestlé.

23. **Asset recognition and measurement.** The hypothetical transactions listed next relate to Ryanair Holdings, Plc. (Ryanair), an Irish airline. Indicate whether each transaction immediately gives rise to an asset under U.S. GAAP and, separately, IFRS. If Ryanair recognizes an asset, state the account title, the amount, and the classification of the asset on the balance sheet as either a current asset or a noncurrent asset. Ryanair reports its results in thousands of euros.

a. Ryanair's board of directors decides to purchase 10 Boeing 777 airplanes, costing €640 million each.

b. Ryanair places an order with Boeing for 10 Boeing 777 airplanes, costing €640 million each.

c. Ryanair pays Boeing €60 million as a deposit on the aircraft it ordered in part **b**.

d. Ryanair spends €50 million to obtain landing rights for the next five years at Beijing Capital International Airport.

e. Ryanair writes a check for €12 million and assumes a mortgage from its bank for another €65 million to purchase new ground equipment costing €77 million.

f. Ryanair issues common stock with a market value of €160 million to acquire used aircraft from a bankrupt regional airline. The carrying value of the equipment on the bankrupt airline's books is €75 million.

24. **Liability recognition and measurement.** The transactions listed next relate to Hana Microelectronic Public Company Limited (Hana Microelectronic), an electronics and semiconductor firm headquartered in Thailand. Indicate whether each transaction immediately gives rise to a liability under U.S. GAAP and, separately, IFRS. If accounting recognizes a liability, state the account title, the amount, and the classification of the liability on the balance sheet as either a current liability or a noncurrent liability. Hana Microelectronic reports its results in millions of baht (Bt).

a. Hana Microelectronic agrees to purchase land and a manufacturing plant from Fujitsu Limited, for Bt3,000 million.

b. Hana Microelectronic receives a check for Bt168 million from a customer for the delivery of merchandise that Hana Microelectronic will produce next month.

c. Refer to the event in part **b**, except now assume that Hana Microelectronic will deliver half of the merchandise next month and the remainder three years from now.

d. During the year, Hana Microelectronic issues 6 million shares of Bt1 par value common stock, for Bt62 million.

e. Hana Microelectronic borrows Bt24 million from a local bank, payable in equal installments over the next three years and bearing interest at the annual rate of 9%.

f. Hana Microelectronic signs a contract to purchase at least Bt45 million of merchandise from a particular supplier over the next two years.

g. Refer to part **f**, and assume Hana Microelectronic places an order for Bt15 million of this merchandise.

25. **Liability recognition and measurement.** The following hypothetical events relate to the Berlin Philharmonic. Indicate whether each transaction immediately gives rise to a

liability under U.S. GAAP and, separately, IFRS. If the Berlin Philharmonic recognizes a liability, state the account title, the amount, and the classification of the liability on the balance sheet as either a current liability or a noncurrent liability. The Berlin Philharmonic reports its results in euros.

a. The Berlin Philharmonic receives €3,040,000 for season tickets sold for next season.

b. The Berlin Philharmonic places an order with a printing company totaling €185,000 for symphony performance programs for next season.

c. The Berlin Philharmonic receives the programs ordered in part **b**, along with an invoice for €185,000.

d. The Berlin Philharmonic receives notice from its attorneys that a loyal customer attending a concert last season and sitting in the first row of the symphony hall has sued the Berlin Philharmonic for €10 million claiming hearing loss. The customer normally sits further back but staff asked her to move forward for this particular concert because of damage to the regular seat.

e. The Berlin Philharmonic signs a three-year contract with its first violinist at a salary of €140,000 per year.

f. The Berlin Philharmonic signs a five-year contract with Sir Simon Rattle, present conductor of the Philharmonic, to be the spokesman for the symphony at the end of his current contract, in 2012. Under the terms of the deal, the Berlin Philharmonic will pay compensation of €2 million a year to Sir Simon, beginning in 2012. Sir Simon will earn this compensation regardless of whether the Berlin Philharmonic asks him to perform any speaking engagements each year.

26. **Recognition and measurement of a loss contingency.** Consider the following hypothetical scenario for Beyond Petroleum (BP), a U.K. oil and gas firm. One of BP's oil rig platforms collapsed, creating damage to the seafloor as well as environmental damage to surrounding ocean water. Given the following additional information, what amount, if any, should BP recognize as a liability were it applying U.S. GAAP and, separately, IFRS? BP reports its results in millions of U.S. dollars.

a. Engineers who have examined the damaged site believe that much of the damage will naturally resolve itself, leading them to conclude that there is a 90% chance that damages are zero. They further estimate there is a 10% chance that the forces of nature will not resolve the damages, which will require additional intervention at a cost of $10 million.

b. Upon further analysis, the engineers in part **a** have revised their assessments. They now believe there is a 51% chance that damages will be $5 million, and a 49% chance damages will be zero.

c. Environmentalists who have examined the damaged site believe that the damage is extensive and requires immediate cleanup, with the following range of damage estimates: $25 million (probability 20%); $300 million (probability 35%); and $4,000 million (probability 45%).

d. Upon further analysis, the environmentalists in part **c** have revised their assessments. They now believe there is an 85% chance that damages will be $5,000 million and a 15% chance they will be zero.

PROBLEMS

27. **Effect of recording errors on the balance sheet equation.** Magyar Telekom is a Hungarian telecommunications company. The company applies IFRS and reports its results in millions of Hungarian forints (HUF). For each of the following hypothetical transactions or events facing Magyar Telekom, indicate the effects on assets, liabilities, and shareholders' equity of *failing to record or recording incorrectly* the transaction or event. Use the notation O/S (overstated), U/S (understated), or No (no effect). For example, Magyar Telekom's failure to record the issuance of common stock for HUF10,000 cash would be shown as follows:

■ Assets—U/S HUF10,000.

■ Liabilities—No.

■ Shareholders' equity—U/S HUF10,000.

(1) Magyar Telekom ordered HUF5,600 million of inventory from a supplier but did not record anything in its accounts.

(2) Magyar Telekom received the merchandise in transaction (1) and recorded it by debiting Inventory and crediting Accounts Payable for HUF6,500 million.

(3) Magyar Telekom acquired new equipment costing HUF17,000 million by paying HUF2,500 million in cash and signing a note payable for the remainder of the purchase price. It recorded the acquisition by debiting Equipment for HUF2,500 million and crediting Cash for HUF2,500 million.

(4) The firm paid the HUF36,000 million annual insurance premium on its headquarters building by debiting Property and crediting Cash for HUF36,000 million. The insurance period begins next month.

(5) Magyar Telekom won a contract to supply telecommunications services to a customer next year. The value of the contract is HUF25,000 million. The customer delivered a check to Magyar Telekom in the amount of HUF6,000 million. The firm made no journal entries for these events.

(6) The firm issued 2 million shares of its HUF100 par value common stock when the shares traded in the stock market at HUF700 per share. It issued the shares to acquire land. It recorded the transaction by debiting Land and crediting Common Stock for HUF200 million.

(7) The firm signed a three-year employment agreement with its chairperson for an annual salary of HUF6.6 million. The employment period begins next month. The firm did not record anything in its accounts related to this agreement.

28. Effect of recording errors on the balance sheet equation. Siderúrgica Venezolana "Sivensa," S.A., is a Venezuelan steel and metalworking company. Assume that during a recent year, Sivensa recorded various transactions with the following journal entries. The company applies IFRS and reports its results in thousands of U.S. dollars. Using the notation O/S (overstated), U/S (understated), or No (no effect), indicate the effects on assets, liabilities, and shareholders' equity of any errors in Sivensa's recording of each of these transactions. For example, if Sivensa recorded the issue of $10,000 of common stock by debiting Cash and crediting Bonds Payable, the effects of the error are as follows:

- Assets—No.
- Liabilities—O/S $10,000.
- Shareholders' equity—U/S $10,000.

(1) Equipment 10,000
      Cash 2,000
      Accounts Receivable 8,000

Assets	=	Liabilities	+	Shareholders' Equity	(Class.)
+10,000					
−2,000					
−8,000					

Sivensa acquired equipment costing $10,000 by paying $2,000 cash and signing a note payable for $8,000. It debited Equipment, credited Cash for $2,000, and credited Accounts Receivable for $8,000.

(2) Equipment.. 4,000
      Note Payable 4,000

Assets	=	Liabilities	+	Shareholders' Equity	(Class.)
+4,000		+4,000			

Sivensa placed an order for equipment valued at $4,000 that it will receive next month. Sivensa made a $1,000 deposit when it made the order and promised to pay the rest on delivery of the equipment. Sivensa debited Equipment for $4,000 and credited Notes Payable for $4,000.

(3) Cash.. 800

    Accounts Receivable 800

Assets	=	Liabilities	+	Shareholders' Equity	(Class.)
+800					
−800					

Sivensa received $800 as a deposit from a customer and debited Cash and credited Accounts Receivable for $800. The customer did not owe Sivensa any amounts at the time of this transaction.

(4) Prepaid Rent 1,000

    Rent Payable 1,000

Assets	=	Liabilities	+	Shareholders' Equity	(Class.)
+1,000		+1,000			

Sivensa signed a rental agreement for warehouse space for a one-year period beginning next month. The monthly rental fee of $1,000 is due on the first day of each month. Sivensa debited Prepaid Rent and credited Rent Payable for $1,000.

(5) Sivensa exchanged common stock with a market value of $2,500 for a patent and made no journal entry to record the exchange.

(6) Merchandise Inventories 4,900

    Cash... 4,900

Assets	=	Liabilities	+	Shareholders' Equity	(Class.)
+4,900					
−4,900					

Sivensa acquired $4,900 of office equipment for cash. It debited Inventory for $4,900 and credited Cash for $4,900.

29. **Balance sheet format, terminology, and accounting methods. Exhibit 3.3** presents the balance sheet of Cathay Pacific Airways Limited (Cathay Pacific), the Hong Kong airline, for the years ended December 31, 2007 and 2006. This balance sheet uses the terminology, format, and accounting methods of Hong Kong Financial Reporting Standards (HKFRS). Cathay reports results in millions of Hong Kong dollars (HKD).

    a. Prepare a balance sheet for Cathay Pacific on December 31, 2007, and December 31, 2006, following the format and terminology commonly used by firms that apply U.S. GAAP.

    b. Prepare a balance sheet for Cathay Pacific on December 31, 2007, and December 31, 2006, following the format and terminology commonly used by firms that apply IFRS.

30. **Balance sheet format, terminology, and accounting methods. Exhibit 3.4** presents the balance sheet prepared by Infosys Technologies Limited (Infosys), the Indian information technology firm, for the years ended March 31, 2008 and March 31, 2007. Infosys applies accounting standards issued by the Institute of Chartered Accountants of India and reports its results in millions of rupees (Rs. Crore).

    a. Prepare a balance sheet for Infosys on March 31, 2008, and March 31, 2007, following the format and terminology commonly used by firms that apply U.S. GAAP.

    b. Prepare a balance sheet for Infosys on March 31, 2008, and March 31, 2007, following the format and terminology commonly used by firms that apply IFRS.

31. **Balance sheet format, terminology, and accounting methods. Exhibit 3.5** presents the balance sheet prepared by Ericsson, the Swedish telecommunications firm, for the years

EXHIBIT 3.3

Cathay Pacific Airways Limited
Balance Sheets
(amounts in millions of HK dollars (HKD))
(Problem 29)

	Year ended December 31,	
	2007	**2006**
ASSETS AND LIABILITIES		
Noncurrent Assets and Liabilities		
Fixed Assets	HKD 62,388	HKD 57,602
Intangible Assets	7,782	7,749
Investments in Associates	10,054	8,826
Other Long-Term Receivables and Investments	3,519	3,406
	HKD 83,743	HKD 77,583
Long-Term Liabilities	HKD(40,323)	HKD(33,956)
Related Pledged Security Deposits	7,833	8,164
Net Long-Term Liabilities	(32,490)	(25,792)
Retirement Benefit Obligations	(268)	(170)
Deferred Taxation	(6,771)	(6,508)
	HKD(39,529)	HKD(32,470)
Net Noncurrent Assets	HKD 44,214	HKD 45,113
Current Assets and Liabilities		
Stock	HKD 882	HKD 789
Trade and Other Receivables	11,376	8,735
Liquid Funds	21,649	15,624
	HKD 33,907	HKD 25,148
Current Portion of Long-Term Liabilities	HKD (4,788)	HKD (7,503)
Related Pledged Security Deposits	910	1,352
Net Current Portion of Long-Term Liabilities	(3,878)	(6,151)
Trade and Other Payables	(14,787)	(10,999)
Unearned Transportation Revenue	(6,254)	(4,671)
Taxation	(2,475)	(2,902)
	HKD(27,394)	HKD(24,723)
Net Current Assets	HKD 6,513	HKD 425
Net Assets	HKD 50,727	HKD 45,538
CAPITAL AND RESERVES		
Share Capital	HKD 788	HKD 787
Reserves	49,761	44,599
Funds Attributable to Cathay Pacific Shareholders	HKD 50,549	HKD 45,386
Minority Interests	HKD 178	HKD 152
Total Equity	HKD 50,727	HKD 45,538

ended December 31, 2007, and December 31, 2006. Ericsson applies IFRS, and reports its results in millions of Swedish kronor (SEK). In addition to the items reported in Ericsson's balance sheet, assume the following hypothetical information is available to you:

■   In 2007 Ericsson revalued land with an acquisition cost of SEK 300 million upward, to its current fair value of SEK 1,200 million.

■   In 2007 Ericsson wrote down the value of equipment, with a net carrying value of SEK 2,400 million, to its fair value of SEK 1,600 million.

■   Included in current provisions for 2007 is the estimated loss on a lawsuit, which a competitor filed, alleging patent infringement. Ericsson estimates the following range

EXHIBIT 3.4

Infosys Technologies Limited Balance Sheet For Years Ended March 31, 2008 and 2007 (Problem 30)

	2008	2007
SOURCES OF FUNDS		
SHAREHOLDERS' FUNDS		
Share capital	286	286
Reserves and surplus	13,204	10,876
	13,490	11,162
APPLICATION OF FUNDS		
FIXED ASSETS		
Original cost	4,508	3,889
Less: Accumulated depreciation	1,837	1,739
Net book value	2,671	2,150
Add: Capital work-in-progress	1,260	957
	3,931	3,107
INVESTMENTS	964	839
DEFERRED TAX ASSETS	99	79
CURRENT ASSETS, LOANS AND ADVANCES		
Sundry debtors	3,093	2,292
Cash and bank balances	6,429	5,470
Loans and advances	2,705	1,199
	12,227	8,961
LESS: CURRENT LIABILITIES AND PROVISIONS		
Current liabilities	1,483	1,162
Provisions	2,248	662
NET CURRENT ASSETS	8,496	7,137
	13,490	11,162

of outcomes for this lawsuit: 10% chance of damages of SEK6,000 million, 10% chance of damages of SEK2,400 million, 30% chance of damages of SEK500 million, 10% chance of damages of SEK40 million, and 40% chance of zero damages.

Prepare a balance sheet for Ericsson on December 31, 2007, following the format, terminology and accounting methods required by U.S. GAAP. Ignore any income tax effects of any revisions to reported amounts.

32. **Interpreting balance sheet changes. Exhibit 3.6** presents a common-size balance sheet for Texas Steakhouse, a restaurant chain, for the fiscal years ended December 31, 2007, and December 31, 2008.

   a. Identify the ways in which the structure of Texas Steakhouse's assets and the structure of its financing correspond to what one would expect of a restaurant chain. What aspects of the structure of its assets and the structure of its financing are not what one would expect?

   b. Identify the major changes in the nature and mix of assets and the nature and mix of financing between 2007 and 2008, and suggest possible reasons for the changes.

   c. "An increase in the common-size balance sheet percentage between two year-ends for a particular balance sheet item (for example, cash) does not necessarily mean that its dollar amount increased." Explain.

33. **Interpreting balance sheet changes. Exhibit 3.7** presents the balance sheet for Cemex S.A., a Mexican construction firm, for two recent years. Cemex applies Mexican reporting standards and reports its results in thousands of pesos ($).

   a. Prepare a common-size balance sheet for Cemex for the years ended December 31, 2006 and 2007.

   b. In what ways is the common-size balance sheet of Cemex on December 31, 2007, typical of a construction company?

   c. Identify the major changes in the nature and mix of assets and the nature and mix of financing between the two year-ends, and suggest possible reasons for the changes.

EXHIBIT 3.5

Ericsson
Balance Sheet
For Years ended December 31, 2007 and 2006
(Problem 31)

December 31, SEK million	Notes	2007	2006
ASSETS			
Non-current assets			
Intangible assets	C10		
Capitalized development expenses		3,661	4,995
Goodwill		22,826	6,824
Intellectual property rights, brands and other intangible assets		23,958	15,649
Property, plant and equipment	C11, C26, C27	9,304	7,881
Financial assets			
Equity in joint ventures and associated companies	C12	10,903	9,409
Other investments in shares and participations	C12	738	721
Customer financing, non-current	C12	1,012	1,921
Other financial assets, non-current	C12	2,918	2,409
Deferred tax assets	C8	11,690	13,564
		87,010	63,373
Current assets			
Inventories	C13	22,475	21,470
Trade receivables	C14	60,492	51,070
Customer financing, current		2,362	1,735
Other current receivables	C15	15,062	15,012
Short-term investments	C20	29,406	32,311
Cash and cash equivalents	C20	28,310	29,969
		158,107	151,567
Total assets		245,117	214,940
EQUITY AND LIABILITIES			
Equity			
Stockholders' equity	C16	134,112	120,113
Minority interest in equity of subsidiaries	C16	940	782
		135,052	120,895
Non-current liabilities			
Post-employment benefits	C17	6,188	6,968
Provisions, non-current	C18	368	602
Deferred tax liabilities	C8	2,799	382
Borrowings, non-current	C19, C20	21,320	12,904
Other non-current liabilities		1,714	2,868
		32,389	23,724
Current liabilities			
Provisions, current	C18	9,358	13,280
Borrowings, current	C19, C20	5,896	1,680
Trade payables	C22	17,427	18,183
Other current liabilities	C21	44,995	37,178
		77,676	70,321
Total equity and liabilities [1]		245,117	214,940

34. **Relating market value to book value of shareholders' equity.** Firms prepare their balance sheets by applying authoritative guidance for the recognition and measurement of assets and liabilities. Accountants refer to the total common shareholders' equity on the balance sheet as the *book value of shareholders' equity*. The *market value of shareholders' equity* equals the number of shares of common stock outstanding times the market price per share. Financial analysts frequently examine the ratio of the market value of shareholders' equity to the book value of shareholders' equity, referred to as the *market-to-book-value ratio*, in assessing current market prices. Theoretical and empirical research suggests that the size of the market-to-book-value ratio is related to (1) a firm's ability to generate higher rates of profitability than its competitors, (2) its rate of growth, and

EXHIBIT 3.6

Texas Steakhouse
Common-Size Balance Sheet
(Problem 32)

	December 31	
	2008	**2007**
ASSETS		
Cash	12.3%	7.6%
Accounts Receivable	0.9	0.9
Inventories	2.6	3.3
Other Current Assets	1.5	1.7
Total Current Assets	17.3%	13.5%
Property, Plant, and Equipment	67.9	68.1
Other Assets	14.8	18.4
Total Assets	100.0%	100.0%
LIABILITIES AND SHAREHOLDERS' EQUITY		
Current Liabilities		
Accounts Payable	4.0%	4.0%
Notes Payable	1.3	1.1
Other Current Liabilities	12.4	10.8
Total Current Liabilities	17.7%	15.9%
Noncurrent Liabilities		
Bonds Payable	1.1%	1.2%
Other Noncurrent Liabilities	3.1	3.9
Total Noncurrent Liabilities	4.2%	5.1%
Total Liabilities	21.9%	21.0%
Shareholders' Equity		
Common Stock	11.1%	15.1%
Retained Earnings	67.0	63.9
Total Shareholders' Equity	78.1%	79.0%
Total Liabilities and Shareholders' Equity	100.0%	100.0%

(3) its use of authoritative guidance in measuring assets and liabilities, which net to the book value of shareholders' equity.

Exhibit 3.8 presents balance sheet information for five firms that report using U.S. GAAP at the end of a recent year. It also shows their market-to-book-value ratios. Additional information regarding the five companies follows:

(1) Coca-Cola (Coke): Coke markets soft drinks worldwide. It has grown primarily by internal expansion rather than by acquiring other soft-drink firms. Coke maintains less than 50% ownership in a large number of its bottlers.

(2) Bristol-Myers Squibb (Bristol): Bristol generates approximately 75% of its revenues from prescription drugs and medical devices and 25% from nonprescription health products, toiletries, and beauty aids.

(3) Bankers Trust (Bankers): Bankers obtains funds primarily from depositors (reported on the Accounts Payable line in **Exhibit 3.8**) and invests them in short-term liquid assets or lends them to businesses and consumers. It also engages in investment activities on its own account.

(4) International Paper (IP): IP has the largest holdings of forestlands of any nongovernmental entity in the United States. It processes timber into wood products for the construction industry and processes pulp from the timber into various types of commodity and specialty papers.

| EXHIBIT 3.7 | Cemex S.A.
Balance Sheets
(amounts in millions of pesos ($))
(Problem 33) |

	Year ended December 31,	
	2007	**2006**
ASSETS		
Current Assets		
Cash and Investments	$ 8,670	$ 18,494
Trade Receivables Less Allowance for Doubtful Accounts	20,719	16,525
Other Accounts Receivable	9,830	9,206
Inventories, net	19,631	13,974
Other Current Assets	2,394	2,255
Total Current Assets	$ 61,244	$ 60,454
Noncurrent Assets		
Investments in Associates	$ 10,599	$ 8,712
Other Investments in Noncurrent Accounts Receivable	10,960	9,966
Property, Machinery and Equipment, net	262,189	201,425
Goodwill, Intangible Assets and Deferred Charges	197,322	70,526
Total Noncurrent Assets	$481,070	$290,629
Total Assets	$542,314	$351,083
LIABILITIES AND STOCKHOLDERS' EQUITY		
Current Liabilities		
Short-Term Debt Including Current Maturities of Long-Term Debt	$ 36,257	$ 14,657
Trade Payables	23,660	20,110
Other Accounts Payable and Accrued Expenses	23,471	17,203
Total Current Liabilities	$ 83,388	$ 51,970
Noncurrent Liabilities		
Long-Term Debt	$180,654	$ 73,674
Pension and Other Retirement Benefits	7,650	7,484
Deferred Income Tax Liability	50,307	30,119
Other Noncurrent Liabilities	16,162	14,725
Total Noncurrent Liabilities	$254,773	$126,002
Total Liabilities	$338,161	$177,972
Minority Interest	$ 40,985	$ 22,484
Shareholders' Equity		
Common Stock	4,115	4,113
Additional Paid in Capital	63,379	56,982
Less: Other Equity Reserves	(104,574)	(91,244)
Retained Earnings	200,248	180,776
Total Shareholders' Equity	$163,168	$150,627
Total Liabilities and Shareholders' Equity	$542,314	$351,083

(5) Walt Disney (Disney): Disney produces motion picture films and operates theme parks.

a. The market-to-book-value ratios differ from 1.0 in part because the rates of profitability and growth of these five firms differ from those of their competitors. This problem does not provide you with sufficient information to assess the impact of these two factors on the market-to-book-value ratio. The ratios also differ from 1.0 because of the

EXHIBIT 3.8

Balance Sheet for Selected Companies
(all dollar amounts in millions)
(Problem 34)

	Coca-Cola	Bristol-Myers Squibb	Bankers Trust	International Paper	Walt Disney
ASSETS					
Cash and Marketable Securities	$ 1,531	$ 2,423	$79,048	$ 270	$ 1,510
Accounts and Notes Receivable	1,525	2,043	11,249	2,241	1,671
Inventories	1,047	1,397	—	2,075	2,264
Other Current Assets	1,102	847	—	244	—
Total Current Assets	$ 5,205	$ 6,710	$90,297	$ 4,830	$ 5,445
Investments in Securities	3,928	—	—	1,032	630
Property, Plant, and Equipment	4,080	3,666	915	9,941	5,814
Other Noncurrent Assets	660	2,534	5,804	2,033	937
Total Assets	$13,873	$12,910	$97,016	$17,836	$12,826
LIABILITIES AND SHAREHOLDERS' EQUITY					
Accounts Payable	$ 2,564	$ 693	$24,939	$ 1,204	$ 2,475
Short-Term Borrowing	2,083	725	55,166	2,083	—
Other Current Liabilities	1,530	2,856	5,502	747	967
Total Current Liabilities	$ 6,177	$ 4,274	$85,607	$ 4,034	$ 3,442
Long-Term Debt	1,426	644	6,455	4,464	2,937
Other Noncurrent Liabilities	1,035	2,288	—	2,824	939
Total Liabilities	$ 8,638	$ 7,206	$92,062	$11,322	$ 7,318
Preferred Stock	—	—	$ 645	—	—
Common Stock	$ 1,600	$ 451	1,401	$ 1,914	$ 945
Retained Earnings	10,708	7,299	3,324	4,711	5,849
Treasury Stock	(7,073)	(2,046)	(416)	(111)	(1,286)
Total Shareholders' Equity	$ 5,235	$ 5,704	$ 4,954	$ 6,514	$ 5,508
Total Liabilities and Shareholders' Equity . . .	$13,873	$12,910	$97,016	$17,836	$12,826
Market Value/Book Value Ratio	12.6	5.2	1.0	1.3	4.4

use of U.S. GAAP for assets and liabilities, which this chapter discussed. Identify the U.S. GAAP requirements that most likely explain the market-to-book-value ratios for each of the five firms (that is, identify which accounting principles cause the book values of assets and liabilities to differ from the market value of shareholders' equity).

b. Discuss the likely rationale for the nature and mix of assets and the nature and mix of financing for each of the five firms.

35. **Relating market value to book value of shareholders' equity.** Firms prepare their balance sheets using authoritative guidance for the recognition and measurement of assets and liabilities. Accountants refer to the total common shareholders' equity appearing on the balance sheet as the *book value of shareholders' equity*. The *market value of shareholders' equity* equals the number of shares of common stock outstanding times the market price per share. Financial analysts frequently examine the ratio of the market value of shareholders' equity to the book value of shareholders' equity, referred to as the *market-to-book-value ratio*, in assessing current market prices. Theoretical and empirical research suggests that the size of the market-to-book-value ratio is related to (1) a firm's ability to generate higher rates of profitability than its competitors, (2) its rate of growth, and (3) its use of authoritative guidance in measuring assets and liabilities, which net to the book value of shareholders' equity.

EXHIBIT 3.9	Common-Size Balance Sheet for Selected Companies (Problem 35)

	Pfizer	Nestlé	Promodes	Deutsche Bank	British Airways	New Oji Paper Co.
ASSETS						
Cash and Marketable Securities	20.5%	11.5%	12.9%	44.2%	6.5%	2.1%
Accounts and Notes Receivable	16.4	18.9	22.6	50.4	13.5	19.8
Inventories	8.1	13.4	18.4	—	0.7	8.5
Other Current Assets	6.3	1.4	—	—	—	1.5
Total Current Assets	51.3%	45.2%	53.9%	94.6%	20.7%	31.9%
Investments in Securities	7.5	7.1	8.7	2.7	6.6	24.5
Property, Plant, and Equipment	28.2	43.7	28.3	1.2	72.7	43.6
Other Noncurrent Assets	13.0	4.0	9.1	1.5	—	—
Total Assets	100.0%	100.0%	100.0%	100.0%	100.0%	100.0%
LIABILITIES AND SHAREHOLDERS' EQUITY						
Accounts Payable	5.1%	11.2%	44.3%	66.5%	9.4%	10.2%
Short-Term Borrowing	12.8	18.1	3.3	16.0	5.3	16.2
Other Current Liabilities	17.8	9.6	12.6	4.9	15.6	10.7
Total Current Liabilities	35.7%	38.9%	60.2%	87.4%	30.3%	37.1%
Long-Term Debt	3.4	6.7	7.7	1.2	36.8	16.9
Other Noncurrent Liabilities	12.9	9.2	4.1	8.0	4.0	4.8
Total Liabilities	52.0%	54.8%	72.0%	96.6%	71.1%	58.8%
Common Stock	27.5%	3.0%	0.8%	1.7%	8.1%	17.3%
Retained Earnings	43.9	42.7	27.2	1.7	20.8	23.9
Treasury Stock	(23.4)	(0.5)	—	—	—	—
Total Shareholders' Equity	48.0%	45.2%	28.0%	3.4%	28.9%	41.2%
Total Liabilities and Shareholders' Equity	100.0%	100.0%	100.0%	100.0%	100.0%	100.0%
Market Value/Book Value Ratio	8.2	3.3	4.6	1.7	2.4	1.4

Exhibit 3.9 presents *common-size* balance sheet information for six firms at the end of a recent year. Some of the six firms apply IFRS and others apply U.S. GAAP. Exhibit 3.9 also shows market-to-book-value ratios for the six firms. Additional information regarding the six companies follows:

(1) Pfizer is a pharmaceutical company headquartered in the United States.

(2) Nestlé is a consumer products company headquartered in Switzerland. In addition to its chocolate products, it manufactures and distributes beverages (Nestea, Poulin Springs mineral water), frozen foods (Stouffer's), milk products (infant formulas), and pet foods (Alpo).

(3) Promodes is a French company that operates supermarket chains (Champion), hypermarkets (Continent, Continente), convenience stores (Promocash, Punt&Cash), and restaurant supply stores (Prodirest).

(4) Deutsche Bank is a German bank that provides both traditional commercial banking services (deposit taking, loan making) and investment banking services (investment management, financial consulting).

(5) British Airways is domiciled in the United Kingdom and provides air transportation services.

(6) New Oji Paper Co. is a Japanese forest-products company. It purchases wood pulp from Canada and the United States and processes it into various papers for sale in Japan.

a. The market-to-book-value ratios differ from 1.0 in part because the rates of profitability and growth of these six firms differ from those of their competitors. This problem does not provide you with sufficient information to assess the impact of these two factors on the market-to-book-value ratio. The ratios also differ from 1.0 because of the use of authoritative guidance for assets and liabilities, which this chapter discussed. Identify the authoritative guidance that most likely explains the market-to-book-value ratios for each of the six firms (that is, identify which accounting principles cause the book values of assets and liabilities to differ from the market value of shareholders' equity).

b. Discuss the likely rationale for the nature and mix of assets and the nature and mix of financing for each of the six firms.

36. **Identifying industries using common-size balance sheet percentages.** Exhibit 3.10 presents common-size balance sheets for five firms. The firms and a description of their activities follow:

   (1) Commonwealth Edison: Generates and sells electricity to businesses and households.

   (2) Hewlett-Packard: Develops, assembles, and sells computer hardware and printers. The firm outsources many of its computer and printer components.

   (3) Household International: Lends money to consumers for periods ranging from several months to several years.

   (4) May Department Stores: Operates department store chains and offers its own credit card.

   (5) Newmont Mining: Mines for gold and other minerals, utilizing heavy equipment.

   Use whatever clues that you can to match the companies listed above with the firms listed in **Exhibit 3.10**. Describe your reasoning.

EXHIBIT 3.10

Common-Size Balance Sheet for Five Companies (Problem 36)

	(1)	(2)	(3)	(4)	(5)
Cash and Marketable Securities	8.5%	0.1%	9.5%	12.1%	1.1%
Receivables	81.9	2.8	1.4	25.7	24.1
Inventories	—	2.0	9.0	23.2	23.6
Property, Plant, and Equipment (net)	1.2	74.3	62.6	20.0	41.4
Other Assets	8.4	20.8	17.5	19.0	9.8
Total Assets	100.0%	100.0%	100.0%	100.0%	100.0%
Current Liabilities	38.8%	8.4%	10.8%	38.3%	29.1%
Long-Term Debt	50.0	47.7	28.1	9.3	28.3
Other Noncurrent Liabilities	—	13.9	6.7	3.9	6.2
Shareholders' Equity	11.2	30.0	54.4	48.5	36.4
Total Liabilities and Shareholders' Equity	100.0%	100.0%	100.0%	100.0%	100.0%

Income Statement: Reporting the Results of Operating Activities

LEARNING OBJECTIVES

1. Understand the classifications of revenues and expenses on the income statement and the importance of those classifications.
2. Understand the timing of revenue and expense recognition and their measurement.
3. Understand the concept of comprehensive income and the relation between net income and comprehensive income.
4. Develop skills to analyze the relations among revenues, expenses, and net income, and understand how differences in business models affect those relations.

The income statement reports **net income** (or **net loss**) for a time period, such as a quarter or a year. Net income (also called **earnings** or **profit**) equals revenues minus expenses plus gains minus losses.[1] We consider gains and losses in later chapters and focus in this chapter on revenues and expenses. **Revenues** reflect the net assets (assets less liabilities) that a firm receives from its customers when it sells goods or renders services. **Expenses** reflect the net assets consumed in generating revenues. The difference between revenues and expenses (plus gains and minus losses), which is net income, therefore reflects the change in net assets as a result of a firm's operating activities during an accounting period. As a measure of operating performance, revenues reflect the goods sold and services rendered by a firm, and expenses reflect the efforts required to create and deliver those goods and services. Users of financial statements analyze net income because it is a summary financial measure of how well a firm transforms efforts (expenses) into salable output (revenues), with larger net income indicating better performance. As we discuss later in this chapter, if you compare firms using net income or income components, you should base the comparisons on ratios, such as the ratio of net income to some denominator, such as sales revenues, book value of shareholders' equity, or total assets. Examining ratios, rather than absolute levels, controls for size effects: larger firms usually generate larger levels of net income because of their larger investment bases.

---

[1]The FASB uses the term *earnings* in *Statement of Financial Accounting Concepts No. 5*, "Recognition and Measurement in Financial Statements of Business Enterprises," 1984, for example, in par. 33–44. The IASB uses the term *profit* in *International Accounting Standard 1*, "Presentation of Financial Statements," revised 2003, for example, in par. 82–88. Many preparers of financial statements use *net income* to refer to this concept, and we will follow this convention with the understanding that net income, profit, and earnings all refer to the same item.

This chapter considers the measurement principles and accounting procedures that underlie the income statement and the insights it provides about operating performance. We discuss typical ways income statements classify and display items. **Chapter 7** introduces criteria for a firm to use in deciding when to recognize revenue (timing) and how much revenue to recognize (measurement). Recognizing revenue often triggers the recognition of expenses associated with those revenues. We therefore discuss the accounting procedures for recognizing both revenues and expenses. We describe the concept of comprehensive income and distinguish net income from comprehensive income. The chapter concludes by describing how to analyze common-size income statements to understand how a given firm performs over time, to explain that performance, and to compare performance across firms. Analysts often refer to comparisons over time as *time-series analysis* and comparisons across firms as *cross-section analysis*.

UNDERLYING CONCEPTS AND TERMINOLOGY

Chapter 2 introduces the income statement, one of the principal financial statements. The income statement is also called the *statement of operations* or the *statement of operating activity,* or the *statement of profit and loss*. Unlike the balance sheet, which displays assets, liabilities, and shareholders' equity at a point in time, the income statement reflects the results of operations during an accounting period. The period that spans the time between the beginning balance sheet and the ending balance sheet is, by definition, the accounting period. For example, **Exhibit 4.1** shows McDonald's Corporation's income statement for the years ending December 31, 2006, 2005, and 2004; McDonald's would also prepare balance sheets as of December 31 of each of these years.[2] Although both the balance sheet and the income statement are dated December 31, the income statement reflects *changes* in net assets *during* the one-year accounting period ending on this date. Stated differently, the income statement presents a summary measure of the *flows* of net assets (the increments from revenues and the decrements from expenses) that occurred *during* the accounting period. In contrast, the balance sheet displays the *levels* of assets, liabilities, and shareholders' equity *as of* the date of the accounting report—the beginning or end of the accounting period. The equation linking the balance sheet and income statement (discussed in **Chapter 2**) captures this distinction:

$$\text{Retained Earnings (beginning)} + \text{Net Income} - \text{Dividends} = \text{Retained Earnings (ending)}$$

or

$$\text{Retained Earnings (ending)} - \text{Retained Earnings (beginning)} = \text{Net Income} - \text{Dividends}$$

or

$$\text{Change in Retained Earnings} = \text{Net Income} - \text{Dividends}$$

This equation shows that the change in the balance sheet account Retained Earnings (that is, the change in retained earnings between two reporting dates) equals the change in net assets, that is, net income adjusted for dividends.

INCOME STATEMENT DISPLAY

Income statements present an ordered list, grouped by broad categories of revenues and expenses. The income statement begins with revenues followed by a list of expenses. U.S. GAAP and IFRS requirements for the presentation of income statements are similar, with some important differences.

- Other than separating revenues from expenses, U.S. GAAP provides little guidance about which items the firm must separately display or their order. IFRS requires, at a minimum,

---

[2]As **Chapter 1** discusses, both U.S. GAAP and IFRS require firms to report balance sheet information for the current year and the prior year, and to report income statement information for the current year and two prior years.

EXHIBIT 4.1 McDonald's Corporation
Consolidated Income Statement

IN MILLIONS, EXCEPT PER SHARE DATA	Years ended December 31, **2006**	2005	2004
REVENUES			
Sales by Company-operated restaurants	**$16,082.7**	$14,726.6	$13,755.2
Revenues from franchised and affiliated restaurants	**5,503.7**	5,105.9	4,838.8
Total revenues	**21,586.4**	19,832.5	18,594.0
OPERATING COSTS AND EXPENSES			
Company-operated restaurant expenses			
Food & paper	**5,349.7**	5,004.9	4,698.2
Payroll & employee benefits	**4,185.4**	3,860.4	3,586.5
Occupancy & other operating expenses	**4,006.6**	3,709.2	3,403.2
Franchised restaurants-occupancy expenses	**1,060.4**	1,021.5	1,002.7
Selling, general & administrative expenses	**2,337.9**	2,167.1	1,939.1
Impairment and other charges (credits), net	**134.2**	(28.4)	281.4
Other operating expense, net	**67.1**	105.3	145.0
Total operating costs and expenses	**17,141.3**	15,840.0	15,056.1
Operating income	**4,445.1**	3,992.5	3,537.9
Interest expense-net of capitalized interest of $5.4, $4.9 and $4.1	**402.0**	356.1	358.4
Nonoperating income, net	**(123.3)**	(38.0)	(21.2)
Income from continuing operations before provision for income taxes	**4,166.4**	3,674.4	3,200.7
Provision for income taxes	**1,293.4**	1,088.0	923.2
Income from continuing operations	**2,873.0**	2,586.4	2,277.5
Income from discontinued operations (net of taxes of $96.8, $11.4 and $0.7)	**671.2**	15.8	1.0
Net income	**$ 3,544.2**	$ 2,602.2	$ 2,278.5
Per common share-basic:			
Continuing operations	**$ 2.33**	$ 2.05	$ 1.81
Discontinued operations	**0.54**	0.01	-
Net income	**$ 2.87**	$ 2.06	$ 1.81
Per common share-diluted:			
Continuing operations	**$ 2.30**	$ 2.03	$ 1.79
Discontinued operations	**0.53**	0.01	-
Net income	**$ 2.83**	$ 2.04	$ 1.79
Dividends per common share	**$ 1.00**	$ 0.67	$ 0.55
Weighted-average shares outstanding-basic	**1,234.0**	1,260.4	1,259.7
Weighted-average shares outstanding-diluted	**1,251.7**	1,274.2	1,273.7

the separate display of revenues, financing costs (for example, interest expense), income tax expense, profit or loss for the period, and certain other items.[3]

■ Both U.S. GAAP and IFRS require the separate display of items whose size, nature, or frequency of occurrence make such separate display necessary for accurately portraying performance.

■ Both U.S. GAAP and IFRS require separate display of items related to discontinued operations, a topic discussed in **Chapter 14**.

■ IFRS requires separate display of the portion of profit or loss attributable to the minority (noncontrolling) interest and the portion attributable to the parent entity, a topic discussed in more detail in **Chapter 13**. U.S. GAAP contains a similar requirement starting in 2009 for most firms.

■ IFRS permits firms to present expenses by either nature or function; although U.S. GAAP is silent on this issue, guidance from the Securities and Exchange Commission requires registrants to classify expenses by function.[4]

---

[3]Those items pertain to discontinued operations and to results of operations of entities accounted for using the equity method (discussed in **Chapter 13**).

[4]All of the income statements presented in this textbook display expenses by function, such as administrative expense or cost of goods sold. Classification by nature groups expenses by their purpose—for example, compensation expense or insurance expense.

To illustrate differences in income statement formats, we examine the income statements of Nordstrom (**Exhibit 1.2** on page 9 of **Chapter 1**), McDonald's (**Exhibit 4.1**), and Scania (**Exhibit 1.6** on page 14 of **Chapter 1**). Both Nordstrom and McDonald's apply U.S. GAAP, and Scania applies IFRS. The following comments relate to the income statement for Nordstrom for its fiscal year ended February 3, 2007, and for McDonald's and Scania for their years ended December 31, 2006.

REPORTING REVENUES

Income statements begin with revenues; for this reason, analysts often refer to revenue growth as "top-line" growth. In **Chapter 2** we define *revenues* (or *sales, sales revenues,* or for some non-U.S. firms, *turnover*) as the inflow of net assets (for example, cash or receivables) received in exchange for providing goods and services. U.S. GAAP and IFRS allow significant latitude with respect to whether and how to aggregate revenues from multiple business lines (segments) on the income statement; there is no requirement that a firm with multiple segments separately disclose *on the income statement* the revenues of each segment.[5]

Nordstrom's income statement for the fiscal year ended February 3, 2007, reports net sales of $8,560.7 million. The word *net* before the word *sales* means that Nordstrom reports sales revenues less discounts, allowances, and returns; we revisit these topics later in this chapter. McDonald's income statement for the year ended December 31, 2006, reports total revenues of $21,586.4 million, composed of revenues from company-operated restaurants of $16,082.7 million and franchise fees from franchised and affiliated restaurants of $5,503.7 million. Thus, McDonald's income statement provides the reader with information about two distinct sources of revenue. Scania's income statement for the year ended December 31, 2006, also shows revenues from two sources: Vehicles and Services has net sales in 2006 of SEK70,738 million, and Customer Finance reports revenues (interest, lease, and fee income) of SEK3,527 million. Scania's income statement begins with information on its main business (Vehicles and Services), followed by information on its secondary business (Customer Finance).

REPORTING EXPENSES

Immediately below revenues, Nordstrom and Scania report information about the cost of sales. **Cost of goods sold** (**cost of services rendered**) is the cost of products sold and services provided during the period. Nordstrom reports cost of sales of $5,353.9 million; Scania reports costs of goods sold of SEK52,255 million for the Vehicles and Services business, and SEK2,608 million for the Customer Finance business (cost of sales for a finance company includes interest and other expenses of the period).

Common terminology, but not definitions in U.S. GAAP and IFRS, often refers to the difference between sales and cost of sales as **gross margin, gross profit**, or **gross income**. Nordstrom reports gross profit of $3,206.7 million; Scania reports gross income of SEK18,483 million for Vehicles and Services and SEK919 million for Customer Finance. Neither U.S. GAAP nor IFRS requires the separate display of this item; both, however, require separate display of sales and cost of sales, so you can always calculate the gross margin yourself.

Most firms do not display the components of cost of sales; for example, both Nordstrom and Scania report only the aggregate number. Some firms, however, disaggregate their cost of sales. For example, McDonald's reports, as separate items in its income statement, the components of cost of sales for company-operated restaurants: food and paper, payroll and employee benefits, and occupancy and other operating expenses. McDonald's does not report its gross profit, but we can calculate this number ourselves. McDonald's reports revenues from company-operated restaurants of $16,082.7 million and company-owned restaurant expenses of $13,541.7 million (the sum of food and paper, payroll and employee benefits and occupancy and other operating expenses). Thus, McDonald's gross profit on company-owned restaurants is $2,541.0 million (= $16,082.7 − $13,541.7). McDonald's also reports its revenues and costs from franchised and affiliated restaurants: franchise fee revenues are $5,503.7

[5]Both U.S. GAAP and IFRS require the disclosure, *in the notes* to the financial statements, of selected information about business segments. Segment reporting is discussed in more detail in **Chapter 6**. The distinction we make here is that the income statement typically does not provide information about the operating results of business segments.

million and franchised restaurant-occupancy costs are $1,060.4 million. Thus, the gross profit on franchised and affiliated operations is $4,443.3 million (= $5,503.7 − $1,060.4). Combining the two sources of revenue and cost,[6] McDonald's total gross profit is $6,984.3 million.

After cost of sales, the income statement typically shows deductions for other expenses associated with operations (other **operating expenses**). Many firms present a subtotal called **operating income** or **operating profit**, the difference between revenues and expenses associated with core operating activities (before items such as interest income and interest expense, and before gains and losses unrelated to operations). In addition to cost of sales, two common types of operating expenses are selling, general, and administrative expenses (SG&A) and research and development expenses (R&D). Nordstrom, for example, reports SG&A expenses of $2,296.9 million as its only operating expense other than cost of sales. In contrast, McDonald's income statement shows the following list of operating expenses, in addition to cost of sales: franchised restaurants occupancy costs, SG&A, impairment and other charges, and other operating costs, net. For its Vehicle and Services business, Scania reports R&D expenses, selling expenses, administrative expenses, and its share of income in associated companies and joint ventures (this last item is discussed in **Chapter 13**). For its Customer Finance business, Scania reports other income and other expenses, as well as selling and administrative expenses and bad debt expense.

Subtracting total operating expenses from sales yields operating profit. Neither U.S. GAAP nor IFRS requires separate display of this item. In addition, neither U.S. GAAP nor IFRS defines *operating* in the context of the income statement, so there is no authoritative guidance on what qualifies as an operating expense, nor is there a list of items considered operating expenses.[7] As a result, items classified as operating expenses reflect management's judgment that the item is a cost of the core business.

All three of the example income statements report operating income. Nordstrom reports operating income of $909.9 million. McDonald's reports operating income (from its combined businesses) of $4,445.1 million. Scania separately reports operating income for each of its two business segments: SEK8,260 million for Vehicles and Services, and SEK493 million for Customer Finance, and total operating income of SEK8,753 million (= SEK8,260 + SEK493).

Other (nonoperating) items follow operating expenses or the subtotal for operating profit. Most firms reporting under U.S. GAAP separately report financing costs, such as interest expense; IFRS requires the separate display of finance costs. In addition, because both U.S. GAAP and IFRS require the separate display of significant items, most firms also separate significant expenses and revenues that do not arise from their core businesses. For example, the decision to sell the headquarters building might generate a gain that would increase income in the year of sale. Selling the headquarters building is not part of the core business, so this item would be aggregated with other noncore, nonoperating items and reported below operating income, probably as Other Income.

Nordstrom's list of nonoperating items includes interest expense (net of interest income) of $42.8 million and other income of $238.5 million. Interest expense reduces income by $42.8 million, while other income increases net income by $238.5 million. McDonald's nonoperating items include interest expense (which reduces income by $402.0 million) and nonoperating income (which increases income by $123.3 million). Finally, Scania's nonoperating items include interest income and interest expense, as well as other financial income and expenses; the net effect of all four nonoperating items reduces Scania's profit by SEK170 million.

Subtracting nonoperating expenses from operating income yields *profit before income taxes*. Multiplying this amount by the applicable tax rate derives the amount of *income tax expense* (usually called the *income tax provision* in the United States; usually called *taxes, taxation,* or *income taxes* in other countries). Subtracting income tax expense from income before taxes yields *net income*. Nordstrom reports income tax expense of $427.6 million on its earnings before income taxes of $1,105.6 million, implying a tax rate of 38.7% (= $427.6/$1,105.6). As discussed in more detail in **Chapter 11**, this rate is the *effective tax rate,* which typically differs from the rate specified by taxing authorities (the *statutory tax rate*). Scania reports income before taxes ("income after financial items") of SEK8,583 mil-

---

[6]McDonald's two measures of gross profit have different interpretations, because the business model of company restaurants is the sale of goods while the business model of franchising is the collection of fees from franchisees. That is, revenue from franchise fees is like a royalty paid for being associated with McDonald's while revenue from company restaurants is earned by providing goods.

[7]Both U.S. GAAP and IFRS do define the term *operating* for purposes of the statement of cash flows.

lion and income tax expense of SEK2,644 million, implying an effective tax rate of 30.8% (= SEK2,644/SEK8,583).

Unlike Nordstrom and Scania, McDonald's reports income from discontinued operations. U.S. GAAP and IFRS require separate income statement display of **income from continuing operations** and **income from discontinued operations**—earnings that will not continue because the firm either sold, or made a decision to sell, a portion of its business. Authoritative guidance reserves the label *discontinued operations* for the sale of entire lines of business, not individual assets.[8] The term *discontinued operations* refers to lines of business the firm has specific plans to discontinue, not just one it has already discontinued. McDonald's reports income from continuing operations before taxes of $4,166.4 million, tax expense of $1,293.4 million (for an effective tax rate of 31.0%), and income from continuing operations, after taxes, of $2,873.0 million. McDonald's separately reports $671.2 million in income, net of taxes, from discontinued operations.

The requirement for separate display of income from continuing operations and income from discontinued operations aids users of the income statement in predicting future earnings. The firm expects income from continuing operations to recur next year, whereas income from discontinued operations will not recur because the firm will soon dispose of those operations (net assets). For similar reasons, the balance sheet separately displays the assets and liabilities of discontinued operations. To illustrate, **Exhibit 4.2** shows McDonald's balance sheet for 2006. At the end of 2005, the balance sheet shows current assets and current liabilities of discontinued operations of $380.0 million and $107.9 million, respectively. Prior to 2005, McDonald's classified many of the assets and possibly some of the liabilities as long-term assets and liabilities. In 2005, McDonald's classified them as current items because it expects to dispose of them within one year. These amounts are zero at the end of 2006. During 2006, McDonald's disposed of these assets and settled these liabilities, reducing the balances in the accounts to zero. Prior to their disposal, however, the current assets continued to generate income, reported in the 2006 income statement as $671.2 million.

The previous discussions describe income statements prepared by Nordstrom and McDonald's using U.S. GAAP as promulgated by the FASB in the United States, and by Scania, using IFRS as promulgated by the IASB. These descriptions illustrate the diverse formats and account names used on income statements. Our discussions so far have focused on the *display* of income statement items, and have left several questions unanswered:

1. What are the criteria for recording (recognizing) revenue and expense? That is, what conditions must a transaction meet for a firm to record revenue?

2. How do firms measure revenues and expenses?

The next section discusses these questions.

REVENUE RECOGNITION AND MEASUREMENT

REVENUE RECOGNITION

Revenue recognition refers to the timing and measurement of revenues. Management applies the revenue recognition criteria of authoritative guidance to decide whether a given transaction meets the criteria and so results in recording revenues (and the related expenses). Revenue recognition is among the most complex issues in financial reporting. As of the writing of this textbook, U.S. GAAP contains over 200 pieces of authoritative guidance for recognizing revenues. The quantity and complexity of this guidance result from several factors. First, misreporting of revenues (either reporting revenues before the firm earns them or reporting nonexistent revenues) is the most common form of discovered accounting fraud.[9] Second, firms

---

[8]The IFRS definition of discontinued operations points to a major line of business or a geographical area of operations with cash flows and operating activities that the firm can clearly distinguish for financial reporting purposes. The U.S. GAAP definition allows for a smaller unit to qualify as a discontinued operation than the IFRS definition; U.S. GAAP defines a discontinued operation as a component of a business that is clearly distinguishable both operationally and for financial reporting, including, possibly, an asset group. See the discussion in **Chapter 14**.

[9]In particular, research shows that the largest category of restated financial statements in the U.S. relates to revenues (Z-V. Palmrose, V. Richardson and S. Scholz, "Determinants of Market Reaction to Restatement Announcements," *Journal of Accounting and Economics*, 37, 1: 59–89). In the United States, firms must restate when they have previously issued financial statements that have not complied with authoritative accounting guidance. Restatements therefore include instances of fraud as well as error.

EXHIBIT 4.2   McDonald's Corporation
Balance Sheet

IN MILLIONS, EXCEPT PER SHARE DATA	December 31, **2006**	2005
ASSETS		
Current assets		
Cash and equivalents	$ 2,136.4	$ 4,260.6
Accounts and notes receivable	904.2	793.9
Inventories, at cost, not in excess of market	149.0	144.3
Prepaid expenses and other current assets	435.7	640.2
Discontinued operations		380.0
Total current assets	3,625.3	6,219.0
Other assets		
Investment in and advances to affiliates	1,036.2	1,035.4
Goodwill, net	2,209.2	1,924.4
Miscellaneous	1,307.4	1,236.7
Total other assets	4,552.8	4,196.5
Property and equipment		
Property and equipment, at cost	31,810.2	29,482.5
Accumulated depreciation and amortization	(10,964.5)	(9,909.2)
Net property and equipment	20,845.7	19,573.3
Total assets	$ 29,023.8	$29,988.8
LIABILITIES AND SHAREHOLDERS' EQUITY		
Current liabilities		
Notes payable	$ -	$ 544.0
Accounts payable	834.1	678.0
Income taxes	250.9	569.6
Other taxes	251.4	233.1
Accrued interest	135.1	158.5
Accrued payroll and other liabilities	1,518.9	1,158.1
Current maturities of long-term debt	17.7	658.5
Discontinued operations		107.9
Total current liabilities	3,008.1	4,107.7
Long-term debt	8,416.5	8,934.3
Other long-term liabilities	1,074.9	851.5
Deferred income taxes	1,066.0	949.2
Shareholders' equity		
Preferred stock, no par value; authorized - 165.0 million shares; issued - none		
Common stock, $.01 par value; authorized - 3.5 billion shares; issued - 1,660.6 million shares	16.6	16.6
Additional paid-in capital	3,445.0	2,720.2
Retained earnings	25,845.6	23,516.0
Accumulated other comprehensive income (loss)	(296.7)	(733.1)
Common stock in treasury, at cost; 456.9 and 397.4 million shares	(13,552.2)	(10,373.6)
Total shareholders' equity	15,458.3	15,146.1
Total liabilities and shareholders' equity	$ 29,023.8	$29,988.8

often bundle products and services and sell them in multiple-element arrangements, and each element of the arrangement has the potential to result in revenue recognition. An example of a multiple-element arrangement is the sale of a machine with an extended five-year warranty, installation services, training for employees to learn how to operate the machine, and software upgrades as they become available. This bundled arrangement can contain five or more elements, delivered at different times, but with a single sales price. The selling firm faces difficult recognition and measurement issues in deciding (1) whether a given element of the arrangement has separable revenues, and (2) when, and in what amounts, to recognize revenues for the separate elements of the arrangement.

Chapter 7 discusses revenue recognition. In this chapter we introduce some of the issues. We also distinguish revenues, which increase net assets, from other transactions that increase net assets but do not involve transactions with customers. For example, we distinguish revenues from **gains**, and we distinguish expenses from **losses**. Earlier in this chapter we discussed the sale of a headquarters building at a gain, meaning that the cash or other assets received were greater than the building's book value, or carrying value, at the time of sale. The gain increases net assets and also increases income, but it is not a transaction with a customer that is part of core operations; therefore, the gain is not revenue.[10] Similarly, a loss (meaning that the cash or assets received in a transaction were less than the carrying value of the assets given up) decreases net assets and decreases net income, but it is not part of the firm's core business and therefore is not part of operating expenses.

Not all transactions that increase net assets affect income. For example, issuing common shares of stock for cash increases net assets, but it does not generate revenue (or income). Exchanges of goods and services for assets, such as cash that occur as part of core operations, constitute revenues.

Revenue recognition involves decisions of both timing (when to recognize revenue) and measurement (the amount of revenue to recognize). With regard to timing, a firm could conceivably recognize revenue at the time it acquired or produced items to sell, at the time it delivered items to customers, at the time it collected cash from customers, at some other point in the process, or even continually. U.S. GAAP and IFRS contain revenue recognition criteria that govern the timing of recording revenues.

CRITERIA FOR REVENUE RECOGNITION

As a general principle, under the accrual basis of accounting, the firm recognizes revenue when the transaction meets both of the following conditions:

1. **Completion of the earnings process.** The seller has done all (or nearly all) that it has promised to do for the customer. That is, the seller has delivered all (or nearly all) of the goods and services it has agreed to provide.

2. **Receipt of assets from the customer.** The seller has received cash or some other asset that it can convert to cash, for example, by collecting an account receivable.

The first criterion focuses on the seller's performance. Firms recognize revenues from many sales of goods and services at the time of sale (delivery) because that is often the point of completion of the earnings process, in the sense that the seller has transferred the promised goods to the customer or has performed the promised services. Even if some items remain unperformed (for example, promises to provide warranty services and promises to accept customer returns), the seller can recognize revenues as long as the unperformed items are not too great a portion of the total arrangement with the customer, and the seller can reasonably measure the cost of the unperformed items.[11]

The second criterion for revenue recognition focuses on measuring the amount of cash the seller will ultimately receive. The exchange price between the customer (buyer) and seller represents the assets exchanged by the customer for goods and services, and provides the initial measure of revenue.

APPLICATION OF REVENUE RECOGNITION CRITERIA

To understand the revenue recognition criteria and to see their importance for financial reporting, we consider several examples of transactions that involve the sale of products and services but which may not result in recognizing revenues.

Example 1 Nordstrom sold a pair of shoes for $100 to a customer who pays with cash. Assume the shoes are marked down and the customer cannot return or exchange them. Nordstrom received cash, so the transaction meets the second criterion. The transaction also meets the first criterion because Nordstrom has no additional obligations after the customer has received the shoes. Nordstrom would, therefore, recognize revenue on this transaction and make the following journal entry:

---

[10]The firm would include the gain in nonoperating income and would likely aggregate it with other similar items.

[11]The issue of how unperformed items in an arrangement with a customer affect revenue recognition presents numerous complexities, as discussed in **Chapter 7**.

```
Cash.................................................................  100
     Sales Revenue ..................................................          100
```

Assets	=	Liabilities	+	Shareholders' Equity	(Class.)
+100				+100	IncSt → RE

Sale of merchandise for $100 cash.

Example 2 Nordstrom sold a pair of shoes for $100 to a customer who paid with a Nordstrom credit card. Again, assume the shoes are marked down and the customer cannot return or exchange them. Nordstrom has received a promise of cash payment (an account receivable), so the transaction meets the second criterion. (We revisit the measurement of accounts receivable in **Chapter 7** when we take up the issue of customers who do not pay.) The transaction also meets the first criterion because Nordstrom has no additional obligations. Nordstrom would, therefore, recognize revenue on this transaction and make the following journal entry:

```
Accounts Receivable .................................................  100
     Sales Revenue ..................................................          100
```

Assets	=	Liabilities	+	Shareholders' Equity	(Class.)
+100				+100	IncSt → RE

Sale of merchandise on account for $100.

Example 3 Nordstrom sells gift cards for cash. Nordstrom has promised to provide merchandise to the holder of the gift card up to the amount stated on the card, so Nordstrom has an obligation. Assume that gift cards expire five years after the issue date so that Nordstrom has no obligation to provide merchandise to the cardholder after the expiration date. If Nordstrom sells a gift card for $100 on the first day of its fiscal year, Nordstrom expects to deliver on its promise of providing merchandise to the cardholder sometime during the next 60 months. Nordstrom has received $100 cash, so the transaction meets criterion 2. However, Nordstrom has not met criterion 1. It has incurred an obligation to perform in the future, equal to the amount of cash received, $100; this is an example of a deferred performance obligation, discussed further in **Chapter 7**. At the time of the gift card purchase, Nordstrom would record the following journal entry:

```
Cash.................................................................  100
     Advances from Customers .............................          100
```

Assets	=	Liabilities	+	Shareholders' Equity	(Class.)
+100		+100			

At the time of the gift card purchase, to record the sale of the gift card for cash.

Nordstrom recognizes revenue as it performs by delivering merchandise to the cardholder. If the cardholder fails to use the entire $100 amount by the expiration date, Nordstrom will recognize as revenue any remaining amount on the card.[12] If the cardholder uses the card

---

[12]This treatment is just one example of several possible accounting treatments for unused gift card balances. In this example, there is a clear expiration date. Some gift cards have no expiration dates, and some states in the United States have laws that either specify a minimum duration for the cards—for example, five years—or forbid expiration altogether. After some period, which varies by jurisdiction and is specified by law, the value of an unused gift card becomes unclaimed property. Jurisdiction-specific laws also specify the treatment of unclaimed property; for example, the property may revert to a governmental body. As a practical matter, many retailers in the United States establish their gift-card operations in states whose laws will allow the retailer to keep unused balances of gift cards.

twice, to purchase a $55 sweater and a $10 pair of socks, Nordstrom would make the following journal entries to recognize revenues.[13]

| Advances from Customers | .... | 55 | |
| Sales Revenue | .... | | 55 |

Assets	=	Liabilities	+	Shareholders' Equity	(Class.)
		−55		+55	IncSt → RE

At the time of the sweater sale, to recognize the revenue on the sale of the sweater.

| Advances from Customers | .... | 10 | |
| Sales Revenue | .... | | 10 |

Assets	=	Liabilities	+	Shareholders' Equity	(Class.)
		−10		+10	IncSt → RE

At the time of the sock sale, to recognize the revenue on the sale of the socks.

At the expiration date, Nordstrom would recognize the remaining amount on the card as revenue with the following journal entry:

| Advances from Customers | .... | 35 | |
| Sales Revenue | .... | | 35 |

Assets	=	Liabilities	+	Shareholders' Equity	(Class.)
		−35		+35	IncSt → RE

To recognize revenue on the unused portion of the gift card at the end of 60 months when the card has expired.

Example 4 Another buyer of a gift card like the one in **Example 3** paid with a Nordstrom credit card. The only difference is that the asset Nordstrom received is an account receivable, not cash. Therefore, the revenue-related journal entries are identical to those shown for **Example 3** except that the first journal entry shows a debit to Accounts Receivable rather than a debit to Cash:

| Accounts Receivable | .... | 100 | |
| Advances from Customers | .... | | 100 |

Assets	=	Liabilities	+	Shareholders' Equity	(Class.)
+100		+100			

At the time of the gift card sale, to record the sale of the gift card on account.

In both **Example 1** and **Example 3** Nordstrom receives cash from a customer, so both transactions meet criterion 2 for revenue recognition. The transaction in **Example 1** also meets criterion 1 because the customer has possession of the shoes, so Nordstrom recognizes revenue, whereas the transaction in **Example 3** does not satisfy criterion 1 until the customer uses the gift card or the gift card expires. In **Examples 2** and **4** Nordstrom did not receive cash from a customer. Even so, in both examples the transactions meet criterion 2 because Nordstrom expects to collect the account receivable in cash. The transaction in **Example 2** meets

---

[13]Nordstrom would also recognize cost of sales; we do not include these journal entries.

criterion 1 because the customer takes possession of the shoes. The transaction in **Example 4**, however, does not yet meet criterion 1. **Examples 1** to **4** illustrate an important concept in accrual accounting—the timing of the receipt of cash from a customer does not usually affect the timing of revenue recognition. What matters is whether the seller has received assets that it can convert to cash and whether it has performed all, or nearly all, of its obligations to deliver goods and services. Whether the parties to the transaction have exchanged cash does not generally affect the timing of revenue recognition.[14]

REVENUE MEASUREMENT

The seller measures revenue as the amount of cash, or the cash-equivalent value of other assets, that it receives from customers. As a starting point, this amount is the exchange price between buyer and seller at the time of sale. If the firm has not performed all of its obligations, however, it will need to adjust the exchange price to reflect those unperformed obligations. Two common examples of adjustments are sales discounts and allowances, and sales returns.

Sales Discounts and Allowances Customers may take advantage of discounts for prompt payment, and the seller may grant allowances for unsatisfactory merchandise. In these cases, the exchange price exceeds the cash collected and retained by the seller. The seller must estimate the amounts for **sales discounts and allowances** and reduce the related revenues recognized by those amounts.

Sales Returns Customers may return goods for cash refunds or, if the customer has not yet paid, for cancellation of the customer's obligation to pay. If so, the seller will collect and keep cash in smaller amounts than the sum of the exchange prices. The seller must estimate the amounts of expected **sales returns** and reduce revenues recognized by those amounts.

Example 5 Based on historical data, Nordstrom estimates that customers will return goods amounting to 1% of its sales. The customers will receive full refunds or store credit. If total sales in an accounting period are $600 million, Nordstrom will recognize an estimated liability for sales returns of $6 (= .01 × $600) million, recorded as follows:

| Sales Revenue | | | | | 6,000,000 |
| Estimated Liability for Sales Returns | | | | | | 6,000,000 |

Assets	=	Liabilities	+	Shareholders' Equity	(Class.)
		+6,000,000		−6,000,000	IncSt → RE

To recognize the estimate of sales that customers will return.

The firm does not record sales returns, allowances, and discounts for individual sales of merchandise. Instead, it records adjustments to sales revenue in adjusting entries at the end of each reporting period, which it bases on total sales of that period. **Chapter 7** considers how Nordstrom will account for returned items.

EXPENSE RECOGNITION AND MEASUREMENT

TIMING OF EXPENSE RECOGNITION

Assets provide future benefits, and expenses measure the consumption of those benefits. Timing of **expense recognition** focuses on *when* the firm consumes the benefits. The critical question

---

[14]The exception, discussed in **Chapter 7**, occurs when the assets received from the customer are so uncertain of collection that the seller cannot reasonably measure the amount of the expected collection. When the firm's ability to collect cash is at substantial risk, the transaction would not meet criterion 2, and the firm would delay revenue recognition until it collects cash.

is, "When does the firm consume the benefits of an asset?" That is, when does the asset leave the balance sheet and become an expense on the income statement?

Balance Sheet   **Income Statement**

Assets ─────────────→ Expenses (which reduce net income and retained earnings on the balance sheet)

CRITERIA FOR EXPENSE RECOGNITION

The firm recognizes an expense when either of the following conditions holds.

1. *The consumption of the asset results from a transaction that leads to the recognition of revenue.* The consumption of the benefit embodied in the asset is an expense in the period when the firm recognizes revenue. For example, a sale of merchandise that results in the seller's recognizing revenue consumes the benefits of the inventory asset and results in an increase in the expense called Cost of Goods Sold. The amount of this expense is determined by the **product costs** associated with the inventory. This treatment, the **matching convention**, matches the timing of some expenses with revenue recognition.

2. *The consumption of the asset results from the passage of time.* When the firm consumes the benefits of an asset over time, that cost becomes an expense of the period when the firm consumes the benefits. For example, the firm consumes benefits of this month's rent on the warehouse during the current month. Therefore, the firm reports the cost as part of this month's expenses (that is, **period expenses**). Most administrative expenditures are period expenses. Another period expense, introduced in **Chapter 2**, results from the expenditures on advertising and research, which the firm must recognize as expense in the period of expenditure, regardless of the firm's expectation of future benefits.

RECOGNITION OF PRODUCT COSTS

Cost of Goods Sold Reports the Decrease in Inventory
A seller of goods can easily associate (or match) the consumption of the benefits of the asset sold with revenues from its sale. Specifically, at the time of sale and revenue recognition, the asset (inventory) leaves the seller's balance sheet. The seller recognizes revenue along with a reduction in an asset (inventory). The firm records the cost of goods sold expense in the same amount as the decrease in the asset, which is the amount by which inventory decreases.

Retail Firms and Merchandise Inventory
A merchandising firm purchases inventory for resale. The merchandiser does not change the physical form of the inventory, so it performs no incremental work and adds nothing to the acquisition cost of the inventory after it is purchased. The inventory appears on the merchandiser's balance sheet initially as an asset, measured at acquisition cost.[15] When the firm sells the items, it recognizes the cost of the inventory as an expense (cost of goods sold) on the income statement.

Manufacturing Firms and Inventory
A manufacturing firm, on the other hand, incurs costs as it produces goods by changing the physical form of raw materials. For a manufacturing firm, product costs are the costs incurred in manufacturing goods for sale. The costs to produce finished goods inventory do not become expenses until the firm sells the product; prior to sale, these costs represent the transformation of assets from one form into another. Three types of manufacturing costs become product costs: (1) direct material costs (or raw material costs), (2) direct labor costs, and (3) manufacturing overhead costs (sometimes called *indirect manufacturing costs*). Conceptually, a firm can readily associate direct material costs and direct labor costs with products.[16] For example, one can measure both the cost of a specific quantity of aluminum used to make a lawn chair and the cost of the labor

---

[15]**Chapter 8** discusses the accounting for inventory in detail. Authoritative guidance requires in some cases, permits in others, the firm to include certain costs, such as transportation costs, along with the acquisition cost in the amount reported for inventory on the balance sheet.

[16]Firms with complex manufacturing processes can track such costs only with difficulty, unless they use estimates and averages.

to make the chair. In contrast, manufacturing overhead includes costs that the firm cannot associate with particular products, for example, expenditures for supervisors' salaries, factory utilities, property taxes, insurance, and depreciation on manufacturing plant and equipment. The firm consumes the benefits of each of these items as it produces inventory for sale, so the costs are called *indirect costs* because they jointly benefit all goods produced during the period, not any one particular item. Once the firm has accumulated all the manufacturing costs incurred during a period in the product cost accounts, such as Work-in-Process, the firm applies allocation mechanisms to apportion the costs to specific products. (Courses in managerial and cost accounting teach these allocation methods.)

Inventory accounts accumulate or accrue the costs of direct material, direct labor, and manufacturing overhead. These inventory items are assets until the firm sells them to customers. The balance sheet reports the costs of incomplete items as Work-in-Process Inventory and the cost of goods ready for sale as Finished Goods Inventory.

To summarize, the direct material, direct labor, and manufacturing overhead costs incurred to produce products for sale are product costs, which represent assets transformed from one form to another, as the manufacturing process converts these assets into finished goods. The cost of completed products remains on the balance sheet as Finished Goods assets until the firm sells the products; upon sale, the cost of the assets becomes a cost of goods sold expense. **Chapter 8** discusses the accounting for manufacturing costs.

RECOGNITION OF PERIOD EXPENSES

Many expenditures benefit specific accounting periods and do not benefit specific revenue transactions. The firm therefore cannot link the timing of recognition of the expenses associated with these expenditures to revenue recognition from specific sales. A common example of a period expense is the cost of management, including the president's salary, accounting and information systems costs, and support activity costs such as legal services, employee training, and corporate planning. These *administrative costs* do not relate directly to products produced or sold, and the firm recognizes them as expenses when it consumes their benefits in the accounting period. The firm treats them, therefore, as period expenses.

Another example of a period expense is the cost of marketing or selling products, for example, salaries and commissions of the sales staff and costs to produce catalogs and other sales literature. The firm recognizes those costs as expenses in the accounting period when it consumes them. The firm incurs some marketing costs, such as advertising, with the intent of providing future benefits. As discussed in **Chapter 2**, U.S. GAAP and IFRS preclude the recognition of these costs as assets. The reasoning for this treatment results from the asset recognition criterion that the firm be able to measure the future benefits with sufficient reliability.

EXPENSE MEASUREMENT

Expenses measure the consumption of assets during an accounting period, so the basis for expense measurement is the same as the measurement of the consumed asset. If the firm measures an asset at acquisition cost on the balance sheet, it also measures expenses based on the acquisition cost of the asset consumed. **Examples 6** and **7** illustrate the concepts of product costs, period expenses, and expense measurement, using journal entries and the dual effects balance sheet equation.

Example 6 In **Example 1** Nordstrom sold a pair of shoes for $100 cash. From **Example 1**, we know this transaction meets the two revenue recognition criteria resulting in the following journal entry:

Cash   100

    Sales Revenue   100

Assets	=	Liabilities	+	Shareholders' Equity	(Class.)
+100				+100	IncSt → RE

Sale of merchandise for $100.

Nordstrom must also show the consumption of the asset sold—the shoes in inventory. If Nordstrom originally purchased the shoes from its shoe vendor for $70, Nordstrom would record the following journal entry to recognize as an expense the product costs associated with the sale of the shoes:

Cost of Goods Sold   70

  Inventory   70

Assets	=	Liabilities	+	Shareholders' Equity	(Class.)
−70				−70	IncSt → RE

To record the reduction of inventory associated with the sale of merchandise.

This transaction affects Nordstrom's income statement; it also affects Nordstrom's balance sheet when revenue and expense accounts are closed to the Retained Earnings account. The revenue part of the transaction increases Retained Earnings by $100, and the expense part of the transaction decreases Retained Earnings by $70. The net effect increases Retained Earnings by $30 (before taxes).

Example 7 Before each of its two big semiannual sales, Nordstrom prints and mails advertisements to its preferred customers and also prints and installs in its stores a variety of signs announcing the sales. Assume that these expenditures cost $2 million per year. Clearly, Nordstrom management believes that spending $2 million to promote the semiannual sales will increase gross margin (sales revenues less cost of sales) by at least $2 million. However, it cannot establish a causal link between any specific promotional expenditure and the sale of a specific item. As a result, Nordstrom treats the promotion costs as period expenses in the period incurred:

Advertising and Promotion Expenses   2,000,000

  Cash.   2,000,000

Assets	=	Liabilities	+	Shareholders' Equity	(Class.)
−2,000,000				−2,000,000	IncSt → RE

To record $2 million of advertising and promotion costs.

PROBLEM 4.1 for Self-Study

Revenue and expense recognition. Crandall SA uses the accrual basis of accounting and recognizes revenues at the time it sells goods or renders services. For each transaction, indicate the amount of revenue or expense that Crandall recognizes *during April*, and show the journal entry or entries that Crandall would make *in April*.

a. Collects €15,000 cash from customers during April for merchandise sold and delivered in March. The cost of the merchandise to the firm was €8,000.

b. Sells merchandise to customers during April for €24,500 cash. The merchandise cost the firm €6,500.

c. Sells to customers, on account, merchandise with a selling price of €105,000. The firm expects to collect the cash during May. The merchandise cost the firm €82,000 when it purchased the items from its supplier last month. The firm has not yet paid the supplier for the merchandise.

d. Pays suppliers €45,500 during April for merchandise received by the firm from its suppliers and sold to customers during March for €109,000.

e. Pays suppliers €50,000 during April for merchandise received from its suppliers and sold to customers during April. Crandall sold the merchandise for €90,400.

(continued)

> **f.** Receives from suppliers and sells to customers during April merchandise that cost €20,000. The selling price of the merchandise to the customer was €38,000, all on account. The firm expects to pay the supplier during May.
>
> **g.** Receives from suppliers during April merchandise that cost €101,000 and that the firm expects to pay for during May. The firm also expects to sell the merchandise in May for €124,000.
>
> **h.** Receives €26,500 from customers for merchandise that the firm will deliver in May. The firm does not yet have the merchandise and expects to acquire it in May for €23,000.

COMPREHENSIVE INCOME

Net income under U.S. GAAP, or profit under IFRS, reports increases in net assets from certain transactions with nonowners such as customers. Net income, or profit, does not include all transactions with nonowners. Both U.S. GAAP and IFRS define net income, or profit, for the current period to exclude certain events and transactions with nonowners that change net assets. Both U.S. GAAP and IFRS use the term **Other Comprehensive Income (OCI)** to refer to changes in net assets that are not transactions with owners and that do not appear on the income statement. Both U.S. GAAP and IFRS specify the items that do not appear in the income statement and that are included in other comprehensive income

The sum of net income and other comprehensive income is **Comprehensive Income**, which includes all changes in net assets for a period except for changes arising from transactions with owners. (Typical transactions with owners include dividends, share issuances, and share repurchases). In all the examples considered in this and preceding chapters, the effect of the event or transaction on net income equals the effect on comprehensive income. Later chapters present items that other comprehensive income, in contrast to net income, includes. Thus,

$$\text{Net Income} + \text{Other Comprehensive Income} = \text{Comprehensive Income}$$

The items reported in other comprehensive income relate to changes in the amount of assets and liabilities resulting from transactions with nonowners—transactions whose effects authoritative guidance has chosen to exclude from net income. Both U.S. GAAP and IFRS require firms to report the cumulative effect of other comprehensive income in a balance sheet account called **Accumulated Other Comprehensive Income (AOCI)**. Accumulated Other Comprehensive Income relates to Other Comprehensive Income just as Retained Earnings relates to Net Income, when the firm declares no dividends.

$$\text{Retained Earnings (beginning)} + \text{Net Income} - \text{Dividends} = \text{Retained Earnings (ending)}$$

$$\begin{array}{c} \text{Accumulated Other} \\ \text{Comprehensive Income} \\ \text{(beginning)} \end{array} + \begin{array}{c} \text{Other} \\ \text{Comprehensive} \\ \text{Income} \end{array} = \begin{array}{c} \text{Accumulated Other} \\ \text{Comprehensive Income} \\ \text{(ending)} \end{array}$$

To see these relations, refer to the balance sheet, and statements of income and other comprehensive income, of Nordstrom in **Exhibits 1.1**, **1.2**, and **1.4** on pages 8, 9, and 11 and those of Scania in **Exhibits 1.5**, **1.7**, and **1.8** on pages 12, 15, and 16. In each accounting period, the net amount of Other Comprehensive Income (Loss) increases (decreases) the balance of Accumulated Other Comprehensive Income, just as in each accounting period the amount of Net Income (Loss) increases (decreases) the balance of Retained Earnings (after adjusting for dividends).

While no general principle describes the nature of items excluded from net income and included in Other Comprehensive Income, they tend to arise from remeasurements of assets and liabilities (often, remeasurements at fair value as described in **Chapter 3**) and not from transactions. For example, IFRS permits but does not require firms to revalue certain noncurrent assets upward to reflect increases in fair value in excess of acquisition cost. Under IFRS, such a revaluation remeasurement increases assets (because the firm now records an existing asset on the balance sheet at a larger number) and increases Other Comprehensive Income. These increases are accumulated in a shareholders' equity account, Revaluation

Surplus.[17] **Chapter 9** discusses the accounting for asset revaluations. As an example, suppose the firm revalues the Land asset by €50; the journal entry to record this revaluation is:

Land.   50

    Other Comprehensive Income   50

Assets	=	Liabilities	+	Shareholders' Equity	(Class.)
+50				+50	OCI → Equity (Revaluation Surplus)

To record an increase in the fair value of land (revaluation) of €50 as permitted by IFRS. OCI stands for Other Comprehensive Income, and the revaluations accumulate in shareholders' equity, in the Revaluation Surplus account.

Both U.S. GAAP and IFRS require the presentation of an income statement and the presentation of the items of Other Comprehensive Income. U.S. GAAP permits three reporting formats, described next. Starting January 1, 2009, IFRS permits free choice between the first two reporting formats.

1. A single statement of comprehensive income that shows *all* the changes in net assets except from transactions with owners;[18]

2. A two-statement presentation that includes an income statement (for example, like Scania's in **Exhibit 1.6**) and a separate statement of comprehensive income.

3. A separate display of the items comprising Other Comprehensive Income within a statement of changes in shareholders' equity. Firms applying U.S. GAAP use this alternative more often than the other two. The **Glossary** illustrates this format at *Other Comprehensive Income*.

Chapter 14 discusses the reporting of comprehensive income.

INTERPRETING AND ANALYZING THE INCOME STATEMENT

Users of financial statements often analyze the ratio of net income to revenues, called the **profit margin percentage**, when evaluating profitability. Consider the following firms and their profit margin percentages for a recent year:

- Nordstrom (retail clothing): 7.9%.
- Scania (engine and truck manufacturing): 8.4%.
- Colgate Palmolive (consumer and pet products): 11.1%.
- Polo Ralph Lauren (clothing design and manufacture): 9.3%.
- McDonald's (retail food): 16.4%.
- Boeing (airplane manufacture): 3.6%.

Can we conclude that Boeing and McDonald's have the worst and best profitability, respectively? Do differences in profit margin percentages signal differences in operating performance, and do they have economic or strategic explanations? Answering these questions requires understanding both the income statement and investments in assets that firms in different industries must have in order to generate revenues. In this section, we focus on tools for understanding the income statement, recognizing that the analysis of profitability and operating performance also requires consideration of the assets used to generate profits.

---

[17]This accounting, which accumulates the increases in a shareholders' equity account, applies to noncurrent assets other than investment properties. The latter are buildings and land held for rental or price appreciation and not for use or sale as part of the firm's normal operations. Revaluations of investment properties are included in net income.

[18]IFRS allows the Statement of Comprehensive Income to be called the Statement of Recognized Income and Expense.

COMMON-SIZE INCOME STATEMENT

One tool for analysis of the income statement, a **common-size income statement**, expresses each expense and net income as a percentage of revenues. (**Chapter 3** introduces the common-size balance sheet, which expresses each balance sheet account as a percentage of total assets.) An analyst can use a common-size income statement to study over-time changes or among-firm differences in the relations among revenues, expenses, and net income and to identify relations that the analyst should explore further.

Time-Series Profitability Analysis To illustrate a **time-series analysis** for a single firm, **Exhibit 4.3** presents a common-size income statement for Nordstrom for fiscal years ended in January or early February of 2007, 2006, and 2005.

Nordstrom experienced an increasing profit margin percentage (= net income divided by sales) over the three years, from 5.5% for the year ended January 29, 2005, to 7.1% for the year ended January 28, 2006, to 7.9% for the year ended February 3, 2007. The increasing profit margin results from four factors:

1. A decreasing cost of goods sold to sales percentage.
2. A decreasing selling, general, and administrative (SG&A) expense to sales percentage.
3. A decreasing interest expense to sales percentage.
4. An increasing other income to sales percentage.

Sales increased by 10.9% between the years ending in 2006 and 2007 and by 8.3% from the years ending in 2005 and 2006. The fact that sales increased year-to-year while both cost of goods sold and SG&A decreased as a percentage of sales suggests that economies of scale affect both of these costs. That is, neither cost increased proportionally with sales; rather, both increased at a rate smaller than the sales increase. If employees do not work at full capacity, for example, the firm need not increase the number of employees at the same rate that sales increase. Or, perhaps the costs of information systems and accounting and legal costs do not increase proportionally with sales. Regardless of the underlying causes, sales increases coupled with less-than-proportional increases in both cost of goods sold and selling and administrative expenses explain the decline in these expense percentages.

Cross-Section Profitability Analysis We illustrate a **cross-section analysis** using the common-size income statements for three other retailing firms: Wal-Mart Stores Inc. (**Exhibit 4.4**), The Gap Inc. (**Exhibit 4.5**), and Saks Inc. (**Exhibit 4.6**). Wal-Mart Stores ("Wal-Mart") is the world's largest retailing firm. Its discount and superstores segment (which includes the retailing firm and its online stores) accounts for about two-thirds of total Wal-Mart sales; the remainder comes from its Sam's Club segment (about 12% of sales) and international operations

EXHIBIT 4.3

Nordstrom Inc.
Common-Size Income Statements
(in thousands)

Fiscal year ending	February 3, 2007		January 28, 2006		January 29, 2005	
Net Sales	$ 8,560,698	100.0%	$ 7,722,860	100.0%	$ 7,131,388	100.0%
Cost of Sales and Related Buying and Occupancy Costs	(5,353,949)	62.5	(4,888,023)	63.3	(4,559,388)	63.9
Gross Profit	$ 3,206,749	37.5%	$ 2,834,837	36.7%	$ 2,572,000	36.1%
Selling, General and Administrative Expenses	(2,296,863)	26.8	(2,100,666)	27.2	(2,020,233)	28.3
Operating Income	$ 909,886	10.6%	$ 734,171	9.5%	$ 551,767	7.7%
Interest Expense, net	(42,758)	0.5	(45,300)	0.6	(77,428)	1.1
Other Income Including Finance Charges, net	238,525	−2.8	196,354	−2.5	172,942	−2.4
Earnings Before Income Taxes	$ 1,105,653	12.9%	$ 885,225	11.5%	$ 647,281	9.1%
Income Tax Expense	(427,654)	5.0	(333,886)	4.3	(253,831)	3.6
Net Earnings	$ 677,999	7.9%	$ 551,339	7.1%	$ 393,450	5.5%

| EXHIBIT 4.4 | Wal-Mart Stores, Inc. Common-Size Income Statements (in millions) |

Fiscal year ending	January 31, 2007		January 31, 2006		January 31, 2005	
Revenues:						
Net Sales	$344,992	99.0%	$308,945	99.0%	$281,488	99.0%
Membership and Other Income	3,658	1.0	3,156	1.0	2,822	1.0
Total Sales Revenue	$348,650	100.0%	$312,101	100.0%	$284,310	100.0%
Costs and Expenses:						
Cost of Sales	264,152	75.8	237,649	76.1	216,832	76.3
Operating Selling, General, and Administrative Expenses	64,001	18.4	55,739	17.9	50,178	17.6
Operating Income	$ 20,497	5.9%	$ 18,713	6.0%	$ 17,300	6.1%
Interest:						
Debt	1,549	0.4	1,171	0.4	931	0.3
Capital Leases	260	0.1	249	0.1	253	0.1
Interest Income	(280)	−0.1	(242)	−0.1	(204)	−0.1
Interest, net	1,529	0.4	1,178	0.4	980	0.3
Income from Continuing Operations Before Income Taxes	$ 18,968	5.4%	$ 17,535	5.6%	$ 16,320	5.7%
Provision for income taxes:						
Current	6,276	1.8	5,932	1.9	5,326	1.9
Deferred	89	0.0	(129)	0.0	263	0.1
	6,365	1.8	5,803	1.9	5,589	2.0
Income from Continuing Operations Before Minority Interest	$ 12,603	3.6%	$ 11,732	3.8%	$ 10,731	3.8%
Minority Interest	(425)	−0.1	(324)	−0.1	(249)	−0.1
Income from Continuing Operations	$ 12,178	3.5%	$ 11,408	3.7%	$ 10,482	3.7%
Loss from discontinued operations, Net of Tax	(894)	−0.3	(177)	−0.1	(215)	−0.1
Net income	$ 11,284	3.2%	$ 11,231	3.6%	$ 10,267	3.6%

| EXHIBIT 4.5 | The Gap Inc. Common-Size Income Statements (in millions) |

Fiscal year ending	February 3, 2007		January 28, 2006		January 29, 2005	
Net Sales	$15,943	100.0%	$16,023	100.0%	$16,267	100.0%
Cost of Sales and Related Buying and Occupancy Costs	10,294	64.6	10,154	63.4	9,886	60.8
Gross Profit	$ 5,649	35.4%	$ 5,869	36.6%	$ 6,381	39.2%
Operating Expenses	4,475	28.1	4,124	25.7	4,296	26.4
Loss on Early Retirement of Debt	—		—		105	0.6
Interest Expense	41	0.3	45	0.3	167	1.0
Interest Income	(131)	−0.8	(93)	0.6	(59)	0.4
Earnings Before Income Taxes	$ 1,264	7.9%	$ 1,793	11.2%	$ 1,872	11.5%
Income Tax Expense	486	3.0	680	4.2	722	4.4
Net Earnings	$ 778	4.9%	$ 1,113	6.9%	$ 1,150	7.1%

EXHIBIT 4.6

Saks Incorporated
Common-Size Income Statements
(in thousands)

Fiscal Year Ending	February 3, 2007		January 28, 2006		January 29, 2005	
Net Sales	$2,940,003	100.0%	$2,778,333	100.0%	$2,766,977	100.0%
Cost of Sales and Related Buying and Occupancy Costs	1,804,294	61.4	1,754,833	63.2	1,681,297	60.8
Gross Margin	$1,135,709	38.6%	$1,023,500	36.8%	$1,085,680	39.2%
Selling, General and Administrative Expenses	819,218	27.9	830,495	29.9	796,574	28.8
Other Operating Expenses:						
Property and Equipment Rentals	114,718	3.9	109,000	3.9	106,677	3.9
Depreciation and Amortization	128,522	4.4	133,556	4.8	130,131	4.7
Taxes Other Than Income Taxes	80,614	2.7	85,016	3.1	80,042	2.9
Store Pre-Opening Costs	597	0.0	1,227	0.0	1,993	0.1
Impairments and Other Dispositions	12,443	0.4	(7,848)	−0.3	20,768	0.8
Operating Loss	$ (20,403)	−0.7%	$ (127,496)	−4.6%	$ (50,505)	−1.8%
Interest Expense	(50,136)	1.7	(77,188)	2.8	(104,773)	3.8
Gain (loss) on Early Extinguishment of Debt	7	0.0	(29,375)	−1.1	—	
Other Income, net	28,407	1.0	7,705	0.3	4,048	0.1
Loss Before Income Taxes	$ (42,125)	−1.4%	$ (226,804)	−8.2%	$ (151,230)	−5.5%
Benefits from Income Taxes	(34,783)	−1.2	(93,161)	−3.4	(71,024)	−2.6
Loss from Continuing Operations	$ (7,342)	−0.2%	$ (133,643)	−4.8%	$ (80,206)	−2.9%
Discontinued Operations:						
Income from Discontinued Operations	$ 193,377	6.6%	$ 321,443	11.6%	$ 235,468	8.5%
Provision for Income Taxes	132,293	4.5	165,452	6.0	94,177	3.4
Income from Discontinued Operations	$ 61,084	2.1%	$ 155,991	5.6%	$ 141,291	5.1%
Net Earnings	$ 53,742	1.8%	$ 22,348	0.8%	$ 61,085	2.2%

(22% of sales). The Gap Inc. ("The Gap") consists of The Gap stores, Old Navy stores, and Banana Republic stores, and the online store formats for each. Saks Inc. ("Saks") consists of Saks Fifth Avenue, Off Fifth, and Club Libby stores. During the fiscal years ended January 28, 2006, and February 3, 2007, Saks sold Proffitt's, McRae's, Northern Department Store Group, and Parisian, so it reported the results for these stores as discontinued operations.

We compare Nordstrom to other retailers. Comparing retailers with nonretailers for profit margin ratios makes little sense; the noncomparability results from the different business models—asset and financial structures—that distinguish Nordstrom from companies such as Scania, Boeing, McDonald's, or Colgate Palmolive. Business models, and their strategic implementations, create across-firm differences in risk and performance, which in turn affect the results reported on financial statements. We use a broad industry, retailing, to hold approximately constant certain factors that we expect to differ across firms with different business models, including the degree of product differentiation, barriers to entry, the extent of competition, and the sensitivity of customer demand to price. **Chapter 6** introduces ratios, such as rates of return on assets or on shareholders' equity, where comparisons across different industries have meaning.

We recognize that our sample of retailers includes variation in business models but less variation than would be present in a sample that included nonretailers. The objective is to hold constant the effects of business models by identifying a peer group, using industry classification as a primary factor, and other factors, such as the size and geographic diversity of operations as possible secondary factors. For example, consider Wal-Mart as a firm comparable to Nordstrom. Both are retailers, but Wal-Mart is over 40 times the size of Nordstrom as measured by revenues, it sells a broader array of products and services than does Nordstrom, it operates more internationally than does Nordstrom, and it has a membership-based discount operation (Sam's Club), which differs markedly from any business in which Nordstrom operates. Without further analysis, one cannot see how these differences affect comparisons between Nordstrom's and Wal-Mart's performances. In addition, Wal-Mart advertises everyday low pricing, which, holding other factors constant, we expect to lead to lower profit margins. Indeed, Wal-Mart obtains 3.2 cents of every sales dollar as net income, compared to 7.9 cents for each Nordstrom sales dollar.

Does the difference in profit margin percentages imply that Nordstrom has larger net income than Wal-Mart? No, as evidenced by Wal-Mart's net income of $11,284 million compared to $678 million for Nordstrom the difference arises because of Wal-Mart's larger investment base; firms with a larger investment base will generally earn larger amounts of income, even if their profit margin percentages are lower.

An analyst might conclude that Wal-Mart is not a good comparison firm for Nordstrom and look instead to The Gap or Saks to judge Nordstrom's performance. Before we perform such a comparison, we introduce a note of caution about formats. Because authoritative guidance does not specify the format, labeling, or aggregation level that firms should use in their income statements, firms often report otherwise similar information differently, impeding direct comparisons of income statement components. Knowing this, a user of financial statements will combine information in a way that allows for consistent comparisons across firms or will limit the analysis to similar items.

We turn now to the income statements of Nordstrom and The Gap. The format and presentation are similar; for example, both firms report cost of sales and occupancy costs as a combined figure, and both report a single class of operating costs apart from cost of sales, albeit with different names (Nordstrom reports selling, general, and administrative expenses; The Gap reports operating expenses). Nothing guarantees that these accounts capture the same items for the two firms, but the fact that neither firm displays other operating expenses suggests that they do.

Nordstrom's profit margin percentage of 7.9% for the year ended February 3, 2007 (the ratio of net income to sales revenues), is about 1.6 times The Gap's ratio of 4.9% for the same fiscal year. Inspection of the components of the two income statements reveals that both operating and nonoperating items contributed to Nordstrom's higher profit margin. Nordstrom has a higher ratio of operating income to sales revenues (10.6%) than does The Gap (7.4%), which we can calculate as operating income of $1,174 (= $5,649 − $4,475) divided by sales revenues of $15,943. Nordstrom's higher operating income ratio comes from both a lower cost of sales ratio (62.5% versus 64.6%) and a lower ratio of other operating expenses to sales (26.8% versus 28.1%). In terms of nonoperating activity, Nordstrom reports other income of 2.8%, compared to The Gap's 0.8%.

Based on an analysis of customers, some analysts would view Saks as more comparable to Nordstrom than The Gap. Differences in format, labels, presentation, and aggregation of income statement items reported by Saks versus Nordstrom, however, make comparisons of these two difficult. For example, in addition to cost of sales and occupancy costs, and selling, general, and administrative costs, Saks reports amounts for four other operating expense items: property and equipment rentals, depreciation and amortization, taxes other than income taxes, and store preopening costs. In aggregate these costs are $324 million, or about 11% of Saks' revenues for the year ended February 3, 2007. That Nordstrom's income statement omits display of these four expense items does *not* mean Nordstrom has no such costs—it almost surely does. Nordstrom likely aggregates these four expenses with other expense items, probably cost of sales and occupancy costs, and selling, general, and administrative expenditures.

One implication of these likely differences in presentation is that the user probably would not want to compare Nordstrom's cost of sales (or SG&A) percentage to Saks' cost of sales (or SG&A) percentage, because the reported line items do not contain the same kinds of costs. If Nordstrom aggregates into its cost of sales and SG&A the four types of other operating expenses reported separately by Saks, then Nordstrom's cost of sales and SG&A percentages will exceed Saks for no economically significant reason. Unfortunately, users of the financial statements cannot usually adjust for these effects because firms do not disclose sufficient disaggregated information. Users can, however, ascertain a level of aggregation of the available data that includes similar cost items in broader categories. For example, the user can calculate and compare the operating income to sales revenue percentages of the two firms;

this comparison is appropriate as long as the user has identified all operating expenses of the two firms. For Nordstrom the operating income to sales percentage is 10.6% and for Saks it is −0.7% (that is, Saks reported an operating loss for the year ended February 3, 2007).

Even for firms in similar lines of business, the formats of income statements may be so noncomparable as to preclude any comparisons of line items and subtotals. In such cases the only appropriate comparison is based on the profit margin percentages because, by definition, net income is comparable across all firms that report under the same accounting standards. Furthermore, because net income aggregates all items on the income statement, it is unaffected by choices concerning format, presentation, labeling, and aggregation of income statement items. For all of these reasons, the profit margin percentage (the ratio of net income to sales revenues) is a widely used ratio in evaluating and comparing operating performance of similar firms. However, profit margin percentages are not comparable unless the firms have similar business models. **Chapter 6** shows how to make meaningful comparisons of dissimilar firms.

SUMMARY

Net income or profit for a period is the difference between revenues from selling goods and services and the expenses incurred to generate those revenues, plus some gains or losses of the period. If the expenses plus losses exceed the revenues plus gains, the result is a net loss. U.S. GAAP and IFRS require the accrual basis of accounting, which detaches the recognition of revenue from the receipt of cash. A seller recognizes revenues when it has performed all, or nearly all, of its obligations to the customer and when it has received cash or an asset that is convertible to cash. The firm recognizes and reports expenses that have a causal link with revenues, such as cost of sales, in the same period as the related revenues. It recognizes and reports other expenses in the period when the firm consumes the benefits of the assets.

Interpreting the income statement involves studying the relations among revenues, expenses, and net income both over time and across firms. These comparisons are likely more valid for the same firm over time than across firms because of the difficulty in identifying truly similar firms. We describe techniques for across-firm comparisons in **Chapter 6**. Numerous factors influence the performance of the firm (as measured by net income) and the components of that performance. In evaluating over-time performance of a given firm, the user must understand both current economic conditions and how those conditions may have changed over the period of analysis. In evaluating across-firm performance, the user should control for the underlying business model by selecting peer firms that are similar, economically, to the firm being analyzed. Most often analysts accomplish this by selecting similar-size firms in the same industry. Even economically comparable firms need not all use the same reporting aggregations and other financial statement presentations, which hinders detailed cross-firm comparisons. The ratio least affected by these presentation issues is the profit margin percentage (the ratio of net income to sales revenues).

SOLUTION TO SELF-STUDY PROBLEM

SUGGESTED SOLUTION TO PROBLEM 4.1 FOR SELF-STUDY

(Revenue and expense recognition.)

a. Crandall recognizes neither revenue nor expense in April. The firm makes a journal entry in April to recognize the cash collected from customers for sales made in March:

Cash	15,000	
Accounts Receivable		15,000

b. In April Crandall recognizes revenue of €24,500 and expenses of €6,500:

Cash	24,500	
Sales Revenue		24,500
Cost of Goods Sold	6,500	
Merchandise Inventory............................		6,500

c. In April Crandall recognizes revenue of €105,000 and expenses of €82,000.

Accounts Receivable	105,000	
Sales Revenue		105,000
Cost of Goods Sold	82,000	
Merchandise Inventory		82,000

d. Crandall recognizes neither revenue nor expense in April. The firm makes the following journal entry made to recognize the cash payment made to suppliers:

Accounts Payable	45,500	
Cash		45,500

e. In April Crandall recognizes revenues of €90,400 and expenses of €50,000.

Merchandise Inventory................................	50,000	
Cash		50,000

Cash	90,400	
Sales Revenue		90,400

Cost of Goods Sold	50,000	
Merchandise Inventory		50,000

f. In April Crandall recognizes revenue of €38,000 and expenses of €20,000.

Merchandise Inventory................................	20,000	
Accounts Payable		20,000
Accounts Receivable	38,000	
Sales Revenue		38,000
Cost of Goods Sold	20,000	
Merchandise Inventory		20,000

g. Crandall recognizes neither revenue nor expense in April. The firm makes the following journal entry in April to recognize the receipt of merchandise and the obligation to pay for that merchandise:

Merchandise Inventory................................	101,000	
Accounts Payable		101,000

h. Crandall recognizes neither revenue nor expense in April. The firm makes the following journal entry in April to recognize the receipt of cash from customers and the obligation it incurs for future delivery of merchandise:

Cash	26,500	
Advances from Customers		26,500

KEY TERMS AND CONCEPTS

Net income or net loss
Earnings
Profit
Revenues
Expenses
Cost of goods sold, cost of services rendered
Gross margin, gross profit, gross income
Operating expenses
Operating income, operating profit
Income from continuing operations
Income from discontinued operations
Revenue recognition
Gain
Loss

Sales discounts and allowances
Sales returns
Expense recognition
Product costs
Matching convention
Period expense
Other comprehensive income (OCI)
Comprehensive income
Accumulated other comprehensive income (AOCI)
Profit margin percentage
Common-size income statement
Time-series analysis
Cross-section analysis

QUESTIONS, EXERCISES, AND PROBLEMS

QUESTIONS

1. Review the meaning of the terms and concepts listed above in Key Terms and Concepts.

2. "The measurement of assets and liabilities relates closely to the measurement of revenues and expenses." Explain.

3. Distinguish between a cost and an expense.

4. Both interest expense on borrowing and dividends on common stock reduce net assets and reduce shareholders' equity. Accountants treat interest as an expense in measuring net income but do not treat dividends on common stock as an expense. Explain the rationale for this apparent inconsistency.

5. Why is it important to separate the income from discontinued operations from the income from continuing operations on the income statement?

6. In an accrual accounting system, firms recognize revenues even if they have not received cash. In a cash basis system, firms recognize revenues when they receive cash from customers. What criteria must sales transactions meet in order for the seller to recognize revenues before collecting cash?

7. In a cash basis system, firms recognize revenues when they receive cash from customers and recognize expenses as they pay cash for goods and services. How does a cash basis system violate the matching convention?

8. Why is it important to separate *gains* from *revenues*?

9. A common-size income statement is an analytical tool that facilitates comparisons across firms and for the same firm over time. However, it can be difficult to prepare a common-size statement for different firms because of differences in income statement classification and display. What one common-size income statement item can an analyst nearly always calculate, regardless of format and display differences?

10. A student says, "It is inconceivable to me that a firm could report increasing net income yet run out of cash." Clarify this seeming contradiction.

EXERCISES

11. **Revenue recognition.** Neiman Marcus, a U.S. retailer, uses the accrual basis of accounting and follows U.S. GAAP. It recognizes revenue at the time it sells merchandise. Indicate the amount of revenue (if any) the firm recognizes during the months of February, March, and April in each of the following hypothetical transactions, in which Neiman Marcus does the following:

  a. Collects $800 cash from a customer during March for a custom-made suit that the firm will make and deliver to the customer in April.

  b. Collects $2,160 cash from customers for meals served in the firm's restaurant during March.

  c. Collects $39,200 cash from customers during March for merchandise sold and delivered in February.

  d. Sells merchandise to customers during March on account, for which the firm will collect $59,400 cash from customers during April.

  e. Rents space in its store to a travel agency for $9,000 a month, effective March 1. Receives $18,000 cash on March 1 for two months' rent.

  f. Same as part **e**, except that it receives the check for the March and April rent on April 1.

12. **Revenue recognition.** Fonterra Cooperative Group Limited (Fonterra), a New Zealand dairy cooperative, uses the accrual basis of accounting and recognizes revenue at the time it sells products or renders services. Fonterra applies New Zealand accounting standards and reports its results in millions of New Zealand dollars (NZ$). In answering this problem, assume Fonterra uses IFRS. Indicate which of the following transactions or events immediately gives rise to Fonterra's recognition of revenue.

  a. Fonterra has completed the pasteurization of an order of 13,000 liters of milk it will deliver to a grocery store chain next week. Fonterra has not yet delivered the milk or invoiced the grocery store. The selling price of the milk is NZ$26,000.

  b. Refer to part **a**, and assume that the grocery store paid Fonterra a deposit of NZ$5,000 on the order of the milk.

  c. Fonterra delivered the milk and billed the grocery store. The grocery store has not yet paid the invoice.

  d. One day after delivery, the grocery store called Fonterra and reported that it has to destroy 3,000 liters of milk because it had spoiled sometime prior to its delivery. The grocer refuses to pay for these 3,000 liters.

  e. Fonterra spent NZ$10 million to develop a technique to transform a by-product of casein (a protein found in milk and cheese) into ethanol. Fonterra expects to use this technique to generate sales of at least NZ$2 million over the next year.

  f. Refer to part **e**, and assume that Fonterra signed contracts worth NZ$400 million for ethanol sales.

13. **Expense recognition.** Sun Microsystems uses the accrual basis of accounting and recognizes revenue at the time it sells goods or renders services. It applies U.S. GAAP and reports in U.S. dollars. Indicate the amount of expenses (if any) the firm recognizes during the months of June, July, and August in each of the following hypothetical transactions. The firm does the following:

  a. Pays $180,000 on July 1 for one year's rent on a warehouse beginning on that date.

  b. Receives a utility bill on July 2 totaling $4,560 for services received during June. It pays the utility bill during July.

  c. Purchases office supplies on account costing $12,600 during July. It pays $5,500 for these purchases during July and the remainder during August. Office supplies on hand on July 1 cost $2,400, on July 31 cost $9,200, and on August 31 cost $2,900.

  d. Pays $7,200 on July 15 for property taxes on office facilities for the current calendar year.

  e. Pays $2,000 on July 15 as a deposit on a custom-made delivery van that the manufacturer will deliver on September 30.

f. Pays $4,500 on July 25 as an advance on the August salary of an employee.

g. Pays $6,600 on July 25 for advertisements that appeared in computer journals during June.

14. **Expense recognition.** Tesco Plc. is a British-based grocer and retailer chain. It uses the accrual basis of accounting and recognizes revenue at the time it sells goods or renders services. It applies IFRS and reports in pounds sterling (£). Indicate the amount of expense recognized during October (if any) from each of the following hypothetical transactions or events. The firm does the following:

   a. Pays £440,000 on October 5 for commercials that appeared on British television during September.

   b. Pays £1,200,000 on October 6 for refrigeration units delivered to its stores on September 30. The firm expects the refrigerators to last for five years and have no salvage value.

   c. Pays £300,000 on October 10 for property taxes for the period from October 1 of this year to September 30 of next year.

   d. Pays £15,500 on October 15 for cleaning supplies purchased on October 10. Cleaning supplies on hand on October 1 cost £3,500 and on October 31 cost £5,400.

   e. Pays £4,000 on October 20 for repairs to a forklift truck on October 1. The truck had a remaining useful life of five years on October 1.

   f. Pays £100,000 on October 25 as a deposit on land Tesco plans to purchase for a new store.

   g. Pays £200,000 on October 31 as rent on a warehouse for October and November.

15. **Relating net income to balance sheet changes.** Comparative balance sheet data for Bombardier Corporation (Bombardier), a Canadian airplane manufacturer, as of January 31, 2007, and January 31, 2008, appear in the following display, based on Bombardier's financial reports as of January 31, 2008. Bombardier applies Canadian accounting standards and reports in millions of U.S. dollars. In answering these questions, assume Bombardier uses either U.S. GAAP or IFRS; for the purposes of this problem, this choice will not matter.

Bombardier Corporation
Balance Sheet Data
January 31, 2007 and 2008

	January 31	
	2008	**2007**
Total Assets	$20,562	$18,577
Liabilities	17,444	15,844
Common Stock	2,078	1,968
Retained Earnings	1,040	765

Bombardier declared and paid dividends of $30 million during the year ended January 31, 2008. During the same year, the firm also reported a positive adjustment to Retained Earnings of $12 million. Net income for 2008 was $293 million.

   a. Compute net income for the year ended January 31, 2008, by analyzing the change in retained earnings.

   b. Demonstrate that the following relation holds:

   Net Income = Increase in Assets − Increase in Liabilities

   − Increase in Contributed Capital + Dividends and Adjustments

16. **Relating net income to balance sheet changes.** Magyar Telekom (Magyar), a Hungarian telecommunications company, reported the following balance sheet information for the years ended December 31, 2006 and 2007. Magyar applies IFRS and reports in millions of Hungarian forints (HUF).

Magyar Telekom
Balance Sheet Data
December 31, 2006 and 2007

	2007	2006
Total Assets	HUF 1,135,578	HUF 1,131,595
Total Liabilities	553,885	538,428
Contributed Capital	129,954	128,728
Minority Interest	66,695	67,128
Retained Earnings	385,044	?

During 2007, Magyar declared and paid dividends of HUF72,729 million and made other adjustments, which increased retained earnings by HUF307 million.

a. Compute Magyar's balance in Retained Earnings for 2006.

b. Compute Magyar's net income for 2007.

17. **Income statement relations.** Selected income statement information for Lenovo Group Limited (Lenovo), a Hong Kong personal computer manufacturer, for two recent years appears in the following display, based on Lenovo's financial statements for the year ended March 31, 2008. Lenovo applies Hong Kong financial reporting standards and reports its results in thousands of U.S. dollars. In answering this question, assume Lenovo uses either U.S. GAAP or IFRS; for purposes of this problem, this choice will not matter.

	2008	2007
Sales	$16,351,503	$13,978,309
Cost of Goods Sold	13,901,523	12,091,433
Selling and Administrative Expenses	1,103,713	1,033,296
Gross Profit	?	?
Profit Before Taxes	?	?
Advertising Expenses	595,902	488,150
Research and Development Expense	229,759	196,225
Other Income (Expense)	?	18,130
Income Tax Expense	47,613	26,197
Net Income	484,708	?

Compute the missing amounts for 2007 and 2008.

18. **Income statement relations.** Selected income statement information for three recent years appears next for ABB, the Swiss engineering firm, based on ABB's financial reports for fiscal 2007. ABB applies U.S. GAAP and reports its results in millions of U.S. dollars.

	2007	2006	2005
Sales of Products	$24,816	?	$17,622
Income Tax Expense	595	?	464
Earnings Before Interest and Taxes	4,023	$2,557	?
Sales of Services	4,367	3,778	3,342
Selling and Administrative Expenses	4,975	?	3,780
Cost of Services Sold	?	2,570	2,305
Income Before Taxes	?	2,076	1,199
Other Operating Income (Expense)	?	139	37
Interest and Other Financial Expense	286	?	407
Gross Profit	8,968	6,744	?
Cost of Products Sold	17,292	13,967	13,205
Other Nonoperating Income (Expense)	?	(321)	(258)
Interest and Dividend Income	273	147	?
Net Income	3,757	1,390	?

Compute the missing amounts for each of the three years.

19. **Income and equity relations.** Selected information based on the comparative balance sheets for James John Corporation (James John), a U.S. clothing designer, manufacturer, and retailer, for the years ended March 31, 2008, 2007, and 2006, appears next. James John applies U.S. GAAP and reports its results in millions of U.S. dollars.

James John Corporation
Balance Sheet Data
March 31, 2008, 2007, and 2006

	March 31		
	2008	2007	2006
Common Stock	?	?	$ 1.1
Accumulated Other Comprehensive Income	?	$(27.2)	0.0
Retained Earnings	$1,742.3	?	1,090.3
Treasury Stock	?	(87.1)	(80.0)
Additional Paid in Capital	872.5	783.6	?
Total Shareholders' Equity	2,334.9	?	1,675.7

James John issued no new shares of common stock after 2006. In 2007 James John reported net income of $308.5 million and declared and paid cash dividends of $19.6 million. In 2008 James John paid $234.4 million to repurchase shares of common stock. Compute the missing amounts for each of the three years.

20. **Income and equity relations.** Selected information based on the comparative balance sheets and income statements of Colgate Palmolive Company (Colgate), a U.S. manufacturer of consumer products, for the years ended December 31, 2007, 2006, and 2005, appears in the following display, based on Colgate's financial reports for fiscal 2007. Colgate applies U.S. GAAP and reports its results in millions of U.S. dollars.

Colgate Palmolive Company
Selected Financial Statement Information

	Year Ended December 31		
	2007	2006	2005
Income Statement Information:			
Net Income	$ 1,737.4	$ 1,353.4	$ 1,351.4
Other Comprehensive Income	414.4	?	1.5
Balance Sheet Information:			
Common Stock	?	?	732.9
Accumulated Other Comprehensive Income	?	(2,081.2)	(1,804.7)
Unearned Compensation	(218.9)	(251.4)	(283.3)
Preferred Stock	197.5	222.7	253.7
Retained Earnings	10,627.5	?	8,968.1
Treasury Stock	?	?	(7,581.0)
Additional Paid-In Capital	1,517.7	1,218.1	?
Total Shareholders' Equity	?	?	1,350.1
Other Information:			
Dividends Declared and Paid	?	677.8	607.2
Share Repurchases	829.8	492.9	615.6
Common Shares Issued	0	0	0

Compute the missing amounts for each of the three years.

21. **Accumulated other comprehensive income relations.** Selected information based on the comparative balance sheets for MosTechi Corporation (MosTechi), a Japanese electronics

manufacturer, appear next for the years ended March 31, 2008, 2007, and 2006. MosTechi applies U.S. GAAP and reports its results in millions of yen (¥).

MosTechi Corporation
Balance Sheet Data
March 31, 2008, 2007, and 2006

	March 31		
	2008	**2007**	**2006**
Common Stock	¥ 626,907	¥ 624,124	¥ 621,709
Accumulated Other Comprehensive Income	?	?	?
Retained Earnings	?	1,602,654	1,506,082
Treasury Stock	?	(3,127)	(6,000)
Additional Paid-In Capital	1,143,423	1,136,638	1,134,222
Total Shareholders' Equity	3,351,500	?	2,870,338

   MosTechi's Other Comprehensive Income for 2007 was ¥229,238; in 2008 it was ¥40,944. During 2008 MosTechi had Net Income of ¥126,328 and declared and paid dividends of ¥25,042. During 2008 MosTechi reported a ¥3,807 decrease to Retained Earnings to adjust for the cumulative effect of an accounting change.
   Compute the missing amounts for each of the three years.

22. **Accumulated other comprehensive income relations.** Selected information based on the comparative balance sheets for Solaronx Company (Solaronx), a U.S. defense manufacturer, appears in the following display for the years ended December 31, 2008, 2007, and 2006. Solaronx applies U.S. GAAP and reports its results in millions of dollars.

Solaronx Company
Balance Sheet Data
December 31, 2008, 2007, and 2006

	December 31		
	2008	**2007**	**2006**
Common Stock	$ 5	$ 5	$ 5
Accumulated Other Comprehensive Income	?	?	(1,919)
Retained Earnings	?	?	2,998
Treasury Stock	(816)	(543)	(73)
Additional Paid-In Capital	10,097	9,722	9,540
Total Shareholders' Equity	?	?	?

   Solaronx's Other Comprehensive Income for 2008 was $774, compared to ($31) in 2007 and $275 in 2006. In addition, in 2008 Solaronx made a one-time adjustment of ($1,338) to Accumulated Other Comprehensive Income. Comprehensive Income for 2008 was $2,057, compared to $840 in 2007 and $692 in 2006. Dividends declared and paid increased from $356 in 2006, to $394 in 2007, to $429 in 2008.
   Compute the missing amounts for each of the three years.

23. **Discontinued operations.** Selected information from Bayer Group's financial statements for the years ended December 31, 2006 and 2007, appear below. Bayer Group (Bayer) is a German pharmaceutical company that applies IFRS and reports its results in millions of euros (€).

   a. What portion of Bayer's total net income in 2007 came from discontinued operations? How does this compare to 2006?

   b. What portion of Bayer's total assets in 2007 is associated with discontinued operations? How does this compare to 2006?

   c. What explains the large decline in Bayer's assets held for discontinued operations in 2007?

Bayer Group
Balance Sheet and Income Statement Data
December 31, 2006 and 2007

	December 31	
	2007	**2006**
Income from Continuing Operations (after taxes)	€ 2,306	€ 1,526
Income from Discontinued Operations (after taxes)	2,410	169
Assets Held for Discontinued Operations	84	2,925
Total Assets	51,378	55,891

24. **Discontinued operations.** Selected financial information for Orascom Telecom Holding S.A.E. (Orascom), an Egyptian telecommunications firm, is shown in the following display for the years ended December 31, 2007 and 2006, based on Orascom's financial reports for fiscal 2007. Orascom applies Egyptian accounting standards and reports its results in thousands of Egyptian pounds (£). In answering this question, assume that Orascom uses either U.S. GAAP or IFRS; for the purposes of this problem, this choice will not matter.

Orascom Telecom Holding S.A.E.
Balance Sheet and Income Statement Data
December 31, 2006 and 2007

	December 31	
	2007	**2006**
Income from Continuing Operations (before taxes)	£ 9,293,448	£ 4,456,900
Assets Held for Discontinued Operations	?	7,327,709
Taxes on Income from Continuing Operations	2,571,426	?
Income from Discontinued Operations (net of tax)	?	1,020,213
Income from Continuing Operations (after tax)	?	3,595,713
Net Income	11,935,088	?
Assets Used in Continuing Operations	34,348,838	?
Total Assets	39,492,853	34,209,746

Compute the missing amounts for each of the two years.

PROBLEMS

25. **Income statement formats.** Information from Cemex, S.A.B.'s income statements for the years ended December 31, 2006 and 2007, is shown in the following display. Cemex is a Mexican construction firm that applies Mexican accounting standards and reports its results in millions of pesos ($).

Cemex, S.A.B.
Income Statement Data
December 31, 2006 and 2007

	December 31	
	2007	**2006**
Net Sales	$236,669	$213,767
Cost of Sales	157,696	?
Gross Profit	?	77,320

(continued)

	December 31	
	2007	2006
Administrative and Selling Expenses	33,120	28,588
Distribution Expenses	13,405	?
Other Expenses, net	3,281	580
Operating Income	?	33,925
Financial Expenses	8,809	?
Financial Income	862	536
Income (Expense) from Financial Instruments	2,387	(161)
Other Financial Income (Expense)	6,647	4,905
Equity in Income of Associates	1,487	1,425
Profit Before Income Tax	?	34,845
Income Tax	?	?
Consolidated Profit	?	?
Portion of Profit Attributable to Minority Interest	837	?
Portion of Profit Attributable to Cemex Shareholders	?	27,855

Assume Cemex had an effective tax rate of 15.11% in 2007, and 16.35% in 2006.

a. Compute the missing amounts for each of the two years.

b. Prepare, in good format, an income statement for Cemex for 2006 and 2007 assuming the firm applies IFRS.

26. **Income statement formats.** Information from GoodLuck Brands's income statements for the years ended December 31, 2008, 2007, and 2006, is shown next. GoodLuck Brands is a U.S.-based manufacturer and distributor. The company applies U.S. GAAP and reports its results in millions of U.S. dollars.

	2008	2007	2006
Net Sales	$8,769.0	$7,061.2	$6,145.2
Cost of Products Sold	4,618.9	3,843.0	3,342.1
Excise Taxes on Spirits and Wine	514.0	326.5	299.7
Advertising, Selling, and Administrative	2,070.1	1,694.4	1,433.6
Amortization of Intangibles	43.5	33.4	35.4
Restructuring Charges	21.2	—	9.8
Operating Income	$1,501.3	$1,163.9	$1,024.6
Interest Expense	332.4	158.9	77.3
Other Financial Expense (Income)	(40.2)	78.9	(47.0)
Income Before Minority Interest and Taxes	$1,209.1	$ 926.1	$ 994.3
Income Taxes	311.1	324.5	261.1
Minority Interests	67.9	20.0	17.2
Income from Continuing Operations	$ 830.1	$ 581.6	$ 716.0
Income from Discontinued Operations, net tax	—	39.5	67.8
Net Income	$ 830.1	$ 621.1	$ 783.8

Prepare, in good format, income statements for GoodLuck Brands for 2006, 2007, and 2008, assuming the firm applies IFRS.

27. **Correcting errors in income statement transactions.** Broyo Corporation (Broyo), a large paper company, reported the following income statement for its year ended December 31, 2008. Broyo applies IFRS and reports its results in millions of euros.

Broyo supplied additional information about the following six transactions or events that happened during 2008, with all euro amounts reported in millions.

a. On October 5, 2008, Broyo signed a sales agreement with Office Supplies International. The agreement calls for delivery of 50,000 boxes of paper at a total price of €200. On this date, Broyo recognized revenues of €200, and recognized cost of sales of €160. No deliveries under the contract had occurred by December 31, 2008.

	2008
Net Sales	€ 4,221
Cost of Products Sold	(3,110)
Gross Profit	€ 1,111
Selling, General, and Administrative Expenses	(794)
Other Operating Income, net	17
Share in Profits of Associated Companies	1
Operating Profit	€ 335
Financial Income and Expenses, net	(43)
Profit on Continuing Operations, before tax	€ 292
Income Taxes	(72)
Profit from Continuing Operations, after tax	€ 220
Profit from Discontinued Operations, net of tax	17
Profit	€ 237
Portion of Profit Owned by Minority Interests	€ 1
Portion of Profit Owned by Shareholders	€ 236

b. On October 18, 2008, Broyo signed a contract with a customer for €45. The customer provided a cash deposit at this time of €20, which Broyo recorded as revenues. Broyo did not recognize any expenses on October 18, 2008.

c. Broyo fulfilled all terms of the contract in part **b** on November 28, 2008. Broyo's cost of the inventory delivered was €36. Because Broyo had recorded revenues in October, it made no entry on November 28.

d. During the fourth quarter of 2008, Broyo spent €11 on research and development. Those expenditures, which were focused on creating a new waterproof paper, were unsuccessful. Broyo capitalized the €11 as a development asset, which it plans to amortize, beginning in 2009, over 10 years.

e. On December 1, 2008, Broyo delivered to a customer €266 of paper products, with a cost of €250. The customer promised to pay Broyo in January 2009. Because Broyo had not received the cash by December 31, 2008, it did not record anything for this transaction.

f. On December 5, 2008, Broyo sold one of its pulp plants for €100. Prior to the sale, the pulp plant had a balance sheet carrying value of €80. Broyo recorded the transaction as follows: debited cash for €100, debited plant and equipment for €80, credited cost of goods sold for €80, and credited revenues for €100.

For each transaction, determine whether revenues and expenses are overstated or understated. Ignore income tax effects.

28. **Correcting errors in income statement transactions.** Dragon Group International Limited (Dragon Group), a diversified electronics firm headquartered in Singapore, reported the following income statement information for its year ended December 31, 2007, based on its financial reports for fiscal 2007. Dragon Group applies Singapore financial reporting standards and reports its results in thousands of Singapore dollars ($). In answering this problem, assume Dragon Group uses either U.S. GAAP or IFRS; for purposes of this problem, this choice will not matter.

	2007
Sales	$ 460,830
Cost of Sales	(416,378)
Gross Profit	$ 44,452
Other Income	1,558
Selling and Marketing Costs	(20,714)
General and Administrative Costs	(20,254)
Development Costs	(1,232)

(*continued*)

	2007
Finance Costs, net.	(6,692)
Gain on Sale of Land	6,546
Share in Results of Associated Companies	(2)
Profit Before Tax	$ 3,662
Taxation	(1,094)
Profit (Loss).	$ 2,568
Portion of Profit Owned by Minority Interests	$ (567)
Portion of Profit Owned by Shareholders	$ 3,135

Assume that Dragon Group supplied additional information about the following six hypothetical transactions or events that happened during 2007, with all monetary amounts reported in thousands of Singapore dollars.

a. In January 2007, Dragon Group collected $1,000 cash from customers who had purchased items on credit in December 2006. Dragon Group had delivered the items by mid-December 2006. Dragon Group recognized January revenues of $1,000.

b. On February 2, 2007, the firm agreed to supply a customer with $25,000 of high-end electronics products. On this date, Dragon Group recognized revenues of $25,000 and cost of sales of $18,000 reflecting the carrying value of the high-end inventory. Dragon Group delivered on the agreement in September 2007.

c. On June 4, 2007, Dragon Group sold some land it had purchased many years earlier, prior to the boom in the real estate market. The carrying value of the land on the firm's books was $454, and Dragon sold it for $7,000. Dragon Group recorded a gain on the sale of the land of $6,546.

d. During 2007, the firm incurred $1,232 in development costs associated with a new product that the firm had developed; the firm expensed these costs. The product design and manufacture is nearly complete. The firm's auditor has decided that Dragon should have capitalized the development costs.

e. In December 2007, Dragon Group recognized interest income on investments in marketable securities of $230. The firm included this income in sales revenues.

f. Dragon Group spent $15,000 for advertising in 2007. Because Dragon Group management believed the advertising would result in future income, it capitalized the expenditures as an asset. No amortization of the asset has yet taken place.

For each transaction, determine whether revenues and expenses are over- or understated.

29. **Interpreting common-size income statements. Exhibit 4.7** presents common-size income statements for Standard Denim and Blue Label Jeans, two apparel retailing firms, for

EXHIBIT 4.7	**Standard Denim and Blue Label Jeans Common-Size Income Statements (Problem 29)**

	Standard Denim			Blue Label Jeans		
	2008	2007	2006	2008	2007	2006
Sales	100.0%	100.0%	100.0%	100.0%	100.0%	100.0%
Other Revenues	1.2	0.1	0.2	0.5	0.6	0.4
Cost of Goods Sold or Services Sold	(56.0)	(56.8)	(59.0)	(62.8)	(64.1)	(66.2)
Selling and Administrative Expenses	(26.7)	(26.5)	(25.8)	(25.3)	(24.6)	(23.1)
Interest Expense	(2.2)	(2.2)	(3.0)	(5.5)	(5.4)	(5.3)
Income Tax Expense	(6.6)	(5.5)	(4.2)	(2.4)	(2.3)	(2.0)
Net Income/Sales	9.7%	9.1%	8.2%	4.5%	4.2%	3.8%

three recent years. In addition to the cost of merchandise sold, both firms include occupancy expense for their stores (rent, utilities, depreciation) in cost of goods sold. Standard Denim tends to rely on print advertising to create demand, whereas Blue Label Jeans relies more heavily on in-store promotions (two-for-one discounts and special daily price reductions). Standard Denim recently expanded into other countries, whereas Blue Label Jeans operates almost exclusively in the United States. Both companies apply U.S. GAAP.

a. Suggest possible reasons for the decreasing cost of goods sold to sales percentages for the two firms during the three-year period.

b. Suggest possible reasons why the cost of goods sold to sales percentages for Standard Denim are less than those for Blue Label Jeans.

c. Suggest possible reasons for the increasing selling and administrative expenses to sales percentages for the two firms for the three-year period.

d. Suggest possible reasons why the selling and administrative expenses to sales percentages for Blue Label Jeans are less than those for Standard Denim.

e. Suggest possible reasons for the different pattern of changes in the interest expense to sales percentages for the two firms during the three-year period.

f. Suggest possible reasons for the increasing income tax expense to sales percentages for the two firms during the three-year period.

30. **Interpreting common-size income statements.** Lyle's Lemonade Company (Lyle's Lemonade) and CitraPop together have a large share of the nonalcoholic beverage market in the United States. Most beverage manufacturing involves adding water to a previously prepared syrup. This mixing process usually occurs at the stage just prior to bottling the beverage. Lyle's Lemonade relies on independent companies to conduct the mixing, bottling, and distribution operations, with Lyle's Lemonade selling the syrup to the bottlers. CitraPop relies more heavily on owning its bottlers and thereby remains involved in both manufacturing and distribution. **Exhibit 4.8** presents common-size income statements for Lyle's Lemonade and CitraPop for three recent years. Both companies apply U.S. GAAP.

a. Suggest possible reasons for the decreasing cost of goods sold to sales percentages for the two firms during the three-year period.

b. Suggest possible reasons for the increasing selling and administrative expenses to sales percentages for the two firms for the three-year period.

c. Suggest possible reasons for the decreasing interest expense top sales percentages for both firms.

d. Lyle's Lemonade's income tax expense to sales percentages are larger than those for CitraPop, suggesting that Lyle's Lemonade has a higher income tax burden. For a different perspective, compute the ratio of income tax expense to net income before

EXHIBIT 4.8	Lyle's Lemonade Company and CitraPop Common-Size Income Statements (Problem 30)					
	Lyle's Lemonade Company			**CitraPop**		
	2008	**2007**	**2006**	**2008**	**2007**	**2006**
Sales	100.0%	100.0%	100.0%	100.0%	100.0%	100.0%
Other Revenues	1.2	3.3	0.9	1.3	0.9	0.8
Cost of Goods Sold	(36.3)	(34.4)	(35.7)	(45.8)	(45.7)	(45.8)
Selling and Administrative Expenses	(35.8)	(35.0)	(34.7)	(34.5)	(35.5)	(36.3)
Interest Expense	(1.0)	(1.6)	(2.6)	(0.7)	(0.9)	(1.2)
Income Tax Expense	(7.8)	(9.6)	(10.0)	(6.5)	(6.4)	(5.6)
Net Income	20.3%	22.7%	17.9%	13.8%	12.4%	11.9%
Sales Growth	8.2%	6.5%	1.8%	6.8%	5.3%	22.7%

Ericsson
Common-Size Income Statements
(in SEK millions)
(Problem 31)

Fiscal year ending December 31	2007		2006		2005	
Net Sales	SEK 187,780	100.0%	SEK 179,821	100.0%	SEK 153,222	100.0%
Cost of Sales	(114,059)	−60.7	(104,875)	−58.3	(82,764)	−54.0
Gross Margin	SEK 73,721	39.3%	SEK 74,946	41.7%	SEK 70,458	46.0%
Research and Development Expenses	(28,842)	−15.4	(27,533)	−15.3	(24,059)	−15.7
Selling and Administrative	(23,199)	−12.4	(21,422)	−11.9	(16,800)	−11.0
Operating Expenses	SEK (52,041)	−27.7%	SEK (48,955)	−27.2%	SEK (40,859)	−26.7%
Other Operating Income and Expenses	1,734	0.9	3,903	2.2	1,090	0.7
Share in Earnings in Associated Companies	7,232	3.9	5,934	3.2	2,395	1.6
Operating Income	SEK 30,646	16.3%	SEK 35,828	19.9%	SEK 33,084	21.6%
Financial Income	1,778	0.9	1,954	1.1	2,653	1.7
Financial Expenses	(1,695)	−0.9	(1,789)	−1.0	(2,402)	−1.6
Income After Financial Items	SEK 30,729	16.4%	SEK 35,993	20.0%	SEK 33,335	21.8%
Taxes	(8,594)	−4.6	(9,557)	−5.3	(8,875)	−5.8
Net Income	SEK 22,135	11.8%	SEK 26,436	14.7%	SEK 24,460	16.0%
Of which:						
Stockholders of the Parent Company	SEK 21,386	11.4%	SEK 26,251	14.6%	SEK 24,315	15.9%
Minority Interest	SEK 299	0.2%	SEK 185	0.1%	SEK 145	0.1%

income taxes for each firm. For example, this percentage for Lyle's Lemonade for 2006 is 35.8% [= 10.0%/(17.9% + 10.0%)]. What insight does this measure provide regarding the income tax burden of Lyle's Lemonade versus CitraPop?

31. **Interpreting common-size income statements.** Ericsson, a Swedish electronics and telecommunications firm, has seen increasing sales in recent years. At the same time, its profit margin has declined. **Exhibit 4.9** presents common-size income statements for Ericsson for three recent years, based on Ericsson's financial reports for fiscal 2007. Ericsson applies IFRS and reports in millions of Swedish kroner (SEK). Discuss the likely reasons for the decreasing profit margin for Ericsson over the three-year period.

32. **Interpreting common-size income statements.** Thales Group (Thales) is a French electronics firm that specializes in information systems, aerospace, and defense. Thales applies IFRS and reports its results in millions of euros. **Exhibit 4.10** presents common-size income statements for Thales for three recent years, based on Thales's financial reports for fiscal 2007. Discuss the likely reasons for Thales' increasing profit margin over the three-year period.

33. **Identifying industries using common-size income statement percentages. Exhibit 4.11** presents common-size income statements for six firms. The six firms and a description of their operations follow. All of these firms apply U.S. GAAP.

    a. Commonwealth Edison: generates and sells electricity to businesses and households in capital-intensive plants.

    b. Delta Air Lines: provides airline transportation services.

    c. Tiffany & Company: designer, manufacturer, and retailer of jewelry and specialty items (including china, timepieces, and silver).

    d. Hewlett-Packard: manufactures and sells computers, printers, and other hardware.

    e. Kroger Stores: operates a chain of grocery stores nationwide.

(continued on page 180)

EXHIBIT 4.10

Thales Group
Common-Size Income Statements
(in € millions)
(Problem 32)

Fiscal year ending December 31	2007		2006		2005	
Revenues	€ 12,295.6	100.0%	€ 10,264.3	100.0%	€ 10,263.2	100.0%
Cost of Sales	(9,560.9)	−77.8	(7,883.6)	−76.8	(7,900.1)	−77.0
Gross Profit	€ 2,734.7	22.2%	€ 2,380.7	23.2%	€ 2,363.1	23.0%
Research and Development Expenses	(443.4)	−3.6	(360.8)	−3.5	(366.0)	−3.6
Marketing and Selling Expenses	(841.0)	−6.8	(805.7)	−7.8	(818.8)	−8.0
General and Administrative Expenses	(560.4)	−4.6	(459.6)	−4.5	(456.5)	−4.4
Amortization of Intangibles	(127.9)	−1.0	—		—	
Income from Operations	€ 762.0	6.2%	€ 754.6	7.4%	€ 721.8	7.0%
Restructuring Costs	(77.9)	−0.6	(193.1)	−1.9	(212.5)	−2.1
Other Operating Income (Expense)	—		—		(84.3)	−0.8
Asset Impairments	(96.5)	−0.8	(8.5)	−0.1	(34.2)	−0.3
Gain (Loss) on Disposal of Assets	432.1	3.5	22.9	0.2	158.3	1.5
Income of Operating Activities	€ 1,019.7	8.3%	€ 575.9	5.6%	€ 549.1	5.4%
Financial Interest on Gross Debt	(100.3)	−0.8	(83.9)	−0.8	(116.2)	−1.1
Financial Income from Cash at Banks	55.2	0.4	42.1	0.4	33.4	0.3
Cost of Net Financial Debt	€ (45.1)	−0.4%	€ (41.8)	−0.4%	€ (82.8)	−0.8%
Other Financial Income (Expense)	(34.0)	−0.3	(31.5)	−0.3	(10.2)	−0.1
Other Components of Pension Charge	65.2	0.5	(19.0)	−0.2	(33.6)	−0.3
Income Tax	(157.7)	−1.3	(100.4)	−1.0	(87.3)	−0.9
Share in Net Income (Loss) of Equity Affiliates	40.6	0.3	7.9	0.1	7.9	0.1
Net Income	€ 888.7	7.2%	€ 391.1	3.8%	€ 343.1	3.3%
Of which:						
Net Income, Group Share	€ 887.4	7.2%	€ 388.0	3.8%	€ 333.9	3.3%
Minority Interests	€ 1.3	0.0%	€ 3.1	0.0%	€ 9.2	0.1%

EXHIBIT 4.11

Common-Size Income Statements for Six Firms
(Problem 33)

	(1)	(2)	(3)	(4)	(5)	(6)
Sales	100.0%	100.0%	100.0%	100.0%	100.0%	100.0%
Other Revenues	—	—	0.5	0.9	—	—
Cost of Goods and Services Sold	(73.6)	(81.4)	(60.6)	(63.0)	(61.3)	(44.5)
Selling and Administrative Expenses	(19.9)	(14.1)	(17.9)	(24.0)	(5.0)	(36.8)
Depreciation	(2.1)	(0.8)	(5.1)	(3.4)	(8.7)	(4.1)
Interest	(1.4)	—	(8.0)	(0.9)	(7.3)	(0.1)
Income Taxes	(1.4)	(1.5)	(3.3)	(2.9)	(6.7)	(6.5)
Net Income	1.6%	2.2%	5.6%	6.7%	11.0%	10.3%

f. Kelly Services: provides temporary office services to businesses and other firms. Sales revenue represents amounts billed to customers for temporary help services, and cost of goods and services sold includes amounts Kelly paid to temporary help employees.

Use whatever clues you can to match the companies in **Exhibit 4.11** with the six firms listed above. Explain your reasoning.

34. **Classification and interpreting income statements.** SeaBreeze Inc., a Taiwan-based semi-conductor manufacturer, reported the following information for 2008. SeaBreeze Inc. applies IFRS and reports in millions of yuan (¥).

	2008
Sales	¥ 1,891,466
Cost of Sales	(1,737,427)
Gross Profit	¥ 154,039
Selling, General and Administrative	(98,524)
Profit Before Tax	¥ 55,515
Income Taxes	(23,594)
Profit	¥ 31,921

Further information available to you reveals the following five items (all financial figures reported in millions of yuan).

a. During 2008 SeaBreeze had ¥$10,000 in gains on sales of assets. The firm included the gains as part of Revenues.

b. SeaBreeze included financial income of ¥$25,800 as part of Revenues, and financial expenses of ¥$12,000 as part of Cost of Sales.

c. The firm included a ¥$6,000 write-down of inventory in Selling, General, and Administrative Expenses. Normally in this industry, such a write-down is included in Cost of Sales.

d. The firm included research and development expenditures of ¥$34,000 in Cost of Sales. None of the expenditures related to proven technologies (and so were correctly not capitalized).

e. During 2008 the firm committed to a plan to discontinue part of its operations. The discontinued operations accounted for ¥$22,000 of gross profit.

Evaluate the way SeaBreeze classified each of the five items on its income statement. If you disagree with the classification, state your reasoning and determine the effect on the firm's gross margin and net income from the alternative classification that you would recommend.

35. **Classification and interpreting income statements.** Dyreng Plc. (Dyreng), a Belgian-based construction firm, reported the following information for 2008. Dyreng applies IFRS and reports in thousands of euros (€).

	2008
Sales	€ 18,957.2
Cost of Sales	(14,161.9)
Gross Profit	€ 4,795.3
Other Operating Income	107.9
Selling, General, and Administrative Expense	(3,929.5)
Other Operating Expenses	(36.5)
Operating Profit	€ 937.2
Finance Costs	(347.2)
Income from Investments	14.5
Profit Before Taxes and Discontinued Operations	€ 604.5
Income Tax Expense	(203.7)
Net Profit from Continuing Operations	€ 400.8
Results of Discontinued Operations (net of tax)	€ 23.7
Net Profit	€ 424.5

Further information available to you reveals the following six items, with all euro amounts reported in thousands.

a. During 2008 Dyreng signed an agreement with the City of London to build a new terminal at Gatwick airport. The construction will commence in 2009. As evidence of its commitment to the project, the City of London gave Dyreng a deposit of €80 toward the contract price of €240. Dyreng recognized revenues in 2008 of €240 on this transaction. Because Dyreng had not yet performed work, it recorded no costs of sales at the time it recognized the revenue.

b. Dyreng recognized revenues of €700 in 2008 related to a contract signed in 2007. It had performed all the work in 2007, but the customer did not remit payment until 2008. It recognized the cost of the work performed, €660, as expense when it recognized the revenue.

c. In 2008 Dyreng consolidated its administrative functions and sold an office building for €560. The carrying value of the building was €600. The firm reported this transaction in revenues and cost of sales, respectively.

d. After preparing its income statement for 2008, Dyreng realized that €45 of income associated with discontinued operations was included in Other Operating Income. Ignore tax effects in evaluating this transaction.

e. During 2008 Dyreng completed a renovation project. The contract price was €450, and the firm expended €230 in materials, labor, and overhead costs. Dyreng sent the bill to the client, but because it did not receive payment in 2008, the firm did not record this transaction in its income statement for 2008.

f. In 2008, a firm offered to pay Dyreng to lease the advertising space on scaffolding that Dyreng was erecting for a renovation project. The client offered Dyreng €960 to lease the advertising space for one year. Dyreng accepted the offer and recorded €960 as a reduction of the cost of sales of the renovation project. At the end of 2008, six months of the lease remained.

Evaluate the way Dyreng classified each of the six items on its income statement. If you disagree with this classification, state your reasoning and determine the effect on the firm's gross profit and pretax profit from continuing operations from the alternative classification that you would recommend.

36. Calculation of tax rates. A multinational computer equipment manufacturer reported the following amounts for two recent years (in millions of U.S. dollars). The firm applies U.S. GAAP.

	2008	2007
Revenues	$ 88,396	$ 87,548
Expenses	(76,862)	(75,791)
Income Before Income Taxes	$ 11,534	$ 11,757
Income Tax Expense	(3,441)	(4,045)
Net Income	$ 8,093	$ 7,712

a. Compute the ratio of net income divided by revenues for each year.

b. Compute the ratio of income before taxes divided by revenues for each year.

c. Compute the ratio of income tax expense divided by income before taxes, a ratio called the *effective tax rate*.

d. What do these ratios suggest as to the principal reason for the change in profitability between 2007 and 2008?

Statement of Cash Flows: Reporting the Effects of Operating, Investing, and Financing Activities on Cash Flows

1. Understand why using the accrual basis of accounting to prepare the balance sheet and income statement creates the need for a statement of cash flows.
2. Understand the types of transactions that result in cash flows from operating, investing, and financing activities.
3. Develop an ability to prepare a statement of cash flows from comparative balance sheets and an income statement.
4. Develop an ability to analyze the statement of cash flows, including the relations among cash flows from operating, investing, and financing activities for businesses in various growth stages.

What do Delta Airlines and Delphi have in common? Both firms filed for bankruptcy during the early 2000s. Firms filing for bankruptcy often operated profitably for most of the years preceding their bankruptcy filings. The bankruptcies occurred because these firms were unable to generate sufficient cash to cover operating costs and debt service payments. The ability to generate cash flows and to manage their timing is critical to the success of business enterprises. For this reason, U.S. GAAP and IFRS require that firms prepare a statement of cash flows showing the sources and uses of cash during the accounting period. This chapter discusses the statement of cash flows, which reports the impact of a firm's operating, investing, and financing activities on cash flows during an accounting period. The statement of cash flows relates to, but differs from, the statement of financial position (balance sheet) and statement of operations (income statement).

NEED FOR A STATEMENT OF CASH FLOWS

How can a profitable firm run out of cash? Two explanations of the relation between cash and income suggest answers.

1. **Net income for a particular period does not equal cash flow from operations. Chapter 1** points out that most firms use the accrual basis of accounting to measure operating performance. For example, firms typically recognize revenue at the time of sale, independent of when they receive the cash from the sale. Some firms, such as airlines and insurance

companies, receive cash before providing services and recognizing revenues. Others, such as manufacturers and distributors, receive cash after they have provided goods and recognized revenues. Thus, revenues on the income statement for any period will not likely equal cash received from customers for that period. As another example, firms recognize expenses either in the period when they recognize associated revenues or in the period when they consume materials or services in operations. The cash outflow related to a specific expense need not occur in the period when the firm recognizes the expense, so expenses on the income statement for any period will not likely equal cash paid to suppliers of materials and services for that period.

Most of the cash outflows for expenses occur before the firm receives the cash inflows from a sale. This lag between cash outflows and cash inflows can lead to cash shortfalls, particularly for a growing firm. Consider the typical firm where cash disbursements to employees and suppliers precede cash collections from customers. The faster such a firm grows, the greater is the shortfall in cash. In this setting, the firm must take steps to obtain the funds necessary to pay suppliers while it awaits cash collections from its own customers; for example, the firm might borrow funds from the bank on a revolving credit arrangement.

The preceding examples highlight the fact that, for any accounting period, the income statement usually will not reflect the cash flows for the period. Stated differently, using the accrual basis of accounting to measure net income creates the need for a separate financial statement that reports the impact of operations on cash flows. That statement helps the reader judge a firm's cash flow needs and how it has dealt with them.

2. **Firms receive cash inflows and disburse cash outflows because of investing and financing activities, which the income statement does not report directly.** Firms building their productive capacity generally use cash to acquire property, plant, and equipment. Short- and long-term borrowing comes due, requiring cash. Firms that regularly pay dividends to shareholders are reluctant to curtail the dividends when cash is tight. None of these transactions affects the income statement in the period they occur. For example, the firm *capitalizes* (that is, records an asset, not an expense) its expenditures for property, plant, equipment, and purchased intellectual property in the period of acquisition. Later periods' income statements will reflect the expensing of these costs, as depreciation or amortization.

Firms use cash for debt service payments. Some of those payments are for interest expense, which the income statement will report. The remainder discharges obligations for principal repayments and is not expense, so it never appears on an income statement. Firms use cash also to pay dividends, which are not expenses reported on the income statement, although they do reduce retained earnings. Dividends are distributions of net assets to owners.

These examples highlight how a profitable firm can collect more cash from customers than it pays for current-period expenditures and still have cash shortages.

Neither the balance sheet nor the income statement displays the firm's sources and uses of cash. The balance sheet reports the balance in cash at the beginning and end of the year but does not explain how cash changed during the period. The income statement measures the increase (or decrease) in net assets from selling goods and services for more (or less) than their costs. Accrual accounting results in an increase in net assets, but seldom all in cash, when the firm earns income. The statement of cash flows helps a reader understand how a firm obtains and uses cash.

OVERVIEW OF THE STATEMENT OF CASH FLOWS

Exhibit 5.1 presents a modified statement of cash flows for Nordstrom Inc. for three years. **Exhibit 5.2** (identical to **Exhibit 1.7** on page 17) shows Scania's statement of cash flows for the years ended December 31, 2006, 2005, and 2004. We modify Nordstrom's statement of cash flows to include some additional information, which we explain below. We refer to the statement of cash flow presentations of Nordstrom and Scania to illustrate key aspects of this financial statement.

EXHIBIT 5.1

Nordstrom, Inc.
Comparative Statement of Cash Flows with Reconciliation
of Net Income to Cash Flow from Operations
(all dollar amounts in millions)

	Fiscal Year		
	2006	2005	2004
Cash Provided by Operating Activities			
Sources of Cash			
Receipts from Customers	$ 8,516.5	$ 7,728.6	$ 7,153.0
Receipts from Other Items	430.3	164.7	100.2
Uses of Cash			
Cash Paid for Goods Available for Sale and Occupancy Costs	(5,308.2)	(4,877.1)	(4,547.3)
Cash Paid for Selling, General, and Administrative Expenses	(1,967.3)	(1,856.8)	(1,766.8)
Cash Paid for Interest	(42.8)	(45.3)	(77.4)
Cash Paid for Income Taxes	(486.1)	(337.9)	(255.4)
Net Cash Provided by Operating Activities	$ 1,142.4	$ 776.2	$ 606.3
Reconciliation of Net Income to Cash Provided by Operating Activities			
Net Earnings	$ 678.0	$ 551.3	$ 393.5
Adjustments to Reconcile Net Earnings to Net Cash Provided by Operating Activities:			
Depreciation and Amortization of Buildings and Equipment	284.5	276.3	264.8
Amortization of Deferred Property Incentives and Other, Net	(36.3)	(33.4)	(31.4)
Stock-Based Compensation Expense	37.4	13.3	8.1
Deferred Income Taxes, Net	(58.3)	(11.2)	(8.0)
Tax Benefit from Stock-Based Payments	43.6	41.1	25.4
Excess Tax Benefit from Stock-Based Payments	(38.3)		—
Provision for Bad Debt Expense	17.1	21.0	24.6
Change in Operating Assets and Liabilities:			
Accounts Receivable	(61.3)	(15.1)	(3.0)
Investment in Asset-Backed Securities	128.0	(135.8)	(150.0)
Merchandise Inventories	(38.6)	(20.8)	(11.8)
Prepaid Expenses	(4.7)	(1.0)	(3.2)
Other Assets	(7.7)	(3.5)	(8.1)
Accounts Payable	84.3	31.7	23.9
Accrued Salaries, Wages, and Related Benefits	48.7	(11.3)	15.1
Other Current Liabilities	23.5	38.7	58.5
Income Taxes Payable	(5.5)	(33.9)	(19.0)
Deferred Property Incentives	30.7	49.5	19.8
Other Liabilities	17.3	19.3	7.1
Net Cash Provided by Operating Activities	$ 1,142.4	$ 776.2	$ 606.3
Investing Activities			
Capital Expenditures	$ (264.4)	$ (271.6)	$ (246.9)
Proceeds from Sale of Assets	0.2	0.1	5.5
Purchases of Short-Term Investments	(109.6)	(542.9)	(3,232.2)
Sales of Short-Term Investments	163.6	530.7	3,366.4
Other, Net	(8.1)	(8.3)	(2.8)
Net Cash Used in Investing Activities	$ (218.3)	$ (292.0)	$ (110.0)
Financing Activities			
Principal Payments on Long-Term Debt	$ (307.6)	$ (101.0)	$ (205.3)
(Decrease) Increase in Cash Book Overdrafts	(50.8)	4.9	(2.7)
Proceeds from Exercise of Stock Options	50.9	73.0	87.1
Proceeds from Employee Stock Purchase Plan	16.3	15.6	12.9
Excess Tax Benefit from Stock-Based Payments	38.3		—
Cash Dividends Paid	(110.2)	(87.2)	(67.2)
Repurchase of Common Stock	(621.5)	(287.1)	(300.0)
Other, Net	0.4	(0.3)	(0.8)
Net Cash Used in Financing Activities	$ (984.2)	$ (382.1)	$ (476.0)
Net (Decrease) Increase in Cash and Cash Equivalents	$ (60.1)	$ 102.1	$ 20.3
Cash and Cash Equivalents at Beginning of Year	462.7	360.6	340.3
Cash and Cash Equivalents at End of Year	$ 402.6	$ 462.7	$ 360.6

EXHIBIT 5.2

Scania
Statement of Cash Flows

January – December, SEK m.	Note	2006	2005	2004
Operating activities				
Income after financial items	24 a	8,583	6,765	6,276
Items not affecting cash flow	24 b	3,236	2,953	2,386
Taxes paid		-2,552	-2,450	-1,784
Cash flow from operating activities before change in working capital		9,267	7,268	6,878
Cash flow from change in working capital				
Inventories		-627	284	-959
Receivables		8	439	-1,664
Provisions for pensions		96	124	250
Trade payables		1,276	646	864
Other liabilities and provisions		1,126	-731	356
Total change in working capital		1,879	762	-1,153
Cash flow from operating activities		11,146	8,030	5,725
Investing activities				
Net investments through acquisitions/ divestments of businesses	24 c	–	-205	-49
Net investments in non-current assets	24 d	-3,810	-3,597	-2,798
Net investments in credit portfolio etc., Customer Finance	24 d	-3,514	-1,410	-478
Cash flow from investing activities		-7,324	-5,212	-3,325
Cash flow before financing activities		3,822	2,818	2,400
Financing activities				
Change in net debt from financing activities	24 e	7,591	62	-1,264
Dividend to shareholders		-3,000	-3,000	-1,200
Cash flow from financing activities		4,591	-2,938	-2,464
Cash flow for the year		8,413	-120	-64
Cash and cash equivalents, 1 January		1,599	1,589	1,663
Exchange rate differences in cash and cash equivalents		-78	130	-10
Cash and cash equivalents, 31 December	24 f	9,934	1,599	1,589

THE STATEMENT EXPLAINS THE REASONS FOR THE CHANGE IN CASH BETWEEN BALANCE SHEET DATES

The last few lines of each statement of cash flows report the amount of cash on each firm's balance sheet at the beginning and the end of each period. Both U.S. GAAP and IFRS require that the statement of cash flows explain changes in cash and cash equivalents. Cash equivalents represent short-term, highly liquid investments in which a firm has temporarily placed excess cash. Throughout this text, we use the term *cash flows* to refer to flows of both cash and cash equivalents.[1] The remaining lines on the statements of cash flows show the inflows and outflows of cash during the period to explain the net change in cash between the two balance sheet dates. Thus, the statement of cash flows reports flows, or changes in cash over time, whereas the balance sheet reports amounts of cash at a single moment.

---

[1]Financial Accounting Standards Board (FASB), *Statement of Financial Accounting Standards No. 95*, "Statement of Cash Flows," 1987 (**Codification Topic 230**); International Accounting Standards Board (IASB), *International Accounting Standard No. 7*, "Statement of Cash Flows," 1992. In 2008 the FASB and IASB tentatively agreed to eliminate the notion of cash equivalents.

EXHIBIT 5.3	Scania
	Note 24 to Financial Statements

NOTE 24 Cash flow statement

In those cases where no allocation by segment is specified, the cash flow statement below refers to Vehicles and Service.

	2006	2005	2004
a. Interest and dividends received/paid			
Dividends received from associated companies	6	4	1
Interest received	550	635	374
Interest paid	-564	-533	-469
b.1 Vehicles and Service: items not affecting cash flow			
Depreciation/amortisation	3,023	2,707	2,158
Bad debts	126	196	205
Associated companies	1	-4	-11
Deferred profit recognition, lease assets	104	65	-42
Other	-100	-81	-9
Total	3,154	2,883	2,301
b.2 Customer Finance: items not affecting cash flow			
Depreciation/amortisation	14	15	15
Bad debts	63	80	89
Other	5	-25	-19
Total	82	70	85
c. Net investment through acquisitions/divestments of businesses[1]			
Divestments of businesses	–	7	0
Acquisitions of businesses	–	-212	-49
Total	–	-205	-49

1 See Note 25, "Businesses acquired/divested".

	2006	2005	2004
d.1 Vehicles and Service: acquisitions of non-current assets			
Investments in non-current assets[2]	-4,618	-4,027	-3,314
Divestments of non-current assets	808	430	516
Total	-3,810	-3,597	-2,798
d.2 Customer Finance: acquisitions of non-current assets			
New financing	-6,713	-4,768	-3,824
Payments of principal and completed contracts	3,199	3,358	3,346
Total	-3,514	-1,410	-478

2 Of which, SEK 180 m. (279 and 316, respectively) in capitalised research and development expenditures.

	2006	2005	2004
e. Change in net debt through financing activities			
Net change in current borrowings	8,827	912	-207
Repayment of non-current borrowings	-6,554	-4,351	-4,446
Increase in non-current borrowings	5,318	3,501	3,389
Total	7,591	62	-1,264
f. Cash and cash equivalents			
Cash and bank balances	1,126	1,106	1,119
Short-term investments comprising cash and cash equivalents	8,808	493	470
Total	9,934	1,599	1,589

THE STATEMENT CLASSIFIES THE REASONS FOR THE CHANGE IN CASH AS AN OPERATING, OR INVESTING, OR FINANCING ACTIVITY

The inflows and outflows of cash during the year appear in the statement of cash flows in one of three categories: operating, investing, and financing. **Figure 5.1** presents the three major types of cash flows, which the following sections describe.

1. Operations A financially healthy company generates sustained cash inflows from selling goods and providing services. Assessed over several years, the cash flow from operations indicates the extent to which operating activities generate more cash than they use. A firm can use the excess **cash flow from operations** to acquire buildings and equipment, pay dividends, retire long-term debt, and conduct other investing and financing activities.

2. Investing The second section of the statement of cash flows shows the amount of **cash flow from investing activities**. The acquisition of noncurrent assets, particularly property, plant, and equipment, usually represents a major ongoing use of cash. A firm must replace such assets as they wear out or become obsolete, and it must acquire additional noncurrent

FIGURE 5.1

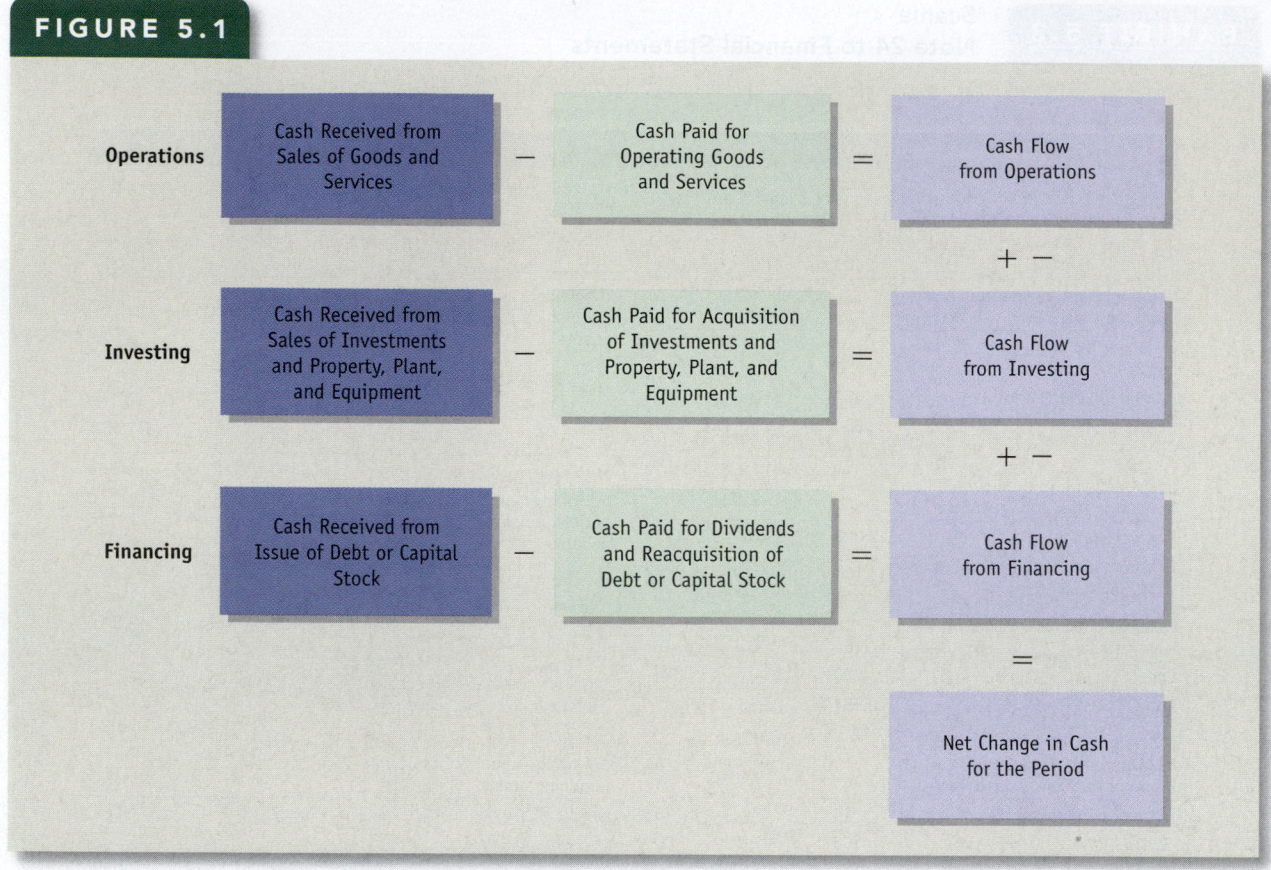

assets if it is to grow. A firm often obtains part of the cash needed to acquire noncurrent assets from sales of existing noncurrent assets. Such cash inflows seldom, however, cover the cost of new acquisitions. Firms not experiencing rapid growth can often finance capital expenditures with cash flow from operations, while rapidly growing firms must often borrow funds or issue common shares to finance their acquisitions of noncurrent assets.

3. Financing Third, a firm obtains cash from borrowing and from issuing common or preferred shares. It uses cash to pay dividends to shareholders, to repay borrowing, and to reacquire outstanding common or preferred shares. These amounts appear as **cash flow from financing activities** in the statement of cash flows.

Ambiguities in Classifying Cash Flows Cash flows do not always fit unambiguously into only one of these three categories. For example, you might think of cash received from investments in securities—received in the form of interest and dividends—as coming from operating activities. The logic for this treatment is that interest and dividends appear as revenues in the income statement. Alternatively, you might view cash received from interest and dividends as coming from investing activities. The logic for this treatment is that cash flows related to the purchase and sale of investments in some securities[2] appear as investing activities in the statement of cash flows. U.S. GAAP requires that firms classify cash receipts from interest and dividend revenues as an operating activity, but classify cash flows related to the purchase and sale of investments in securities as an investing activity. IFRS permits firms to classify cash from interest and dividend revenue as operating, investing, or financing activities, provided the classification is consistently applied across periods.

Similar ambiguities arise with interest expense on debt. Should the cash outflow for interest expense appear as an operating activity (to achieve consistency with its inclusion in the income statement as an expense)? Or, should it appear as a financing activity (to achieve consistency with the classification of debt issues and retirements as a financing activity)? U.S.

---

[2]**Chapter 12** discusses the distinction between the accounting for trading securities and investments in other securities.

GAAP requires that firms classify cash payments for interest expense as an operating activity.[3] IFRS permits firms to select the classification (operating, or investing, or financing) for cash payments of interest expense, again requiring consistent classification from period to period. Under both U.S. GAAP and IFRS, the issue or redemption of debt is a financing activity. Also, cash dividends appear as a financing activity under both U.S. GAAP and IFRS.

Finally, the distinction is not always clear between certain purchases and sales of securities—are these investing or operating activities?—and increases and decreases in certain short-term borrowings—are these financing or operating activities? Later chapters discuss these items more fully, and we return to the question of classification in the last section of this chapter.

READING AND INTERPRETING THE INFORMATION IN THE STATEMENT OF CASH FLOWS

Refer to **Exhibits 5.1** and **5.2**. Both Nordstrom and Scania reported positive cash flow from operations in each of the three years. For example, in the most recent year, Nordstrom reports cash flow from operations of $1,142.4 million, and Scania reports SEK11,146 million. For both firms, the amount of cash flow from operations also exceeded the cash outflows for investing purposes in each of the three years. Business terminology refers to an excess of cash flow from operations over cash flow used for investing as **free cash flow**.[4] Nordstrom's free cash flow for the year ended February 3, 2007, was $924.1 (= $1,142.4 − $218.3) million, and Scania's free cash flow was SEK3,822 (= SEK11,146 − SEK7,324) million for the year ended December 31, 2006.

Firms can use free cash flow to repay borrowing, pay a dividend, repurchase common shares, and add to cash on the balance sheet. In the most recent year, Nordstrom reports that it used its free cash flow primarily to make payments on its long-term debt ($307.6 million cash outflow), to pay dividends ($110.2 million cash outflow), and to reacquire shares of its common stock ($621.5 million cash outflow). In total, Nordstrom's net cash outflow for financing purposes was $984.2 million, or $60.1 million more than the free cash flow generated. Thus, as the last rows of **Exhibit 5.1** show, Nordstrom's cash balance declined by $60.1 million, from $462.6 million at the start of the year to $402.6 million at the end of the year.

Scania reports that for the year ended December 31, 2006, cash flows from financing activities were positive, generating SEK4,591 million in cash inflows. The financing section of its statement of cash flows shows that Scania both issued and repaid debt during 2006, generating a net cash inflow of SEK7,591 million. Payment of a dividend to shareholders of SEK3,000 million reduced this amount. Scania's change in cash for the year was therefore an increase in cash of SEK8,413 (= Scania's free cash flow of SEK3,822 + cash flow from financing of SEK4,591) million. Scania reports that its cash balance increased from a beginning balance of SEK1,599 million to an ending balance of SEK9,934 million in the last lines of **Exhibit 5.2**.

PRESENTATION FORMATS FOR THE STATEMENT OF CASH FLOWS

Both U.S. GAAP and IFRS permit considerable flexibility with respect to the display of information in the statement of cash flows. There are, however, the following requirements:

■ Firms must report cash flows from operations, investing, and financing for the current year and the prior two years.

■ Firms must report the beginning and ending cash balances, and the change in the cash balance. The change in cash must reconcile to the sum of the cash inflows and outflows from operating, investing, and financing activities.

---

[3]The classification of interest expense as an operating activity and dividends paid on common or preferred shares as a financing activity appears inconsistent to some observers as both are payments to suppliers of funds. Authoritative guidance requires the different treatments because interest is an expense in computing net income, whereas dividends represent a distribution of assets generated by net income, not an expense reducing net income.

[4]*Free cash flow* is not a technical term in accounting, but one financial analysts and investment bankers use, so be sure you understand the definition as others use it.

■ If the firm uses the direct method of reporting cash flows from operating activities rather than the indirect method, it must also provide a separate reconciliation of net income to cash flows from operations, as in the blue shaded section of Exhibit 5.1. We discuss the difference between the two methods later in this chapter.

■ Within the investing and financing cash flow categories, the presentation for most items should not net cash inflows against cash outflows. Instead, the firm must show them gross. Gross reporting requires, for example, that firms show the amount of cash spent to acquire property, plant, and equipment for the year separately from the amount of cash received on disposals of property, plant, and equipment during the year.[5]

■ The statement of cash flows does not report *nonmonetary*, sometimes called *noncash, transactions*. That is, the statement does not report transactions that affect recognized assets and liabilities on the balance sheet but that do not result in cash inflows or cash outflows. Examples of nonmonetary transactions are the acquisition of equipment in exchange for shares of common stock and the conversion of a firm's debt into common shares. Under both U.S. GAAP and IFRS, nonmonetary transactions do not appear in the statement of cash flows as investing or financing activities, because they do not help in explaining the change in cash. Firms must disclose nonmonetary investing and financing activities in one of three ways: in the body of the statement of cash flows, or in a separate schedule, or in a note.

To illustrate these requirements, as well as point to differences in formats, refer to Nordstrom's statement of cash flows (**Exhibit 5.1**, which modifies Nordstrom's actual statement in **Exhibit 1.3** to include the direct method for cash flows from operations) and Scania's statement of cash flows (**Exhibit 5.2**). Both firms

■ separately report cash flows from operating, investing, and financing activities;

■ reconcile beginning and ending cash balances to the change in cash flows during the year, and

■ use the indirect method of reporting cash flows, which calculates cash flow from operations by reference to net income.

Their other choices differ in respect to format.

Nordstrom reports gross investing cash flows with separate displays of capital expenditures and proceeds from sale of assets, and separate displays of purchases of short-term investments and sales of short-term investments. In contrast, Scania's statement of cash flows reports many of the cash flow amounts as net amounts (inflows netted against outflows). For example, Scania's cash flow from investing section reports "net investments in non-current assets" of −SEK3,810 for 2006, and its cash flow from financing section reports "change in net debt from financing activities" of +SEK7,591. Scania complies with IFRS rules requiring gross reporting of cash flows, however, because it provides the details of critical line items in note 24 to its financial statements, shown in **Exhibit 5.3**. The data in the note provide the gross reporting required by IFRS. For example, note 24 discloses that in 2006 Scania repaid current borrowings of SEK6,554 million (a financing cash outflow) and increased noncurrent borrowings by SEK5,318 million (a financing cash inflow) for a net cash flow from financing of SEK7,591 million.

The Statement Reconciles Net Income with Cash Flow from Operations

Your first exposure to constructing a statement of cash flows occurred in **Chapter 2**. There you analyzed every entry (change) in the Cash account and placed each change in a statement of cash flows without the required subclassifications. Although the guidance in U.S. GAAP and IFRS states a preference that companies present cash flows from operations as you derived them in **Chapter 2** (the direct method), most companies present cash flows from operations as a reconciliation of net income to operating cash flow (the indirect method).

---

[5]Standard setters view gross reporting as providing a better representation (compared to net reporting) of the firm's operating, investing, and financing activities. The firm may report the net cash flows, however, if gross display of inflows and outflows does not provide more relevant information than does the net change in cash flows. An example might be purchases and sales of highly liquid investments.

The first section of the statement of cash flows derives cash flow from operations. Both U.S. GAAP and IFRS permit firms to report cash flow from operations in either of two ways:

1. **Direct Method** The direct method reports the amounts of cash received from customers less cash disbursed to suppliers, employees, lenders, and taxing authorities. The top panel of **Exhibit 5.1** modifies Nordstrom's published statement of cash flows to illustrate the direct method.

2. **Indirect Method** The indirect method begins with net income for a period and then shows adjustments to net income to convert revenues to cash received from customers and to convert expenses to cash disbursed to various suppliers of goods and services. The boxed section of **Exhibit 5.1** illustrates the indirect method of reporting cash flow from operations. Most companies use this method.

While U.S. GAAP and IFRS permit firms to report cash flow from operations using either the direct or the indirect method, a firm that presents the preferred direct method must also show a reconciliation (see the boxed section of **Exhibit 5.1**) between net income and cash flow from operations. The reconciliation can appear either at the bottom of the statement of cash flows or in a separate note. **Exhibit 5.1** differs from the statement Nordstrom presented in that we show both the direct and indirect methods.

The majority of firms report cash flow from operations using the indirect method. Before the FASB or IASB expressed preference for the direct method, most firms used the indirect method, so both preparers and users had become familiar with it.[6] Experienced financial analysts who use the statement of cash flows generally understand the adjustments required to convert net income to cash flow from operations. The indirect method shows separately changes in inventories, accounts receivable, and accounts payable, whereas the direct method does not. For companies using the direct method, the analyst can refer to the balance sheet to infer the changes. Analysts often look at unusual changes in those three items. A significant increase in inventory might indicate falling sales; a significant increase in accounts receivable might indicate the firm is selling to customers in financial difficulty; an increase in accounts payable might indicate that the firm is unable to pay its vendors on time.

Our experience in teaching the statement of cash flows indicates, however, that on their initial exposure to the statement of cash flows, students have difficulty understanding these adjustments, whereas they find the direct method easier to comprehend. We therefore illustrate the computation of cash flow from operations using both the direct and indirect methods.

Overview of Adjustments to Net Income to Compute Cash Flow from Operations Under the Indirect Method

This section introduces the types of adjustments required to compute cash flow from operations from net income. Later sections of the chapter illustrate these adjustments more fully. The reconciliation of net income to cash flow from operations that a firm using the direct method must provide is essentially the indirect method. In this chapter you will usually see a boxed Reconciliation in the statement of cash flows, which, even though the captions do not explicitly describe it as such, shows the indirect method.

Refer to the reconciliation of net income to cash flow from operations in the boxed section of **Exhibit 5.1**. The first line in the reconciliation shows net income for each year from the income statement. The reconciliation shows the adjustments required to convert net income, measured on an accrual basis, to the amount of net cash flow generated from operations during the period.

Nordstrom shows an addition to net income each year for depreciation (and amortization). To understand this adjustment, first examine the top section, which derives net cash flow as the excess of receipts over disbursements. Depreciation has no place in that section because it uses no cash during that period. Nordstrom used cash in some earlier period to acquire a building or equipment, and in that period reported the use of cash as an investing activity. Depreciation appears as an expense on the income statement because operating retail stores requires using a portion of the service potential of buildings and equipment. The events causing the firm to recognize depreciation expense, however, consume not cash but other assets such as buildings and equipment. Each year Nordstrom recognizes depreciation

---

[6]A recent AICPA survey of 600 large companies reported in the AICPA's annual *Accounting Trends and Techniques* showed that only six to eight companies, about 1%, use the direct method.

expense, which decreases shareholders' equity, and increases accumulated depreciation, which decreases total assets. The reconciliation starts with net income, which included a subtraction for depreciation expense. Because depreciation reduces net income but does not use cash, the reconciliation adds back the depreciation amount to derive cash flow from operations. Subtracting depreciation expense to arrive at the amount of net income reported on the first line of the reconciliation and then adding the same amount of depreciation expense on the second line as a reconciling adjustment to net income results in a zero net effect on cash flow from operations. Thus, the reconciliation's addition for depreciation removes the effect of a noncash expense from operating cash flows.[7]

The reconciliation for Nordstrom shows a subtraction (in each of the three years) for the change (increase) in accounts receivable. How would you derive the amount of cash Nordstrom collected from its customers during a period? Nordstrom made sales in earlier periods as in this period. (For now, assume Nordstrom does not receive cash from customers in the current period as an advance on goods it will deliver in future periods.) Nordstrom received cash this period from customers who purchased before this period; the revenue appeared in that earlier period's income statement when the customers made those purchases. This increased Nordstrom's accounts receivable in the earlier period, followed by a decrease in accounts receivable this period when Nordstrom collected the cash. Nordstrom received additional cash from customers who both purchased and paid this period, resulting in no change in accounts receivable. Finally, Nordstrom made credit sales this period, which it will collect in future periods. As a result accounts receivable increased this period. So, aside from the effects of bad debts, treated in **Chapter 7**, the amount of cash Nordstrom received from customers this period equals the sales for this period, reduced by the increase in accounts receivable during this period or increased by the decrease in accounts receivable during this period.[8]

To see this another way, consider two unrealistic assumptions. First, assume that during a period a firm collects no cash from any of the accounts receivable on the balance sheet at the beginning of the period. Then, the amount of cash the firm receives from customers equals sales revenue less the increase in accounts receivable. Second, assume that a firm has historically made sales on account but that in the current period it makes all its sales for cash. Then, the amount of cash it receives during the period equals sales revenue plus the decrease in accounts receivable.

PROBLEM 5.1 for Self-Study

Classifying cash flows by type of activity. Indicate whether each of the following transactions of the current period would appear as an operating, investing, or financing activity in the statement of cash flows. If any transaction would not appear in the statement of cash flows, suggest the reason.

a. Disbursement of $96,900 to merchandise suppliers.

b. Receipt of $200,000 from issuing common shares.

c. Receipt of $49,200 from customers for sales made this period.

d. Receipt of $22,700 from customers this period for sales made last period.

e. Receipt of $1,800 from a customer for goods the firm will deliver next period.

(continued)

---

[7]To see this another way, imagine a firm whose only activity for a period was the recording of depreciation expense of $100—nothing else. That firm would show negative net income, a loss, of $100, but it would have had no change in cash. Cash flow from operations is zero. So, the reconciliation must start with the −$100 for net income, then add back the $100 depreciation expense, in order to reconcile net loss of −$100 with the zero cash flow from operations. Later chapters explain why the change in the balance sheet account for accumulated depreciation rarely equals the income statement amount for depreciation expense.

[8]A more advanced issue: Nordstrom's balance sheet in **Exhibit 1.1** shows that Accounts Receivable increased from 2005 to 2006 by $44.8 (= $684.4 − $639.6) million. Nordstrom's Statement of Cash Flows in **Exhibit 5.1** shows, however, a larger increase, of $61.3 million. This difference might result from Nordstrom's acquiring some receivables during the year in financing transactions or as part of a corporate acquisition. **Chapters 7** and **11** discuss the raising of cash by selling, or otherwise using, accounts receivable. Sometimes a comparison of the balance sheet and statement of cash flows for changes in accounts receivable, accounts payable, and other items shows a larger (or smaller) balance sheet change than does the statement of cash flows.

f. Disbursement of $16,000 for interest expense on debt.

g. Disbursement of $40,000 to acquire land.

h. Issue of common shares with market value of $60,000 to acquire land.

i. Disbursement of $25,300 as compensation to employees for services rendered this period.

j. Disbursement of $7,900 to employees for services rendered last period but not paid for last period.

k. Disbursement of $53,800 for a patent purchased from its inventor.

l. Acquisition of a building by issuing a note payable to a bank.

m. Disbursement of $19,300 as a dividend to shareholders.

n. Receipt of $12,000 from the sale of equipment that originally cost $20,000 and had $8,000 of accumulated depreciation at the time of sale.

o. Disbursement of $100,000 to redeem bonds at maturity.

p. Disbursement of $40,000 to acquire shares of IBM common stock.

q. Receipt of $200 in dividends from IBM relating to the shares of common stock acquired in transaction **p** above.

PREPARING THE STATEMENT OF CASH FLOWS

Firms could prepare their statements of cash flows directly from entries in their Cash account. To do so would require them to classify each transaction affecting cash as an operating, or investing, or financing activity. As the number of transactions affecting cash increases, however, this approach becomes cumbersome. Most firms design their accounting systems to accumulate the information needed to prepare income statements and balance sheets. They then use a work sheet at the end of the period to transform information from the income statement and balance sheet into a statement of cash flows.

We present a **T-account work sheet** for preparing the statement of cash flows. The work sheet computes cash flow from operations using both the direct and the indirect methods. This T-account work sheet does not show accounts as they appear in the firm's general ledger. Rather, it is like scratch paper, used for computations on the side of the formal record keeping system. Later, we show how to derive the direct method's presentation.

THE CASH CHANGE EQUATION

To understand the preparation of a statement of cash flows, you must understand how changes in cash relate to changes in noncash accounts. The accounting equation states

$$\text{Assets} = \text{Liabilities} + \text{Shareholders' Equity}$$
$$\text{Cash} + \text{Noncash Assets} = \text{Liabilities} + \text{Shareholders' Equity}$$

Balance Sheet Equation (Eq. 1)

This equation must be true for balance sheets constructed at both the start of the period and the end of the period. If the start-of-period and end-of-period balance sheets maintain the accounting equation, then the following equation must also be valid:

$$\begin{array}{c}\text{Change} \\ \text{in Cash}\end{array} + \begin{array}{c}\text{Change in} \\ \text{Noncash} \\ \text{Assets}\end{array} = \begin{array}{c}\text{Change in} \\ \text{Liabilities}\end{array} + \begin{array}{c}\text{Change in} \\ \text{Shareholders'} \\ \text{Equity}\end{array}$$

Balance Sheet Equation (Eq. 2)

Rearranging terms in this equation, we obtain the equation for changes in cash:

$$\begin{array}{c}\text{Change} \\ \text{in Cash}\end{array} = \begin{array}{c}\text{Change in} \\ \text{Liabilities}\end{array} + \begin{array}{c}\text{Change in} \\ \text{Shareholders'} \\ \text{Equity}\end{array} - \begin{array}{c}\text{Change in} \\ \text{Noncash} \\ \text{Assets}\end{array}$$

Cash Change Equation (Eq. 3)

The left-hand side of the **Cash Change Equation** (Eq. 3) represents the change in cash. The right-hand side of the equation, which reflects changes in all noncash accounts, must also equal the change in cash. The equation states that the changes in cash (left-hand side) equal the changes in liabilities plus the changes in shareholders' equity minus the changes in noncash assets (right-hand side). For example, a loan from a bank or another lender increases cash and increases a liability, while the issue of common stock increases cash and increases shareholders' equity. Each of these transactions increases both sides of **Equation 3**.

The purchase with cash of inventory or equipment decreases cash and increases noncash assets. Increases in noncash assets have a negative sign on the right-hand side of the equation, so this transaction decreases both sides of **Equation 3**. *We identify the causes of the change in cash by studying the changes in noncash accounts and classifying each change as operating or investing or financing activities.* The preceding italicized sentence provides the overview of the procedures that underlie the T-account work sheet for the statement of cash flows.

DATA FOR ILLUSTRATIONS

To illustrate the preparation of the statement of cash flows in this chapter, we use information for Solinger Electric Corporation for 2009. **Exhibit 5.4** presents the balance sheet at the beginning and end of 2009. **Exhibit 5.5** presents the income statement for 2009. Solinger Electric Corporation declared and paid $7,000 in dividends during 2009.

T-ACCOUNT WORK SHEET

One can prepare the statement of cash flows by examining every transaction affecting the Cash account, as in **Figure 5.1**, and classifying each one as an operating activity, investing activity, or financing activity.

Given the large number of transactions affecting the Cash account during a period, most firms prepare the statement of cash flows after they have prepared the income statement and the balance sheet. This section presents a step-by-step procedure for preparing the statement of cash flows.

The T-account work sheet for preparing the statement of cash flows, discussed next, provides built-in checks to ensure the full recognition of the effects of each transaction on various accounts. The T-account work sheet uses the T-accounts introduced in **Chapter 2**. After preparing the balance sheet and income statement, you should prepare a T-account work sheet at the end of the period to provide the information for preparing the statement of cash flows. Computer-based business systems do the equivalent of this work, but without T-accounts.

We begin by illustrating the preparation of a T-account work sheet using the data for Solinger Electric Corporation in **Exhibits 5.4** and **5.5**. We then add some complexities to illustrate the use of the T-account work sheet in a more realistic situation.

Step 1 Obtain balance sheets for the beginning and end of the period covered by the statement of cash flows. **Exhibit 5.4** presents the comparative balance sheets of Solinger Electric Corporation for December 31, 2008 and 2009. **Exhibit 5.5** presents the income statement for the year ended December 31, 2009.

Step 2 Prepare a T-account work sheet. An example appears in **Exhibit 5.6**. The top of the work sheet shows a master T-account titled Cash, subdivided into three sections labeled Operations, Investing, and Financing. Enter the beginning and ending amounts of cash in the master T-account. (The beginning and ending cash amounts for Solinger Electric Corporation are $30,000 and $6,000, respectively.) The number at the top of each T-account is the beginning balance; the number at the bottom is the ending balance. The check marks indicate that the figures are balances. The master T-account, Cash, represents the left-hand side of **Equation (3)** for changes in cash.

After preparing the master T-account for Cash (as at the top of **Exhibit 5.6**), complete the work sheet by preparing T-accounts for each liability, shareholders' equity, and noncash asset account. The lower portion of **Exhibit 5.6** shows the T-accounts for each noncash account. Enter the beginning and ending balances in each account for the period given in the balance sheet (see **Exhibit 5.4**). The sum of the changes in these individual T-accounts expresses the right-hand side of **Equation (3)** for changes in cash.

Cash Change Equation (Eq. 3)

Change in Cash	=	Change in Liabilities	+	Change in Shareholders' Equity	−	Change in Noncash Assets

---

Step 3 Explain the change in the master T-account for Cash between the beginning and the end of the period by accounting for the cash effect change from each noncash account during the period. Do this step by reconstructing the entries originally recorded in the accounts during the period and entering them into the same accounts on the T-account work sheet. (You can see how this will appear by looking ahead at **Exhibit 5.7** on page 200.) The only extension is that entries in the master account for cash also require classification as an operating, or investing, or financing activity. Once this procedure has accounted for the net change in each of the noncash accounts, it will have generated sufficient information to account for the net change in cash. In other words, if the reconstructed transactions explain the changes in the right-hand side of the Cash Change Equation (**Eq. 3**), they will have explained the causes of the changes in cash itself on the left-hand side. In constructing the T-account work sheet, we make *analytic entries* that resemble journal entries, but are not part of a firm's record-keeping system. These analytic entries appear only on the work sheet; once we have completed the T-account work sheet and prepared the statement of cash flows, the analytic entries have served their purpose. We can discard them or, perhaps, save them in a file to remind us next period what we did this period.

The debits on the T-account work sheet must equal the credits. Common errors when preparing the T-account work sheet include partial recording of a transaction and recording part of a transaction on the wrong side of a T-account. The errors become evident only on completion of the work sheet when the preparer discovers that the entries in one or more accounts on the T-account work sheet do not explain the change in the account during the period. The preparer must then retrace each of the entries to discover the source of the error. *If you carefully record the analytic entries in the T-account work sheet at the beginning, you will save time later.*

Reconstructing the transactions during the year usually proceeds more easily by accounting first for supplementary information. The following information applies to Solinger Electric Corporation for 2009:

1. Net income is $20,000.

2. Depreciation expense is $10,000.

3. Dividends declared and paid total $7,000.

The analytic entry to record the information concerning net income is as follows:

---

(1) Cash (Operations: Net Income)	20,000	
Retained Earnings.		20,000
Analytic entry recorded in T-account work sheet.		

(Refer to **Exhibit 5.7**, page 200, to see how this analytic entry appears on the T-account work sheet.)

All of the journal entries that together record the process of earning $20,000 in net income are equivalent to the following single journal entry:

Net Assets (= All Assets Minus All Liabilities).	20,000	
Retained Earnings.		20,000

Change in Cash	=	Change in Liabilities	+	Change in Shareholders' Equity	−	Change in Noncash Assets
+20,000		0		+20,000		0
(Opns.)						

Summary entry equivalent to recording earnings of $20,000.

| EXHIBIT 5.4 | Solinger Corporation
Comparative Balance Sheet
December 31, 2009 and 2008 |

	December 31	
	2009	2008
ASSETS		
Current Assets		
Cash	$ 6,000	$ 30,000
Accounts Receivable	55,000	20,000
Merchandise Inventory	50,000	40,000
Total Current Assets	$111,000	$ 90,000
Noncurrent Assets		
Buildings and Equipment (Cost)	$225,000	$100,000
Accumulated Depreciation	(40,000)	(30,000)
Total Noncurrent Assets	$185,000	$ 70,000
Total Assets	$296,000	$160,000
TOTAL SOURCES OF FUNDING		
Current Liabilities		
Accounts Payable—Merchandise Suppliers	$ 50,000	$ 30,000
Accounts Payable—Other Suppliers	12,000	10,000
Salaries Payable	6,000	5,000
Total Current Liabilities	$ 68,000	$ 45,000
Noncurrent Liabilities		
Bonds Payable	$100,000	$ 0
Shareholders' Equity		
Common Stock	$100,000	$100,000
Retained Earnings	28,000	15,000
Total Shareholders' Equity	$128,000	$115,000
Total Sources of Funding	$296,000	$160,000

| EXHIBIT 5.5 | Solinger Electric Corporation
Income Statement
For 2009 |

Sales Revenue	$125,000
Cost of Goods Sold	(60,000)
Depreciation Expense	(10,000)
Salary Expense	(20,000)
Interest Expense	(4,000)
Other Expenses	(11,000)
Net Income	$ 20,000

Both the T-account work sheet and the cash flow from operations section of an actual statement of cash flows (for the indirect method) start with the assumption that all earnings produce cash from operations. Subsequent additions and subtractions correct for transactions where that assumption is invalid.

The preceding journal entry summarizes all the effects on the balance sheet of the income earning activities. That entry shows one debit to Net Assets. We assume at this stage of preparing the statement of cash flows that all of the net assets generated by the earnings process were cash. Thus, in analytic entry **(1)**, the debit shows a provisional increase in cash from operations equal to net income for the period.

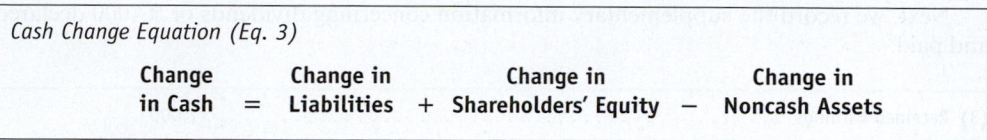

Cash Change Equation (Eq. 3)

Change in Cash	=	Change in Liabilities	+	Change in Shareholders' Equity	−	Change in Noncash Assets

EXHIBIT 5.6   **Solinger Electric Corporation**
T-Account Work Sheet

Cash

| ✓ 30,000 | |

Operations

Investing

Financing

| ✓ 6,000 | |

Accounts Receivable		**Merchandise Inventory**		**Buildings and Equipment (Cost)**	
✓ 20,000		✓ 40,000		✓ 100,000	
✓ 55,000		✓ 50,000		✓ 225,000	

Accumulated Depreciation		**Accounts Payable— Merchandise Suppliers**		**Accounts Payable— Other Suppliers**	
	30,000 ✓		30,000 ✓		10,000 ✓
	40,000 ✓		50,000 ✓		12,000 ✓

Salaries Payable		**Bonds Payable**		**Retained Earnings**	
	5,000 ✓		0 ✓		15,000 ✓
	6,000 ✓		100,000 ✓		28,000 ✓

Not all expenses decrease cash. To calculate the net amount of cash from operations, we must add back to the provisional increase in cash in the amount of any expenses that do not use cash (but instead use noncash net assets in this period). An example is depreciation, illustrated in entry **(2)**:

(2) Cash (Operations: Depreciation Expense Addback)   10,000
       Accumulated Depreciation   10,000
Analytic entry recorded in T-account work sheet.

Depreciation expense, deducted in calculating net income, did not reduce cash this period. Some time ago, the firm used cash to acquire the fixed assets it now depreciates. The use of cash appeared on the statement for the earlier period in the Investing section. This analytic entry adds back depreciation expense to net income in calculating the amount of cash flow from operations.

Next, we record the supplementary information concerning dividends of $7,000 declared and paid:

(3) Retained Earnings	7,000	
Cash (Financing: Dividends)		7,000
Analytic entry recorded in T-account work sheet.		

Dividends reduce retained earnings and cash. Paying dividends appears on the statement of cash flows as a financing activity.

Once the T-account work sheet reflects the supplementary information, one must make inferences about the reasons for the remaining changes in the noncash accounts on the balance sheet. (The preparer of a statement of cash flows for an actual firm will likely not need to make such inferences because sufficient information regarding the change in each account will exist in the firm's accounting records.) Explanations for the changes in noncash accounts appear below, in balance sheet order.

The Accounts Receivable account shows an increase of $35,000. The analytic entry to record this information in the work sheet is as follows:

(4) Accounts Receivable	35,000	
Cash (Operations: Subtractions)		35,000
Analytic entry recorded in T-account work sheet.		

The operations of the period generated sales, but not all of these sales resulted in an increase in cash. Some of the sales increased accounts receivable. Because we start the statement of cash flows with net income, provisionally assuming that all sales generated cash, we must subtract that portion of revenues that did not produce cash (that is, the excess of sales on account over cash collections from customers) in deriving the amount of actual cash from operations.

The next noncash account that changed, Merchandise Inventory, shows an increase of $10,000. The analytic entry in the work sheet to explain the change in Merchandise Inventory is as follows:

(5) Merchandise Inventory	10,000	
Cash (Operations: Subtractions)		10,000
Analytic entry recorded in T-account work sheet.		

Solinger Electric Corporation increased the amount of inventory carried, presumably to support increased future sales. Increasing inventory ordinarily uses cash, and the preparation process provisionally assumes that the firm used cash to acquire all inventory. Later, the process will adjust for the amounts the firm will pay later and for the amounts where the firm has already used cash because it paid in advance. The cost of goods sold reduces the amount of net income; because we start the statement of cash flows with net income, in deriving the amount of cash from operations we must subtract from net income the increase in inventories during the year (that is, the excess of purchases over the cost of goods sold).

The next noncash account, Buildings and Equipment (Cost), shows a net increase of $125,000 (= $225,000 − $100,000). Because we have no other information, we assume that the firm acquired buildings and equipment costing $125,000 during the year. The analytic entry is as follows:

(6) Buildings and Equipment (Cost)	125,000	
Cash (Investing: Acquisitions of Buildings and Equipment)		125,000
Analytic entry recorded in T-account work sheet.		

The next noncash account showing a change is Accounts Payable—Merchandise Suppliers. As the amounts the firm carries in inventory increase, so do amounts it owes to suppliers

$$\begin{array}{l}
\textit{Cash Change Equation (Eq. 3)} \\[4pt]
\begin{array}{ccccc}
\textbf{Change} & & \textbf{Change in} & \textbf{Change in} & \textbf{Change in} \\
\textbf{in Cash} & = & \textbf{Liabilities} + & \textbf{Shareholders' Equity} - & \textbf{Noncash Assets}
\end{array}
\end{array}$$

of inventory. The analytic entry to explain the increase in the amount of Accounts Payable—Merchandise Suppliers is as follows:

(7) Cash (Operations: Additions).....................................	20,000	
Accounts Payable—Merchandise Suppliers		20,000
Analytic entry recorded in T-account work sheet.		

Ordinarily, acquiring inventory requires cash, and in analytic entry **(5)** we assumed that the firm paid cash in the period of acquisition for all inventory it acquired. Suppliers who allow a firm to pay later for goods and services received now in effect supply the firm with cash. Thus, an increase in accounts payable for inventory results from a transaction in which inventory increases but cash will decrease later. This is equivalent to saying that an increase in payables provides cash, even if it is only temporary. Accounting classifies the increase in cash resulting from increased payables for inventory as an operating source of cash.

The next noncash account showing a change is Accounts Payable—Other Suppliers. The analytic entry to explain the increase in the amount of Accounts Payable—Other Suppliers is as follows:

(8) Cash (Operations: Additions)	2,000	
Accounts Payable—Other Suppliers		2,000
Analytic entry recorded in T-account work sheet.		

The reasoning behind this analytic entry is the same as for analytic entry **(7)**. Creditors who permit a firm to increase amounts it owes temporarily provide it with cash.

The same reasoning applies to an increased amount of Salaries Payable, the next noncash account showing a change. The analytic entry to record the increase in Salaries Payable is as follows:

(9) Cash (Operations: Additions)	1,000	
Salaries Payable		1,000
Analytic entry recorded in T-account work sheet.		

Employees who receive salary payments weekly or biweekly or monthly—who do not receive immediate payment for earned salaries—temporarily provide their employer with cash.

Bonds Payable, the final noncash account with a change not yet explained, shows a net increase of $100,000 for the year. We infer that the firm issued long-term bonds during the year, receiving cash of $100,000 in return. The analytic entry is as follows:

(10) Cash (Financing: Long-Term Bond Issue)........................	100,000	
Bonds Payable		100,000
Analytic entry recorded in T-account work sheet.		

Exhibit 5.7 presents the completed T-account work sheet for Solinger Electric Corporation for 2009. The 10 analytic entries explain all changes in the noncash T-accounts and show annotations in the components of change in the Cash account.

Step 4 In the final step we use the information in the master T-account for cash in the completed work sheet to prepare a formal statement of cash flows. **Exhibit 5.8** on page 201 presents the Solinger Electric Corporation statement of cash flows.

EXHIBIT 5.7   Solinger Electric Corporation
T-Account Work Sheet

Cash

✓	30,000			

Operations

Net Income	(1)	20,000	35,000	(4)	Increased Accounts Receivable
Depreciation Expense Addback	(2)	10,000	10,000	(5)	Increased Merchandise Inventory
Increased Accounts Payable to Merchandise Suppliers	(7)	20,000			
Increased Accounts Payable to Other Suppliers	(8)	2,000			
Increased Salaries Payable	(9)	1,000			

Investing

			125,000	(6)	Acquisition of Buildings and Equipment

Financing

Long-Term Bond Issue	(10)	100,000	7,000	(3)	Dividends
	✓	6,000			

Accounts Receivable				Merchandise Inventory				Buildings and Equipment (Cost)		
✓	20,000			✓	40,000			✓	100,000	
(4)	35,000			(5)	10,000			(6)	125,000	
✓	55,000			✓	50,000			✓	225,000	

Accumulated Depreciation			Accounts Payable— Merchandise Suppliers			Accounts Payable— Other Suppliers		
	30,000	✓		30,000	✓		10,000	✓
	10,000	(2)		20,000	(7)		2,000	(8)
	40,000	✓		50,000	✓		12,000	✓

Salaries Payable			Bonds Payable			Retained Earnings			
	5,000	✓		0	✓			15,000	✓
	1,000	(9)		100,000	(10)	(3)	7,000	20,000	(1)
	6,000	✓		100,000	✓			28,000	✓

DEPRECIATION DOES NOT PROVIDE CASH

Because the indirect method adds depreciation expense to net income to calculate cash provided by operations, readers of financial statements might incorrectly conclude that depreciation charges provide cash. The recording of depreciation expense does not affect cash. A noncash asset decreases, and a shareholders' equity account decreases. Cash from operations results from selling goods and services to customers. If a firm makes no sales, there will be no cash provided by operations regardless of the size of the depreciation charge.

We trust you have mastered the concept that *depreciation does not provide cash*, even though the indirect method of presenting cash flow from operations shows an addback for depreciation. When the firm considers income taxes, however, depreciation indirectly affects cash flow. Depreciation affects the calculation of net income reported in the financial statements, and as a deduction, it also reduces taxable income on tax returns. (**Chapter 11** explains why the amounts typically differ.) The larger the amount of depreciation on tax returns, the smaller is the taxable income and the smaller the current payment for income taxes.

Cash Change Equation (Eq. 3)

Change in Cash	=	Change in Liabilities	+	Change in Shareholders' Equity	−	Change in Noncash Assets

EXHIBIT 5.8

**Solinger Electric Corporation
Statement of Cash Flows
For the Year 2009
Indirect Method**

Operations

Net Income		$ 20,000
Additions:		
Depreciation Expense Not Using Cash		10,000
Increased Accounts Payable:		
To Suppliers of Merchandise		20,000
To Other Suppliers		2,000
Increased Salaries Payable		1,000
Subtractions:		
Increased Accounts Receivable		(35,000)
Increased Merchandise Inventory		(10,000)
Cash Flow from Operations		$ 8,000
Investing		
Acquisition of Buildings and Equipment		(125,000)
Financing		
Dividends Paid	$ (7,000)	
Proceeds from Long-Term Bonds Issued	100,000	
Cash Flow from Financing		93,000
Net Change in Cash for Year		$ (24,000)
Cash, January 1, 2009		30,000
Cash, December 31, 2009		$ 6,000

PROBLEM 5.2 for Self-Study

Preparing a T-account work sheet for a statement of cash flows. Exhibit 5.9 presents a comparative balance sheet for Robbie Corporation as of December 31, 2007 and 2008. **Exhibit 5.10** on page 202 shows the income statement for 2008. During 2008 the firm sold no property, plant, and equipment. It declared and paid dividends of $2,000. Prepare a T-account work sheet for the preparation of a statement of cash flows for 2008. Use the format shown in **Exhibit 5.7**.

DIRECT METHOD

Most firms present the operating sections of their statements of cash flows using the indirect method; some of us think this will change within the next decade or so. A firm that uses the direct method in reporting cash flow from operations must also reconcile net income with cash flow from operations, which gives the same information as in the indirect method. Next, we show how you can derive cash flow from operations displayed with the direct method from the T-account work sheet you have constructed to derive cash flow from operations displayed with the indirect method.

Refer to the T-account work sheet in **Exhibit 5.7**. **Exhibit 5.11** on page 203 derives the display for the direct method. The derivation takes three steps shown in three separate panels in **Exhibit 5.11**. After this first illustration, we show all three steps in a single panel.

EXHIBIT 5.9

Robbie Corporation
Comparative Balance Sheet
December 31, 2008 and 2007
(all dollar amounts in thousands)
(Problem 5.2 for Self-Study)

	December 31				December 31	
	2008	2007			2008	2007
ASSETS				**LIABILITIES AND SHAREHOLDERS' EQUITY**		
Current Assets				**Current Liabilities**		
Cash	$ 25	$10		Accounts Payable for Merchandise	$ 37	$30
Accounts Receivable	22	15		Total Current Liabilities	$ 37	$30
Merchandise Inventories	18	20		**Long-Term Debt**		
Total Current Assets	$ 65	$45		Bonds Payable	18	10
Noncurrent Assets				Total Liabilities	$ 55	$40
Property, Plant, and Equipment	$ 66	$50		**Shareholders' Equity**		
Less Accumulated Depreciation	(31)	(25)		Common Stock	$ 20	$10
Total Property, Plant, and Equipment	$ 35	$25		Retained Earnings	25	20
Total Assets	$100	$70		Total Shareholders' Equity	$ 45	$30
				Total Liabilities and Shareholders' Equity	$100	$70

EXHIBIT 5.10

Robbie Corporation
Income Statement
For Year 2008
(all dollar amounts in thousands)
(Problem 5.2 for Self-Study)

Sales Revenue	$180
Cost of Goods Sold	(140)
Selling and Administrative Expenses	(25)
Depreciation Expense	(6)
Interest Expense	(2)
Net Income	$ 7

Step 1 Copy the income statement into the left-hand box. Copy to the bottom left of the middle box the $8,000 of Cash Flow from Operations derived from the indirect method. This number serves as a check on the derivation of the direct method's answer.

Step 2 Copy into the middle box all the additions and subtractions in the *operations section* of the master Cash account in the T-account work sheet, including the $20,000 of net income shown below the box. Place the number next to the income statement item to which the addition or subtraction relates: Accounts Receivable subtraction next to Sales Revenue, Depreciation next to Depreciation Expense, and so on. To do this, you need to understand which income statement item a given addition or subtraction refers to. In placing the number in column **(b)**, use a plus sign if it is on the debit side of the Cash T-account work sheet, which represents a tentative increase in cash. Place the number in column **(b)** with a minus sign if it comes from the credit side of the Cash account, which represents a tentative decrease in cash. To repeat: copy the data from the operations section only.

Add the numbers in column **(b)** to check that you have shown the indirect method's computation of cash flow from operations. Note that column **(b)** resembles the Operating section of the indirect method for the statement of cash flows, except that the numbers have a different order—net income is at the bottom, not at the top—and the other numbers are in income statement order.

EXHIBIT 5.11

Solinger Electric Corporation
Deriving Direct Method Cash Flow from Operations
Using Data from T-Account Work Sheet

Each step is in a separate panel. Later versions condense all work into a single panel.

1. Copy Income Statement and Cash Flow from Operations

		Changes in Related **Balance Sheet Accounts** **from T-Account Work Sheet**		
Operations (a)	(a)	(b)	(c)	(d)
Sales Revenues	$125,000			
Cost of Goods Sold	(60,000)			
Depreciation Expense	(10,000)			
Salary Expense	(20,000)			
Interest Expense	(4,000)			
Other Expense	(11,000)			
Net Income	$ 20,000		Totals	$ —

$ 8,000 = Cash Flow from Operations Derived via Indirect Method

2. Copy Information from T-Account Work Sheet Next to Related Income Statement Item

		Copy from **T-Account** **Work Sheet**	**Changes in Related** **Balance Sheet Accounts** **from T-Account Work Sheet**	
Operations	(a)	(b)	(c)	(d)
Sales Revenues	$125,000	$(35,000)	= Accounts Receivable Increase	
Cost of Goods Sold	(60,000)	(10,000)	= Inventory Increase	
		20,000	= Accounts Payable to Merchandise Suppliers Increase	
Depreciation Expense	(10,000)	10,000	(Expense Not Using Cash)	
Salary Expense	(20,000)	1,000	= Salaries Payable Increase	
Interest Expense	(4,000)	—	Interest Payable (no change in balance sheet)	
Other Expenses	(11,000)	2,000	= Accounts Payable to Other Suppliers Increase	
Net Income	$ 20,000	$ 20,000 = Net Income	Totals	$ —

$ 8,000 = Cash Flow from Operations Derived via Indirect Method

3. Sum Across Rows to Derive Direct Receipts and Expenditures

		Indirect **Method**	**Changes in Related** **Balance Sheet Accounts** **from T-Account Work Sheet**	**Direct** **Method**	**From Operations:** **Receipts Less Expenditures**
Operations	(a)	(b)	(c)	(d)	
Sales Revenues	$125,000	$(35,000)	= Accounts Receivable Increase	$90,000	Receipts from Customers
Cost of Goods Sold	(60,000)	(10,000)	= Inventory Increase	$(50,000)	Payments for Goods Sold
		20,000	= Accounts Payable to Merchandise Suppliers Increase		
Depreciation Expense	(10,000)	10,000	(Expense Not Using Cash)	—	
Salary Expense	(20,000)	1,000	= Salaries Payable Increase	(19,000)	Payments for Salaries
Interest Expense	(4,000)	—	Interest Payable (no change in balance sheet)	(4,000)	Payments for Interest
Other Expenses	(11,000)	2,000	= Accounts Payable to Other Suppliers Increase	(9,000)	Payments for Other Expenses
Net Income	$ 20,000	$ 20,000 Net Income Totals		$ 8,000	= Cash Flow from Operations Derived via Direct Method

$ 8,000 = Cash Flow from Operations Derived via Indirect Method

Note that the information in column (b) is cash flow from operations derived with the indirect method, with items in a different order.

Step 3 Add across the numbers in columns **(a)** and **(b)**, and write the sums in column **(d)**. Give the resulting sum a label—either Receipts or Payments (or Expenditures). The label should describe the nature of the receipt or payment, using any descriptive label that seems appropriate to you. Add the numbers in column **(d)**. If you have done the work correctly, the sum in column **(d)** will match the sum in column **(b)** and both will equal cash flow from operations.

To understand that the indirect and direct methods provide the same data, but in different subtotals, consider the following summary. The indirect method starts with net income, which equals revenues minus expenses. Then, it adds amounts to net income for revenues (or expenses) that produce (or use) cash in amounts different from the revenue (or expense) item. The direct method takes each revenue (and expense) and adds to or subtracts from each of them separately to derive the related receipt or payment. The additions and subtractions for the direct method are the same as for the indirect method. Only the order of computations and presentation differs.

PROBLEM 5.3 for Self-Study

> **Deriving a direct method presentation of cash flows from operations from a T-account work sheet.** Refer to **Problem 5.2 for Self-Study** and its solution. Prepare a derivation of cash flows from operations for Robbie Corporation for 2008 using the direct method and the T-account work sheet in **Exhibit 5.17** on page 215. Use the format of **Exhibit 5.11**, but condense your work into a single panel.

EXTENSION OF THE ILLUSTRATION TO MORE COMPLEX TRANSACTIONS

The illustration for Solinger Electric Corporation considered so far in this chapter is simpler than the typical published statement of cash flows in at least four respects:

1. Only a few balance sheet accounts require explanation.
2. Several types of more complex transactions that affect cash flow from operations do not arise.
3. Each transaction recorded in **Step 3** involves only one debit and one credit.
4. Except for the Retained Earnings account, each explanation of a noncash account change involves only one analytic entry on the work sheet.

Most of the complications that arise in interpreting published statements of cash flows relate to accounting events that later chapters discuss. We illustrate here one complication, arising from an asset disposition that notes to the financial statements will describe. Assume the firm sold some of its equipment during the year at its *carrying value*; that is, the cash proceeds from disposition equal acquisition cost less than the accumulated depreciation of the assets. With this assumption, no gain or loss on the disposition arises.

Disposal of Equipment with No Gain nor Loss Reconsider the Solinger Electric Corporation, assuming that Solinger sold some equipment during 2009 for $3,000 cash. It originally paid $10,000 for this equipment and the accumulated depreciation on the equipment was $7,000. The actual entry made during the year to record the disposal of the equipment was as follows:

Cash   3,000
Accumulated Depreciation   7,000
     Buildings and Equipment (Cost)   10,000

Change in Cash	=	Change in Liabilities	+	Change in Shareholders' Equity	−	Change in Noncash Assets
+3,000		0		0		+7,000
(Invst.)						−10,000

Journal entry for disposal of equipment at carrying value.

Here, we focus on the statement of cash flows, so we show the Cash Change Equation, which we derived from the Balance Sheet Equation.

Assume this is additional information, so that the comparative balance sheets as shown in **Exhibit 5.4** remain the same and thus the net decrease in cash for 2009 is still $24,000. The entries in the T-accounts must change to reflect this new information. To adjust for this new information, we add one new journal entry **(1a)**, replace journal entry **(6)** with **(6a)**, and replace analytic entry **(2)** with **(2a)**. The following analytic entry in the T-account work sheet recognizes the effect of the disposal of equipment:

(1a) Cash (Investing: Disposal of Equipment)	3,000	
Accumulated Depreciation	7,000	
Buildings and Equipment (Cost)		10,000
Analytic entry recorded in T-account work sheet.		

The debit to Cash (Investing: Disposal of Equipment) shows the proceeds of the disposal. As a result of analytic entry **(1a)**, the T-accounts for Buildings and Equipment (Cost) and Accumulated Depreciation appear as follows:

Buildings and Equipment			**Accumulated Depreciation**		
✓ 100,000				30,000	✓
	10,000	**(1a)**	**(1a)** 7,000		
✓ 225,000				40,000	✓

When the time comes to explain the change in Buildings and Equipment (Cost) account, the T-account indicates both a total increase of $125,000 and a credit (decrease) entry **(1a)** of $10,000 to recognize the disposal of equipment. To explain the net increase in the Buildings and Equipment (Cost) account, given the decrease already entered, one must assume that the firm acquired new buildings and equipment for $135,000 (= $125,000 + $10,000) during the period.

The reconstructed analytic entry, which replaces analytic entry **(6)**, and which completes the explanation of the change in this account is as follows:

(6a) Buildings and Equipment (Cost)	135,000	
Cash (Investing: Acquisition of Buildings and Equipment).		135,000
Analytic entry recorded in T-account work sheet.		

Likewise, when the time comes to explain the change in the T-account for Accumulated Depreciation, there is a net credit change of $10,000 and a debit entry of $7,000 **(1a)** to recognize disposal. Thus the depreciation charge for 2009 must have been $17,000 (= $10,000 + $7,000). The reconstructed analytic entry, which replaces analytic entry **(2)** and which completes the explanation of the change in the Accumulated Depreciation account is as follows:

(2a) Cash (Operations: Depreciation Expense Addback).	17,000	
Accumulated Depreciation		17,000
Analytic entry recorded in T-account work sheet.		

Exhibit 5.12 presents a revised T-account work sheet for Solinger Electric Corporation incorporating the new information on the disposal of equipment.

Loss on Disposal of Equipment

Now assume that Solinger Electric Corporation sold the equipment discussed previously for $2,000 instead of $3,000. The entry made during the year to record the disposal of the equipment is as follows:

Cash.	2,000	
Loss on Disposal of Equipment	1,000	
Accumulated Depreciation	7,000	
Buildings and Equipment (Cost)		10,000

(continued)

Assets	=	Liabilities	+	Shareholders' Equity	(Class.)
+2,000				−1,000	IncSt → RE
+7,000					
−10,000					

Change in Cash	=	Change in Liabilities	+	Change in Shareholders' Equity	−	Change in Noncash Assets
+2,000	=	0	+	−1,000	−	−10,000
(Invst.)						+7,000

Journal entry to record disposal of equipment for cash at a loss. We show both the Balance Sheet Equation and the Cash Change Equation.

This entry removes from the accounting records all amounts related to the equipment sold including its acquisition cost of $10,000 and the $7,000 of accumulated depreciation recognized while Solinger Electric Corporation used the equipment. The entry also records the cash Solinger received from disposal of the equipment. The difference between the cash proceeds and the carrying value of the equipment is a loss of $1,000 [= $2,000 − ($10,000 − $7,000)].

The following analytic entry on the T-account work sheet would recognize the effect of the disposal of equipment for $2,000:

(1a) Cash (Investing: Disposal of Equipment) 2,000

Cash (Operations: Loss on Disposal of Equipment Addback) 1,000

Accumulated Depreciation 7,000

    Buildings and Equipment (Cost) 10,000

Analytic entry recorded in T-account work sheet.

The debit to Cash (Investing: Disposal of Equipment) shows the $2,000 proceeds of disposal. The debit to Cash (Operations: Loss on Disposal of Equipment Addback) for $1,000 adds back to net income the loss on disposal of equipment that did not use cash. Like the depreciation expense addback, the debit to Cash (Operations: Loss on Disposal of Equipment Addback) does not represent an operating source of cash (ignoring income taxes). The addback offsets the subtraction of the loss in computing net income. The loss did not use cash this period. The firm spent cash sometime in the past, and it now finds that the assets purchased with that cash have a market value lower than their carrying value.

Consider the impact of reporting the disposal of equipment at a loss on various lines of the statement of cash flows:

Operations

Net Income (Loss on Disposal of Equipment) .... $(1,000)

Loss on Disposal of Equipment Addback 1,000

    Cash Flow from Operations .... $ 0

Investing

Proceeds from Disposal of Equipment .... $ 2,000

Net Change in Cash .... $ 2,000

One might view the recognition of a loss on the disposal of equipment as indicating that the firm recorded insufficient depreciation during the accounting periods before the disposal. If the firm had known for certain that it would receive $2,000 for the equipment, it would have recognized another $1,000 of depreciation expense during the periods when it used the equipment. The disposal of the equipment would then have resulted in no gain or loss. The firm would have shown the $1,000 additional depreciation as an addback to net income in computing cash flow from operations during the periods when it used the equipment.

EXHIBIT 5.12

Solinger Electric Corporation
Revised T-Account Work Sheet

Cash

✓	30,000				

Operations

Net Income	(1)	20,000	35,000	(4)	Increased Accounts Receivable
Depreciation Expense Addback	(2a)	17,000	10,000	(5)	Increased Merchandise Inventory
Increased Accounts Payable to Merchandise Suppliers	(7)	20,000			
Increased Accounts Payable to Other Suppliers	(8)	2,000			
Increased Salaries Payable	(9)	1,000			

Investing

Disposal of Equipment	(1a)	3,000	135,000	(6a)	Acquisition of Buildings and Equipment

Financing

Long-Term Bond Issue	(10)	100,000	7,000	(3)	Dividends
	✓	6,000			

Accounts Receivable

✓	20,000		
(4)	35,000		
✓	55,000		

Merchandise Inventory

✓	40,000		
(5)	10,000		
✓	50,000		

Buildings and Equipment (Cost)

✓	100,000		
(6a)	135,000	10,000	(1a)
✓	225,000		

Accumulated Depreciation

		30,000	✓
(1a)	7,000	17,000	(2a)
		40,000	✓

Accounts Payable— Merchandise Suppliers

		30,000	✓
		20,000	(7)
		50,000	✓

Accounts Payable— Other Suppliers

		10,000	✓
		2,000	(8)
		12,000	✓

Salaries Payable

		5,000	✓
		1,000	(9)
		6,000	✓

Bonds Payable

		0	✓
		100,000	(10)
		100,000	✓

Retained Earnings

		15,000	✓
(3)	7,000	20,000	(1)
		28,000	✓

Gain on Disposal of Equipment

Extending this illustration still further, assume that Solinger Electric Corporation received $4,500 for the equipment. The entry made to record the disposal of equipment is as follows:

Cash	4,500	
Accumulated Depreciation	7,000	
Buildings and Equipment (Cost)		10,000
Gain on Disposal of Equipment		1,500

Journal entry to record disposal of equipment.

Assets	=	Liabilities	+	Shareholders' Equity	(Class.)
+4,500				+1,500	IncSt → RE
+7,000					
−10,000					

Change in Cash	=	Change in Liabilities	+	Change in Shareholders' Equity	–	Change in Noncash Assets
+4,500		0		+1,500		+7,000
(Invst.)						–10,000

This entry, like the one for the disposal at a loss, removes the amounts on the books for the equipment and records the cash proceeds. In this case the cash proceeds exceed the carrying value of the equipment, resulting in a gain on disposal.

The following analytic entry in the T-account work sheet would recognize the effect of the disposal of equipment for $4,500:

(1a) Cash (Investing: Disposal of Equipment)........................	4,500	
Accumulated Depreciation	7,000	
Buildings and Equipment (Cost)		10,000
Cash (Operations: Gain on Disposal		
of Equipment Subtraction)		1,500
Analytic entry recorded in T-account work sheet.		

The debit to Cash (Investing: Disposal of Equipment) shows the $4,500 proceeds of disposal. The credit to Cash (Operations: Gain on Disposal of Equipment Subtraction) reduces net income for the gain on disposals of equipment that did not provide an operating cash inflow. Unless we subtract the $1,500 gain in the operations section of the work sheet, we overstate the amount of cash inflow from this transaction, as the following analysis summarizes:

Operations

Net Income (Gain on Disposal of Equipment)	$ 1,500
Subtraction for Gain on Disposal of Equipment Not Providing an Operating Cash Inflow	$(1,500)
Cash Flow from Operations	$ 0
Investing	
Proceeds from Disposal of Equipment	$ 4,500
Net Change in Cash from Transaction	$ 4,500

PROBLEM 5.4 for Self-Study

Preparing a statement of cash flows. Exhibit 5.13 presents a comparative balance sheet for Gordon Corporation as of December 31, 2007 and 2008. **Exhibit 5.14** on page 209 presents the income statement for 2008.

During 2008 the company declared and paid dividends of $120,000.

During 2008 the company disposed of buildings and equipment that originally cost $55,000 and had accumulated depreciation at the time of disposal of $30,000.

a. Prepare a T-account work sheet for the preparation of the statement of cash flows for 2008 using the indirect method for cash flows from operations.

b. Derive a presentation for cash flows from operations using the format of **Exhibit 5.11**, but using a single panel.

c. Present a statement of cash flows for 2008 using the direct method for cash flows from operations and include a reconciliation of net income to cash flows from operations.

EXHIBIT 5.13

Gordon Corporation
Comparative Balance Sheet
December 31, 2008 and 2007
(all dollar amounts in thousands)
(Problem 5.4 for Self-Study)

	December 31	
	2008	**2007**
ASSETS		
Current Assets		
Cash	$ 40	$ 70
Accounts Receivable	420	320
Merchandise Inventories	470	360
Prepayments	70	50
Total Current Assets.....................	$1,000	$ 800
Property, Plant, and Equipment		
Land..	$ 250	$ 200
Buildings and Equipment (net of accumulated		
depreciation of $840 in 2008 and $800 in 2007)	1,150	1,000
Total Property, Plant, and Equipment	$1,400	$1,200
Total Assets	$2,400	$2,000
LIABILITIES AND SHAREHOLDERS' EQUITY		
Current Liabilities		
Accounts Payable	$ 440	$ 320
Income Taxes Payable	80	60
Other Current Liabilities.....................	360	170
Total Current Liabilities	$ 880	$ 550
Noncurrent Liabilities		
Bonds Payable	200	250
Total Liabilities.........................	$1,080	$ 800
Shareholders' Equity		
Common Stock	$ 540	$ 500
Retained Earnings	780	700
Total Shareholders' Equity	$1,320	$1,200
Total Liabilities and Shareholders' Equity	$2,400	$2,000

EXHIBIT 5.14

Gordon Corporation
Income Statement
For the Year 2008
(all dollar amounts in thousands)
(Problem 5.4 for Self-Study)

Revenues	$1,600
Less:	
Cost of Goods Sold	(900)
Depreciation Expense	(70)
Selling and Administrative Expense	(255)
Interest Expense..	(30)
Loss on Disposal of Buildings and Equipment	(15)
Income Tax Expense	(130)
Net Income	$ 200

USING INFORMATION FROM THE STATEMENT OF CASH FLOWS

The statement of cash flows provides information that helps the reader in (1) assessing the impact of operations on liquidity and (2) assessing the relations among cash flows from operating, investing, and financing activities.

IMPACT OF OPERATIONS ON LIQUIDITY

Perhaps the most important omission from the balance sheet and the income statement is how the operations of a period affected cash flows. Increased earnings do not always generate increased cash flow from operations. When increased earnings result from expanding operations (that is, more *units* sold in contrast to increases in selling price or reductions in cost), the firm usually has decreased cash flow from operations. A growing, successful firm—such as Nordstrom, discussed in connection with **Exhibit 5.1**—may have increasing amounts for accounts receivable and inventories, resulting in a lag between earnings and cash flows. The need to await the collection of accounts receivable but to acquire and pay for additional inventory in anticipation of greater future sales can lead to negative cash from operations. Growing businesses use financing from long-term debt issues or common shares issues to cover short-term cash needs. A failure to obtain long-term financing can lead to chronic liquidity problems.

On the other hand, increased cash flow can accompany reduced earnings. Consider, for example, a firm that is experiencing operating problems and reduces the scope of its activities. Although such a firm likely will report reduced net income or even losses, it might experience positive cash flow from operations. The positive cash flow results from its collecting accounts receivable from prior periods while it does not replace inventories, thus saving cash. See the statements of cash flows in **Exhibit 5.37**, which appears in the end-of-chapter material on page 237, for an example.

RELATIONS AMONG CASH FLOWS FROM OPERATING, INVESTING, AND FINANCING ACTIVITIES

The relations among the cash flows from each of the three principal business activities differ depending on the characteristics of the firm's products and the maturity of its industry. Consider each of the four following patterns of cash flows.

Cash Flows from:	A	B	C	D
Operations	$ (3)	$ 7	$15	$ 8
Investing	(15)	(12)	(8)	(2)
Financing	18	5	(7)	(6)
Net Cash Flow	$ 0	$ 0	$ 0	$ 0

Case A illustrates a new, rapidly growing firm. It is not yet profitable, and it experiences buildups of its accounts receivable and inventories. Thus, it has negative cash flow from operations. To sustain its growth, the firm invests heavily in plant and equipment, and it relies on external sources of cash to finance both its operating and its investing activities.

Case B illustrates a somewhat more seasoned firm than the one in **Case A**, but one that is still growing. It operates profitably and generates positive cash flow from operations. This cash flow from operations, however, falls short of the amount the firm needs to finance acquisitions of plant and equipment. The firm therefore requires external financing.

Case C illustrates the cash flow pattern of a mature, stable firm. It generates sufficient cash flow from operations to acquire new plant and equipment and to repay financing from earlier periods and, perhaps, to pay dividends.

Case D illustrates a firm in the early stages of decline. Its cash from operations has begun to decrease but remains positive because of decreases in accounts receivable and inventories. In the later stages of decline, its cash flow from operations may turn negative as it finds itself unable to sell its products at a positive net cash flow. It cuts back significantly on capital expenditures because it is in a declining industry. It uses some of its excess cash flow to retire outstanding debt and shares, and has the remainder available for investment in new products or other industries.

Now, refer to the statements of cash flows for four actual firms in **Exhibit 5.15**. You will find the statement of cash flows more informative when you study cash flows for several years. These single-year statements illustrate some important relations for firms in different stages of growth.

Amazon.com depicts cash flows of a new and growing firm, operating at a net loss for the year and generating negative cash flow from operations. The firm acquired additional property, plant, and equipment to maintain its growth. It financed the negative cash flow from operations and capital expenditures by selling marketable securities and issuing long-term debt. The firm had issued common stock in an earlier year and invested the cash temporarily in marketable securities. It needed the cash this year and therefore sold a portion of its marketable securities. The proceeds of the new borrowing increased its cash balance on the balance sheet.

Discount Auto Parts depicts cash flows for a growing firm that is somewhat more seasoned than Amazon.com. It reported a positive cash flow from operations for the year. Cash from operations was less than the amounts needed to finance acquisitions of property, plant, and equipment. Discount Auto Parts financed the shortfall with additional long-term borrowing, one appropriate financing method for noncurrent assets.

Anheuser-Busch depicts the cash flow pattern of a mature firm. It reports positive net income, and its cash flow from operations exceeds the amounts needed to finance investments in new property, plant, and equipment. The firm used the excess net cash flow from operating and investing activities to pay dividends and repurchase shares of its common stock.

The cash flows for Levitz Furniture come from a period just prior to its filing for bankruptcy—from a late stage of decline. It operated at a net loss and generated negative cash flow from operations. The investing section indicates the cash inflows from selling property, plant,

---

EXHIBIT 5.15   **Excerpts from Statements of Cash Flows for Four Firms (all dollar amounts in millions)**

	Amazon.com	Discount Auto Parts	Anheuser-Busch	Levitz Furniture
OPERATIONS				
Cash Flow from Operations	$(130)	$ 28	$ 2,258	$ (14)
INVESTING				
Disposal of Fixed Assets	$ —	$ —	$ —	$ 12
Acquisition of Fixed Assets	(135)	(69)	(1,075)	(6)
Sale of Marketable Securities	299	—	—	—
Other Investing Transactions	—	5	(43)	—
Cash Flow from Investing	$ 164	$(64)	$(1,118)	$ 6
FINANCING				
Increase in Short-Term Borrowing	$ —	$ —	$ —	$670
Increase in Long-Term Borrowing	648	40	804	—
Increase in Capital Stock	45	—	135	—
Decrease in Short-Term Borrowing	—	—	—	(659)
Decrease in Long-Term Borrowing	—	—	(514)	(2)
Decrease in Capital Stock	—	—	(986)	—
Dividends	—	—	(571)	—
Other Financing Transactions	(38)	—	—	—
Cash Flow from Financing	$ 655	$ 40	$(1,132)	$ 9
Change in Cash	$ 689	$ 4	$8	$ 1
Cash, Beginning of Year	133	8	152	5
Cash, End of Year	$ 822	$ 12	$ 160	$ 6

and equipment. Given its poor financial condition, Levitz Furniture had to rely on short-term financing. Lenders required the firm to repay financing within one year and replace it with new financing.

These four cases do not, of course, cover all of the patterns of cash flows found in corporate annual reports. They illustrate how the characteristics of a firm's products and industry can affect the interpretation of information in the statement of cash flows.

 # INTERPRETATIVE ISSUES INVOLVING THE STATEMENT OF CASH FLOWS

Some analysts focus attention on cash flow from operations, thinking it as important as, or more important than, net income as a performance measure. Interpreting cash from operations as a measure of operating performance requires considering cash flows along two dimensions:

1. Their timing.
2. Their classification and disclosure in the statement and related notes.

TIMING OF OPERATING CASH FLOWS

Firms have some choice as to when they disburse cash. Delaying payments to suppliers and others during the last several days of an accounting period conserves cash and thereby increases cash flow from operations for that period. The cash payments during the early part of the next period reduce cash flow from operations in that period. Thus, delaying payment increases cash flow from operations during the first period but decreases cash flow from operations during the second period. The firm can repeat the process at the end of the second period—delaying payments from then to the third period—to offset the negative cash flow effects of the payments made early in the second period. A growing firm that delays payments at the end of each period reports larger cash flow from operations each period than if it had not delayed making the cash payments at the end of each period. Such a firm is, in effect, obtaining short-term financing from its suppliers. Absent contracts or other agreements that preclude delayed payments, this business practice is legal; however, sufficiently delayed payments might harm a firm's reputation or its credit rating.

CLASSIFICATION AND DISCLOSURE OF TRANSACTIONS

The first portion of this chapter identified certain ambiguities in the classification of cash flows. While many such items involve complex financial instruments that are beyond the scope of this textbook, others do not. An analyst who wishes to use cash flows from operations as an indicator of performance should be aware that classification decisions can affect cash from operations, perhaps significantly.

Example 1 Rental library firms purchase items such as films and games for short-term rentals to customers. The useful lives of these items range from about six months to two years.

■ Are these items inventory? If so, cash paid to acquire rental library items is an operating cash flow.

■ Or, are the items noncurrent assets? If so, cash paid is an investing cash flow.

Prior to 2006, some firms in the rental library business chose the second alternative, classifying the cash paid for rental library purchases as an investing cash outflow. Practice has now changed, however, to classify these cash payments as part of operations. Note that the total cash paid by the firm has not changed, but cash from operations was larger under the pre-2006 classification than afterwards.

Example 2 Many auto dealers finance their inventories by borrowing from banks and similar lenders, not from the auto manufacturers with conventional trade accounts payable. These arrangements are commonly known as "floor plan financing." Is a floor plan financing an operating cash flow, because it functions like accounts payable in financing inventories, or is it a financing cash flow? Prior to 2006, some auto retailers treated floor plan financing like accounts payable and therefore included it in cash flows from operations. Practice has changed, however, requiring firms to classify the arrangements as financing. While total cash flows have not changed, and the classification change does not affect the substance of the financing arrangement, the change affects cash from operations.

SUMMARY

The statement of cash flows reports the effects of a firm's operating, investing, and financing activities on cash flows. Information in the statement helps in understanding the following concepts:

1. The effect of operations on the liquidity of a firm.
2. The level of capital expenditures needed to support ongoing and growing levels of activity.
3. The major changes in the financing of a firm.

To prepare the statement of cash flows requires analyzing changes in balance sheet accounts during the accounting period, as represented by the Cash Change Equation (**Eq. 3**). As an outcome of correct double-entry recording of all transactions, the net change in cash will equal the net change in all noncash accounts.

The statement of cash flows usually presents cash flow from operations in the indirect format, beginning with net income for the period. The statement then adjusts for revenues not providing cash, for expenses not using cash, and for changes in working capital accounts. The result is cash flow from operations. Some firms use the direct approach to present cash flow from operations, listing all revenues that provide cash and subtracting all expenses that use cash. Firms using this direct approach must also present a reconciliation of net income to cash flow from operations. The cash flows from investing activities and financing activities appear after cash flow from operations.

Interpreting a statement of cash flows requires an understanding of the economic characteristics of the industries in which a firm conducts its activities, including capital intensity, growth characteristics, and similar factors.

PROBLEM 5.5 for Self-Study

Effect of transactions on the statement of cash flows. Exhibit 5.16 on page 214 shows a simplified statement of cash flows for a period. Numbers appear on 11 of the lines in the statement. Other lines (indicated with an "S") are various subtotals and grand totals; ignore these in the remainder of the problem. Assume that the accounting cycle is complete for the period and that the firm has prepared all of the financial statements. It then discovers that it has overlooked a transaction. It records that transaction in the accounts and corrects all of the financial statements. For each of the following transactions, indicate which of the numbered lines of the statement of cash flows change, and state the amount and direction of the change. If net income, line (**3**), changes, be sure to indicate whether it decreases or increases. Ignore income tax effects.

(*Hint*: First, construct the entry the firm would make in its accounts to record the transaction. Then, for each line of the journal entry, identify the line of **Exhibit 5.16** that the transaction affects.)

a. Depreciation expense of $2,000 on an office computer.
b. Purchase of machinery for $10,000 cash.
c. Declaration of a cash dividend of $6,500 on common stock; the firm paid the dividend by the end of the fiscal year.
d. Issue of common shares for $12,000 cash.
e. Proceeds of the sale of an investment in another firm's common shares, a noncurrent asset, for $15,000 cash; the firm sold the investment for its book value of $15,000.

EXHIBIT 5.16	Simplified Statement of Cash Flows (Problem 5.5 for Self-Study)

Operations

Cash Receipts from Customers	(1)
Less: Cash Payments to Suppliers, Employees, and Others	−(2)
Cash Flow from Operations [= (1) − (2)]	S1
Reconciliation of Net Income to Cash Flow from Operations	
Net Income	(3)
Additions to Net Income to Compute Cash Flow from Operations	+(4)
Subtractions from Net Income to Compute Cash Flow from Operations	−(5)
Cash Flow from Operations [= (3) + (4) − (5)]	S1

Investing

Proceeds from Dispositions of "Investing" Assets	+(6)
Cash Used to Acquire "Investing" Assets	−(7)
Cash Flow from Investing [= (6) − (7)]	S2

Financing

Cash Provided by Increases in Debt or Capital Stock	+(8)
Cash Used to Reduce Debt or Capital Stock	−(9)
Cash Used for Dividends	−(10)
Cash Flow from Financing [= (8) − (9) − (10)]	S3
Net Change in Cash [= S1 + S2 + S3]	(11)
Cash, Beginning of the Period	S4
Cash, End of the Period [= (11) + S4]	S5

SOLUTIONS TO SELF-STUDY PROBLEMS

SUGGESTED SOLUTION TO PROBLEM 5.1 FOR SELF-STUDY

(Classifying cash flows by type of activity.)

a. Operating

b. Financing

c. Operating

d. Operating

e. Operating

f. Operating

g. Investing

h. Item does not affect cash flows during the current period and would therefore not appear in the statement of cash flows. The firm must disclose this transaction in a separate schedule or a note to the financial statements.

i. Operating

j. Operating

k. Investing

l. Item does not affect cash flows during the current period and would therefore not appear in the statement of cash flows. The firm must disclose this transaction in a separate schedule or note to the financial statements.

m. Financing

n. Investing

o. Financing

p. Investing

q. Operating

SUGGESTED SOLUTION TO PROBLEM 5.2 FOR SELF-STUDY

(Robbie Corporation; preparing a T-account work sheet for a statement of cash flows.)

Exhibit 5.17 presents a completed T-account work sheet for Robbie Corporation.

EXHIBIT 5.17

Robbie Corporation
T-Account Work Sheet
(all dollar amounts in thousands)
(Problem 5.2 for Self-Study)

	Cash		
✓	10		

	Operations		
(2)	2	7	(1)
(4)	6		
(5)	7		
(8)	7		

	Investing		
		16	(3)

	Financing		
(6)	8	2	(9)
(7)	10		
✓	25		

	Accounts Receivable		
✓	15		
(1)	7		
✓	22		

	Merchandise Inventories		
✓	20		
		2	(2)
✓	18		

	Property, Plant, and Equipment		
✓	50		
(3)	16		
✓	66		

	Accumulated Depreciation		
		25	✓
		6	(4)
		31	✓

	Accounts Payable for Merchandise		
		30	✓
		7	(5)
		37	✓

	Bonds Payable		
		10	✓
		8	(6)
		18	✓

	Common Stock		
		10	✓
		10	(7)
		20	✓

	Retained Earnings		
		20	✓
(9)	2	7	(8)
		25	✓

EXHIBIT 5.18

Robbie Corporation
Deriving Direct Method Cash Flow from Operations
Using Data from T-Account Work Sheet
(Problem 5.3 for Self-Study)

1. Copy Income Statement and Cash Flow from Operations

2. Copy Information from T-Account Work Sheet Next to Related Income Statement Item

3. Sum Across Rows to Derive Direct Receipts and Expenditures

Operations (a)	Indirect Method (b)	Changes in Related Balance Sheet Accounts from T-Account Work Sheet (c)	Direct Method (d)	From Operations: Receipts Less Expenditures
Sales Revenues $180,000	$(7,000)	= Accounts Receivable Increase (1)	$ 173,000	Receipts from Customers
Cost of Goods Sold..... (140,000)	2,000	= Inventory Decrease (2)	$(131,000)	Payments for Merchandise
	7,000	= Accounts Payable for Merchandise Increase (5)		
Selling and Administrative Expenses.......... (25,000)		(No balance sheet account changes.)	(25,000)	Payments for Selling and Administrative Services
Depreciation Expense ... (6,000)	6,000	(Expense Not Using Cash) (4)	—	
Interest Expense ...... (2,000)	—	Interest Payable (no change in balance sheet)	(2,000)	Payments for Interest
Net Income.......... $ 7,000	$ 7,000	= Net Income Totals	$ 15,000	= Cash Flow from Operations Derived via Direct Method
	$15,000	= Cash Flow from Operations Derived via Indirect Method		

Note that the information in column (b) is cash flow from operations derived with the indirect method, with items in a different order.

SUGGESTED SOLUTION TO PROBLEM 5.3 FOR SELF-STUDY

(Robbie Corporation; deriving direct method presentation for cash flows from operations from T-account work sheet.)

Exhibit 5.18 derives the direct method presentation for cash flows from operations from the T-account work sheet in Exhibit 5.17.

SUGGESTED SOLUTION TO PROBLEM 5.4 FOR SELF-STUDY

(Gordon Corporation; preparing a statement of cash flows.)

Exhibit 5.19 presents a completed T-account work sheet for Gordon Corporation. Exhibit 5.20, on page 218, derives a direct method presentation of cash flows for operations. Exhibit 5.21, on page 219, presents a formal statement of cash flows.

(continued)

EXHIBIT 5.19

Gordon Corporation
T-Account Work Sheet
(all dollar amounts in thousands)
(Problem 5.4 for Self-Study)

Cash

✓	70		

Operations

(1)	200	100	(5)
(4)	70	110	(6)
(3)	15	20	(7)
(10)	120		
(11)	20		
(12)	190		

Investing

(3)	10	50	(8)
		245	(9)

Financing

(14)	40	120	(2)
		50	(13)
✓	40		

Accounts Receivable				**Merchandise Inventory**				**Prepayments**		
✓	320			✓	360			✓	50	
(5)	100			(6)	110			(7)	20	
✓	420			✓	470			✓	70	

Land				**Buildings and Equipment**				**Accumulated Depreciation**			
✓	200			✓	1,800					800	✓
(8)	50			(9)	245	55	(3)	(3)	30	70	(4)
✓	250			✓	1,990					840	✓

Accounts Payable				**Income Taxes Payable**				**Other Current Liabilities**		
		320	✓			60	✓		170	✓
		120	(10)			20	(11)		190	(12)
		440	✓			80	✓		360	✓

Bonds Payable				**Common Stock**				**Retained Earnings**			
		250	✓			500	✓			700	✓
(13)	50					40	(14)	(2)	120	200	(1)
		200	✓			540	✓			780	✓

EXHIBIT 5.20

Gordon Corporation
Deriving Direct Method Cash Flow from Operations
Using Data from T-Account Work Sheet
(all dollar amounts in thousands)
(Problem 5.4 for Self-Study)

1. Copy Income Statement and Cash Flow from Operations

2. Copy Information from T-Account Work Sheet Next to Related Income Statement Item

3. Sum Across Rows to Derive Direct Receipts and Expenditures

Operations (a)	Indirect Method (b)	Changes in Related Balance Sheet Accounts from T-Account Work Sheet (c)	Direct Method (d)	From Operations: Receipts Less Expenditures
Revenues $1,600	$(100)	= Accounts Receivable Increase	$1,500	Receipts from Customers
Cost of Goods Sold . . . . (900)	120	= Accounts Payable Increase	(890)	Payments for Merchandise
	(110)	= Merchandise Inventory Increase	—	
Depreciation Expense . . . . . . (70)	70	(Expense Not Using Cash)		
Selling and Administrative Expenses . . . . (255)	190	= Other Current Liabilities Increase	(85)	Payments for Selling and Administrative Services
	(20)	= Prepayment Increase		
Interest Expense . . . . (30)	—	= Interest Payable (no change in balance sheet)	(30)	Payments for Interest
Loss on Disposal of Buildings and Equipment . . . . (15)	15	(Loss Not Using Cash)	—	
Income Tax Expense . . . . . . (130)	20	= Income Taxes Payable Increase	(110)	Payments for Income Taxes
Net Income . . . . $ 200	$ 200	= Net Income Totals	$ 385	= Cash Flow from Operations Derived via Direct Method
	$ 385	= Cash Flow from Operations Derived via Indirect Method		

Note that the information in column **(b)** is cash flow from operations derived with the indirect method, with items in a different order.

EXHIBIT 5.21	**Gordon Corporation** **Statement of Cash Flows** **For Year 2008** **(all dollar amounts in thousands)** **(Problem 5.4 for Self-Study)**

Operations

Receipts from Customers	$1,500	
Payments to Suppliers of Merchandise	(890)	
Payments for Selling and Administrative Expenses	(85)	
Payments to Lenders for Interest	(30)	
Payments for Income Taxes	(110)	
Cash Flow from Operating Activities		$ 385

Reconciliation of Net Income to Cash Provided by Operations

Net Income	$ 200	
Additions:		
Depreciation Expense	70	
Loss on Disposal of Equipment	15	
Increase in Accounts Payable	120	
Increase in Income Taxes Payable	20	
Increase in Other Current Liabilities	190	
Subtractions:		
Increase in Accounts Receivable	(100)	
Increase in Merchandise Inventories	(110)	
Increase in Prepayments	(20)	
Cash Flow from Operations	$ 385	

Investing

Acquisition of Land	$ (50)	
Disposal of Buildings and Equipment	10	
Acquisition of Buildings and Equipment	(245)	
Cash Used for Investing		(285)

Financing

Common Stock Issued	$ 40	
Dividends Paid	(120)	
Repayment of Bonds	(50)	
Cash Used for Financing		(130)
Net Decrease in Cash		$ (30)
Cash, Beginning of 2008		70
Cash, End of 2008		$ 40

SUGGESTED SOLUTION TO PROBLEM 5.5 FOR SELF-STUDY

(Effect of transactions on the statement of cash flows.) Preparing the journal entry for each transaction aids in understanding the effect on the 11 numbered lines in **Exhibit 5.16**.

a. Depreciation Expense 2,000
　　　　Accumulated Depreciation 2,000

Change in Cash	=	Change in Liabilities	+	Change in Shareholders' Equity	–	Change in Noncash Assets
0		0		–2,000		–2,000

　　This entry has no impact on operating cash flows, so it has no effect on lines **(1)** and **(2)**. It involves a debit to an income statement account, so line **(3)** decreases by $2,000. Depreciation expense reduces net income but does not affect cash line **(11)**. Thus, line **(4)** must increase by $2,000 for the addback of depreciation expense to net income. This addback eliminates the effect of depreciation on both cash flow from operations and cash.

b. Machinery 10,000
　　　　Cash 10,000

Change in Cash	=	Change in Liabilities	+	Change in Shareholders' Equity	–	Change in Noncash Assets
–10,000 (Invst.)		0		0		+10,000

　　This entry does not involve receipts from customers nor payments to suppliers, so it does not affect lines **(1)** and **(2)**. It involves a credit to Cash, so line **(11)** decreases by $10,000. Because line **(11)** is the net change in cash for the period, some other line must change as well. Acquisitions of equipment represent Investing activities, so line **(7)** increases by $10,000. Note that line **(7)** has a negative sign, so this means an increase to an amount subtracted; increasing this line reduces cash.

c. Retained Earnings 6,500
　　　　Cash 6,500

Change in Cash	=	Change in Liabilities	+	Change in Shareholders' Equity	–	Change in Noncash Assets
–6,500 (Finan.)		0		–6,500		0

　　This entry involves a credit to Cash, so line **(11)** decreases by $6,500. Dividends are a financing activity, so line **(10)** increases by $6,500.

d. Cash 12,000
　　　　Common Stock 12,000

Change in Cash	=	Change in Liabilities	+	Change in Shareholders' Equity	–	Change in Noncash Assets
+12,000 (Finan.)		0		+12,000		0

　　The debit to Cash means that line **(11)** increases by $12,000. Issuing stock is a financing transaction, so line **(8)** increases by $12,000.

e. Cash...   15,000

    Investment in Securities   15,000

Change in Cash	=	Change in Liabilities	+	Change in Shareholders' Equity	−	Change in Noncash Assets
+15,000 (Invst.)		0		0		−15,000

The debit to Cash means that line **(11)** increases by $15,000. Selling investments in securities is an investing activity, so line **(6)** increases by $15,000.

KEY TERMS AND CONCEPTS

Cash flow from operations	Direct method
Cash flow from investing activities	Indirect method
Cash flow from financing activities	T-account work sheet
Free cash flow	Cash Change Equation

QUESTIONS, EXERCISES, AND PROBLEMS

QUESTIONS

1. Review the meaning of the terms and concepts listed in Key Terms and Concepts.

2. "One can most easily accomplish the reporting objective of the income statement under the accrual basis of accounting and the reporting objective of the statement of cash flows by issuing a single income statement using the cash basis of accounting." Evaluate this proposal.

3. "The accrual basis of accounting creates the need for a statement of cash flows." Explain.

4. "The statement of cash flows provides information about changes in the structure of a firm's assets and sources of financing." Explain.

5. A student remarked: "The direct method of computing cash flow from operations is easier to understand than the indirect method. Why do the majority of firms follow the indirect method in preparing their statements of cash flows?" Respond to this student.

6. The statement of cash flows classifies cash expenditures for interest expense as an operating activity but classifies cash expenditures to redeem debt as a financing activity. Explain this apparent paradox.

7. Under U.S. GAAP, the statement of cash flows classifies cash expenditures for interest on debt as an operating activity but classifies cash expenditures for dividends to shareholders as a financing activity. Explain this apparent paradox.

8. The statement of cash flows classifies changes in accounts payable as an operating activity but classifies changes in short-term bank borrowing as a financing activity. Explain this apparent paradox.

9. The acquisition of equipment by assuming a mortgage is a transaction that firms cannot report in their statement of cash flows but must report in a supplemental schedule or note. Of what value is information about this type of transaction? What is the reason for its exclusion from the statement of cash flows?

10. One writer stated, "Depreciation expense is a firm's chief source of cash for growth." A reader criticized this statement by replying, "The fact remains that if companies had elected, in any year, to charge off $10 million more depreciation than they did charge off, they would not thereby have added one dime to the total of their cash available for expanding plants or for increasing inventories or receivables. Therefore, to speak of depreciation expense as a source of cash is incorrect and misleading." Comment on these statements, taking into account income tax effects.

11. A firm generated net income for the current year, but cash flow from operations was negative. How can this happen?

12. A firm operated at a net loss for the current year, but cash flow from operations was positive. How can this happen?

13. The disposal of equipment for an amount of cash greater than the carrying value of the equipment results in a cash receipt equal to the carrying value of the equipment plus the gain on the disposal, which appears in income. How might the accountant treat this transaction in the statement of cash flows? Consider both the direct and indirect methods.

EXERCISES

14. **Derive sales revenue from data in the statement of cash flows and balance sheet.** Microsoft Corporation reported a balance of $5,196 million in accounts receivable at the beginning of the year and $5,334 million at the end of the year. Its statement of cash flows using the direct method reported cash collections from customers of $33,551 million for the year. Assuming that Microsoft Corporation makes all sales on account, compute the amount of sales during the year.

15. **Derive cost of goods sold from data in the statement of cash flows.** The section showing cash flow from operations, using the indirect method, for General Electric Company reported an increase in inventories during the year of $1,753 million and no change in accounts payable for inventories. The direct method would show cash payments for inventory, purchased and manufactured, totaling $64,713 million. Compute the cost of goods sold for the year.

16. **Derive cost of goods sold from data in the statement of cash flows.** The section showing cash flow from operations, using the indirect method, for Ann Taylor Stores reported an increase in inventories of $5.7 million during the year. It reported also that the balance in accounts payable for inventories increased by $5.9 million. The direct method would show cash payments for merchandise inventory purchased of $646.9 million. Compute the cost of goods sold for the year.

17. **Derive wages and salaries expense from data in the statement of cash flows.** AMR, the parent company of American Airlines, reported in its reconciliation of net income to cash flow from operations a decrease in wages and salaries payable of $21 million during the year. It provided data showing that cash payments for wages and salaries to employees for the year were $8,853 million. Compute the amount of wages and salaries expense for the year.

18. **Derive cash disbursements for dividends.** Johnson & Johnson, a pharmaceutical and medical products company, reported a balance in retained earnings of $26,571 million at the beginning of the year and $28,132 million at the end of the year. Its dividends payable account increased by $233 million during the year. It reported net income for the year of $5,030 million. How much cash did Johnson & Johnson disburse for dividends during the year? Indicate where this information would appear in the simplified statement of cash flows in **Exhibit 5.16**.

19. **Effect of borrowing and interest on statement of cash flows.** Gillette borrowed $250 million on October 1 by issuing bonds. The debt carries an annual interest rate of 6%, which it must pay on April 1 and October 1 of each year. The debt matures 20 years after its issue date. Gillette's accounting period ends on December 31 of each year. Using the format of **Exhibit 5.16**, indicate the effects of all these transactions on Gillette's statement of cash flows for the year of issue, when the bonds were outstanding from October 1 through December 31.

20. **Effect of income taxes on statement of cash flows.** Radio Shack reported a balance in Income Taxes Payable of $78.1 million at the beginning of the year, $60.1 million at the end of the year, and income tax expense for the year of $161.5 million. Using the format of **Exhibit 5.16**, indicate the effects of all these transactions on Radio Shack's statement of cash flows for the year.

21. **Effect of rent transactions on statement of cash flows.** A firm reported a balance in its Prepaid Rent (Advances to Landlord) account of $1,200 on January 1, 2009, for use of the building for the month of January 2009. On February 1, 2009, the firm paid $18,000 as the annual rental for the period from February 1, 2009, to January 31, 2010. It recorded this rental payment by debiting Prepaid Rent (Advances to Landlord) and crediting Cash for $18,000. At the end of 2009, the firm made all proper adjusting entries to correctly report balance sheet and income statement amounts. Using the format of **Exhibit 5.16**, indicate the effects of all these transactions on the firm's statement of cash flows for 2009.

EXHIBIT 5.22

Information Technologies
Data from Income Statement for Current Year
(all dollar amounts in thousands)
(Exercise 22)

Sales	$ 14,508
Cost of Goods Sold	(11,596)
Depreciation Expense	(114)
Other Expenses, Including Salaries and Wages Expense	(2,276)
Income Taxes	(210)
Net Income	$ 312

Data from Beginning- and End-of-Year Balance Sheets

Accounts Receivable	$782 Decrease
Inventories	66 Decrease
Prepayments for Other Costs	102 Decrease
Accounts Payable for Inventories	90 Increase
Current Liabilities for Wages and Salaries Payable	240 Decrease

22. **Calculating components of cash inflow from operations.** Exhibit 5.22 provides items from the financial statements of Information Technologies, a systems engineering firm, for the year. How much cash did Information Technologies collect from its customers during the year?

23. **Calculating components of cash outflow from operations.** Refer to **Exhibit 5.22**, which provides items from the financial statements of Information Technologies.

   a. How much cash did Information Technologies pay during the year to its suppliers of goods?

   b. How much cash did Information Technologies pay during the year to its employees and suppliers of other services?

24. **Spreadsheet for understanding the relation between changes in income statement items and changes in items in the statement of cash flows.** The spreadsheet on the textbook's Web site contains a dynamic version of the spreadsheet reproduced below:

	A	B	C
1 2 3	**Income Statement**		**Lines in Schematic Statement of Cash Flows**
4	Revenues matched with cash inflows this period	$ 25	Line **(1)**
5	Revenues and gains with no cash inflows this period	1	
6	Expenses matched with expenditures this period	(15)	Line **(2)**
7	Expenses and losses with no cash outflow this period	(4)	
8	Net Income	$ 7	Line **(3)**
9	**Direct Method for Deriving Cash Flow from Operations**		
10	Revenues matched with cash inflows this period	$ 25	Line **(1)**
11	Expenses and losses with no cash outflow this period	(15)	Line **(2)**
12	Cash Flow from Operations	$ 10	S1
13	**Indirect Method for Deriving Cash Flow from Operations**		
14	Net Income	$ 7	Line **(3)**
15	Addback Expenses and Losses not Using Cash this Period	4	Line **(4)**
16	Subtract Revenues not Producing Receipts this Period	(1)	Line **(5)**
17	Cash Flow from Operations	$ 10	S1

In the dynamic version of this spreadsheet available on the Web site, you can change any of the numbers in the yellow shaded section and see the effect of the change in the statement of cash flows section for cash flows from operations.

a. Download the spreadsheet and change the first line of the income statement from $25 to $27, increasing income by $2. What is the effect on **S1**?

b. Go back to the original configuration. Change only the second line of the income statement from $1 to $5, increasing income by $4. What are the effects on Lines **(1)** – **(5)** and **S1** of the cash flows from operations sections?

c. Go back to the original configuration. Now, make two changes: change the third line of the income statement from ($15) to ($17) and at the same time, change the fourth line from ($4) to ($2), leaving income unchanged. What are the effects on Lines **(1)** – **(5)** and **S1** of the cash flows from operations sections?

25. **Working backward from changes in the Buildings and Equipment account.** The comparative balance sheets of American Airlines show a balance in the Buildings and Equipment account at cost year-end of $17,369 million; a year earlier, the balance was $16,825 million. The Accumulated Depreciation account shows a balance of $5,465 million at year-end and of $4,914 million a year earlier. The statement of cash flows reports that expenditures for buildings and equipment during the year totaled $1,314 million. The income statement indicates a depreciation charge of $1,253 million during the year. The firm sold buildings and equipment during the year at their carrying value.

   Calculate the acquisition cost and accumulated depreciation of the buildings and equipment that American sold for cash during the year and the proceeds from the disposition.

26. **Preparing a statement of cash flows from changes in balance sheet accounts.** The comparative balance sheets of Southwest Airlines show the following information for a recent year (amounts in thousands):

Change	Amount	Direction
Cash	$ 40,308[a]	Increase
Accounts Receivable	15,351	Decrease
Inventories	15,117	Increase
Prepayments	16,776	Increase
Property, Plant, and Equipment (at cost)	1,134,644[b]	Increase
Accumulated Depreciation	264,088[b]	Increase
Other Nonoperating Assets	8,711	Increase
Accounts Payable	660	Decrease
Other Current Liabilities	114,596	Increase
Long-Term Debt	244,285	Increase
Other Nonoperating Liabilities	140,026	Increase
Common Stock	96,991	Increase
Retained Earnings	340,879[c]	Increase

[a]Cash was $378,511 at the beginning of the year and $418,819 at the end of the year.

[b]Southwest Airlines did not sell any property, plant, and equipment during the year.

[c]Net income was $474,378.

a. Prepare a statement of cash flows for Southwest Airlines for the year. Treat changes in nonoperating assets as investing transactions and changes in nonoperating liabilities as financing transactions.

b. Discuss briefly the pattern of cash flows from operating, investing, and financing activities for Southwest Airlines for the year.

27. **Calculating and interpreting cash flow from operations.** The following items appear in the financial statements of Bamberger Enterprises, a firm offering IT services for Sarbanes-Oxley compliance, for a year (amounts in thousands):

Sales	$ 14,600
Depreciation Expense	(210)
Income Taxes	(200)
Other Expenses	(13,900)
Net Income	$ 290

The changes in the current asset and current liability accounts were as follows:

Accounts Receivable	$780	Decrease
Inventories	80	Decrease
Prepayments	100	Decrease
Accounts Payable	90	Increase
Other Current Liabilities	240	Decrease

a. Compute the amount of cash flow from operations.

b. Comment on the major reasons why cash flow from operations exceeds net income.

28. **Calculating and interpreting cash flow from operations.** Selected data for a Finnish cellular phone manufacturer appear below (amounts in millions of euros):

	2008	2007	2006	2005
Net Income (Loss)	€3,847	€2,542	€1,689	€1,032
Depreciation Expense	1,009	665	509	465
Increase (Decrease) in:				
Accounts Receivable	2,304	982	1,573	272
Inventories	422	362	103	121
Prepayments	(49)	33	17	(77)
Accounts Payable	458	312	140	90
Other Current Liabilities	923	867	1,049	450

a. Compute the amount of cash flow from operations for each of the four years using the indirect method.

b. Discuss briefly the most important reasons why cash flow from operations differs from net income or net loss for each year.

29. **Calculating and interpreting cash flows.** Marketing Communications is a marketing services firm that creates advertising copy for clients and places the advertising in television, magazines, and other media. Accounts receivable represent amounts owed by clients, and accounts payable represent amounts payable to various media. Marketing Communications has purchased other marketing services firms in recent years. Selected data for Marketing Communications for three recent years appear next (amounts in millions):

	2008	2007	2006
Net Income	$ 499	$ 363	$279
Depreciation and Amortization Expense	226	196	164
Increase (Decrease) in Accounts Receivable	514	648	238
Increase (Decrease) in Inventories	98	13	35
Increase (Decrease) in Prepayments	125	(10)	64
Increase (Decrease) in Accounts Payable	277	786	330
Increase (Decrease) in Other Current Liabilities	420	278	70
Acquisition of Property, Plant, and Equipment	150	130	115
Acquisition of Investments in Securities (noncurrent)	885	643	469
Dividends Paid	122	104	88
Long-Term Debt Issued	599	83	208
Common Stock Issued (Reacquired)	(187)	(252)	42

a. Prepare a comparative statement of cash flows for Marketing Communications for the three years. Use the indirect method of computing cash flow from operations.

b. Discuss the relation between net income and cash flow from operations and the pattern of cash flows from operating, investing, and financing activities during the three years.

30. **Effects of gains and losses from sales of equipment on cash flows. Exhibit 5.23** presents an abbreviated statement of cash flows for Largay Corporation for the current year

EXHIBIT 5.23

**Largay Corporation
Statement of Cash Flows
Current Year
(all dollar amounts in thousands)
(Exercise 30)**

Operations

Net Income	$100
Depreciation Expense	15
Changes in Working Capital Accounts	(40)
Cash Flow from Operations	$ 75

Investing

Acquisition of Buildings and Equipment	(30)

Financing

Repayment of Long-Term Debt	(40)
Change in Cash	$ 5
Cash, Beginning of Year	27
Cash, End of Year	$ 32

(amounts in thousands). After preparing this statement of cash flows for the current year, you discover that the firm sold an item of equipment on the last day of the year but failed to record it in the accounts or to deposit the check received from the purchaser. The equipment originally cost $50,000 and had accumulated depreciation of $40,000 at the time of sale. Recast the statement of cash flows in the exhibit, assuming that Largay Corporation sold the equipment for cash in the following amounts (ignore income taxes):

  a. $10,000

  b. $12,000

  c. $8,000

31. **Effect of various transactions on the statement of cash flows. Exhibit 5.16** shows a simplified statement of cash flows for a period. Numbers appear on 11 of the lines in the statement. Other lines are various subtotals and grand totals; ignore these in the remainder of the problem. Assume that the accounting cycle is complete for the period and that the firm has prepared all of the financial statements. It then discovers that it has overlooked a transaction. It records that transaction in the accounts and corrects all of the financial statements. For each of the following transactions, indicate which of the numbered lines of the statement of cash flows change, and state the amount and direction of the change. If net income, line **(3)**, changes, be sure to indicate whether it decreases or increases. Ignore income tax effects. (*Hint*: First, construct the entry the firm would enter in the accounts to record the transaction in the accounts. Then, for each line of the journal entry, identify the line of **Exhibit 5.16** affected.)

  a. Amortization of a patent, treated as an expense, $600.

  b. Acquisition of a factory site financed by issuing capital stock with a market value of $50,000 in exchange.

  c. Purchase of inventory on account for $7,500; assume inventory had increased for the year before the firm recorded this overlooked transaction.

  d. Purchase of inventory for cash of $6,000; assume inventory had increased for the year before the firm recorded this overlooked transaction.

  e. Uninsured fire loss of merchandise inventory totaling $1,500; assume inventory had increased for the year before the firm recorded this overlooked transaction.

  f. Collection of an account receivable totaling $1,450; assume accounts receivable had increased for the year before the firm recorded this overlooked transaction.

  g. Issue of bonds for $10,000 cash.

  h. Disposal of equipment for cash at its carrying value of $4,500.

PROBLEMS

32. **Inferring cash flows from financial statement data. Exhibit 5.24** presents data from the financial statements for Heidi's Hide-Out, a bar and video-game club, with private party rooms for rent. Heidi's deals with

- many employees, to some of whom it has made advances on wages and to some of whom it owes wages for past work;
- many landlords, to some of whom it has made advance payments and to some of whom it owes rent for past months;
- many customers, some of whom have paid for special parties not yet held and some of whom have not yet paid for parties already held; and
- many suppliers of goods, including food and beverages, some of whom Heidi's has paid for orders not yet received and some of whom have delivered goods for which Heidi's has not yet paid.

Heidi's and its customers, suppliers, and employees settle all transactions with cash, never with noncash assets.

a. Calculate the amount of cash received from retail customers during the current year.

b. Calculate the amount of cash Heidi's paid landlords during the current year for the rental of space.

c. Calculate the amount of cash Heidi's paid employees during the current year.

d. Calculate the amount of cash Heidi's paid suppliers of retail merchandise, which includes food and beverages it sells to retail customers, during the current year.

EXHIBIT 5.24

Heidi's Hide-Out
Selected Detail from Financial Statements
Current Year
(Problem 32)

	Beginning of Year	End of Year
BALANCE SHEETS		
Cash	$22,000	$ 10,000
Accounts Receivable from Retail Customers	8,000	8,900
Inventory of Retail Merchandise	11,000	10,000
Advances to Employees	1,000	1,500
Advances to Landlords (Prepaid Rent)	5,000	5,600
Advances to Suppliers of Retail Merchandise	10,000	10,500
Total Assets	$57,000	$ 46,500
Accounts Payable to Suppliers of Retail Merchandise	$8,000	$7,700
Advances from Retail Customers	9,000	10,000
Rent Payable to Landlords	6,000	5,300
Wages Payable to Employees	2,000	1,800
Shareholders' Equity	32,000	21,700
Total Liabilities and Shareholders' Equity	$57,000	$ 46,500
INCOME STATEMENT FOR THE YEAR		
Sales Revenue from Retail Customers		$ 120,000
Cost of Retail Merchandise Sold	$90,000	
Rent Expense	33,000	
Wage Expense	20,000	
Less: Total Expenses		$(143,000)
Net Income (Loss)		$ (23,000)

33. **Inferring cash flows from balance sheet and income statement data.** (Based on a problem prepared by Stephen A. Zeff.) You work for the Plains State Bank in Miles City, Montana, as an analyst specializing in the financial statements of small businesses seeking loans from the bank. Digit Retail Enterprises Inc. provides you with its balance sheet for December 31, 2007 and 2008 (**Exhibit 5.25**), and its income statement for 2008 (**Exhibit 5.26**). Digit Retail Enterprises acquired no new property, plant, and equipment during the year.

   a. Calculate the amount of cash received from customers during the year.

   b. Calculate the acquisition cost of merchandise purchased during the year.

   c. Calculate the amount of cash paid to suppliers of merchandise during the year.

   d. Calculate the amount of cash paid to salaried employees during the year.

   e. Calculate the amount of cash paid to insurance companies during the year.

   f. Calculate the amount of cash paid to landlords for space rented during the year.

   g. Calculate the amount of dividends paid during the year.

EXHIBIT 5.25

Digit Retail Enterprises, Inc.
Balance Sheet
(Problem 33)

	December 31 2008	December 31 2007
ASSETS		
Current Assets		
Cash	$ 50,000	$ 36,000
Accounts Receivable	38,000	23,000
Notes Receivable	—	7,500
Interest Receivable	—	100
Merchandise Inventory	65,000	48,000
Prepaid Insurance	12,000	9,000
Prepaid Rent	—	2,000
Total Current Assets	$165,000	$125,600
Property, Plant, and Equipment		
At Cost	$ 90,000	$100,000
Less Accumulated Depreciation	(35,000)	(20,000)
Net	$ 55,000	$ 80,000
Total Assets	$220,000	$205,600
LIABILITIES AND SHAREHOLDER'S EQUITY		
Current Liabilities		
Accounts Payable—Merchandise Suppliers	$ 20,000	$ 18,000
Salaries Payable	2,800	2,100
Rent Payable	3,000	—
Advances from Customers	6,100	8,500
Note Payable	5,500	—
Dividends Payable	2,600	4,200
Other Current Liabilities	3,700	1,300
Total Current Liabilities	$ 43,700	$ 34,100
Shareholders' Equity		
Common Stock	$164,500	$160,000
Retained Earnings	11,800	11,500
Total Shareholders' Equity	$176,300	$171,500
Total Liabilities and Shareholders' Equity	$220,000	$205,600

EXHIBIT 5.26

Digit Retail Enterprises, Inc.
Income Statement
For Year of 2008
(Problem 33)

Sales Revenue	$270,000
Gain on Sale of Property, Plant, and Equipment	3,200
Interest Revenue	200
Total Revenues	$273,400
Less Expenses:	
Cost of Goods Sold	$145,000
Salaries Expense	68,000
Rent Expense	12,000
Insurance Expense	5,000
Depreciation Expense	20,000
Other Expenses	13,800
Total Expenses	$263,800
Net Income	$ 9,600

  h. Calculate the amount of cash received when property, plant, and equipment were sold during the year.

34. **Preparing and interpreting a statement of cash flows using a T-account work sheet.** Condensed financial statement data for Hale Company for the current year appear in **Exhibits 5.27** and **5.28** on page 230. During the current year, the firm sold for $5,000 equipment costing $15,000 with $10,000 of accumulated depreciation.

  a. Prepare a statement of cash flows for Hale Company for the year using the indirect method of computing cash flow from operations. Support the statement with a T-account work sheet.

  b. Derive a presentation of cash flows from operations using the direct method.

EXHIBIT 5.27

Hale Company
Comparative Balance Sheet
(Problem 34)

	January 1	December 31
ASSETS		
Cash	$ 52,000	$ 58,000
Accounts Receivable	93,000	106,000
Inventory	151,000	162,000
Land	30,000	30,000
Buildings and Equipment (cost)	790,000	830,000
Less Accumulated Depreciation	(460,000)	(504,000)
Total Assets	$ 656,000	$ 682,000
LIABILITIES AND SHAREHOLDERS' EQUITY		
Accounts Payable for Inventory	$ 136,000	$ 141,000
Interest Payable	10,000	8,000
Mortgage Payable	120,000	109,000
Common Stock	250,000	250,000
Retained Earnings	140,000	174,000
Total Liabilities and Shareholders' Equity	$ 656,000	$ 682,000

EXHIBIT 5.28	**Hale Company** **Statement of Income and Retained Earnings** **Current Year** **(Problem 34)**

Sales Revenues...		$1,200,000
Expenses		
Cost of Goods Sold	$788,000	
Wages and Salaries	280,000	
Depreciation	54,000	
Interest	12,000	
Income Taxes..	22,000	
Total Expenses		$1,156,000
Net Income		$ 44,000
Dividends on Common Stock...............................		(10,000)
Addition to Retained Earnings for Year......................		$ 34,000
Retained Earnings, January 1		140,000
Retained Earnings, December 31		$ 174,000

c. Present a statement of cash flows for Hale Company using the direct method for cash flows from operations. Include reconciliation of net income to cash flow from operations.

d. Comment on the pattern of cash flows from operations, investing, and financing activities.

35. **Preparing and interpreting a statement of cash flows using a T-account work sheet.** Financial statement data for Dickerson Manufacturing Company for the current year appear in **Exhibit 5.29** on page 231. Additional information includes the following:

(1) Net income for the year was $568,000; dividends declared and paid were $60,000.

(2) Depreciation expense for the year was $510,000 on buildings and machinery.

(3) The firm sold for $25,000 machinery originally costing $150,000 with accumulated depreciation of $120,000.

(4) The firm retired bonds during the year at their book value.

a. Prepare a statement of cash flows for Dickerson Manufacturing Company for the year using the indirect method to compute cash flow from operations. Support the statement with a T-account work sheet.

b. Comment on the pattern of cash flows from operating, investing, and financing activities.

36. **Preparing direct method of deriving cash flow from operations from data in published annual report.** GTI Inc. manufactures parts, components, and processing equipment for electronics and semiconductor applications in the communication, computer, automotive, and appliance industries. Its sales tend to vary with changes in the business cycle since the sales of most of its customers are cyclical. **Exhibit 5.30** on page 232 presents balance sheets for GTI as of December 31, 2006, 2007, and 2008, and **Exhibit 5.31** on page 232 presents income statements for 2007 and 2008. Notes to the firm's financial statements reveal the following (amounts in thousands):

(1) Depreciation expense, included in Administration Expenses, was $641 in 2007 and $625 in 2008.

(2) Other Noncurrent Assets represent patents. Patent amortization, included in Administrative Expenses, was $25 in 2007 and $40 in 2008.

(3) Changes in Other Current Liabilities and Other Noncurrent Liabilities are both operating transactions relating to Administrative Expenses.

a. Prepare a T-account work sheet for the preparation of a statement of cash flows for GTI Inc. for 2007 and 2008.

EXHIBIT 5.29	Dickerson Manufacturing Company Comparative Balance Sheet (Problem 35)		
		January 1	December 31
ASSETS			
Current Assets			
Cash		$ 358,000	$ 324,000
Accounts Receivable		946,000	1,052,000
Inventory		1,004,000	1,208,000
Total Current Assets		$ 2,308,000	$ 2,584,000
Noncurrent Assets			
Land		$ 594,000	$ 630,000
Buildings and Machinery		8,678,000	9,546,000
Less Accumulated Depreciation		(3,974,000)	(4,364,000)
Total Noncurrent Assets		$ 5,298,000	$ 5,812,000
Total Assets		$ 7,606,000	$ 8,396,000
LIABILITIES AND SHAREHOLDERS' EQUITY			
Current Liabilities			
Accounts Payable		$ 412,000	$ 558,000
Taxes Payable		274,000	290,000
Other Short-Term Payables		588,000	726,000
Total Current Liabilities		$ 1,274,000	$ 1,574,000
Noncurrent Liabilities			
Bonds Payable		1,984,000	1,934,000
Total Liabilities		$ 3,258,000	$ 3,508,000
Shareholders' Equity			
Common Stock		$ 1,672,000	$ 1,704,000
Retained Earnings		2,676,000	3,184,000
Total Shareholders' Equity		$ 4,348,000	$ 4,888,000
Total Liabilities and Shareholders' Equity		$ 7,606,000	$ 8,396,000

b. Prepare a statement of cash flows for GTI Inc. for 2007 and 2008. Present cash flows from operations using the indirect method.

c. Present a derivation of cash flows from operations for 2007 using the direct method.

d. Discuss the relation between net income and cash flow from operations and the pattern of cash flows from operating, investing, and financing activities.

37. **Interpreting a statement of cash flows based on the direct method for presenting cash flow from operations.** Exhibit 5.32 on page 233 shows the consolidated income statements for CVS Caremark Corporation for three recent years. CVS Caremark uses the direct method for presenting its cash flows from operations, which appears in **Exhibit 5.33** on page 233. In the following, we refer to the 52 weeks ending December 29, 2007, as the year 2007.

a. What was the change in accounts receivable during 2007?

b. Accounts payable for inventories increased by $181.4 during 2007. What was the change in inventories during 2007?

c. By how much did the amount paid for interest during 2007 differ from interest expense? Give the amount and indicate whether the amount paid exceeded, or was less than, expense.

d. Note that income increased by a bit more than 10% between 2005 and 2006 but nearly doubled between 2006 and 2007. What cause(s) can you suggest for this dramatic change?

EXHIBIT 5.30

GTI, Inc.
Balance Sheets
(all dollar amounts in thousands)
(Problem 36)

	December 31		
	2008	2007	2006
ASSETS			
Cash	$ 367	$ 475	$ 430
Accounts Receivable	2,545	3,936	3,768
Inventories	2,094	2,966	2,334
Prepayments	122	270	116
Total Current Assets	$ 5,128	$ 7,647	$ 6,648
Property, Plant, and Equipment (net)	4,027	4,598	3,806
Other Noncurrent Assets	456	559	193
Total Assets	$ 9,611	$12,804	$10,647
LIABILITIES AND SHAREHOLDERS' EQUITY			
Accounts Payable (to suppliers of inventory)	$ 796	$ 809	$ 1,578
Notes Payable to Banks	2,413	231	11
Other Current Liabilities	695	777	1,076
Total Current Liabilities	$ 3,904	$ 1,817	$ 2,665
Long-Term Debt	2,084	4,692	2,353
Other Noncurrent Liabilities	113	89	126
Total Liabilities	$ 6,101	$ 6,598	$ 5,144
Preferred Stock	$ 289	$ 289	$ —
Common Stock	86	85	83
Additional Paid-in Capital	4,394	4,392	4,385
Retained Earnings	(1,259)	1,440	1,035
Total Shareholders' Equity	$ 3,510	$ 6,206	$ 5,503
Total Liabilities and Shareholders' Equity	$ 9,611	$12,804	$10,647

EXHIBIT 5.31

GTI, Inc.
Income Statements
(all dollar amounts in thousands)
(Problem 36)

	2008	2007
Sales	$11,960	$22,833
Cost of Goods Sold	(11,031)	(16,518)
Selling and Administrative Expenses	(3,496)	(4,849)
Interest Expense	(452)	(459)
Income Tax Expense	328	(590)
Net Income (Loss)	$(2,691)	$ 417
Dividends on Preferred Stock	(8)	(12)
Net Income (Loss) Available to Common Shareholders	$(2,699)	$ 405

38. **Interpreting a statement of cash flows based on the direct method for presenting cash flow from operations.** Refer to information about CVS Caremark Corporation in the preceding problem. Consider the 52 weeks ending December 30, 2006, as the year 2006.

   a. What was the change in accounts receivable during 2006?

EXHIBIT 5.32

CVS Caremark Corporation
Consolidated Statements of Operations

In millions, except per share amounts	Fiscal Year Ended Dec. 29, 2007 (52 weeks)	Fiscal Year Ended Dec. 30, 2006 (52 weeks)	Fiscal Year Ended Dec. 31, 2005 (52 weeks)
Net revenues	$ 76,329.5	$ 43,821.4	$ 37,006.7
Cost of revenues	60,221.8	32,079.2	27,312.1
Gross profit	16,107.7	11,742.2	9,694.6
Total operating expenses	11,314.4	9,300.6	7,675.1
Operating profit	4,793.3	2,441.6	2,019.5
Interest expense, net	434.6	215.8	110.5
Earnings before income tax provision	4,358.7	2,225.8	1,909.0
Income tax provision	1,721.7	856.9	684.3
Net earnings	2,637.0	1,368.9	1,224.7
Preference dividends, net of income tax benefit	14.2	13.9	14.1
Net earnings available to common shareholders	$ 2,622.8	$ 1,355.0	$ 1,210.6
BASIC EARNINGS PER COMMON SHARE:			
Net earnings	$ 1.97	$ 1.65	$ 1.49
Weighted average common shares outstanding	1,328.2	820.6	811.4
DILUTED EARNINGS PER COMMON SHARE:			
Net earnings	$ 1.92	$ 1.60	$ 1.45
Weighted average common shares outstanding	1,371.8	853.2	841.6
Dividends declared per common share	$ 0.22875	$ 0.15500	$ 0.14500

EXHIBIT 5.33

CVS Caremark Corporation
Excerpts from Statements of Cash Flows
Cash Flow from Operations Presented with the Direct Method

In millions	Fiscal Year Ended Dec. 29, 2007 (52 weeks)	Fiscal Year Ended Dec. 30, 2006 (52 weeks)	Fiscal Year Ended Dec. 31, 2005 (52 weeks)
CASH FLOWS FROM OPERATING ACTIVITIES:			
Cash receipts from revenues	$ 61,986.3	$ 43,273.7	$ 36,923.1
Cash paid for inventory	(45,772.6)	(31,422.1)	(26,403.9)
Cash paid to other suppliers and employees	(10,768.6)	(9,065.3)	(8,186.7)
Interest and dividends received	33.6	15.9	6.5
Interest paid	(468.2)	(228.1)	(135.9)
Income taxes paid	(1,780.8)	(831.7)	(591.0)
Net cash provided by operating activities	3,229.7	1,742.4	1,612.1

b. Inventories increased by $624.1 during 2006. What was the change in accounts payable for inventories during 2006?

c. By how much did the amount paid for interest during 2006 differ from interest expense? Give the amount and indicate whether the amount paid exceeded, or was less than, expense.

d. Note that cash flow from operations increased by about 10% between 2005 and 2006 but nearly doubled between 2006 and 2007. What cause(s) can you suggest for this dramatic change?

39. **Derive cash flow from operations presented with the direct method from annual report presentation that uses the indirect method.** Refer to the Statement of Cash Flows for

---

EXHIBIT 5.34

Quinta Company
All Balance Sheet Accounts
December 31, 2008
(Problem 41)

ASSETS

Cash	$ 25,000
Accounts Receivable	220,000
Merchandise Inventories	320,000
Land	40,000
Buildings and Equipment (at cost)	500,000
Less Accumulated Depreciation	(200,000)
Investments (noncurrent)	100,000
Total Assets	$1,005,000

LIABILITIES AND SHAREHOLDERS' EQUITY

Accounts Payable	$ 280,000
Other Current Liabilities	85,000
Bonds Payable	100,000
Common Stock	200,000
Retained Earnings	340,000
Total Liabilities and Shareholders' Equity	$1,005,000

Nordstrom Inc. in **Exhibit 1.3**. Derive cash flow from operations for a direct method presentation, such as that in **Exhibit 5.1**, for 2006.

Use the information in that exhibit to fill in the spreadsheet template provided on the Web site for this textbook, *www.cengage.com/accounting/stickney*. In that exhibit, we have made some arbitrary choices, such as that all Accounts Payable relate to purchases of inventory and that changes in Other Assets and Other Liabilities relate to Other Income, net.

When you finish, your answer should be the same as that given in **Exhibit 5.1**.

40. **Derive cash flow from operations presented with the direct method from annual report presentation that uses the indirect method.** Repeat the preceding problem for 2005.

41. **Working backward through the statement of cash flows.** Quinta Company presents the balance sheet shown in **Exhibit 5.34** and the statement of cash flows shown in **Exhibit 5.35** (page 235) for 2008. The firm sold investments, equipment, and land for cash at their net book value. The accumulated depreciation of the equipment sold was $20,000.

Prepare a balance sheet for the beginning of the year, January 1, 2008.

42. **Interpreting the statement of cash flows. Exhibit 5.36** (page 236) presents a statement of cash flows for Swoosh Shoes Inc., which we derived from actual reports of Nike, Inc., maker of athletic shoes, for three years.

   a. Why did Swoosh experience increasing net income but decreasing cash flow from operations during this three-year period?

   b. What is the likely explanation for the changes in Swoosh's cash flow from investing during the three-year period?

   c. How did Swoosh finance its investing activities during the three-year period?

   d. Evaluate the appropriateness of Swoosh's use of short-term borrowing during 2008.

43. **Interpreting the statement of cash flows. Exhibit 5.37** (page 237) presents statements of cash flows for Spokane Corporation, a forest products company, for three years from its past when it faced financial difficulty, which you can see by noting the pattern of losses increasing with time. The company has since reorganized and reported positive earnings.

   a. Spokane Corporation operated at a net loss each year but generated positive cash flow from operations. Explain.

EXHIBIT 5.35

Quinta Company
Statement of Cash Flows
For Year of 2008
(Problem 41)

Operations

Net Income	$ 200,000	
Additions:		
Depreciation Expense	60,000	
Increase in Accounts Payable	25,000	
Subtractions:		
Increase in Accounts Receivable	(30,000)	
Increase in Merchandise Inventories	(40,000)	
Decrease in Other Current Liabilities	(45,000)	
Cash Flow from Operations		$ 170,000

Investing

Sale of Investments	$ 40,000	
Sale of Buildings and Equipment	15,000	
Sale of Land	10,000	
Acquisition of Buildings and Equipment	(130,000)	
Cash Flow from Investing		(65,000)

Financing

Common Stock Issued	$ 60,000	
Bonds Issued	40,000	
Dividends Paid	(200,000)	
Cash Flow from Financing		(100,000)
Net Change in Cash		$ 5,000

b. What is the likely explanation for the changes in Spokane Corporation's cash flow from investing activities during the three-year period?

c. What is the likely explanation for the changes in long-term financing during 2006 and 2007?

44. **Interpreting statement of cash flow relations. Exhibit 5.38** (page 238) presents statements of cash flow for eight companies for the same year:

   a. American Airlines (airline transportation)

   b. American Home Products (pharmaceuticals)

   c. Interpublic Group (advertising and other marketing services)

   d. Procter & Gamble (consumer products)

   e. Reebok (athletic shoes)

   f. Texas Instruments (electronics)

   g. Limited Brands (specialty retailing)

   h. Upjohn (pharmaceuticals)

   Discuss the relation between net income and cash flow from operations, and the pattern of cash flows from operating, investing, and financing activities for each firm.

45. **Interpreting direct and indirect methods.** Refer to **Exhibit 5.39** (page 239) for Fierce Fighters Corporation, which shows excerpts from its Statements of Cash Flows, with cash flow from operations presented with the indirect method, for three recent years. We use these years to illustrate a period of successively decreasing cash flows from operations. The columns labeled *Change* and shaded gray do not appear in the original.

EXHIBIT 5.36

Swoosh Shoes, Inc.
Statement of Cash Flows
(all dollar amounts in millions)
(Problem 42)

	2008	2007	2006
Operations			
Net Income	$ 287	$ 243	$ 167
Depreciation and Amortization	34	17	15
Other Addbacks and Subtractions	3	5	(5)
Working Capital Provided by Operations	$ 324	$ 265	$ 177
(Increase) Decrease in Accounts Receivable	(120)	(105)	(38)
(Increase) Decrease in Inventories	(275)	(86)	(25)
(Increase) Decrease in Other Operating Current Assets	(6)	(5)	(2)
Increase (Decrease) in Accounts Payable	59	36	21
Increase (Decrease) in Other Current Operating Liabilities	32	22	36
Cash Flow from Operations	$ 14	$ 127	$ 169
Investing			
Sale of Property, Plant, and Equipment	$ 2	$ 1	$ 3
Acquisition of Property, Plant, and Equipment	(165)	(87)	(42)
Acquisition of Investment	(48)	(3)	(1)
Cash Flow from Investing	$(211)	$ (89)	$ (40)
Financing			
Increase in Short-Term Debt	$ 269	—	—
Increase in Long-Term Debt	5	$ 1	—
Issue of Common Stock	3	2	$ 3
Decrease in Short-Term Debt	—	(8)	(96)
Decrease in Long-Term Debt	(10)	(2)	(4)
Dividends	(41)	(26)	(22)
Cash Flow from Financing	$ 226	$ (33)	$(119)
Change in Cash	$ 29	$5	$ 10
Cash, Beginning of Year	89	84	74
Cash, End of Year	$ 118	$ 89	$ 84

a. Using **Exhibit 5.39**, write a short (no more than 50 words) explanation of why Fierce Fighters' cash flow from operations declined by about 20% per year between 2006 and 2007 and then again between 2007 and 2008. If you cannot explain, then suggest why that might be.

b. Now refer to **Exhibit 5.40** (page 240) for Fierce Fighters, which shows excerpts from its Statements of Cash Flows, with cash flow from operations presented with the direct method, for the same three years as in part **a**. Write a short (no more than 50 words) explanation of why Fierce Fighter's cash flow from operations declined by about 20% per year between 2006 and 2007 and then again between 2007 and 2008. If you cannot explain, then suggest why that might be.

c. Which method of presenting cash flow from operations do you find easier to interpret?

EXHIBIT 5.37	Spokane Corporation Statement of Cash Flows (all dollar amounts in millions) (Problem 43)		
	2008	**2007**	**2006**
Operations			
Net Income (Loss)	$ (63)	$ (77)	$(154)
Depreciation	236	268	266
Other Addbacks (Subtractions)	41	(43)	(56)
(Increase) Decrease in Accounts Receivable	(68)	—	(46)
(Increase) Decrease in Inventories	6	(31)	(3)
Increase (Decrease) in Accounts Payable	55	15	9
Increase (Decrease) in Other Current Liabilities ...	9	(1)	50
Cash Flow from Operations	$ 216	$ 131	$ 66
Investing			
Sale of Property, Plant, and Equipment	$ 171	$ 24	$ 202
Acquisition of Property, Plant, and Equipment	(271)	(222)	(283)
Other Investing Transactions	(75)	9	(31)
Cash Flow from Investing	$(175)	$(189)	$(112)
Financing			
Increase (Decrease) in Short-Term Borrowing	$ 25	$ 27	$ (54)
Increase in Long-Term Debt	139	84	131
Increase in Preferred Stock.........................	—	287	191
Decrease in Long-Term Debt	(116)	(269)	(164)
Dividends	(84)	(67)	(55)
Other Financing Transactions	2	(2)	(5)
Cash Flow from Financing	$ (34)	$ 60	$ 44
Change in Cash	$ 7	$ 2	$ (2)
Cash, Beginning of Year	22	20	22
Cash, End of Year	$ 29	$ 22	$ 20

46. **Issues in manipulating cash flows from operations.** Top financial management wants to increase cash flow from operations. It asks you to implement the following strategies. Which of these, if implemented, will increase cash flow from operations contrasted to the amount if you do not implement the strategy for the firm? Comment on the wisdom and suitability of these strategies.

   a. The firm delays maintaining equipment until after the start of the next period.

   b. The firm delays purchasing new equipment until after the start of the next period.

   c. The firm sells $1 million of accounts receivable for $980,000 cash to a financial institution, but agrees to reimburse the purchaser for the amount by which uncollectible accounts exceed $20,000.

   d. The firm delays paying for its employees' insurance premiums until after the start of the next period.

   e. The firm delays paying some suppliers until after the due date, and until after the start of the next period.

   f. The firm sells goods for cash but promises the customers that they can return the goods for full refund after the start of the next period.

EXHIBIT 5.38

Statements of Cash Flows for Selected Companies
(all dollar amounts in millions)
(Problem 44)

	American Airlines	American Home Products	Interpublic Group	Procter & Gamble	Reebok	Texas Instruments	Limited Brands	Upjohn
Operations								
Net Income (Loss)	$ (110)	$ 1,528	$ 125	$2,211	$ 254	$ 691	$ 455	$ 491
Depreciation	1,223	306	61	1,134	37	665	247	175
Other Addbacks (Subtractions)	166	71	23	196	(4)	(9)	—	7
(Increase) Decrease in Receivables	37	14	(66)	40	(65)	(197)	(102)	6
(Increase) Decrease in Inventories	(27)	(157)	16	25	(82)	(60)	(74)	(21)
Increase (Decrease) in Payables	34	325	59	98	35	330	118	63
Increase (Decrease) in Other Current Liabilities	54	(185)	(15)	(55)	(2)	112	110	(11)
Cash Flow from Operations	$ 1,377	$ 1,902	$ 203	$ 3,649	$ 173	$ 1,532	$ 754	$ 710
Investing								
Capital Expenditures (net)	$(2,080)	$ (473)	$ (79)	$(1,841)	$ (62)	$(1,076)	$(430)	$(224)
Sale (Acquisition) of Marketable Securities	290	24	3	23	—	(47)	—	(287)
Sale (Acquisition) of Other Businesses	—	(9,161)	—	(295)	—	—	(60)	308
Other Investing	36	(5)	(85)	105	(4)	—	—	(1)
Cash Flow from Investing	$(1,754)	$(9,615)	$(161)	$(2,008)	$ (66)	$(1,123)	$(490)	$(204)
Financing								
Increase (Decrease) in Short-Term Borrowing	$ (380)	$ 8,640	$ 35	$ (281)	$ 37	$ (1)	$(322)	$5
Increase in Long-Term Debt	730	—	42	414	—	1	150	15
Increase in Capital Stock	1,081	38	19	36	13	110	17	—
Decrease in Long-Term Debt	(1,069)	—	(15)	(797)	(3)	(88)	—	(46)
Acquisition of Treasury Stock	—	(314)	(37)	(14)	(112)	—	—	(32)
Dividends	(49)	(903)	(36)	(949)	(25)	(79)	(102)	(264)
Other Financing	82	11	(14)	1	(12)	4	—	37
Cash Flow from Financing	$ 395	$ 7,472	$(6)	$(1,590)	$(102)	$ (53)	$(257)	$(285)
Change in Cash	$ 18	$ (241)	$ 36	$ 51	$ 5	$ 356	$7	$ 221
Cash, Beginning of Year	45	1,937	256	2,322	79	404	34	281
Cash, End of Year	$ 63	$ 1,696	$ 292	$ 2,373	$ 84	$ 760	$ 41	$ 502

EXHIBIT 5.39

Fierce Fighters Corporation
Data Taken from Consolidated Statements of Cash Flows
(Shaded Columns Showing Changes Do Not Appear in Original)
(all dollar amounts in millions)
(Problem 45)

Indirect Method

Years ended December 31	2008	Change	2007	Change	2006
Cash Provided by Operating Activities					
Net Income	$ 427	(181)	$ 608	141	$ 467
Adjustments to Reconcile Net Income to Net Cash Provided by Operations:					
Depreciation.	266	91	175	(18)	193
Amortization of Intangible Assets	379	173	206	10	196
Common Stock Issued to Employees	46	38	8	6	2
Loss on Disposal of Discontinued Operations	—	(56)	56	56	—
Loss (Gain) on Disposals of Property, Plant, and Equipment	(7)	(20)	13	(8)	21
Retiree Benefits Income	(269)	223	(492)	(243)	(249)
Decrease (Increase) in					
Accounts Receivable.	1,273	1,952	(679)	(849)	170
Inventoried Costs.	(28)	(105)	77	(95)	172
Prepaid Expenses and Other Current Assets	17	45	(28)	(73)	45
Increase (Decrease) in					
Advances from Customers on Long-Term Contracts	(648)	(1,314)	666	645	21
Accounts Payable and Accruals	(696)	(783)	87	89	(2)
Provisions for Contract Losses	(65)	(85)	20	28	(8)
Deferred Income Taxes	174	(171)	345	115	230
Income Taxes Payable.	(13)	(41)	28	(30)	58
Retiree Benefits	(75)	17	(92)	37	(129)
Other Noncash Transaction	36	24	12	(8)	20
Net Cash Provided by Operating Activities	$ 817	(193)	$1,010	(197)	$1,207

The changes are from right to left, from 2006 to 2007 and from 2007 to 2008. Each number in a change column is the difference: number to the left of the change minus the number to the right of the change.

EXHIBIT 5.40

Fierce Fighters Corporation
Data Taken from Consolidated Statements of Cash Flows
(Shaded Columns Showing Changes Do Not Appear in Original)
(all dollar amounts in millions)
(Problem 45)

Direct Method (without Reconciliation of Net Income to Cash Flow from Operations)

Years ended December 31	2008	Change	2007	Change	2006
Cash Provided by Operating Activities		**Change**		**Change**	
Sources of Cash					
Cash Received from Customers					
Collections from Customers on Long-Term Contracts	$ 3,102	*1,664*	$ 1,438	*(253)*	$ 1,691
Other Collections	11,148	*4,145*	7,003	*(447)*	7,450
Less: Cash Paid to Suppliers and Employees	(13,251)	*(6,001)*	(7,250)	*465*	(7,715)
Net Cash Margin	$ 999	*(192)*	$ 1,191	*(235)*	$ 1,426
Cash Contribution Margin Percentage	7.0%		14.1%		15.6%
Proceeds from Litigation Settlement	$ 220	*220*	$ —	—	$ —
Interest Received	17	—	17	*(1)*	18
Income Tax Refunds Received	23	*8*	15	*(60)*	75
Other Cash Receipts	24	*14*	10	*3*	7
Cash Provided by Operating Activities	$ 1,283	*50*	$ 1,233	*(293)*	$ 1,526
Other Operating Uses of Cash					
Interest Paid	$ 333	*168*	$ 165	*(51)*	$ 216
Income Taxes Paid	126	*69*	57	*(28)*	85
Other Cash Payments	7	*6*	1	*(17)*	18
Cash Used in Operating Activities	$ 466	*243*	$ 223	*(96)*	$ 319
Net Cash Provided by Operating Activities	$ 817	*(193)*	$ 1,010	*(197)*	$ 1,207

The changes are from right to left, from 2006 to 2007 and from 2007 to 2008. Each number in a change column is the difference: number to the left of the change minus the number to the right of the change.

Introduction to Financial Statement Analysis

CHAPTER

6

LEARNING OBJECTIVES

1. Understand the relation between the expected return and risk of investment alternatives and the role financial statement analysis plays in providing information about returns and risk.

2. Understand the usefulness of the rate of return on assets (ROA) as a measure of a firm's operating profitability independent of financing and the insights gained by disaggregating ROA into the profit margin for ROA and the total assets turnover ratios.

3. Understand the usefulness of the rate of return on common shareholders' equity (ROCE) as a measure of profitability that incorporates a firm's financing decisions and the insights gained by disaggregating ROCE into the profit margin for

ROCE, total assets turnover, and the capital structure leverage ratios.

4. Understand the strengths and weaknesses of earnings per common share as a measure of profitability.

5. Understand the distinction between short-term liquidity risk and long-term liquidity risk and the financial statement ratios used to assess each.

6. Develop skills to interpret effectively the results of an analysis of profitability and risk.

7. (Appendix) Develop skills to prepare pro forma financial statements.

8. (Appendix) Understand the usefulness of pro forma financial statements in the valuation of a firm.

Wal-Mart Stores (Wal-Mart) is the largest retailer in the world. As the financial data for a recent year in **Exhibit 6.1** make clear, Wal-Mart's sales exceed the combined sales of its principal competitors, its assets are 67% as large, and its net income exceeds the combined earnings of these competitors.

EXHIBIT 6.1	**Financial Data for Selected Discount and Grocery Retailers (all dollar amounts in millions)**				
Company	Headquarters	Industry	Sales	Assets	Income
Wal-Mart	United States	Hypermarkets	$378,799	$172,400	$12,731
Kohl's	United States	Discount	$ 16,474	$ 10,560	$ 1,084
Target	United States	Discount	63,367	44,560	2,849
Kroger	United States	Grocery	70,235	22,299	1,181
Itochu	Japan	Grocery	25,032	52,800	1,406
Carrefour	France	Hypermarkets	114,004	75,927	3,147
Metro AG	Germany	Hypermarkets	88,056	49,523	1,129
Totals			$377,168	$255,669	$10,796

- What is the source of Wal-Mart's competitive advantage?
- How has Wal-Mart's profitability changed relative to its competitors in recent years?
- What risks does Wal-Mart face that might affect its future operations?

Answering these questions requires that we analyze the financial statements of Wal-Mart and its competitors. This chapter introduces the tools and techniques for analyzing financial statements. **Figure 6.1** presents the typical sequential steps in financial statement analysis and valuation.

1. **Understand the Purpose and Content of the Principal Financial Statements and Related Notes** We begin by understanding the purpose and content of the three principal financial statements and related notes. Chapters 3, 4, and 5 discuss the balance sheet, the income statement, and the statement of cash flows, respectively. Subsequent chapters discuss information that firms disclose in the notes. A later section of this chapter presents the financial statements for Wal-Mart. We do not provide information from the notes to Wal-Mart's financial statements because they would not mean much at this point.

2. **Identify the Industry Economic Characteristics and Firm's Strategy** Next, we identify the economic characteristics of the industry in which a firm participates. Wal-Mart is a discount retailing firm. The principal economic characteristics of the discount retailing industry are as follows:

   - **Nature of Products:** The product offerings of Wal-Mart do not significantly differ from similar offerings by competitors; common terminology refers to such products as *commodities*.

   - **Extent of Competition:** The industry is competitive with many firms offering similar products. Important barriers to entry for new competitors are size, a distribution network, and market penetration.

   - **Growth Characteristics:** The U.S. market is saturated, so any further growth must come from introducing new store concepts and expanding internationally.

Next, we identify the firm's strategy to compete in its industry and gain a competitive advantage. Wal-Mart emphasizes an every-day low price strategy and operates through four principal store concepts:

   - **Wal-Mart Discount Stores:** discount stores that offer clothing, household products, electronics equipment, pharmaceuticals, health and beauty products, sporting goods, and similar items.

   - **Wal-Mart Superstores:** full-line supermarkets offering grocery products combined with Wal-Mart's traditional discount stores. In recent years, Wal-Mart has replaced an increasing number of its traditional discount stores with superstores.

   - **Neighborhood Markets:** smaller stores located in residential areas offering grocery products. This is a relatively new store concept for Wal-Mart.

   - **Sam's Clubs:** members-only warehouse stores that offer products in such categories as food, household, automotive, electronic, and sporting goods in large quantities or sizes at wholesale prices.

Wal-Mart has expanded internationally by acquiring established retail stores in other countries and incorporating operating policies in the acquired stores similar to those it uses in the United States. Sales mix percentages for Wal-Mart for its fiscal years ended January 31, 2006, 2007, and 2008 are as follows:

FIGURE 6.1   **Overview of Financial Statement Analysis**

Understand the Financial Statements → Identify Economic Characteristics → Identify Company Strategy → Analyze Profitability and Risk → Prepare Pro Forma Financial Statements → Value the Firm

Fiscal Year Ended January 31:	2008	2007	2006
Wal-Mart Discount Stores, Superstores, and Neighborhood Markets........	64%	66%	68%
Sam's Clubs..	12	12	13
International	24	22	19
Total	100%	100%	100%

3. **Calculate and Interpret Profitability and Risk Ratios** As a later section makes clear, most financial statement analyses examine a firm's profitability or its risk. Ratios of items in the three principal financial statements provide one analytical tool used to evaluate profitability and risk. This chapter describes and illustrates various profitability and risk ratios. The analysis begins by calculating the financial ratios for the last three or more years and examining why the ratios changed over time (called *over-time* or *times-series analysis*). The analyst also interprets the ratios by comparing them with the corresponding ratios of competitors for the same time period (called *across-firm* or *cross-section analysis*), incorporating information about industry economic characteristics and the firm's strategy.

4. **Prepare Pro Forma, or Projected, Financial Statements** After studying the profitability and risk of a firm in the recent past, the analyst often prepares pro forma, or projected, financial statements for the next three to five years based on a set of assumptions about economic, industry, and firm-specific conditions. The appendix to this chapter illustrates the preparation of pro forma financial statements for Wal-Mart for fiscal year 2009.

5. **Value the Firm** Analysts use projected net income, cash flows, and other items from the financial statements to value the firm. Valuation is a principal topic of courses in finance, but the appendix to this chapter introduces the topic.

OBJECTIVES OF FINANCIAL STATEMENT ANALYSIS

The first question the analyst asks in analyzing a set of financial statements is, "What do I look for?" The response to this question requires an understanding of investment decisions.

To illustrate, assume that you recently inherited $25,000 and must decide what to do with the bequest. You narrow the investment decision to purchasing either a certificate of deposit at a local bank or shares of common stock of Wal-Mart, currently selling for $48 per share. You will base your decision on the **return** you anticipate from each investment and the **risk** associated with that return.

The bank currently pays interest at the rate of 3% annually on certificates of deposit. Because the bank will likely remain in business, you feel confident that you will earn 3% each year. The return from investing in the shares of Wal-Mart's common stock has two components. First, the firm paid a cash dividend in its most recent year of $0.88 per share, and you anticipate that it will continue to pay a dividend at least this large in the future. Also, the market price of Wal-Mart's stock will likely change between the time you purchase the shares and the time in the future when you sell them. The difference between the eventual selling price and the purchase price, often called *price appreciation* (or *price depreciation*, if negative), provides the second component of the return from buying the stock.

The common stock investment involves more risk than does the certificate of deposit investment. The future profitability of Wal-Mart will likely affect future dividends and market price changes. If competitors open new stores or introduce new products or services that erode Wal-Mart's market share, future income might be less than you currently anticipate. In addition, although Wal-Mart has innovated over several decades, one never knows when a new competitor will get a better idea of how to run a similar business. On the other hand, if Wal-Mart opens new stores, or makes acquisitions, or introduces successful new products or services, or is the first to discover new channels of retailing, its future income might be greater than you currently anticipate.

Economy-wide factors, such as inflation, unemployment, and changes in international tensions will also affect the market price of Wal-Mart's shares. Also, specific industry factors, such as changes in exchange rates that affect the cost of merchandise or changes in government regulatory actions, may influence the market price of the shares. Because most individuals prefer less risk to more risk, you will want a higher expected return if you purchase Wal-Mart's shares than if you invest in a certificate of deposit.

FIGURE 6.2	Relation Between Financial Statement Analysis and Investment Decisions

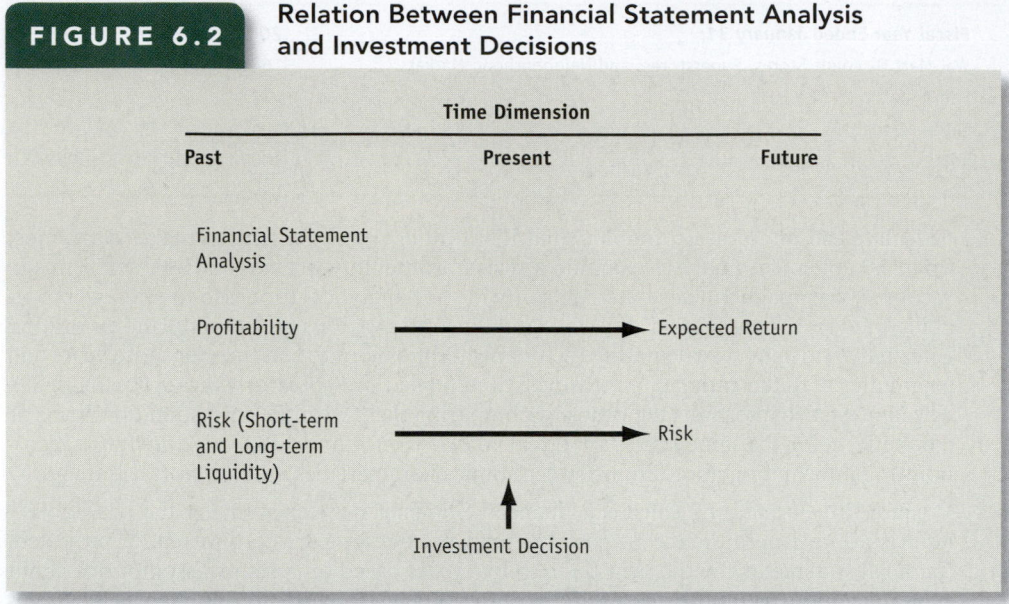

Theoretical and empirical research has shown that the expected return from investing in a firm relates, in part, to the expected profitability of the firm.[1] The analyst studies a firm's past earnings to understand its operating performance and to help forecast its future profitability.

Investment decisions also require that the analyst assess the risk associated with the expected return.[2] A firm may find itself short of cash and unable to repay a short-term loan coming due. Or, it may have so much long-term debt in its financing structure that it has difficulty meeting the required interest and principal payments. The financial statements provide information for assessing how these and other risk elements affect expected return.

Most financial statement analysis, therefore, explores some aspect of a firm's profitability, or its risk, or both. **Figure 6.2** summarizes the relation between financial statement analysis and investment decisions.

USEFULNESS OF RATIOS

Readers cannot easily answer questions about a firm's profitability and risk from the raw information in financial statements. For example, one cannot assess the profitability of a firm by noting the amount of net income—large net income could result from a large firm earning small profits on its transactions or from a small firm earning large profits. Comparing net income with the assets used to generate those earnings will provide more useful information. The analyst expresses these (and other useful) relations between items in the financial statements in the form of ratios. Some ratios compare items within the income statement; some use only balance sheet data; others relate items from more than one of the three principal financial statements. Ratios aid financial statement analysis because they conveniently summarize data in a form easy to understand, interpret, and compare.

Ratios provide little information unless the analyst places them in a context. For example, does a rate of return on common shareholders' equity of 8.6% indicate satisfactory performance? After calculating the ratios, the analyst must compare them with some standard. The following list provides several possible standards:

1. The planned ratio for the period.
2. The corresponding ratio during the preceding period for the same firm.

---

[1]Ray Ball and Phillip Brown, "An Empirical Evaluation of Accounting Income Numbers," *Journal of Accounting Research* (Autumn 1968), 159–178; D. Craig Nicholas and James Wahlen, "How Do Earnings Numbers Relate to Stock Returns? A Review of Classic Accounting Research with Updated Evidence," *Accounting Horizons* (December 2004), 263–286.

[2]Modern finance distinguishes between systematic (market) risk and nonsystematic (firm-specific) risk. The discussion in this chapter does not distinguish between these two dimensions of risk.

EXHIBIT 6.2	Wal-Mart Stores Comparative Income Statement (all dollar amounts in millions)			
		For the Year Ended January 31		
		2008	2007	2006
Sales Revenue		$374,526	$344,992	$308,945
Other Revenues		4,578	3,938	3,398
Total Revenues		$379,104	$348,930	$312,343
Less Expenses:				
Cost of Goods Sold		$286,515	$264,152	$237,649
Selling and Administrative		70,694	64,426	56,063
Interest		2,103	1,809	1,420
Total		$359,312	$330,387	$295,132
Income Before Income Taxes		$ 19,792	$ 18,543	$ 17,211
Income Tax Expense		6,908	6,365	5,803
Net Income		$ 12,884	$ 12,178	$ 11,408

3. The corresponding ratio for a similar firm in the same industry.

4. The average ratio for other firms in the same industry.

A later section of this chapter discusses difficulties encountered in using each of these bases for comparison.

The following sections describe several ratios useful for assessing profitability and various dimensions of risk. To demonstrate the calculation of various ratios, we use data for Wal-Mart for its fiscal years ending January 31, 2006 to 2008, appearing in **Exhibit 6.2** (comparative income statement), **Exhibit 6.3** (comparative balance sheet), and **Exhibit 6.4** (comparative statement of cash flows). We recommend that you trace the amounts in the various financial ratios discussed in this chapter to the amounts in Wal-Mart's financial statements.

Our analysis for Wal-Mart examines changes in its various ratios over the three-year period—a so-called **time-series analysis**. Time-series analysis contrasts with a **cross-section analysis**, which involves comparing a given firm's ratios with those of other firms for a specific period. Several problems at the end of the chapter involve cross-section analysis (see Exercises 11, 12, 14, 15, and 16 and Problems 28 and 29).

ANALYSIS OF PROFITABILITY

A firm engages in operations, such as Wal-Mart selling merchandise in its stores, to generate net income. This section discusses three measures of **profitability**:

1. Rate of return on assets.

2. Rate of return on common shareholders' equity.

3. Earnings per share of common stock.

RATE OF RETURN ON ASSETS

The **rate of return on assets (ROA)** measures a firm's performance in using assets to generate net income independent of how the firm financed the acquisition of those assets. Previous chapters describe three principal business activities: investing, financing, and operating. The rate of return on assets relates the results of *operating* performance to the *investments* (assets) of a firm without regard to how the firm *financed* those investments.

The calculation of ROA is as follows:

$$\text{ROA} = \frac{\text{Net Income} + \text{Interest Expense Net of Income Tax Savings}}{\text{Average Total Assets}}$$

EXHIBIT 6.3

Wal-Mart Stores
Comparative Balance Sheet
(all dollar amounts in millions)

	January 31			
	2008	**2007**	**2006**	**2005**
ASSETS				
Cash	$ 5,569	$ 7,373	$ 6,414	$ 5,488
Accounts Receivable (net)	3,654	2,840	2,662	1,715
Inventories	35,180	33,685	32,191	29,762
Prepayments	3,182	2,690	2,557	1,889
Total Current Assets	$ 47,585	$ 46,588	$ 43,824	$ 38,854
Property, Plant, and Equipment (net)	105,903	94,512	85,652	73,745
Other Noncurrent Assets	18,912	16,165	15,073	13,182
Total Assets	$172,400	$157,265	$144,549	$125,781
LIABILITIES AND SHAREHOLDERS' EQUITY				
Accounts Payable	$ 30,370	$ 28,090	$ 25,373	$ 21,987
Notes Payable	5,040	2,570	3,754	3,812
Current Portion of Long-Term Debt	6,229	5,713	4,894	3,982
Other Current Liabilities	16,815	15,381	14,805	13,401
Total Current Liabilities	$ 58,454	$ 51,754	$ 48,826	$ 43,182
Long-Term Debt	42,288	36,807	36,533	28,885
Other Noncurrent Liabilities	7,050	7,131	6,019	4,318
Total Liabilities	$107,792	$ 95,692	$ 91,378	$ 76,385
Common Stock ($.10 par value)	$ 397	$ 413	$ 417	$ 423
Additional Paid-in Capital	3,028	2,834	2,596	2,425
Retained Earnings	57,319	55,818	49,105	43,854
Accumulated Other Comprehensive Income	3,864	2,508	1,053	2,694
Total Shareholders' Equity	$ 64,608	$ 61,573	$ 53,171	$ 49,396
Total Liabilities and Shareholders' Equity	$172,400	$157,265	$144,549	$125,781

ROA answers the question: how well has the firm done in conducting its operations *independent of financing costs*? The amount in the numerator of ROA excludes any interest expense on debt and distributions to shareholders. The calculation of the numerator amount begins with net income. If the measure of performance in the numerator is to exclude the costs of financing, then the analysis must add back the amount of interest expense because, in computing net income, the firm subtracts interest expense. Because firms can deduct interest expense in calculating taxable income, interest expense does not reduce *after-tax* net income by one dollar for each dollar of interest expense. Rather, each dollar of interest expense reduces after-tax net income by less than a dollar. Thus, to calculate the numerator of ROA (which measures performance independent of financing costs), the analyst adds back interest expense reduced by the income taxes that interest deductions save.

To illustrate, Wal-Mart reported interest expense for 2008[3] (see **Exhibit 6.2**) of $2,103 million. The income tax rate is 35% of pretax income. Because Wal-Mart can deduct interest in computing taxable income, it saved income taxes of $736 million (= 0.35 × $2,103 million). The net after-tax cost of interest expense was $1,367 million (= $2,103 million − $736 million). To compute income before interest expense to lenders, the analyst adds back $1,367 million to net income. The analyst does not add back dividends paid to shareholders because the firm does not deduct them as an expense in calculating net income; net income already measures the results of operations before payments to suppliers of shareholders' equity capital.

Because we are computing ROA for a year, the measure of investment for the denominator should reflect the average amount of assets in use during the year. A crude but usually satisfactory figure for average total assets is one-half the sum of total assets at the beginning and at the end of the year.

---

[3]From this point forward in the chapter, we omit reference to Wal-Mart's use of a fiscal year ending January 31, 2008, and refer to the accounting period as 2008.

| EXHIBIT 6.4 | **Wal-Mart Stores** **Comparative Statement of Cash Flows** **(all dollar amounts in millions)** |

	For the Year Ended January 31		
	2008	**2007**	**2006**
Operations			
Net Income	$ 12,884	$ 12,178	$ 11,408
Additions and Subtractions:			
Depreciation Expense	6,317	5,459	4,717
Other Addbacks and Subtractions	593	1,128	491
(Increase) Decrease in Accounts Receivable	(564)	(214)	(456)
(Increase) Decrease in Inventories	(775)	(1,274)	(1,733)
(Increase) Decrease in Prepayments	(492)	(133)	(668)
Increase (Decrease) in Accounts Payable	865	2,344	2,390
Increase (Decrease) in Other Current Liabilities	1,526	676	1,484
Cash Flow from Operations	$ 20,354	$ 20,164	$ 17,633
Investing			
Acquisitions of Property, Plant, and Equipment	$(14,937)	$(15,666)	$(14,563)
Other Investing Transactions	(733)	1,203	380
Cash Flow from Investing	$(15,670)	$(14,463)	$(14,183)
Financing			
Increase (Decrease) in Short-Term Borrowing	$ 2,376	$ (1,193)	$ (704)
Increase in Long-Term Borrowing	11,167	7,199	7,691
Decrease in Long-Term Borrowing	(9,066)	(6,098)	(2,969)
Acquisition of Common Stock	(7,691)	(1,718)	(3,580)
Dividends	(3,586)	(2,802)	(2,511)
Other Financing Transactions	312	(130)	(451)
Cash Flow from Financing	$ (6,488)	$ (4,742)	$ (2,524)
Net Change in Cash	$ (1,804)	$959	$ 926
Cash, Beginning of Year	7,373	6,414	5,488
Cash, End of Year	$ 5,569	$ 7,373	$ 6,414

CONCEPTUAL Note

Most financial economists would subtract average noninterest-bearing liabilities (for example, accounts payable, salaries payable) from average total assets in the denominator of ROA. **Chapter 8** describes these as operating liabilities and distinguishes them from financial liabilities (liabilities that bear interest). Economists realize that when liabilities do not provide for explicit interest charges (as is the case for operating liabilities), the creditor adjusts the terms of the contract, such as setting a higher selling price or a lower discount from the list price, for those who do not pay cash immediately. ROA requires in the numerator the income amount before

a firm accrues any charges to suppliers of funds. We cannot measure the interest charges implicit in the operating liabilities; items such as cost of goods sold and salary expense are somewhat larger because of these charges. Thus, implicit charges reduce the measure of operating income in the numerator. Subtracting average operating liabilities from average total assets likewise reduces the denominator for assets financed with such liabilities. The examples and problems in this book use average total assets in the denominator of the rate of return on assets, making no adjustment for operating liabilities.

The calculation of ROA for Wal-Mart Corporation for 2008 is as follows:[4]

$$\frac{\begin{array}{c}\text{Net Income +}\\\text{Interest Expense}\\\text{Net of Income Tax Savings}\end{array}}{\text{Average Total Assets}} = \frac{\$12,884 + (1.00 - 0.35)(\$2,103)}{(0.5)(\$157,265 + \$172,400)} = \frac{\$14,251.0}{\$164,832.5} = 8.6\%$$

Thus, for each dollar of assets it used, Wal-Mart earned $0.086 during 2008 before payments to the suppliers of financing. ROA was 9.1% in 2006 and 8.8% in 2007. Thus, ROA decreased between 2006 and 2008.

One might question the rationale for a measure of profitability that excludes the costs of financing. After all, firms must finance their assets and must cover the cost of the financing if they are to be profitable.

ROA has particular relevance to the lenders, or creditors, of a firm. These creditors have a senior claim on net income and assets relative to common shareholders. Creditors receive their return via contractual interest payments. The firm typically pays these amounts before it makes payments, usually as dividends, to other suppliers of financing. When extending credit or providing debt financing to a firm, creditors want to be sure that the firm can generate a ROA from using the financing that exceeds its cost.

Common shareholders find ROA useful in assessing financial leverage, which a later section of this chapter discusses.

DISAGGREGATING THE RATE OF RETURN ON ASSETS

To study changes in ROA, the analyst can disaggregate ROA into the product of two other ratios: the profit margin for ROA ratio and the total assets turnover ratio.

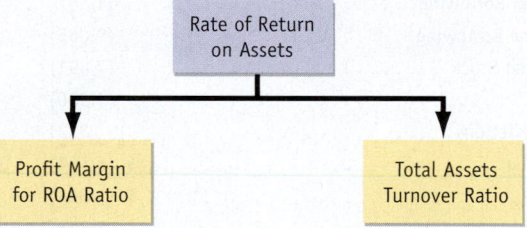

The disaggregation follows:

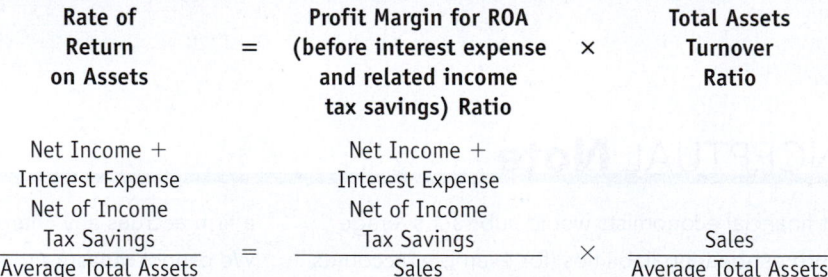

Rate of Return on Assets	=	Profit Margin for ROA (before interest expense and related income tax savings) Ratio	×	Total Assets Turnover Ratio

$$\frac{\begin{array}{c}\text{Net Income +}\\\text{Interest Expense}\\\text{Net of Income}\\\text{Tax Savings}\end{array}}{\text{Average Total Assets}} = \frac{\begin{array}{c}\text{Net Income +}\\\text{Interest Expense}\\\text{Net of Income}\\\text{Tax Savings}\end{array}}{\text{Sales}} \times \frac{\text{Sales}}{\text{Average Total Assets}}$$

The **profit margin for ROA ratio** measures a firm's ability to control the level of expenses relative to sales, to increase selling prices relative to the level of expenses incurred, or a combination of the two. By holding down expenses or increasing selling prices, a firm can increase the profits from a given amount of sales activity and thereby improve its profit margin for ROA ratio.

The **total assets turnover ratio** measures a firm's ability to generate sales from a particular level of investment in assets, or alternatively, to control the amount of assets it uses to generate a particular level of sales. The smaller the amount of assets the firm needs to generate a given level of sales, the better (larger) its assets turnover and the more profitable the firm.

---

[4]Throughout the remainder of this chapter, we omit reference to the fact that the amounts for Wal-Mart are in millions; for example, "$12,884" means "$12,884 million," and "4,066 shares" means "4,066 million shares."

EXHIBIT 6.5	Wal-Mart Stores Disaggregation of ROA for 2006, 2007, and 2008				
	ROA	**=**	**Profit Margin for ROA Ratio**	**×**	**Total Assets Turnover Ratio**
2006	9.1%	=	4.0%	×	2.3
2007	8.8	=	3.9	×	2.3
2008	8.6	=	3.8	×	2.3

The disaggregation of ROA for Wal-Mart for 2008[5] is as follows:

$$\frac{\text{Net Income} + \text{Interest Expense Net of Income Tax Savings}}{\text{Average Total Assets}} = \frac{\text{Net Income} + \text{Interest Expense Net of Income Tax Savings}}{\text{Sales}} \times \frac{\text{Sales}}{\text{Average Total Assets}}$$

$$\frac{\$12,884 + (1 - 0.35)(\$2,103)}{(0.5)(\$157,265 + \$172,400)} = \frac{\$12,884 + (1 - 0.35)(\$2,103)}{\$374,526} \times \frac{\$374,526}{(0.5)(\$157,265 + \$172,400)}$$

$$8.6\% = 3.8\% \times 2.3$$

Exhibit 6.5 presents the disaggregation of ROA for Wal-Mart into the profit margin for ROA and total assets turnover ratios for 2006, 2007, and 2008. The data show that the previously noted decrease in ROA results from a decrease in the profit margin for ROA. The total assets turnover ratio remains steady. To pinpoint the causes of the changes in Wal-Mart's ROA over this three-year period, we must further analyze the changes in the profit margin for ROA and total assets turnover ratios, which we will do in the next section.

Firms improve their ROA by increasing the profit margin for ROA ratio, the rate of assets turnover, or both. Some firms, however, have limited flexibility to alter one or the other of these components. For example, a firm that sells commodity products in a competitive market likely has little opportunity to increase its profit margin for ROA by increasing prices. Such a firm would need to improve its total assets turnover (for example, shortening the holding period for inventories with tighter controls) to increase its ROA. A firm whose activities require substantial investments in property, plant, and equipment and that operates efficiently near its capacity has limited ability to increase its ROA by increasing its total assets turnover. Such a firm might have more flexibility to take actions that increase the profit margin for ROA (for example, creating brand loyalty for its products).

ANALYZING CHANGES IN THE PROFIT MARGIN FOR ROA RATIO

Changes in a firm's expenses relative to sales cause the profit margin for ROA ratio to change. To see the relation, one can express individual expenses and net income as a percentage of sales. **Exhibit 6.6** presents such an analysis, often called a *common-size income statement*, for Wal-Mart. **Exhibit 3.2** shows a similar common-size income statement for Nordstrom. **Exhibit 6.6** alters the conventional income statement format by subtracting interest expense (net of its related income tax effects) as the last expense item. The percentages on the line, Income before Interest and Related Income Tax Effects, correspond to the profit margin for ROA ratios in **Exhibit 6.5**. (A later section discusses the profit margin for ROCE.)

The analysis in **Exhibit 6.6** indicates that Wal-Mart's profit margin for ROA ratio decreased during the three years, primarily because selling and administrative expense as a percentage of sales increased more than cost of goods sold as a percentage of sales decreased. The analyst should explore further with management the reasons for these changing percentages. The following are some possible explanations:

---

[5]In this calculation and similar ones later in this chapter, ROA does not precisely equal profit margin for ROA times total assets turnover due to rounding to one decimal place.

EXHIBIT 6.6

Wal-Mart Stores
Common Size Income Statement
For the Year Ended January 31

	2008	2007	2006
Sales Revenue	100.0%	100.0%	100.0%
Other Revenues	1.2	1.2	1.1
Total Revenues	101.2%	101.2%	101.1%
Less Operating Expenses:			
Cost of Goods Sold	76.5%	76.6%	76.9%
Selling and Administrative	18.9	18.7	18.2
Total	95.4%	95.3%	95.1%
Income Before Income Taxes and Interest	5.8%	5.9%	6.0%
Income Taxes	2.0	2.0	2.0
Income before Interest and Related Tax Effects (= Profit Margin for ROA)	3.8%	3.9%	4.0%
Interest Expense Net of Income Tax Effects	.4	.4	.3
Net Income (= Profit Margin for ROCE)	3.4%	3.5%	3.7%

Decreasing Cost of Goods Sold to Sales Percentage

■ Wal-Mart's increasing size permitted it to purchase merchandise at lower cost, either because of quantity discounts or the ability to exert bargaining power over suppliers.

■ Wal-Mart shifted its sales mix toward products or geographical markets with lower cost of goods sold to sales percentages.

■ Wal-Mart instituted improved controls over the purchase, storage, and delivery of merchandise, reducing the cost of storage and obsolescence. A later section of this chapter indicates that Wal-Mart experienced an increased turnover of its inventories, consistent with improved inventory controls.

Increasing Selling and Administrative Expense to Sales Percentage

■ Increased competition required Wal-Mart to increase advertising and other marketing costs to maintain its market share.

■ Weak economic conditions required Wal-Mart to increase advertising and other marketing costs to stimulate demand.

■ Wal-Mart shifted its sales mix toward products or geographical markets with higher levels of selling or administrative expenses. Wal-Mart's sales mix shifted from domestic to international markets during the three-year period. Efforts to establish and grow international operations could explain the increases in selling and administrative expenses as a percentage of sales.

■ A decrease in the growth of sales required Wal-Mart to spread depreciation and other relatively fixed expenses over a smaller than anticipated sales base. Wal-Mart's sales grew 9.8% in 2006, 11.7% in 2007, but only 8.6% in 2008. Perhaps Wal-Mart anticipated that revenues would grow in 2008 at a rate similar to that in 2006 and 2007 and increased the number of employees, depreciable assets, and other capacity costs accordingly.[6]

Neither the amount nor the trend in a particular ratio should, by itself, cause the analyst to invest in a firm. Ratios simply indicate areas requiring additional analysis.

---

[6]Economists refer to the process of spreading relatively fixed expenses over a larger sales level as *operating leverage,* or *economies of scale.* When firms do not achieve the sales levels anticipated from a particular level of fixed expenses, economists refer to this phenomenon as *diseconomies of scale,* as may have occurred for Wal-Mart in 2008. Managerial accounting and managerial economics textbooks discuss operating leverage more fully.

ANALYZING CHANGES IN THE TOTAL ASSETS TURNOVER RATIO

Changes in the rate of turnover of specific types of assets result in changes in the total assets turnover ratio. The analyst generally calculates separate turnover ratios for three types of assets: accounts receivable, inventory, and fixed assets.

Accounts Receivable Turnover   The rate at which accounts receivable turn over indicates how quickly a firm collects cash. The **accounts receivable turnover ratio** equals sales revenue divided by average accounts receivable during the period. In theory, the numerator should include only sales made on account if the objective is to measure how quickly a firm collects its accounts receivable. Most firms, except some retailers that deal directly with consumers (such as fast food outlets), sell their goods and services on account. Other firms, such as Wal-Mart, sell both for cash and on account. Such firms seldom disclose the proportions of cash and credit sales in their financial statements or notes. Thus, the analyst uses sales revenue in the numerator of the accounts receivable turnover ratio, recognizing that the inclusion of sales made for cash will increase the numerator and thereby overstate the receivables turnover ratio. The accounts receivable turnover ratio therefore indicates how quickly a firm turns its *sales* into cash but not how quickly it collects its *accounts receivable*. The accounts receivable turnover ratio for Wal-Mart for 2008 is as follows:

$$\frac{\text{Net Sales on Account}}{\text{Average Accounts Receivable}} = \frac{\$374,526}{(0.5)(\$2,840 + \$3,654)} = 115.3 \text{ times per year}$$

The analyst often expresses the accounts receivable turnover in terms of the average number of days that elapse between the time the firm makes the sale and the time it later collects the cash, sometimes called *days accounts receivable are outstanding* or *days outstanding for receivables*. To calculate this ratio, divide 365 days by the accounts receivable turnover ratio. The days outstanding for accounts receivable for Wal-Mart during 2008 was 3.2 days (= 365 days/115.3 times per year). Its accounts receivable turnover was 125.4 during 2007 (2.9 days) and 141.2 during 2006 (2.6 days). The rapid accounts receivable turnover and small number of days on average to collect accounts receivable result from two principal causes:

■   Wal-Mart makes a significant portion of its sales for cash, which our calculations include in the numerator but not the denominator of the accounts receivable turnover ratio.

■   Wal-Mart's customers use Visa, MasterCard, and other third-party credit cards for which Wal-Mart receives payment via electronic funds transfer from the credit card company within two to three days.[7]

The decrease in the accounts receivable turnover, which parallels an increase in the number of days receivables are outstanding, might result from the following:

■   Wal-Mart made a higher proportion of sales on account instead of for cash.

■   Wal-Mart experienced a different payment arrangement from credit card companies as it shifted its sales mix from domestic to international markets.

Most firms that sell to other businesses, as opposed to consumers, sell on account and collect within 30 to 90 days. Interpreting any particular firm's accounts receivable turnover and days receivable outstanding requires knowing the terms of sale. If a firm's terms of sale are "net 30 days" and the firm collects its accounts receivable in 45 days, then collections do not accord with the stated terms. Such a result warrants a review of the credit and collection activity to ascertain the cause and to guide corrective action. If the firm offers terms of "net 45 days," a days receivable outstanding of 45 days indicates that the firm handles accounts receivable well.

Many firms sell to customers on account as a strategy to stimulate sales. Customers may purchase more willingly and purchase more if they know they need only sign their name. Such firms may also encourage customers to delay paying for their purchases as a means for the selling firm to generate interest revenue through finance charges on the unpaid amounts. Thus, comparing accounts receivable turnovers over time or between firms requires an analysis of the growth rate in sales, the amount of interest revenue generated, the cost of administering the credit-granting activity, and the losses from uncollectible accounts.

---

[7]If Wal-Mart offered and administered its own credit card, it would likely wait 30 or more days to collect cash from credit customers.

Inventory Turnover The **inventory turnover ratio** indicates how fast firms sell their inventory items, measured in terms of the rate of movement of goods into and out of the firm. Inventory turnover equals cost of goods sold divided by the average inventory during the period. The inventory turnover for Wal-Mart for 2008 is as follows:

$$\frac{\text{Cost of Goods Sold}}{\text{Average Inventory}} = \frac{\$286,515}{(0.5)(\$33,685 + \$35,180)} = 8.3 \text{ times per year}$$

Items remain in inventory an average of 44.0 days (= 365 days/8.3 times per year) before sale. The inventory turnover for Wal-Mart was 7.7 times per year in 2006 (47.4 days) and 8.0 times per year in 2007 (45.6 days). The increased inventory turnover might result from

■ Improved inventory control systems, which reduced the levels of inventory and the cost of storage and obsolescence. This explanation is consistent with the decreased cost of goods sold to sales percentage discussed earlier.

■ A shift in sales mix toward grocery or other products that turn over more quickly.

Managing inventory turnover involves two opposing considerations. On the one hand, for a given amount of gross margin on the goods, firms prefer to sell as many goods as possible with a minimum of assets tied up in inventories. An increase in the rate of inventory turnover between periods indicates reduced costs of financing the investment in inventory. On the other hand, management does not want to have so little inventory on hand that shortages result in lost sales. Increases in the rate of inventory turnover caused by inventory shortages could signal a loss of customers, thereby offsetting any advantage gained by decreased investment in inventory. Firms must balance these opposing considerations in setting the optimum level of inventory and, thus, the rate of inventory turnover.

Some analysts calculate the inventory turnover ratio by dividing sales, rather than cost of goods sold, by the average inventory. As long as the ratio of selling price to cost of goods sold remains relatively constant, either measure will identify changes in the trend of the inventory turnover ratio. Using sales in the numerator, however, will lead to incorrect measures of the inventory turnover ratio for calculating the average number of days that inventory is on hand until sale.

Fixed Asset Turnover The **fixed asset turnover ratio** measures the relation between sales and the investment in fixed assets—property, plant, and equipment. You will likely have more difficulty understanding the notion that fixed assets "turn over" than you do in understanding turnover for inventory. A more appropriate title for the fixed asset turnover ratio might be the *fixed asset productivity ratio*, because it measures the amount of sales generated from a particular level of investments in fixed assets.

The fixed asset turnover ratio for Wal-Mart for 2008 is as follows:

$$\frac{\text{Sales}}{\text{Average Fixed Asssets}} = \frac{\$374,526}{(0.5)(\$94,512 + \$105,903)} = 3.7 \text{ times per year}$$

Thus, $1.00 invested in fixed assets during 2008 generated $3.70 in sales. The fixed asset turnover for Wal-Mart was 3.9 for 2006 and 3.8 for 2007. Thus, the fixed asset turnover declined during the three years. The decline in the fixed asset turnover between 2006 and 2007 likely relates to increased expenditures on property, plant, and equipment as Wal-Mart increased the number of its superstores and expanded internationally. Firms invest in fixed assets prior to experiencing increased sales from those investments. The decreased fixed asset turnover between 2007 and 2008 likely relates to the decrease in the growth rate in sales experienced during 2008. In particular, Wal-Mart may have grown its property, plant, and equipment expecting sales growth rates of the 10% to 11% levels experienced in previous years. The sales growth rate of only 8.6% during 2008 led to a decline in the fixed asset turnover.

Some analysts find the reciprocal of the fixed asset turnover ratio helpful in comparing the operating characteristics of different firms. The reciprocal ratio measures dollars of fixed assets required to generate one dollar of sales. For Wal-Mart, this reciprocal for 2008 is $0.27 (= $1.0/3.7 times). Wal-Mart required $0.27 of fixed assets to generate $1.00 of sales. Compare fixed assets per dollar of sales of AT&T, a telecommunications company, with that of Kroger Stores, a grocery store chain, in a recent year. AT&T has $1.30 of fixed assets per dollar of sales whereas Kroger Stores, with relatively modest fixed assets, requires only $0.17 of fixed assets per dollar of sales. AT&T has large fixed asset requirements to generate sales; Kroger does not.

EXHIBIT 6.7   **Wal-Mart Stores**
Asset Turnover Ratios

	2008	2007	2006
Total Assets Turnover.	2.3	2.3	2.3
Accounts Receivable Turnover.	115.3	125.4	141.2
Inventory Turnover	8.3	8.0	7.7
Fixed Asset Turnover	3.7	3.8	3.9

The analyst should interpret changes in the fixed asset turnover ratio cautiously. Firms often invest in fixed assets (for example, new production facilities) several periods before these assets generate sales from products manufactured in their plants or sold in their stores. Thus, a low or decreasing rate of fixed asset turnover may indicate an expanding firm preparing for future growth. On the other hand, a firm anticipating a decline in product sales could cut back its expenditures on fixed assets. Such an action could increase the fixed asset turnover ratio.

Summary of Asset Turnovers We noted earlier that the total assets turnover ratio for Wal-Mart remained steady between 2006 and 2008. **Exhibit 6.7** presents the four turnover ratios discussed for Wal-Mart over this three-year period. The accounts receivable turnover ratio decreased steadily over the three years, indicating either more sales for credit or slower collection from third-party credit cards. The decreasing accounts receivable turnover ratio will likely not significantly impact the total assets turnover because accounts receivable comprise 2% of total assets. Inventory and fixed assets, on the other hand, together comprise approximately 80% of total assets. The inventory turnover steadily increased, and the fixed asset turnover steadily decreased. The offsetting effects of these two asset turnover ratios led to the constant total assets turnover ratio.

ANALYSIS OF SEGMENT DATA

The analysis of Wal-Mart's operating profitability in the preceding sections used information from its firm-wide income statement and balance sheet. Both U.S. GAAP and IFRS require firms to report certain information about each of their operating segments.[8] These disclosures permit analysis of profitability at an additional level of depth. We consider first the required disclosures and then illustrate their use in the analysis of Wal-Mart's profitability.

Required Segment Information Authoritative guidance requires firms to disclose information on their **operating segments**. The definition of segments takes a management approach. Specifically, U.S. GAAP and IFRS define an operating segment as a unit within a firm for which management prepares separate financial information and which management regularly evaluates in allocating resources and assessing performance. By defining segments in the same way that management operates a business, accounting guidance aims to provide users of the financial reports with the same sort of information that management uses to evaluate business components. Although firms have flexibility in defining their operating segments, this flexibility results from choices management makes to organize and manage the entity. For example, a firm that chooses to organize, manage, and evaluate its business along geographic lines would define its operating segments along geographic lines. As a practical matter, most firms report segment information by products and services, indicating that most firms appear to be organized on these same lines. Firms might also report information by geographical markets (if information is available without undue cost) and by customers who represent more than 10% of revenues (called major customers).

Both U.S. GAAP and IFRS provide quantitative criteria for determining how many segments a firm should report. Firms must report segment information for any operating segments

---

[8]Financial Accounting Standards Board, *Statement of Financial Accounting Standards, No. 131,* "Disclosures About Segments of an Enterprise and Related Information," 1997 (**Codification Topic 280**); International Accounting Standards Board, *International Financial Reporting Standard 8,* "Operating Segments." *IFRS 8* is effective for financial statements prepared for periods beginning on or after January 1, 2009.

EXHIBIT 6.8	Wal-Mart Stores Segment Information (amounts in millions)		

| | For the Year Ended January 31 | | |
	2008	2007	2006
Revenues			
Wal-Mart	$239,529	$226,294	$209,910
Sam's Club	44,357	41,582	39,798
International	90,640	77,116	59,237
Segment and Consolidated Total	$374,526	$344,992	$308,945
Operating Income			
Wal-Mart	$ 17,516	$ 16,620	$ 15,267
Sam's Club	1,618	1,480	1,407
International	4,769	4,265	3,438
Other	(1,907)	(1,868)	(1,399)
Segment and Consolidated Total	$ 21,996	$ 20,497	$ 18,713
Assets			
Wal-Mart	$ 84,286	$ 79,040	$ 72,368
Sam's Club	11,722	11,448	10,588
International	62,961	55,903	48,752
Other	4,545	5,196	4,522
Segment and Consolidated Total	$163,514	$151,587	$136,230
Depreciation			
Wal-Mart	$ 3,813	$ 3,323	$ 2,947
Sam's Club	507	475	436
International	1,684	1,409	1,011
Other	313	252	251
Segment and Consolidated Total	$ 6,317	$ 5,459	$ 4,645

that constitute 10% or more of revenues, assets, or profit and loss; and they must report enough segment information to account for at least 75% of the entity's total revenues.

For each operating segment, firms must report information about revenues, assets, and measures of the segment's operating results,[9] as well as components of operating profit or loss, including depreciation, interest revenue, and interest expense. Firms also generally report information about long-lived assets and capital expenditures. IFRS, but not U.S. GAAP, also requires disclosure of segment liabilities, if management uses this information as part of the normal reporting structure to manage and evaluate the business.

Firms must reconcile data for their operating segments with total revenues, operating income, and assets at a firm-wide level. Segment revenues usually sum to firm-wide revenues. Segment operating income will not equal firm-wide operating income because firms do not allocate all corporate-level expenses (for example, compensation of top management and interest expense) to operating segments. Segment assets will not equal firm-wide assets because firms do not allocate corporate-level assets (for example, corporate headquarters) to operating segments.

Segment Profitability Analysis for Wal-Mart

Exhibit 6.8 presents segment information for Wal-Mart for its 2006, 2007, and 2008 fiscal years. Wal-Mart reports its domestic operations by principal store concepts and groups its international operations into a single geographical segment. Wal-Mart presents revenues, operating income, assets, and depreciation for each segment.

We can compute ROA, profit margin for ROA, and total assets turnover for each segment using the segment disclosures. The amounts for these ratios computed at a segment level differ from those at a corporate level for at least two reasons:

[9]U.S. GAAP and IFRS do not precisely define operating results at either a firm-wide level or segment level. Most firms measure operating income before interest revenue, interest expense, and income tax expense.

1. The numerator of ROA at a firm-wide level includes all revenues and expenses except interest expense net of taxes, whereas the numerator of ROA using the segment data includes operating revenues and expenses only. Segment operating income excludes interest revenue and income taxes, which the firm-wide ROA includes.

2. The denominator of ROA at a firm-wide level is the average of assets at the beginning and end of the year, whereas we use total assets at the end of the year in computing segment ROAs. Although we could use average assets to compute segment ROAs, doing so would require four years of segment asset data. Firms often change the definition of their segments, making it difficult to obtain four years of comparable data for segment assets.

Exhibit 6.9 presents ROA, profit margin for ROA, and total assets turnover ratios for Wal-Mart's segments for fiscal 2006, 2007, and 2008.

We observed at the beginning of the chapter that the sales mix of Wal-Mart shifted from its Wal-Mart and Sam's Club segments to its International segment during the three-year period. A similar mix shift occurred in total assets. The ROA of the Wal-Mart segment decreased slightly during the three years, while the ROA of Sam's Club and the International segment increased. Thus, the declining ROA for Wal-Mart as a whole does not result from declining profitability of its operating segments. Instead, the shift in sales and assets mix toward the International segment, which has the lowest ROA of the three operating segments, explains the declining overall ROA. Because Wal-Mart's strategy includes growing operations internationally, the increasing ROA of the International segment sends an encouraging signal. Wal-Mart can expect downward pressure on its overall ROA as the mix shifts even more to the International segment until the ROA of this segment approaches those of the other two segments.

The declining profit margin for ROA for Wal-Mart as a whole appears due to a decline in the profit margin of the International segment and a shift in the sales mix toward this segment. Firms do not provide information on cost of goods sold or selling and administrative expenses at a segment level. Given the steady profit margins for the Wal-Mart and Sam's Club segments during the three-year period, it appears that the increasing selling and administrative expense to sales percentage for Wal-Mart as a whole occurred in its International segment. Perhaps the expenses incurred in incorporating domestic operating systems into its international operations caused selling and administrative expenses to increase faster than sales abroad.

The steady total assets turnover for Wal-Mart as a whole is the net result of a slightly decreased total assets turnover ratio for the Wal-Mart segment and an increased total assets turnover ratio for the International segment, coupled with a shift in asset mix to the International segment, which has a slower assets turnover.

EXHIBIT 6.9	Wal-Mart Stores Segment ROA and Its Components		
	For the Year Ended January 31		
	2008	**2007**	**2006**
Rate of Return on Assets			
Wal-Mart	20.8%	21.0%	21.1%
Sam's Club	13.8	12.9	13.3
International	7.6	7.6	7.1
Profit Margin for ROA			
Wal-Mart	7.3%	7.3%	7.3%
Sam's Club	3.6	3.6	3.5
International	5.3	5.5	5.8
Total Assets Turnover			
Wal-Mart	2.84	2.86	2.90
Sam's Club	3.78	3.63	3.76
International	1.44	1.38	1.22

SUMMARY OF THE ANALYSIS OF THE RATE OF RETURN ON ASSETS

ROA helps one assess a firm's performance in using assets to generate earnings, independent of the financing of those assets. ROA results from the interaction of its separate components: profit margin for ROA and total assets turnover.

- The profit margin for ROA results from the relation of the various expenses to sales.
- Total assets turnover reflects the effects of turnover ratios for accounts receivable, inventory, and fixed assets.

Thus,

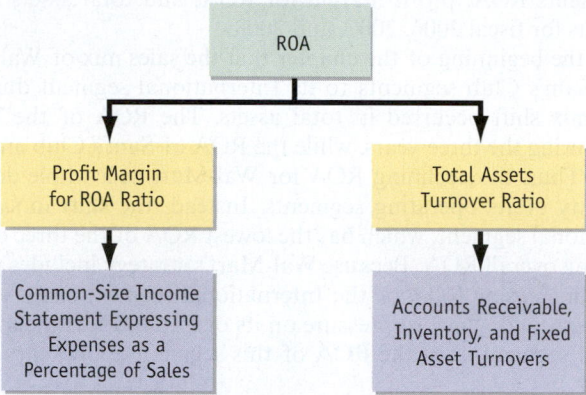

The analysis for Wal-Mart revealed the following:

1. ROA decreased between 2006 and 2008.

2. A decreased profit margin for ROA explains the decreased ROA. The total assets turnover remained steady.

3. Increases in the selling and administrative expense to sales percentage more than offset decreases in the cost of goods sold to sales percentage, thus explaining the decreased profit margin for ROA. Possible explanations for the decreased cost of goods sold to sales percentage include (1) lower purchase, storage, and obsolescence expenses related to Wal-Mart's size or improved inventory control systems, and (2) sales mix changes to higher margin products. Possible explanations for the increased selling and administrative expense to sales percentage include (1) increased marketing expenses due to more intense competition or weak economic conditions, (2) shift in sales mix toward the International segment with its higher levels of marketing and administrative expenses, and (3) the need to spread relatively fixed administrative expenses over a smaller than anticipated level of sales in 2008.

4. The steady total assets turnover primarily reflects the offsetting effects of an increasing inventory turnover and a decreasing fixed asset turnover. Possible reasons for the increasing inventory turnover include

   - improved inventory control systems, and
   - a sales mix shift toward grocery products with faster turnovers.

   Possible reasons for the decreasing fixed asset turnover include

   - increased expenditures on fixed assets to construct superstores and expand abroad, and
   - slower growth in sales during 2008 than that experienced in previous years.

PROBLEM 6.1 for Self-Study

Analyzing the rate of return on assets. Exhibit 6.10 presents profitability ratios for Nordstrom Corporation for its 2004, 2005, and 2006 fiscal years. The rates of return on assets do not precisely equal profit margin for ROA times total assets turnover due to rounding to one decimal place. You may wish to refer to the balance sheet (**Exhibit 1.1**),

(continued)

EXHIBIT 6.10

Nordstrom Corporation
Profitability Ratios
(Problem 6.1 for Self-Study)

		ROA		
	2004	2005	2006	
	9.8%	12.4%	14.7%	

	Profit Margin for ROA				×		Assets Turnover		
	2004	2005	2006				2004	2005	2006
	6.3%	7.6%	8.4%				1.6	1.6	1.8
Sales..................	100.0%	100.0%	100.0%		Accounts Receivable				
Other Revenues	2.5	2.7	3.0		Turnover..........		7.1	6.8	7.4
Cost of Goods Sold	(63.9)	(63.3)	(62.5)		Inventory Turnover		5.0	5.2	5.5
Selling and Administrative ...	(28.3)	(27.2)	(26.8)		Fixed Asset Turnover ...		4.0	4.3	4.8
Income Taxes.............	(4.0)	(4.6)	(5.2)						
Profit Margin for ROA	6.3%	7.6%	8.4%						

the income statement (**Exhibit 1.2**) and the statement of cash flows (**Exhibit 1.3**) of Nordstrom in responding to these questions. Nordstrom includes occupancy cost (that is, rent, depreciation, property taxes, and insurance) in cost of goods sold. Nordstrom offers a credit card in partnership with VISA.

a. Identify the likely reason for the increasing rate of return on assets. Use common-size income statement percentages and individual asset turnover ratios in your interpretations.

b. What is the likely explanation for the decreasing cost of goods sold to sales percentage coupled with the increasing inventory turnover ratio?

RATE OF RETURN ON COMMON SHAREHOLDERS' EQUITY

The **rate of return on common shareholders' equity (ROCE)** measures a firm's performance in using and financing assets to generate earnings. Unlike ROA, the rate of return on shareholders' equity considers financing costs. Thus, this measure of profitability incorporates the results of operating, investing, and financing decisions. The calculation of ROCE is as follows:

$$\text{Rate of Return on Common Shareholders' Equity} = \frac{\text{Net Income} - \text{Dividends on Preferred Stock}}{\text{Average Common Shareholders' Equity}}$$

The Numerator To calculate the amount of net income assignable to common shareholders' equity, the analyst subtracts all amounts required to compensate other providers of financing for the use of their funds. Expenses subtracted in computing net income already include amounts for interest expense, so the calculation of the numerator requires no further adjustment for interest. Because expenses exclude all dividends, the analyst must subtract from net income any earnings allocable to preferred stock equity, usually the dividends on preferred stock declared during the period, to measure the returns solely to the common shareholders. The analyst should not subtract dividends on common stock, because such dividends represent distributions to common shareholders of a portion of the returns generated for them during the period.

The Denominator The capital provided by common shareholders during the period equals the average par value of common stock, capital contributed in excess of par value on common stock, retained earnings, and any other common shareholders' equity accounts for the period. (Alternatively, subtract average preferred shareholders' equity from average total shareholders' equity.)

The ROCE of Wal-Mart for 2008 is as follows:

$$\frac{\text{Net Income} - \text{Dividends on Preferred Stock}}{\text{Average Common Shareholders' Equity}} = \frac{\$12,884 - 0}{(0.5)(\$61,573 + \$64,608)} = 20.4\%$$

ROCE was 22.2% in 2006 and 21.2% in 2007. Thus, the rate of return on common shareholders' equity decreased during the three years.

RELATION BETWEEN RETURN ON ASSETS AND RETURN ON COMMON SHAREHOLDERS' EQUITY

Figure 6.3 graphs the two measures of rate of return discussed thus far for Wal-Mart for 2006, 2007, and 2008. **Figure 6.3** also shows after-tax interest expense as a percentage of the average amount of liabilities each year. In each case, ROCE exceeds ROA. What accounts for this relation, a common one for profitable firms?

ROA measures the profitability of a firm before any payments to the suppliers of financing. Each of the various providers of financing has a claim on some portion of the income in the numerator of ROA. Creditors receive the contractual interest to which they have a claim; the tax savings the firm realizes from deducting interest for tax purposes reduces the interest cost to the firm. Preferred shareholders, if any, receive the stated dividend amounts on the preferred stock. Any remaining income belongs to the common shareholders; that is, common shareholders have a residual claim on all income after creditors and preferred shareholders receive amounts contractually owed them. Thus,

Rate of Return on Asssets	$\rightarrow$	After-Tax Cost of Borrowing (interest)	$\rightarrow$	Return to Preferred Shareholders (dividends)	$\rightarrow$	Rate of Return on Common Shareholders' Equity (residual)

The arrows above indicate that the pool of operating income in the numerator of ROA goes first to lenders in the form of after-tax interest expense, then any remaining amount to preferred shareholders in the form of preferred dividends, and then the residual to the common shareholders.

We can now see that ROCE will exceed ROA whenever ROA exceeds the after-tax cost of borrowing plus any dividends required for preferred shareholders. For 2008, the ROA for Wal-Mart was 8.6% and the after-tax cost of liabilities was 1.3% [= (1.00 − 0.35)($2,103)/ [(0.5)($95,692 + $107,792)]; see **Exhibits 6.2** and **6.3**}. The return that Wal-Mart generated on assets financed with creditors funds (8.6%) in excess of the cost of those funds (1.3%) belongs

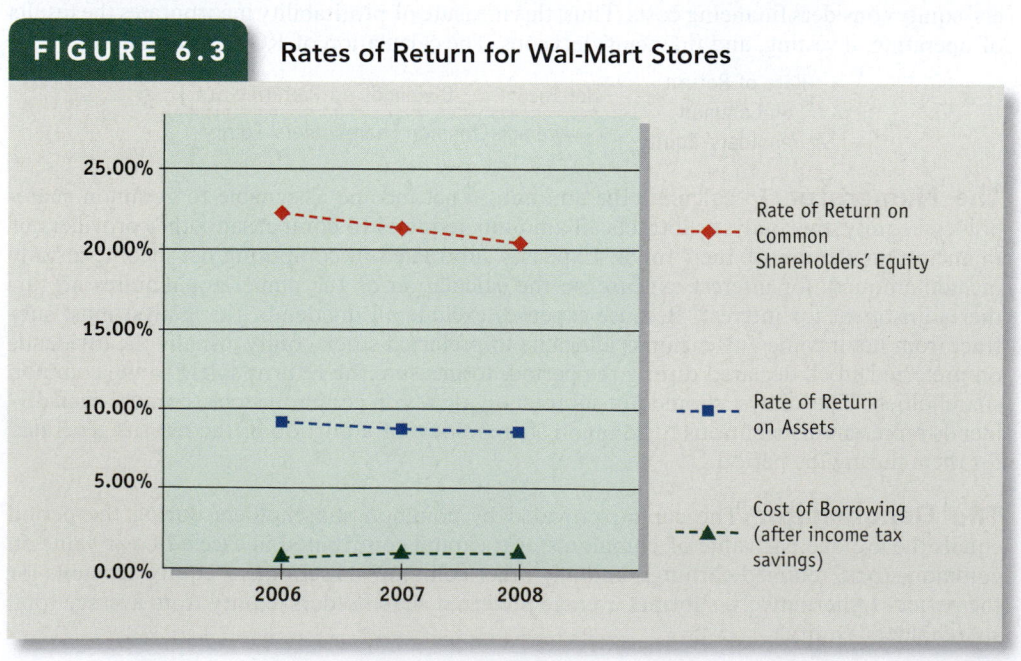

FIGURE 6.3   **Rates of Return for Wal-Mart Stores**

to the common shareholders. This excess return corresponds conceptually to the space in **Figure 6.3** between the line for rate of return on assets and the line for after-tax cost of borrowing. It also corresponds conceptually to the space between the line for the rate of return on assets and the rate of return on common shareholders' equity. Using lower-cost borrowed funds and then earning a rate of return on those funds higher than their cost increases the return to the common shareholders and is a phenomenon called *financial leverage*. The common shareholders earned a higher return, but they undertook more risk in their investment. The risk results from the firm incurring debt obligations with fixed payment amounts and dates. The next section discusses financial leverage.

FINANCIAL LEVERAGE

The term **financial leverage** describes financing with debt and preferred stock to increase the potential return to the residual common shareholders' equity. Financial leverage works as follows:

1. A firm obtains funds from creditors, preferred shareholders, and common shareholders.

2. The firm invests the funds in various assets. Each period the firm generates a return on the assets. ROA measures this return before allocating any amounts to the suppliers of financing.

3. Creditors receive a share of ROA equal to the interest rate on the amount borrowed. The tax deduction for the cost of the interest expense reduces the cost of this debt to the firm.

4. Preferred shareholders receive a share of ROA equal to the preferred dividend rate on the preferred stock outstanding.

5. The common shareholders have a residual claim on all income in excess of the cost of debt and preferred shareholder financing. As long as a firm earns an ROA that exceeds the cost of debt and preferred shareholder financing, the common shareholders benefit. They benefit because the amount earned on assets financed with debt and the preferred shareholders' funds exceeds the amounts the firm must pay for those funds; the excess belongs to the common shareholders. Common shareholders must assess whether the excess return compensates them adequately for the risk they undertake as the residual claimant on the firm's assets.

Illustration of Financial Leverage **Exhibit 6.11** explores this phenomenon. Leveraged Company and No-Debt Company both have $100,000 in assets. Leveraged Company borrows $40,000 at a 10% annual rate. No-Debt Company raises all of its financing from common shareholders. Both companies pay income taxes at the rate of 30%. Consider, first, a good earnings year. Both companies generate an ROA of 10%. The following table summarizes this information. (Note: The arrows indicate an allocation of the net income before financing cost in the numerator of ROA to creditors and to common shareholders. The arrows do not indicate any specific arithmetic relation).

Rate of Return on Assets	→	Return to Creditors	→	Return to Common Shareholders
Leveraged Company				
$ 10,000	→	$ 2,800	→	$ 7,200
$100,000		$40,000		$ 60,000
10%		7%		12%
No-Debt Company				
$ 10,000	→	—	→	$ 10,000
$100,000		—		$100,000
10%		—		10%

Both companies earn $10,000 before interest expense (but after taxes, except for tax effects of interest expense).[10] This represents an ROA for both companies of 10%. The creditors of

---

[10]Income before taxes and before interest expense is $14,286; $10,000 = $(1.0 - 0.3) \times \$14,286$.

EXHIBIT 6.11

Effects of Financial Leverage on Rate of Return on Common Shareholders' Equity (income tax rate of 30% of pretax income)

	Long-Term Financing Equals $100,000		Income after Taxes but Before Interest Expense[a]	After-tax Interest Expense[b]	Net Income	Rate of Return on Assets[c]	Rate of Return on Common Shareholders' Equity
	Borrowing at 10% Per Year	Shareholders' Equity					
Good Earnings Year							
Leveraged Company	$40,000	$ 60,000	$10,000	$2,800	$ 7,200	10.0%	12.0%
No-Debt Company	—	$100,000	$10,000	—	$10,000	10.0%	10.0%
Neutral Earnings Year							
Leveraged Company	$40,000	$ 60,000	$ 7,000	$2,800	$ 4,200	7.0%	7.0%
No-Debt Company	—	$100,000	$ 7,000	—	$ 7,000	7.0%	7.0%
Bad Earnings Year							
Leverage Company	$40,000	$ 60,000	$ 4,000	$2,800	$ 1,200	4.0%	2.0%
No Debt Company	—	$100,000	$ 4,000	—	$ 4,000	4.0%	4.0%

[a]Not including any income tax savings caused by interest expense. Income before taxes and interest for *good year* is $14,286, for *neutral year* is $10,000, and for *bad year* is $5,714.

[b]$40,000 (borrowed) × 0.10 (interest rate) × [1 − 0.30 (income tax rate)]. The numbers shown in the preceding column for after-tax income do not include the effects of interest expense on taxes.

[c]In each year, the rate of return on assets is the same, for both companies, as the rate of return on common shareholders' equity for No-Debt Company: 10%, 7%, and 4%, respectively.

Leveraged Company have a claim on this $10,000 pool of earnings from operations before financing costs of $4,000 (= 0.10 × $40,000) for interest expense. After a tax savings at 30%, the creditors funds cost Leveraged Company $2,800 [= (1 − 0.30)($4,000)]. The remaining income from the pool, $7,200 (= $10,000 − $2,800), belongs to the common shareholders. Thus, the common shareholders provided $60,000 of funds and obtained an ROCE of 12% (= $7,200/$60,000). The common shareholders of No-Debt Company have a claim on the full $10,000 of income from operations because there is no debt in the financing structure. Thus, the common shareholders provided $100,000 of funds and obtained a ROCE of 10%. Leverage increased the ROCE of Leveraged Company because the funds contributed by the long-term lenders earned 10% but required an after-tax interest payment of only 7%. This additional 3% return on each dollar of assets financed by creditors increased ROCE, as the following analysis shows.

RATE OF RETURN TO COMMON SHAREHOLDERS: GOOD EARNINGS YEAR WITH 40% DEBT

Excess Return on Assets Financed with Debt:
    (0.10 − 0.07) × $40,000 .... $ 1,200

Return on Assets Financed by Common Shareholders:
    (0.10) × $60,000.   6,000

    Total Return to Common Shareholders .... $ 7,200

Common Shareholders' Equity. $60,000

Rate of Return on Common Shareholders' Equity:
    $7,200/$60,000. ....   12%

Leverage increased ROCE during the good earnings year, and a larger increase would occur if the firm financed a greater proportion of its assets with long-term borrowing, simultaneously increasing the firm's risk. For example, assume that Leveraged Company financed its assets of $100,000 with $50,000 of long-term borrowing and $50,000 of shareholders' equity. The following summarizes this example.

Rate of Return on Assets	→	Return to Creditors	→	Return to Common Shareholders
Leveraged Company				
$ 10,000	→	$ 3,500	→	$ 6,500
$100,000		$50,000		$ 50,000
10%		7%		13%

Leveraged Company again generates $10,000 of income from operations before financing costs. The cost of the creditors' funds is $3,500 [= (1 − 0.30)(0.10 × $50,000)]. Net income of Leveraged Company in this case would be $6,500 (= $10,000 − $3,500). ROCE would be 13% (= $6,500/$50,000). This compares with a ROCE of 12% when long-term debt was only 40% of the total financing provided. Increasing leverage from 40% to 50%, assuming the interest rate on the borrowings stayed constant, increased the rate of return from 12% to 13%.

This 13% ROCE has the following components:

RATE OF RETURN TO COMMON SHAREHOLDERS: GOOD EARNINGS YEAR WITH 50% DEBT

Excess Return on Assets Financed with Debt:
    (0.10 − 0.07) × $50,000 .... $ 1,500

Return on Assets Financed by Common Shareholders:
    (0.10) × $50,000.   5,000

    Total Return to Common Shareholders .... $ 6,500

Common Shareholders' Equity. $50,000

Rate of Return on Common Shareholders' Equity:
    $6,500/$50,000. ....   13%

Financial leverage increases ROCE when ROA exceeds the after-tax cost of debt. The greater the proportion of debt in the financing structure, however, the greater is the risk the common shareholders bear. As a firm adds more debt to the financing structure, the risk of insolvency or bankruptcy becomes greater. *Insolvency* refers to a condition in which the firm has insufficient cash to pay its current debts, whereas *bankruptcy* refers to a legal condition in which liabilities usually exceed assets. Lenders, including investors in a firm's bonds, require a higher and higher return (interest rate) to compensate for this additional risk. At some point, the after-tax cost of debt will exceed the rate of return earned on assets. At this point, leverage no longer increases the potential rate of return to the common shareholders. For most large manufacturing firms, liabilities represent between 40% and 70% of total financing.

Exhibit 6.11 also demonstrates the effect of financial leverage in a neutral earnings year and in a bad earnings year. In the neutral earnings year, financial leverage neither increases nor decreases ROCE because the ROA is 7% and the after-tax cost of long-term debt is also 7%. In the bad earnings year, ROA falls to 4%, below the 7% after-tax cost of debt. The difference between the cost of debt and the return generated on assets financed with that debt reduces the return to the common shareholders. ROCE then drops below ROA to only 2%. The 2% ROCE has the following components:

RATE OF RETURN TO COMMON SHAREHOLDERS: BAD EARNINGS YEAR WITH 40% DEBT

Deficient Return on Assets Financed with Debt:	
$(0.04 - 0.07) \times \$40,000$	$ (1,200)
Return on Assets Financed by Common Shareholders:	
$(0.04) \times \$60,000$	2,400
Total Return to Common Shareholders	$ 1,200
Common Shareholders' Equity	$ 60,000
Rate of Return on Common Shareholders' Equity:	
$\$1,200/\$60,000$	2%

Clearly, financial leverage—borrowing—can work in two ways. It can enhance the owners' rate of return in good earnings years, but owners run the risk that bad earnings years will be even worse than these years would have been without the borrowing.

DISAGGREGATING THE RATE OF RETURN ON COMMON SHAREHOLDERS' EQUITY

ROCE disaggregates into several components (in a manner similar to the disaggregation of ROA):

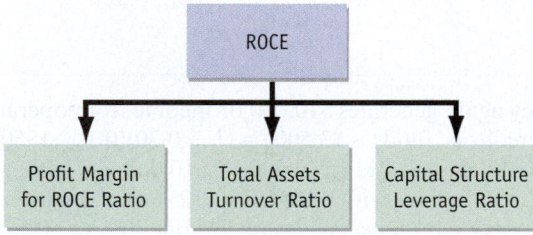

Thus,

Rate of Return on Common Shareholders' Equity	=	Profit Margin for ROCE Ratio	×	Total Assets Turnover Ratio	×	Capital Structure Leverage Ratio
$\dfrac{\text{Net Income} - \text{Dividends on Preferred Stock}}{\text{Average Common Shareholders' Equity}}$	=	$\dfrac{\text{Net Income} - \text{Dividends on Preferred Stock}}{\text{Sales}}$	×	$\dfrac{\text{Sales}}{\text{Average Total Assets}}$	×	$\dfrac{\text{Average Total Assets}}{\text{Average Common Shareholders' Equity}}$

The **profit margin ratio for ROCE ratio** indicates the portion of the sales dollar left over for the common shareholders after covering all operating costs and subtracting claims of creditors and preferred shareholders. It differs from the profit margin for ROA because of the subtraction for the cost of funds provided by creditors and preferred shareholders (see the

EXHIBIT 6.12	Wal-Mart Stores Disaggregated Components of the Rate of Return on Common Shareholders' Equity

	ROCE	=	Profit Margin for ROCE Ratio	×	Total Assets Turnover Ratio	×	Capital Structure Leverage Ratio
2006..................	22.2%	=	3.7%	×	2.3	×	2.6
2007..................	21.2	=	3.5	×	2.3	×	2.6
2008..................	20.4	=	3.4	×	2.3	×	2.6

last line in the profit margin panel in **Exhibit 6.6**). The total assets turnover ratio indicates the sales generated from each dollar of assets and equals the total assets turnover in the disaggregation of ROA. The **capital structure leverage ratio** indicates the proportion of total assets, or total financing, provided by common shareholders contrasted with the financing provided by creditors and preferred shareholders. The higher the capital structure leverage ratio, the lower is the proportion of financing that common shareholders provide and the higher is the proportion that creditors and preferred shareholders provide. Thus, the higher the capital structure leverage ratio, the higher is financial leverage.

The disaggregation of the rate of return on common shareholders' equity ratio for Wal-Mart for 2008 is as follows:

$$\frac{\$12,884}{(0.5)(\$61,573 + \$64,608)} = \frac{\$12,884}{\$374,526} \times \frac{\$374,526}{(0.5)(\$157,265 + \$172,400)} \times \frac{(0.5)(\$157,265 + \$172,400)}{(0.5)(\$61,573 + \$64,608)}$$

$$20.4\% = 3.4\% \times 2.3 \times 2.6$$

Exhibit 6.12 shows the disaggregated components of ROCE for Wal-Mart for 2006, 2007, and 2008. The decrease in ROCE results from a decreasing profit margin for ROCE over the three-year period. The decreasing profit margin for ROCE results from both a decreasing profit margin for ROA and an increasing after-tax cost of debt financing (see **Figure 6.3**). The capital structure leverage ratio remained steady during the three-year period.

PROBLEM 6.2 for Self-Study

Analyzing the rate of return on common shareholders' equity. Refer to the profitability analysis for Nordstrom Corporation in **Problem 6.1 for Self-Study**. Consider the following additional data.

Fiscal Year:	2006	2005	2004
Profit Margin for ROCE Ratio	7.9%	7.1%	5.5%
Total Assets Turnover Ratio	1.8	1.6	1.6
Capital Structure Leverage Ratio...................	2.3	2.5	2.7
ROCE[a]...	31.8%	24.4%	23.0%

[a]Amounts do not exactly equal the product of the three preceding ratios due to rounding.

a. What is the likely explanation for the increasing rate of return on common shareholders' equity?

b. Is financial leverage working to the advantage of the common shareholders in each year?

EARNINGS PER SHARE OF COMMON STOCK

Earnings per share of common stock provides a third measure of profitability. Earnings per share equals net income attributable to common stock divided by the average number of common shares outstanding during the period. The numerator of ROCE and earnings per share

are the same. Earnings per share for Wal-Mart for 2008, based on 4,066 million weighted-average shares outstanding, is \$3.17 (= \$12,884/4,066).

A firm with securities outstanding that holders can convert into, or exchange for, shares of common stock may report two earnings-per-share amounts: **basic earnings per share** (the amount that results from the calculations above) and **diluted earnings per share**. Convertible bonds and convertible preferred stock permit their holders to exchange these securities directly for shares of common stock. Many firms have employee stock-option plans, which allow employees to acquire shares of the company's common stock. When holders convert their securities or when employees exercise their options, the firm will issue additional shares of common stock. Then the amount shown as basic earnings per share will probably decrease, a phenomenon called *dilution*. When a firm has securities outstanding that, if exchanged for shares of common stock, would decrease basic earnings per share by 3% or more, generally accepted accounting principles require a dual presentation: basic earnings per share and diluted earnings per share.[11]

Firms that do not have convertible or other potentially dilutive securities outstanding compute earnings per share in the conventional manner. Firms with outstanding securities that have the potential for materially diluting earnings per share as conventionally computed must present dual earnings-per-share amounts.

Interpreting Earnings per Share Accountants and financial analysts criticize earnings per share as a measure of profitability because it does not consider the amount of assets required to generate that level of earnings. Two firms with the same earnings and earnings per share will differ in profitability if one of the firms requires more assets to generate those earnings than does the other firm.

In comparing firms, earnings-per-share amounts have limited use. For example, assume that two firms have identical earnings, common shareholders' equity, and ROCEs. One firm may have a lower earnings per share simply because it has a larger number of shares outstanding (perhaps due to different earnings retention policies; see **Exercise 20** at the end of this chapter).

Price-Earnings Ratio Financial analysts often compare earnings-per-share amounts with the market price of the stock. They usually express this comparison as a price-earnings ratio (= market price per share/earnings per share). For example, the common stock of Wal-Mart sold for \$48.00 per share on January 31, 2008, Wal-Mart's 2008 fiscal year end. The price-earnings ratio, often called the P/E ratio, is 15.1 (= \$48.00/\$3.17) to 1. The analyst often expresses the relation by saying, "The stock sells at 15.1 times earnings."

Tables of stock prices and financial periodicals often present price-earnings ratios. The analyst must interpret these published P/E ratios cautiously, however. In cases in which a firm's net income includes unusual, nonrecurring gains and losses, the reader must ascertain whether the published ratio uses income only from recurring operations or final net income that includes the unusual items in the denominator. To serve their intended purpose, P/E ratios should use normal, ongoing earnings data in the denominator. The appendix to this chapter discusses the use of earnings per share in the valuation of firms.

SUMMARY OF PROFITABILITY ANALYSIS

This chapter introduces three broad measures for assessing a firm's profitability. Because ROA and ROCE relate income to either the assets or the assets net of liabilities required to generate those earnings, we focus most of our attention on these two profitability measures.

Figure 6.4 summarizes the analysis discussed. At **Level 1**, ROA and ROCE measure overall profitability and the effectiveness of financial leverage. At **Level 2**, we disaggregate the overall measures of profitability into profit margin, asset turnover, and leverage components. At **Level 3**, we further disaggregate the profit margin and asset turnover ratios to gain additional insights into reasons for changes in profitability. We used segment data to analyze profitability at an additional level of depth. The depth of analysis required for an analyst to understand a particular case depends on the relative size of the observed differences or changes in profitability.

[11]Financial Accounting Standards Board, *Statement of Financial Accounting Standards, No. 128*, "Earnings per Share," 1997 (**Codification Topic 260**). International Accounting Standards Board, *International Accounting Standard 33*, "Earnings per Share," revised 2003.

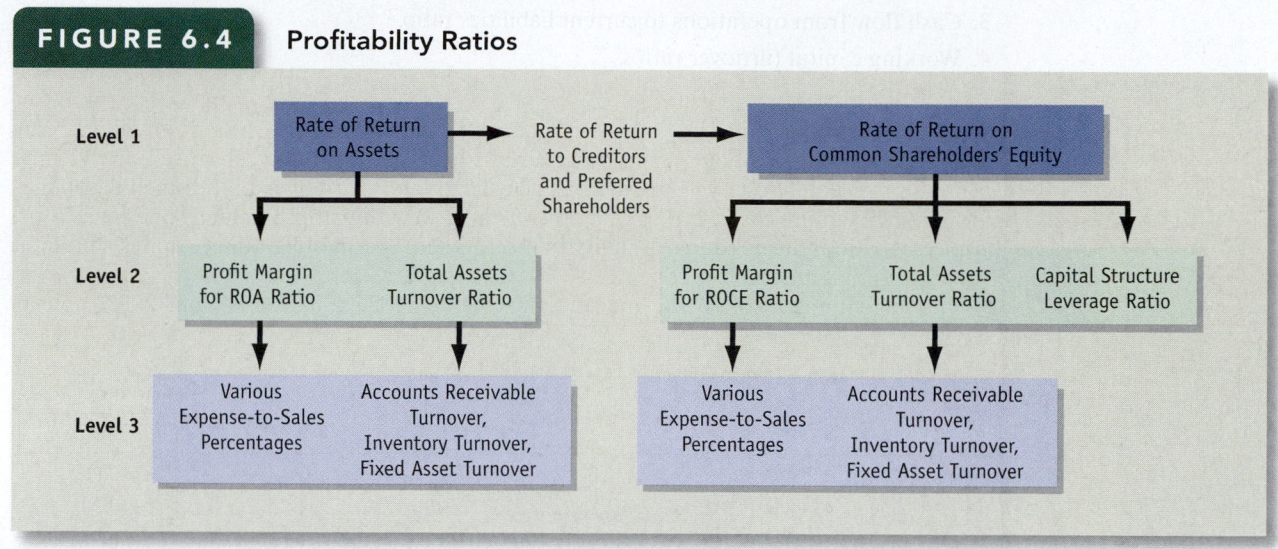

FIGURE 6.4   **Profitability Ratios**

ANALYSIS OF RISK

Analysts deciding between investments must consider the comparative risks. Various factors affect the risk of business firms:

1. Economy-wide factors, such as increased inflation or interest rates, unemployment, and recessions.

2. Industry-wide factors, such as increased competition, lack of availability of raw materials, changes in technology, and increased government regulatory actions, such as antitrust or clean environment policies.

3. Firm-specific factors, such as labor strikes, loss of facilities due to fire or other casualty, and poor health of key managerial personnel.

Analysts assessing risk generally focus on the relative liquidity of a firm. Cash and near-cash assets provide a firm with the resources needed to adapt to the various types of risk; that is, liquid resources provide a firm with financial flexibility. Cash links the operating, investing, and financing activities of a firm, permitting it to run smoothly and effectively.

Assessing liquidity requires a time horizon. Consider the three questions that follow:

1. Does a firm have sufficient cash to repay a loan due tomorrow?

2. Will the firm have sufficient cash to repay the same loan due in six months?

3. Will the firm have sufficient cash to repay the same loan due in five years?

In answering the first question, the analyst probably focuses on the amount of cash on hand and in the bank relative to the obligation coming due tomorrow. In answering the second question, the analyst compares the amount of cash expected from operations during the next six months, as well as from any new borrowings, with the obligations maturing during that period. In answering the third question, the analyst shifts the focus to the longer-run cash-generating ability of a firm relative to the amount of long-term debt that will mature. Ultimately, analysts assess whether a firm will likely become bankrupt; creditors and investors may lose the funds they provided to a bankrupt firm.

MEASURES OF SHORT-TERM LIQUIDITY RISK

This section discusses four measures for assessing **short-term liquidity risk**:

1. Current ratio.
2. Quick ratio.

3. Cash flow from operations to current liabilities ratio.

4. Working capital turnover ratios.

Current Ratio   The **current ratio** equals current assets divided by current liabilities. Current assets comprise cash and assets that a firm expects to turn into cash or sell or consume within approximately one year of the balance sheet date. Current liabilities include obligations that will require cash (or the rendering of services) within approximately one year. Thus, the current ratio indicates a firm's ability to meet its short-term obligations. Analysts prefer a current ratio that at least exceeds 1.0.

The current ratios of Wal-Mart on January 31, 2005, 2006, 2007, and 2008, appear below:

Current Ratio	$=\dfrac{\text{Current Assets}}{\text{Current Liabilities}}$
January 31, 2005: $38,854/$43,182	0.90
January 31, 2006: $43,824/$48,826	0.90
January 31, 2007: $46,588/$51,754	0.90
January 31, 2008: $47,585/$58,454	0.81

Although Wal-Mart's current ratio is less than 1.0, analysts would not likely view Wal-Mart as risky. Wal-Mart sells either for cash or collects sales made on credit within three days. Also, Wal-Mart sells its inventory on average 44 days after purchase. The decrease in the current ratio in 2008 results from increased short-term borrowing (see **Exhibit 6.4**). Thus, Wal-Mart quickly turns its current assets into cash.

Changes in the trend of the current ratio can mislead. For example, when the current ratio exceeds 1.0, an increase of equal amount in both current assets and current liabilities (by acquiring inventory on account) results in a decline in the ratio, whereas equal decreases (by paying an accounts payable) result in an increased current ratio.[12]

In a recessionary period, a business may contract and use cash, a current asset, to pay its current liabilities. When the current ratio exceeds 1, such action will increase it. In a boom period, firms sometimes conserve cash by delaying payment of current liabilities, causing the reverse effect. Thus, a high current ratio may accompany deteriorating business conditions, whereas a falling ratio may accompany profitable operations.

Furthermore, management can take deliberate steps to produce a financial statement that presents a better current ratio at the balance sheet date than the average, or normal, current ratio during the rest of the year. For example, near the end of its accounting period a firm might delay normal purchases on account. Or, it might hasten the collections of a loan receivable, classified as noncurrent assets, and use the proceeds to reduce current liabilities. Such actions will increase the current ratio. Analysts refer to such actions as *window dressing*.

Quick Ratio   A variation of the current ratio is the **quick ratio** (sometimes called the **acid test ratio**). The quick ratio includes in the numerator of the fraction only those current assets that a firm could convert quickly into cash. The numerator customarily includes cash, marketable securities, and accounts receivable. Some businesses can convert their inventory of merchandise into cash more quickly than other businesses can convert their receivables. The facts in each case will indicate whether the analyst should include receivables or exclude inventories. For purposes of this text, assume the numerator includes accounts receivable and excludes inventories. The denominator includes all current liabilities. A quick ratio approximately one-half of the current ratio is typical, although this varies by industry.

Assuming that the quick ratio of Wal-Mart includes accounts receivable but excludes inventory, the quick ratios on January 31 of 2005, 2006, 2007, and 2008, are as follows:

---

[12]The general rule is that adding equal amounts to both the numerator and the denominator of a fraction moves that fraction closer to the number 1, whereas subtracting equal amounts from both the numerator and the denominator of a fraction makes that fraction diverge from the number 1. To be even more general, adding *a* to (subtracting *a* from) the numerator while adding *b* to (subtracting *b* from) the denominator of the fraction makes the fraction converge to (diverge from) the fraction *a/b*.

Quick Ratio	$= \dfrac{\text{Cash, Marketable Securities, Accounts Receivable}}{\text{Current Liabilities}}$
January 31, 2005: ($5,488 + $1,715)/$43,182	0.17
January 31, 2006: ($6,414 + $2,662)/$48,826	0.19
January 31, 2007: ($7,373 + $2,840)/$51,754	0.20
January 31, 2008: ($5,569 + $3,654)/$58,454	0.16

Wal-Mart's quick ratio, like its current ratio, remained relatively steady until January 31, 2008, when it declined because of the increase in short-term borrowing. Its quick ratio appears low, however, relative to its current ratio. Recall though that Wal-Mart, unlike most manufacturing firms, has only small amounts of accounts receivable. Wal-Mart collects cash quickly from sales on account and reinvests the cash in inventory or property, plant, and equipment, pays dividends, or makes other uses of the cash. Thus, the low quick ratios are not a cause for concern.

Cash Flow from Operations to Current Liabilities Ratio

Some analysts criticize the current ratio and the quick ratio to measure short-term liquidity risk because these ratios use balance sheet amounts at a specific time. If financial statement amounts at that time are unusually large or small, the resulting ratios will not reflect normal conditions. If management knows that analysts will evaluate the firm using one of these ratios at a particular time, it can take steps to window dress that ratio by, for example, using cash to pay off a current liability (reducing both numerator and denominator) or acquiring inventory on account (increasing both numerator and denominator).

The **cash flow from operations to current liabilities ratio** overcomes these deficiencies. The numerator of this ratio is cash flow from operations for the year. The denominator is average current liabilities for the year. Healthy mature firms typically have a ratio of 40% or more.

The cash flow from operations to current liabilities ratios for Wal-Mart for 2006, 2007, and 2008 are as follows:

Cash Flow from Operations to Current Liabilities Ratio	$= \dfrac{\text{Cash Flow from Operations}}{\text{Average Current Liabilities}}$
2006: $17,633/[0.5($43,182 + $48,826)]	38.3%
2007: $20,164/[0.5($48,826 + $51,754)]	40.1
2008: $20,354/[0.5($51,754 + $58,454)]	36.9

The cash flow from operations to current liabilities ratio was close to the 40% benchmark. It decreased in 2008 because of the increased short-term borrowing.

Working Capital Turnover Ratios

During the operating cycle, a retailing firm such as Wal-Mart

1. purchases inventory on account from suppliers,
2. sells inventory for cash or on account to customers,
3. collects amounts due from customers, and
4. pays amounts due to suppliers.

This cycle recurs for most businesses. The number of days that a firm holds inventories (that is, 365 days/inventory turnover ratio) indicates the length of the period between the purchase and the sale of inventory during each operating cycle. The number of days that a firm's receivables remain outstanding (that is, 365 days/accounts receivable turnover ratio) indicates the length of the period between the sale of inventory and the collection of cash from customers during each operating cycle.

Firms must finance their investments in inventories and accounts receivable. Suppliers typically provide a portion of the needed financing. The number of days that a firm's accounts payable remain outstanding (that is, 365 days/accounts payable turnover ratio) indicates the length of the period between the purchase of inventory on account and the payment of cash to suppliers during each operating cycle. The **accounts payable turnover ratio** equals purchases on account divided by average accounts payable. Although firms do not disclose their purchases, the analyst can derive the amount as follows:

$$\text{Beginning Inventory} + \text{Purchases} = \text{Cost of Goods Sold} + \text{Ending Inventory}$$

Rearranging terms yields the following:

$$\text{Purchases} = \text{Cost of Goods Sold} + \text{Ending Inventory} - \text{Beginning Inventory}$$

The purchases of Wal-Mart appear below:

	Purchases	=	Cost of Goods Sold	+	Ending Inventory	−	Beginning Inventory
2006	$242,078	=	$237,649	+	$32,191	−	$27,762
2007	$265,646	=	$264,152	+	$33,685	−	$32,191
2008	$288,010	=	$286,515	+	$35,180	−	$33,685

The accounts payable turnover ratios for Wal-Mart for 2006, 2007, and 2008 are as follows:

Accounts Payable Turnover Ratio	$= \dfrac{\text{Purchases}}{\text{Average Accounts Payable}}$
2006: $242,078/[0.5($21,987 + $25,373)].....................................	10.2
2007: $265,646/[0.5($25,373 + $28,090)].....................................	9.9
2008: $288,010/[0.5($28,090 + $30,370)].....................................	9.9

The average number of days that payables were outstanding was 35.8 days (= 365/10.2) for 2006 and 36.9 days (= 365/9.9) for 2007 and for 2008. Thus, the days payable were relatively steady during the three years.

Interpreting the accounts payable turnover ratio involves opposing considerations. An increase in the accounts payable turnover ratio indicates that a firm pays its obligations to suppliers more quickly, requiring cash and even wasting the benefits of cash if the firm makes payments earlier than necessary. On the other hand, a faster accounts payable turnover means a smaller relative amount of accounts payable that the firm must pay in the near future. Most firms want to extend their payables as long as they can, but they also want to maintain their relations with suppliers. Businesses, therefore, negotiate hard for favorable payment terms and then delay paying until just before the last agreed moment.

A comparison of the days outstanding for inventories, accounts receivable, and accounts payable reveals the following:

Year	Days Inventory Held	Days Accounts Receivable Outstanding	Days Accounts Payable Outstanding
2006	47.4	2.6	35.8
2007	45.6	2.9	36.9
2008	44.0	3.2	36.9

Wal-Mart reduced its days inventory but increased it days payable during the three years. Thus, suppliers financed an increasing proportion of Wal-Mart's investment in inventory. Its days receivable increased during the three-year period, decreasing cash flow from operations.

Summary of Short-Term Liquidity Risk Analysis   The current and quick ratios measure liquidity at a particular date. These ratios for Wal-Mart seem low. The cash flow from operations to current liabilities ratio has fluctuated around the 40% benchmark for a mature, financially healthy firm. Wal-Mart sells either for cash or collects its accounts receivable within three days of the sale. It financed an increasing proportion of inventory by delaying payments to suppliers. Thus, Wal-Mart's short-term liquidity risk appears low. Its deterioration in 2008 resulted from increased short-term borrowing.

PROBLEM 6.3 for Self-Study

Analyzing short-term liquidity risk. Refer to the profitability ratios for Nordstrom Corporation in **Problems 6.1** and **6.2 for Self-Study**. Consider the following additional data:

Fiscal Year:	2006	2005	2004
Current Ratio	1.9	1.8	1.9
Quick Ratio	1.1	1.1	1.1
Cash Flow from Operations to Current Liabilities Ratio	74.8%	52.4%	49.2%
Days Accounts Receivable Outstanding	49	54	51
Days Inventories Held	67	70	73
Days Accounts Payable Outstanding	38	38	38

a. What is the likely explanation for the increase in the cash flow from operations to current liabilities ratio?

b. What is your assessment of the short-term liquidity risk of Nordstrom Corporation at the end of fiscal year 2006?

MEASURES OF LONG-TERM LIQUIDITY RISK

Analysts use measures of **long-term liquidity risk** to evaluate a firm's ability to meet interest and principal payments on long-term debt and similar obligations as they come due. If a firm cannot make the payments on time, it becomes insolvent and may have to reorganize or liquidate.

A firm's ability to generate net income over several years provides the best protection against long-term liquidity risk. If a firm is profitable, it will either generate sufficient cash from operations or obtain needed financing from creditors and owners. The measures of profitability discussed previously therefore apply for this purpose as well. Analysts measure long-term liquidity risk with debt ratios, the cash flow from operations to total liabilities ratio, and the interest coverage ratio.

Debt Ratios Several variations in debt ratios commonly appear in financial periodicals and corporate reports. We use three debt ratios in assessing long-term liquidity risk:

1. **Liabilities to Assets Ratio** = Total Liabilities/Total Assets
2. **Long-Term Debt Ratio** = Long-Term Debt/Total Assets
3. **Debt-Equity Ratio** = Long-Term Debt/Shareholders' Equity

The liabilities to assets ratio measures the proportion of assets financed with liabilities. The long-term debt ratio measures the proportion of assets financed with long-term debt. The debt-equity ratio measures the extent of long-term financing obtained from long-term debt relative to shareholders' equity.

Exhibit 6.13 shows these debt ratios for Wal-Mart on January 31, 2005, 2006, 2007, and 2008. The debt ratios for Wal-Mart show similar patterns over time. Because various versions of debt ratios correlate highly, analysts can generally rely on just a couple of these ratios when assessing long-term liquidity risk.

In general, the higher the debt ratios, the higher the likelihood that the firm will be unable to meet fixed interest and principal payments in the future. Most firms must decide how much financial leverage, with its attendant risk, they can afford. Funds obtained from issuing bonds

EXHIBIT 6.13	Wal-Mart Stores Debt Ratios	

Liabilities to Assets Ratio	$\dfrac{\text{Liabilities}}{\text{Assets}}$
January 31, 2005: $76,385/$125,781	60.7%
January 31, 2006: $91,378/$144,549	63.2
January 31, 2007: $95,692/$157,265	60.8
January 31, 2008: $107,792/$172,400	62.5

Long-Term Debt Ratio	$\dfrac{\text{Long-Term Debt}}{\text{Assets}}$
January 31, 2005: $28,885/$125,781	23.0%
January 31, 2006: $36,533/$144,549	25.3
January 31, 2007: $36,807/$157,265	23.4
January 31, 2008: $42,288/$172,400	24.5

Debt-Equity Ratio	$\dfrac{\text{Long-Term Debt}}{\text{Shareholders' Equity}}$
January 31, 2005: $28,885/$49,396	58.5%
January 31, 2006: $36,533/$53,171	68.7
January 31, 2007: $36,807/$61,573	59.8
January 31, 2008: $42,288/$64,608	65.5

or borrowing from a bank have a relatively low interest cost but require fixed, periodic payments that increase the likelihood of insolvency or even bankruptcy.

In assessing the debt ratios, analysts customarily vary the standard in relation to the stability of the firm's earnings and cash flows from operations. The more stable the earnings and cash flows, the higher is the debt ratio they deem acceptable or safe. Public utilities have high liabilities to assets ratios, frequently on the order of 60% to 70%. Banks have even higher liabilities to assets ratios, typically over 90%. The stability of earnings and cash flows of firms in these industries makes these ratios acceptable to many investors. These investors might find such high leverage unacceptable for firms with less stable earnings and cash flows, such as a computer software developer or a biotech firm.

Because several variations of the debt ratio appear in corporate annual reports, the analyst should take care when comparing debt ratios among firms.

Cash Flow from Operations to Total Liabilities Ratio   The debt ratios do not consider the availability of liquid assets to service various levels of debt (that is, to provide for interest and principal payments when due). The **cash flow from operations to total liabilities ratio** overcomes this deficiency. This cash flow ratio resembles the one for assessing short-term liquidity risk, but here the denominator includes all liabilities (both current and noncurrent). A mature, financially healthy company typically has a cash flow from operations to total liabilities ratio of 20% or more.

The cash flow from operations to total liabilities ratios for Wal-Mart are as follows:

Cash Flow from Operations to Total Liabilities Ratio	$=$	$\dfrac{\text{Cash Flow from Operations}}{\text{Average Total Liabilities}}$
2006: $17,633/[0.5($76,385 + $91,378)]		21.0%
2007: $20,164/[0.5($91,378 + $95,692)]		21.6
2008: $20,354/[0.5($95,692 + $107,792)]		20.0

The cash flow from operations to total liabilities ratio was approximately at the 20% benchmark level for the three years, suggesting Wal-Mart has relatively low long-term liquidity risk by this measure.

Interest Coverage Ratio The number of times that income covers interest charges also measures long-term liquidity risk. The **interest coverage ratio** equals income before interest and income tax expenses divided by interest expense. This ratio attempts to indicate the relative protection that operating profitability provides bondholders, permitting them to assess the probability that a firm will fail to meet required interest payments. Analysts typically view an interest coverage ratio below 3.0 as risky, although they prefer a ratio that is stable over time to one that is somewhat higher on average but fluctuates, sometimes being higher and sometimes lower.

Wal-Mart's interest coverage ratios for 2006, 2007, and 2008 are as follows:

Interest Coverage Ratio	$= \dfrac{\text{Net Income Before Interest and Income Taxes}}{\text{Interest Expense}}$
2006: ($11,408 + $5,803 + $1,420)/$1,420	13.1 times
2007: ($12,178 + $6,365 + $1,809)/$1,809	11.3 times
2008: ($12,884 + $6,908 + $2,103)/$2,103	10.4 times

Wal-Mart's decreased profit margins coupled with higher interest expense result in decreasing interest coverage ratios. The ratios easily exceed the 3.0 benchmark, so the decreased interest coverage ratio does not cause concern.

If bond contracts require periodic repayments of principal on long-term liabilities, the denominator of the ratio might include such repayments.

One can criticize the interest or fixed charges coverage ratios as measures for assessing long-term liquidity risk because they use income rather than cash flows in the numerator. Firms pay interest and other fixed payment obligations with cash, not with income. When the amount of the ratio is relatively low (for example, two to three times), the analyst should use some measure of cash flows, such as cash flow from operations, in the numerator.

Summary of Long-Term Liquidity Risk Analysis Long-term liquidity analysis focuses on the amount of debt (particularly long-term debt) in the financing structure of a firm and on the adequacy of net income and cash flows to service this debt. Relatively steady debt ratios coupled with a cash flow from operations to total liabilities ratio at a desired level and a high interest coverage ratio suggest that Wal-Mart's long-term liquidity risk is low.

PROBLEM 6.4 for Self-Study

Analyzing long-term liquidity risk. Refer to the profitability and short-term liquidity risk ratios for Nordstrom Corporation in **Problems 6.1, 6.2,** and **6.3 for Self-Study**. Consider the following additional data:

Fiscal Year:	2006	2005	2004
Liabilities to Assets Ratio	55.0%	57.5%	61.2%
Long-Term Debt Ratio.	12.9%	12.8%	20.2%
Debt-Equity Ratio	28.8%	30.0%	51.9%
Cash Flow from Operations to Total Liabilities Ratio	41.7%	27.5%	21.1%
Interest Coverage Ratio	20.3	16.1	8.6

a. What is the likely explanation for the increase in the cash flow from operations to total liabilities ratio?

b. What is the likely explanation for the increase in the interest coverage ratio?

c. What is your assessment of the long-term liquidity risk of Nordstrom Corporation at the end of fiscal year 2006?

LIMITATIONS OF RATIO ANALYSIS

The analyst should be aware of limitations in the computations discussed in this chapter, such as the following:

1. Because ratios use financial statement data as inputs, the same factors that cause short-comings in financial statements will affect the ratios computed from them. Such short-comings, at least for some purposes, include the use of acquisition cost for assets rather than current replacement cost or net realizable value and the latitude firms have in selecting from among various generally accepted accounting principles.

2. Changes in many ratios correlate with each other. For example, the current ratio and the quick ratio often change proportionally and in the same direction. The analyst need not compute all the ratios to assess a particular dimension of profitability or risk.

3. When comparing the size of a ratio between periods for the same firm, the analyst must recognize conditions that have changed between the periods being compared (for example, different product lines or geographic markets served, changes in economic conditions, changes in prices, changes in accounting principles, and corporate acquisitions).

4. When comparing ratios of a particular firm with those of similar firms, one must recognize differences among the firms (for example, different methods of accounting, different operating methods, and different types of financing).

Financial statement ratios alone do not provide direct indicators of good or poor management. Such ratios indicate areas that the analyst should investigate further. For example, a decrease in the turnover of merchandise inventory, ordinarily considered an undesirable trend, may reflect the accumulation of merchandise to keep retail stores open during anticipated shortages. Such shortages may force competitors to restrict operations or to close down. The analyst must combine ratios derived from financial statements with an investigation of other facts before drawing conclusions.

SUMMARY

For convenient reference, **Exhibit 6.14** summarizes the calculation of the financial statement ratios discussed in this chapter.

This chapter began with the question of whether you should invest your inheritance in a certificate of deposit or in the shares of common stock of Wal-Mart. Analysis of Wal-Mart's financial statements indicates that it has been a growing, profitable company with few indications of either short-term or long-term liquidity problems. You need at least three additional inputs before making the investment decision. First, you should consult sources of information other than the financial statements (for example, articles in the financial press, the firm's statements about its spending plans for long-term assets, analysts' beliefs about spending needs, and new strategies of competitors) to understand a firm's future profitability and risk. Second, you must decide your attitude toward, or willingness to assume, risk. Third, you must decide if you think the stock market price of the shares makes them an attractive current purchase.[13] Before making buy/sell recommendations to investors, analysts compare their assessments of the firm's profitability and risk to the firm's share price. Analysts might recommend the purchase of shares of a poorly run company whose shares they judge underpriced rather than recommend shares of a well-run company whose shares they judge overpriced in the market. At this stage in the investment decision, the analysis requires intuition, judgment, and experience.

---

[13]Finance texts discuss other important factors in the investment decision. Perhaps the most important question is how a particular investment fits in with the investor's entire portfolio. Modern research suggests that the suitability of a potential investment depends more on the attributes of the other components of an investment portfolio and the risk attitude of the investor than it does on the attributes of the potential investment itself.

EXHIBIT 6.14   **Summary of Financial Statement Ratios**

Ratio	Numerator	Denominator
Profitability Ratios		
Rate of Return on Assets (ROA)	Net Income + Interest Expense (net of tax effects)[a]	Average Total Assets during the Period
Profit Margin for ROA Ratio (before interest effects)	Net Income + Interest Expense (net of tax effects)[a]	Sales
Various Expense Ratios	Various Expenses	Sales
Total Assets Ratio Turnover	Sales	Average Total Assets during the Period
Accounts Receivable Turnover Ratio	Sales	Average Accounts Receivable during the Period
Inventory Turnover Ratio	Cost of Goods Sold	Average Inventory during the Period
Fixed Asset Turnover Ratio	Sales	Average Fixed Assets during the Period
Rate of Return on Common Shareholders' Equity (ROCE)	Net Income − Preferred Stock Dividends	Average Common Shareholders' Equity during the Period
Profit Margin for ROCE Ratio (after interest expense and preferred dividends)	Net Income − Preferred Stock Dividends	Sales
Capital Structure Leverage Ratio	Average Total Assets during the Period	Average Common Shareholders' Equity during the Period
Earnings per Share of Common Stock[b]	Net Income − Preferred Stock Dividends	Weighted Average Number of Common Shares Outstanding
Short-Term Liquidity Risk Ratios		
Current Ratio ·	Current Assets	Current Liabilities
Quick or Acid Test Ratio · · · · · · · · · · · · · · · · ·	Highly Liquid Assets (cash, marketable securities, and accounts receivable)[c]	Current Liabilities
Cash Flow from Operations to Current Liabilities Ratio	Cash Flow from Operations	Average Current Liabilities during the Period
Accounts Payable Turnover Ratio	Purchases[d]	Average Accounts Payable during the Period
Days Accounts Receivable Outstanding	365 days	Accounts Receivable Turnover Ratio
Days Inventories Held · · · · · · · · · · · · · · · · · · ·	365 days	Inventory Turnover Ratio
Days Accounts Payable Outstanding · · · · · · · · · ·	365 days	Accounts Payable Turnover Ratio
Long-Term Liquidity Ratios		
Liabilities to Assets Ratio · · · · · · · · · · · · · · · · ·	Liabilities	Assets
Long-Term Debt Ratio · · · · · · · · · · · · · · · · · · ·	Long-Term Debt	Assets
Debt-Equity Ratio ·	Long-Term Debt	Shareholders' Equity
Cash Flow from Operations to Total Liabilities Ratio ·	Cash Flow from Operations	Average Total Liabilities during the Period
Interest Coverage Ratio · · · · · · · · · · · · · · · · · ·	Income before Interest and Income Taxes	Interest Expense

[a]If a parent company does not own all of a consolidated subsidiary, the calculation also adds back to net income the noncontrolling interest share of net income. See **Chapter 13** for discussion of noncontrolling interest.

[b]This calculation is more complicated when there are convertible securities, options, or warrants outstanding.

[c]The calculation could conceivably exclude receivables for some firms and include inventories for others.

[d]Purchases = Cost of Goods Sold + Ending Inventories − Beginning Inventories.

PROBLEM 6.5 for Self-Study

Computing profitability and risk ratios. Exhibit 6.15 presents an income statement for Cox Corporation for 2008, and **Exhibit 6.16** presents comparative balance sheets as of December 31, 2007 and 2008. Using information from these financial statements, compute the following ratios. The income tax rate is 30%. Cash flow from operations totals $3,300.

a. Rate of return on assets (ROA)   c. Cost of goods sold to sales percentage

b. Profit margin ratio for ROA   d. Selling expense to sales percentage   *(continued)*

EXHIBIT 6.15

Cox Corporation
Income and Retained Earnings Statement
For the Year Ended December 31, 2008
(Problem 6.5 for Self-Study)

Sales Revenue		$30,000
Less Expenses:		
Cost of Goods Sold	$18,000	
Selling	4,500	
Administrative	2,500	
Interest	700	
Income Taxes	1,300	
Total Expenses		27,000
Net Income		$ 3,000
Less Dividends:		
Preferred Stock	$ 100	
Common Stock	700	800
Increase in Retained Earnings		$ 2,200
Retained Earnings, December 31, 2007		4,500
Retained Earnings, December 31, 2008		$ 6,700

e. Total assets turnover	**n.** Cash flow from operations to current liabilities ratio
f. Accounts receivable turnover	
g. Inventory turnover	**o.** Accounts payable turnover
h. Fixed asset turnover	**p.** Liabilities to assets ratio (both dates)
i. Rate of return on common share-holders' equity (ROCE)	**q.** Long-term debt ratio (both dates)
j. Profit margin ratio for ROCE	**r.** Debt-equity ratio (both dates)
k. Capital structure leverage ratio	**s.** Cash flow from operations to total liabilities ratio
l. Current ratio (both dates)	**t.** Interest coverage ratio
m. Quick ratio (both dates)	

APPENDIX 6.1: PRO FORMA FINANCIAL STATEMENTS AND VALUATION

Accountants use the term **pro forma financial statements** to refer to financial statements prepared under a particular set of assumptions. One set of assumptions might be that some transactions, actually reported in the firm's income statement for the year under generally accepted accounting principles, had not occurred. Such assumed-away transactions might include unusual or nonrecurring revenues, expenses, gains, and losses. In these cases, firms report pro forma earnings to suggest to financial statement users what the firm views as normal, recurring earnings.

The traditional use of the term *pro forma financial statements* refers to projected financial statements based on some set of assumptions about the future. One set of assumptions might be that historical patterns (for example, growth rates or rates of return) will continue. Alternatively, the pro forma financial statements might reflect new assumptions about growth rates, debt levels, profitability, and so on. For example, a firm might project future sales, net income, assets, and cash flows to ascertain whether operations will generate sufficient cash flows to finance expenditures on long-term assets or whether the firm will need to borrow

EXHIBIT 6.16	Cox Corporation Comparative Balance Sheet December 31, 2007 and 2008 (Problem 6.5 for Self-Study)		

	December 31	
	2008	**2007**
ASSETS		
Current Assets		
Cash	$ 750	$ 600
Accounts Receivable	4,300	3,600
Merchandise Inventories	7,900	5,600
Prepayments	380	300
Total Current Assets	$13,330	$10,100
Property, Plant, and Equipment		
Land	$ 600	$ 500
Buildings and Equipment (net)	10,070	9,400
Total Property, Plant, and Equipment	$10,670	$ 9,900
Total Assets	$24,000	$20,000
LIABILITIES AND SHAREHOLDERS' EQUITY		
Current Liabilities		
Notes Payable.	$ 4,000	$ 2,000
Accounts Payable	3,300	3,500
Other Current Liabilities.	1,900	1,500
Total Current Liabilities	$ 9,200	$ 7,000
Noncurrent Liabilities		
Bonds Payable	2,800	4,000
Total Liabilities.	$12,000	$11,000
Shareholders' Equity		
Preferred Stock.	$ 1,000	$ 1,000
Common Stock	2,500	2,000
Additional Paid-in Capital.	1,800	1,500
Retained Earnings.	6,700	4,500
Total Shareholders' Equity.	$12,000	$ 9,000
Total Liabilities and Shareholders' Equity.	$24,000	$20,000

more. A firm might change its product lines or pricing policies and might want to estimate the impact on rates of return. A firm might project future financial statement amounts for an acquisition target to ascertain the price it should pay. This appendix describes and illustrates procedures for preparing pro forma (projected) financial statements, then shows you how to use them to value firms. In your exposure to managerial and cost accounting concepts, you will encounter the notion of a *budget*. A budget for an entire firm means the same thing as pro forma (projected) financial statements except that the statements projected typically have different uses and formats. Managers and analysts use pro forma financials and budgets for differing reasons, but use similar procedures to prepare them.

PREPARING PRO FORMA FINANCIAL STATEMENTS

The preparation of pro forma financial statements requires the analyst to make assumptions about the future. The usefulness of the pro forma financial statements depends on the reasonableness of those assumptions. Various computer spreadsheet programs ease the calculations required in preparing these statements, but the warning "garbage-in, garbage-out" certainly applies—the results will have quality and validity no better than the input assumptions. Careful analysts bring together, preferably in a single section of their spreadsheet, a list of all assumptions made. Well-prepared pro forma statements allow the analyst to vary critical assumptions to see how the results vary.

The preparation of pro forma financial statements typically begins with the income statement, followed by the balance sheet and then the statement of cash flows. The level of operating activity usually dictates the required amount of assets, which in turn affects the required level of financing. Amounts for the statement of cash flows come directly from the pro forma income statement and comparative balance sheets.

We adhere to the following steps in preparing pro forma financial statements:

1. Project operating revenues.

2. Project operating expenses other than the cost of financing and income taxes.

3. Project the assets required to support the level of projected operating activity.

4. Project the financing (liabilities and contributed capital) required to fund the level of assets in step **3**.

5. Project the cost of financing the debt projected in step **4**, income tax expense, net income, dividends, and the change in retained earnings.

6. Project the statement of cash flows from amounts on the projected balance sheet and income statement.

Exhibit 6.17 summarizes these six steps. To illustrate the preparation of pro forma financial statements, we use the data for Wal-Mart discussed previously in this chapter. We project amounts for 2009.

STEP 1: PROJECT OPERATING REVENUES

The projections begin with sales. The analyst studies the historical pattern of changes in sales and assesses whether this pattern will continue in the future. Among the questions raised are the following:

1. Does the firm plan to change product lines or pricing policies, make acquisitions of other companies, or take other actions that would alter the historical sales pattern?

2. Does the firm expect competitors to alter their strategies or new competitors to enter the market and thereby change the market shares?

3. Will conditions in the economy affect the firm's sales? For example, do the firm's sales fluctuate with economic cycles, do they remain steady, or do they fluctuate with other variables, such as local population growth?

The assumption about sales drives most other items in the pro forma financial statements, which normally makes this the most important assumption.

Exhibit 6.2 indicates that sales revenues for Wal-Mart Corporation increased from $308,945 million to $344,992 million between 2006 and 2007, a growth rate of 11.7% [= ($344,992/$308,945) − 1]. Sales increased from $344,992 million to $374,526 million between 2007 and 2008, a growth rate of only 8.6% [= ($374,526/$344,992) − 1]. The decline in the growth rate occurred in a year when Wal-Mart did not make any large corporate acquisitions and the economy grew slowly. We assume that weak economic conditions will continue in 2009 but that Wal-Mart will convert more discount stores to superstores, open Neighborhood Markets, and expand internationally. We project Wal-Mart's revenues to increase 8% between 2008 and 2009. Thus, projected sales for 2009 are $404,488 (= $374,526 × 1.08) million.

Other revenues have varied between 1.1% and 1.2% of sales during the last three years. We assume that other revenues will equal 1.2% of sales in 2009. Projected other revenues are $4,854 (= 0.012 × $404,488) million.

STEP 2: PROJECT OPERATING EXPENSES

Projecting operating expenses requires understanding the behavior of various operating costs. Does the expense item tend to vary with the level of sales, a behavior pattern characterized as a *variable cost*? Alternatively, does the expense item tend to remain relatively constant for a particular time period regardless of the level of sales, a behavior pattern characterized as

EXHIBIT 6.17	Preparing Pro Forma Financial Statements

Statement of Income and Retained Earnings

Balance Sheet

STEP 1: Project Operating Revenues

Sales Revenue
Other Revenues

STEP 2: Project Operating Expenses

Cost of Goods Sold
Selling and Administrative Expenses
Net Income Before Interest Expense
    and Income Taxes

STEP 5: Project Cost of Financing, Income Tax Expense, and the Change in Retained Earnings

Interest Expense
Income Tax Expense
Net Income
Dividends
Change in Retained Earnings

STEP 3: Project Assets

Cash
Accounts Receivable
Inventories
Other Current Assets
Investments
Fixed Assets
Other Assets

STEP 4: Project Liabilities and Contributed Capital

Accounts Payable
Notes Payable
Other Current Liabilities
Long-Term Debt
Other Liabilities
Contributed Capital

STEP 5: Project Retained Earnings

Retained Earnings

Statement of Cash Flows

STEP 6: Project the Statement of Cash Flows

Operations	**Investing**	**Financing**
Net Income	Acquisition of Fixed Assets	Change in Notes Payable
Depreciation	Sale of Investments	Change in Long-Term Debt
Other Adjustments	Acquisition of Investments	Change in Common Stock
Change in Receivables	Other Investing Transactions	Dividends
Change in Inventories		Other Financing Transactions
Change in Other Current Assets		
Change in Accounts Payable		
Change in Other Current Liabilities		
CASH FLOW FROM OPERATIONS	CASH FLOW FROM INVESTING	CASH FLOW FROM FINANCING

a *fixed cost*? (When you study cost behavior in your managerial accounting and economics courses, you will learn that nearly all costs vary in the long run, but appear fixed in the short run. Deciding on whether a given cost is fixed or variable requires knowing the time period envisioned for the projection.) Does the expense item have both variable- and fixed-cost characteristics, a pattern described as a *mixed cost* or a *step cost*? Does the firm have some discretion to change the amount of a fixed-cost item in the short term in response to current conditions (for example, maintenance or advertising expenditures), or is there little discretion to change the level of fixed costs (for example, depreciation on equipment)? Understanding the behavior of each expense item aids in projecting its amount.

Exhibit 6.6 presents a common-size income statement for Wal-Mart for 2006, 2007, and 2008. We use these common-size percentages in projecting operating expenses.

Cost of Goods Sold Wal-Mart purchases merchandise and then marks it up to sell to customers. Thus cost of goods sold will likely vary with sales. The cost of goods sold percentage has decreased from 76.9% in 2006 to 76.5% in 2008. Assume that the decrease is a result of implementing merchandise purchase and control systems in the non-U.S. retail chains that Wal-Mart acquired in recent years. We assume that Wal-Mart will benefit even further from these inventory systems in 2009, reducing the cost of goods sold to sales percentage to 76.3%. Projected cost of goods sold for 2009 is $308,624 ($= 0.763 \times \$404,488$) million.

Selling and Administrative Expense The ratio of selling and administrative expense to sales increased from 18.2% in 2006 to 18.9% in 2008. Increased competition requiring increased expenditures on marketing partially explains the increasing percentage. Also, the decrease in the growth rate of sales in 2008 likely resulted in spreading fixed costs such as depreciation, rent, and insurance over a smaller-than-anticipated sales base. We project a slower growth rate in sales in 2009 than occurred in 2008. Thus, we assume that selling and administrative expenses will equal 19.0% of sales in 2009. Projected selling and administrative expenses for 2009 are $76,853 (= 0.19 × $404,488) million.

We delay projecting interest expense and income taxes until we project the amount and type of financing required for projected assets.

STEP 3: PROJECT ASSETS

The projection of total assets on the balance sheet requires the analyst to make assumptions consistent with those underlying the pro forma income statement. One approach assumes a total assets turnover (that is, sales/average total assets) similar to that of previous years. For example, the total assets turnover of Wal-Mart was 2.3 during 2008. If the firm maintains this total assets turnover during 2009, then the calculation of its total assets at the end of 2009 results from solving the following equation:

$$\text{Total Assets Turnover} = \frac{\text{Sales}}{\text{Average Total Asssets}} = \frac{\$404,488}{.5(\$172,400 + x)} = 2.3$$

Solving for the unknown in the equation yields projected total assets at the end of 2009 of $179,329. The analyst can then use common-size balance sheet percentages to allocate this total to individual balance sheet accounts.

An alternative approach uses the historical annual growth rate in total assets of 11.1% during the last three years. This approach yields total assets of $191,536 (= $172,400 × 1.111) million. The analyst can then apply common-size balance sheet amounts to allocate this $191,536 million to individual balance sheet items.

A third approach uses a mixture of asset turnovers and growth rates for the various assets and then aggregates projected amounts for individual assets to compute total assets. We illustrate this approach next. We will compute last the amount of cash at the end of 2009 as the residual (or plug) necessary to equate total assets and total liabilities plus shareholders' equity. If the amount for projected cash seems too large or too small relative to prior years, we will go back and alter our assumptions.

Accounts Receivable For most firms, accounts receivable vary with changes in sales. Wal-Mart collects its accounts receivable three days after sale, so accounts receivable comprise only 2% of total assets. We assume that accounts receivable will grow during 2009 at the growth rate in sales. Projected accounts receivable on January 31, 2009, are $3,946 (= $3,654 × 1.08) million.

Inventory We use the inventory turnover to project the ending inventory for 2009. The inventory turnover ratio was 7.7 in 2006, 8.0 in 2007, and 8.3 in 2008. An earlier section suggested that the increased inventory turnover may have resulted from improved inventory controls or a shift in sales mix to products or markets where inventory turns over more quickly. We assume that sales growth will decline between 2008 and 2009 because of recession conditions. We assume that the inventory turnover will remain at 8.3 in 2009, reflecting continued improvement in inventory control systems offset by uncertainty regarding the effects of the recession. We solve for x in the following equation to project inventory at the end of 2009.

$$\frac{\text{Cost of Goods Sold}}{\text{Average Inventory}} = \frac{\$308,624}{(0.5)(\$35,180 + x)} = 8.3$$

Using the inventory turnover of 8.3 times per year projects inventories at the end of 2009 (x in the equation) of $39,187 million.

Prepayments Prepayments include rent, insurance, and similar operating expenses and usually grow at the same rate as sales. We assume that prepayments will grow during 2009 at the projected growth rate in sales of 8%. Thus, prepayments at the end of 2009 are $3,437 (= $3,182 × 1.08) million.

Property, Plant, and Equipment Wal-Mart's fixed assets grew at a rate faster than sales in four of the last five years as it converted discount stores to superstores, opened Neighborhood Markets, and expanded internationally. We assume that the growth rate in fixed assets will again exceed the growth rate in sales during 2009 but that Wal-Mart will decrease the rate of growth in property, plant, and equipment relative to previous years due to the recession. We assume fixed assets will grow 9% in 2009. Thus, projected property, plant, and equipment is $115,434 (= $105,903 × 1.09) million.

Other Noncurrent Assets Other noncurrent assets primarily represent goodwill from corporate acquisitions made in previous years. Neither U.S. GAAP nor IFRS permits firms to amortize goodwill. We assume that Wal-Mart will not record an impairment charge on goodwill in 2009. Thus, other noncurrent assets will not change between the end of 2008 and the end of 2009.

STEP 4: PROJECT LIABILITIES AND CONTRIBUTED CAPITAL

We project next the financing side of the balance sheet. The projection of liabilities and contributed capital flows directly from the projection of the level of operating activity estimated in the first two steps and the projection of total assets estimated in the preceding step.

Accounts Payable The accounts payable turnover varied between 9.9 and 10.2 during the last three years. We project accounts payable at the end of 2009 assuming an accounts payable turnover of 9.9. We solve the following equation to project accounts payable at the end of 2009:

$$\frac{\text{Purchases}}{\text{Average Accounts Payable}} = \frac{\$308,624 + \$39,187 - \$35,180}{(0.5)(\$30,170 + x)} = 9.9$$

Using the turnover of 9.9 times per year projects accounts payable at the end of 2009 of $32,788 million.

Notes Payable Wal-Mart likely uses notes payable to finance inventories and other working capital needs. We assume that notes payable will increase at the growth rate in sales. Thus, projected notes payable is $5,443 (= $5,040 × 1.08) million.

Current Portion of Long-Term Debt Wal-Mart discloses in notes to its financial statements that long-term debt due during 2010, and therefore classified as a current liability on the January 31, 2009, balance sheet, is $5,913 million.

Other Current Liabilities Other current liabilities relate to unpaid salaries, taxes, and other operating costs. These costs tend to vary with the level of operating activity. We project that other current liabilities will grow at the growth rate in sales. We therefore project other current liabilities at the end of 2009 to equal $18,160 (= $16,815 × 1.08) million.

Bonds Payable Wal-Mart uses long-term debt to finance the growth in its stores. We assume that bonds payable will decrease by the amount that Wal-Mart reclassifies from noncurrent liabilities to current liabilities ($5,913 million during 2009). The remaining long-term debt will then grow at twice the growth rate in property, plant, and equipment of 9%. Property, plant, and equipment at the end of 2009 total $105,903 million and long-term debt totals $42,288 million. Wal-Mart finances 40% (= $42,288/$105,903) of its fixed assets with long-term debt. Growing long-term debt at twice the growth rate in property, plant, and equipment approximately maintains this financing pattern. Thus, the projected amount of long-term debt at the end of 2009 is $42,923 [= ($42,288 − $5,913) × 1.18] million.

Other Noncurrent Liabilities Other noncurrent liabilities include obligations for retirement plans and taxes due longer than one year into the future. These obligations vary with the level of operating activity. We therefore assume that other noncurrent liabilities will grow at the growth rate in sales. Projected other noncurrent liabilities at the end of 2009 are $7,614 (= $7,050 × 1.08) million.

Contributed Capital We assume no change in common stock or additional paid-in capital during 2009. If we find that Wal-Mart needs additional financing, we can alter this assumption later.

Accumulated Other Comprehensive Income We assume Accumulated Other Comprehensive Income grows at the growth rate in sales, because most items in this account relate to operations. The projected amount in Accumulated Other Comprehensive Income at the end of 2009 is $4,173 (= $3,864 × 1.08) million.

STEP 5: PROJECT INTEREST EXPENSE, INCOME TAX EXPENSE, NET INCOME, DIVIDENDS, AND THE CHANGE IN RETAINED EARNINGS

Interest Expense Interest expense usually bears a relatively fixed relation to the level of borrowing. Interest expense for Wal-Mart averaged approximately 4.3% of notes and bonds payable during 2009. The average amount of notes payable, current portion of long-term debt, and long-term debt for 2009 equals $53,918 [= 0.5($5,040 + $6,229 + $42,288 + $5,443 + $5,913 + $42,923)]. Projected interest expense is $2,319 [= .043 × $53,918] million.

Income Tax Expense The projections of sales, operating expenses, and interest expense yield income before income taxes of $21,546 (= $404,488 + $4,854 − $308,624 − $76,853 − $2,319) million. Income tax expense varied between 34.3% and 34.9% of income before income taxes during the last three years. We assume an income tax rate of 34.5% for 2009. Projected income tax expense is $7,433 (= 0.345 × $21,546) million.

Retained Earnings Retained earnings increase by the $14,113 million of net income (= $21,546 − $7,433) million and decrease by dividends declared and paid. Wal-Mart's dividends have grown during the last three years at a faster rate than sales or net income. We assume that dividends in 2009 will grow 10%, resulting in a dividend of $3,945 (= $3,586 × 1.10) million. Thus, retained earnings at the end of 2009 are $67,487 (= $57,319 + $14,113 − $3,945) million.

The preparation of pro forma financial statements through the first five steps results in a projected income statement (see **Exhibit 6.18**) and a projected balance sheet (see **Exhibit 6.19**). The only unprojected item on the balance sheet is cash. We set cash as the plug that equates projected total assets with projected liabilities and shareholders' equity. Projected liabilities and shareholders' equity total $187,926 million. Projected assets other than cash equal $180,916 (= $3,946 + $39,187 + $3,437 + $115,434 + $18,912) million. Projected cash is $7,010 (= $187,926 − $180,916) million.

The preparation of pro forma financial statements usually requires the analyst to plug some account to equate assets with liabilities plus shareholders' equity and have income statement amounts articulate with projected balance sheet amounts. Cash is often the plug, but

EXHIBIT 6.18

Wal-Mart Stores
Pro Forma Income Statement
For the Year Ended January 31, 2009
(all dollar amounts in millions)

	2008 Actual	Assumption	2009 Pro Forma
Sales.	$374,526	Growth Rate = 8%	$404,488
Other Revenues.	4,578	1.2% of Sales.	4,854
Total Revenues	$379,104		$409,342
Less Expenses:			
Cost of Goods Sold.	$286,515	76.3% of Sales	$308,624
Selling and Administrative	70,694	19.0% of Sales	76,853
Interest	2,103	4.3% of Interest-Bearing Debt	2,319
Total Expenses.	$359,312		$387,796
Income before Income Taxes.	$ 19,792		$ 21,546
Income Tax Expense	6,908	34.5% of Income Before Income Taxes	7,433
Net Income	$ 12,884	Pro Forma Net Income	$ 14,113

| EXHIBIT 6.19 | **Wal-Mart Stores**
Pro Forma Balance Sheet
For the Year Ended January 31, 2009
(all dollar amounts in millions) |

	January 31, 2008	Assumptions	January 31, 2009
ASSETS			
Cash	$ 5,569	Residual	$ 7,010
Accounts Receivable	3,654	Sale Growth Rate = 8%	3,946
Inventories	35,180	Inventory Turnover = 8.3	39,187
Prepayments	3,182	Sales Growth Rate = 8%	3,437
Total Current Assets.	$ 47,585	Pro Forma Total Current Assets	$ 53,580
Property, Plant, and Equipment (net) . .	105,903	Growth Rate = 9%	$115,434
Other Noncurrent Assets.	18,912	No Change	18,912
Total Assets	$172,400	Pro Forma Total Assets.	$187,926
LIABILITIES AND SHAREHOLDERS' EQUITY			
Accounts Payable	$ 30,370	Accounts Payable Turnover = 9.9	$ 32,788
Notes Payable	5,040	Sales Growth Rate = 8%	5,443
Current Portion of Long-Term Debt . . .	6,229	Given	5,913
Other Current Liabilities.	16,815	Sale Growth Rate = 8%	18,160
Total Current Liabilities	$ 58,454	Pro Forma Total Current Liabilities	$ 62,304
Long-Term Debt	42,288	Property, Plant, and Equipment Growth Rate = 9%	42,923
Other Noncurrent Liabilities	7,050	Sales Growth Rate = 8%	7,614
Total Liabilities	$107,792	Pro Total Liabilities	$112,841
Common Stock	$ 397	No Change	$ 397
Additional Paid-in Capital	3,028	No Change	3,028
Retained Earnings.	57,319	Dividend Growth Rate = 10%	67,487
Accumulated Other Comprehensive Income	3,864	Sales Growth Rate = 8%	4,173
		Pro Forma Total Shareholders'	
Total Shareholders' Equity	$ 64,608	Equity	$ 75,085
Total Liabilities and Shareholders' Equity.	$172,400	Pro Forma Total Liabilities and Shareholders' Equity.	$187,926

not necessarily. The analyst might assume that a firm needs a certain minimum amount of cash. The analyst might assume that the firm will invest cash in excess of this balance in marketable securities or borrow if projected cash flows suggest a cash balance less than the minimum.

STEP 6: PROJECT THE STATEMENT OF CASH FLOWS

The analyst can prepare a pro forma statement of cash flows directly from the pro forma income statement and pro forma balance sheet. **Exhibit 6.20** presents the pro forma statement of cash flows for Wal-Mart for 2009. Note the following:

- We assume that depreciation increases by the growth rate in property, plant, and equipment, 9% in this case to $6,886 (= $6,317 × 1.09).

- We assume that changes in Other Noncurrent Liabilities, which include obligations for retirement plans and taxes due in later years, relate to operations. We also assume that changes in Accumulated Other Comprehensive Income relate to operations. Thus, the $873 million for Other in the Operations section relates to changes in these two accounts.

EXHIBIT 6.20

Wal-Mart Stores
Pro Forma Statement of Cash Flows
For Year Ended January 31, 2009
(all dollar amounts in millions)

OPERATIONS

Net Income	$ 14,113
Depreciation	6,886
Other Addbacks	873
(Increase) Decrease in Accounts Receivable	(292)
(Increase) Decrease in Inventories	(4,007)
(Increase) Decrease in Prepayments	(255)
Increase (Decrease) in Accounts Payable	2,418
Increase (Decrease) in Other Current Liabilities	1,345
Cash Flow from Operations	$ 21,081

INVESTING

Acquisitions of Property, Plant, and Equipment	$(16,417)
Other Investing Activities	0
Cash Flow from Investing	$(16,417)

FINANCING

Increase (Decrease) in Short-Term Borrowing	$403
Increase (Decrease) in Long-Term Borrowing	319
Dividends	(3,945)
Other Financing Activities	0
Cash Flow from Financing	$ (3,223)
Change in Cash	$ 1,441
Cash, January 31, 2008	5,569
Cash, January 31, 2009	$ 7,010

■ We must solve for the amount of property, plant, and equipment acquired. A common error in preparing pro forma financial statements is to fail to reconcile the change in property, plant, and equipment (net) on the balance sheet with the amount for depreciation expense on the income statement (if disclosed) and the statement of cash flows and the amount for acquisitions on the statement of cash flows. The change in property, plant, and equipment during 2009 is as follows:

Property, Plant, and Equipment, January 31, 2008 (actual)	$105,903
Acquisitions of Property, Plant, and Equipment during 2009 (solved for)	16,417
Less Depreciation during 2009 (projected)	(6,886)
Property, Plant, and Equipment, January 31, 2009 (projected)	$115,434

■ The increase in cash during 2009 of $1,441 million on the statement of cash flows reconciles to the change in cash on the pro forma balance sheet.

ANALYSIS OF PRO FORMA FINANCIAL STATEMENTS

The analyst can calculate various financial statement ratios from the pro forma financial statements. **Exhibit 6.21** presents financial statement ratios for Wal-Mart based on its actual amounts for 2006, 2007, and 2008 and on its pro forma amounts for 2009. The pro forma amounts indicate a slight increase in profitability, which ultimately results from our input assumptions. You can see how the assumptions affected profitability by noticing the following. The rate of return on assets increases because of an increased profit margin for ROA.

EXHIBIT 6.21 **Wal-Mart Stores**
Financial Statement Ratio Analysis

	Pro Forma 2009	2008	Actual 2007	2006
Rate of Return on Assets (ROA).....................	8.7%	8.6%	8.8%	9.1%
Profit Margin for ROA	3.9%	3.8%	3.9%	4.0%
Total Assets Turnover...........................	2.2	2.3	2.3	2.3
Cost of Goods Sold/Sales	76.3%	76.5%	76.6%	76.9%
Selling and Administrative Expenses/Sales	19.0%	18.9%	18.7%	18.2%
Interest Expense/Sales	0.6%	0.6%	0.5%	0.5%
Income Tax Expense/Sales	1.8%	1.8%	1.8%	1.9%
Accounts Receivable Turnover.....................	106.4	115.3	125.4	141.2
Inventory Turnover	8.3	8.3	8.0	7.7
Fixed Asset Turnover	3.7	3.7	3.8	3.9
Rate of Return on Common Shareholders' Equity (ROCE)	20.2%	20.4%	21.2%	22.2%
Profit Margin for ROCE..........................	3.5%	3.4%	3.5%	3.7%
Capital Structure Leverage Ratio	2.6	2.6	t2.6	2.6
Current Ratio	0.86	0.81	0.90	0.90
Quick Ratio	0.18	0.16	0.20	0.19
Cash Flow from Operations to Current Liabilities	34.9%	36.9%	40.1%	38.3%
Accounts Payable Turnover.......................	9.9	9.9	9.9	10.2
Liabilities to Assets Ratio	60.0%	62.5%	60.8%	63.2%
Long-Term Debt Ratio	22.8%	24.5%	23.4%	25.3%
Debt-Equity Ratio	57.2%	65.5%	59.8%	68.7%
Cash Flow from Operations to Total Liabilities	19.1%	20.0%	21.6%	21.0%
Interest Coverage Ratio	10.3	10.4	11.3	13.1

The increased profit margin for ROA results from a decline in the cost of goods sold to sales percentage that exceeds the increase in the selling and administrative expense to sales percentage. The total assets turnover declines slightly, the result of an increase in cash. The rate of return on common shareholders' equity decreases because debt levels decline, offsetting the improved operating profitability. The capital structure leverage ratio declines slightly, the result of both reductions in long-term debt and the retention of earnings, but appears not to change when rounded to one decimal place. The risk ratios do not signal any significant changes in either the short-term or long-term liquidity risk of Wal-Mart.

VALUATION

Managers, security analysts, and others analyze financial statements (both historical and pro forma) to form judgments about the market value of a firm. This section briefly describes the relation between financial statement items and market values. The analyst typically values a firm by using several approaches to ascertain if a small range of values emerges. Entire textbooks and courses consider the valuation approaches introduced in the following sections.

Present Value of Future Cash Flows **Chapter 3** defined an asset as a resource with the potential to generate future cash inflows (or to reduce future cash outflows). Likewise, the common stock of a firm has value to an investor because it can generate cash inflows to the investor in the form of dividends and cash proceeds when the investor sells the shares. Dividends and cash proceeds from sales result from the future profitability and cash flows of a firm.

One valuation approach projects the net amount of cash flows a firm will generate for the common shareholders over some number of future years. Cash flow for the common shareholders equals cash flow from operating, investing, and financing activities (other than cash transactions with common shareholders). The analyst then discounts the net amount for

EXHIBIT 6.22	Valuation of Wal-Mart Stores Using Present Value of Cash Flows (amounts in millions)

Year (1)	Cash Flow from Operations (2)	Cash Flow from Investing (3)	Cash Flow from Nonowner Financing (4)	Excess Cash Flow to Common Shareholders (5)	Present Value of Cash Flows to Common Shareholders (6)
2009.	$21,081	$(16,417)	$ 722	$ 5,386	$ 4,809
2010.	23,188	(18,059)	794	5,923	4,722
2011.	25,507	(19,865)	873	6,515	4,637
2012.	25,058	(21,852)	960	7,166	4,554
2013.	30,864	(24,036)	1,056	7,884	4,474
After 2013.				433,620	246,048[b]
Total Present Value					$269,244

[a]Column (5) = Column (2) + Column (3) + Column (4).

[b]Assumes a growth rate in excess cash flows of 10% per year and a discount rate of 12%. See **Problem 44** in the **Appendix**.

each year at an appropriate discount rate to find the present value of these future cash flows. (The **Appendix** to this book discusses the procedure for discounting future cash flows to their equivalent present value.) Corporate finance texts discuss whether the appropriate discount rate should be the required rate of return by the common shareholders, as we assume here, or a weighted average cost of both debt and equity financing.

Refer to the pro forma statement of cash flows for Wal-Mart for 2009 in **Exhibit 6.20**. Cash inflow from operations totals $21,081 million, cash outflow for investing totals $16,417 million, and cash inflow from net nonowner financing is $722 (= $403 + $319) million. Thus, this firm projects a positive net cash inflow for the common shareholders of $5,386 (= $21,081 − $16,417 + $722) million.

Assume for purposes of illustration that pro forma financial statements for Wal-Mart reveal the amounts in columns (2) through (5) of **Exhibit 6.22**. Column (6) shows the present value of the excess cash flow when discounted at 12%, the assumed rate of return demanded by the common shareholders. The analyst expects excess cash flow after 2013 to increase 10% each year. The $246,048 million represents the present value at the end of 2008 of this excess cash flow after 2013. Based on the 3,920 million shares of common stock outstanding (see **Exhibit 6.3**), the analyst estimates a market value of $67.82 (= $269,244 million/3,970 million shares) per share.[14]

Market Multiples
A second valuation approach relies on market multiples of certain financial statement items for similar firms in the market. Identifying similar firms requires the analyst to consider such factors as the type of business, growth characteristics, and size.

Price Earnings Ratios
One common valuation approach relates market prices to multiples of net income. The chain of logic runs as follows:

Market Price = Cash Flows from Stream of Dividends   × Appropriate Discount Factors
               and Residual Value
                         ↓   ↓
= Future Cash Flows of a Firm for All Years × Appropriate Discount Factors
                         ↓   ↓
=   Future One-Year Earnings of a Firm   × Appropriate Market Multiple
                         ↓   ↓
=   Current One-Year Earnings of a Firm   × Appropriate Market Multiple

---

[14]Note that the number of common shares outstanding on January 31, 2008, of 3,970 differs from the average number of shares outstanding during 2008 of 4,066 used in the computation of earnings per share.

The analyst uses current earnings as a surrogate for future earnings and cash flows. Future cash flows of the firm provide the source of cash flows to the investor. The market multiple serves the function of a discount factor in present value calculation.[15]

Assume that firms similar to Wal-Mart sell at 18 times 2008 net income from continuing operations. Based on the earnings of Wal-Mart for 2008 of $12,884 million, a market multiple of 18 yields a total market value of $231,912 million, or $58.42 (= $231,912/ 3,970 shares) per share.

Market-to-Book-Value Ratios Another valuation approach relates market values to the book values of common shareholders' equity of similar firms. Book values tend to exhibit less variability over time than net income and perhaps serve as a better base for estimating market values.

Assume that firms similar to Wal-Mart have average market-to-book-value ratios of 4.0 at the end of 2008. The common shareholders' equity of Wal-Mart is $64,608 million at the end of 2008, suggesting a total market value of $258,432 million, or $65.10 (= $258,432 million/3,970 million) per share.

Summary of Valuation Approaches These valuation approaches yielded market values for Wal-Mart of approximately $58 to $65 per share. We constructed the examples so that the values fell within a narrow range. Analysis of real data will likely show a wider range of market values, so the analyst uses judgment built from practice in choosing an approach to provide a reasonable estimate. The observed market value of Wal-Mart indicated at the beginning of this chapter was $48 per share. If we trust our analysis, we would decide that the shares are selling in the market for less than their fair value. But, we would wonder if the market has considered factors we have overlooked.

SOLUTIONS TO SELF-STUDY PROBLEMS

SUGGESTED SOLUTION TO PROBLEM 6.1 FOR SELF-STUDY

(Nordstrom Corporation; analyzing the rate of return on assets.)

a. The increasing ROA results from an increasing profit margin for ROA in all years and an increase in the total assets turnover in the 2006 fiscal year. The increasing profit margin for ROA results from an increase in other revenues as a percentage of sales and a decrease in both the cost of goods sold to sales percentage and the selling and administrative expense to sales percentage. Sales increased 8.3% in fiscal 2005 and 10.8% in fiscal 2006. Nordstrom likely increased its sales on account and recognized interest revenue on unpaid customer account balances. Cost of goods sold includes occupancy cost, which is primarily a fixed cost. Administrative expenses are also heavily fixed cost in their behavior. Nordstrom spread these relatively fixed costs over a growing sales level, leading to decreases in the expense percentages. Income tax expense as a percentage of income before income taxes was relatively stable during the three years. The increased total assets turnover in fiscal year 2006 results from increases in accounts receivable, inventory, and fixed asset turnovers. Sales grew at a faster rate in fiscal 2006 than in fiscal 2005, perhaps explaining some of the increases in these asset turnovers. The increasing accounts receivable turnover might also result from better screening of credit applications or increased collection efforts. The total assets turnover was stable between fiscal 2004 and fiscal 2005 due to the offsetting effects of a decrease in the accounts receivable turnover and increases in the inventory and fixed asset turnovers.

b. Nordstrom Corporation might have implemented more effective inventory control systems, resulting in an increasing inventory turnover ratio. The more rapid inventory turnover results in fewer write-downs of inventory items for product obsolescence and physical deterioration, thereby decreasing the cost of goods sold to sales percentage.

---

[15]Actually, the discount rate and the market multiple for a no-growth firm have a reciprocal relation. Refer to the discussion of perpetuities in this book's compound interest **Appendix**. There you will see that the current value of an indefinite stream of constant payments, say $1 per period, is $1/r$ when the interest (or discount) rate is r per period. Thus, if the discount rate is 10% per period, the stream has a current value of $10 (= $1/0.10), a multiple of 10, but if the discount rate is 20% per period, then the stream has a current value of only $5 (= $1/0.20), a multiple of 5. Market multipliers for growing firms are larger than $1/r$ because of the need to value the growth in cash flows and earnings. See **Exhibit 14.3** and the discussion of valuation in **Chapter 14**.

SUGGESTED SOLUTION TO PROBLEM 6.2 FOR SELF-STUDY

(Nordstrom Corporation; analyzing the rate of return on common shareholders' equity.)

a. The increasing ROCE results from the net effect of an increasing profit margin for ROCE and a decreasing proportion of debt in the financing structure. The profit margin for ROCE increased for the same reasons as the profit margin for ROA, decreasing cost of goods sold and selling and administrative expense percentages. The profit margin for ROCE also increased because of a decreasing proportion of interest-bearing debt in the capital structure.

b. The rate of return on common shareholders' equity exceeds the rate of return on assets, suggesting that the firm's earnings on assets financed by creditors were greater than the cost of creditors' financing. The excess return benefited the common shareholders.

SUGGESTED SOLUTION TO PROBLEM 6.3 FOR SELF-STUDY

(Nordstrom Corporation; analyzing short-term liquidity risk.)

a. The increasing cash flow from operations to current liabilities ratios results from four factors. First, the profit margin for ROCE increased (see the solution to **Problem 6.2 for Self-Study**), likely resulting in increasing cash flow from operations. Second, the inventory turnover increased, thereby reducing the amount of cash tied up in inventories and increasing cash flow from operations. Third, the accounts receivable turnover increased in fiscal year 2006, thereby reducing the amount of cash tied up in accounts receivable and increasing cash flow from operations. Fourth, the stable days accounts payable were outstanding, despite the decrease in days inventory, suggesting that Nordstrom Corporation did not use the increased cash flow from operations to pay suppliers more quickly.

b. Nordstrom Corporation has a current ratio well above 1.0 and a quick ratio above 1.0. Its cash flow from operations to current liabilities ratio is above the 40% benchmark for a financially healthy firm, and that ratio increased over the three years. These signals suggest a low level of short-term liquidity risk.

SUGGESTED SOLUTION TO PROBLEM 6.4 FOR SELF-STUDY

(Nordstrom Corporation; analyzing long-term liquidity risk.)

a. The response to question **a** in **Problem 6.3 for Self-Study** indicates that increasing profitability and a decreasing inventory turnover in all three years and a decreased accounts receivable turnover in fiscal year 2006 helps explain in part the increase in the cash flow from operations to total liabilities ratio. In addition, total liabilities and long-term debt as a percentage of total assets and shareholders' equity declined, which also leads to a decrease in the cash flow from operations to total liabilities ratio. This decreased borrowing is both short-term and long-term, as the debt ratios indicate.

b. The increasing interest coverage ratio results primarily from decreased interest expense on the decreased debt loads.

c. The cash flow from operations to total liabilities ratio exceeds the 20% level considered desirable for a healthy firm in all years and continually increased. Its interest coverage ratio exceeds the 3.0 level considered troublesome and increased as the firm reduced its debt levels. Thus, the long-term liquidity risk level is low.

SUGGESTED SOLUTION TO PROBLEM 6.5 FOR SELF-STUDY

(Cox Corporation; computing profitability and risk ratios.)

a. Rate of return on assets $= \dfrac{\$3{,}000 + (1 - 0.30)(\$700)}{(0.5)(\$20{,}000 + \$24{,}000)} = 15.9\%$

b. Profit margin ratio for ROA $= \dfrac{\$3{,}000 + (1 - 0.30)(\$700)}{\$30{,}000} = 11.6\%$

c. Cost of goods sold to sales percentage $= \dfrac{\$18{,}000}{\$30{,}000} = 60.0\%$

d. Selling expense to sales percentage $= \dfrac{\$4{,}500}{\$30{,}000} = 15.0\%$

e. Total assets turnover $= \dfrac{\$30,000}{(0.5)(\$20,000 + \$24,000)} = 1.4$ times per year

f. Accounts receivable turnover $= \dfrac{\$30,000}{(0.5)(\$3,600) + \$4,300)} = 7.6$ times per year

g. Inventory turnover $= \dfrac{\$18,000}{(0.5)(\$5,600 + \$7,900)} = 2.7$ times per year

h. Fixed asset turnover $= \dfrac{\$30,000}{(0.5)(\$9,900 + \$10,670)} = 2.9$ times per year

i. Rate of return on common shareholders' equity $= \dfrac{\$3,000 - \$100}{(0.5)(\$8,000 + \$11,000)} = 30.5\%$

j. Profit margin ratio for ROCE $= \dfrac{\$3,000 - \$100}{\$30,000} = 9.7\%$

k. Capital structure leverage ratio $= \dfrac{(0.5)(\$20,000 + \$24,000)}{(0.5)(\$8,000 + \$11,000)} = 2.3$

l. Current ratio (both dates)

December 31, 2006: $= \dfrac{\$10,100}{\$7,000} = 1.4$

December 31, 2008: $= \dfrac{\$13,300}{\$9,200} = 1.4$

m. Quick ratio (both dates)

December 31, 2006: $= \dfrac{\$4,200}{\$7,000} = 0.6$

December 31, 2008: $= \dfrac{\$5,050}{\$9,200} = 0.5$

n. Cash flow from operations to current liabilities ratio $= \dfrac{\$3,300}{(0.5)(\$7,000 + \$9,200)}$ $= 40.7\%$.

o. Accounts payable turnover $= \dfrac{\$18,000 + \$7,900 - \$5,600}{(0.5)(\$3,500 + \$3,300)} = 6.0$ times per year

p. Liabilities to assets ratio (both dates)

December 31, 2006: $= \dfrac{\$11,000}{\$20,000} = 55.0\%$

December 31, 2008: $= \dfrac{\$12,000}{\$24,000} = 50.0\%$

q. Long-term debt ratio (both dates)

December 31, 2006: $= \dfrac{\$4,000}{\$20,000} = 20.0\%$

December 31, 2008: $= \dfrac{\$2,800}{\$24,000} = 11.7\%$

r. Debt-equity ratio (both dates)

December 31, 2006: $= \dfrac{\$4,000}{\$9,000} = 44.4\%$

December 31, 2008: $= \dfrac{\$2,800}{\$12,000} = 23.3\%$

s. Cash flow from operations to total liabilities ratio $= \dfrac{\$3,300}{(0.5)(\$11,000 + \$12,000)}$ $= 28.7\%$

t. Interest coverage ratio $= \dfrac{\$3,000 + \$1,300 + \$700}{\$700} = 7.1$ times

KEY TERMS AND CONCEPTS

Return and risk
Time-series analysis
Cross-section analysis
Profitability
Rate of return on assets (ROA)
Profit margin for ROA ratio
Total assets turnover ratio
Accounts receivable turnover ratio
Inventory turnover ratio
Fixed asset turnover ratio
Operating segments
Rate of return on common shareholders' equity (ROCE)
Financial leverage
Profit margin ratio for ROCE
Capital structure leverage ratio

Earnings per share
Basic and diluted earnings per share
Short-term liquidity risk
Current ratio
Quick ratio or acid test ratio
Cash flow from operations to current liabilities ratio
Accounts payable turnover ratio
Long-term liquidity risk
Liabilities to assets ratio
Long-term debt ratio
Debt-equity ratio
Cash flow from operations to total liabilities ratio
Interest coverage ratio
Pro forma financial statements

QUESTIONS, EXERCISES, AND PROBLEMS

QUESTIONS

1. Review the meaning of the terms and concepts listed in Key Terms and Concepts.

2. "Financial ratios are useful metrics for relating two items in the financial statements. Interpreting changes in a particular financial ratio is difficult, however, because the explanation might relate to changes in the numerator, the denominator, or both." Explain this statement using a change in the cost of goods sold to sales percentage from 65% to 68%.

3. "I can understand why the analyst adds back interest expense to net income in the numerator of the rate of return on assets, but I don't see why an adjustment is made for income taxes." Provide an explanation.

4. A firm's total assets turnover decreased, but its accounts receivable, inventory, and fixed asset turnover increased. Suggest possible explanations.

5. What is the difference between the profit margin for ROA and the profit margin for ROCE? Suggest a scenario when a firm's profit margin for ROA would increase and its profit margin for ROCE would decrease.

6. One company president stated, "The operations of our company are such that we must turn inventory over once every four weeks." A company president in another industry stated, "The operations of our company are such that we can live comfortably with a turnover of four times each year." Explain what these two company presidents probably had in mind.

7. Some have argued that for any given firm at a particular time, there is an optimal inventory turnover ratio. Explain.

8. Under what circumstances will the rate of return on common shareholders' equity exceed the rate of return on assets? Under what circumstances will it be less?

9. A company president stated, "The operations of our company are such that we can effectively use only a small amount of financial leverage." Explain.

10. Define financial leverage. As long as a firm's rate of return on assets exceeds its after-tax cost of borrowing, why doesn't the firm increase borrowing to as close to 100% of financing as it can?

EXERCISES

11. **Calculating and disaggregating the rate of return on assets.** Recent annual reports of CBRL Group (Cracker Barrel) and McDonalds Corporation (McDonalds) reveal the following (amounts in millions):

	Cracker Barrel	McDonalds
Revenues.	$2,352	$22,787
Interest Expense.	59	417
Net Income	76	2,335
Average Total Assets	1,473	29,183

Cracker Barrel operates a chain of restaurants featuring value-priced country meals. Cracker Barrel owns all of its restaurants. McDonalds operates McDonalds, Boston Market, and Chipotle Mexican Grill restaurants worldwide through both company-owned and franchised units. McDonalds owns the land and buildings of most of its franchised restaurants and leases the space to the franchisees. The income tax rate is 35%.

a. Calculate the rate of return on assets for each company.

b. Disaggregate the rate of return on assets in part a into profit margin for ROA and total assets turnover components.

c. Comment on the relative profitability of the two companies.

12. **Profitability analysis for two types of retailers.** Information taken from recent annual reports of two retailers appears as follows (amounts in millions). One of these companies is Family Dollar Stores, a discount store chain, and the other is Abercrombie & Fitch, a specialty retailer of apparel. The income tax rate is 35%. Indicate which of these companies is Family Dollar Stores and which is Abercrombie & Fitch. Explain your reasoning using appropriate financial ratios.

	Company A	Company B
Sales	$3,750	$6,834
Interest Expense.	1	17
Net Income	476	243
Average Total Assets	2,458	2,574

13. **Calculating and disaggregating rate of return on common shareholders' equity.** Information taken from the annual reports of Exxon Mobil, a petroleum company, for three recent years appears below (amounts in millions):

	2007	2006	2005
Revenues.	$404,552	$377,635	$370,680
Net Income	40,610	39,500	36,130
Average Total Assets	230,549	213,675	201,796
Average Common Shareholders' Equity	117,803	112,515	106,471

a. Compute the rate of return on common shareholders' equity for each year. There was no preferred stock outstanding during the three years.

b. Disaggregate the rate of return on common shareholders' equity into profit margin for ROCE, total assets turnover, and capital structure leverage ratio components.

c. How has the profitability of Exxon Mobil changed over the three years?

14. **Profitability analysis for two companies.** The following data show five items from the financial statements of two companies for a recent year (amounts in millions):

	Company A	Company B
For Year		
Revenues.	$3,750	$6,143
Income Before Interest and Related Taxes[a]	476	934
Net Income to Common Shareholders[b]	476	934

(continued)

	Company A	Company B
Average during Year		
Total Assets......................................	2,458	5,594
Common Shareholders' Equity...........................	2,256	2,566

[a]Net Income + [Interest Expense × (1 − Tax Rate)]
[b]Net Income − Preferred Stock Dividends

a. Compute the rate of return on assets for each company. Disaggregate the rate of return on assets into profit margin for ROA and total assets turnover components.

b. Compute the rate of return on common shareholders' equity for each company. Disaggregate the rate of return on common shareholders' equity into profit margin for ROCE, total assets turnover, and capital structure leverage ratio components.

c. The two companies are Harley Davidson (manufacturer of brand-name motorcycles) and Starbucks (operator of specialty retail coffee shops, primarily in rented facilities). Which of the companies corresponds to A and B? What clues did you use in reaching your conclusions?

15. **Profitability analysis for two companies.** The following data show five items from the financial statements of two companies for a recent year (amounts in millions):

	Company A	Company B
For Year		
Revenues..	$38,334	$93,469
Income Before Interest and Related Taxes[a]..................	6,986	6,999
Net Income to Common Shareholders[b].....................	6,976	5,510
Average during Year		
Total Assets......................................	52,010	187,882
Common Shareholders' Equity...........................	39,757	49,558

[a]Net Income + [Interest Expense × (1 − Tax Rate)]
[b]Net Income − Preferred Stock Dividends

a. Compute the rate of return on assets for each company and disaggregate ROA into profit margin for ROA and total assets turnover components.

b. Compute the rate of return on common shareholders' equity for each company and disaggregate ROCE into profit margin for ROCE, total assets turnover, and capital structure leverage components.

c. The two companies are Intel (developer and manufacturer of semiconductors) and Verizon Communications (telecommunication services). Which of the companies corresponds to A and B? What clues did you use in reaching your conclusions?

16. **Analyzing accounts receivable for two companies.** The annual reports of Dell, Inc. and Sun Microsystems, two manufacturers of computers, reveal the information below for the current year (amounts in millions). Dell sells custom-order personal computers, primarily to individuals. Sun Microsystems sells higher-end computers and Internet software, primarily to businesses.

	Dell	Sun Microsystems
Sales	$61,133	$13,873
Accounts Receivable, January 1	6,152	2,702
Accounts Receivable, December 31	7,693	2,964

a. Compute the accounts receivable turnover for each company.

b. Compute the average number of days that accounts receivable are outstanding for each company.

c. Why do the accounts receivable turnovers of these two companies differ?

17. **Analyzing inventories over three years.** The following information relates to the activities of Mattel, a manufacturer of toys (amounts in millions):

	2007	2006	2005
Sales	$5,970	$5,650	$5,179
Cost of Goods Sold	3,193	3,038	2,806
Average Inventory	406	380	415

a. Compute the inventory turnover for each year.

b. Compute the average number of days that inventories are held each year.

c. Compute the cost of goods sold to sales percentage for each year.

d. How well has Mattel managed its inventories over the three years?

18. **Analyzing fixed asset turnover over three years.** The following information relates to The Walt Disney Company (Disney), an entertainment company (amounts in millions):

	2007	2006	2005
Sales	$35,510	$33,747	$31,374
Average Fixed Assets................	16,270	16,174	15,362
Expenditures on Fixed Assets	1,566	1,299	1,823
Depreciation Expense	1,491	1,436	1,339

a. Compute the fixed asset turnover for each year.

b. How well has Disney managed its investment in fixed assets over the three years?

19. **Relating profitability to financial leverage.**

a. Compute the rate of return on common shareholders' equity in each of the following independent cases.

Case	Average Total Assets	Average Interest-Bearing Debt	Average Common Shareholders' Equity	Rate of Return on Assets	After-Tax Cost of Interest-Bearing Debt
A.......................	$200	$100	$100	6%	6%
B.......................	200	100	100	8	6
C.......................	200	120	80	8	6
D.......................	200	100	100	4	6
E.......................	200	50	100	6	6
F.......................	200	50	100	5	6

b. In which cases is financial leverage working to the advantage of the common shareholders?

20. **Interpreting changes in earnings per share.** Company A and Company B both start 2008 with $1 million of shareholders' equity and 100,000 shares of common stock outstanding. During 2008, both companies earn net income of $100,000, a rate of return of 10% on common shareholders' equity at the beginning of 2008. Company A declares and pays $100,000 of dividends to common shareholders at the end of 2008, whereas Company B retains all its earnings and declares no dividends. During 2009, both companies earn net income equal to 10% of shareholders' equity at the beginning of 2009.

a. Compute earnings per share for Company A and for Company B for 2008 and for 2009.

b. Compute the rate of growth in earnings per share for Company A and Company B, comparing earnings per share in 2009 with earnings per share in 2008.

c. Using the rate of growth in earnings per share as the criterion, which company's management appears to be doing a better job for its shareholders? Comment on this result.

21. **Calculating and interpreting short-term liquidity ratios.** Data taken from the financial statements of Nike, a designer and manufacturer of athletic footwear and apparel, appear as follows (amounts in millions):

For the Year	2007	2006	2005
Revenues..................................	$16,326	$14,955	$13,740
Cost of Goods Sold	9,165	8,368	7,624
Net Income	1,492	1,392	1,212
Cash Flow from Operations..................	1,879	1,668	1,571

On May 31	2007	2006	2005	2004
Cash and Marketable Securities..............	$2,847	$2,303	$1,825	$1,229
Accounts Receivable	2,495	2,383	2,262	2,120
Inventories	2,122	2,077	1,811	1,650
Prepayments	613	583	453	529
Total Current Assets....................	$8,077	$7,346	$6,351	$5,528
Accounts Payable	$1,040	$ 952	$ 775	$ 780
Bank Loans	131	299	76	153
Other Current Liabilities...................	1,413	1,362	1,148	1,098
Total Current Liabilities	$2,584	$2,613	$1,999	$2,031

a. Compute the current and quick ratios on May 31 of each year.

b. Compute the cash flow from operations to current liabilities ratio and the accounts receivable, inventory, and accounts payable turnover ratios for 2005, 2006, and 2007.

c. How has the short-term liquidity risk of Nike changed during the three-year period?

22. **Calculating and interpreting short-term liquidity ratios.** Data taken from the financial statements of Nestlé, a consumer foods company headquartered in Switzerland, appear as follows (amounts in millions of euros):

For the Year	2007	2006	2005
Revenues..................................	€89,625	€78,533	€73,135
Cost of Goods Sold	37,530	32,474	30,435
Net Income	8,874	7,277	6,498
Cash Flow from Operations..................	11,030	9,197	8,461

On December 31	2007	2006	2005	2004
Cash and Marketable Securities..............	€ 5,737	€ 7,129	€11,188	€ 9,887
Accounts Receivable	9,316	9,056	9,193	7,640
Inventories	5,602	4,988	5,250	4,545
Prepayments	955	760	1,234	756
Total Current Assets....................	€21,610	€21,933	€26,865	€22,828
Accounts Payable	€ 8,566	€ 7,810	€ 7,151	€ 5,871
Bank Loans	14,826	9,626	12,120	9,525
Other Current Liabilities...................	2,783	2,742	3,792	3,415
Total Current Liabilities	€26,175	€20,178	€23,063	€18,811

a. Compute the current and quick ratios on December 31 of each year.

b. Compute the cash flow from operations to current liabilities ratio and the accounts receivable, inventory, and accounts payable turnover ratios for 2005, 2006, and 2007.

c. How has the short-term liquidity risk of Nestlé changed during the three-year period?

23. **Calculating and interpreting long-term liquidity ratios.** Data taken from the financial statements of Tokyo Electric, a Japanese generator and provider of electric services, appear below (amounts in billions of Japanese yen).

For the Year	2007	2006	2005
Net Income Before Interest and Income Taxes.........	¥ 651	¥635	¥ 538
Cash Flow from Operations.....................	1,074	936	1,411
Interest Expense..........................	155	161	165

(continued)

On December 31	2007	2006	2005	2004
Long-Term Debt	¥ 5,871	¥ 6,278	¥ 7,150	¥ 7,391
Total Liabilities	10,488	10,814	11,247	11,540
Total Shareholders' Equity	3,034	2,780	2,502	2,360

a. Compute the long-term debt ratio and the debt-equity ratio at the end of 2004, 2005, 2006, and 2007.

b. Compute the cash flow from operations to total liabilities ratio and the interest coverage ratio for 2005 through 2007.

c. How has the long-term liquidity risk of Tokyo Electric changed over this three-year period?

24. **Calculating and interpreting long-term liquidity ratios.** Data taken from the financial statements of Arcelor Mittal, a steel manufacturer headquartered in the Netherlands, appear below (amounts in millions of euros). Arcelor Mittal acquired other steel companies during the three-year period.

For the Year	2007	2006	2005
Net Income Before Interest Expense and Income Taxes	€11,538	€6,624	€4,160
Cash Flow from Operations	8,539	6,828	6,034
Interest Expense	676	895	404

On December 31	2007	2006	2005	2004
Long-Term Debt	€15,106	€16,416	€ 6,760	€1,206
Total Liabilities	52,749	53,114	17,448	7,760
Total Shareholders' Equity	38,662	31,947	11,264	4,301

a. Compute the long-term debt ratio and the debt-equity ratio at the end of each year.

b. Compute the cash flow from operations to total liabilities ratio and the interest coverage ratio for 2005 through 2007.

c. How has the long-term liquidity risk of Arcelor Mittal changed over this three-year period?

25. **Effect of various transactions on financial statement ratios.** Indicate the immediate effects (increase, decrease, no effect) of each of the following independent transactions on (1) the rate of return on common shareholders' equity, (2) the current ratio, and (3) the liabilities to assets ratio. State any necessary assumptions.

a. A firm purchases, on account, merchandise inventory costing $205,000.

b. A firm sells for $150,000, on account, merchandise inventory costing $120,000.

c. A firm collects $100,000 from customers on accounts receivable.

d. A firm pays $160,000 to suppliers on accounts payable.

e. A firm sells for $10,000 a machine costing $40,000 and with accumulated depreciation of $30,000.

f. A firm declares dividends of $80,000. It will pay the dividends during the next accounting period.

g. A firm issues common stock for $75,000.

h. A firm acquires a machine costing $60,000. It gives $10,000 cash and signs a note for $50,000 payable five years from now for the balance of the purchase price.

26. **Effect of various transactions on financial statement ratios.** Indicate the effects (increase, decrease, no effect) of the following independent transactions on (1) earnings per share, (2) working capital (= current assets − current liabilities), and (3) the quick ratio, where accounts receivable are included but merchandise inventory is excluded from quick assets. State any necessary assumptions.

a. A firm sells for $300,000, on account, merchandise inventory costing $240,000.

b. A firm declares dividends of $160,000. It will pay the dividends during the next accounting period.

c. A firm purchases, on account, merchandise inventory costing $410,000.

d. A firm sells for $20,000 a machine costing $80,000 and with accumulated depreciation of $60,000.

e. Because of defects, a firm returns to the supplier merchandise inventory purchased for $7,000 cash. The firm receives a cash reimbursement.

f. A firm issues 10,000 shares of $10 par value common stock on the last day of the accounting period for $15 per share. It uses the proceeds to acquire the assets of another firm composed of the following: accounts receivable, $30,000; merchandise inventory, $60,000; plant, and equipment, $100,000. The acquiring firm also agrees to pay current liabilities of $40,000 of the acquired company.

PROBLEMS

27. Calculating and interpreting profitability and risk ratios in a time-series setting. Target Corporation, headquartered in the United States, operates retails chains under two store concepts: Target Discount Stores and Target Superstores. Target Discount Stores offer a wide variety of clothing, household, electronics, sports, toys, and entertainment products at discount prices. Target Superstores add grocery products to the typical product offerings of its Target Discount Stores. On January 31, 2008, Target Corporation operated 1,381 discount stores and 210 superstores.

Target stores attempt to differentiate themselves from competitors by pushing trend merchandising with more brand name products. Target emphasizes customer service, referring to its customers as "guests" and focusing on the theme of "Expect More, Pay Less." Target Corporation also attempts to differentiate itself from competitors by providing wide aisles and a less cluttered store appearance. Target offers its own credit card to customers. Target Corporation grew its number of stores from 1,397 on January 31, 2005 to 1,591 on January 31, 2008. The growth rate in sales of stores open at least two full years was 5.6% for the fiscal year ended January 31, 2006, 4.8% for the fiscal year ended January 31, 2007, and 3.0% for the fiscal year ended January 31, 2008. The financial statements for Target Corporation for its three fiscal years ended January 31, 2006, 2007, and 2008 appear in **Exhibit 6.23** (income statement), **Exhibit 6.24** (balance sheet), and **Exhibit 6.25** (statement of cash flows). **Exhibit 6.26** presents financial statement ratios for Target Corporation for its fiscal years ended January 31, 2006 and 2007.

a. Compute the amounts of the ratios listed in **Exhibit 6.26** for the fiscal year ended January 31, 2008. The income tax rate applicable to interest expense deductions is 35%.

b. What are the likely reasons for the changes in Target Corporation's rate of return on assets during the three-year period? Analyze the financial ratios to the maximum depth possible.

EXHIBIT 6.23

Target Corporation
Comparative Income Statement
(all dollar amounts in millions)
(Problem 27)

	For the Year Ended January 31		
	2008	**2007**	**2006**
Sales Revenue	$61,471	$57,878	$51,271
Other Revenues	1,918	1,637	1,376
Total Revenues	$63,389	$59,515	$52,647
Less Expenses:			
Cost of Goods Sold	$41,895	$39,399	$34,927
Selling and Administrative	16,200	15,022	13,370
Interest	669	597	490
Total	$58,764	$55,018	$48,787
Income Before Income Taxes	$ 4,625	$ 4,497	$ 3,860
Income Tax Expense	1,776	1,710	1,452
Net Income	$ 2,849	$ 2,787	$ 2,408

EXHIBIT 6.24

**Target Corporation
Comparative Balance Sheet
(all dollar amounts in millions)
(Problem 27)**

	January 31			
	2008	**2007**	**2006**	**2005**
ASSETS				
Cash	$ 2,450	$813	$ 1,648	$ 2,245
Accounts Receivable (net)	8,054	6,194	5,666	5,069
Inventories	6,780	6,254	5,838	5,384
Prepayments	1,622	1,445	1,253	1,224
Total Current Assets	$18,906	$14,706	$14,405	$13,922
Property, Plant, and Equipment (net)	25,908	22,681	20,501	18,042
Other Noncurrent Assets.	1,559	1,212	1,552	1,511
Total Assets	$46,373	$38,599	$36,458	$33,475
LIABILITIES AND SHAREHOLDERS' EQUITY				
Accounts Payable	$ 6,721	$ 6,575	$ 6,268	$ 5,779
Current Portion of Long-Term Debt	1,964	1,362	753	504
Other Current Liabilities.	3,097	3,180	2,567	1,937
Total Current Liabilities	$11,782	$11,117	$ 9,588	$ 8,220
Long-Term Debt	16,939	9,925	10,582	10,216
Other Noncurrent Liabilities	2,345	1,924	2,083	2,010
Total Liabilities	$31,066	$22,966	$22,253	$20,446
Common Stock ($.10 par value).	$ 68	$ 72	$ 73	$ 74
Additional Paid-in Capital	2,656	2,387	2,121	1,810
Retained Earnings.	12,761	13,417	12,013	11,148
Accumulated Other Comprehensive Income	(178)	(243)	(2)	(3)
Total Shareholders' Equity.	$15,307	$15,633	$14,205	$13,029
Total Liabilities and Shareholders' Equity.	$46,373	$38,599	$36,458	$33,475

c. What are the likely reasons for the changes in Target Corporation's rate of return on common shareholders' equity during the three-year period?

d. How has the short-term liquidity risk of Target Corporation changed during the three-year period?

e. How has the long-term liquidity risk of Target Corporation changed during the three-year period?

28. **Profitability and risk analysis in a cross-section setting.** This problem compares the profitability and risk ratios of three leading discount chains: Carrefour, Target, and Wal-Mart.

Carrefour, headquartered in France, is Europe's largest retailer and the second largest retailer in the world. Sales in 2008 totaled €820,149 million ($112,461). It segments its activities into four groups (2008 sales mix percentages in parentheses):

(1) Hypermarkets (62%): offer a wide variety of household and food products at competitively low prices under the Carrefour store brand.

(2) Supermarkets (22%): sell traditional grocery products under the Champion, Norte, GS and GB supermarkets, and other store brands.

(3) Hard Discount (10%): offer a limited variety of food products in smaller stores than those of hypermarkets and supermarkets at aggressively low prices under the Dia, Ed, and Minipreco store brands.

(4) Other (6%): includes convenience stores and wholesale stores, the latter targeted at business customers, under the SHOPI, Marche Plus, 8 A Huit, Express, Contact, and Proxi store brands.

EXHIBIT 6.25

Target Corporation
Comparative Statement of Cash Flows
(all dollar amounts in millions)
(Problem 27)

	For the Year Ended January 31		
	2008	2007	2006
Operations			
Net Income	$ 2,849	$ 2,787	$ 2,408
Additions and Subtractions:			
Depreciation Expense	1,659	1,496	1,409
Other Addbacks and Subtractions	485	296	474
(Increase) Decrease in Accounts Receivable	(602)	(226)	(244)
(Increase) Decrease in Inventories	(525)	(431)	(454)
(Increase) Decrease in Prepayments	(38)	(25)	(52)
Increase (Decrease) in Accounts Payable	111	435	489
Increase (Decrease) in Other Current Liabilities	186	530	421
Cash Flow from Operations	$ 4,125	$ 4,862	$ 4,451
Investing			
Acquisitions of Property, Plant, and Equipment	$(4,369)	$(3,928)	$(3,388)
Other Investing Transactions	(1,826)	(765)	(761)
Cash Flow from Investing	$(6,195)	$(4,693)	$(4,149)
Financing			
Increase (Decrease) in Short-Term Borrowing	$ 500	$ —	$ —
Increase in Long-Term Borrowing	7,617	1,256	913
Issue of Common Stock	210	181	231
Decrease in Long-Term Borrowing	(1,326)	(1,155)	(527)
Acquisition of Common Stock	(2,808)	(901)	(1,197)
Dividends	(442)	(380)	(318)
Other Financing Transactions	(44)	(5)	(1)
Cash Flow from Financing	$ 3,707	$(1,004)	$ (899)
Net Change in Cash	$ 1,637	$ (835)	$ (597)
Cash, Beginning of Year	813	1,648	2,245
Cash, End of Year	$ 2,450	$ 813	$ 1,648

Carrefour derived approximately 46% of its 2008 sales within France, 38% within Europe excluding France, 9% in Latin America, and 7% in Asia. In addition to owning most of its stores, Carrefour licenses the rights to other firms to own and operate stores using some of the Carrefour store brand names, for which Carrefour receives license fees.

The chapter describes Wal-Mart's strategy and operations. Problem 27 describes Target's strategy and operations. **Exhibits 6.27** and **6.28** present profitability ratios for Carrefour, Target, and Wal-Mart for fiscal years 2006, 2007, and 2008.[16] **Exhibit 6.29** presents risk ratios for the three firms. **Exhibit 6.30** presents selected other data for these firms. **Exhibit 6.30** expresses amounts for Carrefour in U.S. dollars to enhance comparability with Target and Wal-Mart. The first item in **Exhibit 6.30** shows both the increase in total sales and, in brackets, the increase in sales of stores that have been open for at least two full years. The increase in total sales equals the sum of increases in same store sales and increases in sales due to opening new stores and acquiring new stores through corporate acquisitions. The financial statements

---

[16]Carrefour's accounting period ends on December 31, whereas those of Target and Wal-Mart end on January 31. In the chapter we designated the accounting period of Wal-Mart ending on January 31, 2008, as its 2008 fiscal year. In this problem we designate the year ending December 31, 2007, for Carrefour as its 2008 accounting period to enhance comparisons with Target and Wal-Mart.

EXHIBIT 6.26	Target Corporation Financial Ratio Analysis (Problem 27)

For Fiscal Year:	2008	2007	2006
Rate of Return on Assets		8.5%	7.8%
Profit Margin for ROA		5.5%	5.3%
Total Assets Turnover		1.5	1.5
Other Revenues/Sales		2.8%	2.7%
Cost of Goods Sold/Sales		68.1%	68.1%
Selling and Administrative Expenses/Sales		25.9%	26.1%
Interest Expense/Sales		1.0%	1.0%
Income Tax Expense/Sales		2.3%	2.9%
Accounts Receivable Turnover Ratio		9.8	9.6
Inventory Turnover Ratio		6.5	6.2
Fixed Assets Turnover Ratio		2.7	2.7
Rate of Return on Common Shareholders' Equity		18.7%	17.7%
Profit Margin for ROCE		4.8%	4.7%
Capital Structure Leverage Ratio		2.5	2.6
Current Ratio		1.3	1.5
Quick Ratio		.6	.8
Accounts Payable Turnover Ratio		6.2	5.9
Cash Flow form Operations to Current Liabilities Ratio		47.0%	50.0%
Liabilities to Assets Ratio		59.5%	61.0%
Long-Term Debt Ratio		25.7%	29.0%
Debt-Equity Ratio		63.5%	74.5%
Cash Flow from Operations to Total Liabilities Ratio		21.5%	20.8%
Interest Coverage Ratio		8.5	8.9

include the present value of commitments under all leases in property, plant, and equipment and in long-term debt. Study these financial ratios and respond to the following questions:

a. Wal-Mart and Target follow somewhat different strategies. Wal-Mart consistently has a higher rate of return on assets (ROA) than Target. Using information in **Exhibits 6.27** and **6.30**, suggest reasons for these differences in operating profitability.

b. Wal-Mart and Carrefour follow similar strategies. Wal-Mart consistently outperforms Carrefour on ROA. Using information in **Exhibits 6.27** and **6.30**, suggest reasons for these differences in operating profitability.

c. Refer to **Exhibit 6.28**. Which firm appears to have used financial leverage most effectively in enhancing the rate of return on common shareholders' equity (ROCE)? Explain your reasoning.

d. Refer to **Exhibit 6.29**. Do any of these firms appear unduly risky as of the end of 2008?

29. **Calculating and interpreting profitability and risk ratios.** The Gap and Limited Brands maintain leading market positions in the specialty apparel retailing market. The products of The Gap (jeans, blouses, shirts) are more standardized than those of Limited Brands. The products of Limited Brands are more fashion-oriented and glitzy. **Exhibit 6.31** presents the comparative income statements for fiscal year 2008 and **Exhibit 6.32** presents comparative balance sheets for The Gap and Limited Brands at the end of their 2007 and 2008 fiscal years. Cash flows from operations for fiscal year 2008 were $2,081 million for The Gap and $765 million for Limited Brands. The income tax rate is 35%. Both companies repurchase their own previously issued common stock, called *treasury stock*, a topic discussed in **Chapter 14**. On the basis of this information and appropriate financial statement ratios, which company is

a. more profitable in fiscal year 2008?

EXHIBIT 6.27

Carrefour, Target, and Wal-Mart
Cross-Section ROA Profitability Analysis
(Problem 28)

	ROA		
	2006	**2007**	**2008**
Carrefour	4.5%	4.4%	4.3%
Target	7.8%	8.5%	7.7%
Wal-Mart	9.1%	8.8%	8.6%

	Profit Margin for ROA				Total Assets Turnover		
	2006	**2007**	**2008**		**2006**	**2007**	**2008**
Carrefour	3.1%	3.1%	2.9%		1.5	1.4	1.5
Target	5.3%	5.5%	5.3%		1.5	1.5	1.4
Wal-Mart	4.0%	3.9%	3.8%		2.3	2.3	2.3

	Carrefour			Target			Wal-Mart		
	2006	**2007**	**2008**	**2006**	**2007**	**2008**	**2006**	**2007**	**2008**
Sales	100.0%	100.0%	100.0%	100.0%	100.0%	100.0%	100.0%	100.0%	100.0%
Other Revenues	1.5	1.4	1.5	2.7	2.8	3.1	1.1	1.2	1.2
Cost of Goods Sold	(80.4)	(80.6)	(80.7)	(68.1)	(68.1)	(68.2)	(76.9)	(76.6)	(76.5)
Advertising	(1.5)	(1.4)	(1.5)	(2.0)	(2.0)	(1.9)	(.5)	(.6)	(.5)
Selling and Administrative	(15.2)	(15.1)	(15.1)	(24.1)	(23.9)	(24.4)	(17.7)	(18.1)	(18.4)
Income Taxes	(1.3)	(1.3)	(1.2)	(3.2)	(3.3)	(3.3)	(2.0)	(2.0)	(2.0)
Profit Margin For ROA	3.1%	3.1%	2.9%	5.3%	5.5%	5.3%	4.0%	3.9%	3.8%
Receivable Turnover	13.8	12.8	13.3	9.6	9.8	8.6	141.2	125.4	115.3
Inventory Turnover	10.0	10.2	10.3	6.2	6.5	6.4	7.7	8.0	8.3
Fixed Asset Turnover	3.8	3.9	3.9	2.7	2.7	2.5	3.9	3.8	3.7
Percentage of Total Assets:									
Receivables	11%	12%	10%	16%	16%	17%	2%	2%	2%
Inventory	12	11	12	16	16	15	22	22	20
Fixed Assets	37	37	37	56	59	56	59	60	61
Other	40	40	41	12	9	12	17	16	17
Total	100%	100%	100%	100%	100%	100%	100%	100%	100%

b. less risky in terms of short-term liquidity in fiscal year 2008?

c. less risky in terms of long-term liquidity in fiscal year 2008?

30. **Interpreting profitability and risk ratios.** GlaxoSmithKline plc is a pharmaceutical company headquartered in the United Kingdom. **Exhibit 6.33** presents financial statement ratios for GlaxoSmithKline for 2005, 2006, and 2007. Ignore the line for Minority Interest in Subsidiaries, an account that **Chapter 13** discusses. Respond to each of the following questions.

a. What are the likely reasons for the increase in the profit margin for ROA during the three-year period from 2005 to 2007?

b. What are the likely reasons for the decrease in the total asset turnover from .88 in 2006 to .81 in 2007?

EXHIBIT 6.28	Carrefour, Target, and Wal-Mart Cross-Section ROCE Profitability Analysis (Problem 28)

	ROCE		
	2006	**2007**	**2008**
Carrefour	23.6%	20.8%	18.6%
Target	17.7%	18.7%	18.4%
Wal-Mart	22.2%	21.2%	20.4%

	Profit Margin for ROCE			Total Assets Turnover			Capital Structure Leverage		
	2006	**2007**	**2008**	**2006**	**2007**	**2008**	**2006**	**2007**	**2008**
Carrefour	2.5%	2.4%	2.3%	1.5	1.4	1.5	6.5	6.0	5.6
Target	4.7%	4.8%	4.6%	1.5	1.5	1.4	2.6	2.5	2.7
Wal-Mart	3.7%	3.5%	3.4%	2.3	2.3	2.3	2.6	2.6	2.6

EXHIBIT 6.29	Carrefour, Target, and Wal-Mart Cross-Section Risk Analysis (Problem 28)

	Carrefour			Target			Wal-Mart		
Short-Term Liquidity	**2006**	**2007**	**2008**	**2006**	**2007**	**2008**	**2006**	**2007**	**2008**
Current Ratio	.65	.66	.67	1.50	1.32	1.60	.90	.90	.81
Quick Ratio	.36	.37	.36	.76	.63	.89	.19	.20	.16
Cash Flow from Operations to Current Liabilities Ratio	19.4%	16.4%	19.4%	50.0%	47.0%	36.0%	38.3%	40.1%	36.9%
Days Receivable	26	29	27	38	37	42	3	3	3
Days Inventory	36	36	36	59	56	57	48	46	44
Days Payable	95	96	91	62	59	57	36	37	37
Long-Term Liquidity									
Liabilities to Assets Ratio	82.1%	80.6%	80.0%	61.0%	59.5%	67.0%	63.2%	60.8%	62.5%
Long-Term Debt Ratio	26.3%	25.9%	25.7%	29.0%	25.7%	36.5%	25.3%	23.4%	24.5%
Debt-Equity Ratio	146.8%	133.4%	128.6%	74.5%	63.5%	110.7%	68.7%	59.8%	65.5%
Cash Flow from Operations to Total Liabilities Ratio	11.2%	10.1%	11.8%	20.8%	21.5%	15.3%	21.0%	21.6%	20.0%
Interest Coverage Ratio	6.6	6.5	6.0	8.9	8.5	7.9	13.1	11.3	10.4

c. Did financial leverage work to the advantage of the common shareholders in 2007? Explain in such a way that indicates your understanding of the concept of financial leverage.

d. What are the likely reasons for the decrease in the current ratio from 1.5 in 2006 to 1.3 in 2007?

e. What are the likely reasons for the pattern of changes in the two cash flow ratios during the three-year period from 2005 to 2007?

31. **Interpreting profitability and risk ratios.** Scania is a Swedish company that manufactures trucks and other heavy vehicles and provides financing for its customers' purchases. **Exhibit 6.34** presents financial statement ratios for Scania for 2005, 2006, and 2007.

EXHIBIT 6.30	Carrefour, Target, and Wal-Mart Selected Other Financial Data (Problem 28)		
Growth Rate in Sales [same store]	**2006**	**2007**	**2008**
Carrefour	1.0% [.9%]	5.2% [1.2%]	6.8% [1.8%]
Target	12.2% [5.6%]	12.9% [4.8%]	6.3% [3.0%]
Wal-Mart	9.8% [3.4%]	11.7% [2.0%]	8.6% [1.6%]
Number of Stores			
Carrefour	7,003	7,358	7,906
Target	1,397	1,488	1,591
Wal-Mart	6,141	6,779	7,262
Square Footage (000s)			
Carrefour	156,216	164,354	181,899
Target	178,260	192,064	207,945
Wal-Mart	741,897	806,988	869,341
Sales per Square Foot			
Carrefour	$582	$587	$618
Target	$288	$301	$296
Wal-Mart	$416	$428	$431
Sales per Store			
Carrefour	$12,988,587	$13,103,550	$14,224,804
Target	$36,700,787	$38,896,505	$38,636,706
Wal-Mart	$50,308,582	$50,891,282	$51,573,396
Square Feet per Store			
Carrefour	22,307	22,337	23,008
Target	127,602	129,075	130,701
Wal-Mart	120,810	119,042	119,711
Inventory per Square Foot			
Carrefour	$49	$46	$52
Target	$33	$33	$33
Wal-Mart	$43	$42	$40
Fixed Assets per Square Foot			
Carrefour	$156	$154	$163
Target	$115	$118	$125
Wal-Mart	$115	$117	$122
Sales per Employee			
Carrefour	$242,942	$248,590	$269,992
Target	$178,458	$193,443	$197,592
Wal-Mart	$201,925	$213,617	$209,818
Exchange Rate:			
U.S. Dollars per Euro	$1.245	$1.254	$1.369

The amount on the common-size income statement for Net Financing Income is the difference between interest earned on accounts receivable from customers and interest expense on amounts borrowed to finance those receivables as well as other direct cost of its financing services.

a. What are the likely reasons for the increase in the profit margin for ROA during the three-year period from 2005 to 2007?

EXHIBIT 6.31

The Gap and Limited Brands
Comparative Income Statements
(all dollar amounts in millions)
(Problem 29)

For the Year Ended January 31, 2008:	The Gap	Limited Brands
Sales	$15,763	$10,134
Interest Revenue	117	146
Net Gains from Divestments of Retail Stores	—	230
Total Revenues	$15,880	$10,510
Expenses:		
Cost of Goods Sold	$10,071	$ 6,592
Selling and Administrative	4,377	2,640
Interest	26	149
Income Taxes	539	411
Total Expenses	$15,013	$ 9,792
Net Income	$ 867	$ 718

EXHIBIT 6.32

The Gap and Limited Brands
Comparative Balance Sheets
(all dollar amounts in millions)
(Problem 29)

	The Gap		Limited Brands	
For the Year Ended January 31:	2008	2007	2008	2007
ASSETS				
Cash and Marketable Securities	$1,939	$2,644	$1,018	$ 500
Accounts Receivable	—	—	355	176
Inventories	1,575	1,796	1,251	1,770
Prepayments	572	589	295	325
Total Current Assets	$4,086	$5,029	$2,919	$2,771
Property, Plant, and Equipment (net)	3,267	3,197	1,862	1,862
Other Noncurrent Assets	485	318	2,656	2,460
Total Assets	$7,838	$8,544	$7,437	$7,093
LIABILITIES AND SHAREHOLDERS' EQUITY				
Accounts Payable	$1,006	$772	$517	$593
Current Portion of Long-Term Debt	138	325	7	8
Other Current Liabilities	1,289	1,175	850	1,108
Total Current Liabilities	$2,433	$2,272	$1,374	$1,709
Long-Term Debt	50	188	2,905	1,665
Other Noncurrent Liabilities	1,081	910	939	764
Total Liabilities	$3,564	$3,370	$5,218	$4,138
Common Stock	$ 55	$ 55	$ 262	$ 262
Additional Paid-in Capital	2,783	2,631	1,550	1,565
Retained Earnings	9,223	8,646	4,758	4,277
Accumulated Other Comprehensive Income	125	77	31	(17)
Treasury Stock	(7,912)	(6,235)	(4,382)	(3,132)
Total Shareholders' Equity	$4,274	$5,174	$2,219	$2,955
Total Liabilities and Shareholders' Equity	$7,838	$8,544	$7,437	$7,093

EXHIBIT 6.33	GlaxoSmithKline plc Financial Statement Ratios (Problem 30)		
	2005	**2006**	**2007**
Growth Rate in Sales	7.6%	8.5%	6.3%
Profitability Ratios			
Rate of Return on Assets	20.6%	21.9%	20.5%
Profit Margin for ROA Ratio	23.7%	24.8%	25.1%
Total Assets Turnover Ratio	.87	.88	.81
Rate of Return on Common Shareholders' Equity	72.5%	64.3%	55.8%
Profit Margin for ROCE Ratio	21.6%	23.2%	23.0%
Capital Structure Leverage Ratio	3.9	3.1	3.0
Accounts Receivable Turnover Ratio	5.2	5.3	5.1
Inventory Turnover Ratio	2.2	2.2	2.0
Fixed Asset Turnover Ratio	3.4	3.4	3.1
Common Size Income Statement			
Sales	100.0%	100.0%	100.0%
Investment Income	1.6	1.7	2.2
Other Revenues	1.7	1.2	1.9
Cost of Goods Sold	(22.0)	(21.6)	(23.4)
Selling and Administrative	(33.5)	(31.2)	(30.6)
Research and Development	(14.5)	(14.9)	(14.6)
Other Operating Expenses	(.2)	(.1)	(.1)
Income Taxes	(9.5)	(10.4)	(10.2)
Profit Margin for ROA	23.7%	24.8%	25.1%
Interest Expense (net of tax effect)	(1.5)	(1.1)	(1.7)
Minority Interest in Subsidiaries	(.6)	(.5)	(.4)
Profit Margin for ROCE	21.6%	23.2%	23.0%
Short-Term Liquidity Risk Ratios			
Current Ratio	1.4	1.5	1.3
Quick Ratio	1.0	1.0	.9
Cash Flow from Operations to Current Liabilities	66.1%	52.5%	70.9%
Days Accounts Receivable	70	69	72
Days Inventory	167	168	186
Days Accounts Payable	120	105	100
Long-Term Liquidity Risk Ratios			
Liabilities to Assets Ratio	72.2%	62.2%	68.0%
Long-Term Debt Ratio	19.4%	18.7%	22.8%
Debt-Equity Ratio	69.6%	49.5%	71.3%
Cash Flow from Operations to Total Liabilities Ratio	32.6%	24.7%	33.7%
Interest Coverage Ratio	15.6	22.6	14.0

b. What are the likely reasons for the decreasing cost of goods sold to sales percentage combined with the increasing inventory turnover ratio during the three-year period?

c. What are the likely reasons for the increase in the fixed asset turnover between 2006 and 2007?

d. The total assets turnover remained at .85 between 2005 and 2006, yet the accounts receivable, inventory, and fixed asset turnovers increased. What is the likely explanation for the stable total assets turnover?

e. What are the likely explanations for the increase in the two cash flow ratios between 2005 and 2006?

EXHIBIT 6.34

Scania AB
Financial Statement Ratios
(Problem 31)

	2005	2006	2007
Growth Rate in Sales	11.5%	11.7%	19.4%
Profitability Ratios			
Rate of Return on Assets	7.1%	7.9%	10.1%
Profit Margin for ROA	8.4%	9.3%	10.7%
Total Assets Turnover Ratio	.85	.85	.94
Rate of Return on Common Shareholders' Equity	20.7%	23.8%	33.6%
Profit Margin for ROCE	7.4%	8.4%	10.1%
Capital Structure Leverage Ratio	3.3	3.3	3.5
Accounts Receivable Turnover Ratio	1.97	2.03	2.16
Inventory Turnover Ratio	4.92	5.21	5.79
Fixed Asset Turnover Ratio	2.51	2.65	3.02
Common Size Income Statement			
Sales	100.0%	100.0%	100.0%
Investment Income	1.2	1.0	0.5
Net Financing Income	1.6	1.4	1.3
Cost of Goods Sold	(75.5)	(73.9)	(73.2)
Selling and Administrative	(11.3)	(10.9)	(9.8)
Research and Development	(3.9)	(4.3)	(4.0)
Income Taxes	(3.7)	(4.1)	(4.2)
Profit Margin for ROA	8.4%	9.3%	10.7%
Interest Expense (net of tax effect)	(1.0)	(0.9)	(0.6)
Profit Margin for ROCE	7.4%	8.4%	10.1%
Short-Term Liquidity Risk Ratios			
Current Ratio	1.2	1.2	1.0
Quick Ratio	0.8	0.9	0.7
Cash Flow from Operations to Current Liabilities	35.1%	37.5%	37.7%
Days Accounts Receivable	186	179	169
Days Inventory	74	70	63
Days Accounts Payable	34	38	38
Long-Term Liquidity Risk Ratios			
Liabilities to Assets Ratios	69.7%	70.3%	72.9%
Long-Term Debt Ratio	24.7%	20.3%	21.7%
Debt-Equity Ratio	81.4%	68.6%	80.1%
Cash Flow from Operations to Total Liabilities Ratio	15.5%	19.1%	20.7%
Interest Coverage Ratio	8.8	11.0	18.2

f. What are the likely reasons for the decrease in the current and quick ratios between 2006 and 2007?

g. Did financial leverage work to the advantage of the common shareholders in each year? Explain.

32. **Detective analysis—identify company.** Effective financial statement analysis requires an understanding of a firm's economic characteristics. The relations among various financial statement items provide evidence of many of these economic characteristics. **Exhibit 6.35** presents common-size condensed balance sheets and income statements for 12 firms in different industries. These common-size balance sheets and income statements express various items as a percentage of operating revenues (that is, the statement divides all

EXHIBIT 6.35 Data for Ratio Detective Exercise (Problem 32)

	1	2	3	4	5	6	7	8	9	10	11	12
Balance Sheet at End of Year												
Cash and Marketable Securities	4.7%	16.4%	8.9%	8.4%	16.7%	7.4%	16.1%	21.3%	72.0%	8.3%	1.4%	338.8%
Receivables	8.5	15.9	16.5	27.6	35.9	17.7	81.1	29.6	24.0	10.5	5.9	533.4
Inventories	9.9	2.8	9.9	5.8	6.4	25.7	—	1.3	20.0	2.9	—	15.3
Property, Plant, and Equipment Cost	40.8	20.9	59.0	69.6	88.3	130.9	23.0	110.3	83.3	278.9	535.4	15.3
Accumulated Depreciation	(15.0)	(9.1)	(33.2)	(17.8)	(50.5)	(67.7)	(11.8)	(35.5)	(35.2)	(112.5)	(284.9)	(12.9)
Net	25.8	11.8	25.8	51.8	37.8	63.2	11.2	74.8	48.1	166.4	250.5	2.4
Intercorporate Investments	4.0	14.3	3.0	0.6	18.8	10.3	1.3	10.7	7.7	22.4	16.9	41.9
Other Assets	15.0	10.9	11.7	3.6	7.1	1.9	63.5	42.1	69.1	56.3	5.4	61.9
Total Assets	67.9%	72.1%	75.8%	97.8%	122.7%	126.2%	173.2%	179.8%	240.9%	266.8%	280.1%	978.4%
Current Liabilities	37.3%	25.5%	29.7%	26.4%	42.7%	34.5%	106.0%	65.1%	48.3%	42.6%	51.3%	820.8%
Long-Term Debt	12.0	6.1	6.6	9.1	22.2	23.3	22.7	49.6	56.4	95.8	167.7	76.9
Other Noncurrent Liabilities	2.1	1.8	5.9	2.3	4.2	17.2	10.6	10.9	24.5	27.8	24.7	42.2
Shareholders' Equity	16.5	38.7	33.6	60.0	53.6	51.2	33.9	54.2	111.7	100.6	36.4	38.5
Total Equities	67.9%	72.1%	75.8%	97.8%	122.7%	126.2%	173.2%	179.8%	240.9%	266.8%	280.1%	978.4%
Income Statement for Year												
Operating Revenues	100.0%	100.0%	100.0%	100.0%	100.0%	100.0%	100.0%	100.0%	100.0%	100.0%	100.0%	100.0%
Other Revenues	1.1%	2.7%	1.0%	0.2%	0.7%	2.3%	1.9%	0.3%	13.8%	0.7%	—	—
Cost of Goods Sold (excluding depreciation) or Operating Expenses	87.8	45.2	44.5	64.6	68.0	81.0	55.3	75.5	27.2	45.0	57.3	32.6
Depreciation and Amortization	3.0	4.9	4.1	3.2	5.9	5.3	2.0	7.1	9.9	23.9	19.9	—
Selling and Administrative	6.3	24.8	38.9	24.3	16.4	13.6	27.8	8.1	40.0	15.2	7.3	22.5
Interest	1.4	0.4	2.0	1.3	0.4	3.5	1.9	3.0	5.2	8.6	8.6	35.4
Research and Development	—	9.8	1.3	—	3.7	—	—	—	13.8	—	—	—
Income Taxes	1.3	5.8	3.1	2.4	2.5	0.3	5.9	3.7	4.4	3.9	2.8	2.2
All Other Items (net)	(0.8)	—	0.8	0.3	0.6	(2.1)	0.7	(1.1)	—	0.6	—	1.7
Total Expenses	99.0%	90.9%	94.7%	96.1%	97.5%	101.6%	93.7%	95.8%	100.5%	97.2%	95.9%	94.4%
Net Income	2.1%	11.8%	6.3%	4.1%	3.2%	0.7%	8.2%	4.5%	13.3%	3.5%	4.1%	5.6%

amounts by operating revenues for the year). A dash for a particular financial statement item does not necessarily mean that the amount is zero. It merely indicates that the amount is not sufficiently large for the firm to disclose it. The 12 companies, the country of their headquarters, and a brief description of their activities are as follows.

(1) Accor (France): World's largest hotel group, operating hotels under the names of Sofitel, Novotel, Motel 6, and others. Accor has grown in recent years by acquiring established hotel chains.

(2) Arbed-Acier (Luxembourg): Offers flat-rolled steel products, primarily to the European automobile industry.

(3) Carrefour (France): Operates grocery supermarkets and hypermarkets in Europe, Latin America, and Asia.

(4) Deutsche Telekon (Germany): Europe's largest provider of wired and wireless telecommunication services. The telecommunications industry has experienced increased deregulation in recent years.

(5) Fortis (Netherlands): Offers both insurance and banking services. Operating revenues include insurance premiums received, investment income, and interest revenue on loans. Operating expenses include amounts actually paid or amounts it expects to pay in the future on insurance coverage outstanding during the year.

(6) Interpublic Group (U.S.): Creates advertising copy for clients. Purchases advertising time and space from various media and sells it to clients. Operating revenues represent the commission or fee earned by Interpublic for advertising copy created and media time and space sold. Operating expenses include compensation paid to employees. Interpublic acquired other marketing services firms in recent years.

(7) Marks & Spencer (U.K.): Operates department stores in England and other retail stores in Europe and the United States. It offers its own credit card for customers' purchases.

(8) Nestlé (Switzerland): World's largest food processor, offering prepared foods, coffees, milk-based products, and mineral waters.

(9) Roche Holding (Switzerland): Creates, manufactures, and distributes a wide variety of prescription drugs.

(10) Sun Microsystems (U.S.): Designs, manufactures, and sells engineering workstations and servers used to maintain integrated computer networks. Sun outsources the manufacture of many of its computer components.

(11) Tokyo Electric Power (Japan): Provides electric power services, primarily to the Tokyo community. It maintains almost a monopoly position in its service area.

(12) Toyota Motor (Japan): Manufactures automobiles and offers financing services to its customers.

Use whatever clues you can to match the companies in **Exhibit 6.35** with the companies and industries listed above.

33. **Preparing pro forma financial statements** (requires **Appendix 6.1**). **Problem 27** presents financial statements for Target Corporation for its fiscal years ending January 31, 2006, 2007, and 2008, as well as financial statement ratios.

    a. Prepare a set of pro forma financial statements for Target Corporation for fiscal years 2009 through 2013 using the following assumptions:

INCOME STATEMENT

1. Sales grew 12.2% in 2006 and 12.9% in 2007, primarily as a result of increases in the number of new stores and increases in sales of stores open more than one year. Sales grew only 6.3% in 2008 because of recession conditions. Although Target Corporation will continue to increase the number of stores, economic conditions and competition will likely constrain increases in sales. Thus, assume that sales will grow 9% each year between 2009 and 2013.

2. Other revenues, representing interest on outstanding accounts receivable, have been approximately 3% of sales during the last three years. Assume that other revenues will continue at this historical rate.

3. The cost of goods sold to sales percentage increased slightly from 66.1% in 2006 to 68.2% in 2008. Assume that the cost of goods sold to sales percentage will be 68.1% for 2009 to 2013.

4. The selling and administrative expense percentage has increased slightly from 26.1% of sales in 2006 to 26.2% of sales in 2008. Target will realize economies of scale as its growth rate in sales increases to 9% annually. Assume that the selling and administrative expense to sales percentage will be 26.0% for 2009 to 2013.

5. Target Corporation has borrowed using long-term debt to construct new stores. The average interest rate on interest-bearing debt was approximately 4.4% during 2008. Assume this interest rate for all borrowing outstanding (long-term debt, and current portion of long-term debt) for Target Corporation will be 5% for 2009 to 2013. Compute interest expense on the average amount of interest-bearing debt outstanding each year.

6. Target Corporation's average income tax rate as a percentage of income before income taxes has varied around 38% during the last three years. Assume an income tax rate of 38% of income before income taxes for 2009 to 2013.

7. Target Corporation's dividends increased at an average annual rate of 17.9% between 2006 and 2008. Assume that dividends will grow 16% each year between 2009 and 2013.

BALANCE SHEET

8. Cash will be the amount necessary to equate total assets with total liabilities plus shareholders' equity.

9. Accounts receivable will increase at the growth rate in sales.

10. Inventory will increase at the growth rate in sales.

11. Prepayments relate to ongoing operating costs, such as rent and insurance. Assume that prepayments will grow at the growth rate in sales.

12. Property, plant, and equipment grew 12.4% annually during the most recent three years. The construction of new stores will require additional investments in property, plant, and equipment, but not at the growth rate experienced in recent years. Assume that property, plant, and equipment will grow 10% each year between 2009 and 2013.

13. Other assets changed by only a small amount during the last three years. Assume that other assets will remain the same amount for 2009 to 2013 as the amount at the end of 2008.

14. The accounts payable turnover ratio increased from 5.9 in 2006 to 6.4 during 2008. Assume that Target Corporation will increase its accounts payable turnover to 6.5 times per year for 2009 to 2013.

15. The notes to Target Corporation's financial statements indicate that current maturities of long-term debt on January 31 of each year are as follows: 2008, $1,964 (amount already appears on the January 31, 2008, balance sheet); 2009, $1,951; 2010, $1,251; 2011, $2,236; 2012, $107; 2013, $2,251.

16. Other current liabilities relate to ongoing operating activities and are expected to grow at the growth rate in sales.

17. Target Corporation uses long-term debt to finance acquisitions of property, plant, and equipment. Assume that long-term debt will decrease by the amount of long-term debt reclassified as a current liability each year and then the remaining amount will increase at the growth rate in property, plant, and equipment. For example, the January 31, 2008, balance sheet of Target Corporation shows the current portion of long-term debt to be $1,964. Target Corporation will repay this amount during 2009. During 2009, Target will reclassify $1,951 from long-term debt to current portion of long-term debt (see item 15 above). This will leave a preliminary balance in long-term debt of $14,988 (= $16,939 − $1,951). Target Corporation will increase this amount of long-term debt by the 10% growth rate in property, plant, and equipment. The projected amount for long-term debt on the January 31, 2009, balance sheet is $16,487 (= $14,988 × 1.1).

18. Other noncurrent liabilities include an amount related to retirement benefits and taxes due after more than one year. Assume that other noncurrent liabilities will increase at the growth rate in sales.

19. Assume that common stock and additional paid-in capital will not change.

20. Assume that accumulated other comprehensive income will grow at the growth rate in sales.

STATEMENT OF CASH FLOWS

21. Assume that depreciation expense will increase at the growth rate in property, plant, and equipment.
22. Assume that changes in other noncurrent liabilities and in accumulated other comprehensive income on the balance sheet are operating activities.
23. Assume that the amount for Other Financing Transactions is zero for 2009 to 2013.

    b. Describe actions that Target might take to deal with the shortage of cash projected in part **a**.

    c. What are the likely reasons for the projected changes in the rate of return on common shareholders' equity?

PART 3

FACMU**13**

Measuring and Reporting
Assets and Equities Using
U.S. GAAP and IFRS

Revenue Recognition, Receivables, and Advances from Customers

1. Understand and apply the criteria for recognizing revenue, including the timing of the recognition and measurement of revenue.

2. Understand the relation between revenues (an income statement account) and both accounts receivable (an asset) and advances from customers (a liability).

3. Understand the measurement of accounts receivable, including the allowance for uncollectible accounts and the allowance for sales returns.

REVIEW AND APPLICATION OF INCOME RECOGNITION PRINCIPLES

Chapter 4 describes the accrual basis of accounting, including income recognition. Under accrual accounting, revenue increases income and the related expenses decrease income. Authoritative guidance contains specific criteria for recognizing both revenue and expenses. This chapter reviews and expands the criteria for recognizing and measuring revenues that **Chapter 4** introduces. These criteria in U.S. GAAP and IFRS are broadly similar. **Appendix 7.1** describes certain differences between U.S. GAAP and IFRS guidance for **revenue recognition**. We begin with a general description of the revenue recognition criteria and then present several examples that illustrate the timing and measurement of revenue recognition in order to explore issues in applying the criteria.

Revenue Recognition Both U.S. GAAP and IFRS provide conditions that arrangements with customers must meet in order for firms to recognize revenue. Although the specifics of these conditions differ (as **Appendix 7.1** discusses), we can express the two general conceptual criteria for revenue recognition as follows:

1. The seller must have substantially performed its obligations to the customer (for example, by transferring ownership of goods to the customer).[1]

2. The seller must have obtained an asset from the customer that it can reliably measure. If the asset is not cash, the seller must be reasonably certain of converting it into cash.

Expense Recognition   In **expense recognition**, the firm recognizes expenses when it consumes assets. If an event or transaction leads to the recognition of revenue, firms match the consumption of any assets (the expense), in time, with the revenue recognized. For example, the seller recognizes cost of goods sold when it recognizes the related revenue from selling the goods.

APPLICATION OF INCOME RECOGNITION PRINCIPLES

Example 1   Costco Wholesale Corporation ("Costco") operates discount retail stores. To shop in a Costco store, customers must pay a nonrefundable, annual membership fee in advance, using either cash or an American Express card. A customer purchases an annual membership from Costco for $50, a 20-pack of paper towels for $12.85, and four new tires for $440. The tire purchase includes mounting and aligning by a Costco tire technician at the time of initial installation and alignment and tire rotation services for three years afterward. The customer pays with an American Express card.[2]

When should Costco recognize the $50 membership fee as revenue?   Costco can reliably measure the revenue from sales of membership fees. However, Costco has an obligation to stand ready to provide shopping services at Costco stores. As a result, Costco should recognize 1/12th of the membership fee, or $4.17, each month during the annual membership period.

When should Costco recognize revenue from selling the paper towels?   Because Costco has no further obligations related to the customer's purchase of the paper towels, it will recognize $12.85 in revenue at the time of sale.

When should Costco recognize revenue from selling the tires plus mounting, alignment, and rotation services?   At the time of initial installation, Costco performs its obligation to provide both tires and initial mounting and alignment services. Costco should recognize revenue for the portion of the $440 selling price applicable to the sale of tires and installation services at the time of installation. Costco should delay recognition of revenue for the portion of the $440 selling price applicable to the subsequent alignment and rotation services until it performs the required services.

Example 2   Pol Roget Vineyards processes grapes into champagne, which it bottles, corks, and places on shelves in underground caverns to age for several years. During the aging process, the winemakers hand-turn the bottles a quarter rotation every few months; also, at fixed intervals, they release yeast gases to preclude unwanted fermentation. Assume that Pol Roget contracts to sell a quantity of champagne to a customer for €15 million. Under the terms of the contract, Pol Roget will store the champagne in its caverns and perform all necessary functions associated with the aging process (for example, turning the bottles and releasing yeast gases). The selling price includes the costs of producing the champagne and providing services during the aging process. The customer pays Pol Roget €7.5 million at the beginning of the aging and storage process, and agrees to pay the remainder upon delivery of the champagne.

---

[1]As discussed in **Appendix 7.1**, conceptual guidance in U.S. GAAP refers to the selling entity having earned the revenues (that is, having completed the earnings process). IFRS refers to transferring the risks and rewards of ownership to customers (in the case of revenues involving goods) and to having rendered services (in the case of revenues involving services). In addition, both U.S. GAAP and IFRS indicate that the costs of any obligations that the seller has not performed at the time it recognizes revenue must be measurable with reasonable reliability.

[2]When the customer pays with a credit card, the retailer receives payment from the credit card issuer promptly, typically within a few days. From the retailer's perspective, this is like a cash sale. The credit card issuer bears the risk of nonpayment by the customer, who compensates the issuer by paying finance charges and other fees.

When should Pol Roget recognize revenue from selling the champagne? Pol Roget should delay revenue recognition until it delivers the champagne to the customer. The physical production of the champagne includes the aging process, so Pol Roget has not performed its obligations until the customer takes possession of the champagne. In addition, Pol Roget cannot reliably measure the amount of revenue because, for example, the quality of the champagne might turn out to be poor, in which case the customer might return the champagne (or never take delivery) and refuse to pay the remaining €7.5 million.

Example 3 Microsoft Corporation sells Windows XP to customers, who receive the software and have access to postdelivery telephone support and the right to receive certain upgrades and enhancements if and when Microsoft develops them. Microsoft sells Windows XP for approximately $50; customers pay cash or with a credit card.

When should Microsoft recognize revenue from selling Windows XP? Microsoft can reliably measure the total amount of revenue because customers pay cash when they receive the software, or Microsoft receives cash soon thereafter from the credit card company. Microsoft separates the $50 total revenues into the portion that represents obligations it has performed (delivery of the software) and future obligations (providing telephone service and possible upgrades and enhancements). It recognizes revenue from sale of the software at the time of delivery; it recognizes revenue associated with future obligations over the product's life cycle. We revisit this example later in this chapter.

Example 4 Bombardier Inc., incorporated in Canada, manufactures aircraft and trains. In this industry, the time to manufacture products usually exceeds one year. Assume that Bombardier recently signed a €2 billion contract to provide 25 new high-speed trains to a customer in the European Union. The customer has paid a deposit of €250 million and will pay the remainder in equal installments over the next four years.

When should Bombardier recognize the revenue from this contract? At the time Bombardier signs the contract and receives €250 million cash from the customer, it has not performed any obligations, so it may not recognize revenue. Although application of the first revenue recognition condition might seem to imply that Bombardier should recognize the entire €2 billion as revenue when it delivers the trains, special revenue recognition policies apply to long-term contracts such as this one. If Bombardier can reliably estimate both the revenue from the contract and the costs to complete the contract, it (and other firms selling under multi-year contracts) will recognize revenue (as well as the costs associated with delivering on the contract) over the contract life. We discuss the revenue recognition guidance for long-term contracts like the arrangement in this example later in this chapter.

Example 5 Mitchells & Butlers Plc. is a leading operator of pubs and pub restaurants in the United Kingdom. It operates and franchises about 40 wine restaurants under the name All Bar One, primarily in London. Suppose that in contracting with a franchisee of an All Bar One wine restaurant, Mitchells & Butlers agrees to provide services, including site selection, décor design, marketing, advertising, and recruiting; and the franchisee agrees to pay Mitchells & Butlers £30,000. It is common in the industry to permit the franchisee to pay in equal installments over several years.

When should Mitchells & Butlers recognize revenue from the franchisee contract? At the time it signs the contract with the franchisee, Mitchells & Butlers will likely not have performed all of the promised services. Even if it has done so, the amount of cash that Mitchells & Butlers will collect may not be reliably measurable (because of uncertainty that the franchisee will pay the entire £30,000). Application of the second revenue recognition criterion, which refers to reliable measurement of the asset received by the seller, might delay revenue recognition until the seller can resolve uncertainty about the amount it will collect, regardless of whether the seller has performed all its obligations.

These examples illustrate several features of sales transactions that raise variants of two issues about the timing and measurement of revenues: whether the seller has performed, or substantially completed, all obligations, and whether the seller has received a reliably measurable asset. In many arrangements, the former issue presents the larger problem. We list several issues here that this chapter later discusses in more detail:

- Accounting for customers' promises to pay cash later (accounts receivable).
- Accounting for arrangements where collectibility is uncertain (revenue recognized as cash is received).

- Accounting for customers' cash payments to the seller, before the seller delivers goods and services (advances from customers).
- Accounting for customers' rights to return goods (sales returns).
- Accounting for contracts that contain several components (arrangements with multiple deliverables).
- Accounting for long-term contracts (percentage-of-completion method).

Accrual accounting separates the recognition of revenue from the receipt of cash. Revenue recognition criteria point to the seller's:

1. Performing its obligations to the customer and
2. Receiving assets that are, or can be converted to, cash.

As a result of applying revenue recognition criteria, the seller may recognize revenue before, or after, or at the point of cash collection. A customer may exchange a promise of future payment for goods and services; the seller recognizes such promises as accounts receivable, classified as a current asset on the seller's balance sheet. (The same amount is an account payable on the buyer's balance sheet.) The fact that some customers will not pay their obligations means that the balance sheet carrying value of Accounts Receivable should show, not the gross amount owed, but that amount less an estimate of the portion of accounts receivable that the seller will not collect. Later, this chapter describes the accounting procedures, called the allowance method, for these estimated uncollectible amounts.

Sometimes the customer pays the seller cash before receiving the goods or services; examples include the €7.5 million cash payment in **Example 2** and the €250 million cash payment in **Example 4**. The seller has increased both its assets (specifically its cash) and its obligations (it has not performed its obligations and therefore cannot recognize revenue). The seller recognizes a liability, advances from customers, for products and services in the amount of cash received.[3] When the seller has performed its obligations, it will recognize revenue and reduce its liability.

Some arrangements permit the customer to return goods, as in the case of the tires in **Example 1**. Some transactions create so much uncertainty that the seller delays revenue recognition until the returns period has expired. In other transactions the seller recognizes revenue at the time of the sale and accounts for expected **sales returns** at that time.[4] Arrangements that permit the customer to return goods raise issues of both performance (has the seller performed all its obligations?) and asset measurement.

Customers increasingly demand, and firms increasingly sell, bundles of products and services in a **multiple deliverable contract**. For example, Microsoft's sale of Windows XP (**Example 3**) includes a bundle: the software itself, telephone servicing, and possible upgrades and enhancements. In some cases, such as Microsoft's sale of Windows XP, the seller separates the contract into components or elements for accounting purposes, analyzing each component separately for revenue recognition.[5] In these cases, the seller allocates the total contract revenue among the contract components and decides when it has performed each component. In practice, the seller assigns the amount of revenue to each component based on relative fair values, meaning in this case the price for which the seller would separately sell an individual deliverable component. The allocated revenue for a component is the total contract price

---

[3]The seller performs most of these arrangements within a year, so Advances from Customers is often a current liability. If the arrangement extends beyond one year, the seller apportions the cash advance from the customer into the portion it will discharge over the next year (current liability) and the portion it will discharge after one year (noncurrent liability).

[4]The uncertainty is not whether the seller will collect cash; it is whether the seller has performed its obligations. IFRS does not contain explicit guidance for the seller to decide whether it should delay revenue recognition until the returns period has ended. U.S. GAAP provides six conditions, all of which the transaction must meet for the seller to recognize revenue at the time of sale if the customer has a right of return (Financial Accounting Standards Board, *Statement of Financial Accounting Standards No. 48*, "Revenue Recognition When Right of Return Exists," 1981) (**Codification Topic 605**).

[5]U.S. GAAP provides criteria for the seller to use in deciding when it must separate a multiple deliverable contract into its elements for accounting purposes (*Emerging Issues Task Force Issue No. 00-21*, "Revenue Arrangements with Multiple Deliverables," 2003) (**Codification Topic 605**). (In the United States, separate rules apply to software.) IFRS refers to the need, in certain circumstances, to apply revenue recognition criteria to the separately identifiable components of a single transaction but does not provide criteria for making this separation. The mechanics of separating a contract into multiple elements are beyond the scope of this textbook.

times the ratio of the fair value of that component to the sum of the fair values of all of the bundled components.

Special revenue-recognition guidance applies to long-term contracts such as the Bombardier train contract (**Example 4**). When the seller can reliably estimate both the costs of such contracts and the amounts it will collect, both U.S. GAAP and IFRS require use of the **percentage-of-completion method** to recognize the revenue and costs associated with the contract. One implementation of this method measures revenue for a period as a function of the cost incurred that period, relative to the total estimated contract cost. The percentage of the contract completed this period equals the percentage of total cost incurred this period and that percentage determines the revenue recognized. To illustrate, if in 2009 Bombardier incurred 20% of the total cost of supplying the 25 trains, it would recognize as 2009 revenue 20% of the total contract price, or €400 million (= 20% × €2 billion). Bombardier would also recognize as 2009 expense 20% of total costs (the cost incurred in 2009). Under this approach, Bombardier does not recognize income as it delivers the trains to the customer, but instead recognizes income as it incurs costs, so long as the cost incurrences meet budgeted amounts and completion schedules.

PROBLEM 7.1 for Self-Study

> **Revenue recognition at time of sale, or after sale, or before sale.** Assume Sony Corporation (the seller) ships 5,000 42-inch LCD flat-screen televisions to Best Buy, a U.S.-based electronics retailer (the buyer). For each of the following independent contractual arrangements, apply the two general revenue recognition criteria specified by U.S. GAAP and IFRS to decide when Sony Corporation should recognize revenue.
>
> **a.** The contract between Sony and Best Buy requires that Best Buy pay Sony $2,000 for each television within 30 days of receiving the televisions. Best Buy may return televisions damaged in transit, or found to be defective, to Sony for full refund at any time.
>
> **b.** The contract between Sony and Best Buy requires that Best Buy pay Sony $2,000 per television within 30 days after receiving the televisions. The contract allows Best Buy to return to Sony any of the televisions, for any reason, within six months of the receipt of the televisions.
>
> **c.** The contract between Sony and Best Buy requires that Best Buy sell the televisions, acting on behalf of Sony. Best Buy is responsible for storing and insuring the televisions, marketing them, and setting the selling price, within an agreed upon range of selling prices. The expected selling price is $3,400. In return for performing these services, Sony pays Best Buy $400 per television. At any time it chooses, Best Buy will return unsold televisions to Sony.

INCOME RECOGNITION AT THE TIME OF SALE

Many firms' transactions satisfy the criteria for revenue recognition at the time of sale (that is, at the time of delivery of goods and services). These firms manufacture (or purchase) a product or create a service, identify a customer, deliver the product or service to the customer, and receive cash or some other asset at the time of delivery. To justify recognizing revenue at the time of sale, these firms must account for the effects of certain events that occur *after* the time of sale, including customers not paying the amounts they owe, customers returning unsatisfactory products, and customers receiving promised warranty services. The accounting issues involve measurement of accounts receivable, estimated returns, and estimated warranty costs. We consider the first two accounting issues in this chapter and defer the discussion of the accounting for warranties to **Chapter 8**.

ACCOUNTS RECEIVABLE

Accounts receivable (or **trade receivables**) is the amount owed to a seller by customers who have purchased goods and services on credit. Typically, the seller expects to collect cash within a reasonably short time, such as 30 days, so an account receivable is usually a current asset. Receivables with terms greater than one year are noncurrent assets.

Not all customers ultimately pay the amounts owed. An account receivable that the seller never collects is an **uncollectible account**. A firm does not want to sell products and services to customers who do not pay, but the cost of identifying such customers (assuming this is possible) exceeds the benefits of doing so. Consider, for example, what a retailer would need to do to ensure that *every* credit customer will pay. It would need to gather information about the customer's credit worthiness, for example, a credit history. It would use this information to assess, at the time of sale, the customer's likely ability and willingness to pay the amount owed. This assessment would take time and, if the retailer wanted to avoid bad debts completely, it would most likely deny credit to many customers who would pay their bills, even though they could not pass a stringent credit check designed to eliminate *every* uncollectible credit sale. Those customers will take their business elsewhere, and the retailer will lose sales. As long as the amount collected from credit sales to a given group of customers exceeds the cost of goods sold and the other costs of serving that group of customers, including the costs of uncollectible accounts, the retailer will be better off selling to that group rather than losing the sales.

Most firms find it optimal to bear the cost of some uncollectible receivables. This does not suggest, of course, that a firm should grant credit indiscriminately or not engage in collection efforts. A cost-benefit analysis of credit policy should dictate a strategy that results in uncollectible accounts of an amount that is reasonably predictable before the firm makes any sales.

ALLOWANCE METHOD FOR UNCOLLECTIBLE ACCOUNTS

The two accounting issues for accounts receivable are (1) measurement of the amount on the balance sheet and (2) timing of recognition of the reduction in income caused by the uncollectibility of some accounts. With regard to measurement, both U.S. GAAP and IFRS require that sellers report accounts receivable *net* of the estimated uncollectible amount; that is, at the amount the firm expects to collect from customers, which will be less than the amount that all customers have agreed to pay. With regard to timing, both U.S. GAAP and IFRS require that a seller recognize an expense for estimated uncollectible accounts receivable in the same period when it recognizes the related revenue. The following example illustrates these accounting requirements.

Example 6 Turf Maintenance Company started a lawn services business on January 1, 2008. It sends invoices to its customers for lawn maintenance services at the end of each month, and expects the customer to pay within 30 days. During 2008, Turf Maintenance billed its customers a total of $2,000,000 for services rendered during the year. It made journal entries at the end of each month debiting Accounts Receivable at the gross amount billed and crediting Sales Revenue. The aggregate effect of these entries during 2008 is as follows:

Accounts Receivable, Gross	2,000,000	
Sales Revenue		2,000,000

Assets	=	Liabilities	+	Shareholders' Equity	(Class.)
+2,000,000				+2,000,000	IncSt → RE

To recognize credit sales for 2008.

At the end of 30 days, the firm has not collected all receivables. Turf Maintenance takes steps to collect, such as sending another bill and calling the customer. Both actions will yield some payments from customers, but some customer accounts will continue to remain uncollected. As a business policy, Turf Maintenance treats accounts not collected in cash within six months of billing as uncollectible.

Recognizing revenue before the seller collects cash requires estimating the amount of uncollectible accounts with reasonable accuracy.[6] Both U.S. GAAP and IFRS require the

---

[6]The second criterion for revenue recognition states that the firm must have received cash or *some other asset that it can measure with reasonable reliability*. If the firm has received a promise of payment but cannot measure this promise with reasonable reliability, then the arrangement fails the second criterion, and neither U.S. GAAP nor IFRS would permit revenue to be recognized.

allowance method for uncollectible accounts, which involves *estimating* the amount of uncollectible accounts receivable associated with each accounting period's credit sales. The firm recognizes this estimated amount as an expense in the period of the sale, thereby matching expenses with associated revenue. The credit is to a contra-asset account, **Allowance for Uncollectibles**, that reduces *total* accounts receivable (**Accounts Receivable, Gross**) to the amount of cash the firm expects to collect from customers (**Accounts Receivable, Net**). We next illustrate the accounting procedures of the allowance method, followed by a discussion of how management estimates uncollectible accounts.

Assume that Turf Maintenance estimates that it will not collect 2% of total credit sales in a given month. At the end of each month, it makes an adjusting entry debiting Bad Debt Expense and crediting Allowance for Uncollectibles. The aggregate effect of these entries during 2008 is as follows:[7]

Bad Debt Expense.	40,000	
Allowance for Uncollectibles		40,000

Assets	=	Liabilities	+	Shareholders' Equity	(Class.)
−40,000				−40,000	IncSt → RE

To provide for estimated uncollectible accounts relating to 2008 credit sales ($40,000 = 2% × $2,000,000).

Bad Debt Expense is also called the **Provision for Bad Debts** and the **Provision for Uncollectible Accounts**. *Provision* in this context refers to an expense in U.S. GAAP, not a liability; recall from **Chapter 3** that *provision* in IFRS refers to a liability whose timing or amount, or both, are uncertain. Recognizing bad debt expense of $40,000 matches the amount the firm does not expect to collect in cash from 2008 credit sales with the 2008 credit sales. The firm making the entry is not writing off specific customers' accounts as uncollectible; rather, the firm is measuring accounts receivable at the amount it expects to collect. It does not yet know which accounts it will need to write off because they have not yet proved to be uncollectible.

Chapter 2 introduces the contra-asset account, which appears among the assets on a firm's balance sheet as a subtraction. It typically has a credit balance which, netted against the debit balance in the asset account, reduces asset totals. A credit to the Allowance for Uncollectibles contra account increases the amount subtracted from Accounts Receivable, Gross, reducing the net debit balance in Accounts Receivable, Net.[8]

Accounts Receivable, Gross, is a control account. A **control account** (sometimes called a **controlling account**) aggregates into a single account a group of like accounts.[9] The firm keeps a separate account for each customer, including that customer's name. The sum of the balances in the individual customers' accounts is the balance in the control account, Accounts Receivable, Gross. When the firm receives cash from a customer, it debits Cash and credits the account receivable of that specific customer. When the firm sums the balances in the individual customers' accounts, it derives the balance in the control account, Accounts Receivable, Gross. If Turf Maintenance's customers remitted $1,900,000 in cash during 2008, it would make the following journal entries with the following aggregated amounts:

Cash.	1,900,000	
Accounts Receivable, Gross—specific accounts		1,900,000

(continued)

---

[7]Practice differs as to whether the debit in this journal entry is to an expense account or to a revenue contra account. Some firms debit Bad Debt Expense and include its amount in Selling, General, and Administrative Expenses based on the view that credit sales necessarily involve a certain amount of bad debts. Recording the debit in a revenue contra account measures net sales at the amount of cash the firm expects to collect. Although we find the arguments for using a revenue contra account persuasive, we debit Bad Debt Expense in this book because that is the more common practice.

[8]The balance in the Accounts Receivable, Net, account results from subtracting the credit balance in the Allowance for Uncollectibles contra account from the Accounts Receivable, Gross, account, which measures the amount customers owe. Conventional terminology often drops the word *Gross* from this account title. Account Receivable, Net, measures the amount the firm expects to collect.

[9]Another example of a control account is Property, Plant, and Equipment, because most firms keep separate accounts for each group of machines or for each machine and for each building. Bonds Payable is a control account aggregating information in separate accounts about different bond issues.

Assets	=	Liabilities	+	Shareholders' Equity	(Class.)
+1,900,000					
−1,900,000					

To recognize cash remittances in 2008 on credit sales in 2008.

After this entry, Accounts Receivable, Gross, reflects the individual amounts owed by customers who have not yet paid, a total of $100,000 (= $2,000,000 − $1,900,000). Accounts Receivable, Net, is $60,000 (= $100,000 balance in Accounts Receivable, Gross − $40,000 balance in Allowance for Uncollectibles).

Turf Maintenance does not know, at the time it provides services and sends invoices, which customers will not pay. If it did, it would not sell to them on credit. The firm must, however, account for the estimated expense associated with its *portfolio* of individual accounts receivable. To do this, the firm creates a separate account, Allowance for Uncollectibles, that is contra to Accounts Receivable, Gross. The gross amount less the allowance yields Accounts Receivable, Net, which reflects the amount of cash the firm expects to collect.[10]

When a firm decides that a particular customer account is uncollectible, it removes that account by debiting the Allowance for Uncollectibles and crediting Accounts Receivable, Gross. This process is called **writing off** the account. Turf Maintenance deems uncollectible any customer account not paid after six months. This means that every accounting period, Turf Maintenance ascertains which accounts remained uncollected for six months, and treats these customer accounts as uncollectible by writing them off. If, during 2008, Turf Maintenance identified accounts of specific customers totaling $15,000 with unpaid balances for six months and wrote them off, the journal entry would be as follows:

Allowance for Uncollectibles 15,000

     Accounts Receivable—specific accounts   15,000

Assets	=	Liabilities	+	Shareholders' Equity	(Class.)
+15,000					
−15,000					

To write off customers' accounts totaling $15,000 during 2008.

The write-off of specific customers' accounts using the allowance method has no effect on the income statement. The income effect occurs in the period of sale, when the firm records Bad Debt Expense. The write-off of specific customers' accounts also has no effect on Accounts Receivable, Net, because the write-off amount decreases Accounts Receivable, Gross, and its contra account, the Allowance for Uncollectibles, by exactly the same amount. To see this, note that after the write-off of uncollectible customers' accounts, the balance in Accounts Receivable, Gross, declined by $15,000, as did the balance in the Allowance for Uncollectibles.

The allowance method results in reporting Accounts Receivable, Net, on the balance sheet at the amount the firm expects to collect in cash in future periods. At the end of 2008, Turf Maintenance expects to collect $60,000, measured as follows:

Accounts Receivable, Gross ($2,000,000 − $1,900,000 − $15,000).................	$ 85,000
Less Allowance for Uncollectibles ($40,000 − $15,000).........................	(25,000)
Accounts Receivable, Net	$ 60,000

PROCEDURAL NOTE ON THE ALLOWANCE METHOD

Firms typically write off specific customers' accounts *during* the reporting period as they identify specific customers whose accounts have become uncollectible, and recognize bad debt expense as an adjusting entry at the end of the period. As a result, before it makes this adjusting entry, the firm may have a debit balance in the Allowance for Uncollectibles. After

---

[10]U.S. GAAP and IFRS require that firms disclose sufficient information to allow the reader of financial statements to calculate Accounts Receivable, Gross, Allowance for Uncollectibles, and Accounts Receivable, Net.

EXHIBIT 7.1 **Summary of Accounts Affected by Credit Sales**

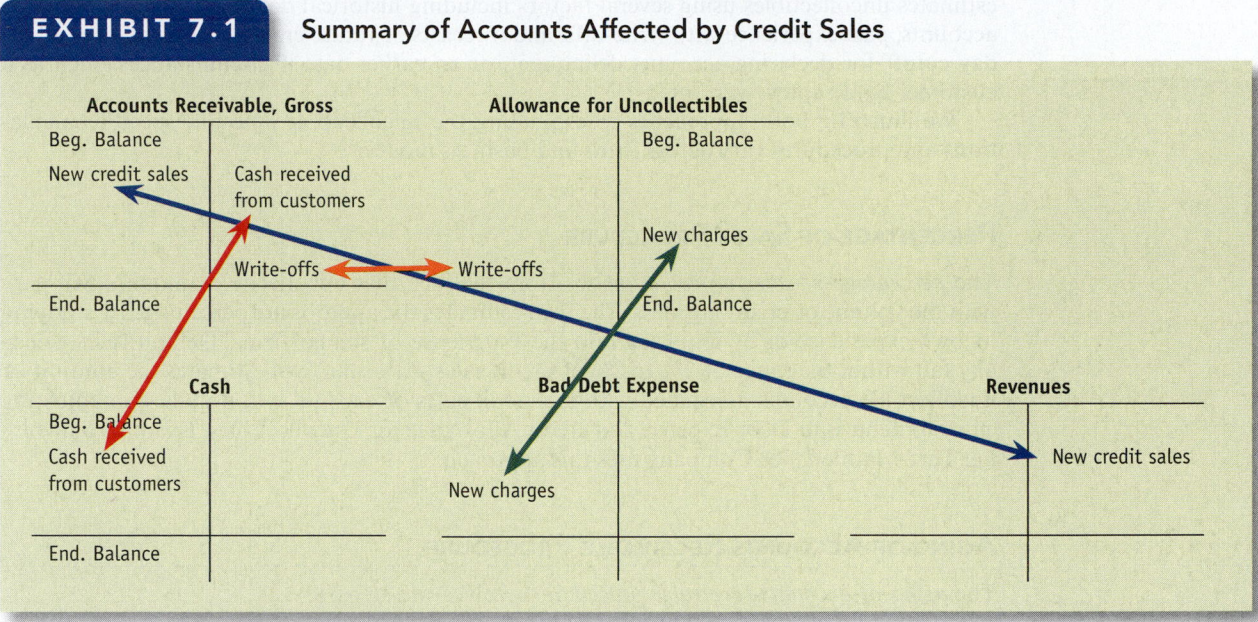

the adjusting entry to recognize bad debt expense, this account always has a credit balance. Because adjusting entries precede balance sheet preparation, a debit balance in the Allowance for Uncollectibles never appears on the balance sheet.

Exhibit 7.1 summarizes the accounting procedures associated with credit sales. The arrows illustrate the four required journal entries:

1. **Blue arrow** shows the sale of goods and services on credit (a debit to Accounts Receivable, Gross, and a credit to Sales Revenue).

2. **Red arrow** shows cash received from customers (a debit to Cash and a credit to Accounts Receivable, Gross).

3. **Green arrow** shows the charge for the estimated amount of uncollectibles (a debit to Bad Debt Expense and a credit to Allowance for Uncollectibles).

4. **Orange arrow** shows the write-off of a particular customer account the firm has classified as uncollectible (a debit to the Allowance for Uncollectibles and a credit to Accounts Receivable, Gross).

ESTIMATING THE AMOUNT OF UNCOLLECTIBLE ACCOUNTS

In **Example 6** we assumed that 2% of credit sales would prove to be uncollectible. We now discuss how management makes this estimate, and illustrate two approaches: the **percentage-of-sales procedure** and the **aging-of-accounts-receivable procedure**. Over time, the two methods, correctly used, will give the same cumulative income and asset totals. U.S. GAAP and IFRS do not require firms to use one or the other, and some firms use both methods. For example, **Exhibit 7.2** reproduces Nordstrom's accounting policy for uncollectible accounts. Nordstrom

EXHIBIT 7.2   Nordstrom Inc.
Critical Accounting Policies

Allowance for Doubtful Accounts
Our allowance for doubtful accounts represents our best estimate of the losses inherent in our private label credit card receivable as of the balance sheet date. We evaluate the collectibility of our accounts receivable based on several factors, including historical trends of aging of accounts, write-off experience and expectations of future performance. We recognize finance charges on delinquent accounts until the account is written off. Delinquent accounts are written off when they are determined to be uncollectible, usually after the passage of 151 days without receiving a full scheduled monthly payment. Accounts are written off sooner in the event of customer bankruptcy or other circumstances that make further collection unlikely.

estimates uncollectibles using several factors including historical data based on aging of the accounts, past experience with write-offs, and forecasts of future credit losses, and uses a 151-day cutoff for declaring accounts delinquent, or an earlier date if circumstances, such as a customer bankruptcy, warrant.

We illustrate both approaches to estimating the uncollectible amount; specific calculations and procedures vary across firms and business models.

PERCENTAGE-OF-SALES PROCEDURE

The *percentage-of-sales procedure* arises from the idea that uncollectible amounts will vary with the volume of credit business. The firm estimates the appropriate percentage by studying its own experience or by inquiring into the experience of similar firms. Default rates generally fall within the range of 1% to 2% of credit sales. After the firm estimates the amount of uncollectible accounts associated with the credit sales of each period, it makes an adjusting entry to debit Bad Debt Expense and credit Allowance for Uncollectibles. **Example 6** involving Turf Maintenance Company uses this approach.

AGING-OF-ACCOUNTS-RECEIVABLE PROCEDURE

The *aging-of-accounts-receivable procedure* involves two steps:

1. Estimating the amount that the firm does not expect to collect from existing accounts receivable, and
2. Adjusting the balance in the Allowance for Uncollectibles so that the balance in this account, when netted against Accounts Receivable, Gross, reflects the amount of cash the firm expects to collect.

Estimating the amount owed by customers that the firm does not expect to collect relies on information about the ages of accounts receivable (the number of days they have been uncollected). **Exhibit 7.3** illustrates a possible classification of individual accounts receivable by age; a firm estimates these amounts from experience.

To illustrate the aging method, assume that the 2008 year-end balance in Accounts Receivable, Gross, for Turf Maintenance is $85,000 (= $2,000,000 from sales on account during 2008 − $1,900,000 of cash collections − $15,000 of accounts written off as uncollectible during 2008). **Exhibit 7.3** presents an aging of these accounts receivable and shows that the estimated uncollectible amount is $24,200.

Before aging the accounts, the Allowance for Uncollectibles has a *debit* balance of $15,000 from writing off actual accounts during 2008. Turf Maintenance would record the following adjusting entry at the end of 2008 to obtain a credit balance in the Allowance for Uncollectibles of $24,200:

EXHIBIT 7.3   Illustration of Aging Accounts Receivable

	Amount	Estimated Uncollectible Percentage	Estimated Uncollectible Amounts
CLASSIFICATION OF ACCOUNTS			
Not yet due	$35,000	8.0%	$ 2,800
1–30 days past due	18,000	20.0	3,600
31–60 days past due	15,000	40.0	6,000
61–180 days past due	13,000	60.0	7,800
More than 180 days past due	4,000	100.0	4,000
	$85,000		$24,200

| Bad Debt Expense. . . . . | | | | 39,200 | |
| Allowance for Uncollectibles . . . . | | | | | 39,200 |

Assets	=	Liabilities	+	Shareholders' Equity	(Class.)
−39,200				−39,200	IncSt → RE

To adjust the balance in the Allowance for Uncollectibles to $24,200
(= −$15,000 + $39,200).

Before this adjusting entry, the Allowance for Uncollectibles had a debit balance of $15,000, so the amount debited to expense and credited to the allowance is the amount required to adjust the balance to the amount of uncollectibles estimated by the aging analysis.

COMPARING PERCENTAGE-OF-SALES AND AGING PROCEDURES

Under the percentage-of-sales procedure, the firm estimates and recognizes its bad debt expense; the offsetting credit increases the balance in the Allowance for Uncollectibles. Under the aging procedure, the firm estimates the ending balance in the Allowance for Uncollectibles account and makes a credit entry to bring the balance to this amount; the offsetting debit is to Bad Debt Expense. If the percentage used under the percentage-of-sales method reasonably reflects collection experience, the balance in the allowance account should be approximately the same at the end of each period under both of these procedures. Many auditors require a periodic aging analysis as a check on the balance in the Allowance for Uncollectibles account, even when the firm uses the percentage method.

Exhibit 7.4 summarizes the differences between the percentage-of-sales method and the aging-of-accounts method. The amount *estimated* by the firm appears in red, and the amount *calculated* (plugged) based on that estimate appears in blue. The percentage-of-sales method requires an estimate of the expense for bad debts (Bad Debt Expense). Using this expense, the beginning balance in the Allowance for Uncollectibles and the amount of write-offs, the firm calculates the ending balance in the Allowance for Uncollectibles. The aging-of-accounts method requires an estimate of the Allowance for Uncollectibles at the end of the year (the ending balance). Using this ending balance, the beginning balance and the amount of write-offs, the firm calculates the amount of Bad Debt Expense for the period.

DEALING WITH CHANGES IN ESTIMATES OF UNCOLLECTIBLE ACCOUNTS

Changes in economic conditions, changes in credit-granting policies, changes in collection efforts, and other similar factors cause differences between estimated and actual uncollectible amounts. These differences necessitate revising the estimates every accounting period to reflect up-to-date information. Both U.S. GAAP and IFRS require firms to reflect any changes in estimates prospectively. That is, firms make no retroactive adjustment to the income statements and balance sheets of previous periods to reflect differences between estimated and actual uncollectible accounts. Rather, the firm adjusts the balance in the Allowance for Uncollectibles going forward. The adjustments for changes in estimates occur naturally under the aging-of-accounts method, because this method first estimates the ending balance in the Allowance for Uncollectibles and then calculates the amount of Bad Debt Expense based on this amount.

EXHIBIT 7.4	Comparison of Methods for Estimating the Provision for Bad Debts

Percentage-of-Sales Method		Aging of Accounts Method	
Allowance for Uncollectibles		**Allowance for Uncollectibles**	
	Beg. Balance		Beg. Balance
	New provision (estimated)		New provision (plug)
Write-offs		Write-offs	
	End. Balance (plug)		End. Balance (estimated)

The prospective application of changes in estimates results from the view that estimates are an essential component of accrual accounting. If firms make conscientious estimates, adjustments for differences between estimated outcomes and actual outcomes will be recurring and small, absent a sudden and substantial change in economic conditions. Retroactive adjustment of previously reported amounts because of differences between estimates and outcomes would lead to continual restatements of prior financial statements, likely confusing users of those financial statements and undermining their credibility.

Examples 7, **8**, and **9** illustrate the accounting for uncollectible accounts. In all of these examples, we compute the ending balance of the Allowance for Uncollectibles using the aging-of-accounts method. Next, we derive the Bad Debt Expense implied by the ending balance and compare this Bad Debt Expense to the amount that would derive from the percentage-of-sales method.

Example 7 At the start of 2009, Coral Designs' Allowance for Uncollectibles balance is €120,000. During 2009, Coral Designs' credit sales were €5,000,000; of this amount, it expected 2% will become uncollectible. During 2009, Coral Designs wrote off €60,000 of accounts receivable. At the end of 2009, Coral Designs estimates, based on an aging of accounts, that the ending balance in the Allowance for Uncollectibles should be €130,000. A T-account representation of this information appears below:

Allowance for Uncollectibles

		120,000	Beg. Bal.
Write-Offs	60,000		
		?	Bad Debt Expense
		130,000	End. Bal.

Under the aging-of-accounts method, Coral Designs solves (plugs) for Bad Debt Expense: €120,000 − €60,000 + Bad Debt Expense = €130,000. The expense is €70,000:

Bad Debt Expense.   70,000
    Allowance for Uncollectibles   70,000

Assets	=	Liabilities	+	Shareholders' Equity	(Class.)
−70,000				−70,000	IncSt → RE

To record the amount of Bad Debt Expense that ensures the ending balance in the Allowance for Uncollectibles is €130,000.

Under the percentage-of-sales method, Bad Debt Expense would be €100,000 (= 2% × €5,000,000), and the ending balance in the Allowance for Uncollectibles would be €160,000, or €30,000 more than the aging-of-accounts method suggests.

Example 8 Assume the same information as in **Example 7** except that management estimates the ending balance in the Allowance for Uncollectibles is €200,000. A T-account representation of this information appears below:

Allowance for Uncollectibles

		120,000	Beg. Bal.
Write-Off	60,000		
		?	Bad Debt Expense
		200,000	End. Bal.

Under the aging-of-accounts method, Coral Designs solves for Bad Debt Expense: €120,000 − €60,000 + Bad Debt Expense = €200,000. The expense is €140,000:

Bad Debt Expense.   140,000
    Allowance for Uncollectibles   140,000

Assets	=	Liabilities	+	Shareholders' Equity	(Class.)
−140,000				−140,000	IncSt → RE

(continued)

To record the amount of Bad Debt Expense that ensures the ending balance in
the Allowance for Uncollectibles is €200,000.

The bad debt expense of €140,000 estimated under the aging-of-accounts method is
€40,000 more than the amount the percentage-of-sales method would compute.

Example 9 Assume the same information as provided in **Example 7** except that management
estimates the ending balance in the Allowance for Uncollectibles is €45,000. A T-account representation of this information follows:

	Allowance for Uncollectibles	
	120,000	Beg. Bal.
Write-Offs 60,000		
	?	Bad Debt Expense
	45,000	End. Bal.

When we solve for the expense, the amount is a *negative* €15,000; in order for the ending balance in the Allowance for Uncollectibles to be €45,000, Coral Designs must record a
€15,000 *debit* to this account and an offsetting *credit* to Bad Debt Expense:

	Allowance for Uncollectibles	
	120,000	Beg. Bal.
Write-Offs 60,000		
Bad Debt Expense ?		
	45,000	End. Bal.

Coral Designs would record the following journal entry:

Allowance for Uncollectibles   15,000

    Bad Debt Expense   15,000

Assets	=	Liabilities	+	Shareholders' Equity	(Class.)
+15,000				+15,000	IncSt → RE

To record the credit to Bad Debt Expense that ensures the ending balance in
the Allowance for Uncollectibles is €45,000.

Example 9 illustrates a setting in which Coral Designs has decided its previous estimates
of uncollectible accounts were too high, given current information. Coral Designs will not
recognize any bad debt expense for 2009 and, in addition, it will reverse €15,000 previously
recognized as bad debt expense. Therefore, Coral Designs' total expenses (of which bad debt
expense is a component) are €15,000 *less* in 2009, and its net assets at year-end are €15,000
larger.

SUMMARY OF ACCOUNTING FOR UNCOLLECTIBLE ACCOUNTS

The accounting for uncollectible accounts using the allowance method involves four steps:

(1) Sale of Goods on Credit

Accounts Receivable, Gross ....   Selling Price

    Sales Revenue ....   Selling Price

Assets	=	Liabilities	+	Shareholders' Equity	(Class.)
+Selling Price				+Selling Price	IncSt → RE

(2) Collection of Cash from Customers

Cash. . . . .   Amount Collected

    Accounts Receivable, Gross . . . .   Amount Collected

Assets	=	Liabilities	+	Shareholders' Equity	(Class.)
+Amount Collected					
−Amount Collected					

(3) Estimate of Expected Uncollectible Accounts

Bad Debt Expense. . . . .   Estimated Uncollectible Amount

    Allowance for Uncollectibles . . . .   Estimated Uncollectible Amount

Assets	=	Liabilities	+	Shareholders' Equity	(Class.)
−Estimated Uncollectible Amount				−Estimated Uncollectible Amount	IncSt → RE

The percentage-of-sales approach estimates the amount of Bad Debt Expense; the offsetting credit is to the Allowance for Uncollectibles. The aging-of-accounts-receivable approach estimates the ending balance in the Allowance for Uncollectibles. The firm credits the Allowance for Uncollectibles by the amount needed to achieve the estimated ending balance; the offsetting debit is to Bad Debt Expense. Estimated amounts of uncollectibles will likely differ from actual amounts. The firm revises its estimates every period in light of new information and adjusts the financial statements prospectively. The revised estimate could increase or decrease the amount recognized as Bad Debt Expense, and in some cases the firm could record a credit to Bad Debt Expense that reverses previously recognized expense.

(4) Write-off of Uncollectible Amounts Using the Allowance Method

Allowance for Uncollectibles . . . .   Actual Uncollectible Amount

    Accounts Receivable, Gross . . . .   Actual Uncollectible Amount

Assets	=	Liabilities	+	Shareholders' Equity	(Class.)
+Actual Uncollectible Amount					
−Actual Uncollectible Amount					

Write-offs occur when the firm decides that a specific customer's account is uncollectible.[11]

---

[11]Some taxing authorities, such as the U.S. Internal Revenue Service, do not permit firms to use the allowance method to calculate the tax deduction for bad debts, but instead require that firms recognize bad debt expense only when they conclude an account is not collectible. This approach, often called the *direct write-off method*, defers the recognition of the costs of bad debts past the period in which the firm recognizes revenue from the sale.

ANALYZING ACCOUNTS RECEIVABLE

This section considers financial statement presentation of accounts receivable, common financial ratios involving accounts receivable, and transfers of accounts receivable in exchange for cash.

Financial Statement Presentation Accounts receivable appear on the balance sheet at the amount the firm expects to collect. This net amount is the gross amount of receivables less the amount in the Allowance for Uncollectibles. **Exhibit 1.1** (on page 8) shows Nordstrom's balance sheets for the years ended February 3, 2007 and January 26, 2006, with ending balances in Accounts Receivable, Net, of $684,376 and $639,558, respectively. **Exhibit 7.5**, from Nordstrom's 10-K filing with the SEC, shows the changes to its allowance accounts, such as the Allowance for Doubtful Accounts (Nordstrom's name for the Allowance for Uncollectibles) during the year.

Using the information in Nordstrom's balance sheet in **Exhibit 1.1** and Schedule II in **Exhibit 7.5**, we can calculate the ending balance in Accounts Receivable, Gross, as of February 3, 2007, and January 28, 2006:

$$
\begin{aligned}
\text{February 3, 2007, Accounts Receivable, Gross} &= \text{Accounts Receivable, Net} \\
&\quad + \text{Allowance for Uncollectibles} \\
&= \$684,376 + \$17,475 \\
&= \$701,851
\end{aligned}
$$

$$
\begin{aligned}
\text{January 28, 2006, Accounts Receivable, Gross} &= \text{Accounts Receivable, Net} \\
&\quad + \text{Allowance for Uncollectibles} \\
&= \$639,558 + \$17,926 \\
&= \$657,484
\end{aligned}
$$

We can derive the adjusting entry Nordstrom made in the year ended February 3, 2007, to record bad debt expense. Schedule II shows an addition to the Allowance for Doubtful Accounts of $17,197; this amount is Nordstrom's bad debt expense. The adjusting entry would be as follows:

Bad Debt Expense...	17,197	
Allowance for Uncollectibles.............................		17,197

Assets	=	Liabilities	+	Shareholders' Equity	(Class.)
−17,197				−17,197	IncSt → RE

EXHIBIT 7.5	**Nordstrom Inc. and Subsidiaries** **Schedule II: Valuation and Qualifying Accounts** **(dollars in thousands)**

Column A	Column B	Column C	Column D	Column E
		Additions		
Description	Balance at beginning of period	Charged to costs and expenses	Deductions	Balance at end of period
Deducted from related balance sheet account				
Allowance for doubtful accounts:				
Year ended:				
February 3, 2007	$17,926	$17,197	$17,648 (A)	$17,475
January 28, 2006	$19,065	$20,918	$22,057 (A)	$17,926
January 29, 2005	$20,320	$24,639	$25,894 (A)	$19,065

(A) Deductions consist of write-offs of uncollectible accounts, net of recoveries.

Schedule II also shows deductions to the Allowance for Uncollectibles account of $17,648, reflecting write-offs of specific customer accounts:

Allowance for Uncollectibles.   17,648
    Accounts Receivable, Gross   17,648

Assets	=	Liabilities	+	Shareholders' Equity	(Class.)
+17,648					
−17,648					

We can also analyze Nordstrom's cash collections from all of its customers, both cash sales and credit sales where the customer has paid. For simplicity, we assume Nordstrom made 100% of its sales on credit; from the income statement, this amount is $8,560,698. The cash collected from credit customers reduces Accounts Receivable, Gross. We can calculate this amount using a T-account showing beginning and ending balances in Accounts Receivable, Gross, (as calculated earlier) and other transactions that affected this account:

	Accounts Receivable, Gross		
Beg. Bal.	657,484		
New Credit Sales	8,560,698	17,648	Write-Off
			Cash Collected from Credit
		8,498,683	Customers
End. Bal.	701,851		

By assumption credit sales equal total revenue of $8,560,698; we previously analyzed write-offs of $17,648. We solve for the Cash Collected from Credit Customers as follows:

Ending Balance = Beginning Balance + New Credit Sales
               − Write-Offs − Cash Collected from Credit Customers

$701,851 = $657,484 + $8,560,698 − $17,648 − Cash Collected from Credit Customers

Cash Collected from Credit Customers in the year ended February 3, 2007 was $8,498,683. You can see from the nature of the entries in the T-account above that for every dollar of assumed cash sales, new credit sales assumed goes down by one dollar and the plug for Cash Collected from Customers also declines by one dollar.

Financial Ratios Involving Accounts Receivable

The financial statements contain information for analyzing the collectibility of accounts receivable and the adequacy of the expense for uncollectible accounts. Typical ratios used for this analysis include the accounts receivable turnover ratio, days receivables outstanding, and the write-off percentage.

The accounts receivable turnover ratio captures the speed of cash collections from credit customers. The ratio is sales revenue divided by average accounts receivable during the period. Although the numerator should include only credit sales, firms seldom disclose the proportions of cash and credit sales. Thus, typically the analyst uses total sales revenue in the numerator of the accounts receivable turnover ratio, recognizing that this assumption overstates the ratio.

Nordstrom's accounts receivable turnover ratio for the year ended February 3, 2007, is as follows:

$$\frac{\text{Sales Revenue}}{\text{Average Accounts Receivable}} = \frac{\$8,560,698}{(0.5)(\$639,558 + \$684,376)} = 12.93 \text{ times per year}$$

The analyst often expresses accounts receivable turnover in terms of the average number of days between a credit sale and cash collection for that sale as **days receivables outstanding**. To calculate this ratio, divide 365 days by the accounts receivable turnover ratio. Days receivables outstanding for Nordstrom during fiscal 2006 was 28 days (= 365 days/12.93 times per year).

Most firms that sell on account to other businesses, as opposed to consumers, collect cash within 30 to 90 days. Interpreting a firm's accounts receivable turnover and days receivables outstanding requires knowing the terms of sale. If the terms of sale are "net 30 days" and the firm collects its accounts receivable in 45 days, collections do not accord with the stated terms. This could be a signal that management should review and possibly change the firm's credit-granting policy and collection activity. If the firm offers terms of "net 60 days," a value of 45 for days receivables outstanding indicates that the firm is collecting its receivables faster than indicated by its contractual terms.

Because firms sell to customers on account as a strategy to stimulate sales, customers may purchase more if they know they need only sign their names. Firms may also permit customers to delay payment and thereby generate interest revenue through finance charges on the unpaid amounts. Thus, comparing accounts receivable turnover ratios over time or across firms requires an analysis of changes in sales revenue, interest revenue, changes in credit-granting and collecting policies, and the losses from uncollectible accounts.

The analyst may also wish to analyze uncollectible accounts specifically. Using information in Nordstrom's Schedule II (shown in **Exhibit 7.5**), we can compare amounts written off to average amounts owed by customers (average gross accounts receivable):

Year Ended	Accounts Written Off as Uncollectible	Accounts Receivable Net	Allowance for Uncollectible Accounts	Accounts Receivable Gross	Write-Offs/ Average Gross Accounts Receivable
February 3, 2007.	$17,648	$684,376	$17,475	$701,851	2.51%
January 28, 2006	$22,057	$639,558	$17,926	$657,484	3.35%

Between the years ending January 28, 2006, and February 3, 2007, Nordstrom decreased its write-offs of uncollectible accounts from 3.35% to 2.51% of gross accounts receivable.

Two ratios used to evaluate the allowance for uncollectibles are the ratio of Bad Debt Expense to Sales Revenue and the ratio of the Allowance for Uncollectibles to Accounts Receivable, Gross. Using the data provided by Nordstrom, we can calculate these ratios as follows:

Year Ended	Bad Debt Expense (1)	Sales (2)	Bad Debt Expense as a % of Sales (1)/(2) = (3)	Balance in Allowance Account (4)	Accounts Receivable, Gross (5)	Allowance Account as a % of Accounts Receivable (4)/(5) = (6)
February 3, 2007.	$17,197	$8,560,698	0.20%	$17,475	$701,851	2.49%
January 28, 2006	$20,198	$7,722,860	0.26%	$17,926	$657,484	2.73%

The ratio of bad debt expense to sales declined between the two years, from 0.26% to 0.20%. The allowance account as a percentage of gross accounts receivable also declined, from 2.73% to 2.49%. Both declines are consistent with the decline in write-offs observed above.

Transfers of Accounts Receivable in Exchange for Cash

In analyzing how a firm converts accounts receivable into cash, it is useful to establish whether the firm collects cash from its customers or transfers to others the receivables (the right to collect cash from customers) in exchange for cash. A firm that transfers its receivables in exchange for cash may show smaller (or no) accounts receivable, depending on the form of the transfer and the related accounting treatment.

At least three forms of transfer are possible. First, a firm may use its accounts receivable as collateral for a loan from a bank or other financial institution. The firm physically maintains control of the accounts receivable, collects cash from customers, and repays the loan. If the firm fails to repay the loan, the lender can claim the receivables. If the firm has used its accounts receivable as collateral for a loan, the firm will continue to show those receivables as an asset (and there will also be a loan payable liability). The firm should disclose the lending arrangement in its financial reports. Second, a firm may *factor* (sell) its accounts receivable to a bank or other financial institution in exchange for cash. In this case, the lender physically controls the receivables and collects cash from customers. Accounts receivable that the firm has factored do not appear on the balance sheet because the firm has sold them. Third, the firm may transfer the accounts receivable to a legally separate entity that issues debt securities to investors; the firm remits to investors the cash received from customers as those cash receipts occur. The firm may be obligated to make payments to investors in securities if the customers fail to make sufficient cash payments to pay the principal and interest on the debt securities. This third arrangement is a **securitization**, a process that transforms an asset (accounts receivable) into securities held by investors.

While a detailed discussion of transfers of accounts receivable in exchange for cash is beyond the scope of this introductory book, we raise the issue here because of its importance in comparing accounts receivable across firms. In particular, if one firm transfers its receivables and a comparison firm does not, the accounts receivable balances and related ratios of the two firms will not be comparable, despite similarities between the two firms in product markets. **Chapter 11** discusses transfers of receivables in more detail, including the difficulties in ascertaining whether a transfer of receivables is a sale of receivables for cash (neither the receivables nor a liability appears on the balance sheet) or a collateralized borrowing (both the receivables and a liability appear on the balance sheet).

PROBLEM 7.2 for Self-Study

Revenue recognition at time of sale. Prepare journal entries for each of the following hypothetical transactions and events affecting Scania during the year ended December 31, 2008.

a. February: Scania sells four truck engines for SEK20,000 per engine. The customer agrees to pay Scania within 60 days.

b. March: Scania signs a contract with a customer for 50 transport containers, with a total selling price of SEK250,000. Scania expects to deliver the containers in June. The customer agrees to pay on delivery.

c. April: The customer pays in full for the four truck engines in part **a**.

d. May: Scania sells a truck to a customer for SEK725,000, which it delivers immediately. The customer pays Scania 20% of the price upon delivery and agrees to pay the remainder in 120 days.

e. June: Scania delivers the containers (from part **b**), and the customer pays as promised.

f. July: The customer in part **d** enters bankruptcy proceedings. Scania does not expect to collect any portion of the remaining receivable from this customer.

g. December: Scania estimates that 2% of its credit sales of SEK70 billion during the year will be uncollectible.

SALES RETURNS: AN APPLICATION OF THE ALLOWANCE METHOD

We have introduced the allowance method in the context of uncollectible accounts receivable. More generally, accountants use the allowance method when, at the time of sale, they can estimate with reasonable reliability the effects of events that will affect future cash flows. Application of the allowance method reduces reported earnings in the period of sale to reflect expected net cash collections.

Sales returns affect net cash collections. When a customer has the right to return a product for a refund, and the firm can reasonably estimate the amount of returns at the time of sale, U.S. GAAP and IFRS require that the firm use the allowance method to estimate and recognize the effects of returns.[12] Specifically, the selling firm debits a revenue contra account (see footnote 7) for expected returns to reduce current period revenues to the estimated amount that will *not* be returned. By reducing current period revenues, the firm measures revenues based on the amount of cash it expects to collect from current period sales. Both U.S. GAAP

---

[12]Not all sales with a right of return qualify for revenue recognition. U.S. GAAP provides explicit criteria for a sale with a right of return to qualify for revenue recognition (Financial Accounting Standards Board, *Statement of Financial Accounting Standards No. 48*, "Revenue Recognition When Right of Return Exists," 1981) **(Codification Topic 605)**. IFRS does not provide explicit criteria. Deciding whether a sale with a right of return qualifies for revenue recognition is beyond the scope of this book.

EXHIBIT 7.6

Nordstrom Inc. and Subsidiaries
**Schedule II: Valuation and Qualifying Accounts
(dollars in thousands)**

Column A	Column B	Column C	Column D	Column E
		Additions		
	Balance at beginning	Charged to costs		Balance at end
Description	of period	and expenses	Deductions	of period
Deducted from related balance sheet account				
Allowance for doubtful accounts:				
Year ended:				
February 3, 2007	$17,926	$17,197	$17,648 (A)	$17,475
January 28, 2006	$19,065	$20,918	$22,057 (A)	$17,926
January 29, 2005	$20,320	$24,639	$25,894 (A)	$19,065
Reserves				
Allowance for sales return, net:				
Year ended:				
February 3, 2007	$51,172	$893,651	$890,277 (B)	$54,546
January 28, 2006	$49,745	$805,288	$803,861 (B)	$51,172
January 29, 2005	$39,841	$725,982	$716,078 (B)	$49,745

(A) Deductions consist of write-offs of uncollectible accounts, net of recoveries.
(B) Deductions consist of actual returns offset by the value of the merchandise returned and the sales commission reversed.

and IFRS preclude revenue recognition when customers have the right to return goods unless the firm can reasonably estimate the amount of returns and it uses an allowance method to incorporate those estimates into income computations. **Exhibit 7.6** reproduces Nordstrom's Schedule II, included in its 10-K filing for the year ended February 3, 2007. This schedule is similar to **Exhibit 7.5**, except that it also shows the activity in the Allowance for Sales Returns account.

The beginning balance in Nordstrom's Allowance for Sales Returns was $51,172; this amount increased during the year by $893,651. The journal entry to record this increase is:

Sales Returns...	893,651	
Allowance for Sales Returns		893,651

Assets	=	Liabilities	+	Shareholders' Equity	(Class.)
−893,651				−893,651	IncSt → RE

The Sales Returns account is a revenue contra account, accumulating subtractions from gross revenue. The debit to Sales Returns reduces Sales Revenue, Net, and therefore reduces income.[13] The Allowance for Sales Returns account is also a contra account; like the Allowance for Uncollectibles, it accumulates subtractions from Accounts Receivable, Gross. The balance in the Allowance for Sales Returns is the firm's estimate of the receivables that it will cancel or the cash that it will pay to satisfy customers who return their merchandise. Nordstrom's Schedule II shows that customer returns (including the effects of sales commissions) were $890,277. Thus, the ending balance in the Allowance for Sales Returns is $54,546 (= $51,172 + $893,651 − $890,277).

Sellers also use the allowance method to account for product warranties, which promise the customer the right to repair or replacement if the purchased product is defective. The firm must be able to reasonably estimate expected warranty costs at the time of sale. If it cannot, it must delay revenue recognition until it can estimate the costs or learns their actual amount. We discuss the accounting for warranties in **Chapter 8**.

---

[13]More precisely, the debit to Sales Returns increases the amount in that account, a contra to revenue. Later, we subtract the balance in Sales Returns from Sales Revenues, which reduces total revenues and net income.

You should master the concepts, procedures, and journal entries associated with the allowance method so that you can apply the method in other, similar transactions. Variants of the allowance method appear in arrangements in which the selling firm recognizes revenue before it has resolved all uncertainty about future cash flows related to the sale.

 # INCOME RECOGNITION AFTER THE SALE

Some businesses provide substantial services after the time of sale, while other businesses involve considerable uncertainty about cash collections. Both of these conditions introduce uncertainty. Under some circumstances this uncertainty is sufficient to preclude the firm's recognizing revenue at the time of sale; instead, it recognizes revenue sometime after the sale.

Here, we repeat the two criteria for revenue recognition:

1. The seller must have substantially performed its obligations to the customer (for example, by transferring ownership of goods to the customer).
2. The seller must have obtained an asset from the customer that it can reliably measure and, if the asset is not cash, the seller must be reasonably certain of converting the asset into cash.

SUBSTANTIAL PERFORMANCE REMAINS

Examples 1-4 describe transactions where the seller receives cash from customers before it completes all, or substantially all, of its performance obligations. **Example 1** is Costco's receipt of $50 for an annual membership; **Example 2** is Pol Roget's receipt of half the €15 million contract price for champagne; **Example 3** is Microsoft's receipt of $50 before it supplies future telephone support service as well as upgrades/enhancements; and **Example 4** is Bombardier's receipt of €250 million before it supplies 25 high-speed trains. Although the seller has received cash (revenue recognition criterion 2), it has not earned all of the revenues represented by the cash by providing goods and services (revenue recognition criterion 1). Instead, the seller has incurred an obligation to provide goods or services. The generic term for these liabilities is **deferred performance obligations**, and a common account title is **Advances from Customers**; other names include **Deferred Revenues** and **Unearned Revenues**.[14] Unlike other liabilities, such as accounts payable, which the firm typically settles by paying cash, it settles these performance obligations by delivering the promised goods or services. The firm recognizes revenue when it settles its obligation to the customer by performing as promised.

To illustrate the firm's accounting for cash received from customers before it has earned revenue by delivering goods or services, consider the sale of the $50.00 annual membership to the Costco customer. If Costco sold one membership one month before its reporting year's end, it would record the receipt of cash from the customer and the related performance obligation (to stand ready to provide access to shopping) as follows:

Cash. 50.00
    Advances from Customers 50.00

Assets	=	Liabilities	+	Shareholders' Equity	(Class.)
+50.00		+50.00			

Costco earns revenue by performing its obligations under the membership arrangement, specifically, by allowing the membership-bearing customer to shop at any Costco store over the next 12 months. Costco recognizes as revenue $4.17, or 1/12 of the $50.00 fee, each month as it performs its obligations:

---

[14]There is no standard terminology for this account, and some industries use names that are specific to that industry. For example, an account title commonly used by airlines is Air Traffic Liability.

Advances from Customers	. . . .		4.17	
Sales Revenue	. . . .			4.17

Assets	=	Liabilities	+	Shareholders' Equity	(Class.)
		−4.17		+4.17	IncSt → RE

After this journal entry, the Advances from Customers account has a balance of $45.83 at the reporting period's year end.

Microsoft's sale of Windows XP follows similar procedures, with two complicating factors. First, the $50 sales price of Windows XP includes two elements:

1. The software itself.

2. The telephone services and future upgrades and enhancements.

Microsoft has earned the revenue from the software when it delivers the software, and it will earn the other revenue over the product's life. Microsoft will allocate the $50 contract price to the two elements of the sales contract, according to the relative fair values of the elements. In this context fair value refers to the price for which the firm (or another firm selling a similar product) separately sells a deliverable component. The allocated revenue for a component is the total contract price times the ratio of the fair value of that component to the sum of the fair values of all of the bundled components in the contract. For example, assume Microsoft sells software separately for $45, the telephone servicing for $3, and the future upgrades/enhancements for $7. The sum of these fair values is $55. Therefore, Microsoft allocates the $50 total revenue as follows:

- $40.91 (= $50 × [$45/$55]) to the software,
- $ 2.73 (= $50 × [$3/$55]) to telephone servicing, and
- $ 6.36 (= $50 × [$7/$55]) to future upgrades/enhancements
- $50.00 (= $40.91 + $2.73 + $6.36)

The second issue concerns the timing of revenue recognition for the separate components of the contract. Microsoft has completed its obligation to deliver software at the time of sale, so it will recognize $40.91 when it sells a copy of Windows XP. The telephone services and the upgrades/enhancements are, at the time of sale, undelivered elements. Microsoft's footnote disclosures state that it recognizes revenue on undelivered elements on a straight-line basis over the product's life cycle, estimated to be 3.5 years for Windows XP. The following journal entries summarize Microsoft's accounting for the sale of one copy of Windows XP. For simplicity, we assume the sale occurs on the first day of Microsoft's fiscal year.

At the Time of Sale

Cash	. . . .	50.00	
Sales Revenue	. . . .		40.91
Advances from Customers[15]	. . . .		9.09

Assets	=	Liabilities	+	Shareholders' Equity	(Class.)
+50.00		+9.09		+40.91	IncSt → RE

To record the sale of Windows XP and related future services for $50.

At the End of One Year

Advances from Customers	. . . .	2.60	
Sales Revenue	. . . .		2.60

Assets	=	Liabilities	+	Shareholders' Equity	(Class.)
		−2.60		+2.60	IncSt → RE

At the end of the year, to recognize revenues associated with telephone services and upgrades/enhancements of $2.60 (= $9.09 × [1.0/3.5]).

---

[15]Microsoft uses the account title "Unearned Revenues."

PROBLEM 7.3 for Self-Study

Revenue recognition after sale when substantial performance remains. Prepare journal entries for each of the following hypothetical transactions and events affecting Scania during the fiscal year ended December 31, 2008.

a. March: Scania signs a contract to deliver 50 transport containers for a total price of SEK250,000. The customer pays Scania the entire amount at the date both parties sign the contract. Scania expects to deliver the containers in June.

b. May: Scania sells a truck to a customer for SEK725,000, which it delivers immediately. The customer pays Scania 20% at delivery and agrees to pay the rest in 60 days. The contract price includes a two-day training session that Scania will design and deliver in June, as well as customer support for three years following delivery of the truck. Sold separately, the truck would cost SEK690,000, the training session would cost SEK40,000, and the customer support would cost SEK50,000.

c. June: Scania delivers the containers (part **a**) and the training session (part **b**).

d. September: Scania and a customer promise to sign a contract in January 2009 for the delivery of 10 buses in exchange for SEK7 million. The customer agrees to pay Scania, in October, a deposit of SEK200,000.

e. October: The customer in part **d** pays SEK200,000 to Scania.

f. December: Scania recognizes eight months (May through December) of customer support provided in connection with the sale of the truck in part **b**.

SUBSTANTIAL UNCERTAINTY ABOUT CASH COLLECTIONS REMAINS

Some sales transactions involve sufficient uncertainty about the ability of a customer to pay that the seller cannot reliably estimate the timing and amounts of cash that it will collect. An example is a franchise arrangement that obligates the franchisee to make substantial cash payments over an extended time period in exchange for goods and services that the seller typically provides well in advance of cash collections, as in **Example 5**. The failure rate among franchises (and other small businesses) is high, and therefore the seller, the franchisor, cannot reliably estimate the portion of the initial franchise fee that it will ultimately collect.

When substantial uncertainty exists at the time of sale regarding the amount, or timing, or both, of cash collections, both U.S. GAAP and IFRS link revenue recognition to the receipt of cash. Two common accounting methods with this characteristic are the installment method and the cost recovery method.[16] We describe these methods and the guidance that determines when a seller can use them.

Installment Method The **installment method** recognizes revenue as the seller collects cash from the customer. The seller applies the **gross margin percentage** on the transaction to calculate the portion of the total **gross margin** recognized in each accounting period. The gross margin equals sales revenue minus cost of goods sold. The gross margin percentage equals gross margin divided by sales revenue.

To illustrate, assume a customer agrees to pay £20,000 over the next three years in three installments of £7,500, £8,750, and £3,750;[17] the retailer's cost of the item purchased is £14,000, so the gross margin is £6,000 (= £20,000 − £14,000). The gross margin percentage is 30% (= £6,000/£20,000) of the total revenue. Immediately after the sale, the customer has physical possession of the inventory, and the seller has a receivable with substantial uncertainty of collection. At the time of sale, the seller recognizes an account receivable and credits inventory and defers the gross margin on the sale until it collects cash.[18] In the example given, the journal entry at the time of sale is:

---

[16]U.S. GAAP describes these methods in para. 12 and related note 8 of Accounting Principles Board, *Opinion No. 10*, "Omnibus Opinion—1966," 1966 (**Codification Topic 605**). IFRS does not use these terms.

[17]This example ignores interest on the customer's delayed payments.

[18]Deferred gross margin (or deferred gross profit) is not a liability, because the seller has performed its obligation to the customer. Conceptually, deferred gross margin is a contra asset account (Financial Accounting Standards Board, *Statement of Financial Accounting Concepts No. 6*, "Elements of Financial Statements," 1985, par. 232–234); however, many firms display it among the current liabilities or between liabilities and shareholders' equity.

Accounts Receivable, Gross	20,000	
Inventory		14,000
Deferred Gross Margin		6,000

Assets	=	Liabilities	+	Shareholders' Equity	(Class.)
+20,000					
−14,000					
−6,000					

To credit the balance sheet Inventory account for inventory that the firm has sold, to recognize accounts receivable and to recognize the deferred gross margin.[19]

The seller recognizes cash received as revenue. The gross margin percentage (30% in this example) times the cash received equals the gross margin recognized. Cost of goods sold is a plug figure (the amount required to make the journal entry balance). The journal entry to record the customer's first £7,500 installment payment, recognize revenue, and recognize cost of goods sold expense is:

Cash	7,500	
Deferred Gross Margin	2,250	
Cost of Goods Sold (plug)	5,250	
Accounts Receivable, Gross		7,500
Sales Revenue		7,500

Assets	=	Liabilities	+	Shareholders' Equity	(Class.)
+7,500				−5,250	IncSt → RE
+2,250				+7,500	IncSt → RE
−7,500					

To record the first installment collection of £7,500, recognize revenue equal to cash received, recognize gross margin, £2,250 (= 0.30 × £7,500), and recognize cost of goods sold (a plug figure). The contribution to income (recognized gross margin) is £2,250 (= £7,500 revenue − £5,250 cost of goods sold).

The journal entry to record the second installment collection of £8,750 is:

Cash	8,750	
Deferred Gross Margin	2,625	
Cost of Goods Sold (plug)	6,125	
Accounts Receivable, Gross		8,750
Sales Revenue		8,750

Assets	=	Liabilities	+	Shareholders' Equity	(Class.)
+8,750				−6,125	IncSt → RE
+2,625				+8,750	IncSt → RE
−8,750					

To record the second installment collection of £8,750, recognize revenue equal to cash received, recognize gross margin, £2,625 (= 0.30 × £8,750), and recognize cost of goods sold (a plug figure). The contribution to income (recognized gross margin) is £2,625.

The journal entry for the third installment collection of £3,750 is:

Cash	3,750	
Deferred Gross Margin	1,125	
Cost of Goods Sold (plug)	2,625	

(continued)

---

[19]We include the deferred gross margin as a reduction of assets following *Concepts Statement 6*.

| Accounts Receivable, Gross | .... | 3,750 | |
| Sales Revenue | .... | | 3,750 |

Assets	=	Liabilities	+	Shareholders' Equity	(Class.)
+3,750				−2,625	IncSt → RE
+1,125				+3,750	IncSt → RE
−3,750					

To record the third installment collection of £3,750, recognize revenue equal to cash received, recognize gross margin, £1,125 (= 0.30 × £3,750), and recognize cost of goods sold (a plug figure). The contribution to income (recognized gross margin) is £1,125.

After the customer makes the third installment payment, the balance in Accounts Receivable, Gross, on the seller's balance sheet is zero, the seller's cumulative revenue is £20,000 (= £7,500 + £8,750 + £3,750), and cumulative cost of goods sold is £14,000 (= £5,250 + £6,125 + £2,625). The cumulative gross margin is £6,000 (= £20,000 − £14,000 = £2,250 + £2,625, + £1,125).

If the customer fails to make all the promised payments, the seller can repossess the sold item and include that item in its inventory at its net realizable value. The seller would also write off the remaining balances in Accounts Receivable, Gross, and in Deferred Gross Margin, recognizing a gain or loss on repossession. In this example, if the customer failed to make the third installment payment and the seller repossessed inventory with net realizable value of £2,600, the seller would make the following journal entry:

Inventory—Repossessed Items	....	2,600	
Deferred Gross Margin	....	1,125	
Loss on Repossession (plug)	....	25	
Accounts Receivable, Gross	....		3,750

Assets	=	Liabilities	+	Shareholders' Equity	(Class.)
+2,600				−25	IncSt → RE
+1,125					
−3,750					

To write off an uncollectible installment account receivable (£3,750) and the related gross margin (£1,125), recognize repossessed inventory at its net realizable value (£2,600), and recognize a loss (£25).

Cost Recovery Method

The **cost recovery method** matches the costs of generating revenue with cash receipts until the seller recovers all its costs. That is, the seller sets expenses equal to revenue in each period until it recovers all its costs. The seller does not recognize gross margin in income until it has recovered all of the costs of the sale. After cumulative cash receipts equal total costs, the seller reports revenue without any matching expenses in its income statement. The seller makes the same journal entry at the time of sale under the cost recovery method as under the installment method. The difference between the two methods arises later when the customer makes installment payments. Instead of applying the gross margin percentage to each cash collection from the customer, the seller sets cost of goods sold equal to revenue until it recovers the entire cost. We illustrate these differences using journal entries, assuming the same transaction terms as in the preceding example. We do not repeat the journal entry at the time of sale, which is the same for the cost recovery method as for the installment method.

The seller's journal entry to record the first cash collection of £7,500 is as follows:

Cash	....	7,500	
Cost of Goods Sold (plug)	....	7,500	
Accounts Receivable, Gross	....		7,500
Sales Revenue	....		7,500

(continued)

Assets	=	Liabilities	+	Shareholders' Equity	(Class.)
+7,500				−7,500	IncSt → RE
−7,500				+7,500	IncSt → RE

To record the first collection of £7,500, recognize revenue equal to cash received, and recognize cost of goods sold equal to revenue. The seller has recovered £7,500 of its total costs of £14,000.

The seller's journal entry to record the second cash collection of £8,750 is as follows:

Cash.	8,750	
Deferred Gross Margin	2,250	
Cost of Goods Sold (plug)	6,500	
Accounts Receivable, Gross		8,750
Sales Revenue		8,750

Assets	=	Liabilities	+	Shareholders' Equity	(Class.)
+8,750				−6,500	IncSt → RE
+2,250				+8,750	IncSt → RE
−8,750					

To record the second collection of £8,750, recognize revenue equal to cash received, and recognize cost of goods sold = £6,500. This amount, combined with the previously recognized £7,500 expense, indicates that the seller has recovered its costs of £14,000. The difference between cumulative cash received, £16,250 (= £7,500 + £8,750) and the £14,000 cost is the recognized gross margin. Income increases by £2,250 (= £8,750 − £6,500).

The seller's journal entry to record the third cash collection of £3,750 is as follows:

Cash.	3,750	
Deferred Gross Margin	3,750	
Accounts Receivable, Gross		3,750
Sales Revenue		3,750

Assets	=	Liabilities	+	Shareholders' Equity	(Class.)
+3,750				+3,750	IncSt → RE
+3,750					
−3,750					

To record the third collection of £3,750 and recognize revenue equal to cash received. The seller has recovered its costs of £14,000, so it recognizes the entire amount of cash received as income.

If the customer fails to make all the promised payments, the seller can repossess the sold item; in this case, the accounting parallels that previously illustrated for the installment method.

Installment Method Compared to Cost Recovery Method In the preceding illustration, the pattern of income recognition differs between the installment method and the cost recovery method. This pattern, where the installment method reports income sooner than does the cost recovery method, holds independent of whether the customer makes all the promised payments. The differences arise from the differing logic supporting the two methods. The logic of the installment method assumes that the seller will receive all the promised cash or, if not, that when collections from the customer cease, the seller can repossess the goods, and, at that time, the goods retain sufficient value to cover the seller's as-yet-uncollected costs. On the other hand, the cost recovery method defers the recognition of any income until the seller has recovered all of its costs.

U.S. GAAP permits firms to use the installment method or the cost recovery method only when receivables are both collectible over an extended period and the seller has no reasonable basis for estimating the amount of cash that it will collect.[20] IFRS does not contain this level of detail; however, its general guidance implies a qualitatively similar criterion. For most sales of goods and services, past experience and an assessment of customers' credit standings provide a sufficient basis for estimating the amount of cash the seller will receive. If the seller can reasonably estimate the amount of cash it will receive, the seller will recognize revenue no later than at the time of sale.

PROBLEM 7.4 for Self-Study

Income recognition when collectibility is uncertain. On January 1, 2008, suppose that Scania agrees to sell two trucks for SEK1,080,000, which cost Scania SEK980,000, to Project Hope, a not-for-profit organization, that plans to open a transportation business. Project Hope has received partial funding for this venture, and its business plan, including forecasted cash flows, indicates significant uncertainty about its financial viability. Scania agrees to deliver the trucks in January and to permit Project Hope to pay in equal installments over 12 months, with the first payment due on June 30, 2008. Assume that Project Hope makes the first three payments and fails to make any other payments; also assume that Scania repossesses the trucks in December 2008 and decides that the net realizable value of the two trucks is SEK690,000. Prepare journal entries for this transaction assuming the following:

a. Scania uses the installment method.

b. Scania uses the cost recovery method.

INCOME RECOGNITION BEFORE DELIVERY

A firm sometimes recognizes revenue and expenses *before* it delivers a product. To satisfy the two criteria for revenue recognition, the transaction must meet the following tests:

- The seller has a firm arrangement with a particular customer.
- The parties have agreed on a selling price.
- The seller can reliably estimate the costs to complete the contract.
- The seller has performed substantial work to create the product.

An example of such an arrangement is a long-term contract, such as Bombardier's sale of trains (**Example 4**). Long-term contracts (for example, producing or constructing airplanes, trains, ships, or buildings) typically have three characteristics:

1. The period of construction (production) spans several accounting periods.
2. The seller identifies a customer, agrees on a contract price in advance (or at least in the early stages of construction), and has little doubt about the ability of the customer to make the agreed-on payments.
3. The buyer makes periodic payments of the contract price as work progresses, sometimes called **progress payments**.

Certain long-term contracts with these characteristics may meet the criteria for recognizing revenue during the period of construction or production. These criteria include:

- The existence of an arrangement (as required by the SEC) that specifies a buyer, a product to be delivered, and an agreed-on price.
- The seller reasonably expects the customer will pay the contract price in cash as construction or production progresses or when the seller completes the work.
- The seller can reliably estimate the costs it will incur in providing these future services.

---

[20]Note 8 to Accounting Principles Board, *Opinion No. 10*, "Omnibus Opinion—1966" (**Codification Topic 605**).

When the arrangement meets these criteria, U.S. GAAP and IFRS require firms to recognize income using the percentage-of-completion method. When the arrangement does not meet the criteria, U.S. GAAP requires firms to recognize income using the completed contract method; IFRS does not permit the completed contract method and instead specifies a variant of the cost recovery method.[21] We discuss each of these methods next.

PERCENTAGE-OF-COMPLETION METHOD

The **percentage-of-completion method** recognizes a portion of the contract price as revenue during each accounting period of construction or production, based on the proportion of total work performed during the accounting period. One commonly used measure of the proportion of total work performed during the accounting period is the ratio of costs incurred to date to the total estimated contract costs.[22] Usually, the firm keeps track of these costs in an inventory account, **Construction in Progress**, or **Construction in Process**. As the firm recognizes revenue for portions of the contract price, it also recognizes equal portions of the total estimated contract cost as expenses. The firm recognizes the expenses by debiting Cost of Goods Sold and crediting Construction in Progress. The percentage-of-completion method follows the accrual basis of accounting and matches expenses with related revenue. The actual schedule of cash collections (that is, progress payments) from the customer does not affect revenue recognition. Even if the contract specifies that the customer will pay the entire contract price when the seller delivers the product, the seller may use the percentage-of-completion method so long as it can reliably estimate the amount of cash it will receive and the costs it expects to incur in completing the job.

To illustrate the percentage-of-completion method, we revisit **Example 4**, in which Bombardier agrees to provide 25 trains over the next four years for a total contract price of €2 billion. The customer pays €250 million on signing the contract and will pay the remaining contract price in four equal installments of €437.5 million at the end of each year for four years.[23] Bombardier estimates the total cost to fulfill this contract is €1.6 billion, to be incurred as follows: first year, €400 million; second year, €600 million; third year, €400 million, and fourth year, €200 million. From these costs, it expects a gross margin of €400 million (= €2 billion − €1.6 billion) on this contract. Bombardier measures the percentage-of-completion as the ratio of total costs incurred to total costs anticipated, so it will recognize revenue and expense from the contract as follows (currency numbers are in millions of euros):[24]

Year	Degree of Completion	Revenue	−	Expense	=	Profit
1	€400/€1,600 = 25.0%	€ 500		€ 400		€100
2	€600/€1,600 = 37.5%	750		600		150
3	€400/€1,600 = 25.0%	500		400		100
4	€200/€1,600 = 12.5%	250		200		50
		€2,000	−	€1,600	=	€400

Bombardier's journal entry when it receives the initial cash collection is as follows:

Beginning of First Year

Cash.	250.0	
Advances from Customers		250.0

Assets	=	Liabilities	+	Shareholders' Equity	(Class.)
+250.0		+250.0			

To record the collection of €250 million at the time of contract signing.

---

[21]U.S. GAAP guidance is *Accounting Research Bulletin No. 45*, "Long-Term Construction-Type Contracts," 1955 (**Codification Topic 605**). IFRS guidance is *International Accounting Standard 11*, "Construction Contracts," 1993.

[22]Another method, which we do not discuss or illustrate, is the engineering estimate method. In that method, experts estimate the fraction of the work done in any period by physical examination of the construction in progress.

[23]This example ignores interest on the customer's delayed payments.

[24]In this simple example, Bombardier's actual costs are identical to its expected costs each year and in total.

At the end of the first year, Bombardier will recognize the receipt of the first installment and the appropriate portion (25%) of revenue and expenses under the percentage-of-completion method:

End of First Year

Cash 437.5

    Advances from Customers 437.5

Assets	=	Liabilities	+	Shareholders' Equity	(Class.)
+437.5		+437.5			

To record the first installment of the remaining contract price, €437.5 million (= 25% × [€2,000 − €250]).

Advances from Customers 500.0

Cost of Goods Sold 400.0

    Sales Revenue 500.0

    Construction in Progress[25] 400.0

Assets	=	Liabilities	+	Shareholders' Equity	(Class.)
−400.0		−500.0		+500.0	IncSt → RE
				−400.0	IncSt → RE

At the end of the first year, the balance in Advances from Customers is €187.5 million (= €250.0 million + €437.5 million − €500.0 million).

At the end of the second year, Bombardier will recognize the receipt of the second installment and the appropriate portion (37.5%) of total revenue and expenses under the percentage-of-completion method:

End of Second Year

Cash 437.5

    Advances from Customers 437.5

Assets	=	Liabilities	+	Shareholders' Equity	(Class.)
+437.5		+437.5			

To record the second installment of the remaining contract price, €437.5 million (= 25% × [€2,000 − €250]).

Accounts Receivable, Gross 125.0

Advances from Customers 625.0

Cost of Goods Sold 600.0

    Sales Revenue 750.0

    Construction in Progress 600.0

Assets	=	Liabilities	+	Shareholders' Equity	(Class.)
+125.0		−625.0		+750.0	IncSt → RE
−600.0				−600.0	IncSt → RE

Before Bombardier recognizes revenue in the second year, the balance in Advances from Customers is €625 million (= Beginning balance of €187.5 + €437.5). Bombardier first reduces the balance in Advances from Customers to zero (by debiting it for €625) and then records the remaining recognized revenue of €125 million (= €750 − €625) as a debit to Accounts Receivable, Gross.[26]

---

[25]For simplicity, we do not show the journal entries that debit Construction in Progress and credit various asset and liability accounts as Bombardier accumulates contract costs.

[26]Bombardier will also apply the allowance method for estimating uncollectible accounts receivable described earlier in this chapter.

At the end of the third year, Bombardier will recognize the receipt of the third installment and the appropriate portion (25.0%) of revenue and expenses under the percentage-of-completion method:

End of Third Year

Cash.. 437.5
    Accounts Receivable, Gross 125.0
    Advances from Customers 312.5

Assets	=	Liabilities	+	Shareholders' Equity	(Class.)
+437.5		+312.5			
−125.0					

To record the third installment of the remaining contract price, €437.5 million (= 25% × [€2,000 − €250]). First Bombardier applies the cash collection to the amounts owed by the customer (Accounts Receivable, Gross) and then records any remainder as Advances from Customers.

Accounts Receivable, Gross 187.5
Advances from Customers 312.5
Cost of Goods Sold 400.0
    Sales Revenue 500.0
    Construction in Progress 400.0

Assets	=	Liabilities	+	Shareholders' Equity	(Class.)
+187.5		−312.5		+500.0	IncSt → RE
−400.0				−400.0	IncSt → RE

Before Bombardier recognizes revenue in the third year, the balance in Advances from Customers is €312.5 million. In recording revenue for the third year, Bombardier first reduces the balance in Advances from Customers to zero (by debiting it for €312.5) and then records the remaining recognized revenue, €187.5 million (= €500 − €312.5), as Accounts Receivable, Gross.

At the end of the fourth year, Bombardier will recognize the receipt of the final installment and the appropriate portion (12.5%) of revenues and expenses under the percentage-of-completion method:

Cash.. 437.5
    Accounts Receivable, Gross 187.5
    Advances from Customers 250.0

Assets	=	Liabilities	+	Shareholders' Equity	(Class.)
+437.5		+250.0			
−187.5					

To record the final installment of the remaining contract price, €437.5 million (= 25% × [€2,000 − €250]). The seller first applies the cash collection to the amounts owed by the customer (Accounts Receivable, Gross) and then records any remainder as Advances from Customers.

Advances from Customers 250.0
Cost of Goods Sold 200.0
    Sales Revenue 250.0
    Construction in Progress 200.0

Assets	=	Liabilities	+	Shareholders' Equity	(Class.)
−200.0		−250.0		+250.0	IncSt → RE
				−200.0	IncSt → RE

COMPLETED CONTRACT METHOD

The **completed contract method** postpones revenue recognition until the seller completes all construction or production and transfers the finished item to the customer. U.S. GAAP specifies the completed contract method when the outcome of the contract is in doubt because of a lack of reliable estimates (of costs or cash to be collected). Continuing the preceding example, if Bombardier used the completed contract method, it would recognize no revenue or expense from the train contract during the first three years. In the fourth year, upon delivery of the 25 trains, it would recognize revenue of €2 billion and cost of goods sold of €1.6 billion. Total gross profit is €400 million under both the percentage-of-completion and the completed contract methods, but the latter defers all revenue recognition until Bombardier completes the project. Applying the completed contract method while it is producing the trains, Bombardier would recognize cash collections from the customer (progress payments) as debits to Cash and credits to Advances from Customers, and would accumulate contract costs in a Construction in Process account.

PERCENTAGE-OF-COMPLETION METHOD COMPARED TO COMPLETED CONTRACT METHOD

The percentage-of-completion method provides information about the seller's performance during the contract period; in contrast, the completed contract method reports all profit only when seller completes the contract. The percentage-of-completion method reflects current performance on a timely basis, relative to the completed contract method. The shorter the contract length, however, the smaller are the accounting differences between the two approaches, so firms might use the completed contract method for short contracts because they find it generally easier to implement and there are no substantial differences in income relative to the percentage-of-completion method.

Because persuasive evidence of an arrangement must exist as a condition for recognizing revenue, firms use the completed contract method if there is no contract with a specific customer, as for example, in the construction of residential housing on speculation. These situations require future marketing effort; moreover, substantial uncertainty may exist regarding the selling price and therefore the amount of cash the seller will collect. In addition, if there is sufficient uncertainty about the total contract costs, the seller may not use the percentage-of-completion method—even when it has a contract with a specified price.

IFRS REQUIREMENTS FOR RECOGNIZING CONTRACT REVENUE WHEN THE SELLER CANNOT RELIABLY ESTIMATE THE OUTCOME

As previously noted, IFRS specifies the percentage-of-completion method when the seller can reliably estimate the outcome of the contract, in terms of revenues and costs. If the seller cannot, then IFRS does not permit the use of the completed contract method. Instead, IFRS requires that the seller recognize revenue to the extent of recoverable contract costs and recognize expenses as incurred. That is, IFRS specifies that the seller recognize revenues equal to recoverable costs incurred and expensed. Therefore, we can think of this approach as a variant of the cost recovery method, which the seller applies when it cannot reliably estimate either the revenues or the costs, or both.

PROBLEM 7.5 for Self-Study

Income recognition for contractor. Suppose that General Electric Company (GE) contracts with the City of Shanghai in June 2008, to build a water treatment plant at a contract price of 145 million yuan (¥). GE plans to begin construction January 1, 2009, and to finish September 2011. GE estimates that the cost of constructing the water treatment plant will be ¥100 million. GE incurred ¥30 million in construction costs during 2009, ¥60 million during 2010, and ¥10 million during 2011. The City of Shanghai agrees to make equal progress payments on the first of each year. GE completed

(continued)

the water treatment facility in September 2011. Calculate GE's gross profit (= revenue less expenses) on the Shanghai contract during 2009, 2010, and 2011, assuming the following:

a. GE uses the percentage-of-completion method.

b. GE uses the completed contract method.

c. GE uses the method specified by IFRS when it cannot reliably estimate the outcome of the contract. Assume that GE decides that all costs incurred are recoverable.

SUMMARY

Revenue is the single largest recurring financial statement item for most firms and a key determinant of operating profitability. Revenue represents inflows of assets from transactions with customers. The timing and measurement of revenue, and the associated expenses, are subject to detailed guidance in U.S. GAAP and general guidance in IFRS, which specifies the conditions for recognizing revenue before, at, and after the time of sale. The seller must have earned revenues in the sense that it has performed, or substantially performed, its obligations to the buyer, and it can reliably estimate the cash or cash equivalent value of assets received from the customer. When either requirement fails, the seller must defer revenue recognition. Accounting guidance also provides special procedures for single arrangements (contracts) that contain multiple deliverables and for long-term contracts.

A firm's gross accounts receivable reflects the amounts customers have promised to pay. The balance sheet displays these receivables net of estimated uncollectible accounts. When the seller decides that a receivable has become uncollectible, it writes off the receivable. Because of their importance for analyzing liquidity and profitability, accounts receivable are an input to several ratios used by financial analysts.

APPENDIX 7.1: COMPARISON OF REVENUE RECOGNITION CRITERIA BETWEEN U.S. GAAP AND IFRS

REVENUE RECOGNITION UNDER U.S. GAAP

Conceptual guidance[27] states that the seller recognizes revenue only when the transaction meets both of the following conditions:

1. The seller has earned the revenue, meaning that the seller has substantially accomplished what it has promised the customer (the "earned" condition).

2. The revenue is realized or realizable, meaning that the seller has received cash or some other asset that it can convert to cash (the "realized or realizable" condition).

In addition, the Securities and Exchange Commission (SEC) of the United States has issued *Staff Accounting Bulletin No. 104 (SAB 104)*, which summarizes the following four conditions for revenue recognition:[28]

1. Persuasive evidence of an arrangement exists.

2. Delivery has occurred or services have been performed.

3. The seller's price to the buyer is fixed or determinable.

4. Collectibility is reasonably assured; that is, the seller can measure the amount of revenue and is reasonably certain to collect it.

---

[27]Financial Accounting Standards Board, *Statement of Financial Accounting Concepts No. 5*, "Recognition and Measurement in Financial Statements of Business Enterprises," 1984, par. 83–84.

[28]Securities and Exchange Commission, *Staff Accounting Bulletin No. 104*, 17 CFR Part 211, December 2003.

Conditions **2**, **3**, and **4** of *SAB 104* are similar to the two conditions stated in *Concepts Statement 5*. *SAB 104* also requires persuasive evidence that the seller has an arrangement with a customer in the form of a contract, or prior business dealings, or customary business practices. The arrangement states the responsibilities of the seller and its customers with respect to the nature and delivery of goods or services, the risks assumed by buyer and seller, the timing of cash payments, and similar factors.

REVENUE RECOGNITION UNDER IFRS

IFRS distinguishes between revenue from sales of goods and revenue from sales of services.[29] With regard to sales of goods, IFRS specifies five conditions for recognizing revenue; conditions **1** and **2** apply only to the sale of goods:

1. The seller has transferred to the buyer the significant risks and rewards of ownership of the goods.

2. The seller has not retained either effective control or the kind of involvement that is associated with ownership.

3. The amount of revenue can be measured reliably.

4. It is probable that the seller will obtain the economic benefits associated with the transaction.

5. The costs incurred or to be incurred can be measured reliably.

With regard to services, IFRS specifies conditions **3**, **4**, and **5**, plus one additional condition: *The stage of completion of the transaction at the end of the reporting period can be measured reliably.*

COMPARISON OF U.S. GAAP WITH IFRS

Within IFRS, conditions **1** and **2** for the sale of goods, and condition **1** for the sale of services, are analogous to the "earned" condition of U.S. GAAP—they specify that the seller has performed its obligations. Conditions **3** and **4** are analogous to the "realized or realizable" condition of U.S. GAAP—they specify that the seller has obtained a reliably measurable asset that will result in benefits. Condition **5** in IFRS pertains to the measurement of cost or expense recognition.

U.S. GAAP and IFRS are consistent in the approach to revenue recognition in that both rely on the idea of an earnings process, which IFRS describes in terms of the transfer of risk and reward of ownership, and the realization principle, which IFRS describes in terms of reliable measurement and the ability to obtain economic benefits. This does not mean, however, that revenue recognition is the same under U.S. GAAP and IFRS. U.S. GAAP provides over 200 specific pieces of detailed guidance, much of which is industry-specific or transaction-specific, while IFRS contains just one general standard and a handful of more specific standards (for example, for construction contracts). So, for example, U.S. GAAP contains specific guidance for revenue recognition for franchise fees and for sales of real estate, while the general IFRS standard for revenue recognition does not address these industry-specific arrangements.[30]

SOLUTIONS TO SELF-STUDY PROBLEMS

SUGGESTED SOLUTION TO PROBLEM 7.1 FOR SELF-STUDY

(Sony Corporation; revenue recognition at time of sale, after sale, or before sale.)

a. At the time of shipment to Best Buy, Sony has incurred most of its costs. Experience should provide Sony with sufficient evidence to estimate the cost of damaged and defective televisions. Thus, the arrangement appears to meet the first criterion for revenue recognition, substantial performance. The second criterion is also met because there is an agreed-on price (of $2,000 per television), and Best Buy agrees to pay within 30 days. Sony

---

[29]International Accounting Standards Committee, *International Accounting Standard 18*, "Revenue," 1993.

[30]Financial Accounting Standards Board, *Statement of Financial Accounting Standards No. 45*, "Accounting for Franchise Fee Revenue," 1981 (**Codification Topic 952**) and *Statement of Financial Accounting Standards No. 66*, "Accounting for Sales of Real Estate," 1982 (**Codification Topic 360**).

may recognize the revenue from this transaction when Best Buy takes possession (that is, ownership) of the televisions, normally either when Best Buy receives the televisions or when Sony ships the televisions.

b. This arrangement is similar to **a**. At the time of shipment, Sony has met the first criterion for revenue recognition. There may be substantial uncertainty, however, about whether Best Buy will return the televisions for a full refund. Sony can recognize revenues on this transaction at the earlier of two dates: (1) Best Buy notifies Sony that it has sold all televisions, or (2) six months from the receipt of the televisions by Best Buy. At both of these times, there is no uncertainty about the return of televisions to Sony (except for defects covered under warranties). Best Buy has committed to pay Sony within 30 days. If Sony can reliably estimate the number of televisions it expects Best Buy to return, then U.S. GAAP might allow Sony to recognize revenue the same way as in part **a**, depending on other factors not discussed here.

c. In this setting, Best Buy acts as a consignee for Sony's televisions; Sony is the consignor. In a consignment arrangement, the consignor (Sony) sends goods (televisions) to a consignee (Best Buy) for sale, with Sony holding title until Best Buy makes a sale. Sony should not recognize revenue when it ships the televisions, because the amount that Sony ultimately receives depends on whether and at what price Best Buy sells the televisions. Therefore, the amount of cash that Sony will collect is uncertain with regard to both amount and timing. Thus, Sony should recognize revenue only when it receives the cash from Best Buy or when Best Buy notifies Sony of the amounts it will remit for sales made this period.

SUGGESTED SOLUTION TO PROBLEM 7.2 FOR SELF-STUDY

(Scania; revenue recognition at time of sale.)

a. To record sale of four truck engines at SEK20,000 per engine, with payment from the customer to be received in 60 days.

| Accounts Receivable, Gross | 80,000 | |
| Sales Revenue | | 80,000 |

Assets	=	Liabilities	+	Shareholders' Equity	(Class.)
+80,000				+80,000	IncSt → RE

b. Scania makes no journal entry at the time it signs the SEK250,000 contract for the 50 transport containers, because there has been no performance and the customer has not made any payments.

c. Customer makes payment in full for four engines from part **a**.

| Cash | 80,000 | |
| Accounts Receivable, Gross | | 80,000 |

Assets	=	Liabilities	+	Shareholders' Equity	(Class.)
+80,000					
−80,000					

d. To record sale of a truck for SEK725,000.

Cash	145,000	
Accounts Receivable, Gross	580,000	
Sales Revenue		725,000

Assets	=	Liabilities	+	Shareholders' Equity	(Class.)
+145,000				+725,000	IncSt → RE
+580,000					

e. To record revenue, delivery of containers, and receipt of customer payment.

Cash.   250,000
    Sales Revenue   250,000

Assets	=	Liabilities	+	Shareholders' Equity	(Class.)
+250,000				+250,000	IncSt → RE

f. To write off an uncollectible account, for SEK580,000.

Allowance for Uncollectibles   580,000
    Accounts Receivable, Gross   580,000

Assets	=	Liabilities	+	Shareholders' Equity	(Class.)
+580,000					
−580,000					

g. To record bad debt expense for the year.

Bad Debt Expense. . . . .   1.4 billion
    Allowance for Uncollectibles . . . .   1.4 billion

Assets	=	Liabilities	+	Shareholders' Equity	(Class.)
−1.4 billion				−1.4 billion	IncSt → RE

SUGGESTED SOLUTION TO PROBLEM 7.3 FOR SELF-STUDY

(Scania; revenue recognition after sale when substantial performance remains.)

a. To record the receipt of SEK250,000 as a customer advance on the contract to deliver 50 containers. Scania has not performed its obligation to deliver containers.

Cash.   250,000
    Advances from Customers   250,000

Assets	=	Liabilities	+	Shareholders' Equity	(Class.)
+250,000		+250,000			

b. To record the sale of the truck, training session, and customer support.

Cash.   145,000
Accounts Receivable, Gross   580,000
    Sales Revenue   641,347
    Advances from Customers   83,653

Assets	=	Liabilities	+	Shareholders' Equity	(Class.)
+145,000		+83,653		+641,347	IncSt → RE
+580,000					

The sum of the fair values of the three contract elements is SEK780,000 (= SEK690,000 + SEK40,000 + SEK50,000). The portion of the contract price attributable to the truck is SEK641,347 (= SEK725,000 × [SEK690,000/SEK780,000]). The portion attributable to the training session is SEK37,179 (= SEK725,000 × [SEK40,000/SEK780,000]), and the portion attributable to the customer support is SEK46,474 (= SEK725,000 × [SEK50,000/SEK780,000]).

c. To record delivery of the containers (part **a**) and delivery of the training session (part **b**).

| Advances from Customers | 250,000 | |
| Sales Revenue | | 250,000 |

Assets	=	Liabilities	+	Shareholders' Equity	(Class.)
		−250,000		+250,000	IncSt → RE

| Advances from Customers | 37,179 | |
| Sales Revenue | | 37,179 |

Assets	=	Liabilities	+	Shareholders' Equity	(Class.)
		−37,179		+37,179	IncSt → RE

d. No journal entry, because there has been only an exchange of promises (an executory contract).

e. To record the payment made by the customer pursuant to the contract in part **d**.

| Cash | 200,000 | |
| Advances from Customers | | 200,000 |

Assets	=	Liabilities	+	Shareholders' Equity	(Class.)
+200,000		+200,000			

f. The adjusting entry for eight months of customer support, May–December (part **b**).

| Advances from Customers | 10,328 | |
| Sales Revenue | | 10,328 |

Assets	=	Liabilities	+	Shareholders' Equity	(Class.)
		−10,328		+10,328	IncSt → RE

From part **b**, the portion of total contract revenue attributable to customer support is SEK46,474 (= SEK725,000 × [SEK50,000/SEK780,000]). Scania will recognize this amount as revenue ratably (equally) over the 3-year (36-months) term of the customer support. 2008 revenue is SEK10,328 (= SEK46,474 × [8 months/36 months]) for support during May–December.

SUGGESTED SOLUTION TO PROBLEM 7.4 FOR SELF-STUDY

(Scania; income recognition when collectibility is uncertain.)

a. Analysis and journal entries under the installment method.

At the time of sale, Scania derecognizes the two trucks, recognizes a receivable, and recognizes a deferred gross margin of SEK100,000 (= SEK1,080,000 − SEK980,000). The gross margin percentage is approximately 9.26% (= SEK100,000/SEK1,080,000). The journal entry at time of sale is:

Accounts Receivable, Gross	1,080,000	
Inventory		980,000
Deferred Gross Margin		100,000

Assets	=	Liabilities	+	Shareholders' Equity	(Class.)
+1,080,000					
−980,000					
−100,000					

By convention, Scania might display the deferred gross margin among its liabilities; we classify it as a reduction of assets following *Concepts Statement 6*.

June–August: Project Hope makes three monthly payments. The journal entry to record each of the three payments is:

Cash	90,000	
Deferred Gross Margin	8,334	
Cost of Goods Sold (plug)	81,666	
Sales Revenue		90,000
Accounts Receivable, Gross		90,000

Assets	=	Liabilities	+	Shareholders' Equity	(Class.)
+90,000				+90,000	IncSt → RE
+8,334				−81,666	IncSt → RE
−90,000					

Scania collects 1/12 of the total contract price, or SEK90,000 (= SEK1,080,000/12 months) and recognizes this amount as revenue. Under the installment method, Scania also recognizes gross margin = gross margin percentage (.0926) × cash received (SEK90,000) or SEK8,334. After Project Hope has made three payments of SEK90,000 each, the balance in Accounts Receivable is SEK810,000 (= SEK1,080,000 − [3 × SEK90,000]). The balance in Deferred Gross Margin is SEK74,998 (= SEK100,000 − [3 × SEK8,334]).

After Project Hope fails to make the promised payments, in December 2008 Scania repossesses the two trucks and judges that their net realizable value is SEK690,000:

Inventory—Repossessed Items	690,000	
Deferred Gross Margin	74,998	
Loss on Repossession (plug)	45,002	
Accounts Receivable, Gross		810,000

Assets	=	Liabilities	+	Shareholders' Equity	(Class.)
+690,000				−45,002	IncSt → RE
+74,998					
−810,000					

Scania writes off the remaining balances in Accounts Receivable and Deferred Gross Margin, recognizes the repossessed inventory at its net realizable value, and recognizes a loss.

b. Analysis and journal entries using the cost recovery method.

At the time of sale, Scania makes the same journal entries under both the installment method and the cost recovery method.

June–August: Project Hope makes three monthly payments. The journal to record each of the three payments is:

Cash	90,000	
Cost of Goods Sold	90,000	
Sales Revenue		90,000
Accounts Receivable, Gross		90,000

Assets	=	Liabilities	+	Shareholders' Equity	(Class.)
+90,000				+90,000	IncSt → RE
−90,000				−90,000	IncSt → RE

(continued)

Scania collects 1/12 of the total contract price, or SEK90,000 (= SEK1,080,000/12 months). Under the cost recovery method, Scania recognizes cost of goods sold equal to revenue until it recovers the entire cost of SEK980,000. Gross margin each month during June–August is zero. After Project Hope has made three payments, the balance in Accounts Receivable is SEK810,000 (= SEK1,080,000 − [3 × SEK90,000]). The balance in Deferred Gross Margin is SEK100,000.

After Project Hope fails to make the promised payments, in December 2008 Scania repossesses the two trucks and judges that their net realizable value is SEK690,000:

Inventory—Repossessed Items	690,000
Deferred Gross Margin	100,000
Loss on Repossession (plug)	20,000
Accounts Receivable, Gross	810,000

Assets	=	Liabilities	+	Shareholders' Equity	(Class.)
+690,000				−20,000	IncSt → RE
+100,000					
−810,000					

Scania writes off the remaining balances in Accounts Receivable and Deferred Gross Margin, recognizes the repossessed inventory at its net realizable value and recognizes a loss.

SUGGESTED SOLUTION TO PROBLEM 7.5 FOR SELF-STUDY

(General Electric Company; income recognition for contractor.)

a. Percentage-of-completion method:

Year	Incremental Percentage Complete	Revenue Recognized	Expenses Recognized	Net Income
2009	30/100 (= 0.30)	¥ 43.5 million	¥ 30.0 million	¥13.5 million
2010	60/100 (= 0.60)	87.0 million	60.0 million	27.0 million
2011	10/100 (= 0.10)	14.5 million	10.0 million	4.5 million
Total	100/100 (= 1.00)	¥145.0 million	¥100.0 million	¥45.0 million

b. Completed contract method:

Year	Revenue Recognized	Expenses Recognized	Net Income
2009	¥ 0	¥ 0	¥ 0
2010	0	0	0
2011	145.0 million	100.0 million	45.0 million
Total	¥145.0 million	¥100.0 million	¥45.0 million

c. IFRS, when GE cannot reliably estimate the contract's outcome:

Year	Revenue Recognized	Expenses Recognized	Net Income
2009	¥ 30.0 million	¥ 30.0 million	¥ 0
2010	60.0 million	60.0 million	0
2011	55.0 million	10.0 million	45.0 million
Total	¥145.0 million	¥100.0 million	¥45.0 million

KEY TERMS AND CONCEPTS

Revenue recognition
Expense recognition
Sales returns
Multiple deliverable contract
Percentage-of-completion method
Accounts receivable, trade receivables
Uncollectible account
Allowance method
Allowance for Uncollectibles account
Accounts Receivable, Gross account
Accounts Receivable, Net account
Bad Debt Expense, Provision for Bad Debts, Provision for Uncollectible Accounts
Control (or controlling) account
Writing off
Percentage-of-sales procedure

Aging-of-accounts-receivable procedure
Accounts receivable turnover ratio
Days receivables outstanding
Securitization
Sales returns
Deferred performance obligations, advances from customers, deferred revenues, unearned revenues
Installment method
Gross margin percentage, gross margin
Cost recovery method
Progress payments
Percentage-of-completion method
Construction in Progress, Construction in Process account
Completed contract method

QUESTIONS, EXERCISES, AND PROBLEMS

QUESTIONS

1. Review the meaning of the terms and concepts listed above in Key Terms and Concepts.

2. The cost recovery method and the completed contract method of recognizing revenues are similar in that both methods delay the recognition of income even if a firm collects cash. In what ways do the two methods differ?

3. The accounting for a multiple element contract separates the contract with a customer into pieces (components or deliverables) and assigns each component a portion of the total contract revenue. The percentage-of-completion method of accounting for a long-term construction contract also separates the contract for accounting purposes. How do the approaches used by the multiple element contract method and the percentage-of-completion method to separate the contract differ from, and resemble, each other?

4. The allowance method of accounting for uncollectible accounts receivable involves the creation of a contra account that shows the estimated amount of uncollectible receivables. Why would financial statement users want to know both this number and the gross amount of accounts receivable?

5. **a.** An old wisdom in tennis holds that if your first serves are always good, you are not hitting them hard enough. An analogous statement in business might be that if you have no uncollectible accounts, you probably are not selling enough on credit. Comment on the validity and parallelism of these statements.

   b. When are more uncollectible accounts better than fewer uncollectible accounts?

   c. When is a higher percentage of uncollectible accounts better than a lower percentage?

6. Under what circumstances will the Allowance for Uncollectible Accounts have a debit balance during the accounting period? The balance sheet figure for the Allowance for Uncollectible Accounts at the end of the period should never show a debit balance. Why?

7. Construction companies often use the percentage-of-completion method. Why doesn't a typical manufacturing firm use this method of income recognition?

8. Both the installment method and the cost recovery method recognize revenue when a firm collects cash. Why, then, does the pattern of income (that is, revenues minus expenses) over time differ under these two methods?

9. "When the total amount of cash that a firm expects to collect from a customer is highly uncertain, the cost recovery method seems more appropriate than the installment method." Explain.

10. A magazine publisher offers a reduced annual subscription fee if customers pay for three years in advance. Under this subscription program, the magazine publisher receives from customers $45,000, which it credits to Advances from Customers. The estimated cost of publishing and distributing magazines for these customers is $32,000. Why does accounting report a liability of $45,000 instead of $32,000?

11. Both bad debt expense and expected returns reduce income in the period of sale. How does the accounting for these two items differ and how is it similar?

12. Conceptually, what kind of account is the Deferred Gross Margin account that arises under the installment method of accounting? How is this account typically classified on balance sheets?

EXERCISES

13. **Revenue recognition for various businesses.** Discuss when each of the following types of businesses is likely to recognize revenue:

   a. A shoe store.

   b. A shipbuilding firm constructing an aircraft carrier under a government contract.

   c. A real estate developer selling lots on long-term contracts with small down payments required.

   d. A barbershop.

   e. A citrus-growing firm.

   f. A producer of television movies working under the condition that it will sell the rights to the movies to a television network for the first three years, and all rights thereafter revert to the producer.

   g. A residential real estate developer who constructs houses only on speculation and later sells the houses to buyers.

   h. A producer of fine whiskey that ages from 6 to 12 years before sale.

   i. A savings and loan association lending money for home mortgages.

   j. A travel agency that sells tickets in one period and to customers who take trips or return tickets in the next period.

   k. A printer who prints only custom-order stationery.

   l. A seller to food stores of trading stamps redeemable by food store customers for various household products.

   m. A wholesale food distributor.

   n. A livestock rancher.

   o. A shipping company that loads cargo in one accounting period, carries cargo across the ocean in a second accounting period, and unloads the cargo in a third period; the shipping is all done under contract, and cash collection of shipping charges is relatively certain.

14. **Income recognition for various business arrangements.** Refer to the conceptual revenue recognition guidance given in **Appendix 7.1**. Applying this conceptual guidance, discuss the timing of revenue recognition and any related measurement issues.

   a. Company A develops software and sells it to customers for an up-front fee. Company A provides these customers with password-protected access to its Web site for two years after delivery of the software. With this access, customers can download certain data and other software. Company A has an obligation to provide updates on its Web site.

   b. Company B develops software and sells it to newly formed storage application service providers (SAPs), who promise to pay for the software over the next two years. These SAPs in turn place the software on their Web sites and sell rights to access the software to their customers.

   c. Company C develops software that it places on its Web site. It sells rights to its customers to access this software online for a period of two years. Customers pay an up-front fee for the right to access the software.

d. Company D maintains an auction site on the Web. It charges customers an up-front fee to list products for sale and a transaction fee when a sale takes place. The transaction fee is refundable if the auction winner fails to honor its commitment to purchase the product.

e. Company E sells products of various supplier companies on its Web site. Company E transmits customers' purchase requests to the supplier companies, who fill the orders. Customers pay for their purchases using third-party credit cards. Company E receives a fee from the supplier companies for each item sold.

f. Company F sells products of various supplier companies on its Web site. It promises to the supplier companies to sell a minimum number of items each month and pays storage and insurance costs for that minimum number of units. Actual storage of these units takes place at the supplier companies' warehouses. The supplier companies also handle shipments to customers. Customers pay for their purchases using third-party credit cards.

g. Company G manufactures and sells personal computers (PCs). Customers receive a $400 rebate on the purchase of the computer if they will purchase Internet access services for three years after the purchase of the computer. Customers mail their rebate coupons to the Internet service provider, called an ISP. Examples are AOL and AT&T. The ISP bears 90% of the initial cost of the rebate, and the PC manufacturer bears the other 10%. If customers do not subscribe for the full three-year period, the parties reallocate the cost of the rebate, $360 (= 0.90 × $400) initially borne by the ISP and $40 (= 0.10 × $400) by the manufacturer, resulting in the PC manufacturer's paying the ISP to reduce the ISP's share of the rebate's cost from $360 to a smaller amount.

h. Company H sells advertising space on its Web site to other companies. For an up-front fee, Company H guarantees to the other companies a certain minimum number of hits, viewings, or click-throughs each month of the one-year contract period. It must return a pro rata portion of the fee if the hits and click-throughs fall short of the guarantee.

i. Company I sells advertising space on its Web site to other companies. It recently received 10,000 shares of common stock of Upstart Company in payment for certain advertising space. Upstart Company intends to make an initial public offering of its common stock in six months. At the most recent financing round, venture capitalists paid $10 per share for the common stock.

j. Company J and Company K both maintain Web sites. Each company sells advertising space to the other company for an agreed-on period, with no funds changing hands.

15. **Meaning of allowance for uncollectible accounts.** Indicate whether each of the following accurately describes the meaning of the Allowance for Uncollectible Accounts account when properly used. If the description does not apply to this account, discuss why it does not.

a. Assets available in case customers don't later pay what they owe.

b. Cash available in case customers don't later pay what they owe.

c. Estimates of the amount that customers who purchased goods this period, but who have not yet paid, and won't later pay.

d. Estimates of the amount of goods purchased by customers, whether paid or not, that the firm estimates those customers will return.

e. Estimates of the amount that customers who purchased goods at any time, but who have not yet paid, and won't later pay.

f. Estimates of amount the firm will owe to others if its customers who purchased goods this period don't later pay what they owe.

g. Estimates of amount the firm will owe to others if its customers who ever purchased goods don't later pay what they owe.

h. Estimates of the amount of sales for the current period that will become bad debt expense for the current period.

i. An amount of deferred revenue.

j. A part of retained earnings.

16. **Revenue recognition at time of sale.** Pret a Manger is a food retailer with stores in the U.K. and the United States and is known for its fast but fresh food menu. A customer shopping

at a London Heathrow store purchased a ham and cheese baguette (£4.50), a small fruit salad (£2.40), and a banana-bran muffin (£1.50). The customer paid with cash.

a. What journal entry will Pret a Manger record for this transaction?

b. Suppose that, in addition to the above items, the customer purchased a Pret a Manger card (to use for future purchases at Pret a Manger stores) for £40.00. What journal entry will Pret a Manger record for this transaction?

c. Suppose that, for the original transaction described in this problem, the customer did not pay with cash but used a Pret a Manger card purchased a month earlier. Assume there is a sufficient balance on the card to cover the cost of his purchases. What journal entry did Pret a Manger record?

17. **Revenue recognition at and after time of sale.** A customer shopping at Bed, Bath & Beyond, a home products retailer in the United States, made the following purchases: $100 for bath towels, $135 for a top-of-the-line iron, $45 for an ironing board, and $250 for a gift certificate sent as a wedding gift. Sales taxes on the purchase amounted to 5% of the total order. The customer paid with cash. What journal entry will Bed, Bath & Beyond make to recognize revenue on this transaction? Ignore the journal entries to recognize the expenses.

18. **Revenue recognition at time of sale.** Marks and Spencer Group, Plc., a U.K. retailer, applies IFRS and reports its results in millions of pounds sterling (£). The notes to its financial statements for the year ended March 29, 2008, provide the following information:

- Revenue comprises sales of goods to customers less an appropriate deduction for returns and discounts. Marks and Spencer records revenues for sales of furniture and items purchased online upon delivery to the customer.

- Marks and Spencer records trade receivables at their nominal amount less an allowance for any doubtful accounts and sales returns. The beginning balance in the allowance for uncollectible accounts and sales returns was £1.1 million, and the ending balance was £3.3 million. There were no recoveries of uncollectible accounts during the year.

For the year ended March 29, 2008, Marks and Spencer reported revenues (before discounts and returns) of £9,022.0 million. The cost of merchandise sold in 2008 was £5,535.2 million. Assume that Marks and Spencer estimates discounts and returns of 1% of sales. Further assume that it made all sales on credit and that it estimates that 1.5% of revenues will be uncollectible.

a. What journal entry did Marks and Spencer record during the year ended March 29, 2008, to recognize revenues and expenses?

b. What journal entry did Marks and Spencer make in the year ended March 29, 2008, to recognize sales returns and bad debts expense?

c. What was the combined amount of sales returns and write-offs of uncollectible accounts during the year ended March 29, 2008?

19. **Revenue recognition at time of sale.** Assume that Lentiva Group Limited provided the following description of its revenue recognition practices in the notes to its 2007 financial statements.

- Lentiva recognizes revenue from the sale of goods (such as sales of hardware and software) when it effectively transfers both ownership and risk of loss to the customer, generally when there is persuasive evidence a sales arrangement exists, the price is fixed or determinable, collectibility is reasonably assured, and delivery has occurred.

- Lentiva defers revenue from contracts to provide training services and amortizes those amounts as earned over the contract period, generally three years.

Assume that on January 1, 2008, Lentiva sold 50,000 laptop computers to the New York City public education system for $75 million. The price of the computers includes a contract for training services, which Lentiva will provide evenly over the next two years. Sold separately, the price of the training services is $100 per laptop, and the price of a laptop is $1,500. Lentiva's cost of a laptop is $1,200, and the expected cost to provide the training is $50 per laptop. At the time of sale, the customer paid Lentiva $15 million, and promised to pay the remaining amount owed in 30 days. Assuming that the arrangement meets the first criterion to recognize revenue, what journal entries will Lentiva make on these dates:

    a. January 1, 2008?

    b. December 31, 2008?

    c. December 31, 2009?

20. Journal entries for coupons. Morrison's Cafeteria sells coupons that customers may use later to purchase meals. Each coupon book sells for $25 and has a face value of $30; that is, the customer can use the book to purchase meals with menu prices of $30. On January 1, 2008, redeemable unused coupons that Morrison's had sold for $4,000 were outstanding. Cash inflows during the next three months appear in the following table:

	March	February	January
Cash-Paying Customers	$50,000	$48,500	$48,000
Sale of Coupon Books	2,400	2,200	2,100
Total Cash Receipts	$52,400	$50,700	$50,100

Customers redeemed coupons with a discounted face value for meals as follows: January, $1,600; February, $2,300; March, $2,100.

    a. Prepare journal entries for January, February, and March to reflect the above information.

    b. What effect, if any, do the coupon sales and redemptions have on the liabilities on the March 31, 2008, balance sheet?

21. Journal entries for service contracts. Abson Corporation began business on January 1, 2008, selling copiers. It also sells service contracts to maintain and repair copiers for $600 per year. When a customer signs a service contract, Abson collects the $600 fee and credits Service Contract Fees Received in Advance. Abson recognizes revenues on a quarterly basis during the year of coverage. For purposes of computing revenue, Abson assumes that all sales of service contracts occur midway through each quarter. Sales of contracts and service expenses for 2008 appear in the following table:

	Sales of Contracts	Service Expenses
First Quarter	$180,000 (300 contracts)	$ 32,000
Second Quarter	300,000 (500 contracts)	71,000
Third Quarter	240,000 (400 contracts)	105,000
Fourth Quarter	120,000 (200 contracts)	130,000

    a. Prepare journal entries for the first three quarters of the year for Abson Corporation. Assume that the firm prepares quarterly reports on March 31, June 30, and September 30, 2008.

    b. What is the balance in the Service Contract Fees Received in Advance account on December 31, 2008?

22. Allowance method for uncollectible accounts. Diversified Technologies opened for business on January 1, 2008. Sales on account during 2008 were $126,900. Collections from customers from sales on account during 2008 were $94,300. Diversified Technologies estimates that it will ultimately not collect 4% of 2008 sales on account. During 2008 the firm wrote off $2,200 of accounts receivable as uncollectible. The firm uses the allowance method for uncollectible accounts.

    a. Compute the amount of bad debt expense for 2008.

    b. Compute the December 31, 2008, balance sheet carrying value of accounts receivable.

23. Aging of accounts receivable. York Company's accounts receivable show the following balances:

Age of Accounts	Balance Receivable
0–30 Days	$1,200,000
31–60 Days	255,000
61–120 Days	75,000
More than 120 Days	30,000

York Company uses the aging-of-accounts-receivable procedure for uncollectible accounts. The credit balance in the Allowance for Uncollectible Accounts is now $16,000. Analysis of collection experience suggests that York should use the following percentages to compute the estimates of amounts that will eventually prove uncollectible: 0–30 days, 0.5%; 31–60 days, 1.0%; 61–120 days, 10%; and more than 120 days, 30%. Prepare the journal entry to provide for estimated uncollectible accounts.

24. **Aging of accounts receivable.** Dove Company's accounts receivable show the following balances by age:

Age of Accounts	Balance Receivable
Not yet due	$1,200,000
0–30 Days	400,000
31–60 Days	90,000
61–120 Days	40,000
More than 120 Days	20,000

The credit balance in the Allowance for Uncollectible Accounts is now $17,200. Dove Company's analyses of its collection experience suggest that Dove should use the following percentages to compute the estimates of amounts that will eventually prove uncollectible: 0–30 days, half of 1.0%; 31–60 days, 1.0%; 61–120 days, 10%; and more than 120 days, 70%. Prepare the journal entry to record Dove's bad debt expense.

25. **Aging of accounts receivable.** Hamilia S.A.'s financial records show the following balances in its accounts receivable for fiscal 2008:

Age of Accounts	Balance Receivable
0–30 Days	€980,000
31–90 Days	130,000
91–150 Days	102,000
More than 150 Days	68,000

Hamilia uses the aging-of-accounts-receivable procedure for uncollectible accounts. At the end of fiscal 2008, the credit balance in the Allowance for Uncollectible Accounts is €96,600. Hamilia's analysis of recent collection experience suggests it should use the following percentages to compute the estimates of amounts that will eventually prove uncollectible: 0–30 days, 0.5%; 31–90 days, 3.0%; 91–150 days, 15%; and more than 150 days, 75%. Prepare the journal entry to provide for estimated uncollectible accounts.

26. **Reconstructing events when using the allowance method.** Selected data from the accounts of Seward Corporation appear next for the year ended December 31, 2008:

	January 1	December 31
Accounts Receivable, Gross	$82,900 Dr.	$ 87,300 Dr.
Allowance for Uncollectible Accounts	8,700 Cr.	9,100 Cr.
Bad Debt Expense	—	4,800 Dr.
Sales Revenue	—	240,000 Cr.

The firm makes all sales on account. There were no recoveries during the year of accounts written off in previous years.

Give the journal entries for the following transactions and events during the year:

a. Sales on account.
b. Recognition of bad debt expense.
c. Write-off of uncollectible accounts.
d. Collection of cash from customers from sales on account.

27. **Allowance method; reconstructing journal entry from events.** (From a problem by S. A. Zeff.) During 2008, Pandora Company wrote off $2,200 of accounts receivable as uncollectible. Pandora Company collected no cash during 2008 for amounts it had written off

in previous years. The balance in the Allowance for Uncollectible Accounts account on the balance sheet was $3,500 at the beginning of 2008 and $5,000 at the end of 2008. Present the journal entry that the company made to provide for estimated uncollectibles during 2008.

28. **Allowance method; reconstructing journal entries from events.** (From a problem by S. A. Zeff.) The balance sheets of Milton Corporation on December 31, 2008 and 2009, showed gross accounts receivable of $15,200,000 and $17,600,000, respectively. The balances in the Allowance for Uncollectible Accounts account at the beginning and end of 2009 were credits of $1,400,000 and $1,550,000, respectively. The income statement for 2009 shows that the expense for estimated uncollectible accounts was $750,000, which was 1% of sales. The firm makes all sales on account. There were no recoveries during 2009 of accounts written off in previous years. Give all the journal entries made during 2009 that affect Accounts Receivable and the Allowance for Uncollectible Accounts.

29. **Reconstructing events from journal entries.** Give the likely transaction or event that would result in making each of the independent journal entries that follow.

a.   Bad Debt Expense   2,300
        Allowance for Uncollectible Accounts   2,300

Assets	=	Liabilities	+	Shareholders' Equity	(Class.)
−2,300				−2,300	IncSt → RE

b.   Allowance for Uncollectible Accounts   450
        Accounts Receivable   450

Assets	=	Liabilities	+	Shareholders' Equity	(Class.)
+450					
−450					

c.   Allowance for Uncollectible Accounts   200
        Bad Debt Expense   200

Assets	=	Liabilities	+	Shareholders' Equity	(Class.)
+200				+200	IncSt → RE

30. **Journal entries for the allowance method.** Data related to sales on account of Heath Company for its first three years of operations, 2006–2008, appear next:

Year	Sales on Account	Accounts Written Off as Uncollectible in Year					
		2006	2007	2008	2009	2010	Total
2006	$ 340,000	$1,800	$5,800	$ 3,000	—	—	$10,600
2007	450,000	—	2,500	8,200	$ 3,400	—	14,100
2008	580,000	—	—	2,900	12,700	$3,300	17,900
	$1,370,000	$1,800	$8,300	$14,100	$16,100	$3,300	$42,600

Heath Company estimates that 3% of sales on account will ultimately become uncollectible. Uncollectible accounts generally occur within three years of the year of sale.

a. Prepare journal entries to recognize bad debt expense and to write off uncollectible accounts for 2006, 2007, and 2008 using the allowance method.

b. Does 3% of sales on account appear to be a reasonable rate for estimating uncollectibles for Heath Company?

31. **Journal entries for the allowance method.** The following data relate to sales made on account by Schneider Corporation for the years ended October 31, 2006, 2007, and 2008:

Year	Sales on Account	Accounts Written Off as Uncollectible in Year					
		2006	2007	2008	2009	2010	Total
2006............	$ 750,000	$1,300	$ 8,700	$ 3,900	—	—	$13,900
2007............	1,200,000	—	2,500	16,600	$ 3,800	—	22,900
2008............	2,400,000	—	—	3,100	37,800	$4,800	45,700
	$4,350,000	$1,300	$11,200	$23,600	$41,600	$4,800	$82,500

Schneider Corporation estimates that 2% of sales on account will ultimately become uncollectible. Uncollectible accounts generally occur within three years of the year of sale.

a. Prepare journal entries to recognize bad debt expense and to write off uncollectible accounts for 2006, 2007, and 2008 using the allowance method.

b. Does 2% of sales on account appear to be a reasonable rate for estimating this firm's uncollectibles?

32. **Reconstructing events when using the allowance method.** Selected data from the accounts of Fujitsu Limited for the years ended March 31, 2007, and March 31, 2006, appear next. Fujitsu follows Japanese accounting standards and reports its results in millions of yen (¥). For purposes of this problem, assume that Fujitsu applies U.S. GAAP or IFRS.

	March 31, 2007	March 31, 2006
Accounts Receivable, Gross..........................	¥1,054,048	¥ 885,300
Allowance for Uncollectible Accounts....................	(6,906)	(6,781)
Sales Revenue	5,100,163	—

Assume Fujitsu estimates that 1% of sales, which are all on account, will become uncollectible. There were no recoveries during the year of accounts written off in previous years. Provide journal entries to record the following:

a. Sales on account during the year.

b. Recognition of bad debt expense.

c. Write-off of actual uncollectible accounts during the year.

d. Collection of cash from customers from sales on account during the year.

33. **Effects of transactions involving suppliers and customers on cash flows.** WollyMartin Limited, a large retailer, provided the following information from its accounting records for the year ended September 30, 2008:

Selected Balance Sheet Accounts	September 30, 2008	September 30, 2007
Accounts Receivable	€ 8,600	€ 8,000
Less: Allowance for Uncollectibles	(750)	(700)
Merchandise Inventory............................	11,200	11,000
Accounts Payable	7,500	7,000

Selected Income Statement Accounts	2008
Sales Revenue	€ 130,000
Bad Debt Expense	(2,000)
Cost of Goods Sold	(85,000)

WollyMartin's business is characterized by many retail customers—some of whom have not paid for goods they have purchased—and many suppliers of goods, some of whom have delivered goods for which the firm has not yet paid. WollyMartin settles all its accounts with customers and suppliers with cash, never with noncash assets.

a. Calculate the amount of cash WollyMartin received from its customers during the year.

b. Calculate the amount of cash WollyMartin paid to its suppliers during the year.

34. **Percentage-of-completion and completed contract methods of income recognition.** The Shannon Construction Company agreed to build a warehouse for $6,000,000. Expected

and actual costs to construct the warehouse were as follows: 2007, $1,200,000; 2008, $3,000,000; and 2009, $600,000. The firm completed the warehouse in 2009. Compute revenue, expense, and income before income taxes for 2007, 2008, and 2009 using the percentage-of-completion method and the completed contract method.

35. **Percentage-of-completion and completed contract methods of income recognition.** Raytheon has agreed to construct a high-tech missile detection system for $900 million. Expected and actual costs to construct the detection system were as follows: 2006, $200 million; 2007, $200 million; and 2008, $300 million. Raytheon completed the system in 2008. Compute revenue, expense, and income before income taxes for 2006–2008 using the percentage-of-completion method and the completed contract method.

36. **Installment and cost recovery methods of income recognition.** During the year ended December 31, 2008, Cunningham Realty Partners sold a tract of land costing $80,000 to a manufacturing firm for $120,000. The manufacturing firm agreed to pay the purchase price in four equal annual installments, with the first payment made on December 31, 2008. Compute revenue, expense, and income before income taxes for each of the four years using the installment method and the cost recovery method.

37. **Installment and cost recovery methods of income recognition.** During the year ended December 31, 2007, Boeing sold a jet to the chief executive officer (CEO) of a local bank for $72 million; assume that manufacturer's cost to produce the jet was $57 million. The CEO agreed to pay Boeing $24 million per year, for three years, with the first payment made on December 31, 2007. Compute revenue, expense, and income before income taxes for each of the three years using the installment method and the cost recovery method.

PROBLEMS

38. **Revenue recognition at and after time of sale.** Assume that during December 2008, Nordstrom sold $20 million of merchandise and another $12 million of gift cards, of which $24 million was on credit and the rest in cash. Nordstrom acquired the merchandise for $7.2 million. Further assume that Nordstrom estimates that 1% of all credit sales in December will be uncollectible, and customers will return 2% of all merchandise sold in December. Gift card sales are not included in merchandise sales for the purposes of estimating sales returns.

   a. What journal entries will Nordstrom make in December 2008 to record December sales?

   b. Assume that Nordstrom closes its books monthly. What adjusting entries will Nordstrom make in December 2008?

   c. Assume no other transactions affecting taxable income for the month. How much income did Nordstrom earn before taxes in December 2008?

   d. In January 2009, customers used gift cards to purchase $6 million of merchandise, with a cost to Nordstrom of $3.6 million. What journal entries will Nordstrom make in January 2009 to account for these sales? Assume the same sales return percentage as in December 2008.

39. **Revenue recognition at and after time of sale.** Hilton Garden Inn, a division of Hilton Hotels, offers its customers two choices when reserving rooms. The customer may purchase a nonrefundable Internet special of $150 per night, or pay at the refundable rate of $220 per night. Whether a customer purchases the nonrefundable Internet special or the refundable room, the customer must charge the entire amount to a credit card at the time of booking. For the Internet special, subsequent cancellation of the reservation results in the customer forfeiting the entire amount of the reservation. For the refundable room, cancellation prior to 3:00 p.m. of the date of arrival results in a refund of the amount of the reservation and cancellation after 3:00 p.m. results in a forfeiture of one day at the reserved rate ($220). What journal entries would Hilton Hotels record for the following transactions assuming it attempts to make correct entries every day? Ignore the journal entries involving expenses. Assume that credit card companies credit Hilton Garden Inn's bank account with cash on the same day that Hilton Garden Inn transmits a charge to a customer's credit card, which is the day of the initial reservation.

a. On February 2, 2008, a customer makes a nonrefundable Internet special reservation for four nights beginning February 16, 2008. The customer arrives at the hotel on February 16, 2008, and departs on February 20, 2008.

b. On February 2, 2008, a customer makes a nonrefundable Internet special reservation for four nights beginning February 16, 2008. On February 14, 2008, the customer cancels the reservation.

c. On February 2, 2008, a customer makes a refundable reservation for four nights beginning February 16, 2008. The customer arrives at the hotel on February 16, 2008, and departs on February 20, 2008.

d. On February 2, 2008, a customer makes a refundable reservation for four nights beginning February 16, 2008. On February 14, 2008, the customer cancels the reservation.

e. On February 2, 2008, a customer makes a refundable reservation for four nights beginning February 16, 2008. At 6:00 p.m. on February 16, 2008, the customer cancels the reservation.

40. **Revenue recognition at and after time of sale.** Stone Pest Control offers extermination services to customers in various arrangements and packages. For example, a customer could call Stone as needed to come out and spray for insects; for this service, Stone charges $80 per service call. For a separate termite inspection, Stone charges $100. Alternatively, the customer can sign an annual $300 contract with Stone for quarterly service visits plus one termite inspection. The contract also permits the customer to request spraying services at any time between quarterly visits, at no extra charge. Stone estimates that the average contract customer requests one service call per year, outside of the scheduled quarterly visits. For each of the following transactions, provide the journal entries that Stone would make to recognize revenues. Ignore the journal entries involving expenses.

a. January 2, 2008, a customer calls Stone to come out and spray for insects. The customer has no contract with Stone. Stone performs the service on January 4, 2008, and the customer pays in cash.

b. January 2, 2008, a customer calls Stone to come out and spray for insects and inspect for termites. The customer has no contract with Stone. Stone performs the services on January 4, 2008, and the customer pays in cash.

c. January 2, 2008, a customer calls Stone to come out and spray for insects and inspect for termites. The customer signs a contract with Stone on January 4, 2008, the same date that Stone provides the first quarterly service and inspects for termites. The customer pays the entire contract price in cash on January 4.

d. How should Stone account for the spraying services that occur between scheduled quarterly services?

e. April 30, 2008, the customer in part **c** calls and asks Stone to come out and spray for ants in the basement.

41. **Analyzing changes in accounts receivable.** Selected data from the financial statements of Kajima Corporation appear next for the years ended March 31, 2004, through March 31, 2007. Kajima applies Japanese accounting standards and reports its results in millions of yen (¥). For purposes of this problem, assume that Kajima applies U.S. GAAP or IFRS.

	2007	2006	2005	2004
Balance Sheet				
Accounts and Notes Receivable, Gross	¥ 630,044	¥ 468,387	¥ 455,517	¥382,692
Allowance for Doubtful Accounts	5,286	10,673	8,341	13,441
Income Statement				
Revenues (assume 100% on credit)	1,891,466	1,775,274	1,687,380	
Bad Debt Expense	1,084	3,152	2,999	

a. Prepare journal entries for 2005, 2006, and 2007 to record the following:

   (1) Revenues.

   (2) Recognition of bad debt expense.

(3) Write-off of actual uncollectible accounts.

(4) Collection of cash from customers.

b. Compute the following ratios, combining Accounts and Notes Receivable:

(1) Accounts receivable turnover ratio for 2005, 2006, and 2007. Use total sales in the numerator and average accounts receivable (net) in the denominator.

(2) Bad debt expense divided by revenues on account for 2005, 2006, and 2007.

(3) Allowance for uncollectible accounts divided by accounts receivable (gross) at the end of 2005, 2006, and 2007.

(4) Write-offs of actual uncollectible accounts divided by average accounts receivable (gross) for 2005, 2006, and 2007.

c. What do the ratios computed in part b suggest about the collection experience of Kajima Corporation during 2005–2007?

42. **Analyzing changes in accounts receivable.** The financial statements and notes for Polaris Corporation reveal the following for the four years ending in March 2005–2008 (amounts in millions of dollars):

	2008	2007	2006	2005
Total Sales	$4,880.1	$4,295.4	$3,746.3	$3,305.4
Bad Debt Expense	36.8	40.1	20.1	20.1

	End of March				
	2008	2007	2006	2005	2004
Accounts Receivable, Gross	$ 680.4	$ 605.6	$ 599.2	$ 566.7	$539.5
Less: Allowance for Uncollectible Accounts . . .	(172.0)	(138.1)	(115.0)	(111.0)	(97.8)
Accounts Receivable, Net	$ 508.4	$ 467.5	$ 484.2	$ 455.7	$441.7

Assume that Polaris's credit sales as a percent of total sales was 75% in each year.

a. Compute the amount of accounts written off as uncollectible during 2005–2008.

b. Compute the amount of cash collections from credit customers during each of the four years ending in March 2005–2008.

c. Compute the total amount of cash collected from customers during each of the four years ended March 2005–2008.

d. Calculate the accounts receivable turnover ratio for the years ended March 2005–2008. Use total sales in the numerator and average accounts receivable, net, in the denominator.

43. **Analyzing disclosures of accounts receivable.** Aracruz Celulose, a Brazilian pulp manufacturer, applies U.S. GAAP and reports its results in thousands of U.S. dollars. For the years ended December 31, 2007 and 2006, Aracruz reported the following information pertaining to accounts receivable:

	December 31, 2007	December 31, 2006
Accounts Receivable, Gross	$365,921	$290,429
Allowance for Doubtful Accounts	4,318	4,634
Write-Offs	433	25

At December 31, 2005, the Allowance for Doubtful Accounts had a balance of $4,067.

a. What is the carrying value of accounts receivable on Aracruz's balance sheets for the years ended December 31, 2007, and December 31, 2006?

b. What is the total amount that customers owe Aracruz as of December 31, 2007, and December 31, 2006?

c. What journal entries did Aracruz make in 2007 and 2006 to recognize Bad Debt Expense?

44. **Analyzing disclosures of accounts receivable.** Metso Corporation is a Finnish engineering firm specializing in design and development for the paper and pulp industry. Metso

applies IFRS and reports its results in millions of euros (€). For the years ended December 31, 2007 and 2006, Metso reported the following information pertaining to accounts receivable:

	December 31, 2007	December 31, 2006
Accounts Receivable, Net	€1,274	€1,218
Allowance for Doubtful Accounts	36	35
Bad Debt Expense	13	10
Other Charges to Allowance	(7)	(4)

The Other Charges to Allowance reflect the effects of business acquisitions and exchange rates. At December 31, 2005, the Allowance for Doubtful Accounts had a balance of €35.

a. What is the carrying value of accounts receivable on Metso's balance sheets for the years ended December 31, 2007, and December 31, 2006?

b. What is the total amount that customers owe Metso as of December 31, 2007, and December 31, 2006?

c. What journal entries did Metso make in 2007 and 2006 to recognize write-offs of uncollectible accounts?

45. **Reconstructing transactions affecting accounts receivable and uncollectible accounts.** The sales, all on account, of Pins Company in 2008, its first year of operations, were $700,000. Collections totaled $500,000. On December 31, 2008, Pins Company estimated that 2% of all sales would probably be uncollectible. On that date, Pins Company wrote off specific accounts in the amount of $8,000.

The balances in selected accounts on December 31, *2009*, are as follows:

Accounts Receivable, Gross (Dr.)	$300,000
Allowance for Uncollectible Accounts (Dr.)	10,000
Sales Revenues (Cr.)	800,000

On December 31, 2009, Pins Company carried out an aging of its accounts receivable balances and estimated that the 2009 ending balance of accounts receivable contained $11,000 of probable uncollectibles. That is, the allowance account should have an $11,000 ending credit balance. It made adjusting entries appropriate for this estimate. Some of the $800,000 sales during 2009 were for cash and some were on account; the problem purposefully does not give the amounts.

a. What was the balance in the Accounts Receivable, Gross, at the end of *2008*? Give the amount and whether it was a debit or a credit.

b. What was the balance in the Allowance for Uncollectible Accounts account at the end of *2008*? Give the amount and whether it was a debit or a credit.

c. What was bad debt expense for *2009*?

d. What was the amount of specific accounts receivable written off as being uncollectible during *2009*?

e. What were total cash collections in *2009* from customers (for cash sales and collections from customers who had purchased on account in either *2008* or *2009*)?

f. What was the net balance of accounts receivable included in the balance sheet asset total for December 31, *2009*?

46. **Effect of errors involving accounts receivable on financial statement ratios.** Indicate—using O/S (overstated), U/S (understated), or NO (no effect)—the pretax effect of each of the following errors on (1) the rate of return on assets, (2) the accounts receivable turnover, and (3) the liabilities to assets ratio. Each of these ratios is less than 100% before discovering the error.

a. A firm using the allowance method neglected to provide for estimated uncollectible accounts at the end of the year.

b. A firm using the allowance method neglected to write off specific accounts as uncollectible at the end of the year.

c. A firm credited a check received from a customer to Advances from Customers even though the customer was paying for purchases previously made on account.

d. A firm recorded as a sale a customer's order received on the last day of the accounting period, even though the firm will not ship the product until the next accounting period.

e. A firm sold goods on account to a particular customer and properly recorded the transactions in the accounts. The customer returned the goods within a few days of the sale, before paying for them, but the firm neglected to record the return of the goods in its accounts. The firm normally treats sales returns as a reduction in Sales Revenue.

47. **Income recognition for a nuclear generator manufacturer.** The French energy company, Areva Group, recently won a $2 billion contract to build a uranium enrichment plant in Idaho Falls, Idaho, U.S. Areva began construction in 2008 and expects to complete it by 2014. Assume that the state government of Idaho agrees to pay as follows: at the time of signing on December 20, 2007, $20 million; on December 31, 2008–2013, $100 million; and at completion on December 31, 2014, $1,380 million. Assume further that Areva incurs the following costs in constructing the generator: 2008, $340 million; 2009–2013, $238 million per year; and 2014, $170 million. Areva uses a Construction in Process account to accumulate costs. Although the costs involve a mixture of cash payments, credits to assets, and credits to liability accounts, assume for purposes of this problem that all costs involve cash.

   a. Calculate the amount of revenue, expense, and income before income taxes that Areva Group will report for years 2008–2014 under each of the following revenue recognition methods:

   (1) Percentage-of-completion method.

   (2) Completed contract method.

   b. Show the journal entries that Areva Group will make for this contract in 2007, 2008, 2009–2013, and 2014 for each of the revenue recognition methods examined in part **a**.

48. **Income recognition for a contractor.** On October 15, 2005, Flanikin Construction Company contracted to build a shopping center at a contract price of $180 million. The schedule of expected and actual cash collections and contract costs is as follows:

Year	Cash Collections from Customers	Estimated and Actual Cost Incurred
2005.	$ 36,000,000	$ 12,000,000
2006.	45,000,000	36,000,000
2007.	45,000,000	48,000,000
2008.	54,000,000	24,000,000
	$180,000,000	$120,000,000

   a. Calculate the amount of revenue, expense, and net income for each of the four years under the following revenue recognition methods:

   (1) Percentage-of-completion method.

   (2) Completed contract method.

   b. Show the journal entries Flanikin will make in 2005, 2006, 2007, and 2008 for this contract. Flanikin accumulates contract costs in a Contract in Process account. Although the costs involve a mixture of cash payments, credits to assets, and credits to liability accounts, assume for purposes of this problem that all costs involve credits to Accounts Payable.

   c. Which method do you believe provides the better measure of Flanikin Construction Company's performance under the contract? Why?

49. **Income recognition when collection from the customer is uncertain.** Furniture Retailers sells furniture to customers who have relatively poor credit quality, offering extended payment terms. In January 2008, a customer buys a full set of dining room and living

room furniture for $8,400 on an installment plan, with no down payment and monthly payments of $400, beginning January 31, 2008. The cost of the furniture to Furniture Retailers is $6,800. Furniture Retailers classifies Deferred Gross Margin as a liability on its balance sheet. Ignore any interest on unpaid accounts receivable. What journal entries will Furniture Retailers make (1) at the time of sale in January 2008, and (2) when it receives each monthly payment from the customer under each of the following methods of recognizing income:

a. Installment method.

b. Cost recovery method.

50. **Revenue recognition when collection is uncertain.** Appliance Sales and Service sells major household appliances to customers, offering extended payment terms. Its fiscal year ends on June 30. In July of 2008, a customer bought a freezer, a refrigerator, and a convection oven on an installment plan, with no down payment and 10 monthly payments of $244, beginning July 31, 2008. The gross margin percentage on this arrangement is 9%. Appliance Sales and Service classifies Deferred Gross Margin as a liability on its balance sheet. Ignore any interest on unpaid accounts receivable.

a. Assume the customer makes all 10 payments. What journal entries will Appliance Sales and Service make (1) at the time of sale in June 2007, and (2) when it receives each monthly payment from the customer under each of the following methods of recognizing revenue:

(1) Installment method.

(2) Cost recovery method.

b. Assume the customer stops making payments after making the November 2008 payment. In December 2008, Appliance Sales and Service repossesses all three appliances and estimates that it could sell the repossessed appliances for $980. What journal entries would Appliance Sales and Services make under each of the following methods of recognizing revenue:

(1) Installment method.

(2) Cost recovery method.

51. **Point-of-sale versus installment method of income recognition.** The J. C. Spangle catalog division began business on January 1, 2007. Activities of the company for the first two years are as follows:

	2008	2007
Sales, All on Account....................................	$300,000	$200,000
Collections from Customers:		
On 2007 Sales	110,000	90,000
On 2008 Sales	120,000	—
Purchase of Merchandise	240,000	180,000
Inventory of Merchandise at 12/31	114,000	60,000
All Expenses Other Than Merchandise, Paid in Cash............	44,000	32,000

a. Prepare income statements for 2007 and 2008, assuming that the company uses the accrual basis of accounting and recognizes revenue at the time of sale.

b. Prepare income statements for 2007 and 2008, assuming that the company uses the accrual basis of accounting and recognizes revenue at the time of cash collection following the installment method of accounting. "All Expenses Other Than Merchandise, Paid in Cash" are period expenses.

52. **Revenue recognition for a franchise.** Pickin Chicken Inc. and Country Delight Inc. both sell franchises for their chicken restaurants. The franchisee receives the right to use the franchisor's products and to benefit from national training and advertising programs. The franchisee agrees to pay $50,000 for exclusive franchise rights in a particular city. Of this amount, the franchisee pays $20,000 on signing the franchise agreement and promises to pay the remainder in five equal annual installments of $6,000 each starting one year after the initial signing payment. Pickin Chicken recognizes franchise revenue as it signs agreements, whereas Country Delight recognizes franchise revenue on an installment basis.

In 2006, each company sold eight franchises. In 2007, each sold five franchises. In 2008, neither company sold a franchise.

a. Calculate the amount of revenue recognized by each company during 2006–2012.

b. When do you think a franchisor should recognize franchise revenue? Why?

53. **Income recognition for various types of business.** Most business firms recognize revenues at the time of sale or delivery of goods and services and, following the principles of the accrual basis of accounting, match expenses either with associated revenues or with the period when they consume resources in operations. Users of financial statements should maintain a questioning attitude as to the appropriateness of recognizing revenues at the time of sale and as to the timing of expense recognition. **Exhibit 7.7** presents common-size income statements for seven firms for a recent year, with all amounts expressed as a percentage of total revenues. **Exhibit 7.7** also indicates the revenues generated by each firm for each dollar of assets in use on average during the year. A brief description of the activities of each firm follows.

Amgen engages in the development, manufacturing, and marketing of biotechnology products. Developing and obtaining approval of biotechnology products takes 10 or more years. Amgen has two principal products that it manufactures and markets and several more products in the development pipeline.

Brown-Forman is a distiller of hard liquors. After combining the ingredients, the company ages the liquors for five or more years before sale.

Deere manufactures farm equipment. It sells this equipment to a network of independent distributors, who in turn sell the equipment to final consumers. Deere provides financing and insurance services both to its distributors and to final consumers.

Fluor engages in construction services on multiyear construction projects. It subcontracts most of the actual construction work and receives a fee for its services.

Golden West is a savings and loan company. It takes deposits from customers and lends funds, primarily to individuals for home mortgages. Customers typically pay a fee (called "points") at the time of loan origination based on the amount borrowed. Their monthly mortgage payments include interest on the outstanding loan balance and a partial repayment of the principal of the loan.

Merrill Lynch (now a part of Bank of America) engages in the securities business. It obtains funds primarily from short-term capital market sources and invests the funds primarily in short-term, readily marketable financial instruments. It attempts to generate an excess of investment returns over the cost of the funds invested. Merrill Lynch also

---

EXHIBIT 7.7	Common-Size Income Statement for Selected Companies (Problem 53)						
	Amgen	**Brown-Forman**	**Deere**	**Fluor**	**Golden West**	**Merrill Lynch**	**Rockwell**
Revenues							
Sales of Goods	98.7%	99.9%	83.6%	—	—	—	99.3%
Sales of Services	—	—	—	99.7%	2.0%	47.5%	—
Interest on Investments	1.3	0.1	16.4	0.3	98.0	52.5	0.7
Total Revenues	100.0%	100.0%	100.0%	100.0%	100.0%	100.0%	100.0%
Expenses							
Cost of Goods or Services Sold	(14.3)	(35.5)	(69.4)	(95.6)	—	(43.3)	(77.4)
Selling and Administrative	(23.4)	(33.1)	(11.4)	(.6)	(15.9)	—	(12.6)
Other Operating[a]	(26.4)	(15.4)	(3.5)	—	(3.3)	—	—
Interest	(0.7)	(1.3)	(11.0)	(0.2)	(60.4)	(47.2)	(0.9)
Income before Income Taxes	35.2%	14.7%	4.7%	3.6%	20.4%	9.5%	9.1%
Income Tax Expense	(16.1)	(5.9)	(1.6)	(1.3)	(8.4)	(3.9)	(3.5)
Net Income	19.1%	8.8%	3.1%	2.3%	12.0%	5.6%	5.6%
Revenues/Average Total Assets . . .	0.9	1.3	0.7	3.1	0.1	0.1	1.2

[a]Represents research and development costs for Amgen and Deere, excise taxes for Brown-Forman, and a provision for loan losses by Golden West.

offers fee-based services, such as financial consulting, buying and selling securities for customers, securities underwriting, and investment management.

Rockwell is a technology-based electronics and aerospace company. It engages in research and development on behalf of its customers, which include the U.S. government (space shuttle program, defense electronics) and private-sector entities. Its contracts tend to run for many years on a constantly renewed basis.

a. When should each of these companies recognize revenue? What unique issues does each company face in the recognition of expenses?

b. Suggest possible reasons for differences in the net income divided by revenues percentages for these companies.

54. **Understanding the purpose of the Allowance for Uncollectible Accounts account.** A member of the Audit Committee of a firm asks the Chief Financial Officer the following question: "How do you know the Allowance for Uncollectible Accounts is adequate?" Discuss the adequacy or inadequacy of each of the following independent responses.

a. "I think it much more likely than not that the amount of cash and marketable securities is adequate to cover any cash shortage caused by customers' not paying what they owe."

b. "I have checked the Bad Debt Expense for sales made this past period and found the amount reasonable."

c. "I have performed an aging of all accounts receivable for all sales this period and found the amount reasonable."

d. "I have performed an aging of all accounts receivable and found the amount reasonable."

e. "We performed a detailed confirmation of receivables from customers whose accounts the firm wrote off as uncollectible this period and found the decision to write them off suitable under the circumstances."

f. "We performed a detailed confirmation of receivables from customers whose accounts the firm has neither collected nor written off by the end of this period and found the decisions suitable under the circumstances."

g. "I know the Allowance account was correct at the end of last period, and I checked the Bad Debt Expense for this period using a percentage of sales recommended for this class of customers by the top two credit reporting agencies."

CHAPTER 8

Working Capital

LEARNING OBJECTIVES

1. Identify the principal components of working capital (other than accounts receivable and advances from customers, discussed in **Chapter 7**, and marketable securities, discussed in **Chapter 12**) and the business transactions that give rise to each: cash, prepayments, inventory, accounts payable, short-term notes, accrued liabilities (such as wages pay-

able and taxes payable), warranties, and restructuring liabilities.

2. Understand inventory components, inventory cost flows, and the accounting for inventory in merchandising and manufacturing firms.

3. Understand the recognition and measurement of warranty liabilities and restructuring liabilities.

UNDERLYING CONCEPTS AND TERMINOLOGY

Chapter 3 introduces the distinction between *current* assets and liabilities and *noncurrent* assets and liabilities. The current–noncurrent distinction refers to whether a firm will convert an asset to cash, or consume it, or sell it within one operating cycle and whether a firm will pay or otherwise settle a liability within one operating cycle. Because the operating cycle for most firms is one year or less, one year is the conventional cutoff for distinguishing a current and a noncurrent asset or liability. This chapter considers certain current assets and current liabilities. **Working capital** is the difference between a firm's current assets and its current liabilities. The **current ratio**, also called the **working capital ratio**, is current assets divided by current liabilities.

Both working capital and the current ratio provide information about **liquidity**—a firm's ability to meet short-term obligations as they come due. A firm with assets that will convert to cash within the next 12 months, in excess of its obligations to pay cash in this same interval, has positive working capital and a current ratio that exceeds one. When current liabilities exceed current assets, working capital is negative and the current ratio is less than one. Although most firms have positive working capital, negative working capital does not mean a firm cannot meet its near-term obligations. A firm may, for example, have a bank line of credit that allows it to borrow cash to meet short-term obligations.

Exhibit 1.1 (page 8) shows Nordstrom's balance sheet for fiscal years ending February 3, 2007, and January 28, 2006; **Exhibit 1.5** (page 12) shows similar information for Scania for the years ending December 31, 2006 and 2005. Nordstrom's balance sheet reveals working capital of $1,309 million, and a current ratio of 1.91, as of February 3, 2007. As of this date, Nordstrom had $1.91 in current assets for each $1.00 of liabilities due within the next year. Scania had working capital of SEK6,237 million, and a current ratio of 1.18, as of December 31, 2006. Scania's lower current ratio does not imply that Scania's financial position is weaker than Nordstrom's. Recall that as of December 31, 2006, Scania obligations due in 2007 were SEK34,103 million, so it needs only SEK34,103 in current assets to cover these payments. Scania does not need additional current assets to meet its current liabilities, and its management may have decided that it can deploy resources more profitably elsewhere, such as acquiring equipment or investing in research and development. Based on such considerations, many firms will seek to have current ratios close to one.

The accountant's definition of working capital (total current assets minus total current liabilities) differs from the definition often used in finance. The difference pertains to the treatment of items that do not clearly relate to the firm's operations; working capital as defined in finance equals current **operating assets** minus current **operating liabilities**, excluding current assets and current liabilities that reflect the financing structure of the firm, called **financial assets** and **financial liabilities**. The general rule to distinguish an operating asset (operating liability) from a financing asset (financial liability) is its purpose: does the firm use the item directly in operations, or use it to finance those operations? On the asset side, current financial assets typically include assets that generate some form of interest or investment income, such as marketable securities and other short-term investments.[1] On the liability side, current financial liabilities typically include obligations that accrue explicit (or implicit) interest, such as short-term bank borrowings and the current portion of long-term debt. In this book, we use the term *working capital* as the accountant uses it, including both operating and financial current assets and current liabilities.

The rest of this chapter focuses on specific current assets (cash, prepayments, and inventory) and specific current liabilities (accounts payable, short-term borrowings, accrued liabilities, income taxes payable, warranties, and restructuring liabilities). **Chapter 7** describes two important working capital accounts associated with revenues (accounts receivable and advances from customers). We defer discussion of other current asset and current liability accounts to later chapters: for example, we describe marketable securities in **Chapter 12**, the current portion of long-term debt in **Chapter 10**, and the current portion of deferred taxes in **Chapter 11**.

PRINCIPAL CURRENT ASSET ACCOUNTS

CASH AND CASH EQUIVALENTS

As defined in **Chapter 2**, **cash** includes currency, money orders, bank checks, checking accounts, and time deposits. The cash account usually includes both cash and **cash equivalents**, the latter term meaning short-term, highly liquid investments in which the firm has temporarily invested excess cash. Generally, investments with maturities of three months or less qualify as cash equivalents. Firms classify instruments with longer maturities as short-term investments or marketable securities. The measurement of cash is the cash value of the instruments included in this category.

PREPAYMENTS

Prepayments (also called **prepaid assets**[2]) are assets that represent services the firm has paid for before consuming them, such as rent and insurance. For example, suppose that on August 1, the firm pays £18,000 for insurance coverage for the next 12 months. On August 1, the firm records the following journal entry:

---

[1]One problem with defining all marketable securities and short-term investments as financial assets is that a user of the financial statements is not able to see management's intent in holding these assets. For example, investments in marketable securities and short-term investments might be used to support an operating strategy. In such a case, these current assets would be classified as operating assets.

[2]Since all assets are prepaid, we prefer the term *prepayments*, but practice often refers to *prepaid assets*.

Prepaid Insurance. 18,000

    Cash. 18,000

Assets	=	Liabilities	+	Shareholders' Equity	(Class.)
+18,000					
−18,000					

To record the cash paid for insurance coverage over the next 12 months.

At the end of each of the next 12 months, the firm records the following adjusting entry:

Insurance Expense 1,500

    Prepaid Insurance. 1,500

Assets	=	Liabilities	+	Shareholders' Equity	(Class.)
−1,500				−1,500	IncSt → RE

To record £1,500 (= £18,000/12 months) of insurance services consumed during the month.

If the firm prepared a balance sheet as of December 31, the prepaid asset would be £10,500 (= £18,000 − [5 months × £1,500/month]).

INVENTORY

Inventory refers to goods and other items that a firm owns and holds for sale or for further processing as part of its operations. Inventory is also called "stock" in some countries; do not confuse this usage with common stock, which is an entity's contributed equity capital. When the firm sells inventory, the carrying amount of that inventory becomes an expense, Cost of Goods Sold (sometimes called Cost of Sales). Inventories are a major asset for merchandising and manufacturing firms, and cost of goods sold is typically their largest single expense.

The *inventory equation* describes changes in inventory. The following equation measures all quantities in physical units:

$$\underbrace{\text{Beginning Inventory} + \text{Additions}}_{\text{Goods Available for Sale (or Use)}} - \text{Withdrawals} = \text{Ending Inventory}$$

If we begin a period with 2,000 pounds of sugar (beginning inventory) and purchase (add) 4,500 pounds during the period, there are 6,500 (= 2,000 + 4,500) pounds available for sale or use. The term *goods available for sale* (or *use*) refers to the sum of Beginning Inventory plus Additions. If we use (withdraw) 5,300 pounds during the period, 1,200 pounds of sugar remain at the end of the period (ending inventory).

The inventory equation can also be written as follows:

$$\underbrace{\text{Beginning Inventory} + \text{Additions}}_{\text{Goods Available for Sale (or Use)}} - \text{Ending Inventory} = \text{Withdrawals}$$

If we begin the period with 2,000 pounds of sugar, purchase 4,500 pounds during the period, and observe 1,200 pounds on hand at the end of the period, the firm used 5,300 (= 2,000 + 4,500 − 1,200) pounds of sugar during the period.

Financial statements report financial amounts (such as dollars, euros, and pesos), not physical amounts (such as units, kilograms, and cubic feet). The accountant transforms physical quantities of inventories into financial amounts by assigning costs to those physical quantities. When acquisition costs of inventory are constant, all inventory items carry the same per-unit cost; physical quantities and financial amounts change together so that variation in the monetary amounts recorded for inventories results from changes in quantities. The major problems in inventory accounting arise because the per-unit acquisition costs of inventory items change over time.

The remainder of this section discusses three issues in inventory accounting:

1. The types of costs included in the acquisition cost of inventory.
2. The treatment of changes in the market value of inventories subsequent to acquisition.
3. The cost flow assumption used to trace the movement of costs into and out of inventory, including the effects of per-unit inventory costs changing over time.

ISSUE 1: COSTS INCLUDED IN INVENTORY

The principle for cost inclusion is that the balance sheet amount for inventory should include all costs incurred to acquire goods and prepare them for sale.

Merchandising Firms **Merchandising firms**, such as Nordstrom, acquire inventory items in a physical condition ready for sale. Acquisition cost includes the invoice price less any cash discounts taken for prompt payment, plus the cost of transporting, receiving, unpacking, inspecting, and shelving, as well as any costs incurred to record the purchases in the accounts.

Manufacturing Firms **Manufacturing firms**, such as Scania, do not acquire inventory items in a physical form ready for sale. Instead, such firms transform raw materials, purchased parts, and components into finished products in their factories. The acquisition cost of manufactured inventories includes three categories of costs:

- **Direct Materials** (also called **Raw Materials**): The cost of materials that the manufacturing firm can trace directly to units of product it manufactures. For example, direct materials for Scania would include the steel, plastic, nuts, bolts, assembled CD/radios and navigation systems, and other parts that physically become part of a manufactured truck.
- **Direct Labor**: The cost of labor to transform raw materials into a finished product. This cost for Scania includes the compensation of factory workers on the production line.
- **Manufacturing Overhead:** A variety of indirect costs. Examples include depreciation, insurance and taxes on manufacturing facilities, supervisory factory labor, and supplies for factory equipment that the firm cannot directly trace to products manufactured but that are essential for production to occur. Manufacturing overhead for Scania includes such items as depreciation, insurance, and property taxes on the factory building and equipment; compensation of supervisory factory labor; and electricity to light, heat, and cool the factory.

Until a manufacturing firm sells its products and recognizes revenue, it treats all manufacturing costs as **product costs**, which are assets, and accumulates the costs in various inventory accounts. The inventory accounts include three broad inventory components: raw materials, work in process (also called work in progress), and finished goods. (Refer to **flow of costs** in the **Glossary** for a diagram showing how the process accumulates product costs and assigns them to finished goods.) The U.S. SEC requires firms with significant amounts of inventory whose shares are publicly traded in the U.S. to disclose this information in their financial reports, usually in a note. IFRS notes that information about inventory components "is useful to financial statement users."[3] As an illustration, Scania's balance sheet (**Exhibit 1.5**, page 12) reports a carrying value for inventory of SEK10,100 for the year ended December 31, 2006; **Exhibit 8.1** shows the components of Scania's inventory by category, as revealed in Note 14 to its financial statements (in millions of SEK).

A manufacturing firm, like a merchandising firm, also incurs marketing costs (for example, sales commissions, depreciation, insurance and taxes on the sales staff's automobiles) and administrative costs (for example, salary of the chief executive officer, depreciation on computers used in human resources). Both merchandising and manufacturing firms treat selling and administrative costs as **period expenses**. Period expenses are not assets and, therefore, do not accumulate in inventory accounts; firms recognize them as expenses in the period when they consume the goods or services.

---

[3]International Accounting Standards Board, *International Accounting Standard 2*, "Inventories," revised 2003, par. 37.

EXHIBIT 8.1   Scania
Note 14: Inventories

NOTE 14 Inventories	2006	2005	2004
Raw materials, components and supplies	960	970	937
Work in progress	1,392	1,114	1,109
Finished goods	7,748	7,865	7,441
Total	**10,100**	9,949	9,487

Overview of the Accounting Process for a Manufacturing Firm Figure 8.1
summarizes the nature and flow of costs for a manufacturing firm, and **Figure 8.2** shows the
flow of manufacturing costs through the various inventory and other accounts.

A manufacturing firm maintains separate inventory accounts to accumulate product costs
associated with inventories at various stages of completion. The **Raw Materials Inventory**
account includes the cost of raw materials purchased but not yet transferred to the factory
floor; the manufacturing firm records purchases of raw materials as debits to the Raw Materials Inventory account. When the manufacturer physically transfers raw materials to the factory floor, it also transfers the cost of the raw materials from the Raw Materials Inventory
account to the Work-in-Process Inventory account. It records this transfer as a credit to the
Raw Materials Inventory account for the cost of the raw materials transferred and a debit to
the Work in Process Inventory account. The balance in Raw Materials Inventory is the cost
of raw materials on hand in the storeroom or warehouse.

The **Work-in-Process Inventory** account (also called **Work-in-Progress Inventory**) accumulates the cost of raw materials transferred to the factory floor, the cost of direct labor used
in production, and manufacturing overhead costs. At the completion of the manufacturing
process, the firm physically transfers completed units from the factory floor to the finished
goods storeroom. It also transfers the product costs of those completed units to **Finished
Goods Inventory**. The firm credits the Work-in-Process Inventory account for the manufacturing costs assigned to the finished units transferred to the finished goods storeroom and
debits the Finished Goods Inventory account. This journal entry reduces the balance in

FIGURE 8.1   Diagram of Cost Flows

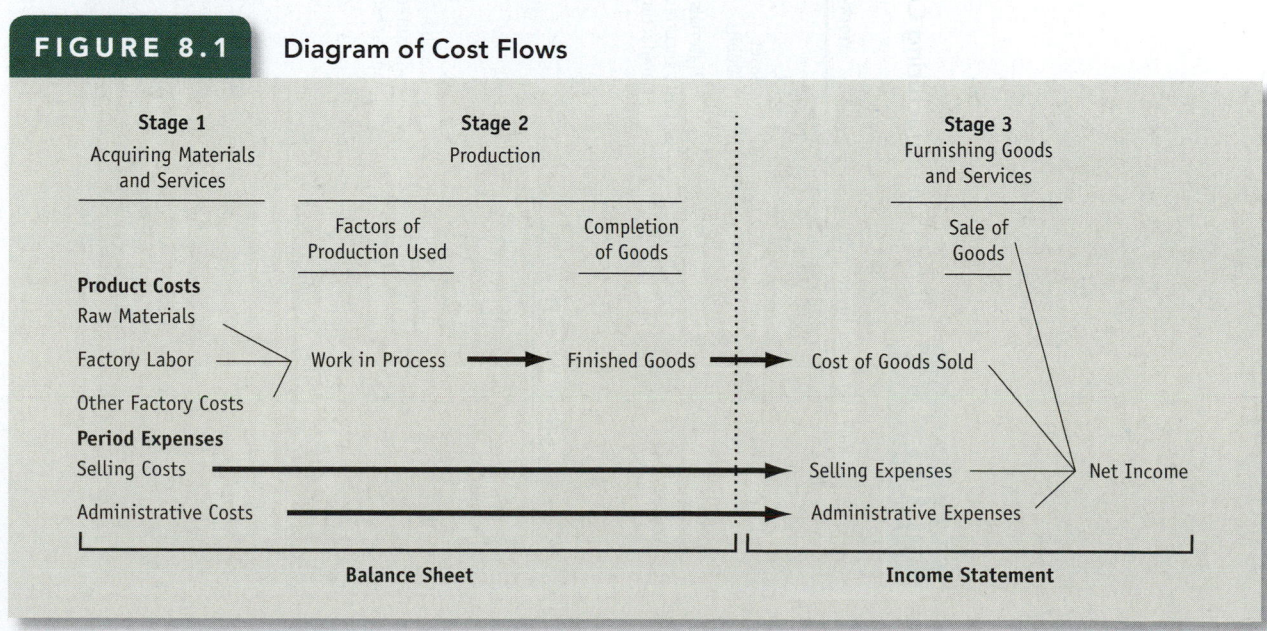

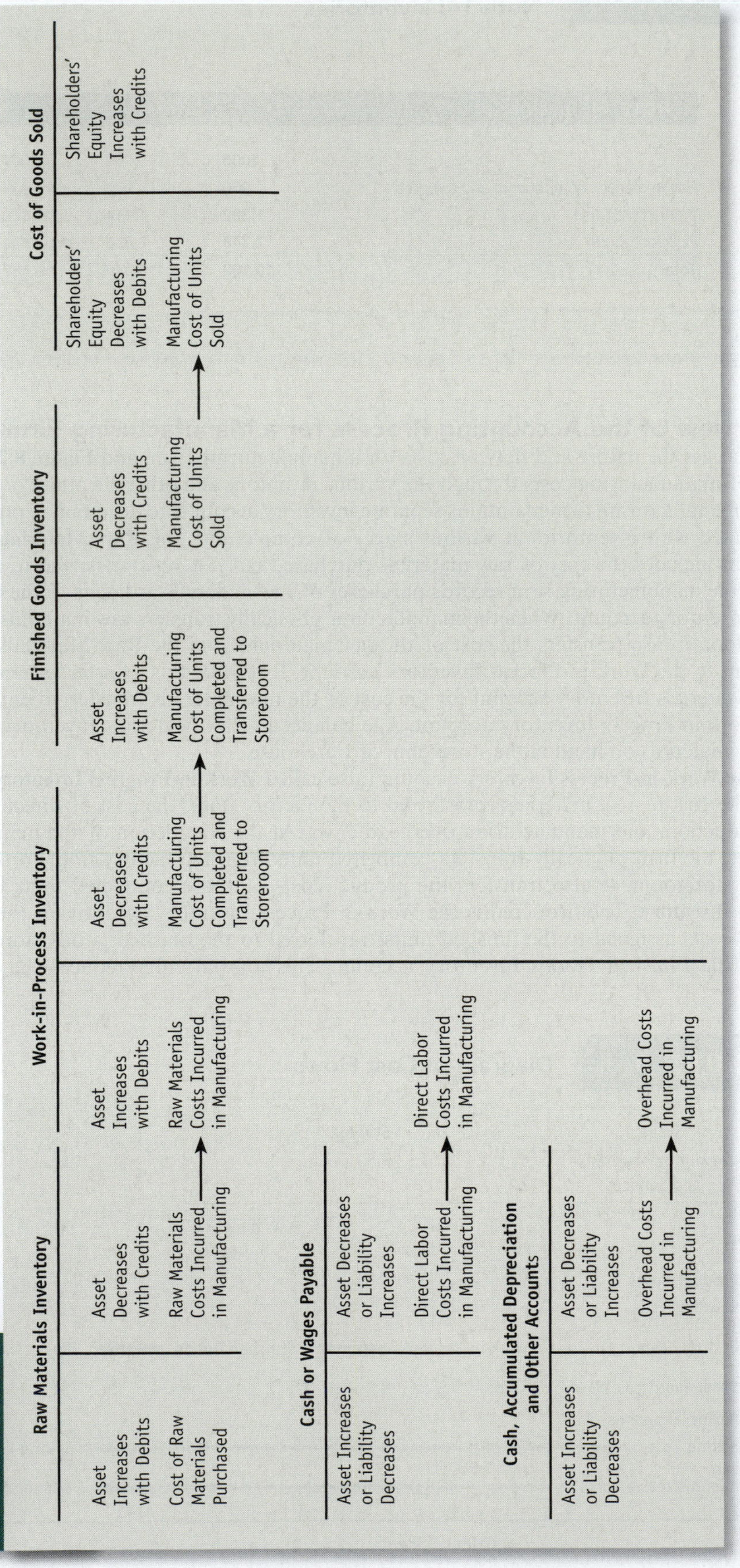

FIGURE 8.2 Flow of Manufacturing Costs Through the Accounts

Work-in-Process Inventory and increases the balance in Finished Goods Inventory. The balance in the Work-in-Process Inventory account measures the product costs incurred for units not yet finished.

The Finished Goods Inventory account measures the total manufacturing cost of units completed but not yet sold. The sale of manufactured goods to customers results in a transfer of their cost from the Finished Goods Inventory account to **Cost of Goods Sold**, an expense reducing net income and ultimately retained earnings. The journal entry is a debit to Cost of Goods Sold and a credit to Finished Goods Inventory.

Example 1 Moon Products began its Belgian operations on January 1 by issuing 10,000 shares of €10 par value common stock for €30 per share. Transactions during January and the related journal entries follow:

(1) The firm rents a building and pays 12 months rent in advance, in cash. The amount is €250,000.

| Prepaid Rent | | 250,000 | |
| Cash | | | 250,000 |

Assets	=	Liabilities	+	Shareholders' Equity	(Class.)
+250,000					
−250,000					

To record payment of 12 months rent.

(2) The firm purchases on account raw materials costing €25,000.

| Raw Materials Inventory | | 25,000 | |
| Accounts Payable | | | 25,000 |

Assets	=	Liabilities	+	Shareholders' Equity	(Class.)
+25,000		+25,000			

To record purchase of inventory on account.

(3) The firm issues, to producing departments, raw materials costing €20,000.

| Work-in-Process Inventory | | 20,000 | |
| Raw Materials Inventory | | | 20,000 |

Assets	=	Liabilities	+	Shareholders' Equity	(Class.)
+20,000					
−20,000					

To record the transfer of raw materials to producing departments.

(4) The total payroll for January is €60,000: €40,000 paid to factory workers and €20,000 paid to marketing and administrative personnel.

Work-in-Process Inventory		40,000	
Salaries Expense		20,000	
Cash			60,000

Assets	=	Liabilities	+	Shareholders' Equity	(Class.)
+40,000				−20,000	IncSt → RE
−60,000					

To record payroll costs: €40,000 product cost and €20,000 period expense.

A manufacturing firm records nonmanufacturing costs as expenses of the period when the firm consumes the services. It consumes the services of marketing and administrative personnel in the same period when employees provide those services. Journal entry **(4)** illustrates the difference between recording a product cost and recording a period expense. The debits may appear similar, but note that the first increases an asset account and the second increases an expense, thereby reducing shareholders' equity. Entries **(5)** and **(6)** also split a single item (either a payment for utilities or the consumption of prepaid rental services) between a product cost and a period expense.

(5)   Expenditures for utilities during January are €1,200. Of this amount, €1,000 is for manufacturing activities and €200 is for marketing and administrative activities.

Work-in-Process Inventory   1,000
Utilities Expense   200
    Cash.   1,200

Assets	=	Liabilities	+	Shareholders' Equity	(Class.)
+1,000				−200	IncSt → RE
−1,200					

To record utilities costs: €1,000 product cost and €200 period expense.

(6)   Refer to entry **(1)**, where Moon Products prepaid rent for the year. Rental expense for the month of January is €20,833 (= €250,000/12 months). Of the rented space, the firm uses 70% for manufacturing purposes and 30% for administrative (nonmanufacturing) purposes.

Work-in-Process Inventory   14,583
Rent Expense   6,250
    Prepaid Rent   20,833

Assets	=	Liabilities	+	Shareholders' Equity	(Class.)
+14,583				−6,250	IncSt → RE
−20,833					

To record the consumption of prepaid rent services: €14,583 product cost and €6,250 period expense.

(7)   Units completed during January and transferred to the finished goods storeroom have a manufacturing cost of €48,500.

Finished Goods Inventory   48,500
    Work-in-Process Inventory   48,500

Assets	=	Liabilities	+	Shareholders' Equity	(Class.)
+48,500					
−48,500					

To record the transfer of completed units to finished goods inventory.

(8)   Sales during January total €75,000, of which €25,000 is on account.

Cash.   50,000
Accounts Receivable   25,000
    Sales Revenue   75,000

Assets	=	Liabilities	+	Shareholders' Equity	(Class.)
+50,000				+75,000	IncSt → RE
+25,000					

To record sales of €75,000.

(9) The cost of the goods sold during January is €42,600.

| Cost of Goods Sold | | | | 42,600 | |
| Finished Goods Inventory | | | | | 42,600 |

Assets	=	Liabilities	+	Shareholders' Equity	(Class.)
−42,600				−42,600	IncSt → RE

To record cost of sales of €42,600.

Exhibit 8.2 presents a statement of income before taxes for Moon Products for the month of January. **Exhibit 8.3** shows the T-accounts summarizing the journal entries affecting the inventory accounts during the month. Moon Products earned income before taxes of €5,950 in January. At the end of January, Moon Products has a balance of €5,000 in Raw Materials Inventory, €27,083 in Work-in-Process Inventory, and €5,900 in Finished Goods Inventory. Thus, Moon Products' balance sheet for January would show a carrying value for Inventories of €37,983 (= €5,000 + €27,083 + €5,900).

EXHIBIT 8.2

Moon Products
Income Statement
For the Month of January

Sales Revenue		€75,000
Less Expenses:		
Cost of Goods Sold	€42,600	
Salaries Expense	20,000	
Utilities Expense	200	
Rent Expense	6,250	
Total Expenses		69,050
Income Before Taxes		€ 5,950

EXHIBIT 8.3

Moon Products
T-Accounts Showing Inventory Transactions
During January

Raw Materials Inventory

✓	0		
(2)	25,000	20,000	(3)
✓	5,000		

Work-in-Process Inventory

✓	0		
(3)	20,000		
(4)	40,000	48,500	(7)
(5)	1,000		
(6)	14,583		
✓	27,083		

Finished Goods Inventory

✓	0		
(7)	48,500	42,600	(9)
✓	5,900		

Cost of Goods Sold

(9)	42,600		

Summary of the Accounting Process for Manufacturing Operations The accounting procedures for the marketing and administrative costs of manufacturing firms resemble those for merchandising firms. The firm expenses these costs in the same period that it consumes the services. The accounting procedures for a manufacturing firm differ from those for a merchandising firm in the treatment of inventories. A merchandising firm acquires products in finished form ready for sale. It debits purchases of merchandise to the Inventory account and credits the Inventory account when it sells the merchandise. A manufacturing firm incurs costs in transforming raw materials into work in process and then into finished products. Although a manufacturing firm consumes raw materials, labor services, and factory overhead services in the manufacturing process, the consumption results in the creation of an asset—partially completed and completed units of inventory. Until the manufacturing firm sells the units produced, it accumulates manufacturing costs in asset accounts—the Raw Materials Inventory account, the Work-in-Process Inventory account, and the Finished Goods Inventory account—depending on the stage of completion of each inventory item. The firm therefore debits product costs to inventory (asset) accounts until it sells the units produced.

PROBLEM 8.1 for Self-Study

Flow of manufacturing costs through the accounts. The following data relate to the manufacturing activities of Haskell Ltd. during March:

	March 1	March 31
Raw Materials Inventory	£42,400	£ 46,900
Work-in-Process Inventory	75,800	63,200
Finished Goods Inventory	44,200	46,300

Factory Costs Incurred during the Month	
Raw Materials Purchased	60,700
Labor Services Received	137,900
Heat, Light, and Power	1,260

Expirations of Previous Factory Acquisitions and Prepayments	
Rental Charges for Factory Equipment	1,800
Rental Charges on Factory Building	4,100
Prepaid Insurance Expired	1,440

Other Data Relating to the Month	
Sales Revenue	400,000
Selling and Administrative Expenses	125,000

a. Calculate the cost of raw materials used during March.
b. Calculate the cost of units completed during March and transferred to the finished goods storeroom.
c. Calculate the cost of units sold during March.
d. Calculate income before taxes for March.

ISSUE 2: VALUATION SUBSEQUENT TO ACQUISITION

Both U.S. GAAP and IFRS require firms to initially record inventories at acquisition cost (**Issue 1** discussed above). The market value of inventories may change, however, while the firm holds the inventory awaiting its sale to customers. This section discusses the treatment of increases and decreases in the market value of inventories subsequent to acquisition. Market value generally means **replacement cost**, the amount the firm would have to pay to replace the inventory.[4]

Increases in Market Value

Increases in Market Value Inventories may increase in market value subsequent to acquisition for various reasons. A shortage of a key raw material (such as oil or nickel) may increase the market value of that raw material and therefore increase the replacement cost of inventory of which the raw material is a component. A new labor agreement may increase labor cost and thereby increase the replacement cost of manufactured inventories. If a firm were to remeasure its inventories to the higher replacement cost, or market value, it would make an entry such as the following:

Inventories X				
Unrealized Holding Gain on Inventories				X

Assets	=	Liabilities	+	Shareholders' Equity	(Class.)
+Increase in Value				+Increase in Value	IncSt → RE*

*Alternatively, the firm might include this increase in Other Comprehensive Income.

Neither U.S. GAAP nor IFRS permit firms to remeasure inventories upward to an amount exceeding their acquisition cost.[5] The reasoning is that acquisition cost leads to a more conservative measure of inventories and net income during the periods prior to sale. Although an increase in the market value of inventory likely permits the firm to raise its selling price, the firm realizes the benefit of that increase in the period of sale when the firm actually obtains a higher selling price. Both U.S. GAAP and IFRS delay recognition in net income until the period of sale.

Decreases in Market Value

Decreases in Market Value Inventories can decrease in market value for various reasons. A competitor may introduce a technologically superior product; a product may include materials found to contain a health hazard; the introduction of a lower-cost raw material lowers the manufacturing cost of a product using that raw material as a component.

In contrast to the treatment of increases in market value, both U.S. GAAP and IFRS require firms to write down (that is, reduce the balance sheet carrying value of) inventories when their replacement cost, or market value, declines below acquisition cost. Accountants refer to the inventory as *impaired* and to this valuation as the **lower-of-cost-or-market basis**.[6] The journal entry to record the inventory impairment results in a loss and a new balance sheet carrying value that is the lower of cost or market value. U.S. GAAP does not permit firms to recognize subsequent value increases, even if the new value remains less than the original acquisition cost. In contrast, IFRS permits firms to reverse previous impairments, up to the amount of the original acquisition cost of the inventory, if the circumstances that caused the inventory impairment no longer exist.

To illustrate a typical impairment of inventory, if Nordstrom experienced a decline of $5,000 in the market value of inventory with an acquisition cost of $119,000, it would make the following journal entry to recognize the impairment:

---

[4]U.S. GAAP specifies that, in the context of inventories, *market* means replacement cost, except that market may not exceed net realizable value (estimated selling price less cost to complete and sell the inventory) and may not be less than net realizable value reduced by a normal profit margin (chapter 4 of AICPA, Committee on Accounting Procedures, *Accounting Research Bulletin No. 43*, "Inventory Pricing," 1953) (**Codification Topic 330**). IFRS specifies that, in the context of inventories, *market* means net realizable value (International Accounting Standards Board, *International Accounting Standard 2*, "Inventories," revised 2003).

[5]An exception to this rule exists in *International Accounting Standard 41*, "Agriculture," 2001. This standard requires that firms measure agricultural assets, including both plants and animals, at fair value less estimated point-of-sale costs, unless they cannot measure fair value reliably. We do not consider this exception in this textbook.

[6]AICPA, Committee on Accounting Procedures, *Accounting Research Bulletin No. 43*, "Inventory Pricing," 1953 (**Codification Topic 330**); International Accounting Standards Board, *International Accounting Standard 2*, "Inventories," revised 2003.

| Unrealized Holding Loss on Inventory | 5,000 | |
| Inventory | | 5,000 |

Assets	=	Liabilities	+	Shareholders' Equity	(Class.)
−5,000				−5,000	IncSt → RE

To record an impairment loss of 5,000 on inventory.

The Unrealized Holding Loss on Inventory (sometimes called Impairment Loss) is an expense of the period and can appear on the income statement on a separate line. Many firms include the unrealized holding loss in cost of goods sold.

Consider, for example, the calculations in **Exhibit 8.4** where beginning inventory is $19,000, purchases are $100,000, and ending inventory has a cost of $25,000 and a market value of $20,000. Cost of Goods Sold is $5,000 larger when the firm records ending inventory at lower of cost or market than when it records the inventory at acquisition cost. The loss of $5,000 increases Cost of Goods Sold by $5,000 and therefore reduces net income by $5,000, compared to the acquisition cost basis. The firm should disclose the existence of large write-downs included in Cost of Goods Sold in the notes so that users of financial statements understand the components of the Cost of Goods Sold account.

Now suppose the same inventory increased $3,000 in market value in the subsequent period. Under U.S. GAAP, the firm would continue to record the inventory at $20,000, the lower of cost or market. However, if Nordstrom prepared its financial statements in accordance with IFRS, it would reverse a portion of its previous impairment by making the following journal entry:

| Inventory | 3,000 | |
| Unrealized Holding Gain on Inventory | | 3,000 |

Assets	=	Liabilities	+	Shareholders' Equity	(Class.)
+3,000				+3,000	IncSt → RE

To record a partial recovery of previous inventory impairment.

Firms in industries that frequently experience inventory price fluctuations often use an allowance account to record lower-of-cost-or-market adjustments. As an illustration of the allowance approach applied to inventory, **Exhibit 8.5** shows the inventory note disclosure to Nestlé Group's financial statements prepared for the year ended December 31, 2007 (amounts reported in millions of Swiss francs, CHF):

Nestlé's balance sheet for 2007 shows inventories with a carrying value of CHF9,272 million. The *gross* amount of Nestlé's inventory is CHF9,547 million, equal to the *net* inventory amount of CHF9,272 million plus the ending balance in the Allowance for Write-Downs of CHF275 million. Nestlé estimates the amount of any impairment in inventory arising from application of the lower-of-cost-or-market rule, and records these impairments in an inventory contra account, the Allowance for Write-Down at Net Realizable Value. If Nestlé had lower-of-cost-or-market adjustments of CHF100 million in 2007, it would have recorded the following journal entry:

EXHIBIT 8.4   Calculating Cost of Goods Sold Using Different Bases of Inventory Valuation

	Cost Basis	Lower-of-Cost-or-Market Basis
Beginning Inventory	$ 19,000	$ 19,000
Purchases	100,000	100,000
Goods Available for Sale	$119,000	$ 119,000
Less Ending Inventory	(25,000)	(20,000)
Cost of Goods Sold	$ 94,000	$ 99,000

| EXHIBIT 8.5 | Nestlé Group
Note 10: Inventory
Year Ended December 31, 2007 |

10. Inventories

In millions of CHF	2007	2006
Raw materials, work in progress and sundry supplies	3 590	3 102
Finished goods	5 957	5 164
Allowance for write-down at net realisable value	(275)	(237)
	9 272	8 029

Unrealized Holding Loss on Inventory 100

    Allowance for Write-Down at Net Realizable Value 100

Assets	=	Liabilities	+	Shareholders' Equity	(Class.)
−100				−100	IncSt → RE

To record an impairment loss of 100 on inventory.

Under IFRS, the firm would reverse the write-downs in the Allowance for Inventory Impairment, as long as those reversals do not exceed the cumulative amount of prior write-downs. Further, because the firm makes lower-of-cost-or-market adjustments for each type or class of inventory, a firm using IFRS might record *both* an impairment charge on one class of inventory *and* a reversal on a different class of inventory in the same year.

The lower-of-cost-or-market basis for inventory valuation is a conservative accounting policy because (1) it recognizes losses from decreases in market value before a sale occurs, but recognizes gains from increases in market value above original acquisition cost only when a sale occurs, and (2) it reports inventories on the balance sheet at amounts that are never greater, but may be less, than acquisition cost.[7]

Subsequent Sale of Inventory Adjusted to Lower-of-Cost-or-Market Assume that the inventory that the firm has written down (or marked down) remains salable. The firm will record revenues on the eventual sale of the items. The firm will debit Cost of Goods Sold and credit Inventory at the time it recognizes revenue. The difference between the amount of revenue and the amount of cost of goods sold is the gross margin on the transaction. Holding the selling price constant, the lower-of-cost-or-market adjustment reduces the carrying value of the inventory in the period of write-down but increases the gross margin recognized on the eventual sale of the inventory in a future period.

When both the write-down (or mark-down) and the sale of the marked-down inventory occur in the same reporting period, the income statement for that period captures both effects: the impairment loss (mark-down) will offset the lower market value of inventory recognized as cost of goods sold. If the firm does not sell the marked-down inventory until a later reporting period, the impairment loss will reduce income in an earlier period, but the later, higher gross margin in the period of sale will offset the loss. For example, suppose Nordstrom estimates that unsold women's clothing with a carrying value of $400 million has minimal market value given a change in fashion. To reflect the minimal market value of the merchandise, Nordstrom would record an impairment loss of $400 million, reducing the carrying value of this inventory to zero. If Nordstrom sells the clothes for $85 million in a subsequent accounting period, it would recognize zero cost of goods sold and a gross margin of $85 million on

---

[7]Consult the **Glossary** for the definition of conservatism in accounting. Conservative accounting policies result in both lower asset totals and lower retained earnings totals, thus implying lower cumulative net income totals. Conservatism does not mean reporting lower income in every period. Over long-enough time spans, an accounting policy that results in lower income in earlier periods must result in higher income in some subsequent periods. The conservative accounting policy results in lower income in the early periods.

the sale, for a net margin of $-$315 (= $-$400 + $85) million over the two periods. Had Nordstrom not used lower of cost or market, the net margin in the period of sale would have been the same $-$315 million. Lower of cost or market does not change total net income over the life of the item but does result in lower reported income in the earlier periods.

Summary of the Effects of Inventory Remeasurements For any one unit of inventory, there is only one total gain or loss figure: the difference between its selling price and its acquisition cost. Inventory remeasurement rules determine *when* this gain or loss appears in the financial statements over the accounting periods between acquisition and final disposition. If a firm remeasures inventory upward to current replacement cost (not permitted by U.S. GAAP or IFRS), income in the period of the inventory write-up would be higher than if the firm had used the acquisition cost basis, but income in the later period, when the firms sells the inventory, will be lower. The later, lower income results from the inventory having a higher balance sheet carrying value and therefore causing a larger cost of goods sold expense. When a firm uses the lower-of-cost-or-market basis, income in the period of an inventory write-down will be lower than if the firm had used the acquisition cost basis, but income in a later period, when the firm sells the inventory, will be higher. Thus, income for each accounting period considered in isolation depends on the valuation of inventory on the balance sheet.

ISSUE 3: COST-FLOW ASSUMPTIONS

The accounting records typically contain information on the cost of the beginning inventory for a period, which was the ending inventory of last period, and information on purchases made or production costs incurred during the current period. Thus, firms can easily measure the cost of goods available for sale or use. Firms can usually match units sold and units in ending inventory with specific purchases by using product bar codes or other identifiers.[8] Using the identifier, the firm can trace the unit back to its purchase invoice or cost record.[9] This is an example of the **specific identification** system for computing cost of goods sold.

To illustrate the specific identification system, assume a cycling store has a beginning inventory of one bi-level touring bicycle 1, for which it paid $2,500. Suppose that during the period the store purchases bicycle 2 for $2,900 and bicycle 3 for $3,000, and that it sells one bicycle for $5,500. The three bicycles are physically identical; the store acquired them at different times as their acquisition costs changed, so only their costs differ.

We can write the inventory equation as follows, measuring all quantities in dollars of cost:

$$\text{Beginning Inventory} + \text{Purchases} - \text{Cost of Goods Sold} = \text{Ending Inventory}$$
$$\$2,500 \quad + \quad \$5,900 \quad - \quad ? \quad = \quad ?$$

Suppose the cycling store uses the specific identification system, and uses serial numbers or product bar codes to identify bicycle 2 as the unit sold. The cost of goods sold is $2,900, and the ending inventory consisting of bicycles 1 and 3 is $5,500 (= $2,500 + $3,000).

Suppose a firm does not have a system for the specific identification of units sold and units remaining in inventory. It will have records of the cost of the beginning inventory and the cost of purchases, but it will not have records for the cost of goods sold or for ending inventory. It can use a physical count of the ending inventory to obtain the number of units in ending inventory, but it will not have records of the costs of those units. Instead, it has records of the costs of units available for sale during the period (the cost of beginning inventory plus the cost of purchases). It could compute the cost of the units in ending inventory (or, conversely, cost of goods sold) using the most recent costs, the oldest costs, or the average cost of the units available for sale. Once it determines a cost for one unknown quantity—either ending inventory or cost of goods sold—the inventory equation automatically

---

[8]In theory, similar identifiers apply to production runs; in practice, however, it is difficult to use specific identification for a manufacturing firm, especially a firm that produces products that contain thousands of parts, each created by its own manufacturing operation. Most such firms use standard cost systems to allocate costs to products. Standard costing is an important topic in managerial accounting.

[9]When a firm computes the cost of goods sold each time it sells an inventory item, it uses a *perpetual inventory system*. When a firm computes the cost of goods sold at the end of each period by taking a physical inventory and assumes that it sold any items not in ending inventory, it uses a *periodic inventory system*. See the **Glossary** for a description of these two inventory systems. We assume use of a periodic system throughout this book.

EXHIBIT 8.6	Comparison of Cost-Flow Assumptions Historical Cost Basis

Assumed Data

Beginning Inventory:	Bicycle 1 Cost	$2,500
Purchases:	Bicycle 2 Cost	2,900
	Bicycle 3 Cost	3,000
Cost of Goods Available for Sale		$8,400
Sales: One bicycle		$5,500

	Cost Flow Assumption		
	FIFO	**Weighted Average**	**LIFO**
Financial Statements	**(1)**	**(2)**	**(3)**
Sales	$5,500	$5,500	$5,500
Cost of Goods Sold	2,500[a]	2,800[b]	3,000[c]
Gross Margin on Sales	$3,000	$2,700	$2,500
Ending Inventory	$5,900[d]	$5,600[e]	$5,400[f]

[a]Bicycle 1 costs $2,500.
[b]Average bicycle costs $2,800 (= $8,400/3).
[c]Bicycle 3 costs $3,000.

[d]Bicycles 2 and 3 cost $2,900 + $3,000 = $5,900.
[e]Two bicycles at average cost 2 × $2,800 = $5,600.
[f]Bicycles 1 and 2 cost $2,500 + $2,900 = $5,400.

determines the cost for the other quantity. The sum of the two unknowns, Cost of Goods Sold and Ending Inventory, must equal the cost of goods available for sale (= Beginning Inventory + Purchases). The higher the cost assigned to one unknown, the lower must be the cost assigned to the other.

In short, the firm must know, or make an assumption about, which units it has sold or which units remain in inventory. Specific identification avoids making an assumption but is not feasible for all firms. Inventory items of some firms are sufficiently similar and fluid that the firm cannot feasibly use specific identification, for example, for gasoline in a storage tank or rock salt in a quarry. Even when technology, such as product bar codes, allows firms to track the cost of each item in inventory, it may not be cost effective to do so. For example, a home improvements store likely does not develop and implement a bar code system to track pieces of lumber or hammers sold.

Neither U.S. GAAP nor IFRS requires firms to use specific identification; both allow firms to select a **cost-flow assumption**. That cost-flow assumption need not match the actual physical flow of units within the firm. Typical cost-flow assumptions are as follows:

1. Weighted average.
2. First-in, first-out (FIFO).
3. Last-in, first-out (LIFO), which U.S. GAAP permits, but IFRS does not.[10]

We illustrate each of these cost-flow assumptions using the data provided in **Exhibit 8.6**.

Under the **weighted-average** cost-flow assumption, a firm calculates the average of the costs of all goods available for sale (or use) during the accounting period, including the cost applicable to the beginning inventory. This weighted-average cost applies to the units sold during the period and to the units on hand at the end of the period. Column (2) in **Exhibit 8.6** illustrates the weighted-average cost-flow assumption. The weighted-average cost of each bicycle available for sale during the period is $2,800 [= $\frac{1}{3}$ × ($2,500 + $2,900 + $3,000)]. Cost of Goods Sold is thus $2,800, and ending inventory is $5,600 (= 2 × $2,800).

The **first-in, first-out (FIFO)** cost-flow assumption assigns the costs of the earliest (or *first*) units acquired to the withdrawals and assigns the costs of the most recent acquisitions

---

[10]As this book goes to press, the SEC has proposed that U.S. companies adopt IFRS by 2016. An impediment to U.S. companies switching from U.S. GAAP to IFRS may come from the IFRS prohibition of LIFO. See the discussion in the following section about income tax implications of the cost-flow assumptions.

to the ending inventory. This cost flow assumes that the firm uses/sells the oldest materials and goods first—a good business practice, especially in managing the physical flow of items that deteriorate or become obsolete. Column **(1)** of **Exhibit 8.6** illustrates FIFO, which assumes that the firm sells bicycle 1 while bicycles 2 and 3 remain in inventory. FIFO is like a conveyor belt: the first items put on the conveyor belt come off first for use or sale, while the last items put on the conveyor belt remain there at the end of the period.

The **last-in, first-out (LIFO)** cost-flow assumption assigns the costs of the latest (or *last*) units acquired to the withdrawals and assigns the costs of the oldest units to the ending inventory. Some argue that LIFO matches current costs to current revenues and, therefore, that LIFO better measures income. Column **(3)** of **Exhibit 8.6** illustrates LIFO, which assumes that the firm sells bicycle 3 costing $3,000 while the costs of bicycles 1 and 2 remain in inventory. LIFO is like a stack of trays in a cafeteria: the last tray deposited on the stack is the first one taken off, and the lowest tray in the stack remains there as long as any trays remain. Note that LIFO does not reflect typical physical inventory flows; that is, the next product a firm sells is typically not the last one that it purchased or produced. As described next, firms use LIFO because it produces a cost of goods sold figure based on more recent purchase prices and, therefore, results in lower net income and reduced tax payments.

As noted earlier, IFRS prohibits use of the LIFO cost-flow assumption. The U.S. taxing authorities permit a firm to use LIFO for tax purposes as long as it also uses LIFO for financial reporting purposes.[11] In periods of rising purchase prices and increasing inventory quantities, LIFO results in a higher cost of goods sold, a lower reported periodic income, and lower current income taxes than either FIFO or the weighted-average cost-flow assumption. The data in **Exhibit 8.6** illustrate this pattern, which shows that, during this period characterized by increasing bicycle costs (from $2,500 to $2,900 to $3,000), LIFO results in the smallest gross margin ($2,500) of the three cost-flow assumptions. You might tentatively conclude, therefore, that LIFO always provides a lower amount of net income. Such a conclusion is incorrect, however, as we discuss in **Appendix 8.1** to this chapter, because inventory quantities or acquisition costs of inventory need not always increase.

COMPARISON OF AND CHOICE AMONG COST-FLOW ASSUMPTIONS

Note from **Exhibit 8.6** that cost of goods sold plus ending inventory equals $8,400, the total cost of goods available for sale, in all three cases. When purchase prices change, no cost-flow assumption places up-to-date costs on both the income statement and the balance sheet. For example, consider a period of rising prices as in **Exhibit 8.6**. If cost of goods sold for the income statement includes recent, higher acquisition prices, as occurs under LIFO, then older, lower acquisition prices must appear in the cost of ending inventory on the balance sheet. As long as accounting standards require firms to use acquisition costs for valuing inventory, either the income statement or the balance sheet will reflect current cost figures, but not both.

Of the three cost-flow assumptions, FIFO results in balance sheet figures that are closest to current cost because the latest purchases dominate the ending inventory amounts. However, the FIFO cost of goods sold will be out of date because FIFO assumes that the earlier acquisition costs of the beginning inventory and the earliest inventory acquisitions during the period become expenses. When prices rise, FIFO usually leads to the highest reported net income of the three methods, and when purchase prices fall, it leads to the smallest.

LIFO ending inventory can contain costs of items acquired many years previously. When inventory costs have been rising and inventory amounts increasing, LIFO produces balance sheet figures that are usually much lower than current costs. However, LIFO's cost of goods sold figure approximates current costs. Of the three cost-flow assumptions, LIFO usually results in the smallest net income when inventory costs are rising (highest cost of goods sold) and the largest net income when inventory costs are falling (lowest cost of goods sold). Also, LIFO results in the least fluctuation in gross margins in businesses in which selling prices tend to change as acquisition costs of inventories change.

---

[11]The requirement that U.S. firms using LIFO for tax reporting purposes must also use LIFO for financial reporting purposes is called the *LIFO conformity rule*. U.S. disclosure rules require that a LIFO firm must disclose ending inventory either at its current cost or on a FIFO cost-flow basis. Coupled with other financial statement information, this disclosure provides sufficient information to permit financial statement users to calculate the values of inventory and cost of goods sold under current a FIFO cost flow assumption or an approximation thereto, such as current cost.

The weighted-average cost-flow assumption falls between the other two in its effects, but it resembles FIFO more than LIFO in its effects on the financial statements. When inventory turns over rapidly, the weighted-average inventory cost-flow assumption provides amounts virtually identical to FIFO's amounts. The remaining discussion treats FIFO and weighted average as being the same in terms of income statement effects.

Differences in cost of goods sold and inventories under different cost-flow assumptions relate in part to the rate of change in the acquisition costs of inventory items. Using older purchase prices for inventories under LIFO or using older purchase prices for cost of goods sold under FIFO has little impact if prices are stable. As the rate of price change increases, the effect of using older versus more recent prices increases, resulting in larger differences in cost of goods sold and inventories between FIFO and LIFO.

Differences in cost of goods sold also relate in part to the rate of *inventory turnover*—that is, the speed with which the firm sells its products. As inventory turnover increases, current-period inventory acquisitions make up an increasing proportion of the cost of goods available for sale. Because purchases are the same regardless of the cost-flow assumption, cost of goods sold amounts will not vary as much with the choice of cost-flow assumption. Even with rapid inventory turnover, inventory amounts on the balance sheet can still differ significantly depending on the cost-flow assumption. The longer a firm uses LIFO, the greater will be the difference between inventories based on LIFO and FIFO cost-flow assumptions. **Appendix 8.1** to this chapter provides a more detailed examination of financial statement effects introduced by the difference in inventories accounted for under LIFO versus FIFO.

PROBLEM 8.2 for Self-Study

Computing cost of goods sold and ending inventory under various cost-flow assumptions. Exhibit 8.7 presents data on beginning inventory, purchases, withdrawals, and ending inventory for June and July.

a. Compute the cost of goods sold and the ending inventory for June using (1) FIFO, (2) LIFO, and (3) weighted-average cost-flow assumptions.

b. Compute the cost of goods sold and the ending inventory for July using (1) FIFO, (2) LIFO, and (3) weighted-average cost-flow assumptions.

EXHIBIT 8.7 — Data for Inventory Calculations (Problem 8.2 for Self-Study)

	Units	Unit Cost	Total Cost
ITEM X			
Beginning Inventory, June 1	—	—	—
Purchases, June 1	100	$10.00	$1,000
Purchases, June 7	400	11.00	4,400
Purchases, June 18	100	12.50	1,250
Total Goods Available for Sale	600		$6,650
Withdrawals During June	(495)		?
Ending Inventory (June 30) and Beginning Inventory (July 1)	105		$?
Purchases, July 5	300	13.00	3,900
Purchases, July 15	200	13.50	2,700
Purchases, July 23	250	14.00	3,500
Total Goods Available for Sale	855		$?
Withdrawals During July	(620)		?
Ending Inventory (July 31)	235		$?

ANALYZING INVENTORY DISCLOSURES

The financial statements and notes provide information for analyzing the effects of inventories and cost of goods sold on assessments of profitability and risk. This section illustrates several such analyses.

Two ratios introduced in **Chapter 6** that pertain to inventory management are the **cost of goods sold percentage** and the **inventory turnover ratio**. The cost of goods sold percentage is the ratio of cost of goods sold to sales revenue. The larger this ratio, the greater the portion of sales revenue required to cover the costs of the product and, therefore, the less is available to contribute to profitability. Industry economic characteristics, business strategies, and operating environments largely determine cost of goods sold percentages. Highly competitive markets force firms to set prices closer to the cost of the product (resulting in a high cost of goods sold percentage) than do less competitive markets. The inventory turnover ratio, equal to cost of goods sold divided by the average inventory during the period, measures how quickly firms sell their inventory.

We can calculate the cost of goods sold percentage and the inventory turnover ratio for Nordstrom for the fiscal year ending February 3, 2007, using data from its balance sheet shown in **Exhibit 1.1** (page 8) and from its income statement shown in **Exhibit 1.2** (page 9). Nordstrom's cost of goods sold percentage is 62.5%:

$$\frac{\text{Cost of Goods Sold}}{\text{Sales Revenue}} = \frac{\$5,353,949}{\$8,560,698} = 62.5\%$$

Its inventory turnover ratio is 5.5:

$$\frac{\text{Cost of Goods Sold}}{\text{Average Inventory}} = \frac{\$5,353,949}{0.5 \times (\$955,978 + \$997,289)} = 5.5$$

An inventory turnover ratio of 5.5 implies that items remain in Nordstrom's inventory for an average of 66 days (= 365 days / 5.5 times per year) before Nordstrom sells them.

Firms experience changes in their cost of goods sold percentages and their inventory turnover ratios simultaneously. Both ratios use cost of goods sold, so there can, but need not, be a relation between them. **Chapter 6** presented the disaggregation of the rate of return on assets (ROA) into the product of the profit margin for ROA multiplied by total asset turnover. Changes in the cost of goods sold percentage affect the profit margin. Changes in inventory turnover affect the total asset turnover. The following sections describe possible explanations for various combinations of changes in the cost of goods sold percentage and the inventory turnover ratio.

Increasing Cost of Goods Sold Percentage and Increasing Inventory Turnover Ratio

This combination results in a lower profit margin and an increased total asset turnover. The net effect on ROA depends on which of the two effects dominates. The firm may have shifted its sales mix toward faster-moving but more commodity-like products that generate smaller gross margins. The firm may also have increased the proportion of manufacturing outsourced to other manufacturers. Outsourcing reduces raw materials and work-in-process inventories, but the firm must share some of the profit margin with the supplier, the outsourcing firm.

Decreasing Cost of Goods Sold Percentage and Increasing Inventory Turnover Ratio

This combination increases both the profit margin and the total asset turnover and thereby increases ROA. How might this combination occur?

A firm institutes improved inventory control systems that increase its inventory turnover. The savings in storage costs and costs of obsolescence reduce the cost of goods sold percentage.

Another possibility is that a firm experiences an increase in demand for its products, and inventory moves more quickly. The increased demand permits the firm to raise prices and thereby lower the cost of goods sold percentage. If the firm is a capital-intensive manufacturer with a high proportion of fixed costs in its cost structure, and if the firm has excess capacity to meet the increase in demand, then cost of goods sold will increase, but unit costs will decline because the firm will not incur additional fixed costs. As a result, its cost of goods sold percentage will decline.

Increasing Cost of Goods Sold Percentage and Decreasing Inventory Turnover Ratio

This combination decreases both the profit margin and the total asset turnover and lowers ROA. This combination might occur if a firm experiences a buildup of obsolete inventory because competitors introduce technologically superior products. The firm has to write down the cost of the inventory to lower-of-cost-or-market or reduce selling prices. Consider, also, the capital-intensive manufacturing firm. Demand weakens, so production slows, as does the turnover of inventory; per-unit manufacturing cost increases because the firm must spread, or allocate, the same amount of fixed cost over fewer units produced.

Decreasing Cost of Goods Sold Percentage and Decreasing Inventory Turnover Ratio This combination increases the profit margin but decreases the total asset turnover. The net effect on ROA depends on which effect dominates. This combination could occur if a firm reduced the amount of outsourcing and thereby captured more of the gross margin, while the need for more raw materials and work-in-process inventories slows the inventory turnover. Or, the firm shifts its sales mix toward higher-margin differentiated products that turn over more slowly.

Other explanations could cause the various combinations discussed above. Additional combinations of changes in one of the two ratios and not in the other are also possible.

PROBLEM 8.3 for Self-Study

Effect of cost-flow assumptions on financial ratios. Refer to the data in **Problem 8.2 for Self-Study.** Assume the following:

	July 31	June 30
Current Assets Excluding Inventories	$3,480	$1,650
Current Liabilities	4,820	2,290

a. Compute the current ratio for June 30 and July 31 using (1) FIFO, (2) LIFO, and (3) weighted-average cost-flow assumptions for inventories. Assume for this part that there are no differences in income taxes payable related to the three cost-flow assumptions.

b. Compute the inventory turnover ratio (= cost of goods sold/average inventory) for July using (1) FIFO, (2) LIFO, and (3) weighted-average cost-flow assumptions.

PRINCIPAL CURRENT LIABILITY ACCOUNTS

Current liabilities are those due within the next operating cycle, normally one year. They include accounts payable, short-term notes payable, accrued liabilities (such as for payroll and income taxes), deferred performance obligations (including advances from customers and warranty liabilities), and restructuring liabilities. Current liabilities also include the portion of long-term debt requiring payment within the year after the balance sheet date. We defer discussion of this item until **Chapter 10**.

A firm continually discharges current liabilities and replaces them with new ones in the course of business operations. Because the firm will not pay these obligations for several weeks or months after the current balance sheet date, they have a present value less than the amount to be paid. The firm reports these items at the full amount owed because, considering the small difference between the amount owed and its present value, a separate accounting for this difference (as interest expense) would not be cost-effective. In some countries, such as Argentina as this book goes to press, the rate of inflation is so high that the accounting procedures have a shorter cutoff, such as a month, for ignoring the difference between nominal amounts and their present values.

ACCOUNTS PAYABLE

A firm typically defers payment for goods and services received until it receives a bill (invoice) from the supplier, at which point it records a liability called **accounts payable** (sometimes called **trade payables**). Even then, the firm may not pay the bill immediately but instead accumulate it with other bills until a specified time of the month when it pays all bills. Because these accounts do not accrue explicit interest, management tries to obtain as much funding as possible from its creditors by delaying payment as long as possible. Failure to keep scheduled promises to creditors can lead to poor credit ratings and to restrictions on future credit.

Chapter 6 introduces the accounts payable turnover ratio—the ratio of purchases during the period to average accounts payable. Recall the inventory equation, with terms rearranged:[12]

$$\text{Beginning Inventories} + \text{Purchases} = \text{Cost of Goods Sold} + \text{Ending Inventories}$$

Using the information in Nordstrom's balance sheet (**Exhibit 1.1**, page 8) and its income statement (**Exhibit 1.2**, page 9) for the fiscal year ended February 3, 2007, we can calculate Nordstrom's purchases using the preceding equation (dollar amounts in thousands):

$$\$955,978 + \text{Purchases} = \$5,353,949 + \$997,289$$

$$\text{Purchases} = \$5,395,270$$

Nordstrom's accounts payable turnover ratio is, then:

$$\frac{\text{Purchases}}{\text{Average Accounts Payable}} = \frac{\$5,395,270}{0.5 \times (\$540,019 + \$576,796)} = 9.7$$

An accounts payable turnover ratio of 9.7 means that Nordstrom's accounts payable turn over about 10 times per year. A more intuitive measure of the efficiency of accounts payable management divides the accounts payable ratio into 365, to obtain days accounts payable. Nordstrom's days accounts payable for the year ended February 3, 2007, is 37.6 days (= 365/9.7), implying that Nordstrom pays its suppliers on average every 38 days.

We now introduce the concept of the **cash cycle** (also called the **earnings cycle** or the **operating cycle**). The cash cycle is the time that elapses between the firm's first acquiring inventory (or components thereof), then making and selling the product, and ultimately receiving cash from customers and paying cash to suppliers. The analyst can measure the cash cycle as Days Inventory + Days Accounts Receivable − Days Accounts Payable. Using the data for Nordstrom for the fiscal year ended February 3, 2007, we can calculate the cash cycle as follows:

$$\underset{\text{(Days Inventory)}}{28 \text{ days}} + \underset{\text{(Days Accounts Receivable)}}{67 \text{ days}} - \underset{\text{(Days Accounts Payable)}}{38 \text{ days}} = 57 \text{ days}$$

This means that Nordstrom's operations require cash funding for 57 days. If Nordstrom were to reduce the number of days units sit in inventory (that is, increase inventory turnover), or collect from customers more quickly (increase receivables turnover), or pay its suppliers more slowly (reduce accounts payable turnover), its cash cycle, and its need to raise cash from suppliers of funds, would decrease. All else equal, the shorter the cash cycle, the more profitable the firm.

Most, but not all firms, have positive cash cycles. Dell Inc., a manufacturer and distributor of laptop and desktop computers, has a *negative* cash cycle, collecting cash on average before it spends it. For the year ended February 1, 2008, Dell reported financial information that reveals an accounts receivable turnover of 11.6 (or days accounts receivable of 31.5), inventory turnover of 53.8 (or days inventory of 6.8), and accounts payable turnover of 4.4 (or days accounts payable of 83.0). Dell's cash cycle is, therefore, −44.7 days (= 31.5 days + 6.8 days − 83.0 days). Dell's negative cash cycle means that, on net, Dell receives interest-free financing from its suppliers for a period of about 45 days. Dell's cash cycle is unusual in part because of its high inventory turnover ratio. Because Dell does not build a laptop or desktop until the customer places the order, it does not have much inventory (especially finished goods inventory) on its balance sheet. The time lag between production of the computer and sale of the computer is small, so the inventory turnover ratio is high.

SHORT-TERM NOTES AND INTEREST PAYABLE

Firms obtain financing for less than a year from banks or other lenders by signing a short-term **note payable**. In return for the cash it receives from the lender, the borrower records a liability, Notes Payable. For example, suppose that on June 1, 2008, Nordstrom borrows

---

[12]Our discussion of the accounts payable turnover ratio assumes that all credits to Accounts Payable relate to purchases of inventory, and all debits relate to payments made to suppliers of that inventory. In reality, other transactions might also affect Accounts Payable, including recognition of a liability for the purchase of administrative items, such as office supplies or professional services.

$1,000,000 from the local bank, promising to pay interest at the rate of 6% per year. On June 1, 2008, it records the following journal entry:

| Cash.. | 1,000,000 | |
| Notes Payable .... | | 1,000,000 |

Assets	=	Liabilities	+	Shareholders' Equity	(Class.)
+1,000,000		+1,000,000			

To record $1,000,000 bank loan.

As time passes, the borrower makes entries, usually adjusting entries, debiting Interest Expense and crediting Interest Payable, to reflect interest that has been accrued but not yet paid. For example, on January 31, 2009 (the end of its 2008 fiscal year), Nordstrom would make the following adjusting journal entry to record accrued interest:

| Interest Expense...................................... | 40,000 | |
| Interest Payable.................................... | | 40,000 |

Assets	=	Liabilities	+	Shareholders' Equity	(Class.)
		+40,000		−40,000	IncSt → RE

To record interest at 6% per year for eight months (June–January); 6% × 1,000,000 × (8/12) = $40,000.

When the borrower makes payments, the entry credits Cash and debits Interest Payable and, perhaps, Notes Payable. Payments go first to reduce the liability for Interest Payable and then, if the amount exceeds the balance in the Interest Payable account, to reduce the principal for Notes Payable. If Nordstrom pays, in full, its obligations to the bank on May 30, 2009, it would show the following two journal entries:

| Interest Expense .... | 20,000 | |
| Interest Payable.................................... | | 20,000 |

Assets	=	Liabilities	+	Shareholders' Equity	(Class.)
		+20,000		−20,000	IncSt → RE

To record the remaining interest at 6% per year for the final four months (February–May), 6% × 1,000,000 × (4/12) = $20,000.

Notes Payable	1,000,000	
Interest Payable.......................................	60,000	
Cash...		1,060,000

Assets	=	Liabilities	+	Shareholders' Equity	(Class.)
−1,060,000		−1,000,000			
		−60,000			

To record payment of the interest and repayment of principal.

WAGES, SALARIES, AND OTHER PAYROLL ITEMS

The end of a firm's reporting period often does not coincide with the end of the cycle governing wage and salary payments to employees. For example, a firm might end its fiscal reporting period on December 31, but not have paid all workers for time and efforts spent prior to this date. To ensure that their financial statements reflect the obligations owed to employees, firms debit Wages and Salaries Expense and credit **Wages and Salaries Payable** for the amount employees have earned but firms have not yet paid as of the end of the reporting period.

Employees owe part of their wages to governments for income and other taxes. They may also owe other amounts for union dues and insurance plans. These amounts are part of the employer's wage expense, but the employer withholds those amounts from each employee's gross pay and then pays them on each employee's behalf to the governments, unions, and insurance companies. In addition, the employer must itself pay various payroll taxes and may have agreed to pay for other fringe benefits, such as paid vacations. Employers often provide paid vacations to employees who have worked for a specified period, such as six months or one year. The employer must accrue the costs of the earned but unused vacations (including the payroll taxes and fringe benefits on them) at the time the employees earn them, not at the later time when employees take vacations and receive their wages. This treatment results in charging each month of the year with a portion of the cost of vacations rather than allocating all costs to the summer, when most employees take the majority of their vacation days.

Example 2 Assume that the Sacramento Radio Shack's employees earn $100,000 and that the employer (Sacramento Radio Shack) withholds taxes averaging 40% of these amounts for federal income taxes, state income taxes, Social Security taxes, and Medicare taxes. In addition, employees in aggregate owe $500 for union dues to be withheld by the employer and $3,000 for health insurance. Sacramento Radio Shack must also pay various payroll taxes averaging 18% of gross wages, as well as $4,500 to Fireman's Fund for payments to provide life and health insurance coverage. Employees have earned vacation pay estimated to be $4,000; Sacramento Radio Shack estimates employer payroll taxes and fringe benefits to be 18% of the gross amount of vacation pay.

The journal entries that follow record these wages. If production workers had earned some of the wages, the firm would debit some of the amounts to Work-in-Process Inventory rather than to Wages and Salaries Expense.

Wages and Salaries Expense	100,000	
Taxes Payable to Various Governments		40,000
Withheld Dues Payable to Union		500
Insurance Premiums Payable		3,000
Wages and Salaries Payable		56,500

Assets	=	Liabilities	+	Shareholders' Equity	(Class.)
		+40,000		−100,000	IncSt → RE
		+500			
		+3,000			
		+56,500			

To record wage expense; plug for $56,500 actually payable to employees.

Wages and Salaries Expense	18,000	
Insurance Expense	4,500	
Payroll Taxes Payable		18,000
Insurance Premiums Payable		4,500

Assets	=	Liabilities	+	Shareholders' Equity	(Class.)
		+18,000		−18,000	IncSt → RE
		+4,500		−4,500	IncSt → RE

To record employer's expense for amounts not payable directly to employees.

Wages and Salaries Expense	4,720	
Estimated Vacation Wage and Fringes Payable		4,720

Assets	=	Liabilities	+	Shareholders' Equity	(Class.)
		+4,720		−4,720	IncSt → RE

To record estimate of vacation pay and fringes thereon earned during the current period of $4,720 (=$4,000 + [18% × $4,000]).

INCOME TAXES PAYABLE

Most businesses organized as corporations pay federal income taxes based on their taxable income from business activities.[13] Some jurisdictions do not levy taxes on income earned by corporations, and in those jurisdictions no income taxes would accrue for business activities. Taxable income (which usually differs from pretax income reported in financial statements) and corporate income tax rates determine the amount of income taxes payable. That is, in many jurisdictions the income reported to the taxing authorities, which we always refer to as *taxable income*, differs from the amount of income reported on the income statement, which we always refer to as *pretax income*. The difference between taxable income and pretax income (sometimes called "book income") arises from several factors, as **Chapter 11** describes.

For now, we note that a firm reports the amount of taxes it must pay to the taxing authorities in the current liability account, **Income Taxes Payable**. This account may go by a more general name, **Taxes Payable**, reflecting the fact that it incorporates other types of taxes (for example, property taxes, sales taxes, city and state taxes). A typical entry to record taxes payable would debit tax expense and credit taxes payable.

PRODUCT WARRANTIES

Chapter 7 introduces deferred performance liabilities in the form of advances from customers. A deferred performance liability arises when a firm accepts payments from a customer but has not delivered the product or rendered the service to the customer. Such a deferred performance liability arises when a firm agrees to provide a **warranty** for service or repairs for some period after a sale. At the time of the sale, the firm will estimate the likely amount of the **warranty liability**. (Firms using IFRS would use the term **warranty provision** instead of warranty liability.[14])

As time passes, firms gain information about both actual warranty usage and actual warranty expenditures. To illustrate the accounting for warranty costs, assume that Scania sold truck engines for SEK280 million during the accounting period. Scania estimates that it will eventually spend approximately 4% of the sales revenue to satisfy warranty claims for the engines. The current period expense for warranties is, therefore, SEK11.2 ($= 4\% \times$ SEK280) million. Scania will make the following entry at the time of the sale of the trucks:

Accounts Receivable	280.0	
Warranty Expense	11.2	
Sales Revenue		280.0
Warranty Liability		11.2

Assets	=	Liabilities	+	Shareholders' Equity	(Class.)
+280.0		+11.2		+280.0	IncSt → RE
				−11.2	IncSt → RE

To record sales and estimated liability for warranties on items sold.

Scania recognizes warranty expense, and a related warranty liability, in the same period that it recognizes revenue, even though it will make the repairs in a later period. The selling price of a warranted product includes amounts for the product sold and for the future warranty services. Recognizing warranty expense in the period of sale results in matching of warranty expense against the related sales revenue. In this case, both the amount and the timing of the liability are uncertain, but Scania can estimate them with reasonable precision. Recall from **Chapter 3** that both U.S. GAAP and IFRS require that firms accrue the expense and the related warranty liability when they can "reasonably estimate" the amount.

---

[13]In contrast, businesses organized as partnerships or sole proprietorships do not pay income taxes. Instead most taxing authorities tax the income of the business entity as income of the individual partners or the sole proprietor. Each partner or sole proprietor adds his or her share of business income to income from all other (nonbusiness) sources in preparing an individual income tax return.

[14]The word *provision* usually refers to an expense account in the United States, but to a liability account abroad. See the **Glossary**.

In a subsequent period, Scania makes expenditures of SEK4.8 million for actual repairs under the warranty. At this time, it would make the following journal entry:

Warranty Liability. 4.8
    Cash (or other assets consumed for repairs) 4.8

Assets	=	Liabilities	+	Shareholders' Equity	(Class.)
−4.8		−4.8			

To record repairs made. The firm does not recognize expense when it provides warranty services, because it recognized the expense at the time of sale.

Note that expenditures to satisfy warranty claims do not affect net income. The net income effect occurs in the period of sale when Scania estimates the *expected* expenditures to satisfy warranty claims arising from products sold in that period. With experience, the firm will adjust the percentage of sales charged to Warranty Expense to maintain the Warranty Liability account at each balance sheet date with a credit balance that reasonably estimates the actual cost of repairs it will make under warranties outstanding at that time. The accounting for warranties resembles the allowance method for uncollectible accounts receivable discussed in **Chapter 7** and is, therefore, sometimes referred to as the "allowance method for warranties." Under the **allowance method for warranties**, current period income reflects an estimate of the cost of future warranty expenditures; the firm revises this estimate over time so that it recognizes an appropriate amount of future warranty expense to satisfy the remaining warranty obligations.[15] The firm treats any reversal of previously accrued warranty charges as a change in accounting estimate, which increases net income immediately. This treatment resembles the treatment of reversals of estimates of uncollectible accounts receivable in the allowance method for uncollectibles. Such reversals will rarely occur because for one to occur, the expected warranty costs from this period's sales plus the costs incurred this period to service warranties outstanding at the beginning of this period would have to be less than the balance of the Warranty Liability at the start of this period. While this can happen in principle, in practice we would expect not to see it often.

When the warranty period is one year or less, the warranty liability is a current liability. When the warranty period exceeds one year, the firm will record both a current portion of the liability and a noncurrent portion. Firms using IFRS classify both amounts as Provisions on the balance sheet. Many firms, like Scania (see **Exhibit 1.5**, page 12) report both Current Provisions and Noncurrent Provisions. U.S. GAAP provides no common terminology for warranty liabilities. Often, firms aggregate them in Other Liabilities.

PROBLEM 8.4 for Self-Study

Warranty liabilities. During the year ended December 31, 2006, Scania reported the following information (in Note 18 to its financial statements) for its liability for Product Obligations (amounts in millions of SEK). For purposes of this exercise, ignore exchange rate differences. Scania uses IFRS terminology where *Provision* means liability.

	Product obligations
2006	
1 January	1,028
Provisions during the year	1,339
Provisions used during the year	-1,056
Provisions reversed during the year	-230
Exchange rate differences	-24
31 December	**1,057**

(continued)

[15]Firms may not use the allowance method in U.S. tax reporting. In tax reporting, taxpayers recognize expense in the period when they use cash or other assets to discharge the obligation. The difference between the financial reporting treatment and the tax treatment creates a temporary difference between financial statement pretax income and taxable income, as discussed in **Chapter 11**.

a. What amount did Scania report for Product Obligations on its balance sheet at the end of 2006?

b. What journal entry did Scania make to record warranty expense during 2006? What effect did this journal entry have on Scania's net income for 2006?

c. What journal entry did Scania make in 2006 for actual expenditures under warranty? What effect did this journal entry have on Scania's net income for 2006?

d. During 2006, what journal entry, if any, did Scania make to reverse previously accrued warranty charges? What effect did this journal entry have on Scania's net income for 2006?

RESTRUCTURING LIABILITIES

Periodically, a firm may decide to restructure all or some portion of its operations. A **restructuring** involves substantial changes to the scope or conduct of the business—for example, sale or closing of divisions or plants, combining offices, moving operations from one location to another, terminating employees or leases, and selling assets. Firms restructure their operations because they believe the restructured firm will operate more efficiently and profitably.

Both U.S. GAAP and IFRS require that firms estimate the costs of a restructuring effort and record this estimate as an expense, with an associated **restructuring liability** (U.S. GAAP terminology) and **restructuring provision** (IFRS terminology).[16] Restructuring efforts can extend beyond one year, so one often sees restructuring liabilities or provisions (IFRS) included as both current liabilities and noncurrent liabilities on a firm's balance sheet.

U.S. GAAP and IFRS differ with respect to the timing of recognition. Under U.S. GAAP firms recognize restructuring charges only under the following conditions:

1. Management has committed to the plan of restructuring.

2. The restructuring costs meet the definition of a liability—a present obligation that the firm has little or no discretion to avoid.

Under IFRS, firms recognize restructuring costs when the firm has committed to and approved a restructuring plan that management will control. The commitment requires that management has estimated the timing and costs of actions and that it has identified and notified employees whom the plan will terminate. IFRS does not require that the restructuring costs meet the definition of a liability, so firms usually recognize restructuring costs earlier under IFRS than they do under U.S. GAAP.

Under both U.S. GAAP and IFRS, the accounting for restructuring charges is similar to the accounting for warranty expenditures using the allowance method. To illustrate the journal entries, consider Scania's financial statements, which show a Restructuring Provision (Liability) of SEK38 million as of December 31, 2006 (recall that Scania uses IFRS terminology where *Provision* means liability); Note 18 to its financial statements shows the following (in millions of SEK):

2006	
1 January	45
Provisions during the year	14
Provisions used during the year	−18
Provisions reversed during the year	−2
Exchange rate differences	−1
31 December	38

The beginning balance in the Restructuring Liability account was SEK45 million. During 2006, Scania recognized restructuring charges of SEK14 million (described as "Provisions during the year") and made the following journal entry:

---

[16]Financial Accounting Standards Board, *Statement of Financial Accounting Standards No. 146*, "Accounting for Costs Associated with Exit or Disposal Activities," 2002 (**Codification Topic 420**); International Accounting Standards Board, *International Accounting Standard 37*, "Provisions, Contingent Assets and Contingent Liabilities," 1998.

| Restructuring Expense | . . . . | 14 | |
| Restructuring Liability | . . . . | | 14 |

Assets	=	Liabilities	+	Shareholders' Equity	(Class.)
		+14		−14	IncSt → RE

To record restructuring charges for the year.

Scania also reports that during 2006 it made expenditures of SEK18 million for the restructuring efforts (described as "Provisions used during the year"):

| Restructuring Liability | . . . . | 18 | |
| Cash (or other assets consumed for restructuring) | . . . . | | 18 |

Assets	=	Liabilities	+	Shareholders' Equity	(Class.)
−18		−18			

To record restructuring expenditures.

Finally, Scania also reports that during 2006 it reversed SEK2 million of previously recorded restructuring charges (described as "Provisions reversed during the year"):

| Restructuring Liability | . . . . | 2 | |
| Restructuring Expense | . . . . | | 2 |

Assets	=	Liabilities	+	Shareholders' Equity	(Class.)
		−2		+2	IncSt → RE

To reverse previously recorded restructuring charges.

PROBLEM 8.5 for Self-Study

Journal entries for transactions involving current liabilities. Prepare journal entries for each of the following transactions of Ashton S.A. during the year ended December 31, 2008. Ashton uses IFRS to prepare its financial reports.

a. January 2: The firm borrows €10,000 on a 9%, 90-day note from First National Bank.

b. January 3: The firm acquires merchandise costing €8,000 from suppliers on account.

c. January 10: The firm receives €1,500 from a customer as a deposit on merchandise that Ashton expects to deliver in February.

d. Month of January: The firm sells merchandise costing €6,000 to customers on account for €12,000.

e. Month of January: The firm pays suppliers €8,000 of the amount owed for purchases of merchandise on account and collects €7,000 of amounts owed by customers.

f. January 31: Products sold during January include a two-year warranty. Ashton S.A. estimates that warranty claims will equal 8% of sales. No customer made warranty claims during January.

g. January 31: Employees earned wages of €4,000 for the month of January. The firm withholds the following from the amounts it pays to employees: 20% for income taxes, 10% for pension and welfare taxes, and €200 for union dues. In addition,

(continued)

the employer must pay pension and welfare taxes of 10% and employment taxes of 3.5%. These wages and taxes remain unpaid at the end of January.

h. January 31: The firm accrues interest expense on the bank loan (see transaction **a**).

i. January 31: The firm accrues income tax expense, but makes no payment, at a rate of 40% on net income during January.

j. February 1: Ashton pays employees their January wages net of withholdings.

k. February 10: The firm delivers merchandise costing €800 to the customer in transaction **c** in full satisfaction of its order.

l. February 15: The firm remits payroll taxes and union dues to government and union authorities.

m. February 20: A customer who purchased merchandise during January returns goods for warranty repairs. The repairs cost the firm €220, which it paid in cash.

n. March 14: Ashton decides to restructure its operations and has committed to a restructuring plan that management has approved and will control. Management has identified and notified employees whose employment will be terminated. The estimated costs for the restructuring plan activities are €50,000.

o. June 20: Ashton begins closing plants pursuant to the March restructuring plan and incurs cash payments of €20,000. At this time, Ashton also realizes that its estimate of total restructuring costs is too high, by €12,500.

SUMMARY

Working capital is the difference between a firm's current assets and its current liabilities. Current assets include cash, accounts receivable (discussed in **Chapter 7**), marketable securities (discussed in **Chapter 12**), prepayments, and inventory; current liabilities include accounts payable, short-term notes payable, the current portion of long-term debt (discussed in **Chapter 10**), advances from customers (discussed in **Chapter 7**), certain short-term accrued liabilities (such as wages payable and taxes payable), the current portion of deferred taxes (discussed in **Chapter 11**), certain short-term warranties, and the portion of restructuring liabilities management expects to settle in the next year.

Of the working capital accounts discussed in this chapter, inventory is the most complex. Inventory measurements affect the income statement (through cost of goods sold and through impairment charges) and the balance sheet, which reports the carrying value of inventory at the end of the reporting period. The sum of cost of goods sold and the ending inventory balance must equal the sum of the beginning inventory balance plus purchases or other acquisitions of inventory during the period. The amount allocated to expense (cost of goods sold) and the inventory asset (ending inventory balance) results in part from the firm's choices of the cost-flow assumption (FIFO, LIFO, and weighted average). When prices are rising and inventory amounts are increasing, LIFO (the last-in, first-out cost-flow assumption) results in the largest cost of goods sold and the smallest balance sheet carrying value of inventory. FIFO (the first-in, first-out cost-flow assumption) results in balance sheet carrying values that approximate current cost.

APPENDIX 8.1: A CLOSER LOOK AT LIFO'S EFFECTS ON FINANCIAL STATEMENTS

LIFO usually presents a cost of goods sold figure that reflects current costs. In periods of rising prices, it also generally results in reporting lower taxable income and, therefore, incurring lower income tax payments. At the same time, U.S. firms that use LIFO reported lower net income to shareholders than they would have reported if they had still used FIFO (because of the LIFO conformity rule described in footnote 11). The deferral of income taxes increased the present value of the cash flows for these firms, despite reporting lower earnings to shareholders.

| EXHIBIT 8.8 | Data for Illustration of LIFO Layers (Inventory at January 1, 2009) |

LIFO Layers		Cost	
Year Purchased	Number of Units	Per Unit	Total Cost
2005.........................	100	$ 50	$ 5,000
2006.........................	110	60	6,600
2007.........................	120	80	9,600
2008.........................	130	100	13,000
	460		$34,200

LIFO Layers In any year when inventory purchases exceed sales, the quantity of units in inventory increases. The amount added to inventory for that year is called a **LIFO inventory layer**. For example, assume that a firm acquires 100 cell phones each year and sells 98 cell phones each year for four years, starting in 2005. Its inventory at the end of the fourth year, 2008, contains 8 units. The cost of the 8 units under LIFO is the cost of phones numbered 1 and 2 (2005), 101 and 102 (2006), 201 and 202 (2007), and 301 and 302 (2008). Common terminology would say that this firm has four LIFO layers, each labeled with its year of acquisition. The physical units on hand would almost certainly be the units most recently acquired in 2008, units numbered 393 through 400, but they would appear on the balance sheet at costs incurred for purchases during each of the four years.

To take another example, the data in **Exhibit 8.8** illustrate four LIFO inventory layers, one for each of the years shown.

Dipping into LIFO Layers A U.S. firm using LIFO must consider the implications of dipping into old LIFO layers, also called **LIFO liquidation**. LIFO reduces current taxes in periods of rising purchase prices and rising inventory quantities. If inventory quantities decline, however, the opposite effect occurs in the year of the decline: older, lower costs per unit of prior years' LIFO layers leave the balance sheet and become expenses. If a firm reduces end-of-period physical inventory quantities below the beginning-of-period quantities, cost of goods sold will reflect the current period's purchases plus a portion of the older and lower costs in the beginning inventory. Such a firm will have lower cost of goods sold as well as larger reported income and larger income taxes in that period than if the firm had maintained its ending inventory at beginning-of-period levels.

To illustrate, assume that LIFO inventory at the beginning of 2009 consists of 460 units with a total cost of $34,200, as in **Exhibit 8.8**. Assume that the cost at the end of 2009 is $120 per unit and that the income tax rate is 40%. If 2009 ending inventory drops to 100 units, all 360 units purchased in 2006, 2007, and 2008 will enter cost of goods sold. These 360 units cost $29,200 (= $6,600 + $9,600 + $13,000), but the current cost of comparable units is $43,200 (= 360 units × $120 per unit). Cost of goods sold will be $14,000 smaller (= $43,200 − $29,200) than if quantities had not declined because the firm dipped into old LIFO layers. Income subject to income taxes will be $14,000 larger, and income after taxes will be $8,400 (= [1 − .40] × $14,000) larger than if quantities had not declined from 460 to 100 units. LIFO results in firms deferring taxes as long as they do not dip into LIFO layers.

LIFO Balance Sheet LIFO usually leads to a balance sheet amount for inventory that is far below the current cost of that inventory. The U.S. Securities and Exchange Commission (SEC) has worried that this out-of-date information might mislead readers of financial statements. As a result, the SEC requires SEC registrants that use LIFO to disclose, in notes to the financial statements, the amounts by which inventories based on FIFO or current cost exceed their amounts as reported with a LIFO cost-flow assumption. Some managers refer to the excess of FIFO or current cost over LIFO cost of inventories as the **LIFO reserve**. Another term, less commonly used, is "LIFO valuation allowance."

Converting Financial Statement Information from LIFO to FIFO Using disclosures of the excess of FIFO or current cost inventories over LIFO inventories, the analyst can compute inventories and cost of goods sold assuming a FIFO cost flow and thereby obtain comparable data between a LIFO firm and its FIFO competitor. To illustrate the con-

EXHIBIT 8.9   **Colgate Palmolive Company Consolidated Income Statement**

For the years ended December 31,	2007
Net sales	$13,789.7
Cost of sales	6,042.3
Gross profit	7,747.4
Selling, general and administrative expenses	4,973.0
Other (income) expense, net	121.3
Operating profit	2,653.1
Interest expense, net	156.6
Income before income taxes	2,496.5
Provision for income taxes	759.1
Net income	$ 1,737.4
Earnings per common share, basic	$ 3.35
Earnings per common share, diluted	$ 3.20

EXHIBIT 8.10   **Colgate Palmolive Company Excerpt from Consolidated Balance Sheet**

As of December 31,	2007	2006
Assets		
Current Assets		
Cash and cash equivalents	$ 428.7	$ 489.5
Receivables (net of allowances of $50.6 and $46.4, respectively)	1,680.7	1,523.2
Inventories	1,171.0	1,008.4
Other current assets	338.1	279.9
Total current assets	3,618.5	3,301.0
Property, plant and equipment, net	3,015.2	2,696.1
Goodwill, net	2,272.0	2,081.8
Other intangible assets, net	844.8	831.1
Other assets	361.5	228.0
Total assets	$10,112.0	$ 9,138.0

version, consider the information reported by Colgate Palmolive Company (Colgate) for the year ended December 31, 2007. **Exhibit 8.9** shows Colgate's income statement, **Exhibit 8.10** shows the asset portion of the balance sheet, and **Exhibit 8.11** shows excerpts from the disclosures that relate to inventories, which the U.S. SEC requires of LIFO firms.

Colgate's disclosures reveal that it uses the FIFO method for about 80% of its inventories and LIFO for the remainder (20%). When a firm reports using LIFO for a material portion of its inventory, common practice in the United States describes it as a LIFO firm—even though in this case Colgate uses FIFO for most (80%) of its inventories.

Exhibit 8.12 shows the conversion of inventories and cost of goods sold from a LIFO to a FIFO cost-flow assumption. The inventory amounts in the first column under LIFO appear on Colgate's balance sheet, and cost of goods sold and sales come from the income statement. We compute purchases using the inventory equation. The amounts disclosed for the excess of FIFO over LIFO permit the computation of beginning and ending inventories under FIFO in the third column. Colgate reports that at the end of 2007, the excess of FIFO cost over LIFO cost was $47.4 million ($46.9 million at the end of 2006). This means that if Colgate had used FIFO to measure all inventories, the inventories would have been $47.4

EXHIBIT 8.11

Colgate Palmolive Company
Excerpts from Inventory Disclosures

Inventories

Inventories are stated at the lower of cost or market. The cost of approximately 80% of inventories is determined using the first-in, first-out (FIFO) method. The cost of all other inventories, predominantly in the U.S. and Mexico, is determined using the last-in, first-out (LIFO) method.

16. Supplemental Balance Sheet Information

Inventories	2007	2006
Raw materials and supplies	$ 258.2	$ 248.3
Work-in-process	43.7	45.4
Finished goods	869.1	714.7
Total Inventories	$1,171.0	$1,008.4

Inventories valued under LIFO amounted to $258.8 and $238.2 at December 31, 2007 and 2006, respectively. The excess of current cost over LIFO cost at the end of each year was $47.4 and $46.9, respectively. The liquidations of LIFO inventory quantities had no effect on income in 2007, 2006 and 2005.

EXHIBIT 8.12

Colgate Palmolive Company
Derivation of FIFO Income from Financial Statements and Notes (all dollar amounts in millions)

(Amounts shown in **boldface** appear in Colgate's financial statements. We derive other amounts as indicated.)

	LIFO Cost-Flow Assumption (actually used)	+	Excess of FIFO over LIFO Amount	=	FIFO Cost-Flow Assumption (hypothetical)
Beginning Inventory	$ 1,008.4		$46.9		$ 1,055.3
Purchases	6,204.9ª		0.0		6,204.9
Cost of Goods Available for Sale	$ 7,213.3		$46.9		$ 7,260.2
Less Ending Inventory	1,171.0		47.4		1,218.4
Cost of Goods Sold	$ 6,042.3		$ (0.5)		$ 6,041.8
Sales	13,789.7		0.0		13,789.7
Less Cost of Goods Sold	6,042.3		(0.5)		6,041.8
Gross Margin on Sales	$ 7,747.4		$ 0.5		$ 7,747.9

ªComputation of Purchases not presented in financial statements:

Purchases	=	Cost of Goods Sold	+	Ending Inventory	−	Beginning Inventory
$6,204.9	=	$6,042.3	+	$1,171.0	−	$1,008.4

million higher than reported at the end of 2007 and $46.9 million higher than reported at the beginning of 2007. Purchases are the same under LIFO and FIFO. Using the inventory equation, we calculate cost of goods sold under FIFO as $6,041.8 million, compared to $6,042.3 million under LIFO. The gross margin under LIFO is $7,747.4, as compared to $7,747.9

under FIFO. The larger gross margin under FIFO suggests that inventory costs increased during the year.

We can also compute inventory turnover ratios under LIFO and FIFO as follows:

LIFO: $6,042.3/0.5($1,008.4 + $1,171.0) = 5.5 times per year

FIFO: $6,041.8/0.5($1,055.3 + $1,218.4) = 5.3 times per year

The inventory turnover ratio under LIFO is misleading because it uses relatively current costs in the numerator and the older cost of LIFO layers in the denominator. The inventory turnover under FIFO more accurately measures the actual turnover of inventory because it uses relatively current cost data in both the numerator and the denominator.

Consider also the current ratio (= current assets/current liabilities). Financial statement analysts use the current ratio to assess short-term liquidity. If a firm uses LIFO in periods of rising prices while inventory quantities increase, the amount of inventory included in the numerator of the current ratio will be smaller than it would be if the firm measured inventory at more current costs using FIFO. Hence, the unwary reader may underestimate the liquidity of a company that uses a LIFO cost-flow assumption.

The LIFO–FIFO Choice U.S. firms face the choice between the LIFO and FIFO cost-flow assumptions because U.S. tax authorities allow LIFO for tax purposes. (Recall that IFRS forbids LIFO for financial reporting.) For U.S. firms, the decision as to which cost-flow assumption to use will depend on several factors:

1. **The extent of changes in manufacturing or purchase costs:** When such costs do not change significantly, then the three cost-flow assumptions provide similar amounts for inventories and cost of goods sold.

2. **The rate of inventory turnover:** The faster the rate of inventory turnover, the smaller are the differences in inventories and cost of goods sold among the three cost-flow assumptions.

3. **The direction of expected changes in costs:** FIFO results in higher net income and income taxes when total costs increase and lower net income and income taxes when costs decrease.

4. **The relative emphasis on reporting higher earnings to shareholders versus saving income taxes:** U.S. issue only.

5. **The increased record-keeping costs of LIFO (for example, keeping track of LIFO layers for all of a firm's products) and its inconsistency with the usual physical flow of inventories.**

6. **The requirement that U.S. firms must use LIFO for financial reporting if they use LIFO for income tax reporting.**

An annual survey of the choices that U.S. firms make in their selection of accounting principles reported for a recent year that more than a third of the companies surveyed used a combination of cost-flow assumptions. More than 65% use FIFO for a significant portion of their inventories, and about 35% use LIFO for a significant portion. Less than 30% use weighted average or specific identification.[17] The industries with the largest percentages of firms using LIFO include firms in the chemical industry and firms that manufacture industrial and farm equipment. Retailing firms also use LIFO extensively. The industries with the smallest proportion of firms using LIFO include technology-based firms, which experience decreasing production costs, such as computers and other electronic equipment. Most foreign tax authorities do not allow LIFO for income tax reporting, so most companies that use LIFO for U.S. inventories use FIFO for inventories abroad.

PROBLEM 8.6 for Self-Study

Assessing the impact of a LIFO layer liquidation. Refer to the data in **Problem 8.2 for Self-Study.** During August the firm purchased 600 units for $15 each and sold 725 units.

a. Compute the cost of goods sold and the ending inventory for August using (1) FIFO, (2) LIFO, and (3) weighted-average cost-flow assumptions.

b. Calculate the effect of the LIFO liquidation on net income before income taxes for the year.

---

[17]American Institute of Certified Public Accountants, *Accounting Trends and Techniques*, 2008, page 159.

SOLUTIONS TO SELF-STUDY PROBLEMS

SUGGESTED SOLUTION TO PROBLEM 8.1 FOR SELF-STUDY

(Haskell Ltd; flow of manufacturing costs through the accounts.)

a. Beginning Raw Materials Inventory	£ 42,400
Raw Materials Purchased	60,700
Raw Materials Available for Use	£ 103,100
Subtract Ending Raw Materials Inventory	(46,900)
Cost of Raw Materials Used	£ 56,200

b. Beginning Work-in-Process Inventory	£ 75,800
Cost of Raw Materials Used (from part **a**)	56,200
Direct Labor Costs Incurred	137,900
Heat, Light, and Power Costs	1,260
Rental Charges for Factory Equipment	1,800
Rental Charges for Factory Building	4,100
Prepaid Insurance Costs Consumed	1,440
Total Beginning Work-in-Process and Manufacturing Costs Incurred	£ 278,500
Subtract Ending Work-in-Process Inventory	(63,200)
Cost of Units Completed and Transferred to Finished Goods Storeroom	£ 215,300

c. Beginning Finished Goods Inventory	£ 44,200
Cost of Units Completed and Transferred to Finished Goods Storeroom (from part **b**)	215,300
Subtract Ending Finished Goods Inventory	(46,300)
Cost of Goods Sold	£ 213,200

Income before taxes is £61,800 (= £400,000 − £213,200 − £125,000).

SUGGESTED SOLUTION TO PROBLEM 8.2 FOR SELF-STUDY

(Computing cost of goods sold and ending inventory under various cost-flow assumptions.)

a. See **Exhibit 8.13**.

EXHIBIT 8.13   Suggested Solution to Problem 8.2 for Self-Study, Part a

			Total Cost		
	Units	**Unit Cost**	**FIFO**	**LIFO**	**Weighted Average**
Beginning Inventory	—	—	—	—	—
Purchases, June 1	100	$10.00	$ 1,000	$ 1,000	$ 1,000
Purchases, June 7	400	11.00	4,400	4,400	4,400
Purchases, June 18	100	12.50	1,250	1,250	1,250
Total Goods Available for Sale	600		$ 6,650	$ 6,650	$ 6,650
Withdrawals During June	(495)		(5,345)[a]	(5,595)[c]	(5,486)[e]
Ending Inventory	105		$ 1,305[b]	$ 1,055[d]	$ 1,164[f]

[a](100 × $10.00) + (395 × $11.00) = $5,345.
[b](100 × $12.50) + (5 × $11.00) = $1,305.
[c](100 × $12.50) + (395 × $11.00) = $5,595.
[d](100 × $10.00) + (5 × $11.00) = $1,055.
[e]495 × ($6,650/600) = $5,486.
[f]105 × ($6,650/600) = $1,164.

b. See **Exhibit 8.14**.

| **EXHIBIT 8.14** | Suggested Solution to Problem 8.2 for Self-Study, Part b |

			Total Cost		
	Units	**Unit Cost**	**FIFO**	**LIFO**	**Weighted Average**
Beginning Inventory, July 1	105	See **Exhibit 8.13**	$ 1,305	$ 1,055	$ 1,164
Purchases, July 5	300	$13.00	3,900	3,900	3,900
Purchases, July 15	200	13.50	2,700	2,700	2,700
Purchases, July 23	250	14.00	3,500	3,500	3,500
Total Goods Available for Sale	855		$11,405	$11,155	$11,264
Withdrawals During July.	(620)		(8,115)[a]	(8,410)[c]	(8,168)[e]
Ending Inventory	235		$ 3,290[b]	$ 2,745[d]	$ 3,096[f]

[a]$1,305 + (300 × $13.00) + (200 × $13.50) + (15 × $14.00) = $8,115.

[b](235 × $14.00) = $3,290.

[c](250 × $14.00) + (200 × $13.50) + (170 × $13.00) = $8,410.

[d]$1,055 + (130 × $13.00) = $2,745.

[e]620 × ($11,264/855) = $8,168.

[f]235 × ($11,264/855) = $3,096.

SUGGESTED SOLUTION TO PROBLEM 8.3 FOR SELF-STUDY

(Effect of cost-flow assumptions on financial ratios.)

a. **Current Ratio**

	FIFO	**LIFO**	**Weighted Average**
June 30			
($1,650 + $1,305)/$2,290	1.29		
($1,650 + $1,055)/$2,290		1.18	
($1,650 + $1,164)/$2,290			1.23
July 31			
($3,480 + $3,290)/$4,820	1.40		
($3,480 + $2,745)/$4,820		1.29	
($3,480 + $3,096)/$4,820			1.36

b. **Inventory Turnover Ratio**

July	**FIFO**	**LIFO**	**Weighted Average**
$8,115/0.5($1,305 + $3,290)	3.53		
$8,410/0.5($1,055 + $2,745)		4.43	
$8,168/0.5($1,164 + $3,096)			3.83

SUGGESTED SOLUTION TO PROBLEM 8.4 FOR SELF-STUDY

(Scania; warranty liabilities.)

a. Scania's balance sheet for the year ended December 31, 2006, shows an ending balance in Product Obligations of SEK1,057 million.

b. Journal entry made to record warranty expense during 2006 (described as "Provisions during the year"):

Warranty Expense   1,339
    Warranty Liability.   1,339

Assets	=	Liabilities	+	Shareholders' Equity	(Class.)
		+1,339		−1,339	IncSt → RE

This journal entry reduced Scania's 2006 income by SEK1,339 million.

c. Journal entry made in 2006 for actual expenditures under warranty (described as Provisions used during the year"):

Warranty Liability   1,056
    Cash (or other assets consumed for repairs)   1,056

Assets	=	Liabilities	+	Shareholders' Equity	(Class.)
−1,056		−1,056			

This journal entry had no effect on Scania's 2006 income.

d. Journal entry made to reverse previously accrued warranty charges (described as "Provisions reversed during the year"):

Warranty Liability   230
    Warranty Expense   230

Assets	=	Liabilities	+	Shareholders' Equity	(Class.)
		−230		+230	IncSt → RE

This journal entry increased Scania's 2006 income by SEK230 million.

SUGGESTED SOLUTION TO PROBLEM 8.5 FOR SELF-STUDY

(Ashton S.A.; journal entries for transactions involving current liabilities.)

a. *January 2*
Cash.   10,000
    Note Payable   10,000

Assets	=	Liabilities	+	Shareholders' Equity	(Class.)
+10,000		+10,000			

To record 90-day, 9% bank loan.

b. *January 3*
Merchandise Inventory   8,000
    Accounts Payable   8,000

Assets	=	Liabilities	+	Shareholders' Equity	(Class.)
+8,000		+8,000			

To record purchases of merchandise on account.

c. *January 10*
Cash.   1,500
    Advances from Customers.   1,500

Assets	=	Liabilities	+	Shareholders' Equity	(Class.)
+1,500		+1,500			

To record advance from customer on merchandise scheduled for delivery in February.

---

d. *Month of January*

Accounts Receivable   12,000

    Sales Revenue   12,000

Assets	=	Liabilities	+	Shareholders' Equity	(Class.)
+12,000				+12,000	IncSt → RE

To record sales on account during January.

Cost of Goods Sold   6,000

    Merchandise Inventory   6,000

Assets	=	Liabilities	+	Shareholders' Equity	(Class.)
−6,000				−6,000	IncSt → RE

To record the cost of merchandise sold.

---

e. *Month of January*

Accounts Payable   8,000

    Cash.   8,000

Assets	=	Liabilities	+	Shareholders' Equity	(Class.)
−8,000		−8,000			

To record payments to suppliers for purchases on account.

Cash.   7,000

    Accounts Receivable   7,000

Assets	=	Liabilities	+	Shareholders' Equity	(Class.)
+7,000					
−7,000					

To record collections from customers for sales on account.

---

f. *January 31*

Warranty Expense   960

    Warranty Liability.   960

Assets	=	Liabilities	+	Shareholders' Equity	(Class.)
		+960		−960	IncSt → RE

To record estimated warranty cost for goods sold during January; $0.08 \times \$12,000 = €960$.

---

g. *January 31*

Wages Expense.   4,000

    Withholding Taxes Payable.   800

    Pension and Welfare Taxes Payable   400

    Withheld Union Dues Payable.   200

    Wages Payable   2,600

(continued)

Assets	=	Liabilities	+	Shareholders' Equity	(Class.)
		+800		−4,000	IncSt → RE
		+400			
		+200			
		+2,600			

To record January wages net of taxes and union dues withheld.

Wages Expense.   540

    Pension and Welfare Taxes Payable   400

    Unemployment Taxes Payable   140

Assets	=	Liabilities	+	Shareholders' Equity	(Class.)
		+400		−540	IncSt → RE
		+140			

To record employer's share of payroll taxes.

h. *January 31*

Interest Expense   75

    Interest Payable.   75

Assets	=	Liabilities	+	Shareholders' Equity	(Class.)
		+75		−75	IncSt → RE

To record interest expense on notes payable for January; €10,000 × 0.09 × 30/360 = €75.

i. *January 31*

Income Tax Expense   170

    Income Tax Payable   170

Assets	=	Liabilities	+	Shareholders' Equity	(Class.)
		+170		−170	IncSt → RE

To accrue income taxes payable for January: 0.40 × (€12,000 − €6,000 − €960 − €4,000 − €540 − €75) = €170.

j. *February 1*

Wages Payable.   2,600

    Cash.   2,600

Assets	=	Liabilities	+	Shareholders' Equity	(Class.)
−2,600		−2,600			

To pay employees their January wages net of withholdings.

k. *February 10*

Advances from Customers.   1,500

    Sales Revenue   1,500

Assets	=	Liabilities	+	Shareholders' Equity	(Class.)
		−1,500		+1,500	IncSt → RE

To record the delivery of merchandise to customer, resulting in revenue being recognized.

(continued)

Cost of Goods Sold   800

    Merchandise Inventory   800

Assets	=	Liabilities	+	Shareholders' Equity	(Class.)
−800				−800	IncSt → RE

To record the cost of merchandise sold.

---

l. *February 15*

Withholding Taxes Payable   800

Pension and Welfare Taxes Payable   800

Unemployment Taxes Payable   140

Withheld Union Dues Payable   200

    Cash   1,940

Assets	=	Liabilities	+	Shareholders' Equity	(Class.)
−1,940		−800			
		−800			
		−140			
		−200			

To record payment of payroll taxes and union dues.

---

m. *February 20*

Warranty Liability   220

    Cash   220

Assets	=	Liabilities	+	Shareholders' Equity	(Class.)
−220		−220			

To record the cost of warranty repairs on products sold during January.

---

n. *March 14*

Restructuring Expense   50,000

    Restructuring Liability   50,000

Assets	=	Liabilities	+	Shareholders' Equity	(Class.)
		+50,000		−50,000	IncSt → RE

To record restructuring expense.

---

o. *June 20*

Restructuring Liability   20,000

    Cash   20,000

Assets	=	Liabilities	+	Shareholders' Equity	(Class.)
−20,000		−20,000			

To record payments for closing of plants pursuant to restructuring plan.   *(continued)*

| Restructuring Liability | | | | 12,500 | |
| Restructuring Expense | | | | | 12,500 |

Assets	=	Liabilities	+	Shareholders' Equity	(Class.)
		−12,500		+12,500	IncSt → RE

To reverse restructuring charges.

SUGGESTED SOLUTION TO PROBLEM 8.6 FOR SELF-STUDY

(Assessing the impact of a LIFO layer liquidation.)

a. See **Exhibit 8.15**.

EXHIBIT 8.15   Suggested Solution to Problem 8.6 for Self-Study, Part a

	Units	Unit Cost	Total Cost FIFO	LIFO	Weighted Average
Beginning Inventory	235	See Exhibit 8.14	$ 3,290	$ 2,745	$ 3,096
Purchases During August	600	$15	9,000	9,000	9,000
Total Goods Available for Sale	835		$ 12,290	$ 11,745	$ 12,096
Withdrawals During August	(725)		(10,640)[a]	(10,625)[c]	(10,503)[e]
Ending Inventory	110		$ 1,650[b]	$ 1,120[d]	$ 1,593[f]

[a]$3,290 + (490 × $15) = $10,640.
[b](110 × $15) = $1,650.
[c](600 × $15) + (125 × $13) = $10,625.
[d]$1,055 + (5 × $13) = $1,120.
[e]($12,096/835) × 725 = $10,503.
[f]($12,096/835) × 110 = $1,593.

b. 125 × ($15 − $13) = $250.

KEY TERMS AND CONCEPTS

Working capital
Current ratio, working capital ratio
Liquidity
Operating assets, operating liabilities
Financial assets, financial liabilities
Cash
Cash equivalents
Prepayments, prepaid assets
Inventory
Merchandising firm
Manufacturing firm
Direct materials, raw materials
Direct labor
Manufacturing overhead
Product costs
Period expenses
Raw materials inventory

Work-in-process inventory, work-in-progress inventory
Finished goods inventory
Cost of goods sold
Replacement cost
Lower-of-cost-or-market basis
Specific identification
Cost-flow assumption
Weighted average
First-in, first-out (FIFO)
Last-in, first-out (LIFO)
Cost of goods sold percentage
Inventory turnover ratio
Accounts payable, trade payables
Cash cycle, earnings cycle, operating cycle
Note payable
Wages and salaries payable

Income taxes payable, taxes payable
Warranty
Warranty liability, warranty provision
Allowance method for warranties
Restructuring

Restructuring liability, restructuring
   provision
LIFO inventory layer
LIFO liquidation
LIFO reserve

QUESTIONS, EXERCISES, AND PROBLEMS

QUESTIONS

1. Review the meaning of the terms and concepts listed above in Key Terms and Concepts.

2. What are the characteristics of prepayments that qualify as assets? What is the accounting for prepayments?

3. Identify the underlying principle that guides the measurement of the acquisition cost of inventories. What is the rationale for this accounting principle?

4. "Firms may treat depreciation on equipment either as a product cost or as a period expense, depending on the type of equipment." Explain.

5. Compare and contrast the Merchandise Inventory account of a merchandising firm and the Finished Goods Inventory account of a manufacturing firm.

6. "Inventory computations require cost-flow assumptions only because specific identification of items sold is costly. Specific identification is theoretically superior to any cost-flow assumption and eliminates the possibility of income manipulation available with some cost-flow assumptions." Comment.

7. Assume no changes in physical quantities during the period. During a period of rising purchase prices, will a FIFO or a LIFO cost-flow assumption result in the higher ending inventory balance sheet carrying value? The lower balance sheet carrying value? Which cost-flow assumption will result in the higher cost of goods sold? Which will result in the lower cost of goods sold?

8. "Firms should obtain as much financing as possible from suppliers through accounts payable because it is a free source of funds." Do you agree? Why or why not?

9. The Francis W. Parker School, a private lower school, has a reporting year ending June 30. It hires teachers for a 10-month period: September of one year through June of the following year. It contracts to pay teachers in 12 monthly installments over the period September of one year through August of the next year. For the current academic year, suppose that the school will pay teachers total contractual salaries of $3,600,000. How should the school account for this amount in the financial statements issued June 30 at the end of the academic year?

10. A noted accountant once remarked that the optimal number of faulty TV sets for Sony to sell is "not zero," even if Sony promises to repair all faulty Sony sets that break down, for whatever reason, within two years of purchase. Why could the optimal number be "not zero"?

11. Describe the similarities and differences between the allowance method for uncollectibles (see **Chapter 7**) and the allowance method for warranties.

12. What does it mean for a firm to reverse a portion of a previously accrued charge, such as the expense creating a warranty liability or a restructuring liability? What is the effect of a reversal on the firm's income statement, balance sheet, and statement of cash flows in the period of the reversal?

EXERCISES

13. **Accounting for prepayments.** Delhaize Group (Delhaize), a Belgian food distributor, reported ending balances in Prepayments of €30.7 million, €25.8 million, and €42.1 million for the years ended December 31, 2007, 2006, and 2005, respectively. Assume that Prepayments pertain to insurance premiums on warehouses and merchandise. During

each of the three years, Delhaize paid insurance premiums of €50 million. Delhaize follows IFRS and reports its results in millions of euros (€).

a. What journal entries did Delhaize make in each of the three years to recognize prepayments?

b. What journal entries did Delhaize make in 2006 and 2007 to recognize insurance on its warehouse and inventory?

14. **Accounting for prepayments.** LG Corporation, a Korean multinational firm, reported an ending balance for Prepayments of KRW345,609 million for the year ending December 31, 2007. For the year ended December 31, 2006, the ending balance in this account was KRW260,324. Suppose that at the beginning of 2007, the Prepayments balance consisted of three months of prepaid rent on factory warehouses; at the end of the three months, LG prepaid one year of rent. LG follows Korean generally accepted accounting principles and reports its results in million of Korean won (KRW). For purposes of this problem, assume that LG uses either U.S. GAAP or IFRS (the choice will not matter).

a. What journal entry did LG make in each of the three months, January–March of 2007, associated with its prepaid rent?

b. What journal entry did LG make at the end of March 2007 to reflect its prepayment of one year of rent?

c. What journal entry did LG make in each of the months April–December of 2007 associated with its prepaid rent?

15. **Identifying inventory cost inclusions.** Harnet Winery is a large U.S.-based winery. In 2008 Harnet spent $2.2 million to acquire grapes (including transportation costs of $200,000). Harnet incurred processing costs of $50,000 in materials (such as barrels, bottles, and corks), $145,000 in labor, $100,000 in machine costs, and $250,000 in utility charges. During the two- to three-year maturing period, Harnet incurred additional costs for storage ($600,000), insurance ($120,000), indirect labor ($180,000), and taxes ($28,000). Harnet also spent $400,000 on research and development and $200,000 on advertising during this period. Identify the costs Harnet should include in its Wine Inventory account.

16. **Identifying inventory cost inclusions.** Trembly Department Store commenced operations on January 1, 2008. It engaged in the following transactions during January. Identify the amount that the firm should include in the valuation of merchandise inventory.

a. Purchases of merchandise on account during January totaled $300,000.

b. The freight cost to transport merchandise to Trembly's warehouse was $13,800.

c. The salary of the purchasing manager was $3,000.

d. Depreciation, taxes, insurance, and utilities for the warehouse totaled $27,300.

e. The salary of the warehouse manager was $2,200.

f. The cost of merchandise that Trembly purchased in part **a** and returned to the supplier was $18,500.

g. Cash discounts taken by Trembly from purchases on account in part **a** totaled $4,900.

17. **Effect of inventory valuation on the balance sheet and net income.** ResellFast purchases residential and commercial real estate for resale. ResellFast has a December 31 year-end and prepares financial statements quarterly. On February 5, 2008, ResellFast acquired an open-air mall in Miami, Florida, with space for 15 retail businesses, for $20 million. On April 12, 2008, a storm flooded a portion of the mall, reducing the mall's fair value to $16.5 million. On August 14, 2008, a large retailer announced plans to build a new store adjacent to the open-air mall; this announcement, combined with ResellFast's repairs, attracted several smaller retailers to inquire about acquiring space in the open-air mall. By September 30, 2008, the fair value of the open-air mall had increased to $26 million. On November 8, 2008, ResellFast sold the mall for $27.5 million. Compute the carrying value of the open-air mall on ResellFast's balance sheet and the related income statement effect for each quarter of 2008. ResellFast follows U.S. GAAP.

18. **Inventory and accounts payable journal entries.** Target Corporation, a U.S.-based retailer, follows U.S. GAAP and reports its results in millions of U.S. dollars ($). Its balance sheet for the years ended February 2, 2008, and February 3, 2007, contains the following information:

(Millions of $)	February 2, 2008	February 3, 2007
Merchandise Inventory.............................	$6,780	$6,254
Accounts Payable	6,721	6,575

Target's income statement reports Cost of Goods Sold of $41,895 million for the year ended February 2, 2008. Assume that Accounts Payable relates only to inventory.

a. How much merchandise inventory did Target purchase during the year ended February 2, 2008?

b. What journal entry did Target make related to part **a**? Assume that Target made all purchases on account.

c. What journal entry did Target make in the year ended February 2, 2008, to record its payments to vendors?

19. **Inventory and accounts payable journal entries.** Tesco Plc. is the U.K.'s largest grocery store chain. It applies IFRS and reports its results in millions of pounds sterling (£). For the years ended February 23, 2008, and February 24, 2007, Tesco reported the following balances in Trade Payables and Merchandise Inventory:

(Millions of £)	February 23, 2008	February 24, 2007
Merchandise Inventory.............................	£2,420	£1,911
Trade Payables	3,936	3,317

During the year ended February 23, 2008, Tesco paid its suppliers £43,558 million. Assume that Trade Payables relates only to inventory.

a. What journal entry did Tesco make to record the payments to suppliers during the year ended February 23, 2008?

b. How much merchandise inventory did Tesco purchase during the year ended February 23, 2008, and what journal entry did it make to record those purchases?

c. What was Tesco's Cost of Goods Sold for the year ended February 23, 2008? What journal entry did it record to reflect this cost?

20. **Income computation for a manufacturing firm.** Fun-in-the-Sun Tanning Lotion Company manufactures suntan lotion made from organic materials. During its first year of operations, it purchased raw materials costing $78,200, of which it used $56,300 in manufacturing suntan lotions. It incurred manufacturing labor costs of $36,100 and manufacturing overhead costs of $26,800 during the year. Inventories taken at the end of the year revealed unfinished suntan lotions costing $12,700 and finished suntan lotions costing $28,500. Compute the amount of cost of goods sold for the year.

21. **Income computation for a manufacturing firm.** The following data relate to GenMet, a U.S.-based consumer goods manufacturing firm, for the fiscal year ending October 31, 2008. Reported amounts are in millions of U.S. dollars ($).

	October 31, 2008	October 31, 2007
Raw Materials Inventory.............................	$101.5	$ 73.7
Work-in-Process Inventory	119.1	100.8
Finished Goods Inventory.............................	322.3	286.2

GenMet incurred manufacturing costs (direct material, direct labor, manufacturing overhead) during fiscal 2008 totaling $2,752.0. Sales revenue was $6,700.2, selling and administrative expenses were $2,903.7, and interest expense was $151.9. The income tax rate is 35%. Compute GenMet's net income for fiscal year 2008.

22. **Income computation for a manufacturing firm.** The following data relate to Crystal Chemical Corporation for the year ended December 31, 2008 (amounts in millions of euros):

	December 31, 2008	December 31, 2007
Raw Materials Inventory.............................	€ 373	€ 452
Work-in-Process Inventory	837	843
Finished Goods Inventory.............................	2,396	2,523

The company incurred manufacturing costs (direct material, direct labor, and manufacturing overhead) during the year totaling €28,044. Sales revenue was €32,632, marketing and administrative expenses were €2,436, and interest expenses were €828. The income tax rate is 35%. Compute net income for the year.

23. **Effect of inventory errors.** Warren Company uses a FIFO cost-flow assumption and calculates Cost of Goods Sold as Beginning Inventory + Purchases – Ending Inventory. It uses a physical count of merchandise on hand to determine the balance in Ending Inventory. On December 30, 2008, Warren Company received merchandise from a supplier and placed that merchandise in its merchandise warehouse. Warren Company included the merchandise in its December 31, 2008 physical count of inventory. Although Warren Company had not yet received the invoice for this merchandise it knew the cost was $1,000 from the purchase order confirmation provided by the seller. When the firm received the actual invoice on January 4, 2009, it recorded the merchandise purchase. In summary, Warren Company received merchandise in December 2008, included the merchandise in its physical count of ending inventory at the end of December 2008 but made no journal entry in December to record the purchase of the inventory. Instead, the firm recorded the merchandise purchase in January 2009. Assume that the firm never discovered its error. Indicate the effect (overstatement (OS), understatement (US), none (NO)) on each of the following amounts (ignore income taxes):

   a. Inventory, 12/31/2008.

   b. Inventory, 12/31/2009.

   c. Cost of goods sold, 2008.

   d. Cost of goods sold, 2009.

   e. Net income, 2008.

   f. Net income, 2009.

   g. Accounts payable, 12/31/2008.

   h. Accounts payable, 12/31/2009.

   i. Retained earnings, 12/31/2009.

24. **Lower of cost or market for inventory.** Cemex S.A., a Mexican cement and construction firm, reported ending inventory, net for the year ended December 31, 2007, of $19,631 million (all amounts reported in millions of Mexican pesos). During fiscal 2007, Cemex reported that application of the lower-of-cost-or-market rule to inventories resulted in an impairment of $131 million. Cemex's allowance account for inventory impairments had an ending balance of $556 million.

   a. What was the gross value of Cemex's inventory at December 31, 2007?

   b. What journal entry did Cemex make in 2007 to record the impairment charge for inventory?

25. **Lower of cost or market for inventory.** Ericsson, a Swedish networks and communications firm, reported a gross value of inventory of SEK25,227 on December 31, 2007. It also reported an ending balance in the allowance for impairments of SEK2,752 million. During 2007, Ericsson recognized a write-down of inventory in the amount of SEK1,276 million. Assume the acquisition cost of the inventory written down is SEK3,500 million. Ericsson applies IFRS and reports its results in millions of Swedish kronor (SEK).

   a. What was the carrying value of Ericsson's inventory as of December 31, 2007?

   b. What journal entry did Ericsson make in 2007 to record the write-down (impairment) of inventory?

   c. Suppose that in January 2008, the market value of the impaired inventory increased to SEK2,800. What journal entry, if any, would Ericsson make?

   d. How, if at all, would your answers to parts **a–c** differ if Ericsson applied U.S. GAAP?

26. **Computations involving different cost-flow assumptions.** Sun Health Food's purchases of vitamins during 2008, its first year of operations, were as follows:

	Quantity	Cost per Unit	Total Cost
January 5 Purchase	460	$4.30	$ 1,978
April 16 Purchase	670	4.20	2,814

(continued)

	Quantity	Cost per Unit	Total Cost
August 26 Purchase..................	500	4.16	2,080
November 13 Purchase...............	870	4.10	3,567
Totals........................	2,500		$10,439

The inventory on December 31, 2008, was 420 units. Compute the cost of the inventory on December 31, 2008, and the cost of goods sold for 2008 under each of the following cost-flow assumptions:

a. FIFO.

b. Weighted average.

c. LIFO.

27. **Computations involving different cost flow assumptions.** Arnold Company's raw material purchases during January, its first month of operations, were as follows:

	Quantity	Cost per Unit	Total Cost
1/2 Purchased	1,200 pounds	$2.20	$ 2,640
1/8 Purchased	2,200 pounds	2.25	4,950
1/15 Purchased	2,800 pounds	2.28	6,384
1/23 Purchased	1,500 pounds	2.30	3,450
1/28 Purchased	3,000 pounds	2.32	6,960
Total Goods Available for Use	10,700 pounds		$24,384

The inventory at January 31 was 3,500 pounds. Compute the cost of the inventory on January 31 and the cost of raw materials issued to production for January under each of the following cost-flow assumptions:

a. FIFO.

b. Weighted average.

c. LIFO.

28. **Effect of LIFO on financial statements over several periods.** Harmon Corporation commenced operations on January 1, 2008. It uses a LIFO cost-flow assumption. Its purchases and sales for the first three years of operations appear next:

	Purchases		Sales	
	Units	Unit Cost	Units	Unit Price
2008.........................	83,000	$20.00	64,000	$32.00
2009.........................	92,000	$25.00	101,000	$40.00
2010.........................	120,000	$30.00	110,000	$48.00

a. Compute the amount of ending inventory for each of the three years.

b. Compute the amount of income for each of the three years.

29. **LIFO provides opportunity for income manipulation.** EKG Company, a manufacturer of medical supplies, began the year with 10,000 units of product that cost $8 each. During the year, it produced another 60,000 units at a cost of $15 each. Sales for the year were expected to total 70,000 units. During November, the company needs to plan production for the remainder of the year. The company might produce no additional units beyond the 60,000 units already produced. On the other hand, the company could produce up to 100,000 additional units; the cost would be $22 per unit regardless of the quantity produced. Assume that sales are 70,000 units for the year at an average price of $30 per unit.

a. What production level for the remainder of the year gives the largest cost of goods sold for the year? What is that cost of goods sold?

b. What production level for the remainder of the year gives the smallest cost of goods sold for the year? What is that cost of goods sold?

c. Compare the gross margins implied by the two production plans devised in the preceding parts.

30. **Conversion from LIFO to FIFO.** Caterpillar Incorporated is a U.S. firm that manufactures machinery and engines for the construction, agriculture, and forestry industries. It follows U.S. GAAP and reports its results in millions of U.S. dollars ($). For the year ended December 31, 2007, it reported LIFO inventories of $7,204 million, compared to $6,351 million as of December 31, 2006. Caterpillar's cost of goods sold for 2007 was $32,626 million. Caterpillar reports in the notes to its 2007 financial statements that inventories would have been $2,617 million higher as of December 31, 2007, had it used the FIFO cost-flow assumption, and $2,403 million higher as of December 31, 2006. Compute Caterpillar's cost of goods sold for 2007 if the firm had used FIFO instead of LIFO.

31. **Analysis of LIFO and FIFO disclosures.** Ford Motor Company, a U.S. automotive manufacturer, reports that it uses the LIFO cost-flow assumption for inventory. For the year ended December 31, 2007, Ford's cost of goods sold was $142,587 million. It reported the following information in the notes to its 2007 financial statements:

	December 31, 2007	December 31, 2006
Total Inventories under FIFO	$11,221	$11,032
Less: LIFO Adjustment	(1,100)	(1,015)
Total Inventories under LIFO	$10,121	$10,017

a. What was the carrying value of Ford's inventory as of December 31, 2007, and as of December 31, 2006?

b. What would Ford's cost of goods sold for 2007 have been had the firm used FIFO?

32. **Journal entries for payroll.** During the year ended June 30, 2008, McGee Associates' office employees earned wages of $700,000. McGee withheld 30% of this amount for payments for various income and payroll taxes. In addition, McGee must pay 10% of gross wages for the employer's share of various taxes. McGee has promised to contribute 4% of gross wages to a profit-sharing fund, which workers will share as they retire. Employees earned vacation pay estimated to be $14,000; estimated fringe benefits are 20% of that amount.

a. Prepare journal entries for these wage-related items.

b. What is total wage and salary expense?

33. **Accounting for uncollectible accounts and warranties.** Hurley Corporation sells household appliances (for example, refrigerators, dishwashers) to customers on account. The firm also provides warranty services on products sold. Hurley estimates that 2% of sales will ultimately become uncollectible and that warranty costs will equal 6% of sales. Actual uncollectible accounts and warranty expenditures generally occur within three years of the time of sale. Amounts in selected accounts appear next:

December 31:	2010	2009	2008
Accounts Receivable, Net of Allowance for Uncollectible Accounts of $245 on December 31, 2010, $405 on December 31, 2009, and $355 on December 31, 2008 . . .	$6,470	$7,750	$7,000
Estimated Warranty Liability	1,720	1,535	1,325

For the Year:	2010	2009	
Sales Revenue	$16,000	$18,000	

a. Prepare an analysis that explains the change in the Allowance for Uncollectible Accounts account during 2009 and 2010.

b. Prepare an analysis that explains the change in the Warranty Liability account during 2009 and 2010.

34. **Journal entries for warranty liabilities and subsequent expenditures.** Miele Company is a German family-owned appliance business. Assume that Miele provides a two-year warranty on its products and that Miele estimates 2008 warranty costs to be 4% of sales revenues. At the end of 2007, Miele's balance sheet carrying value of estimated warranty

liabilities was €30,000. Miele will incur actual warranty costs over the two years follow-ing the time of sale. Assume that sales (all on account) and actual warranty expenditures (all paid in cash) were as follows:

	Sales	Actual Warranty Expenditures
2008	€1,200,000	€12,000
2009	1,500,000	50,000

   a. Prepare journal entries to recognize sales revenues, warranty costs, and warranty expenditures in 2008 and 2009. Closing entries are not required.

   b. What is the balance in the Warranty Liability account at the end of 2009?

35. **Journal entries for warranty liabilities and subsequent expenditures.** Kingspeed Bikes offers three-year warranties against defects on the sales of its high-end racing bikes. The firm estimates that the total cost of warranty claims over the three-year warranty period on bikes sold will equal 6% of sales revenue. Kingspeed will incur actual warranty costs over the three-year period following the time of sale. Sales (all for cash) and actual warranty costs incurred on bikes under warranty (60% in cash and 40% in parts) appear next for years 2008–2010:

	Sales	Actual Warranty Costs Incurred During Year on Racing Bikes Under Warranty
2008	$ 800,000	$22,000
2009	1,200,000	55,000
2010	900,000	52,000

   a. Prepare journal entries for the events of 2008, 2009, and 2010. Closing entries are not required.

   b. What is the balance in the Warranty Liability account at the end of 2010?

36. **Journal entries for restructuring liabilities and subsequent expenditures.** For the fiscal year ended September 30, 2007, Sappi Paper Limited, a South African paper company, reported an ending balance in its Restructuring Provision, the balance sheet account, of ZAR16 million (ZAR denotes the South Africa Rand currency). The beginning balance in this account was ZAR41 million. During the year, Sappi made cash expenditures of ZAR32 million to settle previously accrued costs of severance charges and plant closings. Sappi did not change any restructuring estimates during 2007. Prepare journal entries related to Sappi's restructuring provision during fiscal 2007.

37. **Journal entries for restructuring liabilities and subsequent expenditures.** On December 31, 2007, Delhaize Group reported a balance in Restructuring Provisions of €50.9 million, of which €12.5 was expected to be paid in 2008, with the remainder to be settled dur-ing 2009–2010. The balance in this account at the start of the year was €84.0 million. During 2007, assume that Delhaize accrued restructuring charges of €14.2 million, and reversed €7.3 million of previous charges.

   a. Prepare all journal entries Delhaize made during 2007 related to its restructuring activities.

   b. How will Delhaize report its Restructuring Provision on its balance sheet for the year ended December 31, 2007?

   c. What is the effect of Delhaize's 2007 restructuring activities on its income statement? How are these activities displayed on the statement of cash flows? Ignore tax effects.

PROBLEMS

38. **Preparation of journal entries and income statement for a manufacturing firm.** Katherine's Outdoor Furniture, a manufacturer specializing in lawn, deck, and poolside furniture, showed the following amounts in its inventory accounts on January 1, 2008:

Raw Materials Inventory	$226,800
Work-in-Process Inventory	427,900
Finished Goods Inventory	182,700

Katherine's Outdoor Furniture engaged in the following transactions during January 2008:

(1) Acquired raw materials costing $667,200 on account.

(2) Issued, to producing departments, raw materials costing $689,100.

(3) Paid salaries and wages during January for services received during the month as follows:

Factory Workers	$432,800
Sales Personnel	89,700
Administrative Officers	22,300

(4) Calculated depreciation on buildings and equipment during January as follows:

Manufacturing Facilities	$182,900
Selling Facilities	87,400
Administrative Facilities	12,200

(5) Incurred and paid other operating costs in cash as follows:

Manufacturing	$218,500
Selling	55,100
Administrative	34,700

(6) The cost of goods manufactured and transferred to the finished goods storeroom totaled $1,564,500.

(7) Sales on account during January totaled $2,400,000.

(8) A physical inventory taken on January 31 revealed a finished goods inventory of $210,600.

a. Present journal entries to record the transactions and events that occurred during January.

b. Prepare an income statement for Katherine's Outdoor Furniture for January. Ignore income taxes.

39. Flow of manufacturing costs through the accounts. The following data relate to the manufacturing activities of the Lord Crompton Plc. during June 2008:

	June 30, 2008	June 1, 2008
Raw Materials Inventory	£ 43,600	£ 46,900
Factory Supplies Inventory	7,700	7,600
Work-in-Process Inventory	115,200	110,900
Finished Goods Inventory	71,400	76,700

It incurred factory costs during the month of June as follows:

Raw Materials Purchased	£429,000
Supplies Purchased	22,300
Labor Services Received	362,100
Heat, Light, and Power	10,300
Insurance	4,200

It also experienced expirations of previous factory acquisitions and prepayments as follows:

Depreciation on Factory Equipment....................................	£36,900
Prepaid Rent Expired...	3,600

Other information included the following:

Sales	£1,350,000
Selling and Administrative Expenses	246,900
Interest Expense	47,100
Income Tax Rate	40%

a. Calculate the cost of raw materials and factory supplies used during June.

b. Calculate the cost of units completed during June and transferred to the finished goods storeroom.

c. Calculate the cost of goods sold during June.

d. Calculate the amount of net income for the month of June.

40. **Flow of manufacturing costs.** Toyota Corporation, a Japanese automobile manufacturer, follows U.S. GAAP and reports its results in millions of yen (¥). On March 31, 2008 and 2007, Toyota reported the following information pertaining to its inventories:

	March 31	
(Millions of Yen)	**2008**	**2007**
Raw Materials and Supplies Inventory	¥ 374,210	¥ 362,686
Work-in-Process Inventory	239,937	236,749
Finished Goods Inventory.............................	1,211,569	1,204,521

Toyota reported Cost of Products Sold for the year ended March 31, 2008, of ¥20,452,338. Toyota reported no write-downs of inventory to lower of cost or market during either fiscal year.

a. What is the carrying value of Toyota's total inventory, as of March 31, 2008?

b. What was the cost of units completed by Toyota during 2007?

c. Suppose that Toyota's direct labor and overhead were ¥12,000,000 million for the year ended March 31, 2008. How much in raw materials and supplies costs did Toyota charge to Work in Process during the year ended March 31, 2008? What journal entry did it make to record this charge?

d. What was the cost of Toyota's raw material and supplies purchased for the year ended March 31, 2008? Assuming all purchases were made on credit, what journal entry did Toyota make to record those purchases?

41. **Flow of manufacturing costs.** The Sandvik Group is a Swedish-based, high-technology engineering firm. It follows IFRS and reports its results in millions of Swedish kronor (SEK). For the years ended December 31, 2007 and 2006, Sandvik reported the following information pertaining to its inventories:

	December 31	
(SEK millions)	**2007**	**2006**
Raw Materials Inventory.............................	SEK6,964	SEK5,690
Work-in-Process Inventory	5,157	4,093
Finished Goods Inventory.............................	13,180	8,955

Sandvik reported Cost of Sales for 2007 of SEK57,222 million. The notes to its financial statements state that 2007 Cost of Sales includes a SEK281 million write-down of Finished Goods inventory.

a. What is the carrying value of Sandvik's total inventory as of December 31, 2007?

b. What journal entry did Sandvik make in 2007 to reflect inventory write-downs?

c. What was Sandvik's Cost of Sales prior to the write-down of inventory to its lower of cost or market value?

d. What was the cost of units completed by Sandvik during 2007?

e. Suppose that Sandvik's direct labor and overhead costs are 300% of direct material costs. That is, for every SEK1 of direct material costs, Sandvik incurs an additional SEK3 in direct labor and overhead costs. How much in direct materials costs did Sandvik charge to Work in Process during 2007? What journal entry did it make to record this charge?

f. What was the cost of Sandvik's raw materials purchased in 2007?

42. **Lower-of-cost-or-market valuation for inventory; U.S. GAAP versus IFRS.** Fortune Brands reported a carrying value of its total inventory as of December 31, 2007, of $2,047.6 million; the corresponding figure for December 31, 2006, was $1,937.8. Fortune Brands applies U.S. GAAP and reports its results in millions of U.S. dollars ($).

a. Suppose that on January 1, 2008, the market value of Fortune Brands' inventory increased to $2,300.0 million. What journal entry, if any, should Fortune Brands record on January 1?

b. Suppose that on January 1, 2008, the market value of Fortune Brands' inventory decreased to $1,880.6 million. What journal entry, if any, should Fortune Brands record on January 1?

c. Continuing the scenario in part **b**, suppose that the market value of the inventory previously written down increased to $1,962.3 million on February 16, 2008. What journal entry, if any, should Fortune Brands record on this date?

d. Would your answers to parts **a**, **b**, and **c** differ if Fortune Brands applies IFRS?

43. **Detailed comparison of various choices for inventory accounting.** Burton Corporation commenced retailing operations on January 1, 2007. Purchases of merchandise inventory during 2007 and 2008 appear next:

	Quantity Purchased	Unit Price	Acquisition Cost
1/10/2007	600	$10	$ 6,000
6/30/2007	200	12	2,400
10/20/2007	400	15	6,000
Total 2007	1,200		$14,400

	Quantity Purchased	Unit Price	Acquisition Cost
2/18/2008	500	$14	$ 7,000
7/15/2008	500	12	6,000
12/15/2008	800	10	8,000
Total 2008	1,800		$21,000

Burton Corporation sold 1,000 units during 2007 and 1,500 units during 2008.

a. Calculate the cost of goods sold for 2007 using a FIFO cost-flow assumption.

b. Calculate the cost of goods sold for 2007 using a LIFO cost-flow assumption.

c. Calculate the cost of goods sold for 2007 using a weighted-average cost-flow assumption.

d. Calculate the cost of goods sold for 2008 using a FIFO cost-flow assumption.

e. Calculate the cost of goods sold for 2008 using a LIFO cost-flow assumption.

f. Calculate the cost of goods sold for 2008 using a weighted-average cost-flow assumption.

g. Will FIFO or LIFO result in reporting the larger net income for 2007? Explain.

h. Will FIFO or LIFO result in reporting the larger net income for 2008? Explain.

44. **Effect of FIFO and LIFO on income statement and balance sheet.** Hanover Oil Products (HOP) operates a gasoline outlet. It commenced operations on January 1, 2008. It prices its gasoline at 10% above its average purchase price for gasoline. Purchases of gasoline during January, February, and March appear next:

	Gallons Purchased	Unit Price	Acquisition Cost
January 1	4,000	$1.40	$ 5,600
January 13.........................	6,000	1.46	8,760
January 28........................	5,000	1.50	7,500
Total...............................	15,000		$21,860

	Gallons Purchased	Unit Price	Acquisition Cost
February 5	7,000	$1.53	$10,710
February 14	6,000	1.47	8,820
February 21	10,000	1.42	14,200
Total...............................	23,000		$33,730

	Gallons Purchased	Unit Price	Acquisition Cost
March 2...........................	6,000	$1.48	$ 8,880
March 15	5,000	1.54	7,700
March 26	4,000	1.60	6,400
Total...............................	15,000		$22,980

Sales for each month were as follows:

January: $20,840 (13,000 gallons)

February: $35,490 (22,000 gallons)

March: $28,648 (17,000 gallons)

a. Compute the cost of goods sold for January using both a FIFO and a LIFO cost-flow assumption.

b. Repeat part **a** for February.

c. Repeat part **a** for March.

d. Why does the cost-flow assumption that provides the largest cost of goods sold amount change each month?

e. Compute the cost of goods sold percentage for each month using both a FIFO and a LIFO cost-flow assumption.

f. Which cost-flow assumption provides the most stable cost of goods sold percentage over the three months? Explain why this is the case.

g. HOP deliberately allowed its inventory to decline to 1,000 gallons at the end of March because of the high purchase cost. Assume for this part that HOP had purchased 6,000 gallons on March 26 instead of 4,000, thereby maintaining an ending inventory equal to the beginning inventory for the month of 3,000 gallons. Compute the amount of cost of goods sold for March using both a FIFO and a LIFO cost-flow assumption. Why are your answers the same as, or different from, those in part **c** above? Explain.

45. **Reconstructing underlying events from ending inventory amounts.** (Adapted from CPA examination.) Burch Corporation began a merchandising business on January 1, 2006. It acquired merchandise costing $100,000 in 2006, $125,000 in 2007, and $135,000 in 2008. Information about Burch Corporation's inventory as it would appear on the balance sheet under different inventory methods follows:

	Balance Sheet Inventory Amounts		
December 31	LIFO Cost	FIFO Cost	Lower of Cost or Market
2006.........................	$40,200	$40,000	$37,000
2007.........................	36,400	36,000	34,000
2008.........................	41,800	44,000	44,000

In answering each of the following questions, indicate how you deduced the answer. You may assume that in any one year, prices moved only up or down but not both.

a. Did prices go up or down in 2006?

b. Did prices go up or down in 2008?

c. Which inventory method would show the highest income for 2006?

d. Which inventory method would show the highest income for 2007?

e. Which inventory method would show the highest income for 2008?

f. Which inventory method would show the lowest income for all three years considered as a single period?

g. For 2008, how much higher or lower would income be on the FIFO cost-flow assumption than on the lower-of-cost-or-market basis?

46. **LIFO layers influence purchasing behavior and provide opportunity for income manipulation.** Wilson Company sells chemical compounds made from expensium. The company has used a LIFO inventory flow assumption for many years. The inventory of expensium on December 31, 2008, comprised 4,000 pounds from 1999 through 2008 at prices ranging from $30 to $52 per pound:

Year Acquired	Purchase Price	Pounds	Cost
1999.........................	$30	2,000	$ 60,000
2004.........................	46	200	9,200
2005.........................	48	400	19,200
2008.........................	52	1,400	72,800
Total.........................		4,000	$161,200

Expensium costs $62 per pound during 2009, but the purchasing agent expects its price to fall back to $52 per pound in 2010. Sales for 2009 require 7,000 pounds of expensium. Wilson Company wants to carry a stock of 4,000 pounds of inventory. The purchasing agent suggests that the firm decrease the inventory of expensium from 4,000 to 600 pounds by the end of 2009 and replenish it to the desired level of 4,000 pounds early in 2010.

The controller argues that such a policy would be foolish. If the firm allows inventories to decrease to 600 pounds, the cost of goods sold will be extraordinarily low (because Wilson will consume older LIFO layers) and income taxes will be extraordinarily high. The controller suggests that the firm plan 2009 purchases to maintain an end-of-year inventory of 4,000 pounds.

Assume that sales for 2009 do require 7,000 pounds of expensium, that the prices for 2009 and 2010 are as forecast, and that the income tax rate for Wilson Company is 40%.

a. Calculate the cost of goods sold and the end-of-year LIFO inventory for 2009, assuming that the firm follows the controller's advice and that inventory at the end of 2009 is 4,000 pounds.

b. Calculate the cost of goods sold and the end-of-year LIFO inventory for 2009, assuming that the firm follows the purchasing agent's advice and that inventory at the end of 2009 is 600 pounds.

c. Assume the firm follows the advice of the controller, not the purchasing agent. Calculate the tax savings for 2009 and the extra cash costs for inventory.

d. What should Wilson Company do? Consider quality of earnings issues in your response.

e. Management of Wilson Company wants to know what discretion it has to vary income for 2009 by planning its purchases of expensium. If the firm follows the controller's policy, after-tax income for 2009 will be $50,000. What is the range, after taxes, of income that the firm can achieve by the purposeful management of expensium purchases?

47. **Interpreting inventory disclosures.** Refer to the information in **Problem 40** concerning Toyota Corporation's inventory for the years ended March 31, 2008 and 2007. The notes to Toyota's financial statements for the year ended March 31, 2008, state that some of Toyota's inventory is valued using the last-in, last-out (LIFO) method. Specifically, Toyota reported that for the year ended March 31, 2008, ¥283,735 million of inventory was valued using LIFO, compared to ¥357,055 for the year ended March 31, 2007. The LIFO inventory amounts exceeded their FIFO amounts by ¥13,780 million for the year ended March 31, 2008, and by ¥30,360 million for the year ended March 31, 2007.

a. What would have been the carrying value of Toyota's inventory at March 31, 2008 and 2007, had the firm used FIFO to value all inventories?

b. What would have been Toyota's Cost of Products Sold for the year ended March 31, 2008, if it had used FIFO for all of its inventories? Note: Convention assigns any LIFO reserve entirely to Finished Goods Inventory.

48. **Allowance method for warranties; reconstructing transactions.** Assume that Central Appliance sells appliances, all for cash. It debits all acquisitions of appliances during a year to the Merchandise Inventory account. The company provides warranties on all its products, guaranteeing to make required repairs, within one year of the date of sale, for any of its appliances that break down. The company has many years of experience with its products and warranties.

The following table shows summary data and financial statement excerpts for Central Appliance for the end of 2007 and for some of the events during 2008. The firm made entries to the Warranty Liability account during 2008 as it made repairs, which converted the credit balance at the end of 2007 into a debit balance of $15,000 at the end of 2008. That is, before the firm makes its entry to recognize warranty expense for the entire year, the Warranty Liability account has a *debit* balance of $15,000. Also, the Merchandise Inventory account, to which the firm has debited all purchases of inventory, has a balance of $820,000 before the adjusting entry for Cost of Goods Sold, so that Goods Available for Sale totaled $820,000. Central Appliance makes its adjusting entries and closes its books only once each year, at the end of the year.

Balance Sheet Excerpts		End of 2007
Merchandise Inventory.		$ 100,000
All Other Asset Accounts		110,000
Total Assets		$ 210,000
Warranty Liability		$ 6,000
All Other Liability and Shareholders' Equity Accounts		204,000
Total Liabilities and Shareholders' Equity		$ 210,000

Income Statement Excerpts	2008	2007
Sales Revenue	$1,000,000	$800,000
Warranty Expense	?	18,000

At the end of 2008, the management of Central Appliance analyzes the appliances sold within the preceding 12 months. It classifies all appliances still covered by warranty as follows: those sold on or before June 30 (more than six months old), those sold after June 30 but on or before November 30 (more than one month but less than six months old), and those sold on or after December 1. Assume that it estimates that one-half of 1% of the appliances sold more than six months ago will require repair, 5% of the appliances sold one to six months before the end of the year will require repair, and 8% of the appliances sold within the last month will require repair. From this analysis, management estimates that $5,000 of repairs will still have to be made in 2009 on the appliances sold in 2008. Items remaining in ending inventory on December 31, 2008, had cost $120,000.

    a. What were the total acquisitions of merchandise inventory during 2008?

    b. What was the cost of goods sold for 2008?

    c. What was the dollar amount of repairs made during 2008?

    d. What was the warranty expense for 2008?

    e. Give journal entries for repairs made during 2008, for the warranty expense for 2008, and for cost of goods sold for 2008.

49. **Interpreting restructuring disclosures.** The notes to the financial statements of Bayer Group, a German pharmaceutical company, report a balance of €154 million for Restructuring Provisions on December 31, 2007; for the prior year, the ending balance in this liability account was €196 million. During 2007, Bayer reports Utilizations (that is, expenditures) of €134 million, and Reversals of €$31 million. Other effects (such as exchange rate differences and changes in the scope of consolidation) reduced the balance in this account by €5 million during 2007.

    a. What journal entry did Bayer make in 2007 to record Utilizations and Reversals?

    b. What journal entry did Bayer make in 2007 to record new additions to the Restructuring Provision account?

Long-Lived Tangible and Intangible Assets

CHAPTER

9

1. Understand the concepts distinguishing expenditures on long-lived assets that qualify for asset recognition from expenditures that firms treat as expenses in the period incurred.

2. Understand the concepts underlying the measurement of acquisition cost.

3. Understand the distinction between finite-lived and indefinite-lived assets and the implications for depreciation or amortization.

4. Develop the skills to compute depreciation based on initial estimates of useful life and residual value and to adjust depreciation for changes in those estimates over time.

5. Develop the skills to compute an impairment loss on long-lived assets.

6. Develop the skills to record the disposal of assets at various selling prices.

Consider the following transactions of eBay Inc., an online provider of trading, payment, and communication services.

Example 1 eBay acquired all of the common stock of Skype Technologies SA on October 14, 2005, for $2,590 million. eBay identified the following tangible net assets and intangible assets acquired and measured those items initially at their fair value:

Tangible Assets Net of Liabilities	$ (20)
Identifiable Intangible Assets:	
Customer List and User Base	27
Trade Names and Trademarks	244
Developed Technologies	8
Network Access Agreements	1
Goodwill	2,330
Total	$2,590

The amount of goodwill represents the excess of the total purchase price over the fair value of identifiable tangible and intangible net assets. Goodwill refers to other unidentifiable assets, such as operating synergies or a trained labor force, acquired in a business combination.

Example 2 eBay concluded that each of the identifiable intangible assets had a finite useful life. It estimated the useful lives as follows:

Customer List and User Base	6 years
Trade Names and Trademarks	5 years
Developed Technologies	2 years
Network Access Agreements	1 year

eBay amortized each intangible asset over its useful life, using the straight-line method. As discussed later in this chapter, goodwill has an indefinite life, so the firm did not amortize it.

Example 3   During the third quarter of 2007, eBay tested the goodwill from the Skype Technologies acquisition for possible impairment. Based on that assessment, eBay decreased the balance sheet carrying value of goodwill and recognized an impairment loss of $1,390 million. eBay reported a net *loss* of $936 million for the third quarter. Excluding the impairment loss, eBay would have reported net *income* of $454 million.

These examples illustrate several issues in the accounting for long-lived assets. Long-lived assets include both **tangible assets**, such as land, buildings, and equipment, and **intangible assets**, such as patents, brand names, trademarks, customer lists, airport landing rights, and franchise rights. Long-lived financial assets also include investments in securities, a topic discussed in **Chapters 12** and **13**. Both U.S. GAAP and IFRS provide guidance in the following areas of the accounting for long-lived tangible and intangible assets:

1. Deciding which expenditures with potential long-term benefits firms should recognize as assets on the balance sheet and which they should recognize as expenses on the income statement in the year of the expenditure.

2. Deciding which expenditures recognized as assets firms should depreciate or amortize as expenses each period.

3. For assets that firms depreciate or amortize, determining the length of time and pattern of charges to measure depreciation or amortization.

4. The accounting treatment of changes in expected useful lives and salvage values.

5. The accounting treatment of changes in fair values of long-lived assets.

6. The accounting for disposals of long-lived assets.

Long-lived assets can have useful lives extending for decades and provide uncertain benefits because of technological change, introduction of new products, changing consumer tastes, changing government regulations, and similar factors. In addition, intangible long-lived assets have no physical substance. These characteristics of long-lived assets create special accounting challenges, including the need to estimate long useful lives and how, if at all, to recognize changes in fair value. For many firms, investments in long-lived assets represent the single largest balance sheet item as well as a significant use of cash. Management's ability to use these assets is a key determinant of financial success or failure. In order to analyze this aspect of performance, therefore, users of financial statements need to understand both the financial reporting standards applicable to long-lived assets and the judgments and estimates that firms make to apply those standards.

TREATMENT OF EXPENDITURES AS ASSETS VERSUS AS IMMEDIATE EXPENSES

The first question we address is: *In the year of expenditure, should firms treat expenditures with potential long-term benefits as assets on the balance sheet or as expenses on the income statement?*

Recall from **Chapter 3** that an expenditure qualifies as an asset if it (1) meets the definition of an asset, and (2) satisfies the criteria for asset recognition. These requirements are similar in U.S. GAAP and IFRS. FASB *Statement of Financial Accounting Concepts No. 6*[1] states that an asset has three essential characteristics:

---

[1]Financial Accounting Standards Board, *Statement of Financial Accounting Concepts No. 6,* "Elements of Financial Statements," 1985, paragraph 26.

1. It embodies a probable future benefit.

2. A particular entity can obtain the benefit and control others' access to it.

3. The transaction or other event giving rise to the entity's right to, or control of, the benefit has already occurred.

FASB *Statement of Financial Accounting Concepts No. 5*[2] imposes an additional recognition criterion: the item must have a relevant attribute that a firm can measure with sufficient reliability. That relevant attribute is the fair value of the asset at the time of initial recognition.

Thus, firms treat expenditures as assets when they

■ Have acquired rights to the future use of a resource as a result of a past transaction or event.

■ Can reliably measure the cost of the expected benefits at the time of initial recognition.

The exchange of cash for a resource with future service potential typically satisfies the first criterion. Satisfying the second criterion is more difficult because of the extended time that must elapse before expected benefits materialize. Satisfying the second criterion is more challenging for intangibles than for tangibles because of the difficulty of observing the realization of benefits. Expenditures that do not meet the criteria for an asset are expenses in the period incurred.

CONCEPTUAL **Note**

As this book goes to press, the Financial Accounting Standards Board and the International Accounting Standards Board are reconsidering the definition of an asset and the criteria for asset recognition. Their proposed asset definition emphasizes the *present* existence of an economic resource and de-emphasizes the notions of a *past* exchange and the probability of *future* benefits. Resources satisfying the definition of an asset would be recognized if they (1) are separable from the entity (capable of being sold, exchanged, licensed, or otherwise disposed), which implies a market in which a firm can measure the fair value of the resource, or (2) arise from contractual or other legal rights, suggesting that negotiations between independent parties in establishing the rights permit estimation of fair value, even if the item cannot be exchanged. The future development of these tentative definitions and concepts and the changes in reporting that might result are difficult to predict at this time.

The following examples illustrate the application of the current criteria for asset recognition.

Example 4   General Motors pays cash to acquire land and a building. The land and building provide General Motors with future benefits. The exchange between an independent buyer and seller establishes the cost of the expected benefits at the time of acquisition. The land and building therefore are assets on the balance sheet of General Motors.

Example 5   Wal-Mart self-constructs new stores using both its employees and outside contractors. The new stores, when completed, will provide Wal-Mart with future benefits. This example differs from **Example 4** in that Wal-Mart (1) incurs part of the cost internally, and (2) makes expenditures over time to construct the stores instead of acquiring a completed asset. The store buildings in process provide evidence of the likelihood of future benefits; during the construction process the accumulated construction costs measure the cost of those benefits. All expenditures during the construction process are part of the cost of the self-constructed asset. When Wal-Mart completes construction of the stores, it will compare the accumulated construction costs with the fair value of the stores. If accumulated construction costs exceed fair value, Wal-Mart will decrease the recorded amount of the asset and recognize a loss. If

---

[2]Financial Accounting Standards Board, *Statement of Financial Accounting Concepts No. 5,* "Recognition and Measurement in Financial Statements of Business Enterprises," 1984, paragraph 65.

fair value exceeds accumulated construction costs, Wal-Mart will not increase the recorded amount of the asset and recognize a gain.

Example 6   Merck, a pharmaceutical firm, acquires a patent on a new drug from its creator for $120 million. This patent gives Merck an exclusive right to manufacture and market the drug for 20 years from the patent's initial filing date, although the time-consuming drug approval process likely reduces the expected useful life of the patent.[3] The transaction between Merck and the seller fixes both Merck's right to use the patent and the cost of the expected benefits. The patent is an asset on Merck's balance sheet.

Example 7   Merck spends $4.8 billion during the current year on research to identify, develop, and test new drugs to combat diseases and illnesses. This example differs from **Example 6** in that Merck (1) incurs the costs internally, and (2) does not acquire a completed asset. Merck would not engage in research if it did not expect future benefits. U.S. GAAP requires firms to expense research and development (R&D) costs in the period incurred. This requirement rests on reasoning that the costs do not satisfy the second criterion for asset recognition because the firm cannot measure the expected future benefits with sufficient reliability.[4] The difficulty is identifying the portion of each year's expenditure that leads to future benefits and the portion that does not. Thus, Merck recognizes the $4.8 billion as an expense of the current year.

International Accounting Standard No. 38 treats *research* costs the same as U.S. GAAP but treats *development* costs as assets.[5] When a research project reaches the stage of technical feasibility and the firm intends to continue developing the technology for ultimate use or sale, the research project moves from the research phase to the development phase. Thus, under IFRS, reliable measurement of the cost of future benefits commences at the development phase. A later section illustrates the difference in accounting for development costs under U.S. GAAP and IFRS.

Example 8   Microsoft Corporation incurs costs internally to develop new computer software products. U.S. GAAP treats costs incurred prior to establishing technological feasibility like other internally incurred R&D costs: Microsoft must expense the costs in the period incurred.[6] However, under U.S. GAAP the accounting for costs of developing software after the point of technological feasibility is similar to the IFRS treatment of development costs generally: the costs are recognized as assets.

Example 9   Refer to **Example 1**. eBay paid $2,590 million for Skype Technologies. eBay used appraisals and other means to establish the fair value of the identifiable assets and liabilities acquired, including intangibles that Skype developed internally and therefore did not appear as assets on the balance sheet of the acquired firm. An identifiable asset must either (1) be separable (that is, capable of being separated from the acquired entity and sold, transferred, licensed, rented, or exchanged), or (2) arise from contractual or other legal rights.[7] **Example 1** lists the separately identifiable intangible assets eBay acquired. Network access agreements derive from contractual rights and therefore meet the second criterion. The customer list, user base, trade names, trademarks, and developed technologies meet the separability criterion.[8]

---

[3]The laws governing patent protection are both jurisdiction-specific and subject to change, as is the process for obtaining approval to market a new drug. As a general rule, the longer the drug approval process, the shorter is the useful life of the patent. If, for example, four years elapse from the initial filing date to the approval date, the useful life of the drug in the United States would be 16 years.

[4]Financial Accounting Standards Board, *Statement of Financial Accounting Standards No. 2,* "Accounting for Research and Development Costs," 1974 (**Codification Topic 730**).

[5]International Accounting Standards Board, *International Accounting Standard 38,* "Intangible Assets," 1998.

[6]Financial Accounting Standards Board, *Statement of Financial Accounting Standards No. 86,* "Accounting for the Costs of Computer Software to Be Sold, Leased or Otherwise Marketed," 1985 (**Codification Topic 985**).

[7]Financial Accounting Standards Board, *Statement of Financial Accounting Standards No. 141 (revised),* 2007 (**Codification Topic 805**); International Accounting Standards Board, *International Financial Reporting Standard 3,* "Business Combinations," 2007.

[8]The criteria for asset recognition envisioned by current discussions within the FASB and IASB as described in the Conceptual Note are consistent with the criteria for asset recognition in business combinations.

FIGURE 9.1   **Treatment of Expenditures with Potential Long-Term Benefits**

	Nature of Resource	
	Tangible	**Intangible**
Acquired Internally	Self-constructed Buildings and Equipment (asset)	Research and Development (expense under U.S. GAAP; research is an expense and development is an asset under IFRS)
		Advertising (expense)
		Employee Training (expense)

		Software Development Costs:
		    Pre-technological Feasibility (expense)
		    Post-technological Feasibility (asset)

Acquired Externally	Land, Buildings, and Equipment (asset)	Proved Technologies (asset)
		In-Process Technologies (asset)
		Patents, Trademarks, Customer Lists, and Other Identifiable Resources (asset)
		Trained Labor Force and Other Unidentifiable Resources (part of goodwill)
		Goodwill (asset)

Example 10 Refer to **Examples 1** and **9**. eBay recognized an acquired asset for developed technologies. Assume that Skype Technologies had incurred costs to develop computer software but that the software had not reached the stage of technological feasibility at the time of the acquisition (an example of **in-process research and development**, or, **IPR&D**). For many technology and pharmaceutical firms, a large portion of their value to an acquirer might relate to IPR&D. Firms recognize IPR&D acquired in a business combination that meets the **separability criterion** as an asset and measured initially at fair value, even though the firm that *developed* the IPR&D expensed the costs as they were incurred.[9] IPR&D appears as an asset on the balance sheet only when it arises from a business combination.

Example 11 Refer to **Example 1**. Of the $2,590 million purchase price of Skype Technologies, only $260 million relates to identifiable assets and liabilities. The remainder of the purchase price, $2,330 million, relates to goodwill. In a corporate acquisition, the purchase price measures the fair value of the acquired enterprise, and goodwill reflects the fair value of assets that eBay cannot separately identify and therefore cannot recognize. Goodwill is an asset because it is part of the fair value of the acquired firm.

Figure 9.1 summarizes the accounting treatment of expenditures on resources with potential long-term benefits. We can make the following generalizations:

1. Firms recognize expenditures to acquire or self-construct tangible assets as assets because the physical nature of tangible assets provides evidence of probable future benefits. The cost to acquire the tangible asset is the best evidence of the fair value at the time of the acquisition.

2. Firms treat expenditures to develop intangibles internally as expenses when incurred because of the absence of an external market validation of the existence of an asset and its fair value. Exceptions occur for software development costs incurred after the point of technological feasibility under U.S. GAAP and for development costs generally after the point of technological feasibility under IFRS.

3. Firms recognize expenditures to acquire intangibles externally from third parties as assets if the intangibles are either separable or arise from contractual or other legal rights. The

---

[9]Financial Accounting Standards Board, *Statement of Financial Accounting Standards No. 141 (revised 2007),* "Business Combinations," 2007 (**Codification Topic 805**); International Accounting Standards Board, *International Financial Reporting Standard 3,* "Business Combinations," 2007.

market transaction validates the existence of an intangible asset, whether completed or in process, and its fair value.

4. In a business combination, the excess of the purchase price over the fair value of the identifiable net tangible and intangible assets is goodwill, an asset.

The accounting for expenditures with potential long-term benefits has been, and continues to be, controversial. Inconsistencies between the treatment of tangibles and intangibles and between costs incurred internally and externally permeate U.S. GAAP and IFRS. The user of the financial statements should recognize such inconsistencies when comparing a manufacturing firm with significant tangible assets and a technology or service firm with significant unrecognized intangibles, or when comparing a firm that develops brand names and other intangibles internally and one that acquires such intangibles from other firms.

 # MEASUREMENT OF ACQUISITION COST

Firms record long-lived assets, whether tangible or intangible, at acquisition cost (which equals fair value on the date of acquisition). Acquisition cost includes all costs incurred to prepare an asset for rendering services. The acquisition cost of equipment, for example, is the sum of the invoice price (less any discounts), transportation costs, installation charges, and any other costs incurred before the equipment is ready for use.[10] Also consider the following more complex example.

Example 12   Refer to **Example 4**. General Motors incurs the following costs in searching for and acquiring the land and building:

1. Purchase price of land with an existing building, $1,000,000.
2. Fees paid to attorney in handling purchase contracts, $10,000.
3. Transfer taxes paid to local real estate taxing authorities, $2,000.
4. Salaries earned by management personnel during the search for the site and the negotiation of its purchase, $8,000.
5. Operating expenditures for company automobiles used during the search, $375.
6. Depreciation charges for company automobiles used during the search, $440.
7. Fees paid to consulting engineer for a report on the structural soundness of the building, its fair value, and the estimated cost of making needed repairs, $15,000.
8. Uninsured costs to repair automobiles damaged in a multi-vehicle accident during the search, $3,000.
9. Profits lost on sales the company failed to make because, during the search, management paid insufficient attention to a potential new customer, $20,000.

The first six cost items relate to the search for, and acquisition of, the land and building. General Motors will accumulate these items in a temporary Land and Building account. Some firms would treat items **5** and **6** as expenses of the period because they are immaterial, but strict application of accounting theory would capitalize these costs as an asset. After completing the acquisition of the land and building, General Motors should allocate the accumulated costs of $1,020,815 (= $1,000,000 + $10,000 + $2,000 + $8,000 + $375 + $440) between these two assets based on the relative fair values of the land and the building. General Motors will recognize depreciation on the building but not on the land. For example, if the engineer in item **7** estimates the fair value of the current building to be $250,000, General Motors will allocate 25% (= $250,000/$1,000,000) of the combined cost of $1,020,815 to the building and 75% to the land.

Item **7** relates to the building only, so the cost of the engineer's services is part of the cost of the building.

---

[10]However, firms must expense when incurred the transactions cost of acquiring a firm in a business combination under both U.S. GAAP and IFRS.

Some accountants would treat item **8**, repair costs for the accident, as an asset on the basis that it was incurred in the process of searching for the land and building. Others would treat this cost as an expense on the basis that it was not a necessary cost to acquire the land and building.

Item **9**, forgone profits, is not a cost incurred in an arm's-length transaction with outsiders. U.S. GAAP and IFRS do not recognize this cost, called an *opportunity cost*.

Example 13   Refer to **Example 6**. Merck's acquisition cost for the patent includes $120 million paid to its creator, $800,000 in legal fees to evaluate its legal rights under the patent, and $1,800 to register the patent. Merck's acquisition cost is therefore $120,801,800 (= $120,000,000 + $800,000 + $1,800).

Noncash Consideration   Firms sometimes acquire assets by exchanging an asset other than cash or by issuing common stock. In these cases, acquisition cost is either the fair value of the consideration given or the fair value of the asset received, depending on which firms can more reliably measure.

Self-Constructed Asset   When a firm, such as Wal-Mart Stores in **Example 5**, constructs its own buildings or equipment, it recognizes the labor, material, and overhead costs incurred as an asset. U.S. GAAP and IFRS require firms to include, or capitalize, **interest costs during construction** in the cost of a self-constructed asset.[11] The rationale for capitalization is that firms must incur financing costs in self-constructing an asset just as they must incur labor and material costs.

Firms base the amount of interest costs capitalized on the amount borrowed to self-construct the asset. The amount represents the interest cost incurred during periods of construction that the firm could have avoided by not constructing the asset. If the costs of self-construction exceed the amount of any new borrowing, the firm uses the weighted-average rate it pays for its other borrowings to measure the amount capitalized. The total amount capitalized cannot exceed total interest costs for the period. Interest capitalization stops when construction ends.

The capitalization of interest in the acquisition cost of assets during construction reduces otherwise reportable interest expense and thereby increases net income during periods of construction. In later periods, the self-constructed asset will have higher depreciation charges, reducing net income. Total expense over the life of the asset equals the cash expenditure; capitalizing interest delays expense recognition from the times of borrowing to the times of using the asset.

Example 14   Refer to **Example 5**. Assume the following long-term debt structure for Wal-Mart Stores:

Construction Loan at 5% on Building Under Construction	$1,000,000
Other Borrowings at 6% Average Rate	3,600,000
Total Long-Term Debt	$4,600,000

The account Building Under Construction has an average balance during the year of $3,000,000. Wal-Mart Stores bases the amount of interest capitalized on the new construction-related borrowing, $1,000,000, and enough of the other borrowing, $2,000,000, to bring the total to $3,000,000. Wal-Mart computes interest capitalized as follows:

$1,000,000 × .05	$ 50,000
2,000,000 × .06	120,000
$3,000,000	$170,000

---

[11]Financial Accounting Standards Board, *Statement of Financial Accounting Standards No. 34,* "Capitalization of Interest Costs," 1979 (**Codification Topic 835**); International Accounting Standards Board, *International Accounting Standard 23 (revised 2007),* "Borrowing Costs."

The entries to record interest and to capitalize the required amounts are as follows:

Interest Expense. 266,000
    Interest Payable.   266,000

Assets	=	Liabilities	+	Shareholders' Equity	(Class.)
		+266,000		−266,000	IncSt → RE

To record all interest as expense: $266,000 [= (.05 x $1,000,000) + (.06 x $3,600,000)] = $50,000 + $216,000.

Building Under Construction. 170,000
    Interest Expense.   170,000

Assets	=	Liabilities	+	Shareholders' Equity	(Class.)
+170,000				+170,000	IncSt → RE

To capitalize the portion of interest related to self-constructed building. The amount capitalized reduces interest expense and increases the recorded cost of the building.

The firm might combine the preceding two entries into one as follows:

Interest Expense. 96,000
Building Under Construction. 170,000
    Interest Payable.   266,000

Assets	=	Liabilities	+	Shareholders' Equity	(Class.)
+170,000		+266,000		−96,000	IncSt → RE

To record interest cost for the year as either an expense or capitalized into the cost of the self-constructed building.

The firm must disclose in notes to the financial statements both total interest costs for the year, $266,000, and the amount capitalized, $170,000. Interest expense on the income statement is $96,000 in this example.

PROBLEM 9.1 for Self-Study

Calculating the acquisition cost of fixed assets. Jensen Company purchased land with a building as the site for a new plant it planned to construct. The company received bids from several independent contractors for demolition of the old building and construction of the new one. It rejected all bids and undertook demolition and construction using company labor, facilities, and equipment.

Jensen Company debited or credited amounts for all transactions relating to these properties to a single account, Construction in Process. Descriptions of various items in the Construction in Process account appear below. At the completion of construction, Jensen Company will remove all amounts in the Construction in Process account and close that account. It will reclassify the amounts into the following accounts:

1. Land account.
2. Building account.
3. Revenue, gain, expense, or loss account.
4. Some balance sheet account other than Land or Building.

(continued)

Reclassify the amounts of the following transactions into one or more of these accounts. If you use **4** (some other balance sheet account), indicate the nature of the account.

a. Cost of land, including old building.

b. Legal fees paid to bring about purchase of land and to transfer its title.

c. Invoice cost of materials and supplies used in construction of the new building.

d. Direct labor and materials costs incurred in demolishing the old building.

e. Direct costs of excavating raw land to prepare it for the foundation of the new building.

f. Discounts earned for prompt payment of item **c**.

g. Interest for the year on notes issued to finance construction.

h. Amounts equivalent to interest on Jensen Company's own funds that it used in construction but that it would have invested in marketable securities if it had used an independent contractor; it debited the amount to Construction in Process and credited Interest Revenue so that the cost of the real estate would be comparable to the cost if it had purchased the building from an independent contractor.

i. Depreciation during the construction period on trucks used both in construction and in other company operations.

j. Proceeds of sale of materials salvaged from the old buildings; the firm debited these to Cash and credited Construction in Process.

k. Cost of building permits.

l. Salaries of certain corporate engineering executives; these represent costs for both Salary Expense and Construction in Process, with the portion debited to Construction in Process representing an estimate of the portion of the time spent during the year on planning and construction activities for the new building.

m. Payments for property taxes on the plant site (its former owner owed these taxes, but Jensen Company assumed responsibility to pay them).

n. Payments for property taxes on plant site during construction period.

o. Insurance premiums to cover workers engaged in demolition and construction activities; the insurance policy requires the company to pay the first $5,000 of damages from any accident.

p. Cost of injury claims for $2,000 paid by the company because the amount was less than the deductible amount in the policy.

q. Costs of new machinery to be installed in the new building.

r. Installation costs for the machinery in item **q**.

s. Profit on construction of the new building (computed as the difference between the lowest independent contractor's bid and the actual construction cost); the firm debited this to Construction in Process and credited Construction Revenue.

TREATMENT OF ACQUISITION COST OVER LIFE OF ASSET

The second question we address in accounting for long-term assets is: *Should firms write off a portion of the acquisition costs of long-lived assets as expenses each period?* The guiding principles to respond to this question are as follows:

- The cost of long-lived assets with a **finite life**, that is, ones for which a firm consumes the asset's services over time in generating revenues, is recognized as an expense each period. The balance sheet carrying value decreases over time as the firm recognizes the cost of the asset as an expense. Management must estimate the asset's finite life, that is, its service life or useful life. Examples include buildings, equipment, patents, copyrights, landing rights, and customer lists.

■   The cost of long-lived assets with an **indefinite life**, that is, ones for which a firm does not consume the asset's services as time passes or cannot estimate the length of the benefit period, is not recognized as an expense each period. Instead, the asset remains on the balance sheet at acquisition cost (unless an asset impairment occurs). Examples include trade names, trademarks, certain renewable licenses, and goodwill arising from a business combination. Long-lived assets with extremely long useful lives, such as land and works of art, are treated as having an indefinite life.

■   **Depreciation** is the accounting term used to refer to the periodic write-off of the acquisition cost of a tangible long-lived asset with a finite service life, such as buildings and equipment. **Amortization** is the periodic write-off of intangible assets.

Example 15   Refer to **Examples 5** and **14**. Wal-Mart Stores consumes the services of the store building over time in generating revenues. It depreciates the acquisition cost minus estimated salvage value of the building over the building's useful life. Salvage value is the estimated value of the building at the end of its useful life. Firms do not depreciate salvage values. Instead, firms compare the proceeds of selling the building at the end of its useful life with its carrying value (that is, its salvage value) to compute a gain or loss on the sale.

Example 16   Refer to **Examples 6** and **13** where Merck acquires a patent from its creator. Although a patent has a legal life of up to 20 years, management's expectations of technological change may lead to a shorter economic life. Merck should amortize the acquisition cost of the patent over its expected useful life, equal to the shorter of the economic life and the legal life.

Example 17   Refer to **Examples 2** and **11** for eBay. eBay recognized intangible assets (customer lists and user base, trade names and trademarks, developed technologies, and network access agreements) in its acquisition of Skype Technologies. eBay measured each asset initially at fair value and estimated the useful life of the assets as the number of years over which it would receive benefits. For each of these assets, eBay will amortize the initial fair value of the intangible over its useful life.

Example 18   Refer to **Examples 1** and **11** for eBay. The recognized goodwill represents the excess of the purchase price of Skype Technologies as a whole over the amounts that eBay attributed to identifiable assets and liabilities. Goodwill reflects the value of knowledgeable employees, a reputation for quality products, and other items not separately recognized. Under both U.S. GAAP and IFRS, goodwill has an *indefinite* life, and firms do not amortize the amount recognized as goodwill.[12] Firms must, however, test goodwill annually for a loss in value, a topic discussed later in the section on impairment losses.

FUNDAMENTAL CONCEPTS OF DEPRECIATION AND AMORTIZATION

The third question we address in accounting for long-term assets is: *How should firms spread the acquisition cost of long-lived assets over their expected service lives?* We address this question by discussing the fundamental concepts underlying depreciation and amortization and then describing and illustrating several acceptable depreciation and amortization methods.

Depreciation and Amortization: A Process of Cost Allocation   The acquisition cost of a long-lived asset is the cost of a series of future services. The asset is a prepayment, similar to prepaid rent or insurance, a payment in advance for services a firm will consume in the future. As the firm uses the asset in each accounting period, it treats a portion of the cost of the asset as the cost of the service received.

Long-lived assets benefit several accounting periods, so their cost is a **joint cost** of these accounting periods. Each of the periods of the asset's use benefits from its services. There is usually no single correct way to allocate a joint cost. Firms select a depreciation or amortization method for a long-lived asset that allocates the acquisition cost minus salvage value to each period of expected useful life in a systematic, predetermined manner.

---

[12]Financial Accounting Standards Board, *Statement of Financial Accounting Standards No. 142,* "Goodwill and Other Intangible Assets," 2001 (**Codification Topic 350**); International Accounting Standards Board, *International Accounting Standard 38,* "Intangible Assets," 1998.

Depreciation and Amortization: Not a Measure of the Decline in Economic Value   Depreciation and amortization involve cost allocation, not valuation. In ordinary conversation and in economics, *depreciation* and *amortization* frequently mean a decline in value. Over the service life of a long-lived asset, the asset's value usually declines from acquisition until the firm retires it from service. The charge to each accounting period does not measure that decline in value, nor does it intend to. Depreciation and amortization represent a systematic process of cost allocation. If, in a given period, an asset increases in value, the firm still records depreciation and amortization during that period. In such a time period, there are two offsetting processes: (1) a holding gain on the asset for the increase in value, and (2) an allocation of the asset's acquisition cost to the period of benefit in the form of depreciation and amortization. U.S. GAAP precludes recognition of the holding gain. IFRS permits recognition of the holding gain under certain circumstances; we discuss this treatment later in the chapter.

MEASUREMENT OF DEPRECIATION AND AMORTIZATION

Calculating depreciation or amortization of long-lived assets requires management to

1. Measure the depreciable or amortizable basis of the asset.
2. Estimate its service (useful) life.
3. Decide the pattern of expiration of asset cost over its service life.

This section discusses each of these three items.

Depreciable or Amortizable Basis of Long-Lived Assets: Acquisition Cost Less Salvage Value   Firms base depreciation and amortization charges on the acquisition cost less the estimated salvage value of long-lived assets. The terms **salvage value** and **residual value** refer to the estimated proceeds on the disposition of an asset less all removal and selling costs. Firms recover salvage value through the proceeds of sale, so it is not part of the depreciable or amortizable basis of an asset.

For buildings, common practice assumes a zero salvage value on the assumption that the costs a firm will incur in tearing down the building will approximate the sales value of the scrap materials recovered. Other tangible assets may have substantial salvage value. For example, a car-rental firm will replace its automobiles at a time when other owners can use the cars for several years more. The car rental firm expects to recover a substantial part of acquisition cost from selling used cars. Intangible assets related to a contractual right, such as landing rights at an airport or franchise rights to sell a franchiser's products, generally expire at a specific time and therefore have zero residual value. Identifiable intangibles acquired in a business combination that are separable, such as customer lists or brand names, may have significant salvage values.

Some assets are not readily salable at the end of their useful lives, and retiring them may impose substantial costs. Consider, for example, the cost of dismantling a nuclear power plant at the end of its service life. Firms must estimate the fair value of the dismantling costs and include that amount in the initial measurement of the asset. The firm must also recognize a liability, referred to as an *asset retirement obligation*, of equal amount. The firm computes depreciation based on the combined cost of the plant assets, including the fair value of the dismantling obligation, because the firm must recover this cost through depreciation during the asset's useful life.[13] The firm also recognizes interest expense on the increase in the fair value of the liability.

Estimating Service Life   The second factor in calculating depreciation and amortization is the expected **service life**. Both **physical and functional factors** limit service lives. Physical factors for tangible assets include ordinary wear and tear from use, chemical action such as rust, and the effects of wind and rain. The most important functional factor for both tangible and intangible assets is obsolescence. Changes in production processes, for example, might reduce the unit cost of production to the point where a firm finds continued operation of old equipment uneconomical, even though the equipment remains usable. Computers may work as well as ever, but firms replace them because new, smaller computers occupy less space and

[13]Financial Accounting Standards Board, *Statement of Financial Accounting Standards No. 143,* Accounting for Asset Retirement Obligations," 2001 (**Codification Topic 410**); International Accounting Standards Board, *International Accounting Standard 16,* "Property, Plant and Equipment," 1998.

compute faster. Although display cases and storefronts may not have worn out, retail stores replace them to make the store look better. Technology-based intangibles can become obsolete overnight. Although the legal life of a drug patent is 20 years, the expected economic life of the drug is often less than half of that period.

Estimating service lives presents the most difficult task in the depreciation and amortization calculation. Because obsolescence typically results from external forces, its effect on the service life is particularly uncertain. As a result, firms must review their estimates of service lives each year. A change in this estimate will change the depreciation and amortization amounts going forward, a later topic in this chapter.

IFRS, but not U.S. GAAP, requires firms to calculate depreciation separately for significant portions of plant and equipment if those portions have different service lives. Therefore, management must analyze the components of fixed assets to determine if those components have different service lives; if they do, firms must use a component's service life to depreciate the cost of that component. For example, the airframe and the engines of an aircraft likely have different service lives, and the firm would therefore depreciate them separately.

Pattern of Depreciation and Amortization

An asset's acquisition cost, salvage value, and service life determine both the total of depreciation or amortization charges and the time span over which to charge those costs. The firm must also select the pattern for allocating those charges to the specific years of the service life.

Depreciation of tangible assets follows one of three basic patterns.

1. Straight line over time.
2. Straight line with respect to usage.
3. Accelerated over time (with higher depreciation in the early years of the service life).

Amortization of intangible assets is usually straight line over time.

The next section describes and illustrates the depreciation and amortization patterns. When acquiring or retiring a long-lived asset during an accounting period, a firm calculates depreciation and amortization only for that portion of the period during which it uses the asset.

Straight-Line (Time) Method

The **straight-line (time) method** is the most common method for financial reporting. This method divides the acquisition cost of an asset (including the cost to dismantle and retire) less its estimated salvage value by the estimated service life to calculate depreciation or amortization.

$$\text{Annual Depreciation or Amortization} = \frac{\text{Cost Less Estimated Salvage Value}}{\text{Estimated Life in Years}}$$

For example, if a machine costs $5,000, has an estimated salvage value of $200, and has an expected service life of five years, the annual depreciation is $960 [= ($5,000 – $200)/5]. If a patent acquired for $30,000 has an expected service life of five years and zero salvage value, the annual amortization is $6,000 (= $30,000/5).

Straight-Line (Use) Method

For assets whose use is not uniform over time, the straight-line (time) method of depreciation may result in depreciation patterns unrelated to usage patterns. For example, manufacturing plants often have seasonal variations in operations, so they use certain machines 24 hours a day at one time of the year and 8 hours or less a day at another time of the year. Trucks do not receive the same amount of use in each year of their service lives.

A **straight-line (use) method** is appropriate for such assets. For example, a firm could base depreciation of a truck for a period on the ratio of miles driven during the period to total expected driving miles over the truck's life. The depreciation cost per unit (mile) of use is as follows:

$$\text{Depreciation or Amortization Cost per Unit} = \frac{\text{Cost Less Estimated Salvage Value}}{\text{Estimated Units of Use}}$$

Assume that a truck cost $54,000, has an estimated salvage value of $4,000, and will provide 200,000 miles of use before retirement. The depreciation per mile is $0.25 [= ($54,000 – $4,000)/200,000]. If the truck operates 24,000 miles in a given year, the depreciation charge is $6,000 (= 24,000 × $0.25).

Accelerated Depreciation   The service capacity of some depreciable assets declines with age or use. Cutting tools lose some of their precision; printing presses require more frequent shutdowns for repairs; rent receipts from an old office building fall below those from a new one. Some assets provide more and better services in the early years of their lives and require increasing amounts of maintenance as they grow older. These cases justify accelerated depreciation methods, which recognize larger depreciation charges in early years and smaller depreciation charges in later years. However, authoritative guidance does not *require* the use of an accelerated method. As a later section discusses, U.S. GAAP and IFRS provide firms considerable flexibility in choosing their depreciation method.

Two common accelerated depreciation methods are the **declining-balance method** and the **sum-of-the-years'-digits method**. **Problem 20** at the end of this chapter describes and illustrates these accelerated depreciation methods.

PROBLEM 9.2 for Self-Study

Calculating periodic depreciation. Markam Corporation acquires a new machine costing $20,000 on January 1, 2008. The firm expects

- To use the machine for five years.
- To operate it for 24,000 hours during that time.
- To recoup an estimated salvage value of $2,000 at the end of five years.

Calculate the depreciation charge for each of the five years using the following:

a. The straight-line (time) method.

b. The straight-line (use) method. The expected operating times are 5,000 hours each year for four years and 4,000 hours in the fifth year.

FACTORS IN CHOOSING THE DEPRECIATION AND AMORTIZATION METHOD

Depreciation and amortization affect both net income reported in the financial statements and taxable income on tax returns. Taxing authorities in most jurisdictions specify allowable depreciation methods for tax reporting. When permitted to do so by the taxing authority, firms often use different depreciation methods for financial and tax reporting. When this happens, the difference between depreciation expense in the financial statements and the depreciation deduction on the tax return leads to an issue in accounting for income taxes, which **Chapter 11** discusses.

Tax Reporting   If permitted a choice of depreciation methods for tax reporting, a firm should try to maximize the present value of the reductions in tax payments from claiming depreciation. When tax rates stay constant over time and the firm is sufficiently profitable to benefit from tax deductions, earlier deductions have greater value than later ones because taxes saved today have greater value than taxes saved tomorrow. When taxing authorities permit a choice among alternative depreciation methods, a firm should choose the alternative that allows it to pay the least amount of tax, as late as possible, within the law.

Financial Reporting   The objective of financial reporting for long-lived assets is to realistically measure the expiration of the assets' benefits and provide a reasonable pattern of cost allocation. However, the cost of the long-lived asset jointly benefits all the periods of use, and there is no single correct way to allocate such joint costs. As a consequence, authoritative guidance requires that financial statements report depreciation charges based on reasonable estimates; in practice, the straight-line (time) method is the most common.

ACCOUNTING FOR PERIODIC DEPRECIATION AND AMORTIZATION

Recording periodic depreciation and amortization results in a debit to either an expense account or a product cost account. Depreciation of factory buildings and equipment used in manufacturing operations becomes part of the cost of work-in-process and finished goods inventories; that is, using the language introduced in **Chapter 8**, these depreciation charges are product costs. The amortization of a patent on a semiconductor that a firm embeds in its product is likewise a product cost. Firms classify the amortization of a customer list as either amortization expense or selling expense, depending on whether the firm classifies expenses by their nature or by their function. Firms classify the depreciation of office equipment in the corporate headquarters as either depreciation expense or administrative expense. The amortization of the customer list and depreciation of the office equipment do not relate to product manufacturing and are, therefore, period costs.

The recording of amortization of intangibles generally results in a credit directly to the asset account that is being amortized, such as Patent or Customer List. The recording of depreciation of tangible assets could, in principle, likewise result in a credit directly to the asset account, such as Buildings or Equipment. In practice, however, most firms credit a contra-asset account called Accumulated Depreciation. Using the contra account leaves the acquisition cost of the asset undisturbed and permits the analyst to compute both the amount written off through depreciation and the undepreciated acquisition cost. If the firm credited the asset account directly, an analysis of the accounts would reveal only the net effect of the two. A later section of this chapter shows how the analyst can use this information to make useful inferences.

The entry to record periodic depreciation of $1,500 on office facilities is as follows:

Depreciation (or Administrative) Expense 1,500
    Accumulated Depreciation 1,500

Assets	=	Liabilities	+	Shareholders' Equity	(Class.)
−1,500				−1,500	IncSt → RE

The entry to record periodic depreciation of $1,500 on manufacturing facilities is as follows:

Work-in-Process Inventory 1,500
    Accumulated Depreciation 1,500

Assets	=	Liabilities	+	Shareholders' Equity	(Class.)
+1,500					
−1,500					

The entry to record patent amortization of $1,500 embedded in a product is as follows:

Work-in-Process Inventory 1,500
    Patent 1,500

Assets	=	Liabilities	+	Shareholders' Equity	(Class.)
+1,500					
−1,500					

The entry to record amortization of a customer list is as follows:

Amortization (or Selling) Expense 1,500
    Customer List 1,500

Assets	=	Liabilities	+	Shareholders' Equity	(Class.)
−1,500				−1,500	IncSt → RE

The Work-in-Process Inventory account is an asset. Product costs, such as depreciation on manufacturing facilities, accumulate in the Work-in-Process Inventory account until the firm completes the goods and transfers them to Finished Goods Inventory. The Accumulated Depreciation account appears either on the balance sheet or in the notes. The balance in this account is a deduction from the asset account to which it is contra. The balance in the Accumulated Depreciation account usually represents the total charges in all accounting periods up through the balance sheet date for the depreciation on assets currently in use. The difference between the balance in the asset account (the gross value) and the balance in the Accumulated Depreciation account is the asset's *net carrying value* or *net book value*.

IMPACT OF NEW INFORMATION ABOUT LONG-LIVED ASSETS

This chapter has considered thus far the acquisition and depreciation or amortization of long-lived assets based on transactions and knowledge at the time of initial acquisition. New information often comes to light over the life of tangible or intangible assets that affects the accounting for these assets. This section discusses the following items:

1. Changes in expected service lives or salvage values.
2. Additional expenditures to maintain or improve the assets.
3. Changes in the fair value of assets.

CHANGES IN SERVICE LIVES OR SALVAGE VALUES

The original depreciation or amortization schedule for long-lived assets sometimes requires changing. Each period a firm must evaluate its estimates of service life and salvage value and assess if these estimates require changing in light of new information. If changing from the old estimates to the new estimates would have a material impact, the firm must change the depreciation or amortization schedule prospectively. That is, the firm makes no adjustment for the past misestimate but spreads the remaining carrying value less the new estimate of salvage value over the new estimate of the remaining service life of the asset.[14]

The reasoning for adjusting current and future depreciation or amortization charges instead of retrospectively revising past charges rests on the nature and role of estimates in accounting. Management's estimates of depreciable lives and salvage values, uncollectible accounts, warranty costs, and similar items use the available information at the time of the estimate. Changes in estimates occur regularly; many of them do not materially affect the financial statements. Requiring the restatement of previously issued financial statements for changes in estimates might confuse users and undermine the credibility of the statements. **Chapter 14** discusses these issues more fully.

To understand the **treatment of changes in periodic depreciation or amortization**, assume the following facts, illustrated in **Figure 9.2**. A firm

- purchases an office machine for $9,200,
- estimates that it will use the machine for 15 years, and
- estimates a salvage value of $200.

The depreciation charge recorded for each of the first five years under the straight-line method is $600 [= ($9,200 − $200)/15]. On December 31 of the sixth year, before closing the books for the year, the firm analyzes its estimates of useful life and salvage value. In light of new information, the firm estimates that

- the machine will have a total useful life of only 10 years, and
- the salvage estimate of $200 remains reasonable.

This decrease in service life changes future depreciation charges so that the correct total will accumulate in the Accumulated Depreciation account by the end of the revised service life. The firm makes no adjustments of amounts previously recorded. In our example, the acquisition cost yet to be depreciated before the change in the sixth year is $6,000 [= ($9,200 − $200) − (5 × $600)]. The new estimate of the remaining life is five years (the year just ended plus the next four). This change in estimate changes the amount recorded for

---

[14]Financial Accounting Standards Board, *Statement of Financial Accounting Standards No. 154,* "Accounting Changes and Error Corrections," 2005, par. 19 (**Codification Topic 250**); International Accounting Standards Board, *International Accounting Standard 16,* "Property, Plant and Equipment," 1998.

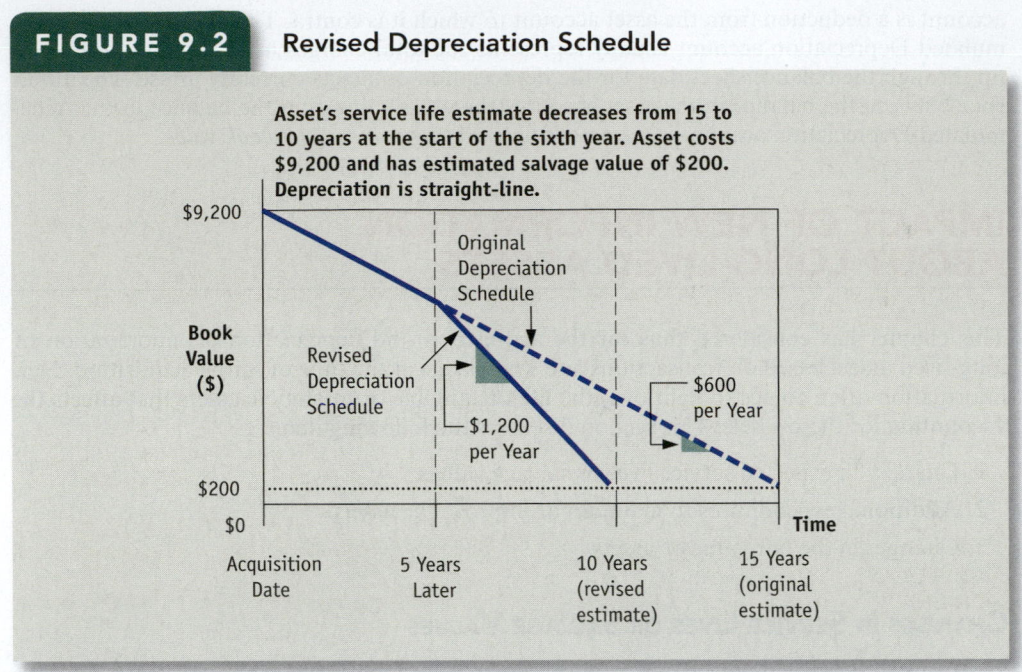

FIGURE 9.2   **Revised Depreciation Schedule**

Asset's service life estimate decreases from 15 to 10 years at the start of the sixth year. Asset costs $9,200 and has estimated salvage value of $200. Depreciation is straight-line.

annual depreciation in the current and future years from $600 to $1,200 (= $6,000/5). The depreciation entry on December 31 of the sixth year and each year thereafter is as follows:

Depreciation Expense.	1,200	
Accumulated Depreciation		1,200

Assets	=	Liabilities	+	Shareholders' Equity	(Class.)
−1,200				−1,200	IncSt → RE

To record depreciation for the sixth year based on revised estimates.

Figure 9.2 illustrates the revised depreciation path.

PROBLEM 9.3 for Self-Study

Adjustments for changes in estimates. Central States Electric Company constructs a nuclear power plant at a cost of $200 million. It estimates the service life of the plant to be 50 years and the cost to dismantle and retire the asset from service to be $20 million. These "decommissioning" costs include the costs to dismantle the plant and dispose of the radioactive materials. The firm computes and charges straight-line depreciation once per year, at year-end.

During the company's 11th year of operating the plant, Congress enacts new regulations governing nuclear waste disposal. The estimated decommissioning costs increase from $20 million to $24 million. During the 31st year of operation, the firm revises the estimated service life of the plant to 60 years in total.

a.   What is the depreciation charge for the first year?
b.   What is the depreciation charge for the 11th year?
c.   What is the depreciation charge for the 31st year?

ADDITIONAL EXPENDITURES TO MAINTAIN OR IMPROVE LONG-LIVED ASSETS

Firms often incur costs to maintain, repair, and improve their tangible assets. Distinguishing between these purposes affects reported income because U.S. GAAP and IFRS require firms to treat expenditures for maintenance and repairs as expenses of the period as incurred but treat expenditures for improvements as assets (which firms subsequently depreciate or amortize).

Maintenance and Repairs   A firm incurs costs to keep its tangible assets in their expected operating condition. **Maintenance** includes routine costs such as for cleaning and adjusting. **Repairs** include the costs of restoring an asset's service potential after breakdowns or other damage. Expenditures for these items do not extend the estimated service life or increase its productive capacity beyond original expectations. Therefore, U.S. GAAP and IFRS treat such expenditures as expenses of the period when the firm makes the expenditure. In practice, distinguishing repairs from maintenance is difficult but typically not necessary because expenditures for both are period expenses.

Improvements   Expenditures for **improvements**, sometimes called *betterments*, increase an asset's performance by, for example, increasing the service life, or reducing the operating costs, or increasing the rate of output. Expenditures that increase service potential meet the definition and recognition criteria for an asset under both U.S. GAAP and IFRS. That is, a firm accounts for the expenditures as if it had acquired new benefits. When the firm makes the expenditure, it capitalizes the cost of the improvement by debiting the existing asset account (or a new asset account). Regardless, subsequent depreciation charges will increase because of the increased investment in depreciable assets.

Example 19   Assume a firm suffers a loss to its building in a fire and spends $200,000 on repairs and improvements. It judges that $160,000 of the expenditure replaces long-lived assets lost in the fire, and $40,000 represents improvements to the building. It could make the following single journal entry.

Building				40,000	
Loss from Fire				160,000	
Cash					200,000

Assets	=	Liabilities	+	Shareholders' Equity	(Class.)
+40,000				−160,0000	IncSt → RE
−200,000					

To record loss and subsequent expenditure.

The following two entries are equivalent and may be easier to understand:

| Loss from Fire | | | | 160,000 | |
| Building | | | | | 160,000 |

Assets	=	Liabilities	+	Shareholders' Equity	(Class.)
−160,000				−160,000	IncSt → RE

To record loss from fire.

| Building | | | | 200,000 | |
| Cash | | | | | 200,000 |

Assets	=	Liabilities	+	Shareholders' Equity	(Class.)
+200,000					
−200,000					

To record expenditures on building.

Distinguishing Maintenance and Repairs from Improvements   Expenditures on maintenance and repairs have different income effects than expenditures on improvements. Some expenditures may both repair and improve. Consider expenditures to replace a roof damaged in a hurricane. If the new roof is purposefully designed to be stronger than the old one so that it will support the air conditioning equipment the firm plans to install, part of the expenditure represents repair and part represents improvement. Firms must make judgments and allocate costs between maintenance and repairs and improvements using professional judgment and all available evidence.

PROBLEM 9.4 for Self-Study

Distinguishing repairs from improvements. Purdy Company acquired two used trucks from Foster Company. Although the trucks were not identical, they both cost $15,000. Purdy knew when it negotiated the purchase price that the first truck required extensive engine repair, estimated to cost $4,000. The repair was made the week after acquisition and actually cost $4,200. Purdy Company thought the second truck was in normal operating condition when it negotiated the purchase price but discovered, after taking possession of the truck, that it required new bearings. The firm made this repair, costing $4,200, during the week after acquisition.

a. What costs should Purdy Company record in the accounts for the two trucks?

b. If the amounts recorded in part a are different, distinguish between the two repairs.

CHANGES IN THE FAIR VALUE OF LONG-LIVED ASSETS

A firm acquires assets for their future benefits. The world changes, and expected future benefits change, sometimes increasing and sometimes decreasing. U.S. GAAP does not permit firms to increase the balance sheet carrying values of tangible and intangible long-lived assets when the fair values of their assets increase. This prohibition means that firms will recognize the increase in the fair value of the asset only as the firm realizes the value increase through either sale or continuing use.

In contrast, IFRS permits upward **asset revaluations**, the recognition of unrealized increases in the fair value of long-lived assets under certain conditions.[15] In the case of an intangible asset, firms must base the revaluation on the price in an active market; in addition, the firm must perform the revaluation regularly and at the same time for all assets in a class of assets. These conditions are sufficiently restrictive that revaluations of intangible assets are rare. In the case of tangible long-lived assets, firms need not base fair value on the price in an active market; however, firms must keep the revaluations up to date. For both tangible and intangible assets, firms credit the increase in a revalued asset's balance sheet carrying value to other comprehensive income, not net income. However, firms would credit income if the increase reverses a revaluation decrease (discussed next) that was previously recognized as a loss.

ASSET IMPAIRMENTS

Although U.S. GAAP and IFRS differ in the recognition of unrealized increases in fair values, both require firms to recognize decreases in fair values as an **impairment loss**. U.S. GAAP and IFRS distinguish three categories of long-lived assets for purposes of measuring and recognizing impairment losses:

Category 1. Long-lived assets except intangible assets not subject to amortization and goodwill. Category 1 includes property, plant, equipment, patents, franchise rights, and similar assets. These assets provide benefits over predictable, finite periods of time and are therefore subject to depreciation or amortization. This category, however, also includes land, which provides benefits for an indefinite period of time and is not depreciated.

Category 2. Intangibles, other than goodwill, not subject to amortization. Category 2 includes brand names, trademarks, and renewable licenses or other legal rights. Firms do not amortize these intangibles if they provide benefits over an *indefinite* period of time.

Category 3. Goodwill.

---

[15]International Accounting Standards Board, *International Accounting Standard 16*, "Property, Plant and Equipment," 1998.

Although both U.S. GAAP and IFRS distinguish the same three categories of long-lived assets for impairment analysis, the procedures for assessing an asset for impairment and measuring the impairment loss differ. For each category of asset, we separately describe U.S. GAAP[16] and IFRS[17] procedures. For both sets of reporting standards, management assesses the firm's assets for impairment at each reporting date by determining if impairment indicators are present. Impairment indicators include, for example, a decline in the market value of an asset significantly beyond what would be expected because of use or the passage of time; significant adverse changes in the entity's technological, market, economic, or legal environment; significant increases in expected return on investment.

U.S. GAAP Treatment of Asset Impairment for Long-Lived Assets Other Than Nonamortized Intangibles and Goodwill (Category 1)
U.S. GAAP provisions require a three-step procedure for measuring and recording impairments for long-lived assets other than nonamortized intangibles and goodwill.

1. The test for an impairment loss for this category compares the sum of the undiscounted cash flows from the assets with their carrying values. An asset impairment loss arises when the carrying values of the assets exceed the sum of the undiscounted cash flows.

2. The amount of the impairment loss is the excess of the carrying values of the assets over their fair values.

3. At the time the firm judges that an impairment loss has occurred, the firm reduces the carrying value of the asset to its current fair value. **Chapter 3** discusses the measurement of fair value.

In requiring that the firm use undiscounted cash flows to test for an asset impairment in **Step 1**, the FASB reasoned that a loss has not occurred if the firm can recover in future cash flows an amount at least equal to or larger than the carrying value. The use of undiscounted, instead of discounted, cash flows seems theoretically unsound. The economic value of an asset may decline below its carrying value, but the firm would recognize no impairment loss because the undiscounted future cash flows from the asset exceed its carrying value.

IFRS Treatment of Asset Impairment for Long-Lived Assets Other Than Nonamortized Intangibles and Goodwill (Category 1)
The test for an impairment loss for assets in this category compares the balance sheet carrying value with the asset's **recoverable amount**, defined as the higher of (1) fair value less cost to sell, and (2) value in use, defined as the present value of future cash flows of the asset in its current use by the firm. The impairment loss is the excess of the carrying value over the assets' recoverable amount. The IASB requirements differ from those of U.S. GAAP in two ways:

1. Under IFRS, firms need not compare the carrying value to the sum of the undiscounted cash flows to determine if an impairment loss has occurred. An impairment loss occurs whenever the carrying value exceeds the recoverable amount.

2. Firms measure the impairment loss under IFRS by comparing the carrying value to the higher of the fair value less costs to sell and the value in use.

We illustrate the application of the impairment test and the subsequent revaluations with examples.

Basic Impairment Example: Background
Miller Company owns an apartment building that originally cost $20 million and by the end of the current period has accumulated depreciation of $5 million, with net carrying value of $15 (= $20 − $5) million. Miller Company had originally expected to collect rentals of $1.67 million each year for 30 years before selling the building for $8 million. Unanticipated placement of a new shopping center has caused Miller Company to reassess the future rentals. Miller Company expects the building to provide rentals for only 15 more years before Miller will sell it. Miller Company uses a discount rate of 8% per year in discounting expected rentals from the building.

---

[16]Financial Accounting Standards Board, *Statement of Financial Accounting Standards No. 144,* "Accounting for Impairment of Long-Lived Assets," 2001 (**Codification Topic 360**).

[17]International Accounting Standards Board, *International Accounting Standard 36,* "Impairment of Assets," revised 2004.

Example 20   Miller now expects to receive annual rentals of $1.35 million per year for 15 years and to sell the building for $5.0 million after 15 years; these payments, in total, have a present value of $13.1 million when discounted at 8% per year. The building's fair value is $12.5 million today. Costs to sell are estimated at $500,000.

Under U.S. GAAP, no impairment loss has occurred because the expected undiscounted future cash flows of $25.25 [= ($1.35 × 15.0) + $5.00] million exceed the carrying value of $15 million. Thus, although Miller has suffered an economic loss (because the fair value of the building of $12.5 million is less than the carrying value of $15.0 million), it will not recognize an impairment loss.

In contrast, applying IFRS, Miller would compare the asset's carrying value of $15.0 million to the higher of the fair value less cost to sell of $12.0 million (= $12.5 million less $500,000) and the value in use of $13.1 million. The impairment loss is $1.9 million (= $15.0 million − $13.1 million).

Example 21   Now assume that Miller expects to receive annual rentals of $600,000 per year for 15 years and to sell the building for $3.0 million after 15 years; these payments, in total, have a present value of $6.1 million when discounted at 8% per year. The building's fair value is $5.5 million today and costs to sell are $300,000.

Under U.S. GAAP, Miller has an asset impairment loss because the carrying value of $15.0 million exceeds the expected undiscounted future cash flows of $12.0 [= ($0.6 × 15) + $3.0] million. Miller recognizes an impairment loss of $9.5 million, equal to the excess of the carrying value of the building of $15 million over its fair value of $5.5 million.

Under IFRS, Miller compares the carrying value of $15.0 million to the recoverable amount of $6.1 million (that is, the higher of the value in use of $6.1 million and the fair value less cost to sell of $5.2 million; $5.2 million = $5.5 million less $300,000) and recognizes an impairment loss of $8.9 million (= $15.0 million − $6.1 million).

The recording of an impairment loss is similar under U.S. GAAP and IFRS. We illustrate this accounting using **Example 21**. The accounting involves first removing the building's acquisition cost and the accumulated depreciation from the accounts and then establishing a new asset cost: fair value under U.S. GAAP and recoverable amount under IFRS. The journal entries applying U.S. GAAP (with amounts in millions) would be as follows:

Accumulated Depreciation	5.0	
Apartment Building (New Valuation)	5.5	
Loss on Impairment.	9.5	
Apartment Building (Acquisition Cost)		20.0

Assets	=	Liabilities	+	Shareholders' Equity	(Class.)
+5.0				−9.5	IncSt → RE
+5.5					
−20.0					

Applying IFRS would change the new valuation amount to the recoverable amount of $6.1 million and the impairment loss to $8.9 million. Under both U.S. GAAP and IFRS, the firm includes the loss in net income, unless the firm had previously revalued the assets upward under IFRS. In that case the loss is a revaluation decrease (a debit to other comprehensive income) up to the amount of the revaluation, with any excess loss recognized in net income.

U.S. GAAP Treatment of Asset Impairment on Nonamortized Intangibles, Other Than Goodwill (Category 2)

Because these assets have an indefinite life, firms cannot feasibly apply the undiscounted cash flow test for asset impairment. That is, the indefinite life precludes estimation of total future cash flows. U.S. GAAP requires firms to recognize an impairment loss on a nonamortized intangible other than goodwill whenever the carrying value of the asset exceeds its fair value.

IFRS Treatment of Asset Impairment on Nonamortized Intangibles, Other Than Goodwill (Category 2)

The treatment for these assets parallels that for amortized or depreciated assets (Category 1) except that firms perform the impairment test annually (regardless of the presence of impairment indicators). The measurement of the loss and the new balance sheet carrying value are the same as for Category 1 assets.

Example 22 Assume that Miller Company's balance sheet shows a trade name acquired as part of a business combination with a carrying value of $15 million. The trade name has an indefinite life and therefore Miller does not amortize it. Negative publicity regarding the product carrying the trade name has reduced its fair value to $12 million and its value in use to $11 million. Miller compares the carrying value of the trade name of $15 million with its fair value of $12 million and recognizes a $3 million impairment loss. The entry is (with amounts in millions) as follows:

Loss on Impairment 3.0
   Trade Name 3.0

Assets	=	Liabilities	+	Shareholders' Equity	(Class.)
−3.0				−3.0	IncSt → RE

Asset Impairment for Goodwill (Category 3)

As previously discussed, firms do not amortize goodwill under either U.S. GAAP or IFRS. Both standard-setting bodies require firms to test annually for impairment losses on goodwill, as well as whenever there is an indication of impairment due, for example, to changes in the legal or economic climate, adverse regulatory conditions, unanticipated competition, and loss of key personnel.

Goodwill is not a separable asset, so it is evaluated for impairment as part of a **reporting unit** (U.S. GAAP) or a **cash generating unit** (IFRS). These units are identifiable groups of assets that generate identifiable cash flows,[18] which firms use to measure fair value (U.S. GAAP) or recoverable amount (IFRS).

U.S. GAAP Treatment of Goodwill Impairment

Before testing for goodwill impairment, firms must first apply the procedures described earlier for measuring and recognizing impairment losses on assets other than goodwill. Firms then follow these two steps:[19]

Step 1. Test for Impairment of Goodwill. Ascertain the current fair value of a reporting unit that includes goodwill. Recall from **Chapter 3** that fair value is an exit value, the price a firm would receive if it sold the reporting unit in an orderly transaction at the measurement date. If the fair value of a reporting unit that includes goodwill is less than the carrying value of its assets (including goodwill) less liabilities, then an impairment loss on goodwill may have occurred and the firm proceeds to **Step 2**.

Step 2. Measure the Amount of the Goodwill Impairment Loss. Measuring the amount of the impairment loss of goodwill involves the following:

a. Allocate the fair value from **Step 1** to identifiable assets and liabilities of the reporting unit based on their current fair values.

b. Allocate any excess fair value to goodwill.

c. Compare the amount allocated to goodwill in **Step 2b** with the balance sheet carrying value of goodwill.

d. Recognize an impairment loss on goodwill to reduce the carrying value of goodwill to its fair value computed in **Step 2b**.

This computation parallels the initial computation of goodwill when the reporting unit first recognized it at the time of a business combination. However, goodwill impairment does not involve a remeasurement on the balance sheet of the identifiable assets and liabilities. The accountant uses the allocations described in **Steps 2a** and **2b** solely for purposes of measuring

[18]*SFAS No. 142*, defines a reporting unit as a segment or a component of a segment that is a business with separate financial information that management regularly reviews. *IAS 36* defines a cash generating unit as the smallest identifiable group of assets that generates cash inflows that are largely independent of the cash inflows from other assets or groups of assets.

[19]Financial Accounting Standards Board, *Statement of Financial Accounting Standards No. 142*, "Goodwill and Other Intangible Assets," 2001 (**Codification Topic 350**).

the amount of the impairment loss to goodwill. The following example illustrates the application of this procedure.

Example 23   Burns, Philp and Company Limited (B-P), a food ingredients company, spent $100 million to acquire the long-lived tangible assets and brand names of Tone's Spices. B-P intended to sell Tone's Spices in warehouse stores like Sam's Club and Costco. The fair values of the identifiable assets at the acquisition date were $15 million of long-lived tangible assets, $35 million of brand names with indefinite lives, and $50 million of goodwill. Soon after the acquisition, market pressure from its competitor, McCormick Spices, forced B-P to offer higher-than-anticipated cash discounts and slotting fees (for the rights to put spices into the club stores and warehouses) to its large customers, reducing the fair value of Tone's Spices as an entity to $60 million.

B-P first applies the U.S. GAAP requirements for identifying and measuring an impairment loss on the long-lived tangible assets. B-P estimates that the undiscounted cash flows related to long-lived tangible assets total $25 million and that their fair value is $15 million. The long-lived tangible assets are not impaired because the undiscounted cash flows of $25 million exceed their carrying value of $15 million.

B-P next applies the U.S. GAAP requirement for identifying and measuring an impairment loss on the brand names. B-P estimates the fair value of the brand names is now $25 million, which is less than the carrying value of $35 million. B-P recognizes a $10 million impairment loss on the brand names. This loss reduces the carrying value of Tone's Spices to $90 million (= $15 million for long-lived tangible assets + $25 million for brand names + $50 million for goodwill).

B-P may have incurred a goodwill impairment loss because the fair value of Tone's Spices of $60 million is less than the carrying value of $90 million after the impairment loss on the brands (**Step 1** above).

B-P remeasures the fair values of Tone's Spices' long-lived tangible assets ($15 million—already measured) and brand names ($25 million—already measured). The residual of $20 million is assigned to goodwill solely for the purpose of measuring the amount of the goodwill impairment loss. The balance sheet carrying value of goodwill of $50 million exceeds its implied fair value of $20 million by $30 million. B-P therefore recognizes a $30 million goodwill impairment loss. The journal entries would be as follows (with amounts in millions). B-P makes the first entry at the time of acquisition and the second entry on discovery of the impairment:

Land, Buildings, and Equipment	15	
Brand Names	35	
Goodwill on Acquisition of Tone's Spices	50	
Cash		100

Assets	=	Liabilities	+	Shareholders' Equity	(Class.)
+15					
+35					
+50					
−100					

To record the acquisition of Tone's Spices for $100 million cash.

Loss on Impairments	40	
Brand Names		10
Goodwill on Acquisition of Tone's Spices		30

Assets	=	Liabilities	+	Shareholders' Equity	(Class.)
−10				−40	IncSt → RE
−30					

To record asset impairment losses.

The loss appears on the income statement. Recording this loss reduces the carrying value of Tone's Spices to $60 (= $15 + $25 + $20) million, its current fair value.

IFRS Treatment of Goodwill   The impairment test under IFRS is applied at the level of a *cash generating unit*, defined as the smallest identifiable group of assets that generates cash flows that are largely independent of the cash flows of other assets. If the recoverable amount of the unit is less than the balance sheet carrying value, the firm recognizes an impairment loss. The credit to offset the debit for the impairment loss is allocated first to goodwill and second to the other assets, the latter prorated based on their carrying amounts. In each instance, the asset (whether goodwill or a separately identifiable asset) is written down to its recoverable amount or zero, whichever is larger. Although the amounts will be different, because both the impairment test and the subsequent balance sheet carrying value will be different, the journal entries for recognizing goodwill impairments under IFRS are similar to those shown previously for B-P. However, unlike U.S. GAAP, IFRS requires that firms assess, every reporting period, whether there has been a recovery of a goodwill impairment loss. Firms must recognize a recovery if one has occurred.

Example 24   Refer to **Example 23** for Tone's Spices. Assume that B-P views Tone's Spices as a cash-generating unit. Assume also the following carrying values and recoverable amounts[20] for Tone's Spices for purposes of measuring the asset impairment loss (amounts in millions):

	Carrying Value	Recoverable Amount
Land, Buildings, and Equipment	$ 15	$15
Brand Names	35	25
Goodwill	50	20
Total for Cash Generating Unit	$100	$60

B-P recognizes an impairment loss of $40 million because the carrying value of the cash-generating unit exceeds its recoverable amount of $60 million. B-P first reduces the carrying value of goodwill by $30 million to its recoverable amount. B-P would next allocate the remaining impairment loss of $10 million to the land, building, and equipment and brand names based on their relative carrying values. However, the carrying amount of land, buildings, and equipment equal their recoverable amount. The allocation of the excess impairment loss cannot decrease an asset below its recoverable amount. Thus, B-P reduces the brand names for the remaining $10 million impairment loss, decreasing its carrying value to $25 million, which is also its recoverable amount. The journal entry is the same as that shown in **Example 23**.

SUMMARY OF ACCOUNTING FOR ASSET IMPAIRMENTS

Accounting for the impairment of long-lived assets is complex because GAAP requirements differ for various assets and for U.S. GAAP and IFRS. **Exhibit 9.1** summarizes the requirements for measuring asset impairments.

PROBLEM 9.5 for Self-Study

Measuring impairment losses. Real Estate Financing Corporation (REFC) acquired the assets of Key West Financing Corporation (KWFC) on June 1, 2006, for $250 million. On the acquisition date, KWFC's assets consisted of loans receivable with a fair value of $120 million and real estate leased to businesses and individuals with a fair value of $60 million. The remainder of the purchase price of $70 (= $250 – $120 – $60) million represents goodwill. On October 15, 2008, a hurricane hit Key West and severely damaged many homes and businesses. Information related to the assets of KWFC on October 15, 2008, is as follows (amounts in millions):

(continued)

[20]We simplify this illustration by assuming that the recoverable amounts under IFRS in **Example 24** equal the fair values under U.S. GAAP in **Example 23**. These amounts usually differ.

EXHIBIT 9.1	Summary of Accounting for Impairments of Long-Lived Assets

	U.S. GAAP	IFRS
Long-lived assets except intangible assets not subject to amortization and goodwill	An asset impairment occurs when the carrying value of the asset exceeds its undiscounted future cash flows. The amount of the impairment loss is the excess of the carrying value over the fair value of the asset. Fair value is the amount a firm would receive if it sold the asset in an arm's-length transaction on the measurement date.	An asset impairment occurs and is measured by the excess of the carrying value of the asset over its recoverable amount. The recoverable amount is the larger of the fair value less cost to sell and the present value of the cash flows the firm expects the asset to generate in its current use.
Intangibles not subject to amortization except goodwill	An asset impairment occurs and is measured by the excess of the carrying value over the fair value of the asset.	The requirements are the same as for long-lived assets subject to depreciation or amortization.
Goodwill	First, compare the carrying value of a *reporting unit* that has goodwill to the fair value of that reporting unit. If the carrying value of the reporting unit exceeds its fair value, continue to the next step; otherwise stop. Second, compare the carrying value of the *goodwill* with its fair value. To measure the fair value of goodwill, determine the fair value of the reporting unit to which the goodwill applies. Allocate this total fair value to identifiable assets and liabilities on the balance sheet based on their fair values. The remaining fair value of the reporting unit is the fair value of goodwill. A firm allocates the total fair value of the reporting unit only for the purpose of measuring the fair value of goodwill. If the carrying value of the goodwill exceeds its fair value from this second step, recognize a goodwill impairment loss.	A goodwill impairment loss occurs when the carrying value of the net assets of a *cash-generating unit* with goodwill exceeds the recoverable amount for that unit. First, reduce the carrying value of goodwill by the amount of the impairment loss but not below its recoverable amount. Second, reduce all other assets pro rata based on their carrying values but not below their recoverable amounts for any remaining impairment loss.

	Carrying Value	Undiscounted Cash Flows	Fair Value
Loans Receivable	$140	$160	$125
Real Estate	80	65	50
Goodwill	70		
Total	$290		

a. Assume that the fair value of KWFC on October 15, 2008, after the hurricane is $310 million. Compute the amount of any asset impairment losses under U.S. GAAP.

b. Assume that the market value of KWFC on October 15, 2008, after the hurricane is $220 million. Compute the amount of any asset impairment losses under U.S. GAAP.

DISPOSAL OF ASSETS

The final question we address regarding long-lived assets is: *How does disposal of an asset through sale, abandonment, or trade-in on another asset affect net income?*

Sale of Asset   The firm records the consideration received from the sale (usually cash), eliminates all debits and credits in the accounts related to the asset sold, and recognizes a gain or loss. Because sales of long-lived assets are usually peripheral to a firm's principal business activities, the firm records the gain or loss net instead of gross. That is, the firm does not record the amount received as revenue and the carrying value of the asset sold as an expense. Rather, the firm nets the two amounts and reports only the gain or loss.

Before recording the sale, the firm recognizes depreciation and amortization for the current year up to the date of the sale. When a firm retires an asset from service, it removes the cost of the asset and, in the case of tangible, depreciable assets, the related amount of accumulated depreciation from the books. As part of this entry, the firm records the amount received from the sale, a debit, and the amount of net carrying value removed from the books, a net credit (that is, a credit to the asset account and a smaller debit to the accumulated depreciation account). Typically, the amount of the debit for cash proceeds differs from the net credit to remove the asset from the accounts. The excess of the proceeds received on retirement over the carrying value is a gain (if positive) or a loss (if negative, that is, if net carrying value exceeds proceeds).

To illustrate, assume office equipment costs $5,000, has an expected life of four years and a salvage value of $200. The firm has depreciated this asset on a straight-line basis at $1,200 [= ($5,000 – $200)/4] per year. The firm has recorded depreciation for two years and sells the equipment at midyear in the third year. The firm records the depreciation from the start of the accounting period to the date of sale: $600 [= 1/2 × ($5,000 – $200)/4].

| Depreciation Expense | 600 | |
| Accumulated Depreciation | | 600 |

Assets	=	Liabilities	+	Shareholders' Equity	(Class.)
−600				−600	IncSt → RE

To record depreciation charges up to the date of sale.

The carrying value of the asset is now its cost less two and a half years of straight-line depreciation of $1,200 per year, or $2,000 [= $5,000 – (2 1/2 × $1,200) = $5,000 – $3,000]. The entry to record the sale of the asset depends on the amount of the selling price.

1. If the firm sells the equipment for cash at its carrying value of $2,000, the entry to record the sale would be as follows:

Cash	2,000	
Accumulated Depreciation	3,000	
Equipment		5,000

Assets	=	Liabilities	+	Shareholders' Equity	(Class.)
+2,000					
+3,000					
−5,000					

There is no gain or loss on the sale of a long-lived asset at its carrying value or at the end of its service life for an amount equal to the expected salvage value used in computing depreciation or amortization.

2. If the firm sells the equipment for $2,300 cash, more than its carrying value, the entry to record the sale would be as follows:

Cash	2,300	
Accumulated Depreciation	3,000	
Equipment		5,000
Gain on Sale of Equipment		300

(continued)

Assets	=	Liabilities	+	Shareholders' Equity	(Class.)
+2,300				+300	IncSt → RE
+3,000					
−5,000					

The gain appears in net income and, after closing entries, increases Retained Earnings.

3. If the firm sells the equipment for $1,500 cash, less than its carrying value, the entry to record the sale would be as follows:

Cash	1,500	
Accumulated Depreciation	3,000	
Loss on Sale of Equipment	500	
Equipment		5,000

Assets	=	Liabilities	+	Shareholders' Equity	(Class.)
+1,500				−500	IncSt → RE
+3,000					
−5,000					

The firm includes the loss in net income, reducing Retained Earnings.

Abandonment of Asset

Firms will sometimes abandon assets if there is no market for the asset. Examples include an automobile severely damaged in an accident or a machine requiring an overhaul that is not cost effective. The firm eliminates the carrying value of the asset and recognizes a loss in an amount equal to the carrying value.

Trading in an Asset

A firm may retire an asset from service by trading it in on a new asset. U.S. GAAP and IFRS require that firms record trade-in transactions at fair value, unless they lack commercial substance. An exchange lacks commercial substance if the asset's future cash flows are not expected to change significantly as a result of replacing the old asset with the new one.[21] Firms record trade-ins that lack commercial substance at the carrying value of the exchanged asset.

Example 25   Roadway Express Inc. owns a moving van that originally cost $250,000 and currently has $225,000 of accumulated depreciation. The fair value of the moving van is $60,000. Roadway Express Inc. exchanges the van plus $240,000 in cash for a new moving van costing $300,000; the exchange has commercial substance and is accounted for at fair value. The entry to record the transaction is as follows:

Equipment (new van)	300,000	
Accumulated Depreciation (old van)	225,000	
Equipment (old van)		250,000
Cash		240,000
Gain on Trade-in of Old Van		35,000

Assets	=	Liabilities	+	Shareholders' Equity	(Class.)
+300,000				+35,000	IncSt → RE
+225,000					
−250,000					
−240,000					

To record the trade-in of a van with a carrying value of $25,000 and a fair value of $60,000 for a new van costing $300,000 and the disbursement of $240,000 cash.

---

[21] Financial Accounting Standards Board, *Statement of Financial Accounting Standards No. 153*, "Exchanges of Nonmonetary Assets," 2004. (**Codification Topic 845**). International Accounting Standards Board, *International Accounting Standard 16*, "Property, Plant, and Equipment," revised 1998.

FINANCIAL STATEMENT PRESENTATION

This section discusses the presentation of long-lived assets in the balance sheet and income statement.

BALANCE SHEET

The balance sheet separates noncurrent from current assets. Tangible long-lived assets typically appear under the title Property, Plant, and Equipment, among the noncurrent assets. Firms generally disclose the assets' acquisition cost and accumulated depreciation in one of three ways, illustrated with the following data from a recent annual report of General Electric Company (with dollar amounts in millions):

1. All information is displayed on the balance sheet.

Property, Plant, and Equipment:	
Acquisition Cost	$25,168
Less Accumulated Depreciation	(11,557)
Property, Plant, and Equipment—Net........................	$13,611

2. Acquisition cost is omitted from the balance sheet.

Property, Plant, and Equipment, less Accumulated Depreciation of $11,557..............	$13,611

3. Acquisition cost and accumulated depreciation are omitted from the balance sheet but are detailed in the notes.

Property, Plant, and Equipment—Net (Note 10)	$13,611

Note 10 to the Financial Statements
Property, plant, and equipment have an acquisition cost of $25,168 and accumulated depreciation of $11,557.

Firms typically disclose the amounts for various classes of long-lived depreciable assets (for example, land, buildings, and equipment) separately in notes to the financial statements.

In practice, most firms present intangibles on the balance sheet in a format similar to the last one above, with details in the notes.

Exhibit 9.2 presents the disclosures on long-lived assets for PepsiCo for a recent year.

EXHIBIT 9.2	Excerpts from the Balance Sheet of PepsiCo For the Years Ended December 31, 2006 and 2007 (all dollar amounts in millions)	
	December 31, 2007	**December 31, 2006**
Current Assets (detail omitted)	$10,151	$ 9,130
Property, Plant and Equipment, net	11,228	9,687
Amortizable Intangible Assets, net	796	637
Goodwill	5,169	4,594
Other Nonamortizable Intangible Assets	1,248	1,212
Investments in Noncontrolled Affiliates	4,354	3,690
Other Assets	1,682	980
Total Assets	$34,628	$29,930

PepsiCo's amortizable intangible assets are brand names with limited lives. The nonamortizable intangibles are brand names with indefinite lives, which PepsiCo calls *perpetual brands*. These assets, as well as goodwill, arise from PepsiCo's acquisition of other firms.

INCOME STATEMENT

Depreciation and amortization expenses appear in the income statement, sometimes disclosed separately, sometimes included in selling and administrative expenses, and sometimes, particularly for manufacturing firms, included as part of cost of goods sold expense. United States Steel Corporation lists depreciation expense separately from other costs of goods sold, noting that cost of goods sold excludes depreciation. General Electric includes depreciation expense in cost of goods sold and selling and administrative expense and separately discloses the amount of depreciation in the notes. Asset impairment losses sometimes appear on a separate line on the income statement and sometimes are included in selling and administrative expenses. Gains and losses on disposals of property, plant, and equipment and intangible assets appear on the income statement, often in "Other income and expense."

ANALYZING FINANCIAL STATEMENT DISCLOSURES OF LONG-LIVED ASSETS

PROPERTY, PLANT, AND EQUIPMENT

The financial statements and notes provide information for analyzing changes in property, plant, and equipment. **Exhibit 9.3** presents information for Wal-Mart Stores for three recent years. This section illustrates insights provided by these disclosures.

Fixed Asset Turnover **Chapter 6** discusses the fixed asset turnover, a measure of the amount of sales generated from property, plant, and equipment. The computation of the fixed asset turnover for Wal-Mart Stores is as follows:

2006: $308,945/0.5($65,400 + $74,600)	4.4
2007: $344,992/0.5($74,600 + $85,390)	4.3
2008: $374,526/0.5($85,390 + $93,875)	4.2

The fixed assets turnover declined slightly during the three years. Sales increased 11.7% between fiscal 2006 and fiscal 2007 but only 8.6% between fiscal 2007 and fiscal 2008. In addi-

EXHIBIT 9.3	Selected Data for Wal-Mart Stores (all dollar amounts in millions)

January 31:	2008	2007	2006	2005
Balance Sheet				
Land.	$ 19,879	$ 18,612	$16,174	$14,472
Buildings	72,533	64,052	55,206	46,574
Fixtures and Transportation Equipment	30,236	27,134	24,157	22,991
Total	$122,648	$109,798	$95,537	$84,037
Less Accumulated Depreciation	(28,773)	(24,408)	(20,937)	(18,637)
Total	$ 93,875	$ 85,390	$74,600	$65,400

	For the Year Ended January 31:		
Income Statement	**2008**	**2007**	**2006**
Sales	$374,526	$344,992	$308,945
Depreciation Expense	6,317	5,459	4,645

tion, Wal-Mart continues to construct new superstores, but sales in the new stores increase with a lag. The decreased growth in sales coupled with continued investment in new stores lead to the slight decline in the fixed asset turnover.

Proportion of Depreciable Assets Consumed Wal-Mart Stores uses the straight-line depreciation method. We can compare the amount in accumulated depreciation with the acquisition cost of depreciable assets to approximate the fraction of the useful life, or service capacity, of its assets that Wal-Mart Stores has consumed.

2005: $18,637/($46,574 + $22,991)	26.8%
2006: $20,937/($55,206 + $24,157)	26.4%
2007: $24,408/($64,052 + $27,134)	26.8%
2008: $28,773/($72,533 + $30,236)	28.0%

Over the four years, the proportion of depreciable assets consumed is approximately 26% to 28%. If Wal-Mart Stores added new depreciable assets each year in the same dollar amount that it retired fully depreciated assets, then the proportion of fixed assets depreciated would remain stable at 50%. However, the data in **Exhibit 9.3** show that the cost of depreciable assets increased each year. Wal-Mart is adding new depreciable assets at a higher rate, or a higher cost, or both, than the cost of depreciable assets retired. The proportion of fixed assets consumed is less than 50%, because more depreciable assets are in the early years of their lives.

Average Life of Depreciable Assets The average total life of depreciable assets equals the average acquisition cost of depreciable assets divided by depreciation expense. The computations are as follows:

2006: 0.5($46,574 + $22,991 + $55,206 + $24,157)/$4,645	16.0 years
2007: 0.5($55,206 + $24,157 + $64,052 + $27,134)/$5,459	15.6 years
2008: 0.5($64,052 + $27,134 + $72,533 + $30,236)/$6,317	15.4 years

Because depreciation expense is an amount for the year, we use the average amount of depreciable assets at acquisition cost during the year. We exclude land because firms do not depreciate it. The average total life varied between 15.4 years and 16.0 years over the three years. An examination of the data in **Exhibit 9.3** indicates that expenditures on longer-lived buildings increased at a faster pace than expenditures on shorter-lived fixtures and transportation equipment. Thus, the average total life of depreciable assets should have increased. Perhaps Wal-Mart Stores increased the estimated lives of fixtures and transportation equipment or decreased the lives of buildings in a mixture to cause the relatively stable average service life.

Average Age of Depreciable Assets The average age of depreciable assets equals the average amount of accumulated depreciation divided by depreciation expense each year. The computations are as follows:

2006: 0.5($18,637 + $20,937)/$4,645	4.3
2007: 0.5($20,937 + $24,408)/$5,459	4.2
2008: 0.5($24,408 + $28,773)/$6,317	4.2

The stable average age is consistent with the stable proportion of depreciable assets consumed and the stable average total life.

INTANGIBLES

The analysis of intangible assets is more challenging than the analysis of tangible long-lived assets for the following reasons:

1. Except for software development costs under U.S. GAAP and development costs under IFRS, firms generally do not recognize internally developed intangibles as assets on the

EXHIBIT 9.4

Excerpts from the Balance Sheets of PepsiCo and Coke For the Year Ended December 31, 2007 (all dollar amounts in millions)

	PepsiCo		Coke	
	Amount	Percentage	Amount	Percentage
Current Assets (detail omitted)	$10,151	29.3%	$12,105	28.0%
Property, Plant and Equipment, net	11,228	32.4	8,493	19.6
Amortizable Intangible Assets, net	796	2.3	493	1.1
Goodwill	5,169	14.9	4,256	9.8
Other Nonamortizable Intangible Assets	1,248	3.6	7,470	17.3
Investments in Noncontrolled Affiliates	4,354	12.6	7,777	18.0
Other Assets	1,682	4.9	2,675	6.2
Total Assets	$34,628	100.0%	$43,269	100.0%

balance sheet. To value nonrecognized intangibles, an analyst must use information not reported in the financial statements. **Problem 36** at the end of this chapter illustrates a possible approach to such valuations.

2. Firms that grow through corporate acquisitions will likely report intangible assets on the balance sheet. U.S. GAAP and IFRS require firms to measure the fair values of identifiable intangibles acquired in a business combination and assess whether they have finite lives or indefinite lives.

Exhibit 9.4 presents excerpts from the balance sheets for PepsiCo and for The Coca-Cola Company (Coke) at the end of 2007.

Intangibles comprise a higher proportion of Coke's total assets, 28.2% (= 1.1% + 9.8% + 17.3%), than PepsiCo's total assets, 20.8% (= 2.3% + 14.9% + 3.6%). Coke reports a higher proportion of identifiable nonamortizable assets, 17.3% versus 3.6%, and PepsiCo allocates a higher proportion to goodwill, 14.9% versus 9.8%. Neither firm reports significant proportions of amortizable intangible assets.

3. Differences between U.S. GAAP and IFRS in the treatment of development costs mean that comparisons of firms that apply U.S. GAAP with firms that apply IFRS require consideration of and adjustment for those differences.

Exhibit 9.5 presents excerpts from the financial statements of Nokia Corporation, a Finnish-based manufacturer of mobile telecommunication devices. Nokia Corporation applies IFRS.

EXHIBIT 9.5

Excerpts from the Financial Statements of Nokia Corporation (all amounts in millions of Euros)

December 31:	2007	2006
Capitalized Development Costs	€ 378	€ 251
Goodwill	1,384	532
Other Intangible Assets	2,358	298
Property, Plant, and Equipment	1,912	1,602
Other Noncurrent Assets	2,273	1,348
Total Noncurrent Assets	€8,305	€4,031

Note 13: Research and Development Research and development costs are expensed as they are incurred, except for certain development costs, which are capitalized when it is probable that a development project will generate future economic benefits, and certain criteria, including commercial and technological feasibility, have been met. Capitalized development costs, comprising direct labor and related overhead, are amortized on a systematic basis over their expected useful lives between two and five years.

Nokia's balance sheet shows the development costs recognized as an asset, including both capitalized software development costs, which U.S. GAAP also recognizes as an asset, and other capitalized development costs.

SUMMARY

This chapter started by setting forth a series of questions regarding the accounting for long-lived assets. We repeat those questions here and summarize U.S. GAAP and IFRS responses to each.

1. Should firms treat expenditures with potential long-term benefits as assets on the balance sheet or as expenses on the income statement in the year of the expenditure? Firms capitalize an expenditure as an asset if it meets the definition of an asset and the recognition criteria as follows:

   - The expenditure results in a future economic benefit that the firm obtains and controls as a result of a past transaction or exchange.
   - The firm can measure the future benefits with a reasonable degree of precision.

   Firms easily apply these criteria to tangible assets, such as buildings and equipment, because of their physical attributes. Considerable controversy surrounds the recognition of many intangibles, particularly expenditures for research and development, brand names, and software development costs.

2. For expenditures treated as assets, should firms depreciate or amortize a portion of the assets as expenses each period? Firms depreciate or amortize the cost of long-lived assets whose service benefits diminish over time (that is, assets with finite useful lives). Examples are buildings, equipment, and patents. Firms do not depreciate or amortize the cost of long-lived assets when service benefits do not diminish with time or have an indefinite life, such as for land and goodwill. Firms must test these, and all other, assets for impairment in value.

3. For assets with finite lives, over what period and using what pattern should firms depreciate or amortize the cost of the assets? Firms depreciate or amortize the cost of assets over their expected service life. Most firms choose to depreciate or amortize an equal amount each year using the straight-line method. Some firms use accelerated methods for tangible assets.

4. How should firms treat new information about expected useful lives or salvage value? Both U.S. GAAP and IFRS require firms to depreciate or amortize the remaining carrying value at the time of the change in estimate over the revised remaining useful life.

5. How should firms treat changes in the fair values of long-lived assets? The treatment of changes in fair value under U.S. GAAP is asymmetric. Firms cannot increase long-lived assets for increases in fair value but must test assets for impairment in value and recognize losses. U.S. GAAP specifies different impairment tests for assets with finite lives and intangibles with indefinite lives. IFRS also requires impairment testing and the recognition of impairment losses but permits upward revaluations of assets to recognize both unrealized fair value increases and recoveries of impairment losses.

6. What impact does the disposal of long-lived assets have on net income? Firms record any proceeds of disposal, eliminate the carrying value of the asset, and record a gain or loss for the difference (except for some trade-ins).
   Both U.S. GAAP and IFRS require significant judgment and estimates in accounting for long-lived assets. Firms must estimate service lives and salvage values for depreciation and amortization, choose depreciation methods, and estimate fair values of identifiable assets in business combinations and in measuring asset impairments.

SOLUTIONS TO SELF-STUDY PROBLEMS

SUGGESTED SOLUTION TO PROBLEM 9.1 FOR SELF-STUDY

(Jensen Company; calculating the acquisition cost of fixed assets.)

1. a, b, d, j, m, o, p.
2. c, e, f, g, i, k, l, n, o, p.
3. h, i, l, p.
4. i, q, r.

COMMENTS AND EXPLANATIONS

d. Removing the old building makes the land ready to accept the new one. These costs apply to the land, not to the new building.

f. The reduction in the cost of materials and supplies will reduce the cost of the building. The actual accounting entries depend on the method used to record the potential discount. This book does not discuss these issues.

h. Explicit interest is capitalized but not opportunity-cost interest or interest imputed on one's own funds. The adjusting entry credits Construction in Process and debits Interest Revenue. The debit reduces income, removing the revenue that the company had recognized.

i. Computation of the amounts to be allocated requires an estimate. Once the firm estimates amounts, it debits them to Building or to Depreciation Expense and Work-in-Process Inventory, as appropriate, for the regular company operations.

j. Credit to Land account, reducing its cost.

l. Allocate to Building and to expense, based on an estimate of how time was spent. Given the description, most of these costs are probably for the building.

m. Include as part of the cost of the land.

n. Capitalize as part of the Building account for the same reasons that a firm capitalizes interest during construction.

o. Allocate the costs for insuring workers to the same accounts as the wages for those workers.

p. Probably as an expense or a loss for the period. An alternative and justifiable treatment is to include this as part of the cost of the building, paralleling the treatment of explicit insurance cost. If, however, the company was irrational in acquiring insurance policies with deductible clauses, this item would be an expense or loss. Accounting usually assumes that most managements make rational decisions most of the time.

q. Debit to Machinery and Equipment account, an asset account separate from Building.

r. Treat the same as the preceding item; installation costs are part of the cost of the asset; see **Chapter 3**.

s. Recognizing revenue is incorrect. Credit the Construction in Process account and debit the Construction Revenue account.

SUGGESTED SOLUTION TO PROBLEM 9.2 FOR SELF-STUDY

(Markam Corporation; calculating periodic depreciation.)

a. Straight-Line (Time) Method:

Years 2008 to 2012: ($20,000 − $2,000)/5 = $3,600 each year
Total: $3,600 × 5 = $18,000

b. Straight-Line (Use) Method:

Years 2008 to 2011: 5,000 × $0.75^a = $3,750 per year
Year 2012: 4,000 × $0.75^a = $3,000

(continued)

Total [($3,750 × 4) + $3,000] = $18,000
ª($20,000 − $2,000)/24,000 = $0.75 per hour

SUGGESTED SOLUTION TO PROBLEM 9.3 FOR SELF-STUDY

(Central States Electric Company; adjustments for changes in estimates.)
(All dollar amounts in millions.)

a. $4.4 per year = ($200 + $20)/50 years

b. $4.5 per year = [$200 + $20 + $4 − ($4.4 per year × 10 years)]/40 years remaining life
         = ($224 − $44)/40 = $180/40

c. $3.0 per year = [$180 − ($4.5 × 20 years)]/30 years remaining life
         = ($180 − $90)/30 = $90/30

SUGGESTED SOLUTION TO PROBLEM 9.4 FOR SELF-STUDY

(Purdy Company; distinguishing repairs from improvements.)

a. Record the first truck at $19,200. Record the second truck at $15,000; debit $4,200 to expense or loss.

b. When Purdy Company acquired the first truck, it knew it would have to make the "repair," which is an improvement. The purchase price was lower because of the known cost to be incurred. At the time of acquisition, the firm anticipated the cost as required to produce the expected service potential of the asset. The fact that the cost was $4,200, rather than "about $4,000," does not seem to violate Purdy Company's expectations at the time it acquired the truck. If the repair had cost significantly more than $4,000—say, $7,000—then the excess could be a loss or an expense.

    Purdy Company believed that the second truck was operable when it agreed on the purchase price. Purdy Company incurred the cost of the repair to achieve the level of service potential it thought it had acquired. There are no more future benefits after the repair than it had anticipated at the time of acquisition. Therefore, the $4,200 is an expense or a loss.

SUGGESTED SOLUTION TO PROBLEM 9.5 FOR SELF-STUDY

(Real Estate Financing Corporation; measuring impairment losses.)

a. The undiscounted cash flows related to the loans receivable of $160 million exceed their carrying value of $140 million, so no impairment loss arises for the receivables. For real estate, the carrying value of $80 million exceeds their undiscounted cash flows of $65 million, so Real Estate Financing Corporation recognizes an impairment loss of $30 (= $50 − $80) million. The carrying value of the firm after recognizing the impairment loss is $260 million (= $140 for loans receivable + $50 million for real estate + $70 million for goodwill). The fair value of the firm of $310 million exceeds the carrying value of $260 million, so no impairment loss on goodwill arises.

b. The answers for the loans receivable and the real estate in part **a** apply here as well. In this case, however, the carrying value of the firm of $260 million exceeds the fair value of $220 million, so an impairment loss of goodwill arises. To measure the impairment loss, the accountant attributes $125 million of the fair value of $220 million to loans receivable, $50 million to real estate, and $45 million to goodwill. Comparing the fair value of goodwill of $45 million to the carrying value of goodwill of $70 million yields an impairment loss of $25 million.

KEY TERMS AND CONCEPTS

Tangible assets	Separability criterion
Intangible assets	Interest costs during construction
In-process research and development	Finite life
(IPR&D)	Indefinite life

Depreciation	Maintenance
Amortization	Repairs
Joint cost	Improvements
Salvage value	Asset revaluations
Residual value	Impairment loss
Service life	Recoverable amount
Physical and functional factors	Reporting unit
Straight-line (time and use) methods	Cash generating unit
Declining-balance methods	
Sum-of-the-years'-digits method	
Treatment of changes in periodic depreciation and amortization (estimates of useful lives and residual values of long-lived assets)	

QUESTIONS, EXERCISES, AND PROBLEMS

QUESTIONS

1. Review the meaning of the terms and concepts listed in Key Terms and Concepts.

2. A firm that makes expenditures to self-construct a building treats the expenditures as an asset. When that same firm makes research and development expenditures to create a new patented technology, it must treat the expenditures as an expense. When that same firm makes expenditures to create computer software for eventual sale to customers, it might treat some of those expenditures as an asset and some as an expense. Explain U.S. GAAP's rationale for the different treatment of these expenditures.

3. A pharmaceutical firm that makes expenditures to research new drugs must treat the expenditures as an expense. If that same pharmaceutical firm acquires a patent for a new drug from its creator, it must treat the expenditure as an asset. If that same pharmaceutical firm acquires another firm with in-process R&D, it must treat the portion of the purchased price allocated to the in-process R&D as an asset. Explain U.S. GAAP's rationale for the different treatment of these expenditures.

4. a. What is the effect of capitalizing interest on reported net income summed over all the periods of the life of a given self-constructed asset, from building through use until eventual retirement? Contrast with a policy of expensing interest as incurred.

   b. Consider a company engaging in increasing dollar amounts of self-construction activity each period during periods when interest rates do not decline. What is the effect on reported income each year of capitalizing interest in contrast to expensing interest as incurred?

5. Contrast the terms *finite life, infinite life,* and *indefinite life* as they apply to depreciation of tangible long-lived assets and amortization of intangible assets.

6. When PepsiCo (see **Exhibit 9.2**) acquires another firm, it allocates a portion of the purchase price to brand names, some of which it amortizes and some of which it does not amortize. How does PepsiCo likely justify this different treatment of brand names?

7. An airline has depreciated its new aircraft in the past over 25 years. New fuel usage and safety standards indicate that a shorter useful life is now appropriate for all of its existing aircraft. Depending on the circumstances, the airline might (a) spread the undepreciated cost of the aircraft over the remaining life of the aircraft, or (b) recognize an asset impairment loss immediately and then spread the carrying value over the remaining life of the aircraft. Under what circumstances might each of these two treatments be appropriate?

8. A firm expects to use a delivery truck for five years. At the end of three years, the transmission wears out and requires replacement at a cost of $4,000. The firm argues that it should capitalize the expenditure because without it the useful life is zero and with it the useful life will be another three years. Comment on the firm's reasoning relative to U.S. GAAP and IFRS.

9. Relate the concept of return of capital to the criterion under U.S. GAAP for deciding whether an impairment loss on long-lived assets other than nonamortized intangibles has occurred.

10. Why does the cash recoverability criterion apply to impairment losses on amortized intangibles but not on nonamortized intangibles under U.S. GAAP?

11. The text states, "The use of undiscounted, instead of discounted, cash flows [for identifying asset impairment losses on depreciable and amortizable long-lived assets under U.S. GAAP] seems theoretically unsound." Explain this statement.

12. Competition among acquiring firms to make a corporate acquisition may result in the successful firm paying more than the fair value of another firm. The acquiring firm will allocate the excess purchase price to goodwill, along with amounts attributable to unidentifiable intangible benefits. Because U.S. GAAP and IFRS do not require firms to amortize goodwill, the excess purchase price will not affect net income. Do you agree? Why or why not?

EXERCISES

13. **Calculating acquisition costs of long-lived assets.** Outback Steakhouse opened a new restaurant on the site of an existing building. It paid the owner $260,000 for the land and building, of which it attributes $52,000 to the land and $208,000 to the building. Outback incurred legal costs of $12,600 to conduct a title search and prepare the necessary legal documents for the purchase. It then paid $35,900 to renovate the building to make it suitable for Outback's use. Property and liability insurance on the land and building for the first year was $12,000, of which $4,000 applied to the period during renovation and $8,000 applied to the period after opening. Property taxes on the land and building for the first year totaled $15,000, of which $5,000 applied to the period during renovation and $10,000 applied to the period after opening. Calculate the amounts that Outback Steakhouse should include in the Land account and in the Building account.

14. **Classifying expenditure as asset or expense.** For each of the following expenditures or acquisitions, indicate the type of account debited. Classify the account as (1) asset other than product cost, (2) product cost (Work-in-Process Inventory), or (3) expense. If the account debited is an asset account, specify whether it is current or noncurrent.

    a. $150 for repairs of office machines.

    b. $1,500 for emergency repairs to an office machine.

    c. $250 for maintenance of delivery trucks.

    d. $5,000 for a machine acquired in return for a three-year note.

    e. $4,200 for research and development staff salaries.

    f. $3,100 for newspaper ads.

    g. $6,400 for wages of factory workers engaged in production.

    h. $3,500 for wages of factory workers engaged in installing equipment the firm has purchased.

    i. $2,500 for salaries of the office workforce.

    j. $1,000 for legal fees incurred in acquiring an ore deposit.

    k. $1,200 for a one-year insurance policy beginning next month.

    l. $1,800 for U.S. Treasury notes, to be sold to pay the next installment due on income taxes.

    m. $4,000 for royalty payment for the right to use a patent used in manufacturing.

    n. $10,000 for purchase of a trademark.

    o. $100 filing fee for copyright registration application.

    p. $1,850 to purchase computer software used in recordkeeping.

    q. $8,600 to purchase from its creator initial research on a possible drug to treat hypertension.

15. **Cost of self-constructed assets.** Assume that Bolton Company purchased a plot of land for $90,000 as a factory site. A small office building sits on the plot, conservatively appraised at $20,000. The company plans to use the office building after making some modifications and renovations (item (4) below). The company had plans drawn for a factory and

received bids for its construction. It rejected all bids and decided to construct the factory itself. Management believes that plant asset accounts should include the following additional items:

(1)	Materials and Supplies for Factory Building	$200,000
(2)	Excavation of Land	12,000
(3)	Labor on Construction of Factory Building	140,000
(4)	Cost of Remodeling Old Building into Office Building	13,000
(5)	Interest Paid on Cash Borrowed by Bolton to Construct Factory[a]	6,000
(6)	Interest Forgone on Bolton's Own Cash Used	9,000
(7)	Cash Discounts on Materials Purchased for Factory Building	7,000
(8)	Supervision by Management on Factory Building	10,000
(9)	Workers' Compensation Insurance Premiums on Labor in (3)	8,000
(10)	Payment of Claims for Injuries During Construction of Factory Building Not Covered by Insurance	3,000
(11)	Clerical and Other Expenses on Construction of Factory Building	8,000
(12)	Paving of Streets and Sidewalks	5,000
(13)	Architect's Plans and Specifications of Factory Building	4,000
(14)	Legal Costs of Conveying Land	2,000
(15)	Legal Costs of Injury Claim During Construction of Factory Building	1,000
(16)	Income Credited to Retained Earnings Account (the difference between the forgone cost and the lowest contractor's bid)	11,000

[a]This interest is the entire amount of interest paid during the construction period.

Show in detail the items Bolton should include in the following accounts: Land, Factory Building, Office Building, and Site Improvements. Explain the reason for excluding any of these items from the four accounts.

16. **Cost of self-developed product.** Duck Vehicle Manufacturing Company incurs various costs in developing a new, amphibious vehicle for use in providing tours on land and water. Indicate the accounting treatment for each of the following expenditures.

(1)	Salaries of Company Engineers to Design the New Vehicle	$325,000
(2)	Cost of Prototype of New Vehicle Built by External Contractor	278,200
(3)	Cost of Supplies and Salaries of Personnel to Test Prototype	68,900
(4)	Fees Paid to Environmental Protection Agency to Test Emissions of New Vehicle	15,200
(5)	Legal Fees Incurred to Register and Establish a Patent on the New Vehicle	12,500
(6)	Cost of Castings, or Molds, for Metal Parts of New Vehicle	46,000
(7)	Cost of Local Permits to Commence Manufacturing the New Vehicle	5,000
(8)	Cost of Manufacturing the First Vehicle for a Customer	167,600

17. **Calculating interest capitalized during construction.** Bulls Eye Stores constructed new stores during the current year. The average balance in the Construction-in-Process account excluding the current year's capitalized interest costs was $3,400,000. Bulls Eye Stores engaged in borrowing directly related to these stores in the amount of $2,000,000, which carries an interest rate of 6%. Bulls Eye Stores has other borrowing outstanding totaling $8,000,000 at an average interest rate of 7%. Compute the amount of interest capitalized in the Construction-in-Process account during the current year.

18. **Amount of interest capitalized during construction.** Nexor, a steel manufacturer, self-constructs a new manufacturing facility in Vermont. At the start of 2008, the Construction-in-Process account had a balance of $30 million. Construction activity occurred uniformly throughout the year. At the end of 2008, the balance was $60 million before capitalization of interest for the year. The outstanding borrowings of the company during the year were as follows:

New Construction Loans at 8% per Year	$ 25,000,000
Old Bond Issues Averaging 6% Rate	100,000,000
Total Interest-Bearing Debt	$125,000,000

    a. Compute the amount of interest capitalized in the Construction-in-Process account for 2008.

    b. Present journal entries for interest for 2008.

    c. On December 31, 2009, Nexor completed the manufacturing facility and put it to work. Average Construction-in-Process for 2009 was $110 million. The debt listed above remained outstanding throughout the construction project and the firm did not issue any additional interest-bearing debt during this time. Present journal entries for 2009 related to interest expense and interest capitalization.

19. **Calculations for various depreciation methods.** Alcoa acquires a machine for $88,800. It expects the machine to last six years and to operate for 30,000 hours during that time. Estimated salvage value is $4,800 at the end of the machine's useful life. Calculate the depreciation charge for each of the first three years using each of the following methods:

    a. The straight-line (time) method.

    b. The straight-line (use) method, with the following operating times: first year, 4,500 hours; second year, 5,000 hours; third year, 5,500 hours.

20. **Calculations for various depreciation methods.** On January 1, 2008, Luck Delivery Company acquired a new truck for $30,000. It estimated the truck to have a useful life of five years and no salvage value. The company closes its books annually on December 31. Indicate the amount of the depreciation charge for each year of the asset's life under the following methods:

    a. The straight-line method.

    b. The declining-balance method at twice the straight-line rate, with a switch to straight-line in 2011. The declining balance method multiplies the book value (that is, acquisition cost minus accumulated depreciation) of the asset by a depreciation rate. A depreciation rate of twice the straight-line rate equals 2/n, or 2/5 in this case. Because a firm will never fully depreciate an asset using the declining-balance method, firms switch to the straight-line method at some time prior to the end of an asset's useful life, 2011 in this case.

    c. The sum-of-the-years'-digits method. The sum-of-the-years'-digits method begins by summing the digits of an asset's useful life. The sum for a five-year asset is 15 (= 5 + 4 + 3 + 2 + 1). The depreciation rate for the first year of useful life is 5/15, for the second year is 4/15, and so forth. The depreciation base is the same as for the straight-line method, acquisition cost minus salvage value. Multiplying the depreciation base by the depreciation rate yields the amount of depreciation for each year.

    d. The truck belongs to a category of property for tax purposes requiring the following proportions of the asset's cost to be depreciated each year: 0.20, 0.32, 0.192, 0.115, 0.115, 0.058. (*Hint:* Charge depreciation for each of six calendar years. These fractions result from assuming one-half year of use in the first year, a full year of use in each of the next four years, and a final half year of use in the sixth year.) The tax law allows firms to ignore salvage value in calculating depreciation.

21. **Change in depreciable life and salvage value.** Thompson Financial acquired a computer on January 1, 2006, for $10,000,000. The computer had an estimated useful life of six years and $1,000,000 estimated salvage value. The firm uses the straight-line depreciation method. On January 1, 2008, Thompson Financial discovers that new technologies make it likely that the computer will last only four years in total and that the estimated salvage value will be only $600,000. Compute the amount of depreciation expense for 2008 for this change in depreciable life and salvage value. Assume that the change does not represent an impairment loss.

22. **Journal entries for revising estimate of life.** Give the journal entries for the following selected transactions of Florida Manufacturing Corporation. The company uses the straight-line method of calculating depreciation and reports on a December 31 year-end.

a. The firm purchases a cutting machine on November 1, 2008, for $180,000. It estimates that the machine will have a useful life of 12 years and a salvage value of $7,200 at the end of that time. Give the journal entry for the depreciation at December 31, 2008.

b. Record the depreciation for the year ending December 31, 2009.

c. In August 2014 the firm estimates that the machine will probably have a total useful life of 14 years and a $3,840 salvage value. Record the depreciation for the year ending December 31, 2014.

d. The firm sells the machine for $40,000 on March 31, 2019. Record the entries of that date, assuming that the firm records depreciation as indicated in part c.

23. **Distinguishing repairs versus betterments.** Disney World experienced damage from a tornado at Space Mountain, one of its most popular attractions. It paid $30,200 to replace steel reinforcements to the structure damaged by the tornado, $86,100 for a new roof torn off by the tornado, $26,900 for a new air conditioning system that was housed on the roof, and $12,600 to replace carpeting damaged by water. Disney World estimates that higher quality steel used as replacements added 20% more structural support in terms of weight-bearing capacity. The new air conditioning system provides 25% more cooling power than the unit previously installed in the attraction. Compute the amount of these expenses that Disney World should treat as a repair and the amount it should treat as a betterment.

24. **Computing the amount of an impairment loss on tangible long-lived assets.** Wildwood Properties owns an apartment building that has a carrying value of $15,000,000 on January 1, 2008. The highway department has decided to construct a new highway near the building, which substantially decreases its attractiveness to tenants. Wildwood Properties estimates that it will now collect rentals from the building of $1,400,000 a year for the next six years and that it will sell the building at the end of that time for $4,000,000. Wildwood Properties will use the present value of expected cash flows to measure the fair value of the building under U.S. GAAP and the recoverable amount under IFRS. An appropriate interest rate to discount cash flows is 10%. Assume that all cash flows occur at the end of the year. Compute the amount of any impairment loss that Wildwood Properties should recognize under U.S. GAAP and under IFRS.

25. **Computing the amount of impairment loss.** Tillis Corporation acquired the assets of Kieran Corporation (Kieran) on January 1, 2006, for $2,400,000. On this date the fair values of the assets of Kieran were as follows: land, $400,000; building, $600,000; equipment, $900,000. On June 15, 2008, a competitor introduced a new product that will likely significantly affect future sales of Kieran's products. It will also affect the value of Kieran's property, plant, and equipment because of their specialized nature in producing Kieran's existing products. The following information relates to the property, plant, and equipment of Kieran on June 15, 2008:

	Carrying Value	Undiscounted Cash flows	Fair Value
Land	$ 550,000	$575,000	$550,000
Building.	580,000	600,000	580,000
Equipment	1,200,000	950,000	800,000

The fair value of Kieran as an entity on June 15, 2008, is $2,200,000.

Compute the amount of impairment loss recognized on each of Kieran's property, plant, and equipment and on goodwill on June 15, 2008, under U.S. GAAP.

26. **Computing the gain or loss on sale of equipment.** Fedup Express acquired a delivery truck on January 1, 2004, for $48,000. It estimated that the truck would have a six-year useful life and $6,000 salvage value. Fedup Express uses the straight-line depreciation method. On July 1, 2008, Fedup Express sells the truck for $14,000. Give the journal entries that Fedup Express makes on July 1, 2008, to recognize depreciation for 2008 and the sale of the truck.

27. **Working backward to derive proceeds from disposition of plant assets.** The balance sheets of Wilcox Corporation at the beginning and end of the year contained the following data:

	Beginning of Year	End of Year
Property, Plant, and Equipment (at cost)...............	$400,000	$550,000
Accumulated Depreciation............................	180,000	160,000
Net Carrying Value	$220,000	$390,000

During the year, Wilcox Corporation sold machinery and equipment at a gain of $4,000. It purchased new machinery and equipment at a cost of $230,000. Depreciation charges on machinery and equipment for the year amounted to $50,000. Calculate the proceeds Wilcox Corporation received from the sale of the machinery and equipment.

28. **Journal entries to correct accounting errors.** Give correcting entries for the following situations. In each case, the firm uses the straight-line method of depreciation and closes its books annually on December 31. Recognize all gains and losses currently.

   a. A firm purchased a computer for $3,000 on January 1, 2006. It depreciated the computer at a rate of 25% of acquisition cost per year. On June 30, 2008, it sold the computer for $800 and acquired a new computer for $4,000. The bookkeeper made the following entry to record the transaction:

Equipment..	3,200	
Cash..		3,200

Assets	=	Liabilities	+	Shareholders' Equity	(Class.)
+3,200					
−3,200					

   b. A firm purchased a used truck for $7,000. Its cost, when new, was $12,000. The bookkeeper made the following entry to record the purchase:

Truck..	12,000	
Accumulated Depreciation		5,000
Cash..		7,000

Assets	=	Liabilities	+	Shareholders' Equity	(Class.)
+12,000					
−5,000					
−7,000					

   c. A firm purchased a testing mechanism on April 1, 2006, for $1,200. It depreciated the testing mechanism at a 10% annual rate. A burglar stole the testing mechanism on June 30, 2008. The firm had not insured against this theft. The bookkeeper made the following entry:

Theft Loss	1,200	
Testing Machine		1,200

Assets	=	Liabilities	+	Shareholders' Equity	(Class.)
−1,200				−1,200	IncSt → RE

PROBLEMS

29. **Recording transactions involving tangible and intangible assets.** Present journal entries for each of the following transactions of Moon Macrosystems:

   a. Acquired computers costing $400,000 and computer software costing $40,000 on January 1, 2006. Moon expects the computers to have a service life of 10 years and $40,000 salvage value. It expects the computer software to have a service life of four years and zero salvage value.

b. Paid $20,000 to install the computers in the office. Paid $10,000 to install and test the computer software.

c. Recorded depreciation and amortization using the straight-line method for 2006 and 2007. Moon records a full year of depreciation in the year of acquisition. Treat depreciation and amortization as a period expense.

d. On January 1, 2008, new software offered on the market made the software acquired in part **a** completely obsolete. Give any required journal entry.

e. On January 2, 2008, Moon revised the depreciable life of the computers to a total of 14 years and the salvage value to $56,000. Give the entry to record depreciation for 2008.

f. On December 31, 2009, Moon sold the computers for $260,000. Give the required journal entries for 2009.

30. **Effect on net income of changes in estimates for depreciable assets.** American Airlines has $3 billion of assets, including airplanes costing $2.5 billion with net carrying value of $1.6 billion. It earns net income equal to approximately 6% of total assets. American Airlines depreciates its airplanes for financial reporting purposes on a straight-line basis over 10-year lives to a salvage value equal to 10% of acquisition cost. American announces a change in depreciation policy; it will use 14-year lives and salvage values equal to 12% of acquisition cost. The airplanes are all four years old. Assume an income tax rate of 35%.

Calculate the approximate impact on net income of the change in depreciation policy. Compute both dollar and percentage effects.

31. **Recognizing and measuring impairment losses.** Give the journal entry to recognize an impairment loss, if appropriate, in each of the following cases under U.S. GAAP. If a loss does not qualify as an impairment loss, explain the reason, and indicate the appropriate accounting.

a. Commercial Realty Corporation leases office space to tenants in Boston. One of its office buildings originally cost $80 million and has accumulated depreciation of $20 million. The city of Boston has announced its intention to construct an exit ramp from a nearby expressway on one side of the office building. Rental rates in the building will likely decrease as a result. The expected future undiscounted cash flows from rentals and from disposal of the building decreased from $120 million before the announcement to $50 million afterward. The fair value of the building decreased from $85 million before the announcement to $32 million afterward.

b. Refer to part **a**. Assume that the undiscounted cash flows totaled $70 million and that the fair value totaled $44 million after the announcement.

c. Medical Services Corporation plans, and then builds, its own office building and clinic. It originally anticipated that the building would cost $15 million. The physicians in charge of overseeing construction had medical practices so busy that they did not closely track costs, which ultimately reached $25 million. The expected future cash flows from using the building total $22 million, and the fair value of the building totals $16 million.

d. Medco Pharmaceuticals acquired New Start Biotechnology two years ago for $40 million. Medco allocated $25 million to a patent held by New Start and $15 million to goodwill. By the end of the current period, Medco has amortized the carrying value of the patent to $20 million. A competitor recently received approval for a biotechnology drug that will reduce the fair value of the patent that Medco acquired from New Start. The expected future undiscounted cash flows from sales of the patented drug total $18 million, and the fair value of the patent is $12 million. The fair value of the former New Start Biotechnology operation owned by Medco is now $25 million.

e. Chicken Franchisees Inc. acquires franchise rights in the Atlanta area for Chicken Delight Restaurants, a national restaurant chain. The franchise rights originally cost $15 million; since acquisition, Chicken Franchisees has amortized the book value to $10 million. Chicken Delight Restaurants recently received negative publicity because the chickens it delivered to its franchisees contained potentially harmful pesticides. As a result, business has declined. Chicken Franchisees estimates that the future undiscounted cash flows associated with the Chicken Delight name total $6 million and that the franchise rights have fair value of $3 million.

32. **Expensing versus capitalizing research and development costs.** Pfizer, a pharmaceutical company, plans to spend $90 million on research and development (R&D) at the beginning of each of the next several years to develop new drugs. As a result of the R&D expenditure for a given year, it expects pretax income (not counting R&D expense) to increase by $36 million a year for three years, including the year of the expenditure itself. Pfizer has other pretax income of $30 million per year. The controller of Pfizer is curious about the effect on the financial statements of following one of two accounting policies with respect to R&D expenditures:

    (1) Expensing the R&D costs in the year of expenditure (the policy required in the United States).

    (2) Capitalizing the R&D costs and amortizing them over three years, including the year of the expenditure itself.

    Assume that the company does spend $90 million at the beginning of each of four years and that the planned increase in income occurs. Ignore income tax effects.

    a. Prepare a four-year condensed summary of income before income taxes, assuming that Pfizer follows policy (1) and expenses R&D costs as incurred.

    b. Prepare a four-year condensed summary of income before income taxes, assuming that Pfizer follows policy (2) and capitalizes R&D costs, then amortizes them over three years. Also compute the amount of Deferred R&D Costs (asset) appearing on the balance sheet at the end of each of the four years.

    c. In what sense is policy (1) a conservative policy?

    d. Ascertain the effect on income before income taxes and on the balance sheet if Pfizer continues to spend $90 million each year and the pretax income effects continue as in the first four years.

33. **Interpreting disclosures regarding long-lived assets.** **Exhibit 9.6** presents a partial balance sheet for General Mills Inc., a consumer foods processing company, for its fiscal years ending May 28, 2006, and May 27, 2007.

    a. General Mills is not in the business of developing computer software. Why then does computer software appear as an asset on its balance sheet?

    b. Is it likely that General Mills recognizes depreciation on its computer software? Explain.

EXHIBIT 9.6

Partial Balance Sheet for General Mills Inc.
(all dollar amounts in millions)
(Problem 9.33)

	May 27, 2007	May 28, 2006
Current Assets	$ 3,054	$ 3,041
Land	$ 61	$ 54
Buildings	1,518	1,430
Equipment	4,016	3,859
Capitalized Software	225	211
Construction in Progress	276	252
Total Land, Buildings, and Equipment	$ 6,096	$ 5,806
Less Accumulated Depreciation	(3,082)	(2,809)
Total Land, Buildings, and Equipment—Net	$ 3,014	$ 2,997
Intangibles Subject to Amortization:		
Patents and Trademarks—Net	$ 12	$ 12
Intangibles Not Subject to Amortization:		
Brands	3,682	3,595
Goodwill	6,835	6,652
Total Intangibles	$10,529	$10,259
Other Assets	$ 1,587	$ 1,778
Total Assets	$18,184	$18,075

c. General Mills computes depreciation on its depreciable assets using the straight-line method and recognized depreciation of $421 million during fiscal 2007. Compute the average total life and the average age of depreciable assets for fiscal 2007.

d. Did General Mills likely dispose of any depreciable assets during fiscal 2007? Explain.

e. Does General Mills appear to be a firm that primarily grows by internal expansion or by acquiring other consumer foods companies? Explain.

f. Is it likely that General Mills made a corporate acquisition during fiscal 2007? Explain.

g. What is General Mills' likely rationale for treating patents and trademarks as intangibles subject to amortization?

h. What is General Mills' likely rationale for treating brand names as an intangible not subject to amortization?

i. The income statement of General Mills reports Interest Expense—Net. Based on the information in **Exhibit 9.6**, what item has General Mills likely netted against interest expense?

34. **Interpreting disclosures regarding long-lived assets. Exhibit 9.7** presents a partial balance sheet for Amgen Inc., a creator and manufacturer of biotechnology pharmaceutical products, for December 31, 2006 and 2007.

a. Does Amgen likely recognize depreciation on the amount in the Construction in Progress account each year? Explain.

b. Amgen depreciates its assets using the straight-line method and recognized $593 million of depreciation during 2007. Compute the average total life and average age of Amgen's depreciable assets for 2007.

c. Did Amgen appear to dispose of any depreciable assets during 2007? Explain.

d. Describe the likely reasons that Amgen treats Developed Product Technology, Core Technology, Trade Name, and Acquired Technology Rights as intangibles subject to amortization. Consider each of these four items separately.

EXHIBIT 9.7

Partial Balance Sheet for Amgen Inc.
(all dollar amounts in millions)
(Problem 9.34)

	December 31, 2007	December 31, 2006
Current Assets	$11,712	$ 9,235
Land	$ 398	$ 294
Buildings and Improvements	2,776	2,485
Equipment	4,243	3,584
Construction in Progress	1,271	958
Total Land, Buildings, and Equipment	$ 8,688	$ 7,321
Less Accumulated Depreciation	(2,767)	(2,283)
Total Land, Buildings, and Equipment—Net	$ 5,921	$ 5,038
Intangibles Subject to Amortization:		
Developed Product Technology	$ 2,877	$ 3,077
Core Technology	1,348	1,348
Trade Name	190	190
Acquired Technology Rights	350	—
Other Intangible Assets	454	335
Total Intangibles Subject to Amortization	$ 5,219	$ 4,950
Less Accumulated Amortization	(1,472)	(1,208)
Total Intangibles Subject to Amortization—Net	$ 3,747	$ 3,742
Goodwill	11,302	10,495
Other Assets	$ 1,106	$ 787
Total Assets	$33,788	$29,297

e. Amgen uses the straight-line amortization method and recognized $370 million of amortization for 2007. Compute the average total life and average age of Amgen's intangibles subject to amortization for 2007.

f. Describe the likely reasons why Developed Product Technology decreased from $3,077 million to $2,877 million during 2007, whereas the amounts for Core Technology and Trade Name remained the same.

g. Given the nature of Amgen's business, suggest the likely items that comprise Goodwill on the balance sheet.

h. The income statement of Amgen shows Interest Expense—Net. Based on the information in **Exhibit 9.7**, what item has Amgen likely netted against interest expense?

35. **Interpreting disclosures regarding long-lived assets. Exhibit 9.8** presents a partial balance sheet for Hewlett-Packard Company (HP), a creator and manufacturer of computer hardware and software and related services, for its fiscal years ending October 31, 2006 and 2007.

a. HP uses the straight-line method to depreciate its buildings, leasehold improvements, machinery, and equipment. It recognized depreciation expense of $1,922 million during fiscal 2007. Compute the average total life and average age of its depreciable assets during fiscal 2007.

b. Did HP appear to abandon or dispose of any depreciable assets during fiscal 2007? Explain.

c. What is the likely rationale for treating Customer Contracts, Core Technology, Patents, and Product Trademarks as intangibles subject to amortization? Consider each of these four items separately.

d. HP uses the straight-line amortization method for intangibles subject to amortization and recognized $783 million of amortization during fiscal 2007. Compute the average total life and average age of intangibles subject to amortization for fiscal 2007.

EXHIBIT 9.8

Partial Balance Sheet for Hewlett-Packard Company (all dollar amounts in millions) (Problem 9.35)

	October 31, 2007	October 31, 2006
Current Assets	$47,402	$48,264
Land	$ 464	$ 534
Buildings and Leasehold Improvements	6,044	5,771
Machinery and Equipment	9,903	8,719
Total Land, Buildings, and Equipment	$16,411	$15,024
Less Accumulated Depreciation	(8,613)	(8,161)
Total Land, Buildings, and Equipment—Net	$ 7,798	$ 6,863
Intangibles Subject to Amortization:		
Customer Contracts, Customer Lists, and Distribution Agreements	$ 3,239	$ 2,586
Developed and Core Technology and Patents	2,768	1,923
Product Trademarks	115	103
Total Intangibles Subject to Amortization	$ 6,122	$ 4,612
Less Accumulated Amortization	(3,465)	(2,682)
Intangibles Subject to Amortization—Net	$ 2,657	$ 1,930
Intangibles Not Subject to Amortization:		
Compaq Brand Name	1,422	1,422
Goodwill	21,773	16,853
Total Intangibles	$25,852	$20,205
Other Assets	$ 7,647	$ 6,649
Total Assets	$88,699	$81,981

    e. HP acquired Compaq Computer seven years ago. Why does HP treat the Compaq brand name as an intangible not subject to amortization?

    f. Did HP appear to make a corporate acquisition during fiscal 2007? Explain.

36. **Valuation of brand name.** When an acquiring firm purchases another firm with established brand names, it will likely allocate a portion of the purchase price to the brand names. Measuring the fair value of a brand name involves estimating the likely net cash flows from the branded product over the expected number of years the brand name will persist and then computing the present value of the expected cash flows using a risk-adjusted discount rate. **Exhibit 9.9** illustrates one approach to valuing brand names.

1. The first step is to estimate the cash flow that the brand is expected to generate. This illustration uses projected net income from the brand for the next year, although a more precise calculation would adjust net income for changes in receivables and payables to derive expected cash flow.

2. The second step subtracts an amount for the cost of inventory, fixed assets, and other items of physical capital required to manufacture and distribute the branded products. Assume the cost of capital is 12% and that the brand requires $188.1 million of physical capital.

3. The third step subtracts the estimated amount of income taxes. Assume an income tax rate of 37%.

4. The fourth step applies a capitalization factor to compute the present value of the expected cash flows (based on net brand name profit in this illustration). The **Appendix** at the back of the book discusses the computation of the present value of cash flows, including the present value of perpetuities starting at **Example 12**. This illustration assumes that the appropriate discount rate is 12% and that the expected cash flows will last in perpetuity. The capitalization factor is 8.33 (= 1/.12), yielding $217.4 million (= $26.1 × 8.33) as the estimated brand value. If the appropriate discount rate is 10%, the capitalization factor is 10 (= 1/.10), and the estimated brand value is $261 million (= $26.1 × 10). If the brand name was expected to yield profits for a finite number of years, then the calculation involves using a factor for the present value of cash flows for that number of years. Assume, for example, that the brand name is expected to provide benefits for 20 years and that the discount rate is 12%. **Table 4** at the back of the book indicates the factor for the present value of an annuity for 20 years at 12% is 7.46944. The estimated value of the brand is therefore $195 million (= $26.1 × 7.46944). These examples indicate that the value of brand names is sensitive to the discount rate and expected period of benefit.

    Ross Laboratories sells various formulations of infant baby food around the world under the brand name Similac. In a recent year, worldwide sales less operating expenses were $600 million. Ross Laboratories employed $500 million of physical capital to produce and sell this food. Estimate the fair value of the Similac brand assuming the following:

    a. Ross Laboratories charges 10%, before taxes, for physical capital, pays income taxes at the rate of 40% of pretax income, and uses a capitalization factor of 17.

    b. Ross Laboratories charges 20%, before taxes, for physical capital, pays income taxes at the rate of 40% of pretax income, and uses a capitalization factor of 8.

EXHIBIT 9.9	**Illustration of Steps to Estimate the Value of a Brand Name** (all dollar amounts in millions) (Problem 9.36)

Worldwide Sales of Branded Product for Next Year	$312.7
Cost of Goods Sold and Operating Expenses	(248.6)
[1] Operating Margin	$ 64.1
[2] Subtract Return Required on Physical Capital Employed: .12 × $188.1	(22.6)
Pretax Profit Generated by Brand Name	$ 41.5
[3] Subtract Income Taxes at 37%	(15.4)
Net Brand Name Profit	$ 26.1
[4] Multiply by After-Tax Capitalization Factor	× 8.33
Estimated Brand Value	$217.4

Notes, Bonds, and Leases

10

L E A R N I N G
O B J E C T I V E S

1. Develop the skills to compute the issue price, carrying value, and current fair value of notes and bonds payable in an amount equal to the present value of the future contractual cash flows by applying the appropriate discount rate.

2. Understand the effective interest method, and apply it to debt amortization.

3. Understand the application of the fair value option to financial liabilities.

4. Develop an ability to distinguish between capital or finance leases and operating leases based on their economic characteristics, accounting criteria, and financial statement effects.

5. Develop the skills to account for capital or finance leases and operating leases.

Chapter 8 indicated that firms typically finance current operating assets, such as accounts receivable and inventories, with short-term borrowing or trade credit (delayed payments to suppliers). Firms use the cash received from customers within the next several months to repay short-term lenders and suppliers. Firms typically finance long-term assets, particularly property, plant, and equipment, with long-term borrowing or funds provided directly or indirectly by shareholders. This chapter discusses the accounting for long-term borrowing arrangements (that is, those requiring repayment later than one year from the date of the balance sheet).

The more long-term debt in a firm's capital structure, the greater the risk that the firm will experience difficulty making the required payments when due and, therefore, the greater is the risk of default or bankruptcy. Financial analysts use several financial statement ratios to assess risk related to long-term borrowing. One financial ratio is the long-term debt ratio. This ratio relates the amount of long-term debt to the amount of total financing.

$$\text{Long-Term Debt Ratio} = \frac{\text{Long-Term Debt}}{\text{Liabilities} + \text{Shareholders' Equity}}$$

The debt-equity ratio relates long-term debt to shareholders' equity,[1] indicating the relative mix of long-term financing obtained from lenders versus owners.

$$\text{Debt-Equity Ratio} = \frac{\text{Long-Term Debt}}{\text{Shareholders' Equity}}$$

---

[1]In classic usage, the word *equity* refers to any item on the right-hand side of the balance sheet—any source of funding for a firm. Modern business usage has come to restrict the word *equity* to mean only shareholders' equity, both contributed capital and retained earnings. Still, current usage is sufficiently diverse that you should understand the meaning others have in mind when they use it.

EXHIBIT 10.1   Debt Ratios for Four Firms

Firm	Long-Term Debt Ratio	Debt-Equity Ratio	Property, Plant, and Equipment/Total Assets
Tokyo Electric	43.4%	193.5%	81.5%
Boise Cascade	44.9%	59.1%	54.1%
WPP Group	8.3%	24.1%	2.8%
Intel	3.8%	5.0%	36.4%

Exhibit 10.1 presents these two debt ratios, as well as the ratio of property, plant, and equipment to total assets, for four firms in different industries. We use these ratios to assess the relations among a firm's industry economic characteristics; its use of property, plant, and equipment; and its use of long-term debt financing.

Tokyo Electric Tokyo Electric is a regulated monopoly providing electric services in Japan. Property, plant, and equipment dominate the asset side of the balance sheet. It relies more on long-term debt than shareholders' equity to finance these facilities (as a debt-equity ratio exceeding 100% indicates). The regulated monopoly status practically eliminates the risk of default or bankruptcy, so Tokyo Electric faces a relatively low borrowing cost. Its production and transmission facilities also serve as collateral for the debt, meaning that lenders can sell the facilities and use the cash proceeds to repay the debt in the event Tokyo Electric does not do so.

Boise Cascade Boise Cascade, a United States-based company, processes wood pulp into paper products in fixed-asset intensive facilities. It has the second largest ratio of property, plant, and equipment to total assets and the second largest debt-equity ratio of the four firms. Boise Cascade carries higher levels of risk than Tokyo Electric. First, Boise Cascade does not have the regulated, monopoly status of Tokyo Electric. Thus, market forces and not regulation set the prices for its products. Second, the sales of Boise Cascade are more sensitive to changes in the level of business activity than those of Tokyo Electric. Third, Boise Cascade has fewer assets to serve as collateral for borrowing. The higher risk of Boise Cascade raises its borrowing costs and decreases its reliance on debt financing.

WPP Group WPP Group is a United Kingdom-based communication services firm whose employees provide advertising, market research, public relations, and other services worldwide. Other than relatively small amounts of equipment, it owns virtually no property, plant, and equipment (it leases most of its office space). Of the four firms considered in this example, it exhibits the lowest fixed asset intensity and the second lowest debt-equity ratio. WPP Group creates value from employees' services, not from operating assets, so there is neither the need nor the ability to borrow long-term using property, plant, and equipment as collateral.

Intel Intel is a United States-based designer and manufacturer of semiconductors. It manufactures semiconductors in fixed-asset intensive plants. The moderate fraction of its total assets that are property, plant, and equipment results from depreciating its technology-intensive manufacturing facilities over periods as short as four years. Intel has the smallest long-term debt and debt-equity ratios of the four firms in this example. There are at least two reasons for this relatively low reliance on debt financing. First, Intel is exceptionally profitable and therefore generates funds from operations. Second, Intel incurs substantial technology risk from product obsolescence, with product life cycles of less than two years. Heavy reliance on debt financing would add financing risk and thereby increase borrowing costs even more.

These examples illustrate the importance of understanding a firm's industry economic characteristics when analyzing long-term debt and assessing risk. This chapter discusses the recognition and measurement of long-term debt. Which obligations of a firm do U.S. GAAP and IFRS recognize as long-term debt? How do U.S. GAAP and IFRS measure the amount that firms report as debt on the balance sheet? With a few exceptions, the accounting for debt under U.S. GAAP and IFRS is similar. We consider notes, bonds, and leases in this chapter. The next section discusses notes and bonds. A later section discusses leases.

OVERVIEW OF LONG-TERM DEBT MARKETS

This section provides a brief description of debt markets to enhance understanding of the accounting for long-term debt discussed in later sections. Debt markets have a unique vocabulary, so be prepared to encounter new terms.

SOURCES OF LONG-TERM DEBT FINANCING

Firms that need cash for long-term purposes, such as acquiring buildings and equipment or financing a business acquisition, and that wish to use debt as a means of obtaining cash, will do one of two things:

1. Borrow from commercial banks, insurance companies, or other financial institutions.
2. Issue bonds in the capital markets.

Loans from commercial banks and other financial institutions often require firms to pledge assets as collateral. For example, a firm borrowing to finance the acquisition of equipment would likely pledge the equipment as collateral. If the firm fails to maintain specified levels of financial health while the loan is outstanding or does not pay principal and interest on the loan when due, the lender has the right to seize the collateral and sell it to satisfy the amounts due. Common terminology refers to the financial contract underlying bank loans as a **note**, so that these loans usually appear on the balance sheet under the title **Notes Payable**. Notes of business firms generally have maturity dates less than approximately ten years and arise from borrowing from a single lender. Borrowing from a single lender avoids some of the reporting requirements of more public issues of debt. However, no public market for the debt exists in this case, so the borrower will have difficulty disengaging from the borrowing arrangement prior to maturity.

Most firms issue **bonds** on the market to satisfy their long-term needs for cash. A bond is a financial contract, similar in concept to borrowing agreements with banks or insurance companies, in which the borrower and the lender agree to certain conditions about repayment of the bonds, operating policies, other borrowing activities while the bonds are outstanding, and other provisions. **Bond indenture** refers to the financial contract underlying bonds. Bonds appear on the balance sheet under the title **Bonds Payable**. In contrast to notes, bonds typically carry maturity dates longer than approximately ten years and involve many lenders instead of a single lender. Firms classify the portion of bonds due within the next year as a current liability and the remaining portion as a noncurrent liability. Firms must also disclose a list of their long-term debt obligations in notes to the financial statements.

VARIETY OF BOND PROVISIONS

Bond issues vary with respect to their specific provisions. For example, particular collateral might back up bonds (a secured borrowing), or firms might issue bonds based only on their credit worthiness as an entity. Such **unsecured borrowing** means that lenders must rely on assets not pledged as collateral for other loans in the event the firm cannot repay the bonds. Unsecured borrowing might carry **senior rights** or **subordinated rights** in the event of bankruptcy. Senior debt holders have a higher priority for payment in the event of bankruptcy than subordinated (junior) unsecured lenders.

Bonds also vary in terms of their payment provisions. The typical **debenture bond** pays interest periodically, usually every six months, during the life of the bond and repays the principal amount borrowed at maturity. A **serial bond** requires periodic payments of interest plus a portion of the principal throughout the life of the bond. A **zero coupon bond** provides for no periodic payments of interest while the bond is outstanding; the bond requires payment of all principal and interest at maturity. A later section defines *principal* and *interest* more precisely.

Convertible bonds permit the holder to exchange the bonds for shares of the firm's common stock under certain conditions. This conversion option has value because the holder can benefit from some of the later increases in the market value of the firm's common stock after issuance of the bonds. If holders do not convert the bonds into common stock prior to maturity, the issuing firm repays the debt at maturity, the same as for nonconvertible bonds. We discuss convertible bonds more fully in **Chapter 14**.

Some bonds are **callable**, which means the issuing firm has the right to repurchase the bonds prior to maturity at a specified price. An issuing firm might exercise this call provision if interest rates decline after the initial issuance of the bonds. The firm can borrow at the lower interest rate and use the proceeds to finance the repurchase of the bonds initially issued.

Investors in bonds sometimes hold a **put option**, meaning they can force the issuing company to repay the bonds prior to maturity under specified contractual conditions. Investors might exercise this put option if interest rates increase, and investors can reinvest the cash proceeds in debt securities with a higher yield.

Bonds can carry either **fixed interest rates** or **variable interest rates**. Bonds with fixed interest rates pay interest at that fixed rate throughout the life of the bond. Bonds with variable interest rates pay interest at rates that change during the life of the bond. The bond indenture specifies the formula for the periodic calculation of the variable interest rate.

Industry economic characteristics, the financial health of a firm, and the particular provisions of a bond issue combine to determine the risk of investing in the bond, which in turn affects the interest rate investors demand and therefore the bond's price. The next section discusses the measurement of financial instruments in general. Subsequent sections discuss the measurement of notes, bonds, and leases. To understand the calculations illustrated in the remainder of this chapter, you will need to understand compound interest and its use in computing the **present value of future cash flows**. The **Appendix** at the back of the book discusses compound interest.

MEASUREMENT OF FINANCIAL INSTRUMENTS: GENERAL PRINCIPLES

We use the term **financial instrument** to refer to a financial arrangement in which a firm contracts to receive or make specified payments in the future in return for cash or other resources paid or received currently. Notes, bonds, and leases are financial instruments. Derivatives, discussed in **Chapter 12**, are also financial instruments. A characteristic of these examples of financial instruments is that they specify the means of calculating the amounts that firms will receive or pay at specified times in the future.

The accounting measurement of notes and bonds payable follows two general principles:

1. The amount borrowed initially and the market value of a note or bond at any date subsequent to the initial borrowing equals the present value of the future, or remaining, cash flows discounted at an appropriate interest rate (discussed next).

2. The **internal rate of return**, often called **yield to maturity**, is the discount rate that equates the future cash flows to the market value at any date. Common terminology also refers to this rate as the **market interest rate**. When a financial instrument does not specify the internal rate of return, the investor can solve for this rate, called the **implicit interest rate**, following procedures described in the **Appendix**. On the date of initial issuance, the market value will equal the initial issue proceeds—the amount borrowed. To understand the accounting for notes and bonds, we need two additional definitions:

   - **Historical Market Interest Rate**: The discount rate prevailing at the date of the initial borrowing. Discounting the contractual cash flows at this rate equates the present value of future cash flows to the amount initially borrowed—the market value on the initial issue date.

   - **Current Market Interest Rate**: The discount rate at any date subsequent to the date of the initial borrowing. Discounting the contractual cash flows at this rate equates the present value of remaining cash flows to the market value at the subsequent measurement date.

Later sections of this chapter indicate that U.S. GAAP and IFRS permit firms to account for notes and bonds under one of two approaches:

1. **Amortized Cost** Use the historical market interest rate to compute the carrying value of notes and bonds while these obligations are outstanding and disclose in the notes to the financial statements the fair value of these financial instruments based on the current

market interest rate. This approach dominates current financial reporting, so this chapter focuses on it.

2. **Fair Value**   Measure notes and bonds at fair value each period, in effect using the current market interest rate instead of the historical market interest rate to discount the remaining cash flows. The FASB and the IASB refer to this approach as the **fair value option**.[2] A later section of this chapter describes and illustrates the fair value option.

ACCOUNTING FOR NOTES

Firms typically borrow from banks, insurance companies, and other financial institutions by signing a note, which specifies the terms of the borrowing arrangement.

Example 1   Newsom Company borrows $800,000 from its bank to purchase a tract of land on January 1, 2008. The firm pledges the land as collateral for the loan. Interest accrues on the unpaid balance of the loan at a rate of 6% compounded semiannually (that is, 3% each six months). The borrower must make payments of $93,784.41 on June 30 and December 31 of each year for five years.[3]

Initial Valuation   The initial valuation of this loan is the $800,000 amount borrowed. This amount equals the present value of the future cash payments discounted at the yield required by the lender, which we assume is also 6% compounded semiannually (final calculations taken to more decimal points than shown):[4]

Present Value of an Annuity of $93,784.41 per Period for 10 Periods at

   3% per Period: $93,784.41 × 8.53020. . . . . $800,000.00

These calculations illustrate an important concept: *When the stated interest rate for a loan (6% compounded semiannually in this example) equals the yield required by the lender (also 6% compounded semiannually), then the amount borrowed equals the principal amount of the loan (also called the* face value *in the case of bonds).* The significance of this concept will become more apparent when we consider how to measure the carrying value of bonds.

The entries to record the loan and the purchase of land on the books of Newsom Company are as follows:

January 1, 2008

Cash.	800,000	
Note Payable		800,000

Assets	=	Liabilities	+	Shareholders' Equity	(Class.)
+800,000		+800,000			

To record $800,000 loan received from bank for five years at 6% compounded semiannually requiring payments of $93,784.41 at the end of each six months.

---

[2]Financial Accounting Standards Board, *Statement of Financial Accounting Standards No. 159,* "The Fair Value Option for Financial Assets and Financial Liabilities," 2007 (**Codification Topic 825**); International Accounting Standards Board, *International Accounting Standard 39,* "Financial Instruments: Recognition and Measurement," 1999, revised 2003.

[3]**Example 9** in the **Appendix** shows the derivation of the $93,784.41 payment.

[4]The illustrations in this chapter use present value factors using 15 significant digits in the computer, but rounded to five digits after the decimal for presentation here. The **Appendix** illustrates the use of Excel® to perform these calculations. The inputs into Excel for the present value of an annuity are =PV(interest rate, number of periods, periodic payment, future value, type). The inputs for this note are =PV(.03,10,93784.41,0,0), although Excel does not require the last two zeros.

January 1, 2008

| Land. . . . . | | | 800,000 | |
| Cash. . . . . | | | | 800,000 |

Assets	=	Liabilities	+	Shareholders' Equity	(Class.)
+800,000					
−800,000					

To record the purchase of land for $800,000 cash.

Measurement Subsequent to the Date of the Initial Loan

During the first six months, interest of $24,000 (= .03 × $800,000) accrues on the loan. The firm then makes the required cash payment of $93,784.41. The entry to record interest expense, the loan payment, and the reduction in the amount of the Note Payable is as follows:

June 30, 2008

Interest Expense	24,000.00	
Note Payable	69,784.41	
Cash.		93,784.41

Assets	=	Liabilities	+	Shareholders' Equity	(Class.)
−93,784.41		−69,784.41		−24,000	IncSt → RE

To record interest expense, cash payment, and reduction in Note Payable for first six months.

Thus, the carrying value of the loan changes during this first six months as follows:

Balance in Note Payable on January 1, 2008	$800,000.00
Plus Interest for First Six Months: .03 × $800,000	24,000.00
Less Cash Payment on June 30, 2008	(93,784.41)
Balance in Note Payable on June 30, 2008	$730,215.59

The carrying value of the loan on June 30, 2008, equals the present value of the *remaining* cash flows discounted at 6% compounded semiannually (except for minor rounding differences), as the following computations show:

Present Value of an Annuity of $93,784.41 per Period for 9 Periods at 3% per Period: $93,784.41 × 7.78611.	$730,215.62

These calculations illustrate a second important concept: *The amount reported on the balance sheet throughout the life of a loan (that is, its carrying value) equals the present value of the remaining cash flows discounted at the historical market interest rate (6% compounded semiannually in this example). The current market interest rate usually differs from the historical market interest rate during the life of the loan. A firm that does not account for long-term notes and bonds using the fair value option (discussed later), uses the historical market interest rate to account for the loan while it is outstanding.*

Amortization Schedule

Exhibit 10.2 presents an **amortization schedule** for this loan. It shows the amount of interest expense and cash payments each six months and the resulting reduction in the carrying value of the loan during the ten periods. The interest expense equals the required yield (3% each six months) times the unpaid balance of the loan at the beginning of each six-month period. Common terminology refers to the calculations illustrated in **Exhibit 10.2** for amortizing a financial instrument to its maturity value over time as the **effective interest method**. The effective interest method has the following features:

1. The note, bond, or other financial instrument will appear on the balance sheet both initially and at each subsequent date at the present value of the remaining cash flows discounted at the historical market interest rate (that is, its initial yield to maturity).

	Amortization Schedule for $800,000 Loan, Repaid
EXHIBIT 10.2	**in 10 Semiannual Installments of $93,784.41.** **Interest Rate Is 6% Compounded Semiannually** **(3% compounded each six months)**

Period (1)	Balance at Beginning of Period (2)	Interest Expense for Period (3)	Cash Payment (4)	Portion of Payment Reducing Principal (5)	Balance at End of Period (6)
1	$800,000.00	$24,000.00	$93,784.41	($69,784.41)	$730,215.59
2	$730,215.59	$21,906.47	$93,784.41	($71,877.94)	$658,337.65
3	$658,337.65	$19,750.13	$93,784.41	($74,034.28)	$584,303.37
4	$584,303.37	$17,529.10	$93,784.41	($76,255.31)	$508,048.06
5	$508,048.06	$15,241.44	$93,784.41	($78,542.97)	$429,505.09
6	$429,505.09	$12,885.15	$93,784.41	($80,899.26)	$348,605.83
7	$348,605.83	$10,458.17	$93,784.41	($83,326.24)	$265,279.60
8	$265,279.60	$ 7,958.39	$93,784.41	($85,826.02)	$179,453.58
9	$179,453.58	$ 5,383.61	$93,784.41	($88,400.80)	$ 91,052.77
10	$ 91,052.77	$ 2,731.64	$93,784.41	($91,052.77)	0

Column (2) = Column (6) from previous period.

Column (3) = .03 × Column (2), except for period 10, where it is the amount such that
       Column (3) = Column (4) − Column (5).

Column (4) is given.

Column (5) = Column (4) − Column (3).

Column (6) = Column (2) − Column (5).

2. The amount of interest expense each period equals the historical market interest rate times the carrying value of the financial instrument at the beginning of each period.

We can illustrate again the general principal that the carrying value of this loan at the end of any period equals the present value of the remaining cash flows. Take, for example, the loan balance of $265,279.60 at the end of Period 7. At the end of Period 7, three semiannual payments of $93,784.41 remain (for Periods 8, 9, and 10). Following is the present value of these cash flows:

Present Value of an Annuity of $93,784.41 per Period for 3 Periods at
   3% per Period: $93,784.41 × 2.82861 . . . . $265,279.64

As before, minor differences in measurement arise because of rounding.

The carrying value of the note changes each period, increasing to reflect the nearer in time of all remaining cash flows and decreasing for the payment of interest and principal. This pattern appears in **Exhibit 10.3**.

PROBLEM 10.1 for Self-Study

Implicit interest rate and amortization schedule for interest-bearing note. Vera Company receives cash of $97,375.69 in return for a three-year $100,000 note, promising to pay $6,000 at the end of one year, $6,000 at the end of two years, and $106,000 at the end of three years.

a. Demonstrate that the required yield, or implicit interest rate, on this loan is 7% compounded annually.

b. Prepare an amortization schedule for this loan similar to that in Exhibit 10.2.

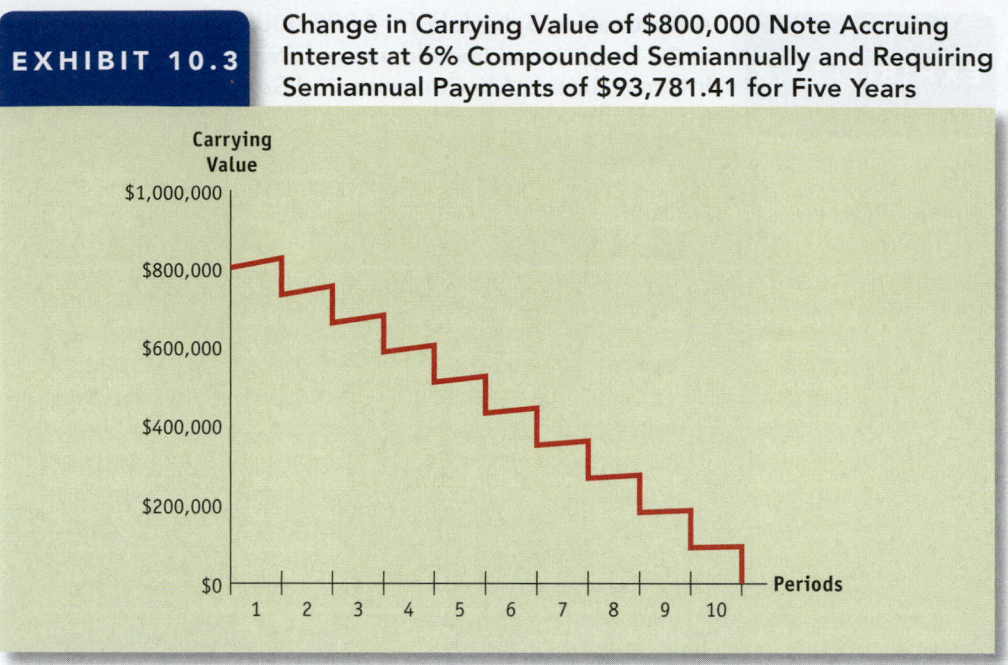

EXHIBIT 10.3 Change in Carrying Value of $800,000 Note Accruing Interest at 6% Compounded Semiannually and Requiring Semiannual Payments of $93,781.41 for Five Years

 # ACCOUNTING FOR BONDS

Firms typically issue bonds on the market to large numbers of debt investors to obtain cash for long-term purposes. As previously explained, the provisions of bond issues vary widely, depending on the firm's cash needs over time and the preferences of investors in the bonds. Investment bankers often advise corporate borrowers on the sorts of financial instruments the lending market appears to prefer at the time the firm wants to borrow.

CASH FLOW PATTERNS FOR BONDS

Bonds vary with respect to the pattern of cash payments made by the borrower to debt investors. Three common types of bonds are coupon bonds, serial bonds, and zero coupon bonds.

Example 2 Ford Motor Company issues $250 million of 8%, semiannual, 20-year coupon bonds. The bond indenture requires Ford to make coupon payments of $10 million (= .08 × $250 million × 6/12) every six months for 20 years and to repay the $250 million principal at the end of 20 years. Common terminology refers to the $250 million as the **principal** or **face value** of the bond and the 8% rate as the **coupon interest rate**. In this case the $250 million is also the **maturity value** of the bonds. The term *face value* refers to the principal amount printed on the face of the bond certificate. The principal or face value is the base for computing the amount of each semiannual coupon payment.[5] At one time the bond certificate would have coupons attached, with each coupon equal to 4% of the principal amount and each dated, with dates six months apart. Investors would clip the predated coupons from the bond certificate each six months and deposit them in their bank accounts, just as they would deposit a check they had received. Although checks or electronic funds transfers have replaced coupons, the term *coupon* remains in use. Thus, the 8% coupon rate multiplied times the $250 million principal equals the annual cash payment of $20 million, which Ford pays in two semiannual installments of $10 million each.

---

[5]Almost everyone in business refers to the periodic payment as "interest payments." The term causes confusion because, as you will soon see, the amount of interest expense for a period almost never equals the amount of these same payments for that same period. The periodic payment will always include some amount to pay interest to the lender, but not necessarily all interest accrued since the last payment. If the payment exceeds all interest, then the payment will discharge some of the principal amount. Both payment of interest and payment of principal serve to reduce the debt, so one all-purpose term used for the payments is *debt service payments*.

Example 3 Chrysler Corporation issues $180 million of 15-year serial bonds. The bond indenture requires Chrysler to pay $10,409,418 every six months for 15 years. Each periodic payment includes interest plus repayment of a portion of the principal. The principal or face value of this bond is $180 million. This bond does not specify a stated interest rate, but each payment includes implicit interest. We discuss serial bonds more fully later in this chapter.

Example 4 General Motors Corporation issues $300 million of 10-year zero coupon bonds. These bonds do not require periodic payments of interest. Instead the $300 million maturity value includes both principal and interest. Although these bonds do not state an interest rate, there is an implicit interest rate embedded in the maturity value. We consider zero coupon bonds in greater depth later in this chapter.

REVIEW OF BOND TERMINOLOGY

Let's take a moment to review to this point:

1. The bond contract specifies the basis for computing all future cash flows for that bond issue. Identifying those cash flows is the starting point to account for the bond both initially and at each subsequent measurement date.

2. Terminology with respect to bonds includes the following:
   a. **Face Value**: The amount printed on the face of the bond certificate that serves as the basis for computing periodic coupon payments on coupon bonds.[6] The face value equals the maturity value on coupon bonds and on zero coupon bonds but not on serial bonds.
   b. **Principal**: The same as face value on coupon bonds and serial bonds but not on zero coupon bonds.
   c. **Maturity Value**: The amount paid by the issuer at the maturity date of bonds. The maturity value equals the face value on coupon bonds and on zero coupon bonds.
   d. **Market Value**: The amount at which bonds sell in the market either at date of issue or at any subsequent date while the bonds are outstanding. Firms that account for bonds using the fair value option, discussed in a later section, can use market value to measure fair value.
   e. **Coupon Interest Rate**: The interest rate stated in the bond contract that when multiplied times the face value or principal amount of coupon bonds equals the required annual cash payment. The stated coupon rate is always an annual rate. The issuer might pay this required annual amount in more than one installment during the year, typically semiannually. For example, if the coupon rate is 6% payable semiannually, the issuer pays interest of 3% every six months. The frequency of payment affects the yield on the bond and the amortization calculations. The coupon rate need not equal the historical market interest rate, a possibility we discuss more fully later in the chapter.
   f. **Historical Market Interest Rate or Initial Yield to Maturity**: The interest rate that discounts all future cash flows such that their present value equals the initial issue price of the bond.
   g. **Current Market Interest Rate**: The interest rate that discounts all future cash flows such that their present value equals the current market price of the bond.

INITIAL MEASUREMENT OF BONDS

The initial issue price of a bond depends on two factors:

1. The promised cash payments indicated in the bond contract as discussed in the preceding section.
2. The yield to maturity required by investors to induce them to purchase the bonds, which the next section discusses and illustrates.

---

[6]Common terminology also refers to the face value of bonds as *par value*. To reduce ambiguity, we use face value in reference to bonds and par value in reference to common and preferred shares in this book.

Example 2 (continued) The bonds of Ford in **Example 2** require Ford to pay $10 million at the end of every six months and to repay the $250 million principal at the end of 20 years. The time line (see **Appendix** for description of time lines) for this semiannual coupon bond covers 40 six-month periods as depicted in the following graph (amounts in millions):

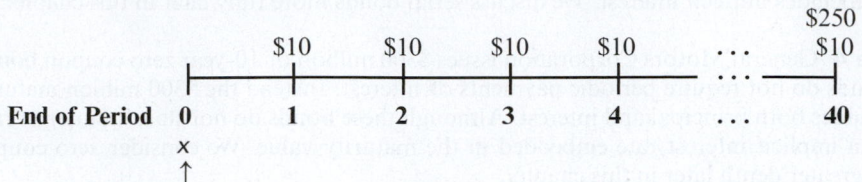

Assume that the market requires a yield to maturity for the bonds of Ford of 8% compounded semiannually. Thus, the initial issue price for these bonds is $250 million, computed as follows (calculations based on spreadsheet computational accuracy, then rounded to the nearest dollar):

Present Value of an Annuity of $10 million for 40 Periods at
    4% per Period: $10 million × 19.79277 . . . . $197,927,739[7]

Present Value of $250 million for 40 Periods at 4% per Period:
    $250 million × .20829 . . . .   52,072,261[8]

Initial Issue Price . . . . $250,000,000[9]

Note the concept described earlier in **Example 1**: when the coupon rate equals the historical market interest rate or initial yield to maturity, then the initial issue price equals the face value of the bonds.

Example 3 (continued) Now consider the valuation of the serial bonds of Chrysler. Chrysler must pay $10,409,418 at the end of every six months for 15 years. The time line is as follows (amounts in millions):

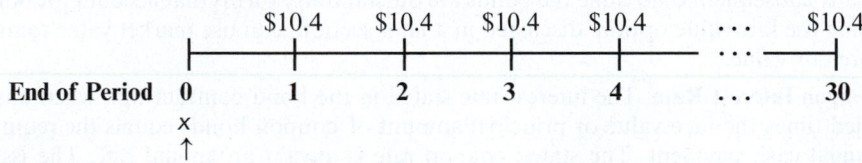

Assume that the market requires a yield to maturity of 8% compounded semiannually to induce investors to purchase these bonds. The computation of the initial issue price is as follows:

Present Value of an Annuity of $10,409,418 for 30 Periods at
    4% per Period: $10,409,418 × 17.29203 . . . . $180,000,000

An initial issue price equal to the face value of the bonds means that the implicit interest rate equals the yield to maturity.

Example 4 (continued) The bonds of General Motors require a payment of $300 million at the end of 10 years. The time line is as follows (amounts in millions):

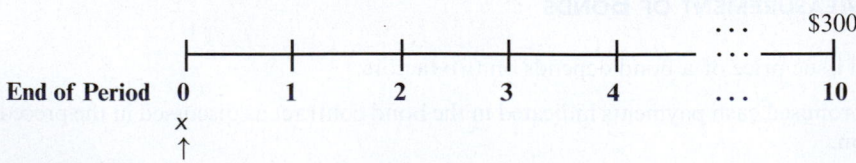

---

[7]The inputs in an Excel spreadsheet are =PV(.04,40,10000000,0,0).

[8]The inputs in an Excel spreadsheet are =PV(.04,40,0,250000000,0).

[9]The inputs in an Excel spreadsheet to solve simultaneously for the present value of the interest and principal payments are =PV(.04,40,10000000,250000000,0).

Assume that, like Ford and Chrysler, the market requires the bonds of General Motors to yield 8% compounded semiannually. The computation of the initial issue price is as follows:

Present Value of $300 million for 20 Periods at 4% per Period:
$300 million × .45639 .... $136,916,084

The face value and maturity value of the bonds exceed the issue price. The difference between the face value and the present value of $163,083,916 (= $300,000,000 − $136,916,084) represents interest on the $136,916,084 amount borrowed. To see this, note that the future value of $136,916,084 for 20 periods at 4% is $300,000,000 (= $136,916,084 × 2.19112). Bond investors pay General Motors $136,916,084 today for the right to receive $300,000,000 ten years from today. This calculation demonstrates that investors earn interest on the amounts invested, but they receive it all at maturity. The interest rate on zero coupon bonds is an implicit interest rate, because it is implied by the difference between the face amount paid at maturity and the initial issue price.

PROBLEM 10.2 for Self-Study

Amortization Schedules for Bonds

a. Using a spreadsheet program such as Excel, prepare amortization schedules such as that in Exhibit 10.2 for each of the three bond issues in Examples 2, 3 and 4 above.

b. Why does the amount of the coupon bond at the end of each six-month period continue to equal $250 million?

c. Why does the amount of the serial bond at the end of each six-month period decline to zero over the 15 years?

d. Why does the amount of the zero coupon bond increase to $300 million over the 10-year period?

Example 2 (continued) Extended for Bonds Issued for More or Less Than Face Value It is unusual that the coupon rate on a bond exactly equals the yield to maturity that debt investors require on the date of a new bond issue. Preparing a new bond issue for the market requires months of effort. Market interest rates will likely change between the time the issuing firm specifies the coupon rate in the bond contract and in other documents and the day when the firm issues the bond. The difference in rates is usually small (except for zero coupon bonds), but the accounting for the bond must address the differences. Whenever the coupon rate differs from the market-required yield to maturity, the issue price will differ from the face value of the bonds. The following generalizations apply:

1. When the market-required yield to maturity exceeds the coupon rate, the bonds initially sell for less than, or a **discount to**, **face value**.

2. When the market-required yield to maturity is less than the coupon rate, the bonds initially sell for more than, or a **premium to**, **face value**.

For example, assume that the market-required yield to maturity of the bonds of Ford is 10% compounded semiannually. The initial issue price is as follows:

Present Value of an Annuity of $10 million for 40 Periods at
5% per Period: $10 million × 17.15909 .... $171,590,860
Present Value of $250 million for 40 Periods at 5% per Period:
$250 × .14205 35,511,421
Initial Issue Price $207,102,281

If lenders paid the $250 million face value for Ford's bonds, they would realize a yield to maturity of 8%. Lenders who require a yield of 10% would not pay $250 million because the value of the promised payments discounted at 10% is only $207,102,281. The lack of investor demand for the bonds at this price results in a decline in the market price to $207,102,281, at which price the bonds provide the required yield to maturity of 10% compounded semiannually. The difference between the $207,102,281 initial issue price and the $250,000,000 maturity value represents additional interest that Ford pays at maturity. Thus, total interest expense on this bond equals $442,897,719 [= ($10 million × 40) + ($250,000,000 − $207,102,281)]. The promised cash flows do not change; the bond contract specifies them. The only factor that changes is the required yield to maturity and thereby the initial issue price.

This example shows that when the yield that investors require (10% in this example) exceeds the stated coupon rate (8%), the bonds sell at a discount to face value. The difference between the proceeds and the face value compensates investors for the difference in interest rates. A zero coupon bond, such as that for General Motors in **Example 4**, is an extreme example of a bond issued at a discount. The coupon rate is zero, so the difference between the required yield and the coupon rate equals the required yield.

Let's examine what happens in the opposite case when the coupon rate exceeds the yield that investors require. Assume now that bond investors require a return of 6% compounded semiannually on Ford's bonds. The computation of the initial issue price is as follows:

Present Value of an Annuity of $10 million for 40 Periods at 3% per Period: $10 million × 23.11477	$231,147,720
Present Value of $250 million for 40 Periods at 3% per Period: $250 × .30656	76,639,211
Initial Issue Price	$307,786,931

If investors paid $250 million for this bond issue, they would realize a yield to maturity of 8% compounded semiannually. If investors require a yield of 6% compounded semiannually, competition among investors to purchase the bonds would force the market price of the bonds up to $307,786,931. At this point the yield to maturity will equal the 6% compounded semiannually required by the market. The difference between the $307,786,931 cash proceeds at issuance and the $250,000,000 paid at maturity represents a reduction in interest expense. Thus, total interest expense over the life of the bonds equals $342,213,069 [= ($10 million × 40) − ($307,786,931 − $250,000,000)]. As before, the contractual cash flows do not change; only the yield required by the market changes and thereby the initial issue price.

As a practical matter, one would not expect to encounter coupon rates that differ by 2 percentage points (referred to as *200 basis points*) from the yield to maturity (except in the case of zero coupon bonds). Thus, discounts and premiums encountered in practice seldom differ from the face value as much as these examples indicate.

PROBLEM 10.3 for Self-Study

Amortization Schedules for Bonds Issued at a Discount and a Premium

a. Using a spreadsheet program such as Excel, prepare amortization schedules similar to those in **Exhibit 10.2** for the bonds of Ford issued as a discount and issued at a premium using the initial issue prices shown above.

b. Does the additional interest expense for bonds issued at a discount and the reduction in interest expense for bonds issued at a premium affect the amount of interest expense each period or only in the 40th period? Explain.

JOURNAL ENTRIES TO ACCOUNT FOR BONDS

The entries to account for bonds resemble those illustrated previously for notes. The carrying value of bonds increases each period for interest and decreases for any cash payments made.

Bonds Issued for Less Than Face Value Consider **Example 2** discussed previously where Ford issues 20-year, 8% bonds for less than face value to yield 10% compounded semiannually. The entries at the time of issue and for the first two six-month periods are as follows:

January 1, 2008

Cash...	207,102,281	
Bonds Payable		207,102,281

Assets	=	Liabilities	+	Shareholders' Equity	(Class.)
+207,102,281		+207,102,281			

To record the issue of $250 million face value, 8% semiannual coupon bonds priced on the market to yield 10% compounded semiannually.

June 30, 2008

Interest Expense	10,355,114	
Bonds Payable		355,114
Cash..		10,000,000

Assets	=	Liabilities	+	Shareholders' Equity	(Class.)
−10,000,000		+355,114		−10,355,114	IncSt → RE

To record interest expense of $10,355,114 (=.05 × $207,102,281), a cash payment of $10,000,000, and an increase in the carrying value of the bond for the difference. The carrying value of the bond at the end of the first six-month period is $207,457,395 (= $207,102,281 + $10,355,114 − $10,000,000).

Following is the entry for the second six months:

December 31, 2008

Interest Expense	10,372,870	
Bonds Payable		372,870
Cash..		10,000,000

Assets	=	Liabilities	+	Shareholders' Equity	(Class.)
−10,000,000		+372,870		−10,372,870	IncSt → RE

To record interest expense of $10,372,870 (=.05 × $207,457,395), a cash payment of $10,000,000, and an increase in the carrying value of the bond for the difference. The carrying value of the bond at the end of the second six-month period is $207,830,265 (= $207,457,395 + $10,372,870 − $10,000,000).

Interest expense each period exceeds the cash payment of $10 million. The additional amount of interest expense of $372,870 in the second six-month period represents amortization, using the effective interest method, of the difference between the initial issue price of $207,102,281 and the $250,000,000 maturity value. Interest expense increases each period because the carrying value of the liability at the beginning of each period, the base for computing interest expense, increases.

Bonds Issued for More Than Face Value Consider now the entries if Ford issues the bonds for more than face value to yield 6%, compounded semiannually. The entries at the time of issue and for the first two six-month periods are as follows:

January 1, 2008

Cash...	307,786,931	
Bonds Payable		307,786,931

Assets	=	Liabilities	+	Shareholders' Equity	(Class.)
+307,786,931		+307,786,931			

To record the issue of $250 million face value, 8% semiannual coupon bonds priced on the market to yield 6% compounded semiannually.

June 30, 2008

Interest Expense	9,233,608	
Bonds Payable	766,392	
Cash		10,000,000

Assets	=	Liabilities	+	Shareholders' Equity	(Class.)
−10,000,000		−766,392		−9,233,608	IncSt → RE

To record interest expense of $9,233,608 (=.03 × $307,786,931), a cash payment of $10,000,000, and a decrease in the carrying value of the bond for the difference. The carrying value of the bond at the end of the first six-month period is $307,020,539 (= $307,786,931 + $9,233,608 − $10,000,000).

Following is the entry for the second six months:

December 31, 2008

Interest Expense	9,210,616	
Bonds Payable	789,384	
Cash		10,000,000

Assets	=	Liabilities	+	Shareholders' Equity	(Class.)
−10,000,000		−789,384		−9,210,616	IncSt → RE

To record interest expense of $9,210,616 (=.03 × $307,020,539), a cash payment of $10,000,000, and a decrease in the carrying value of the bond for the difference. The carrying value of the bond at the end of the second six-month period is $306,231,155 (= $307,020,539 + $9,210,616 − $10,000,000).

Interest expense each period is less than the $10 million cash payment. The reduction in the amount of interest expense represents amortization, using the effective interest method, of the difference between the initial cash proceeds of $307,786,931 and the $250,000,000 maturity value. Interest expense decreases each period as the carrying value of the liability at the beginning of each period decreases.

RETIREMENT OF DEBT

Many bonds remain outstanding until the stated maturity date. Refer to the amortization table for Ford's bonds issued for less than face value in the solution to **Problem 10.2 for Self-Study**. The entries for the 40th six-month period are as follows:

December 31, 2027

Interest Expense	12,380,973	
Bonds Payable		2,380,973
Cash		10,000,000

Assets	=	Liabilities	+	Shareholders' Equity	(Class.)
−10,000,000		+2,380,973		−12,380,973	IncSt → RE

To record interest expense of $12,380,973 [= (.05 × $247,619,027) + $22 for rounding], a cash payment of $10,000,000, and an increase in the carrying value of the bond for the difference. The carrying value of the bond at the end of the 40th six-month period is $250,000,000 (= $247,619,027 + $12,380,973 − $10,000,000).

Following is the entry to repay the principal amount of the bonds at maturity:

December 31, 2027

Bonds Payable		250,000,000	
Cash			250,000,000

Assets	=	Liabilities	+	Shareholders' Equity	(Class.)
−250,000,000		−250,000,000			

To record repayment of bonds at maturity.

Firms sometimes reacquire their bonds on the open market before maturity (referred to as *early retirement* or *early extinguishment of debt*). Because interest rates change frequently, the market price will seldom equal the carrying value of the bonds. Assume, for example, that the bonds of Ford at the end of Period 30 trade on the market to yield 7% compounded semiannually. A current market interest rate of 7% implies a market price for the bonds of $260,395,757, as the following computations show:

Present Value of an Annuity of $10 million for 10 Periods at 3.5% per Period: $10 million × 8.31661	$ 83,166,053
Present Value of $250 million for 10 Periods at 3.5% per Period: $250 million × .70892	177,229,703
Market Price at the End of Period 30	$260,395,757

The carrying value of these bonds at the end of Period 30 is $230,695,649 (see the amortization table for Ford's bonds issued for less than face value in the solution to **Problem 10.3 for Self-Study**). Following is the entry to record the purchase for cash and retirement of these bonds at the end of Period 30:

December 30, 2022

Bonds Payable	230,695,649	
Loss on Retirement of Bonds	29,700,108	
Cash		260,395,757

Assets	=	Liabilities	+	Shareholders' Equity	(Class.)
−260,395,757		−230,695,649		−29,700,108	IncSt → RE

To purchase and retire bonds with a carrying value of $230,695,649 for $260,395,757 and record a loss on the retirement.

Ford incurs a loss on early retirement of these bonds because the current market price (that is, the price at which investors are willing to buy and sell the bonds) exceeds the carrying value of the bonds on Ford's balance sheet. The current market price is higher than the carrying value because the market interest rate on the bonds declined from 10% to 7% since Ford issued them. A decline in interest rates means that investors now own a bond that provides a 10% return when the market demands a return of only 7%. Investors will not sell a bond yielding 10% unless the borrower compensates the investor for the difference between the yield of 10% and the 7% yield the investor will earn from reinvesting the cash proceeds. In this case the amount of additional compensation is $29,700,108, or the difference between the market price of the bonds and their carrying value. At this price, investors are indifferent between holding the original 10% bonds and exchanging those bonds and reinvesting the proceeds in bonds yielding 7%.

DISCLOSURES OF CARRYING AND FAIR VALUES OF DEBT

Authoritative guidance requires firms that account for notes and bonds using the historical market interest rate to report the carrying values, or book values, on the balance sheet and

EXHIBIT 10.4	Target Corporation Disclosures of Long-Term Debt

The carrying value and maturities of our debt portfolio, including swap valuation adjustments for our fair value hedges, was as follows:

Debt Maturities

(dollars in millions)	February 2, 2008		February 3, 2007	
	Rate *(a)*	Balance	Rate *(a)*	Balance
Due fiscal 2007-2011	4.9%	$ 5,614	6.2%	$ 5,931
Due fiscal 2012-2016	4.9	3,893	5.4	2,302
Due fiscal 2017-2021	5.4	2,661	6.8	362
Due fiscal 2022-2026	8.7	64	8.7	64
Due fiscal 2027-2031	6.8	680	6.8	680
Due fiscal 2032-2037	6.8	4,051	6.3	551
Total notes and debentures *(b)*	5.5	16,963	6.1	9,890
Capital lease obligations		127		147
Less: amounts due within one year		(1,964)		(1,362)
Long-term debt		$15,126		$ 8,675

(a) Reflects the weighted average stated interest rate as of year-end, including the impact of interest rate swaps.
(b) The estimated fair value of total notes and debentures, excluding swap valuation adjustments, using a discounted cash flow analysis based on our incremental interest rates for similar types of financial instruments, was $17,117 million at February 2, 2008 and $10,058 million at February 3, 2007. See Note 20 for the estimated fair value of our interest rate swaps.

Required principal payments on notes and debentures over the next five years, excluding capital lease obligations and fair market value adjustments recorded in long-term debt, are as follows:

Required Principal Payments

(millions)	2008	2009	2010	2011	2012
Required principal payments	$1,951	$1,251	$2,236	$107	$2,251

Most of our long-term debt obligations contain covenants related to secured debt levels. In addition to a secured debt level covenant, our credit facility also contains a debt leverage covenant. We are, and expect to remain, in compliance with these covenants.

to disclose the fair value of these notes and bonds in notes to the financial statements.[10] The fair value of long-term debt is the amount the firm would have to pay to repurchase the debt on the market in an orderly transaction on the measurement date. The measurement date is typically the date of the balance sheet. The fair value of bonds traded in an active market is the market price of the bonds on that date. The fair value of bonds not actively traded is the present value of the contractual cash payments discounted at the interest rate a lender would require on the measurement date.

Exhibit 10.4 presents disclosures of long-term debt from the notes to the financial statements of Target Corporation, a retailer. Target Corporation combines notes and debentures (that is, bonds) and groups them by maturity dates. The firm also indicates the weighted average stated interest rate for each group of debt and for all of its long-term debt. (The stated interest rate is similar to the coupon rate and is not the required yield.) Note (b) indicates the fair value of this debt based on the present value of the contractual cash flows and the incremental borrowing rate of Target Corporation for similar debt. The carrying value of long-term notes and debentures of $16,963 million on February 2, 2008, is less than the fair value of $17,117 million (see Target Corporation's note (b) in **Exhibit 10.4**), suggesting that Target Corporation's borrowing costs have decreased, relative to the stated interest rates on existing

---

[10]Financial Accounting Standards Board, *Statement of Financial Accounting Standards No. 107,* "Disclosures about Fair Value of Financial Instruments," 1991 (**Codification Topic 825**); *Statement of Financial Accounting Standards No. 157,* "Fair Value Measurements," 2006 (**Codification Topic 820**); International Accounting Standards Board, *International Financial Reporting Standard 7,* "Financial Instruments: Disclosures," 2005.

debt. Target Corporation includes in long-term debt a minor amount of capital leases, a topic discussed later in this chapter. The note separates the amount of long-term debt that Target Corporation must pay within one year and includes the amount in the Current Liabilities section of the balance sheet using the label, current portion of long-term debt. Finally, Target Corporation shows the principal amount of long-term debt payable each year for the next five years to assist the analyst in projecting likely cash needs.

FAIR VALUE OPTION

An earlier section indicated that U.S. GAAP and IFRS allow firms to account for certain financial assets and certain financial liabilities, including notes and bonds, using either (1) amortized cost, with measurements based on the historical market interest rate, as illustrated in previous sections of this chapter, or (2) fair value, with measurements based on current market conditions, including the current market interest rate.[11] **Chapter 3** introduced fair value measurement. This section discusses fair value measurement in greater depth and discusses its implication for measuring financial assets and financial liabilities on the balance sheet and recognizing unrealized gains and losses from changes in fair value on the income statement. This discussion of the fair value option applies to other items discussed in later chapters as well, including investments in debt and equity securities and derivatives in **Chapter 12**.

Authoritative guidance has taken the position that measurements of financial assets and financial liabilities at fair value provide more relevant and reliable information than cost-based measurements. Accounting for notes and bonds using the historical market interest rate under the amortized cost approach is a cost-based approach. U.S. GAAP and IFRS already require firms to report certain financial instruments related to hedging activities at fair value,[12] a topic discussed in **Chapter 12**. Standard-setting bodies, however, are not yet prepared to require fair value measurement for all financial assets and financial liabilities. Thus, they view the option to account for selected financial assets and financial liabilities as an interim step toward reporting all financial instruments at fair value.

Firms can choose between fair value measurement and the amortized cost approach based on historical market interest rates on a case-by-case (instrument-by-instrument) basis. Firms make this choice when they first adopt the FASB *Statement No. 159* or *IAS 39* or when they subsequently acquire a financial asset or incur a financial liability. The choice to use the fair value option is generally irrevocable.

Statement No. 157[13] sets forth the requirements for measuring fair value. Perhaps because it views the fair value option as an interim step, the FASB did not provide detailed requirements for applying fair value measurements to the calculation of net income. A later section illustrates one possible way to calculate the income effects of notes and bonds under the fair value option.

Underlying Concepts for Fair Value Option

Fair value is the amount a firm would receive if it sold an asset or would pay if it transferred, or settled, a liability in an orderly transaction at the measurement date. Determining fair value

---

[11]Financial Accounting Standards Board, *Statement of Financial Accounting Standards No. 159,* "The Fair Value Option for Financial Assets and Financial Liabilities," 2007 (**Codification Topic 825**); International Accounting Standards Board, *International Accounting Standard 39,* "Financial Instruments: Recognition and Measurement," 1999, revised 2003.

[12]Financial Accounting Standards Board, *Statement of Financial Accounting Standards No. 133,* "Accounting for Derivative Instruments and Hedging Activities," 1998 (**Codification Topic 815**); International Accounting Standards Board, *International Accounting Standard 39,* "Financial Instruments: Recognition and Measurement."

[13]Financial Accounting Standards Board, *Statement of Financial Accounting Standards No. 157,* "Fair Value Measurements," 2006 (**Codification Topic 820**). IFRS contains no analogous guidance. As of the writing of this textbook, the IASB has undertaken a project that will analyze all the IFRS guidance that requires a fair value measurement to ascertain whether the guidance intended those measurements to be exit values (similar to the definition of fair value in U.S. GAAP). The IASB will also consider how IFRS should define fair value and will create a single source of measurement guidance. The IASB plans to complete this project in 2010. The IASB discusses the differences between fair value measurement in IFRS and U.S. GAAP in its Discussion Paper, *Fair Value Measurements,* issued in November 2006 and available on the IASB's Web site (*iasb .org.uk*).

rests on the assumption that the transaction would occur in the principal market for the asset or liability or, in the absence of a principal market, in the most advantageous market from the viewpoint of the reporting entity. Thus, a firm that normally obtains and repays long-term debt in public capital markets would measure fair value based on the amount it would pay to repay bonds in those markets. However, a firm that obtained long-term financing from both public capital markets and private placements with insurance companies could choose the market that would provide the most advantageous terms to settle the debt.

Measuring fair value also rests on the assumption that the market participants in the principal (or most advantageous) market are independent of the reporting entity, knowledgeable about the asset or liability, and willing and able to engage in a transaction with the reporting entity. Fair value must reflect assumptions that market participants, as opposed to the reporting entity, would make about the best use of a financial asset or the best terms for settling a financial liability. The best use for a financial asset might be to combine it with other assets, as when an automobile manufacturer uses customer financing, which generates receivables, to enhance sales of its automobiles. The best use for a financial asset might be as a stand-alone asset, as when an investment bank purchases and sells automotive receivables for profit.

Inputs to measuring fair value fall into three categories:

1. Level 1: Observable quoted market prices in active markets for identical assets or liabilities that the reporting entity is able to access at the measurement date.

2. Level 2: Observable inputs other than quoted market prices within Level 1. This category might include quoted prices for similar assets or liabilities in active markets or quoted market prices for identical assets or liability in markets that are not active. This category also includes observable factors that would be of particular relevance in using present values of cash flows to measure fair value, including interest rates, yield curves, foreign exchange rates, credit risks, and default rates.

3. Level 3: Unobservable inputs reflecting the reporting entity's own assumptions about the assumptions market participants would use in pricing an asset or settling a liability.

Firms should use Level 1 inputs if available to measure fair value, then Level 2 inputs, and finally Level 3 inputs.[14]

ILLUSTRATION OF FAIR VALUE OPTION

Refer to **Example 2** in which Ford issues $250 million face value of 8% semiannual coupon bonds. Assume as in the initial illustration that the market requires a yield of 8% compounded semiannually. Thus, Ford issues the bonds on January 1, 2008, for the $250 million face value. Interest expense for the first period is $10 million (= .08 × 1/2 × $250 million). The entry to record interest expense is the same as the one illustrated earlier:

June 30, 2008

Interest Expense	10,000,000	
Cash.		10,000,000

Assets	=	Liabilities	+	Shareholders' Equity	(Class.)
−10,000,000				−10,000,000	IncSt → RE

To record interest expense of $10,000,000 (= .04 × $250,000,000) and the required cash payment of $10,000,000. The carrying value of the bonds at the end of the first period is $250 million (= $250 million initial valuation + $10 million interest expense − $10 million cash payment).

Assume now that the market interest rate on these bonds at the end of the first period increases to 9%. The market price of the bonds decreases to $227,212,930 as the following computations show:

---

[14]For a discussion of the difficulties firms encounter in measuring fair values using Level 2 and Level 3 inputs, see Securities and Exchange Commission, "Report and Recommendations Pursuant to Section 133 of the Emergency Economic Stabilization Act of 2008: Study on Mark-to-Market Accounting."

Present Value of an Annuity of $10 million for 39 Periods at 4.5% per Period:	
$10 million × 18.22966	$182,296,557
Present Value of $250 million for 39 Periods at 4.5% per Period:	
$250 million × .17967	44,916,373
Present Value (Market Value) at End of Period 1	$227,212,930

For purposes of this illustration, assume that the market price of $227,212,930 is fair value. If Ford had elected the fair value option for this bond at the time of issue, Ford would now recognize an unrealized gain at the end of the first period of $22,787,070 (= $250,000,000 − $227,212,930), equal to the change in fair value during the period. Ford's entry to record the unrealized gain is as follows:

June 30, 2008

Bonds Payable	22,787,070	
Unrealized Gain from Remeasurement of Bonds		22,787,070

Assets	=	Liabilities	+	Shareholders' Equity	(Class.)
		−22,787,070		+22,787,070	IncSt → RE

To remeasure bonds from a carrying value of $250,000,000 to a fair value of $227,212,930 and recognize an unrealized gain of $22,787,070.

Ford would include the unrealized gain in net income for this first period.

Continuing this illustration, let's consider the second period. Interest expense for the second period based on the current market yield at the beginning of the period of 9% compounded semiannually is $10,224,582 (= .09 × 1/2 × $227,212,930). Following is the entry to record interest expense and the cash payment:

December 31, 2008

Interest Expense	10,224,582	
Cash..		10,000,000
Bonds Payable		224,582

Assets	=	Liabilities	+	Shareholders' Equity	(Class.)
−10,000,000		+224,582		−10,224,582	IncSt → RE

To record interest expense of $10,224,582 (= .045 × $227,212,930), the required cash payment of $10,000,000, and an increase in bonds payable for the difference. The carrying value of the bond at the end of the second period before revaluation to fair value is $227,437,512 (= $227,212,930 + $10,224,582 − $10,000,000).

Assume now that the yield required by the market on this bond decreases to 7% at the end of the second six months. The fair value of this bond increases to $276,051,359, as the following computations show:

Present Value of an Annuity of $10 million for 38 Periods at	
3.5% per Period: $10 million × 20.84109	$208,410,874
Present Value of $250 million for 38 Periods at 3.5% per Period:	
$250 million × .27056	67,640,485
Fair Value at End of Period 2	$276,051,359

Ford must now recognize an unrealized loss of $48,613,847, because the fair value of these bonds of $276,051,359 exceeds their carrying value of $227,437,512. The entry is as follows:

December 31, 2008

Unrealized Loss from Remeasurement of Bonds	48,613,847
Bonds Payable	48,613,847

Assets	=	Liabilities	+	Shareholders' Equity	(Class.)
		+48,613,847		−48,613,847	IncSt → RE

To remeasure bonds from a carrying value of $227,437,512 to a fair value of $276,051,359 and recognize an unrealized loss of $48,613,847.

The total of interest expense and unrealized gains and losses for 2008 is as follows:

Period	Interest Expense	Unrealized Gain (Loss)	Total
1	($10,000,000)	$22,787,070	$12,787,070
2	(10,224,582)	(48,613,847)	(58,838,429)
Total.	($20,224,582)	($25,826,777)	($46,051,359)

The effect on net income before taxes of −$46,051,359 equals the cash payments for interest of $20,000,000 (= $10,000,000 × 2) plus the −$26,051,359 increase in fair value of the debt from $250,000,000 at the beginning of the year to $276,051,359 at the end of the year. An increase (decrease) in the fair value of a *liability* implies an unrealized loss (gain).

The FASB stated that it would not specify how firms applying the fair value option should measure interest expense. An alternative to using the effective interest method illustrated above might be to set interest expense equal to the cash payments of $20,000,000. This approach would result in $224,582 (= $20,224,582 − $20,000,000) less interest expense, a $224,582 smaller carrying value of the bonds at the end of the second period before remeasurement, and a $224,582 larger unrealized loss. Thus, the effect on net income before taxes is the same regardless of the allocation between interest expense and net unrealized loss.

DISCLOSURES RELATED TO THE FAIR VALUE OPTION

Because the fair value option offers a free choice between measurement at fair value and measurement at amortized cost, firms will likely report some financial instruments using historical market interest rates (amortized cost measurement) and some using fair values. The disclosure requirements attempt to provide sufficient information to enable the user of the financial statements to understand the effect of this mixture of accounting measurements.

A firm must identify the financial assets and financial liabilities on the balance sheet for which it used the fair value option and disclose the reasons for choosing to measure those items at fair value. If a line item on the balance sheet (for example, Bonds Payable) includes items measured at amortized cost along with items measured at fair value, the firm must disclose the amounts measured under both approaches. Finally, a firm must also disclose the difference between the aggregate fair value and the aggregate unpaid principal amount on long-term receivables and long-term payables.

With respect to the income statement, a firm must describe its method of computing interest expense and the unrealized gain or loss on financial instruments measured at fair value and indicate the amount and line items on the income statement that include these items. The fair value of a financial instrument can change because of changes in interest rates in general or because of changes in instrument-specific credit risk. Firms must therefore estimate and disclose the proportion of the unrealized gain or loss due to changes in instrument-specific credit risk.

Notes to the financial statements must indicate whether the basis for measuring fair value for each major category of asset or liability comes from Level 1, Level 2, or Level 3 inputs. If firms rely on inputs from more than one of the three levels for a particular category of asset or liability, then the firm classifies the asset or liability as coming from the lowest level for which the input had a significant influence on the determination of fair value. For fair value measurements using significant unobservable inputs (Level 3), firms must reconcile the beginning and ending balances of those fair value measurements with descriptions of the transactions or events that caused those fair value amounts to change during a period.

EXHIBIT 10.5 Fair Value Disclosures by PepsiCo for the First Quarter of 2008

FAIR VALUE

In September 2006 the Financial Accounting Standards Board (FASB) issued Statement of Financial Accounting Standards (SFAS) 157, *Fair Value Measurements* (SFAS 157), which defines fair value, establishes a framework for measuring fair value, and expands disclosures about fair value measurements. The provisions of SFAS 157 are effective as of the beginning of our 2008 fiscal year. We adopted SFAS 157 at the beginning of our 2008 fiscal year, and our adoption did not have a material impact on our financial statements.

The fair value framework requires the categorization of assets and liabilities into three levels based upon the assumptions (inputs) used to price the assets or liabilities. Level 1 provides the most reliable measure of fair value, whereas Level 3 generally requires significant management judgment. The three levels are defined as follows:

- *Level 1:* Unadjusted quoted prices in active markets for identical assets and liabilities.
- *Level 2:* Observable inputs other than those included in Level 1. For example, quoted prices for *similar* assets or liabilities in active markets *or* quoted prices for identical assets or liabilities in inactive markets.
- *Level 3:* Unobservable inputs reflecting management's own assumptions about the inputs used in pricing the asset or liability.

As of March 22, 2008, the fair values of our financial assets and liabilities are categorized as follows:

	Total	Level 1	Level 2	Level 3
ASSETS				
Short-term investments (a)	$181	$181	$ —	$ —
Available-for-sale securities (b)	71	71	—	—
Forward exchange contracts (c)	46	—	46	—
Commodity contracts (d)	6	—	6	—
Interest rate swaps (e)	78	—	78	—
Prepaid forward contracts (f)	63	—	63	—
Total assets at fair value	$445	$252	$193	$ —
LIABILITIES				
Forward exchange contracts (c)	$ 49	$ —	$ 49	$ —
Commodity contracts (d)	10	—	10	—
Cross currency interest rate Swaps (g)	8	—	8	—
Deferred compensation (h)	547	182	365	—
Total liabilities at fair value	$614	$182	$432	$ —

(a) Based on price changes in index funds.
(b) Based on the price of common stock.
(c) Based on observable market transactions of spot and forward rates.
(d) Based on average prices on futures exchanges and recently reported transactions in the marketplace.
(e) Based on the LIBOR index.
(f) Based on the price of our common stock.
(g) Based on observable local benchmarks for currency and interest rates.
(h) Based on the fair value of investments corresponding to employees' investment elections.

Exhibit 10.5 presents fair value disclosures for PepsiCo for the first quarter of 2008. PepsiCo did not use Level 3 inputs so did not need to report a reconciliation between fair value measurements at the beginning and end of the quarter based on Level 3 inputs.

As this book goes to press, it is unclear how widely firms will choose the fair value option.

ACCOUNTING FOR LEASES

An alternative to borrowing cash to purchase buildings, equipment, and certain other assets is signing a contract to lease the property from its owner, called the *lessor*. Leases vary in their characteristics but all convey to the lessee the right to use an asset. In some cases the lessor enjoys the rewards and bears most of the risks of ownership, whereas in other cases the lessee, or user of the property, enjoys the rewards and bears most of these risks. U.S. GAAP and IFRS provide for two methods of accounting for long-term leases: the **operating lease method** and the **capital** or **finance lease method**.[15] As subsequent sections discuss, the operating lease method is appropriate when the lessor enjoys most of the rewards and bears most of the risks of ownership. The leased property is an asset on the books of the lessor. The **capital lease method** is appropriate when the lessee enjoys most of the rewards and bears most of the risks of ownership. The lessee records both the leased asset and a lease liability, much the same as if it had borrowed to purchase the asset. Capital leases are economically similar to purchasing assets with funds obtained from issuing long-term bonds and result in similar accounting.

To understand these two methods, suppose that Food Barn wants to acquire a computer that has a three-year life and a purchase price of $45,000. Assume that Food Barn must pay 8% per year to borrow funds for three years. The computer manufacturer will sell the computer to Food Barn for $45,000 or lease it for three years for $17,461.51 per year, payable at the end of each year.[16] In practice, lessees usually make payments in advance, but assuming the payments occur at year-end simplifies the computations. Food Barn must pay for property taxes, maintenance, and repairs of the computer whether it purchases or leases. Food Barn signs the lease on January 1, 2008.

OPERATING LEASE METHOD

In an operating lease, the owner, or lessor, enjoys the rewards and bears most of the risks of ownership. For example, if a lease requires the lessee to make fixed periodic payments, the lessor benefits from decreases in interest rates (the lessor receives the fixed periodic amount) but bears the risk of interest rate increases (the lessor cannot increase the fixed periodic payment). If the lease specifies that the lessee must return the leased asset to the lessor at the end of the lease term, the lessor must then re-lease or sell the asset. The lessor bears the risk of technological change and other factors that would affect its ability to lease or sell the asset. If the computer manufacturer, and not Food Barn, bears most of the risks of ownership, accounting considers the lease to be an executory contract and treats it as an operating lease. Food Barn would make no entry on January 1, 2008, when it signs the lease. It makes the following entry on December 31 of each year:

December 31 of Each Year

Rent Expense. 17,461.51

    Cash. 17,461.51

Assets	=	Liabilities	+	Shareholders' Equity	(Class.)
−17,461.51				−17,461.51	IncSt → RE

To record annual expense of leasing computer under the operating lease method.

CAPITAL LEASE METHOD

In a capital lease, the lessee enjoys the rewards and bears most of the risks of ownership. If the periodic rental payments vary with changes in interest rates, then Food Barn, not the

---

[15]Financial Accounting Standards Board, *Statement of Financial Accounting Standards No. 13,* "Accounting for Leases," 1975 (reissued and interpreted 1980) (**Codification Topic 840**); International Accounting Standards Board, *International Accounting Standard 17,* "Leases" 1982, revised 1997 and 2003. U.S. GAAP uses the term *capital lease method* and IFRS uses the term *finance lease method.* We use the term *capital lease method* throughout this section on leases.

[16]The present value of an annuity of $17,461.51 for three years at a discount rate of 8% is $45,000.

computer manufacturer, bears interest rate risk. If the lease period approximately equals the useful life of the leased asset, then Food Barn bears the risk of factors that affect the market value of the asset. If Food Barn—not the computer manufacturer—bears most of the risks of ownership, accounting views the arrangement as a form of borrowing to purchase the computer. Food Barn must account for it as a capital lease. This treatment recognizes the signing of the lease as the simultaneous acquisition of a long-term asset and the incurring of a long-term liability for lease payments. At the time Food Barn signs the lease, it records both the leased asset and the lease liability at the present value of the required cash payments, $45,000 in this example. The entry at the time Food Barn signs the three-year lease is as follows:

January 1, 2008

Leased Assets—Computer 45,000	
Lease Liability	45,000

Assets	=	Liabilities	+	Shareholders' Equity	(Class.)
+45,000		+45,000			

To record leased asset and lease liability under the capital lease method.

At the end of each year, Food Barn must account for the leased asset and the lease liability. To recognize depreciation expense on the leased asset, assuming Food Barn uses the straight-line depreciation method and zero salvage value, Food Barn makes the following entry at the end of each year:

December 31 of Each Year

Depreciation Expense (on Computer) 15,000	
Accumulated Depreciation—Computer	15,000

Assets	=	Liabilities	+	Shareholders' Equity	(Class.)
−15,000				−15,000	IncSt → RE

To record depreciation expense on leased asset under the capital lease method.

The second entry made by Food Barn at the end of each year recognizes that the lease payment both pays interest and reduces the lease liability. Separating the portion of the lease payment that represents interest from the portion reducing the liability follows the effective interest method illustrated for notes and bonds earlier in this chapter. The amortization schedule for this lease appears in **Exhibit 10.6**.

EXHIBIT 10.6

Amortization Schedule for $45,000 Lease Liability, Accounted for as a Capital Lease, Repaid in Three Annual Installments of $17,461.51 Each, Interest Rate 8%, Compounded Annually

Period (1)	Balance at Beginning of Period (2)	Interest Expense for Period (3)	Cash Payment (4)	Portion of Payment Reducing Principal (5)	Balance at End of Period (6)
1	$ 45,000.00	$ 3,600.00	$17,461.51	($13,861.51)	$ 31,138.49
2	$ 31,138.49	$ 2,491.08	$17,461.51	($14,970.43)	$ 16,168.06
3	$ 16,168.06	$ 1,293.45	$17,461.51	($16,168.06)	0

The entries made for the debt service payments at the end of each year are as follows:

December 31, 2008

Interest Expense	3,600.00	
Lease Liability	13,861.51	
Cash		17,461.51

Assets	=	Liabilities	+	Shareholders' Equity	(Class.)
−17,461.51		−13,861.51		−3,600.00	IncSt → RE

To recognize lease payment, interest on the lease liability for the first year of $3,600.00 (= .08 × $45,000), and the plug for the reduction in the liability. The present value of the lease liability after this entry is $31,138.49 (= $45,000 − $13,861.51).

December 31, 2009

Interest Expense	2,491.08	
Lease Liability	14,970.43	
Cash		17,461.51

Assets	=	Liabilities	+	Shareholders' Equity	(Class.)
−17,461.51		−14,970.43		−2,491.08	IncSt → RE

To recognize lease payment, interest on the lease liability for the second year of $2,491.08 (= .08 × $31,138.49), and the plug for the reduction in the liability. The present value of the lease liability after this entry is $16,168.06 (= $31,138.49 − $14,970.43).

December 31, 2010

Interest Expense	1,293.45	
Lease Liability	16,168.06	
Cash		17,461.51

Assets	=	Liabilities	+	Shareholders' Equity	(Class.)
−17,461.51		−16,168.06		−1,293.45	IncSt → RE

To recognize lease payment, interest on the lease liability for the third year of $1,293.45, which differs slightly due to rounding from $1,293.44 (= .08 × $16,168.06), and the plug for the reduction in the liability. The present value of the lease liability after this entry is zero (= $16,168.06 − $16,168.06).

EFFECT OF THE OPERATING AND CAPITAL LEASE METHODS ON THE FINANCIAL STATEMENTS OF THE LESSEE

Both the leased asset and the lease liability appear on the lessee's balance sheet under the capital lease method, whereas neither appears on the lessee's balance sheet under the operating lease method.

Exhibit 10.7 summarizes the nature and amount of expenses under the operating and capital lease methods. The total rent expense under the operating lease method equals $52,384.53 (= $17,461.51 × 3). Total depreciation expense of $45,000 (= $15,000 × 3) plus total interest expense of $7,384.53 (= $3,600.00 + $2,491.08 + $1,293.45) also equals $52,384.53. Total expenses under the operating lease method and the capital lease method are the same and equal the total cash expenditures. The operating lease method and the capital lease method differ in the timing, but not in the total amount, of expense. For the lessee, the capital lease method recognizes expenses earlier than the operating lease method.

The operating lease method classifies all of the lease payment each period as an operating use of cash on the statement of cash flows. The capital lease method classifies the portion of the lease payment related to interest expense as an operating use of cash and the portion

| EXHIBIT 10.7 | Comparison of Expense Recognized Under Operating and Capital Lease Methods for Lessee |

	Expense Recognized Each Year Under:	
Year	Operating Lease Method	Capital Lease Method
1	$17,461.51	$18,600.00 (= $15,000 + $3,600.00)
2	17,461.51	17,491.08 (= 15,000 + 2,491.08
3	17,461.51	16,293.45 (= 15,000 + 1,293.45)
Total	$52,384.53	$52,384.53 (= $45,000 + $7,384.53)

related to a reduction in the lease liability as a financing use of cash. In addition, the lessee adds depreciation expense to net income or net loss to compute cash flow from operations.

CHOOSING THE ACCOUNTING METHOD FOR LEASES

The capital lease method results in larger long-term debt and debt-equity ratios during the life of a lease than the operating lease method. A larger debt ratio makes a firm appear more risky. Thus, given a choice, lessees tend to prefer the operating lease method to the capital lease method. The operating lease method also recognizes expense more slowly over the life of the lease than the capital lease method. These financial statement effects often lead lessees to structure leases so that they take the form of an operating lease.

Meanwhile, standard-setting bodies have tried to specify rules precluding the use of the operating lease method when leases transfer the rewards and risks of ownership from the lessor to the lessee.

U.S. GAAP Criteria for Lease Accounting U.S. GAAP specifies criteria for a capital lease. If a particular lease meets any one of the following four conditions, the lessor and lessee account for the lease as a capital lease. If the lease meets none of the four conditions, firms treat the lease as an operating lease.

1. The lease transfers ownership of the leased asset to the lessee at the end of the lease term.

2. Transfer of ownership at the end of the lease term seems likely because the lessee has a *bargain purchase option*. A bargain purchase option gives the lessee the right to purchase the leased asset at a specified future time for a price less than the currently predicted fair value of the property at that future time.

3. The lease extends for at least 75% of the asset's expected useful life.

4. The present value of the contractual minimum lease payments equals or exceeds 90% of the fair value of the asset at the time the lessee signs the lease. The present value computation uses a discount rate appropriate for the creditworthiness of the lessee.

These criteria attempt to identify who enjoys the benefits and bears the economic risks of the leased property. If the leased asset, either automatically or for a bargain price, becomes the property of the lessee at the end of the lease period, then the lessee enjoys all of the economic benefits of the asset and incurs all risks of ownership. If the life of the lease extends for most of the expected useful life of the asset (U.S. GAAP specifies 75% or more), then the lessee enjoys most of the benefits, particularly when we measure them in present values, and incurs most of the risk of technological obsolescence.

Lessors and lessees can usually structure leasing contracts to avoid the first three conditions. Avoiding the fourth condition is more difficult because it requires the lessor to bear more risk than it might desire. The fourth condition compares the present value of the lessee's contractual minimum lease payments with the fair value of the leased asset at the time the lessee signs the lease. The lessor presumably could either sell the asset for its fair value or lease it to the lessee for a set of lease payments. The present value of the minimum lease payments has the economic character of a loan in that the lessee has committed to make payments just as it would commit to make payments on a loan with a bank. When the present value of the contractual minimum lease payments equals at least 90% of the amount that the lessor would receive if it sold the asset instead of leasing it, then the lessor receives most of its return from the leasing arrangement. That is, 90% of the fair value of the asset is not at risk, and the lessor need receive only 10% of the fair value of the asset at the inception of the lease from selling or re-leasing the asset at the end of the lease term.

Under these conditions, the fourth criterion views the lessee as enjoying most of the rewards and bearing most of the risk of ownership, and the lease therefore qualifies as a capital lease. If, on the other hand, the lessor has more than 10% of the asset's initial fair value at risk, then the criterion views the lessor as enjoying most of the benefits and bearing most of the risks of ownership and would classify the lease as an operating lease. This fourth criterion has presented the most difficulties in practice because small changes in the amount or timing of lease payments can shift the present value of the lease payments to just below or just above the 90% threshold.

IFRS Criteria for Lease Accounting

IFRS uses the same general criterion for classifying leases: *Which party to the lease enjoys the rewards and bears the risk in a leasing arrangement?* Unlike U.S. GAAP, IFRS does not specify strict percentages, such as the 75% useful life criterion or the 90% present value criterion. Instead, IFRS identifies several indicators about which entity enjoys the rewards and bears the risk in the leasing arrangement and permits firms and their independent accountants to apply their professional judgment to classify a lease as an operating lease versus a capital lease. The criteria are similar to those of U.S. GAAP but not as specific:

1. Does ownership transfer from the lessor to the lessee at the end of the lease?
2. Is there a bargain purchase option?
3. Does the lease extend for the major part of the asset's economic life?
4. Does the present value of the minimum lease payments equal substantially all of the asset's fair value?
5. Is the leased asset specialized for use by the lessee?

A lease for which the present value of the minimum lease payments was 89.9% of the fair value of the leased asset at inception of the lease could escape capital lease treatment under U.S. GAAP but might not under IFRS.

ACCOUNTING BY THE LESSOR

The entries to account for operating leases and capital leases for the lessor mirror those for the lessee, but there are some important differences.

Lessor Accounting for Operating Leases

The leased asset appears on the books of the lessor in an operating lease. If the lessor also manufactured the leased property, the leased asset will appear at the cost of manufacturing the item. If the lessor is a financial institution that purchased the property that it subsequently leases, the leased asset will appear at the acquisition cost to the financial institution. Assume that the lessor's manufacturing cost of the computer it leased to Food Barn is $39,000. The first entry made by the lessor reclassifies the leased asset from inventory, a current asset, to equipment, a noncurrent asset.

January 1, 2008

| Equipment (Computer Leased to Customers) . . . . | 39,000 | |
| Inventory . . . . | | 39,000 |

Assets	=	Liabilities	+	Shareholders' Equity	(Class.)
+39,000					
−39,000					

To reclassify computer from inventory to equipment at its manufacturing cost of $39,000.

Each year the lessor records the cash received as Rent Revenue, mirroring the lessee's entries for Rent Expense.

December 31 of Each Year

| Cash... | 17,461.51 | |
| Rent Revenue .... | | 17,461.51 |

Assets	=	Liabilities	+	Shareholders' Equity	(Class.)
+17,461.51				+17,461.51	IncSt → RE

To record annual revenue of leasing computer under the operating lease method.

The lessor must also recognize depreciation expense on the leased asset, as it would on other equipment it uses in operations. The lessor uses its acquisition cost of $39,000 to compute depreciation (analogous to the lessee using its acquisition cost of $45,000 to compute depreciation under the capital lease method illustrated previously). The lessor also uses the expected useful life of the leased asset, which might exceed the lease period. We assume the computer has a three-year useful life with zero salvage value and the lessor uses the straight-line depreciation method.

December 31 of Each Year

| Depreciation Expense .... | 13,000 | |
| Accumulated Depreciation—Computer .... | | 13,000 |

Assets	=	Liabilities	+	Shareholders' Equity	(Class.)
−13,000				−13,000	IncSt → RE

To record depreciation expense on rented computer of $13,000 (= $39,000/3).

Lessor Accounting for Capital Leases The lessor initially records a capital lease as if it had *sold* the leased asset to the lessee. (Recall that the lessee records a capital lease as if it had *purchased* the leased asset with financing provided by the lessor.) The lessor receives a promise by the lessee to make future lease payments, which gives rise to a Lease Receivable. Continuing with the assumption that the lessor manufactured the computer leased to Food Barn, the lessor makes the following two entries at the time of signing the lease contract on January 1, 2008:

January 1, 2008

| Lease Receivable .... | 45,000 | |
| Sales Revenue .... | | 45,000 |

Assets	=	Liabilities	+	Shareholders' Equity	(Class.)
+45,000				+45,000	IncSt → RE

To record the "sale" of a computer for a series of future cash flows with a present value of $45,000. We place "sale" in quotation marks, because the lessor does not formally sell the asset, but transfers so much of its future benefits and risk to the user that the economics resemble a sale.

January 1, 2008

| Cost of Goods Sold .... | 39,000 | |
| Inventory .... | | 39,000 |

(continued)

Assets	=	Liabilities	+	Shareholders' Equity	(Class.)
−39,000				−39,000	IncSt → RE

To record the cost of a computer "sold" as an expense.

Thus, the computer manufacturer recognizes $6,000 (= $45,000 − $39,000) gross margin on signing the lease contract. We revisit this topic shortly.

The lessor makes entries each year that mirror those of the lessee for the lease payment, for the portion of the payment representing Interest Revenue, and for the portion representing a reduction of Lease Receivable. The following entries use the amounts from the amortization table in **Exhibit 10.6**.

December 31, 2008

Cash	17,461.51	
Interest Revenue		3,600.00
Lease Receivable		13,861.51

Assets	=	Liabilities	+	Shareholders' Equity	(Class.)
+17,461.51				+3,600.00	IncSt → RE
−13,861.51					

To recognize lease payment received, interest on the lease receivable for the first year of $3,600.00 (= .08 × $45,000), and the plug for the reduction in the receivable. The present value of the lease receivable after this entry is $31,138.49 (= $45,000.00 + $3,600.00 − $17,461.51).

December 31, 2009

Cash	17,461.51	
Interest Revenue		2,491.08
Lease Receivable		14,970.43

Assets	=	Liabilities	+	Shareholders' Equity	(Class.)
+17,461.51				+2,491.08	IncSt → RE
−14,970.43					

To recognize lease payment received, interest on the lease receivable for the second year of $2,491.08 (= .08 × $31,138.49), and the plug for the reduction in the receivable. The present value of the lease receivable after this entry is $16,168.06 (= $31,138.49 + $2,491.08 − 17,461.51).

December 31, 2010

Cash	17,461.51	
Interest Revenue		1,293.45
Lease Receivable		16,168.06

Assets	=	Liabilities	+	Shareholders' Equity	(Class.)
+17,461.51				+1,293,45	IncSt → RE
−16,168.06					

To recognize lease payment received, interest on the lease receivable for the third year of $1,293.45, which differs slightly due to rounding from $1,293.44 (= .08 × $16,168.06), and the plug for the reduction in the receivable. The present value of the lease receivable after this entry is zero (= $16,168.06 + $1,293.45 − $17,461.51).

EXHIBIT 10.8	Comparison of Income Recognized Under Operating and Capital Lease Methods for Lessor

	Income Recognized Each Year Under:	
Year	**Operating Lease Method**	**Capital Lease Method**
1	$ 4,461.51 (= $17,461.51 − $13,000)	$ 9,600.00 (= $6,000 + $3,600.00)
2	4,461.51 (= 17,461.51 − 13,000)	2,491.08 (= 0 + 2,491.08)
3	4,461.51 (= 17,461.51 − 13,000)	1,293.45 (= 0 + 1,293.45)
Total	$13,384.53 (= $52,384.53 − $39,000)	$13,384.53 (= $6,000 + $7,384.53)

EFFECT OF THE OPERATING AND CAPITAL LEASE METHODS ON THE FINANCIAL STATEMENTS OF THE LESSOR

Both assets and liabilities increase for a lessee using the capital lease method as compared to the operating lease method. For a lessor, however, either the leased asset (operating lease method) or a lease receivable (capital lease method) appears on the balance sheet. The amount in the Lease Receivable account exceeds the amount in the Equipment account by the gross margin (that is, sales minus cost of goods sold) recognized by the lessor from the "sale" of the lease asset. The balance sheet effects of the operating and capital lease methods do not differ as much for lessors as they do for lessees.

The effects of the operating versus capital lease methods on the income statement of the lessor are more pronounced. The lessor recognizes a gross margin from the "sale" of the leased asset at the time of signing the lease ($6,000 in this case) and then recognizes interest revenue over the life of the lease. Total income over the life of the lease of $13,384.53 equals the cash inflow from lease payments received of $52,384.53 (= $17,461.51 × 3) minus the $39,000 cost of manufacturing the computer. **Exhibit 10.8** summarizes these differences in income.

Although lessors tend to prefer recognizing income from the "sale" of the computer at the time of signing under the capital lease method, they recognize the preferences of lessees to structure leases as operating leases. Because the lessor and lessee apply the same criteria to classify leases as either an operating lease or a capital lease, lessors tend to accommodate the preferences of lessees, their customers, but set rental payments to compensate for any additional risk the lessor bears.

PROBLEM 10.4 for Self-Study

Operating and Capital Lease Methods for Lessee and Lessor. On January 1, 2008, Holt Book Store will acquire a delivery van that a local automobile dealer sells for $40,000. The dealer purchased the van from the manufacturer for $36,000. The dealer offers Holt Book Store the option of leasing the van for four years, with rentals of $11,543.65 due on December 31 of each year. Holt Book Store must return the van at the end of four years, although the automobile dealer anticipates that the resale value of the van after four years will be negligible. The automobile dealer considers 6% an appropriate interest rate to charge Holt Book Store to finance the acquisition.

a. Does this lease qualify as an operating lease or as a capital lease for financial reporting according to the four criteria specified in U.S. GAAP? Explain.

b. Assume for this part that the lease qualifies as an operating lease. Give the journal entries made by Holt Book Store over the first two years of the life of the lease.

c. Repeat part b for the automobile dealership. Use straight-line depreciation and zero estimated salvage value.

d. Assume for this part that the lease qualifies as a capital lease. Give the journal entries made by Holt Book Store over the first two years of the life of the lease.

e. Repeat part d for the automobile dealership.

(continued)

f. Compute the amount of expenses that Holt Book Store recognizes during each of the four years under the operating and capital lease methods.

g. Compute the amount of revenues and expenses that the automobile dealership recognizes during each of the four years under the operating and capital lease methods.

h. Why are the lessee's total expenses the same under the operating and capital lease methods? Why is the lessor's total income (revenue minus expenses) the same under the operating and capital lease methods?

i. Why do total expenses of the lessee differ from total income of the lessor?

LEASE DISCLOSURES

Firms must disclose in notes to the financial statements the cash flows associated with capital leases and with operating leases for each of the succeeding five years and for all years after five years in the aggregate. Firms must also indicate the present value of the cash flows for capital leases.[17] **Exhibit 10.9** presents Target Corporation's lease disclosures.

Target Corporation includes $4 million of capital leases in current liabilities and $123 million in long-term debt. Target Corporation, like most firms, does not indicate the weighted-average interest rate it used to compute the present value of capital leases.

Most of Target Corporation's leases are operating leases. Thus, neither the leased assets nor the lease liabilities appear on the balance sheet. The user of the financial statements might follow one of two approaches when dealing with operating leases:

1. Leave the operating lease commitments off the balance sheet on the assumption underlying GAAP's criteria that Target Corporation does not receive most of the rewards nor bear most of the risks of the leased assets.

2. Attempt to place a present value on the lease commitments and include that amount in noncurrent assets and long-term debt on the assumption that noncancelable leases result

EXHIBIT 10.9   Lease Disclosures for Target Corporation

Future minimum lease payments required under noncancelable lease agreements existing at February 2, 2008 were as follows:

Future Minimum Lease Payments (millions)	Operating Leases	Capital Leases
2008	$ 239	$ 12
2009	187	16
2010	173	16
2011	129	16
2012	123	17
After 2012	2,843	155
Total future minimum lease payments	$3,694 *(a)*	232
Less: Interest *(b)*		(105)
Present value of future minimum capital lease payments		$ 127 *(c)*

(a) Total contractual lease payments include $1,721 million related to options to extend lease terms that are reasonably assured of being exercised and also includes $98 million of legally binding minimum lease payments for stores that will open in 2008 or later.
(b) Calculated using the interest rate at inception for each lease.
(c) Includes the current portion of $4 million.

---

[17]Firms cannot currently apply the fair value options to assets and liabilities recognized under capital leases. See Financial Accounting Standards Board, *Statement of Financial Accounting Standards No. 159,* "The Fair Value Option for Financial Assets and Financial Liabilities," par. 8, 2007 (**Codification Topic 825**); International Accounting Standards Board, *International Accounting Standard 39*, "Financial Instruments: Recognition and Measurement," revised 2003.

in the acquisition of a noncurrent asset and constitute an obligation that firms should treat as long-term debt, a process called **constructive capitalization**.

Placing a present value on the operating lease commitments requires two estimates:

1. The discount rate to apply to the operating lease payments.
2. The timing of the aggregate cash flows after the fifth year.

The discount rate should reflect a long-term interest rate for collateralized borrowing. **Exhibit 10.4** indicates that the weighted-average borrowing rate on Target Corporation's long-term notes and debentures on February 2, 2008, was 5.5%. Target Corporation does not disclose the collateralized portion of this long-term debt. We will use a discount rate of 5.5% to illustrate the constructive capitalization of operating leases.

The cash flows for operating leases for the first five years decline each year. One might assume a continuing decline in some pattern for the years after 2012. An alternative approach assumes that Target Corporation will continue to make payments on operating leases in an amount equal to that in 2012, or $123 million a year, until it pays the $2,843 aggregate remaining amount. Thus, Target Corporation will continue to pay $123 million for 23.1 (= $2,843/$123) additional years. The estimated total years of these operating leases of 28.1 (= 5.0 + 23.1) years suggest that these leases are primarily for retail stores.

Exhibit 10.10 shows the computation of the present value of Target Corporation's operating lease commitments on February 2, 2008. The calculation of the present value of the cash flows after 2012 involves the present value of a deferred annuity.

Constructive capitalization of Target Corporation's operating leases adds $1,982 million to property, plant, and equipment; $227 million to the current portion of long-term debt; and $1,755 (= $1,982 − $227) million to long-term debt classified as a noncurrent liability on the balance sheet. The long-term debt and the debt-equity ratios of Target Corporation on February 2, 2008, based on reported amounts and as adjusted for the capitalization of operating leases are as follows:

Long-Term Debt Ratio

Reported Amounts: $15,126/$44,560 = 33.9%

Adjusted Amounts: ($15,126 + $1,755)/($44,560 + $1,982) = 36.3%

Debt-Equity Ratio

Reported Amounts: $15,126/$15,307 = 98.8%

Adjusted Amounts: ($15,126 + $1,755)/$15,307 = 110.3%

The debt ratios for Target Corporation increase with the capitalization of operating leases but not significantly. Larger increases in debt ratios typically occur for airlines, railroads, trucking companies, and other retailers, many of whom use operating leases extensively.

EXHIBIT 10.10   **Present Value of Operating Lease Commitments**

Year	Payments	Present Value Factor at 5.5%	Present Value
2008	$ 239	.94787	$ 227
2009	$ 187	.89845	168
2010	$ 173	.85161	147
2011	$ 129	.80722	104
2012	$ 123	.76513	94
After 2012	$2,843[a]	13.19369[b] x .76513[c]	1,242
Total			$1,982

[a]Assume that Target Corporation makes the $2,843 million payments after 2012 at the rate of $123 million a year. Target Corporation makes these payments for 23.1 (= $2,843/$123) years.

[b]Factor for the present value of an annuity of $123 million for 23.1 periods.

[c]Factor for the present value of $1 for five periods.

SUMMARY

This chapter discussed the accounting for long-term notes, bonds, and leases. The accounting for these obligations depends on whether a firm uses either of the following:

1. Amortized cost measurement, based on the historical market interest rate.
2. Fair value measurement, based on the current market interest rate.

The fair value option in U.S. GAAP and IFRS allows firms to use either method for many kinds of long-term notes and bonds, but not for long-term leases.

Exhibit 10.11 summarizes the balance sheet presentation of long-term liabilities considered in this chapter and the procedures for computing both balance sheet amounts and interest expense under both amortized cost and fair value measurements. First, we describe the amounts on the balance sheet, a "state description" (like a blueprint). Then we describe a process for computing the amounts, a "process description" (like a recipe). Following the process description produces liabilities on the balance sheet at the state description.

PROBLEM 10.5 for Self-Study

Unifying principles of accounting for long-term liabilities when using the historical market interest rate. This problem illustrates the state and process descriptions for long-term liabilities when using the historical market interest rate as summarized in the left column of **Exhibit 10.11**. Assume that a firm closes its books once each year, making adjusting entries once each year. On the date the firm borrows, the market-required yield is 10% per year, compounded annually for all loans spanning a two-year period. Note the following steps:

EXHIBIT 10.11 Summary of Accounting for Long-Term Debt Obligations

Amortized Cost Measurement Using Historical Market Interest Rate	Fair Value Measurement Using Current Market Interest Rate
State Description	**State Description**
Long-term liabilities appear on the balance sheet at the present value of the remaining cash flows discounted at the historical market interest rate on the date the borrower incurred the obligation.	Long-term liabilities appear on the balance sheet at fair value, which equals either the current market price or the present value of the remaining cash flows discounted at the market interest rate on the date of the balance sheet.
Process Description	**Process Description**
1. Initially record the liability at the cash (or cash equivalent) value received. This amount equals the present value of the future contractual payments discounted using the historical market interest rate for the borrower on the date the loan begins. (Sometimes the borrower must compute an implicit historical market interest rate by finding the internal rate of return.)	1. Initially record the same amount as that at the left. On the date that a loan begins, the historical market interest rate and the current market interest rate are the same.
2. At any subsequent time when the firm makes a cash payment or an adjusting entry for interest, it computes interest expense as the carrying value of the liability at the beginning of the period (which includes interest added in prior periods) multiplied by the historical market interest rate. The accountant debits this amount to Interest Expense and credits it to the liability. If the firm makes a cash payment, the accountant debits the liability account and credits Cash.	2. At each subsequent balance sheet date, compute the present value of the remaining contractual cash flows using the current market interest rate on that date. The difference between the amount of the liability at the beginning and end of the period is the net of the cash payment, interest expense, and unrealized gain or loss. Authoritative guidance does not specify a procedure for allocating the net change in value between the two income elements.

1. Compute the initial issue proceeds received by the firm issuing the obligation (that is, borrowing the cash) on the date of issue.

2. Give the journal entry for issue of the liability and receipt of cash.

3. Give the journal entry or entries for interest accrual and cash payment, if any, at the end of the first year, and recompute the carrying value of all liabilities related to the borrowing at the end of the first year. Combine the liability accounts for the main borrowing and accrued interest into a single account called Financial Liability.

4. Give the journal entry or entries for interest accrual and cash payment at the end of the second year, and recompute the carrying value of the liability related to the borrowing at the end of the second year.

Perform the above steps for each of the following borrowings:

a. The firm issues a single-payment note on the first day of the first year, promising to pay $1,000 on the last day of the second year.

b. The firm issues a 10% annual coupon bond, promising to pay $100 on the last day of the first year and $1,100 (= $1,000 + $100) on the last day of the second year.

c. The firm issues an 8% annual coupon bond, promising to pay $80 on the last day of the first year and $1,080 (= $1,000 + $80) on the last day of the second year.

d. The firm issues a 12% annual coupon bond, promising to pay $120 on the last day of the first year and $1,120 (= $1,000 + $120) on the last day of the second year.

e. The firm issues a level-payment note, promising to pay $576.19 on the last day of the first year and another $576.19 on the last day of the second year.

SOLUTIONS TO SELF-STUDY PROBLEMS

SUGGESTED SOLUTION TO PROBLEM 10.1 FOR SELF-STUDY

(Vera Company; implicit interest rate and amortization schedule for interest-bearing note.)

a.

Year	Cash Payment	Present Value Factor at 7%	Present Value[a]
1	$ 6,000	.93458	$ 5,607.48
2	$ 6,000	.87344	5,240.63
3	$106,000	.81630	86,527.58
Total			$97,375.69

[a]Present value calculations use present value factors with more decimal places than shown.

b. The amortization schedule appears in **Exhibit 10.12**.

EXHIBIT 10.12	Amortization Schedule for $100,000, 6% Note Discounted at a Required Yield of 7% Compounded Annually (Problem 10.1 for Self-Study)

Period (1)	Balance at Beginning of Period (2)	Interest Expense for Period (3)	Cash Payment (4)	Increase (Decrease) in Liability (5)	Balance at End of Period (6)
1	$97,375.69	$6,816.30	$6,000.00	$816.30	$ 98,191.99
2	$98,191.99	$6,873.44	$6,000.00	$873.44	$ 99,065.43
3	$99,065.43	$6,934.57[a]	$106,000.00	$934.57	0

[a]Amount reduced by $.01 to compensate for rounding.

SUGGESTED SOLUTION TO PROBLEM 10.2 FOR SELF-STUDY

(Amortization schedules for bonds.)

a. See **Exhibits 10.13**, **10.14**, and **10.15**.

b. The coupon rate equals the initial yield to maturity, so the present value of the remaining cash flows equals the face value of the bonds both initially and at the end of each period.

EXHIBIT 10.13

Amortization Schedule for $250 Million Face Value 8% Semiannual Coupon Bonds Priced Initially to Yield 8% Compounded Semiannually (Problem 10.2 for Self-Study)

Period (1)	Balance at Beginning of Period (2)	Interest Expense for Period (3)	Cash Payment (4)	Change in Liability (5)	Balance at End of Period (6)
1	$250,000,000	$10,000,000	$10,000,000	$0	$250,000,000
2	$250,000,000	$10,000,000	$10,000,000	$0	$250,000,000
3	$250,000,000	$10,000,000	$10,000,000	$0	$250,000,000
4	$250,000,000	$10,000,000	$10,000,000	$0	$250,000,000
5	$250,000,000	$10,000,000	$10,000,000	$0	$250,000,000
6	$250,000,000	$10,000,000	$10,000,000	$0	$250,000,000
7	$250,000,000	$10,000,000	$10,000,000	$0	$250,000,000
8	$250,000,000	$10,000,000	$10,000,000	$0	$250,000,000
9	$250,000,000	$10,000,000	$10,000,000	$0	$250,000,000
10	$250,000,000	$10,000,000	$10,000,000	$0	$250,000,000
11	$250,000,000	$10,000,000	$10,000,000	$0	$250,000,000
12	$250,000,000	$10,000,000	$10,000,000	$0	$250,000,000
13	$250,000,000	$10,000,000	$10,000,000	$0	$250,000,000
14	$250,000,000	$10,000,000	$10,000,000	$0	$250,000,000
15	$250,000,000	$10,000,000	$10,000,000	$0	$250,000,000
16	$250,000,000	$10,000,000	$10,000,000	$0	$250,000,000
17	$250,000,000	$10,000,000	$10,000,000	$0	$250,000,000
18	$250,000,000	$10,000,000	$10,000,000	$0	$250,000,000
19	$250,000,000	$10,000,000	$10,000,000	$0	$250,000,000
20	$250,000,000	$10,000,000	$10,000,000	$0	$250,000,000
21	$250,000,000	$10,000,000	$10,000,000	$0	$250,000,000
22	$250,000,000	$10,000,000	$10,000,000	$0	$250,000,000
23	$250,000,000	$10,000,000	$10,000,000	$0	$250,000,000
24	$250,000,000	$10,000,000	$10,000,000	$0	$250,000,000
25	$250,000,000	$10,000,000	$10,000,000	$0	$250,000,000
26	$250,000,000	$10,000,000	$10,000,000	$0	$250,000,000
27	$250,000,000	$10,000,000	$10,000,000	$0	$250,000,000
28	$250,000,000	$10,000,000	$10,000,000	$0	$250,000,000
29	$250,000,000	$10,000,000	$10,000,000	$0	$250,000,000
30	$250,000,000	$10,000,000	$10,000,000	$0	$250,000,000
31	$250,000,000	$10,000,000	$10,000,000	$0	$250,000,000
32	$250,000,000	$10,000,000	$10,000,000	$0	$250,000,000
33	$250,000,000	$10,000,000	$10,000,000	$0	$250,000,000
34	$250,000,000	$10,000,000	$10,000,000	$0	$250,000,000
35	$250,000,000	$10,000,000	$10,000,000	$0	$250,000,000
36	$250,000,000	$10,000,000	$10,000,000	$0	$250,000,000
37	$250,000,000	$10,000,000	$10,000,000	$0	$250,000,000
38	$250,000,000	$10,000,000	$10,000,000	$0	$250,000,000
39	$250,000,000	$10,000,000	$10,000,000	$0	$250,000,000
40	$250,000,000	$10,000,000	$10,000,000	$0	$250,000,000

EXHIBIT 10.14	Amortization Schedule for $180 Million Serial Bonds Requiring Payments of $10,409,418 Every Six Months for 15 Years Priced Initially to Yield 8% Compounded Semiannually (Problem 10.2 for Self-Study)

Period (1)	Balance at Beginning of Period (2)	Interest Expense for Period (3)	Cash Payment (4)	Reduction in Liability (5)	Balance at End of Period (6)
1	$180,000,000	$7,200,000	$10,409,418	($ 3,209,418)	$176,790,582
2	$176,790,582	$7,071,623	$10,409,418	($ 3,337,795)	$173,452,787
3	$173,452,787	$6,938,111	$10,409,418	($ 3,471,307)	$169,981,481
4	$169,981,481	$6,799,259	$10,409,418	($ 3,610,159)	$166,371,322
5	$166,371,322	$6,654,853	$10,409,418	($ 3,754,565)	$162,616,757
6	$162,616,757	$6,504,670	$10,409,418	($ 3,904,748)	$158,712,009
7	$158,712,009	$6,348,480	$10,409,418	($ 4,060,938)	$154,651,072
8	$154,651,072	$6,186,043	$10,409,418	($ 4,223,375)	$150,427,696
9	$150,427,696	$6,017,108	$10,409,418	($ 4,392,310)	$146,035,386
10	$146,035,386	$5,841,415	$10,409,418	($ 4,568,003)	$141,467,384
11	$141,467,384	$5,658,695	$10,409,418	($ 4,750,723)	$136,716,661
12	$136,716,661	$5,468,666	$10,409,418	($ 4,940,752)	$131,775,909
13	$131,775,909	$5,271,036	$10,409,418	($ 5,138,382)	$126,637,528
14	$126,637,528	$5,065,501	$10,409,418	($ 5,343,917)	$121,293,611
15	$121,293,611	$4,851,744	$10,409,418	($ 5,557,674)	$115,735,937
16	$115,735,937	$4,629,437	$10,409,418	($ 5,779,981)	$109,955,957
17	$109,955,957	$4,398,238	$10,409,418	($ 6,011,180)	$103,944,777
18	$103,944,777	$4,157,791	$10,409,418	($ 6,251,627)	$ 97,693,150
19	$ 97,693,150	$3,907,726	$10,409,418	($ 6,501,692)	$ 91,191,458
20	$ 91,191,458	$3,647,658	$10,409,418	($ 6,761,760)	$ 84,429,699
21	$ 84,429,699	$3,377,188	$10,409,418	($ 7,032,230)	$ 77,397,469
22	$ 77,397,469	$3,095,899	$10,409,418	($ 7,313,519)	$ 70,083,949
23	$ 70,083,949	$2,803,358	$10,409,418	($ 7,606,060)	$ 62,477,889
24	$ 62,477,889	$2,499,116	$10,409,418	($ 7,910,302)	$ 54,567,587
25	$ 54,567,587	$2,182,703	$10,409,418	($ 8,226,715)	$ 46,340,872
26	$ 46,340,872	$1,853,635	$10,409,418	($ 8,555,783)	$ 37,785,089
27	$ 37,785,089	$1,511,404	$10,409,418	($ 8,898,014)	$ 28,887,075
28	$ 28,887,075	$1,155,483	$10,409,418	($ 9,253,935)	$ 19,633,140
29	$ 19,633,140	$ 785,326	$10,409,418	($ 9,624,092)	$ 10,009,047
30	$ 10,009,047	$ 400,371[a]	$10,409,418	($10,009,047)	$ 0

[a] Amount increased $9 to compensate for effects of rounding.

c. A portion of each payment reduces the balance of the liability.

d. The time until payment at maturity decreases, resulting in an increase in the present value.

SUGGESTED SOLUTION TO PROBLEM 10.3 FOR SELF-STUDY

(Amortization schedules for bonds issued at a discount and a premium.)

a. See **Exhibits 10.16** and **10.17**.

b. Amortization of the discount or premium affects interest expense each period and not only in the 40th period. Interest expense each period equals the historical market interest rate times the carrying value of the liability at the beginning of each period. For bonds issued at a discount, interest expense exceeds the coupon payment. The excess of interest expense over the coupon payment increases the liability from its initial discount amount over time so that at maturity the carrying value of the liability equals its face

EXHIBIT 10.15	Amortization Schedule for $300 Million Face Value 10-Year Zero Coupon Bonds Priced Initially to Yield 8% Compounded Semiannually (Problem 10.2 for Self-Study)

Period (1)	Balance at Beginning of Period (2)	Interest Expense for Period (3)	Cash Payment (4)	Increase in Liability (5)	Balance at End of Period (6)
1	$136,916,084	$ 5,476,643	$0	$ 5,476,643	$142,392,727
2	$142,392,727	$ 5,695,709	$0	$ 5,695,709	$148,088,436
3	$148,088,436	$ 5,923,537	$0	$ 5,923,537	$154,011,974
4	$154,011,974	$ 6,160,479	$0	$ 6,160,479	$160,172,453
5	$160,172,453	$ 6,406,898	$0	$ 6,406,898	$166,579,351
6	$166,579,351	$ 6,663,174	$0	$ 6,663,174	$173,242,525
7	$173,242,525	$ 6,929,701	$0	$ 6,929,701	$180,172,226
8	$180,172,226	$ 7,206,889	$0	$ 7,206,889	$187,379,115
9	$187,379,115	$ 7,495,165	$0	$ 7,495,165	$194,874,280
10	$194,874,280	$ 7,794,971	$0	$ 7,794,971	$202,669,251
11	$202,669,251	$ 8,106,770	$0	$ 8,106,770	$210,776,021
12	$210,776,021	$ 8,431,041	$0	$ 8,431,041	$219,207,062
13	$219,207,062	$ 8,768,282	$0	$ 8,768,282	$227,975,344
14	$227,975,344	$ 9,119,014	$0	$ 9,119,014	$237,094,358
15	$237,094,358	$ 9,483,774	$0	$ 9,483,774	$246,578,132
16	$246,578,132	$ 9,863,125	$0	$ 9,863,125	$256,441,258
17	$256,441,258	$10,257,650	$0	$10,257,650	$266,698,908
18	$266,698,908	$10,667,956	$0	$10,667,956	$277,366,864
19	$277,366,864	$11,094,675	$0	$11,094,675	$288,461,539
20	$288,461,539	$11,538,462	$0	$11,538,462	$300,000,000

and maturity value. For bonds issued at a premium, the coupon payment exceeds interest expense. The excess of the coupon payment over the amount of interest expense reduces the liability from its initial premium amount over time so that at maturity the carrying value of the liability equals its face and maturity value.

SUGGESTED SOLUTION TO PROBLEM 10.4 FOR SELF-STUDY

(Holt Book Store and automobile dealer; operating and capital lease methods for lessee and lessor.)

a. Application of the four criteria is as follows:

(1) Ownership transferred to lessee at end of lease term: not satisfied.

(2) Lease contains a bargain purchase option: not satisfied.

(3) Lease period extends for at least 75% of asset's life: satisfied.

(4) Present value of contractual minimum lease payments equals or exceeds 90% of the fair market value of the asset at the time lessee signs the lease: satisfied. The present value of the lease payments when discounted at 6% is $40,000 (= $11,543.65 × 3.46511), which equals the $40,000 market value of the asset on January 1, Year 1.

The lease is therefore a capital lease because it meets at least one of the four criteria (in fact, it meets two conditions).

EXHIBIT 10.16	Amortization Schedule for $250 Million Face Value 8% Semiannual Coupon Bonds Priced Initially to Yield 10% Compounded Semiannually (Problem 10.3 for Self-Study)

Period (1)	Balance at Beginning of Period (2)	Interest Expense for Period (3)	Cash Payment (4)	Increase in Liability (5)	Balance at End of Period (6)
1	$207,102,281	$10,355,114	$10,000,000	$ 355,114	$207,457,395
2	$207,457,395	$10,372,870	$10,000,000	$ 372,870	$207,830,265
3	$207,830,265	$10,391,513	$10,000,000	$ 391,513	$208,221,778
4	$208,221,778	$10,411,089	$10,000,000	$ 411,089	$208,632,867
5	$208,632,867	$10,431,643	$10,000,000	$ 431,643	$209,064,510
6	$209,064,510	$10,453,226	$10,000,000	$ 453,226	$209,517,736
7	$209,517,736	$10,475,887	$10,000,000	$ 475,887	$209,993,623
8	$209,993,623	$10,499,681	$10,000,000	$ 499,681	$210,493,304
9	$210,493,304	$10,524,665	$10,000,000	$ 524,665	$211,017,969
10	$211,017,969	$10,550,898	$10,000,000	$ 550,898	$211,568,867
11	$211,568,867	$10,578,443	$10,000,000	$ 578,443	$212,147,311
12	$212,147,311	$10,607,366	$10,000,000	$ 607,366	$212,754,676
13	$212,754,676	$10,637,734	$10,000,000	$ 637,734	$213,392,410
14	$213,392,410	$10,669,621	$10,000,000	$ 669,621	$214,062,031
15	$214,062,031	$10,703,102	$10,000,000	$ 703,102	$214,765,132
16	$214,765,132	$10,738,257	$10,000,000	$ 738,257	$215,503,389
17	$215,503,389	$10,775,169	$10,000,000	$ 775,169	$216,278,558
18	$216,278,558	$10,813,928	$10,000,000	$ 813,928	$217,092,486
19	$217,092,486	$10,854,624	$10,000,000	$ 854,624	$217,947,110
20	$217,947,110	$10,897,356	$10,000,000	$ 897,356	$218,844,466
21	$218,844,466	$10,942,223	$10,000,000	$ 942,223	$219,786,689
22	$219,786,689	$10,989,334	$10,000,000	$ 989,334	$220,776,024
23	$220,776,024	$11,038,801	$10,000,000	$1,038,801	$221,814,825
24	$221,814,825	$11,090,741	$10,000,000	$1,090,741	$222,905,566
25	$222,905,566	$11,145,278	$10,000,000	$1,145,278	$224,050,844
26	$224,050,844	$11,202,542	$10,000,000	$1,202,542	$225,253,387
27	$225,253,387	$11,262,669	$10,000,000	$1,262,669	$226,516,056
28	$226,516,056	$11,325,803	$10,000,000	$1,325,803	$227,841,859
29	$227,841,859	$11,392,093	$10,000,000	$1,392,093	$229,233,952
30	$229,233,952	$11,461,698	$10,000,000	$1,461,698	$230,695,649
31	$230,695,649	$11,534,782	$10,000,000	$1,534,782	$232,230,432
32	$232,230,432	$11,611,522	$10,000,000	$1,611,522	$233,841,953
33	$233,841,953	$11,692,098	$10,000,000	$1,692,098	$235,534,051
34	$235,534,051	$11,776,703	$10,000,000	$1,776,703	$237,310,753
35	$237,310,753	$11,865,538	$10,000,000	$1,865,538	$239,176,291
36	$239,176,291	$11,958,815	$10,000,000	$1,958,815	$241,135,106
37	$241,135,106	$12,056,755	$10,000,000	$2,056,755	$243,191,861
38	$243,191,861	$12,159,593	$10,000,000	$2,159,593	$245,351,454
39	$245,351,454	$12,267,573	$10,000,000	$2,267,573	$247,619,027
40	$247,619,027	$12,380,973[a]	$10,000,000	$2,380,973	$250,000,000

[a]Amount increased by $22 to compensate for effects of rounding.

EXHIBIT 10.17	Amortization Schedule for $250 Million Face Value 8% Semiannual Coupon Bonds Priced Initially to Yield 6% Compounded Semiannually (Problem 10.3 for Self-Study)

Period (1)	Balance at Beginning of Period (2)	Interest Expense for Period (3)	Cash Payment (4)	Decrease in Liability (5)	Balance at End of Period (6)
1	$307,786,931	$9,233,608	$10,000,000	($ 766,392)	$307,020,539
2	$307,020,539	$9,210,616	$10,000,000	($ 789,384)	$306,231,155
3	$306,231,155	$9,186,935	$10,000,000	($ 813,065)	$305,418,090
4	$305,418,090	$9,162,543	$10,000,000	($ 837,457)	$304,580,632
5	$304,580,632	$9,137,419	$10,000,000	($ 862,581)	$303,718,051
6	$303,718,051	$9,111,542	$10,000,000	($ 888,458)	$302,829,593
7	$302,829,593	$9,084,888	$10,000,000	($ 915,112)	$301,914,481
8	$301,914,481	$9,057,434	$10,000,000	($ 942,566)	$300,971,915
9	$300,971,915	$9,029,157	$10,000,000	($ 970,843)	$300,001,073
10	$300,001,073	$9,000,032	$10,000,000	($ 999,968)	$299,001,105
11	$299,001,105	$8,970,033	$10,000,000	($1,029,967)	$297,971,138
12	$297,971,138	$8,939,134	$10,000,000	($1,060,866)	$296,910,272
13	$296,910,272	$8,907,308	$10,000,000	($1,092,692)	$295,817,580
14	$295,817,580	$8,874,527	$10,000,000	($1,125,473)	$294,692,108
15	$294,692,108	$8,840,763	$10,000,000	($1,159,237)	$293,532,871
16	$293,532,871	$8,805,986	$10,000,000	($1,194,014)	$292,338,857
17	$292,338,857	$8,770,166	$10,000,000	($1,229,834)	$291,109,023
18	$291,109,023	$8,733,271	$10,000,000	($1,266,729)	$289,842,293
19	$289,842,293	$8,695,269	$10,000,000	($1,304,731)	$288,537,562
20	$288,537,562	$8,656,127	$10,000,000	($1,343,873)	$287,193,689
21	$287,193,689	$8,615,811	$10,000,000	($1,384,189)	$285,809,500
22	$285,809,500	$8,574,285	$10,000,000	($1,425,715)	$284,383,785
23	$284,383,785	$8,531,514	$10,000,000	($1,468,486)	$282,915,298
24	$282,915,298	$8,487,459	$10,000,000	($1,512,541)	$281,402,757
25	$281,402,757	$8,442,083	$10,000,000	($1,557,917)	$279,844,840
26	$279,844,840	$8,395,345	$10,000,000	($1,604,655)	$278,240,185
27	$278,240,185	$8,347,206	$10,000,000	($1,652,794)	$276,587,391
28	$276,587,391	$8,297,622	$10,000,000	($1,702,378)	$274,885,012
29	$274,885,012	$8,246,550	$10,000,000	($1,753,450)	$273,131,563
30	$273,131,563	$8,193,947	$10,000,000	($1,806,053)	$271,325,510
31	$271,325,510	$8,139,765	$10,000,000	($1,860,235)	$269,465,275
32	$269,465,275	$8,083,958	$10,000,000	($1,916,042)	$267,549,233
33	$267,549,233	$8,026,477	$10,000,000	($1,973,523)	$265,575,710
34	$265,575,710	$7,967,271	$10,000,000	($2,032,729)	$263,542,982
35	$263,542,982	$7,906,289	$10,000,000	($2,093,711)	$261,449,271
36	$261,449,271	$7,843,478	$10,000,000	($2,156,522)	$259,292,749
37	$259,292,749	$7,778,782	$10,000,000	($2,221,218)	$257,071,532
38	$257,071,532	$7,712,146	$10,000,000	($2,287,854)	$254,783,678
39	$254,783,678	$7,643,510	$10,000,000	($2,356,490)	$252,427,188
40	$252,427,188	$7,572,812[a]	$10,000,000	($2,427,188)	$250,000,000

[a] Amount decreased by $4 to compensate for effects of rounding.

b.

December 31 of Each Year

Rent Expense. 11,543.65

   Cash. 11,543.65

Assets	=	Liabilities	+	Shareholders' Equity	(Class.)
−11,543.65				−11,543.65	IncSt → RE

To recognize annual rent expense on rental of delivery van accounted for as an operating lease.

c.

January 1, 2008

Equipment (delivery van leased to customer)   36,000

   Inventory   36,000

Assets	=	Liabilities	+	Shareholders' Equity	(Class.)
+36,000					
−36,000					

To record transfer of delivery van from inventory to equipment.

December 31 of Each Year

Cash. 11,543.65

   Rent Revenue 11,543.65

Assets	=	Liabilities	+	Shareholders' Equity	(Class.)
+11,543.65				+11,543.65	IncSt → RE

To recognize annual rent revenue from rental of delivery van accounted for as an operating lease.

December 31 of Each Year

Depreciation Expense   9,000

   Accumulated Depreciation   9,000

Assets	=	Liabilities	+	Shareholders' Equity	(Class.)
−9,000				−9,000	IncSt → RE

To recognize annual depreciation of $9,000 (= $36,000/4) on leased van accounting for as an operating lease.

d.

January 1, 2008

Leased Asset—Delivery Van   40,000

   Lease Liability   40,000

Assets	=	Liabilities	+	Shareholders' Equity	(Class.)
+40,000		+40,000			

To record "acquisition" of delivery van and related liability accounted for as a capital lease.

December 31, 2008

Interest Expense (.06 × $40,000)	2,400.00	
Lease Liability	9,143.65	
Cash		11,543.65

Assets	=	Liabilities	+	Shareholders' Equity	(Class.)
−11,543.65		−9,143.65		−2,400.00	IncSt → RE

To recognize interest expense for 2008, the cash payment, and the reduction in the liability under the capital lease method. The carrying value of the liability at the end of 2008 is $30,856.35 (= $40,000 + $2,400.00 − $11,543.65).

December 31, 2008

Depreciation Expense	10,000	
Accumulated Depreciation		10,000

Assets	=	Liabilities	+	Shareholders' Equity	(Class.)
−10,000				−10,000	IncSt → RE

To record depreciation expense for 2008 of $10,000 (= $40,000/4) for lessee.

December 31, 2009

Interest Expense (.06 × $30,856.35)	1,851.38	
Lease Liability	9,692.27	
Cash		11,543.65

Assets	=	Liabilities	+	Shareholders' Equity	(Class.)
−11,543.65		−9,692.27		−1,851.38	IncSt → RE

To recognize interest expense for 2009, the cash payments, and the reduction in the liability under the capital lease method. The carrying value of the liability at the end of 2009 is $21,164.08 (= $30,856.35 + $1,851.38 − $11,543.65).

December 31, 2009

Depreciation Expense	10,000	
Accumulated Depreciation		10,000

Assets	=	Liabilities	+	Shareholders' Equity	(Class.)
−10,000				−10,000	IncSt → RE

To record depreciation expense for 2009 of $10,000 (= $40,000/4) for lessee.

e.

January 1, 2008

Lease Receivable	40,000	
Sales Revenue		40,000

Assets	=	Liabilities	+	Shareholders' Equity	(Class.)
+40,000				+40,000	IncSt → RE

To record "sale" of delivery van accounted for as a capital lease.

January 2, 2008

Cost of Goods Sold	36,000	
Inventory		36,000

Assets	=	Liabilities	+	Shareholders' Equity	(Class.)
−36,000				−36,000	IncSt → RE

To record cost of delivery van "sold" under capital lease arrangement.

December 31, 2008

Cash.....................................	11,543.65	
Interest Revenue		2,400.00
Lease Receivable		9,143.65

Assets	=	Liabilities	+	Shareholders' Equity	(Class.)
+11,543.65				+2,400	IncSt → RE
−9,143.65					

To record interest revenue, cash received, and reduction in lease receivable for 2008. The amounts mirror those of the lessee.

December 31, 2009

Cash.....................................	11,543.65	
Interest Revenue		1,851.38
Lease Receivable		9,692.27

Assets	=	Liabilities	+	Shareholders' Equity	(Class.)
+11,543.65				+1,851.38	IncSt → RE
−9,692.27					

To record interest revenue, cash received, and reduction in lease receivable for 2009. The amounts mirror those of the lessee.

f.

Expense Recognized Each Year Under:

Year	Operating Lease Method	Capital Lease Method
2008	$11,543.65	$12,400.00 (= $10,000 + $2,400.00)
2009	11,543.65	11,851.38 (= 10,000 + 1,851.38)
2010	11,543.65	11,269.84 (= 10,000 + 1,269.84)
2011	11,543.65	10,653.38 (= 10,000 + 653.38)
Total	$46,174.60	$46,174.60 (= $40,000 + $6,174.60)

g.

Income Recognized Each Year Under:

Year	Operating Lease Method	Capital Lease Method
2008	$ 2,543.65 (= $11,543.65 − $ 9,000)	$ 6,400.00 (= $4,000 + $2,400.00)
2009	2,543.65 (= 11,543.65 − 9,000)	1,851.38 (= 0 + 1,851.38)
2010	2,543.65 (= 11,543.65 − 9,000)	1,269.84 (= 0 + 1,269.84)
2011	2,564.65 (= 11,543.65 − 9,000)	653.38 (= 0 + 653.38)
	$10,174.60 (= $46,174.60 − $36,000)	$10,174.60 (= $4,000 + $6,174.60)

h. The lessee's total expenses equal cash outflows, and the lessor's income equals cash inflows minus cash outflows. The operating and the capital lease methods recognize the revenues, expenses, and income associated with these cash flows in different periods.

EXHIBIT 10.18

Accounting for Long-Term Financial Liabilities Based on the Present Value of Future Cash Flows (Problem 10.5 for Self-Study)

	a. Single-Payment Note of $1,000 Maturing in Two Years			b. Two-Year Annual Coupon Bond—10% ($100) Coupons		
	Amount	Dr.	Cr.	Amount	Dr.	Cr.
(1) Compute Present Value of Future Contractual Payments Using Historical Interest Rate on Day Financial Liability is First Recorded.						
Rate is 10.0%.						
(a) 1 Year Hence	$ 0			$ 100.00		
(b) 2 Years Hence	$1,000.00			$1,100.00		
Multiply Payment by Present Value Factors (Table 2).						
0.90909 × (a)	$ 0			$ 90.91		
0.82645 × (b)	826.45			909.09		
(c) Total Present Value	$ 826.45			$1,000.00		
(2) Record Initial Liability and Cash or Other Assets Received from Step 1.						
Cash or Other Assets		826.45			1,000.00	
Financial Liability			826.45			1,000.00
(3) First Recording (payment date or end of period): End of First Year						
(a) Compute Interest Expense as Financial Liability × Historical Interest Rate.						
Amount on Line 1(c) × 0.10	$ 82.64			$ 100.00		
(b) Record Interest Expense.						
Interest Expense		82.64			100.00	
Financial Liability			82.64			100.00
(c) Record Cash Payment (if any).						
Financial Liability		—			100.00	
Cash			—			100.00
(d) Compute Book Value of Financial Liability.						
Beginning Balance	$ 826.45			$1,000.00		
Add Interest Expense	82.64			100.00		
Subtotal	$ 909.09			$1,100.00		
Subtract Cash Payment (if any)	—			(100.00)		
= Ending Balance	$ 909.09			$1,000.00		
(4) Second Recording: End of Second Year						
(a) Compute Interest Expense as Financial Liability × Historical Interest Rate.						
Amount on Line 3(d) × 0.10	$ 90.91			$ 100.00		
(b) Record Interest Expense.						
Interest Expense		90.91			100.00	
Financial Liability			90.91			100.00
(c) Record Cash Payment (if any).						
Financial Liability		1,000.00			1,100.00	
Cash			1,000.00			1,100.00
(d) Compute Book Value of Financial Liability.						
Beginning Balance	$ 909.09			$1,000.00		
Add Interest Expense	90.91			100.00		
Subtotal	$1,000.00			$1,100.00		
Subtract Cash Payment (if any)	(1,000.00)			(1,100.00)		
= Ending Balance	$ 0			$ 0		

c. Two-Year Annual Coupon Bond—8% ($80) Coupons			d. Two-Year Annual Coupon Bond—12% ($120) Coupons			e. Two-Year Level-Payment Note— Annual Payments of $576.19		
Amount	Dr.	Cr.	Amount	Dr.	Cr.	Amount	Dr.	Cr.
$ 80.00			$ 120.00			$ 576.19		
$1,080.00			$1,120.00			$ 576.19		
$ 72.73			$ 109.09			$ 523.81		
892.57			925.62			476.19		
$ 965.30			$1,034.71			$1,000.00		
	965.30			1,034.71			1,000.00	
		965.30			1,034.71			1,000.00
$ 96.53			$ 103.47			$ 100.00		
	96.53			103.47			100.00	
		96.53			103.47			100.00
	80.00			120.00			576.19	
		80.00			120.00			576.19
$ 965.30			$1,034.71			$1,000.00		
96.53			103.47			100.00		
$1,061.83			$1,138.18			$1,100.00		
(80.00)			(120.00)			(576.19)		
$ 981.83			$1,018.18			$ 523.81		
$ 98.18			$ 101.82			$ 52.38		
	98.18			101.82			52.38	
		98.18			101.82			52.38
	1,080.00			1,120.00			576.19	
		1,080.00			1,120.00			576.19
$ 981.83			$1,018.18			$ 523.81		
98.18			101.82			52.38		
$1,080.01			1,120.00			$ 576.19		
(1,080.00)			(1,120.00)			(576.19)		
$ 0[a]			$ 0			$ 0		

[a]Rounding error of $0.01.

i. The lessee's total expenses equal its total cash outflows of $46,174.60 (= $11,543.65 × 4). The lessor's income equals its total cash inflows of $46,174.60 ($11,543.60 × 4) minus its cash outflow to purchase the van of $36,000.

SUGGESTED SOLUTION TO PROBLEM 10.5 FOR SELF-STUDY

(Unifying principles of accounting for long-term liabilities when using the historical market interest rate.)

Exhibit 10.18 shows the accounting for five types of long-term monetary liabilities stated at the present value of future cash flows in columns labeled **a** through **e**. The accounting for each of these monetary liabilities follows a common procedure.

1. Compute the initial amount of cash received by the borrower as well as the historical market interest rate. Sometimes you will know both of these. Sometimes you will know the cash received and you must calculate the interest rate. Sometimes, as **Exhibit 10.18** illustrates in all five cases, you will know the interest rate and must compute the initial cash received.

    a. To compute the initial amount of cash received, given the contractual payments and the historical market interest rate, multiply each of the contractual payments by the present value factor (as from **Table 2** at the back of the book) for a single payment of $1 to be received in the future. **Exhibit 10.18** shows the present value factors at 10% interest for payments to be received in one year (0.90909) and in two years (0.82645).

    b. Computing the historical market interest rate, given the initial cash proceeds and the series of contractual payments, requires finding the *internal rate of return* of the series of cash flows. The **Appendix** at the back of the book illustrates this process. **Exhibit 10.18** shows that only the 10% coupon bond and the level-payment note have initial cash proceeds equal to $1,000. The difference in amounts arises because each of the items has a different present value, in spite of the fact that some people might, loosely speaking, call each a "$1,000 liability."

2. Record a journal entry debiting cash and crediting the financial liability with the amount of cash received. This presentation showing the common theme uses the generic account title Financial Liability, although in practice a firm would use more descriptive titles.

3. At every contractual payment date and at the end of an accounting period, compute interest expense as the book value of the liability at the beginning of the period (which includes the principal liability account and the Interest Payable account if the firm keeps these amounts in separate accounts) multiplied by the historical market interest rate. Debit the computed amount to Interest Expense and credit the Financial Liability account.

    If the borrower makes a cash payment, credit cash and debit the Financial Liability account. The book value of the liability is now equal to the beginning balance plus interest expense recorded less cash payments made, if any.

    Exhibit 10.18 does not illustrate this fact directly, but if you were to return to step **1** at this point and compute the present value of the remaining contractual payments using the historical market interest rate (10% in the examples), that present value would equal the book value computed after step **3**.

4. At each payment date, or at each period-end closing date, repeat step **3**. Eventually, when the borrower makes the final payment (as illustrated at the bottom of **Exhibit 10.18**), it will have discharged the entire amount of the liability plus interest. The remaining liability is zero. The accounting has amortized the liability to zero at the same time that the firm has extinguished its obligation.

KEY TERMS AND CONCEPTS

Note	Unsecured borrowing
Notes Payable	Senior rights
Bond	Subordinated rights
Bond indenture	Debenture bond
Bonds payable	Serial bond

Zero coupon bond
Convertible bond
Callable bond
Put option
Fixed or variable interest rate
Present value of future cash flows
Financial instrument
Internal rate of return or yield to maturity
Market interest rate
Implicit interest rate
Historical market interest rate
Current market interest rate
Amortized cost

Fair value
Fair value option
Amortization schedule
Effective interest method
Principal or face value
Coupon interest rate
Maturity value
Market value
Discount and premium to face value
Operating lease method
Capital (or finance) lease method
Constructive capitalization

QUESTIONS, EXERCISES, AND PROBLEMS

QUESTIONS

1. Review the meaning of the terms and concepts listed in Key Terms and Concepts.

2. "Using amortized cost based on the historical market interest rate to account for bonds in periods subsequent to their initial issuance provides a carrying value for bonds that is consistent with using historical, or acquisition, cost measurements for assets." Explain.

3. "Applying the effective interest method using the historical market interest rate gives a constant amount of interest expense on bonds each period." Do you agree? If not, how would you change the statement to make it accurate?

4. A firm issues two bonds with identical issue prices, market-required yields, and final maturity dates. One bond is a semiannual coupon bond, and the other bond is a serial bond. Will the total interest expense over the life of these two bonds be the same or different? Explain.

5. Firm A issues $1,000,000 face value, 9% semiannual coupon bonds at a price to yield 8% compounded semiannually. Firm B issues $1,000,000 face value, 7% semiannual coupon bonds at a price to yield 8% compounded semiannually. Both bond issues mature in 20 years. Will these firms receive the same initial issue price for these bonds? Explain.

6. "The total effect on income before income taxes over the life of a bond that a firm repays at maturity will be the same whether the firm accounts for the bond using amortized cost measurement based on the historical market interest rate or fair value measurement based on the current market interest rate." Do you agree? Explain.

7. Refer to question 6. Would your answer differ if the firm repaid the bond prior to maturity?

8. Why is the identification of the entity in a lease transaction that enjoys the benefits and incurs the risk of the leased asset important in accounting for the lease?

9. A retailer leases space in a shopping center on a ten-year lease. The lessee pays a small fixed amount per month plus 10% of sales for the previous month. The retailer will likely treat this lease as an operating lease and not a capital lease. Why?

10. A trucking company leases a hauling rig from the manufacturer for a three-year period. The trucking company pays a monthly rental and guarantees a certain minimum resale value of the rig at the end of the three years. The trucking company will likely treat this lease as a capital lease and not an operating lease. Why?

11. In what ways is the economic substance of a lessee's capital lease similar to, and different from, that of purchasing the equipment using the proceeds of a loan repayable in installments?

12. "The lessor recognizes the same amount of income (revenue minus expenses) over the term of a lease as the lessee recognizes as expenses." Do you agree or disagree? Explain.

13. "If permitted, a lessee generally prefers to account for leases using the operating lease method for financial reporting and the capital lease method for tax reporting." Explain.

14. "If permitted, a lessor generally prefers to account for leases using the capital lease method for financial reporting and the operating lease method for tax reporting." Explain.

EXERCISES

15. **Amortization schedule for note where stated interest rate differs from historical market rate of interest.** Hager Company acquires a computer from Volusia Computer Company. The cash price (fair value) of the computer is $37,938. Hager Company gives a three-year, interest-bearing note with a maturity value of $40,000. The note requires annual payments of 6% of face value, or $2,400 per year, payable at the end of each year. The interest rate implicit in the note is 8% per year.

   a. Prepare an amortization schedule for the note similar to **Exhibit 10.2**.

   b. Prepare journal entries for Hager Company over the life of the note. Ignore entries for depreciation expense on the computer.

16. **Computing the issue price of bonds.** Compute the issue price of each of the following bonds.

   a. $10,000,000 face value, zero coupon bonds due in 20 years, priced on the market to yield 8% compounded semiannually.

   b. $10,000,000 face value, serial bonds repayable in equal 40 semi-annual installments of $500,000, which includes coupon payments and repayment of principal, for 20 years, priced on the market to yield 6% compounded annually.

17. **Computing the issue price of bonds.** Compute the issue price of each of the following bonds.

   a. $1,000,000 face value, zero coupon bonds due in 20 years, priced on the market to yield 10% compounded semiannually.

   b. $1,000,000 face value, serial bonds repayable in equal semiannual installments of $50,000 for 20 years, priced on the market to yield 6% compounded semiannually.

   c. $1,000,000 face value, 10% semiannual coupon bonds with interest payable each six months and the principal due in 20 years, priced on the market to yield 8% compounded semiannually.

   d. $1,000,000 face value semiannual coupon bonds, with an annual coupon rate of 6% for the first ten years and 8% for the second ten years and the principal due in 20 years, priced on the market to yield 10% compounded semiannually.

18. **Amortization schedule for bonds.** On January 1 of the current year, Womack Company issues 10% semiannual coupon bonds maturing five years from the date of issue. The firm issues the bonds to yield 8% compounded semiannually. The bonds have a face value of $100,000.

   a. Compute the initial issue proceeds of these bonds.

   b. Construct an amortization schedule, similar to that in **Exhibit 10.2**, for this bond issue, assuming that Womack Company uses amortized cost measurement based on the historical market interest rate to account for the bonds.

   c. Assume that at the end of the bonds' third year of life, Womack Company reacquires $10,000 face value of these bonds for 103% of face value and retires them. Give the journal entry to record the retirement.

19. **Amortization schedule for bonds.** On January 1, 2008, Seward Corporation issues $100,000 face value, 8% semiannual coupon bonds maturing three years from the date of issue. The coupons, dated for June 30 and December 31 of each year, each promise 4% of the face value, 8% total for a year. The firm issues the bonds to yield 10%, compounded semiannually.

   a. Compute the initial issue proceeds of these bonds.

   b. Construct an amortization schedule, similar to that in **Exhibit 10.2**, for this bond issue, assuming that Seward Company uses amortized cost measurement based on the historical market interest rate to account for the bonds.

   c. Give the journal entries related to these bonds for 2008. Seward uses the calendar year as its reporting period.

d. On January 1, 2010, Seward Corporation reacquires $20,000 face value of these bonds for 102% of face value and retires them. Give the journal entry to record the retirement.

20. **Accounting for bonds using amortized cost measurement based on the historical market interest rate.** O'Brien Corporation issues $8,000,000 face value, 8% semiannual coupon bonds maturing in 20 years. The market initially prices these bonds to yield 6% compounded semiannually. O'Brien Corporation accounts for these bonds using amortized cost measurement based on the historical market interest rate.

   a. Compute the issue price of these bonds.

   b. Compute the interest expense on these bonds for the first six months.

   c. Compute the interest expense on these bonds for the second six months.

   d. Compute the carrying value of these bonds at the end of the second six-month period.

   e. Use present value computations to verify the carrying value of the bonds at the end of the second six-month period as computed in part **d** above.

21. **Accounting for bonds using amortized cost measurement based on the historical market interest rate.** Robinson Company issues $5,000,000 face value, 8% semiannual coupon bonds maturing in 10 years. The market initially prices these bonds to yield 10% compounded semiannually. Robinson Company accounts for these bonds using amortized cost measurement based on the historical market interest rate.

   a. Compute the issue price of these bonds.

   b. Compute the interest expense for the first six months.

   c. Compute the interest expense for the second six months.

   d. Compute the carrying value of these bonds at the end of the second six-month period.

   e. Use present value computations to verify the carrying value of the bonds at the end of the second six-month period as computed in part **d** above.

22. **Accounting for bonds using amortized cost measurement based on the historical market interest rate.** Several years ago, Huergo Dooley Corporation (HDC) issued $2,000,000 face value, 8% semiannual coupon bonds on the market initially priced to yield 10% compounded semiannually. The bonds require HDC to make semiannual payments of 4% of face value on June 30 and December 31 of each year. The bonds mature on December 31, 2012.

   a. Compute the carrying value of these bonds on January 1, 2008, assuming that HDC has used amortized cost measurement based on the historical market interest rate to account for these bonds.

   b. Give HDC's journal entry to recognize interest expense and cash payment on June 30, 2008.

   c. Give HDC's journal entry to recognize interest expense and cash payment on December 31, 2008.

   d. On January 1, 2009, these bonds trade in the market at a price to yield 6%, compounded semiannually. On this date, HDC repurchased 20% of these bonds on the open market and retired them. Give the journal entry to record the repurchase.

23. **Accounting for bonds using the fair value option based on the current market interest rate.** Stroud Corporation issues $10,000,000 face value, 10-year, 6% semiannual coupon bonds on January 1, 2008. The bonds require coupon payments on June 30 and December 31 of each year. The market initially priced the bonds to yield 6% compounded semiannually. The current market yield on these bonds was 6.2% compounded semiannually on June 30, 2008, and 6.6% compounded semiannually on December 31, 2008. Stroud Corporation computes interest expense for each six-month period using the market yield at the beginning of the period.

   a. Compute the carrying value of these bonds on January 1, June 30, and December 31 of 2008 using the fair value option.

   b. Compute the amount of interest expense and the amount of the unrealized gain or loss for the first six months of 2008.

c. Compute the amount of interest expense and the amount of the unrealized gain or loss for the second six months of 2008.

d. Give the journal entries for these bonds on January 1, June 30, and December 31 of 2008.

24. **Accounting for bonds using the fair value option based on the current market interest rate.** Restin Corporation issues $20,000,000 face value, 10 year, 8% semiannual coupon bonds on January 1, 2008. The bonds promise coupon payments on June 30 and December 31 of each year. The market initially priced the bonds to yield 7% compounded semiannually. The current market yield on these bonds was 6.8% compounded semiannually on June 30, 2008, and 6.4% on December 31, 2008. Restin Corporation computes interest expense for each six-month period using the market yield at the beginning of the period.

    a. Compute the carrying value of these bonds on January 1, June 30, and December 31 of 2008 using the fair value option.

    b. Compute the amount of interest expense and the amount of the unrealized gain or loss for the first six months of 2008.

    c. Compute the amount of interest expense and the amount of the unrealized gain or loss for the second six months of 2008.

    d. Give the journal entries for these bonds on January 1, June 30, and December 31 of 2008.

25. **Applying the capital lease criteria.** Boeing manufactures a jet aircraft at a cost of $50 million. The usual selling price for this aircraft is $60 million, and its typical useful life is 25 years. American Airlines desires to lease this aircraft from Boeing. The parties contemplate the following alternatives for structuring the lease. Indicate whether each arrangement qualifies as an operating lease or a capital lease. Assume that all cash flows occur at the end of each year.

    a. American Airlines will lease the aircraft for 20 years at an annual rental of $6 million. At the end of 20 years, American will return the aircraft to Boeing. The interest rate appropriate to a 20-year collateralized loan for American Airlines is 10%.

    b. American Airlines will lease the aircraft for 15 years at an annual rental of $7.2 million. At the end of 15 years, American Airlines will return the aircraft to Boeing. The interest rate appropriate for a 15-year collateralized loan for American Airlines is 10%.

    c. American Airlines will lease the aircraft for 10 years at an annual rental of $5.5 million. At the end of 10 years, American Airlines has the option of returning the aircraft to Boeing or purchasing it for $55 million. The interest rate appropriate for a 10-year collateralized loan for American Airlines is 8%.

    d. American Airlines will lease the aircraft for 18 years at an annual rental of $6.2 million, and will return the aircraft at the end of the lease term. In addition, American Airlines will pay a fee of $1,500 per hour for each hour over 5,000 hours per year that American Airlines flies the aircraft. American Airlines' average usage of its aircraft is currently 6,200 hours per year. The interest rate appropriate for an 18-year collateralized loan for American Airlines is 10%.

26. **Preparing lessee's journal entries for an operating lease and a capital lease.** General Motors Corporation (GM) sells a luxury minivan for $25,000. FedUp Delivery Services agrees to lease a minivan for a monthly rental of $750 for three years. FedUp Delivery Services will return the minivan to GM at the end of the lease period. GM expects to lease the minivan to Rent-a-Wreck for the remaining two years of its useful life. The appropriate interest rate for a three-year collateralized loan for FedUp Delivery Services is 6%, compounded monthly. Assume that FedUp Delivery Services makes all rental payments at the end of each month.

    a. Does this lease qualify as an operating lease or a capital lease? Explain.

    b. Assume that this lease is an operating lease. Give the journal entries for FedUp Delivery Services at the time it signs the lease and at the end of the first two months of the lease period.

    c. Repeat part **b** assuming that the lease is a capital lease. FedUp Delivery Services uses the straight-line depreciation method and records depreciation monthly.

27. **Preparing lessor's journal entries for an operating lease and a capital lease.** Sun Micro-systems manufacturers an engineering workstation for $7,200 and sells it for $12,000. Although the workstation has a physical life of approximately ten years, rapid techno-logical change limits its expected useful life to three years. Sun leases a workstation to Design Consultants for the three-year period beginning January 1, 2008. The annual rental payments of $4,386.70 are due at the beginning of each year. The interest rate appropriate for discounting cash flows is 10%, compounded annually. Sun uses a calen-dar year as its reporting period.

   a. Does this lease qualify as an operating lease or a capital lease? Explain.

   b. Assume that this lease qualifies as an operating lease. Give the journal entries for Sun Microsystems over the three-year period.

   c. Repeat part **b** assuming that the lease qualifies as a capital lease.

28. **Preparing lessee's journal entries for an operating lease and a capital lease.** On January 1, 2008, Baldwin Products, as lessee, leases a machine used in its operations. The annual lease payment of $10,000 is due on December 31 of 2008, 2009, and 2010. The machine reverts to the lessor at the end of the three years. The lessor can either sell the machine or lease it to another firm for the remainder of its expected total useful life of five years. Baldwin Products could borrow on a three-year collateralized loan at 8%. The market value of the machine at the inception of the lease is $30,000. Round all amounts to the nearest dollar.

   a. Does this lease qualify as an operating lease or a capital lease?

   b. Assume that this lease qualifies as an operating lease. Give the journal entries for Baldwin Products over the three-year period.

   c. Assume this lease qualifies as a capital lease. Repeat part **b**.

   d. Compute the total expenses for the three-year period under the operating and capital lease methods.

PROBLEMS

29. **Accounting for long-term bonds.** The notes to the financial statements of Aggarwal Cor-poration for 2008 reveal the following information with respect to long-term debt. *All interest rates in this problem assume semiannual compounding and the effective interest method of amortization using amortized cost measurement based on the historical market interest rate.*

	December 31	
	2008	**2007**
$800,000 zero coupon notes due December 31, 2017, initially priced to yield 10%	?	$ 301,512
$1,000,000 7% bonds due December 31, 2012. Interest is payable on June 30 and December 31. The bonds' initial price implies a yield of 8%..................	$966,336	?
$1,000,000, 9% bonds due December 31, 2023. Interest is payable on June 30 and December 31. The bonds' initial price implies a yield of 6%	?	$1,305,832

   a. Compute the carrying value of the zero coupon notes on December 31, 2008. A zero coupon note requires no periodic cash payments; only the face value is payable at maturity. Do not overlook the italicized sentence above.

   b. Compute the amount of interest expense for 2008 on the 7% bonds.

   c. On July 1, 2008, Aggarwal Corporation acquires half of the 9% bonds ($500,000 face value) in the market for $526,720 and retires them. Give the journal entry to record this retirement.

   d. Compute the amount of interest expense on the 9% bonds for the second half of 2008.

30. **Accounting for zero coupon debt.** When Time Warner Inc. announced its intention to borrow about $500 million by issuing 20-year zero coupon (single payment) notes, *The Wall Street Journal* reported the following:

> New York—Time Warner announced an offering of debt that could yield the company as much as $500 million. . . . The media and entertainment giant said that it would offer $1.55 billion principal amount of zero-coupon . . . notes due [in 20 years] . . . through Merrill Lynch. . . . Zero-coupon debt is priced at a steep discount to principal, [which] is fully paid at maturity. . . . A preliminary prospectus . . . didn't include the issue price and yield on the notes.[18]

Assume Time Warner borrows funds at the beginning of 2008 and pays $1.55 billion in a single payment at the end of 2027.

a. Assume the initial yield on the notes is 6% per year, compounded annually. What initial issue proceeds will Time Warner Inc. realize from issuing these notes?

b. Assume the initial issue proceeds from these notes are $500 million. What is the initial yield on these notes?

c. Assume the initial issue proceeds from these notes are $400 million and their annual yield is 7% compounded annually. What interest expense will Time Warner Inc. record for 2008, the first year the notes are outstanding, assuming that it uses the amortized cost method based on the historical market interest rate?

d. Assume the initial issue proceeds from these notes are $400 million and their annual yield is 7% compounded annually. What interest expense will Time Warner Inc. record for 2027, the last year the notes are outstanding, assuming that it uses the amortized cost method based on the historical market interest rate?

e. Assume that Time Warner Inc. initially issued the notes to yield 6% compounded annually and that the bonds traded in the market on December 31, 2017, to yield 8% compounded annually. Give the journal entry that Time Warner Inc. would make if it repurchased and retired $700 million face value of these zero coupon notes on this date. Round amounts to the nearest one million.

31. **Understanding and using bond tables. Exhibit 10.19** presents a bond table for 8%, semi-annual bonds for various market yields and years to maturity. The amounts given are percentages of face value.

a. Why are the amounts in the 8.0% market yield column equal to 100% regardless of the number of years to maturity?

b. Why are the amounts in the columns to the left of the 8.0% column greater than 100% and the amounts in the columns to the right of the 8.0% column less than 100% for all years to maturity?

c. Why do the amounts in the columns to the left of the 8.0% column decrease toward 100% and the amounts in the columns to the right of the 8.0% column increase toward 100% as the years to maturity decrease?

Assume for the remaining parts of this problem that a firm issues $1 million face value, 8% semiannual coupon bonds on January 1, 2008, at a price to yield 7% compounded semiannually. The firm uses the historical market interest rate to account for these bonds for parts **d** to **f** and the fair value option for parts **g** to **i**.

d. What are the initial issue proceeds for these bonds if they mature in 25 years?

e. What is the carrying value of these bonds after five years?

f. Use the bond table to compute the amount of interest expense for 2013. Independently verify this amount of interest expense for 2013 by multiplying the historical market interest rate times the liability at the beginning of each six-month period during 2013.

g. At the end of the 15th year, this firm adopts the fair value option. Any difference between the carrying value and the market value of these bonds is an adjustment to retained earnings. If the market interest rate on these bonds at the end of the 15th year is 7.8%, compute the pretax adjustment to retained earnings, and indicate whether the adjustment increases or decreases retained earnings.

---

[18]*The Wall Street Journal,* December 8, 1992, p. A6.

EXHIBIT 10.19	Bond Values in Percent of Face Value 8% Semiannual Coupon Bonds[a] (Problem 31)

Market Yield Percent per Year Compounded Semiannually

Years to Maturity	6.0	7.0	7.8	8.0	8.3	9.0
0.5	100.9709	100.4831	100.0962	100	99.8560	99.5215
1.0	101.9135	100.9498	100.1889	100	99.7177	99.0637
1.5	102.8286	101.4008	100.2780	100	99.5849	98.6255
2.0	103.7171	101.8365	100.3638	100	99.4574	98.2062
2.5	104.5797	102.2575	100.4464	100	99.3350	97.8050
5.0	108.5302	104.1583	100.8151	100	98.7924	96.0436
9.0	113.7535	106.5948	101.2763	100	98.1240	93.9200
9.5	114.3238	106.8549	101.3246	100	98.0548	93.7034
10.0	114.8775	107.1062	101.3711	100	97.9883	93.4960
15.0	119.6004	109.1960	101.7504	100	97.4528	91.8556
19.0	122.4925	110.4205	101.9649	100	97.1564	90.9750
19.5	122.8082	110.5512	101.9874	100	97.1257	90.8852
20.0	123.1148	110.6775	102.0091	100	97.0962	90.7992
25.0	125.7298	111.7278	102.1855	100	96.8588	90.1190
30.0	127.6756	112.4724	102.3059	100	96.7007	89.6810
40.0	130.2008	113.3744	102.4440	100	96.5253	89.2173

[a]The amounts of the entries of this exhibit result from using the present value function in Excel and then dividing the result by 10,000 to express as a percentage. For example, the computation of the value of 100.9709 in the 6% yield and 0.5 years to maturity is as follows: =-PV(.03,1,40000,1000000,0)/10000.

h. The market interest rate on June 30, 2023, is 8.3%. Compute the amount of interest expense for the first six months of 2023 and the amount of any unrealized gain or loss for this six-month period. Assume the firm computes interest expense using the market interest rate at the beginning of the six-month period.

i. The market interest rate on December 31, 2023, is 9.0%. Compute the amount of interest expense for the second six months of 2023 and the amount of any unrealized gain or loss for this six-month period.

32. **Interpreting disclosures of long-term debt.** **Exhibit 10.20** presents excerpts from the notes to the financial statements of Lowe's.

a. The amounts shown for Debentures, Notes, and the Medium-Term Notes appear as the same amounts on February 3, 2006, and February 2, 2007. What is the likely interpretation for the identical reported amounts at the beginning and end of the year?

b. The Senior Notes comprise two debt issues on February 3, 2006, and an additional two debt issues on February 2, 2007. Indicate the amounts in each of the following cells. *Hint:* Given the face value, term to maturity, and coupon rate, use Excel to solve for the historical market interest rate. Solving for the historical market interest rate involves inputting various interest rates until the present value is within $1 million of the issue price. Be sure to consider semiannual payments and semiannual compounding. Express the coupon interest rate and the historical market interest rate in the following cells as annual rates based on semiannual compounding.

Issue Date	Face Value	Term to Maturity at Issue Date	Issue Price	Coupon Interest Rate	Historical Market Interest Rate
October 2005					
October 2005					
October 2006					
October 2006					

c. The amount on the balance sheet for Senior Notes on February 2, 2007, of $1,980 million slightly exceeds the total issue price of the four Senior Notes of $1,979 million (= $988 + $991). Why do the amounts differ and why is the difference so small?

d. Why are the interest rates on the convertible notes so much lower than those on Lowe's other debt?

e. Refer to Note 7 on Financial Instruments. Is the weighted-average historical market interest rate on long-term debt higher or lower than the weighted-average current market interest rate on February 3, 2006, and February 2, 2007? Explain.

f. Assume that Lowe's had elected the fair value option of FASB Statement No. 159 on February 2, 2006, and February 2, 2007. Compute the amount that Lowe's would include in net income before taxes for the fiscal year ending February 2, 2007, related to long-term debt.

33. **Accounting for lease by lessor and lessee.** IBM manufactures a particular computer for $6,000 and sells it for $10,000. Adair Corporation needs this computer in its operations and contemplates three ways of acquiring it on January 1, 2008. The computer has a three-year estimated useful life and zero salvage value. Both firms use the straight-line depreciation method.

(1) Outright Purchase: Adair Corporation will borrow $10,000 from its bank and purchase the computer from IBM. The bank loan bears interest at 8% annually and requires payments of $3,880, which includes principal and interest, on December 31 of 2008, 2009, and 2010.

(2) Operating Lease: Adair Corporation will lease the computer from IBM and account for it as an operating lease. IBM sets the annual payment due on December 31, 2008, 2009, and 2010 at $3,810.

(3) Capital Lease: Adair Corporation will lease the computer from IBM and account for it as a capital lease, using an annual interest rate of 7%. The annual payment due on December 31 of 2008, 2009, and 2010 is $3,810.

a. Give the journal entries on the books of Adair Corporation on January 1, 2008, December 31, 2008, and December 31, 2009, related to the loan and acquisition of the equipment assuming the outright purchase alternative.

b. Repeat part **a** assuming the operating lease alternative.

c. Repeat part **a** assuming the capital lease alternative.

d. Give the journal entries on the books of IBM on January 1, 2008, December 31, 2008, and December 31, 2009, related to the sale of the equipment assuming the outright sale alternative.

e. Repeat part **d** assuming the operating lease alternative.

f. Repeat part **d** assuming the capital lease alternative.

g. Prepare a schedule of the total expenses incurred by Adair Corporation for 2008, 2009, and 2010 under each of the three alternatives.

h. Prepare a schedule of the total revenues and total expenses recognized by IBM for 2008, 2009, and 2010 under each of the three alternatives.

34. **Comparison of borrow/buy with operating and capital leases.** Carom Sports Collectibles Shop plans to acquire, as of January 1, 2008, a computerized cash register system that costs $100,000 and has a five-year life and no salvage value. The company considers two plans for acquiring the system:

(1) Outright purchase. To finance the purchase, the firm will issue $100,000 of face value, 10% semiannual coupon bonds on January 1, 2008, at par. The bonds mature in five years.

(2) Lease. The lease requires five annual payments on December 31, 2008, 2009, 2010, 2011, and 2012. The lease payments are such that they have a present value of $100,000 on January 1, 2008, when discounted at 10% per year.

The firm will use the straight-line method for all depreciation and amortization computations for assets.

a. Verify that the amount of the required lease payment is $26,380 by constructing an amortization schedule for the five payments. Note that there will be a $2 rounding error in the fifth year. Nevertheless, you may treat each payment as being $26,380 in the rest of the problem.

EXHIBIT 10.20

Excerpts from Notes to the Financial Statements of Lowe's (in millions) (Problem 32)

NOTE 6—LONG-TERM DEBT:

	Interest Rates %	Fiscal Year of Final Maturity	February 2, 2007	February 3, 2006
Secured debt				
Mortgage notes..................	6.57 to 8.25	2028	$ 30	$ 38
Unsecured debt				
Debentures	6.50 to 6.88	2029	693	693
Notes	8.25	2010	498	498
Medium-term notes— series A.....................	7.35 to 8.20	2023	27	27
Medium-term notes— series B.....................	6.70 to 7.61	2037	267	267
Senior notes	5.00 to 5.80	2036	1,980	988
Convertible notes	0.86 to 2.50	2021	518	596
Capital leases and other...........		2030	400	424
Total long-term debt			4,413	3,531
Less current maturities			88	32
Long-term debt, excluding current maturities			$4,325	$3,499

SENIOR NOTES

In October 2005, the Company issued $1 billion of unsecured senior notes, comprised of two $500 million tranches maturing in October 2015 and October 2035, respectively. The first $500 million tranche of 5.0% Senior Notes was sold at a discount of $4 million. The second $500 million tranche of 5.5% Senior Notes was sold at a discount of $8 million. Interest on the Senior Notes is payable semiannually in arrears in April and October of each year until maturity. The discount associated with the issuance is included in long-term debt and is being amortized over the respective terms of the Senior Notes. The net proceeds of approximately $988 million were used for the repayment of $600 million in outstanding notes due December 2005, for general corporate purposes, including capital expenditures and working capital needs, and to finance repurchases of common stock.

In October 2006, the Company issued $1 billion of unsecured senior notes, comprised of two tranches: $550 million of 5.4% Senior Notes maturing in October 2016 and $450 million of 5.8% Senior Notes maturing in October 2036. The 5.4% Senior Notes and the 5.8% Senior Notes were each issued at a discount of approximately $4.4 million. Interest on the Senior Notes is payable semiannually in arrears in April and October of each year until maturity, beginning in April 2007. The discount associated with the issuance is included in long-term debt and is being amortized over the respective terms of the Senior Notes. The net proceeds of approximately $991 million were used for general corporate purposes, including capital expenditures and working capital needs, and to finance repurchases of common stock.

NOTE 7 — FINANCIAL INSTRUMENTS:

The fair value of the Company's long-term debt excluding capital leases and other is as follows:

	February 2, 2007		February 3, 2006	
(in millions)	Carrying Amount	Fair Value	Carrying Amount	Fair Value
Liabilities:				
Long-Term Debt (excluding capital leases and other)	$4,013	$4,301	$3,107	$3,578

Interest rates that are currently available to the Company for issuance of debt with similar terms and remaining maturities are used to estimate fair value for debt issues that are not quoted on an exchange.

b. What balance sheet accounts are affected if the firm selects plan (1)? What if the firm uses plan (2) and the firm uses the operating lease method? What if the firm selects plan (2) and it uses the capital lease method?

c. What is the total depreciation and interest expense for the five years under plan (1)?

d. What is the total expense for the five years under plan (2) if the firm could account for the lease as an operating lease? As a capital lease?

e. Why are the answers in part d the same? Why do the answers in part c differ from those in part d?

f. What is the total expense for the first year under plan (1)? Under plan (2) accounted for as an operating lease? Under plan (2) accounted for as a capital lease?

g. Repeat part f for 2012.

35. **Financial statement effects of capital and operating leases.** Excerpts from the notes to the financial statements of Northern Airlines for two recent years reveal the following (amounts in millions).

	December 31	
	2008	2007
Capitalized Leased Asset	$ 865	$ 1,019
Capital Lease Liability	$ 927	$ 1,088
Long-Term Debt (including Capital Lease Liability)	$12,041	$13,456
Total Assets	$29,145	$29,495

Future minimum commitments under leases with lease periods extending beyond one year taken from notes to the financial statements for the year ending December 31, *2007*, appear in the following table.

Year	Capital Leases	Operating Leases
2008	$ 263	$ 1,065
2009	196	1,039
2010	236	973
2011	175	872
2012	140	815
After 2012	794	7,453
Total	$1,804	$12,217
Less Interest Portion	(716)	
Lease Liability	$1,088	

Future minimum commitments under leases with lease periods extending beyond one year taken from notes to the financial statements for the year ending December 31, *2008*, appear next.

Year	Capital Leases	Operating Leases
2009	$ 196	$ 1,098
2010	236	1,032
2011	175	929
2012	140	860
2013	142	855
After 2013	652	6,710
Total	$1,541	$11,484
Less Interest Portion	(614)	
Lease Liability	$ 927	

a. Assume that Northern Airlines makes all lease payments at the end of each year. Prepare an analysis that explains how the capital lease liability decreased from $1,088 million on December 31, 2007, to $927 million on December 31, 2008.

b. Compute the weighted-average interest rate that Northern Airlines apparently used to compute the present value of capital lease commitments on December 31, 2007.

c. Prepare an analysis that explains how the capitalized leased asset decreased from $1,019 million on December 31, 2007, to $865 million on December 31, 2008.

d. Give the journal entries to account for capital leases during 2008.

e. Give the journal entries to account for operating leases during 2008.

f. Assume that 10% is an appropriate interest rate to compute the present value of operating lease commitments on December 31, 2007, and December 31, 2008. Compute the present value of operating lease commitments on each date. Assume that the operating lease payment in the fifth year continues at that amount ($815 million for the lease commitments on December 31, 2007, and $855 million for the lease commitments on December 31, 2008) until the firm has paid all commitments for years after 2012 and after 2013, respectively.

g. Compute the long-term debt ratio on December 31, 2007, and December 31, 2008, based on the reported amounts (that is, without capitalization of operating leases).

h. Repeat part **g** but capitalize the operating lease commitments.

36. **Financial statement effects of capital and operating leases.** Excerpts from the notes to the financial statements of FedUp Corporation for two recent years reveal the following (amounts in millions).

	May 31	
	2008	**2007**
Capitalized Leased Asset	$ 150	$ 273
Capital Lease Liability	$ 310	$ 401
Long-Term Debt (including Capital Lease Liability)	$ 1,592	$ 2,427
Total Assets	$22,690	$20,404
Total Shareholders' Equity	$11,511	$ 9,588

Future minimum commitments under leases with lease periods extending beyond one year taken from notes to the financial statements for the year ending May 31, *2007*, appear next.

Fiscal Year	Capital Leases	Operating Leases
2008	$121	$ 1,646
2009	22	1,518
2010	99	1,356
2011	11	1,191
2012	96	1,045
After 2012	130	7,249
Total	$479	$14,005
Less Interest Portion	(78)	
Lease Liability	$401	

Future minimum commitments under leases with lease periods extending beyond one year taken from notes to the financial statements for the year ending May 31, *2008*, appear next.

Fiscal Year	Capital Leases	Operating Leases
2009	$ 24	$ 1,672
2010	100	1,478
2011	12	1,290

(continued)

Fiscal Year	Capital Leases	Operating Leases
2012	96	1,120
2013	8	984
After 2013	144	6,780
Total	$384	$13,324
Less Interest Portion	(74)	
Lease Liability	$310	

a. Assume that FedUp Corporation makes all lease payments at the end of each year. The interest rate implicit in capital leases is approximately 5%. Prepare an analysis that explains how the capital lease liability decreased from $401 million on May 31, 2007, to $310 million on May 31, 2008.

b. Prepare an analysis that explains how the capitalized leased asset decreased from $273 million on May 31, 2007, to $150 million on May 31, 2008.

c. Give the journal entries to account for capital leases during fiscal 2008.

d. Give the journal entries to account for operating leases during fiscal 2008.

e. Assume that 5% is an appropriate interest rate to compute the present value of operating lease commitments on May 31, 2007, and May 31, 2008. Compute the present value of operating lease commitments on each date. Assume that the operating lease payment in the fifth year continues at that amount ($1,045 million for the lease commitments on May 31, 2007, and $984 million for the lease commitments on May 31, 2008) until the firm has paid all commitments for years after 2012 and after 2013, respectively.

f. Compute the long-term debt ratio and the debt-equity ratio on May 31, 2007, and May 31, 2008, based on the reported amounts (that is, without capitalization of operating leases).

g. Repeat part g but capitalize the operating lease commitments.

37. **Measuring interest expense.** GSB Corporation issued semiannual coupon bonds with a face value of $110,000 several years ago. The annual coupon rate is 8%, with two coupons due each year, six months apart. The historical market interest rate was 10% compounded semiannually when GSB Corporation issued the bonds, equal to an effective interest rate of 10.25% [= (1.05 × 1.05) − 1]. GSB Corporation accounts for these bonds using amortized cost measurement based on the historical market interest rate. The current market interest rate at the beginning of the current year on these bonds was 6% compounded semiannually, for an effective interest rate of 6.09% [= (1.03 × 1.03) − 1]. The market interest rate remained at this level throughout the current year. The bonds had a book value of $100,000 at the beginning of the current year. When the firm made the payment at the end of the first six months of the current year, the accountant debited a liability for the exact amount of cash paid. Compute the amount of interest expense on these bonds for the last six months of the life of the bonds, assuming all bonds remain outstanding until the retirement date.

Liabilities: Off-Balance-Sheet Financing, Retirement Benefits, and Income Taxes

1. Understand (a) why and how firms structure financing to keep debt off the balance sheet, and (b) how standard setters have refined the concept of an accounting liability to reduce the number of off-balance-sheet financing obligations.

2. Understand the accounting issues in measuring and recognizing the cost of retirement benefits (such as pension benefits and health care benefits) and in reporting on the balance sheet an asset for overfunded benefits and a liability for underfunded benefits.

3. Understand why firms may recognize revenues and expenses for financial reporting in a period different from that used for tax reporting and the effect of such differences on the measurement of income tax amounts on the income statement and the balance sheet.

Chapter 3 introduces the concept of an accounting liability. **Chapter 8** discusses current liabilities and **Chapter 10** discusses long-term notes, bonds, and leases. This chapter explores three additional topics related to the recognition and measurement of liabilities:

1. Off-balance-sheet financing.
2. Retirement benefits.
3. Income taxes.

Each of these topics affects the amounts that firms report as liabilities on the balance sheet and therefore risk assessments. These items also affect reported expenses on the income statement and, therefore, assessments of profitability. For each topic we discuss both U.S. GAAP and IFRS.

OFF-BALANCE-SHEET FINANCING

Off-balance-sheet financing refers to obtaining cash, goods, or services without a formal borrowing arrangement that U.S GAAP or IFRS recognizes as a liability on the balance sheet. This section explores the rationale for off-balance-sheet financing, transaction structures that typically achieve off-balance-sheet financing, and the responses of standard-setting bodies that require firms to recognize an increasing number and variety of off-balance-sheet financing arrangements.

RATIONALE FOR OFF-BALANCE-SHEET FINANCING

Managers frequently cite these reasons, among others, for using off-balance sheet financing:

1. Some managers believe that it lowers the cost of borrowing. Lower borrowing costs might result if lenders ignore off-balance-sheet financing, or are unaware of it because borrowers do not disclose it, leading lenders to set interest rates for loans lower than the underlying risk levels warrant.

2. Off-balance-sheet financing may avoid violating debt covenants that include items recognized only in the financial statements. Covenants in existing debt contracts may preclude increases in debt ratios, but an off-balance-sheet arrangement that does not affect those ratios would allow the firm to borrow more.

The first suggested reason for off-balance-sheet financing assumes that some lenders, credit-rating agencies, and others who assess financial risks do not possess the knowledge, skills, and information needed to identify and deal with those financing arrangements. Even though there is little evidence that financial statement users systematically ignore these obligations, managers sometimes structure financing arrangements as though they believe that assumption. The second reason suggested for off-balance-sheet financing results from some lawyers' inability to understand that some of a firm's obligations do not appear on the balance sheet as liabilities.

STRUCTURING OFF-BALANCE-SHEET FINANCING

Recall from the discussion in **Chapter 3** that liabilities are present obligations of an entity to transfer assets or provide services to other entities in the future as a result of past transactions and events.[1] Many off-balance-sheet financings fall into one of two categories that accounting typically does not recognize as liabilities: executory contracts and contingent obligations.

Executory Contracts Firms frequently sign contracts promising to pay defined amounts in the future in return for future benefits. For an obligation to qualify as an accounting liability, the firm must have received a past or current benefit, which gives rise to a current obligation. If the firm has not received past or current benefits, but will receive the benefits in the future, accounting treats the obligation as an **executory contract** and typically does not recognize a liability.

Example 1 Operating lease commitments, discussed in **Chapter 10**, are the most frequently encountered example of an executory contract. If American Airlines (American) needs additional aircraft to expand internationally, it could borrow the needed funds and purchase the aircraft. This arrangement places additional debt on the balance sheet. Instead, American signs an operating lease agreement in which it agrees to pay the owner of the aircraft certain amounts each year for 12 years. The aircraft has an estimated service life of 18 years. American paints its name on the aircraft, uses the aircraft in operations, and makes the required lease payments. The assumption underlying an operating lease is that American receives benefits when it uses the aircraft, not when it initially signs the lease. That is, American has future benefits, not past or current benefits. Thus, American obtains financing for its flight equipment without showing a liability on the balance sheet.[2]

Example 2 Louisiana-Pacific Corporation and Weyerhaeuser Company (forest products companies) need additional pulp-processing capacity. Each firm could borrow the needed funds and build its own manufacturing plant. Instead, they form a joint venture to build a pulp-processing plant. Each firm agrees to use half of the new plant's capacity each year for 20 years and to pay half of all operating and debt service costs. The joint venture uses

---

[1]Financial Accounting Standards Board, *Statement of Financial Accounting Concepts No. 6*, "Elements of Financial Statements," 1985; International Accounting Standards Board, *Framework for the Preparation and Presentation of Financial Statements*, 1989.

[2]As this book goes to press, both the FASB and the IASB are reconsidering the accounting for leases. Initial discussions suggest that both standard-setting bodies will eliminate the operating and capital lease methods of accounting for leases and require firms to report rights acquired and obligations incurred under all long-term leasing arrangements as assets and liabilities at the time of signing, effectively eliminating this means of off-balance-sheet financing. The principal issue in these discussions is the definition of an asset and a liability.

the purchase commitments of Louisiana-Pacific Corporation and Weyerhaeuser Company to obtain a loan to build the facility. Accounting views the purchase commitments as executory contracts—all benefits occur in the future—and therefore neither firm will recognize a liability for its portion of the loan. The loan will appear as a liability on the balance sheet of the joint venture. Thus, each firm obtains financing for the services of the plant without showing a liability on its balance sheet.[3]

Contingent Obligations As an alternative to borrowing and using a particular asset as collateral, a firm might obtain cash by selling (transferring) an asset to a purchaser (transferee). In some cases, the arrangement includes a requirement that the seller will pay cash to the purchaser under certain conditions, for example, if the asset sold generates less cash for the purchaser than anticipated at the time of sale. In this arrangement, the seller has relinquished its claim to the cash flows that the transferred asset will generate and has assumed an obligation to stand ready to make a cash payment if the stated condition is met. These are the accounting issues:

1. Should the transferor account for the transfer of the asset as a sale or as a secured borrowing?
2. If the transferor accounts for the transfer as a sale, how should it account for the obligation (referred to as a **contingent obligation** by U.S. GAAP and as a **provision** by IFRS) to stand ready to make a future cash payment?

We present two examples to illustrate these arrangements now, and return to these questions later in the chapter.

Example 3 Sears extends credit to its customers to purchase appliances, furniture, and other goods. Sears could borrow from a bank using its accounts receivable as collateral, thereby placing debt on the balance sheet. Sears would then use the cash collections from the receivables to repay the bank loan with interest. Instead, Sears sells the accounts receivable to the bank for an amount that is less than the cash the bank expects to collect from receivables purchased. The amount takes account of expected defaults, which would reduce the cash generated by the receivables. This difference between the amount paid to Sears by the bank for the receivables and the amount that the bank expects to collect from the receivables provides the bank with its expected return. In this scenario, Sears has no further obligation and will treat this transaction as a sale, with no incremental debt on the balance sheet.

Example 4 Seagram Company, a distiller of liquors, ages its whiskeys for approximately 10 years. The firm must pay the costs to produce the whiskey and to store it during the aging process. Using the whiskey as collateral, Seagram could borrow to finance the costs incurred during the aging process; doing so would, however, lead to Seagram reporting increased liabilities. Instead, Seagram sells the whiskey to a bank and agrees to oversee the aging process on the bank's behalf. At the completion of the aging, Seagram assists the bank in finding a buyer but is not responsible for ensuring that a sale occurs at a specific price, or at all. Under this arrangement, the bank bears the risk of changes in selling prices for the whiskey. Seagram will probably treat this transaction as a sale, with no incremental debt on the balance sheet.

TREATMENT OF OFF-BALANCE-SHEET FINANCING ARRANGEMENTS UNDER U.S. GAAP AND IFRS

U.S. GAAP and IFRS provide guidance for deciding whether a given financing arrangement appears as a liability on the balance sheet or disclosed in the notes. Many financing arrangements are complex, and the authoritative guidance tends to relate to specific financing arrangements (for example, transfers of receivables, transfers of inventory) and tied to facts and circumstances of a particular arrangement. Two themes appear in much of this authoritative guidance:

---

[3]These firms would likely structure the arrangement so that neither firm controlled the joint venture and therefore neither firm would prepare consolidated financial statements with the joint venture. As **Chapter 13** explains more fully, consolidating the financial statements of the joint venture with those of either joint owner would result in reporting the loan to finance the pulp-processing plant on the consolidated balance sheet of the firm with control.

- Identifying the party that enjoys the economic benefits of the resource in each transaction and that bears the economic risk of holding it.
- Identifying the party that obtains financing.

If the entity that *obtains* financing also controls the benefits and risks, the typical outcome is the recognition of a liability by that entity. If the entity that *provides* the financing also controls the benefits and risks, the typical outcome is no recognition of a liability by the entity needing financing—the financing remains off-balance-sheet.

Example 5 Refer to **Example 1**. Recall from **Chapter 10** that the criteria for a capital lease identify the entity, either lessor or lessee, that enjoys the benefits and incurs the risk of the leased asset. When the *lessor* enjoys the benefits and incurs the risk, the lease is an operating lease and no liability appears on the balance sheet of the lessee. When the *lessee* enjoys the benefits and incurs the risk, the lease is a capital lease and a lease liability appears on the balance sheet of the lessee. The lease life in the American Airlines example of 12 years is less than 75% of the 18-year useful life of the aircraft, making it likely that this lease is an operating lease under U.S. GAAP. If, instead, the lease life were 18 years and the minimum lease payments compensated the lessor for the cost of the aircraft and provided a reasonable return for the risk involved, then the parties would likely treat the lease as a capital lease under both U.S. GAAP and IFRS. The lessee (in this case, American Airlines) would therefore recognize a lease liability on its balance sheet.

Example 6 Refer to **Example 2**. If the lender relies only on the purchase commitments and neither Louisiana-Pacific nor Weyerhaeuser guarantees repayment of the loan, then no liability will appear on the balance sheet of either company. If, however, the lender requires either or both Louisiana-Pacific and Weyerhaeuser to guarantee payment of the loan in case the joint venture defaults, this arrangement creates a financial guarantee, discussed in **Chapter 3**. Under both U.S. GAAP and IFRS, the guarantors would recognize the fair value of the guarantee when they signed the loan. If it becomes probable that the joint venture will default, then the guarantor would apply loss contingency accounting (U.S. GAAP) or provision accounting (IFRS) and recognize a liability.

Example 7 Refer to **Example 3**. Assume that Sears must transfer additional uncollected receivables to the lender/purchaser bank under either of two conditions: (1) if any receivables become uncollectible, and (2) if interest rates rise above a specified level. In this case, Sears bears both credit risk and interest rate risk and should treat the transfer of receivables as a loan, with debt appearing on its balance sheet.

Example 8 Refer to **Example 4**. Assume that Seagram guarantees an ultimate selling price that pays the lender both the original purchase price and a reasonable return over that amount. In this case, Seagram bears the economic risks and must show a liability on its balance sheet. If, however, the lender does not require Seagram to guarantee a minimum selling price for the whiskey, the lender bears both the risk of market prices changes and the uncertainty about the quality of the aged whiskey. In this case, Seagram will likely record the transaction as a sale and not a loan.

TRANSFER OF RECEIVABLES IN EXCHANGE FOR CASH

A transfer of receivables is a common form of financing that sometimes achieves off-balance-sheet financing. **Example 3** and **Example 7** involve transfers of receivables to a bank. In more complicated financing arrangements, firms such as Ford Motor Company, Scania, General Electric, and Fannie Mae often sell batches of receivables to a legally separate entity whose sole purpose is to hold the receivables and issue claims on their cash flows. Common terminology refers to such an entity as a **special purpose entity**, or **SPE**, or a **variable interest entity**, or **VIE**[4] and to the firm that sells the receivables as the *transferor*. The entity (VIE or SPE) holding the receivables issues securities to investors in return for cash and transfers the cash to the transferor in payment for the receivables. The investors in securities issued by the entity

---

[4]**Chapter 13** discusses the conditions with which firms must prepare consolidated financial statements with such entities.

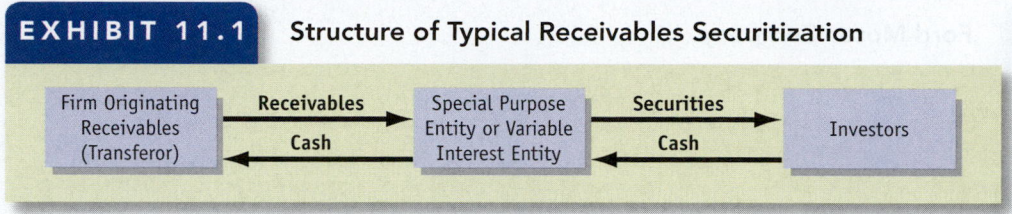

EXHIBIT 11.1   **Structure of Typical Receivables Securitization**

receive payments out of the cash flow from the transferred receivables. Common terminology refers to this process as **securitization** of the receivables. **Exhibit 11.1** depicts a typical securitization structure.

Securitization transactions have become so complex that it is often difficult to ascertain whether the transaction is a collateralized loan or a sale of the receivables. For example, the transferor may continue to service the receivables on behalf of the purchasing entity (servicing involves, for example, collecting cash and pursuing customers who do not pay on time or at all). The transferor may also retain some credit risk, perhaps by agreeing to transfer additional receivables to the entity if uncollectible accounts exceed a specified level. Finally, the transferor may or may not retain some or all of the interest rate risk. U.S. GAAP and IFRS provide the accounting rules transferors must apply to account for transfers like the one illustrated in **Exhibit 11.1**. Even if the transferor accounts for the transaction as a sale, the transferor must still recognize assets it controls and liabilities it has incurred. For example, if the transferor promises to service the receivables for the purchaser, it would recognize that servicing right on its balance sheet.[5]

Exhibit 11.2 presents disclosures from notes to the financial statements of Ford Motor Company describing its securitizations.

Note the following items in Ford's disclosures:

1. The first paragraph indicates that most of Ford Credit's transfers of receivables do not qualify as sales. Consequently, the receivables remain on the books of Ford Credit, a wholly owned subsidiary of Ford Motor Company. The borrowing done by the special purpose entity appears as a liability on the consolidated balance sheet.

2. The second paragraph describes the criteria that Ford Credit uses to assess if a transfer qualifies for off-balance-sheet treatment, which means the transaction is a sale of the receivables. The wording of the three criteria is almost identical to the criteria in FASB *Statement No. 140*. These criteria require that Ford Credit transfer control of the receivables to the special purpose entity. That is, Ford will treat the transfer as a sale for accounting purposes if it transfers the receivables to another party (the transferee) and retains no ability to determine what happens to the receivables thereafter. This condition implies that the benefits and risks of the receivables reside with the transferee.

3. The third paragraph indicates that Ford Credit retains certain interests in transferred receivables and therefore allocates the cost of its investment in the receivables between the receivables sold and the rights retained based on their relative fair values. This paragraph describes Ford Credit's application of the financial components approach required by FASB *Statement No. 140*.

4. The fourth paragraph describes Ford Credit's accounting for its servicing rights and responsibilities. Ford Credit recognizes an asset for the expected benefit of servicing fees and recognizes the obligation associated with providing those services.

SUMMARY OF THE ACCOUNTING TREATMENT OF OFF-BALANCE-SHEET FINANCING ARRANGEMENTS

The accounting for transfers of receivables has come under the scrutiny of standard setters, as has the accounting for transfers involving inventories and research and development

---

[5]The guidance is Financial Accounting Standards Board, *Statement of Financial Accounting Standards No. 140*, "Accounting for Transfers and Servicing of Financial Assets and Extinguishments of Liabilities," 2000 (**Codification Topic 860**); *Statement of Financial Accounting Standards No. 156*, "Accounting for Servicing of Financial Assets," 2006 (**Codification Topic 860**); International Accounting Standards Board, *International Accounting Standard 39*, "Financial Instruments: Recognition and Measurement," revised 2003.

EXHIBIT 11.2	**Ford Motor Company**

DISCLOSURES RELATED TO SECURITIZATIONS OF RECEIVABLES

Sales of Receivables

Ford Credit securitizes finance receivables and net investment in operating leases and sells retail installment sale contracts in whole-loan sale transactions to fund operations and to maintain liquidity. Most of its securitizations do not meet the criteria for off-balance-sheet treatment. As a result, the securitized assets and associated debt remain on its balance sheet and no gain or loss is recorded for these transactions.

Ford Credit records its sales of receivables as off-balance-sheet when each of the following criteria is met:

- The receivables are isolated from the transferor (i.e., Ford Credit transfers the receivables to bankruptcy-remote special purpose entities [SPEs] or other independent entities).
- The receivables are transferred to an entity that has the right to pledge or exchange the assets, or to a qualifying SPE whose beneficial interest holders have the right to pledge or exchange their beneficial interests. In its off-balance-sheet transactions, Ford Credit generally uses a qualifying SPE, or it sells the receivables to an independent entity. In either case, Ford Credit does not restrict the transferee from pledging or exchanging the receivables or beneficial interests.
- The transferor does not maintain control over the receivables (i.e., Ford Credit is not permitted to regain control over the transferred receivables or cause the return of specific receivables, other than through a "cleanup" call, an optional repurchase of the remaining transferred financial assets at a point where the cost of servicing the outstanding assets becomes burdensome in relation to the benefits).

For off-balance-sheet sales of receivables, gains or losses are recognized in the period in which the sale occurs. Ford Credit retains certain interests in receivables sold in off-balance-sheet securitization transactions. In determining the gain or loss on each sale of finance receivables, the investment in the sold receivables pool is allocated between the portions sold and retained based on their relative fair values at the date of sale. Retained interests may include residual interests in securitizations, restricted cash held for the benefit of securitization investors, and subordinated securities. These interests are recorded at fair value with unrealized gains recorded, net of tax, as a separate component of *Accumulated Other Comprehensive Income/(Loss)*. Residual interests in securitizations represent the present value of monthly collections on the sold finance receivables in excess of amounts needed for payment of the debt and other obligations issued or arising in the securitization transactions. Ford Credit does not retain any interests in the whole-loan sale transactions but continues to service the sold receivables.

In both off-balance-sheet securitization transactions and whole-loan sales, Ford Credit also retains the servicing rights and generally receives a servicing fee. The fee is recognized as collected over the remaining term of the related sold finance receivables. Ford Credit establishes a servicing asset or liability when the servicing fee does not adequately compensate for retaining the servicing rights. Interest supplement payments due from affiliates related to receivables sold in off-balance-sheet securitizations or whole-loan sale transactions are recorded, on a present value basis, as a receivable in *Other Assets* on its balance sheet at the time the receivables are sold. Present value accretion is recognized in *Financial Services revenues*.

arrangements.[6] Both the FASB and IASB seem to understand the implications of attempts to structure transfers of assets and other transactions to keep debt off the balance sheet. A goal in formulating appropriate reporting standards is to reflect the economic effect of such arrangements and the trend in recent standards is to recognize more obligations as liabilities that were previously off-balance-sheet.

PROBLEM 11.1 for Self-Study

Off-balance-sheet financing. Assume that International Paper Company (IP) wishes to obtain $75 million of additional financing without recording additional debt on its balance sheet. To do this, it creates a trust to which, on January 1, it transfers cutting rights to a mature timber tract. The trust will pay for these rights by borrowing $75 million for five years from a bank, with interest at 8%. The trust promises to make five equal installment payments, one on December 31 of each year.

The trust will harvest and sell timber each year to obtain cash to make the loan payments and to pay operating costs. At current prices, the value of the standing wood

(continued)

---

[6]The U.S. GAAP guidance for transfers involving inventories is Financial Accounting Standards Board, *Statement of Financial Accounting Standards No. 49*, "Accounting for Product Financing Arrangements," 1981 (**Codification Topic 470**); for research and development arrangements, the U.S. GAAP guidance is Financial Accounting Standards Board, *Statement of Financial Accounting Standards No. 68*, "Research and Development Arrangements," 1982 (**Codification Topic 730**). The IFRS guidance is more general, covering a wide class of arrangements that pertain to off-balance-sheet financing using off-balance-sheet entities. That guidance is International Accounting Standards Board, *SIC Interpretation 12*, "Consolidation—Special Purpose Entities," 1998.

exceeds by 10% the amounts the trust will need to service the loan and to pay ongoing operating costs (including wind, fire, and erosion insurance). The future selling price of timber will determine the trust's actions, as follows:

- If the selling price of timber declines, the trust will harvest more timber and sell it to service the debt and to pay operating costs.

- If the selling price of timber increases, the trust will harvest timber at the level originally planned and invest cash receipts that exceed debt service and operating costs to provide a cushion for possible future price decreases. At the end of five years, the trust will distribute the value of any cash and uncut timber to IP.

IP will guarantee the debt in the event cash flows from selling the timber are inadequate to pay operating costs and service the debt. The bank has the right to inspect the tract at any time and to replace IP's forest-management personnel with managers of its own choosing if it feels that IP is mismanaging the tract.

a. Identify IP's economic returns and risks in this arrangement.

b. Identify the bank (lender's) economic returns and risks in this arrangement.

c. Should IP treat this transaction as a loan (a liability will appear on IP's balance sheet) or as a sale (no liability will appear on IP's balance sheet)? Explain your reasoning.

RETIREMENT BENEFITS

Many employers provide retirement benefits to their employees, including pensions, health insurance, and life insurance. This section discusses the measurement and recognition of the cost of retirement plans and the reporting of assets and obligations of retirement plans on the balance sheet. The discussion focuses on the accounting for pension plans, although similar principles and procedures apply to health and life insurance benefits. U.S. GAAP and IFRS have similar provisions,[7] although both standard-setting bodies currently have projects underway to make changes in the required accounting.

RECOGNITION OF PENSION EXPENSE

The employer must recognize the cost of pension plans as an expense in some period. An important conceptual question is whether the employer should recognize this cost as an expense:

1. During the years while employees render services, or
2. Later, when retired employees receive benefits during retirement.[8]

The first approach records the cost of pension benefits as an expense in the period when a firm receives employee services, so the accounting for this type of **deferred compensation** is similar to the accounting for current compensation (that is, salaries and wages). Employees agree to render services currently for a package of compensation, some of which they receive immediately and some of which they receive later. The second approach records the cost of pension benefits as an expense long after the firm has received employee services. Typically accounting records a cost as an expense when a firm receives services (in this case, when employees earn pension benefits in return for working) regardless of when a firm actually pays cash to settle the obligation (in this case, when the employees receive the benefits). Both

---

[7]Financial Accounting Standards Board, *Statement of Financial Accounting Standards No. 87,* "Employers' Accounting for Pensions," 1985 (**Codification Topic 715**); International Accounting Standards Board, *International Accounting Standard 19,* "Employee Benefits," revised 1998.

[8]To simplify the discussion, we make no distinction between pension plan costs that are product costs (for employees involved in manufacturing) versus period expenses (for employees involved in selling and administrative activities). The conceptual question applies whether the pension plan cost is a product cost or a period expense.

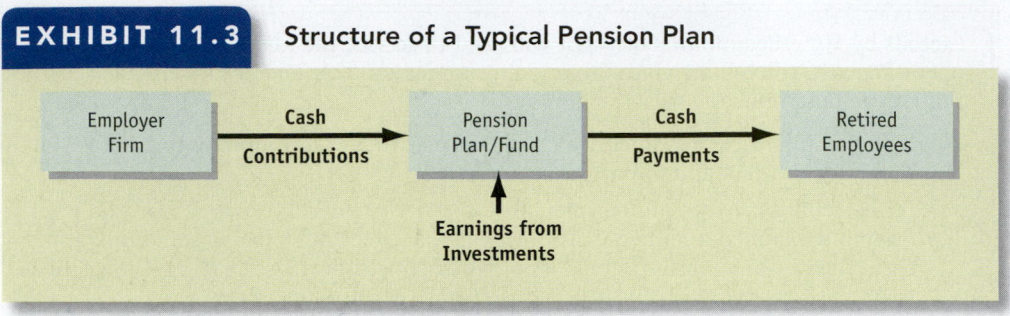

EXHIBIT 11.3 Structure of a Typical Pension Plan

U.S. GAAP and IFRS require firms to recognize the cost of pension plans as an expense during the years when employees render services.

PENSION PLAN STRUCTURE AND DEFINITIONS

Exhibit 11.3 presents the structure of a typical pension plan, the elements of which we discuss next.

1. The employer sets up a pension plan that is legally separate from the employer. The pension plan specifies the eligibility of employees, the types of promises to employees, the method of funding, and the pension plan administrator.[9] Some employers promise to contribute a certain amount to the pension plan each period for each employee (usually based on an employee's salary), without specifying the benefits the employee will receive during retirement. The amounts employees eventually receive depend on the investment performance of the pension plan. Common terminology refers to such plans as **defined contribution pension plans**. In most defined contribution plans, employees have a say regarding how the administrator invests the amounts contributed on their behalf. Other employers specify the benefit that employees will receive during retirement. Employer contributions plus earnings from investments made with those contributions pay the specified benefit. Common terminology refers to such plans as **defined benefit pension plans**. For reasons discussed later, the assets in a defined benefit pension plan will usually not equal the liabilities of the plan, resulting in an overfunded or underfunded plan.

2. Each period the employer transfers cash to the pension plan, which is usually organized as a trust. The plan administrator serves in a fiduciary capacity for the benefit of employees. The employer cannot access assets in the pension plan except under specific conditions that vary, as a matter of pension law, by jurisdiction. Under current accounting guidance, the employer does not consolidate the assets and liabilities of the pension plan with its own assets and liabilities.[10] The total amount of cash that the employer contributes to the pension plan over time is the total amount of pension expense that the employer must recognize in measuring net income. The pension expense for a particular period is the amount of the cash contribution for defined contribution pension plans. For defined benefit pension plans, the cash contribution rarely equals pension expense. We discuss the measurement of pension expense for such plans later in this section.

3. The pension plan receives cash each period from the employer and invests the cash in bonds, common stock, real estate, and other investments. The plan pays cash to retired employees each period. The assets in the pension plan usually change each period as follows:

	Assets at Beginning of the Period
+/−	Actual Earnings on Pension Plan Investments
+	Contributions Received from the Employer
−	Payments to Retirees
=	Assets at End of the Period

---

[9]Although pension law distinguishes the *plan administrator* (who has the fiduciary responsibility for the plan) from the *funding agent* (who receives cash payments and invests them), we do not make this distinction.

[10]**Chapter 13** discusses consolidated financial statements.

U.S. GAAP and IFRS require firms to report pension plan assets at fair value. Thus, actual earnings from pension plan investments include not only interest and dividends but also realized and unrealized changes in the fair value of plan investments.

4. The pension plan computes the amount of the pension liability each period. The pension liability for a defined contribution plan equals the assets in the pension plan. The computation of the pension liability for a defined benefit plan uses the pension benefit formula underlying the pension plan and requires management to estimate employee turnover, mortality, interest rates, and other factors, commonly referred to collectively as *actuarial estimates* or *actuarial assumptions*. The liability of the pension plan equals the present value of the expected amounts payable to employees (that is, the employees' expected benefits). The discount rate that firms use in measuring the liability is the rate of return on high-quality fixed-income investments with a maturity approximately equal to the period to maturity of the pension benefits.

The typical benefit formula for a defined benefit plan takes into account both the employee's length of service and salary. For example, the employer might promise to pay an employee during retirement an annual pension equal to a stated percentage (say, 2%) of the average annual salary during the employee's five highest-paid working years. In this example, an employee with 40 years of service receives an annual pension equal to 80% of that employee's average salary during the five highest-paid working years.

U.S. GAAP defines the primary measurement of the pension liability of the pension plan as the **projected benefit obligation (PBO)**—the present value of the amount the pension plan expects to pay to employees during retirement based on accumulated service but using the level of salary expected to serve as a basis for computing pension benefits. IFRS uses similar measurement methods and terminology.

A related measure of the pension obligation, found in U.S. GAAP, is the **accumulated benefit obligation (ABO)**—the present value of amounts the pension plan expects to pay to employees during retirement based on accumulated service and current salary at the time of measuring the pension liability. The difference between the PBO and the ABO relates to future salary increases, which the PBO incorporates but the ABO does not include.

U.S. GAAP and IFRS require firms to base both pension expense and funded status on the PBO (discussed later). The liability of the pension plan usually changes each period as follows:

	Projected Benefit Obligation (PBO) at Beginning of the Period
+	Increase in PBO for Interest
+	Increase in PBO for Current Employee Service (service cost)
+/−	Actuarial Gains and Losses
−	Payments to Retirees
=	Projected Benefit Obligation (PBO) at End of the Period

The projected benefit obligation changes during a period for several reasons:

- Like other long-term liabilities, it increases each period because interest accrues as the payment dates approach (that is, the payments are one year nearer to becoming cash outflows).
- It increases because employees work another period and earn rights to a larger pension.
- It changes because of changes in assumptions about employee turnover, mortality, interest (discount) rates, and similar factors.

SUMMARY OF PENSION PLAN STRUCTURE AND DEFINITIONS

Keep the following ideas from the preceding section in mind as this discussion proceeds:

1. The employer firm and the pension plan are legally separate entities, each with its own financial reports.
2. The balance sheet of a defined benefit pension plan includes the assets in the pension plan measured at fair value and the projected benefit obligation measured using a current interest rate on high-quality fixed-income investments. The difference between the assets and the liabilities indicates the extent to which a pension plan is overfunded or underfunded.

EXHIBIT 11.4 Illustrative Data for Defined Benefit Pension Plan

	Pension Plan Assets			
	2008	**2009**	**2010**	**2011**
Pension Plan Assets at Beginning of Year	$ 0	$100	$228	$379
Contributions from Employer	100	120	140	160
Income from Investments	0	8	11	30
Payments to Retirees	0	0	0	0
Pension Plan Assets at End of Year	$100	$228	$379	$569

	Pension Plan Liabilities			
	2008	**2009**	**2010**	**2011**
Pension Plan Liability at Beginning of Year.............	$ 0	$100	$228	$421
Increase from Current Service Cost	100	120	140	160
Increase from Interest...........................	0	8	18	34
Changes in Actuarial Assumptions	0	0	5	0
Change Due to Prior Service	0	0	30	0
Payments to Retirees............................	0	0	0	0
Pension Plan Liability at End of Year	$100	$228	$421	$615

3. Total pension expense over time for the employer equals the amount of cash contributed to the pension plan, although the cash contribution each period rarely equals pension expense for that period for a defined benefit plan.

ILLUSTRATION OF THE ACCOUNTING BY A DEFINED BENEFIT PENSION PLAN

This section illustrates the accounting by a defined benefit pension plan. The next section illustrates the accounting by the employer. **Exhibit 11.4** presents the assets and liabilities of a simplified pension plan for its first four years.

2008 Assume that this firm commences business on January 1, 2008, and establishes a defined benefit plan for its employees. On December 31, 2008, the firm computes the present value of retirement benefits earned by employees during the year based on one year of service and using the expected future salary levels on which the plan will ultimately pay pension benefit to employees. These computations take into consideration estimates of employee turnover, mortality, and other actuarial factors. The computation of the projected benefit obligation uses an 8% discount rate in this illustration. We assume that the employer contributes cash to the pension plan equal to the increase in the projected benefit obligation for current employees' services, $100 in 2008. Common terminology refers to this amount as the **service cost**. The assets in the pension plan equal the liabilities at the end of 2008 (that is, the plan is fully funded).

2009 During 2009 the projected benefit obligation increases by $8 (= .08 × $100) because the benefits earned during 2008 are one year closer to being paid. Common terminology refers to this amount as the **interest cost**. The projected benefit obligation also increases by $120 for current employee service, suggesting either that the firm hired additional employees during 2009 or projected salary levels increased above those anticipated at the end of 2008. The pension plan invested the cash on hand on January 1, 2009. We assume an actual return on plan assets of 8%, resulting in investment income of $8. The pension plan also receives a contribution from the employer of $120, equal to the present value of the expected benefits earned by employees for services during 2009. The assets in the pension plan at the end of 2009 equal the projected benefit obligation (that is, the pension plan remains fully funded). This result occurs because (1) the assets in the pension plan equal the projected benefit obligation at the beginning of the year, (2) the rate of return on assets equals the discount rate used to compute the projected benefit obligation, (3) the employer's contribution equals the increase in the projected benefit obligation for current services, and (4) there were no changes in actuarial estimates of employee turnover, mortality, or other factors. It is unrealistic to assume that these outcomes actually occur in practice. A divergence in any one of the first three or a change in the fourth will cause the amount of assets in the pension plan to differ from the projected benefit obligation.

2010 We make several changes in the illustration for 2010:

- The actual rate of return on pension investments is 4.8% (= $11/$228), instead of 8% during 2009. The expected return on assets is $18 (= .08 × $228).

- Changes in some of its actuarial assumptions increase the projected benefit obligation by $5.

- The employer, as part of a new labor contract, changes the pension benefit formula and agrees to give employees credit under the new benefit formula for the time they have already worked. This retroactive benefit increases the projected benefit obligation by $30. Common terminology refers to the cost of this increased benefit as **prior service cost**.

We continue to use an 8% discount rate to compute the projected benefit obligation. The service cost increases during 2010 to $140 because of more employees or higher projected salary levels, and the employer contributes this amount to the pension plan.

Exhibit 11.4 indicates that the assets in the pension plan at the end of 2010 are less than the projected benefit obligation by $42 (= $379 − $421). The pension plan is underfunded by $42 for the following reasons:

Actual Return on Investments of $11 Is Less Than the $18 Expected	$ 7
Change in Actuarial Assumptions	5
Change in Pension Benefit Formula Increasing Prior Service Cost	30
Total Amount of Underfunding	$42

In a defined benefit plan, the employer is ultimately responsible for either contributing cash or obtaining a return on pension investments sufficient to pay promised amounts to retired employees. Thus, the employer must increase its cash contribution, pension investments must generate higher returns, or changes in the projected benefit obligation in the future must offset the increased obligation.

2011 During 2011, pension fund investments earn 8% (= $30/$379), up from 4.8% in 2010. There are no changes in the interest rate used to compute the projected benefit obligation (8%), in actuarial assumptions, or in the pension benefit formula. Thus, at the end of 2011, the pension plan is underfunded by $46 (= $569 − $615) for the following reasons:

Deficient Return on Assets of $7 in 2010 plus Deficient Return on Assets of $4 [= .08 × ($7 + $5 + $30)] in 2011 Due to Lost Earnings on $7 Deficient Return in 2010 and Lost Earnings Because Employer Did Not Immediately Contribute Cash for the Change in Actuarial Assumptions and Prior Service Cost from 2010.	$11
Change in Actuarial Assumptions Carried Over from 2010	5
Change in Pension Benefit Formula Increasing Prior Service Cost Carried Over from 2010	30
Total Amount of Underfunding	$46

In this example, the pension plan carries forward the effects of underfunding in that liabilities continue to increase for interest cost but, because assets are less than liabilities, investment returns are less than the interest cost. As previously indicated in the discussion for 2010, the employer is ultimately responsible for the promised payments to retirees; this claim on the employer's assets helps explain the employer's accounting for pension arrangements and related disclosures discussed next.

ILLUSTRATION OF EMPLOYER (SPONSOR) ACCOUNTING FOR A DEFINED BENEFIT PENSION PLAN

This section discusses the employer's accounting for its pension plan. This accounting uses information for the pension plan discussed and illustrated in the previous section. This discussion considers the balance sheet, measurement of pension expense, and the relation between pension accounting on the balance sheet and the income statement.

Reporting the Funded Status on the Balance Sheet Both U.S. GAAP and IFRS require employers to recognize the funded status of a defined benefit pension plan as either an asset (pension plan is overfunded) or as a liability (pension plan is underfunded).[11] A firm with multiple plans for different groups of employees nets the pension assets and pension liabilities for each pension plan and may further combine all plans that are overfunded and, separately, all plans that are underfunded. A firm with both net underfunded plans and net overfunded plans would show both an asset (for the net overfunded plans) and a liability (for the net underfunded plans). Applying U.S. GAAP, the firm debits or credits Other Comprehensive Income, a shareholders' equity account that is not part of net income, for the offsetting amount. Applying IFRS, the firm has several options for recognizing this amount, the details of which are beyond the scope of this book. Let's continue the example from the previous section as summarized in **Exhibit 11.4**, adopting the approach of including the offset to net funded status in Other Comprehensive Income.

2008 and 2009 Pension assets equal pension liabilities at the end of 2008 and 2009. The net asset (or liability) is thus zero, and the employer's balance sheet shows neither an asset nor a liability.

2010 At the end of 2010, the pension plan is underfunded by $42, and the employer makes the following entry on its books:

December 31, 2010

Other Comprehensive Income: Performance and Actuarial Losses	12
Other Comprehensive Income: Prior Service Cost	30
Liability for Pension Benefits	42

Assets	=	Liabilities	+	Shareholders' Equity	(Class.)
		+42		−12	OCI → AOCI
				−30	OCI → AOCI

To recognize both a liability for an underfunded pension plan of $42 and offsetting entries in other comprehensive income.

The $12 debit to Other Comprehensive Income includes the deficient earnings on pension investments of $7 and the actuarial loss of $5 from changes in actuarial assumptions. Recall from the discussion in **Chapter 4** that Other Comprehensive Income and Accumulated Other Comprehensive Income report and accumulate amounts that subsequently affect net income. Other Comprehensive Income does not appear on the income statement (U.S. GAAP and IFRS do not view it as revenues, expenses, gains, or losses). Many entries in Other Comprehensive Income represent changes in fair value, in this case in the pension plan, that receive delayed recognition in net income.

Before illustrating the entry at the end of 2011, we discuss the measurement of pension expense.

Recognition of Pension Expense in the Income Statement Pension expense (or credit) for a defined benefit pension plan, under both U.S. GAAP and IFRS, comprises the following:[12]

---

[11]Financial Accounting Standards Board, *Statement of Financial Accounting Standards No. 158*, "Employers' Accounting for Defined Benefit Pension and Other Postretirement Plans," 2006 (**Codification Topics 715 and 958**). International Accounting Standards Board, *International Accounting Standard 19*, "Employee Benefits," revised 1998.

[12]Pension expense for a defined contribution plan equals the employer's contribution to the plan.

	Interest Cost (the increase in the obligation because of the passage of time)
+	Service Cost (the increase in the obligation because of an additional year of employee service)
−	Expected Return on Pension Investments
+/−	Amortization of Performance and Actuarial Gains and Losses
+/−	Amortization of Prior Service Cost
=	Net Pension Expense (or Credit)

Including interest cost as a positive amount and the expected return on pension investments as a negative amount illustrates the extent to which expected earnings from pension investments cover the increase in the pension liability caused by the passage of time. If the expected return is large enough, the firm will report a pension credit to income, as opposed to an expense. When pension assets equal pension liabilities and the expected rate of return on pension investments equals the discount rate used to compute the projected benefit obligation, as was the case for 2009 in the example above, then the amounts on these two lines offset each other. Such an outcome is unlikely. When the interest cost exceeds the expected return on pension investments, as occurred in 2010, either employer contributions or future earnings on pension plan investments must make up the difference.[13] Computing pension expense (or credit) using the expected return (not the actual return) rests on the view that pension plans should take a long-term perspective and generate earnings from investments based on a long-term expected rate of return. Annual deviations from this long-run expected rate should not flow through to net income as they occur. Finally, including service cost as a positive amount (that is, as an increase in the expense) parallels inclusion of wage and salary costs as an expense.

One of the principles underlying the accounting for pensions and other postretirement benefits is deferred recognition of the effects of deviations of actual from expected investment performance, actuarial gains and losses, and changes in prior service cost. U.S. GAAP and IFRS require firms to include these effects in Other Comprehensive Income as they occur and amortize them into net income over time. Thus, at the end of 2010, the employer's financial reports show debits to Other Comprehensive Income of $12 for performance and actuarial losses and $30 for prior service cost.

The rules for amortization of these amounts under U.S. GAAP and IFRS are complex and beyond the scope of this book,[14] but we provide a simple illustration here. Assume, for example, that the firm in the illustration amortizes $2 of performance and actuarial losses and $4 of the prior service cost during 2011. Pension expense for each of the four years is as follows:

	2008	2009	2010	2011
Interest Cost	$ 0	$ 8	$ 18	$ 34
Service Cost	100	120	140	160
Expected Return on Pension Investments . . .	(0)	(8)	(18)	(30)
Amortization of Performance and Actuarial Gains and Losses	0	0	0	2
Amortization of Prior Service Cost	0	0	0	4
Net Pension Expense	$100	$120	$140	$170

During 2008, 2009, and 2010, the firm debits Pension Expense and credits Cash for $100, $120, and $140, respectively. The entry for 2011 is as follows:

December 31, 2011

Pension Expense.	170	
Other Comprehensive Income: Performance and Actuarial Losses		2
Other Comprehensive Income: Prior Service Cost		4
Cash.		160
Liability for Pension Benefits		4

(continued)

---

[13]Employer contributions to defined benefit pension plans are subject to several forms of government regulation, none of which we consider.

[14]Firms must amortize these amounts only if they exceed a minimum threshold, which we do not consider in these illustrations.

Assets	=	Liabilities	+	Shareholders' Equity	(Class.)
−160		+4		−170	IncSt → RE
				+2	OCI → AOCI
				+4	OCI → AOCI

To recognize pension expense for 2011, credits to Other Comprehensive Income for amounts amortized, and the increase in the underfunded pension liability at the end of 2011.

The two credits to Other Comprehensive Income represent amounts carried over as debits from the end of 2010 that the firm amortized during 2011 and included in the debit to Pension Expense. The firm must therefore eliminate these amortized amounts from Other Comprehensive Income and Accumulated Other Comprehensive Income.

The credit of $4 to Liability for Pension Benefits requires further explanation. The pension plan was underfunded by $42 at the end of 2010 and by $46 at the end of 2011. The increase in underfunding occurs because the assets available for investment at the beginning of 2011 were less than the projected benefit obligation. The plan assets earned the expected rate of return of 8%, but that return was on a smaller asset base than if the firm had fully funded the plan by the end of 2010.

SUMMARY OF ACCOUNTING FOR DEFINED BENEFIT PENSION PLANS

The funded status of a defined benefit pension plan on the employer's balance sheet mirrors the overfunded or underfunded status on the books of the pension plan on each balance sheet date. Differences between pension assets and pension liabilities relate to funding policies of the employer, investment performance, changes in actuarial assumption, and changes in the pension benefit formula. Pension plans measure and report pension assets at fair values and measure and report pension liabilities using a current market interest rate for high-quality, fixed-income investments. Thus, the amounts reported on the balance sheet of the employer and of the pension fund reflect value changes as they occur.

U.S. GAAP and IFRS do not require the employer to recognize these value changes in measuring net income as the value changes occur. Instead, employers include unamortized performance and actuarial gains and losses and unamortized prior service cost in Other Comprehensive Income.[15] When firms amortize these items and include them in Pension Expense (or less commonly Pension Credit), they eliminate the amounts previously recorded in Other Comprehensive Income.

OTHER POSTRETIREMENT BENEFIT PLANS

The accounting and reporting of health care, life insurance, and other postretirement plans follow the concepts and procedures discussed and illustrated for defined benefit pension plans. For many firms, the liability for the underfunded health care obligation exceeds the liability for underfunded pensions. This occurs both because the projected rate of increase in health care costs is higher than that for salaries and because many employers do not fund (that is, make cash contributions to) their postretirement health care obligations.[16]

INTERPRETING RETIREMENT BENEFIT DISCLOSURES

Firms report extensive information about their retirement plans in notes to the financial statements. We illustrate certain of these disclosures taken from the notes to the financial

---

[15]Firms cannot currently apply the fair value option to retirement plan obligations. If those provisions did apply, firms would report unamortized items in net income as they arose. See Financial Accounting Standards Board, *Statement of Financial Accounting Standards No. 159*, "The Fair Value Option for Financial Assets and Financial Liabilities," 2007; International Accounting Standards Board, *International Accounting Standard 39*, "Financial Instruments: Recognition and Measurement," revised 2003.

[16]Both the regulatory treatment and the tax treatment of employer contributions differ substantially between postretirement health plans and defined benefit pension plans. Briefly, both regulations and tax treatments create stronger incentives to contribute to the defined benefit pension plans than to postretirement health plans. In general, the regulatory and tax treatments of employer contributions to postretirement benefit arrangements, including pensions, are jurisdiction-specific.

| EXHIBIT 11.5 | AMR Corporation Funded Status of Pension and Other Benefit Plans (amounts in millions) |

	Pension Plans		Other Benefit Plans	
	2007	2006	2007	2006
Benefit Obligation, January 1	$11,048	$11,003	$ 3,256	$ 3,384
Service Cost	370	399	71	78
Interest Cost	672	641	194	194
Plan Amendments	—	—	—	(27)
Actuarial Loss (Gain)	(1,021)	(390)	(693)	(212)
Benefits Paid	(618)	(605)	(156)	(161)
Benefit Obligation, December 31	$10,451	$11,048	$ 2,672	$ 3,256
Fair Value of Plan Assets, January 1	$ 8,565	$ 7,778	$ 202	$ 161
Actual Return on Assets	766	1,063	9	31
Employer Contributions	386	329	168	171
Benefits Paid	(618)	(605)	(155)	(161)
Fair Value of Plan Assets, December 31	$ 9,099	$ 8,565	$ 224	$ 202
Net Funded Asset (Liability)	$ (1,352)	$(2,483)	$(2,448)	$(3,054)
Recognized in:				
Current Liabilities	$ (6)	$ (8)	$ (170)	$ (187)
Noncurrent Liabilities	(1,346)	(2,475)	(2,278)	(2,867)
Net Asset (Liability) Recognized	$(1,352)	$(2,483)	$(2,448)	$(3,054)
Recognized in Shareholders' Equity:				
Prior Service Cost (Credit)	$ 137	$ 153	$ (65)	$ (78)
Net Actuarial Loss	$ 246	$ 1,311	$ (605)	$ 72

statements of AMR Corporation (AMR), the parent company of American Airlines, which applies U.S. GAAP. Disclosures from applying IFRS are similar.

Exhibit 11.5 shows the disclosures related to the funded status of pension plans and other benefit plans (health and life insurance) for two recent years. Both the pension plan and other benefit plans are underfunded. The underfunded amounts for these plans appear in current liabilities and noncurrent liabilities on the balance sheet of AMR at the end of 2006 and 2007. To provide some perspective on the amount of underfunding, AMR reports long-term debt of $9,413 million on December 31, 2007, and pension and other benefit obligations of $3,800 (= $1,352 + $2,448) million.

The amounts that AMR includes in Accumulated Other Comprehensive Income, a shareholders' equity account, represent unamortized prior service costs and net actuarial losses.

Exhibit 11.6 shows the components of net pension cost and net other benefits cost for 2005, 2006, and 2007. The interest cost and expected return on assets for pension plans largely

| EXHIBIT 11.6 | AMR Corporation Elements of Pension and Other Benefits Expense (amounts in millions) |

	Pension Plans			Other Benefit Plans		
	2007	2006	2005	2007	2006	2005
Service Cost	$370	$399	$372	$ 70	$ 78	$ 75
Interest Cost	672	641	611	194	194	197
Expected Return on Assets	(747)	(669)	(658)	(18)	(15)	(14)
Transition Asset	—	(1)	(1)	—	—	—
Prior Service Cost	16	16	16	(13)	(10)	(10)
Actuarial Loss	25	81	52	(7)	1	2
Net Expense	$336	$467	$392	$226	$248	$250

EXHIBIT 11.7

AMR Corporation
Actuarial Assumptions for Pension and Other Benefit Plans

Actuarial Assumptions:	Pension Plans		Other Benefit Plans	
	2007	2006	2007	2006
Discount Rate	6.00%	5.75%	6.0%	6.0%
Expected Return on Assets	8.75%	8.75%	8.75%	8.75%
Rate of Compensation Increase	3.78%	3.78%	—	—
Initial Health Care Cost Trend Rate	—	—	7.0%	9.0%
Ultimate Health Care Cost Trend Rate	—	—	4.5%	4.5%
Number of Years to Ultimate Trend Rate	—	—	3 years	4 years

offset, whereas interest cost significantly exceeds the expected return on assets for other benefit plans. AMR only recently began funding its other benefit plans, so the liabilities of these plans exceed the assets by a substantial amount.

The amortization of the transition asset relates to the overfunded status of AMR's pension plan when it adopted FASB *Statement of Financial Accounting Standards No. 87* in the late 1980s. The transition asset is fully amortized by the end of 2006. Observe also that amortization of the prior service cost for pensions increases net pension expense whereas amortization of prior service cost for other benefit plans decreases the net other benefits expense. AMR likely changed its pension benefit formula, increasing its pension obligation, and reduced benefits under its health care plan (for example, larger employee deductibles or co-payments), decreasing its other benefits obligation.

Exhibit 11.7 presents the estimates AMR used as inputs in accounting for its pension and other benefit plans. The discount rate used to compute the pension obligations increased from 5.75% at the end of 2006 to 6.0% at the end of 2007; this change in estimate decreases the pension obligations. **Exhibit 11.5** shows that AMR reported an actuarial gain of $1,021 million for its pension plan and $693 million for its other benefits plans for 2007 as a result of decreases in its obligations.

AMR decreased the assumed initial rate of increase in health care costs from 9% at the end of 2006 to 7% at the end of 2007. AMR also reduced the number of years before hitting the lower long-term trend rate in health care costs. These changes decrease its health care obligation and increase the actuarial gain during 2007.

Firms typically do not assume that recent rates of inflation in health care costs will continue for the remaining average working life of employees; doing so would result in a very large liability. The analyst should study carefully both the ultimate health care inflation rate estimate and the estimated pace of decline to that steady-state rate.

We next use the disclosures in **Exhibits 11.5**, **11.6**, and **11.7** to analyze the retirement benefit plans of AMR more fully.

CHANGE IN PRIOR SERVICE COSTS

Exhibit 11.5 indicates the amounts of unamortized prior service cost for pension and other benefit plans at the end of 2006 and 2007. The following analysis explains the reasons for the changes in these amounts for 2007.

	Pension Plans	Other Benefit Plans
Unamortized Prior Service Cost (Credit) at End of 2006	$153	$(78)
Plus Increase (Less Decrease) in Prior Service Cost from Plan Amendments	0	0
Amortization of Prior Service Cost for 2007	(16)	13
Unamortized Prior Service Cost (Credit) at End of Year 6	$137	$(65)

Exhibit 11.5 discloses the amounts for the change in prior service cost or credit from plan amendments when explaining the change in the benefit obligations. **Exhibit 11.6** discloses

the amounts for amortization of prior service cost as they affect net pension expense and net other benefits expense for 2007.

CHANGE IN ACTUARIAL LOSSES

We can analyze the change in unamortized actuarial losses similarly.

	Pension Plans	Other Benefit Plans
Unamortized Actuarial Loss at End of 2006	$ 1,311	$ 72
Less Actuarial Gains for 2007	$(1,021)	(693)
Less Excess of Actual Return over Expected Return on Investments: $766 − $747; $9 − $18	(19)	9
Amortization of Actuarial Loss (Gain) for 2007	(25)	7
Unamortized Actuarial Loss (Gain) at End of 2007	$ 246	$(605)

The amounts for the actuarial gain for 2007 appear in the analysis of the change in the pension and other benefits obligations in **Exhibit 11.5**. **Exhibits 11.5** and **11.6** include the amounts for the actual and expected returns on investments, respectively. **Exhibit 11.6** includes the amounts for amortization of the actuarial loss and gain for 2007.

JOURNAL ENTRY TO RECORD CHANGE IN BENEFIT OBLIGATIONS

We can now reconstruct the journal entry AMR made to record the change in the underfunded pension obligation for 2007 as follows:

2007

Pension Expense	336	
Pension Liability (Current Liability: $8 − $6)	2	
Pension Liability (Noncurrent Liability: $2,475 − $1,346)	1,129	
Cash		386
Other Comprehensive Income (Prior Service Cost:		
$153 − $137)		16
Other Comprehensive Income (Actuarial Loss: $1,311 − $246)		1,065

Assets	=	Liabilities	+	Shareholders' Equity	(Class.)
−386		−2		−336	IncSt → RE
		−1,129		+16	OCI → AOCI
				+1,065	OCI → AOCI

To record pension expense, pension funding, and the change in balance sheet accounts related to the pension plan.

Exhibits 11.5 and **11.6** provide the amounts for pension contribution and pension expense, respectively. The entries for the underfunded pension liability reported in current liabilities and noncurrent liabilities adjust the amounts on the balance sheet at the end of 2006 to their amounts at the end of 2007. The entries in Other Comprehensive Income reflect the changes in unamortized prior service cost and actuarial loss during 2007. The preceding two sections, pages 532–533, provide the amounts for the changes in prior service cost and actuarial loss.

Recall that neither U.S. GAAP nor IFRS requires the recognition of changes in the plan assets or benefit obligations in measuring pension or other benefits expense as those changes occur. Firms initially include incurred but not yet amortized amounts in Other Comprehensive Income and then remove them from Other Comprehensive Income when they include them in pension or other benefits expense. For example, AMR amortized $16 million of prior service cost related to its pension plan during 2007. The preceding entry credits Other Comprehensive Income to remove this portion of the amount previously debited to this account when AMR changed its pension plan. The offsetting debit is to Pension Expense, which **Exhibit 11.6** indicates includes the $16 amortization of prior service cost for 2007.

The journal entry for other benefit plans for 2007 is as follows:

2007

Other Benefits Expense	226	
Other Benefits Liability (Current Liability: $187 − $170)	17	
Other Benefits Liability (Noncurrent Liability: $2,867 − $2,278)	589	
Other Comprehensive Income (Prior Service Credit: $78 − $65)	13	
Cash...		168
Other Comprehensive Income (Actuarial Gain: $(605) − $72)		677

Assets	=	Liabilities	+	Shareholders' Equity	(Class.)
−168		−17		−226	IncSt → RE
		−589		−13	OCI → AOCI
				+677	OCI → AOCI

To record other benefits expense, other benefits funding, and the change in balance sheet accounts related to other benefit plans during 2007.

The explanation of the amounts in this entry is identical to those above for the entry for AMR's pension obligation.

PROBLEM 11.2 for Self-Study

Interpreting Retirement Plan Disclosures. Exhibit 11.8 presents the elements of pension, health care, and life insurance expense for General Electric (GE) for 2005, 2006, and 2007. **Exhibit 11.9** presents the funded status of pension, health care, and life insurance plans for 2006 and 2007, as well as a listing of the actuarial assumptions made.

a. Refer to the disclosures in **Exhibit 11.9** of GE's benefit obligation for its principal pension plans. What is the likely explanation for the actuarial gain of $3,205 million in 2007?

b. Refer to the disclosures in **Exhibit 11.9** for the amount of prior service cost for both pension plans and health care and life insurance plans. What is the likely explanation for the increase in prior service cost for 2007?

c. Evaluate the performance of GE's pension, health care, and life insurance plan investments in 2006 and 2007 relative to expectations.

d. Why does GE include the net funded asset for its principal pension plans in both assets and liabilities on its balance sheet?

(continued)

EXHIBIT 11.8

General Electric Inc.
Elements of Pension (Principal Plans),
Health Care, and Life Insurance Expense
(amounts in millions)
(Problem 11.2 for Self-Study)

	Principal Pension Plans			Health Care and Life Insurance Plans		
	2007	2006	2005	2007	2006	2005
Service Cost.........................	$ 1,355	$ 1,402	$ 1,359	$ 286	$ 229	$ 243
Interest Cost	2,416	2,304	2,248	577	455	507
Expected Return on Assets	(3,950)	(3,811)	(3,885)	(125)	(127)	(138)
Prior Service Cost	241	253	256	603	363	326
Actuarial Loss	693	729	351	(17)	64	70
Net Expense.........................	$ 755	$ 877	$ 329	$1,324	$ 984	$1,008

EXHIBIT 11.9

General Electric Inc.
Funded Status of Pension (Principal Plans),
Health Care, and Life Insurance Plans
(amounts in millions)
(Problem 11.2 for Self-Study)

	Principal Pension Plans		Health Care and Life Insurance Plans	
	2007	2006	2007	2006
Benefit Obligation, January 1	$43,293	$43,331	$ 8,262	$ 9,084
Service Cost	1,355	1,402	286	229
Interest Cost	2,416	2,304	577	455
Plan Amendments	1,470	80	4,257	—
Actuarial Loss (Gain)	(3,205)	(1,514)	320	(707)
Participant Contributions	173	162	47	43
Benefits Paid	(2,555)	(2,472)	(796)	(810)
Other	—	—	30	(32)
Benefit Obligation, December 31	$42,947	$43,293	$ 12,983	$ 8,262
Fair Value of Plan Assets, January 1	$54,758	$49,096	$ 1,710	$ 1,619
Actual Return on Assets	7,188	7,851	221	222
Employer Contributions	136	121	622	636
Participant Contributions	173	162	47	43
Benefits Paid	(2,555)	(2,472)	(796)	(810)
Fair Value of Plan Assets, December 31	$59,700	$54,758	$ 1,804	$ 1,710
Net Funded Asset (Liability)	$16,753	$11,465	$(11,179)	$(6,552)
Recognized in:				
Noncurrent Assets	$20,190	$15,019	$ —	$ —
Current Liabilities	(111)	(106)	(675)	(681)
Noncurrent Liabilities	(3,326)	(3,448)	(10,504)	(5,871)
Net Asset (Liability) Recognized	$16,753	$11,465	$(11,179)	$(6,552)
Recognized in Shareholders' Equity:				
Prior Service Cost	$ 2,060	$ 831	$ 5,700	$ 2,046
Net Actuarial Loss (Gain)	$(4,974)	$ 2,162	$210	$(31)
Actuarial Assumptions:				
Discount Rate	6.34%	5.70%	6.31%	5.75%
Expected Return on Assets	8.50%	8.50%	8.50%	8.50%
Rate of Compensation Increase	5.00%	5.00%	—	—
Initial Health Care Cost Trend Rate	—	—	9.10%	9.20%
Ultimate Health Care Cost Trend Rate	—	—	6.00%	5.00%
Number of Years to Ultimate Trend Rate	—	—	18 years	7 years

e. Prepare an analysis that explains the change in the prior service cost included in shareholders' equity from $831 at the end of 2006 to $2,060 at the end of 2007 for GE's principal pension plans and from $2,046 at the end of 2006 to $5,700 at the end of 2007 for its health care and life insurance plans.

f. Prepare an analysis that explains the change in the net actuarial loss (gain) included in shareholders' equity from a loss of $2,162 at the end of 2006 to a gain of $4,974 at the end of 2007 for GE's principal pension plans and from a gain of $31 at the end of 2006 to a loss of $210 at the end of 2007 for its health care and life insurance plans.

g. Give the journal entry that GE made on its books to recognize pension expense, pension funding, and the change in the net funded asset for 2007.

h. Give the journal entry that GE made on its books to recognize health care and life insurance expense and funding and the change in the net funded liability for 2007.

INCOME TAXES

Previous chapters have discussed the recognition and measurement of various revenues and expenses without giving much consideration to the impact of these revenues and expenses on income tax expense. Yet, income tax expense affects assessments of profitability as much as any other expense. A common ratio for analyzing the effect of income taxes on profitability is the effective tax rate, equal to income tax expense[17] divided by financial reporting income before income taxes:

$$\text{Effective Tax Rate} = \frac{\text{Income Tax Expense}}{\text{Pretax Book Income}}$$

Consider the data for three pharmaceutical companies in **Exhibit 11.10**.

EXHIBIT 11.10 **Effective Income Tax Rates and Profit Margin Data for Three Pharmaceutical Companies**

	Merck	Johnson & Johnson	Pfizer
Effective Tax Rate	28.7%	24.2%	15.3%
Income Before Income Taxes/Revenues	27.5%	27.4%	26.9%
Net Income/Revenues	19.6%	20.7%	22.8%

Merck has the highest ratio of income before income taxes to revenues but the lowest ratio of net income to revenues because it has the highest effective tax rate. Pfizer on the other hand has the lowest ratio of income before income taxes to revenues but the highest ratio of net income to revenues because it has the lowest effective tax rate.

This section discusses the measurement of income tax expense and how information about income tax positions appears in the notes to the financial statements. We consider both U.S. GAAP[18] and IFRS,[19] which provide similar authoritative guidance.

MEASUREMENT OF INCOME TAX EXPENSE

One might think that income tax expense for a period equals the income taxes imposed by governmental entities on the taxable income shown on a firm's income tax returns for that period. That is, income tax *expense* equals income tax *payable* for the period. The measurement of income tax expense is more complicated, however, because the amounts of revenues and expenses recognized for financial reporting purposes will usually differ from the amounts of revenues and expenses reported for income tax purposes. In the discussion that follows, we use these terms:

- *Book purposes* and *tax purposes* to distinguish the financial statements from the tax return.

- *Pretax book income* to refer to financial statement income and *taxable income* to refer to income on the tax return.

- *Book basis* to refer to the unamortized cost of an item for financial reporting and *tax basis* to refer to the unamortized cost of an item for tax reporting.

The difference between pretax book income and taxable income arises from two factors.

1. **Permanent Differences**—book income includes revenues (such as tax-exempt interest revenue) or expenses (such as certain fines) that taxable income never includes.

---

[17]Firms often use the terminology *provision for income taxes* instead of *income tax expense* in their financial reports. See the **Glossary**. In U.S. GAAP, *provision* means an expense account; in IFRS, *provision* means a liability account. We urge you not to use *provision* in an account title for this reason.

[18]Financial Accounting Standards, *Statement of Financial Accounting Standards No. 109*, "Accounting for Income Taxes," 1992 (**Codification Topic 740**).

[19]International Accounting Standards Board, *International Accounting Standard 12*, "Income Taxes," (revised 1996).

2. **Temporary Differences**—book income includes revenues and expenses (such as depreciation on long-lived assets and bad debt expense) in one period whereas taxable income includes them in a different period.

Firms compute **income tax payable** for a period using taxable income as the base. Taxable income excludes permanent differences and uses the accounting methods that the income tax law and regulations either require or permit firms to use for tax reporting. The number and nature of permanent differences and temporary differences are jurisdiction-specific.

A more controversial issue concerns the appropriate base for computing **income tax expense**, the amount reported on the financial statements. The issue: should income tax expense equal

1. The income taxes actually payable each period based on taxable income, or

2. The income taxes actually payable each period plus (minus) the income taxes a firm expects to pay (save) in the future when temporary differences between book income and taxable income of the current period reverse?

Advocates of the first approach view income taxes similar to other taxes (such as property taxes, sales taxes, and payroll taxes). Government entities define the tax base (for example, assessed value of property, sales revenue, or payroll costs) and apply a tax rate to this tax base to measure the taxes due each period. One possible approach to financial reporting for income taxes would set income taxes expense equal to income taxes currently payable.

Advocates of the second approach focus on two financial reporting objectives: recognizing the amount of taxes payable in the current year and recognizing **deferred tax assets** and **deferred tax liabilities** for the future income tax consequences of temporary differences. Under this approach, a temporary difference that implies a future tax deduction gives rise to a deferred tax asset, and a temporary difference that implies a future increase in income tax payable gives rise to a deferred tax liability. The accountant computes income tax expense using pretax amounts for financial reporting, not the amounts on income tax returns. Note that permanent differences never reverse, never affect cash outflows for income taxes, and therefore never affect income tax expense for any period. The second approach forms the basis for both U.S. GAAP and IFRS requirements for income tax accounting for financial reporting purposes.[20]

ILLUSTRATION OF TEMPORARY DIFFERENCES

Exhibit 11.11, which shows data for Burns Corporation for a six-year period, illustrates some of the issues in accounting for income taxes for a firm with temporary differences. Burns Corporation acquires equipment that cost $120,000 and that has a six-year life with no expected salvage value. Columns **(1)** and **(5)** show that Burns Corporation's income *before depreciation expense and income tax expense* is $100,000 for each of the six years of the asset's life.

Columns **(1)** through **(4)** show data from the income tax return of Burns Corporation for each of the six years. The firm computes depreciation using an allowable depreciation method under the U.S. tax code, which results in accelerated depreciation deductions relative to the straight-line depreciation method. Column **(3)** shows the amount of taxable income after subtracting accelerated depreciation. Column **(4)** shows the amount of income taxes payable for each year using an income tax rate of 40%.

The data in columns **(5)** through **(7)** come from the financial statements of Burns Corporation. Column **(6)** shows depreciation expense computed using the straight-line method. Column **(7)** shows the amounts of pretax book income.

Assume, contrary to U.S. GAAP and IFRS, that Burns Corporation reported income tax expense equal to income tax payable, so that income tax expense equals the amounts in column **(4)**, resulting in the hypothetical net income numbers in column **(8)**. The caption on column **(8)** does not say *Net Income* because U.S. GAAP and IFRS do not measure income tax expense in this way. Column **(8)** shows pretax book income minus income taxes payable.

Note the over-time behavior of the hypothetical income numbers in column **(8)**: up 11.6% from the first year to the second year, down 11.3% from the second year to the third year, and down in each of the next three years by varying amounts. Recall, from **Chapter 4**, that one purpose of the income statement is to assist a user of financial reports to understand *why*

[20]Financial Accounting Standards Board, *Statement of Financial Accounting Standards No. 109,* "Accounting for Income Taxes," 1996 (**Codification Topic 740**); International Accounting Standards Board, *International Accounting Standard 12,* "Income Taxes," 1996, 2001. The two standards have broadly similar requirements, but differences exist that are beyond the scope of this book.

EXHIBIT 11.11

Burns Corporation
Computation of Income Taxes over Six-Year Life of Equipment
(Equipment Costs $120,000 and Has Six-Year Life)

Information from (or Based on) Tax Returns

Year	Income Before Depreciation and Taxes [1]	Depreciation Deduction on Tax Return [2]	Taxable Income [3]	Income Taxes Payable [4]
1	$100,000	$24,000	$76,000	$30,400
2	100,000	38,400	61,600	24,640
3	100,000	22,800	77,200	30,880
4	100,000	14,400	85,600	34,240
5	100,000	13,200	86,800	34,720
6	100,000	7,200	92,800	37,120
Totals		$120,000	$480,000	$192,000

Information from (or Based on) Financial Statements

				Accounting Not Allowed by U.S. GAAP and IFRS		Accounting Required by U.S. GAAP and IFRS	
Year	Income Before Depreciation and Taxes [5]	Depreciation Expense [6]	Pretax Income = $100,000 − $20,000 [7]	Pretax Income Less Income Taxes Payable [8]	Percentage Change in Column [8] [9]	Pretax Income Less Income Taxes at 40% of Pretax Income [10]	Percentage Change in Column [10] [11]
1	$100,000	$20,000	$80,000	$49,600	—	$48,000	—
2	100,000	20,000	80,000	55,360	11.6%	48,000	—
3	100,000	20,000	80,000	49,120	−11.3%	48,000	—
4	100,000	20,000	80,000	45,760	−6.8%	48,000	—
5	100,000	20,000	80,000	45,280	−1.0%	48,000	—
6	100,000	20,000	80,000	42,880	−5.3%	48,000	—
Totals		$120,000	$480,000	$288,000		$288,000	

[1] = Given   [3] = [1] − [2]   [5] = Given   [7] = [5] − [6]   [9] = ([8] this year/[8] last year) − 1

[2] = Given   [4] = .40 × [3]   [6] = $120,000/6   [8] = [7] − [4]   [10] = (1.00 − .40) × [7]

EXHIBIT 11.12	Burns Corporation Summary Computation of Income Tax Expense

Year (1)	Income Taxes Payable (2)	Tax Depreciation (3)	Book Depreciation (4)	Temporary Difference (5)	40% of Temporary Difference (6)	Income Tax Expense (7)
1.............	$ 30,400	$ 24,000	$ 20,000	$ 4,000	$ 1,600	$ 32,000
2.............	24,640	38,400	20,000	18,400	7,360	32,000
3.............	30,880	22,800	20,000	2,800	1,120	32,000
4.............	34,240	14,400	20,000	(5,600)	(2,240)	32,000
5.............	34,720	13,200	20,000	(6,800)	(2,720)	32,000
6.............	37,120	7,200	20,000	(12,800)	(5,120)	32,000
Totals..........	$192,000	$120,000	$120,000	$ 0	$ 0	$192,000

Column (5) = Column (3) − Column (4).

Column (6) = .40 × Column (5).

Column (7) = Column (2) + Column (6).

income behaves over time as it does. When operations remain the same year after year and tax rates do not change, the user of financial reports will expect net income to remain the same. The numbers in column **(8)**, however, portray instability, even though Burns Corporation does the same thing for six years, and its performance remains constant over the six-year period. If income tax expense equaled income taxes payable, reported earnings would vary from year to year simply because temporary differences cause book income before taxes to differ from taxable income.

U.S. GAAP and IFRS require firms to calculate income tax expense based on pretax book income. Thus, when pretax book income remains the same, $80,000 (= $100,000 − $20,000) in this example, income tax expense also remains the same, $32,000 (= .40 × $80,000). Net income is $48,000 (= $80,000 − $32,000) each year, as column **(10)** shows. This example assumes there are no permanent differences.

Exhibit 11.12 summarizes the computation of income tax expense for each year in this example. Income tax expense in column **(7)** equals income taxes currently payable in column **(2)** plus (minus) the income tax the firm expects to pay (save) in the future on the temporary depreciation difference in column **(5)**. Total income tax expense of $192,000 for the six years equals total cash payments for income taxes of $192,000. Note also that the time-series pattern of expense recognition differs from the pattern of cash outflows.

RECORDING INCOME TAX EXPENSE

Exhibits 11.11 and **11.12** illustrate that income tax expense differs from income tax payable each year. The difference in the first year in this example gives rise to a deferred tax liability. The temporary difference associated with accelerated depreciation for tax purposes and straight-line depreciation for financial reporting purposes means that Burns Corporation will pay lower income taxes in the early years of the asset's life, but this temporary difference will reverse over the entire six years, resulting in higher taxes in later years. The journal entry to record income taxes for the first year is as follows:

December 31, First Year

Income Tax Expense	32,000	
Income Tax Payable		30,400
Deferred Tax Liability		1,600

Assets	=	Liabilities	+	Shareholders' Equity	(Class.)
		+30,400		−32,000	IncSt → RE
		+1,600			

To record income tax expense for the first year.

The credit to the Deferred Tax Liability account represents the income taxes saved (today) because Burns Corporation claimed more depreciation for tax purposes than for book purposes. Burns Corporation will make similar entries for the second and third years, adding $7,360 to the Deferred Tax Liability account for the second year and $1,120 for the third year. The balance in the Deferred Tax Liability account at the end of the third year is $10,080 (= $1,600 + $7,360 + $1,120). This amount equals the 40% tax rate times the cumulative difference between tax depreciation of $85,200 (= $24,000 + $38,400 + $22,800) and book depreciation of $60,000 (= $20,000 × 3).

The temporary differences for depreciation begin to reverse in the fourth year. The journal entry to recognize income tax expense for the fourth year is as follows:

December 31, Fourth Year

Income Tax Expense	32,000	
Deferred Tax Liability	2,240	
Income Tax Payable		34,240

Assets	=	Liabilities	+	Shareholders' Equity	(Class.)
		+34,240		−32,000	IncSt → RE
		−2,240			

To record income tax expense for the fourth year.

Depreciation recognized for financial reporting, $20,000, exceeds the depreciation deduction for tax purposes, $14,400. The portion of the deferred tax liability that is currently payable is $2,240 [= .40 × ($20,000 − $14,400)]. Burns Corporation will make similar entries in the fifth year, reducing (debiting) the deferred tax liability by $2,720 [= .40 × ($20,000 − $13,200)], and in the sixth year, reducing the deferred tax liability by $5,120 [= .40 × ($20,000 − $7,200)]. The reductions in the Deferred Tax Liability account in these three years total $10,080 (= $2,240 + $2,720 + $5,120), resulting in a zero balance at the end of the sixth year. Total lifetime depreciation amounts on the equipment for both financial reporting and tax reporting are the same: $120,000; only the timing differs. **Exhibit 11.13** illustrates the entries for the six years in a T-account for the deferred tax liability.

EXHIBIT 11.13

Burns Corporation
Deferred Tax Liability Account
(amounts with check mark appear on the balance sheet)

Deferred Tax Liability		
	0 √	Balance at Beginning of First Year
	1,600 [1]	Entry for First Year
	1,600 √	Balance at End of First Year
	7,360 [2]	Entry for Second Year
	8,960 √	Balance at End of Second Year
	1,120 [3]	Entry for Third Year
	10,080 √	Balance at End of Third Year
Entry for Fourth Year [4] 2,240		
	7,840 √	Balance at End of Fourth Year
Entry for Fifth Year [5] 2,720		
	5,120 √	Balance at End of Fifth Year
Entry for Sixth Year [6] 5,120		
	0 √	Balance at End of Sixth Year

PROBLEM 11.3 for Self-Study

Computing income tax expense. Wade Corporation acquires a machine on January 1 of the current year, costing $80,000 and having a four-year useful life and zero salvage value. Wade deducts depreciation on its income tax return as follows:

- 33% of the cost of the machine in First Year
- 44% in Second Year
- 15% in Third Year
- 8% in Fourth Year

The firm uses the straight-line method for financial reporting. Income before depreciation and income taxes is $100,000 each year, and the income tax rate is 40%.

a. Compute the amount of income taxes currently payable for each year.

b. Compute the amount of income tax expense for each year.

c. Give the journal entries for income taxes for each year.

A FURTHER LOOK AT FINANCIAL REPORTING REQUIREMENTS FOR INCOME TAXES

The illustration for Burns Corporation in the previous section showed that income tax expense each period equals pretax book income multiplied by the income tax rate; in each year, income tax expense is $32,000 (= .40 × $80,000). Income tax expense for Burns Corporation also equals income taxes currently payable plus the change in the deferred tax liability. For example, income tax expense for the first year equals income taxes currently payable of $30,400 plus the $1,600 increase in the deferred tax liability. Income tax expense for the fourth year equals income taxes currently payable of $34,240 reduced by the $2,240 debit (reduction) to the deferred tax liability. The deferred tax liability changed each year by the amount of the tax effect of the temporary differences between depreciation for financial reporting and depreciation for tax reporting.

U.S. GAAP and IFRS require a more complex procedure for accounting for income taxes than this simple example for Burns Corporation illustrates. The principal complexities are as follows:

1. Income tax rates change over time, so the deferred tax liability need not represent the amount of taxes that the firm must pay later.

2. Some temporary differences create deferred tax assets. A deferred tax asset arises when a firm recognizes an expense earlier for financial reporting than for tax reporting. For example, firms provide for estimated uncollectible accounts when they recognize sales on account but delay the tax deduction until later, when firms judge that particular customers' accounts are uncollectible. As another example, firms provide for estimated warranty cost in the year they sell warranted products but delay the tax deduction until later, when firms make actual expenditures for warranty repairs.

3. Firms recognize deferred tax assets only to the extent that they expect to generate sufficient taxable income to realize the assets in the form of tax savings in the future. U.S. GAAP requires use of a **deferred tax asset valuation allowance** (similar in concept to an allowance for uncollectible accounts) to reduce the balance in the Deferred Tax Asset account to the amount the firm expects to realize in tax savings in the future. IFRS requires that firms recognize the expected realizable amount of deferred tax assets, with explanatory disclosures.

Thus, the Deferred Tax Asset or Deferred Tax Liability accounts on the balance sheet can change each period for the following reasons:

1. Temporary differences originate or reverse during the current period.

2. Income tax rates expected to apply in future periods when temporary differences reverse change during the current period.

3. A firm's expectations of future taxable income, which affect whether a firm can realize the deferred tax assets through an actual reduction in cash outflows, change during the current period.

The example for Burns Corporation in **Exhibit 11.11** illustrates only the first factor, temporary differences. In such cases, we can measure income tax expense using pretax book income amounts and add or subtract the difference between income tax expense and income tax payable to deferred tax assets or deferred tax liability accounts. Because the second and third factors often occur, U.S. GAAP and IFRS require firms to measure income tax expense following a procedure more complex than the one illustrated for Burns Corporation.[21]

PROBLEM 11.4 for Self-Study

Working backward to components of book and taxable income. Dominiak Company reports the following information for financial and tax reporting for a year:

Depreciation Expense for Financial Reporting	$270,000
Pretax Book Income for Financial Reporting	160,000
Income Tax Expense for Financial Reporting	36,000
Income Tax Payable for Tax Reporting	24,000

The federal and state governments combine to tax taxable income at a rate of 40%. Permanent differences result from municipal bond interest that appears as revenue for book purposes but is exempt from income taxes. Temporary differences result from the use of accelerated depreciation for tax purposes and the straight-line method for financial reporting.

Reconstruct the income statement for financial reporting and for tax reporting for the year, identifying temporary differences and permanent differences.

DISCLOSURE OF INCOME TAXES IN THE FINANCIAL STATEMENTS

Notes to the financial statements provide additional information about income tax expense and deferred tax assets and deferred tax liabilities. **Exhibit 11.14** illustrates these disclosures for Pfizer Inc., a pharmaceutical company, that applies U.S. GAAP. Disclosures under IFRS would be similar. Firms report four items of information:

1. **Components of Income Before Income Taxes** This disclosure shows the amounts of book income before income taxes from Pfizer's domestic operations and its international operations.

   Pfizer derived approximately three-fourths of its pretax book income from countries other than the United States in 2006. Its lower domestic pretax book incomes in 2005 and 2007 resulted from restructuring charges and other charges related to acquisitions of other companies.

2. **Components of Income Tax Expense** This section indicates the amount of income taxes currently payable and the amount deferred because of temporary differences for both domestic operations and international operations.

   The information disclosed in these first two sections permits the calculation of the effective tax rate for domestic, international, and domestic and international operations combined. The effective taxes rates for Pfizer for 2007 are as follows:

   Domestic: $(350)/$242 = not meaningful

   International: $1,373/$9,036 = 15.2%

   Combined: $1,023/$9,278 = 11.0%

   The next section discusses the effective tax rate more fully.

3. **Reconciliation from Statutory to Effective Tax Rate** The **effective tax rate** equals income tax expense divided by book income before income taxes. This section gives the reasons

<hr>

[21]The Web site for this book contains a file titled "Further Issues in Accounting for Income Taxes" that discusses and illustrates this more complex procedure.

the effective tax rate differs from the 35% statutory federal income tax rate. The reasons generally fall into one of two categories: (1) income tax rate differences, and (2) permanent differences.

The disclosures for Pfizer indicate that a recurring and important reason for an effective tax rate lower than the 35% statutory tax rate is lower tax rates on earnings generated in other countries. The assumption on the first line of the tax reconciliation is that government entities worldwide impose a 35% tax rate. The tax reconciliation indicates the effect (in Pfizer's case, a reduction) on the effective tax rate that results from taxes imposed by foreign governments at rates other than 35%. Research tax credits also reduce Pfizer's effective tax rate on an ongoing basis. Another recurring item in the reconciliation for Pfizer is an addition for acquired in-process research and development (IPR&D). Recall from the discussion in **Chapter 9** that firms recognize the fair value of acquired IPR&D as an asset and then amortize it over the expected period of benefit. However, the income tax law generally does not permit the acquiring firm to deduct this amount on its income tax return. This difference in financial reporting and tax reporting gives rise to a permanent difference between book income and taxable income. The assumption on the first line of the tax reconciliation is that all items of revenue and expense are subject to a 35% tax rate. Because IPR&D is never deductible for tax purposes, the reconciliation shows an addition to the effective tax rate. The remaining items in the tax reconciliation for Pfizer result from events affecting only one or two years and therefore do not appear to have a continuing tax impact.

4. **Components of Deferred Tax Assets and Liabilities** This section discloses the types of temporary differences that result in deferred tax assets and deferred tax liabilities on the balance sheet at the end of each period.

Pfizer is not unusual in showing a variety of reconciling items that affect both deferred tax assets and deferred tax liabilities. The relatively large deferred tax liabilities for intangibles and property, plant, and equipment result from more rapid amortization and depreciation for tax purposes than for book purposes. The deferred tax liability for unremitted earnings results because Pfizer recognizes earnings when the foreign entity earns income, but reports taxable income only when it receives a cash distribution from the foreign entity (also called a *repatriation of foreign-source income*) for tax purposes. The deferred tax asset for employee benefits results from Pfizer having underfunded employee benefit plans. Pfizer recognizes retirement benefits expense in its financial statements earlier than it contributes cash to its retirement plans and receives an income tax deduction. The deferred tax asset reflects the future tax benefits when Pfizer claims an income tax deduction for retirement benefits. Note that Pfizer reports a small valuation allowance on its deferred tax assets to reduce the deferred tax asset to the amount that Pfizer expects to realize in the form of reductions in taxable income. Pfizer's valuation allowance likely relates to the probability of its being able to realize all the tax benefits of net operating loss and credit carryforwards. The last panel of data shows where Pfizer reports deferred tax assets and deferred tax liabilities on its balance sheet.

We noted earlier that income tax expense equals income taxes currently payable plus, or minus as appropriate, the changes in the deferred tax asset and deferred tax liability accounts. Unfortunately, most disclosures do not permit us to illustrate this concept. The difficulty arises from the omission of detailed amounts reported for deferred tax assets and deferred tax liabilities. These amounts include the tax effects of temporary differences that affect book income during the current period as well as the tax effects of temporary differences that affect Other Comprehensive Income of the current period (and will affect book income of later periods).

SUMMARY OF ACCOUNTING FOR INCOME TAXES

The central question in accounting for income taxes is the recognition and measurement of the tax effects of temporary differences between book and taxable income: when do they originate, and when do they reverse? In measuring income tax expense, U.S. GAAP and IFRS require recognition of the tax effect when temporary differences originate. Any difference between income tax expense and income taxes payable for a given reporting period results in a deferred tax asset or deferred tax liability. The notes to the financial statements provide information on the components of book income before taxes, the current and deferred portions of income tax expense, a reconciliation between income taxes at the statutory rate and the effective rate, and the components of deferred tax assets and deferred tax liabilities.

EXHIBIT 11.14

Pfizer Inc.
Disclosures in the Income Tax Note

1. INCOME BEFORE TAXES

Income from continuing operations before provision for taxes on income, minority interests and the cumulative effect of a change in accounting principles consists of the following:

(millions of dollars)	Year Ended December 31,		
	2007	2006	2005
United States	$ 242	$ 3,266	$ 985
International	9,036	9,762	9,815
Total Income from Continuing Operations Before Provision for Taxes on Income, Minority Interests and Cumulative Effect of a Change in Accounting Principles	$9,278	$13,028	$10,800

2. TAXES ON INCOME

The provision for taxes on income from continuing operations before minority interests and the cumulative effect of a change in accounting principles consists of the following:

	Year Ended December 31,		
	2007	2006	2005
United States:			
Taxes Currently Payable:			
Federal	$ 1,393	$ 1,399	$ 2,572
State and Local	243	205	108
Deferred Income Taxes	(1,986)	(1,371)	(1,295)
Total U.S. Tax (Benefit)/Provision	(350)	233	1,385
International:			
Taxes Currently Payable	2,175	1,913	1,963
Deferred Income Taxes	(802)	(154)	(170)
Total International Tax Provision	1,373	1,759	1,793
Total Provision for Taxes on Income	$ 1,023	$ 1,992	$ 3,178

3. TAX RATE RECONCILIATION

Reconciliation of the U.S. statutory income tax rate to our effective tax rate for continuing operations before the cumulative effect of a change in accounting principles follows:

	Year Ended December 31,		
	2007	2006	2005
U.S. Statutory Income Tax Rate	35.0%	35.0%	35.0%
Earnings Taxed at Other Than U.S. Statutory Rate	(21.6)	(15.7)	(20.6)
Resolution of Certain Tax Positions	—	(3.4)	(5.4)
Tax Legislation Impact	—	(1.7)	—
U.S. Research Tax Credit and Manufacturing Deduction	(1.5)	(0.5)	(0.8)
Repatriation of Foreign Earnings	—	(1.0)	15.4
Acquired IPR&D	1.1	2.2	5.4
All Other—net	(2.0)	0.4	0.4
Effective Tax Rate for Income from Continuing Operations Before Cumulative Effect of a Change in Accounting Principles	11.0%	15.3%	29.4%

(continued)

EXHIBIT 11.14   **(Continued)**

4. DEFERRED TAXES

Deferred taxes arise because of different timing treatment between financial statement accounting and tax accounting, known as "temporary differences." We record the tax effect of these temporary differences as "deferred tax assets" (generally items that we can use as a tax deduction or credit in future periods) or "deferred tax liabilities" (generally items for which we received a tax deduction, but have not yet recorded in the consolidated statement of income).

The tax effect of the major items recorded as deferred tax assets and liabilities, shown before jurisdictional netting, as of December 31, is as follows:

(millions of dollars)	2007 Deferred Tax		2006 Deferred Tax	
	Assets	(Liabilities)	Assets	(Liabilities)
Prepaid/Deferred Items	$1,315	$ (431)	$ 1,164	$ (312)
Intangibles	897	(6,737)	841	(7,704)
Property, Plant, and Equipment	300	(957)	104	(1,105)
Employee Benefits	2,552	(740)	3,141	(804)
Restructurings and Other Charges	717	(11)	573	(19)
Net Operating Loss/Credit Carryforwards	1,842	—	1,061	—
Unremitted Earnings	—	(3,550)	—	(3,567)
State and Local Tax Adjustments	529	—	—	—
All Other	848	(37)	912	(392)
Subtotal	9,000	(12,463)	7,796	(13,903)
Valuation Allowance	(158)	—	(194)	—
Total Deferred Taxes	$8,842	$(12,463)	$ 7,602	$(13,903)
Net Deferred Tax Liability		$ (3,621)		$ (6,301)

Valuation allowances are provided when we believe that our deferred tax assets are not recoverable, based on an assessment of estimated future taxable income that incorporates ongoing, prudent, feasible tax planning strategies.

Deferred tax assets and liabilities in the preceding table, netted by taxing jurisdiction, are in the following captions in our consolidated balance sheets:

(millions of dollars)	As of December 31,	
	2007	2006
Current Deferred Tax Asset[a]	$ 1,664	$ 1,384
Noncurrent Deferred Tax Assets[b]	2,441	354
Current Deferred Tax Liability[c]	(30)	(24)
Noncurrent Deferred Tax Liability[d]	(7,696)	(8,015)
Net Deferred Tax Liability	$(3,621)	$(6,301)

(a) Included in *Prepaid Expenses and Taxes*.

(b) Included in *Other Assets, Deferred Taxes and Deferred Charges*.

(c) Included in *Other Current Liabilities*.

(d) Included in *Deferred Taxes*.

SOLUTIONS TO SELF-STUDY PROBLEMS

SUGGESTED SOLUTION TO PROBLEM 11.1 FOR SELF-STUDY

(International Paper Company; off-balance-sheet financing.)

a. IP receives an immediate benefit of $75 million cash on January 1. IP retains a residual interest in the cash and uncut timber at the end of five years. IP's principal risk is that the 10% timber cushion will be inadequate to service the debt and pay operating costs and IP will have to make debt service payments.

b. The bank has rights to a future revenue stream of 8% of the unpaid balance of the loan and repayment of the loan as it matures. The bank bears relatively little risk because of the loan guarantee of IP and the 10% excess timber.

c. IP should initially recognize a liability equal to the fair value of its guarantee of the debt. The expected adequacy of the 10% timber cushion affects the fair value amount. If timber prices decrease or the quality of the timber declines such that IP has to make debt service payments, then the provisions for recognition of a loss contingency come into play and require IP to recognize a liability for the debt. Note: U.S. GAAP provisions might treat the timber trust as a variable interest entity (VIE), a topic discussed in **Chapter 13**. If so, and if IP qualifies as the primary beneficiary of the VIE, IP would prepare consolidated financial statements with the trust and include the debt to the bank as a liability on the consolidated balance sheet. We do not explore this possibility further at this point.

SUGGESTED SOLUTION TO PROBLEM 11.2 FOR SELF-STUDY

(General Electric; interpreting retirement plan disclosures.)

a. General Electric (GE) increased the discount rate it uses to compute the present value of the benefit obligation from 5.7% to 6.34%, which decreased the liability and resulted in an actuarial gain. Another possibility is that GE changed some of its actuarial assumptions and the changes decreased the liability.

b. GE might have sweetened the benefit formula or made other plan amendments that increased the benefits provided to retired employees. The analysis of changes in the benefit obligation in **Exhibit 11.9** indicates that plan amendments increased the obligation for both pensions and health care and life insurance benefits.

c. The actual return on investments exceeded the expected return in each year and for each type of plan. The actual return for 2007 on GE's principal pension plan of $7,188 million compares to an expected return of $3,950 million.

d. GE has multiple pension plans for its various groups of employees, some of which were overfunded and some of which were underfunded. Because GE cannot use the assets in an overfunded plan to finance the obligation in an underfunded plan, authoritative guidance requires GE to report both the net assets of overfunded plans and the net liabilities of underfunded plans.

e.

	Principal Pension Plans	Health Care and Life Insurance Plans
Prior Service Cost, December 31, 2006	$ 831	$2,046
Plus Additional Prior Service Cost for 2007	1,470	4,257
Minus Amortization of Prior Service Cost for 2007	(241)	(603)
Prior Service Cost, December 31, 2007	$ 2,060	$5,700

f.

	Principal Pension Plans	Health Care and Life Insurance Plans
Net Actuarial Loss (Gain), December 31, 2006	$ 2,162	$(31)
Minus Deferral of Excess of Actual Return on Investments over Expected Return for 2007: ($7,188 − $3,950) and ($221 − $125)	(3,238)	(96)
Actuarial (Gain) Loss for 2007	(3,205)	320
Amortization of Actuarial (Loss) Gain for 2007	(693)	17
Net Actuarial Loss (Gain), December 31, 2007	$(4,974)	$ 210

g.

December 31, 2007

Pension Expense....................................	755	
Pension Asset (Noncurrent Asset: $20,190 − $15,019).............	5,171	
Pension Liability (Noncurrent Liability: $3,326 − $3,448)..............	122	
Other Comprehensive Income (Prior Service Cost and Amortization of Prior Service Cost: $1,470 − $241)	1,229	
Cash..		136
Pension Liability (Current Liability: $111 − $106)..............		5
Other Comprehensive Income (Excess Return on Pension Plan Investments: $7,188 − $3,950)		3,238
Other Comprehensive Income (Actuarial Gain and Amortization of Actuarial Loss: $3,205 + $693)		3,898

Assets	=	Liabilities	+	Shareholders' Equity	(Class.)
+5,171		−122		−755	IncSt → RE
−136		+5		−1,229	OCI → AOCI
				+3,238	OCI → AOCI
				+3,898	OCI → AOCI

h.

December 31, Year 6

Health Care and Life Insurance Expense	1,324	
Health Care and Life Insurance Liability (Current Liability: $675 − $681)..	6	
Other Comprehensive Income (Prior Service Cost and Amortization of Prior Service Cost: $4,257 − $603)	3,654	
Other Comprehensive Income (Actuarial Loss and Amortization of Actuarial Gain: $320 + $17)...........................	337	
Other Comprehensive Income (Other).........................	30	
Cash..		622
Health Care and Life Insurance Liability (Noncurrent Liability: $10,504 − $5,871).................................		4,633
Other Comprehensive Income (Excess Return on Health Care and Life Insurance Plan Investments: $221 − $125)		96

Assets	=	Liabilities	+	Shareholders' Equity	(Class.)
−622		−6		−1,324	IncSt → RE
		+4,633		−3,654	OCI → AOCI
				−337	OCI → AOCI
				−30	OCI → AOCI
				+96	OCI → AOCI

SUGGESTED SOLUTION TO PROBLEM 11.3 FOR SELF-STUDY

(Wade Corporation: computing income tax expense.)

a.

Year	Income Before Depreciation and Income Taxes [1]	Deduction on Tax Return [2]	Taxable Income [3]	Income Tax Payable [4]
1............	$100,000	$26,400	$ 73,600	$ 29,440
2............	$100,000	35,200	64,800	25,920
3............	$100,000	12,000	88,000	35,200
4............	$100,000	6,400	93,600	37,440
Totals.........	$400,000	$80,000	$320,000	$128,000

Column [1] is given.
Column [2] = $80,000 × 0.33 for first year, 0.44 for second year, 0.15 for third year, and 0.08 for fourth year.
Column [3] = [1] − [2].
Column [4] = 0.40 × [3].

b.

Year	Income Before Depreciation and Income Taxes [1]	Depreciation Expense [2]	Income Before Income Taxes [3]	Income Tax Expense [4]
1.............	$100,000	$20,000	$ 80,000	$ 32,000
2.............	100,000	20,000	80,000	32,000
3.............	100,000	20,000	80,000	32,000
4.............	100,000	20,000	80,000	32,000
Totals.........	$400,000	$80,000	$320,000	$128,000

Column [1] is given.
Column [2] = $80,000/4 = $20,000.
Column [3] = [1] − [2].
Column [4] = .40 × [3].

c.

First Year

Income Tax Expense	32,000	
Income Tax Payable		29,440
Deferred Tax Liability		2,560

Assets	=	Liabilities	+	Shareholders' Equity	(Class.)
		+29,440		−32,000	IncSt → RE
		+2,560			

To recognize income tax expense, income tax payable, and the change in deferred taxes for first year.

Second Year

Income Tax Expense	32,000	
Income Tax Payable		25,920
Deferred Tax Liability		6,080

Assets	=	Liabilities	+	Shareholders' Equity	(Class.)
		+25,920		−32,000	IncSt → RE
		+6,080			

To recognize income tax expense, income tax payable, and the change in deferred taxes for second year.

Third Year

Income Tax Expense	32,000	
Deferred Tax Liability	3,200	
Income Tax Payable		35,200

Assets	=	Liabilities	+	Shareholders' Equity	(Class.)
		−3,200		−32,000	IncSt → RE
		+35,200			

To recognize income tax expense, income tax payable, and the change in deferred taxes for third year.

Fourth Year

Income Tax Expense	32,000	
Deferred Tax Liability	5,440	
Income Tax Payable		37,440

Assets	=	Liabilities	+	Shareholders' Equity	(Class.)
		−5,440		−32,000	IncSt → RE
		+37,440			

To recognize income tax expense, income tax payable, and the change in deferred taxes for fourth year.

SUGGESTED SOLUTION TO PROBLEM 11.4 FOR SELF-STUDY

(Dominiak Company; working backward to components of book and taxable income.) See **Exhibit 11.15**.

EXHIBIT 11.15	**Dominiak Company** **Temporary and Permanent Differences** **(Suggested Solution to Problem 11.4 for Self-Study)**

	Financial Statements	Type of Difference	Income Tax Return
Operating Income Except Depreciation	$360,000 (6)	—	$360,000 (4)
Depreciation	(270,000) (g)	Temporary	(300,000) (3)
Municipal Bond Interest	70,000 (5)	Permanent	—
Taxable Income			$ 60,000 (2)
Pretax Book Income	$160,000 (g)		
Income Tax Payable at 40%			$ 24,000 (g)
Income Tax Expense at 40% of $90,000 = $160,000 − $70,000, Which Is Book Income Excluding Permanent Differences	(36,000) (g)		
Net Income	$124,000 (1)		

Order and derivation of computations:

(g) Given.

(1) $124,000 = $160,000 − $36,000.

(2) $60,000 = $24,000/0.40.

(3) Temporary difference for depreciation is ($36,000 − $24,000)/0.40 = $30,000. Because income taxes payable are less than income tax expense, we know that depreciation deducted on tax return exceeds depreciation expense on financial statements. Thus the depreciation deduction on the tax return is $300,000 = $270,000 + $30,000.

(4) $360,000 = $300,000 + $60,000.

(5) Financial statement income before taxes, excluding permanent differences, is $90,000 = $36,000/0.40. Financial statement income before taxes, including permanent differences, is $160,000. Hence permanent differences are $160,000 − $90,000 = $70,000.

(6) $160,000 + $270,000 − $70,000 = $360,000. See also (4), for check.

KEY TERMS AND CONCEPTS

Off-balance-sheet financing
Executory contract
Contingent obligation or provision
Special purpose entity (SPE)
Variable interest entity (VIE)
Securitization
Deferred compensation
Defined contribution pension plan
Defined benefit pension plan
Projected benefit obligation (PBO)
Accumulated benefit obligation (ABO)

Service cost
Interest cost
Prior service cost
Permanent difference
Temporary difference
Income tax payable
Income tax expense
Deferred tax asset
Deferred tax liability
Deferred tax asset valuation allowance
Effective tax rate

QUESTIONS, EXERCISES, AND PROBLEMS

QUESTIONS

1. Review the meaning of the terms and concepts listed in Key Terms and Concepts.

2. Compare and contrast the financial statement effects of achieving off-balance-sheet financing through an executory contract versus an asset sale with recourse, where the seller of the assets will reimburse the buyer for any shortfall in collections from the purchased asset.

3. Identifying the entity that enjoys the economic benefits and incurs the risk in a business transaction is not always clear-cut. How does the financial components approach attempt to deal with this difficulty?

4. "Recognizing the rights and obligations under all executory contracts (for example, leases, purchase commitments, employment contracts) would eliminate a major means of off-balance-sheet financing." How might such an action confuse and possibly mislead financial statement users?

5. What role does a special purpose entity or variable interest entity serve in achieving off-balance-sheet financing involving the sale of receivables?

6. "The principal accounting issue involving deferred compensation plans relates to when firms recognize compensation cost as an expense." Explain.

7. Suggest reasons why the total assets and total liabilities of a defined benefit pension plan do not appear, but their net amount does appear, on the employer's balance sheet.

8. Over sufficiently long periods of time, why is the total amount of an employer's pension expense equal to the cash the employer pays into a pension plan instead of the cash the pension plan pays retired employees?

9. Under what circumstances would an employer firm report both a net pension asset and a net pension liability on its balance sheet? Why don't U.S. GAAP and IFRS permit the firm to net these amounts and show only a single net pension asset or net pension liability?

10. When an employer firm recognizes the change in either a pension asset or pension liability for a period, the offsetting credit or debit is usually to Other Comprehensive Income. Why doesn't this amount immediately affect pension expense as a credit or debit instead?

11. Describe the rationale for reducing pension expense for the return on pension investments.

12. Describe the rationale for reducing pension expense by the expected return on investments instead of the actual return.

13. "The principal issue in accounting for income taxes concerns when firms recognize the tax effects of temporary differences between income for book purposes and income for tax purposes." Explain.

14. "One might view a deferred tax liability as an interest-free loan from the government." Do you agree? Why or why not?

15. Under what circumstances will a firm report a deferred tax asset on the balance sheet? Under what circumstances will a firm report a deferred tax liability on the balance sheet?

16. "The required accounting for deferred taxes delays recognizing in net income the benefits and costs of temporary differences from the period when they originate to the period when they reverse." Explain.

17. Of what value is information in the tax reconciliation about the reasons for differences between the statutory tax rate and the effective tax rate?

18. Of what value is information about the components of deferred tax assets and deferred tax liabilities, given that firms calculate income tax expense on income before taxes and not on individual revenues and expenses?

EXERCISES

19. **Using accounts receivable to achieve off-balance-sheet financing.** Cypres Appliance Store has $100,000 of accounts receivable on its books on January 2, 2008. These receivables

are due on December 31, 2008. The firm wants to use these accounts receivables to obtain financing.

a. Prepare journal entries during 2008 for the transactions in parts (i) and (ii) below:

(i) The firm borrows $92,593 from its bank, using the accounts receivable as collateral. The loan is repayable on December 31, 2008, with interest at 8%.

(ii) The firm sells the accounts receivable to the bank for $92,593. It collects amounts due from customers on these accounts and remits the cash to the bank.

b. Compare and contrast the income statement and balance sheet effects of these two transactions.

c. How should Cypres Appliance Store structure this transaction to ensure that it qualifies as a sale instead of a collateralized loan?

20. **Using inventory to achieve off-balance-sheet financing.** P. J. Lorimar Company grows and ages tobacco. On January 2, 2008, the firm has aging tobacco with a cost of $200,000 and a current market value of $300,000. P. J. Lorimar Company wants to use this tobacco to obtain financing. The firm uses a December 31 year-end.

a. Prepare journal entries during 2008 and 2009 for the transactions in parts (i) and (ii) below:

(i) The firm borrows $300,000 from its bank, using the tobacco inventory as collateral. The loan is repayable on December 31, 2009, with interest at 10% per year compounded annually. Assume zero storage costs. The firm expects to sell the tobacco on December 31, 2009, for $363,000.

(ii) The firm sells the tobacco inventory to the bank for $300,000. It promises to sell the inventory on behalf of the bank at the end of two years and remit the proceeds to the bank.

b. Compare and contrast the income statement and balance sheet effects of these two transactions.

c. How should P. J. Lorimar Company structure this transaction to ensure that it qualifies as a sale instead of a collateralized loan?

21. **Preparing journal entry for pension plan.** An aerospace manufacturer reports the following information related to its only pension plan for 2008 (amounts in millions).

Pension Plan Assets, Beginning of 2008.	$43,484
Plus Actual Return on Investments	4,239
Plus Employer Contribution	526
Less Benefits Paid	(2,046)
Pension Plan Assets, End of 2008	$46,203
Pension Plan Liability, Beginning of 2008	$45,183
Plus Service Cost	908
Plus Interest Cost	2,497
Less Actuarial Gain	(960)
Less Benefits Paid	(2,046)
Pension Plan Liability, End of 2008	$45,582
Service Cost	$ 908
Interest Cost	2,497
Expected Return on Pension Plan Investments	(3,456)
Amortization of Actuarial Losses	1,101
Net Pension Expense	$ 1,050

Give a single journal entry on the books of the aerospace manufacturer to recognize pension expense, the pension plan contribution, and the change in the net pension asset or net pension liability for 2008. Be sure to consider needed entries in Other Comprehensive Income, supporting the entry in this account with amounts from the disclosures above. Ignore income taxes.

22. **Preparing journal entry for pension plan.** A consumer foods company reports the following information related to its only pension plan for 2008 (amounts in millions).

Pension Plan Assets, Beginning of 2008	$5,086
Plus Actual Return on Investments	513
Plus Employer Contribution	19
Less Benefits Paid	(233)
Pension Plan Assets, End of 2008	$5,385
Pension Plan Liability, Beginning of 2008	$5,771
Plus Service Cost	245
Plus Interest Cost	319
Less Actuarial Gain	(155)
Less Benefits Paid	(233)
Pension Plan Liability, End of 2008	$5,947
Service Cost	$ 245
Interest Cost	319
Expected Return on Pension Plan Investments	(391)
Amortization of Actuarial Losses	167
Net Pension Expense	$ 340

Give a single journal entry for the consumer foods company to recognize pension expense, the pension plan contribution, and the change in the net pension asset or net pension liability for 2008. Be sure to consider needed entries in Other Comprehensive Income, supporting the entry in this account with amounts from the disclosures above. Ignore income taxes.

23. **Preparing journal entry for health care plan.** An automobile manufacturer reports the following information related to its health care plan for 2008 (amounts in millions).

Health Care Plan Assets, Beginning of 2008	$ 6,497
Plus Actual Return on Investments	510
Plus Employer Contribution	0
Less Benefits Paid	(1,547)
Health Care Plan Assets, End of 2008	$ 5,460
Health Care Plan Liability, Beginning of 2008	$39,274
Plus Service Cost	617
Plus Interest Cost	2,004
Less Actuarial Gain	(9,485)
Less Benefits Paid	(1,547)
Health Care Plan Liability, End of 2008	$30,863
Service Cost	$ 617
Interest Cost	2,004
Expected Return on Health Care Plan Investments	(479)
Amortization of Actuarial Losses	41
Net Health Care Benefits Expense	$ 2,183

Give a single journal entry for the automobile manufacturer to recognize health care benefits expense, the health care plan contribution, and the change in the net health care benefits asset or net health care benefits liability for 2008. Be sure to consider needed entries in Other Comprehensive Income, supporting the entry in this account with amounts from the preceding disclosures. Ignore income taxes.

24. **Preparing journal entries for income tax expense.** An athletic shoe company reports the following information about its income taxes for three recent years (amounts in millions):

Components of Income Tax Expense	2008	2007	2006
Currently Payable	$775.6	$622.8	$495.4
Deferred	(26.0)	25.4	9.0
Total Income Tax Expense	$749.6	$648.2	$504.4

a. Give the journal entries to record income tax expense for 2006, 2007, and 2008.

b. Describe the likely reasons for the pattern of taxes currently payable and deferred for each year. Assume that the deferred taxes relate primarily to retirement benefits. The effective tax rate was relatively stable for the three years.

25. **Preparing journal entries for income tax expense.** An electric utility reports the following information about its income taxes for three recent years (amounts in millions):

Components of Income Tax Expense	2008	2007	2006
Currently Payable	$ 46	$415	$ (96)
Deferred	344	(74)	368
Total Income Tax Expense	$390	$341	$272

a. Give the journal entries to record income tax expense for 2006, 2007, and 2008.

b. Describe the likely reasons for the pattern of taxes currently payable and deferred for each year. Assume that deferred taxes relate primarily to depreciation temporary differences. The effective tax rate was relatively stable for the three years.

26. **Deriving permanent and temporary differences from financial statement disclosures.** Pownall Company reports the following information for a year:

Book Income Before Income Taxes	$318,000
Income Tax Expense	156,000
Income Taxes Payable for the Year	48,000
Income Tax Rate on Taxable Income	40%

The company has both permanent and temporary differences between book income and taxable income.

a. What is the amount of temporary differences for the year? Give the amount, and indicate whether the effect is to make book income larger or smaller than taxable income.

b. What is the amount of permanent differences for the year? Give the amount, and indicate whether the effect is to make book income larger or smaller than taxable income.

27. **Reconstructing information about income taxes.** Lilly Company reports the following information about its financial statements and tax return for a year:

Depreciation Expense from Financial Statements	$322,800
Financial Statement Pretax Book Income	190,800
Income Tax Expense from Financial Statements	42,000
Income Taxes Payable from Tax Returns	27,600

Together the federal and state governments tax taxable income at a rate of 40%. Permanent differences result from municipal bond interest that appears as revenue in the financial statements but is exempt from income taxes. Temporary differences result from the use of accelerated depreciation for tax returns and straight-line depreciation for financial reporting.

Reconstruct the income statement for financial reporting and for tax reporting for the year, identifying temporary differences and permanent differences.

28. **Effect of temporary differences on income taxes.** Woodward Corporation purchases a new machine for $50,000 on January 1, 2008. The machine has a four-year estimated service life and an estimated salvage value of zero. After paying the cost of running and maintaining the machine, the firm enjoys a $25,000-per-year excess of revenues over expenses

(except depreciation and taxes). In addition to the $25,000 from the machine, other pretax income each year is $35,000. Woodward uses straight-line depreciation for financial reporting and depreciates the machine for tax reporting using the following percentages: 33% in the first year, 44% in the second, 15% in the third, and 8% in the fourth. Depreciation is Woodward's only temporary difference. Woodward pays combined federal and local income taxes at a rate of 40% of taxable income.

a. Compute the amount of income taxes currently payable for each of the four years.

b. Compute the carrying value of the machine for financial reporting and the tax basis of the machine for tax reporting at the end of each of the four years. The tax basis is the amortized cost for income tax purposes.

c. Compute the amount of income tax expense for each of the four years.

d. Give the journal entries to record income tax expense and income tax payable for 2008 through 2011.

PROBLEMS

29. **Interpreting disclosures regarding sales of accounts receivable.** Federated Department Stores Inc. owns various chains of retail department stores, including Macy's and Bloomingdales. On August 30, 2005, it acquired May Department Stores, thereby acquiring Filenes, Marshall Field, Kaufmann's, Lord & Taylor, and other retail chains. It then changed the name of the entire company to Macy's. It subsequently sold all of the credit card receivables of its department store chains to Citibank. **Exhibit 11.16** reports the sale of these receivables.

a. Using information in **Exhibit 11.16**, discuss why the sales of receivables to Citibank likely qualified as a sale and not as a collateralized loan.

EXHIBIT 11.16

Macy's
Note on Sale of Receivables
(Problem 29)

5. Sale of Credit Card Accounts and Receivables

On October 24, 2005, the Company sold to Citibank certain proprietary and nonproprietary credit card accounts owned by the Company, together with related receivables balances, and the capital stock of Prime Receivables Corporation, a wholly owned subsidiary of the Company, which owned all of the Company's interest in the Prime Credit Card Master Trust (the foregoing and certain related assets being the "FDS Credit Assets"). The sale of the FDS Credit Assets for a cash purchase price of approximately $3.6 billion resulted in a pretax gain of $480 million. The net proceeds received, after eliminating related receivables-backed financings, were used to repay debt associated with the acquisition of May.

On May 1, 2006, the Company terminated the Company's credit card program agreement with GE Capital Consumer Card Co. ("GE Bank") and purchased all of the "Macy's" credit card accounts owned by GE Bank, together with related receivables balances (the "GE/Macy's Credit Assets"), as of April 30, 2006. Also on May 1, 2006, the Company sold the GE/Macy's Credit Assets to Citibank, resulting in a pretax gain of approximately $179 million. The net proceeds of approximately $180 million were used to repay short-term borrowings associated with the acquisition of May.

On May 22, 2006, the Company sold a portion of the acquired May credit card accounts and related receivables to Citibank, resulting in a pretax gain of approximately $5 million. The net proceeds of approximately $800 million were primarily used to repay short-term borrowings associated with the acquisition of May.

On July 17, 2006, the Company sold the remaining portion of the acquired May credit card accounts and related receivables to Citibank, resulting in a pretax gain of approximately $7 million. The net proceeds of approximately $1,100 million were used for general corporate purposes.

In connection with the sales of credit card accounts and related receivable balances, the Company and Citibank entered into a long-term marketing and servicing alliance pursuant to the terms of a Credit Card Program Agreement (the "Program Agreement") with an initial term of 10 years expiring on July 17, 2016, and, unless terminated by either party as of the expiration of the initial term, an additional renewal term of three years. The Program Agreement provides for, among other things, (i) the ownership by Citibank of the accounts purchased by Citibank, (ii) the ownership by Citibank of new accounts opened by the Company's customers, (iii) the provision of credit by Citibank to the holders of the credit cards associated with the foregoing accounts, (iv) the servicing of the foregoing accounts, and (v) the allocation between Citibank and the Company of the economic benefits and burdens associated with the foregoing and other aspects of the alliance.

b. Exhibit 11.16 indicates that Federated and Citibank allocated the "economic benefits and burdens associated with the foregoing and other aspects of the alliance." Identify the likely economic benefits and burdens of the arrangement to Federated Department Stores (subsequently Macy's).

c. What were the likely functions of Prime Receivables Corporation and Prime Credit Card Master Trust that Federated Department Stores owned or used prior to the sale of the receivables to Citibank?

30. **Interpreting notes on off-balance-sheet financing.** Louisiana-Pacific Corporation (LP) sold certain timber assets and received cash and notes receivable from the purchaser. LP then engaged in a transaction to turn the notes receivable into cash without recognizing a liability on the balance sheet. **Exhibit 11.17** presents the notes from LP's financial statements describing this transaction.

   Based on the disclosures in **Exhibit 11.17**, discuss the likely reasons why this transaction qualified as a sale and not as a collateralized loan.

31. **Interpreting retirement plan disclosures. Exhibits 11.18** and **11.19** present selected information from the notes to the financial statements of a beverage company regarding its U.S. pension and health care retirement plans.

   a. What is the likely reason for the actuarial gains in the pension and health care obligations during 2008?

   b. Did the pension plan investments perform up to expectations during 2007 and 2008? Explain.

   c. Why is the expected return on health care assets equal to zero in each year?

   d. Prepare an analysis that explains the change in prior service cost for pension plans from $5 million at the end of 2007 to $13 million at the end of 2008.

(*continued on page 557*)

EXHIBIT 11.17

**Louisiana-Pacific Corporation
Note on Sale of Notes Receivable
(Problem 30)**

12. Off-Balance-Sheet Arrangement

In connection with the sale of LP's southern timber and timberlands in 2003, LP received cash of $26.4 million and notes receivable of $410.0 million from the purchasers of such timber and timberlands. In order to borrow funds in a cost-effective manner, (i) LP contributed the notes receivable to a Qualified Special Purpose Entity (QSPE) as defined under SFAS No. 140, (ii) the QSPE issued to unrelated third parties bonds supported by a bank letter of credit, which are secured by the notes receivable, and (iii) the QSPE distributed to LP, as a return of capital, substantially all of the proceeds realized by the QSPE from the issuance of its bonds. The QSPE has no sources of liquidity other than the notes receivable, the cash flow generated by the notes receivable generally will be dedicated to the payment of the bonds issued by the QSPE, and the QSPE's creditors generally will have no recourse to LP for the QSPE's obligations (subject to the limited exception described below).

Pursuant to the arrangement described above, during 2003, LP contributed the $410.0 million of notes receivable to the QSPE, the QSPE issued $368.7 million of its bonds to unrelated third parties and distributed $365.8 million to LP as a return of capital.

The principal amount of the QSPE's borrowings is approximately 90% of the principal amount of the notes receivable contributed by LP to the QSPE. LP's retained interest in the excess of the notes receivable contributed to the unconsolidated subsidiary over the amount of capital distributed by the unconsolidated subsidiary, in the form of an investment in the QSPE, represented $44.5 million of the Investments in and advances to affiliates on the Consolidated Balance Sheets as of December 31, 2006. Management believes the book value of this investment approximates market value, as the interest rates on the notes receivable are variable.

In accordance with SFAS No. 140, the QSPE is not included in LP's consolidated financial statements and the assets and liabilities of the QSPE are not reflected on the Consolidated Balance Sheets. The QSPE's assets have been removed from LP's control and are not available to satisfy claims of LP's creditors except to the extent of LP's retained interest, if any, remaining after the claims of QSPE's creditors are satisfied. In general, the creditors of the QSPE have no recourse to LP's assets, other than LP's retained interest. However, under certain circumstances, LP may be liable for certain liabilities of the QSPE (including liabilities associated with the marketing or remarketing of its bonds and reimbursement obligations associated with the letter of credit supporting the bonds) in an amount not to exceed 10% of the aggregate principal amount of the notes receivable pledged by the QSPE. LP's maximum exposure in this regard was approximately $41 million as of December 31, 2006. The estimated fair value of this guarantee is not material.

EXHIBIT 11.18

Elements of U.S. Pension and Health Care Expense
(amounts in millions)
(Problem 31)

	U.S. Pension Plans			Health Care Plans		
	2008	2007	2006	2008	2007	2006
Service Cost..............	$ 245	$ 213	$ 193	$ 46	$ 40	$ 38
Interest Cost	319	296	271	72	78	72
Expected Return on Assets	(391)	(344)	(325)	—	—	—
Prior Service Cost	3	3	6	(13)	(11)	(8)
Actuarial Loss	164	106	81	21	26	19
Net Expense..............	$ 340	$ 274	$ 226	$126	$133	$121

EXHIBIT 11.19

Funded Status of U.S. Pension and Health Care Plans
(amounts in millions)
(Problem 31)

	U.S. Pension Plans		Health Care Plans	
	2008	2007	2008	2007
Benefit Obligation, January 1	$5,771	$4,968	$ 1,312	$ 1,319
Service Cost	245	213	46	40
Interest Cost	319	296	72	78
Plan Amendments	11	—	—	(8)
Actuarial Loss (Gain)	(163)	517	(34)	(45)
Benefits Paid	(233)	(241)	(75)	(74)
Other	(3)	18	49	2
Benefit Obligation, December 31................	$5,947	$5,771	$ 1,370	$ 1,312
Fair Value of Plan Assets, January 1	$5,086	$4,152	$ —	$ —
Actual Return on Assets....................	513	477	—	—
Employer Contributions	19	699	75	74
Benefits Paid	(233)	(241)	(75)	(74)
Other	(7)	(1)	—	—
Fair Value of Plan Assets, December 31	$5,378	$5,086	$ —	$ —
Net Funded Asset (Liability)	$ (569)	$ (685)	$(1,370)	$(1,312)
Recognized in:				
Noncurrent Assets	$ 185	$2,068	$ —	$ —
Current Liabilities	(25)	—	(100)	—
Noncurrent Liabilities....................	(729)	(2,753)	(1,270)	(1,312)
Net Asset (Liability) Recognized.............	$ (569)	$ (685)	$(1,370)	$(1,312)
Recognized in Shareholders' Equity:				
Prior Service Cost (Credit)...................	$ 13	$5	$ (101)	$ (114)
Net Actuarial Loss	$1,836	$2,285	$ 364	$ 419
Actuarial Assumptions:				
Discount Rate	5.8%	5.7%	5.8%	5.7%
Expected Return on Assets...................	7.8%	7.8%	—	—
Rate of Compensation Increase	4.5%	4.4%	—	—
Initial Health Care Cost Trend Rate	—	—	9.0%	10.0%
Ultimate Health Care Cost Trend Rate.............	—	—	5.0%	5.0%
Number of Years to Ultimate Trend Rate	—	—	5 years	5 years

e. Prepare an analysis that explains the change in the net actuarial loss for pension plans from $2,285 million at the end of 2007 to $1,836 million at the end of 2008.

f. Prepare an analysis that explains the change in the prior service credit for health care plans from $114 million at the end of 2007 to $101 million at the end of 2008.

g. Prepare an analysis that explains the change in the net actuarial loss for health care plans from $419 million at the end of 2007 to $364 million at the end of 2008.

h. Give the journal entry that this firm would make at the end of 2008 to recognize net pension expense, pension funding, and the change in balance sheet accounts for its pension plan.

i. Give the journal entry that this firm would make at the end of 2008 to recognize net health care expense, health care funding, and the change in balance sheet accounts for its health care plan.

32. **Interpreting retirement plan disclosures. Exhibits 11.20** and **11.21** present selected information from the notes to the financial statements of a tire manufacturing company regarding its U.S. pension and health care retirement plans.

a. Refer to **Exhibit 11.20**. Why does the interest cost of the U.S. pension plans exceed the expected return on assets for 2006 and 2007, but these amounts are identical for 2008?

b. What is the likely reason for the decline in the net expense for this firm's health care plans between 2006 and 2007?

c. Why does this firm show no subtraction for the expected return on investments in computing net health care expense for each year?

d. What are the likely reasons that this firm reports an actuarial gain in its pension obligation and health care obligation for 2008?

e. Prepare an analysis that explains the change in the prior service cost for U.S. pension plans from $314 at the end of 2007 to $366 at the end of 2008.

f. Prepare an analysis that explains the change in the net actuarial loss for U.S. pension plans from $1,646 at the end of 2007 to $1,252 at the end of 2008.

g. Prepare an analysis that explains the change in the prior service cost for health care plans from $339 at the end of 2007 to $299 at the end of 2008.

h. Prepare an analysis that explains the change in the actuarial loss for health care plans from $340 at the end of 2007 to $221 at the end of 2008.

i. Give the journal entry that this firm would make at the end of 2008 to recognize net pension expense, pension funding, and the change in balance sheet accounts for its pension plan.

j. Give the journal entry that this firm would make at the end of 2008 to recognize net health care expense, health care funding, and the change in balance sheet accounts for its health care plan.

EXHIBIT 11.20 Elements of U.S. Pension and Health Care Expense (amounts in millions) (Problem 32)

	U.S. Pension Plans			Health Care Plans		
	2008	2007	2006	2008	2007	2006
Service Cost	$ 103	$ 56	$ 41	$ 25	$ 23	$ 25
Interest Cost	295	294	300	135	149	188
Expected Return on Assets	(295)	(258)	$(234)	—	—	—
Prior Service Cost	59	63	71	41	43	45
Actuarial Loss	91	86	79	9	10	35
Net Expense	$ 253	$ 241	$ 257	$210	$225	$293

EXHIBIT 11.21

Funded Status of U.S. Pension and Health Care Plans
(amounts in millions)
(Problem 32)

	U.S. Pension Plans		Health Care Plans	
	2008	2007	2008	2007
Benefit Obligation, January 1	$ 5,407	$ 5,191	$ 2,629	$ 3,218
Service Cost	103	56	25	23
Interest Cost	295	294	135	149
Plan Amendments	111	—	1	—
Actuarial Loss (Gain)	(120)	174	(110)	(532)
Participant Contributions	10	11	26	19
Benefits Paid	(409)	(334)	(255)	(260)
Other	20	15	27	12
Benefit Obligation, December 31	$ 5,417	$ 5,407	$ 2,478	$ 2,629
Fair Value of Plan Assets, January 1	$ 3,404	$ 3,046	$ —	$ —
Actual Return on Assets	478	261	—	—
Employer Contributions	567	420	233	241
Benefits Paid	10	11	26	19
Other	(409)	(334)	(255)	(260)
Fair Value of Plan Assets, December 31	$ 4,050	$ 3,404	$ 4	$ —
Net Funded Asset (Liability)	$(1,367)	$(2,003)	$(2,474)	$(2,629)
Recognized in:				
Current Liabilities	$ (19)	$ (736)	$ (231)	$ (254)
Noncurrent Liabilities	(1,348)	(1,267)	(2,243)	(2,375)
Net Asset (Liability) Recognized	$(1,367)	$(2,003)	$(2,474)	$(2,629)
Recognized in Shareholders' Equity:				
Prior Service Cost (Credit)	$ 366	$ 314	$ 299	$ 339
Net Actuarial Loss	$ 1,252	$ 1,646	$ 221	$ 340
Actuarial Assumptions:				
Discount Rate	5.75%	5.50%	5.75%	5.50%
Expected Return on Assets	8.50%	8.50%	—	—
Rate of Compensation Increase	4.04%	4.04%	—	—
Initial Health Care Cost Trend Rate	—	—	11.20%	11.50%
Ultimate Health Care Cost Trend Rate	—	—	5.00%	5.00%
Number of Years to Ultimate Trend Rate	—	—	8 years	8 years

33. **Interpreting income tax disclosures. Exhibit 11.22** presents selected information from the notes to the financial statements of a manufacturer of equipment for farming, construction, and residential uses for the years ending October 31, 2008, 2007, and 2006.

   a. Present the journal entry to recognize income tax expense and income taxes payable for the year ended October 31, 2007. Be sure to consider the effect on deferred tax asset and deferred tax liability accounts.

   b. Repeat part **a** for the year ended October 31, 2008.

   c. Why do state and local taxes appear as an addition in the tax reconciliation between income taxes at the statutory tax rate and income tax expense?

   d. This firm combines the effect of nondeductible costs and other items in its income tax reconciliation. Will nondeductible costs have the effect of increasing or decreasing the effective tax rate? Explain.

   e. Explain why a recognized health care liability and a recognized pension liability give rise to deferred tax assets, whereas a recognized prepaid pension asset gives rise to a deferred tax liability.

EXHIBIT 11.22	Income Tax Disclosures (amounts in millions) (Problem 33)		

	2008	2007	
Income Before Income Taxes	$2,174	$2,107	
Income Tax Expense:			
Current	$ 736	$ 738	
Deferred.	6	(39)	
Total Income Tax Expense	$ 742	$ 699	
Income Taxes on Income Before Income Taxes at the Statutory Tax Rate of 35%.	$ 761	$ 737	
State and Local Taxes (net of federal tax benefit)	22	10	
Foreign Tax Rates	8	(6)	
Nondeductible Costs and Other	(49)	(42)	
Income Tax Expense	$ 742	$ 699	

October 31:	2008	2007	2006
COMPONENTS OF DEFERRED TAXES			
Deferred Tax Assets:			
Health Care Liability	$ 825	$ 997	$1,017
Sales Allowances	327	324	304
Pension Liability.	246	250	156
Tax Loss and Tax Credit Carryforwards.	132	93	55
Other	362	225	257
Valuation Allowance	(50)	(25)	(1)
Total Deferred Tax Assets	$1,842	$1,864	$1,788
Deferred Tax Liabilities:			
Prepaid Pension Asset	$ 845	$ 860	$ 778
Depreciation	214	231	263
Deferred Lease Income.	144	154	159
Other	122	96	104
Total Deferred Tax Liabilities	$1,325	$1,341	$1,304

  f. Sales allowances relate to amounts that this firm pays after the time of sale for warranty repairs, rebates, and returned equipment. Why do sales allowances give rise to a deferred tax asset?

  g. What is the likely reason that the valuation allowance on deferred tax assets increased continually during the three years?

  h. What is the likely explanation for the direction of the change in the deferred tax liability relating to depreciation?

  i. This firm leases equipment to its customers, which gives rise to a deferred tax liability. Does this firm likely account for these leases as operating leases or as capital leases for financial reporting? Which method of accounting for these same leases does the firm likely use for tax reporting?

34. Interpreting income tax disclosures. Exhibit 11.23 presents information from the income tax note to the financial statements for a computer manufacturer for the years ending December 31, 2008, 2007, and 2006.

  a. Present the journal entry to recognize income tax expense and income taxes payable for the year ended December 31, 2007. Use a single deferred tax account instead of separate accounts for deferred tax assets and deferred tax liabilities.

  b. Repeat part **a** for the year ended December 31, 2008.

EXHIBIT 11.23	**Income Tax Disclosures (amounts in millions) (Problem 34)**

	2008	2007
Income Before Income Taxes	$13,317	$12,226
Income Tax Expense:		
Current	$ 2,177	$2,047
Deferred	1,724	2,185
Total Income Tax Expense	$ 3,901	$ 4,232
Income Taxes at the Statutory Tax Rate of 35%	35%	35%
State and Local Taxes (net of federal tax benefit)	1	1
Foreign Tax Rates	(5)	(5)
Other	(2)	4
Effective Tax Rate	29%	35%

October 31:	2008	2007	2006
COMPONENTS OF DEFERRED TAXES			
Deferred Tax Assets:			
Stock-Based and Other Compensation	$ 3,147	$ 3,022	$ 3,122
Retirement Benefits	3,002	3,039	3,908
Capitalized Research and Development	1,355	1,728	1,794
Bad Debts and Warranties	724	937	1,050
Other	3,128	3,471	4,855
Valuation Allowance	(510)	(562)	(603)
Total Deferred Tax Assets	$10,846	$11,635	$14,126
Deferred Tax Liabilities:			
Retirement Benefits	$ 2,906	$ 7,267	$ 7,057
Deferred Lease Income	1,385	964	622
Software Development Costs	505	348	381
Other	1,340	1,502	1,324
Total Deferred Tax Liabilities	$ 6,136	$10,081	$ 9,384

c. Why do the amounts for deferred taxes in the entries in parts **a** and **b** not equal the change in deferred tax assets and deferred tax liabilities in **Exhibit 11.23** for each year?

d. Why do state and local taxes appear as an addition in the reconciliation between the statutory tax rate and the effective tax rate?

e. Why does this firm show both deferred tax assets and deferred tax liabilities for retirement benefits?

f. What does the reporting of a deferred tax asset for bad debts and warranties suggest about when this firm recognizes expenses for these items for financial reporting and for tax reporting?

g. This firm leases equipment to its customers, which gives rise to a deferred tax liability. Does this firm likely account for these leases as operating leases or as capital leases for financial reporting? Which method of accounting for these same leases does this firm likely use for tax reporting?

h. What does the reporting of a deferred tax liability for software development costs suggest about when this firm recognizes an expense for this item for financial reporting and for tax reporting?

35. **Interpreting income tax disclosures. Exhibit 11.24** presents information from the income tax note for a discount retailer for its fiscal years ending January 31, 2008, 2007, and 2006.

   a. Present the journal entry to recognize income tax expense and income taxes payable for the year ended January 31, 2006. Use a single deferred tax account instead of separate accounts for deferred tax assets and deferred tax liabilities.

   b. Repeat part **a** for the year ended January 31, 2007.

   c. Repeat part **a** for the year ended January 31, 2008.

   d. Why do the amounts for deferred taxes in the entries in parts **a**, **b**, and **c** not equal the changes in deferred tax assets and deferred tax liabilities in **Exhibit 11.24** for each year?

   e. Why do state and local taxes appear as an addition in the reconciliation between the statutory tax rate and the effective tax rate?

   f. What does the reporting of a deferred tax asset for health care benefits and a deferred tax liability for pensions suggest about the funding status of its health care and pension plans?

   g. The deferred tax liability for property, plant, and equipment remained relatively steady between January 31, 2006, and January 31, 2007. What does this behavior of the deferred tax liability suggest about this firm's expenditures on property, plant, and equipment?

   h. What is the interpretation of the absence of a deferred tax asset valuation allowance?

EXHIBIT 11.24	**Income Tax Disclosures** (amounts in millions) (Problem 35)

Fiscal Year Ended January 31:	2008	2007	2006
Income Before Income Taxes	$4,500	$3,862	$3,032
Income Tax Expense:			
Current	$1,911	$1,574	$1,052
Deferred	(201)	(122)	94
Total Income Tax Expense	$1,710	$1,452	$1,146
Income Taxes at the Statutory Tax Rate of 35%	35.0%	35.0%	35.0%
State and Local Taxes (net of federal tax benefit)	4.0	3.3	3.3
Other	(1.0)	(.7)	(.5)
Effective Tax Rate	38.0%	37.6%	37.8%

	January 31:			
	2008	2007	2006	2005
COMPONENTS OF DEFERRED TAXES				
Deferred Tax Assets:				
Stock-Based Compensation	$ 466	$ 399	$ 332	$297
Self-Insured Benefits	238	217	179	143
Bad Debts	191	167	147	133
Health Care Benefits	39	39	38	42
Other	192	152	175	97
Total Deferred Tax Assets	$1,126	$ 974	$ 871	$ 712
Deferred Tax Liabilities:				
Property, Plant, and Equipment	$1,041	$1,080	$1,136	$ 806
Pensions	100	287	268	218
Other	135	114	96	84
Total Deferred Tax Liabilities	$1,276	$1,481	$1,500	$1,108

36. **Behavior of deferred income tax account when a firm acquires new assets every year.** Equilibrium Company has adopted a program of purchasing a new machine each year. It uses a prescribed method of depreciation on its income tax return and straight-line depreciation on its financial statements. Each machine costs $12,000 installed and has an economic life of six years for financial reporting. Equilibrium Company depreciates this equipment for tax purposes using the following percentages of acquisition cost each year: 20%, 32%, 19%, 12%, 11%, and 6% of cost in each of the six years, respectively.

    a. Calculate the total depreciation deduction on the tax return for each of the first seven years.

    b. Calculate depreciation for each year using the straight-line method of depreciation.

    c. Calculate the annual difference in depreciation charges using the results from parts **a** and **b**.

    d. Calculate the annual increase in the Deferred Tax Liability account for the balance sheet by multiplying the tax rate, 40%, by the amount found in part **c**.

    e. Calculate year-end balances for the Deferred Tax Liability account on the balance sheet.

    f. If Equilibrium Company continues to follow its policy of buying a new machine every year for $12,000, what will happen to the balance in the Deferred Tax Liability account on the balance sheet?

37. **Attempts to achieve off-balance-sheet financing.** (Adapted from materials by R. Dieter, D. Landsittel, J. Stewart, and A. Wyatt.) Shiraz Company wants to raise $50 million cash but, for various reasons, does not want to do so in a way that results in a newly recorded liability. It is sufficiently solvent and profitable that its bank will lend up to $50 million at the prime interest rate. Shiraz Company's financial executives have devised six different plans, described in the following paragraphs.

    Plan 1: Transfer of Receivables with Recourse. Shiraz Company will transfer to Credit Company its long-term accounts receivable, which call for payments over the next two years. Credit Company will pay an amount equal to the present value of the receivables less an allowance for uncollectibles as well as a discount, because it pays now but will collect cash later. Shiraz Company must repurchase from Credit Company at face value any receivables that become uncollectible in excess of the allowance. In addition, Shiraz Company may repurchase any of the receivables not yet due at face value less a discount specified by formula and based on the prime rate at the time of the initial transfer. (This option permits Shiraz Company to benefit if an unexpected drop in interest rates occurs after the transfer.) The accounting issue is whether the transfer is a sale (Shiraz Company debits Cash, credits Accounts Receivable, and debits an expense or loss on transfer) or whether the transfer is merely a loan collateralized by the receivables (Shiraz Company debits Cash and credits Notes Payable at the time of transfer).

    Plan 2: Product Financing Arrangement. Shiraz Company will transfer inventory to Credit Company, who will store the inventory in a public warehouse. Credit Company may use the inventory as collateral for its own borrowings, whose proceeds will be used to pay Shiraz Company. Shiraz Company will pay storage costs and will repurchase all the inventory within the next four years at contractually fixed prices plus interest accrued for the time elapsed between the transfer and later repurchase. The accounting issue is whether Shiraz has sold the inventory to Credit Company, with later repurchases treated as new acquisitions for Shiraz's inventory, or whether Shiraz has merely borrowed from Credit Company, with the inventory remaining on Shiraz's balance sheet.

    Plan 3: Throughput Contract. Shiraz Company wants a branch line of a railroad built from the main rail line to carry raw material directly to its own plant. It could, of course, borrow the funds and build the branch line itself. Instead, it will sign an agreement with the railroad to ship specified amounts of material each month for 10 years. Even if it does not ship the specified amounts of material, it will pay the agreed shipping costs. The railroad will take the contract to its bank and, using it as collateral, borrow the funds to build the branch line. The accounting issue is whether Shiraz Company should debit an asset for future rail services and credit a liability for payments to the railroad. The alternative is to make no accounting entry except when Shiraz makes payments to the railroad.

Plan 4: Construction Joint Venture. Shiraz Company and Mission Company will jointly build a plant to manufacture chemicals that both companies need in their production processes. Each will contribute $5 million to the project, called Chemical. Chemical will borrow another $40 million from a bank, with Shiraz only guaranteeing the debt. Shiraz and Mission are each to contribute equally to future operating expenses and debt-service payments of Chemical, but in return for guaranteeing the debt, Shiraz will have an option to purchase Mission's interest for $20 million four years later. The accounting issue is whether Shiraz Company, which will ultimately be responsible for all debt-service payments, should recognize a liability for the funds that Chemical borrowed. Alternatively, the debt guarantee is merely a commitment that Shiraz Company must disclose in notes to its financial statements.

Plan 5: Research and Development Partnership. Shiraz Company will contribute a laboratory and preliminary finding about a potentially profitable gene-splicing discovery to a partnership, called Venture. Venture will raise funds by selling the remaining interest in the partnership to outside investors for $2 million and by borrowing $48 million from a bank, with Shiraz Company guaranteeing the debt. Although Venture will operate under the management of Shiraz Company, it will be free to sell the results of its further discoveries and development efforts to anyone, including Shiraz Company. Shiraz Company has no obligation to purchase any of Venture's output. The accounting issue is whether Shiraz Company should recognize the liability. (Would it make any difference if Shiraz Company did not guarantee the loan but had either the option to purchase or an obligation to purchase the results of Venture's work?)

Plan 6: Hotel Financing. Shiraz Company owns and operates a profitable hotel. It could use the hotel as collateral for a conventional mortgage loan. Instead, it considers selling the hotel to a partnership for $50 million cash. The partnership will sell ownership interests to outside investors for $5 million and borrow $45 million from a bank on a conventional mortgage loan, using the hotel as collateral. Shiraz Company guarantees the debt. The accounting issue is whether Shiraz Company should record the liability for the guaranteed debt of the partnership.

Discuss whether Shiraz Company should recognize any of these obligations or commitments as a liability on its balance sheet.

Marketable Securities and Derivatives

1. Understand why firms acquire securities of other firms and how the purpose of the investment governs the accounting for that investment.

2. Develop skills to account for short-term and long-term investments in marketable securities at fair value.

3. Understand why firms use derivative contracts to hedge the risk of changes in interest rates, exchange rates, commodity prices, and other factors and for other purposes.

4. Develop skills to apply hedge accounting to derivative contracts.

5. Develop the ability to apply the fair value option to marketable securities and hedging contracts.

For various reasons, firms often acquire the **marketable securities** (bonds, preferred stock, and common stock) of other entities. The following examples illustrate some such acquisitions.

Example 1 Goldman Sachs, an investment bank, has trading operations that focus on short-term price changes of securities. It acquired shares of common stock of Toyota Motor Corporation for $45.66 per share on the New York Stock Exchange and sold the shares three days later for $46.25.

Example 2 Southwest Airlines sells airline tickets and receives cash prior to providing transportation services. Rather than let the cash remain idle in its bank account, Southwest Airlines acquires U.S. Treasury Notes. The firm earns interest while it holds the notes and will sell the notes when it needs the cash for operations.

Example 3 Roche Holding, a pharmaceutical company, acquires shares of common stock of several firms engaged in biotechnology research. Roche will benefit from increases in the market prices of these shares if the research efforts succeed.

Firms also enter into financial contracts with other entities to hedge various risks.

Example 4 Nestlé, a consumer foods company, purchases cocoa beans for its chocolate candies from Ghana. Based on its production plan, Nestlé intends to purchase 2,000 metric tons of cocoa beans, with delivery in six months. Nestlé can either acquire the cocoa beans in the spot market six months from now or buy the beans today for delivery in six months using a *forward purchase contract*. The former arrangement exposes Nestlé to changes in cocoa bean prices, while the latter fixes the price today. If Nestlé locks in the price today using a forward contract, it will benefit if cocoa bean prices increase during the next six months, and it will suffer an opportunity loss if prices decline.

Example 5 A retailer in Germany places an order for 5,000 T-shirts to be screen-painted in Mexico and delivered in six months. The German retailer agrees to pay the supplier 64 Mexican pesos per T-shirt. The current exchange rate between the euro and the Mexican peso is about €.06 = 1 peso, so this implies the current price of the 5,000 shirts in euros is €19,200 (= 64 pesos × 5,000 × €.06). However, the euro–peso exchange rate is volatile, and the retailer worries that the exchange rate will change before it takes delivery in six months, and the shirts will cost more than the current €19,200 equivalent of P320,000 (= 64 pesos × 5,000). The retailer acquires a *forward foreign exchange contract* from its bank to purchase P320,000 for €25,600 in six months, implying an exchange rate of €.08 to P1. If the euro declines in value such that the exchange rate rises above €.08 per peso, the bank will pay the retailer the difference. If the exchange rate is €.08 or less, the forward exchange contract expires, and the retailer exchanges the necessary euros to purchase P320,000. Thus, the retailer benefits if the exchange rate declines below €.08, incurs the cost for exchange rates between €.06 and €.08—the return to the bank for selling the forward foreign exchange contract—and neutralizes its risk for exchange rates above €.08

Example 6 Arcelor Mittal, a steel manufacturer, has €50 million of variable interest rate bonds outstanding. The interest rate that Arcelor Mittal pays on these bonds varies with the bank prime interest rate in the Netherlands, currently 6%. To fix the interest rate on its borrowing at 6%, Arcelor Mittal enters into an *interest rate swap contract* with its bank. If the variable interest rate rises above 6%, say to 8%, Arcelor Mittal must pay its bondholders interest at 8%. However, the bank will pay Arcelor Mittal 2% of the amount borrowed, fixing Arcelor Mittal's net borrowing cost at 6%. If the interest rate declines below 6%, say to 5%, Arcelor will pay its bondholders interest at 5%. However, Arcelor Mittal must pay the bank 1% of the amount borrowed, again fixing its borrowing cost at 6%.

The financial assets described in **Examples 1**, **2**, and **3** appear either in the current assets section or the noncurrent assets section of the balance sheet, depending on the expected holding period. These financial assets are marketable securities. The financial contracts in **Examples 4**, **5**, and **6** are *derivatives*, which can be either assets or liabilities, depending on movement in the financial variable (for example, interest rates) linked to the financial contract. This chapter discusses the accounting for investments in marketable securities and derivatives. The discussion proceeds as follows:

1. We begin with a general discussion of measurement issues and reporting the effects of remeasurements of marketable securities and derivatives.

2. We then describe the requirements of U.S. GAAP and IFRS to account for investments in marketable securities.

3. We next describe the requirements of U.S. GAAP and IFRS to account for derivatives.

4. We conclude by discussing and illustrating the fair value option, which provides firms with the choice to measure certain financial assets at fair value.

 # ISSUES IN ASSET MEASUREMENT AND INCOME RECOGNITION

As background to the accounting guidance in U.S. GAAP and IFRS for marketable securities and derivatives, we first identify the accounting issues involved in the measurement of financial assets on the balance sheet and the recognition of income on the income statement.

Example 7 To illustrate these accounting issues, assume the following:

1. **January 1, 2009**: Ford Motor Company (Ford) purchases 100 shares of Duke Power Corporation common stock for $50 per share as an investment.

		2009	2010	2011

EXHIBIT 12.1 Illustration of Asset Measurement and Income Recognition

	2009	2010	2011
Method 1: Acquisition Cost			
Balance Sheet	$5,000	$5,000	$ 0
Other Comprehensive Income → Accumulated Other Comprehensive Income	$ 0	$ 0	$ 0
Net Income → Retained Earnings	$ 0	$ 0	$ 3,000
Method 2: Fair Value with Unrealized Gains and Losses in Other Comprehensive Income			
Balance Sheet	$6,000	$8,000	$ 0
Other Comprehensive Income → Accumulated Other Comprehensive Income	$1,000	$2,000	$(3,000)
Net Income → Retained Earnings	$ 0	$ 0	$ 3,000
Method 3: Fair Value with Unrealized Gains and Losses in Net Income			
Balance Sheet	$6,000	$8,000	$ 0
Other Comprehensive Income → Accumulated Other Comprehensive Income	$ 0	$ 0	$ 0
Net Income → Retained Earnings	$1,000	$2,000	$ 0

2. **December 31, 2009**: The market price of Duke Power's common stock is $60 per share. Ford continues to hold the shares.

3. **December 31, 2010**: The market price of Duke Power's common stock is $80 per share. Ford continues to hold the shares.

4. **January 2, 2011**: Ford sells the 100 shares of Duke Power Corporation for $80 per share.

Setting aside requirements of U.S. GAAP and IFRS, Ford might measure the Duke Power shares on its balance sheet using either (1) acquisition cost, or (2) fair value. If Ford uses fair value, it might recognize the changes in fair value either (1) in other comprehensive income as the fair values change and in net income when it sells the shares, or (2) in net income as fair values change. **Exhibit 12.1** illustrates the amounts on the balance sheet and in other comprehensive income and net income under these three methods. The arrows signify the closing of net income to Retained Earnings or the closing of other comprehensive income to Accumulated Other Comprehensive Income.

METHOD 1: ACQUISITION COST MEASUREMENT

Measuring the investment at acquisition cost for all periods until Ford sells it results in reporting marketable securities at $5,000 on the balance sheet at the end of 2009 and 2010. At the time of sale in 2011, Ford realizes a gain of $3,000 (= $8,000 − $5,000), which it includes in net income for that year. The acquisition cost method does not confront issues in measuring fair values each year, which could be a problem for equity securities of private companies and for certain derivatives. The acquisition cost method does not *recognize* gains and losses before they arise in a market transaction at the time of sale. Thus, this method ignores unrealized holding gains and losses while a firm holds the securities, and reports only *realized* gains and losses in the income statement. An important shortcoming of the acquisition cost method is that it does not report the fair value of securities on the balance sheet, although users of financial statements likely find fair values more relevant than acquisition cost.

METHOD 2: FAIR VALUE MEASUREMENT WITH UNREALIZED GAINS AND LOSSES IN OTHER COMPREHENSIVE INCOME

The second method measures and reports the securities at fair value on the balance sheet at the end of each reporting period. Thus, Ford would report the marketable securities at $6,000 on its December 31, 2009, balance sheet and at $8,000 on its December 31, 2010, balance sheet. Measuring securities at fair value provides financial statement users with information about the amount the firm would receive by selling the securities on the balance sheet date. The second method does not report changes in fair value in the income statement until the firm realizes the gain by selling the securities. Thus, net income for 2011 will include the $3,000 realized gain, the total gain since acquisition, on sale of the securities.

To maintain the balance sheet equality in this illustration, this second method must have an offsetting credit for the debit to Marketable Securities arising from the increase in fair value each year. This second method increases Other Comprehensive Income, which firms close to Accumulated Other Comprehensive Income, another shareholders' equity account, at the end of each reporting period. Thus, the $1,000 increase in fair value during 2009 increases Other Comprehensive Income by $1,000 and results in a balance in Accumulated Other Comprehensive Income of $1,000 at the end of 2009. The $2,000 increase in fair value during 2010 increases Other Comprehensive Income by $2,000 and results in a balance in Accumulated Other Comprehensive Income of $3,000 (= $1,000 + $2,000) at the end of 2010. When the firm sells the securities in 2011, it makes the following entry:

January 2, 2011

Cash...	8,000	
Other Comprehensive Income	3,000	
Marketable Securities		8,000
Realized Gain on Sale of Marketable Securities		3,000

Assets	=	Liabilities	+	Shareholders' Equity	(Class.)
+8,000				−3,000	OCI → AOCI
−8,000				+3,000	NI → RE

To record the sale for $8,000 of marketable securities with a carrying value of $8,000 and transfer previously recognized unrealized holding gains of $3,000 from Accumulated Other Comprehensive Income to net income as a realized gain.

METHOD 3: FAIR VALUE MEASUREMENT WITH UNREALIZED HOLDING GAINS AND LOSSES IN NET INCOME

The third method, like the second, reports marketable securities at fair value each period. However, it recognizes the unrealized holding gain (or loss) in net income as the fair value changes, instead of waiting until Ford sells the shares. Under the third method, readers of the financial statements that use net income to assess performance will have the needed information about a firm's decisions to purchase, hold, and sell marketable securities reported in the income statement. Advocates of this method, as compared to the second method, argue that if fair values are sufficiently reliable to measure assets, then they should be sufficiently reliable to recognize unrealized gains and losses on those assets in net income.

Each of these three methods has perceived advantages and disadvantages. U.S. GAAP and IFRS use a combination of these three methods in specifying the required accounting for marketable securities and for derivatives.

ACCOUNTING AND REPORTING OF MARKETABLE SECURITIES

Firms acquire marketable securities for trading purposes, as **Example 1** describes for Goldman Sachs, or as a short-term investment of excess cash, as **Example 2** describes for Southwest Airlines. They classify the investments as current assets on the balance sheet. Firms that acquire marketable securities as a long-term investment, as **Example 3** describes for Roche, classify the **investments in securities** as a noncurrent asset. The term *marketable securities* implies the existence of a market where the securities actively trade, permitting relatively easy and reliable measurement of fair values. Firms that do not elect the fair value option for financial assets (discussed later in this chapter) follow the provisions of FASB *Statement 115* (U.S. GAAP) or *IAS 39* (IFRS) in accounting and reporting marketable securities.[1] We discuss and illustrate the provisions of U.S. GAAP and IFRS next.

CLASSIFICATION OF MARKETABLE SECURITIES

The provisions of U.S. GAAP and IFRS require firms to classify marketable securities into three categories:

1. **Debt securities held to maturity** (U.S. GAAP) or **held-to-maturity investments** (IFRS) for which a firm has both the intent and the ability to hold to maturity—shown on the balance sheet at an amount based on acquisition cost, but subject to impairment (following a variation of the first method illustrated in **Exhibit 12.1**).

2. Debt and equity securities held as **trading securities** (U.S. GAAP) or as **financial assets at fair value through profit or loss** (IFRS)—shown on the balance sheet at fair value, with changes in fair value of securities held at the end of the accounting period reported each period in net income (following the third method illustrated in **Exhibit 12.1**).

3. Debt and equity securities held as **securities available for sale** (U.S GAAP) or as **available-for-sale financial assets** (IFRS)—shown on the balance sheet at fair value, with unrealized changes in fair value of securities held at the end of the accounting period included in other comprehensive income, and realized changes in fair value included in net income when a firm sells the securities (following the second method illustrated in **Exhibit 12.1**).

MEASUREMENT OF SECURITIES AT ACQUISITION

A firm initially records the purchase of marketable securities at acquisition cost, which includes the purchase price plus any commissions, taxes, and other costs incurred.[2] For example, if a firm acquires securities classified as marketable securities for $10,000, the entry is as follows:

| Marketable Securities | | | | | 10,000 | |
| Cash | | | | | | 10,000 |

Assets	=	Liabilities	+	Shareholders' Equity	(Class.)
+10,000					
−10,000					

To record the acquisition of marketable securities costing $10,000.

The investor recognizes dividends on equity securities as revenue when the firm's board of directors declares dividends and recognizes interest on debt securities when interest accrues over time. Assume that a firm holds equity securities earning $250 through dividend declarations and debt securities earning $300 from interest earned and that it has not yet received these amounts in cash. The entry is as follows:

Dividends and Interest Receivable	550	
Dividend Revenue		250
Interest Revenue		300

(continued)

---

[1]Financial Accounting Standards Board, *Statement of Financial Accounting Standards No. 115*, "Accounting for Certain Investments in Debt and Equity Securities," 1993 (**Codification Topic 320**); International Accounting Standards Board, *International Accounting Standard 39*, "Financial Instruments: Recognition and Measurement," revised 2003. We use the term *marketable securities* to refer to the financial instruments that firms classify as held-to-maturity, trading, or available for sale securities (discussed in the next section), recognizing that the term does not have a precise definition in U.S. GAAP or IFRS.

[2]U.S. GAAP and IFRS exclude transactions costs from the acquisition cost of trading securities, treating such costs as expenses of the period.

Assets	=	Liabilities	+	Shareholders' Equity	(Class.)
+550				+250	IncSt → RE
				+300	IncSt → RE

To record dividends and interest revenue from Marketable Securities.

The measurement of marketable securities at the date of acquisition and the recording of dividends and interest present no new issues. Measuring securities after acquisition, however, departs from acquisition cost accounting.

MEASUREMENT OF SECURITIES AFTER ACQUISITION

Debt Securities Held to Maturity Firms sometimes acquire debt securities with the intention of holding these securities until maturity, as in the next example.

Example 8 Consolidated Edison (ConEd), an electric utility, has $100 million of bonds payable outstanding that mature in five years. The utility acquires U.S. government securities whose periodic interest payments and maturity value exactly equal those on the utility's outstanding bonds. The firm intends to use the cash received from the government bonds to make required interest and principal payments on its own bonds.

Note that ConEd could also have used its cash to purchase its bonds in the marketplace. **Example 8** illustrates a mechanism that firms might use instead of bond repurchases for bond issues that are widely held. The mechanism avoids the considerable transaction costs of identifying and locating all of the bondholders and persuading them to sell their bonds to ConEd before maturity.

U.S. GAAP and IFRS require firms to measure marketable securities for which firms have an intent and ability to hold to maturity at **amortized acquisition cost**. A firm initially records these debt securities at acquisition cost. This acquisition cost will differ from the maturity value of the debt if the coupon rate on the bonds differs from the required market yield on the bonds at the time the firm acquired them. The firm must use the effective interest method to amortize any difference between acquisition cost and maturity value over the life of the debt as an adjustment to interest revenue. The amortization procedure involves the same compound interest computations that **Chapter 10** discussed for the issuer of the bonds and illustrated in **Exhibit 10.2**.

The amortization procedure involves the following steps:

1. The holder of the debt securities (the investor) records interest revenue each period at an amount equal to the carrying value of the debt at the start of the period multiplied by the market rate of interest applicable to that debt on the day the firm acquired the debt. It debits the Marketable Securities account and credits Interest Revenue, which after closing entries increases Retained Earnings.

2. If the investor receives cash each period, it debits Cash and credits the Marketable Securities account. The result of this process is a new carrying value (called the *amortized cost*) for use in the computations during the next period.

Example 9 Refer to **Example 8**. Assume that the U.S. government will pay the investor $2,500,000 each six months, equal to 2.5% of the $100 million face amount of the bonds (5% annual coupon rate, paid in two installments each year), and will repay the $100 million at the end of five years. Assume that at the time ConEd purchases the bonds, the market prices these bonds to yield the investor 6% annually (3% each six months). Because the market requires a higher yield (6%) than the stated interest rate (5%) on the bonds, the bonds will sell on the market for a discount (that is, for less than their face amount). ConEd will pay $95,734,898[3] for these bonds. **Exhibit 12.2** shows the amortization table for these bonds for the ten six-month periods prior to maturity in five years.

---

[3]The amount equals the present value of an annuity of $2.5 million for 10 periods plus the present value of $100 million paid at the end of 10 periods, both cash flows discounted at 3% per period.

EXHIBIT 12.2 Amortization Table for $100 Million Bonds with a Stated Interest Rate of 5% and a Market Required Yield of 6%

Period (1)	Marketable Security at Beginning of Period (2)	Interest Revenue at 3% per Period (3)	Cash Received for Period (4)	Increase in Carrying Value of Marketable Security (5)	Marketable Security at End of Period (6)
1	$95,734,898	$2,872,047	$2,500,000	$372,047	$ 96,106,945
2	$96,106,945	$2,883,208	$2,500,000	$383,208	$ 96,490,153
3	$96,490,153	$2,894,705	$2,500,000	$394,705	$ 96,884,858
4	$96,884,858	$2,906,546	$2,500,000	$406,546	$ 97,291,404
5	$97,291,404	$2,918,742	$2,500,000	$418,742	$ 97,710,146
6	$97,710,146	$2,931,304	$2,500,000	$431,304	$ 98,141,450
7	$98,141,450	$2,944,244	$2,500,000	$444,244	$ 98,585,694
8	$98,585,694	$2,957,571	$2,500,000	$457,571	$ 99,043,265
9	$99,043,265	$2,971,298	$2,500,000	$471,298	$ 99,514,563
10	$99,514,563	$2,985,437	$2,500,000	$485,437	$100,000,000

Column (2) equals Column (6) from the previous period, except for the first period, when it equals the purchase price of the bonds.

Column (3) = .03 × Column (2).

Column (4) is given.

Column (5) = Column (3) − Column (4).

Column (6) = Column (2) + Column (5).

ConEd makes the following entry at the time it purchases the U.S. government securities:

Beginning of Period 1

| Marketable Securities | | | 95,734,898 | |
| Cash | | | | 95,734,898 |

Assets	=	Liabilities	+	Shareholders' Equity	(Class.)
+95,734,898					
−95,734,898					

To record the purchase of $100 million face amount of bonds classified as held to maturity for $95,734,898.

ConEd would classify this investment as a noncurrent asset on its balance sheet because it intends to hold the securities for more than one year.

At the end of the first six-month period, ConEd makes the following entry:

End of First Six-Month Period

| Marketable Securities | | | 2,872,047 | |
| Interest Revenue | | | | 2,872,047 |

Assets	=	Liabilities	+	Shareholders' Equity	(Class.)
+2,872,047				+2,872,047	IncSt → RE

To recognize interest revenue on bonds; $2,872,047 = .03 × $95,734,898.

End of First Six-Month Period

| Cash | 2,500,000 | |
| Marketable Securities | | 2,500,000 |

Assets	=	Liabilities	+	Shareholders' Equity	(Class.)
+2,500,000					
−2,500,000					

To record cash received from investment in U.S. government bonds.

ConEd could combine the two preceding entries into one:

End of First Six-Month Period

Cash	2,500,000	
Marketable Securities	372,047	
Interest Revenue		2,872,047

Assets	=	Liabilities	+	Shareholders' Equity	(Class.)
+2,500,000				+2,872,047	IncSt → RE
+372,047					

ConEd makes similar entries each six months during the five years using the amounts in the amortization table in **Exhibit 12.2**. At the end of five years, the carrying value of the bonds will be $100 million. ConEd makes the following entry at the maturity of the bonds when it receives cash:

End of Last Six-Month Period

| Cash | 100,000,000 | |
| Marketable Securities | | 100,000,000 |

Assets	=	Liabilities	+	Shareholders' Equity	(Class.)
+100,000,000					
−100,000,000					

To record cash received at the maturity of the bonds.

The accounting for debt securities held to maturity relies on the acquisition cost method illustrated in **Exhibit 12.1** in that both the initial amount recorded and adjustments for amortization each period rely on the initial purchase price of $95,734,898. The amount that results from the application of this measurement approach is sometimes called *amortized cost*. U.S. GAAP and IFRS require firms to account for debt securities designated as held to maturity at amortized cost, except that they are also subject to impairment. That is, firms do not recognize increases in fair value (unrealized gains) but might recognize decreases in fair value (unrealized losses).[4]

The argument for measuring held-to-maturity debt securities at amortized cost and ignoring most changes in fair value during the contractual term of the debt is that changes in fair value are not relevant if the firm has the intention and ability to hold the securities to maturity; firms would recognize impairment losses because of conservatism and because impairments due to changes in default risk reflect changes in the amount the investor is likely to receive. The counter argument is, first, that any change in economic circumstances—changes in interest rates, or the credit risk of the borrower, or the investor's need for cash—could change the investor's willingness or ability to hold the securities until maturity; and second,

---

[4]If a held-to-maturity security is deemed to be impaired, the investor recognizes (debits) an impairment loss (included in net income) and reduces (credits) the balance sheet carrying value of the investment. This book does not address the different U.S. GAAP and IFRS requirements for a firm to use in deciding if an impairment loss has occurred and, if so, how to measure it.

that the fair value of the security reflects the economic opportunity cost of continuing to hold the securities.

PROBLEM 12.1 for Self-Study

Accounting for an investment in bonds. General Electric Capital Services (GECS) pays $105,346 to acquire bonds of Sapra Company. GECS classifies these bonds as held to maturity investments. GECS will receive $8,000 at the end of the first year, $8,000 at the end of the second year, and $108,000 at the end of the third year. The market required yield at the time GECS purchased the bonds is 6%.

a. Prepare an amortization table, similar to that in **Exhibit 12.2**, for the life of the bonds.

b. Prepare journal entries that GECS would make on the date of purchase and at the end of the first year after the date of purchase.

Trading Securities Firms sometimes purchase and sell debt and equity securities for the short-term profit potential—some would say for *speculation*. The term *trading* implies active and frequent buying and selling with the objective of generating profits from short-term changes in market prices. Acquisition and disposition of trading securities are usually operating activities. Investment banks, for example, often trade securities in different capital markets worldwide to take advantage of temporary differences in market prices. Other financial firms, such as thrift institutions, insurance companies, and brokerage firms, also trade securities. Manufacturers, retailers, and other nonfinancial firms also invest funds for trading purposes, but less frequently and in relatively smaller amounts than do financial services firms. Firms include trading securities in marketable securities in the current assets section of the balance sheet.

Firms initially record trading securities at fair value, excluding transactions costs (which firms expense as they incur them). U.S. GAAP and IFRS require firms to report trading securities at fair value on the balance sheet. For these securities, active securities markets provide objective measures of fair values, and fair values provide financial statement users with the most relevant information for assessing the success of a firm's trading activities over time.

The income statement reports the debit (loss) for decreases in the fair value and the credit (gain) for increases in the fair value of trading securities in an account with a title such as *Unrealized Holding Loss* (or *Gain* or *Gains and Losses, net*) *on Trading Securities.*

Example 10 First Insurance acquired shares of Sun Microsystems' common stock on December 28, 2008, for $400,000 and classified them as trading securities. The fair value of these securities on December 31, 2008, was $402,000. First Insurance sold these shares on January 3, 2009, for $405,000. The journal entries to record these transactions appear below.

December 28, 2008

Marketable Securities	400,000	
Cash		400,000

Assets	=	Liabilities	+	Shareholders' Equity	(Class.)
+400,000					
−400,000					

To record acquisition of trading securities.

December 31, 2008

Marketable Securities	2,000	
Unrealized Holding Gain on Trading Securities		2,000

(continued)

Assets	=	Liabilities	+	Shareholders' Equity	(Class.)
+2,000				+2,000	IncSt → RE

To measure trading securities at fair value and recognize unrealized holding gain in net income.

January 3, 2009

Cash 405,000

       Marketable Securities 402,000

       Realized Gain on Sale of Trading Securities 3,000

Assets	=	Liabilities	+	Shareholders' Equity	(Class.)
+405,000				+3,000	IncSt → RE
−402,000					

To record the sale of trading securities at a gain.

The total income from the purchase and sale of these securities is $5,000 (= $405,000 of cash inflows − $400,000 of cash outflows). Measurement of trading securities at fair value reflects this income when it occurs in the form of a change in fair value, not when the investor realizes a gain or loss at the time of sale. In 2008 the income effect is $2,000, the change in fair value during that year, and in 2009 the income effect is $3,000, the change in fair value during that year. This accounting follows the third method illustrated in **Exhibit 12.1**.

Securities Available for Sale U.S. GAAP and IFRS require firms to classify marketable securities that are neither debt securities held to maturity nor trading securities as securities available for sale. Securities available for sale that a firm intends to sell within one year appear in marketable securities in the current assets section of the balance sheet. All others appear in investments in securities in noncurrent assets. Acquisition and disposition of securities available for sale are usually investing activities on the statement of cash flows. U.S. GAAP and IFRS require firms to report these securities at fair value on the balance sheet.

Firms initially record investments in securities available for sale at acquisition cost, including transaction costs. If a firm classifies debt securities as available for sale, it must amortize any difference between the purchase price and the maturity value of the debt over the remaining term to maturity, the same as if the firm classified the debt as held to maturity. This amortization makes interest revenue on these debt securities differ from the cash receipts for debt service payments. On the date of each balance sheet, firms measure securities classified as available for sale at fair value. The difference between amortized cost for debt securities or the carrying value for equity securities and the fair value of these securities is an unrealized holding gain or loss. The unrealized holding gain or holding loss increases or decreases Other Comprehensive Income (a shareholders' equity account), which firms close to Accumulated Other Comprehensive Income (another shareholders' equity account) at the end of the period. Accumulated Other Comprehensive Income includes the sum of all increases and decreases in fair value of securities available for sale that have not yet appeared in net income. Holding gains and losses on securities available for sale affect net income only when the firm sells these securities; that is, when the firm realizes the gain or loss. The accounting for securities available for sale follows the second method illustrated in **Exhibit 12.1**.

Example 11 Nike acquires common stock of Merck for $400,000 on November 1, 2008, and designates this investment as available for sale. The fair value of these shares is $435,000 on December 31, 2008. Nike sells these shares on August 15, 2009, for $480,000. The journal entries to record these transactions are as follows:

November 1, 2008

Marketable Securities 400,000

       Cash 400,000

(continued)

Assets	=	Liabilities	+	Shareholders' Equity	(Class.)
+400,000					
−400,000					

To record acquisition of securities available for sale.

December 31, 2008

Marketable Securities	35,000	
Unrealized Holding Gain on Securities Available for Sale.		35,000

Assets	=	Liabilities	+	Shareholders' Equity	(Class.)
+35,000				+35,000	OCI → AOCI

To measure securities available for sale at fair value and recognize an unrealized holding gain in other comprehensive income.

August 15, 2009

Cash	480,000	
Unrealized Holding Gain on Securities Available for Sale	35,000	
Marketable Securities		435,000
Realized Gain on Sale of Securities Available for Sale		80,000

Assets	=	Liabilities	+	Shareholders' Equity	(Class.)
+480,000				−35,000	OCI → AOCI
−435,000				+80,000	NI → RE

To record the sale of securities available for sale at a realized gain and reduce amount previously recognized as an unrealized holding gain.

The total income from the purchase and sale of these securities is $80,000 (= $480,000 of cash inflows − $400,000 of cash outflows). The entire gain affects net income in the year of sale, even though the balance sheet reports changes in fair value of the assets as they occur.

Like securities classified as held-to-maturity debt securities, firms must also test securities classified as available for sale for impairment. If the securities are impaired, the firm treats the unrealized loss in Accumulated Other Comprehensive Income as if it were realized. For example, if a firm decides that an available-for-sale security with an unrealized loss of $5,000 is impaired as of December 31, the journal entry would be:

December 31, 2008

Impairment Loss	5,000	
Unrealized Holding Loss on Securities Available for Sale		5,000

Assets	=	Liabilities	+	Shareholders' Equity	(Class.)
				−5,000	NI → RE
				+5,000	AOCI → NI

To record an impairment loss on securities available for sale.

The required accounting for trading securities and for securities classified as available for sale differs with respect to the income statement but not with respect to the balance sheet. The unrealized gain or loss on trading securities appears in net income in the period when fair value changes occur. The unrealized holding gain or loss on securities available for sale appears in other comprehensive income period by period, and its cumulative amount resides in the Accumulated Other Comprehensive Income account on the balance sheet. Management can sell securities with unrealized holding gains (or losses) and transfer through net income to Retained Earnings the entire unrealized holding gain (or loss)—that is, management can affect the timing of gain or loss recognition in net income for securities available for sale but not for trading securities. This timing ability is, however, asymmetric in that impairment rules preclude indefinite deferrals of the recognition in income of unrealized losses, but not unrealized gains. Users of the financial statements should be alert to this accounting effect in evaluating the profitability of firms with both types of securities.

RECLASSIFICATION OF SECURITIES

The firm's purpose for holding certain securities may change, requiring it to transfer securities from one of the three categories to another. The firm transfers the securities at fair value at the time of the transfer. FASB *Statement No. 115* and IASB *IAS 39* prescribe the accounting for any unrealized gain or loss at the time of the transfer, a topic beyond the scope of this textbook. Note, however, that a transfer of a held-to-maturity investment in debt securities to either trading securities or securities available for sale would call into question the original designation of that investment.

PROBLEM 12.2 for Self-Study

Accounting for securities available for sale. Transactions involving Conlin Corporation's marketable securities appear in **Exhibit 12.3**.

a. Give the journal entries to account for these securities during 2008 and 2009 assuming Conlin Corporation classifies them as securities available for sale.

b. How would the journal entries in part **a** differ if Conlin Corporation classified these securities as trading securities?

EXHIBIT 12.3

Conlin Corporation
(Problem 12.2 for Self-Study)

| | | | | | Fair Value | |
| | | | | | December 31, | December 31, |
Security	Date Acquired	Acquisition Cost	Date Sold	Selling Price	2008	2009
A	2/3/2008	$ 40,000	—	—	$ 38,000	$ 33,000
B	7/15/2008	75,000	9/6/2009	$78,000	79,000	—
C	11/27/2008	90,000	—	—	93,000	94,000
		$205,000			$210,000	$127,000

DISCLOSURES ABOUT MARKETABLE SECURITIES

U.S. GAAP and IFRS require disclosures about marketable securities each period. We illustrate these disclosures next using information from the balance sheet and notes for Starbucks Corporation presented in **Exhibit 12.4**. These disclosures reflect U.S. GAAP requirements. IFRS requirements are similar but can result in less detailed disclosures.[5]

1. The aggregate fair value, gross unrealized holding gains, gross unrealized holding losses, and amortized cost for debt securities held to maturity and for debt and equity securities available for sale.

Starbucks Corporation's short-term investments comprise securities available for sale and trading securities, and its long-term investments include securities classified as available for sale. It reports no debt securities held to maturity. The available-for-sale securities comprise debt securities of various governmental entities. The amortized cost column in **Exhibit 12.4**

---

[5]Financial Accounting Standards Board, *Statement of Financial Accounting Standards No. 115*, "Accounting for Certain Investments in Debt and Equity Securities," 1993 (**Codification Topic 320**); International Accounting Standards Board, *International Financial Reporting Standard 7*, "Financial Instruments: Disclosure," 2005.

EXHIBIT 12.4

Starbucks Corporation
Disclosures Related to Marketable Securities
(amounts in thousands)

Balance Sheet	September 30, 2007	October 1, 2006
Current Assets:		
Marketable Securities Available for Sale	$83,845	$87,542
Marketable Securities Held as Trading Securities	73,588	53,496
Noncurrent Assets:		
Long-Term Investments—Available-for-Sale Securities	21,022	5,811

	Fiscal Year 2007	Fiscal Year 2006
Statement of Cash Flows: Investing Activities		
Purchases of Available-for-Sale Securities	$(237,422)	$(639,192)
Maturities of Available-for-Sale Securities	178,167	269,134
Sales of Available-for-Sale Securities	47,497	431,181

Note 3: Short-Term Investments
The Company's short-term investments consist of the following:

	Amortized Cost	Gross Unrealized Holding Gains	Gross Unrealized Holding Losses	Fair Value
September 30, 2007				
Short-Term Investments—Available-for-Sale Securities:				
State and Local Government Obligations	$ 81,366	—	$ (21)	$ 81,345
U.S. Government Agency Obligations	2,500	—	—	2,500
Total	$ 83,866	—	$ (21)	$ 83,845
Short-Term Investments—Trading Securities	67,837			73,588
Total Short-Term Investments	$ 151,703			$157,433
Long-Term Investments—Available-for-Sale Securities:				
U.S. Government Agency Obligations	$ 21,000	$ 22	—	$ 21,022
October 1, 2006				
Short-Term Investments—Available-for-Sale Securities:				
State and Local Government Obligations	$ 75,379	$ 9	$(332)	$ 75,056
U.S. Government Agency Obligations	10,000	—		10,000
Corporate Debt Securities	2,488	—	(2)	2,486
Total	$ 87,867	$ 9	$(334)	$ 87,542
Short-Term Investments—Trading Securities	55,265			53,496
Total Short-Term Investments	$ 143,132			$141,038
Long-Term Investments—Available-for-Sale Securities:				
State and Local Government Obligations	$ 5,893	$ —	$ (82)	$ 5,811

For available-for-sale securities, proceeds from sales were $47 million, $431 million, and $626 million in fiscal years 2007, 2006, and 2005, respectively. Gross realized gains from sales were $3.8 million and $0.1 million in fiscal years 2006 and 2005, respectively. Gross realized losses from sales were $0.1 million and $1.7 million in fiscal years 2006 and 2005, respectively. For fiscal 2007, there were no realized losses and an immaterial amount of realized gains.

In fiscal years 2007 and 2006, the changes in net unrealized holding gains/losses in the trading portfolio included in earnings were a net gain of $7.5 million and a net loss of $4.2 million, respectively.

shows the carrying value of debt securities after amortizing any difference between the purchase price of these securities and their maturity value. The fair value column shows the fair value of these securities at each balance sheet date. The two middle columns show the gross unrealized gains and gross unrealized losses on securities available for sale. Requiring the separate disclosure of unrealized gains and unrealized losses provides information that would not appear if firms could net these amounts. The differences between amortized cost and fair value appear relatively small on both balance sheet dates.

2. The proceeds from sales of securities available for sale, and the gross realized gains and gross realized losses on those sales.

The statement of cash flows shows the cash expenditures to purchase available-for-sale securities and the cash receipts from maturities and sales of available-for-sale securities. For Starbucks, the cash receipts largely offset expenditures each year, and their amounts are larger than the balance sheet amount of available-for-sale securities at the beginning and end of the year. This implies that Starbucks turns over its portfolio of available-for-sale securities several times each year. The paragraph under the panel of data in **Exhibit 12.4** also discloses the proceeds from selling available-for-sale securities, as well as the gross realized gains and gross realized losses. As with disclosures about unrealized gains and losses on the balance sheet, requiring the separate disclosure of realized gains and realized losses provides information that would not appear if firms were permitted to net these amounts.

3. The change during the period in the net unrealized holding gain or loss on securities available for sale included in a separate shareholders' equity account.

The statement of changes in shareholders' equity shows that Accumulated Other Comprehensive Income increased by $1,767 thousand in fiscal 2006 and decreased by $20,380 thousand in fiscal 2007 because of net unrealized gains and losses. Starbucks Corporation does not indicate how much of these changes in Accumulated Other Comprehensive Income relates to marketable securities and how much relates to cash flow hedges, a topic discussed in the next section.

4. The change during the period in the net unrealized holding gain or loss on trading securities included in earnings.

The second paragraph under the panel of data in **Exhibit 12.4** indicates the amount of the gain in fiscal year 2007 and the amount of the net loss in fiscal year 2006 from changes in unrealized holding gains and losses on trading securities.

DERIVATIVE INSTRUMENTS

Firms incur risks in carrying out their business activities. A fire might destroy a warehouse of a retail chain and disrupt the flow of merchandise to stores. An automobile accident involving a member of the sales staff may injure the employee or others and damage the firm's automobile. A firm's products might injure customers and subject the firm to lawsuits. Most firms purchase property, medical, and liability insurance against such risks. The insurance shifts the risk of the loss beyond the deductible amount and up to the limits in the insurance policy to the insurance company. The firm pays insurance premiums for the right to shift the insured risk.

Firms engage in other transactions that subject them to specific financial risks. Consider the following scenarios.

Example 12 Firm A, a U.S. firm, orders a machine on June 30, 2008, for delivery on June 30, 2009, from a British supplier for £10,000 (currency is Great Britain pounds sterling). The exchange rate between the U.S. dollar and the British pound is currently $1.60 per £1, indicating a purchase price of $16,000. If the value of the U.S. dollar declines between June 30, 2008, and June 30, 2009, when it must convert U.S. dollars into British pounds, Firm A will pay more than $16,000 to purchase the machine.

Example 13 Firm B issued a note to a supplier dated January 1, 2008, for the purchase of manufacturing equipment. The note has a face value of $100,000 and bears interest at the rate of 8% each year. Interest is payable annually on December 31, and the note matures on December 31, 2010. If interest rates change, the market value of the note will change.

Example 14 Firm C gives a note payable to a supplier on January 1, 2008, to acquire manufacturing equipment. The note has a face value of $100,000 and bears interest at the prime lending rate, which is 8% on January 1, 2008. The supplier resets the interest rate each

December 31 to establish the interest charge for the next calendar year. Interest is payable on December 31 of each year, and the note matures on December 31, 2010. If interest rates rise above 8% during the term of the note, Firm C will have to pay interest at that higher rate.

Example 15 Firm D holds 10,000 gallons of whiskey in inventory on October 31, 2008. Firm D expects to complete aging this whiskey by March 31, 2009, at which time it intends to sell the whiskey. Uncertainties about the quality of the aged whiskey and economic conditions at the time, however, make predicting the selling price on March 31, 2009, difficult.

Most firms face risks—that is, variability of outcome—from changes in interest rates, foreign exchange rates, and commodity prices. Firms can purchase financial instruments to reduce these business risks, that is, to reduce the volatility of certain outcomes. Some of these instruments trade in relatively active markets, like marketable securities, while others have specialized terms and do not trade at all. The general term used for the types of financial instruments that firms might buy to mitigate the risks described in **Examples 12–15** is a **derivative**. The accounting for derivative financial instruments follows some of the principles governing the accounting for marketable securities discussed in the previous section, with some exceptions. This section discusses the nature, use, accounting, and reporting of derivative instruments. FASB *Statements 133* and *138* and *IAS 39* provide accounting and disclosure guidance for derivatives.[6]

NATURE AND USE OF DERIVATIVE INSTRUMENTS

A derivative is a financial instrument whose value changes in response to changes in an underlying observable variable, such as a stock price, an interest rate, a currency exchange rate, or a commodity price. Unlike equity securities, which have no definite settlement date, firms settle a derivative at a date that the terms of the instrument specify. Finally, a derivative requires an investment that is small, relative to the investment in a contract that is similarly exposed to changes in market factors, or requires no investment at all.[7] An option to purchase a share of stock derives its value from movements in the market price of that stock. A commitment to purchase a certain amount of foreign currency in the future derives its value from changes in the exchange rate for that currency. Firms use derivative instruments to hedge the risks that arise from changes in interest rates, foreign exchange rates, and commodity prices. The general idea behind hedging is that changes in the fair value of the derivative instrument offset changes in the fair value of an asset or liability or changes in future cash flows, thereby neutralizing, or at least reducing, the effects of those changes. Let's reconsider the previous four examples.

Example 16 Refer to **Example 12**. Firm A desires to incur a cost now to eliminate the effect of changes in the exchange rate between the U.S. dollar and the British pound while it awaits delivery of the equipment. It purchases a **forward foreign exchange contract** from a bank on June 30, 2008, in which it promises to pay a fixed U.S. dollar amount on June 30, 2009, in exchange for £10,000 received on that date. The forward exchange rate between U.S. dollars and British pounds on June 30, 2008, for settlement on June 30, 2009, establishes the number of U.S. dollars it must deliver. If the forward rate on June 30, 2008, for settlement of the forward contract on June 30, 2009, is $1.64 per £1, Firm A can purchase a forward contract and thereby lock in the cost of the equipment at $16,400 (= £10,000 × $1.64 per pound). By purchasing a forward foreign exchange contract, Firm A avoids volatility in the price of the equipment due to currency movements; it forgoes the possibility of benefit if the U.S. dollar strengthens against the pound but avoids the possibility of loss if the U.S. dollar weakens.

---

[6]Financial Accounting Standards Board, *Statement of Financial Accounting Standards No. 133*, "Accounting for Derivative Instruments and Hedging Activities," 1998 (**Codification Topic 815**); Financial Accounting Standards Board, *Statement of Financial Accounting Standards No. 138*, "Accounting for Certain Derivative Instruments and Certain Hedging Activities," 2000 (**Codification Topic 815**); International Accounting Standards Board, *International Accounting Standard 39*, "Financial Instruments: Recognition and Measurement," revised 2003.

[7]The definitions of a derivative in U.S. GAAP and IFRS are similar. However, the nature and complexity of financial instruments makes it difficult to discern, in certain cases, whether a given instrument is a derivative. In addition, both U.S. GAAP and IFRS contain exceptions—instruments that seem to meet the definition of a derivative are nonetheless not accounted for as derivatives.

Example 17 Refer to **Example 13**. Firm B wants to neutralize the effect of changes in the market value of the note payable caused by changes in market interest rates. It engages in an **interest rate swap** with its bank. The swap has the effect of allowing Firm B to exchange its fixed interest rate obligation for a variable interest rate obligation. The market value of the note and the related swap contract remain at $100,000 as long as the variable interest rate in the swap is the same as the variable rate used to revalue the note while it is outstanding.

Example 18 Refer to **Example 14**. Firm C wants to neutralize the effects of changes in interest rates. It engages in an interest rate swap with its bank. The swap has the effect of allowing Firm C to exchange its variable interest rate obligation for a fixed interest rate obligation, and therefore a fixed cash payment, of 8% times the $100,000 face value of the note. Firm C cannot benefit from decreases in interest rates below 8%, but it no longer bears risks—with attendant costs—if the interest rate rises above 8%.

Example 19 Refer to **Example 15**. Firm D would like to fix the price at which it can sell the whiskey in its inventory on March 31, 2009. It acquires a **forward commodity contract** in which it promises to sell 10,000 gallons of whiskey on March 31, 2009, at a fixed price. The forward price of whiskey on October 31, 2008, for delivery on March 31, 2009, is $320 per gallon. Thus, Firm D locks in a total cash inflow of $3,200,000 from selling the whiskey.

The forward contracts and swap contracts described in these examples illustrate two types of derivative instruments. Some derivative contracts contain standardized terms and trade in relatively active markets. Others contain terms tailored to suit the needs of the contracting parties and do not trade at all. The nature and complexity of derivatives vary widely. We use swap contracts to illustrate the accounting and reporting of derivatives.

TERMINOLOGY FOR DERIVATIVES

Consider the following elements of a derivative:

1. A derivative has one or more **underlyings**. An underlying is an observable variable such as a specified interest rate, or commodity price, or foreign exchange rate. The underlying in **Example 16** is the foreign exchange rate, in **Examples 17** and **18** is an interest rate, and in **Example 19** is the price of whiskey.

2. A derivative has one or more **notional amounts**. A notional amount is a number of currency units, bushels, shares, or other units specified in the contract. The notional amount in **Example 16** is £10,000, in **Examples 17** and **18** is the $100,000 face value of the note, and in **Example 19** is 10,000 gallons of whiskey.

3. A derivative sometimes requires no initial investment. The firm usually acquires a derivative by exchanging promises with a **counterparty**, such as a commercial or investment bank. The exchange of promises is a mutually unexecuted contract.

4. Derivatives typically require, or permit, **net settlement**, which means that when the counterparties settle the derivative contract, one of the contracting parties pays the other the fair value of the contract. For example, Firm A in **Example 16** will not deliver $16,400 and receive in exchange £10,000. Firm A will actually purchase £10,000 in the market on June 20, 2009, at the exchange rate on that date, when it needs the British pounds to purchase the equipment. Then, Firm A will receive cash from the counterparty (that is, the bank) to the extent that the exchange rate on June 30, 2009, exceeds $1.64 per £1 or will pay the counterparty on this date to the extent that the exchange rate is less than $1.64 per £1. The difference between the June 30, 2009, exchange rate and the $1.64 per £1 determines the fair value on that date. Firm B in **Example 17** will pay the supplier the 8% interest established in the fixed rate note. If the variable interest rate used in the interest rate swap contract increases to 10%, Firm B will pay the counterparty an amount equal to 2% (= 10% − 8%) of the notional amount of the note, $100,000. Paying interest of 8% to the supplier and 2% to the counterparty results in interest payments of 10%. If the variable interest rate decreases to 5%, Firm B still pays the supplier interest of 8% as specified in the original note, but would receive from the counterparty 3% (= 8% − 5%), resulting in net payments equal to the variable rate of 5%.

Because many derivatives require no initial investment, that is, no initial cash payment to the counterparty, measurement at acquisition cost makes little sense for these instruments.

That is, a derivative may have zero initial cost, but potentially large positive or negative fair values later. Both U.S. GAAP and IFRS require that firms record derivatives at their fair values on the balance sheet date.

ACCOUNTING FOR DERIVATIVES

A firm must recognize derivatives on its balance sheet as assets or liabilities, depending on the rights and obligations under the contract. The forward contract in **Example 16** is either an asset or a liability to Firm A, depending on the exchange rate. The swap contracts in **Examples 17** and **18** may be assets or liabilities, depending on interest rates—that is, whether at the balance sheet date the holder of the derivative would be entitled to receive cash or have to pay cash to the counterparty. The forward contract in **Example 19** may be an asset or liability, depending on the price of whiskey.

Firms must remeasure derivatives to fair value each period. The change in fair value either increases or decreases the balance sheet carrying value of the derivative asset or liability, and also affects either (1) net income immediately (like a trading security), or (2) other comprehensive income immediately and net income later (like securities available for sale).

The income effect of a change in the fair value of a derivative depends on the purpose for which a firm acquires the derivative and whether the firm chooses to apply **hedge accounting**. In both U.S. GAAP and IFRS, hedge accounting is elective; firms need not designate any derivatives as accounting hedges, regardless of the degree to which the derivatives mitigate the volatility of outcomes of other arrangements.

U.S. GAAP and IFRS require firms to classify derivatives as (1) fair value hedges, (2) cash flow hedges, or (3) not a hedging instrument.[8] Derivatives designated as cash flow hedges or fair value hedges receive special accounting treatment. The choice between the two designations depends on the firm's general hedging strategy and its purpose in acquiring the particular derivative instrument. If a firm does not designate a particular derivative as either a fair value hedge or a cash flow hedge, authoritative guidance requires that the firm account for the derivative as if it were a trading security (U.S. GAAP) or a security at fair value through profit and loss (IFRS). Firms measure derivatives that they do not designate as hedges at fair value each period and include the resulting gain or loss in net income. This accounting is the same as the third method illustrated in **Exhibit 12.1**.

Fair Value Hedges   Derivative instruments acquired to hedge exposure to changes in the fair values of assets or liabilities are **fair value hedges**. Fair value hedges are either (1) hedges of a *recognized* asset or liability (or an identified portion of a recognized asset or liability), or (2) hedges of an *unrecognized* firm commitment (or an identified portion of that commitment). Firm B in **Examples 13** and **17** entered into the interest swap agreement to neutralize the effect of changes in interest rates on the fair value of its notes payable, a recognized liability. Firm A in **Examples 12** and **16** acquired the forward foreign exchange contract to neutralize the effect of changes in exchange rates on its commitment to purchase the equipment. Firm A and Firm B can designate these derivatives as fair value hedges.

Cash Flow Hedges   Derivative instruments acquired to hedge exposure to variability in cash flows are **cash flow hedges**. Cash flow hedges are of two general types: (1) hedges on some or all of the cash flows of a *recognized* asset or liability, and (2) hedges on some or all of the cash flows of *forecasted* transactions. Firm C in **Examples 14** and **18** entered into the interest swap agreement to neutralize changes in cash flows for interest payments on its variable rate notes payable, a recognized liability. Firm D in **Examples 15** and **19** acquired the forward contract on whiskey to protect itself from changes in the selling price of whiskey on March 31, 2009, a recognized asset. Firm C and Firm D can designate these derivative instruments as cash flow hedges.

Firms might use a particular derivative either to hedge fair value or to hedge cash flows, but not both. Both the forward foreign exchange contract in **Example 16** and the forward whiskey price contract in **Example 19** fix, or lock in, cash flows and the firm could therefore

---

[8]These terms are the same in U.S. GAAP and IFRS. In addition, U.S. GAAP and IFRS allow firms to designate derivatives as hedges of a net investment in a foreign operation. We do not consider such hedges in this textbook.

designate the derivatives as cash flow hedges for accounting purposes. Alternatively, Firm A in **Example 16** could acquire the forward contract to fix, or lock in, the fair value of the equipment acquired and therefore designate that derivative as a fair value hedge. Firm D in **Example 19** could acquire the derivative to lock in the fair value of the inventory and therefore designate the contract as a cash flow hedge.

The four examples described thus far in this section illustrate the accounting for the following possible scenarios:

Example	Type of Hedge	Derivative Instruments Used
12 and 16	Fair Value—Firm Commitment	Forward Foreign Exchange Contract
13 and 17	Fair Value—Recognized Liability	Swap Contract—Variable for Fixed Interest Rate
14 and 18	Cash Flow—Interest Payments	Swap Contract—Fixed for Variable Interest Rate
15 and 19	Cash Flow—Forecasted Transaction	Forward Commodity Contract

TREATMENT OF HEDGING GAINS AND LOSSES

U.S. GAAP and IFRS allow firms to choose whether to designate a particular derivative as a hedge, and therefore eligible for hedge accounting. Firms remeasure derivatives not designated as a hedge to fair value at every balance sheet date and include changes in fair value in net income. For a derivative designated as a hedge, firms must further designate it as hedging the risk of a change in fair value (fair value hedges) or a change in cash flows (cash flow hedges). The accounting for fair value hedges and cash flows hedges is similar under U.S. GAAP and IFRS. For fair values hedges, U.S. GAAP and IFRS require firms to remeasure both the hedged item and the related derivative instrument (the hedging instrument) to fair value each period and to recognize gains and losses from changes in the fair value of both in *net income*. If the hedge is fully effective, the gain (loss) on the derivative will precisely offset the loss (gain) on the asset or liability hedged. The net effect on earnings is zero. If the hedge is not fully effective, the net gain or loss increases or decreases earnings to the degree the offset is incomplete. This accounting follows the third method illustrated in **Exhibit 12.1** in the sense that *both sides* of the hedging relationship are measured at fair value, with changes in fair value recognized in earnings.

For cash flow hedges, U.S. GAAP and IFRS require firms to remeasure the derivative instrument (the hedging instrument) to fair value each period but to include gains and losses from changes in fair values in other comprehensive income each period to the extent the hedging instrument is "highly effective" in neutralizing the risk of the hedged item. Firms must include the ineffective portion in net income currently. At the end of the period, the firm closes the Other Comprehensive Income account to the balance sheet account for Accumulated Other Comprehensive Income. The firm removes the amount in Accumulated Other Comprehensive Income related to a particular hedging instrument and transfers it to net income either periodically during the life of the hedging instrument or at the time of settlement, depending on the type of derivative instrument used as a hedge. This accounting follows the second method illustrated in **Exhibit 12.1**.

The matching convention provides both the basis for hedge accounting, as well as the logic for the treating gains and losses from changes in fair value of fair value hedges differently from cash flow hedges. In a fair value hedge of a recognized asset or liability, both the hedged asset (or liability) and its related derivative (hedging instrument) appear on the balance sheet. Remeasuring both the hedged asset (or liability) and its related derivative to fair value each period and including the gain or loss on the hedged asset (or liability) and the loss or gain on the derivative in net income results in a *net* gain or loss that indicates the effectiveness of the hedge in neutralizing the risk. If the hedge is completely effective, there is a zero net effect on income (the gain or loss on the hedged item exactly offsets the loss or gain on the hedging instrument). In a cash flow hedge of a forecasted transaction, the hedged cash flow commitment does not appear on the balance sheet but the derivative instrument does appear. Recognizing a gain or loss on the derivative instrument in net income each period but not recognizing the loss or gain on the anticipated transaction each period results in poor matching. Application of the matching convention results in classifying the gain or loss on the derivative instrument in other comprehensive income until the forecasted transaction occurs, at which time net income will include the gain or loss.

EXHIBIT 12.5	**Effects on Various Accounts of $100,000 Fixed Rate Note and Related Interest Rate Swap Accounted for as a Fair Value Hedge**

	Cash	Equipment: at Cost	Notes Payable: at Fair Value	Swap Contract: at Fair Value	Income Statement
2008					
(1) Issue Note for Equipment	$ —	$100,000	$(100,000)	$ —	$ —
(2) Enter Swap Contract	—	—	—	—	—
(3) Record Interest on Note	(8,000)	—	—	—	8,000
(4) Remeasure Note Payable	—	—	(3,667)	—	3,667
(5) Remeasure Swap Contract	—	—	—	3,667	(3,667)
December 31, 2008	$ (8,000)	$100,000	$(103,667)	$ 3,667	$ 8,000
2009					
(6) Record Interest on Note	(8,000)	—	1,780	—	$ 6,220
(7) Record Interest on Swap Contract	—	—	—	220	(220)
(8) Record Swap Interest Received	2,000	—	—	(2,000)	—
(9) Remeasure Note Payable	—	—	3,705	—	(3,705)
(10) Remeasure Swap Contract	—	—	—	(3,705)	3,705
December 31, 2009	$ (14,000)	$100,000	$ (98,182)	$(1,818)	$ 6,000
2010					
(11) Record Interest on Note	(8,000)	—	(1,818)	—	$ 9,818
(12) Record Interest on Swap Contract	—	—	—	(182)	182
(13) Record Swap Interest Paid	(2,000)	—	—	2,000	—
(14) Repay Note Payable	(100,000)	—	100,000	—	—
December 31, 2010	$(124,000)	$100,000	$ —	$ —	$10,000

Note: Amounts in parentheses are credits to the various accounts.

ILLUSTRATIONS OF ACCOUNTING FOR DERIVATIVES

This section illustrates the accounting for the derivatives used in the two examples involving interest rate swaps. (**Problem 12.3 for Self-Study** examines the accounting for the forward foreign exchange contract in **Example 16**. **Problem 28** at the end of the chapter examines the forward commodity contract in **Example 19**.)

Fair Value Hedge: Interest Rate Swap to Convert Fixed Rate Debt to Variable Rate Debt This section illustrates the accounting for an interest rate swap designated as a fair value hedge. Refer to **Examples 13** and **17**. Assume that Firm B wishes to hedge the effects of interest rate changes on the fair value of its fixed rate note payable of $100,000. Firm B enters into an interest rate swap contract to convert the 8% fixed rate debt to variable rate debt and designates the swap contract as a fair value hedge. To enhance understanding of the accounting for this fair value hedge, **Exhibit 12.5** summarizes the effects of the journal entries discussed next on the balance sheet and the income statement. You may wish to refer to **Exhibit 12.5** as you study these journal entries.

(1) Firm B issues the note to the supplier on January 1, 2008, and makes the following entry:

January 1, 2008

Equipment	100,000	
Note Payable		100,000

(continued)

Assets	=	Liabilities	+	Shareholders' Equity	(Class.)
+100,000		+100,000			

To record the acquisition of equipment by giving a $100,000 note payable with a fixed interest rate of 8%.

(2) The swap contract is a mutually unexecuted contract on January 1, 2008. The variable interest rate on this date is 8%, the same as the fixed rate for the note payable to the equipment supplier. The swap contract has a fair value of zero on this date. Thus, Firm B makes no entry to record the swap contract.

(3) On December 31, 2008, Firm B makes the required interest payment on the note for 2008:

December 31, 2008

Interest Expense	8,000	
Cash		8,000

Assets	=	Liabilities	+	Shareholders' Equity	(Class.)
−8,000				−8,000	IncSt → RE

To recognize interest expense and cash payment at the fixed interest rate of 8%; $8,000 = .08 × $100,000.

(4) Interest rates decline during 2008. On December 31, the variable interest rate on the swap contract resets the interest rate for 2009 to 6%. Firm B remeasures the note payable to fair value and records the change in the fair value of the swap contract caused by the decline in the interest rate.

The present value of the remaining cash flows on the note payable when discounted at 6% is:

Present Value of Interest Payments: $8,000 × 1.83339	$ 14,667
Present Value of Principal: $100,000 × .89000	89,000
Total Present Value	$103,667

Firm B makes the following entry to record the change in fair value:

December 31, 2008

Loss on Remeasurement of Note Payable	3,667	
Note Payable		3,667

Assets	=	Liabilities	+	Shareholders' Equity	(Class.)
		+3,667		−3,667	IncSt → RE

To measure Note Payable at fair value with cash flows discounted at 6%.

For the most part, firms do not remeasure their liabilities, such as this note payable, to fair value when interest rates change. They continue to account for the liabilities using the interest rate at the time of the initial recording of the financial instrument in the accounts. Fair value hedge accounting, however, *requires* the recognition of changes in fair values of a financial instrument that firms have designated as a hedged item (the note payable), and *requires* recognition of changes in the fair value of the hedging instrument (the swap contract).

(5) The decline in interest rates to 6% means that Firm B will save $2,000 [= (.08 − .06) × $100,000] each year in interest payments. The present value of a $2,000 annuity for two periods at 6% is $3,667 (= $2,000 × 1.83339). Thus, the fair value of the swap contract increased from zero at the beginning of 2008 to $3,667 at the end of the year. Firm B makes the following entry:

December 31, 2008

Swap Contract		3,667	
Gain on Remeasurement of Swap Contract			3,667

Assets	=	Liabilities	+	Shareholders' Equity	(Class.)
+3,667				+3,667	IncSt → RE

To measure the swap contract at fair value and recognize an asset on the balance sheet and a gain in net income.

The fair value loss on the note payable exactly offsets the fair value gain on the swap contract, indicating that the swap contract was fully effective. That is, the Loss on Remeasurement of Note Payable is 100% offset by the Gain on Remeasurement of Swap Contract.

(6) Firm B follows a similar process at the end of 2009. First, it records interest expense on the note payable:

December 31, 2009

Interest Expense		6,220	
Note Payable		1,780	
Cash			8,000

Assets	=	Liabilities	+	Shareholders' Equity	(Class.)
−8,000		−1,780		−6,220	IncSt → RE

To record interest expense at 6% of the carrying value of the note payable at the beginning of the year ($6,220 = .06 × $103,667), the cash payment at the contractual interest rate of 8% on the face amount of the note ($8,000 = .08 × $100,000), and the reduction in the carrying value of the note payable for the difference.

Firm B uses the effective interest method to compute interest expense for the year. The effective interest rate for 2009 is 6%, and the carrying value of the note payable at the beginning of the year is $103,667. The cash payment of $8,000 is the amount specified in the original borrowing arrangement with the equipment supplier.

(7) Second, Firm B records interest revenue for the change in the present value of the swap contract for the year.

December 31, 2009

Swap Contract		220	
Interest Revenue			220

Assets	=	Liabilities	+	Shareholders' Equity	(Class.)
+220				+220	IncSt → RE

To record interest revenue for the increase in the carrying value of the swap contract for the passage of time; $220 = .06 × $3,667.

Interest expense (net) as a result of the two entries is $6,000 (= $6,220 − $220), which is the same as the variable rate for 2009 of 6% times the face value of the note.

(8) Third, Firm B receives $2,000 under the swap contract with its counterparty because interest rates decreased from 8% to 6%.

December 31, 2009

Cash	2,000	
Swap Contract		2,000

Assets	=	Liabilities	+	Shareholders' Equity	(Class.)
+2,000					
−2,000					

To record cash received from the counterparty because the interest rate declined from 8% to 6%.

The $2,000 cash received from the counterparty is the benefit to Firm B for 2009, because interest rates declined to 6%.

(9) Fourth, Firm B must remeasure the note payable and the swap contract for changes in fair value at the end of 2009. Assume that interest rates increased during 2009, so the interest rate in the swap agreement resets to 10% for 2010. The present value of the remaining payments on the note at 10% is:

Present Value of Interest Payment: $8,000 × .90909	$ 7,273
Present Value of Principal: $100,000 × .90909	90,909
Total Present Value	$98,182

The carrying value of the note payable before remeasurement is $101,887 (= $103,667 − $1,780). The entry to measure the note payable at fair value is:

December 31, 2009

Note Payable	3,705	
Gain on Remeasurement of Note Payable		3,705

Assets	=	Liabilities	+	Shareholders' Equity	(Class.)
		−3,705		+3,705	IncSt → RE

To measure the note payable at fair value using an interest rate of 10% to discount the remaining cash flows to their present value; $3,705 = $101,887 − $98,182.

(10) The fair value of the swap contract decreases, and Firm B now pays the counterparty $2,000 in 2010 because of the swap contract. Thus, the swap contract is a liability instead of an asset. The present value of $2,000 when discounted at 10% is $1,818 (= $2,000 × .90909). The carrying value of the swap contract before remeasurement is an asset of $1,887 (= $3,667 + $220 − $2,000). The entry to remeasure the swap contract is:

December 31, 2009

Loss on Remeasurement of Swap Contract	3,705	
Swap Contract (Asset)		1,887
Swap Contract (Liability)		1,818

Assets	=	Liabilities	+	Shareholders' Equity	(Class.)
−1,887		+1,818		−3,705	IncSt → RE

To measure the swap contract at fair value using a discount rate of 10% and recognize a loss from the decrease in fair value.

The gain on remeasurement of the note exactly offsets the loss on remeasurement of the swap contract, so the swap contract hedges the change in interest rates.

(11) The first entry for 2010 recognizes interest expense and the cash payment for interest.

December 31, 2010

Interest Expense	9,818	
Note Payable		1,818
Cash		8,000

Assets	=	Liabilities	+	Shareholders' Equity	(Class.)
−8,000		+1,818		−9,818	IncSt → RE

To record interest expense at 10% of the carrying value of the note payable at the beginning of the year ($9,818 = .10 × $98,182), the cash payment at the contractual interest rate of 8% on the face amount of the note ($8,000 = .08 × $100,000), and the increase in the carrying value of the note payable for the difference.

(12) Firm C must also recognize interest on the swap contract:

December 31, 2010

Interest Expense	182	
Swap Contract (Liability)		182

Assets	=	Liabilities	+	Shareholders' Equity	(Class.)
		+182		−182	IncSt → RE

To record interest expense for the increase in the carrying value of the swap contract for the passage of time; $182 = .10 × $1,818.

Interest expense (net) after these two entries is $10,000 (= $9,818 + $182), which equals the variable interest rate of 10% times the face value of the note.

(13) Firm B pays the counterparty 2% of the face value of the note, because the variable interest rate of 10% exceeds the fixed interest rate of 8%.

December 31, 2010

Swap Contract (Liability)	2,000	
Cash		2,000

Assets	=	Liabilities	+	Shareholders' Equity	(Class.)
−2,000		−2,000			

To record cash paid to the counterparty because the variable interest rate of 10% exceeded the fixed interest rate of 8%.

(14) Firm B repays the note and closes out the Swap Contract account.

December 31, 2010

Note Payable	100,000	
Cash		100,000

Assets	=	Liabilities	+	Shareholders' Equity	(Class.)
−100,000		−100,000			

To record repayment of note payable at maturity.

The Swap Contract account has a zero balance on December 31, 2010, after the firm makes the entries above (= $1,818 + $182 − $2,000).

Refer back to **Exhibit 12.5**, which summarizes the effects of these entries on various accounts (credit entries in parentheses). Net income reflects the variable interest rate each year, 8% for 2008, 6% for 2009, and 10% for 2010. The sum of the balance sheet carrying amounts for the note payable and the swap contract (the net value) is $100,000 at the end of each year. Firm B recognizes gains and losses from changes in the fair value of both the hedged item and its derivative in net income as their fair values change.

Summary of the Accounting for a Fair Value Hedge of a Recognized Asset or Liability   The following summarizes the accounting for a fair value hedge of a recognized asset or liability.

1. A firm recognizes the hedged asset or liability, even in the absence of hedge accounting. In the absence of hedge accounting, the measurement of the hedged item depends on the required accounting for that item (for example, lower of cost or market for inventories, present value of future cash flows for long-term receivables and payables).

2. On the date a firm enters the derivative contract and designates that contract as a fair value hedge, it recognizes the derivative as an asset if it makes an initial payment. It recognizes the derivative as a liability if it receives an initial payment. Otherwise, no amount appears on the balance sheet for the derivative.

3. At the end of each period, the firm remeasures the hedged asset or liability to fair value and includes the resulting gain or loss in net income.

4. At the end of each period, the firm remeasures the derivative instrument (hedging instrument) to fair value and includes the resulting loss or gain in net income.

5. The firm reports both the hedged asset or liability and its related hedging instrument separately on the balance sheet without netting.

6. When the firm settles the derivative contract and the hedged item, the firm removes the hedged asset or liability and its related derivative from the accounts.

Cash Flow Hedge: Interest Rate Swap to Convert Variable Rate Debt to Fixed Rate Debt   This section illustrates the journal entries for an interest rate swap accounted for as a cash flow hedge. Refer to **Examples 14** and **18**. Firm C desires to hedge the risk of changes in interest rates on its cash payments for interest. It enters into a swap contract with a counterparty to convert its variable rate note payable (currently at 8%) to a fixed rate note. Firm C designates the swap contract as a cash flow hedge. The facts for the case resemble those for Firm B. The note has a $100,000 face value, an initial variable interest rate of 8%, reset to 6% for 2009 and 10% for 2010. The note matures on December 31, 2010. **Exhibit 12.6** summarizes the effects of the journal entries discussed next on the balance sheet and income statement. You may use **Exhibit 12.6** as you study these journal entries.

(1) The entry to record the note payable is:

January 1, 2008

Equipment	100,000	
Note Payable		100,000

Assets	=	Liabilities	+	Shareholders' Equity	(Class.)
+100,000		+100,000			

To record the acquisition of equipment by giving a $100,000 note payable with a variable interest rate of 8%.

(2) The swap contract has a fair value of zero on January 1, 2008, so Firm C makes no entry on this date.

| EXHIBIT 12.6 | Effects on Various Accounts of $100,000 Variable Rate Note and Related Interest Rate Swap Accounted for as a Cash Flow Hedge |

	Cash	Equipment: at Cost	Notes Payable: at Carrying Value	Swap Contract: at Fair Value	Income Statement	Other Comprehensive Income
2008						
(1) Issue Note for Equipment	$ —	$100,000	$(100,000)	$ —	$ —	$ —
(2) Enter Swap Contract	—	—	—	—	—	—
(3) Record Interest on Note	(8,000)	—	—	—	8,000	—
(4) Remeasure Swap Contract	—	—	—	(3,667)	—	3,667
December 31, 2008...............	$ (8,000)	$100,000	$(100,000)	$(3,667)	$ 8,000	$ 3,667
2009						
(5) Record Interest on Note	(6,000)	—	—	—	6,000	—
(6) Record Interest on Swap Contract	—	—	—	(220)	—	220
(7) Record Swap Interest Paid	(2,000)	—	—	2,000	—	—
(8) Reclassify Portion of Other Comprehensive Income	—	—	—	—	2,000	(2,000)
(9) Remeasure Swap Contract	—	—	—	3,705	—	(3,705)
December 31, 2009...............	$ (16,000)	$100,000	$(100,000)	$ 1,818	$ 8,000	$(1,818)
2010						
(10) Record Interest on Note	(10,000)	—	—	—	10,000	—
(11) Record Interest on Swap Contract	—	—	—	182	—	(182)
(12) Record Swap Interest Received	2,000	—	—	(2,000)	—	—
(13) Reclassify Portion of Other Comprehensive Income	—	—	—	—	(2,000)	2,000
(14) Repay Note Payable	(100,000)	—	100,000	—	—	—
(15) Close Out Swap Contract	—	—	—	—	—	—
December 31, 2010...............	$(124,000)	$100,000	$ —	$ —	$ 8,000	$ —

Note: Amounts in parentheses are credits to the various accounts.

(3) Firm C records interest on the note for 2008.

December 31, 2008

| Interest Expense .... | 8,000 | |
| Cash .... | | 8,000 |

Assets	=	Liabilities	+	Shareholders' Equity	(Class.)
−8,000				−8,000	IncSt → RE

To recognize interest expense and cash payment at the variable interest rate of 8%; $8,000 = .08 × $100,000.

---

(4) The fair value of the note in this case will not change as interest rates change because the note carries a variable interest rate. The fair value of the swap contract varies with changes in interest rates. The fair value of the swap contract on December 31, 2008, after the interest rate resets to 6%, is $3,667. This amount is the present value of the $2,000 that Firm C will pay the counterparty on December 31 of 2009 and 2010 if the interest rate remains at 6%. This amount is the same as in the previous illustration for a fair value hedge. The entry, however, differs from the one made previously.

December 31, 2008

Loss from Remeasurement of Swap Contract			3,667	
Swap Contract				3,667

Assets	=	Liabilities	+	Shareholders' Equity	(Class.)
		+3,667		−3,667	OCI → AOCI

To measure the swap contract at fair value and recognize a liability on the balance sheet and a loss in other comprehensive income.

The swap contract is a liability because Firm C must pay the counterparty $2,000 at the end of 2009 and 2010. In the previous illustration, the swap contract at the end of 2008 is an asset because Firm B had the right to receive $2,000 at the end of 2009 and 2010 from the counterparty. The $3,667 amount results in a decrease in other comprehensive income, whereas Firm B recognized a gain in net income.

The carrying value of the note payable of $100,000 plus the carrying value of the swap contract of $3,667 is $103,667. This amount is the present value of the expected cash flows under the fixed rate note and swap contract combined, discounted at 6%.

(5) The entry on December 31, 2009, to recognize and pay interest on the variable rate note is:

December 31, 2009

Interest Expense			6,000	
Cash				6,000

Assets	=	Liabilities	+	Shareholders' Equity	(Class.)
−6,000				−6,000	IncSt → RE

To recognize interest expense and cash payment at the variable interest rate; $6,000 = .06 × $100,000.

(6) Firm C must also recognize interest on the swap contract due to the passage of time.

December 31, 2009

Interest on Fair Value of Swap Contract			220	
Swap Contract				220

Assets	=	Liabilities	+	Shareholders' Equity	(Class.)
		+220		−220	OCI → AOCI

To record interest for the increase in the carrying value of the swap contract for the passage of time; $220 = .06 × $3,667.

The interest charge does not affect net income immediately but instead decreases other comprehensive income.

(7) Firm C pays the counterparty the $2,000 [= $100,000 × (.08 − .06)] required by the swap contract. The entry is:

December 31, 2009

Swap Contract			2,000	
Cash				2,000

Assets	=	Liabilities	+	Shareholders' Equity	(Class.)
−2,000		−2,000			

To record cash paid to the counterparty because the interest rate declined from 8% to 6%.

(8) Because the swap contract hedged cash flows related to interest rate risk during 2009, Firm C reclassifies a portion of other comprehensive income to net income. The entry is:

December 31, 2009

Interest Expense					2,000	
Other Comprehensive Income						2,000

Assets	=	Liabilities	+	Shareholders' Equity	(Class.)
				−2,000	NI → RE
				+2,000	OCI → AOCI

To reclassify a portion of other comprehensive income to net income for the hedged portion of interest expense on the note payable.

Interest expense on the income statement includes (1) interest at 6% of the note payable paid to the holder of the note under the variable rate borrowing agreement, and (2) interest at 2% arising from the swap contract for total interest expense for 2009 of $8,000. Firm C entered into the swap arrangement to fix its cash payment at 8% of the note payable, which it accomplishes with this hedging arrangement.

At this point the Swap Contract account has a credit balance of $1,887 (= $3,667 + $220 − $2,000). Other comprehensive income related to this transaction has a debit amount of $1,887.

(9) Resetting the interest rate on December 31, 2009, to 10% changes the swap contract from a liability to an asset. The present value of the $2,000 that Firm C will receive from the counterparty at the end of 2010 when discounted at 10% is $1,818. The entry to remeasure the swap contract is:

December 31, 2009

Swap Contract (Liability)					1,887	
Swap Contract (Asset)					1,818	
Gain from Remeasurement of Swap Contract						3,705

Assets	=	Liabilities	+	Shareholders' Equity	(Class.)
+1,818		−1,887		+3,705	OCI → AOCI

To measure the swap contract at fair value and recognize an asset on the balance sheet and a gain in other comprehensive income.

Other comprehensive income has a credit amount of $1,818, which equals the debit balance in the Swap Contract account.

(10) The entry at the end of 2010 to recognize and pay interest on the variable rate note is:

December 31, 2010

Interest Expense					10,000	
Cash						10,000

Assets	=	Liabilities	+	Shareholders' Equity	(Class.)
−10,000				−10,000	IncSt → RE

To recognize interest expense and cash payment at the variable interest rate of 10%; $10,000 = .10 × $100,000.

---

(11) Firm C also increases the carrying value of the swap contract for the passage of time.

December 31, 2010

| Swap Contract | | | | | 182 | |
| Interest on Swap Contract | | | | | | 182 |

Assets	=	Liabilities	+	Shareholders' Equity	(Class.)
+182				+182	OCI → AOCI

To record interest for the increase in the book value of the swap contract for the passage of time; $182 = .10 \times \$1,818$.

(12) The swap contract requires the counterparty to pay the firm $2,000 under the swap contract.

December 31, 2010

| Cash | | | | | 2,000 | |
| Swap Contract | | | | | | 2,000 |

Assets	=	Liabilities	+	Shareholders' Equity	(Class.)
+2,000					
−2,000					

To record cash received from the counterparty because the interest rate increased from 6% to 10%.

(13) Because the swap contract hedged cash flows related to interest rate risk during 2010, Firm C reclassifies a portion of other comprehensive income to net income. The entry is:

December 31, 2010

| Other Comprehensive Income | | | | | 2,000 | |
| Interest Expense | | | | | | 2,000 |

Assets	=	Liabilities	+	Shareholders' Equity	(Class.)
				−2,000	OCI → AOCI
				+2,000	IncSt → RE

To reclassify a portion of other comprehensive income to net income for the hedged portion of interest expense on the note payable.

Thus, interest expense (net) for 2010 is $8,000 (= $10,000 − $2,000), which equals the net cash outflow for interest that Firm C hedged with the interest rate swap.

(14) Firm C repays the note on December 31, 2010:

December 31, 2010

| Note Payable | | | | | 100,000 | |
| Cash | | | | | | 100,000 |

Assets	=	Liabilities	+	Shareholders' Equity	(Class.)
−100,000		−100,000			

To record repayment of note payable at maturity.

The Swap Contract account has a balance of zero on December 31, 2010 (= $1,818 + $182 − $2,000). If the swap contract had been highly effective, but not perfectly effective, in neutralizing the interest rate risk, then Accumulated Other Comprehensive Income would have a balance related to the swap contract, which Firm C reclassifies to net income.

Refer again to **Exhibit 12.6.** Interest expense is $8,000 each year, the fixed rate of 8% that Firm C accomplished by entering into the swap contract. The amounts in Other Comprehensive Income reflect changes in the fair value of the swap contract. The Swap Contract account begins and ends with a zero value.

Summary of Accounting for a Cash Flow Hedge of a Recognized Asset or Liability
The following summarizes the accounting for a cash flow hedge of an recognized asset or liability:

1. A firm recognizes the hedged asset or liability on the balance sheet and its measurement depends on the required accounting for the particular asset or liability (for example, lower of cost or market for inventories, present value of future cash flows for long-term receivables and payables).

2. The firm recognizes the derivative as an asset on the date of acquisition to the extent it makes an initial investment or as a liability to the extent it receives cash. Otherwise, no amount appears on the balance sheet for the derivative. The firm designates the derivative as a hedging instrument.

3. At the end of each period, the firm remeasures the derivative instrument (the hedging instrument) to fair value and includes the resulting loss or gain in other comprehensive income.

4. The firm reclassifies gains and losses from other comprehensive income to net income when the gain or loss on the hedged item affects net income. If the derivative is not highly effective in neutralizing the gain or loss on the hedged item, then the firm must reclassify the ineffective portion to net income immediately and not wait until the gain or loss on the hedged items affects net income.

5. The firm reports the hedged asset and liability and the hedging instrument separately on the balance sheet and the cumulative amount of net changes in fair value of the hedging instrument in accumulated other comprehensive income.

6. The firm removes the hedged asset or liability and its related derivative from the accounts at the time of settlement (for example, at the time of interest payments).

SUMMARY OF ACCOUNTING FOR DERIVATIVES

Derivatives appear on the balance sheet at fair value. Their effect on net income depends on whether a firm designates the derivative as a hedge, and if so, whether it is a fair value hedge or cash flow hedge.

- Gains and losses on derivatives not designated as hedges of a specific risk, gains and losses on fair value hedges, and the ineffective portion of cash flow hedges affect net income simultaneously with changes in fair value. This accounting follows the third method illustrated in **Exhibit 12.1** at the beginning of the chapter.

- Gains and losses on effective cash flow hedges initially affect other comprehensive income, not net income. The holder of the hedging instrument will exclude from current earnings, but include in Accumulated Other Comprensive Income, the gains and losses used effectively to hedge cash flows. Firms reclassify these gains and losses from accumulated other comprehensive to net income when the gain or loss on the hedged item affects net income. This accounting follows the second method illustrated in **Exhibit 12.1** at the beginning of the chapter.

DISCLOSURES RELATED TO DERIVATIVE INSTRUMENTS

U.S. GAAP and IFRS require firms to disclose the fair value of financial instruments in a note to the financial statements. U.S. GAAP also requires firms to disclose the following information (among others) with respect to derivatives (IFRS requires similar but not identical disclosures).

1.   A description of the firm's risk management strategy and how particular derivatives help accomplish the firm's hedging objectives. The description should distinguish among derivative instruments designated as fair value hedges, cash flow hedges, and all other derivatives.

This disclosure helps the user of the financial statements to understand the types of risks that a firm faces and how it uses derivatives to hedge those risks.

2.   For fair value and cash flow hedges, firms must disclose the net gain or loss recognized in earnings resulting from the hedge's ineffectiveness (that is, not offsetting the risk hedged) and the line on the income statement that includes this net gain or loss.

Without this required disclosure, firms might be reluctant to divulge that their hedging activities were ineffective and include the amount of any gain or loss from such ineffectiveness in an account with other revenues, gains, expenses, and losses.

3.   For cash flow hedges, firms must describe the transactions or events that will result in reclassifying gains and losses from accumulated other comprehensive income to net income and the estimated amount of such reclassifications during the next 12 months.

Accumulated other comprehensive income includes unrealized gains and losses that will affect net income of future periods. Most derivatives do not give management discretion as to when these unrealized gains and losses will affect earnings, unlike marketable securities classified as available for sale where management has some discretion in timing earnings effects, as we discussed previously. This disclosure for derivatives requires firms to disclose their expectations as to the amount that the firm will transfer from accumulated other comprehensive income to net income within the next year to assist users of the financial statements forecast the next year's earnings.

4.   The net amount of gains and losses recognized in earnings because a hedged firm commitment no longer qualifies as a fair value hedge or a hedged forecasted transaction no longer qualifies as a cash flow hedge.

A firm might use a derivative to hedge an unrecognized commitment or forecasted transaction. If events unfold so that the firm does not need to fulfill its commitment or engage in the forecasted transaction, any unrealized gains and losses on derivatives related to those commitments and forecasted transactions affect net income. Standard setters were perhaps concerned that firms would acquire a particular derivative for speculation but designate it as hedging a commitment or forecasted transaction. This required disclosure alerts users of the financial statements of the gains and losses that result because the derivative no longer qualifies, if it ever did, as a fair value or cash flow hedge.

Exhibit 12.7 shows the disclosures of PepsiCo regarding the fair value of financial instruments and the additional disclosures regarding its use of derivatives.

The panel of data indicates the carrying value and fair value of all financial assets and financial liabilities, including derivatives. The notes to this panel of data indicate the classification of each asset and liability on the balance sheet (that is, current assets, current liabilities, other assets, and other liabilities). The book value, or balance sheet carrying value, and the fair value of most financial instruments are the same. One exception is long-term debt obligations, measured at amortized cost unless the firm either hedges risks associated with the debt and classifies it as a fair value hedge or chooses the fair value option discussed in the next section of this chapter. Commodity contracts, forward exchange contracts, and swap contracts appear on both the asset and liability sides of the balance sheet, indicating that some contracts are assets (they give rise to a right to receive cash from the counterparties) and some contracts are liabilities (they require PepsiCo to pay cash to the counterparties).

The narrative in PepsiCo's note preceding the panel of data indicates the nature of the risks (commodity prices, foreign exchange, and interest rates) for which it acquires derivative instruments and the way PepsiCo uses derivatives to hedge these risks. PepsiCo uses both fair value hedges and cash flow hedges. It also acquires some derivatives that it does not designate (PepsiCo uses the terminology *does not qualify*) for hedge accounting treatment.

The paragraphs describing commodity price hedging and foreign exchange hedging indicate that the hedges were effective, or not materially ineffective, for the periods presented. The paragraph describing commodity price hedging indicates that PepsiCo expects to reclassify $1 million from accumulated other comprehensive income to net income within the next 12 months when it transacts anticipated commodity purchases. PepsiCo gives no indication that it included gains or losses in earnings because a hedged firm commitment no longer qualified as a fair value hedge or a hedged forecasted transaction no longer qualified as a cash flow hedge.

PROBLEM 12.3 for Self-Study

Accounting for a Forward Foreign Exchange Contract as a Fair Value Hedge. Refer to **Examples 12** and **16** in the chapter. Firm A places its firm order for the equipment on June 30, 2008. It simultaneously signs a forward foreign exchange contract for £10,000. The forward rate on June 30, 2008, for settlement on June 30, 2009, is $1.64 per £1. Firm A designates the forward foreign exchange contract as a fair value hedge of the firm commitment.

a. U.S. GAAP and IFRS guidance does not require Firm A to record either the purchase commitment or the forward foreign exchange contract on the balance sheet as a liability or an asset on June 30, 2008. What is the logic for this accounting?

b. On December 31, 2008, the forward foreign exchange rate for settlement on June 30, 2009, is $1.73 per £1. Give the journal entries to record the change in the fair value of the purchase commitment and the change in the fair value of the forward contract for 2008. Assume an 8% interest rate for discounting cash flows to their present values on December 31, 2008.

c. Give the journal entries on June 30, 2009, to record the change in the present value of the purchase commitment and the forward foreign exchange contract for the passage of time.

d. On June 30, 2009, the spot foreign exchange rate is $1.75 per £1. Give the journal entries to record the change in the fair value of the purchase commitment and the change in the fair value of the forward contract due to changes in the exchange rate during the first six months of 2009.

e. Give the journal entry on June 30, 2009, to purchase £10,000 with U.S. dollars and acquire the equipment.

f. Give the journal entry on June 30, 2009, to settle the forward foreign exchange contract.

g. How would the entries in parts **b** through **f** differ if Firm A had chosen to designate the forward foreign exchange contract as a cash flow hedge of a forecasted transaction instead of a fair value hedge of a firm commitment?

h. Suggest a scenario that would justify Firm A treating the forward foreign exchange contract as a fair value hedge, and a scenario that would justify the firm treating the contract as a cash flow hedge.

THE FAIR VALUE OPTION APPLIED TO MARKETABLE SECURITIES AND DERIVATIVES

Both U.S. GAAP and IFRS provide for the option of reporting selected financial assets and financial liabilities at fair value and recognizing gains and losses in net income as fair values change.[9] Firms can apply the **fair value option** on an instrument-by-instrument basis,

---

[9]The fair value option under IFRS is in International Accounting Standards Board, *International Accounting Standard 39*, "Financial Instruments: Recognition and Measurement," revised 2003. The fair value option under U.S. GAAP is in Financial Accounting Standards Board, *Statement of Financial Accounting Standards No. 159*, "The Fair Value Option for Financial Assets and Financial Liabilities, Including an Amendment of FASB Statement No. 115," 2007 (**Codification Topic 825**). U.S. GAAP provides guidance for fair value measurements in *SFAS No. 157*, "Fair Value Measurement," 2006. IFRS contains no analogous guidance. As of the writing of this textbook, the IASB has undertaken a project that will analyze all the IFRS guidance that requires a fair value measurement to decide whether those measurements were intended to be exit values (similar to the definition of fair value in U.S. GAAP). The IASB will also consider how IFRS will define fair value and will create a single source of measurement guidance. The IASB plans to complete the project in 2010. The IASB's Discussion Paper, "Fair Value Measurements," issued in November 2006 and available on the IASB's Web site (*iasb.org.uk*) discusses the differences between fair value measurement in IFRS and U.S. GAAP.

EXHIBIT 12.7   PepsiCo's Disclosures Relating to Derivatives and Other Financial Instruments (amounts in millions)

NOTE 10—RISK MANAGEMENT

We are exposed to market risks arising from adverse changes in the following areas:

- Commodity prices, affecting the cost of our raw materials and energy.
- Foreign exchange risks.
- Interest rates.

In the normal course of business, we manage these risks through various strategies, including the use of derivatives. Certain derivatives are designated as either cash flow or fair value hedges and qualify for hedge accounting treatment, while others do not qualify and are marked to market through earnings.

For cash flow hedges, changes in fair value are deferred in accumulated other comprehensive loss within shareholders' equity until the underlying hedged item is recognized in net income. For fair value hedges, changes in fair value are recognized immediately in earnings, consistent with the underlying hedged item. Hedging transactions are limited to an underlying exposure. As a result, any change in the value of our derivative instruments would be substantially offset by an opposite change in the value of the underlying hedged items. Hedging ineffectiveness and a net earnings impact occur when the change in the value of the hedge does not offset the change in the value of the underlying hedged item. If the derivative instrument is terminated, we continue to defer the related gain or loss and include it as a component of the cost of the underlying hedged item. Upon determination that the underlying hedged item will not be part of an actual transaction, we recognize the related gain or loss in net income in that period.

We also use derivatives that do not qualify for hedge accounting treatment. We account for such derivatives at market value with the resulting gains and losses reflected in our income statement. We do not use derivative instruments for trading or speculative purposes, and we limit our exposure to individual counterparties to manage credit risk.

Commodity Prices

We are subject to commodity price risk because our ability to recover increased costs through higher pricing may be limited in the competitive environment in which we operate. This risk is managed through the use of fixed-price purchase orders, pricing agreements, geographic diversity, and derivatives. We use derivatives, with terms of no more than two years, to economically hedge price fluctuations related to a portion of our anticipated commodity purchases, primarily for natural gas, diesel fuel, and fruit. For those derivatives that qualify for hedge accounting, any ineffectiveness is recorded immediately. However, such commodity cash flow hedges have not had any significant ineffectiveness for all periods presented. We classify both the earnings and cash flow impact from these derivatives consistent with the underlying hedged item. During the next 12 months, we expect to reclassify net gains of $1 million related to cash flow hedges from accumulated other comprehensive loss into net income. Derivatives used to hedge commodity price risks that do not qualify for hedge accounting are marked to market each period and reflected in our income statement.

Foreign Exchange

Our operations outside of the United States generate 44% of our net revenue, with Mexico, the United Kingdom, and Canada comprising 19% of our net revenue. As a result, we are exposed to foreign currency risks. On occasion, we enter into hedges, primarily forward contracts with terms of no more than two years, to reduce the effect of foreign exchange rates. Ineffectiveness of these hedges has not been material.

Interest Rates

We centrally manage our debt and investment portfolios considering investment opportunities and risks, tax consequences, and overall financing strategies. We may use interest rate and cross currency interest rate swaps to manage our overall interest expense and foreign exchange risk. These instruments effectively change the interest rate and currency of specific debt issuances. These swaps are entered into concurrently with the issuance of the debt that they are intended to modify. The notional amount, interest payment and maturity date of the swaps match the principal, interest payment, and maturity date of the related debt. These swaps are entered into only with strong creditworthy counterparties and are settled on a net basis.

when the firm first adopts the standard that provides for the fair value option, when the firm acquires an eligible instrument, and at certain remeasurement events, such as business combinations. Once elected, the fair value option is irrevocable (for the instrument to which the firm applies it). This option results in the accounting illustrated under the third method in **Exhibit 12.1**. Both U.S. GAAP and IFRS require measurement at fair value with changes included in income for three items discussed previously in this chapter:[10]

1. Trading securities
2. Fair value hedges
3. Derivatives not designated as hedges

---

[10]U.S. GAAP and IFRS specify the items eligible for the fair value option. The qualifying criteria differ between the two sets of guidance. We do not consider all these items in this textbook.

EXHIBIT 12.7

PepsiCo's Disclosures Relating to Derivatives and Other Financial Instruments (amounts in millions) (Continued)

Fair Value

All derivative instruments are recognized on our balance sheet at fair value. The fair value of our derivative instruments is generally based on quoted market prices. Book and fair values of our derivative and financial instruments are as follows:

	2007		2006	
	Book Value	Fair Value	Book Value	Fair Value
ASSETS				
Cash and Cash Equivalents[a]	$ 910	$ 910	$1,651	$1,651
Short-Term Investments[b]	1,571	1,571	1,171	1,171
Forward Exchange Contracts[c]	32	32	8	8
Commodity Contracts[d]	10	10	2	2
Prepaid Forward Contracts[e]	74	74	73	73
Interest Rate Swaps[f]	36	36	—	—
Cross Currency Interest Rate Swaps[f]	—	—	1	1
LIABILITIES				
Forward Exchange Contracts[c]	61	61	24	24
Commodity Contracts[d]	7	7	29	29
Debt Obligations	4,203	4,352	2,824	2,955
Interest Rate Swaps[g]	—	—	4	4
Cross Currency Interest Rate Swaps[g]	8	8	—	—

The above items are included on our balance sheet under the captions noted or as indicated below. In addition, derivatives qualify for hedge accounting unless otherwise noted below.

(a) Book value approximates fair value due to the short maturity.

(b) Principally short-term time deposits and includes $189 million at December 29, 2007, and $145 million at December 30, 2006, of mutual fund investments used to manage a portion of market risk arising from our deferred compensation liability.

(c) The 2007 asset includes $20 million related to derivatives that do not qualify for hedge accounting, and the 2007 liability includes $4 million related to derivatives that do not qualify for hedge accounting. The 2006 liability includes $10 million related to derivatives that do not qualify for hedge accounting. Assets are reported within current assets and other assets, and liabilities are reported within current liabilities and other liabilities.

(d) The 2007 asset includes $10 million related to derivatives that do not qualify for hedge accounting, and the 2007 liability includes $7 million related to derivatives that do not qualify for hedge accounting. The 2006 liability includes $28 million related to derivatives that do not qualify for hedge accounting. Assets are reported within current assets and other assets, and liabilities are reported within current liabilities and other liabilities.

(e) Included in current assets and other assets.

(f) Asset included within other assets.

(g) Reported in other liabilities.

Thus, firms can elect the fair value option for the following items discussed in this chapter:

1. Bonds held to maturity
2. Available-for-sale securities
3. Cash flow hedges

Applying the fair value option to investments in debt securities classified as held to maturity results in accounting for the investments as if they were a trading security, with changes in fair value recognized in income each period. Applying the fair value option to available-for-sale securities and to cash flow hedges results in reporting unrealized gains and losses from remeasurement to fair value in net income as fair value changes, instead of initially in other comprehensive income.

Refer to the disclosures regarding financial instruments of PepsiCo in **Exhibit 12.7**. PepsiCo indicates elsewhere in notes to its financial statements that Accumulated Other Comprehensive Income on December 31, 2007, includes $35 million after taxes of unrealized losses on cash flow hedges and $49 million after taxes for unrealized gains on marketable securities. If PepsiCo adopted the fair value option for all marketable securities and cash flow hedges on January 1, 2008, it would transfer these amounts out of Accumulated Other Comprehensive Income and adjust the beginning balance in Retained Earnings for 2008. Subsequent unrealized gains and losses on securities and derivatives for which it chose the fair value option would affect net income; they would no longer affect other comprehensive income and accumulated other comprehensive income.

SUMMARY

Firms acquire securities issued by other entities for various reasons. Businesses also acquire derivatives or engage in various arrangements with other entities to hedge risks of changes in interest rates, exchange rates, and commodity prices. U.S. GAAP and IFRS currently require the following accounting for marketable securities and derivatives if a firm does not elect the fair value option:

Accounting Method	Applicable To:
Method 1: Amortized Acquisition Cost	Debt Securities Held to Maturity
Method 2: Fair Value with Unrealized Gains and Losses Recognized in Other Comprehensive Income as Fair Values Change and Later in Net Income	Marketable Securities Classified as Available for Sale Cash Flow Hedges
Method 3: Fair Value with Unrealized Gains and Losses Recognized in Net Income as Fair Values Change	Marketable Securities Classified as Trading Securities Fair Value Hedges Derivatives Not Classified as Hedges

The delayed inclusion of unrealized gains and losses in net income for items in the second category above results in measuring available for sale securities and cash flow hedges at fair value without recognizing the net income effect until the firm realizes the gain or loss. Firms that adopt the fair value option will not delay recognizing the net income effect as fair values change. The accounting is the same as for items in the third method above.

SOLUTIONS TO SELF-STUDY PROBLEMS

SUGGESTED SOLTUON TO PROBLEM 12.1 FOR SELF-STUDY

(General Electric Capital Services and Sapra Company; accounting for an investment in bonds.)

a. See **Exhibit 12.8**.

EXHIBIT 12.8	Amortization Table for $100,000 Bonds with a Stated Interest Rate of 8% and a Market Required Yield of 6%

Period (1)	Marketable Securities at Beginning of Period (2)	Interest Revenue at 6% per Period (3)	Cash Received (4)	Portion of Cash Received Reducing Carrying Value (5)	Marketable Securities at End of Period (6)
1	$105,346	$6,321	$8,000	$(1,679)	$103,667
2	$103,667	$6,220	$8,000	$(1,780)	$101,887
3	$101,887	$6,113	$108,000	$(101,887)	$ 0

b.

Date of Purchase

Marketable Securities	105,346	
Cash		105,346

Assets	=	Liabilities	+	Shareholders' Equity	(Class.)
+105,346					
−105,346					

To record the purchase of bonds for $105,346.

End of First Year

Marketable Securities	6,321	
Interest Revenue		6,321

Assets	=	Liabilities	+	Shareholders' Equity	(Class.)
+6,321				+6,321	IncSt → RE

To accrue interest revenue for the first year after purchase.

End of First Year

Cash	8,000	
Marketable Securities		8,000

Assets	=	Liabilities	+	Shareholders' Equity	(Class.)
+8,000					
−8,000					

To record cash received at end of the first year and the reduction in Marketable Securities.

Note that GECS could combine the last two entries as follows:

End of First Year

Cash	8,000	
Interest Revenue		6,321
Marketable Securities		1,679

Assets	=	Liabilities	+	Shareholders' Equity	(Class.)
+8,000				+6,321	IncSt → RE
−1,679					

SUGGESTED SOLUTION TO PROBLEM 12.2 FOR SELF-STUDY

(Conlin Corporation; accounting for securities available for sale.)

a.

(1) February 2, 2008

Marketable Securities	40,000	
Cash		40,000

Assets	=	Liabilities	+	Shareholders' Equity	(Class.)
+40,000					
−40,000					

To record acquisition of Security A.

(2) July 15, 2008

Marketable Securities	75,000	
Cash		75,000

Assets	=	Liabilities	+	Shareholders' Equity	(Class.)
+75,000					
−75,000					

To record acquisition of Security B.

(3) November 27, 2008

Marketable Securities	90,000	
Cash		90,000

Assets	=	Liabilities	+	Shareholders' Equity	(Class.)
+90,000					
−90,000					

To record acquisition of Security C.

(4) December 31, 2008

Unrealized Holding Loss on Securities A	2,000	
Marketable Securities		2,000

Assets	=	Liabilities	+	Shareholders' Equity	(Class.)
−2,000				−2,000	OCI → AOCI

To measure Security A at fair value.

(5) December 31, 2008

Marketable Securities	4,000	
Unrealized Holding Gain on Security B		4,000

Assets	=	Liabilities	+	Shareholders' Equity	(Class.)
+4,000				+4,000	OCI → AOCI

To measure Security B at fair value.

(6) December 31, 2008

Marketable Securities	3,000	
Unrealized Holding Gain on Security C......................		3,000

Assets	=	Liabilities	+	Shareholders' Equity	(Class.)
+3,000				+3,000	OCI → AOCI

To measure Security C at fair value.

Note: Entries **(4)**, **(5)**, and **(6)** above could be combined as follows:

December 31, 2008

Marketable Securities	5,000	
Net Unrealized Holding Gain on Marketable Securities		5,000

Assets	=	Liabilities	+	Shareholders' Equity	(Class.)
+5,000				+5,000	OCI → AOCI

To measure the portfolio of marketable securities available for sale to fair value.

(7) September 6, 2009

Cash	78,000	
Unrealized Holding Gain on Security B	4,000	
Marketable Securities		79,000
Realized Gain on Sale of Marketable Securities		3,000

Assets	=	Liabilities	+	Shareholders' Equity	(Class.)
+78,000				−4,000	OCI → AOCI
−79,000				+3,000	IncSt → RE

To record sale of Marketable Security B.

(8) December 31, 2009

Unrealized Holding Loss on Security A.......................	5,000	
Marketable Securities		5,000

Assets	=	Liabilities	+	Shareholders' Equity	(Class.)
−5,000				−5,000	OCI → AOCI

To measure Security A at fair value.

(9) December 31, 2009

Marketable Securities	1,000	
Unrealized Holding Gain on Security C...................		1,000

Assets	=	Liabilities	+	Shareholders' Equity	(Class.)
+1,000				+1,000	OCI → AOCI

To measure Security C at fair value.

Note: Entries **(8)** and **(9)** could be combined as follows:

(8a/9a) December 31, 2009

Net Unrealized Holding Loss on Marketable Securities	4,000	
Marketable Securities		4,000

Assets	=	Liabilities	+	Shareholders' Equity	(Class.)
−4,000				−4,000	OCI → AOCI

b. The first three journal entries are identical. The unrealized holding gain or loss accounts in entries **(4)**, **(5)**, **(6)**, **(8)**, and **(9)** are income statement accounts when the firm classifies the securities as trading securities. Entry **(7)** is as follows:

(7) September 6, 2009

Cash	78,000	
Realized Loss on Sale of Marketable Securities	1,000	
Marketable Securities		79,000

Assets	=	Liabilities	+	Shareholders' Equity	(Class.)
+78,000				−1,000	IncSt → RE
−79,000					

To record sale of trading security for less than its carrying value at the time of sale.

SUGGESTED SOLUTION TO PROBLEM 12.3 FOR SELF-STUDY

Accounting for Forward Foreign Exchange Contract as a Fair Value Hedge.

a. The purchase commitment and the forward foreign exchange contract are mutually unexecuted contracts as of June 30, 2008. U.S. GAAP and IFRS do not currently require firms to recognize mutually unexecuted contracts in the accounts.

b. The change in the value of the undiscounted cash flows related to the purchase commitment and the forward foreign exchange contract is $900 [= (10,000 × $1.73) − (10,000 × $1.64)]. The present value of $900 discounted at 8% for six months is $865 (= $900/(1 + .08/2).

December 31, 2008

Loss on Firm Commitment	865	
Commitment to Purchase Equipment		865

Assets	=	Liabilities	+	Shareholders' Equity	(Class.)
		+865		−865	IncSt → RE

To record a loss on a previously unrecognized firm commitment because the U.S. dollar decreased in value relative to the British pound.

December 31, 2008

Forward Foreign Exchange Contract	865	
Gain on Forward Foreign Exchange Contract		865

Assets	=	Liabilities	+	Shareholders' Equity	(Class.)
+865				+865	IncSt → RE

To measure the forward foreign exchange contract at fair value and recognize a gain in net income.

c.

June 30, 2009

Interest Expense	35	
Commitment to Purchase Equipment		35

Assets	=	Liabilities	+	Shareholders' Equity	(Class.)
		+35		−35	IncSt → RE

To recognize interest on the commitment because of the passage of time; $35 = .04 × $865.

June 30, 2009

Forward Foreign Exchange Contract	35	
Interest Revenue		35

Assets	=	Liabilities	+	Shareholders' Equity	(Class.)
+35				+35	IncSt → RE

To record interest on the forward foreign exchange contract because of the passage of time; $35 = .04 × $865.

d. The change in the value of the purchase commitment and the forward foreign exchange contract due to exchange rate changes is $200 [= (10,000 × $1.75) − (10,000 × $1.73)].

June 30, 2009

Loss on Firm Commitment	200	
Commitment to Purchase Equipment		200

(continued)

Assets	=	Liabilities	+	Shareholders' Equity	(Class.)
		+200		−200	IncSt → RE

To record a loss on the purchase commitment because the value of the U.S. dollar declined relative to the British pound.

June 30, 2009

| Forward Foreign Exchange Contract . . . . | 200 | |
| Gain on Forward Foreign Exchange Contract . . . . | | 200 |

Assets	=	Liabilities	+	Shareholders' Equity	(Class.)
+200				+200	IncSt → RE

To record the increase in the fair value of the forward foreign exchange contract because the U.S. dollar declined in value relative to the British pound.

e.

June 30, 2009

Equipment	16,400	
Commitment to Purchase Equipment	1,100	
Cash		17,500

Assets	=	Liabilities	+	Shareholders' Equity	(Class.)
+16,400		−1,100			
−17,500					

To record the amount paid in U.S. dollars to acquire £10,000 ($17,500 = 10,000 × 1.75), to eliminate the balance in the Commitment to Purchase Equipment account of $1,100 (= $865 + $35 + $200), and to record the acquisition cost of the equipment for $16,400.

f.

June 30, 2009

| Cash . . . . | 1,100 | |
| Forward Foreign Exchange Contract . . . . | | 1,100 |

Assets	=	Liabilities	+	Shareholders' Equity	(Class.)
+1,100					
−1,100					

To record cash received from the counterparty and eliminate the balance in the Forward Foreign Exchange Contract account of $1,100 (= $865 + $35 + $200).

g. Firm A would not recognize changes in the fair value of the purchase commitment. Each of the entries related to changes in the fair value of the derivative and involving income statement accounts in parts **b** to **d** would instead affect Other Comprehensive Income, which the firm would close to Accumulated Other Comprehensive Income. Assuming that the hedge was highly effective, any balance in Accumulated Other Comprehensive Income related to the forward foreign exchange contract on June 30, 2009, would affect the income statement on this date.

h. To treat this hedge as a fair value hedge, Firm A must desire to protect the amount it pays for the equipment. Perhaps Firm A has committed to resell the equipment to a customer on June 30, 2009, for a fixed price in U.S. dollars and wants to protect its expected profit margin from the sale. To treat this hedge as a cash flow hedge, Firm A must desire to protect the amount of cash it pays to the British supplier.

KEY TERMS AND CONCEPTS

Marketable securities	Interest rate swap
Investments in securities	Forward commodity contract
Debt securities held to maturity or held-to-maturity investments	Underlyings
Trading securities or financial assets at fair value through profit or loss	Notional amounts
	Counterparty
	Net settlement
Securities available for sale or available-for-sale financial assets	Hedge accounting
	Fair value hedge
Amortized acquisition cost	Cash flow hedge
Derivative	Fair value option
Forward foreign exchange contract	

QUESTIONS, EXERCISES, AND PROBLEMS

QUESTIONS

1. Review the meaning of the terms and concepts listed above in Key Terms and Concepts.

2. Distinguish between the following pairs of terms:

   a. Debt securities classified as "held to maturity" versus "available for sale."

   b. Equity securities classified as "trading securities" versus "available for sale."

   c. Amortized acquisition cost versus fair value of debt securities.

   d. Unrealized holding gain or loss on trading securities versus on securities available for sale.

   e. Realized gain or loss on trading securities versus on securities available for sale.

3. What is the justification of authoritative guidance for including unrealized holding gains and losses on trading securities in income but reporting unrealized holding gains and losses on securities available for sale in Accumulated Other Comprehensive Income, a separate shareholders' equity account?

4. "Reporting marketable securities available for sale at fair value on the balance sheet but not including the unrealized holding gains and losses in income is inconsistent and provides an opportunity for earnings management." Do you agree? Why or why not?

5. When is a derivative also an accounting hedge? When is it not also an accounting hedge? Can management manipulate earnings by its choice of whether to use hedge accounting?

6. Distinguish between a fair value hedge and a cash flow hedge.

7. "The recognition of a derivative classified as a fair value hedge of a firm commitment as an asset but not recognizing the commitment that the derivative is hedging as a liability is inconsistent." Do you agree? Why or why not?

8. Both U.S. GAAP and IFRS require the immediate recognition in net income of unrealized gains and losses on derivatives hedging recognized assets and liabilities treated as fair value hedges. Both U.S. GAAP and IFRS delay recognition in net income of unrealized gains and losses on derivatives hedging recognized assets and liabilities treated as cash flow hedges. What is the likely rationale for these different treatments?

9. Suggest reasons why a firm would acquire a derivative and not treat it as an accounting hedge.

10. "Adopting the fair value option for marketable securities and derivatives collapses the accounting methods discussed in this chapter to a single accounting method." Do you agree? Why or why not?

EXERCISES

11. **Classifying securities.** Firms that do not elect the fair value option classify marketable securities along two dimensions:

- Purpose of investment: debt securities held to maturity, trading securities, or securities available for sale.

- Length of expected holding period: current asset (Marketable Securities) or noncurrent asset (Investment in Securities).

Classify each of the securities below along each of these two dimensions.

a. A forest products company plans to construct a pulp-processing plant beginning in April of next year. It issues common stock for $200 million on December 10 of this year to help finance construction. The company invests this $200 million in U.S. government debt securities to generate income until it needs the cash for construction.

b. An electric utility has bonds payable outstanding for $100 million that mature in five years. The electric utility acquires U.S. government bonds that have a maturity value of $100 million in five years. The firm plans to use the proceeds from the government bonds to repay its own outstanding bonds.

c. A commercial bank acquires bonds of the state of New York to generate tax-exempt interest revenue. The bank plans to sell the bonds when it needs cash for loans and other ongoing operating needs.

d. A pharmaceutical company acquires common stock of a biogenetic engineering company that conducts research in human growth hormones. The pharmaceutical company hopes the investment will lead to strategic alliances or joint ventures in the future.

e. A commercial bank maintains a department that regularly purchases and sells securities on stock exchanges around the world. This department acquires common stock of Nissan Motors on the New York Stock Exchange because it thinks the market price does not fully reflect favorable news about Nissan.

f. A U.S. computer company has bonds outstanding that are payable in Swiss francs. The bonds mature in installments during the next five years. The computer company purchases a Swiss winery's bonds, denominated in Swiss francs, that mature in seven years. The computer company will sell a portion of the bonds of the Swiss winery each year to obtain the Swiss francs needed to repay its franc-denominated bonds.

12. **Accounting principles for marketable securities and derivatives.** For each of the items **a** to **d** below, describe its accounting using one of the following four systems, assuming that the firm does not elect the fair value option:

   (1) Measured at fair value with changes recognized in net income.

   (2) Measured at amortized cost.

   (3) Measured at fair value with changes recognized initially in other comprehensive income.

   (4) Measurement depends on whether firm uses hedge accounting.

   a. A derivative judged to be effective used to hedge forecasted sales.

   b. Derivatives appearing as liabilities; these derivatives do not hedge assets or liabilities or forecasted transactions.

   c. Traded debt issued by others that the firm has purchased with the ability to hold to maturity, but the intent after the current year is uncertain. The firm frequently buys and sells debt of this sort.

   d. Marketable equity securities held for an indefinite period as securities available for sale.

13. **Accounting for bonds held to maturity.** Murray Company acquired $100,000 face value of the outstanding bonds of Campbell Company on January 1, 2008. The bonds pay interest semiannually on June 30 and December 31 at an annual rate of 6% and mature on December 31, 2011. The market priced these bonds on January 1, 2008, to yield 8% compounded semiannually. Murray Company classifies these bonds as held to maturity.

   a. Compute the amount that Murray Company paid for these bonds, excluding commissions and taxes.

   b. Prepare an amortization table for these bonds similar to that in **Exhibit 12.2**.

c. Give the journal entries that Murray Company would make to account for these bonds during 2008.

d. Give the journal entries that Murray Company would make to account for these bonds on December 31, 2011.

14. **Accounting for bonds held to maturity.** Kelly Company acquired $500,000 face value of the outstanding bonds of Steedly Company on January 1, 2008. The bonds pay interest semiannually on June 30 and December 31 at an annual rate of 7% and mature on December 31, 2010. The bonds were priced on the market on January 1, 2008, to yield 6% compounded semiannually. Kelly Company classifies these bonds as held to maturity.

a. Compute the amount that Kelly Company paid for these bonds, excluding commissions and taxes.

b. Prepare an amortization table for these bonds similar to that in **Exhibit 12.2**.

c. Give the journal entries that Kelly Company would make to account for these bonds during 2008.

d. Give the journal entries that Kelly Company would make to account for these bonds on December 31, 2010.

15. **Accounting for securities available for sale.** Events related to Elston Corporation's investments of temporarily excess cash appear below. The firm classifies these investments as securities available for sale and does not adopt the fair value option.

Security	Date Acquired	Acquisition Cost	Fair Value on December 31		Date Sold	Selling Price
			2008	**2009**		
A	10/15/2008	$28,000	$25,000	—	2/10/2009	$24,000
B	11/2/2008	$49,000	$55,000	$53,000	7/15/2010	$57,000

Elston received no dividends on Security A. It received dividends from Security B of $1,000 on December 31, 2008, and $1,200 on December 31, 2009. Prepare dated journal entries for the following events related to these investments, assuming that the accounting period is the calendar year.

a. Acquisition of securities

b. Receipt of dividends

c. Revaluation on December 31

d. Sale of securities

16. **Accounting for securities available for sale.** Events related to Simmons Corporation's investments of temporarily excess cash appear below. The firm classifies these investments as securities available for sale and does not elect the fair value option.

Security	Date Acquired	Acquisition Cost	Fair Value on December 31		Date Sold	Selling Price
			2008	**2009**		
S	6/13/2008	$12,000	$13,500	$15,200	2/15/2010	$14,900
T	6/13/2008	$29,000	$26,200	$31,700	8/22/2010	$28,500
U	6/13/2008	$43,000	—	—	10/11/2008	$39,000

None of these three securities paid dividends. Prepare dated journal entries for the following events related to these investments, assuming that the accounting period is the calendar year.

a. Acquisition of securities

b. Revaluation on December 31

c. Sale of securities

17. **Working backward from data on marketable securities transaction.** (Adapted from a problem by S. A. Zeff.) During 2008, Fischer/Black Co. purchased equity securities classified

as securities available for sale. On May 22, 2009, the company recorded the following correct journal entry to record the sale of the equity securities:

Cash	16,000	
Realized Loss	5,000	
Unrealized Holding Loss		3,000
Marketable Securities		18,000

Assets	=	Liabilities	+	Shareholders' Equity	(Class.)
+16,000				−5,000	IncSt → RE
−18,000				+3,000	OCI → AOCI

a. What was the acquisition cost of these securities in 2008?

b. What was the market price of these securities at the end of 2008?

c. What is the total amount of securities gain or loss that Fischer/Black reports on the income statement for 2009?

18. **Working backward from data on marketable securities transaction.** (Adapted from a problem by S. A. Zeff.) On December 12, 2008, Canning purchased 2,000 shares of Werther. By December 31, the market price of these shares had dropped by $1,000. On March 2, 2009, Canning sold the 2,000 shares for $18,000 and reported a realized gain on the transaction of $4,000.

a. What was the acquisition cost of these securities if Canning had accounted for them as trading securities?

b. What was the acquisition cost of these securities if Canning had accounted for them as securities available for sale?

19. **Reconstructing events from journal entries.** Give the likely transaction or event that would result in making each of the independent journal entries that follow:

a.

Unrealized Loss on Securities Available for Sale...................	4,000	
Marketable Securities		4,000

Assets	=	Liabilities	+	Shareholders' Equity	(Class.)
−4,000				−4,000	OCI → AOCI

b.

Cash	1,100	
Realized Loss on Sale of Securities Available for Sale	200	
Marketable Securities		1,300

Assets	=	Liabilities	+	Shareholders' Equity	(Class.)
+1,100				−200	IncSt → RE
−1,300					

c.

Marketable Securities	750	
Unrealized Holding Gain on Securities Available for Sale		750

Assets	=	Liabilities	+	Shareholders' Equity	(Class.)
+750				+750	OCI → AOCI

d.

Cash					1,800	
Marketable Securities						1,700
Realized Gain on Sale of Securities Available for Sale						100

Assets	=	Liabilities	+	Shareholders' Equity	(Class.)
+1,800				+100	IncSt → RE
−1,700					

20. **Reconstructing transactions involving short-term securities available for sale.** During 2008, Zeff Corporation sold marketable securities for $14,000 that had a carrying value of $13,000 at the time of sale. The financial statements of Zeff Corporation reveal the following information with respect to securities available for sale:

	December 31	
	2008	**2007**
Balance Sheet		
Marketable Securities at Fair Value	$195,000	$187,000
Net Unrealized Holding Gain on Securities Available for Sale	$ 10,000	$ 12,000

	2008
Income Statement	
Realized Gain on Sale of Securities Available for Sale	$4,000

a. What was the acquisition cost of the marketable securities sold?

b. What was the unrealized holding gain on the securities sold at the time of sale?

c. What was the unrealized holding gain during 2008 on securities still held by the end of 2008?

d. What was the cost of marketable securities purchased during 2008?

21. **Accounting for forward foreign exchange contract as a fair value hedge.** On September 1, 2008, Turner Corporation places an order with a Japanese supplier for manufacturing equipment for delivery on June 30, 2009. The purchase is denominated in Japanese yen in the amount of ¥5,200,000. Turner Corporation purchases a forward foreign exchange contract on September 1, 2008, for the purchase of ¥5,200,000 at a forward foreign exchange rate for settlement on June 30, 2009, of $1 = ¥102. Turner Corporation designates the forward foreign exchange contract as a fair value hedge. The forward foreign exchange rate on December 31, 2008, for settlement on June 30, 2009, is $1 = ¥100, and the actual exchange rate on June 30, 2009, is $1 = ¥95. The following summarizes this information:

Date	Type of Exchange Rate	Exchange Rate	Amount in Japanese Yen	Equivalent U.S. Dollar Amount
September 1, 2008	Forward Rate for June 30, 2009, Settlement	$1 = ¥102	¥5,200,000	$50,980
December 31, 2008.	Forward Rate for June 30, 2009, Settlement	$1 = ¥100	¥5,200,000	$52,000
June 30, 2009	Actual	$1 = ¥95	¥5,200,000	$54,737

a. Using a discount rate of 8% per year, what is the fair value of the foreign exchange contract on December 31, 2008? Is the amount an asset or a liability?

b. What amount would Turner Corporation report on its December 31, 2008, balance sheet related to its commitment to purchase the equipment?

c. What is the fair value of the foreign exchange contract on June 30, 2009, just before settling the transaction?

d. Give the journal entry on June 30, 2009, to purchase the equipment.

e. Give the journal entry on June 30, 2009, to settle the forward foreign exchange contract.

22. **Accounting for forward foreign exchange contract as a cash flow hedge.** On October 1, 2008, Biddle Corporation purchases equipment from a supplier in France on account at a purchase price of €40,000 and denominates the transaction in euros. Biddle Corporation must pay the €40,000 on March 31, 2009. To protect its cash flows, Biddle Corporation purchases a forward foreign exchange contract on October 1, 2008, for €40,000 at a forward foreign exchange rate for settlement on March 31, 2009, of €1 = $1.32. Biddle Corporation designates the forward foreign exchange contract as a cash flow hedge. The forward foreign exchange rate on December 31, 2008, for settlement on March 31, 2009, is €1 = $1.35, and the actual exchange rate on March 31, 2009, is €1 = $1.40. Ignore discounting of cash flows in this exercise. The following summarizes this information:

Date	Type of Exchange Rate	Exchange Rate	Amount in Euros	Equivalent U.S. Dollar Amount
October 1, 2008	Forward Rate for March 31, 2009, Settlement	€1 = $1.32	€40,000	$52,800
December 31, 2008 . . .	Forward Rate for March 31, 2009, Settlement	€1 = $1.35	€40,000	$54,000
March 31, 2009.	Actual	€1 = $1.40	€40,000	$56,000

a. What is the fair value of the foreign exchange contract on December 31, 2008? Is the amount an asset or a liability?

b. What amount would Biddle Corporation report on its December 31, 2008, balance sheet for its Note Payable to the supplier?

c. What is the fair value of the foreign exchange contract on March 31, 2009, just before settling the transaction?

d. Give the journal entry on March 31, 2009, to pay cash to the supplier.

e. Give the journal entry on March 31, 2009, to settle the forward foreign exchange contract.

PROBLEMS

23. **Journal entries and financial statement presentation of short-term securities available for sale.** The following information summarizes data about Dostal Corporation's marketable securities held as current assets and classified as securities available for sale:

					Fair Value	
Security	Date Acquired	Acquisition Cost	Date Sold	Selling Price	Dec. 31, 2008	Dec. 31, 2009
A	2/5/2008	$60,000	6/5/2009	$72,000	$66,000	—
B	8/12/2008	$25,000	—	—	$20,000	$20,000
C	1/22/2009	$82,000	—	—	—	$79,000
D	2/25/2009	$42,000	6/5/2009	$39,000	—	—
E	3/25/2009	$75,000	—	—	—	$80,000

a. Give all journal entries relating to these marketable equity securities during 2008 and 2009, assuming that the accounting period is the calendar year.

b. Provide a suitable presentation of marketable securities in the balance sheet and related notes on December 31, 2008.

c. Provide a suitable presentation of marketable securities in the balance sheet and related notes on December 31, 2009.

24. **Journal entries and financial statement presentation of long-term securities available for sale.** The following information summarizes data about Rice Corporation's investments in equity securities held as noncurrent assets and classified as securities available for sale:

					Fair Value	
Security	Date Acquired	Acquisition Cost	Date Sold	Selling Price	Dec. 31, 2008	Dec. 31, 2009
A	3/5/2008	$40,000	10/5/2009	$52,000	$45,000	—
B	5/12/2008	$80,000	—	—	$70,000	$83,000
C	3/22/2009	$32,000	—	—	—	$27,000
D	5/25/2009	$17,000	10/5/2009	$16,000	—	—
E	5/25/2009	$63,000	—	—	—	$67,000

a. Give all journal entries relating to these equity securities during 2008 and 2009, assuming that the accounting period is the calendar year.

b. Provide a suitable presentation of investments in securities in the balance sheet and related notes on December 31, 2008.

c. Provide a suitable presentation of investments in securities in the balance sheet and related notes on December 31, 2009.

25. **Analysis of financial statement disclosures for securities available for sale.** Exhibit 12.9 reproduces data about the marketable equity securities held as securities available for sale for Moonlight Mining Company. Assume that Moonlight held no current marketable securities at the end of 2008, sold no current marketable securities during 2009, purchased no noncurrent marketable securities during 2009, and transferred no noncurrent marketable securities to the current portfolio during 2009. The income statement for 2009 shows a realized loss on sale of noncurrent marketable securities of $3,068,000.

a. What amount of net unrealized holding gain or loss on noncurrent marketable securities appears on the balance sheet for the end of 2008?

b. What amount of net unrealized gain or loss on noncurrent securities appears on the balance sheet for the end of 2009?

c. What were the proceeds from the sale of noncurrent marketable securities during 2009?

d. What amount of unrealized holding gain or loss on marketable securities appears on the income statement for 2009?

26. **Effect of various methods of accounting for marketable equity securities.** Information related to marketable equity securities of Callahan Corporation appears on the next page.

EXHIBIT 12.9

Moonlight Mining Company
Data on Marketable Equity Securities
(all dollar amounts in thousands)
(Problem 25)

Marketable Equity Securities	Acquisition Cost	Fair Value
At December 31, 2009:		
Current Marketable Securities	$7,067	$4,601
Noncurrent Marketable Securities	$6,158	$8,807
At December 31, 2008:		
Noncurrent Marketable Securities	$21,685	$11,418

Security	Acquisition Cost in 2008	Dividends Received During 2008	Fair Value on Dec. 31, 2008	Selling Price in 2009	Dividends Received During 2009	Fair Value on Dec. 31, 2009
G	$18,000	$ 800	$16,000	$14,500	$ 200	—
H	25,000	1,500	24,000	26,000	500	—
I	12,000	1,000	14,000	—	1,500	$17,000
	$55,000	$3,300	$54,000	$40,500	$2,200	$17,000

a. Assume that these securities are trading securities. Indicate the nature and amount of income recognized during 2008 and 2009 and the presentation of information about these securities on the balance sheet on December 31, 2008 and 2009.

b. Repeat part **a** assuming that these securities are securities available for sale held as temporary investments of excess cash by Callahan Corporation.

c. Repeat part **a** assuming that these securities represent long-term investments by Callahan Corporation held as securities available for sale.

d. Compute the combined income for 2008 and 2009 under each of the three treatments of these securities in parts **a**, **b**, and **c**. Why do the combined income amounts differ? Will total shareholders' equity differ? Why or why not?

27. **Analysis of financial statement disclosures related to marketable securities and quality of earnings.** A commercial bank reports the following information relating to its marketable securities classified as securities available for sale for a recent year (amounts in millions):

	December 31	
	2009	2008
Marketable Securities at Acquisition Cost	$13,968	$14,075
Gross Unrealized Holding Gains	1,445	957
Gross Unrealized Holding Losses	(218)	(510)
Marketable Securities at Fair Value	$15,195	$14,522

Cash proceeds from sales and maturities of marketable securities totaled $37,600 million in 2009. Gross realized gains totaled $443 million, and gross realized losses totaled $113 million during 2009. The carrying value of marketable securities sold or matured totaled $37,008 million. Interest and dividend revenue during 2009 totaled $1,081 million. Purchases of marketable securities totaled $37,163 million during 2009.

a. Give the journal entries to record the sale of marketable securities during 2009.

b. Analyze the change in the net unrealized holding gain from $447 million on December 31, 2008, to $1,227 million on December 31, 2009.

c. Compute the total income (both realized and unrealized) *occurring during 2009* on the bank's investments in securities.

d. How might the judicious selection of marketable securities sold during 2009 permit the bank to report an even larger net realized gain?

28. **Accounting for forward commodity price contract as a cash flow hedge.** Refer to **Examples 15** and **19** in the chapter. Firm D holds 10,000 gallons of whiskey in inventory on October 31, 2008, that costs $225 per gallon. Firm D contemplates selling the whiskey on March 31, 2009, when it completes the aging process. Uncertainty about the selling price of whiskey on March 31, 2009, leads Firm D to acquire a forward contract on whiskey. The forward contract does not require an initial investment of funds. Firm D designates the forward commodity contract as a cash flow hedge of a forecasted transaction. The forward price on October 31, 2008, for delivery on March 31, 2009, is $320 per gallon.

a. Give the journal entry, if any, that Firm D would make on October 31, 2008, when it acquires the forward commodity price contract.

b. On December 31, 2008, the end of the accounting period for Firm D, the forward price of whiskey for March 31, 2009, delivery is $310 per gallon. Give the journal entry to record the change in the value of the forward commodity price contract. Ignore the discounting of cash flows in this part and for the remainder of the problem.

c. Give the journal entry, if any, that Firm D must make on December 31, 2008, for the decline in value of the whiskey inventory.

d. On March 31, 2009, the price of whiskey declines to $270 per gallon. Give the journal entry that Firm D must make to revalue the forward contract.

e. Give the entry, if any, that Firm D must make on March 31, 2009, to reflect the decline in value of the inventory.

f. Give the journal entry that Firm D would make on March 31, 2009, to settle the forward contract.

g. Assume that Firm D sells the whiskey on March 31, 2009, for $270 a gallon. Give the journal entries to record the sale and recognize the cost of goods sold.

h. How would the entries in parts **b** through **g** differ if Firm D had chosen to designate the forward commodity price contract as a fair value hedge instead of a cash flow hedge?

i. Suggest a scenario that would justify the firm treating the forward commodity price contract as a fair value hedge, and a scenario that would justify treating it as a cash flow hedge.

29. **Accounting for forward foreign exchange contract as a fair value hedge and a cash flow hedge.** On October 1, 2008, Owens Corporation places an order with a European supplier for manufacturing equipment for delivery on June 30, 2009. The purchase is denominated in euros in the amount of €60,000. Owens Corporation purchases a forward foreign exchange contract on October 1, 2008, for the purchase of €60,000 at a forward foreign exchange rate for settlement on June 30, 2009, of €1 = $1.32. Owens Corporation designates the forward foreign exchange contract as a fair value hedge. The forward foreign exchange rate on December 31, 2008, for settlement on June 30, 2009, is €1 = $1.35, and the actual exchange rate on June 30, 2009, is €1 = $1.40. The following summarizes this information:

Date	Type of Exchange Rate	Exchange Rate	Amount in Euros	Equivalent U.S. Dollar Amount
October 1, 2008	Forward for June 30, 2009, Settlement	€1 = $1.32	€60,000	$79,200
December 31, 2008	Forward for June 30, 2009, Settlement	$1 = €1.35	€60,000	$81,000
June 30, 2009	Actual	€1 = $1.40	€60,000	$84,000

a. Using a discount rate of 8% per year, give the journal entries that Owens Corporation would make on October 1, 2008; December 31, 2008; and June 30, 2009; to account for the purchase commitment and the forward foreign exchange contract. Owens Corporation's accounting period is the calendar year.

b. How would the journal entries in part **a** differ if Owens Corporation designates the foreign exchange contract as a cash flow hedge instead of a fair value hedge?

c. Suggest a scenario that would justify the firm treating the forward foreign exchange contract as a fair value hedge, and a scenario that would justify treating it as a cash flow hedge.

30. **Accounting for an interest rate swap as a fair value hedge.** Sandretto Corporation issues a note payable on January 1, 2008, to a supplier in return for equipment. The note has a face value of $50,000 and bears interest at 6% each year. Interest is payable annually on December 31, and the note matures on December 31, 2010. Sandretto Corporation has the option of repaying the note at any time prior to maturity at its fair value. Sandretto Corporation will pay early only if interest rates drop. In that event, the fair value of the note would exceed $50,000, and Sandretto Corporation will not capture the benefits of the lower interest rate. Sandretto Corporation wants to neutralize the effects of changes in the fair value of the note payable. It therefore enters into an interest rate swap with its bank. The swap has the effect of allowing Sandretto Corporation to exchange its fixed interest rate liability for a variable rate obligation. Assume that the variable interest rate

is 6% on January 1, 2008, and the rate is reset to 8% on December 31, 2008, and to 4% on December 31, 2009.

a. Give the journal entries that Sandretto Corporation will make on January 1, 2008; December 31, 2008; and December 31, 2009.

b. Sandretto Corporation decides to repay this note early on January 1, 2010. Give the journal entries for the repayment of the note and to close out the swap agreement, assuming that Sandretto Corporation does not incur any additional costs for the early payment or closing out the swap contract.

c. How would the entries in part **a** differ if Sandretto Corporation elected the fair value option for the note payable and interest rate swap?

31. **Accounting for an interest rate swap as a cash flow hedge.** Avery Corporation issues a note payable on January 1, 2008, to a supplier in return for equipment. The note has a face value of $50,000 and bears interest at a variable interest rate; the variable interest rate is 6% on January 1, 2008. Interest is payable annually on December 31, and the note matures on December 31, 2010. Avery Corporation desires to protect its cash flows from changes in the variable interest rate. It therefore enters into an interest rate swap with its bank. The swap has the effect of allowing Avery Corporation to exchange its variable interest rate liability for a 6% fixed rate obligation. Assume the variable interest rate increases to 8% on December 31, 2008, and decreases to 4% on December 31, 2009. Avery Corporation designates the interest rate swap as a cash flow hedge. Give the journal entries that Avery Corporation will make on January 1, 2008; December 31, 2008; December 31, 2009; and December 31, 2010.

Intercorporate Investments in Common Stock

1. Understand why firms invest in the common stock issued by other entities and how the purpose of the investment determines the method of accounting for those investments.

2. Develop skills to apply the equity method to minority, active investments, contrasting its financial statement effects with those of measuring marketable securities at fair value.

3. Understand the concepts underlying consolidated financial statements for majority, active investments, contrasting the financial statement effects of consolidation with those of the equity method.

4. Understand the accounting for a joint venture, an entity in which no owner has control.

5. Understand consolidation policy for a variable interest entity (VIE), an entity for which the analysis of voting interests does not reveal whether another entity controls the VIE.

L E A R N I N G O B J E C T I V E S

For various reasons, corporations often acquire common stock issued by other entities.

Example 1 Citigroup, a commercial bank, has trading operations that focus on short-term changes in the prices of securities. Citigroup purchases shares of common stock of Roche Holding, Ltd., a pharmaceutical company, on December 28, 2009, with the expectation of selling them early in 2010 when Roche releases news about a new drug discovery.

Example 2 Microsoft Corporation acquires 5% of the shares of common stock of a technology start-up company, with the intent of benefitting from increases in the market prices of these shares if the technology company is successful.

Example 3 The Coca-Cola Company (Coke) owns 40% of the common stock of Coca-Cola Enterprises, a bottler of its soft drinks. This ownership percentage permits The Coca-Cola Company to exert significant influence over the operations of Coca-Cola Enterprises and keep the affiliate's capital-intensive bottling assets and its debt off Coke's balance sheet.

Example 4 The Walt Disney Company owns all the common stock of ESPN, Inc. and can therefore control both the broad policy and the day-to-day business decisions of ESPN, Inc.

OVERVIEW OF THE ACCOUNTING FOR AND REPORTING OF INVESTMENTS IN COMMON STOCK

The accounting for investments in common stock depends on (1) the expected holding period, and (2) the purpose of the investment, as determined by both the percentage held and management intent.

EXPECTED HOLDING PERIOD

The expected holding period determines the balance sheet classification of investments in securities as current assets or as noncurrent assets. Securities that firms expect to sell within the next year appear as **marketable securities** in current assets on the balance sheet. In **Example 1**, Citigroup would include its investment in Roche Holding, Ltd. in marketable securities as a current asset. Securities that firms expect to hold for more than one year from the date of the balance sheet appear in **investments in securities**, classified as a noncurrent asset on the balance sheet. Microsoft's investment in the technology start-up company in **Example 2** and The Coca-Cola Company's investment in Coca-Cola Enterprises in **Example 3** appear in investments in securities. A later section explains that Walt Disney in **Example 4** would prepare consolidated financial statements with ESPN, Inc. The consolidation procedure requires Walt Disney to replace its Investment in ESPN, Inc. account with accounts showing that firm's individual assets and liabilities. The Investment in ESPN, Inc. account does not appear on the consolidated balance sheet. Although we and others use the phrase *investment in securities* to refer broadly to all investments in the bonds, capital stock, and other financial instruments of other entities, in this book we reserve the word *investment* for holdings with a long-term purpose.

PURPOSE OF AN INVESTMENT IN COMMON STOCK

This section describes how the purpose of an investment in common stock and the percentage of common stock held combine to determine the accounting for that investment. Refer to **Figure 13.1**, which identifies three types of investments.

1. In **minority, passive investments**, an investor acquires the common stock of another entity (the investee) for the interest, dividends, and capital gains (increases in market prices) anticipated from share ownership. The acquiring (investor) company's ownership percentage is sufficiently small that it cannot control or exert **significant influence** over the other company. Citigroup's investment in Roche Holding, Ltd. in **Example 1** and Microsoft Corporation's 5% ownership investment in the technology start-up company in **Example 2** are minority, passive investments. Occasionally, an investor that owns a small percentage of the shares of the investee has the contractual right to elect one or more members of the board of directors of the investee entity. If so, the investor, even though a small percentage holder, could exercise significant influence. U.S. GAAP and IFRS view investments of less than 20% of the voting shares of another company as

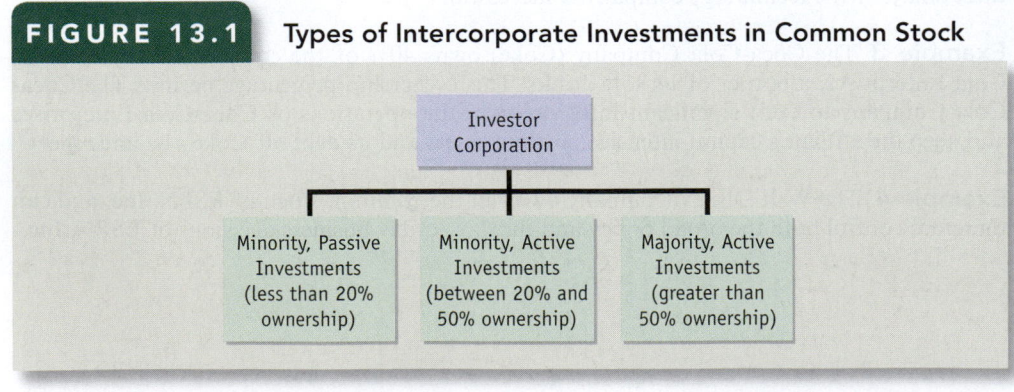

FIGURE 13.1 Types of Intercorporate Investments in Common Stock

minority, passive investments in most cases.[1] An investor who intends to hold the shares for less than a year would classify them as current assets; if the expected holding period is longer, the investor would classify them as noncurrent assets (Investments in Securities). **Chapter 12** discusses the accounting for minority, passive investments in marketable securities, including both debt securities and equity securities.

2. In **minority, active investments**, an investor acquires common shares of an investee with the intent of exerting significant influence over the investee's activities, perhaps through representation on the investee's board of directors. Because many different individuals or entities own most publicly held corporations, and those owners typically do not collaborate in voting their shares, an investor can exert significant influence over an investee with ownership of less than a majority of the voting stock. The Coca-Cola Company's investment in the shares of Coca-Cola Enterprises in **Example 3** is a minority, active investment. U.S. GAAP and IFRS view investments of between 20% and 50% of the voting stock of another company as minority, active investments unless evidence indicates that the investor cannot exert significant influence.[2] Minority, active investments appear as noncurrent assets on the balance sheet.

3. In **majority, active investments**, an investor acquires shares of an investee so that the investor can control the investee both at the broad policy-making level and at the day-to-day operational level. Refer to **Example 4**. Walt Disney acquired ESPN, Inc. to add sports television broadcasting to its entertainment capabilities. U.S. GAAP and IFRS view ownership of more than 50% of an investee as implying an ability to control the investee, unless evidence indicates to the contrary.[3] For example, an investor cannot exercise control of a majority-owned investee if a court effectively controls the investee in bankruptcy proceedings or if the investee is a foreign company whose government restricts the withdrawal of assets from the country.

This chapter describes and illustrates the accounting for minority, active investments in common shares and majority, active investments in common shares. Throughout our discussion, we will designate the acquiring corporation (the investor) as P, for purchaser or for parent, depending on the context, and the acquired corporation (the investee) as S, for seller or for subsidiary.

MINORITY, ACTIVE INVESTMENTS

When an investor owns less than a majority of the voting stock of another corporation, the accountant must judge when the investor can exert significant influence. For the sake of uniformity, U.S. GAAP and IFRS presume that significant influence exists at 20% ownership (that is, when the investor owns 20% or more of the voting stock of the investee). Significant influence can exist at lower ownership levels, provided management has a contractual or other basis to demonstrate that influence.

U.S. GAAP and IFRS require firms to account for minority, active investments, generally those where the investor owns between 20% and 50%, using the **equity method**. Under the equity method, the investor recognizes as revenue (expense) each period its share of the net income (loss) of the investee. The investor recognizes dividends received from the investee as a return (reduction) of investment, not as income.

Equity Method: Rationale

To understand the rationale for the equity method, review the accounting for available-for-sale marketable securities, discussed in **Chapter 12**. P measures its investments in available-for-sale

---

[1]Accounting Principles Board, *Opinion No. 18,* "The Equity Method of Accounting for Investments in Common Stock," 1971 (**Codification Topic 323**); International Accounting Standards Board, *International Accounting Standard 28,* "Investments in Associates," 1989.

[2]Financial Accounting Standards Board, *Interpretation No. 35,* "Criteria for Applying the Equity Method of Accounting for Investments in Common Stock," 1981 (**Codification Topic 323**).

[3]Financial Accounting Standards Board, *Statement of Financial Accounting Standards No. 94,* "Consolidation of All Majority-owned Subsidiaries," 1987 (**Codification Topic 810**); International Accounting Standards Board, *International Accounting Standard 28,* "Investments in Associates," 1989.

marketable securities at fair value on the balance sheet and recognizes income only when it receives a dividend (revenue) or sells some of the securities at a gain or loss. (P recognizes unrealized changes in the fair value of available-for-sale securities in other comprehensive income, not in earnings.) Suppose, as often happens, that S follows a policy of financing its own operations using assets generated through the retention of earnings, consistently declaring dividends less than its net income or no dividends at all. The fair value of S's shares will probably increase to reflect this retention of assets, but P reports income only from the dividends it receives—the increase in the fair value of S's common stock will not appear in earnings until P realizes the fair value increase. Because P, by assumption, exerts significant influence over S, it can affect S's dividend policy, which in turn affects P's net income. For example, if P would like to increase its income for a particular period, it can pressure S to raise S's dividend for the period or pay a special dividend. When P can so easily manage its own net income (via influencing the dividend policy of S), measuring its investment in S at fair value and reporting unrealized gains and losses in other comprehensive income will not reasonably reflect P's net income from investing in S. The rationale for the equity method is that it better measures an investor's income from investing activities when, because of its ownership interest, it can exert significant influence over the operations and dividend policy of the investee.

EQUITY METHOD: PROCEDURES

The equity method records the initial purchase of an investment at acquisition cost, just as for minority, passive investments. Each period, P treats as revenue its share of the periodic earnings,[4] not the dividends, of S. P treats dividends declared by S as a reduction of P's Investment in Stock of S account.

Example 5 Suppose that P acquires 30% of the outstanding shares of S for $600,000. The entry to record the acquisition is as follows:

(1) Investment in Stock of S 600,000
 Cash   600,000

Assets	=	Liabilities	+	Shareholders' Equity	(Class.)
+600,000					
−600,000					

Investment in 30% of the common shares of Company S.

P typically acquires an investment in S by buying previously issued shares of S from other investors. S does not make a journal entry to reflect P's acquisition of some of its shares.

Between the time of the acquisition and the end of P's next accounting period, S reports earnings of $80,000. P, using the equity method, records the following journal entry:

(2) Investment in Stock of S 24,000
 Equity in Earnings of Affiliate   24,000

Assets	=	Liabilities	+	Shareholders' Equity	(Class.)
+24,000				+24,000	IncSt → RE

To record 30% of the earnings of S accounted for using the equity method; $24,000 = 0.30 × $80,000.

The Equity in Earnings of Affiliate account is a revenue account.[5] Firms that apply IFRS more commonly use an alternative title, Equity in Earnings of Associate (or Associated Companies).

---

[4]If the earnings of the investee include profit or loss from transactions between the investor and investee, the investor eliminates these amounts from earnings before accruing its share of the investee's earnings. We do not illustrate this refinement here.

[5]In this example, S has earnings of $80,000. If, instead, S had a loss of $20,000, P would make an entry debiting Equity in Loss of Affiliate and crediting Investment in Stock of S for $6,000 (= 0.30 × $20,000). That is, just as S's earnings increase P's income, so too do its losses decrease P's income.

If S declares and pays a dividend of $30,000 to holders of its common stock, P receives $9,000 (= 0.30 × $30,000) and records the following journal entry:

---

(3) Cash.   9,000
    Investment in Stock of S.   9,000

Assets	=	Liabilities	+	Shareholders' Equity	(Class.)
+9,000					
−9,000					

To record 30% of the dividend declared and paid by S, accounted for using the equity method.

P records income earned by S as an increase in investment, while the dividend returns part of the investment and decreases the Investment in Stock of S account.

Hint: To understand journal entry **(3)**, which shows a credit to an asset account by the investor when the investee company pays a dividend, consider an ordinary savings account at a bank. Assume that you put $600,000 in a savings account, that later the bank adds interest of 4% (or $24,000) to the account, and that still later you withdraw $9,000 from the savings account. You can record journal entries **(1)** through **(3)** for these three events, with slight changes in the account titles: Investment in Stock of S changes to Savings Account, and Equity in Earnings of Affiliate changes to Interest Revenue. The cash withdrawal of $9,000 reduces the amount invested in the savings account. Similarly, the payment of a cash dividend by an investee accounted for with the equity method reduces the investor's investment because it reduces the investee's retained earnings. The investor, P, owns a sufficiently large percentage of the voting shares that it can often require S to pay a dividend, just as you can require the savings bank to remit cash to you almost whenever you choose.

Suppose that S reports earnings of $100,000 and pays dividends of $40,000 during the next accounting period. P's entries are as follows:

---

(4) Investment in Stock of S.   30,000
    Equity in Earnings of S   30,000

Assets	=	Liabilities	+	Shareholders' Equity	(Class.)
+30,000				+30,000	IncSt → RE

To record 30% of the earnings of S, accounted for using the equity method; $30,000 = 0.30 × $100,000.

---

(5) Cash.   12,000
    Investment in Stock of S.   12,000

Assets	=	Liabilities	+	Shareholders' Equity	(Class.)
+12,000					
−12,000					

To record 30% of the dividend declared and paid by S, accounted for using the equity method; $12,000 = 0.30 × $40,000.

P's Investment in Stock of S account now has a balance of $633,000 as follows:

	Investment in Stock of S		
(1)	600,000	9,000	**(3)**
(2)	24,000	12,000	**(5)**
(4)	30,000		
Bal.	**633,000**		

Assume now that P sells one-fourth of its investment in S for $165,000. The entry is as follows:

(6) Cash	165,000	
Investment in Stock of S		158,250
Gain on Sale of Investment in Stock of S		6,750

Assets	=	Liabilities	+	Shareholders' Equity	(Class.)
+165,000				+6,750	IncSt → RE
−158,250					

To record the sale of one-fourth of the investment in S. The balance sheet carrying value of the investment sold is $158,250 = 1/4 × $633,000.

After the sale, the balance in the Investment in Stock of S account is $474,750, as follows:

Investment in Stock of S

(1)	600,000	9,000	(3)	
(2)	24,000	12,000	(5)	
(4)	30,000			
Bal. 633,000				
		158,250	(6)	
Bal. 474,750				

Excess Purchase Price on Acquisition of Equity Method Investment

P's investment in S represents a proportionate share (in this case, 30%) of the shareholders' equity of S. P may pay more than the carrying value for this investment. That is, P's payment for S may exceed its 30% interest in the balance sheet carrying value of the net assets (= assets − liabilities), or shareholders' equity, of S at the date of acquisition. For example, assume that when P acquired 30% of S's common shares for $600,000, S's total shareholders' equity was $1.5 million. P's cost exceeds the carrying value of the net assets acquired by $150,000 [= $600,000 − (0.30 × $1,500,000)]. P may pay this premium because the fair values of S's net assets differ from their carrying values, or because of unrecorded assets (for example, trade secrets).

The investor's accounting for the excess purchase price embedded in the Investment in Stock of S account is similar to the treatment of an excess purchase price in a business combination. As **Chapter 9** discusses, the investor identifies any recorded assets and liabilities with fair values that differ from their carrying values, as well as any unrecorded assets and liabilities. The investor attributes the excess purchase price to these assets and liabilities, based on the investor's proportionate ownership interest, and any remaining excess purchase price to goodwill. For example, assume that P attributes the $150,000 excess purchase price in the preceding example as follows: $100,000 to remeasure buildings and equipment to fair value and $50,000 to goodwill. P does not reclassify this excess out of its Investment in Stock of S account to Buildings and Equipment and to Goodwill. However, P must amortize (or depreciate) any amount attributed to assets with limited lives. Thus, P must depreciate the $100,000 attributed to buildings and equipment over their remaining useful lives. U.S. GAAP and IFRS do not permit the investor to amortize the excess purchase price attributed to goodwill and other assets with indefinite lives. Instead, the investor must test the investment account annually for possible impairment. Impairment occurs when the balance sheet carrying value exceeds the fair value of the investment. The investor applies the impairment test to its investment in the investee, not to the investee's individual assets and liabilities.

Recognizing the Investor's Share of the Investee's Other Comprehensive Income

In addition to recognizing the investor's share of the investee's net income, the investor also recognizes its share of the investee's other comprehensive income.[6] The inves-

---

[6]Financial Accounting Standards Board, *Statement of Financial Accounting Standards No. 130,* "Reporting Comprehensive Income," 1997, par. 121 (**Codification Topic 220**).

tor can combine its share of the elements of other comprehensive income of the investee with similar items arising from its own operations. For instance, in the preceding example assume that S's other comprehensive income during the first period is as follows:

Unrealized Holding Gains from Marketable Securities	$ 3,000
Unrealized Losses from Cash Flow Hedges	(2,000)
Other Comprehensive Income	$ 1,000

P would make the following entry to recognize its share of the items of other comprehensive income of S, based on its 30% ownership of S.

Investment in Stock of S	300	
Unrealized Holding Losses from Cash Flow Hedges (Other Comprehensive Income)	600	
Unrealized Holding Gains from Marketable Securities (Other Comprehensive Income)		900

Assets	=	Liabilities	+	Shareholders' Equity	(Class.)
+300				−600	OCI → AOCI
				+900	OCI → AOCI

To recognize P's share of S's Other Comprehensive Income.

Fair Value Option for Equity Method Investments Firms can elect to report certain qualifying financial assets and financial liabilities at fair value each period and recognize unrealized holding gains and losses in net income.[7] **Chapter 10** discusses the application of the fair value option to notes and bonds, and **Chapter 12** discusses its application to marketable securities and derivatives. Firms may likewise apply the fair value option to certain equity method investments.

Summary of Accounting for Investments Under the Equity Method On the balance sheet, an investment accounted for with the equity method appears among noncurrent assets. The amount shown generally equals the acquisition cost of the shares, plus P's share of S's undistributed earnings (or losses) since the date P acquired the shares, plus or minus amortization of any excess cost at the date of acquisition attributable to assets with limited lives. On the income statement, P reports each period its share of S's income (or loss) as revenue (or expense), as well as any amortization of excess cost. P also recognizes its share of the investee's other comprehensive income. The accounting method that the investor, P, uses does not affect the separate financial statements of the investee, S.

EQUITY METHOD DISCLOSURES

Exhibit 13.1 presents the note from Scania's financial statements concerning its investments in associated companies and joint ventures. Scania accounts for both investments using the equity method. We discuss the accounting for joint ventures later in this chapter.

The first panel shows the names, ownership percentages, and the balance sheet carrying values of Scania's investments in four associated companies and two joint ventures. The second panel shows the reasons for changes in those carrying values. The carrying value of the investments increased for Scania's share of the net income of each associate and decreased for dividends. Scania also reports the effects of exchange rate changes. Note that Scania aggregates other items, including in a single line impairment losses, acquisitions, capital contributions, and divestments. In 2006, for example, Scania established its joint venture with Cummins and contributed SEK83 million in return for an ownership interest; because this

---

[7]Financial Accounting Standards Board, *Statement of Financial Accounting Standards No. 159,* "The Fair Value Option for Financial Assets and Financial Liabilities," 2007 (**Codification Topic 825**); International Accounting Standards Board, *International Accounting Standard 39,* "Financial Instruments: Recognition and Measurements," revised 2003.

EXHIBIT 13.1 Scania's Note on Investments in Associated Companies and Joint Ventures

Associated Company or Joint Venture/Country of Registration	Ownership %	Value of Scania's Share in Consolidated Financial Statements		
		2006	2005	2004
Cummins-Scania High Pressure Injection L.L.C., USA	30	23	32	30
BitsData AB, Sweden	25	4	3	1
ScaMadrid S.A., Spain	49	21	22	19
ScaValencia S. A., Spain	26	14	13	16
Holdings in Associated Companies		62	70	66
Cummins-Scania XPI, USA	50	83	—	—
Other	1	3	1	—
Holdings in Joint Ventures		86	1	—
Holdings in Associated Companies and Joint Ventures		148	71	66

	2006	2005	2004
Carrying Amount, 1 January	71	66	66
Acquisitions, Capital Contributions, Divestments, Impairment Losses[1]	83	−6	−4
Reclassifications	—	1	—
Exchange Rate Differences	−5	7	−3
Share in Income for the Year	5	8	8
Dividends	−6	−5	−1
Carrying Amount, 31 December	148	71	66

[1]SEK83 million refers to a capital contribution to Cummins-Scania XPI, which Cummins and Scania started in 2006. Scania has entered into a joint venture with Cummins related to development projects.

Share of Assets, Liabilities, and Income	2006	2005	2004
Noncurrent Assets	104	47	46
Current Assets	120	76	73
Noncurrent Liabilities	11	14	16
Current Liabilities	65	37	34
Scania's Share of Net Assets	148	72	69
Sales Revenue	736	464	455
Income After Financial Items	7	11	12
Taxes	−2	−3	−4
Net Income for the Year	5	8	8

amount fully accounts for the sum of impairment losses, acquisitions, capital contributions, and divestments, we know that Scania recorded no impairments, acquisitions, or divestments in that year. The third panel shows Scania's share of the net assets and net income from its investments in associated companies and joint ventures. The amounts for net income on the last line of the third panel match the amounts that Scania discloses in the second panel for its share of income each year. The amounts for Scania's share of the net assets do not equal the carrying value of the investments each year, perhaps because Scania recognized impairment losses on its investments that the associated companies did not recognize on their books. The disclosures in the third panel indicate the mixture of current and noncurrent assets and liabilities of Scania's associated companies and joint ventures, as well as sufficient information to compute the pretax and after-tax profit margins of these other entities.

PROBLEM 13.1 for Self-Study

Journal entries to apply the equity method for long-term investments in securities. Exhibit 13.2 summarizes data about the minority, active investments of Equity Investing Group. Assume that any excess of acquisition cost over the carrying value of the net assets acquired relates to equipment with a 10-year remaining life on January 1, 2008. Prepare the journal entries to do the following:

a. Record the acquisition of these securities on January 1, 2008.

b. Apply the equity method for 2008.

c. Apply the equity method for 2009.

d. Record the sale of Security E on January 2, 2010, for $190,000.

EXHIBIT 13.2	Equity Investing Group (Problem 13.1 for Self-Study)

Security	Date Acquired	Acquisition Cost	Ownership Percentage	Carrying Value of Net Assets on January 1, 2008	Earnings (Loss) 2008	Earnings (Loss) 2009	Dividends 2008	Dividends 2009
D	1/1/2008	$ 80,000	40%	$200,000	$ 40,000	$ 50,000	$10,000	$12,000
E	1/1/2008	190,000	30	500,000	120,000	(40,000)	30,000	—
F	1/1/2008	200,000	20	800,000	200,000	50,000	60,000	60,000

MAJORITY, ACTIVE INVESTMENTS

When one firm, P, owns more than 50% of the voting stock of another company, S, P can control the activities of S in terms of both broad policy making and day-to-day operations. Common usage refers to the majority investor as the **parent** and to the majority-owned company as the **subsidiary**. U.S. GAAP and IFRS require the parent to combine the financial statements of majority-owned companies with those of the parent in **consolidated financial statements**.[8]

REASONS FOR LEGALLY SEPARATE CORPORATIONS

Business firms have several reasons for preferring to operate as a group of legally separate corporations, rather than as a single entity. From the standpoint of the parent company, the more important reasons for maintaining legally separate subsidiary companies include the following:

1. **To reduce the parent's legal or operational risk.** Separate corporations may mine raw materials, transport them to a manufacturing plant, produce the product, and sell the finished product to the public. If any one part (subsidiary) of the total process proves to be unprofitable or inefficient, losses from insolvency will fall only on the owners and creditors of the one subsidiary corporation. (Some drug firms acquire subsidiaries to make and market medical products in the hope that if something goes wrong in future years, the parent firm will not be liable for harm to the subsidiary's customers. Individuals who believe the subsidiary's products have harmed them often sue the parent and sometimes succeed in obtaining legal relief from the parent.)

2. **To reduce the costs of dealing with jurisdiction-specific differences in corporate laws and tax rules.** An organization that does business in a number of localities faces overlapping and inconsistent taxation and regulations. Organizing legally separate corporations to

---

[8]Financial Accounting Standards Board, *Statement of Financial Accounting Standards No. 94*, "Consolidation of All Majority-Owned Subsidiaries," 1987 (**Codification Topic 810**); International Accounting Standards Board, *International Accounting Standard 27*, "Consolidated and Separate Financial Statements," revised 2003.

conduct operations in the various locales can reduce the administrative costs of dealing with location-specific rules.

3. **To expand or diversify.** A firm may enter a new line of business, or expand an existing line, by acquiring a controlling interest in another company's voting stock. This approach may be faster, less expensive, and less risky than constructing a new plant or starting a new line of business.

4. **To reduce the costs of divesting assets.** Firms generally save costs if they sell the common stock of a subsidiary rather than trying to sell each of its assets separately. In addition, a sale of shares transfers all known and, perhaps, unknown liabilities to a buyer.

PURPOSE OF CONSOLIDATED STATEMENTS

For various reasons, then, a single **economic entity** may exist in the form of a parent and several legally separate subsidiaries, often referred to as an *affiliated group*. (General Electric Company, for example, comprises more than 50 large, legally separate companies.) A consolidation of the financial statements of the parent and each of its subsidiaries presents the results of operations, financial position, and cash flows of an affiliated group of companies under the control of a parent as if the group of companies composed a single entity. The parent and each subsidiary are legally separate entities that operate as one centrally controlled economic entity. Consolidated financial statements generally provide more useful information to the shareholders of the parent corporation than do separate financial statements for the parent and each subsidiary.

Consolidated financial statements also provide more helpful information than does the equity method, because they include all the assets, liabilities, revenues, and expenses of the controlled subsidiaries, not just the investment account that represents the parent's investment in the subsidiary's common shareholders' equity and not just the parent's share of the subsidiary's net income. The parent, because of its voting interest, can control the use of *all* of the subsidiary's assets. The parent needs to own only a majority of the voting stock, not necessarily 100%, to control the use of 100% of the subsidiary's assets. Consolidation of the individual assets, liabilities, revenues, and expenses of both the parent and the subsidiary provides a more realistic picture of the operations and financial position of the single economic entity.

The separate financial statements of the parent and its subsidiaries form the base for consolidated financial statements. In a legal sense, therefore, consolidated statements supplement, and do not replace, the separate statements of the individual corporations. Published annual reports may contain only the consolidated statements.

Example 6 Ford, General Electric, IBM, and Scania, among others, have wholly owned finance subsidiaries that make loans to customers who want to purchase the products of the parent company. The parent company consolidates the financial statements of these subsidiaries. These subsidiaries have billions of dollars of assets, mostly receivables; consolidation combines the parent's assets—largely noncurrent manufacturing plant and equipment—with the more liquid assets of the finance subsidiary. Although a focus on liquidity analysis would suggest preparing separate statements for the manufacturing parent and for the financial subsidiary, these entities in fact operate as a single integrated unit so that consolidated financial statements more accurately depict their combined operations. However, nothing prevents the separate display of the finance subsidiary's financial statements; General Electric follows this practice.

Example 7 A major mining company owns a mining subsidiary in South America, where the government enforces stringent control over cash payments outside the country. The parent cannot control all the assets of the subsidiary, despite owning a majority of the voting shares, so it does not prepare consolidated statements with the subsidiary.

THE PURCHASE TRANSACTION

In a business combination, one corporation either

1. Acquires the assets and assumes the liabilities of another corporation, or

2. Acquires all, or a majority, of another corporation's common shares and thereby acquires a controlling interest in the net assets of the other corporation.

In both cases, U.S. GAAP and IFRS require firms to account for the business combination using the **acquisition**, or **purchase, method**.[9] The acquisition method views a business combination as conceptually identical to the purchase of any single asset (for example, inventory or a machine). Application of the acquisition method involves two steps:

1. Measure the identifiable tangible and intangible assets and liabilities of the acquired company at their fair values. In some cases the acquired firm did not recognize identifiable assets or liabilities in its accounting records. For example, the acquired company may own patents and trademarks not recorded on its balance sheet. The acquirer would recognize those assets at their fair values.

2. The acquirer compares the fair value of the cash, common stock, or other consideration given with the fair value of the identifiable assets less liabilities acquired. The excess of the fair value of the consideration over the fair value of the acquired firm's identifiable assets net of identifiable liabilities is **goodwill**. If the fair value of the identifiable assets less liabilities exceeds the fair value of the consideration, the excess is a gain from a **bargain purchase**, which the purchaser immediately includes in net income.

PROBLEM 13.2 for Self-Study

Financial statement effects of the acquisition method. Exhibit 13.3 presents balance sheet data for Powell Corporation and Steele Corporation as of January 1, 2008. On this date, Powell Corporation exchanges 2,700 shares of its common stock, selling for $20 per share, for all of the individual assets and liabilities of Steele Corporation.

a. Give the journal entry on the books of Powell Corporation to record the acquisition of the assets and liabilities of Steele Corporation.

b. Prepare a balance sheet for Powell Corporation after the acquisition of Steele Corporation on January 1, 2008, using the acquisition method.

EXHIBIT 13.3	Powell Corporation and Steele Corporation Financial Statement Data for January 1, 2008 (Problem 13.2 for Self-Study)		
	Carrying Value		**Fair Value**
	Powell Corp.	**Steele Corp.**	**Steele Corp.**
ASSETS			
Current Assets	$10,000	$ 7,000	$ 7,000
Property, Plant, and Equipment (net).........	30,000	18,000	23,000
Goodwill	—	—	40,000
Total Assets	$40,000	$25,000	$70,000
LIABILITIES AND SHAREHOLDERS' EQUITY			
Liabilities	$25,000	$16,000	$16,000
Common Stock ($1 par value)..............	1,000	1,000	1,000
Additional Paid-In Capital	9,000	5,000	5,000
Retained Earnings	5,000	3,000	3,000
Unrecorded Excess of Fair Value over Carrying Value	—	—	45,000
Total Liabilities and Shareholders' Equity	$40,000	$25,000	$70,000

[9]Financial Accounting Standards Board, *Statement of Financial Accounting Standards No. 141R (revised 2007)*, "Business Combinations," 2007 (**Codification Topic 805**); International Accounting Standards Board, *International Financial Reporting Standard 3*, "Business Combinations," revised 2008.

Understanding Consolidated Financial Statements

Recording the Acquisition In **Problem 13.2 for Self-Study**, Powell Corporation acquired the assets and liabilities of Steele Corporation and recognized them at their fair values. After the acquisition, the assets of Steele Corporation would consist of only the consideration received from Powell Corporation. Steele Corporation might then distribute this consideration to its shareholders and no longer remain a legally separate corporation. In contrast, firms prepare consolidated financial statements when a firm purchases either all or a majority of the common stock of the acquired firm. In this case, the acquiring firm records the acquisition in the Investment in Stock account on its own (parent company) books in the same net amount as it would had it purchased the identifiable assets net of liabilities. Thus, Powell Corporation records its investment in Steele Corporation as follows:

January 1, 2009

Investment in Steele Corporation	54,000	
Common Stock.		2,700
Additional Paid-In Capital		51,300

Assets	=	Liabilities	+	Shareholders' Equity	(Class.)
+54,000				+2,700	ContriCap
				+51,300	ContriCap

The first two columns of **Exhibit 13.4** present balance sheets of Powell Corporation and Steele Corporation on January 1, 2008, immediately after Powell Corporation's acquisition of Steele Corporation's common stock.

Powell Corporation's balance sheet includes the Investment in Steele Corporation account measured on January 1, 2008, at the consideration given, equal to the fair value of the identifiable net assets of Steele Corporation plus the $40,000 of goodwill, or $54,000 in total.

Preparing a Consolidated Balance Sheet at Date of Acquisition To prepare a consolidated balance sheet with Steele Corporation on January 1, 2008, Powell Corporation would construct a **consolidation work sheet** like that in **Exhibit 13.4**. The first two columns show the amounts from the separate balance sheets of each company. Adding these amounts together would double-count both the net assets and the shareholders' equity of the two entities. Powell Corporation's balance sheet contains an asset for its investment in the net assets of Steele Corporation. The books of Steele Corporation contain the individual net assets. Likewise, Powell

EXHIBIT 13.4	Consolidated Work Sheet for Powell Corporation and Steele Corporation January 1, 2008

	Powell Corp.	Steele Corp.	Debit	Credit	Consolidated
ASSETS					
Current Assets	$10,000	$ 7,000			$ 17,000
Property, Plant, and Equipment (net)	30,000	18,000	5,000		53,000
Investment in Powell Corp.	54,000			54,000	—
Goodwill	—	—	40,000		40,000
Total Assets	$94,000	$25,000			$110,000
LIABILITIES AND SHAREHOLDERS' EQUITY					
Liabilities	$25,000	$16,000			$ 41,000
Common Stock ($1 par value)	3,700	1,000	1,000		3,700
Additional Paid-In Capital	60,300	5,000	5,000		60,300
Retained Earnings	5,000	3,000	3,000		5,000
Total Liabilities and Shareholders' Equity	$94,000	$25,000			$110,000

Corporation's shareholders' equity provides the equity financing for its assets, one of which is its investment in Steele Corporation, while Steele Corporation's balance sheet includes the shareholders' equity owned by Powell Corporation. Thus, to prepare a consolidated balance sheet that reflects the assets, liabilities, and shareholders' equity as if the two companies were one economic entity, we must eliminate the double-counting. We make this elimination entry on the consolidation work sheet, not on the books of either company. This entry involves eliminating the Investment in Steele Corporation of $54,000, the shareholders' equity accounts of Steele Corporation in the amount of $9,000 (= $1,000 + $5,000 + $3,000), and allocating the difference of $45,000 (= $54,000 − $9,000) to property, plant, and equipment (net) for $5,000 and to goodwill for $40,000. The entry on the consolidation work sheet is as follows:

January 1, 2008

Common Stock	1,000
Additional Paid-In Capital	5,000
Retained Earnings	3,000
Property, Plant, and Equipment (net)	5,000
Goodwill	40,000
Investment in Steele Corporation	54,000

Assets	=	Liabilities	+	Shareholders' Equity	(Class.)
+5,000				−1,000	ContriCap
+40,000				−5,000	ContriCap
−54,000				−3,000	RE

Work sheet entry to eliminate the investment account and the shareholders' equity accounts of Steele Corporation, and to allocate the excess purchase price to property, plant, and equipment (net) and goodwill.

The amounts in the Consolidated column of the work sheet are identical to those in **Exhibit 13.9** in the solution to **Problem 13.2 for Self-Study**, in which Powell Corporation acquires the assets and liabilities of Steele Corporation directly.

Accounting for the Investment Subsequent to the Date of Acquisition

Powell Corporation will account for its investment in Steele Corporation subsequent to the acquisition on its separate-company books using the equity method. Assume that during 2008, Steele Corporation's net income is $2,500 and that it declares and pays a dividend of $400. Also assume that the average remaining life of Steele Corporation's depreciable assets at the acquisition date was 10 years. Powell Corporation makes the following entries on its books to apply the equity method during 2008:

December 31, 2008

Investment in Steele Corporation	2,500
Equity in Earnings of Steele Corporation	2,500

Assets	=	Liabilities	+	Shareholders' Equity	(Class.)
+2,500				+2,500	IncSt → RE

To recognize Powell Corporation's share of Steele Corporation's earnings.

December 31, 2008

Cash	400
Investment in Steele Corporation	400

Assets	=	Liabilities	+	Shareholders' Equity	(Class.)
+400					
−400					

To recognize Powell Corporation's share of the dividends of Steele Corporation.

December 31, 2008

Depreciation Expense	500	
Investment in Steele Corporation		500

Assets	=	Liabilities	+	Shareholders' Equity	(Class.)
−500				−500	IncSt → RE

To record additional depreciation expense from the excess of fair value over carrying value of property, plant, and equipment of Steele Corporation on January 1, 2008; $500 = $5,000/10.

The Investment in Steele Corporation account has a balance of $55,600 (= $54,000 + $2,500 − $400 − $500) on December 31, 2008.

Preparing Consolidated Financial Statements Subsequent to the Date of Acquisition Exhibit 13.5 presents information from the separate-company accounting records of Powell Corporation in column (1) and Steele Corporation in column (2) on

EXHIBIT 13.5 Illustrative Data for Preparation of Consolidated Financial Statements

	Powell Corp. (1)	Steele Corp. (2)	Combined (3)	Consolidated (4)
CONDENSED BALANCE SHEET ON DECEMBER 31, 2008				
Assets				
Current Assets	$ 12,000	$ 8,200	$ 20,200	$ 14,200
Property, Plant, and Equipment (net)	35,400	20,000	55,400	59,900
Investment in Steele Corp.	55,600	—	55,600	—
Goodwill	—	—	—	40,000
Total Assets	$103,000	$28,200	$131,200	$114,100
Liabilities and Shareholders' Equity				
Liabilities	$ 26,500	$17,100	$ 43,600	$ 37,600
Common Stock ($1 par value)	3,700	1,000	4,700	3,700
Additional Paid-In Capital	60,300	5,000	65,300	60,300
Retained Earnings	12,500	5,100	17,600	12,500
Total Liabilities and Shareholders' Equity	$103,000	$28,200	$131,200	$114,100
CONDENSED INCOME STATEMENT FOR 2008				
Revenues				
Sales	$200,000	$50,000	$250,000	$230,000
Equity in Earnings of Steele Corporation	2,500	—	2,500	—
Total Revenues	$202,500	$50,000	$252,500	$230,000
Expenses				
Cost of Goods Sold	$125,000	$30,000	$155,000	$135,000
Selling and Administrative	50,000	11,800	61,800	61,800
Interest	2,000	1,500	3,500	3,500
Income Taxes	10,200	4,200	14,400	14,400
Total Expenses	$187,200	$47,500	$234,700	$214,700
Net Income	$ 15,300	$ 2,500	$ 17,800	$ 15,300
Dividend Declared	(7,800)	(400)	(8,200)	(7,800)
Increase in Retained Earnings for the Year	$ 7,500	$ 2,100	$ 9,600	$ 7,500

December 31, 2008. Column **(3)** combines the amounts from the separate-company accounting records of Powell Corporation and Steele Corporation. These amounts do not represent the correct amounts for consolidated statements for the reasons discussed next. Column **(4)** shows the correct consolidated amounts. We use **Exhibit 13.5** to gain additional understanding of consolidated financial statements. We consider three topics:

1. The need for intercompany eliminations.
2. The meaning of consolidated net income.
3. The nature of noncontrolling interest.

Need for Intercompany Eliminations Corporation laws typically require each legally separate corporation to maintain its own accounting records. Thus, during the accounting period, each corporation will record transactions of that entity with all other entities (both affiliated and nonaffiliated). At the end of the period, each corporation will prepare its own financial statements. The consolidation, or combining, of these financial statements involves summing the amounts for various financial statement items across the separate company statements and then adjusting these sums to eliminate double-counting resulting from **intercompany transactions**.

The guiding principle of consolidation procedures is that consolidated financial statements reflect the results that the affiliated group would report if it were a single company. Consolidated financial statements reflect the transactions between the consolidated group of entities and others outside the consolidated group. Thus, if one subsidiary in a consolidated group sells goods to another, the consolidation procedure must remove from the financial statements the effects of this intercompany transaction.

Eliminating Double-Counting of Intercompany Payables Separate company records indicate that $6,000 of Powell Corporation's receivables represent amounts receivable from Steele Corporation. Column **(3)** of **Exhibit 13.5** counts the current assets underlying this transaction twice: once as a receivable on Powell Corporation's books and a second time as cash that Steele Corporation will use to pay Powell Corporation. Also, the liability shown on Steele Corporation's books appears in the combined amount for liabilities in column **(3)**. The consolidated group does not owe this $6,000 to an outsider. To eliminate double-counting on the asset side and to report liabilities at the amounts payable to outsiders, the consolidation process eliminates $6,000 from the amounts for receivables and liabilities in column **(3)**. The work sheet entry is as follows:

December 31, 2008

Liabilities	6,000	
Current Assets		6,000

Assets	=	Liabilities	+	Shareholders' Equity	(Class.)
−6,000		−6,000			

To eliminate intercompany receivable and payable.

In column **(4)**, the consolidated Current Assets, which include receivables, and consolidated Liabilities, which include the payable to Powell Corporation, both total $6,000 less than their sum in column **(3)**.

If a parent or subsidiary invests in bonds or long-term notes issued by the other, the consolidation process eliminates the investment and related liability in the consolidated balance sheet, and eliminates the borrower's interest expense and the lender's interest revenue from the consolidated income statement.

Eliminating Double-Counting of Investment Powell Corporation's balance sheet shows an asset, Investment in Steele Corporation, which represents Powell Corporation's investment in Steele Corporation's net assets. The subsidiary's balance sheet shows its individual assets and liabilities. When column **(3)** adds the two balance sheets, the sum shows both Powell Corporation's investment in Steele Corporation's assets and Steele Corporation's actual assets. The consolidation process eliminates Powell Corporation's account, Investment in Steele Corporation, $55,600, from the sum of the balance sheets. The work sheet entry is as follows:

December 31, 2008

Common Stock	1,000	
Additional Paid-In Capital	5,000	
Retained Earnings	3,000	
Equity in Earnings of Steele Corporation	2,500	
Property, Plant, and Equipment (net)	4,500	
Goodwill	40,000	
Dividend Declared		400
Investment in Steele Corporation		55,600

Assets	=	Liabilities	+	Shareholders' Equity	(Class.)
+4,500				−1,000	ContriCap
+40,000				−5,000	ContriCap
−55,600				−3,000	RE
				−2,500	IncSt → RE
				+400	RE

To eliminate the Investment in Steele Corporation account and the shareholders' equity accounts of Steele Corporation, and recognize the unamortized difference between the fair values of Steele Corporation's net assets at acquisition and their carrying values at that time.

This elimination entry is similar to the work sheet entry made on January 1, 2008, at the time of the acquisition, except for the following:

1. The balance in the Investment in Steele Corporation account changed during 2008 as a result of applying the equity method. We eliminate the Investment in Steele Corporation account on Powell Corporation's books and the related shareholders' equity accounts on Steele Corporation's books. The latter include Common Stock, Additional Paid-In Capital, Retained Earnings, and Dividends Declared. We also eliminate the Equity in Earnings of Steele Corporation account of $2,500. Steele Corporation's records show individual revenues and expenses that net to $2,500. When column **(3)** sums the revenues and expenses of the two companies, it counts that income twice. The consolidation process eliminates the account Equity in Earnings of Steele Corporation. Likewise, Steele Corporation paid the dividend it declared to Powell Corporation, not to an outsider, so we eliminate the intercompany dividend.

2. The amount added to property, plant, and equipment (net) equals the difference between the fair value and the carrying value of these assets on January 1, 2008, of $5,000 less one year of amortization of $500.

3. Because Powell Corporation does not amortize goodwill, its carrying value on December 31, 2008, is the same as on January 1, 2008, $40,000. Powell Corporation will test the amount of goodwill for possible impairment. We assume no such impairment in this example.

Eliminating Intercompany Sales   The consolidation process eliminates intercompany transactions from the sum of the income statements so that the consolidated income statement presents only the consolidated entity's transactions with outsiders. Consider intercompany sales. Separate company records indicate that Powell Corporation sold merchandise at its cost of $20,000 to Steele Corporation for $20,000 during the year. None of this inventory remains in Steele Corporation's inventory on December 31, 2008. Therefore, the merchandise inventory sold appears in Sales Revenue both on Powell Corporation's books (sale to Steele Corporation) and on Steele Corporation's books (sale to outsiders). Thus, column **(3)** overstates sales of the consolidated entity to outsiders. Likewise, Cost of Goods Sold of both companies in column **(3)** counts twice the cost of the goods sold, first by Powell Corporation to Steele Corporation and then by Steele Corporation to outsiders. The consolidation process eliminates the effects of the intercompany sale with the following work sheet entry:

December 31, 2008

| Sales .... | 20,000 | |
| Cost of Goods Sold .... | | 20,000 |

Assets	=	Liabilities	+	Shareholders' Equity	(Class.)
				−20,000	IncSt → RE
				+20,000	IncSt → RE

To eliminate intercompany sale of merchandise.

A Realistic Complication We simplified the example by having Powell Corporation sell the goods to Steele Corporation at cost, $20,000, so that you can easily see that the consolidation process reduces both sales and cost of goods sold by $20,000. However, sales revenue usually exceeds cost of goods sold. Assume now that Powell Corporation sold goods costing $15,000 to Steele Corporation for $20,000, and Steele Corporation later sold the goods to outsiders for $23,000. The consolidation process eliminates the intercompany sale of $20,000 from both the combined sales and the combined cost of goods sold. The transactions remaining in the consolidated income statement will be Steele Corporation's sales to outsiders for $23,000 and Powell Corporation's cost of goods sold of $15,000, just as if they were a single company selling, for $23,000, goods that cost $15,000.

It is possible that Steele Corporation has not yet, by the end of the accounting period, sold all the goods it bought from Powell Corporation. In that case, Powell Corporation's single-company income statement contains a profit on the goods remaining in inventory, which the consolidation must eliminate. We do not illustrate this complication.

Consolidated Income The amount of consolidated net income (or loss) for a period exactly equals the amount that the parent would show on its separate company books if it used the equity method for all its subsidiaries. That is, consolidated net income is as follows:

Parent Company's Net Income from Its Own Activities	+	Parent Company's Share of Subsidiaries' Net Income	−	Profit (or + Loss) on Intercompany Transactions

Powell Corporation used the equity method to account for its investment in Steele Corporation and reported net income for 2008 of $15,300, including $2,500 for Equity in Earnings of Steele Corporation. The work sheet entry to eliminate the Investment in Steele Corporation account eliminated the Equity in Earnings of Steele Corporation account in the amount of $2,500 and replaced it in consolidation with the revenues and expenses of Steele Corporation for 2008 netting to $2,500. A consolidated income statement differs from a parent's income statement using the equity method only in the components presented.

TERMINOLOGY **Note**

Accountants sometimes refer to the equity method as a *one-line consolidation* because the revenues less the expenses of the subsidiary appear in the one account, Equity in Earnings of Subsidiary, and the assets and liabilities of the subsidiary appear on one line, Investment in Subsidiary. Application of the equity method therefore rests on this guiding principle: treat the items in such a way that the parent's net income equals the same amount that it would report if it consolidated the investee firm instead of using the equity method.

Noncontrolling Interest in Consolidated Subsidiary Often, the parent does not own 100% of the voting stock of a consolidated subsidiary. The parent refers to the owners of the remaining shares of voting stock as a **noncontrolling**, or **minority**, **interest**.[10] By virtue

[10]Common practice in the United States has been to use the term *minority interest*. IFRS does not use this term, and U.S. GAAP has eliminated it; however, you may continue to encounter it in financial reports.

of their ownership of shares, these shareholders have provided a portion of the subsidiary's equity financing and have a claim to this portion of the net assets (= total assets − total liabilities) of the subsidiary and this portion of its earnings. Do not confuse this noncontrolling interest in a consolidated subsidiary with a firm's own minority investments, discussed earlier. The noncontrolling interest represents share ownership by others outside the consolidated group. In contrast, a firm's minority investments represent less than 50% ownership of shares of other companies.

The Noncontrolling Interest in Net Assets on the Consolidated Balance Sheet Assume that Powell Corporation acquired 80% of the outstanding stock of Steele Corporation instead of the 100% illustrated to this point. The noncontrolling shareholders own 20% of Steele Corporation.

Powell Corporation, with its controlling voting interest, can direct the use of *all* Steele Corporation's assets and liabilities, not merely the 80% it owns of Steele Corporation's voting shares. The consolidated balance sheet reports the ownership interest of the noncontrolling shareholders in the consolidated, but less-than-wholly-owned, subsidiary as part of shareholders' equity.

The amount of the noncontrolling interest appearing in the balance sheet *at the date of acquisition* differs between U.S. GAAP and IFRS. Under U.S. GAAP, the consolidated balance sheet shows all assets and liabilities at fair value and the noncontrolling interest at its ownership percentage times this fair value.[11] Refer to the information for Steele Corporation on January 1, 2008, in **Exhibit 13.3**. The fair value of the net assets of Steele Corporation is $54,000 (= $70,000 − $16,000). A 20% noncontrolling interest would appear on the consolidated balance sheet at $10,800 (= 0.20 × $54,000) on January 1, 2008.[12]

In contrast, IFRS permits firms a choice: firms can use either the carrying value or the fair value of the subsidiary's net assets as the basis for measuring the noncontrolling interest.[13] Thus, under IFRS, the noncontrolling interest would appear on the balance sheet at either $1,800 [= 0.20 × ($25,000 − $16,000)] or $10,800 as measured under U.S. GAAP.

The consolidated income statement shows all of the parent's and the subsidiary's revenues less all of the parent's and the subsidiary's expenses, plus or minus intercompany sales, expenses, gains, and losses, which equals consolidated income. The consolidated income statement shows the portion of this consolidated income to which the noncontrolling shareholders have a claim, typically an amount equal to the subsidiary's net income multiplied by the noncontrolling shareholders' ownership percentage, and the portion to which the parent company shareholders have a claim.

PROBLEM 13.3 for Self-Study

Understanding consolidation concepts. Exhibit 13.6 presents income statement data, and **Exhibit 13.7** presents balance sheet data for Parent and its 80%-owned Sub. The first two columns in each exhibit show amounts taken from the separate-company accounting records of each firm. The third column sums the amounts in the first two columns. The fourth column shows consolidated amounts for Parent and Sub after making intercompany eliminations.

a. Does the account Investment in Sub (equity method) on the Parent's books include any excess acquisition cost relative to the fair value of the shareholders' equity of Sub?

(continued)

---

[11]Financial Accounting Standards Board, *Statement of Financial Accounting Standards No. 160,* "Noncontrolling Interests in Consolidated Financial Statements," 2007 (**Codification Topic 810**).

[12]U.S. GAAP permits the acquirer to include a control premium in measuring the fair value of the subsidiary and to incorporate a discount for lack of control when measuring the fair value of the noncontrolling interest. Thus, the fair value per share of the controlling and noncontrolling interests may differ. See, Financial Accounting Standards Board, *Statement of Financial Accounting Standards No. 141R,* "Business Combinations," 2007 (**Codification Topic 805**). We do not incorporate this provision in the examples and problems in this book.

[13]International Accounting Standards Board, *International Financial Reporting Standard 3,* "Business Combinations," revised 2008.

EXHIBIT 13.6

Parent and Sub
Income Statement Data for 2008
(Problem 13.3 for Self-Study)

	Parent (1)	Sub (2)	Combined (3) = (1) + (2)	Consolidated (4)
Revenues				
Sales	$4,000	$2,000	$6,000	$5,500
Equity in Earnings of Sub	80	—	80	—
Total Revenues	$4,080	$2,000	$6,080	$5,500
Expenses				
Cost of Goods Sold	$2,690	$1,350	$4,040	$3,540
Selling and Administrative	1,080	480	1,560	1,560
Interest	30	20	50	50
Income Taxes	70	50	120	120
Total Expenses	$3,870	$1,900	$5,770	$5,270
Income Before Noncontrolling Interest	$ 210	$ 100	$ 310	$ 230
Noncontrolling Interest in Earnings of Sub	—	—	—	(20)
Net Income	$ 210	$ 100	$ 310	$ 210

EXHIBIT 13.7

Parent and Sub
Balance Sheet Data, December 31, 2008
(Problem 13.3 for Self-Study)

	Parent (1)	Sub (2)	Combined (3) = (1) + (2)	Consolidated (4)
ASSETS				
Cash	$ 125	$ 60	$ 185	$ 185
Accounts Receivable	550	270	820	795
Inventories	460	210	670	670
Investment in Sub (equity method)	192	—	192	—
Property, Plant, and Equipment (net)	680	380	1,060	1,060
Total Assets	$2,007	$920	$2,927	$2,710
LIABILITIES AND SHAREHOLDERS' EQUITY				
Accounts Payable	$ 370	$170	$ 540	$ 515
Notes Payable	400	250	650	650
Other Current Liabilities	245	60	305	305
Long-Term Debt	300	200	500	500
Total Liabilities	$1,315	$680	$1,995	$1,970
Noncontrolling Interest in Net Assets of Sub	$ —	$ —	$ —	$ 48
Common Stock	200	50	250	200
Retained Earnings	492	190	682	492
Total Shareholders' Equity	$ 692	$240	$ 932	$ 740
Total Liabilities and Shareholders' Equity	$2,007	$920	$2,927	$2,710

b. Suggest four ways in which the data in **Exhibits 13.6** and **13.7** confirm that Parent owns 80% of Sub.

c. Why does the amount for accounts receivable in column **(3)** of **Exhibit 13.7** differ from the amount in column **(4)**?

d. Explain why the account Investment in Sub does not appear on the consolidated balance sheet.

e. Why does the total shareholders' equity of $740 on the consolidated balance sheet exceed the shareholders' equity on Parent's separate-company accounting records of $692?

f. Compute the amount of intercompany sales during the year.

g. Explain why the $80 for Equity in Earnings of Sub does not appear on the consolidated income statement.

h. Why does the Noncontrolling Interest in Earnings of Sub account appear on the consolidated income statement but not on the income statements of either Parent or Sub?

DISCLOSURE OF CONSOLIDATION POLICY

The summary of significant accounting principles, a required part of the financial statement notes, must include a statement about the parent's **consolidation policy**. If an investor does not consolidate a significant majority-owned subsidiary, the notes will disclose that fact.

The notes to the financial statements of Scania describe its accounting for the acquisition of subsidiaries and the preparation of consolidated financial statements.

Consolidated Financial Statements

The consolidated financial statements encompass Scania AB and all subsidiaries. "Subsidiaries" refers to companies in which Scania directly or indirectly owns more than 50% of the voting rights of the shares or otherwise has a controlling influence.

Subsidiaries are reported according to the purchase method of accounting. This means that identifiable assets and liabilities in the acquired company are accounted for at fair values assigned by the purchaser. The acquisition analysis establishes the cost of the shares or business, as well as the fair value on the acquisition date of the company's identifiable assets, debts assumed and contingent liabilities. The cost of shares in subsidiaries or of the business, respectively, consists of the fair values on the transfer date of assets, liabilities that have arisen or are assumed and equity instruments issued as payment in exchange for the acquired net assets as well as transaction costs directly attributable to the acquisition. In case of acquisition of a business in which the acquisition cost exceeds the fair value of the company's identified assets, liabilities assumed and contingent liabilities, the difference is reported as goodwill. When the difference is negative, this is recognized directly in the income statement. Only earnings arising after the date of acquisition are included in the equity of the Group. Divested companies are included in the consolidated financial statements until and including the divestment date. Intra-Group receivables and liabilities, revenue or expenses and unrealized gains or losses that arise from intra-Group transactions between Group companies are eliminated in their entirety during the preparation of the consolidated financial statements. The same applies to associated companies.

Minority interests in equity are reported separately from share capital owned by the Parent Company's shareholders. A separate disclosure of the minority share of the year's earnings is provided.

The first paragraph indicates that Scania consolidates all majority-owned subsidiaries. The second paragraph describes the accounting for the acquisition of a subsidiary following the purchase, or acquisition, method and the elimination of the effects of intercompany transactions for both consolidated subsidiaries and investments in associated companies accounted for using the equity method. The third paragraph describes Scania's disclosure of the minority (noncontrolling) interest in consolidated subsidiaries. Refer to the balance sheet of Scania in **Exhibit 1.5** (page 12). Scania shows the minority (noncontrolling) interest in the net assets of consolidated subsidiaries as the last item in shareholders' equity, distinguishing Scania's share of the net assets and that of the noncontrolling shareholders. For the year ended December 31, 2006, Scania reported a carrying value for minority interest of SEK5 million. Refer also to Scania's income statement in **Exhibit 1.6** (page 14). Scania computes an amount labeled net income and then shows the portion of that net income attributable to Scania's shareholders and the portion attributable to the minority (noncontrolling) interests. For the year ended December 31, 2006, Scania reported that none of its net income (or equivalently, an immaterial amount of its net income) of SEK5,939 was attributable to minority interest holders.

LIMITATIONS OF CONSOLIDATED STATEMENTS

The consolidated statements, provided for the parent's shareholders, do not replace the statements of individual corporations.

- Creditors must rely on the resources of the entity to which they lend funds and are therefore interested in the unconsolidated (single-company) financial statements of that entity.

- A corporation can declare dividends against only its own retained earnings.

- When the parent company does not own all of the shares of the subsidiary, the noncontrolling shareholders can judge the dividend constraints, both legal and financial, only by inspecting the subsidiary's statements.

JOINT VENTURE INVESTMENTS

Firms frequently join in business ventures with other firms to share resources, personnel, or technologies and to spread risks. **Exhibit 13.1** indicates that Scania entered into a joint venture with Cummins Inc., a U.S.-based designer and manufacturer of diesel- and gas-powered engines. Scania owns 50% of the joint venture. The notes to the financial statements of Cummins Inc. show that it also owns 50%. This arrangement is a typical **joint venture** in which neither firm has control; they share joint control.

Firms might account for joint ventures in three possible ways:

1. Use the equity method.
2. Fully consolidate the joint venture and report the interest of the joint owner as an external interest, similar to the noncontrolling interest in a consolidated subsidiary.
3. Partially consolidate the joint venture to the extent of the 50% ownership percentage, a method referred to as **proportionate consolidation**. That is, consolidate 50% of each asset, liability, revenue, and expense.

U.S. GAAP requires firms to account for joint ventures using the equity method (unless the firm elects the fair value option for investments in joint ventures).[14] The ownership percentage in the joint venture permits each owner to exert significant influence but not control. Thus U.S. GAAP does not permit either full consolidation or proportionate consolidation.

IFRS permits firms to account for jointly controlled entities using either the equity method or proportionate consolidation.[15] Scania follows IFRS in preparing its financial statements. **Exhibit 13.1** indicates that Scania accounts for its investment in the joint venture with Cummins Inc. using the equity method and includes this investment in the account, Investments in Associated Companies and Joint Ventures. For the year ended December 31, 2006, Scania reports that the joint venture with Cummins has a carrying value of SEK83 million on Scania's balance sheet. If Scania had proportionately consolidated the joint venture, it would have eliminated its investment in the joint venture and replaced it with its share of the individual assets and liabilities of the joint venture. Scania discloses aggregated balance sheet and income statement information showing its share of the assets, liabilities, revenue, and net income of associated companies and joint ventures. With this information, the analyst could convert the financial statements of Scania from the equity method to proportionate consolidation for these other entities.

---

[14]Accounting Principles Board, *Opinion No. 18*, "The Equity Method of Accounting for Investments in Common Stock," 1971 (**Codification Topic 323**).

[15]International Accounting Standards Board, *International Accounting Standard 28*, "Investments in Associates," 1989, revised 2003.

VARIABLE INTEREST ENTITIES, SPECIAL PURPOSE ENTITIES, AND QUALIFYING SPECIAL PURPOSE ENTITIES

VARIABLE INTEREST ENTITIES

The usual criterion for preparing consolidated financial statements is voting control in the form of majority ownership of common stock. However, for some entities common stock ownership does not indicate control because the common stock of the entity lacks one or more of the economic characteristics associated with equity. To see this, consider the following business arrangement of Company P, which wants to borrow to finance the acquisition of an airplane.

1. Company P pays $100,000 to an unrelated party to induce that party to own 100% of the shares of Company S. The unrelated party buys these shares for $60,000 cash, contributing the cash to Company S in return for the shares, and keeps the remaining $40,000

2. Company S borrows $50 million from a group of Lenders to buy the airplane that Company P wants to use. It agrees to repay the loan in 120 monthly installments at the rate of $717,500 per month. The implicit interest rate is 1% per month, and the loan is fully paid after 120 payments.

3. Company P provides a written guarantee to the Lenders that it will make any debt service payment that Company S fails to make on time. Without the guarantee, the Lenders would not lend to Company S, as the airplane itself does not provide sufficient collateral for the loan.

4. Company P agrees to pay $717,500 per month to rent the airplane, plus a small additional fee to cover Company S's transactions costs. Company S must use the rental payments from Company P to repay the $50 million loan. Company P takes possession of the airplane, including responsibility for using and maintaining it. The governing documents that established Company S preclude it from engaging in any transactions other than the borrowing and repayment of the loan and the rental arrangement involving Company P.

Figure 13.2 depicts this structure.

In this arrangement, the unrelated party owns 100% of Company S, but Company P controls the use of Company S's only asset (the airplane) and has responsibility for timely repayment of the loan. The unrelated party that owns Company S has no management responsibility and no opportunity for gain or loss. Company P enjoys the risks and rewards of using the airplane. If the airplane becomes obsolete, Company P bears the cost. If the rental arrangement turns out to be a bargain, Company P will enjoy the gains. Firms have organized entities such as Company S to turn accounts receivable into cash without explicit borrowing and to finance research and development efforts.

U. S. GAAP refers to entities such as Company S in our illustration as a **variable interest entity (VIE)**.[16] A variable interest entity is an entity that meets one or both of the following criteria:

1. The invested equity is so small that the entity requires other financial support to sustain its activities.[17]

2. The equity owners lack meaningful decision rights.

If the entity qualifies as a VIE, U.S. GAAP requires the **primary beneficiary** (if one exists) of the VIE to consolidate the VIE. Company S in our example qualifies as a VIE because its owners have no meaningful decision rights. A company, such as Company P in the illustration, will be the primary beneficiary of the VIE if it absorbs (or receives) the majority of the variability of the outcomes of the VIE. In the preceding example, Company P guarantees all the debt of the VIE and is the primary beneficiary. Thus, Company P must consolidate the VIE.

---

[16]Financial Accounting Standards Board, *Interpretation No. 46R,* "Consolidation of Variable Interest Entities," 2003 (**Codification Topic 810**).

[17]The FASB specifies 10% as the minimum equity investment, absent evidence that a smaller equity investment is sufficient to absorb the expected losses of the entity.

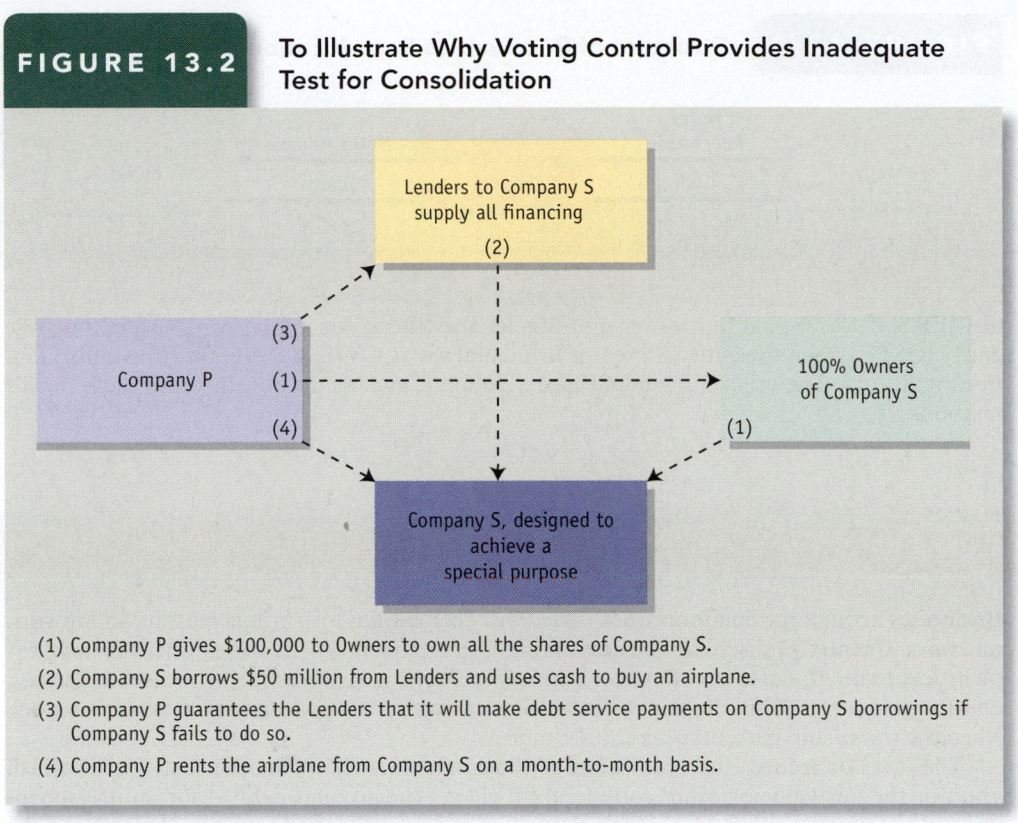

FIGURE 13.2 **To Illustrate Why Voting Control Provides Inadequate Test for Consolidation**

(1) Company P gives $100,000 to Owners to own all the shares of Company S.

(2) Company S borrows $50 million from Lenders and uses cash to buy an airplane.

(3) Company P guarantees the Lenders that it will make debt service payments on Company S borrowings if Company S fails to do so.

(4) Company P rents the airplane from Company S on a month-to-month basis.

IFRS does not contain the concept of a VIE. Rather, IFRS describes a **special purpose entity (SPE)** in general terms that suggest certain similarities to a VIE but does not provide either a specific definition of an SPE or specific criteria for an entity to qualify as an SPE. IFRS requires that an entity must consolidate a SPE if it controls the SPE.[18]

QUALIFYING SPECIAL PURPOSE ENTITIES

Both U.S. GAAP and IFRS address the accounting for sales of financial assets in exchange for cash when the seller or transferor has continuing involvement. In some cases, the transferee (the entity that receives the transferred financial assets) has some of the characteristics of a VIE. However, U.S. GAAP specifically excludes from consideration as a VIE a transferee that is a **qualifying special purpose entity (QSPE)**. To illustrate the concept of a QSPE, assume that Scania has notes receivable from its customers related to the sale of trucks and that it wishes to obtain financing. It could borrow from a financial institution, using the notes receivable as collateral, and show the debt on its balance sheet. Alternatively, Scania sells the receivables to a specially created entity for cash. To obtain the financing needed to pay Scania, this entity borrows from banks or other lenders and uses the customers' notes as collateral. **Figure 13.3** depicts this arrangement.

If this arrangement qualifies as a sale of the receivables to the entity and if Scania does not consolidate the entity, then Scania will de-recognize the receivables that it has transferred to the entity, and it will not show the entity's borrowing on its balance sheet. U.S. GAAP and IFRS set forth criteria for deciding whether the transfer of assets to the entity qualifies as a sale for accounting purposes.[19] **Chapter 11** discusses these criteria. Under U.S. GAAP but

---

[18]The IFRS guidance for analysis of special purpose entities is in International Accounting Standards Board, *Standing Interpretations Committee Interpretation 12,* "Special Purpose Entities," 1998. This Interpretation contains a list of indicators of control.

[19]Financial Accounting Standards Board, *Statement of Financing Accounting Standards No. 140,* "Accounting for Transfers and Servicing of Financial Assets and Extinguishments of Liabilities," 2000 (**Codification Topic 860**); International Accounting Standards Board, *International Accounting Standard 39,* "Financial Instruments: Recognition and Measurement," revised 2003.

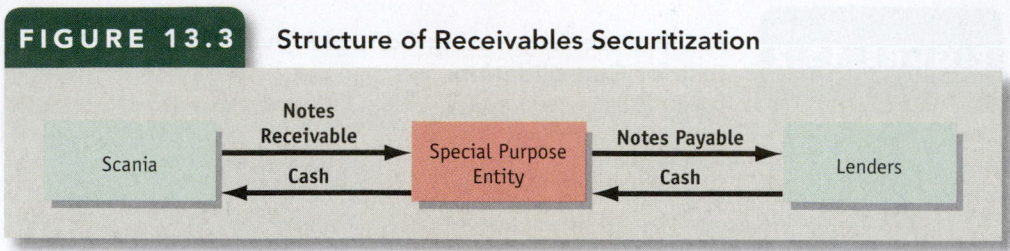

FIGURE 13.3   **Structure of Receivables Securitization**

not IFRS, if the special purpose entity satisfies the criteria for a qualifying special purpose entity (QSPE), then the entity is exempt from analysis as a VIE and exempt from consolidation by Scania. The criteria for a QSPE are complex, and we do not illustrate them in this textbook.[20]

SUMMARY

Businesses acquire the common stock issued by other entities for various reasons and in various ways. **Chapter 12** discusses the accounting for investments in securities when the investor owns less than 20% of the voting stock of another entity, for investments in debt securities, and for derivatives. This chapter discusses the accounting for investments in common stock when the ownership percentage is 20% or more.

The investor records the acquisition of the common stock of another entity at the cash given or the fair value of other consideration given. The account debited for an investment in equity securities, either Marketable Securities or Investment in Securities, depends on the expected holding period.

Investment in S	X	
Cash or Other Consideration Given		X

The accounting for investments in equity securities subsequent to acquisition depends on the ownership percentage:

- The fair value method generally applies when the investor owns less than 20%.

- The equity method generally applies when the investor owns at least 20% but not more than 50% of the common stock of another company (the investee). The equity method applies also when the investor can exercise significant influence over the investee even though it owns less than 20%. Firms have the option to use the fair value method instead of the equity method for certain investments.

- The investor generally prepares consolidated statements when it owns more than 50% of the voting shares of another company.

Exhibit 13.8 summarizes the accounting for investments subsequent to acquisition studied in **Chapters 12** and **13**.

Consolidated statements and the equity method have the same effect on net income. The investor shows as income its proportional share of the investee's periodic income since acquisition, after eliminating the effects of intercompany transactions. In the equity method, this share appears on a single line of the income statement. Income statement amounts of revenues and expenses are larger in consolidation because the consolidated income statement combines the revenues and expenses of the acquired company with those of the parent, net of the effects of intercompany transactions. Balance sheet components under consolidation will exceed those under the equity method; the consolidated balance sheet replaces the parent company's Investment in Subsidiary account with the individual assets and liabilities of the acquired company.

---

[20]As this book goes to press, the FASB is reconsidering the accounting for qualifying special purpose entities, specifically whether such entities qualify for possible consolidation as variable interest entities.

EXHIBIT 13.8	Effects of Various Methods of Accounting for Short- and Long-Term Investments in Corporate Securities

Method of Accounting	Balance Sheet	Income Statement
Fair value method for securities available for sale (generally used when ownership percentage is less than 20%) and for cash flow hedges.[a]	Investment account or derivative appears at fair value. Unrealized holding gains and losses appear in Other Comprehensive Income.	Dividends declared by investee included in revenue of investor. Gains and losses (from acquisition cost) included in income only when realized in arm's-length transactions with outsiders.
Fair value method for trading securities (generally used when ownership percentage is less than 20%) and for fair value hedges.	Investment account or derivative appears at fair value. Unrealized holding gains and losses appear in income statement, and the effects increase or decrease the Retained Earnings account.	Dividends declared by investee included in revenue of investor. Gains and losses (from then-current carrying values) included in income when fair values change.
Amortized cost method (used only for debt where holder has both intention and ability to hold to maturity).[a]	Acquisition cost plus accrued interest not yet received in cash.	Carrying value at start of period multiplied by historical market interest rate on the date of acquisition of debt security.
Equity method (generally used when ownership percentage is at least 20% but not more than 50%).[a]	Investment account appears at acquisition cost plus share of investee's net income less share of investee's dividends since acquisition minus amortization of excess of purchase price over fair value of identifiable assets with limited lives.	Equity in investee's net income is part of revenue in the period that investee earns income. Reduce (increase) by the amount, if any, of intercompany gains (losses).
Consolidation (generally used when ownership percentage exceeds 50%).	Eliminate investment account, and replace it with individual assets and liabilities of subsidiary. Show noncontrolling interest in shareholders' equity. Eliminate intercompany assets and liabilities.	Combine individual revenues and expenses of subsidiary with those of parent, and eliminate intercompany items. Subtract noncontrolling interest in subsidiary's net income.

[a]Firms can elect the fair value option to account for these securities. The effects on the balance sheet and income statement are the same as those described for trading securities and fair value hedges.

SOLUTIONS TO SELF-STUDY PROBLEMS

SUGGESTED SOLUTION TO PROBLEM 13.1 FOR SELF-STUDY

(Equity Investing Group; journal entries to apply the equity method for long-term investments in securities.)

a.

January 1, 2008

Investment in Securities [D]	80,000	
Investment in Securities [E]	190,000	
Investment in Securities [F]	200,000	
Cash		470,000

Assets	=	Liabilities	+	Shareholders' Equity	(Class.)
+80,000					
+190,000					
+200,000					
−470,000					

b.

December 31, 2008

Investment in Securities [D] (0.40 × $40,000)...............	16,000	
Investment in Securities [E] (0.30 × $120,000)	36,000	
Investment in Securities [F] (0.20 × $200,000)	40,000	
Equity in Earnings of Affiliates.........................		92,000

Assets	=	Liabilities	+	Shareholders' Equity	(Class.)
+16,000				+92,000	IncSt → RE
+36,000					
+40,000					

December 31, 2008

Cash...	25,000	
Investment in Securities [D] (0.40 × $10,000)...............		4,000
Investment in Securities [E] (0.30 × $30,000)...............		9,000
Investment in Securities [F] (0.20 × $60,000)...............		12,000

Assets	=	Liabilities	+	Shareholders' Equity	(Class.)
+25,000					
−4,000					
−9,000					
−12,000					

December 31, 2008

Amortization Expense	8,000	
Investment in Securities [E]		4,000
Investment in Securities [F]		4,000

Assets	=	Liabilities	+	Shareholders' Equity	(Class.)
−4,000				−8,000	IncSt → RE
−4,000					

Security	Carrying Value of Investee's Net Assets on January 1, 2008	Ownership Percentage	Share of Carrying Value Acquired	Acquisition Cost of Investment	Excess Acquisition Cost	Annual Amortization for 10 Years
D	$200,000	40%	$ 80,000	$ 80,000	—	—
E	500,000	30	150,000	190,000	$40,000	$4,000
F	800,000	20	160,000	200,000	40,000	4,000

c.

December 31, 2009

Investment in Securities [D] (0.40 × $50,000)....................	20,000	
Investment in Securities [F] (0.20 × $50,000)	10,000	
Investment in Securities [E] (0.30 × $40,000)...............		12,000
Equity in Net Earnings of Affiliates		18,000

Assets	=	Liabilities	+	Shareholders' Equity	(Class.)
+20,000				+18,000	IncSt → RE
+10,000					
−12,000					

December 31, 2009

Cash..	16,800	
Investment in Securities [D] (0.40 × $12,000)...............		4,800
Investment in Securities [F] (0.20 × $60,000)...............		12,000

Assets	=	Liabilities	+	Shareholders' Equity	(Class.)
+16,800					
−4,800					
−12,000					

December 31, 2009

Amortization Expense	8,000	
Investment in Securities [E]		4,000
Investment in Securities [F]		4,000

Assets	=	Liabilities	+	Shareholders' Equity	(Class.)
−4,000				−8,000	IncSt → RE
−4,000					

d.

January 2, 2010

Cash..	190,000	
Loss on Sale of Investment in Securities	7,000	
Investment in Securities [E]		197,000

Assets	=	Liabilities	+	Shareholders' Equity	(Class.)
+190,000				−7,000	IncSt → RE
−197,000					

$$\$197,000 = \$190,000 + \$36,000 - \$9,000 - \$4,000 - \$12,000 - \$4,000.$$

SUGGESTED SOLUTION TO PROBLEM 13.2 FOR SELF-STUDY

(Powell Corporation and Steele Corporation; financial statement effects of the acquisition method.)

a.

January 1, 2008

Current Assets	7,000	
Property, Plant, and Equipment (net).......................	23,000	
Goodwill	40,000	
Liabilities		16,000
Common Stock (2,700 × $1)		2,700
Additional Paid-In Capital (2,700 × $19)....................		51,300

Assets	=	Liabilities	+	Shareholders' Equity	(Class.)
+7,000		+16,000		+2,700	ContriCap
+23,000				+51,300	ContriCap
+40,000					

b. Exhibit 13.9 presents the consolidated balance sheet of January 1, 2008, using the acquisition method.

EXHIBIT 13.9

**Powell Corporation and Steele Corporation
Consolidated Balance Sheet, January 1, 2008
(Problem 13.2 for Self-Study)**

ASSETS	
Current Assets	$ 17,000
Property, Plant, and Equipment (net)	53,000
Goodwill	40,000
Total Assets	$110,000

LIABILITIES AND SHAREHOLDERS' EQUITY	
Liabilities	$ 41,000
Common Stock	3,700[a]
Additional Paid-In Capital	60,300[b]
Retained Earnings	5,000
Total Equities	$110,000

[a]$3,700 = \$1,000 + (2,700 \times \$1)$.

[b]$60,300 = \$9,000 + (2,700 \times \$19)$.

SUGGESTED SOLUTION TO PROBLEM 13.3 FOR SELF-STUDY

(Parent and Sub; understanding consolidation concepts.)

a. No. The investment account shows a balance of $192, which equals 80% of Sub's share-holders' equity ($192 = 0.80 \times \$240$). If there was an excess of the fair value over the carrying value of Sub's net assets on the date of acquisition, Parent has either fully amortized the excess or recognized impairment losses, which eliminated the excess.

b. **(1)** The Investment in Sub account has a balance of $192, which equals 80% of the shareholders' equity of Sub. This clue supports the 80% ownership only because no unamortized excess acquisition cost exists (see the response to question **a**).

   (2) The noncontrolling interest in the net assets of Sub is $48, which equals 20% of the shareholders' equity of Sub ($48 = 0.20 \times \$240$).

   (3) The Equity in Earnings of Sub account on Parent's books has a balance of $80 for 2008, which equals 80% of the net income of Sub for 2008 ($80 = 0.80 \times \$100$).

   (4) The Noncontrolling Interest in Earnings account of Sub has a balance of $20 for 2008 ($20 = 0.20 \times \$100$).

c. Parent and Sub have intercompany accounts receivable and accounts payable. Combined accounts receivable exceed consolidated accounts receivable by $25 (= $820 − $795), the same as the excess of combined accounts payable over consolidated accounts payable ($25 = $540 − $515).

d. Double-counting results if both the investment account and the individual assets and liabilities of Sub appear on the consolidated balance sheet.

e. Consolidated shareholders' equity includes the shareholders' equity of Parent plus the 20% noncontrolling interest in Sub.

f. $500 (= $6,000 − $5,500 or $4,040 − $3,540).

g. Consolidated amounts include individual revenues, expenses, and noncontrolling interest in earnings, which net to $80. Double-counting this earnings results if the accountant does not eliminate the equity in earnings account.

h. The separate-company income statements report the total revenues and expenses of each entity without regard to who owns the common stock of each company. The consolidated income statement shows the earnings allocable to the noncontrolling shareholders and to the shareholders of the parent company. The shareholders of Parent have a claim on all of the earnings of Parent but on only 80% of the earnings of Sub. Consolidated revenues and expenses include the combined amounts for both companies, adjusted for intercompany transactions. The noncontrolling interest in net income of Sub shows the portion of Sub's net income not subject to a claim by Parent's shareholders.

KEY TERMS AND CONCEPTS

Marketable securities	Goodwill
Investments in securities	Bargain purchase
Minority, passive investments	Consolidation work sheet
Significant influence	Intercompany transactions
Minority, active investments	Noncontrolling (minority) interest
Majority, active investments	Consolidation policy
Equity method	Joint venture
Parent	Proportionate consolidation
Subsidiary	Variable interest entity (VIE)
Consolidated financial statements	Primary beneficiary
Economic entity	Special purpose entity (SPE)
Acquisition, or purchase, method	Qualifying special purpose entity (QSPE)

QUESTIONS, EXERCISES, AND PROBLEMS

QUESTIONS

1. Review the meaning of the terms and concepts listed above in Key Terms and Concepts.

2. Distinguish between *significant influence* and *control*, and describe how these concepts relate to the method of accounting for intercorporate investments.

3. "Dividends received or receivable from another company are a revenue in calculating net income, a return of investment, or eliminated, depending on the method of accounting the investor uses." Explain.

4. Describe the rationale for why an investor using the equity method must amortize any excess purchase price attributable to undervalued assets with a limited life.

5. Describe the rationale for why an investor using the equity method must eliminate any intercompany profit or loss on transactions between the investor and the investee.

6. Describe the rationale for why an investor using the equity method must recognize its share of Other Comprehensive Income of the investee.

7. Why is the equity method sometimes described as a *one-line consolidation*? Consider both the balance sheet and the income statement in your response.

8. "Accounting for an investment in a subsidiary using the equity method and not consolidating it yields the same net income as consolidating the subsidiary. Total assets will differ, however, depending on whether or not the investor consolidates the subsidiary." Explain.

9. Distinguish between minority investments in other companies and the noncontrolling, or minority, interest in a consolidated subsidiary.

10. Define the concept of an *economic entity* and explain its importance in preparing consolidated financial statements of a parent company with its controlled subsidiaries.

11. The Investment in Subsidiary account is an asset. Why must an investor eliminate this account when preparing consolidated financial statements with the subsidiary?

12. Distinguish between the noncontrolling, or minority, interest in net income and the noncontrolling, or minority, interest in net assets of a consolidated subsidiary.

13. Does accounting for an investment in a joint venture using (1) the equity method or (2) proportionate consolidation reflect better the nature of the relation between each joint owner and the joint venture? Explain, giving examples as needed to support your reasoning.

14. Under what circumstances might majority ownership of another entity not serve as an indicator of control?

EXERCISES

15. **Equity method entries.** Hanna Company purchased 100% of the common stock of Denver Company on January 2 for $550,000. The common stock of Denver Company at this date was $200,000, and the retained earnings balance was $350,000. During the year, net income of Denver Company was $120,000 and dividends declared were $30,000. Hanna Company uses the equity method to account for the investment. Give the journal entries that Hanna Company made during the year to account for its investment in Denver Company.

16. **Equity method entries.** Weber Corporation acquired significant influence over Albee Computer Company on January 2 by purchasing 20% of its outstanding stock for $100 million. Weber Corporation attributes the entire excess of acquisition cost over the carrying value of Albee Computer Company's net assets to a patent, which it amortizes over 10 years. The shareholders' equity accounts of Albee Computer Company appeared as follows on January 2 and December 31 of the current year (amounts in millions):

	Jan. 2	Dec. 31
Common Stock	$300	$300
Retained Earnings	120	190

Albee Computer Company had earnings of $100 million and declared dividends of $30 million during the year. The accounts receivable of Weber Corporation at December 31 included $600,000 due from Albee Computer Company. Weber Corporation accounts for its investment in Albee Computer Company using the equity method. Give the journal entries to record the acquisition of the shares of Albee Computer Company and to apply the equity method during the year on the books of Weber Corporation.

17. **Journal entries to apply the equity method of accounting for investments in securities.** Wood Corporation made three long-term intercorporate investments on January 2. Data relating to these investments for the year appear next.

Company	Percentage Acquired	Carrying Value and Fair Value of Identifiable Net Assets on January 2	Acquisition Cost	Net Income (Loss) for the Year	Dividends Declared During the Year
Knox Corporation	50%	$700,000	$350,000	$ 70,000	$30,000
Vachi Corporation	30	520,000	196,000	40,000	15,000
Snow Corporation	20	400,000	100,000	(24,000)	—

Give the journal entries to record the acquisition of these investments and to apply the equity method during the year. There are no goodwill impairments.

18. **Journal entries to apply the equity method of accounting for investments in securities.** The following information summarizes data about the minority, active investments of Stebbins Corporation.

Security	Date Acquired	Acquisition Cost	Ownership Percentage	Carrying Value of Identifiable Net Assets on January 1, 2008
R	1/1/2008	$250,000	25%	$800,000
S	1/1/2008	325,000	40	750,000
T	1/1/2008	475,000	50	950,000

Security	Earnings (Loss)		Dividends	
	2008	2009	2008	2009
R	$ 200,000	$225,000	$125,000	$130,000
S	120,000	75,000	80,000	80,000
T	(150,000)	50,000	—	—

Company R owns a building with 10 years of remaining life and with a fair value exceeding its carrying value by $160,000. $40,000 of this amount applies to the share Stebbins Corporation owns. Stebbins Corporation attributes the rest of any excess of acquisition cost over carrying value acquired to goodwill. The building has a 10-year remaining life. The fair values of the recorded net assets of Company S and Company T equal their carrying values. There are no goodwill impairments.

a. Give the journal entries to record the acquisition of these investments and to apply the equity method during 2008 and 2009.

b. Stebbins Corporation sells Security R on January 1, 2010, for $275,000. Give the journal entry to record the sale.

19. **Working backward to consolidation relations.** Laesch Company, as parent, owns shares in Lily Company. Laesch has owned the shares since it formed Lily. Lily has never declared a dividend. Laesch has retained earnings from its own operations independent of intercorporate investments of $100,000. The consolidated balance sheet shows no goodwill and shows retained earnings of $156,000. Consider each of the following questions independently of the others:

a. If Laesch owns 80% of Lily, its consolidated subsidiary, what are the retained earnings of the subsidiary?

b. If Lily has retained earnings of $77,000, what fraction of Lily does Laesch own?

c. If Laesch had not consolidated Lily but instead had accounted for it using the equity method, how much revenue would Laesch have recognized from the investment?

20. **Working backward from consolidated income statements.** Dealco Corporation published a consolidated income statement for the year, shown in **Exhibit 13.10**. The unconsolidated affiliate retained 25% of its earnings of $140 million during the year, having paid out the rest as dividends. The consolidated subsidiary earned $280 million during the year and declared no dividends.

a. What percentage of the unconsolidated affiliate does Dealco Corporation own?

b. What amount of dividends did Dealco Corporation receive from the unconsolidated affiliate during the year?

c. What percentage of the consolidated subsidiary does Dealco Corporation own?

EXHIBIT 13.10

Dealco Corporation
Consolidated Income Statement
(Exercise 20)

REVENUES		
Sales		$1,400,000
Equity in Earnings of Unconsolidated Affiliate		56,000
Total Revenues		$1,456,000
EXPENSES		
Cost of Goods Sold (excluding depreciation)		$ 910,000
Administrative Expense		140,000
Depreciation Expense		161,000
Amortization of Goodwill		7,000
Income Tax Expenses:		
Currently Payable	$58,800	
Deferred	14,000	72,800
Total Expenses		$1,290,800
Income of the Consolidated Group		$ 165,200
Less Noncontrolling Interest in Earnings of Consolidated Subsidiary		(42,000)
Net Income to Shareholders		$ 123,200

21. **Consolidation policy and principal consolidation concepts.** CAR Corporation manufactures computers in the United States. It owns 75% of the voting stock of Charles Electronics, 80% of the voting stock of Alexandre du France Software Systems (in France), and 90% of the voting stock of R Credit Corporation (a finance company). CAR Corporation prepares consolidated financial statements consolidating Charles Electronics, uses the equity method for R Credit Corporation, and treats its investment in Alexandre du France Software Systems as securities available for sale. Data from the annual reports of these companies appear next. There are no intercompany transactions.

	Percentage Owned	Net Income	Dividends	Accounting Method
CAR Corporation Consolidated	—	$1,200,000	$ 84,000	—
Charles Electronics	75%	120,000	48,000	Consolidated
Alexandre du France Software Systems[a]	80	96,000	60,000	Fair Value (Securities Available for Sale)
R Credit Corporation	90	144,000	120,000	Equity

[a]Fair value of shares exceeds acquisition cost.

a. Which, if any, of the companies does CAR incorrectly account for according to U.S. GAAP?

Assuming the accounting methods and accounting itself for the three subsidiaries shown above are correct, answer the following questions:

b. How much of the net income reported by CAR Corporation Consolidated results from the operations of the three subsidiaries?

c. What is the amount of the noncontrolling, or minority, interest now shown on the consolidated income statement, and how does it affect net income of CAR Corporation Consolidated?

d. If CAR had consolidated all three subsidiaries, what would have been the net income of CAR Corporation Consolidated?

e. If CAR had consolidated all three subsidiaries, what noncontrolling, or minority, interest would appear on the income statement?

22. **Equity method entries.** Vogel Company is a subsidiary of Joyce Company. Joyce Company accounts for its investment in Vogel Company using the equity method on its single-company books. Present journal entries for the following selected transactions. Record the set of entries on the books of Vogel Company separately from the set of entries on the books of Joyce Company.

(1) On January 2, Joyce Company acquired on the market, for cash, 100% of the common stock of Vogel Company. The outlay was $420,000. The total contributed capital of Vogel Company's stock outstanding was $300,000; the retained earnings balance was $80,000. Joyce attributes the excess of acquisition cost over the carrying value of the net assets acquired to an internally developed patent that has a 10-year remaining useful life on January 2.

(2) Vogel Company purchased materials for $29,000 from Joyce Company on account at the latter's cost.

(3) Vogel Company obtained an advance of $6,000 from Joyce Company. Vogel Company deposited the funds in the bank.

(4) Vogel Company paid $16,000 on the purchases in (2).

(5) Vogel Company repaid $4,000 of the loan received from Joyce Company in (3).

(6) Vogel Company declared and paid a dividend of $20,000 during the year.

(7) The net income of Vogel Company for the year was $30,000.

23. **Working backward from data that has eliminated intercompany transactions.** (Adapted from a problem by S. A. Zeff.) Alpha owns 100% of Omega and consolidates Omega in an entity called Alpha/Omega. Beginning in 2008, Alpha sold merchandise to Omega at

a price 50% larger than Alpha's costs. Omega sold some, but not all, of these goods to customers at a further markup. Excerpts from the single-company statements of Alpha and Omega and from the consolidated financial statements of Alpha/Omega appear next.

	Single-Company Statements		Consolidated Financial Statements
	Alpha	**Omega**	
Sales Revenue	$450,000	$250,000	$620,000
Cost of Goods Sold	300,000	210,000	430,000
Merchandise Inventory	60,000	50,000	100,000

a. What was the total sales price at which Alpha sold goods to Omega during 2008?

b. What was Omega's cost of the goods it had purchased from Alpha but has not yet sold by the end of 2008? What was Alpha's cost of those goods? Which of those two numbers appears in the total Merchandise Inventory on the consolidated balance sheet?

24. **Working backward from purchase data.** (Adapted from a problem by S. A. Zeff.) On May 1, 2008, Homer acquired the assets and agreed to take on and pay off the liabilities of Tonga in exchange for 10,000 of Homer's common shares. Homer accounted for the acquisition of the net assets of Tonga using the purchase method. On the date of acquisition, Tonga's carrying value of depreciable assets exceeded Homer's estimate of their fair value, but Homer judged all other items on Tonga's books to reflect fair value on that date so that the purchase price exceeded the fair value of the identifiable assets, generating goodwill. On the date of the acquisition, Tonga's shareholders' equity was $980,000, and its liabilities totaled $80,000. Tonga reported no goodwill on its balance sheet.

Homer made the following journal entry to record the acquisition:

Current Assets	210,000	
Depreciable Assets (net)	700,000	
Goodwill	120,000	
Liabilities		80,000
Common Stock—Par		150,000
Additional Paid-In Capital		800,000

Assets	=	Liabilities	+	Shareholders' Equity	(Class.)
+210,000		+80,000		+150,000	ContriCap
+700,000				+800,000	ContriCap
+120,000					

a. What was the carrying value on Tonga's books of its total assets just before the acquisition?

b. What was the carrying value of depreciable assets of Tonga just before the acquisition?

25. **Effect of equity method versus consolidation. Exhibit 13.11** presents a spreadsheet that we use to compare the effects of using the equity method with using consolidated financial statements. The Web site for this book contains an Excel spreadsheet that duplicates the one in **Exhibit 13.11.** Download this spreadsheet in preparing your solution to this exercise. You will change only the cell marked in yellow.

a. For this part, assume that Parent owns 80% of Sub. Respond to the following questions:

   (1) Why is net income the same independent of whether Parent uses the equity method or prepares consolidated financial statements with Sub?

   (2) Why is the ratio of liabilities to assets higher if Parent prepares consolidated financial statements with Sub than when it uses the equity method?

b. For this part, change Parent's ownership interest in Sub from 80% to 60%. Respond to the following questions:

EXHIBIT 13.11

Spreadsheet for Studying the Effects of the
Equity Method and Consolidation
(Exercise 25)

	A	B	C	D
1				[Third column not meaningful unless ownership exceeds 50%]
2	To see how things change, alter this number ⟶		80.0%	
3		Equity Method Parent Only	Percent Owned Sub	
4	**Income Statement**			Consolidated
5	Revenues	$1,000	$ 400	$ 1,400
6	Equity in Earnings of Sub	80		
7	Expenses	(700)	(300)	(1,000)
8	Noncontrolling Interest in Net Income of Sub [Note A]			(20)
9	Net Income	$ 380	$ 100	$ 380
10	Note A: Noncontrolling Interest Owns (1—Parent's Fraction)		20.0%	
11	**Balance Sheet**			
12	Assets, Other Than Investment in Sub	$3,000	$2,000	$ 5,000
13	Investment in Sub	400	—	—
14	Total Assets	$3,400	$2,000	$ 5,000
15	Total Liabilities	$1,800	$1,500	$ 3,300
16	Noncontrolling Interest in Net Assets of Sub	—	—	100
17	Shareholders' Equity	1,600	500	1,600
18	Total Liabilities and Shareholders' Equity	$3,400	$2,000	$ 5,000

(1) Why does net income decrease for the change in ownership percentage, independent of whether Parent uses the equity method or prepares consolidated financial statements?

(2) Why do total assets using the equity method decrease but total assets on the consolidated balance sheet remain the same with the decrease in the ownership percentage?

(3) Why do total liabilities using the equity method remain the same with the decrease in the ownership percentage?

(4) Why do total liabilities on the consolidated balance sheet remain the same with the decrease in the ownership percentage?

(5) Why does total shareholders' equity decrease using the equity method but remain the same on the consolidated balance sheet with the decrease?

(6) Why does the ratio of liabilities to assets on the consolidated balance sheet remain the same with the decrease in the ownership percentage?

26. **Effect of errors on financial statements.** Using the notation O/S (overstated), U/S (understated), or NO (no effect), indicate the effects on assets, liabilities, shareholders' equity, and net income of each of the independent errors that follow. Ignore income tax effects.

a. In applying the equity method, P correctly accrues its share of S's net income for the year. However, when receiving a dividend, P credits Dividend Revenue.

b. P acquired 30% of S on January 1 of the current year for an amount in excess of the carrying value of S's net assets. The excess relates to patents. P correctly accounted for its share of S's net income and dividends for the year but neglected to amortize any of the excess purchase price.

c. During the current year, P sold inventory items to S, its wholly owned subsidiary, at a profit. S sold these inventory items, and S paid P for them before the end of the year. The firms made no elimination entry for this intercompany sale on the consolidation work sheet.

d. Refer to part **c.** Assume that S owes P $10,000 for intercompany purchases at year-end. The firm made no elimination entry for this intercompany debt.

e. P owns 90% of S. P treats the noncontrolling interest in consolidated subsidiaries as a liability. In preparing a consolidated work sheet, the firms made no entry to accrue the noncontrolling interest's share of S's net income or of S's net assets.

27. **Accounting for a joint venture. Exhibit 13.12** presents selected balance sheet data for Parrot Corporation and for a joint venture in which it has a 50% ownership interest.

    a. Prepare a balance sheet of Parrot Corporation in which it accounts for its investment in the joint venture using proportionate consolidation instead of the equity method.

    b. Compute the liabilities-to-assets ratio and the debt-equity ratio for Parrot Corporation assuming Parrot Corporation accounts for its investment in the joint venture using (1) the equity method, and (2) proportionate consolidation.

    c. Explain the reason for the differences in the debt ratios computed in part **b** for each accounting method.

PROBLEMS

28. **Preparing a consolidated balance sheet.** The first two columns of **Exhibit 13.13** present information from the accounting records of Ely Company and Sims Company at the end of the current year. Ely Company acquired 100% of the common stock of Sims Company on January 1 of the current year for $70,000 cash. On this date, the balance in the Retained Earnings account of Sims Company was $42,000. Any excess purchase price relates to goodwill. Ely Company has not recorded a goodwill impairment. The receivables of Ely Company and the liabilities of Sims Company contain an advance from Ely Company to Sims Company of $7,500. Enter the appropriate amounts in the Consolidated column for a consolidated balance sheet of Ely Company and Sims Company on December 31 of the current year.

29. **Preparing a consolidated balance sheet.** The first two columns of **Exhibit 13.14** present information from the accounting records of Company P and Company S on December 31, 2009. Company P acquired 100% of the common stock of Company S on January 1, 2008, when the balance in Company S's retained earnings was $40,000. Company P attributes any excess of acquisition cost over the carrying value of the net assets of Company

---

EXHIBIT 13.12 **Parrot Corporation and Joint Venture (Exercise 27)**

	Parrot Corporation	Joint Venture
Current Assets	$ 300	$200
Property, Plant, and Equipment (net)	500	600
Investment in Joint Venture (equity method)	200	—
Total Assets	$1,000	$800
Current Liabilities	$ 250	$150
Long-Term Debt	450	250
Total Liabilities	$ 700	$400
Shareholders' Equity	300	400
Total Liabilities and Shareholders' Equity	$1,000	$800

EXHIBIT 13.13

Ely Company and Sims Company
Information from the Accounting Records on
December 31 of the Current Year
(Problem 28)

	Ely Company	Sims Company	Consolidated
ASSETS			
Cash	$ 12,000	$ 5,000	
Receivables	25,000	15,000	
Investment in Sims Company	78,000	—	
Other Assets	85,000	80,000	
Total Assets	$200,000	$100,000	
LIABILITIES AND SHAREHOLDERS' EQUITY			
Current Liabilities	$ 45,000	$ 40,000	
Common Stock	50,000	10,000	
Retained Earnings	105,000	50,000	
Total Liabilities and Shareholders' Equity	$200,000	$100,000	

EXHIBIT 13.14

Company P and Company S
Information from the Accounting Records on
December 31 of the Current Year
(Problem 29)

	Company P	Company S	Consolidated
ASSETS			
Cash	$ 36,000	$ 26,000	
Accounts and Notes Receivable	180,000	50,000	
Inventories	440,000	250,000	
Investment in Company S (using the equity method)	726,000	—	
Property, Plant, and Equipment (net)	600,000	424,000	
Total Assets	$1,982,000	$750,000	
LIABILITIES AND SHAREHOLDERS' EQUITY			
Accounts and Notes Payable	$ 110,000	$ 59,000	
Other Liabilities	286,000	21,000	
Common Stock	1,200,000	500,000	
Additional Paid-In Capital	—	100,000	
Retained Earnings	386,000	70,000	
Total Liabilities and Shareholders' Equity	$1,982,000	$750,000	

S to a building with a 10-year remaining life as of Janaury 1, 2008. Company P holds a note issued by Company S in the amount of $16,400 on December 31, 2009.

a. Enter the appropriate amounts in the Consolidated column for a consolidated balance sheet of Company P and Company S on December 31, 2009.

b. Compute the acquisition cost of Company P's investment in Company S on January 1, 2008.

c. Prepare an analysis that explains the changes in the Investment in Company S account between January 1, 2008, and December 31, 2009.

30. **Equity method and consolidated financial statements.** The first two columns of **Exhibit 13.15** present information from the accounting records of Peak Company and Valley

	EXHIBIT 13.15	Peak Company and Valley Company Information from the Accounting Records on December 31 of the Current Year Acquisition Cost is $50,000 (Problem 30)

	Peak Company	Valley Company	Consolidated
ASSETS			
Cash	$ 33,000	$ 6,000	
Accounts Receivable	42,000	20,000	
Investment in Valley Company (using equity method)	56,000	—	
Other Assets	123,000	85,000	
Total Assets	$ 254,000	$111,000	
LIABILITIES AND SHAREHOLDERS' EQUITY			
Accounts Payable	$ 80,000	$ 25,000	
Bonds Payable	50,000	30,000	
Common Stock	10,000	5,000	
Retained Earnings.	114,000	51,000	
Total Liabilities and Shareholders' Equity.	$ 254,000	$111,000	
Sales Revenue	$ 400,000	$125,000	
Equity in Earnings of Valley Company	10,000	—	
Cost of Goods Sold	(320,000)	(90,000)	
Selling and Administrative Expense	(44,000)	(20,000)	
Income Tax Expense	(12,000)	(5,000)	
Net Income	$ 34,000	$ 10,000	

Company on December 31 of the current year. Peak Company acquired 100% of the common stock of Valley Company on January 1 of this year for $50,000 cash. The shareholders' equity of Valley Company on January 1 comprised $5,000 of common stock and $45,000 of retained earnings. Valley Company earned $10,000 and declared and paid dividends of $4,000 during the current year. Advances from Peak Company to Valley Company on December 31 total $8,000; Peak includes the advances in its Accounts Receivable; Valley shows the advances in its Accounts Payable.

a. Give the journal entries that Peak Company made on its books on January 1 of the current year to acquire the common stock of Valley Company and to apply the equity method during the current year.

b. Insert the amounts in the Consolidated column of **Exhibit 13.15** for a consolidated balance sheet and a consolidated income statement for Peak Company and Valley Company.

c. Assume for parts **c, d,** and **e** that Peak Company paid $70,000, instead of $50,000, for all of the common stock of Valley Company. The fair values of Valley Company's recorded assets and liabilities equaled their carrying values. Valley Company holds a patent that resulted from the firm's internal research and development efforts. The patent has a zero carrying value, a $20,000 fair value, and a 10-year remaining life on the date of the acquisition. Give the journal entries that Peak Company would make on its books on January 1 of the current year to acquire the common stock of Valley Company and to apply the equity method during the year. Peak Company included amortization of the patent in Selling and Administrative Expenses. The amortization of the patent is a permanent difference between book income and taxable income. That is, for financial reporting, Peak will amortize the cost of the patent to expense, but for tax reporting, none of that cost is ever a deduction. If Peak were to sell the patent, it would compute taxable gain or loss on sale as proceeds less the fair value

EXHIBIT 13.16

Peak Company and Valley Company
Information from the Accounting Records on
December 31 of the Current Year
Acquisition Cost is $70,000
(Problem 30)

	Peak Company	Valley Company	Consolidated
ASSETS			
Cash	$ 13,000	$ 6,000	
Accounts Receivable	42,000	20,000	
Investment in Valley Company (using equity method)	?	—	
Other Assets	123,000	85,000	
Total Assets	$?	$111,000	
LIABILITIES AND SHAREHOLDERS' EQUITY			
Accounts Payable	$ 80,000	$ 25,000	
Bonds Payable	50,000	30,000	
Common Stock	10,000	5,000	
Retained Earnings	?	51,000	
Total Liabilities and Shareholders' Equity.....	$?	$111,000	
Sales Revenue	$ 400,000	$125,000	
Equity in Earnings of Valley Company	?	—	
Cost of Goods Sold	(320,000)	(90,000)	
Selling and Administrative Expense	?	(20,000)	
Income Tax Expense	(12,000)	(5,000)	
Net Income	$?	$ 10,000	

allocated to the patent at the time of acquisition. Thus, income tax expense will not change as a result of the patent amortization.

d. **Exhibit 13.16** presents information for Peak Company and Valley Company at the end of the current year assuming that Peak Company paid $70,000 for all of the common stock of Valley Company on January 1 of the current year. Enter the amounts indicated by a question mark (?) on the books of Peak Company as of December 31 of the current year. *Hint: Refer to the amounts in the entries in part c.*

e. Insert the amounts in the Consolidated column of **Exhibit 13.16** for a consolidated balance sheet and a consolidated income statement for Peak Company and Valley Company.

31. **Equity method and consolidated financial statements with noncontrolling interest.** The first two columns of **Exhibit 13.17** present information from the accounting records of Parent Company and Sub Company on December 31 of the current year. Parent Company acquired 80% of the common stock of Sub Company on January 1 of the current year for $96,000 cash. The shareholders' equity of Sub Company on January 1 comprised $50,000 of common stock and $70,000 of retained earnings. Sub Company earned $20,000 and declared and paid dividends of $8,000 during the current year. Insert the amounts in the Consolidated column of **Exhibit 13.17** for a consolidated balance sheet and a consolidated income statement for Parent Company and Sub Company.

32. **Effect of intercorporate investment policies on financial statements.** The Coca-Cola Company (Coke) follows a policy of holding less than a 50% ownership interest in the corporations that bottle its beverages. **Exhibit 13.18** presents selected balance sheet data for Coke and for its bottling affiliates on December 31, 2007. The first column shows amounts for Coke as reported, with Coke using the equity method to account for investments in its bottlers. The second column shows amounts for Coke's bottlers as reflected in a note to Coke's financial statements. Coke's investment in its bottlers exceeds its share

EXHIBIT 13.17	Parent Company and Sub Company Information from the Accounting Records on December 31 of the Current Year (Problem 31)		

	Parent Company	Sub Company	Consolidated
ASSETS			
Cash	$ 38,000	$ 12,000	
Accounts Receivable	63,000	32,000	
Investment in Sub Company (using equity method)	105,600	—	
Other Assets	296,400	160,000	
Total Assets	$ 503,000	$204,000	
LIABILITIES AND SHAREHOLDERS' EQUITY			
Accounts Payable	$ 85,000	$ 32,000	
Bonds Payable	150,000	40,000	
Total Liabilities	$ 235,000	$ 72,000	
Noncontrolling Interest in Net Assets of Sub Company	—	—	
Common Stock	$ 20,000	$ 50,000	
Retained Earnings	248,000	82,000	
Total Shareholders' Equity	$ 268,000	$132,000	
Total Liabilities and Shareholders' Equity	$ 503,000	$204,000	
Sales Revenue	$ 800,000	$145,000	
Equity in Earnings of Sub Company	16,000	—	
Cost of Goods Sold	(620,000)	(85,000)	
Selling and Administrative Expense	(135,000)	(30,000)	
Income Tax Expense	(24,000)	$ (10,000)	
Net Income of Consolidated Entity	$ 37,000	$ 20,000	
Noncontrolling Interest in Net Income of Sub Company	—	—	
Net Income	$ 37,000	$ 20,000	

of the carrying value of its share of the net assets of these bottlers by $785 million on December 31, 2007.

a. Suggest reasons why the amount for other noncurrent assets in the consolidated column exceeds the sum of the amounts for noncurrent assets on the accounting records of Coke and of its bottling affiliates.

b. Compute the liabilities-to-assets ratio and the debt-equity ratio for Coke assuming Coke (1) accounts for its investments using the equity method, and (2) consolidates its bottlers.

c. Suggest reasons why Coke might choose to own less than 50% of its bottlers.

33. **Accounting for joint ventures.** Smithfield Foods produces and processes beef, pork, and other meat products. It operates through 50/50 joint ventures with other consumer foods companies for sales in certain markets. Smithfield Foods accounts for its investments in the joint ventures using the equity method. The excess of the carrying value of these investments over Smithfield Foods' proportionate interest in the shareholders' equity of the joint ventures relates to brand names, which Smithfield Farms does not amortize. **Exhibit 13.19** presents selected balance sheet and income statement information for Smithfield Foods and for its joint ventures on December 31, 2007.

a. Prepare a balance sheet and income data for Smithfield Foods and its investments in the joint ventures in three columns, as follows: (continued on page 655)

EXHIBIT 13.18

The Coca-Cola Company
Condensed Balance Sheet Data
(amounts in millions)
(Problem 32)

	Coke as Reported	Bottling Affiliates	Consolidated
ASSETS			
Current Assets	$12,105	$14,251	$26,356
Investments in Bottling Affiliates	7,289	—	—
Other Noncurrent Assets	23,875	44,636	71,116
Total Assets	$43,269	$58,887	$97,472
LIABILITIES AND SHAREHOLDERS' EQUITY			
Current Liabilities	$13,225	$13,930	$27,155
Noncurrent Liabilities	8,300	23,374	31,674
Total Liabilities	$21,525	$37,304	$58,829
Shareholders' Equity	$21,744	$21,583	$21,744
Noncontrolling Interest in Bottling Affiliates	—	—	16,899
Total Shareholders' Equity	$21,744	$21,583	38,643
Total Liabilities and Shareholders' Equity	$43,269	$58,887	$97,472

EXHIBIT 13.19

Selected Information for Smithfield Foods
and Joint Ventures
(amounts in millions)
(Problem 33)

BALANCE SHEET	Smithfield Foods	Joint Ventures
ASSETS		
Current Assets	$ 2,733.7	$ 1,367.9
Investments in Joint Venture	420.8	—
Other Noncurrent Assets	3,814.1	703.4
Total Assets	$ 6,968.6	$ 2,071.3
LIABILITIES AND SHAREHOLDERS' EQUITY		
Current Liabilities	$ 1,361.2	$ 947.5
Noncurrent Liabilities	3,352.7	893.8
Total Liabilities	$ 4,713.9	$ 1,841.3
Shareholders' Equity	2,254.7	230.0
Total Liabilities and Shareholders' Equity	$ 6,968.6	$ 2,071.3
INCOME STATEMENT		
Sales	$ 11,911.1	$ 2,912.8
Equity in Earnings of Joint Venture	10.9	—
Expenses	(11,733.6)	(2,891.0)
Net Income	$ 188.4	$ 21.8

Column (1): Equity method (given in **Exhibit 13.19**).

Column (2): Proportionate consolidation.

Column (3): Full consolidation, with separate disclosure of the interest of the other joint owners.

b. Compute the following ratios for each of the three accounting methods in part **a**:

(1) Liabilities-to-assets ratio

(2) Debt-equity ratio

(3) Net income to sales ratio

c. Which accounting method do you think best portrays the operating relations between Smithfield Foods and its joint ventures?

34. **Accounting for a variable interest entity.** Papa John's International operates a chain of pizza restaurants, using a combination of company-owned units and franchised units. Franchisees own the franchised units, although they rely on Papa John's International for a portion of their financing. An important ingredient in pizza is cheese, which has price variations depending on supply and demand conditions in the market. Papa John's International and its franchisees have entered into a purchasing arrangement with BIBP for the purchase of cheese. **Exhibit 13.20** presents the disclosure by Papa John's International of its relation to BIBP, a variable interest entity. Discuss whether Papa John's International should prepare consolidated financial statements with BIBP.

EXHIBIT 13.20

Disclosures by Papa John's International Relating to a Variable Interest Entity
(Problem 34)

5. Accounting for Variable Interest Entities

FASB Interpretation No. 46, Consolidation of Variable Interest Entities, an Interpretation of Accounting Research Bulletin No. 51 (FIN 46), provides a framework for identifying variable interest entities (VIEs) and determining when a company should include the assets, liabilities, noncontrolling interests and results of activities of a VIE in its consolidated financial statements. In general, a VIE is a corporation, partnership, limited liability company, trust, or any other legal structure used to conduct activities or hold assets that either (1) has an insufficient amount of equity to carry out its principal activities without additional subordinated financial support, (2) has a group of equity owners that are unable to make significant decisions about its activities, or (3) has a group of equity owners that do not have the obligation to absorb losses or the right to receive returns generated by its operations.

FIN 46 requires a VIE to be consolidated if a party with an ownership, contractual or other financial interest in the VIE (a variable interest holder) is obligated to absorb a majority of the risk of loss from the VIEs activities, is entitled to receive a majority of the VIEs residual returns (if no party absorbs a majority of the VIEs losses), or both. A variable interest holder that consolidates the VIE is called the primary beneficiary. Upon consolidation, the primary beneficiary generally must initially record all of the VIE's assets, liabilities and noncontrolling interests at fair value and subsequently account for the VIE as if it were consolidated based on majority voting interest.

We have a purchasing arrangement with BIBP, a special-purpose entity, for the sole purpose of reducing cheese price volatility to domestic systemwide restaurants. BIBP is an independent, franchisee-owned corporation. BIBP purchases cheese at the market price and sells it to our distribution subsidiary, PJ Food Service, Inc. (PJFS), at a fixed quarterly price based in part upon historical average market prices. PJFS in turn sells cheese to Papa John's restaurants (both Company-owned and franchised) at a set quarterly price. PJFS purchased $138.2 million, $144.1 million and $151.9 million of cheese from BIBP during 2007, 2006 and 2005, respectively. We recognize the operating losses generated by BIBP if BIBP's shareholders' equity is in a net deficit position. Further, we recognize the subsequent operating income generated by BIBP up to the amount of any losses previously recognized. We recognized a pre-tax loss of $31.7 million, a pre-tax gain of $19.0 million, and a pre-tax gain of $4.5 million in 2007, 2006 and 2005, respectively, reflecting BIBP's operating income (losses), net of BIBP's shareholders' equity.

BIBP has a $20.0 million line of credit with a commercial bank, which is not guaranteed by Papa John's. Papa John's has agreed to provide additional funding in the form of a loan to BIBP. As of December 30, 2007, BIBP had borrowings of $8.7 million and a letter of credit of $3.0 million outstanding under the commercial line of credit facility and $20.5 million under the line of credit from Papa John's. As of December 31, 2006, BIBP had borrowings of $525,000 and a letter of credit of $3.0 million outstanding under the commercial line of credit facility (no outstanding borrowings from Papa John's). BIBP had outstanding borrowings of $13.6 million under the commercial bank facility and $23.6 million under the line of credit from Papa John's as of February 19, 2008.

Shareholders' Equity: Capital Contributions, Distributions, and Earnings

1. Understand the different priority claims of common and preferred shareholders on the assets of a firm and the disclosure of those claims in the shareholders' equity section of the balance sheet.

2. Understand the accounting for the issuance of common and preferred stock, particularly shares issued under various option arrangements.

3. Understand the accounting for (a) cash, property, and stock dividends, and (b) stock splits and reverse stock splits.

4. Understand the accounting for the acquisition and reissue of treasury stock.

5. Understand why the format for reporting income matters, and master the concept that different kinds of income require different formats.

6. Understand the distinction between *net income* (or *profit*) and *comprehensive income*.

7. Understand the required adjustments for errors and accounting changes.

8. Develop the skills to interpret disclosures about changes in shareholders' equity accounts.

Chapters 7–13 discussed the accounting for assets and liabilities under U.S. GAAP and IFRS. Changes in assets and liabilities often cause shareholders' equity[1] to change. Changes in shareholders' equity result from three types of transactions:

1. **Capital Contributions:** Firms issue equity instruments such as common or preferred stock to obtain funds to finance operating and investing activities or as compensation for employees.

2. **Distributions:** Firms distribute assets to shareholders as dividends or by repurchasing common or preferred stock.

3. **Earnings (or Losses):** Firms use assets financed by creditors and owners to generate net income, profit, or earnings—or in some cases net losses.

Exhibit 14.1 presents the shareholders' equity section of the balance sheet of Citigroup, Inc, a commercial banking firm. Previous chapters discussed the items marked in boldface. Let's review the important concepts:

1. Shareholders' equity is a residual interest. It represents the shareholders' claim on the assets of a firm after the firm satisfies all higher-priority claims. The balance sheet of Citigroup shows assets of $2,187,631 million, liabilities of $2,074,033 million, and shareholders' equity of $113,598 million at the end of 2007. Thus, lenders finance approximately 95% (= $2,074,033/$2,187,631) of Citigroup's assets. This percentage is common for commercial banks but would be high for nonfinancial firms.

---

[1]Common business practice uses the terms *shareholders' equity* and *stockholders' equity* interchangeably. Outside of the United States, stock sometimes means inventory. To minimize confusion, we use the term *shareholders' equity* throughout this chapter.

EXHIBIT 14.1	Citigroup, Inc. Disclosures of Shareholders' Equity (dollar amounts in millions)		
		December 31	
		2007	2006
Preferred Stock ($1.00 par value; authorized shares: 30 million); at aggregate liquidation value		$ 0	$ 1,000
Common Stock ($0.01 par value; authorized shares: 15 billion), issued shares: 2007 and 2006: 5,477,416,086 shares. . .		55	55
Additional Paid-In Capital		18,007	18,253
Retained Earnings		121,920	129,267
Treasury Stock, at cost: 2007: 482,834,568 shares; 2006: 565,422,201 shares		(21,724)	(25,092)
Accumulated Other Comprehensive Income (Loss)		(4,660)	(3,700)
Total Shareholders' Equity		$113,598	$119,783

2. All corporations issue common stock. Firms may also issue preferred stock, which has a claim that is senior to that of the common shareholders. Citigroup had preferred stock outstanding in 2006, which it redeemed and retired in 2007, as indicated by the zero balance in preferred stock on the December 31, 2007, balance sheet.

3. Common and preferred stock usually have a par or stated value. Citigroup's preferred stock had a $1.00 par value per share, and its common stock has a $0.01 par value per share. Firms report amounts received from issuing common stock in excess of the par or stated value as Additional Paid-In Capital, or Capital in Excess of Par Value, or a similar account title. The amounts in Additional Paid-In Capital for Citigroup exceed the amounts in Common Stock, indicating that Citigroup issued common stock for substantially more than $0.01 par value, a common practice among publicly traded firms.

4. Firms accumulate information about revenues and expenses during a reporting period to enable the preparation of the income statement. Net income for a period increases net assets (= assets minus liabilities) and retained earnings; a net loss reduces net assets and retained earnings.[2]

5. Firms may periodically distribute net assets generated by earnings to shareholders as a dividend. Firms reduce net assets and retained earnings for the distribution. Citigroup declared dividends of $45 million on its preferred stock and $10,733 million on its common stock during 2007.

6. Retained earnings on the balance sheet provides a measure of the cumulative net assets generated by earnings in excess of dividends declared. Retained earnings for Citigroup exceeds the capital provided by issuing common stock. The retention of net assets generated by operations represents the primary source of funds for most successful businesses.

This chapter explores these concepts in greater depth and expands the discussion of shareholders' equity by considering the following:

1. The reasons for issuing preferred stock and the different rights firms might grant to preferred stockholders.

2. The use of options in connection with the issuance of additional common stock.

3. The reasons for repurchasing shares of common or preferred stock and the accounting for such share repurchases. **Exhibit 14.1** indicates that Citigroup had repurchased $25,092 million of its own stock as of December 31, 2006, and $21,724 million as of December 31, 2007. These repurchases substantially reduced total shareholders' equity.

4. The reporting of earnings transactions, particularly the distinction between net income (or profit) and other comprehensive income. **Exhibit 14.1** indicates that Citigroup reports a reduction in shareholders' equity for negative amounts of Accumulated Other Comprehensive Income (that is, losses) at the end of each year. What is the purpose of

---

[2]A debit balance in Retained Earnings is an *accumulated deficit*.

classifying items in other comprehensive income instead of net income or profit? What types of transactions or events give rise to other comprehensive income?

As in previous chapters, we discuss both U.S. GAAP and IFRS. We begin with capital contributions. We then move to distributions and finish the chapter with the reporting of earnings transactions.

TERMINOLOGY **Note**

The term *capital* can mean any of the following things:

- It can mean *cash* ("The firm raised capital with a stock issue"),

- or *long-term assets* ("The firm's capital assets have depreciable lives between 7 and 10 years"),

- or all sources of funding, that is, all items on the right side of the balance sheet ("The firm's weighted-average cost of capital is 11%"),

- or shareholders' equity,

- or, as in this chapter, *contributed capital*, that part of shareholders' equity arising from owners' contributions of cash and other assets in exchange for shares.

We recommend that you use this word to mean only contributed capital, but the rest of the world will continue to use the word to mean whatever is convenient for the speaker at the time. You should be attuned to the various meanings and understand what a particular user means at a particular time by the word *capital*. See the discussion in the **Glossary** for *capital*.

CAPITAL CONTRIBUTIONS

Most publicly traded firms operate as **corporations**. The corporate form has at least three advantages:

1. The corporate form provides the owner (shareholder) with **limited liability**; that is, should the corporation become insolvent, creditors can claim only the assets of the corporate entity and cannot claim the assets of the individual owners. In contrast, to settle debts of general partnerships and sole proprietorships, creditors have a claim on the owners' business and personal assets. In recent years, many partnerships and sole proprietorships have become limited liability companies (LLCs), or limited liability partnerships (LLPs), to limit their owners' personal liability for business debts and other obligations arising from unpleasant surprises involving the business, such as lawsuits filed by customers.

2. The corporate form allows the firm to raise funds by issuing shares to investors in varying amounts.

3. The corporate form facilitates the transfer of ownership interests because owners can sell their shares without affecting the ongoing operations of the firm. The transfer is a transaction between shareholders and does not involve the firm whose shares change hands.

The corporation has legal status separate from its owners. Investors make capital contributions under a contract between themselves and the corporation. Various laws and contracts govern the rights and obligations of a shareholder:

1. The corporation laws of the jurisdiction in which incorporation takes place.

2. The articles of incorporation or the **corporate charter**. This contract sets out the agreement between the firm and the jurisdiction in which the business incorporates. The jurisdiction grants to the firm the privileges of operating as a corporation for certain stated purposes and of obtaining its capital through the issue of shares of stock.

3. The **corporate bylaws**. The board of directors adopts bylaws, which are the rules and regulations governing the internal affairs of the corporation.

4. The **capital stock contract**. Each type of **capital stock** has its own provisions on matters such as voting, sharing in earnings, distributing assets generated by earnings, and sharing in assets in case of dissolution of the firm. Both U.S. GAAP and IFRS require the disclosure of information about the rights of each type of capital stock outstanding.[3]

PREFERRED SHAREHOLDERS' EQUITY

Owners of **preferred stock** have a claim on the assets of a firm that is senior to the claim of common shareholders. Preferred shares also carry special rights. The senior status and special rights may induce certain investors to purchase preferred shares of a firm, even though they would be unwilling to purchase common shares of the same firm. The senior status and special rights reduce the risks of preferred shareholders relative to common shareholders. Preferred shareholders should therefore expect a lower return than common shareholders. Preferred shares vary with respect to the rights and obligations of the issuing firm and of the investor in the preferred shares.

Dividend Rights Preferred shares usually entitle their holders to dividends at a certain rate, which the firm must pay before it can pay dividends to common shareholders. Firms may sometimes postpone or omit preferred dividends. Most preferred shares, however, have **cumulative dividend rights**, which means that a firm must pay all current and previously postponed preferred dividends before it can pay any dividends on common shares.

Call Provisions **Callable preferred shares** provide the issuer with the right (that is, the option)—but not the obligation—to repurchase preferred shares at a specified price, which may vary according to a preset time schedule. If financing becomes available at a cost lower than the rate fixed for the preferred shares, the issuing firm can reduce its financing costs by issuing new securities and then exercising its option to reacquire the outstanding preferred shares at a fixed price. The call option is valuable to the issuing firm but makes the shares less attractive to potential owners of the shares. Other things equal, a firm will receive a smaller amount from issuing callable shares than from issuing noncallable shares.

Convertible Feature **Convertible preferred shares** give the holder of preferred shares the right (that is, the option)—but not the obligation—to convert the preferred shares into a specified number of common shares under certain specified conditions. Convertible preferred shares provide the security holders with a relatively assured dividend, a claim that is senior to that of common shareholders, and the possibility of capital appreciation by converting the preferred shares into common shares if the market price of the common shares rises sufficiently. Because of the conversion option, changes in the market price of convertible preferred shares will often parallel changes in the market price of common shares. The issuing firm benefits from issuing convertible preferred shares, because these shares carry a lower dividend rate than purchasers otherwise would have required to buy the shares for a given price.

Redemption Right or Obligation Preferred shares may provide for redemption by the issuing firm in the future. **Redeemable preferred shares** carry one of three types of redemption rights or obligations:

1. **Redemption Right of the Issuer** The issuing firm has the right (that is, the option)—but not the obligation—to redeem the preferred stock under certain conditions. Redeemable preferred stock is identical to callable preferred stock discussed above.

2. **Redemption Obligation of the Issuer at a Specified Time or upon a Specified Event Certain to Occur** Common terminology refers to this preferred stock as *mandatorily redeemable preferred stock*. This preferred stock has attributes of both long-term debt and shareholders' equity. The specified redemption time is analogous to the maturity date of long-term debt. An example of an event certain to occur that would trigger redemption is the death of the preferred shareholder.

---

[3]Financial Accounting Standards Board, *Statement of Financial Accounting Standards No. 129,* "Disclosure of Information about Capital Structure," 1997 (**Codification Topic 505**); International Accounting Standards Board, *International Accounting Standard 1,* "Presentation of Financial Statements," revised 2003.

3. **Redemption Obligation of the Issuer Conditional on a Specified Event Not Certain to Occur** Some preferred stock is redeemable at the option of the holder; the owner of the preferred stock has a **put option**, the right to require the issuing firm to repurchase the shares. This is an example of an event not certain to occur. The preferred shareholder may not demand redemption.

The balance sheet classification of redeemable preferred stock depends on the provisions relating to redemption. U.S. GAAP and IFRS classify preferred stock subject to redemption only at the option of the issuing firm as shareholders' equity. Preferred stock subject to mandatory redemption is a liability. Preferred stock subject to redemption at the option of the preferred shareholders appears between liabilities and shareholders' equity in U.S. GAAP and as a liability in IFRS.[4]

The following examples illustrate disclosures related to preferred stock.

Example 1 Citigroup reports the following information about its preferred stock shown in **Exhibit 14.1** (amounts in millions).

Preferred Stock   The preferred stock of Citigroup includes the following series:

	Dividend Rate	Redeemable on or after:	Redemption Amount	Book Value
Series F	6.365%	6/17/2007	$250	$400
Series G	6.213%	7/1/2007	$250	$200
Series H	6.231%	9/8/2007	$250	$200
Series M	5.864%	10/8/2007	$250	$200

The preferred dividends are cumulative. Citigroup redeemed each series of preferred stock during 2007.

This preferred stock was callable, or redeemable, at the option of Citigroup and therefore appeared in the shareholders' equity section of its balance sheet at the end of 2006.

Example 2 A note to the financial statements of Rite Aid, a drug store chain, describes its redeemable preferred stock.

12. Redeemable Preferred Stock
In March 1999 and February 1999, Rite Aid Lease Management Company, a wholly owned subsidiary of the Company, issued 63,000 and 150,000 shares of Cumulative Preferred Stock, Class A, par value $100 per share, respectively. The Class A Cumulative Preferred Stock is mandatorily redeemable on April 1, 2019, at a redemption price of $100 per share plus accumulated and unpaid dividends. The Class A Cumulative Preferred Stock pays dividends quarterly at a rate of 7.0% per annum of the par value of $100 per share when and if declared by the Board of Directors of Rite Aid Lease Management Company in its sole discretion. The amount of dividends payable in respect of the Class A Cumulative Preferred Stock may be adjusted under certain events. The outstanding shares of the Class A Preferred Stock were recorded at their estimated fair value of $19,253 for the fiscal 2000 issuances, which equaled the sale price on the date of issuance. Because the fair value of the Class A Preferred Stock was less than the mandatory redemption amount at issuance, periodic accretions to stockholders' equity using the interest method are made so that the carrying amount equals the redemption amount on the mandatory redemption date. Accretion was $102 in fiscal 2007, 2006, and 2005. The amount of this instrument is $20,072 and $19,970 and is recorded in Other Noncurrent Liabilities as of March 3, 2007, and March 4, 2006, respectively.

Rite Aid's preferred stock is mandatorily redeemable on a specified date. Both U.S. GAAP and IFRS require Rite Aid to include the preferred shares among liabilities. Analogous to bonds issued at a discount to face value, Rite Aid must amortize the difference between the issue price and the redemption amount. The amortization involves a debit to interest expense and a credit to preferred stock.

---

[4]Financial Accounting Standards Board, *Statement of Financial Accounting Standards No. 150*, "Accounting for Certain Financial Instruments with Characteristics of Both Liabilities and Equity," 2003 (**Codification Topic 480**); Financial Accounting Standards Board, *EITF Topic D-98*, "Classification and Measurement of Redeemable Securities" (**Codification Topic 480**); Securities and Exchange Commission, *Accounting Series Release No. 268*, "Presentation in Financial Statements of Redeemable Preferred Stock"; International Accounting Standards Board, *International Accounting Standard 32*, "Financial Instruments: Presentation," revised 2003. As this book goes to press, the FASB is reconsidering the classification of redeemable preferred stock conditional on an event not certain to occur and its classification between liabilities and shareholders' equity on the balance sheet.

Example 3 Nike, a sports footwear and apparel company, discloses the following information about its redeemable preferred stock.

Note 9—Redeemable Preferred Stock

Sojitz America is the sole owner of the Company's authorized Redeemable Preferred Stock, $1 par value, which is redeemable at the option of Sojitz America or the Company at par value aggregating $0.3 million. A cumulative dividend of $0.10 per share is payable annually on May 31, and no dividends may be declared or paid on the common stock of the Company unless dividends on the Redeemable Preferred Stock have been declared and paid in full. As the holder of the Redeemable Preferred Stock, Sojitz America does not have general voting rights but does have the right to vote as a separate class on the sale of all or substantially all of the assets of the Company and its subsidiaries, on merger, consolidation, liquidation or dissolution of the Company or on the sale or assignment of the NIKE trademark for athletic footwear sold in the United States.

Nike's preferred stock is redeemable at the option of either Sojitz America or Nike at its par value of $0.3 million. U.S. GAAP views this preferred stock as conditionally redeemable and requires classification on the balance sheet between liabilities and shareholders' equity. IFRS would require classification as a liability because the holder of the preferred stock has the right to require the issuer to redeem the shares.

The dividend of $0.10 per share is cumulative. Nike must pay this dividend for the current year and any unpaid dividends from prior years before it can pay dividends on its common stock. The preferred stock has voting rights only on major changes in Nike.

COMMON SHAREHOLDERS' EQUITY

Corporations need not issue preferred stock. All corporations, however, must issue **common stock**. Common shareholders have a claim on the assets of a firm after creditors and preferred shareholders have received amounts promised to them. Frequently, corporations grant voting rights only to common shares, giving their holders the right to elect members of the board of directors and to decide certain broad corporate policies (spelled out in the stock contract). Some firms issue more than one class of common shares, with each class granted different voting rights.

Example 4 Nike reports its common stock as follows (amounts in millions):

Common Stock (Note 10)	May 31, 2007	May 31, 2006
Class A Convertible, 117.6 and 127.8 shares outstanding	.1	.1
Class B, 384.1 and 382.2 shares outstanding	2.7	2.7

Note 10—Common Stock

The authorized number of shares of Class A Common Stock, no par value, and Class B Common Stock, no par value, are 350 million and 1.5 billion, respectively. Each share of Class A Common Stock is convertible into one share of Class B Common Stock. Voting rights of Class B Common Stock are limited in certain circumstances with respect to the election of directors.

The Class B shares trade in public securities markets, whereas the Class A shares do not trade. A small group of individuals owns the Class A shares and has senior rights with respect to electing members of the board of directors relative to the Class B shares. The two classes of common stock receive identical dividends per share.

ISSUING CAPITAL STOCK

Firms may issue capital stock (preferred or common) for cash or for noncash assets. Some issuances of common stock result from various option arrangements.

Issue for Cash Firms usually issue shares for cash at the time of their initial incorporation and at periodic intervals as they need additional shareholder funds. Firms sometimes issue shares to employees as compensation. The issue price for preferred stock usually approximates its par value. Firms generally issue common shares, both at the time of initial incorporation and in subsequent years, for amounts greater than **par (or stated) value**.[5] The firm credits the excess of issue proceeds over par (or stated) value to the **Additional Paid-In Capital** account.

To illustrate, assume a firm issues 1,000 common shares with a par value of $10 per share for $100,000. The journal entry is as follows:

Cash	100,000	
Common Stock—$10 Par Value		10,000
Additional Paid-In Capital		90,000

Assets	=	Liabilities	+	Shareholders' Equity	(Class.)
+100,000				+10,000	ContriCap
				+90,000	ContriCap

To record the issue of common shares for cash in an amount greater than par value.

Issue for Noncash Assets Firms also issue common stock for assets other than cash, for example, to acquire another firm. The firm records the shares exchanged for noncash assets at the fair value of the shares given or, if the firm cannot make a reasonable estimate, at the fair value of the assets received.[6]

Assume that a firm issues 1,000 shares of its common stock with a par value of $10 per share and a fair value of $100 per share to acquire another firm's assets having the following fair values: accounts receivable, $6,000; inventories, $12,000; land, $10,000; building, $62,000; and equipment, $10,000. The journal entry to record the exchange is as follows:

Accounts Receivable	6,000	
Inventories	12,000	
Land	10,000	
Building	62,000	
Equipment	10,000	
Common Stock—$10 Par Value		10,000
Additional Paid-In Capital		90,000

Assets	=	Liabilities	+	Shareholders' Equity	(Class.)
+6,000				+10,000	ContriCap
+12,000				+90,000	ContriCap
+10,000					
+62,000					
+10,000					

To record the issue of common shares for noncash assets in amount greater than par value. The amount for Additional Paid-In Capital is the excess of the fair value of the shares issued over their aggregate par value.

Issue for Services Received If a firm issues common stock in return for services other than from employees (discussed later), the firm records the transaction at the fair value of the services received if it can more reliably measure this amount than the fair value of the shares issued. Otherwise, the firm records the transaction at the fair value of the shares

[5]Not all common shares have a par or stated value; some firms issue no-par shares. The laws of the jurisdiction in which a firm incorporates largely determine whether the firm issues par value or no-par value shares. Par or stated values have less relevance now than they did years ago when the par value established the lower limit on the amount for which a firm could issue shares.

[6]Financial Accounting Standards Board, *Statement of Financial Accounting Standards No. 141R (revised 2007)*, "Business Combinations," 2007 (**Codification Topic 805**); International Accounting Standards Board, *International Financial Reporting Standard 3*, "Business Combinations," revised 2008.

issued. For example, if a firm issues 100 shares with $10 par value to attorneys for $10,000 of legal services, instead of paying cash, the entry would be as follows:

Legal Expense	10,000	
Common Stock—$10 Par Value		1,000
Additional Paid-In Capital		9,000

Assets	=	Liabilities	+	Shareholders' Equity	(Class.)
				−10,000	IncSt → RE
				+1,000	ContriCap
				+9,000	ContriCap

To record the issue of common shares with a fair value of $10,000 to attorneys for legal services received.

ISSUE UNDER OPTION ARRANGEMENTS

Corporations often sell, or exchange for goods and services, various **call options** on their shares. A call option gives the holder the right to acquire shares of common stock at a fixed or determinable price, called the **strike price** or **exercise price**. If the market price of the shares increases above the exercise price, the holder of the option can benefit by exercising the option to purchase shares. The excess of the market price over the exercise price is the option's **intrinsic value**.

Stock Options and Stock Purchase Rights Many firms pay part of the compensation of some employees by issuing call options on their own shares. Common terminology refers to these arrangements as **employee stock options (ESOs)**. These stock options typically permit the employees to purchase shares of the employer's common stock at a fixed exercise price that the employer often sets equal to the market price of the stock at the time it grants the stock option. Firms adopt stock option plans to motivate employees to take actions that will increase the market value of the firm's common shares, to conserve cash and, in the United States, to take advantage of the favorable tax treatment that income tax laws accord this form of compensation. Firms may also grant or sell **stock purchase rights** to current shareholders, which give the shareholders the right to purchase shares of common or preferred stock at a specified price. Firms may also sell or exchange call options for goods and services with counterparties other than employees.

Stock Warrants Firms sometimes issue bonds with **stock warrants** that have the same features as call options. The bond contract gives the holder the right to receive periodic interest payments and the principal amount at maturity. The stock warrant permits the holder to exchange the warrant and a specified amount of cash for shares of the firm's common stock. Attaching a stock warrant permits the firm to issue bonds at a lower interest cost than the market would require for bonds without such a warrant attached.

Firms may also issue preferred stock with stock warrants attached. Attaching a stock warrant permits the firm to issue preferred stock with a lower dividend rate. The preferred shareholders benefit if the market price of the common stock increases. A conversion provision, previously discussed in the context of convertible preferred stock, also functions like a stock warrant. That is, a conversion provision has the same economic features as a call option.

Example 5 The following excerpt from the notes to the financial statements of Priceline.com describes its preferred stock with stock warrants attached.

> In 2001, the Company issued Delta Air Lines, Inc. ("Delta") 80,000 shares of Series B Redeemable Preferred Stock, par value $0.01 per share ("Series B Preferred Stock") and warrants (the "Warrants") to purchase approximately 4.5 million shares of the Company's common stock at an exercise price of $17.81 per share. The exercise price of the Warrants is paid by surrendering .0178125 shares of Series B Preferred Stock for each share of the Company's common stock purchased.

The terms of these stock warrants effectively permit the preferred shareholders to convert their preferred stock into common stock. Alternatively, the warrants are the equivalent of a call option with an exercise price of $17.81 per share.

FIGURE 14.1   **Graphic Depiction of Stock Option Arrangement**

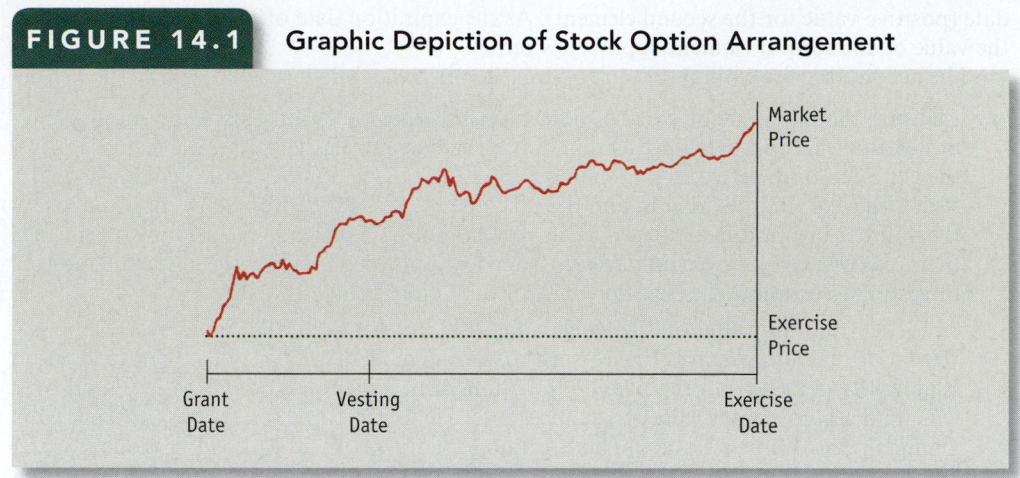

Arrangements such as stock options, stock rights, and stock warrants that give the holder the right to obtain common shares at a fixed exercise price have economic value. However, accounting recognition of this value lacks consistency, particularly when the arrangement is part of another financial instrument such as a bond (that is, convertible debt). A later section discusses the accounting for bonds issued with stock warrants attached and for convertible debt. Both U.S. GAAP and IFRS require firms to recognize the fair value of employee stock options in the accounting records,[7] as discussed next.

Employee Stock Option Plans An understanding of the accounting for employee stock options (ESOs) requires several definitions. Refer to **Figure 14.1**. The *grant date* is the date a firm awards a stock option to employees. The *vesting date* is the first date employees can exercise their stock options. The *vesting period* is the period between the grant date and the vesting date. A vesting period that depends only on the passage of time is a service condition; a vesting period that depends on achieving a specified level of profitability or meeting some other nonshare-price-based target is a performance condition; and a vesting period that depends on the firm's stock price reaching a specified target is a market condition. The purpose of these conditions is to increase the likelihood that the employee continues to work for the firm and to motivate the employee to take actions that will increase the stock price.

The *exercise date* is the date employees exchange the option and cash for shares of common stock. The *exercise price* is the price specified in the stock option contract for purchasing the common stock. The *market price* is the price of the stock as it trades in the market.

The value of a stock option results from two elements:

1. The benefit realized on the exercise date, because the market price of the stock exceeds the exercise price (the **benefit element**) equal to the intrinsic value of the option on the exercise date.

2. The length of the period during which the holder can exercise the option (the **time value element**).

One cannot measure the amount of the benefit element before the exercise date. Stock options with exercise prices less than the current market price of the stock (described as *in the money*) have a higher value, other things equal, than stock options with exercise prices exceeding the current market price of the stock (described as *out of the money*). The time value element results from the possibility of increases in the market price of the stock during the exercise period. Time value is larger the longer the exercise period and the more volatile the market price of the stock. A stock option whose exercise price exceeds the current market price (zero intrinsic value and therefore zero value for the benefit element) has economic value because of the possibility that the market price will exceed the exercise price on the exercise

---

[7]Financial Accounting Standards Board, *Statement of Financial Accounting Standards No. 123R*, "Share-Based Payment," 2004 (**Codification Topic 718**); International Accounting Standards Board, *International Financial Reporting Standard 2*, "Share-Based Payment," 2004.

date (positive value for the second element). As the expiration date of the option approaches, the value of the second element approaches zero.[8]

The accounting for employee stock options involves the following:

1. Measure the fair value of stock options on the date of the grant using an option-pricing model that incorporates information about the current market price, the exercise price, the expected time between grant and exercise, the expected market price volatility of the stock, the expected dividends, and the risk-free interest rate. Total compensation cost is the number of options the firm expects to vest times the fair value per option. Firms use their historical experience on forfeitures due to employees terminating employment prior to vesting to estimate the expected number of options that will vest.

2. Amortize the fair value of the stock options on the date of the grant over the *requisite service period*, which is the expected period of benefit. The requisite service period, usually the period from the date of the grant to the date of vesting, is the period over which an employee must provide services in order to vest in the options. The firm debits Compensation Expense and credits Additional Paid-In Capital (Stock Options) for the amount amortized. The firm does not recompute the fair value of the option at each succeeding balance sheet date to reflect new information about stock prices, volatility, dividend yield, or risk-free interest rates.

3. When employees exercise their options, the firm debits Cash for the proceeds, debits Additional Paid-In Capital (Stock Options) for any amounts credited to that account in step **2** above, credits Common Stock for the par value of the shares issued, and credits Additional Paid-In Capital for any excess of the cash received plus the amount amortized in step **2** above over the par value of the shares issued.

Example 6 Fiala Corporation awards options to employees on January 1, 2008, to acquire 1,000 shares of $5 par value common stock at an exercise price of $35 per share. The firm uses an option-pricing model to value the options at $8,000. The requisite service period (the period during which Fiala Corporation expects to receive employee services) is two years; this is an example of a service condition. All of the options vest, and employees exercise the options on December 31, 2011, when the market price of the stock is $50 per share. Fiala Corporation makes the following entries:

January 1, 2008
No entry

December 31, 2008

Compensation Expense	4,000
Additional Paid-In Capital (Stock Options)	4,000

Assets	=	Liabilities	+	Shareholders' Equity	(Class.)
				−4,000	IncSt → RE
				+4,000	ContriCap

December 31, 2009

Compensation Expense	4,000
Additional Paid-In Capital (Stock Options)	4,000

Assets	=	Liabilities	+	Shareholders' Equity	(Class.)
				−4,000	IncSt → RE
				+4,000	ContriCap

December 31, 2011

Cash (1,000 × $35)	35,000	
Additional Paid-In Capital (Stock Options)	8,000	
Common Stock—Par Value (1,000 × $5)		5,000
Additional Paid-In Capital [8,000 + (1,000 × ($35 − $5))]		38,000

(continued)

---

[8]For an elaboration on the theory of option pricing, see Fischer Black and Myron Scholes, "The Pricing of Options and Corporate Liabilities," *Journal of Political Economy* (May–June 1973), pp. 637–654.

Assets	=	Liabilities	+	Shareholders' Equity	(Class.)
+35,000				−8,000	ContriCap
				+5,000	ContriCap
				+38,000	ContriCap

This accounting recognizes an expense as the firm receives the benefits ($4,000 each in both 2008 and 2009) and increases contributed capital for both the cash equivalent value of employees' services rendered to obtain the common stock ($8,000) and the cash received when employees exercise their options ($35,000).

The accounting for stock options is more complex than this illustration suggests because firms often include combinations of service, performance, and market conditions and because firms can restructure their plans.

Example 7 **Exhibit 14.2** presents information about the stock option plan of Panera Bread Company (Panera) for its 2005, 2006, and 2007 fiscal years.

The first paragraph indicates that Panera uses the Black-Scholes option-pricing model to derive option values of $21.19 for fiscal 2005, $19.18 for fiscal 2006, and $15.69 for fiscal 2007. The first paragraph also indicates the assumptions Panera made with respect to stock price volatility, expected term, expected dividend, and risk-free interest rate.

The panel of data indicates the recent history of total options granted, exercised, cancelled, and outstanding, along with the number of options and weighted-average exercise

EXHIBIT 14.2   **Panera Bread Company**
Stock Options Disclosures

STOCK OPTIONS

The weighted-average fair value of options granted during fiscal 2007, 2006 and 2005 of $15.69, $19.18, and $21.19, respectively, was estimated on the date of grant using the Black-Scholes option-pricing model with the following assumptions: expected volatility of 30% in fiscal 2007 and 2006 and 36% in fiscal 2005, expected term of 5 years in fiscal 2007, 2006, and 2005, risk-free interest rate of 4.73% in fiscal 2007, 4.84% in fiscal 2006, and 4.04% in fiscal 2005, and expected dividend yield of 0% in fiscal 2007, 2006, and 2005.

A summary of stock option activity under the Company's stock-based compensation plans is set forth below:

	Options (in thousands)	Weighted-Average Exercise Price	Weighted-Average Remaining Contractual Term (in years)	Aggregate Intrinsic Value (in thousands)
Outstanding at December 25, 2004	3,045	28.72		
Granted	340	55.55		
Exercised	(657)	19.24		
Cancelled	(159)	36.70		
Outstanding at December 27, 2005	2,569	34.20		
Granted	146	54.27		
Exercised	(305)	25.25		
Cancelled	(99)	37.74		
Outstanding at December 26, 2006	2,311	36.36		
Granted	140	44.58		
Exercised	(310)	21.40		
Cancelled	(55)	40.88		
Outstanding at December 25, 2007	2,086	39.05	2.3	$5,000
Exercisable at December 25, 2007	1,316	36.65	1.9	$4,425

Of the options at December 25, 2007; December 26, 2006; and December 27, 2005; 1,315,512; 1,152,382; and 927,972, respectively, were vested and exercisable with a weighted-average exercise price of $36.65, $32.40, and $30.01, respectively.

The total intrinsic value of options exercised during the fiscal years ended December 25, 2007; December 26, 2006; and December 27, 2005; was $10.1 million, $12.3 million, and $25.5 million, respectively. Stock option expense was $3.9 million for fiscal 2007 and $5.9 million for fiscal 2006. As of December 25, 2007, the total unrecognized compensation cost related to nonvested options was $7.8 million, which is net of a $1.4 million forfeiture estimate and is expected to be recognized over a weighted-average period of approximately 2.6 years.

price for each category. This panel of data also indicates the number of options and weighted-average exercise price for options exercisable on December 25, 2007. Exercisable options are those that have vested for employees. The weighted-average remaining contractual term indicates the time remaining for employees to exercise the options. The intrinsic value is the difference between the market price and the exercise price on December 25, 2007, for the number of options outstanding and exercisable.

The first paragraph under the panel of data indicates the number of outstanding and exercisable options and the weighted-average exercise price at the end of fiscal 2005, 2006, and 2007 for comparison with the disclosures on the last two lines in the panel of data.

The last paragraph discloses the following:

1. **The total intrinsic value of options exercised during the last three years.** These amounts represent the benefits actually realized by employees who exercised their options at a price less than the market price on the date of exercise.

2. **The amount of stock option expense for fiscal 2006 and 2007.** The amount of stock option expense for fiscal 2007 would include amortized portions of compensation cost from options granted in fiscal years prior to and including 2007.

3. **The amount of compensation cost Panera expects to amortize over the weighted-average remaining period of 2.6 years.** The $7.8 million amount, net of estimated forfeitures, likely includes portions of compensation cost from options granted in fiscal 2007 and prior years. One might expect stock option expense of at least $3 million (= $7.8 million/2.6 years) in fiscal 2008. Stock option expense will exceed $3 million, however, because Panera will amortize a portion of the cost of options granted in fiscal 2008.

Stock Rights Like stock options, stock rights give their holder the right to acquire shares of stock at a specified price. The major differences between stock options and stock rights are as follows:

- **Firms grant stock options to employees.** Employees receive them as a form of compensation and in general may not transfer or sell them to others; therefore, they do not trade in public markets.

- **Firms grant stock rights to current shareholders.** Shareholders may exercise the stock rights or sell them to others. The rights usually trade in public markets.

Firms often issue stock rights to raise new capital from current shareholders. The granting of stock rights to current shareholders requires no accounting entries. U.S. GAAP and IFRS do not require recognition of the rights on the date of the grant. When holders exercise the rights, the firm records the issue of shares at the price paid just as it records the issue of new shares for cash.

Stock Warrants Firms issue stock warrants to the general investing public for cash or attached to bonds. Assume that a firm issues warrants for $15,000 cash. The warrants allow holders to purchase 10,000 shares for $20 each. The entry is as follows:

Cash..	15,000	
Additional Paid-In Capital (Stock Warrants)		15,000

Assets	=	Liabilities	+	Shareholders' Equity	(Class.)
+15,000				+15,000	ContriCap

To record the sale of common stock warrants to the public.

When warrant holders exercise their rights, the firm issues 10,000 shares of $5 par value common stock in exchange for the warrants plus $200,000 and makes the following entry:

Cash..	200,000	
Additional Paid-In Capital (Stock Warrants)	15,000	
Common Stock—$5 Par Value.............................		50,000
Additional Paid-In Capital		165,000

(*continued*)

Assets	=	Liabilities	+	Shareholders' Equity	(Class.)
+200,000				−15,000	ContriCap
				+50,000	ContriCap
				+165,000	ContriCap

To record the issue of 10,000 shares for $200,000 and the redemption of warrants.

If the warrants expire before the holders exercise them, the firm records the following entry:

Additional Paid-In Capital (Stock Warrants)	15,000	
Additional Paid-In Capital		15,000

Assets	=	Liabilities	+	Shareholders' Equity	(Class.)
				−15,000	ContriCap
				+15,000	ContriCap

Holders of a bond or preferred stock with common stock warrants attached can detach and redeem the warrants separately from the bond or preferred stock. The holder receives periodic interest or preferred dividends and holds a call option to purchase common shares. U.S. GAAP and IFRS require the firm to measure the fair value of the stock warrants separately from the value of the associated bond or preferred stock and allocate the issue price between the two securities.[9]

To illustrate, assume that a firm issues 20-year, $1,000,000 bonds with 7% semiannual coupons. The bonds contain stock warrants, which their holders can either sell on the open market or exercise to acquire 10,000 shares of common stock for $200,000. The issue price for the bonds and warrants is $1,050,000. Immediately after issue, the bonds sell on the market for $1,035,000, and the warrants sell for $15,000. The journal entry to record the issue of the bonds is as follows:

Cash..	1,050,000	
Bonds Payable		1,035,000
Additional Paid-In Capital (Stock Warrants)		15,000

Assets	=	Liabilities	+	Shareholders' Equity	(Class.)
+1,050,000		+1,035,000		+15,000	ContriCap

To record the issue of bonds with stock warrants.

The subsequent accounting for the bonds follows the procedures discussed in **Chapter 10** for bonds issued above or below par value. The accounting for the warrants follows the procedures illustrated above for warrants issued for cash.

Convertible Bonds or Preferred Stock **Convertible bonds** and **convertible preferred stock** permit the owner either to hold the security as a bond or preferred stock or to convert the security into shares of common stock. The owner cannot detach and transfer, or separately exercise, the conversion option as the owner can for a bond or preferred stock issued with a separable stock warrant. The issue price of a convertible bond or convertible preferred stock is payment for both debt or preferred stock and for the conversion option, but no one can observe the fair value of these separate components..

Issue of Convertible Bonds or Convertible Preferred Stock: U.S. GAAP In most cases U.S. GAAP requires firms to allocate the full issue price to the bonds or preferred stock and none of the price to the conversion feature.[10] Suppose, for example, that Johnson

---

[9]Accounting Principles Board, *Opinion No. 14,* "Accounting for Convertible Debt and Debt Issued with Stock Purchase Warrants," 1969 (**Codification Topic 470**); International Accounting Standards Board, *International Accounting Standard 32,* "Financial Instruments: Presentation," revised 2003.

Company's credit rating would allow it to issue either $100,000 of 10-year, 8% semiannual coupon bonds at par or $100,000 of convertible 6% semiannual coupon bonds that permit the holder of each $1,000 bond to convert it into 50 shares of Johnson Company $5 par value common stock. (Holders in aggregate can convert the entire issue into 5,000 shares.) The conversion price, which is the exercise price on the call option embedded in the conversion feature, is $20 per share (=$1,000/50 shares). U.S. GAAP requires the following entry:

Cash..	100,000	
Convertible Bonds Payable............................		100,000

Assets	=	Liabilities	+	Shareholders' Equity	(Class.)
+100,000		+100,000			

To record the issue of convertible bonds at par under U.S. GAAP.

This entry effectively treats convertible bonds like nonconvertible bonds, and it records the value of the conversion feature at zero.

Issue of Convertible Bonds or Convertible Preferred Stock: IFRS

IFRS[11] requires firms to allocate a portion of the issue price to the conversion feature. The calculation of this amount requires knowing the proceeds of an issue of nonconvertible bonds that otherwise resemble the convertible bonds. In this case, that amount would be the present value of 6%, 10-year, semiannual (nonconvertible) coupon bonds discounted at 8%, or $86,410. That is, the firm can borrow at 8% without a conversion feature and at 6% with a conversion feature. For this firm to issue 6% convertible bonds at par, the conversion feature must be worth $13,590 (= $100,000 − $86,410). That is, the bond buyers have paid $13,590 for the conversion feature. The entry under IFRS is as follows:

Cash..	100,000	
Convertible Bonds Payable............................		86,410
Additional Paid-In Capital (Convertible Bonds)		13,590

Assets	=	Liabilities	+	Shareholders' Equity	(Class.)
+100,000		+86,410		+13,590	ContriCap

To record under IFRS the issue of 6% semiannual coupon convertible bonds at a time when the firm could issue nonconvertible bonds for $86,410. U.S. GAAP does not allow this entry.[12]

After issue, the firm, following IFRS, will use the amortized cost method, as explained in **Chapter 10**, with an historical interest rate of 8%.

Conversion of Convertible Bonds and Convertible Preferred Stock

Accounting for the conversion of bonds or preferred stock into common stock uses either carrying values or fair values to record the conversion, although practice is evolving.

The usual entry to record the conversion of convertible bonds or preferred stock into common shares ignores current market prices and shows the swap of common shares for bonds or preferred stock at their carrying value. For example, assume that the market price of Johnson Company's common stock increases to $30 a share, so that the holder of one $1,000 bond, convertible into 50 shares, can convert it into shares with a market value of $1,500. If holders convert all the convertible bonds into common shares at this time, the firm would issue 5,000 shares of $5 par value stock on conversion and make the following journal entry when using carrying values of the bonds:

---

[10]Accounting Principles Board, *Opinion No. 14*, "Accounting for Convertible Debt and Debt Issued with Stock Purchase Warrants," 1969 (**Codification Topic 470**).

[11]International Accounting Standards Board, *International Accounting Standard 32*, "Financial Instruments: Presentation," revised 2003.

[12]As this book goes to press, the FASB is reconsidering the accounting for convertible bonds. Given the FASB's recent moves to recognize the fair value of various options, the required accounting for convertible bonds in the future may follow the IFRS treatment.

Convertible Bonds Payable	. . .	100,000	
Common Stock—$5 Par Value	. . .		25,000
Additional Paid-In Capital	. . .		75,000

Assets	=	Liabilities	+	Shareholders' Equity	(Class.)
		−100,000		+25,000	ContriCap
				+75,000	ContriCap

To record the conversion of convertible bonds with a carrying value of $100,000 into 5,000 shares of $5 par value stock.[13]

An allowable alternative treatment recognizes that market prices provide information useful in quantifying the market value of the shares issued. Under the alternative treatment, with $30 market price per share and $150,000 fair market value of the 5,000 shares issued on conversion, the journal entry would be as follows:

Convertible Bonds Payable	. . .	100,000	
Loss on Conversion of Bonds	. . .	50,000	
Common Stock—$5 Par Value	. . .		25,000
Additional Paid-In Capital	. . .		125,000

Assets	=	Liabilities	+	Shareholders' Equity	(Class.)
		−100,000		−50,000	IncSt → RE
				+25,000	ContriCap
				+125,000	ContriCap

To record the conversion of convertible bonds with a carrying value of $100,000 into 5,000 shares of common stock at a time when the market price is $30 per share.

Relative to the usual entry, the alternative entry results in a loss on the income statement and the same total shareholders' equity, with smaller retained earnings but larger contributed capital. The alternative entry treats the conversion as if the following two separate transactions occurred:

Cash	. . .	150,000	
Common Stock—$5 Par Value	. . .		25,000
Additional Paid-In Capital	. . .		125,000

Assets	=	Liabilities	+	Shareholders' Equity	(Class.)
+150,000				+25,000	ContriCap
				+125,000	ContriCap

To record the issue of 5,000 shares of $5 par value common stock at $30 per share.

Convertible Bonds Payable	. . .	100,000	
Loss on Retirement of Bonds	. . .	50,000	
Cash	. . .		150,000

Assets	=	Liabilities	+	Shareholders' Equity	(Class.)
−150,000		−100,000		−50,000	IncSt → RE

To record the retirement by purchase for $150,000 of convertible bonds with a carrying value of $100,000.

---

[13]The carrying value of the bonds under IFRS will be less than $100,000 because a portion of the issue price was initially allocated to the conversion option. A firm following IFRS and using carrying values to record the conversion would use the carrying value of the debt at the time of conversion in this entry.

PROBLEM 14.1 for Self-Study

Journal entries for capital contributions. Prepare journal entries to record the following transactions for Healy Corporation during the current year under U.S. GAAP. The accounting period of Healy Corporation ends on December 31.

a. Issued 100,000 of $10 par value common stock for $14 per share on January 2.

b. Issued 10,000 shares of common stock on January 2 in the acquisition of a patent. The firm has no separate information about the fair value of the patent.

c. Issued 2,000 shares of $100 convertible preferred stock on March 1 for $100 per share. Holders may convert each share of preferred stock into four shares of common stock.

d. Sold 10,000 common warrants on the open market on June 1 for $5 per warrant. Holders can exchange each warrant and $24 in cash for a share of common stock.

e. Holders of 600 shares of convertible preferred stock (see **c**) exchanged their shares for common stock on September 15. The market price of the common stock on this date was $26 per share. Record the conversion using the carrying values.

f. Holders of 4,000 common stock warrants exchanged their warrants (see **d**) and $96,000 in cash for common stock on November 20. The market price of the common stock on this date was $32 per share.

g. Granted options to employees to purchase 5,000 shares of common stock for $35 per share on January 2. The fair value of these options is $30,000 and the requisite service period is three years. The firm expects all the options to vest.

CORPORATE DISTRIBUTIONS

Firms use net assets (= assets − liabilities) to generate more net assets through the earnings process. Firms typically retain some or all of the net assets generated by earnings, causing net assets to increase, along with retained earnings, which is the component of shareholders' equity showing the cause of that increase in net assets. The retention of net assets generated by earnings generally increases the market price of the firm's common shares. Some firms pay periodic dividends to the common shareholders. Each common shareholder receives the same dividend per share as all other common shareholders, unless a firm has more than one class of common stock and their dividend rights differ. This section discusses corporate dividend policies and the accounting for dividends.

Firms may also choose to use the net assets generated by earnings to repurchase common shares. Repurchases result in cash outflows for a firm, similar to paying a cash dividend. In the case of share repurchases, only those shareholders that choose to sell their shares to the firm receive cash. This section discusses business reasons for stock repurchases and the accounting for such repurchases.

DIVIDENDS

The board of directors has the legal authority to declare dividends. When considering whether to declare dividends, directors must conclude that declaring a dividend is both legal (under law and contract) and financially desirable.

Legal Limits on Dividends—Statutory (by Law) Jurisdiction-specific corporate laws limit directors' freedom to declare dividends. Without these limits, directors might dissipate the firm's assets for the benefit of common shareholders, harming other nonshareholding stakeholders, in particular creditors.

One example of a limitation of the declaration of dividends provides that the board may not declare dividends "out of capital," that is, debited against the contributed capital accounts, which result from fund-raising transactions with owners, but must declare them "out of earnings" by debiting them against the Retained Earnings account, which results from earnings transactions. The wording and the interpretation of this rule vary among jurisdictions. "Capital" may mean the par or stated value of outstanding common shares or the total amount paid in by shareholders. Some jurisdictions allow corporations to declare dividends out of the earnings of the current period even if the Retained Earnings account has a debit (negative) balance because of accumulated losses from previous periods.

Statutory limits generally do not influence the accounting for shareholders' equity and dividends. A balance sheet does not provide the details of amounts legally available for dividends, but it should disclose information necessary for the user to apply the legal rules of the corporation's jurisdiction of incorporation.

Legal Limits on Dividends—Contractual Contracts with bondholders, other lenders, and preferred shareholders often limit dividend payments and thereby compel the retention of earnings. For example, a bond contract may require that total liabilities not exceed the total amount of shareholders' equity or that firms retire debt "out of earnings." Such a provision involves curtailing dividends so that the necessary debt service payments, plus any dividends, do not exceed the amount of earnings for the period. This provision forces the shareholders to increase their investment in the business by limiting the amount of dividends that the board might otherwise declare for them. Financial statement notes must disclose significant limitations on dividend declarations.[14]

Example 8 The notes to a financial statement of Sears contain the following disclosure:

> Dividend payments are restricted by several statutory and contractual factors, including: Certain indentures relating to the long-term debt of Sears, which represent the most restrictive contractual limitation on the payment of dividends, provide that the company cannot take specified actions, including the declaration of cash dividends, which would cause its consolidated unencumbered assets, as defined [in the indentures, not in the annual report], to fall below 150% of its consolidated liabilities, as defined. At . . . [year-end], $11.2 billion in retained income [of a total of $12.7 billion of retained earnings] could be paid in dividends to shareholders under the most restrictive indentures. [Sears declared dividends for the year of approximately $700 million.]

Dividends and Corporate Financial Policy Directors usually declare dividends less than the legal maximum and thereby allow retained earnings to increase as a matter of corporate financial policy for several reasons:

1. Available cash did not increase by as much as the amount of earnings, so paying the maximum legally permitted dividends would require raising more cash.
2. Restricting dividends in prosperous years may permit continued level or steadily growing dividend payments in poor years.
3. The firm may need funds for expansion of working capital or for plant and equipment.
4. Reducing the amount of borrowings, rather than paying dividends, may seem prudent.
5. The firm can distribute the funds to shareholders with lower tax burdens for them by using the cash to repurchase shares.

Example 9 Refer to the information for Citigroup in **Exhibit 14.1**. Citigroup declared dividends on its common stock of $9,761 million in 2006 and $10,733 million in 2007. Net income was $21,249 million in 2006 and $3,617 million for 2007. Despite the decline in net income between 2006 and 2007, Citigroup increased its dividends. Firms typically do not consistently pay dividends in amounts larger than net income. The increase in dividends in 2007, despite the reduced earnings, might signal that Citigroup expects the reduced net income to be temporary.

ACCOUNTING FOR DIVIDENDS

A firm may pay dividends in cash, other assets, or shares of its common stock.

---

[14]Financial Accounting Standards Board, *Statement of Financial Accounting Standards No. 5*, "Accounting for Contingencies," 1975 (**Codification Topic 450**). The required disclosure is implicit in International Accounting Standards Board, *International Accounting Standard 1*, "Presentation of Financial Statements," revised 2003.

Cash Dividends When the board of directors declares a **cash dividend**, the entry is as follows:

| Retained Earnings (Dividends Declared) | . . . . | 150,000 | |
| Dividends Payable | . . . . | | 150,000 |

Assets	=	Liabilities	+	Shareholders' Equity	(Class.)
		+150,000		−150,000	RE

To record declaration of dividends.

Once the board of directors declares a dividend, the dividend becomes a legal liability of the corporation. Dividends Payable appears as a current liability on the balance sheet if the firm has not yet paid the dividends by the end of the accounting period. When the firm pays the dividends, the entry is as follows:

| Dividends Payable | . . . . | 150,000 | |
| Cash | . . . . | | 150,000 |

Assets	=	Liabilities	+	Shareholders' Equity	(Class.)
−150,000		−150,000			

To record payment of previously declared dividend.

Property Dividends Corporations sometimes distribute assets other than cash when paying a dividend; such a dividend is known as a **dividend in kind** or a **property dividend**.

Example 10 Millenium Holding Group reported the following information about a property dividend:

> Millenium Holding Group Inc. today announced a dividend of 750,000 shares of Pacific First Corporation's common stock to the shareholders of the Company. Pacific First Corporation is a real estate development and full service real estate company. Millenium was engaged to assist Pacific First Corporation in achieving certain strategic objectives, consulting, and performing advisory services. Compensation is the stock being distributed to the Millenium shareholders.

The accounting for property dividends resembles that for cash dividends, except that when the firm pays the dividend, it credits the asset given up, rather than Cash. The amount debited to Retained Earnings equals the fair value of the assets distributed. When this fair value differs from the carrying value of the assets distributed, the firm recognizes a gain or loss in net income.[15]

Stock Dividends The retention of earnings may lead to a substantial increase in shareholders' equity, as the firm accumulates net assets that it keeps invested in the business on a relatively permanent basis. The permanency results from the firm's having committed the net assets generated by the earnings process for the long term, for example, by investing in fixed assets. To indicate such a permanent commitment of assets generated by reinvested earnings, the board of directors may declare a **stock dividend**. The accounting involves a debit to the Retained Earnings account and credits to contributed capital accounts. The stock dividend does not affect total shareholders' equity. It reallocates amounts from Retained Earnings to the contributed capital accounts. When the firm declares a stock dividend, shareholders receive additional shares of stock in proportion to their existing holdings. If, for example, the firm issues a 5% stock dividend, each shareholder receives one additional share for every 20 shares held before the dividend.

---

[15]Financial Accounting Standards Board, *Opinion No. 29*, "Accounting for Nonmonetary Transactions," 1973 (**Codification Topic 845**). This accounting is consistent with IASB pronouncements on related topics.

Example 11 The financial statements of Canyon Bancorp, a commercial bank holding company located in Palm Springs, California, disclosed the following:

Stock Dividend

The board of directors of Canyon Bancorp, the parent company of Canyon National Bank, approved a 5% stock dividend on November 27, 2007, payable to shareholders of record on December 11, 2007. The stock dividend will be issued on December 26, 2007.

U.S. GAAP requires firms to record the shares issued in a stock dividend at their fair value.[16] Canyon Bancorp had 2,316,620 shares outstanding prior to the stock dividend. The 5% stock dividend resulted in the issuance of 115,831 (= .05 × 2,316,620) additional shares. Canyon Bancorp recorded the stock dividend using a market price per share of $18.73. The entry was as follows (amounts in thousands):

Retained Earnings (Dividends Declared)............................	2,169	
Common Stock—No Par Value............................		2,169

Assets	=	Liabilities	+	Shareholders' Equity	(Class.)
				−2,169	RE
				+2,169	ContriCap

To record the declaration and issue of a stock dividend; $2,169 = 115.831 × $18.73.

The stock dividend relabels a portion of the retained earnings that had been legally available for dividend declarations as a more permanent form of shareholders' equity, because the firm has used some funds represented by past earnings to expand plant facilities or to replace assets at increased prices or to retire bonds. The firm does not have this cash available for cash dividends. The stock dividend does not affect the availability of cash on hand or cash that the firm has already invested; rather, the stock dividend signals to readers of the balance sheet, perhaps more clearly than before, the commitment to investment.

Stock dividends have little economic substance for shareholders. A proportionate increase in the number of shares held by each shareholder does not change that shareholder's ownership interest or proportionate voting power. Although the book value per common share (total common shareholders' equity divided by the number of common shares outstanding) decreases, each shareholder has a proportionately larger number of shares, so the total book value of each shareholder's interest remains unchanged. The market value per share should decline commensurate with the proportional increase in shares, but all else equal, the total market value of an individual's shares should not change. To describe such a distribution of shares as a "dividend"—meaning a distribution of assets generated by earnings—may mislead some readers, but the terminology is generally accepted.

STOCK SPLITS

Stock splits (or, more technically, split-ups) resemble stock dividends. The corporation issues additional shares of stock to shareholders in proportion to their existing holdings. The firm receives no additional assets. Firms typically execute a stock split following one of two approaches:

1. **Reduce the par value of the common stock in proportion to the new number of shares issued.** A corporation may, for example, have 1,000 shares of $10 par value stock outstanding and, by a stock split, exchange those shares for 2,000 shares of $5 par value stock (a two-for-one split) or for 4,000 shares of $2.50 par value stock (a four-for-one split).

2. **Make no change in par value but issue additional shares of the same par value.** For example, a corporation executing a two-for-one stock split would issue additional shares equal to the number of shares already outstanding.

---

[16]Committee on Accounting Procedure, *Accounting Research Bulletin No. 43, 1953*, "Restatement and Revision of Accounting Research Bulletins Nos. 1–42," 1953 (**Codification Topic 505**). This accounting is consistent with IASB pronouncements on related topics.

A stock split accomplished by altering the par value in direct proportion to the number of new shares does not require a journal entry. If the change in par value is not proportional to the new number of shares or if the firm does not change the par value, the firm decreases Additional Paid-In Capital or Retained Earnings. The amount shown in the Common Stock account represents a different number of shares. Of course the firm must record the new number of shares held by each shareholder in the subsidiary capital stock records.

Example 12 Deere, Inc., a manufacturer of home, farm, and construction equipment, discloses the following:

> On November 14, 2007, the stockholders of the company approved a two-for-one stock split effected in the form of a 100% stock dividend to stockholders of record on November 26, 2007, distributed on December 3, 2007. This stock split has been recorded as of October 31, 2007, by a transfer of $268 million from retained earnings to common stock, representing a $1 par value for each additional share issued. The number of common shares the company is authorized to issue was also increased from 600 million to 1,200 million. The number of shares of common stock issuable upon exercise of outstanding stock options, vesting of other stock awards, and the number of shares reserved for issuance under various employee benefit plans were proportionately increased in accordance with terms of the respective plans.

Deere did not change the par value of its shares. It increased the amount in the common stock account by $268 million for the par value of the additional shares issued and reduced retained earnings by an equal amount. Its use of the terminology "effected in the form of a 100% stock dividend" means that it reduced retained earnings as it would for a stock dividend. However, unlike a stock dividend, Deere transferred amounts from retained earnings equal to the par value, not the fair value, of the additional shares issued.

Distinguishing a stock dividend from a stock split can sometimes cause difficulties. For example, consider a 50% increase in the number of shares. Does the firm account for this distribution as a stock dividend, using the market value of the stock, or as a 1.5-for-one stock split, using the par value of the stock? Usually firms treat small-percentage distributions, say less than a 25% increase in the number of shares, as stock dividends and larger ones as stock splits.

Firms may also execute a **reverse stock split**. In this case, firms reduce the number of outstanding shares, either by increasing the par value of the stock or by simply cancelling outstanding shares.

Example 13 Sun Microsystems disclosed the following information regarding a reverse stock split (share amounts in millions).

Reverse Stock Split
The Company executed a 4-for-1 reverse stock split effective November 12, 2007. Nine hundred shares of $.001 par value common stock were exchanged for the 3,600 shares of $.00067 par value common stock outstanding. All reported amounts have been restated retroactively to reflect the new par value and number of shares.

Poor operating performance in recent years led to a decline in the market price per share of Sun Microsystems' common stock. The reverse stock split should increase the market price per share but not the total market value of Sun Microsystems' shares outstanding.

Sun accounted for the reverse stock split as follows (amounts in millions):

Common Stock—$.00067 Par Value (3,600 shares)	2.412
Common Stock—$.001 Par Value (900 shares)	.900
Additional Paid-In Capital (plug)	1.512

Assets	=	Liabilities	+	Shareholders' Equity	(Class.)
				−2.412	ContriCap
				.900	ContriCap
				1.512	ContriCap

To record a four-for-one reverse stock split and change in par value from $.00067 per share to $.001 per share.

A stock split (or a stock dividend) usually reduces the market value per share, all else equal, in inverse proportion to the split (or dividend). If so, a two-for-one split results in a 50% reduction in the market price per share. Likewise, a reverse stock split usually increases the market value per share in inverse proportion to the reverse split. Therefore, managers and governing boards might use stock splits and reverse stock splits to keep the market price per share within some target trading range. For example, the board of directors might think that a market price of $60 to $80 is an effective trading range for its stock. If the share price has risen to $150 in the market, the board of directors may declare a two-for-one split.

PROBLEM 14.2 for Self-Study

Journal entries for dividends and stock splits. The shareholders' equity section of the balance sheet of Baker Corporation on January 1 of the current year appears below:

Shareholders' Equity	
Common Stock, $10 par value, 25,000 shares issued and outstanding	$250,000
Additional Paid-In Capital	50,000
Retained Earnings	150,000
Total	$450,000

Prepare journal entries for each of the following transactions of Baker Corporation for the current year. Ignore income taxes.

a. March 31: The board of directors declares a cash dividend of $0.50 per share. The firm will pay the dividend on April 15.

b. April 15: The firm pays the dividend declared on March 31.

c. June 30: The board of directors declares and distributes a 10% stock dividend. The market price per share on this date is $15.

d. December 31: The board of directors declares a two-for-one stock split and changes the par value of the common shares from $10 to $5.

STOCK REPURCHASES

Treasury stock or **treasury shares** are shares a firm has previously issued and later reacquired. Treasury shares do not receive dividends, do not have voting rights, and do not enter the calculation of earnings per share, because corporation laws do not consider them outstanding shares for these purposes.

Refer to the disclosure of shareholders' equity for Citigroup in **Exhibit 14.1**. Citigroup has repurchased shares of its common stock in an amount equal to approximately 16% of its total shareholders' equity before treasury stock transactions at the end of 2007. Reasons for reacquiring outstanding common stock include the following:

1. **To use in option arrangements.** To fulfill commitments to deliver shares to its employees under employee stock option plans, the employer can reacquire shares so that the number of shares outstanding remains approximately constant. Doing so avoids diluting existing shareholders' voting interest and perhaps maintaining earnings per share. The firm would project the expected number of shares needed for the exercise of employee stock options and repurchase that amount of shares in the open market.

2. **To invest excess cash.** Some firms believe that their own shares provide a good investment. Evidence supports the notion that share prices often increase after a firm announces a share repurchase program.

3. **To defend against an unfriendly takeover bid.** Two different motives appear to be at work here:

   ■ Share repurchases reduce common shareholders' equity and increase the proportion of debt in the capital structure, making the firm more risky and therefore less attractive to an unfriendly bidder. Some firms even borrow cash to repurchase shares, which affects the debt ratios even more than using already available cash to reacquire shares.

- Share repurchases use up available cash and thereby reduce the attractiveness of the company to outsiders who believe that the available cash makes the company an attractive target.

4. **To distribute cash to shareholders in a tax-advantaged way.** Rather than pay dividends to all shareholders, many of whom will owe personal income taxes on the entire dividend amount, the firm can buy back shares from those who wish to receive cash. Some shareholders will have lower tax rates on receipts from sales of shares than on dividend receipts.

Example 14 **Exhibit 14.1** indicates that Citigroup reduced the number of treasury shares from 565,422,201 at the end of 2006 to 484,834,568 at the end of 2007. The following analysis shows the reasons for the change in the number of shares.

	Number of Shares (in 000s)
Treasury Shares, December 31, 2006	565,422
Shares Reissued in Employee Benefit Plans	(68,839)
Shares Reissued in Corporate Acquisitions	(25,364)
Treasury Shares Acquired	12,463
Other	(847)
Treasury Shares, December 31, 2007	482,835

Citigroup used treasury shares in employee benefit plans and for corporate acquisitions, but it did not actually reissue the same shares that it had previously purchased. It issued new stock certificates and cancelled the shares held as treasury shares. Thus, accounting views treasury shares as issued shares but not as outstanding shares.

ACCOUNTING FOR TREASURY SHARES

U.S. GAAP and IFRS on accounting for repurchases and reissuances of treasury shares follow the principle that a corporation does not report a gain or loss on transactions involving its own shares.[17] Even though the firm may sell (technically, reissue) the shares for more, or less, than their acquisition cost, accounting does not report the economic gain, or economic loss, as a component of accounting income. The required accounting views treasury stock purchases and sales as financing, not operating, transactions and therefore debits (for economic losses) or credits (for economic gains) the contributed capital accounts for the adjustments for reissue of treasury shares. The amounts bypass net income, other comprehensive income and Accumulated Other Comprehensive Income, and often Retained Earnings (depending on the specific accounting method used).

U.S. GAAP provides for three approaches to the accounting for treasury shares:

1. The cost method.
2. The par value method.
3. The constructive retirement method.

All three approaches reduce shareholders' equity but the specific accounts affected differ. All three approaches are consistent with IFRS, which requires only that firms reduce shareholders' equity for the acquisition cost of the shares and report no gain or loss on treasury share transactions.[18]

---

[17]Accounting Principles Board, *APB Opinion No. 6*, "Status of Accounting Research Bulletins," 1965 (**Codification Topic 505**); International Accounting Standards Board, *International Accounting Standard 32*, "Financial Instruments: Presentation," revised 2003.

[18]Committee on Accounting Procedure, *Accounting Research Bulletin 43*, "Restatement and Revision of Accounting Research Bulletins 1–42," 1953 (**Codification Topic 505**); International Accounting Standards Board, *International Accounting Standard 32*, "Financial Construments: Presentation", revised 2003. Many jurisdictions with widely varying laws and regulations use IAS 32. Its lack of precise accounting requirements as to which elements of equity firms debit for purchases of treasury stock can accommodate those various legal requirements.

To illustrate these three approaches, assume that a firm originally sold 1,000 $1 par value common shares for $40 per share and later reacquired them for $50 each.

Cost Method for Repurchased Shares

When a firm reacquires common shares under the cost method, it debits the Treasury Shares—Common account with the total amount paid to reacquire the shares.

| Treasury Stock—Common | | | | | 50,000 | |
| Cash | | | | | | 50,000 |

Assets	=	Liabilities	+	Shareholders' Equity	(Class.)
−50,000				−50,000	ContriCap

To record $50,000 paid to reacquire 1,000 common shares using the cost method.

The Treasury Stock—Common account has a debit balance and therefore reduces total shareholders' equity.

Par Value Method for Repurchased Shares

When a firm uses the par value method to account for treasury shares, it debits the Treasury Stock—Common account for the par value of the repurchased shares, debits Additional Paid-In Capital for the difference between the original issue price of the shares and par value, and plugs Retained Earnings for any difference between the repurchase price ($50 in this case) and the original issue price ($40 in this case). The par value method requires specific identification of the date and initial proceeds of the shares repurchased, which is why firms seldom use this method.

The entry to record the acquisition is as follows:

Treasury Stock—Common	1,000	
Additional Paid-In Capital	39,000	
Retained Earnings	10,000	
Cash		50,000

Assets	=	Liabilities	+	Shareholders' Equity	(Class.)
−50,000				−1,000	ContriCap
				−39,000	ContriCap
				−10,000	RE

To record $50,000 paid to reacquire 1,000 common shares using the par value method.

Constructive Retirement Method for Repurchased Shares

The constructive retirement method differs from the par value method in only one way: the debit is to Common Stock, not Treasury Stock—Common. Firms use this method when management and the governing board do not intend to reissue shares within a reasonable amount of time or when jurisdiction-specific corporation laws define reacquired shares as retired shares. The journal entry under the constructive retirement method is as follows:

Common Stock	1,000	
Additional Paid-In Capital	39,000	
Retained Earnings	10,000	
Cash		50,000

Assets	=	Liabilities	+	Shareholders' Equity	(Class.)
−50,000				−1,000	ContriCap
				−39,000	ContriCap
				−10,000	RE

To record $50,000 paid to reacquire 1,000 common shares using the constructive retirement method.

Cost Method for Reissued Treasury Shares   Under the cost method, if the firm later reissues treasury shares for cash, it debits Cash with the amount received and credits the Treasury Shares—Common account with the cost of the shares. If it reissues treasury shares at the conversion of bonds or preferred stock into common stock, it debits the Convertible Bonds or Preferred Stock instead of debiting Cash. The reissue price will usually differ from the amount paid to acquire the treasury shares. If the reissue price exceeds the acquisition price, the credit to make the entry balance is to the Additional Paid-In Capital account. If the firm reissued the 1,000 shares in this example for $55 a share, the entry under the cost method is as follows:

Cash.	55,000	
Treasury Stock—Common		50,000
Additional Paid-In Capital		5,000

Assets	=	Liabilities	+	Shareholders' Equity	(Class.)
+55,000				+50,000	ContriCap
				+5,000	ContriCap

To reissue 1,000 shares of treasury stock at a price greater than acquisition cost accounted for using the cost method. The $5,000 economic gain does not appear on the income statement as an accounting gain.

Par Value Method for Reissued Treasury Shares   When a firm uses the par value method, it credits the Treasury Stock—Common account for the par value of the treasury shares and increases Additional Paid-In Capital for the excess of the reissue price over the par value of the shares. The journal entry in this example is as follows:

Cash.	55,000	
Treasury Stock—Common		1,000
Additional Paid-In Capital		54,000

Assets	=	Liabilities	+	Shareholders' Equity	(Class.)
+55,000				+1,000	ContriCap
				+54,000	ContriCap

To reissue 1,000 shares of treasury stock at a price greater than par value accounted for using the par value method. The $5,000 economic gain does not explicitly appear in this journal entry as it does under the cost method.

Constructive Retirement Method for Reissued Treasury Shares   The entry under the constructive retirement method credits Common Stock for the par value of the reissued shares and credits Additional Paid-In Capital for the excess of the reissue price over the par value. The journal entry is as follows:

Cash.	55,000	
Common Stock.		1,000
Additional Paid-In Capital		54,000

Assets	=	Liabilities	+	Shareholders' Equity	(Class.)
+55,000				+1,000	ContriCap
				+54,000	ContriCap

To reissue 1,000 shares of treasury stock at a price greater than par value accounted for using the constructive retirement method. The $5,000 economic gain does not explicitly appear in this journal entry as it does under the cost method.

In some cases, particularly when the reissue results from the exercise of employee stock options, the amount paid by the firm to reacquire the treasury shares exceeds the subsequent reissue price. If the firm uses the cost method, it debits the balance to Additional Paid-In Capital so long as that account has a sufficiently large credit balance. To the extent the required debit exceeds the credit balance in the Additional Paid-In Capital account, the firm reduces that account to zero and debits the excess to Retained Earnings. If the firm applied the par value method or the constructive retirement method, it is unlikely that the reissue price would be so low as to require a debit to Additional Paid-In Capital (that is, the reissue price is almost surely greater than par value).

PROBLEM 14.3 for Self-Study

Journal entries for treasury stock transactions. Prepare journal entries for the following transactions of Crissie Corporation using the cost method to account for treasury stock transactions:

a. Reacquired 2,000 shares of $10 par value common stock on January 15 for $45 per share.

b. Issued 1,200 shares of treasury stock to employees upon the exercise of stock options at a price of $28 per share on April 26.

c. Reacquired 3,000 shares of $10 par value common stock for $52 per share on August 15.

d. Issued 1,600 shares of treasury stock to holders of 800 shares of convertible preferred stock, which had a carrying value of $80,000 on November 24. Crissie Corporation uses a first-in, first-out assumption on reissues of treasury stock and uses carrying values to record conversions of preferred stock.

e. Sold 1,500 shares of treasury stock on the open market for $47 per share on December 20.

REPORTING EARNINGS TRANSACTIONS

The primary purpose of the income statement is not to show the amount of net income for the period. The reader of the financial statements can generally ascertain net income by subtracting the beginning balance of the Retained Earnings account from its ending balance and adjusting for dividends and possibly treasury stock transactions. Income statements help managers and investors understand the nature and amounts of a firm's revenues, gains, expenses, and losses. This information permits the reader to compare a company's performance with other companies (cross-section analysis) or with the company itself over time (time-series analysis) and to make more informed projections about the future.

Previous chapters concentrated on *measuring* the results of income transactions. This section focuses on *reporting*, or *disclosing*, income transactions in the financial statements. To motivate an understanding of the issues involved in reporting income transactions, consider the data for Bernard Company in **Exhibit 14.3**. To simplify the illustration, we assume that revenues result in immediate cash receipts, and expenses require immediate cash expenditures, and we ignore taxes. Thus, income flows equal cash flows.

Suppose that an analyst wished to value Bernard Company using the present value of the cash flows of its individual activities, some recurring and some not. Assume the discount rate appropriate for finding the present value of Bernard Company's cash flows is 10% per year. Corporate finance classes discuss the issues related to choosing the discount rate, and the **Appendix** to this book introduces the techniques of present value analysis. You need not have studied the **Appendix** if you will take on faith the derivation of the numbers in the right-hand column of **Exhibit 14.3**.

Bernard Company engages in six activities, numbered 1 through 6, shown in **Exhibit 14.3**.

Activity 1. The first activity generates $100 per year, with the cash flow at the end of each year, indefinitely. The present value of this activity is $1,000 (= $100/0.10). (See the discussion of the present value of a perpetuity in the **Appendix**.) Investors sometimes call this process

EXHIBIT 14.3	Bernard Company
	Measurement of Firm's Market Value from Cash Flow Data

	Cash Flows Occur at the End of Each Period									Present Value of Activity Using Discount Rate of 10%
Activities of the Firm	Period Number									
	1	2	3	4	5	6	7	8		
1. Recurring	$100	$100	$100	$100	$100	$100	$100	$100	...	$1,000.00
2. Recurring, but Growing at 6% per Year	30	32	34	36	38	40	43	45	...	750.00
3. Cyclic	115	0	115	0	115	0	115	0	...	602.38
4. Nonrecurring	120	0	0	0	0	0	0	0	...	109.09
5. Recurring	(40)	(40)	(40)	(40)	(40)	(40)	(40)	(40)	...	(400.00)
6. Nonrecurring	(70)	0	0	0	0	0	0	0	...	(63.64)
Net Income for Year 1	$255									
			Present Value [= Fair Market Value] of Entire Firm ...							$1,997.83

of deriving market value from a series of future cash flows as *capitalizing earnings*. The analyst might say that the earnings of $100 have a *price/earnings ratio* of 10 or that the earnings "deserve [or carry] a multiple of 10."

Activity 2. The second activity generates $30 at the end of the first year, and a cash flow that grows by 6% per year thereafter. The present value of this activity is $750 [= $30/ (0.10 − 0.06)]. (See the discussion of the valuation of a growing perpetuity in the **Appendix**.) The price/earnings ratio (or multiple) for these cash flows is 25, because of their growth. That is, investors put higher values on growing-earnings companies than on stable-earnings companies.

Activity 3. The third activity is cyclic, generating $115 per year at the end of each odd-numbered year. The present value of this activity is $602.38.

Activity 4. The fourth activity is nonrecurring, generating a single cash flow of $120 at the end of the first year, with present value of $109.09 (= $120/1.10) at the start of the first year.

Activity 5. The fifth activity, an expenditure (outflow), uses $40 of cash each year, at the end of each year. The present value of this activity is −$400 (= −$40/0.10).

Activity 6. The sixth activity, a single expenditure (outflow), uses $70 cash at the end of the first year and has present value of −$63.64 (= −$70/1.10).

The value of the firm is the sum of the present values of its individual activities, $1,997.83 in **Exhibit 14.3**. In this example, most of the value of this firm comes from the recurring activities. In deriving firm values, investors generally care about recurring activities more than nonrecurring ones, because recurring activities add value each year whereas nonrecurring activities, by definition, happen once or infrequently.

Exhibit 14.3 shows net income of $255 (which recall we assume also equals cash flows). How can analysts and investors deduce the value of the company from this one year's income statement? They can't. This firm is too complex for even a sophisticated user to derive the value from a single column of data, without further data. To estimate a firm's value, investors and analysts need information about the components of a firm's net income and their recurring versus nonrecurring nature. Because recurring items are easier to predict, analysts feel more confident estimating the value of firms with recurring activities than with nonrecurring activities. Analysts may also want to include changes in the fair value of a firm's assets and liabilities in their valuations even though U.S. GAAP and IFRS may not include these fair value changes in net income.

OVERVIEW OF GAAP REPORTING OF INCOME TRANSACTIONS

The sections that follow discuss the reporting of various income items. We begin by providing an overview of this reporting.

1. U.S. GAAP and IFRS require firms to initially report the results of most income transactions in the income statement instead of bypassing the income statement and reporting the amounts in some other shareholders' equity account. This reporting reflects the emphasis most analysts and investors place on the income statement when evaluating a firm's operating performance and the concern that statement users may overlook income transactions reported elsewhere.

2. U.S. GAAP and IFRS recognize that some income transactions are central to a firm's principal business activities and recur, while others are either peripheral or nonrecurring. Firms must report items in their income statements in various categories to inform statement users about the nature of income items.

3. Changes in the fair values of assets and liabilities affect the value of a firm as they occur. U.S. GAAP and IFRS recognize some of these fair value changes in net income as they occur even though the firm has not yet sold the asset for cash or settled the liability—events that confirm the amount of the value change. Firms must delay reporting fair value changes of other assets and liabilities in net income until confirming events occur. In the meantime, firms include such value changes in Other Comprehensive Income and then close them to Accumulated Other Comprehensive Income, a component of shareholders' equity.

4. Firms sometimes discover errors in amounts previously reported, change their accounting principles, or change estimates made in applying their accounting principles. U.S. GAAP and IFRS require firms to retrospectively restate previously reported amounts for material corrections of errors and some changes in accounting principles, and to adjust current and future amounts for changes in accounting estimates and some changes in accounting principles.

We examine the reporting of four types of earnings transactions, which succeeding sections discuss and illustrate more fully:

1. Recurring versus nonrecurring.
2. Central versus peripheral.
3. Unrealized versus realized gains and losses from changes in the fair values of assets and liabilities.
4. Adjustments for errors and changes in accounting principles and accounting estimates.

The accounting for these four items affects the user's interpretation of reported net income and the forecasting of future net income. U.S. GAAP and IFRS aid this analysis process by requiring firms to classify income transactions in particular ways in the financial statements.

REPORTING RECURRING/NONRECURRING AND CENTRAL/PERIPHERAL ACTIVITIES

An analyst likely asks two questions when using a firm's past profitability to project its likely future profitability:

1. Does the income item result from an activity in which a firm will likely continue its involvement, or does the income item result from an unusual transaction or event that is unlikely to recur regularly?
2. Does the income item result from a firm's primary operating activity (creating and selling a good or service for customers) or from an activity incidental or peripheral to the primary operating activity (for example, periodic sales of equipment previously used by the firm in manufacturing)?

Figure 14.2 depicts these distinctions, with examples of each. A financial statement user who wants to evaluate a firm's ongoing operating profitability will likely focus on income items in the upper left cell. A financial statement user who wants to project net income of prior periods into the future would likely focus on the two *recurring income* cells. Income

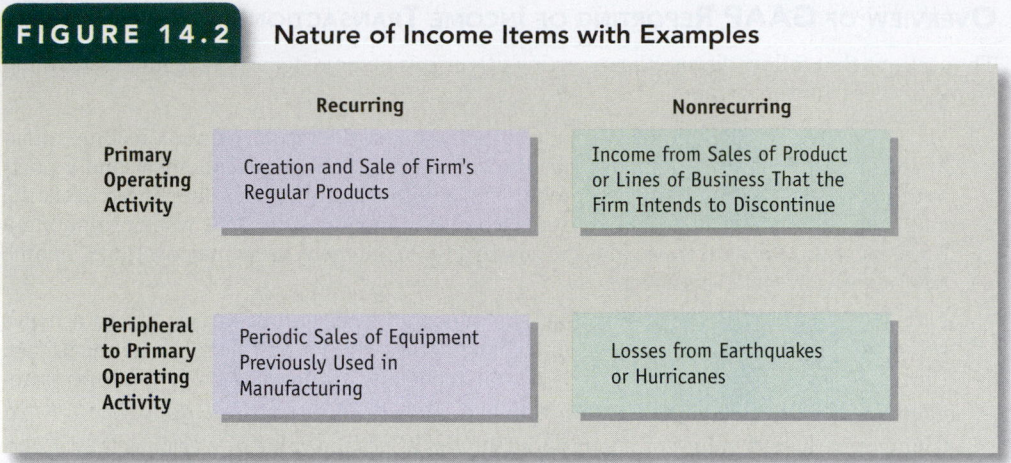

FIGURE 14.2 Nature of Income Items with Examples

items in the nonrecurring cells should not affect long-term assessments of profitability. The following discussion considers the reporting of each type of income item.

MEASUREMENT OF INCOME EFFECT

U.S. GAAP and IFRS distinguish between revenues and expenses on the one hand and gains and losses on the other. Revenues and expenses result from the recurring, primary operating activities of a business (upper left cell in **Figure 14.2**). Income items in this first category are the ordinary, recurring operating activities of the firm. Gains and losses result from either peripheral activities (lower left cell) or nonrecurring activities (upper and lower right cells). A second distinction is the reporting of revenues and expenses at gross amounts, whereas firms report gains and losses at net amounts. The following examples illustrate this distinction.

Example 15 IBM sells a computer to a customer for $400,000. The computer cost IBM $300,000 to manufacture. IBM records this sale as follows:

| Cash | | | | | 400,000 | |
| Sales Revenue | | | | | | 400,000 |

Assets	=	Liabilities	+	Shareholders' Equity	(Class.)
+400,000				+400,000	IncSt → RE

To record sale.

| Cost of Goods Sold | | | | | 300,000 | |
| Finished Goods Inventory | | | | | | 300,000 |

Assets	=	Liabilities	+	Shareholders' Equity	(Class.)
−300,000				−300,000	IncSt → RE

To record the cost of goods sold.

This transaction fits into the upper left cell of **Figure 14.2** (primary/recurring). The income statement reports both sales revenue and cost of goods sold, providing information to the financial statement user regarding both the manufacturing cost of the computer and IBM's ability to mark up this cost in setting selling prices. Retained earnings increase by $100,000 as a result of this transaction. Notice that the $100,000 amount does not itself appear in the income statement. Rather, income increases by $100,000 as a result of sales of $400,000 offset with cost of goods sold of $300,000.

Example 16 The GAP, a retail clothing chain, sells computers previously used for processing data in its stores. This sale relates only peripherally to The GAP's primary operating activity, which is to sell casual clothes. Assume that the computers originally cost $500,000 and have $200,000 of accumulated depreciation at the time of sale. Thus, the computers have a net carrying value of $300,000. The sale of these computers for $400,000 results in the following journal entry on The GAP's books:

Cash..	400,000	
Accumulated Depreciation	200,000	
Equipment		500,000
Gain on Sale of Equipment		100,000

Assets	=	Liabilities	+	Shareholders' Equity	(Class.)
+400,000				+100,000	IncSt → RE
+200,000					
−500,000					

Disposal of computers for $100,000 more than carrying value.

This transaction fits into the lower left cell of **Figure 14.2** (peripheral/recurring). The income statement reports only the $100,000 gain on the sale, not the selling price of $400,000 and the carrying value of $300,000. The income statement reports gains and losses at net, instead of gross, amounts because, presumably, financial statement users do not need information about the individual components comprising peripheral or nonrecurring income items. The gain on the sale increases retained earnings by $100,000.

Note that both revenues and gains appear as credits in journal entries and increase Retained Earnings. Both expenses and losses appear as debits in journal entries and reduce Retained Earnings. To repeat, revenues and expenses report operating or central items as gross amounts; gains and losses report nonrecurring or peripheral items as net amounts.

CLASSIFICATIONS IN THE INCOME STATEMENT

Income statements contain some or all of the following sections or categories, depending on the nature of a firm's earnings for the period:[19]

1. Income from continuing operations.

2. Income, gains, and losses from discontinued operations.

3. For financial statements prepared under U.S. GAAP, extraordinary gains and losses. IFRS does not use the term *extraordinary* but does require the separate disclosure of material income items, along with suggested circumstances and items that would qualify for separate disclosure.[20]

Many income statements include only the first section. **Exhibit 14.4** presents an income statement for Hypothetical Company that includes all three sections.

Income from Continuing Operations Revenues, gains, expenses, and losses from the continuing areas of business activity of a firm appear in the first section of the income statement, **Income from Continuing Operations**. This section includes income derived from a firm's primary business activities as well as from activities peripherally related to operations. The firm expects these sources of earnings to continue. Firms without the nonrecurring categories of earnings for a particular year (discussed next) need not use the title *Income from Continuing Operations* in their income statements. In these cases, absence of nonrecurring types of income implies that all reported revenues, gains, expenses, and losses relate to continuing operations. Firms often show a subtotal within the continuing operations section of

---

[19]Accounting Principles Board, *Opinion No. 30*, "Reporting the Results of Operations," 1973 (**Codification Topic 225**); Financial Accounting Standards Board, *Statement of Financial Accounting Standards No. 130*, "Reporting Comprehensive Income," 1997 (**Codification Topic 225**); International Accounting Standards Board, *International Accounting Standard 1*, "Presentation of Financial Statements," revised 2003.

[20]International Accounting Standards Board, *International Accounting Standard 1*, "Presentation of Financial Statements," revised 2003, para. 87 explicitly precludes the presentation of any item of comprehensive income as extraordinary.

		Hypothetical Company
EXHIBIT 14.4		**Income Statement**
		(all except per share amounts in millions)

	2008	2007	2006
INCOME FROM CONTINUING OPERATIONS			
Sales	$ 295	$ 265	$ 240
Cost of Goods Sold	(165)	(154)	(144)
Selling and Administrative Expenses	(67)	(58)	(50)
Operating Income	$ 63	$ 53	$ 46
Interest Revenue	7	5	4
Interest Expense	(22)	(19)	(15)
Gain on Sale of Equipment	3	9	4
Income from Continuing Operations Before Taxes	$ 51	$ 48	$ 39
Income Taxes	(17)	(16)	(13)
Income from Continuing Operations	$ 34	$ 32	$ 26
INCOME, GAINS, AND LOSSES FROM DISCONTINUED OPERATIONS			
Income (Loss) from Operations of Division Sold			
in 2008 (net of income taxes)	$ 2	$ (4)	$ 16
Gain on Sale of Division (net of income taxes)	40	—	—
Income from Discontinued Operations	$ 42	$ (4)	$ 16
EXTRAORDINARY GAINS AND LOSSES			
Loss from Hurricane (net of income taxes)	—	$ (12)	—
Net Income	$ 76	$ 16	$ 42
EARNINGS PER COMMON SHARE			
Continuing Operations	$3.09	$3.04	$2.60
Discontinued Operations	3.82	(0.38)	1.60
Extraordinary Items	—	(1.14)	—
Net Income	$6.91	$1.52	$4.20

the income statement, labeled *operating income.* U.S. GAAP and IFRS do not define *operating* and *nonoperating*, so firms have discretion as to the classification of particular revenues and expenses. **Exhibit 14.4** includes revenues and expenses from the firm's primary business activity of creating and selling goods or services as *operating income*. Revenues from marketable securities and investments in securities, interest expense on borrowings, and gains and losses from peripheral activities appear separately as *nonoperating income* in the continuing operations section of the income statement in this example.

Firms almost always report asset impairment charges or restructuring charges in Income from Continuing Operations. Although these charges may not appear every year and therefore appear to be nonrecurring, the business activity to which they relate is a continuing operation of the firm; hence their classification in Income from Continuing Operations.

Income, Gains, and Losses from Discontinued Operations Sometimes a firm sells or otherwise disposes of a major division or segment of its business during the year or contemplates its sale or disposal within a foreseeable time after the end of the accounting period. If so, it must disclose separately any income, gains, and losses related to that division or segment. The separate disclosure appears in the next section of the income statement, **Income, Gains, and Losses from Discontinued Operations**, alerting the financial statement reader that the firm does not expect this source of earnings to continue. Firms report the income, gain, or loss net of income tax effects. This section follows the section presenting Income from Continuing Operations.

U.S. GAAP and IFRS are similar in the accounting for discontinued operations, although the definition of a discontinued operation differs. Under U.S. GAAP, a discontinued operation is a *component of an entity*, comprising operations and cash flows that clearly differ from the rest of the entity, both operationally and for financial reporting.[21] Segments, divisions, subsidiaries, and groups of assets can qualify as a component of an entity. IFRS uses the idea of a *disposal group*, a group of assets and directly associated liabilities that a firm will dispose of as a group in a single transaction.[22] The disposal group notion of IFRS envisions a larger unit than the component notion of U.S. GAAP.

In the year that a firm decides to sell or otherwise dispose of a unit that qualifies as a discontinued operation, it aggregates the assets and liabilities of that unit on the balance sheet into four groups:

1. Current assets of discontinued operations.
2. Noncurrent assets of discontinued operations.
3. Current liabilities of discontinued operations.
4. Noncurrent liabilities of discontinued operations.

The firm measures these assets and liabilities at the lower of their carrying values or their fair values. It reports any gain or loss that results because the carrying value exceeds fair value in the Discontinued Operations section of the income statement. The Discontinued Operations section also includes income or loss from operating the unit for that year. Financial statements for prior years included for comparative purposes classify those amounts also as a discontinued operation.

The firm continues to report income from operating that unit prior to disposal in the Discontinued Operations section of the income statement. When the firm sells or disposes of the unit, it includes any gain or loss on the sale in the Discontinued Operations section.

Example 17 Altria Group Inc. owns Kraft Foods (consumer foods), Philip Morris (tobacco), and other companies. Altria Group uses U.S. GAAP. During 2006 Altria Group contemplated spinning off Kraft Foods to its shareholders as a dividend but took no formal action to do so. However, in preparation for the spin-off, Altria Group recognized impairment losses of the assets of Kraft Foods totaling $1,002 million. The recognition of the impairment losses resulted in measuring the assets of Kraft Foods at fair value. The journal entry to recognize the impairment losses in 2006 is as follows (amounts in millions and pretax):

| Impairment Losses on Assets | | | | | 1,002 | |
| Various Specific Assets | | | | | | 1,002 |

Assets	=	Liabilities	+	Shareholders' Equity	(Class.)
−1,002				−1,002	IncSt → RE

To recognize impairment losses on specific assets.

Altria reported the impairment loss in Income from Continuing Operations in 2006 because it has not yet considered Kraft Foods to be a discontinued operation.

Example 18 On January 31, 2007, the board of directors voted to spin off Kraft Foods as a dividend to shareholders. The distribution was to occur on March 30, 2007. Because Kraft Foods qualified as a component of Altria with separable operations and cash flows, Altria treated Kraft Foods as a discontinued operation under U.S. GAAP. Altria reclassified the assets and liabilities of Kraft Foods into the following four accounts:

1. Current Assets of Discontinued Operations: $7,647 million.
2. Noncurrent Assets of Discontinued Operations: $48,805 million.
3. Current Liabilities of Discontinued Operations: $9,866 million.
4. Noncurrent Liabilities of Discontinued Operations: $19,629 million.

Altria Group measured the assets of Kraft Foods approximately at fair value, given the asset impairment charges recognized during 2006.

---

[21]Financial Accounting Standards Board, *Statement of Financial Accounting Standards No. 144*, "Accounting for the Impairment or Disposal of Long-lived Assets," 2001 (**Codification Topic 360**).

[22]International Accounting Standards Board, *International Financial Reporting Standard 5*, "Non-current Assets Held for Sale and Discontinued Operations," 2004.

Example 19 On March 30, 2007, Altria Group spun off Kraft Foods to its shareholders as a dividend. Recall that firms debit Retained Earnings for the fair value of the net assets distributed and recognize a gain or loss for any difference between the fair value and the carrying value of the net assets. Altria Group did not recognize a gain or loss in connection with the spin-off, evidence that Kraft Foods' carrying values of assets and liabilities reflected fair values. Based on the information reported by Altria Group for this transaction, we can recreate the journal entry to record the spin-off as follows:

March 30, 2007

Current Liabilities of Discontinued Operations	9,866	
Noncurrent Liabilities of Discontinued Operations	19,629	
Retained Earnings	29,520	
Current Assets of Discontinued Operations		7,647
Noncurrent Assets of Discontinued Operations		48,805
Accumulated Other Comprehensive Income.		2,109
Other		454

Assets	=	Liabilities	+	Shareholders' Equity	(Class.)
−7,647		−9,866		−29,520	RE
−48,805		−19,629		−2,109	AOCInc
−454					

To record spin-off of Kraft Foods to shareholders of Altria Group.

Accumulated Other Comprehensive Income included $2,109 million of losses related to retirement plans and foreign currency translation for Kraft Foods. The preceding entry removes these amounts from Accumulated Other Comprehensive Income. The $454 million is a plug to equate the debits and credits. This amount likely reflects changes in the fair value of assets and liabilities between January 31, 2007, and March 30, 2007.

Example 20 The income statement of Altria Group for the year ended December 31, 2007, reports the income of Kraft Foods as a discontinued operation for 2005, 2006, and 2007, even though the income statements originally issued for 2005 and 2006 included the income of Kraft Foods as part of continuing operations. **Exhibit 14.5** summarizes the reporting.

The income from discontinued operations originally reported for 2005 relates to another unit sold, not Kraft Foods.

Extraordinary Gains and Losses A separate section of an income statement prepared under U.S. GAAP presents **Extraordinary Gains and Losses**. For an item to be extraordinary, it must generally meet both of the following:

EXHIBIT 14.5

**Altria Group
Partial Income Statements
For the Years Ended
December 31, 2007, 2006, and 2005**

	2007	2006	2005
As Originally Reported for 2006 and 2005			
Income from Continuing Operations	—	$12,022	$10,668
Income from Discontinued Operations	—	—	(233)
Net Income	—	$12,022	$10,435
As Reported in 2007 Annual Report			
Income from Continuing Operations	$9,161	$ 9,329	$ 8,170
Income from Discontinued Operations	625	2,693	2,265
Net Income	$9,786	$12,022	$10,435

1. Unusual in nature.
2. Infrequent in occurrence.

An example of an item likely to be extraordinary for most firms is a loss from an earthquake or confiscation of assets by a foreign government. Firms report extraordinary items net of their tax effects. IFRS guidance would require the separate disclosure of the item but would not permit the use of the label *extraordinary*.

Example 21 Verizon Communications reported the following information for 2007 about an extraordinary loss from the nationalization of its investment in a Venezuelan company:

Extraordinary Item

In January 2007, the Bolivarian Republic of Venezuela (the Republic) declared its intent to nationalize certain companies, including CANTV. On February 12, 2007, we entered into a Memorandum of Understanding (MOU) with the Republic, which provided that the Republic offer to purchase all of the equity securities of CANTV, including our 28.5% interest, through public tender offers in Venezuela and the United States. Under the terms of the MOU, the prices in the tender offers would be adjusted downward to reflect any dividends declared and paid subsequent to February 12, 2007. During the second quarter of 2007, the tender offers were completed and Verizon received an aggregate amount of approximately $572 million, which included $476 million from the tender offers as well as $96 million of dividends declared and paid subsequent to the MOU. Based upon our investment balance in CANTV, we recorded an extraordinary loss of $131 million, including taxes of $38 million.

UNREALIZED GAINS AND LOSSES FROM CHANGES IN FAIR VALUES OF CERTAIN ASSETS AND LIABILITIES

The FASB and IASB have increasingly required or permitted firms to report certain assets and liabilities at their fair values (or the lower of fair value or carrying value) at the end of each period instead of their historical (or acquisition) costs. Examples discussed in previous chapters include the following:

1. Measurement of inventories at lower of cost or market (**Chapter 8**).
2. Measurement of fixed assets and intangibles at fair value when recognizing an asset impairment loss (**Chapter 9**).
3. Measurement of marketable equity securities at fair value (**Chapter 12**).
4. Measurement of derivatives, and financial instruments in certain designated hedges, at fair value (**Chapter 12**).

When a firm increases or decreases the carrying values of assets and liabilities to reflect fair values, the question arises as to how it should treat the offsetting credit (gain) or debit (loss). At the time of the remeasurement, the firm has not yet **realized** the gains or losses. That is, the firm has not yet sold the asset or settled (or transferred) the liability. In some cases U.S. GAAP and IFRS require firms to **recognize** the gains and losses in measuring net income in the period of the revaluation, even though the firm has not yet realized the gain or loss in a cash transaction. For example, firms include losses from decreases in the carrying values of inventories, fixed assets, and intangibles in computing net income in the period of the remeasurement. As the fair value of the hedged financial instrument and its derivative change, firms include gains and losses from the remeasurement of financial instruments classifed as fair value hedges in net income.

U.S. GAAP and IFRS do not require firms to include in net income all unrealized gains and losses from the remeasurement of assets and liabilities. Doing so would probably increase the volatility of reported income. For example, including all unrealized gains and losses on marketable equity securities in net income each period would cause reported net income to fluctuate in response to fluctuations in market prices. Many managers prefer to report stable or steadily growing net income in contrast to fluctuating net income, perhaps because they believe that lower income volatility will lead to a higher market price of the firm's shares.

To address concerns that users of financial statements might overlook fair value changes in certain items if they appear on the comparative balance sheet only and not in the income statement, U.S. GAAP and IFRS require firms to disclose unrealized gains and losses that historically have bypassed the income statement in a category called **other comprehensive income**.[23]

---

[23]Financial Accounting Standards Board, *Statement of Financial Accounting Standards No. 130*, "Reporting Comprehensive Income," 1997 (**Codification Topic 220**); International Accounting Standards Board, *International Accounting Standard 1*, "Presentation of Financial Statements," revised 2003.

Other comprehensive income *for a reporting period* includes changes in the fair value of marketable equity securities available for sale and changes in the fair value of derivatives used as cash flow hedges (discussed in **Chapter 12**). Other comprehensive income also includes gains and losses related to retirement plans not yet recognized in measuring retirement benefits expense (discussed in **Chapter 11**). **Accumulated Other Comprehensive Income**, a shareholders' equity account on the balance sheet, reports the *cumulative* amounts of other comprehensive income as of the date of the balance sheet. **Comprehensive income** equals net income on the traditional income statement plus other comprehensive income for the period.

Firms have considerable flexibility as to how they report other comprehensive income each period. Under U.S. GAAP, they can

1. Include it with net income in a single statement of comprehensive income.

2. Include it in a separate statement of other comprehensive income that is one of the notes to the financial statements.

3. Include it in a statement of changes in shareholders' equity.

IFRS permits the first and second alternatives. Many firms that apply U.S. GAAP follow the third format and include the elements of other comprehensive income in a statement explaining the reasons for changes in shareholders' equity accounts, which we illustrate later in this chapter in **Exhibit 14.6**.[24]

ADJUSTMENTS FOR ERRORS AND ACCOUNTING CHANGES

Firms occasionally obtain new information about amounts included in net income of prior periods or change either their accounting principles or estimates used in applying their accounting principles. Consider the following examples:

1. Ace Hardware discovered that it overstated its ending inventory for the current year. As a consequence, Ace Hardware understated cost of goods sold and overstated its net income for the year.

2. JC Penney has used a LIFO cost-flow assumption for inventories and cost of goods sold for many years. It decides during the current year to change to a FIFO cost-flow assumption. Net income of prior years would differ if JC Penney had used a FIFO, instead of a LIFO, cost-flow assumption.

3. American Airlines depreciates its aircraft over a 20-year life. More fuel-efficient aircraft now available on the market leads American Airlines to begin slowly replacing its existing aircraft with the new aircraft. American Airlines reduces the depreciable life of its existing aircraft, which increases current and future depreciation charges relative to the recent past.

Each of these three examples requires the accountant to apply U.S. GAAP and IFRS guidance to determine whether to (1) retrospectively restate prior years' net income (*retrospective restatement*), (2) include an adjustment for the correction or accounting change in the current year's net income, or (3) correct or adjust net income of the current and future periods (*prospective adjustment*).

Advocates of retrospective restatement view past net income numbers as useful to the extent they permit predictions of future net income. Retrospective restatement results in recomputing net income for prior years on the same basis as net income of the current and future years, thereby enhancing earnings predictions.

Advocates of including adjustments for these items in the income statement of the current year argue that all income items should initially appear in the income statement of some period. In this way, the cumulative series of income statements includes all income items. The financial statement reader will less likely overlook the items if they appear in the income statement than if they appear as an adjustment of prior years' net income. Adequate disclosure of the nature of each item in the income statement will permit the financial statement user to assess its importance when evaluating the firm's profitability. Probably with good reason, some on this side of the argument suggest that if managers have the discretion to leave such items out of the current year's income statement, many of them will find ways to jus-

---

[24]As this book goes to press, the Securities and Exchange Commission has recommended that firms follow the first format. See Securities and Exchange Commission, "Report and Recommendations Pursuant to Section 133 of the Emergency Economic Stabilization Act of 2008: Study on Mark-To-Market Accounting."

tify restating prior years' net income for income-reducing adjustments and including in net income of the current period only income-enhancing adjustments.

Advocates of adjusting earnings prospectively argue that restating previously reported amounts reduces the credibility of the financing reporting process. Advocates also argue that adjustments such as those in the three examples are a normal, recurring part of the accounting process. Prospective adjustment avoids the implication that the firm has computed prior years' earnings incorrectly.

U.S. GAAP and IFRS distinguish the accounting for (1) corrections of errors, (2) adjustments for changes in accounting principles, and (3) adjustments for changes in accounting estimates.[25]

Reporting Correction of Errors Errors result from such actions as miscounting inventories and misapplying accounting principles. The following excerpt from a press release by Ace Hardware describes more fully its error in accounting for inventories described earlier.

> Ace Hardware restated previously issued income and equity for fiscal 2006, 2005, and 2004. The restatement was primarily the result of the discovery of a $152 million shortfall due to an inventory accounting error. Net income for 2006 was restated as $94.5 million, previously reported as $107.4 million. The 2005 figures were adjusted to $79.5 million, down from $100.4 million. The 2004 net income was adjusted to $65.0 million, down from $101.9 million. Equity was restated as $174.0 million at the end of 2006, down from $319.9 million.

Although Ace Hardware does not explain the exact nature of the error, given its recurring nature, it is likely that the firm included items in the cost of ending inventory each year that it should have treated as expenses of the period.

U.S. GAAP and IFRS require firms to account for **correction of errors**, if material, by retrospectively restating net income of prior periods and adjusting the beginning balance in Retained Earnings for the current period. The cumulative effect of the inventory error at the end of 2006 was an overstatement of retained earnings of $145.9 million (= $319.9 − $174.0). The overstatement of inventory, described in the press release as a "shortfall," totaled $152 million. The firm makes the following entry at the beginning of 2007 to correct the error (amounts in millions):

Retained Earnings	145.9	
Income Tax Receivable or Deferred Tax Asset	6.1	
Inventory		152.0

Assets	=	Liabilities	+	Shareholders' Equity	(Class.)
−152.0				−145.9	RE
+6.1					

To correct inventory error.

The small income tax effect results from the taxation of Ace Hardware as a dealer-owned cooperative, a topic beyond the scope of this textbook.

Reporting Changes in Accounting Principles JC Penney's change from a LIFO to a FIFO cost-flow assumption is a **change in accounting principle**. If it is practical to recalculate income for prior periods under the new accounting principle, U.S. GAAP and IFRS require firms to retrospectively apply the new accounting principle to recalculate prior years' net income. Assume that inventory at the end of last year for JC Penney was $450 million under LIFO and $525 million under FIFO. The entry to record the balance sheet effect of the change in accounting principle, ignoring income taxes, is as follows (in millions):

Merchandise Inventory	75	
Retained Earnings		75

(continued)

---

[25]Financial Accounting Standards Board, *Statement of Financial Accounting Standards No. 154*, "Accounting Changes and Error Corrections," 2005 (**Codification Topic 250**); International Accounting Standards Board, *International Accounting Standard 8*, "Accounting Policies, Changes in Accounting Estimates, and Errors," revised 2003.

Assets	=	Liabilities	+	Shareholders' Equity	(Class.)
+75				+75	RE

To retrospectively apply the FIFO accounting principle.

JC Penney would also recalculate net income for each prior year reported in its financial statements using a FIFO cost-flow assumption.

Reporting Changes in Accounting Estimates Accrual accounting requires frequent, ongoing changes in estimates. As time passes and conditions change, new information becomes available that causes management to change the estimates required to apply accounting principles. Examples of such estimates include the amount of uncollectible accounts and the useful lives of depreciable assets. The previous example for American Airlines is a change in accounting estimate. Earlier chapters have pointed out that firms do not recalculate revenues and expenses of previous periods to incorporate new information involving estimates. Instead, firms report the effect of the change in estimate prospectively, in current and future periods' earnings. Refer, for example, to **Figure 9.2**, which illustrates the effect of a change in depreciable life on depreciation expense. Rather than adjust Retained Earnings directly, the firm adjusts current and future depreciation charges—but not past ones—to take into account the carrying value at the time the new information arrives as well as the new information itself.

Changes in estimates do not always relate to recurring accrual accounting measurements, such as depreciable lives. Some changes in estimates concern unusual or nonrecurring events. Consider, for example, a litigation situation in which a court this period finds a firm responsible for an act that occurred several years previously and caused injury. The damage award differs from the amount that the firm previously recognized with a debit to a loss and a credit to a liability. The court's decision provides new information regarding measurements made in previous periods. Even though the events do not recur, U.S. GAAP and IFRS treat them similarly to changes in estimates for recurring items. Firms report the income effect of these items in the income statement of the current period, appropriately disclosed, not in retained earnings as a direct adjustment.

PROBLEM **14.4** for Self-Study

Journal entries for net income and retained earnings transactions. Prepare journal entries for each of the following transactions of Able Corporation for 2008. Ignore income taxes.

a. January 15: As a result of a computer software error the preceding December, the firm failed to record depreciation on office facilities totaling $35,000.

b. March 20: An earthquake in California causes an uninsured loss of $70,000 to a warehouse.

c. December 31: The firm acquired its office building six years before December 31, 2008. The building cost $400,000, had zero estimated salvage value, and had a 40-year life. The firm uses the straight-line depreciation method. Able Corporation now estimates that the building will have a total useful life of 30 years instead of 40 years. Record depreciation expense on the building for 2008 and any required adjustment to depreciation of previous years.

EARNINGS AND BOOK VALUE PER SHARE

Publicly held firms that apply U.S. GAAP or IFRS must show **earnings per common share** data in the body of the income statement.[26] Earnings per common share result from dividing

---

[26]Financial Accounting Standards Board, *Statement of Financial Accounting Standards No. 128*, "Earnings per Share," 1997 (**Codification Topic 250**); International Accounting Standards Board, *International Accounting Standard 33*, "Earnings per Share," revised 2003.

net income minus preferred stock dividends by the weighted-average number of outstanding common shares during the accounting period. Firms reporting multiple categories of income items must disclose earnings per common share for each reported category. See **Exhibit 14.4** for categories and the disclosure. Issues in calculating earnings per common share go beyond the scope of this book. **Problem 39** at the end of this chapter illustrates some of the calculations.

Some firms voluntarily disclose **book value per common share** in their annual reports. Book value per common share equals total common shareholders' equity divided by the number of shares outstanding on the date of the balance sheet.

Appendix 6.1 indicates that investors often apply multiples to earnings per common share and book value per common share in deciding on a reasonable market price for a firm's shares.

DISCLOSURE OF CHANGES IN SHAREHOLDERS' EQUITY

The annual reports to shareholders must explain the changes in all shareholders' equity accounts.[27] The reconciliation of retained earnings may appear in the balance sheet, in a statement of earnings and retained earnings, or in a separate statement. The reconciliation of Other Comprehensive Income may also appear in a separate statement.

Exhibit 14.6 shows the consolidated statement of shareholders' equity for Citigroup for 2005, 2006, and 2007. This statement explains the reasons for the changes in shareholder's equity accounts between balance sheet dates. The three-year statement shows separate amounts for preferred stock, common stock, and additional paid-in capital, retained earnings, treasury stock, and accumulated other comprehensive income. It also shows the components of comprehensive income for each year. We explore each of these items for 2007, in part to provide a review of the various topics discussed in this chapter.

PREFERRED STOCK

Citigroup redeemed its remaining outstanding preferred stock during 2007. Citigroup reported the preferred stock on its balance sheet at redemption value, so no gain or loss results from the redemption. Citigroup made the following entry to redeem its preferred stock (amounts in millions).

| Preferred Stock | 1,000 | |
| Cash | | 1,000 |

Assets	=	Liabilities	+	Shareholders' Equity	(Class.)
−1,000				−1,000	ContriCap

To redeem preferred stock.

COMMON STOCK AND ADDITIONAL PAID-IN CAPITAL

Employee Benefit Plans   Citigroup reports amounts related to employee benefit plans under both common stock and additional paid-in capital and under treasury stock. Consider first the amounts under treasury stock. Citigroup issued common stock to employees under various stock option and stock purchase plans and reduced the number of treasury shares for the number of common shares issued. The cost of these treasury shares was $2,853 million. The statement of cash flows indicates that Citigroup issued common stock to employees for $1,060 million. The entry to record the issue of common stock to employees is (in millions):

---

[27]Accounting Principles Board, *Opinion No. 12*, "Omnibus Opinion—1967," 1967 (**Codification Topic 215**); International Accounting Standards Board, *International Accounting Standard 1*, Presentation of Financial Statements," revised 2003.

EXHIBIT 14.6

Citigroup, Inc.
Statement of Changes in Shareholders' Equity
(amounts in millions)

	2007	2006	2005
Preferred Stock at Aggregate Liquidation Value			
Balance, Beginning of Year	$ 1,000	$ 1,125	$ 1,125
Redemption or Retirement of Preferred Stock	(1,000)	(125)	—
Balance, End of Year	$ 0	$ 1,000	$ 1,125
Common Stock and Additional Paid-In Capital			
Balance, Beginning of Year	$ 18,308	$ 17,738	$ 16,960
Employee Benefit Plans	455	769	524
Issuance of Shares in Corporate Acquisitions	192	—	—
Present Value of Stock Purchase Contract Payments	(888)	—	—
Other	(5)	1	54
Balance, End of Year	$ 18,062	$ 18,308	$ 17,538
Retained Earnings			
Balance, Beginning of Year	$129,267	$117,555	$102,154
Adjustment to Opening Balance (net of taxes) for New FASB Pronouncements	(186)	—	—
Adjusted Balance, Beginning of Year	$129,081	$117,555	$102,154
Net Income	3,617	21,538	24,589
Common Dividends	(10,733)	(9,761)	(9,120)
Preferred Dividends	(45)	(65)	(68)
Balance, End of Year	$121,920	$129,267	$117,555
Treasury Stock, at Cost			
Balance, Beginning of Year	$ (25,092)	$ (21,149)	$ (10,644)
Issuance of Shares in Employee Benefit Plans	2,853	3,051	2,203
Treasury Stock Acquired	(663)	(7,000)	(12,794)
Issuance of Shares in Corporate Acquisitions	1,140	—	—
Other	38	6	86
Balance, End of Year	$ (21,724)	$ (25,092)	$ (21,149)
Accumulated Other Comprehensive Income			
Balance, Beginning of Year	$ (3,700)	$ (2,532)	$ (304)
Adjustment to Opening Balance (net of taxes) for New FASB Pronouncements	149	—	—
Adjusted Balance, Beginning of Year	$ (3,551)	$ (2,532)	$ (304)
Net Change in Unrealized Gains and Losses on Marketable Securities (net of taxes)	(621)	(141)	(1,549)
Net Change in Cash Flow Hedges (net of taxes)	(3,102)	(673)	439
Net Change in Foreign Currency Translation Adjustment (net of taxes)	2,024	1,294	(980)
Pension Liability Adjustment (net of taxes)	590	(1)	(138)
Adjustment to Apply SFAS 158 (net of taxes)	—	(1,647)	—
Net Change in Accumulated Other Comprehensive Income	$ (1,109)	$ (1,168)	$ (2,228)
Balance, End of Year	$ (4,660)	$ (3,700)	$ (2,532)
Comprehensive Income			
Net Income	$ 3,617	$ 21,538	$ 24,589
Net Change in Accumulated Other Comprehensive Income	(1,109)	(1,168)	(2,228)
Comprehensive Income	$ 2,508	$ 20,370	$ 22,361

Cash	1,060	
Additional Paid-In Capital	1,793	
Treasury Stock—At Cost		2,853

Assets	=	Liabilities	+	Shareholders' Equity	(Class.)
+1,060				−1,793	ContriCap
				+2,853	ContriCap

To record issue of common stock to employees for an amount less than the cost of the treasury stock.

Consider next the entry for employee benefit plans under common stock and additional paid-in capital. There is a credit to Common Stock and Additional Paid-In Capital of $455 million for 2007. Citigroup's disclosures in its annual report indicate that the amount for employee benefit plans under common stock and additional paid-in capital did not increase the number of shares. Thus, the $455 million for 2007 does not relate to the issuance of previously unissued common stock. The amount necessary to reconcile to a net credit to Additional Paid-In Capital of $455 million, given the debit of $1,793 in the entry above, is a credit of $2,248 million (= $1,793 + $455). This amount represents the amortized cost of stock options for 2007. The entry is (in millions):

| Compensation Expense .... | 2,248 | |
| Additional Paid-In Capital .... | | 2,248 |

Assets	=	Liabilities	+	Shareholders' Equity	(Class.)
				−2,248	IncSt → RE
				+2,248	ContriCap

To recognize amortization of the cost of stock options.

Corporate Acquisitions

Corporate acquisitions likewise affected both common stock and additional paid-in capital and treasury stock. Citigroup issued common stock in the acquisition of other companies and reduced the number of treasury shares for the new shares issued. U.S. GAAP and IFRS require firms to record the net assets acquired at their fair values and to increase or decrease additional paid-in capital for any difference between that fair value and the cost of the treasury stock. The $192 million increase in additional paid-in capital indicates that the fair value of the net assets acquired exceeded the cost of the treasury stock. The entry is (in millions):

Net Assets Acquired	1,332	
Treasury Stock—At Cost		1,140
Additional Paid-In Capital		192

Assets	=	Liabilities	+	Shareholders' Equity	(Class.)
+1,332				+1,140	ContriCap
				+192	ContriCap

To record the acquisition of other companies and reduction in the number of treasury shares.

Stock Purchase Contract Payments

This transaction is beyond the scope of this book, but we provide a brief explanation. Citigroup had contracted with an investment banking firm to repurchase shares of its common stock over a specified future time span. The annual report does not indicate whether Citigroup has already paid cash or incurred a liability. Thus, the entry is:

| Common Stock and Additional Paid-In Capital. . . . . | 888 | |
| Cash or Liability. . . . . | | 888 |

Assets	=	Liabilities	+	Shareholders' Equity	(Class.)
−888	or	+888		−888	ContriCap

RETAINED EARNINGS

Citigroup applies U.S. GAAP and adopted several reporting standards in 2007 that required remeasurement of certain assets and liabilities and an adjustment of the beginning balance in Retained Earnings. The adjustment is a debit of $186 million.

The entry to close out revenue and expense accounts and record net income of $3,617 million for 2007 is as follows (in millions):

Revenue and Gains	159,229	
Expenses and Losses		155,612
Retained Earnings		3,617

Assets	=	Liabilities	+	Shareholders' Equity	(Class.)
				−159,229	IncSt → RE
				+155,612	IncSt → RE
				+3,617	IncSt → RE

To close income accounts to retained earnings.

Citigroup declared and paid dividends of $10,733 million on common stock and $45 million on its preferred stock during 2007.

| Retained Earnings . . . . | 10,778 | |
| Cash . . . . | | 10,778 |

Assets	=	Liabilities	+	Shareholders' Equity	(Class.)
−10,778				−10,778	RE

To record the declaration and payment of dividends on common and preferred stock.

TREASURY STOCK

A previous section discussed the changes in treasury stock related to employee benefit plans and corporate acquisitions. Citigroup also repurchased common stock during the year in the amount of $663 million:

| Treasury Stock—At Cost . . . . | 663 | |
| Cash . . . . | | 663 |

Assets	=	Liabilities	+	Shareholders' Equity	(Class.)
−663				−663	ContriCap

To record the purchase of common stock held as treasury stock.

ACCUMULATED OTHER COMPREHENSIVE INCOME

Adjustment of Beginning Balance The adoption of new reporting standards in 2007 required Citigroup to remeasure certain assets and liabilities. The offsetting debits and credits affected accumulated other comprehensive income at that time, not retained earnings.

Unrealized Gains and Losses on Marketable Securities Recall from **Chapter 12** that firms measure marketable equity securities classified as available for sale at fair value and record the unrealized changes in fair value as an element of other comprehensive income. The fair value of Citigroup's portfolio of marketable equity securities declined during 2007, which, net of taxes, reduced comprehensive income and accumulated other comprehensive income by $621 million.

Cash Flow Hedges **Chapter 12** indicates that firms remeasure derivatives designated as cash flow hedges to fair value at the end of each period and report the unrealized gain or loss in other comprehensive income. Citigroup experienced a decrease in the fair value of its cash flows hedges during 2007, which, net of taxes, reduced other comprehensive income and accumulated other comprehensive income by $3,102 million.

Foreign Currency Translation Firms translate the reported results of their foreign operations from local currencies into U.S. dollars in order to prepare consolidated financial statements, a topic not discussed in this book. The adjustment for changes in the value of the U.S. dollar relative to foreign currencies was an unrealized gain, net of taxes, of $2,024 million for 2007.

Pension Liability Recall from **Chapter 11** that firms must include gains and losses from changes in actuarial assumptions, actuarial performance, and prior service cost in other comprehensive income prior to their amortization as an adjustment to pension expense. These items caused the pension liability to decrease, net of taxes, by $590 million during 2007, which resulted in an increase in other comprehensive income and accumulated other comprehensive income for the year.

COMPREHENSIVE INCOME

Comprehensive income equals net income as reported on the income statement plus (minus) the increase (decrease) in other comprehensive income for the year. Comprehensive income for Citigroup for 2007 equals net income of $3,617 million (see this amount in the reconciliation of the change in retained earnings) minus the decrease in accumulated other comprehensive income for 2007 of $1,109 million (see this amount in the reporting of changes in other comprehensive income).

SUMMARY

The shareholders' equity section of the balance sheet reports the sources of financing provided by preferred and common shareholders and their claims on the net assets of the firm. The equity of the preferred shareholders usually approximates the liquidation value of the preferred shares. The remaining shareholders' equity accounts relate to the equity of the common shareholders. The equity of the common shareholders equals the sum of the amounts appearing in the Common Stock, Additional Paid-In Capital, Retained Earnings, Accumulated Other Comprehensive Income, Treasury Stock, and other common-share equity accounts. The user of the financial statements gains insight into capital contributions, net income, other comprehensive income, dividends, and treasury stock transactions only by studying changes in the individual accounts.

SOLUTIONS TO SELF-STUDY PROBLEMS

SUGGESTED SOLUTION TO PROBLEM 14.1 FOR SELF-STUDY

(Healy Corporation; journal entries for capital contributions.)

a. *January 2*

Cash..	1,400,000	
Common Stock—$10 Par Value.........................		1,000,000
Additional Paid-In Capital		400,000

Assets	=	Liabilities	+	Shareholders' Equity	(Class.)
+1,400,000				+1,000,000	ContriCap
				+400,000	ContriCap

To record issue of 100,000 shares of $10-par value common stock for $14 per share.

b. *January 2*

Patent	140,000	
Common Stock—$10 Par Value.........................		100,000
Additional Paid-In Capital		40,000

Assets	=	Liabilities	+	Shareholders' Equity	(Class.)
+140,000				+100,000	ContriCap
				+40,000	ContriCap

To record issue of 10,000 shares of $10-par value common stock in exchange for a patent. The value of the patent is not easily measurable, so use the issue price of $14 per share from part **a**.

c. *March 1*

Cash..	200,000	
Preferred Stock		200,000

Assets	=	Liabilities	+	Shareholders' Equity	(Class.)
+200,000				+200,000	ContriCap

To record issue of 2,000 shares of convertible preferred stock at par value.

d. *June 1*

Cash..	50,000	
Additional Paid-In Capital (Stock Warrants)		50,000

Assets	=	Liabilities	+	Shareholders' Equity	(Class.)
+50,000				+50,000	ContriCap

To record issue of 10,000 common stock warrants for $5 per warrant.

e. *September 15*

Preferred Stock	60,000	
Common Stock—$10 Par Value.........................		24,000
Additional Paid-In Capital		36,000

(continued)

Assets	=	Liabilities	+	Shareholders' Equity	(Class.)
				−60,000	ContriCap
				+24,000	ContriCap
				+36,000	ContriCap

To record the conversion of 600 preferred shares into 2,400 common shares at carrying value.

---

f. *November 20*

Cash...	96,000	
Additional Paid-In Capital (Stock Warrants)	20,000	
Common Stock—$10 Par Value.........................		40,000
Additional Paid-In Capital		76,000

Assets	=	Liabilities	+	Shareholders' Equity	(Class.)
+96,000				−20,000	ContriCap
				+40,000	ContriCap
				+76,000	ContriCap

To record issue of 4,000 shares of common stock in exchange for 4,000 stock warrants and $96,000 cash.

---

g.

Compensation Expense	10,000	
Additional Paid-In Capital (Stock Options)		10,000

Assets	=	Liabilities	+	Shareholders' Equity	(Class.)
				−10,000	IncSt → RE
				+10,000	ContriCap

To amortize cost of employee stock options; $10,000 = $30,000/3.

SUGGESTED SOLUTION TO PROBLEM 14.2 FOR SELF-STUDY

(Baker Corporation; journal entries for dividends and stock splits.)

---

a. *March 31*

Retained Earnings	12,500	
Dividends Payable		12,500

Assets	=	Liabilities	+	Shareholders' Equity	(Class.)
		+12,500		−12,500	RE

To record declaration of cash dividend of $0.50 per share on 25,000 shares.

---

b. *April 15*

Dividends Payable	12,500	
Cash		12,500

Assets	=	Liabilities	+	Shareholders' Equity	(Class.)
−12,500		−12,500			

To pay cash dividend declared on March 31.

c. *June 30*

Retained Earnings   37,500

    Common Stock—$10 Par Value   25,000

    Additional Paid-In Capital   12,500

Assets	=	Liabilities	+	Shareholders' Equity	(Class.)
				−37,500	RE
				+25,000	ContriCap
				+12,500	ContriCap

To record issuance of 10% stock dividend: 0.10 × 25,000 = 2,500 shares; 2,500 × $15 = $37,500.

d. *December 31*

Common Stock—$10 Par Value   275,000

    Common Stock—$5 Par Value   275,000

Assets	=	Liabilities	+	Shareholders' Equity	(Class.)
				−275,000	ContriCap
				+275,000	ContriCap

To record two-for-one stock split by decreasing the par value of the common stock.

Alternatively, the firm need make no entry because the reduction in par value is directly proportional to the additional number of shares.

SUGGESTED SOLUTION TO PROBLEM 14.3 FOR SELF-STUDY

(Crissie Corporation; journal entries for treasury stock transactions.)

a. *January 15*

Treasury Stock—Common   90,000

    Cash   90,000

Assets	=	Liabilities	+	Shareholders' Equity	(Class.)
−90,000				−90,000	ContriCap

To record the reacquisition of 2,000 common shares at $45 per share.

b. *April 26*

Cash   33,600

Additional Paid-In Capital   20,400

    Treasury Stock—Common   54,000

Assets	=	Liabilities	+	Shareholders' Equity	(Class.)
+33,600				−20,400	ContriCap
				+54,000	ContriCap

To record reissue of 1,200 shares of treasury stock costing $45 per share; treasury shares reissued to employees under stock option plan with an exercise price of $28 per share.

c. *August 15*

Treasury Stock—Common   156,000

    Cash   156,000

(continued)

Assets	=	Liabilities	+	Shareholders' Equity	(Class.)
−156,000				−156,000	ContriCap

To record reacquisition of 3,000 common shares at $52 a share.

---

d. *November 24*

Preferred Stock	80,000	
Treasury Stock—Common		77,600
Additional Paid-In Capital		2,400

Assets	=	Liabilities	+	Shareholders' Equity	(Class.)
				−80,000	ContriCap
				+77,600	ContriCap
				+2,400	ContriCap

To record reissue of 1,600 shares of treasury stock with a cost of $77,600 [= (800 × $45) + (800 × $52)] in exchange for convertible preferred stock with a carrying value of $80,000.

---

e. *December 20*

Cash	70,500	
Additional Paid-In Capital	7,500	
Treasury Stock—Common		78,000

Assets	=	Liabilities	+	Shareholders' Equity	(Class.)
+70,500				−7,500	ContriCap
				+78,000	ContriCap

To record reissue of 1,500 shares of treasury stock costing $52 per share; treasury shares sold on the open market for $47 per share.

SUGGESTED SOLUTION TO PROBLEM 14.4 FOR SELF-STUDY

(Able Corporation; journal entries for net income and retained earnings transactions.)

---

a. *January 15*

Retained Earnings	35,000	
Accumulated Depreciation		35,000

Assets	=	Liabilities	+	Shareholders' Equity	(Class.)
−35,000				−35,000	RE

To correct error in prior year's depreciation, increasing accumulated depreciation and reducing retained earnings.

---

b. *March 20*

Loss from Earthquake	70,000	
Building		70,000

Assets	=	Liabilities	+	Shareholders' Equity	(Class.)
−70,000				−70,000	IncSt → RE

To record loss from earthquake in an income statement account.

The firm would likely classify the loss as an extraordinary item if it reported using U.S. GAAP but not use the term *extraordinary* if it reported under IFRS.

c. *December 31*

Depreciation Expense   14,000
    Accumulated Depreciation   14,000

Assets	=	Liabilities	+	Shareholders' Equity	(Class.)
−14,000				−14,000	IncSt → RE

To record a change in depreciable life of a building from 40 years to 30 years. Original depreciation: $400,000/40 = $10,000 per year. Carrying value on January 1, 2008, is $350,000 [= $400,000 − ($10,000 × 5)]. Depreciation for 2008 is $14,000 (= $350,000/25).

KEY TERMS AND CONCEPTS

Corporation
Limited liability
Corporate charter
Corporate bylaws
Capital stock contract
Capital stock
Preferred stock
Cumulative dividend rights
Callable preferred shares
Convertible preferred shares
Redeemable preferred shares
Put option
Common stock
Par (or stated) value
Additional Paid-In Capital
Call options
Strike price or exercise price
Intrinsic value of stock option
Employee stock options (ESOs)
Stock purchase rights
Stock warrants
Benefit element in stock option

Time value element in stock option
Convertible bonds or convertible preferred stock
Cash dividend
Dividend in kind or property dividend
Stock dividend
Stock split
Reverse stock split
Treasury stock, treasury shares
Income from Continuing Operations
Income, Gains, and Losses from Discontinued Operations
Extraordinary Gains and Losses
Realize v. recognize
Other comprehensive income
Accumulated other comprehensive income
Comprehensive income
Correction of errors
Change in accounting principle
Changes in estimates
Earnings per common share
Book value per common share

QUESTIONS, EXERCISES, AND PROBLEMS

QUESTIONS

1. Review the meaning of the terms and concepts listed above in Key Terms and Concepts.

2. A firm contemplates issuing 10,000 shares of $100 par value preferred stock. The preferred stock promises a $4 per share annual dividend. The firm considers making this preferred stock callable, or convertible, or subject to mandatory redemption. Will the issue price be the same in each of these three cases? Explain.

3. Redeemable preferred stock might appear among liabilities, or among shareholders' equity, or between liabilities and shareholders' equity on the balance sheet under U.S. GAAP. Describe the circumstances when redeemable preferred stock would appear in each of these three places on the balance sheet.

4. Compare and contrast a stock option, a stock right, and a stock warrant. How does the accounting for these three differ?

5. Stock option valuation models indicate that the value of a stock option increases with the volatility of the stock, increases with the time between the grant date and the expected exercise date, and decreases with increases in the discount rate. Explain.

6. U.S. GAAP and IFRS require firms to amortize the fair value of stock options as an expense over the periods the firm expects to receive employee services as a result of granting the options. What is the theoretical rationale for this amortization?

7. "The accounting for stock options, stock dividends, and treasury stock clouds the distinction between capital transactions and income transactions." Explain.

8. Compare the position of a shareholder who receives a cash dividend, a property dividend, and a stock dividend.

9. A firm that sells inventory for more than its acquisition cost realizes an economic gain that accountants include in net income, but a firm that sells treasury stock for more than its acquisition cost realizes an economic gain that accountants exclude from net income. What is the rationale for the difference in treatment of these economic gains?

10. A security analyst states, "Accountants could increase the usefulness of income statements if they included only recurring income items in the income statement and reported nonrecurring items directly in retained earnings, bypassing the income statement." Do you agree?

11. Why do U.S. GAAP and IFRS exclude from net income such items of other comprehensive income as holding gains and losses on securities available for sale?

12. Distinguish between the nature of, and accounting for, (1) a correction of an error in previously issued financial statements, (2) the adjustment for a change in accounting principle, and (3) the adjustment for a change in an accounting estimate made in preparing previously issued financial statements.

EXERCISES

13. **Classification of redeemable preferred stock.** The Washington Post Company has preferred stock outstanding with a par and redemption value of $1,000 per share. The Company can redeem this preferred stock anytime on or after October 1, 2015. The holders of the preferred stock can require the Company to purchase their shares at the redemption value during a particular 60-day period each year. Discuss the classification of this preferred stock on the balance sheet of the Company.

14. **Classification of redeemable preferred stock.** Bank of America has 81,000 shares, or $2.0 billion, of Bank of America Corporation Floating Rate Noncumulative Preferred Stock outstanding. The preferred stock contract requires Bank of America to pay a quarterly cash dividend on the liquidation preference of $25,000 per share at an annual rate equal to the greater of (a) three-month LIBOR plus 0.35%, and (b) 4.00%, payable quarterly in arrears. On any dividend date on or after November 15, 2011, the Corporation may redeem this preferred stock, in whole or in part, at its option, at $25,000 per share, plus accrued and unpaid dividends. Discuss the classification of this preferred stock on the balance sheet of Bank of America.

15. **Accounting for stock options.** Intel granted stock options to employees on December 31, 2007, permitting them to purchase 24.6 million shares of Intel common stock for $22.63 per share. An option-pricing model indicates that the value of each option on this date is $5.79. Intel expects to receive the benefit of enhanced employee services for the next three years. On December 31, 2012, employees exercise these options when the market price of the stock is $40 per share. Compute the pretax effect of this option plan on the net income of Intel for 2008 through 2012.

16. **Journal entries for employee stock options.** Morrissey Corporation grants 50,000 stock options to its managerial employees on December 31, 2008, to purchase 50,000 shares of its $1 par value common stock for $60 per share. The market price of a share of common stock on this date is $50 per share. Employees must wait two years before the options vest and they can exercise the options, and this two-year period is the expected period of benefit from the stock options. An option-pricing model indicates that the value of these options on the grant date is $400,000. On June 30, 2011, holders of 30,000 options exercise their options at a time when the market price of the stock is $65 per share. On November 15, 2011, holders of the remaining options exercise them at a time when the market price of the stock is $72 per share.

Present journal entries to record the effects of the transactions related to stock options during 2008, 2009, 2010, and 2011. The firm reports on a calendar-year basis. Ignore income tax effects.

17. **Journal entries for employee stock options.** Watson Corporation grants 20,000 stock options to its managerial employees on December 31, 2008, to purchase 20,000 shares of its $10 par value common stock for $25 per share. The market price of a share of common stock on this date is $18 per share. Employees must work for another three years before they can exercise the options. An option-pricing model indicates that the value of these options on the grant date is $75,000. On April 30, 2012, holders of 15,000 options exercise their options at a time when the market price of the stock is $30 per share. On September 15, 2013, holders of the remaining options exercise them at a time when the market price of the stock is $38 per share.

    Present journal entries to record these transactions on December 31, 2009, 2010, and 2011; on April 30, 2012; and on September 15, 2013. Assume that the firm receives any benefits of the stock option plan during 2009, 2010, and 2011 and that the firm reports on a calendar-year basis. Ignore income tax effects.

18. **Journal entries for convertible bonds.** Higgins Corporation issues $1 million of 20-year, $1,000 face value, 10% semiannual coupon bonds at par on January 2, 2008. Each $1,000 bond is convertible into 40 shares of $1 par value common stock. Assume that Higgins Corporation's credit rating is such that it could issue 15% semiannual, nonconvertible bonds at par. On January 2, 2012, holders convert their bonds into common stock. The common stock has a market price of $45 per share on January 2, 2012.

    a. Present the journal entries made under U.S. GAAP on January 2, 2008, and January 2, 2012, to record the issue and conversion of these bonds. Use the carrying value method to record the conversion.

    b. Present the journal entries made under IFRS on January 2, 2008, to issue the bonds.

19. **Accounting for conversion of bonds.** Symantec has convertible bonds outstanding with a face value of $10,000,000 and a carrying value of $10,255,000. Holders of the bonds convert them into 100,000 shares of $10 par value common stock. The common stock sells for $105 per share on the market. Give the journal entries to record the conversion of the bonds using (1) the carrying value method, and (2) the fair value method.

20. **Journal entries for stock warrants.** Kiersten Corporation sells 60,000 common stock warrants for $4 each on February 26, 2008. Each warrant permits its holder to purchase a share of the firm's $10 par value common stock for $30 per share at any time during the next two years. The market price of the common shares was $20 per share on February 26, 2008. Holders of 40,000 warrants exercised their warrants on June 6, 2010, at a time when the market price of the stock was $38 per share. Kiersten Corporation experienced a major uninsured loss from a fire late in 2010, and its market price fell immediately to $22 per share. The market price remained around $22 until the stock warrants expired on February 26, 2012. Present journal entries on February 26, 2008; June 6, 2010; and February 26, 2012, relating to these stock warrants.

21. **Journal entries for stock warrants.** On December 7, 2002, Altus Pharmaceuticals issued shares of convertible preferred stock and warrants to purchase additional shares of preferred stock for an aggregate issue price of $46,180,000 in a private placement of securities. Investment bankers estimated the fair value of the warrants on this date to be $2,730,000. The Company therefore allocated $43,450,000 to the preferred stock and $2,730,000 to the warrants. Between the issue date and January 15, 2007, dividends of $19,083,000 accrued on the preferred stock but remain unpaid. The preferred stock carries cumulative dividends rights. Because of a deficit in Retained Earnings, the Company debited the dividends to Additional Paid-In Capital each year and credited Convertible Preferred Stock. On January 15, 2007, Altus Pharmaceuticals made its initial public offering of common stock. Holders of the preferred stock converted their shares into 5,269,705 shares of $.01 par value common stock. The warrants to purchase preferred stock became warrants to purchase common stock. Give the journal entry on December 7, 2002, to issue the preferred stock and warrants and the entry on January 15, 2007, to convert the preferred stock to common stock. Use the carrying value method to record the conversion. The warrants remain outstanding.

22. **Journal entries for dividends.** Give journal entries, if required, for the following transactions, which are unrelated unless otherwise specified:

    a. A firm declares the regular quarterly dividend on its 6%, $100 par value preferred stock. There are 30,000 shares authorized and 15,000 shares issued, of which the firm has previously reacquired 2,000 shares and holds them in the treasury.

    b. The firm pays the dividend on the preferred stock (see part **a**).

    c. A company declares and issues a stock dividend of $300,000 of no-par common stock to its common shareholders.

    d. The shares of no-par stock of the corporation sell on the market for $200 a share. To bring the market value down to a more popular price and thereby broaden the distribution of its stockholdings, the board of directors votes to issue four extra shares to shareholders for each share they already hold. The corporation issues the shares.

23. **Journal entries for dividends.** Prepare journal entries for the following transactions of Watt Corporation. The firm has 20,000 shares of $15 par value common stock outstanding on January 1, 2008. The balance in the Additional Paid-In Capital account on this date is $200,000.

    a. Declares a cash dividend of $0.50 per share on March 31, 2008.

    b. Pays the dividend in part **a** on April 15, 2008.

    c. Declares and distributes a 10% stock dividend on June 30, 2008. The market price of the stock is $20 on this date.

    d. Declares a cash dividend of $0.50 per share on September 30, 2008.

    e. Pays the dividend in part **d** on October 15, 2008.

    f. Declares a three-for-two stock split on December 31, 2008, but does not alter the par value.

24. **Journal entries for treasury stock transactions.** Prepare journal entries under the cost method to record the following treasury stock transactions of Danos Corporation.

    a. Purchases 10,000 shares of its own $10 par value common stock for $30 per share.

    b. Issues 6,000 treasury shares to employees under stock option plans. The exercise price is $32 per share. Assume that the market price of the common stock on the exercise date is $35 per share. The stock options had a value of $6 per option when issued, which the firm has already amortized to expense.

    c. Purchases 7,000 shares of its own common stock for $38 per share.

    d. Issues 8,000 treasury shares in the acquisition of land valued at $300,000. Danos Corporation uses a FIFO assumption for reissues of treasury stock.

    e. Sells the 3,000 remaining shares of treasury stock for $36 per share.

25. **Journal entries for treasury stock transactions.** Prepare journal entries under the cost method to record the following treasury stock transactions of Melissa Corporation.

    a. Purchases 10,000 shares of its own $5 par value common stock for $12 per share.

    b. Issues 6,000 treasury shares upon the conversion of bonds with a carrying value of $72,000. Melissa Corporation records bond conversions using the carrying value method.

    c. Purchases 20,000 shares of its own $5 par value common stock for $15 per share.

    d. Issues 24,000 treasury shares and 6,000 newly issued shares of common stock in the acquisition of land with a market value of $540,000.

26. **Treatment of accounting errors, changes in accounting principles, and changes in accounting estimates.** A firm computes net income for 2008 of $1,500 and for 2009 of $1,800, its first two years of operations. Before issuing its financial statements for 2009, the firm discovers that an item requires an income-reducing adjustment of $400 after taxes. Indicate the amount of net income for 2008 and 2009 assuming (1) the item is an error in the computation of depreciation expense for 2008 (2009 depreciation expense is correct as computed), (2) the item is the change in net income for 2008 as a result of adopting a new method of accounting for stock options in 2009 (2009 stock option expense reflects the new accounting principle), and (3) the item is the change in estimated uncollectible accounts for 2008 as a result of worsened credit losses experienced in 2009; the firm included the adjustment amount in bad debt expense for 2009.

27. **Journal entries to correct errors and adjust for changes in estimates.** Prepare journal entries to record each of the following items for Uncertainty Corporation for 2008. Uncertainty Corporation uses a calendar year reporting period. Ignore income tax effects.

a. Discovers on January 15, 2008, that it neglected to amortize a patent during 2007 in the amount of $12,000.

b. Discovers on January 20, 2008, that it recorded the sale of a machine on December 30, 2007, for $6,000 with the following journal entry:

Cash	6,000	
Loss on Sale of Machine	4,000	
Machine (acquisition cost)		10,000

Assets	=	Liabilities	+	Shareholders' Equity	(Class.)
+6,000				−4,000	IncSt → RE
−10,000					

The machine had accumulated depreciation of $7,000 on the date of the sale.

c. Changes the depreciable life of a building as of December 31, 2008, from a total use-ful life of 30 years to a total of 42 years. The building has an acquisition cost of $2,400,000 and is 11 years old as of December 31, 2008. The firm has not recorded depreciation for 2008. It uses the straight-line method and zero estimated salvage value.

d. The firm has used 2% of sales as its estimate of uncollectible accounts for several years. Its actual losses have averaged only 1.50% of sales. Consequently, the Allow-ance for Estimated Uncollectibles account has a credit balance of $25,000 at the end of 2008 before making the provision for 2008. An aging of customers' accounts sug-gests that the firm needs $35,000 in the allowance account at the end of 2008 to cover estimated uncollectibles. Sales for 2008 are $1,000,000.

PROBLEMS

28. **Journal entries to record the issuance of capital stock.** Prepare journal entries under U.S. GAAP to record the issuance of capital stock in each of the following independent cases. You may omit explanations for the journal entries. A firm does the following:

a. Issues 50,000 shares of $5 par value common stock for $30 per share.

b. Issues 20,000 shares of $100 par value convertible preferred stock at par.

c. Issues 16,000 shares of $10 par value common stock in the acquisition of a patent. The shares of the firm traded on a stock exchange for $15 per share on the day of the transaction. The seller listed the patent for sale at $250,000.

d. Issues 25,000 shares of $1 par value common stock in exchange for convertible pre-ferred stock with a par and carrying value of $400,000. The common shares traded on the market for $18 per share on the date of the transaction. Use the carrying value method to record the conversion.

e. Issues 5,000 shares of $10 par value common stock to employees as a bonus for reach-ing sales goals for the year. The shares traded for $12 per share on the day of the transaction.

29. **Journal entries for the issuance of capital stock.** Prepare journal entries to record the issu-ance of capital stock in each of the following independent cases. You may omit explana-tions for the journal entries. A firm does the following:

a. Issues 20,000 shares of $10 par value common stock in the acquisition of inven-tory with a market value of $175,000, land valued at $220,000, a building valued at $1,400,000, and equipment valued at $405,000.

b. Issues 10,000 shares of $100 par value preferred stock at par. The preferred stock is subject to mandatory redemption in five years.

c. Issues 5,000 shares of $1 par value common stock upon the exercise of stock war-rants. The firm had issued the stock warrants several years previously for $8 per warrant and properly recorded the sale of the warrants in the accounts. The exercise price is $24 plus one warrant for each share of common stock.

d. Issues 20,000 shares of $10 par value common stock upon the conversion of 10,000 shares of $50 par value convertible preferred stock originally issued for par. Record the conversion using carrying values.

30. **Transactions to incorporate and run a business.** The following events relate to shareholders' equity transactions of Wilson Supply Company during the first year of its existence. Present journal entries for each of the transactions.

a. January 2: The firm files articles of incorporation with the State Corporation Commission. The authorized capital stock consists of 5,000 shares of $100 par value preferred stock that offers an 8% annual dividend, and 50,000 shares of no-par common stock. The original incorporators acquire 300 shares of common stock at $30 per share; the firm collects cash for the shares. It assigns a stated value of $30 per share to the common stock.

b. January 6: The firm issues 2,000 shares of common stock for cash at $30 per share.

c. January 8: The firm issues 4,000 shares of preferred stock at par.

d. January 9: The firm issues certificates for the shares of preferred stock.

e. January 12: The firm acquires the tangible assets and goodwill of Richardson Supply, a partnership, in exchange for 1,000 shares of preferred stock and 12,000 shares of common stock. It values the tangible assets acquired as follows: inventories, $50,000; land, $80,000; buildings, $210,000; and equipment, $120,000.

f. July 3: The directors declare the semiannual dividend on preferred stock outstanding, payable July 25, to shareholders of record on July 12.

g. July 5: The firm operated profitably for the first six months, and it decides to expand. The company issues 25,000 shares of common stock for cash at $33 per share.

h. July 25: It pays the dividend on preferred stock declared on July 3.

i. October 2: The directors declare a dividend of $1 per share on the common stock, payable October 25, to shareholders of record on October 12.

j. October 25: The firm pays the dividend on common stock declared on October 2.

31. **Reconstructing transactions involving shareholders' equity.** Fisher Company began business on January 1. Its balance sheet on December 31 contained the shareholders' equity section in **Exhibit 14.7**. During the year, Fisher Company engaged in the following transactions:

(1) Issued shares for $15 each.

(2) Acquired a block of 600 shares for the treasury in a single transaction.

(3) Reissued some of the treasury shares.

(4) Sold for $10,000 securities available for sale with original acquisition cost of $6,000. At the end of the year, securities available for sale, still on hand, had originally cost $12,000 and had a fair value of $14,000.

Assuming that these were all of the common stock transactions during the year and that the firm used the cost method to account for treasury stock transactions, answer the following questions:

a. How many shares did Fisher Company issue for $15?

b. What was the price at which it acquired the treasury shares?

EXHIBIT 14.7	**Fisher Company** **Shareholders' Equity as of December 31** **(Problem 31)**

Common Stock ($10 par value)	$60,000
Additional Paid-In Capital	31,440
Retained Earnings	12,000
Plus Unrealized Holding Gain on Securities Available for Sale	2,000
Less 360 Shares Held in Treasury—At Cost	(7,200)
Total Shareholders' Equity	$98,240

    c. How many shares did it reissue from the block of treasury shares?

    d. What was the price at which it reissued the treasury shares?

    e. What journal entries did it make during the year for items (1) to (4)?

    f. In which statement or statements will Fisher Company report the various gains and losses on its holdings of securities available for sale?

32. **Reconstructing transactions involving shareholders' equity.** Shea Company began business on January 1. Its balance sheet on December 31 contained the shareholders' equity section shown in **Exhibit 14.8**. During the year, Shea Company engaged in the following transactions:

    (1) Issued shares for $30 each.

    (2) Acquired a block of 2,000 shares for the treasury in a single transaction.

    (3) Reissued some of the treasury shares.

    (4) Sold for $12,000 securities available for sale that had originally cost $14,000. At the end of the year, securities available for sale, still on hand, that had originally cost $25,000 had a fair value of $18,000.

    Assuming that these were the only common stock transactions during the year and that the firm used the cost method to account for treasury stock transactions, answer the following questions:

    a. How many shares did Shea Company issue for $30 each?

    b. What was the price at which it acquired the treasury shares?

    c. How many shares did it reissue from the block of treasury shares?

    d. What was the price at which it reissued the treasury shares?

    e. What journal entries did it make during the year for items (1) to (4)?

    f. In which statement or statements will Shea Company report the various gains and losses on its holdings of securities available for sale?

EXHIBIT 14.8

Shea Company
Shareholders' Equity as of December 31
(Problem 32)

Common Stock ($5 par value)	$100,000
Additional Paid-In Capital	509,600
Retained Earnings	50,000
Less Unrealized Holding Loss on Securities Available for Sale	(7,000)
Less 1,200 Shares Held in Treasury—At Cost	(33,600)
Total Shareholders' Equity	$619,000

---

33. **Accounting for stock options.** Lowe Corporation grants stock options to its managerial employees on December 31 of each year. Employees may acquire one share of common stock with each stock option. Lowe Corporation sets the exercise price equal to the market price of its common stock on the date of the grant. Employees must continue working for two years after the date of the grant before the options vest and employees can exercise them. This two-year period is the period of benefit. **Exhibit 14.9** presents information for the stock options granted by Lowe Corporation on December 31 of each year.

    Calculate the effect of the stock options on net income before income taxes for 2008 to 2012.

34. **Accounting for stock options.** The Procter & Gamble Company (P&G) grants stock options to its managerial employees on December 31 of each year. Employees may acquire one share of common stock with each stock option. P&G sets the exercise price equal to the market price of its common stock on the date of the grant. Employees must continue working for two years after the date of the grant before the options vest and employees can exercise them. This two-year period is the period of benefit. **Exhibit 14.10** presents information for the stock options granted by P&G on December 31 of each year.

EXHIBIT 14.9	Lowe Corporation Stock Option Data (Problem 33)			
Year		**Options Granted at End of Year**	**Exercise Price per Share**	**Fair Value per Option**
2008		5,000	$18	$2.40
2009		6,000	$22	$3.00
2010		7,000	$25	$3.14
2011		8,000	$30	$3.25
2012		9,000	$38	$5.33

EXHIBIT 14.10	Procter & Gamble Company Stock Option Data (Problem 34)			
Year		**Options Granted at End of Year**	**Exercise Price per Share**	**Fair Value per Option**
2003		35,759	$35.75	$10.99
2004		40,866	$51.06	$12.50
2005		29,100	$53.75	$14.34
2006		33,904	$59.97	$16.30
2007		33,091	$63.33	$17.29

Calculate the effect of the stock options on net income before income taxes for 2004 to 2008.

35. **Reconstructing transactions affecting shareholders' equity. Exhibit 14.11** reproduces a portion of the statement of changes in shareholders' equity for Microsoft Corporation for 2007. When Microsoft repurchases its common stock, it cancels the outstanding shares. Prepare journal entries for each of the seven listed transactions in **Exhibit 14.11**. Record the effect of items affecting accumulated other comprehensive income using the amounts in **Exhibit 14.11** (that is, treating those net-of-tax amounts as if they were pre-tax amounts).

36. **Journal entries for changes in shareholders' equity. Exhibit 14.12** presents a portion of the statement of changes in shareholders' equity for Sirius Satellite Radio Inc. for 2007. Prepare journal entries for each of the six listed transactions in **Exhibit 14.12**. Transactions **(4)** and **(5)** were not with employees. Transaction **(5)** did not require the tendering of cash. Record the conversion of the notes in transaction **(6)** at carrying value.

37. **Journal entries for changes in shareholders' equity. Exhibit 14.13** presents a portion of the statement of changes in shareholders' equity for Anheuser-Busch Companies for 2007. Prepare journal entries for each of the eight transactions listed in **Exhibit 14.13**. Record the effect of items affecting accumulated other comprehensive income using the amounts in **Exhibit 14.13** (that is, as if they were pretax amounts).

38. **Treasury shares and their effects on performance ratios. Exhibit 14.14** presents the changes in common shareholders' equity of Monk Corporation for 2006 through 2008. Monk regularly purchases shares of its common stock and reissues them in connection with stock option plans. It will usually issue a small number of new common shares when it requires fractional shares to complete a stock option transaction. Earnings per common share were $2.70 for 2006, $3.20 for 2007, and $3.83 for 2008.

a. Give the journal entries for 2008 to record (1) the issue of common shares in connection with stock option plans, and (2) the purchase of treasury stock.

b. Compute the percentage change in net income and in earnings per share between 2006 and 2007, and between 2007 and 2008. Why do the percentage changes in earnings per share exceed the percentage changes in net income in both 2007 and 2008?

EXHIBIT 14.11

Microsoft Corporation
Excerpt from Statement of Changes
in Shareholders' Equity
(amounts in millions)
(Problem 35)

	2007
Common Stock and Additional Paid-In Capital	
Balance, Beginning of Year	$ 59,005
(1) Common Stock Issued	6,783
(2) Common Stock Repurchased	(6,162)
(3) Stock-Based Compensation Expense	889
Other	42
Balance, End of Year	$ 60,557
Retained Earnings	
Balance, Beginning of Year	$(20,130)
(4) Net Income	14,065
(5) Common Dividends	(3,837)
(2) Common Stock Repurchased	(21,212)
Balance, End of Year	$(31,114)
Accumulated Other Comprehensive Income	
Balance, Beginning of Year	$ 1,229
(6) Net Change in Unrealized Gains and Losses on Marketable Securities (net of taxes)	326
(7) Net Change in Unrealized Gains and Losses on Derivatives (net of taxes)	14
Net Change in Foreign Currency Translation Adjustment (net of taxes)	85
Balance, End of Year	$ 1,654
Comprehensive Income	
Net Income	$ 14,065
Net Change in Accumulated Other Comprehensive Income	425
Comprehensive Income	$ 14,490

EXHIBIT 14.12

Sirius Satellite Radio Inc.
Excerpt from Statement of Changes in Shareholders' Equity
(amounts in thousands)
(Problem 36)

	Number of Common Shares	Par Value of Common Stock	Additional Paid-In Capital
Balance, Beginning of Year	1,434,635,501	$1,435	$3,443,214
(1) Common Stock Issued to Third Parties	22,058,824	22	82,919
(2) Common Stock Issued to Employees	4,279,097	4	19,242
(3) Stock-Based Compensation Expense			52,683
(4) Exercise of Options	2,859,232	3	3,529
(5) Exercise of Warrants	4,988,726	5	(5)
(6) Exchange of Convertible Notes	2,322,190	2	3,182
Balance, End of Year	1,471,143,570	$1,471	$3,604,764

c. Compute the book value per outstanding common share at the end of 2006, 2007, and 2008, and the percentage change in book value per share between 2006 and 2007, and between 2007 and 2008. Why are the percentage changes in book value per common share less than the percentage changes in both net income and earnings per share?

EXHIBIT 14.13	Anheuser-Busch Companies Excerpt from Statement of Changes in Shareholders' Equity (amounts in millions, except per share amounts) (Problem 37)

	2007
Common Stock, $1 Par Value	
Balance, Beginning of Year	$ 1,473.7
(1) Shares Issued Under Stock Plans	8.8
Balance, End of Year	$ 1,482.5
Additional Paid-In Capital	
Balance, Beginning of Year	$ 2,962.5
(1) Shares Issued Under Stock Plans	283.5
(2) Stock Compensation Related	136.1
Balance, End of Year	$ 3,382.1
Retained Earnings	
Balance, Beginning of Year	$ 16,741.0
(3) Net Income	2,115.3
(4) Common Dividends	(932.4)
Balance, End of Year	$ 17,923.9
Treasury Stock, at Cost	
Balance, Beginning of Year	$(16,007.7)
(5) Treasury Stock Acquired	(2,707.2)
(2) Stock Compensation Related	0.2
Balance, End of Year	$(18,714.7)
Accumulated Other Comprehensive Income	
Balance, Beginning of Year	$ (1,230.8)
(6) Net Change in Unrealized Gains and Losses on Marketable Securities (net of taxes)	(.3)
(7) Net Change in Cash Flow Hedges (net of taxes)	(2.0)
Net Change in Foreign Currency Translation Adjustment (net of taxes)	105.2
(8) Pension Liability Adjustment (net of taxes)	205.2
Net Change in Accumulated Other Comprehensive Income	308.1
Balance, End of Year	$ (922.7)
Comprehensive Income	
Net Income	$ 2,115.3
Net Change in Accumulated Other Comprehensive Income	308.6
Comprehensive Income	$ 2,423.9

d. Compute the rate of return on common shareholders' equity for 2005, 2006, and 2007.

e. Does Monk appear to acquire the treasury stock primarily to satisfy commitments under stock option plans? Explain.

39. **Case introducing earnings-per-share calculations for a complex capital structure.** The Layton Ball Corporation has a relatively complicated capital structure—that is, it raises funds using various financing devices. In addition to common shares, it has issued stock options, warrants, and convertible bonds. **Exhibit 14.15** summarizes some pertinent information about these items. Net income for the year is $9,500, and the income tax rate used in computing income tax expense is 40% of pretax income.

a. First, ignore all items of capital except for the common shares. Calculate earnings per common share.

EXHIBIT 14.14

Monk Corporation
Analysis of Changes in Common Shareholders' Equity
(all dollar amounts in millions)
(Problem 38)

	Common Stock[a]		Retained Earnings	Treasury Stock		Total
	Shares	Amount		Shares	Amount	
December 31, Year 2005	1,483.168	$4,667.8	$10,942.0	(235.342)	$(4,470.8)	$11,139.0
Net Income	—	—	3,376.6	—	—	3,376.6
Dividends	—	—	(1,578.0)	—	—	(1,578.0)
Stock Options Exercised	0.295	74.7	—	14.104	294.3	369.0
Treasury Stock Purchased	—	—	—	(33.377)	(1,570.9)	(1,570.9)
December 31, 2006	1,483.463	$4,742.5	$12,740.6	(254.615)	$(5,747.4)	$11,735.7
Net Income	—	—	3,870.5	—	—	3,870.5
Dividends	—	—	(1,793.4)	—	—	(1,793.4)
Stock Options Exercised	0.156	225.0	—	15.982	426.0	651.0
Treasury Stock Purchased	—	—	—	(38.384)	(2,493.3)	(2,493.3)
December 31, 2007	1,483.619	$4,967.5	$14,817.7	(277.017)	$(7,814.7)	$11,970.5
Net Income	—	—	4,596.5	—	—	4,596.5
Dividends	—	—	(2,094.8)	—	—	(2,094.8)
Stock Options Exercised	0.307	286.5	—	14.183	427.6	714.1
Treasury Stock Purchased	—	—	—	(27.444)	(2,572.8)	(2,572.8)
December 31, 2008	1,483.926	$5,254.0	$17,319.4	(290.278)	$(9,959.9)	$12,613.5

EXHIBIT 14.15

Layton Ball Corporation
Information on Capital Structure
for Earnings-per-Share Calculations
(Problem 39)

Assume the following data about the capital structure and earnings for the Layton Ball Corporation for the year:

Number of Common Shares Outstanding Throughout the Year	2,500 shares
Market Price per Common Share Throughout the Year	$ 25
Options Outstanding During the Year:	
Number of Shares Issuable on Exercise of Options	1,000 shares
Exercise Price per Share	$ 15
Warrants Outstanding During the Year:	
Number of Shares Issuable on Exercise of Warrants	2,000 shares
Exercise Price per Share	$ 30
Convertible Bonds Outstanding:	
Number (issued 15 years ago)	100 bonds
Proceeds per Bond at Time of Issue (= face value)	$1,000
Coupon Rate (per year)	4%

b. In past years, Layton Ball has issued to employees options to purchase shares of stock. **Exhibit 14.15** indicates that the price of the common stock throughout the current year has remained steady at $25 but that holders of the stock options could exercise them at any time for $15 for each share. That is, the option allows the holder to surrender it along with $15 cash and receive one share in return. Thus the number of shares would increase, which would decrease the earnings-per-share figure. The company would, however, have more cash. Assume that the holders of options tender them, along with $15 each, to purchase shares. Assume that the company uses the cash to purchase shares for its own treasury at a price of $25 each. Compute a new earnings-per-share figure. The firm does not count shares in its own treasury in the denominator of the earnings-per-share calculation.

c. **Exhibit 14.15** indicates that there were also warrants outstanding in the hands of the public. The warrant allows the holder to turn in that warrant, along with $30 cash, to purchase one share of stock. If holders exercised the warrants, the number of outstanding shares would increase, which would reduce earnings per share. However, the company would have more cash, which it could use to purchase shares for the treasury, reducing the number of shares outstanding. Assume that all holders of warrants exercise them. Assume that the company uses the cash to purchase outstanding shares for the treasury. Compute a new earnings-per-share figure. Ignore the information about options and the calculations in part **b** at this point. Note however that this is an unlikely hypothetical scenario because rational warrants holders would not exercise the warrants for $30 when they can purchase shares for $25 each.

d. The firm also has convertible bonds outstanding. Each convertible bond entitles the holder to exchange that bond for 10 shares. If holders convert the bonds, the number of shares would increase, which would tend to reduce earnings per share. On the other hand, the company would not have to pay interest and thus would have no interest expense on the bond because it would no longer be outstanding. This would tend to increase income and earnings per share. Assume that all holders of convertible bonds convert their bonds into shares. Compute a new net income figure (do not forget income tax effects on income of the interest saved) and a new earnings-per-share figure. Ignore the information about options and warrants and the calculations in parts **b** and **c** at this point.

e. Now consider all the previous calculations. Which combined set of assumptions from parts **b**, **c**, and **d** would lead to the lowest possible earnings per share? Compute a new earnings per share under the most restrictive set of assumptions about reductions in earnings per share.

f. Accountants publish several earnings-per-share figures for companies with complicated capital structures and complicated events during the year. *The Wall Street Journal*, however, publishes only one figure in its daily columns (where it reports the price-earnings ratio—the price of a share of stock divided by its earnings per share). Which of the figures computed previously for earnings per share do you think *The Wall Street Journal* should report as the earnings-per-share figure? Why?

40. **Case for discussion: Value of stock options.** (The text does not give an explicit answer to this question but provides a sufficient basis to enable students to discuss the question.) Below is an excerpt from an article from the San Francisco Examiner, a leading Silicon Valley newspaper, which appeared at the height of the controversy over the accounting for employee stock options.

> For example, if StartUp Inc. recruits the brilliant software designer Joe Bithead . . . by offering him the option to buy 10,000 shares of StartUp's stock at its current price of a penny a share, what's the value of Joe's grant? If StartUp goes belly up, as 80% of new high-tech firms do, the grant is worthless. . . . If, on the other hand, after five years of struggle, StartUp manages to create a successful product and outperforms its competitors, the company's stock might sell for $10 a share on the public market. For a penny each, Joe can buy the 10,000 shares. . . . He unloads them in the market for a $100,000 profit.

The accounting question is, What cost, if any, does StartUp incur on Day 1 of the grant to Joe Bithead of an option to acquire 10,000 shares five years hence for $0.01 per share? StartUp shares trade in public stock markets on the date of grant at $0.01 per share. Because the word **cost** has so many meanings (see **cost terminology** in the **Glossary**), make the question operational and specific by considering the following.

Imagine that you are the financial executive of StartUp and that Goldman Sachs offers to relieve you of the obligation to deliver the shares to Joe Bithead. That is, Goldman will take a payment from you today and will deliver the shares to Bithead if he exercises the options but will do nothing otherwise, except keep your cash. How much are you willing to pay Goldman today to relieve you of your obligation to Bithead? That is, you pay Goldman now and they later deliver shares to Bithead if he exercises his options.

No one can be sure of the exact answer, given the sketchy data, but which of the following ranges do you think most likely?

a. $0 to $10.

b. $10 to $100.

c. $100 to $1,000.

d. $1,000 to $10,000.

e. $10,000 to $100,000.

f. Some other answer (indicate answer).

PART 4

FACMU13

Synthesis

Statement of Cash Flows: Another Look

15

1. Review the rationale for the statement of cash flows, emphasizing why net income differs from cash flows.
2. Review the T-account procedure, introduced in Chapter 5, for preparing the statement of cash flows.
3. Solidify your understanding of the cash flow effects of various transactions presented in Chapters 7 through 14.
4. Develop skills in analyzing and interpreting the statement of cash flows.

Chapter 5 introduces the statement of cash flows, discussing its rationale and illustrating a T-account approach for its preparation. Subsequent chapters describe the effect of various transactions on the income statement and the balance sheet but did not consider their effect on the statement of cash flows. This chapter discusses the effect of these transactions on the statement of cash flows, using a comprehensive example.

REVIEW OF CONCEPTS UNDERLYING THE STATEMENT OF CASH FLOWS

Chapter 5 discusses the following concepts underlying the statement of cash flows:

1. The statement of cash flows explains the reasons for the change in cash and cash equivalents during a period. This statement classifies the reasons as relating to operating or investing or financing decisions.

2. Revenues from sales of goods or services to customers during a particular period do not necessarily equal cash received from customers during the same period. The receipt of cash can precede, coincide with, or follow the recognition of revenue. Expenses incurred to generate revenues during a particular period do not necessarily equal cash expended for the goods and services consumed in operations during the same period. The expenditure of cash can precede, or coincide with, or follow the recognition of expenses. Thus, net income for a particular period will likely differ from cash flow from operations for the same period.

3. Firms typically report cash flows from operations using the indirect method. The indirect method starts with net income, then adds any expense amount that does not use cash, and subtracts any revenue amount that does not provide cash. The adjustments to convert net income to cash flow from operations generally involve (1) adding the amount by which an expense exceeds the related cash expenditure for the period (for depreciation, adding the entire amount as there was no cash expenditure in the current period), (2) subtracting (in rare cases, adding) the amount by which a revenue exceeds (or is less than) the related cash receipt for the period (such as equity method earnings exceeding [or being less than] dividends), (3) adding credit changes[1] in operating non-cash working capital accounts, such as accounts receivable, inventories, and accounts payable, and (4) subtracting debit changes in operating working capital accounts.

4. Cash flow from investing activities includes cash purchases and cash sales of marketable securities; property, plant, and equipment; intangibles; and investments in securities.

5. Cash flow from financing activities includes cash issues and cash redemptions of long-term borrowings, cash sales and cash repurchases of common and preferred shares, and cash dividends.

REVIEW OF T-ACCOUNT PROCEDURE FOR PREPARING THE STATEMENT OF CASH FLOWS

The accountant prepares the statement of cash flows after completing the balance sheet and the income statement. **Chapter 5** describes and illustrates a procedure for preparing the statement of cash flows using a T-account work sheet. A summary of the procedure follows:

Step 1 Obtain a balance sheet for the beginning and the end of the period for which you wish to prepare the statement of cash flows.

Step 2 Prepare a T-account work sheet. A master T-account for cash appears at the top of the work sheet. This master T-account has three sections labeled, respectively, Operations, Investing, and Financing. Enter the beginning and the ending balances in cash and cash equivalents in the master T-account. *Cash equivalents* represent short-term, highly liquid investments in which a firm has temporarily placed excess cash. Generally, only investments with maturities of three months or less qualify as cash equivalents. We use the term *cash flows* to refer to changes in cash and cash equivalents. Complete the T-account work sheet by preparing a T-account for each balance sheet account other than cash and cash equivalents, and enter the beginning and the ending balances.

Step 3 Explain the change in the master Cash account between the beginning and the end of the period by explaining, or accounting for, the changes in the other balance sheet accounts. Do this by reconstructing the entries originally made in the accounts during the period and entering them in appropriate T-accounts on the work sheet. By explaining the changes in balance sheet accounts other than cash and cash equivalents, this process also explains the change in cash and cash equivalents. We make such extensive use of the Cash Change Equation in this chapter that we abbreviate words into symbols, as follows:

Cash Change Equation (Equation 3, Chapter 5)

$$\text{Change in Cash} = \text{Change in Liabilities} + \text{Change in Shareholders' Equity} - \text{Change in Noncash Assets}$$

$$\Delta\text{Cash} = \Delta L + \Delta SE - \Delta N\$A$$

Step 4 Prepare a statement of cash flows using information in the T-account work sheet.

---

[1]With respect to a single account, the term *credit change* means a decrease in an asset account or an increase in a liability (or shareholders' equity) account. So, "credit changes in operating working capital accounts" means "a decrease in a current operating asset account or an increase in a current operating liability account." In parallel, with respect to a single account, the term *debit change* means an increase in an asset account or a decrease in a liability (or shareholders' equity) account.

COMPREHENSIVE ILLUSTRATION OF THE STATEMENT OF CASH FLOWS

The comprehensive illustration that follows uses data for Ellwood Corporation for 2008. **Exhibit 15.1** presents an income statement for 2008; **Exhibit 15.2** presents a comparative balance sheet for December 31, 2008 and 2007; and **Exhibit 15.3** presents a statement of cash flows. The calculation of cash flow from operations first presents the indirect method. The sections that follow explain each of the line items in **Exhibit 15.3**. **Exhibit 15.4** shows the T-account work sheet. Cash and cash equivalents decreased by $790 during the year, from $2,670 (= $1,150 + $1,520) to $1,880 (= $1,090 + $790).

LINE 1: NET INCOME

The income statement indicates net income of $760 for the period. The work sheet entry presumes that cash provisionally increases by the amount of net income.

(1a) Cash (Operations—Net Income)	760	
Retained Earnings		760

The effect of net income on the Cash Change Equation is as follows:

$$\Delta \text{Cash} \quad = \quad \Delta L \quad + \quad \Delta SE \quad - \quad \Delta N\$A$$
$$\text{Operations} + \$760\ (1a) \quad = \quad \$0 \quad + \quad \$760\ (1a) \quad - \quad \$0$$

Throughout this chapter, entries with a number followed by the letter *a* indicate entries on the statement of cash flows work sheet. Entries with a number and not followed with the letter *a* indicate entries made during the year in the accounting records of Ellwood Corporation.

LINE 2: DEPRECIATION OF BUILDINGS AND EQUIPMENT

Internal records indicate that depreciation on manufacturing facilities totaled $450 and on selling and administrative facilities totaled $250 during the year. The firm included these amounts in cost of goods sold and selling and administrative expenses, respectively, in the

EXHIBIT 15.1	**Ellwood Corporation** **Consolidated Income Statement** **For the Year 2008**

REVENUES	
Sales	$10,500
Interest and Dividends	320
Equity in Earnings of Affiliate	480
Gain on Disposal of Equipment	40
Total Revenues	$11,340
EXPENSES	
Cost of Goods Sold	$ 6,000
Selling and Administrative Expense	3,550
Compensation Expense (Employee Stock Options)	170
Impairment Loss on Land	80
Loss on Sale of Marketable Equity Securities	30
Interest Expense	450
Income Tax Expense	300
Total Expenses and Losses	$10,580
Net Income	$ 760

EXHIBIT 15.2

**Ellwood Corporation
Consolidated Balance Sheet**

	December 31	
	2008	**2007**
ASSETS		
Current Assets		
Cash	$ 1,090	$ 1,150
Certificate of Deposit	790	1,520
Marketable Equity Securities Available for Sale	190	280
Accounts Receivable (net)	4,300	3,400
Inventories	2,350	1,500
Prepayments	600	800
Total Current Assets	$ 9,320	$ 8,650
Investments		
Investment in Company A (15%—Available for Sale)	$ 1,280	$ 1,250
Investment in Company B (40%)	2,420	2,100
Total Investments	$ 3,700	$ 3,350
Property, Plant, and Equipment		
Land	$ 920	$ 1,000
Buildings	8,900	8,600
Equipment.	11,540	10,840
Less Accumulated Depreciation	(6,480)	(6,240)
Total Property, Plant, and Equipment	$14,880	$14,200
Intangible Assets		
Patent	$ 2,550	$ 2,550
Less Accumulated Amortization	(750)	(600)
Total Intangible Assets	$ 1,800	$ 1,950
Total Assets	$29,700	$28,150
LIABILITIES AND SHAREHOLDERS' EQUITY		
Current Liabilities		
Bank Notes Payable	$ 2,750	$ 2,000
Accounts Payable (for inventory)	3,230	2,450
Warranty Liability	900	1,200
Advances from Customers	1,000	600
Total Current Liabilities	$ 7,880	$ 6,250
Noncurrent Liabilities		
Bonds Payable	$ 1,370	$ 2,820
Capitalized Lease Obligation.	2,100	1,800
Deferred Income Taxes	650	550
Total Noncurrent Liabilities	$ 4,120	$ 5,170
Shareholders' Equity		
Preferred Shares	$ 1,200	$ 1,000
Common Shares	2,110	2,000
Additional Paid-In Capital	4,400	4,000
Accumulated Other Comprehensive Income:		
Unrealized Holding Loss on Marketable Securities	(40)	(30)
Unrealized Holding Gain on Investments in Securities	80	50
Retained Earnings	10,330	9,960
Total	$18,080	$16,900
Less Cost of Treasury Shares	(380)	(250)
Total Shareholders' Equity	$17,700	$16,730
Total Liabilities and Shareholders' Equity	$29,700	$28,150

EXHIBIT 15.3

Ellwood Corporation
Consolidated Statement of Cash Flows
For the Year 2008

OPERATIONS

(1) Net Income	$ 760

Noncash Revenues, Expenses, Gains, and Losses Included in Income:

(2) Depreciation of Buildings and Equipment	700
(3) Amortization of Patent	150
(4) Compensation Expense (in Form of Employee Stock Options)	170
(5) Loss on Impairment of Land	80
(6) Loss on Sale of Marketable Equity Securities	30
(7) Deferred Income Taxes	100
(8) Excess of Coupon Payments over Interest Expense	(50)
(9) Gain on Disposal of Equipment	(40)
(10) Equity in Undistributed Earnings of Affiliate	(320)
(11) Decrease in Prepayments	200
(12) Increase in Accounts Payable (for inventory)	780
(13) Increase in Advances from Customers	400
(14) Increase in Accounts Receivable (net)	(900)
(15) Increase in Inventories	(850)
(16) Decrease in Warranty Liability	(300)
Cash Flow from Operations	$ 910

INVESTING

(17) Sale of Marketable Equity Securities	$50
(18) Sale of Equipment	180
(19) Acquisition of Equipment	(1,300)
Cash Flow from Investing	(1,070)

FINANCING

(20) Short-Term Bank Borrowing	$750
(21) Long-Term Bonds Issued	400
(22) Preferred Shares Issued	200
(23) Retirement of Long-Term Debt at Maturity	(1,500)
(24) Acquisition of Common Shares	(130)
(25) Dividends	(390)
(26) Common Shares (Issued on Exercise of Employee Options)	40
Cash Flow from Financing	(630)
Net Change in Cash	$ (790)
Cash, Beginning of 2008	2,670
Cash, End of 2008	$ 1,880

income statement in **Exhibit 15.1**. None of this $700 of depreciation required an operating cash flow during 2008. The firm reported cash expenditures for these assets as investing activities in the earlier periods when it acquired them. Thus, the work sheet entry to explain the change in the Accumulated Depreciation account adds back depreciation to net income in deriving cash flow from operations.

(2a) Cash (Operations—Depreciation Expense Addback)	700	
Accumulated Depreciation		700

Addback for Depreciation as a Product Cost The addback for the $450 of depreciation on manufacturing facilities requires elaboration. **Chapter 8** explains that accountants treat such depreciation charges as a product cost, not a period expense. The accountant debits

EXHIBIT 15.4   Ellwood Corporation
T-Account Work Sheet

Cash

✓	2,670				

Operations

Net Income	(1a)	760	50	(8a)	Excess Coupon Payments
Depreciation Expense	(2a)	700	40	(9a)	Gain on Sale of Equipment
Amortization Expense	(3a)	150	320	(10a)	Equity in Undistributed Earnings
Employee Stock Option Compensation	(4a)	170	900	(14a)	Increase in Accounts Receivable (net)
Impairment Loss on Land	(5a)	80	850	(15a)	Increase in Inventories
Loss on Sale of Marketable Securities	(6a)	30	300	(16a)	Decrease in Warranty Liability
Deferred Income Taxes	(7a)	100			
Decrease in Prepayments	(11a)	200			
Increase in Accounts Payable	(12a)	780			
Increase in Advances from Customers	(13a)	400			

Investing

Sale of Marketable Securities	(6a)	50	1,300	(19a)	Acquisition of Equipment
Sale of Equipment	(9a)	180			

Financing

Short-Term Borrowing	(20a)	750	1,500	(23a)	Retirement of Long-Term Debt
Long-Term Bonds Issued	(21a)	400	130	(24a)	Acquisition of Common Shares
Preferred Shares Issued	(22a)	200	390	(25a)	Dividends
Common Shares Issued	(26a)	40			
✓	1,880				

Marketable Equity Securities Available for Sale

✓	280			
(6b)	10	80	(6a)	
		20	(27a)	
✓	190			

Accounts Receivable (net)

✓	3,400		
(14a)	900		
✓	4,300		

Inventories

✓	1,500		
(15a)	850		
✓	2,350		

Prepayments

✓	800		
		200	(11a)
✓	600		

Investment in Company A Available for Sale

✓	1,250		
(28a)	30		
✓	1,280		

Investment in Company B

✓	2,100		
(10a)	320		
✓	2,420		

Land

✓	1,000		
		80	(5a)
✓	920		

Buildings

✓	8,600		
(29a)	300		
✓	8,900		

Equipment

✓	10,840			
(19a)	1,300	600	(9a)	
✓	11,540			

(continued)

EXHIBIT 15.4

**Ellwood Corporation
T-Account Work Sheet (Continued)**

Accumulated Depreciation			
	6,240	✓	
(9a) 460	700	(2a)	
	6,480	✓	

Patent		
✓ 2,550		
✓ 2,550		

Accumulated Amortization		
	600	✓
	150	(3a)
	750	✓

Bank Notes Payable		
	2,000	✓
	750	(20a)
	2,750	✓

Accounts Payable (for inventory)		
	2,450	✓
	780	(12a)
	3,230	✓

Warranty Liability		
	1,200	✓
(16a) 300		
	900	✓

Advances from Customers		
	600	✓
	400	(13a)
	1,000	✓

Bonds Payable		
	2,820	✓
(8a) 50	400	(21a)
(23a) 1,500		
(30a) 300		
	1,370	✓

Capitalized Lease Obligation		
	1,800	✓
	300	(29a)
	2,100	✓

Deferred Income Taxes		
	550	✓
	100	(7a)
	650	✓

Preferred Shares		
	1,000	✓
	200	(22a)
	1,200	✓

Common Shares		
	2,000	✓
	100	(30a)
	10	(26a)
	2,100	✓

Additional Paid-In Capital		
	4,000	✓
	170	(4a)
	200	(30a)
	30	(26a)
	4,400	✓

Unrealized Holding Loss on Marketable Securities		
✓ 30		
	10	(6b)
(27a) 20		
✓ 40		

Unrealized Holding Gain on Investments in Securities		
	50	✓
	30	(28a)
	80	✓

Retained Earnings		
	9,960	✓
(25a) 390	760	(1a)
	10,330	✓

Treasury Shares		
✓ 250		
(24a) 130		
✓ 380		

Work-in-Process Inventory for this $450 and credits Accumulated Depreciation. If, during the period, the firm sells all the goods it produces, cost of goods sold includes this $450. Because cost of goods sold includes an amount that does not use cash, the addback to net income cancels the portion of depreciation charges that cost of goods sold includes.

Suppose, however, that the firm does not sell all the goods it produces during the period. The ending inventory of Work-in-Process Inventory or Finished Goods Inventory includes a portion of the $450 depreciation charge. Assume, for example, that the firm sold 80% of the units produced during the period. Cost of goods sold includes $360 (= .80 × $450) of the depreciation, and inventory accounts include the remaining $90. The statement of cash flows adds back to net income the entire $450 of depreciation on manufacturing facilities for the period. The $90 of depreciation included in the cost of units not sold caused the inventory accounts to increase by $90. Under the indirect method of computing cash flow from operations, the accountant subtracts this increase in inventories in computing cash flow from operations. The $450 addition for depreciation less the $90 subtraction for the increase in inventories nets to a $360 addition to income. Because cost of goods sold includes only $360 of depreciation, the addition required to cancel the depreciation included in cost of goods sold equals $360. Thus, the work sheet entry **2a** shows an addback for the full amount of depreciation for the period (both as a product cost and as a period expense), not just the amount included in cost of goods sold; then, line **15** of the statement of cash flows includes a subtraction for the $90 increase in inventories caused by adding depreciation to work in process.

LINE 3: AMORTIZATION OF PATENT

The effect of patent amortization on cash flow is conceptually identical to that for depreciation charges, both for period expenses and product costs. Company records indicate that cost of goods sold for 2008 includes patent amortization of $150. The work sheet entry to explain the change in the Accumulated Amortization account is as follows:

(3a) Cash (Operations—Amortization Expense Addback) 150	
Accumulated Amortization.	150

LINE 4: STOCK OPTION COMPENSATION EXPENSE

Notes to the financial statements of Ellwood Corporation indicate that part of the compensation to executives took the form of options to buy shares of Ellwood Corporation. **Chapter 14** discusses that firms use an option pricing model to measure the cost of stock options and then amortize this cost over the expected period of benefit. Ellwood Corporation amortized $170 as compensation expense during 2008. Following is the entry in the accounting records to record the expense:

(4) Compensation Expense 170	
Additional Paid-In Capital	170

Assets	=	Liabilities	+	Shareholders' Equity	(Class.)
				−170	IncSt → RE
				+170	ContriCap

The $170 of compensation reduced net income but did not require a cash outflow during 2008. The entry explains part of the change in the Additional Paid-In Capital account. The work sheet entry for the amortization of stock options is as follows:

(4a) Cash (Operations—Compensation Expense Addback). 170	
Additional Paid-In Capital	170

Income Tax Effects of Employee Stock Option Income tax laws, depending on the jurisdiction, may permit firms to claim an income tax deduction for stock options. For example, the income tax law in the United States currently permits firms to deduct the intrinsic value (= market price − exercise price) of a nonqualified stock option in the year employees exercise stock options. The issues raised by the income tax benefits and their effects on the statement of cash flows are too advanced to include in the example for Ellwood Corporation in **Exhibit 15.3**.

LINE 5: IMPAIRMENT LOSS ON LAND

Notes to the financial statements of Ellwood Corporation indicate that the sum of the expected rentals on land that the company rents to others plus the amounts it expects to receive on eventual sale of the land has dropped so much that the land has become impaired.

The difference between the carrying value of the land and its fair value at the end of 2008 is $80. The following entry is made in the accounting records to record the loss:

(5) Loss on Impairment of Land.. 80
     Land 80

Assets	=	Liabilities	+	Shareholders' Equity	(Class.)
−80				−80	IncSt → RE

The $80 of impairment loss reduced net income and the carrying value of land, but did not require a cash outflow during 2008. The work sheet entry to reflect the change in the Land account is as follows:

(5a) Cash (Operations—Asset Impairment Loss Addback)................. 80
     Land 80

LINE 6: LOSS ON SALE OF MARKETABLE EQUITY SECURITIES

The accounting records indicate that Ellwood Corporation sold marketable equity securities held as securities available for sale during 2008. Ellwood Corporation acquired these securities for $80 during 2007, wrote them down to their market value of $70 at the end of 2007, and sold them during 2008 for $50. The firm made the following entry in the accounting records to record this sale:

(6) Cash... 50
    Realized Loss on Sale of Marketable Equity Securities (IncSt) 30
       Marketable Equity Securities 70
       Unrealized Holding Loss on Securities Available for Sale
        (Other Comprehensive Income) 10

Assets	=	Liabilities	+	Shareholders' Equity	(Class.)
+50				−30	IncSt → RE
−70				+10	OCI → AOCI

ΔCash	=	ΔL	+	ΔSE	−	ΔN$A
+50 (Invst.)		0		−20		−70

Recall that journal entry numbers without letters, such as this one numbered **(6)**, refer to actual entries Ellwood recorded in its books. For some such entries, we give the effect on the Cash Change Equation, derived from the balance sheet equation. For some complex transactions, such as this one, we give the Balance Sheet Equation. For some, we give both.

The work sheet entries to reflect this transaction are as follows:

(6a) Cash (Investing—Sale of Marketable Equity Securities)............... 50
    Cash (Operations—Loss on Sale of Marketable
      Equity Securities Addback) 30
       Marketable Equity Securities 70
       Unrealized Holding Loss on Securities Available
        for Sale (Other Comprehensive Income) 10

The statement of cash flows classifies all $50 cash proceeds as an investing activity on line **17** and none as an operating activity. Net income on line **1** in **Exhibit 15.3** includes a subtraction for the loss on the sale of marketable equity securities. To avoid understating the amount of cash flow from operations, the accounting adds back the loss to net income. This addback offsets the loss included in the calculation of net income and eliminates its effect on cash flow from operations. Line **17** shows the entire cash proceeds from the sale as an investing activity. The analyst might reasonably view purchases and sales of marketable equity securities as operating activities because these transactions involve the use of temporarily excess cash. Most, but not all, firms consider these transactions sufficiently peripheral to the firms' principal operating activity—selling goods and services to customers—that they classify such purchases and sales as investing activities.

LINE 7: DEFERRED INCOME TAXES

Notes to the financial statements of Ellwood Corporation indicate that income tax expense of $300 comprises $200 currently payable taxes and $100 deferred to future periods. Ellwood Corporation made the following entry during the year to recognize income tax expense.

(7) Income Tax Expense	300	
Cash.		200
Deferred Income Tax Liability		100

Assets	=	Liabilities	+	Shareholders' Equity	(Class.)
−200		+100		−300	IncSt → RE

ΔCash	=	ΔL	+	ΔSE	−	ΔN$A
−200 (Opns.)		+100		−300		0

In the United States, a common account title for the debit is "Provision for Income Taxes," but see the **Glossary** entry for *provision*.

The $100 of deferred income taxes reduced net income but did not require a cash outflow during 2008. To explain the change in the Deferred Income Tax Liability account, the work sheet must add back deferred income taxes to net income to derive cash flow from operations.

(7a) Cash (Operations—Deferred Tax Addback)	100	
Deferred Income Tax Liability		100

We have prepared the statement of cash flows for Ellwood Corporation using U.S. GAAP where it differs from IFRS. IFRS requires the firm to split income tax expense into operating, investing, and financing portions depending on the activity that caused the portion of income tax expense and to report each portion in the corresponding section of the statement.

LINE 8: EXCESS OF COUPON PAYMENTS OVER INTEREST EXPENSE

Bonds Payable on the balance sheet includes one series of bonds initially issued at a premium (that is, the coupon rate exceeded the required market rate of interest when Ellwood Corporation issued the bonds, so the initial issue proceeds exceeded the face value of the bonds). The amortization of the bond premium causes the amount of interest expense recognized over the life of the bonds to be less than the periodic debt service payments for the coupons. The entry made in the accounting records for interest expense during the period was as follows:

(8) Interest Expense	450	
Bonds Payable	50	
Cash		500

(continued)

ΔCash	=	ΔL	+	ΔSE	–	ΔN$A
−500 (Opns.)		−50		−450		0

The firm spent $500 of cash even though it subtracted only $450 of interest expense in computing net income. To explain the change in the Bonds Payable account, the work sheet subtracts an additional $50 from net income to derive cash flow from operations.

(8a) Bonds Payable	50	
Cash (Operations—Excess Coupon Payments Subtraction)		50

The statement of cash flows classifies cash used for interest expense as an operating activity because it views interest as a cost of carrying out operations. Some security analysts suggest that this $50 use of cash for principal repayment is a financing activity for debt service, not an operating activity, and would place it in the financing section. IFRS allows, but does not require, showing interest payments as a financing use of cash. The Financial Accounting Standards Board *Statement of Financial Accounting Standards No. 95*, however, classifies the $50 cash outflow as an operating activity, which IFRS allows.

LINE 9: GAIN ON DISPOSAL OF EQUIPMENT

The accounting records indicate that Ellwood Corporation sold for $180 during 2008 a machine originally costing $600, with accumulated depreciation of $460. The journal entry made to record this disposal was as follows:

(9) Cash	180	
Accumulated Depreciation	460	
Equipment		600
Gain on Disposal of Equipment		40

Assets	=	Liabilities	+	Shareholders' Equity	(Class.)
+180				+40	IncSt → RE
+460					
−600					

ΔCash	=	ΔL	+	ΔSE	–	ΔN$A
+180 (Invst.)		0		+40		+460 −600

Line **18** shows all the cash proceeds of $180 as an increase in cash from an investing activity. Net income reported in line **1** includes the $40 gain on sale. To avoid overstating the amount of cash derived from this sale, the accountant subtracts the $40 gain from net income in computing cash flow from operations.

(9a) Cash (Investing—Sale of Equipment)	180	
Accumulated Depreciation	460	
Equipment		600
Cash (Operations—Gain on Sale of Equipment Subtraction)		40

The statement of cash flows classifies all cash proceeds from selling equipment as an investing activity and none as an operating activity. Most firms acquire and sell fixed assets with the objective of providing the capacity to carry out operations rather than as a means of generating operating income.

Illustration of Loss, Alternative to Main Elwood Example. Fixed assets disposed of at a loss instead of a gain require an addback to net income in deriving cash flow from operations.

The work sheet entry, assuming the same data as in the preceding entry except that Ellwood Corporation sells the equipment for $110, would be as follows:

Cash (Investing—Disposal of Equipment)	110	
Accumulated Depreciation	460	
Cash (Operations—Loss on Disposal of Equipment Addback)	30	
Equipment		600

LINE 10: EQUITY IN UNDISTRIBUTED EARNINGS OF AFFILIATE

The balance sheet indicates that Ellwood Corporation owns 40% of the common stock of Company B. During 2008 Company B earned $1,200 and paid $400 of dividends. Ellwood Corporation made the following entries on its books during the year:

(10) Investment in Company B	480	
Equity in Earnings of Affiliate		480

Assets	=	Liabilities	+	Shareholders' Equity		(Class.)
+480				+480		IncSt → RE

ΔCash	=	ΔL	+	ΔSE	–	ΔN$A
0		0		+480		+480

Records equity in earnings of $480 (= 0.40 × $1,200).

Cash	160	
Investment in Company B		160

Assets	=	Liabilities	+	Shareholders' Equity		(Class.)
+160						
−160						

ΔCash	=	ΔL	+	ΔSE	–	ΔN$A
+160 (Opns.)		0		0		−160

Records dividends received of $160 = 0.40 × $400.

Net income of Ellwood Corporation on line **1** of **Exhibit 15.3** includes $480 of equity income, but Ellwood Corporation received only $160 of cash. Thus, the work sheet subtracts $320 (= $480 − $160) from net income in deriving cash from operations.

(10a) Investment in Company B	320	
Cash (Operations—Equity in Undistributed		
Earnings Subtraction)		320

LINE 11: DECREASE IN PREPAYMENTS

Because prepayments decreased by $200 during 2008, the firm paid cash during 2008 for new prepayments in an amount smaller than the amount it expensed for prepayments of earlier years. Assume that all prepayments relate to selling and administrative activities. The journal entries that Ellwood Corporation made in the accounting records during the year had the following combined effect:

(11) Selling and Administrative Expenses	....	3,550	
Cash	....		3,350
Prepayments	....		200

ΔCash	=	ΔL	+	ΔSE	−	ΔN$A
−3,350 (Opns.)		0		−3,550		−200

To explain the change in the work sheet for prepayments, add back $200 to net income for the credit change[2] in an operating current asset account so that cash flow from operations reports the amount for expenditures.

| (11a) Cash (Operations—Decrease in Prepayments) | .... | 200 | |
| Prepayments | .... | | 200 |

LINE 12: INCREASE IN ACCOUNTS PAYABLE

An increase in accounts payable indicates that new purchases on account during 2008 exceeded payments during 2008 for previous purchases on account. This increase in accounts payable, an operating current liability account, implicitly provides cash. Suppliers have provided financing so that Ellwood Corporation can acquire goods on account. You might think of it this way: Imagine a firm borrows cash from a supplier, debiting Cash and crediting Notes Payable. Then the firm uses the cash to acquire inventory or other items. You can see that the supplier has provided cash, and the firm increases a current liability account. A firm buying on account has achieved the same result, except that it credits Accounts Payable, not Notes Payable. Because the supplier ties the financing to the purchase of goods used in operations, accounting classifies this source of cash in the operating, not financing, section of the statement of cash flows.

| (12a) Cash (Operations—Increase in Accounts Payable) | .... | 780 | |
| Accounts Payable (for inventory) | .... | | 780 |

We explore the effect that the adjustment for the change in accounts payable has on the equation for the change in cash when we discuss the adjustment for inventory.

LINE 13: INCREASE IN ADVANCES FROM CUSTOMERS

The $400 increase in customer advances means that the firm received $400 more cash during 2008 than it recognized as revenue. The work sheet adds this excess to net income in deriving cash flow from operations.

| (13a) Cash (Operations—Increase in Advances from Customers) | .... | 400 | |
| Advances from Customers | .... | | 400 |

We consider the effect that the adjustment for the change in advances for customers has on the equation for the change in cash next, when we discuss the adjustment for accounts receivable.

LINE 14: INCREASE IN ACCOUNTS RECEIVABLE

The increase in accounts receivable indicates that the firm collected less cash from customers than the amount shown for sales on account. The work sheet subtracts the increase in accounts receivable in deriving cash flow from operations.

---

[2]Because prepayments declined, the amount of the decline is an addback. Had prepayments increased, a debit change, the amount of the increase would be a subtraction.

(14a) Accounts Receivable (net)	900	
Cash (Operations—Increase in Accounts Receivable)		900

Note that this entry automatically incorporates the effect of any change in the Allowance for Uncollectible Accounts. The work sheet could show separate entries for the change in gross accounts receivable and the change in the allowance for uncollectible accounts.

We can now summarize the effect that changes in accounts receivable and advances from customers have on the equation for changes in cash. Ellwood Corporation made entries during the year with the following combined effect:

(actual journal entries for transactions in 13 and 14, above, combined into one)

Cash.	10,000	
Accounts Receivable, Net.	900	
Advances from Customers		400
Sales Revenue		10,500

Assets	=	Liabilities	+	Shareholders' Equity	(Class.)
+10,000		+400		+10,500	IncSt → RE
+900					

ΔCash	=	ΔL	+	ΔSE	–	ΔN$A
+10,000 (Opns.)		+400		+10,500		+900

LINE 15: INCREASE IN INVENTORIES

The increase in inventories indicates the firm purchased more raw materials and supplies than it sold during 2008. The work sheet subtracts this change in inventory in deriving cash flow from operations.

(15a) Inventories	850	
Cash (Operations—Increase in Inventories)		850

We can now consider the effect on cash of the change in inventories and the change in accounts payable. Ellwood Corporation made entries during the year that had the following combined effect:

(actual journal entries for transactions in 12 and 15, above, combined into one)

Cost of Goods Sold	6,000	
Inventories	850	
Accounts Payable (for inventory)		780
Cash.		6,070

Assets	=	Liabilities	+	Shareholders' Equity	(Class.)
+850		+780		−6,000	IncSt → RE
−6,070					

ΔCash	=	ΔL	+	ΔSE	–	ΔN$A
−6,070 (Opns.)		+780		−6,000		+850

LINE 16: DECREASE IN WARRANTY LIABILITY

As **Chapter 8** explains, firms estimate future warranty costs on current sales using the allowance method for warranties. The Warranty Liability account increases for the estimated cost of future warranty services on products sold during the period and decreases by the actual cost of warranty services performed during the same period. During 2008 the firm paid $300 more in warranty claims than it reported as expenses on the income statement. Ellwood Corporation estimated warranty expense of $920 and included that amount in selling and administrative expenses in its income statement in **Exhibit 15.1**. The firm made entries during the year with the following combined effect:

(16) Selling and Administrative Expenses		920	
Warranty Liability		300	
Cash			1,220

ΔCash	=	ΔL	+	ΔSE	−	ΔN$A
−1,220 (Opns.)		−300		−920		0

The work sheet subtracts this decrease in Warranty Liability so that cash flow from operations reports the amount of cash expenditures, not the amount for expenses.

(16a) Warranty Liability		300	
Cash (Operations—Decrease in Warranty Liability)			300

Cash flow from operations, summed for the transactions recorded as affecting operating activities, is $910 for 2008.

LINES 17 AND 18

See the discussion for lines **6** and **9**.

LINE 19: ACQUISITION OF EQUIPMENT

The firm acquired equipment costing $1,300 during 2008. The entry for this investing activity is as follows:

(19a) Equipment		1,300	
Cash (Investing—Acquisition of Equipment)			1,300

Cash flow from investing, summed for the transactions recorded as affecting financing activities for 2008, is a net outflow of $1,070.

LINE 20: SHORT-TERM BANK BORROWING

Ellwood Corporation borrowed $750 during 2008 from its bank under a short-term borrowing arrangement. Even though this loan is short term, the statement of cash flows classifies it as a financing instead of an operating activity. The entry on the work sheet is as follows:

(20a) Cash (Financing—Short-Term Bank Borrowing)		750	
Bank Note Payable			750

LINE 21: LONG-TERM BONDS ISSUED

The firm issued long-term bonds totaling $400 during 2008.

(21a) Cash (Financing—Long-Term Bonds Issued)	400	
Bonds Payable		400

LINE 22: PREFERRED SHARES ISSUED

The firm issued preferred shares totaling $200 during the year.

(22a) Cash (Financing—Preferred Shares Issued)	200	
Preferred Shares		200

LINE 23: RETIREMENT OF LONG-TERM DEBT AT MATURITY

Ellwood Corporation retired $1,500 of long-term debt at maturity. The income statement in **Exhibit 15.1** shows no gain or loss on retirement of this debt. Thus, Ellwood Corporation must have retired the debt at its carrying value. We make the following work sheet entry:

(23a) Bonds Payable	1,500	
Cash (Financing—Retirement of Long-Term Debt)		1,500

If the firm had retired the debt prior to maturity, the firm would likely have recognized a gain or loss. The work sheet would eliminate the gain or loss from net income in computing cash flow from operations and classify as a financing activity the full amount of cash used to retire the debt.

LINE 24: ACQUISITION OF COMMON SHARES

The firm acquired shares of its own common stock at a cost of $130 during 2008. The entry on the work sheet is as follows:

(24a) Treasury Stock	130	
Cash (Financing—Acquisition of Common Shares)		130

LINE 25: DIVIDENDS

Ellwood Corporation declared and paid $390 of dividends to its shareholders during 2008. The entry is as follows:

(25a) Retained Earnings	390	
Cash (Financing—Dividends)		390

IFRS allows firms to show cash used for dividends as an operating use.

LINE 26: EXERCISE BY EMPLOYEES OF THEIR STOCK OPTIONS

During 2008, employees of Ellwood Corporation exercised their stock options. In a previous year the employees had received options for which Ellwood Corporation had charged $20 for compensation expense (and credited Additional Paid-In Capital). (See entry **(4)** for the same sort of entry made this year.) During 2008, the employees exercised those options by paying $40 cash to acquire common shares with par value of $10. The entry made in the accounting records to record the exercise is as follows:

(26) Cash	40	
Additional Paid-In Capital	20	

(continued)

Common Shares   10
Additional Paid-In Capital   50

Assets	=	Liabilities	+	Shareholders' Equity	(Class.)
+40				−20	ContriCap
				+10	ContriCap
				+50	ContriCap

ΔCash	=	ΔL	+	ΔSE	−	ΔN$A
40		0		−20		0
				+10		
				+50		

The accountant reflects this financing transaction on the T-account work sheet by making the following entry:

(26a)	Cash (Financing—Common Shares Issued)	40	
	Additional Paid-In Capital	20	
	Common Shares		10
	Additional Paid-In Capital		50

Summing the transactions that affect financing activities, we compute a net cash outflow for financing of $630 for the year.

NONCASH INVESTING AND FINANCING TRANSACTIONS

Some investing and financing transactions do not involve cash and therefore do not appear on the statement of cash flows. These transactions nevertheless help explain changes in balance sheet accounts. The accountant must enter these transactions in the T-account work sheet to account fully for all balance sheet changes and to compute correctly the portion of the changes affecting cash.

Write-Down of Marketable Equity Securities During 2008, Ellwood Corporation wrote down marketable equity securities to market value. The journal entry made for this write-down is as follows:

(27)	Unrealized Holding Loss on Marketable Equity Securities Available for Sale	20	
	Marketable Equity Securities Available for Sale		20

Assets	=	Liabilities	+	Shareholders' Equity	(Class.)
−20				−20	OCI → AOCI

ΔCash	=	ΔL	+	ΔSE	−	ΔN$A
0		0		−20		−20

This entry does not affect cash and therefore does not appear in the statement of cash flows. It does, however, help to explain the change during the year in the marketable equity securities account above, and it requires the following entry in the T-account work sheet:

(27a)	Unrealized Holding Loss on Marketable Equity Securities Available for Sale	20	
	Marketable Equity Securities Available for Sale		20

Write-Up of Investment in Securities During 2008, Ellwood Corporation also wrote up its Investment in Company A, a security available for sale, to reflect market value. The journal entry for the write-up is as follows:

(28) Investment in Company A 30
           Unrealized Holding Gain on Investment in Securities 30

Assets	=	Liabilities	+	Shareholders' Equity	(Class.)
+30				+30	OCI → AOCI

ΔCash	=	ΔL	+	ΔSE	−	ΔN$A
0		0		+30		+30

This entry does not affect cash flows but explains the change during the year in the Investment in Company A account and requires the following entry in the T-account work sheet:

(28a) Investment in Company A 30
           Unrealized Holding Gain on Investment in Securities 30

Capitalization of Leases

During 2008, Ellwood Corporation signed a long-term lease for a building. It classified the lease as a capital lease and recorded it in the accounts as follows:[3]

(29) Building (or Leasehold) 300
           Capitalized Lease Obligation 300

Assets	=	Liabilities	+	Shareholders' Equity	(Class.)
+300		+300			

ΔCash	=	ΔL	+	ΔSE	−	ΔN$A
0		+300		0		+300

Note that this entry does not affect cash. It does affect the investing and financing activities of Ellwood Corporation and requires disclosure in a supplementary schedule or notes to the financial statements. The accountant makes the following entry in the T-account work sheet:

(29a) Building (or Leasehold) 300
           Capitalized Lease Obligation 300

The firm must disclose transactions such as this in notes, not in the statement of cash flows. Even though they involve investing activities, they do not involve cash.

Conversion of Debt into Equity

During 2008, investors in bonds of Ellwood Corporation exercised their option to convert their debt securities into shares of common stock. The entry made in the accounting records to record the conversion is as follows:

(30) Bonds Payable 300
           Common Stock.. 100
           Additional Paid-In Capital 200

Assets	=	Liabilities	+	Shareholders' Equity	(Class.)
		−300		+100	ContriCap
				+200	ContriCap

(continued)

---

[3]Technically, the account debited is not Building, but Leasehold on Building. Our research into actual practice suggests that many firms call it, merely, Building.

ΔCash	=	ΔL	+	ΔSE	−	ΔN$A
0		−300		+100		0
				+200		

The accountant reflects this financing transaction on the T-account work sheet by making the following entry:

(30a) Bonds Payable	300	
Common Stock		100
Additional Paid-In Capital		200

Exhibit 15.4 presents a T-account work sheet for Ellwood Corporation for 2008.

PROBLEM 15.1 for Self-Study

Effects of transactions on the statement of cash flows. Exhibit 5.16 in **Chapter 5** presents a simplified statement of cash flows. For each of the transactions that follow, indicate the number(s) of the line(s) in **Exhibit 5.16** affected by the transaction and the amount and direction (increase or decrease) of the effect. Expand the definition of Line (1) to include receipts from other operating revenue sources. If the transaction affects net income, be sure to indicate whether it increases or decreases. Ignore income tax effects.

a. A firm sells for $12,000 equipment that originally cost $30,000 and has accumulated depreciation of $16,000 at the time of sale.

b. A firm owns 25% of the common stock of an investee acquired several years ago at its net book value and uses the equity method. The investee had net income of $80,000 and paid dividends of $20,000 during the period.

c. A firm, as lessee (tenant), records lease payments of $50,000 on capital leases for the period, of which $35,000 represents interest expense.

d. Income tax expense for the period totals $120,000, of which the firm pays $90,000 immediately and defers the remaining $30,000 because of temporary differences between the accounting principles used for financial reporting and those used for tax reporting.

e. A firm owns 10% of the common stock of an investee acquired at its net carrying value several years ago and accounts for it as an available for sale security classified as a long-term investment. The investee had net income of $100,000 and paid dividends of $40,000 during the period. The market value at the end of the period equaled the market value at the beginning of the period.

ILLUSTRATION OF THE DIRECT METHOD FOR CASH FLOW FROM OPERATIONS

Exhibit 15.5 derives Cash Flow from Operations presented with the direct method for Ellwood Corporation. While the direct method's presentation of cash flow requires less understanding of the contrast between cash and accrual accounting, its derivation requires the same understanding as does the indirect method. Every addback and subtraction in the indirect presentation appears in the direct method's derivation.

To see the relation between the indirect and direct methods, consider the following contrast of the equivalent arithmetic used for the two derivations of cash flow from operations.

■ The indirect method starts with the total for net income. Then it adds amounts for expenses not using cash in the amount of the expense and subtracts for revenues not producing cash in the amount of the revenue. Then it removes the effects of nonoperating gains and losses—subtracting the amount of the gains and adding back the amount of the losses. Finally, it adds or subtracts balance sheet changes involving non-cash operating accounts.

■ The direct method starts with the components of income, the individual revenues and expenses, but not gains and losses, then adds or subtracts the same balance sheet changes involving the same operating accounts. Take an income statement line, then list next to it, horizontally, additions and subtractions.

The indirect method presents the net of revenues less expenses, then adds to, and subtracts from, that total. The direct method starts with a line of the income statement, then adds to, and subtracts from, that component. Because the amounts for balance sheet changes added and subtracted are the same, the final result—cash flow from operations—must be the same.

We think you will better understand cash flow from operations if you master the direct method, because its presentation, if not its derivation, will match your intuition. In addition, understanding the cause of changes from period to period in cash flow from operations comes easier from the direct method's presentation. Few firms, however, use the direct method in their public presentations.

EXHIBIT 15.5

Ellwood Corporation
Deriving Direct Method Cash Flow from Operations
Using Data from T-Account Work Sheet

1. Copy Income Statement [column (a)] and Cash Flow from Operations [column (b)]

2. Copy Information from T-Account Work Sheet Next to Related Income Statement Item [columns (b) and (c)]

3. Sum Across Rows to Derive Direct Receipts and Expenditures [columns (d) and (e)]

Operations Income Statement: Revenues, Gains, Expenses, and Losses (a)	Indirect Method (b)	Changes in Related Balance Sheet Accounts from T-Account Work Sheet (c)	Direct Method (d)	From Operations: Receipts less Expenditures (e)
Sales $10,500	$ 400	= Advances from Customers Increase	$10,000	Receipts from Customers
	(900)	= Accounts Receivable Increase		
Interest and Dividends 320			320	Receipts from Investments
Equity in Earnings of Affiliate 480	(320)	Dividends Received were only $160	160	Receipts from Equity Method Investments
Gain on Disposal of Equipment 40	(40)	Gain Produces No Cash from Operations	—	
Cost of Goods Sold .... (6,000)	450	Depreciation on Manufacturing Facilities	(5,470)	Payments for Inventory
	150	Amortization of Patents Used in Manufacturing		
	780	= Accounts Payable Increase		
	(850)	= Inventory Increase		
Selling and Administrative Expenses .... (3,550)	250	Depreciation on Administrative Buildings and Equipment	(3,400)	Payments for Selling and Administrative Services
	200	= Prepayments Decrease		
	(300)	= Warranties Payable Decrease		
Compensation Expense Employee Stock Options .... (170)	170	Compensation Paid in Options	—	
Loss on Impairment of Land ... (80)	80	Loss Reduces Land Carrying Amount	—	
Loss on Sale of Marketable Equity Securities .... (30)	30	Loss Uses No Cash	—	
Interest Expense .... (450)	(50)	Coupon Payments in Excess of Interest Expense	(500)	Payments for Debt Service
Income Tax Expense .... (300)	100	Deferred Income Taxes Use No Cash This Period	(200)	Payments for Income Taxes
Net Income .... $ 760 =	760	Totals	$ 910	= Cash Flow from Operations Derived via Direct Method
	$ 910	= Cash Flow from Operations Derived via Indirect Method		

INTERPRETING THE STATEMENT OF CASH FLOWS

Chapter 5 points out that the proper interpretation of information in the statement of cash flows requires:

- An understanding of the economic characteristics of the industries in which a firm conducts operations, and
- A multi-period view.

This section discusses the interpretation of the statement of cash flows more fully.

RELATION BETWEEN NET INCOME AND CASH FLOW FROM OPERATIONS

Net income (= Revenues − Expenses) differs from Cash Flow from Operations (= Receipts from operations − Expenditures for operations). The balance sheet reflects these differences in the changes in current and noncurrent accounts:

1. Changes in noncurrent assets and noncurrent liabilities.
2. Changes in operating working capital accounts.

Changes in Noncurrent Assets and Noncurrent Liabilities

The extent to which a firm adjusts net income for changes in noncurrent assets and noncurrent liabilities in deriving cash flow from operations depends on the nature of its operations. Capital-intensive firms will likely show a substantial addback to net income for depreciation expense, whereas service firms will show a smaller amount. Rapidly growing firms usually show an addback for deferred tax expense, whereas firms that stop growing or that shrink show a subtraction. Firms that grow or diversify by acquiring minority ownership positions in other businesses will often show a subtraction from net income for equity in undistributed earnings. Firms that decrease in size will usually show additions or subtractions for losses and gains on the disposal of assets.

Changes in Operating Working Capital Accounts

The adjustment for changes in operating working capital accounts depends in part on a firm's rate of growth. Rapidly growing firms usually experience significant increases in accounts receivable and inventories. Some firms use suppliers or other creditors to finance these working capital needs (classified as operating activities), whereas other firms use short- or long-term borrowing or equity financing (classified as financing activities).

RELATIONS AMONG CASH FLOWS FROM OPERATING, INVESTING, AND FINANCING ACTIVITIES

The product life-cycle concept from microeconomics and marketing provides useful insights into the relations among cash flows from operating, investing, and financing activities.

During the introduction phase, cash outflow exceeds cash inflow from operations because operations are not yet earning profits while the firm must invest in accounts receivable and inventories. Investing activities result in a net cash outflow to build productive capacity. Firms must rely on external financing during this phase to overcome the negative cash flow from operations and investing.

The growth phase portrays cash flow characteristics similar to the introduction phase. The growth phase reflects sales of successful products, and net income turns positive. A growing firm makes more sales, but it also needs to acquire more goods to sell. Because it usually must pay for the goods it acquires before it collects for the goods it sells, the growing firm finds itself often short of cash from operations. The faster it grows (even though profitable), the more cash it needs. Banks do not like to lend for such needs. They view such needs (even though for current assets) as a permanent part of the firm's financing needs. Thus, banks want firms to use shareholders' equity or long-term debt to finance growth in nonseasonal inventories and receivables.

The maturing of a product alters these cash flow relations. Net income usually reaches a peak, and working capital stops growing. Operations generate positive cash flow, enough to finance expenditures on property, plant, and equipment. Capital expenditures usually maintain, rather than increase, productive capacity. Firms use the excess cash flow to repay borrowing from the introduction and growth phases and to begin paying dividends to shareholders.

Weakening profitability—from reduced sales or reduced profit margins on existing sales—signals the beginning of the decline phase, but ever-declining accounts receivable and inventories can produce positive cash flow from operations. In addition, sales of unneeded property, plant, and equipment can result in positive cash flow from investing activities. Firms can use the excess cash flow to repay remaining debt or diversify into other areas of business.

Biotechnology firms are in their growth phase, consumer foods companies are in their mature phase, and U.S. auto manufacturers are in the late maturity or the decline phase.

THE EFFECTS OF TRANSACTIONS INVOLVING DERIVATIVES AND THE FAIR VALUE OPTION ON THE STATEMENT OF CASH FLOWS

Chapter 12 introduces the reasons firms engage in transactions involving derivatives and shows the accounting for them. For the most part, the complex parts of these transactions occur after the firm has acquired the derivative, but those subsequent transactions do not affect cash flows until, possibly, their settlement. The following discussion refers to a statement of cash flows that uses the indirect method for presenting cash flows from operations.[4]

■ The firm acquires a derivative for cash. Most such derivative acquisitions represent marketable securities held as current assets. The cash flow from operations section shows a subtraction for the increase in the current asset accounts in an amount equal to the firm's expenditure to acquire the derivative. If the firm classifies the derivative as a nonoperating asset, then the cash outflow appears in the investing section of the statement of cash flows.

■ Subsequent to acquisition, the firm may report (see **Chapter 12** for the situations) changes in the fair value of the derivative in income. Those changes do not affect cash flow. A subtraction in the operating section of cash flows from operations offsets the amount of any gain reported in income. An addition in the operating section offsets the amount of any loss reported in income.

■ Subsequent to acquisition, the firm may report (see **Chapter 12** for the situations) changes in fair value of derivatives in Other Comprehensive Income. These changes have no effect on any lines of the statement of cash flows.

■ As the derivative transaction settles, there can be various effects. Some of these settlements involve net cash flow, such as for a derivative that is not a hedge. Derivatives with cash settlement can involve cash flows even when the firm uses them as a hedge; often, however, the cash inflow or outflow from the derivative usually offsets another cash outflow or inflow from the other side of the hedge. Other settlements involve the receipt of assets such as inventory or equipment, which do not involve cash. A discussion of all the possibilities goes beyond the scope of this textbook.

Chapter 12 discusses, as well, the fair value option for marketable securities and derivatives. Firms using the fair value option mark the carrying value of the asset to fair value each period.

■ If the change in fair value increases carrying value, then the firm reports a gain in income equal to the amount of the increase in carrying value during the current period. The cash flow from operations section starts with the resulting higher income. That higher income does not, however, result in increased cash inflows during the current period, so the cash flow from operations sections shows a subtraction for the amount of the gain.

---

[4]The owner of an exchange-traded derivative must maintain margin in an account equivalent to a cash account. That is, if the fair value of the derivative goes down, the owner must put more cash in the margin account, and if the fair value increases, it can reduce that amount of cash in that account. Since the margin account is a cash equivalent, transfer of cash between a checking account and a margin account doesn't appear in the statement of cash flows. Over-the-counter derivatives may require payments, depending on the arrangement between counterparties.

■ If the change in fair value of the derivative decreases carrying value, then the firm reports the amount of that decrease as a loss during the current period. The cash flow from operations section shows lower income as a result. The loss does not, however, result in outflows or in decreased cash inflows during the current period, so the cash flow from operations sections shows an addback for the loss.

THE EFFECTS OF TRANSACTIONS INVOLVING INVESTMENTS ON THE STATEMENT OF CASH FLOWS

Chapter 13 discusses the accounting for investments. **Exhibit 13.8** summarizes the effect on the balance sheet and income statement of the various forms of investment. Here, we summarize the effects on the statement of cash flows in U.S. GAAP.

Accounting Method	Effects on Statement of Cash Flows
• Fair value method for securities available for sale and cash flow hedges. Realized gains and losses appear in net income. Unrealized gains and losses appear in Other Comprehensive Income.	• Dividends received from investee included in investor's cash flow from operations. In indirect method, add back realized holding losses, and subtract realized holding gains included in income for the period to derive cash flow from operations. All proceeds of sale of securities available for sale appear as [dis-]investing source of cash.
• Fair value method for trading securities trading securities and fair value hedges. Both realized and unrealized gains and losses appear in net income.	• Dividends received from investee included in investor's cash flow from operations. In indirect method, add back both realized and unrealized holding losses, and subtract both realized and unrealized holding gains included in income for the period. All proceeds of sale of trading securities appear as [dis-]investing source of cash.
• Amortized cost method for debt where investor has both ability and intent to hold to maturity. Investor reports interest revenue using methods like those illustrated in **Exhibit 12.2**.	• If investor acquired the debt at a price below par, then cash flow from operations includes only the interest coupon received. If the investor acquired the investment in debt at a price below par, then cash flow from operations will include the amount of interest revenue for the period, with source of the remainder of the cash received appearing as a [dis-]investing activity, the same as the proceeds of selling an investment.
• Equity method, where investor reports its share of investee's income.	• Investor's cash flow from operations increases by only the amount of dividends received. In the indirect method, deduct the investor's share of the undis-tributed earnings of the investee.
• Consolidation, where investor reports all income of consolidated subsidiaries and subtracts the minority's interest in income of less than 100%-owned subsidiaries.	• In indirect method, add back the subtraction for minority interest in earnings of consolidated, but less than 100%-owned subsidiaries to derive cash flow from operations.

SUMMARY

This chapter provides a comprehensive example of the statement of cash flows, which includes many of the transactions that the text introduces after **Chapter 5**.

SOLUTION TO SELF-STUDY PROBLEM

SUGGESTED SOLUTION TO PROBLEM 15.1 FOR SELF-STUDY

(Effects of transactions on the statement of cash flows.)

a. The journal entry to record this transaction is as follows:

Cash.   12,000
Accumulated Depreciation   16,000
Loss on Sale of Equipment   2,000
    Equipment   30,000

Assets	=	Liabilities	+	Shareholders' Equity	(Class.)
+12,000				−2,000	IncSt → RE
+16,000					
−30,000					

ΔCash	=	ΔL	+	ΔSE	−	ΔN$A
+12,000 (Invst.)		0		−2000		+16,000
						−30,000

    The debit to Cash results in an increase on line **(11)** of $12,000. Selling equipment is an investing transaction, so line **(6)** increases by $12,000. The loss on the sale reduces net income, so line **(3)** decreases by $2,000. Because the loss does not use cash, line **(4)** increases by $2,000 to add back the loss to net income when computing cash flow from operations.

b. The journal entry to record this transaction is as follows:

Cash.   5,000
Investment in Securities   15,000
    Equity in Earnings of Affiliate   20,000

Assets	=	Liabilities	+	Shareholders' Equity	(Class.)
+5,000				+20,000	IncSt → RE
+15,000					

ΔCash	=	ΔL	+	ΔSE	−	ΔN$A
+5,000 (Opns.)		0		+20,000		+15,000

    The debit to Cash results in an increase on line **(11)** of $5,000. Line **(1)** increases by $5,000 for the receipt from the investment, considered an operating source of cash. Line **(3)** increases by $20,000 for the equity in earnings of the affiliate. Because the firm receives only $5,000 in cash, line **(5)** must increase by $15,000 to subtract from earnings the excess of equity in earnings over the dividends received.

c. The journal entry to record this transaction is as follows:

Interest Expense   35,000
Capitalized Lease Obligation   15,000
    Cash   50,000

Assets	=	Liabilities	+	Shareholders' Equity	(Class.)
−50,000		−15,000		−35,000	IncSt → RE

ΔCash	=	ΔL	+	ΔSE	−	ΔN$A
−50,000 (Opns.)		−15,000		−35,000		0

    The credit to Cash reduces line **(11)** by $50,000. Line **(2)** increases by $35,000 for the increased use of cash, the expenditure for the portion of the debt-service payment for interest. The recognition of interest expense reduces net income on line **(3)** by $35,000.

This amount represents an operating use of cash and therefore requires no addback or subtraction in computing cash flow from operations. The remaining cash payment of $15,000 is a financing use of cash, so line **(9)** increases by $15,000.

d. The journal entry to record this transaction is as follows:

Income Tax Expense					120,000	
Deferred Tax Liability						30,000
Cash						90,000

Assets	=	Liabilities	+	Shareholders' Equity	(Class.)
−90,000		+30,000		−120,000	IncSt → RE

ΔCash	=	ΔL	+	ΔSE	−	ΔN$A
−90,000 (Opns.)		+30,000		−120,000		0

The credit to Cash results in a reduction on line **(11)** of $90,000. Line **(2)** increases by $90,000 for the expenditure related to income taxes. The recognition of income tax expense reduces net income on line **(3)** by $120,000. Because the firm used only $90,000 in cash for income taxes this period, line **(4)** increases by $30,000 for the portion of the expense that did not use cash.

e. The journal entry to record this transaction is as follows:

Cash					4,000	
Dividend Revenue						4,000

Assets	=	Liabilities	+	Shareholders' Equity	(Class.)
+4,000				+4,000	IncSt → RE

ΔCash	=	ΔL	+	ΔSE	−	ΔN$A
+4,000 (Opns.)		0		+4,000		0

The debit to Cash results in an increase on line **(11)** of $4,000. The recognition of dividend revenue increases net income on line **(3)** by $4,000. Because dividends received from investments in securities are operating transactions and the amount of the dividends revenue equals the amount of cash received, the accountant makes no adjustment to net income when computing cash flow from operations. IFRS allows the firm to show the cash received from dividend investments either as from operations or from investing activities.

PROBLEMS

1. **Effects of transactions on statement of cash flows. Exhibit 5.16** in **Chapter 5** provides a simplified statement of cash flows. For each of the transactions that follow, indicate the number(s) of the line(s) in **Exhibit 5.16** affected by the transaction and the amount and direction (increase or decrease) of the effect. If the transaction affects net income on line **(3)** or cash on line **(11)**, be sure to indicate if it increases or decreases the line. Expand the definition of Line **(1)** to include receipts from other operating revenue sources. Ignore income tax effects. Indicate the effects of each transaction on the Cash Change Equation.

    a. A firm declares cash dividends of $15,000, of which it pays $12,000 immediately to its shareholders; it will pay the remaining $3,000 early in the next accounting period.

    b. A firm borrows $75,000 from its bank.

    c. A firm sells for $20,000 machinery originally costing $40,000 and with accumulated depreciation of $35,000.

    d. A firm as lessee records lease payments on operating leases of $28,000 for the period.

    e. A firm acquires, with temporarily excess cash, marketable equity securities costing $39,000.

    f. A firm writes off a fully depreciated truck originally costing $14,000.

    g. A marketable equity security (available for sale) acquired during the current period for $90,000 has a fair value of $82,000 at the end of the period. Indicate the effect of any year-end adjusting entry to apply the market value method.

    h. A firm records interest expense of $15,000 for the period on bonds issued several years ago at a discount, comprising a $14,500 cash payment and a $500 addition to Bonds Payable.

    i. A firm records an impairment loss of $22,000 for the period on goodwill arising from the acquisition several years ago of an 80% investment in a subsidiary.

2. **Effects of transactions on statement of cash flows. Exhibit 5.16** in **Chapter 5** provides a simplified statement of cash flows. For each of the transactions that follow, indicate the number(s) of the line(s) in **Exhibit 5.16** affected by the transaction and the amount and direction (increase or decrease) of the effect. If the transaction affects net income on line **(3)** or cash on line **(11)**, be sure to indicate if it increases or decreases the line. Expand the definition of Line **(1)** to include receipts from other operating revenue sources. Ignore income tax effects. Indicate the effects of each transaction on the Cash Change Equation.

    a. A firm acquires a building costing $400,000, paying $40,000 cash and signing a promissory note to the seller for $360,000.

    b. A firm using the allowance method records $32,000 of bad debt expense for the period.

    c. A firm using the allowance method writes off accounts totaling $28,000 as uncollectible.

    d. A firm owns 30% of the common stock of an investee acquired several years ago at carrying value. The investee had net income of $40,000 and paid dividends of $50,000 during the period.

    e. A firm sells for $22,000 marketable equity securities (available for sale) originally costing $25,000 and with a carrying value of $23,000 at the time of sale.

    f. Holders of a firm's preferred stock with a carrying value of $10,000 convert their preferred shares into common stock with a par value of $2,000. Use the book value method.

    g. A firm gives land with an acquisition cost and market value of $5,000 in settlement of the annual legal fees of its corporate attorney.

    h. A firm reduces the liability account Rental Fees Received in Advance for $8,000 when it provides rental services.

    i. A firm reclassifies long-term debt of $30,000, maturing within the next year, as a current liability.

3. **Effects of transactions on statement of cash flows. Exhibit 5.16** in **Chapter 5** provides a simplified statement of cash flows. For each of the transactions that follow, indicate the number(s) of the line(s) in **Exhibit 5.16** affected by the transaction and the amount and direction (increase or decrease) of the effect. If the transaction affects net income on line **(3)** or cash on line **(11)**, be sure to indicate if it increases or decreases the line. Expand the definition of Line **(1)** to include receipts from other operating revenue sources. Ignore income tax effects. Indicate the effects of each transaction on the Cash Change Equation.

    a. A firm using the percentage-of-completion method for long-term contracts recognizes $15,000 of revenue for the period.

    b. A local government donates land with a fair value of $50,000 to a firm as an inducement to locate manufacturing facilities in the area.

    c. A firm writes down long-term investments in securities by $8,000 to reflect a decrease in fair value.

    d. A firm records $60,000 depreciation on manufacturing facilities for the period. The firm has sold all goods it manufactured this period.

e. A firm using the allowance method recognizes $35,000 as warranty expense for the period.

f. A firm using the allowance method makes expenditures totaling $28,000 to provide warranty services during the period.

g. A firm recognizes income tax expense of $80,000 for the period, comprising $100,000 paid currently and a $20,000 reduction in the Deferred Income Tax Liability account.

h. A firm writes down inventories by $18,000 to reflect the lower-of-cost-or-market valuation.

4. **Working backward from the statement of cash flows. Exhibit 15.6** presents an income statement and a statement of cash flows for Metals Company for 2009. Give the entry made on the T-account work sheet for each of the numbered line items. For example, the work sheet entry for line **(1)** is as follows (amounts in millions):

Cash (Operations—Net Income)	1,367.4	
Retained Earnings.		1,367.4

5. **Deriving direct method presentation of cash flow from operations using data from the T-account work sheet.** Refer to the data in **Exhibit 15.6** for Metals Company for 2009. Derive a presentation of cash flow from operations using the direct method.

6. **Working backward from the statement of cash flows. Exhibit 15.7** presents a statement of cash flows from Ingers Company for 2008. Give the entry made on the T-account work sheet for each of the numbered line items. For example, the work sheet entry for line **(1)** is as follows (amounts in millions):

Cash (Operations—Net Income)	270.3	
Retained Earnings		270.3

7. **Preparing a statement of cash flows.** (Adapted from CPA examination.) The management of Warren Corporation, concerned over a decrease in cash, provides you with the comparative analysis of changes in account balances between June 30, 2008, and June 30, 2009, appearing in **Exhibit 15.8.**

During the year ended June 30, 2009, Warren Corporation engaged in the following transactions:

(1) Purchased new machinery for $463,200. In addition, it sold certain obsolete machinery, having a carrying value of $73,200, for $57,600. It made no other entries in Machinery and Equipment or related accounts other than provisions for depreciation.

(2) Paid $2,400 of legal costs in a successful defense of a new patent, which it correctly debited to the Patents account. It recorded patent amortization amounting to $5,040 during the year ended June 30, 2009.

(3) Purchased 120 preferred shares, par value $100, at $110 and subsequently canceled the shares. Warren Corporation debited the premium paid to Retained Earnings.

(4) On June 10, 2009, the board of directors declared a cash dividend of $0.24 per share, payable to holders of common stock on July 10, 2009.

(5) The following illustration presents a comparative analysis of retained earnings as of June 30, 2008, and June 30, 2009:

	June 30	
	2009	**2008**
Balance, June 30, 2008	$321,600	$157,200
Net Income	234,000	206,400
Subtotal	$555,600	$363,600
Dividends Declared	(48,000)	(42,000)
Premium on Preferred Stock Repurchased	(1,200)	—
Balance, June 30, 2009	$506,400	$321,600

	Metals Company
EXHIBIT 15.6	(Problem 4)

Income Statement for 2009 (all dollar amounts in millions)

Sales Revenues	$20,465.0
Gain on Sale of Marketable Securities	20.8
Equity in Earnings of Affiliates	214.0
Total Revenues and Gains	$20,699.8
Cost of Goods Sold	$ 9,963.3
General and Administrative Expenses	5,570.2
Interest Expense	2,887.3
Income Tax Expense	911.6
Total Expenses	$19,332.4
Net Income	$ 1,367.4

Statement of Cash Flows for 2009 (all dollar amounts in millions)

OPERATIONS

(1)	Net Income	$ 1,367.4

Adjustments for Noncash Transactions:

(2)	Depreciation	664.0
(3)	Increase in Deferred Tax Liability	82.0
(4)	Equity in Undistributed Earnings of Affiliates	(47.1)
(5)	Gain from Sale of Marketable Securities Available for Sale	(20.8)
(6)	(Increase) Decrease in Accounts Receivable	74.6
(7)	(Increase) Decrease in Inventories	(198.9)
(8)	(Increase) Decrease in Prepayments	(40.3)
(9)	Increase (Decrease) in Accounts Payable for Inventory	33.9
(10)	Increase (Decrease) in Other Current Liabilities	(110.8)
	Cash Flow from Operations	$ 1,804.0

INVESTING

(11)	Sale of Marketable Securities Available for Sale	$ 49.8
(12)	Acquisition of Marketable Securities Available for Sale	(73.2)
(13)	Acquisition of Property, Plant, and Equipment	(875.7)
(14)	Acquisition of Subsidiaries	(44.5)
	Cash Flow from Investing	$ (943.6)

FINANCING

(15)	Common Stock Issued to Employees	$ 34.4
(16)	Repurchase of Common Stock	(100.9)
(17)	Dividends Paid to Shareholders	(242.9)
(18)	Additions to Short-Term Borrowing	127.6
(19)	Additions to Long-Term Debt	121.6
(20)	Payments on Long-Term Debt	(476.4)
	Cash Flow from Financing	$ (536.6)
	Change in Cash	$ 323.8
	Cash, Beginning of Year	506.8
	Cash, End of Year	$ 830.6

SUPPLEMENTARY INFORMATION

(21)	Acquisition of Property, Plant, and Equipment by Mortgaged Borrowing	$ 76.9
(22)	Acquisition of Property, Plant, and Equipment by Capital Leases	98.2
(23)	Conversion of Debt into Common Stock	47.8
(24)	Other Current Liabilities represents obligations for General and Administrative Expenses.	

EXHIBIT 15.7	Ingers Company Statement of Cash Flows 2008 (all dollar amounts in millions) (Problem 6)	

OPERATIONS

(1)	Net Income	$ 270.3
Adjustments for Noncash Transactions:		
(2)	Depreciation	179.4
(3)	Gain on Sale of Property, Plant, and Equipment	(3.6)
(4)	Equity in Earnings of Affiliates	(41.5)
(5)	Deferred Income Taxes	15.1
(6)	(Increase) Decrease in Accounts Receivable	50.9
(7)	(Increase) Decrease in Inventories	(15.2)
(8)	(Increase) Decrease in Other Current Assets	(33.1)
(9)	Increase (Decrease) in Accounts Payable	(37.9)
(10)	Increase (Decrease) in Other Current Liabilities	19.2
Cash Flow from Operations		$ 403.6
(11)	Capital Expenditures	$(211.7)
(12)	Proceeds from Sale of Property, Plant, and Equipment	26.5
(13)	(Increase) Decrease in Marketable Securities	(4.6)
(14)	Advances from Equity Companies	18.4
Cash Flow from Investing		$(171.4)

FINANCING

(15)	Decrease in Short-Term Borrowing	$ (81.5)
(16)	Issue of Long-Term Debt	147.6
(17)	Payment of Long-Term Debt	(129.7)
(18)	Proceeds from Exercise of Stock Options	47.9
(19)	Proceeds from Sale of Treasury Stock	59.3
(20)	Dividends Paid	$ (78.5)
Cash Flow from Financing		$ (34.9)
Change in Cash		197.3
Cash, Beginning of Year		48.3
Cash, End of Year		$ 245.6

SUPPLEMENTARY INFORMATION

(21)	New Capital Leases Signed	$ 147.9
(22)	Conversion of Preferred Stock into Common Stock	62.0
(23)	Issue of Common Stock to Acquire Investments in Securities	94.3

(6) Warren Corporation wrote off accounts totaling $3,600 as uncollectible during 2009.

a. Prepare a T-account work sheet for the preparation of a statement of cash flows.

b. Prepare a formal statement of cash flows for Warren Corporation for the year ending June 30, 2009, using the indirect method for presenting cash flow from operations.

8. **Preparing a statement of cash flows.** (Adapted from CPA examination.) Roth Company has prepared its financial statements for the year ended December 31, 2008, and for the three months ended March 31, 2009. You will prepare a statement of cash flows for the three months ended March 31, 2009. **Exhibit 15.9** presents the company's balance sheet at December 31, 2008, and March 31, 2009, and **Exhibit 15.10** presents its income statement for the three months ended March 31, 2009. You believe that the amounts presented are correct.

EXHIBIT 15.8

**Warren Corporation
Changes in Account Balances
Between June 30, 2008 and June 30, 2009
(Problem 7)**

	June 30	
	2009	2008
DEBIT BALANCES		
Cash	$ 174,000	$ 223,200
Accounts Receivable	306,000	327,600
Inventories	579,600	645,600
Securities Held for Plant Expansion Purposes	180,000	—
Machinery and Equipment	1,112,400	776,400
Leasehold Improvements	104,400	104,400
Patents	33,360	36,000
Totals	$2,489,760	$2,113,200
CREDIT BALANCES		
Allowance for Uncollectible Accounts	$ 19,200	$ 20,400
Accumulated Depreciation of Machinery and Equipment	499,200	446,400
Accumulated Amortization of Leasehold Improvements	69,600	58,800
Accounts Payable	279,360	126,000
Cash Dividends Payable	48,000	—
Current Portion of 6% Serial Bonds Payable	60,000	60,000
6% Serial Bonds Payable (noncurrent portion)	300,000	360,000
Preferred Stock	108,000	120,000
Common Stock	600,000	600,000
Retained Earnings	506,400	321,600
Totals	$2,489,760	$2,113,200

Your discussion with the company's controller and a review of the financial records reveal the following information:

(1) On January 8, 2009, the company sold marketable securities for cash. The firm had purchased these securities on December 31, 2008. The firm purchased no marketable securities during 2008.

(2) The company's preferred stock is convertible into common stock at a rate of one share of preferred for two shares of common. The preferred stock and common stock have par values of $2 and $1, respectively.

(3) On January 17, 2009, the local government condemned three acres of land. Roth Company received an award of $48,000 in cash on March 22, 2009. It does not expect to purchase additional land as a replacement.

(4) On March 25, 2009, the company purchased equipment for cash.

(5) Interest expense on bonds payable exceeded the cash coupon payments by $225 during the three-month period. On March 29, 2009, the company issued bonds payable for cash.

(6) Roth Company declared $12,000 in dividends during the three months.

a. Prepare a T-account work sheet for the preparation of a statement of cash flows, defining funds as cash and cash equivalents.

b. Prepare a formal statement of cash flows for Roth Company for the three months ending March 31, 2009. Use the indirect method.

c. Derive a presentation of cash flows from operations using the direct method.

| | | EXHIBIT 15.9 | Roth Company Balance Sheet (Problem 8) |

EXHIBIT 15.9

Roth Company
Balance Sheet
(Problem 8)

	March 31, 2009	December 31, 2008
Cash	$131,100	$37,950
Marketable Securities Available for Sale	10,200	24,000
Accounts Receivable (net)	73,980	36,480
Inventory	72,885	46,635
Total Current Assets	$288,165	$145,065
Land	28,050	60,000
Building	375,000	375,000
Equipment	122,250	—
Accumulated Depreciation	(24,375)	(22,500)
Investment in 30%-Owned Company (using equity method)	100,470	91,830
Other Assets	22,650	22,650
Total Assets	$912,210	$672,045
Accounts Payable	$ 25,995	$ 31,830
Dividend Payable	12,000	—
Income Taxes Payable	51,924	—
Total Current Liabilities	$ 89,919	$ 31,830
Other Liabilities	279,000	279,000
Bonds Payable	169,275	71,550
Deferred Income Tax	1,269	765
Preferred Stock	—	45,000
Common Stock	165,000	120,000
Unrealized Holding Loss on Marketable Securities	(750)	(750)
Retained Earnings	208,497	124,650
Total Liabilities and Shareholders' Equity	$912,210	$672,045

EXHIBIT 15.10

Roth Company
Income Statement Data
For the Three Months Ended March 31, 2009
(Problem 8)

Sales	$364,212
Gain on Sale of Marketable Securities	3,600
Equity in Earnings of 30%-Owned Company	8,640
Gain on Condemnation of Land	16,050
Total Revenues	$392,502
Cost of Sales	$207,612
General and Administrative Expenses	33,015
Depreciation	1,875
Interest Expense	1,725
Income Taxes	52,428
Total Expenses	$296,655
Net Income	$ 95,847

9. **Preparing a statement of cash flows.** (Adapted from CPA examination.) **Exhibit 15.11** presents a comparative statement of financial position for Biddle Corporation as of December 31, 2008 and 2009. **Exhibit 15.12** presents an income statement for 2009. Additional information follows:

(1) On February 2, 2009, Biddle issued a 10% stock dividend to shareholders of record on January 15, 2009. The market price per share of the common stock on February 2, 2009, was $15.

(2) On March 1, 2009, Biddle issued 1,900 shares of common stock for land. The common stock and land had current fair values of approximately $20,000 on March 1, 2009.

(3) On April 15, 2009, Biddle repurchased long-term bonds with a face and carrying value of $25,000. It reported a gain of $6,000 on the income statement.

(4) On June 30, 2009, Biddle sold equipment costing $26,500, with a carrying value of $11,500, for $9,500 cash.

(5) On September 30, 2009, Biddle declared and paid a $0.04 per share cash dividend to shareholders of record on August 1, 2009.

(6) On October 10, 2009, Biddle purchased land for $42,500 cash.

(7) Deferred income taxes represent temporary differences relating to the use of different depreciation methods for income tax and financial statement reporting.

a. Prepare a T-account work sheet for the preparation of a statement of cash flows.

b. Prepare a formal statement of cash flows for Biddle Corporation for the year ended December 31, 2009. Use the indirect method.

EXHIBIT 15.11

Biddle Corporation
Statement of Financial Position
(Problem 9)

	December 31	
	2009	2008
ASSETS		
Cash	$ 50,000	$ 45,000
Accounts Receivable (net of allowance for doubtful accounts of $10,000 and $8,000, respectively)	105,000	70,000
Inventories	130,000	110,000
Total Current Assets	$285,000	$225,000
Land	162,500	100,000
Plant and Equipment	290,000	316,500
Less Accumulated Depreciation	(45,000)	(50,000)
Patents	15,000	16,500
Total Assets	$707,500	$608,000
LIABILITIES AND SHAREHOLDERS' EQUITY		
Liabilities		
Accounts Payable	$130,000	$100,000
Accrued Liabilities	100,000	105,000
Total Current Liabilities	$230,000	$205,000
Deferred Income Taxes	70,000	50,000
Long-Term Bonds (due December 15, 2020)	65,000	90,000
Total Liabilities	$365,000	$345,000
Shareholders' Equity		
Common Stock, Par Value $5, Authorized 50,000 Shares, Issued and Outstanding 21,000 and 25,000 Shares, Respectively	$125,000	$105,000
Additional Paid-In Capital	116,500	85,000
Retained Earnings	101,000	73,000
Total Shareholders' Equity	$342,500	$263,000
Total Liabilities and Shareholders' Equity	$707,500	$608,000

EXHIBIT 15.12

Biddle Corporation
Income Statement
For the Year Ended December 31, 2009
(Problem 9)

Sales	$500,000
Gain on Repurchase of Bonds	6,000
Total Revenues	$506,000
Expenses:	
Cost of Goods Sold	$280,000
Salary and Wages	95,000
Depreciation	10,000
Patent Amortization	1,500
Loss on Sale of Equipment	2,000
Interest	8,000
Miscellaneous	4,000
Expenses Before Income Taxes	$400,500
Income Before Income Taxes	$105,500
Income Taxes	
Current	$ 25,000
Deferred	20,000
Provision for Income Taxes	$ 45,000
Net Income	$ 60,500
Earnings per Share	$ 2.45

10. **Preparing a statement of cash flows.** (Adapted from CPA examination.) **Exhibit 15.13** presents the comparative balance sheets for Plainview Corporation for 2008 and 2009. The following additional information relates to 2009 activities:

(1) The Retained Earnings account changed as follows:

Retained Earnings, December 31, 2008		$758,200
Add Net Income		236,580
Subtotal		$994,780
Deduct:		
Cash Dividends	$130,000	
Loss on Reissue of Treasury Stock	3,000	
Stock Dividend	100,200	233,200
Retained Earnings, December 31, 2009		$761,580

(2) On January 2, 2009, Plainview Corporation sold for $127,000 marketable securities with an acquisition cost and a carrying value of $110,000. The firm used the proceeds from this sale, the funds in the bond sinking fund, and the amount received from the issuance of the 8% debentures to retire the 6% mortgage bonds.

(3) The firm reissued treasury stock on February 28, 2009. It treats "losses" on the reissue of treasury stock as a charge to Retained Earnings.

(4) The firm declared a stock dividend on October 31, 2009, when the market price of Plainview Corporation's stock was $12 per share.

(5) On April 30, 2009, a fire destroyed a warehouse that cost $100,000 and on which depreciation of $65,000 had accumulated. The firm carried no insurance of this loss. Plainview Corporation properly included the loss in the Continuing Operations section of the income statement.

(6) Plant and equipment transactions consisted of the sale of a building at its carrying value of $4,000 and the purchase of machinery for $28,000.

EXHIBIT 15.13

Plainview Corporation
Comparative Balance Sheets
December 31, 2009 and 2008
(Problem 10)

	2009	2008
ASSETS		
Cash	$ 142,100	$ 165,300
Marketable Securities (at fair value)	122,600	129,200
Accounts Receivable (net)	312,200	371,200
Inventories	255,200	124,100
Prepayments	23,400	22,000
Bond Sinking Fund	—	63,000
Investment in Subsidiary (at equity)	134,080	152,000
Plant and Equipment (net)	1,443,700	1,534,600
Total Assets	$2,433,280	$2,561,400
SOURCES OF FINANCING		
Accounts Payable	$ 238,100	$ 213,300
Notes Payable—Current	—	145,000
Accrued Payables	16,500	18,000
Income Taxes Payable	97,500	31,000
Deferred Income Taxes (noncurrent)	127,900	128,400
6% Mortgage Bonds Payable (due Year 17)	—	310,000
8% Debentures Payable (due Year 25)	125,000	—
Common Stock, $10 Par Value	1,033,500	950,000
Additional Paid-In Capital	67,700	51,000
Accumulated Other Comprehensive Income		
Unrealized Holding Gain on Marketable Securities	2,500	2,500
Retained Earnings	759,080	755,700
Treasury Stock—at Cost of $3 per Share	(34,500)	(43,500)
Total Sources of Financing	$2,433,280	$2,561,400

(7) The firm wrote off accounts receivable as uncollectible totaling $16,300 in 2008 and $18,500 in 2009. It recognized expired insurance of $4,100 in 2008 and $3,900 in 2009.

(8) The subsidiary, which is 40% owned, reported a loss of $44,800 for 2009.

a. Prepare a T-account work sheet for Plainview Corporation for 2009 for preparing a statement of cash flows.

b. Prepare a formal statement of cash flows using the indirect method for the year ending December 31, 2009.

11. **Preparing and interpreting the statement of cash flows. Exhibit 15.14** presents a comparative balance sheet and **Exhibit 15.15** presents a comparative income statement for Airlines Corporation for 2008 and 2009. Expenditures on new property, plant, and equipment were $1,568 million in 2008 and $2,821 million in 2009. Changes in other noncurrent assets are investing activities, and changes in other noncurrent liabilities are financing activities.

a. Prepare T-account work sheets for 2008 and 2009 for a statement of cash flows.

b. Prepare a comparative statement of cash flows for 2008 and 2009 using the indirect method.

c. Comment on the relations between cash flows from operating, investing, and financing activities for 2008 and 2009.

12. **Preparing and interpreting the statement of cash flows.** Irish Paper Company (Irish) manufactures and markets various paper products around the world. Paper manufacturing is a capital-intensive activity. A firm that does not adequately use its manufacturing capacity will experience poor operating performance. Sales of paper products tend to be cyclical with general economic conditions, although consumer paper products are less cyclical than business paper products.

  Exhibit 15.16 on page 753 presents comparative income statements and **Exhibit 15.17** on page 754 presents comparative balance sheets for Irish Paper Company for 2007, 2008, and 2009. Additional information appears below (amounts in millions).

(1)

Cash Flow Information	2009	2008	2007
Investments in Affiliates[a]	$ (13)	$ 86	$ (92)
Expenditures on Property, Plant, and Equipment	(315)	(931)	(775)
Long-Term Debt Issued	36	890	449

[a]Excludes earnings and dividends.

(2) Depreciation expense was $306 million in 2007, $346 million in 2008, and $353 million in 2009.

(3) During 2007, Irish purchased outstanding stock warrants for $201 million. It recorded the transaction by debiting the Common Stock account.

(4) During 2007, Irish sold timberlands at a gain. It received cash of $5 million and a long-term note receivable for $220 million, which it includes in Other Assets on the balance sheet.

(5) In addition to the preceding cash expenditures, Irish acquired property, plant, and equipment during 2008 costing $221 million by assuming a long-term mortgage payable.

(6) During 2009, Irish resold treasury stock for an amount greater than its cost.

(7) Changes in Other Assets are investing activities.

a. Prepare T-account work sheets for a statement of cash flows for Irish for 2007, 2008, and 2009.

b. Prepare a comparative statement of cash flows for Irish for 2007, 2008, and 2009 using the indirect method.

c. Comment on the pattern of cash flows from operating, investing, and financing activities for each of the three years.

13. **Preparing a statement of cash flows.** (Adapted from a problem prepared by Stephen A. Zeff.) Selected information from the accounting records of Breda Enterprises Inc. appears next. The firm uses a calendar year as its reporting period. Prepare a statement of cash flows for Breda Enterprises Inc. for 2009. Use the indirect method. Key all figures in the statement of cash flows to the numbered items below.

(1) Net income for 2009 is $90,000.

(2) Beginning and ending balances in three accounts relating to the firm's customers were as follows:

	December 31, 2009	December 31, 2008
Accounts Receivable (gross)	$53,000	$41,000
Allowance for Uncollectible Accounts	3,200	1,800
Advances from Customers	1,000	3,700

  On November 1, 2009, a customer gave the firm a six-month, 8%, $15,000 note in satisfaction of an account receivable of $15,000. Interest is payable at maturity. This was the only note receivable held by the company during 2009.

(3) The balances in Merchandise Inventory and Accounts Payable were as follows:

EXHIBIT 15.14

Airlines Corporation
Comparative Balance Sheet
(all dollar amounts in millions)
(Problem 11)

	December 31		
	2009	**2008**	**2007**
ASSETS			
Cash	$ 221	$ 465	$ 1,087
Marketable Securities	1,066	1,042	—
Accounts Receivable (net)	913	888	741
Inventories	323	249	210
Prepayments	209	179	112
Total Current Assets	$ 2,732	$ 2,823	$ 2,150
Property, Plant, and Equipment	8,587	7,704	7,710
Accumulated Depreciation	(3,838)	(3,805)	(3,769)
Other Assets	605	570	610
Total Assets	$ 8,086	$ 7,292	$ 6,701
LIABILITIES AND SHAREHOLDERS' EQUITY			
Accounts Payable	$ 552	$ 596	$ 540
Short-Term Borrowing	447	446	121
Current Portion of Long-Term Debt	89	84	110
Advances from Customers	843	661	619
Other Current Liabilities	1,826	1,436	1,485
Total Current Liabilities	$ 3,757	$ 3,223	$ 2,875
Long-Term Debt	1,475	1,334	1,418
Deferred Tax Liability	368	364	352
Other Noncurrent Liabilities	721	719	715
Total Liabilities	$ 6,321	$ 5,640	$ 5,360
Common Stock	$ 120	$ 119	$ 119
Additional Paid-In Capital	52	48	48
Accumulated Other Comprehensive Income			
Unrealized Holding Gain on Marketable Securities	92	85	—
Retained Earnings	1,613	1,512	1,188
Treasury Stock	(112)	(112)	(14)
Total Shareholders' Equity	$ 1,765	$ 1,652	$ 1,341
Total Liabilities and Shareholders' Equity	$ 8,086	$ 7,292	$ 6,701

	December 31, 2009	December 31, 2008
Merchandise Inventory	$43,000	$47,000
Accounts Payable	39,000	27,000

(4) During 2009 the firm sold, for $25,000 cash, equipment with a carrying value of $38,000. The firm also purchased equipment for cash. Depreciation expense for 2009 was $42,000. The balance in the Equipment account at acquisition cost decreased $26,000 between the beginning and end of 2009. The balance in the Accumulated Depreciation account increased $11,000 between the beginning and end of 2009.

(5) The balances in the Leasehold Asset and Lease Liability accounts were as follows on various dates:

EXHIBIT 15.15

Airlines Corporation
Comparative Income Statement
(all dollar amounts in millions)
(Problem 11)

	2009	2008
REVENUES		
Sales	$11,037	$ 9,794
Interest Revenue	123	121
Gains on Dispositions of Property, Plant, and Equipment	286	106
Total Revenues	$11,446	$10,021
EXPENSES		
Compensation	$ 3,550	$ 3,158
Fuel	1,811	1,353
Commissions	1,719	1,336
Depreciation	560	517
Other Operating Costs	3,514	2,950
Interest	121	169
Income Taxes	70	214
Total Expenses	$11,345	$ 9,697
Net Income	$ 101	$ 324

EXHIBIT 15.16

Irish Paper Company
Comparative Income Statements
(all dollar amounts in millions)
(Problem 12)

	2009	2008	2007
Sales	$4,976	$5,356	$5,066
Equity in Earnings of Affiliates	30	38	31
Interest Income	60	23	34
Gain (Loss) on Sale of Property, Plant, and Equipment	(34)	19	221
Total Revenues	$5,032	$5,436	$5,352
Cost of Goods Sold	$3,388	$3,721	$3,493
Selling Expenses	1,005	925	857
Administrative Expenses	581	414	303
Interest Expense	221	199	158
Income Tax Expense	(21)	8	165
Total Expenses	$5,174	$5,267	$4,976
Net Income	$ (142)	$ 169	$ 376

	December 31, 2009	December 31, 2008	December 31, 2007
Leasehold Asset (net)	$71,000	$76,000	$0
Lease Liability	73,600	76,000	0

On December 31, 2008, the firm signed a long-term lease, which, by its terms, qualified as a capital lease. The firm made a payment under the lease of $10,000 on December 31, 2009.

EXHIBIT 15.17

Irish Paper Company
Comparative Balance Sheets
(all dollar amounts in millions)
(Problem 12)

	2009	2008	2007	2006
ASSETS				
Cash	$ 184	$ 114	$ 49	$ 374
Accounts Receivable (net)	670	829	723	611
Inventories	571	735	581	522
Prepayments	56	54	54	108
Total Current Assets	$ 1,481	$ 1,732	$ 1,407	$ 1,615
Investments in Affiliates	333	322	375	254
Property, Plant, and Equipment	7,172	7,079	5,969	5,272
Accumulated Depreciation	(2,977)	(2,698)	(2,392)	(2,160)
Other Assets	484	465	387	175
Total Assets	$ 6,493	$ 6,900	$ 5,746	$ 5,156
LIABILITIES AND SHAREHOLDERS' EQUITY				
Accounts Payable	$ 1,314	$ 1,178	$ 992	$ 920
Current Portion of Long-Term Debt	158	334	221	129
Other Current Liabilities	38	83	93	98
Total Current Liabilities	$ 1,510	$ 1,595	$ 1,306	$ 1,147
Long-Term Debt	2,333	2,455	1,678	1,450
Deferred Income Taxes	661	668	694	607
Total Liabilities	$ 4,504	$ 4,718	$ 3,678	$ 3,204
Preferred Stock	$ 7	$ 7	$ 7	$ 7
Common Stock	439	432	428	629
Retained Earnings	1,557	1,758	1,648	1,331
Treasury Stock	(14)	(15)	(15)	(15)
Total Shareholders' Equity	$ 1,989	$ 2,182	$ 2,068	$ 1,952
Total Liabilities and Shareholders' Equity	$ 6,493	$ 6,900	$ 5,746	$ 5,156

(6) The firm declared cash dividends during 2009 of $26,000, of which $10,000 remains unpaid on December 31, 2009. During 2009 the firm paid $8,000 cash for dividends declared during 2008.

(7) The firm classifies all marketable securities as available for sale. It purchased no marketable securities during 2009 but sold marketable equity securities that had originally cost $4,500 for $9,100 cash in November 2009. The fair values of marketable equity securities were $4,000 on December 31, 2008, and $10,500 on December 31, 2009. These amounts were also the carrying values of the securities on these two dates.

(8) Investors in $100,000 face value of convertible bonds of Breda Enterprises Inc. converted them into 8,000 shares of the firm's $12 par value common stock during 2009. The common stock had a market value of $15 per share on the conversion date. Breda Enterprises Inc. had originally issued the bonds at a premium. Their carrying value on the date of the conversion was $105,000. The firm chose the generally accepted (alternative) accounting principle of recording the issuance of the common stock at market value and recognizing a loss of $15,000. The loss is not an extraordinary item. The firm amortized $1,500 of the bond premium between January 1, 2009, and the date of the conversion.

14. **Interpreting the statement of cash flows. Exhibit 15.18** presents a statement of cash flows for Gear Locker, manufacturer of athletic shoes and sportswear, for three recent years.

EXHIBIT 15.18	Gear Locker Statement of Cash Flows (all dollar amounts in thousands) (Problem 14)		

	2009	2008	2007
OPERATIONS			
Net Income	$ 55,059	$ 22,030	$ 4,371
Depreciation	1,199	446	133
Noncash Compensation to Employees	558	—	—
Increase in Accounts Receivable	(51,223)	(34,378)	(12,410)
Increase in Inventories	(72,960)	(50,743)	(1,990)
Increase in Prepayments	(8,624)	(2,432)	(599)
Increase in Accounts Payable	17,871	7,197	1,656
Increase (Decrease) in Other Current Liabilities	10,587	11,193	(537)
Cash Flow from Operations	$(47,533)	$(46,687)	$ (9,376)
INVESTING			
Sale of Marketable Securities	—	—	$5,661
Acquisition of Property, Plant, and Equipment	$ (6,168)	$ (2,546)	(874)
Acquisition of Other Noncurrent Assets	(246)	(406)	(241)
Cash Flow from Investing	$ (6,414)	$ (2,952)	$ 4,546
FINANCING			
Increase (Decrease) in Short-Term Borrowing	$(19,830)	$ 50,104	$ 4,566
Issue of Common Stock	69,925	495	—
Cash Flow from Financing	$ 50,095	$ 50,599	$ 4,566
Change in Cash	$ (3,852)	$ 960	$ (264)
Cash, Beginning of Year	4,205	3,245	3,509
Cash, End of Year	$ 353	$ 4,205	$ 3,245

a. What is the likely reason for the negative cash flow from operations?

b. How did Gear Locker finance the negative cash flow from operations during each of the three years? Suggest reasons for Gear Locker's choice of financing source for each year.

c. Expenditures on property, plant, and equipment substantially exceeded the addback for depreciation expense each year. What is the likely explanation for this difference in amounts?

d. The addback for depreciation expense is a relatively small proportion of net income. What is the likely explanation for this situation?

e. Gear Locker had no long-term debt in its capital structure during 2007 through 2009. What is the likely explanation for such a financial structure?

15. **Interpreting the statement of cash flows. Exhibit 15.19** presents a statement of cash flows for Canned Soup Company for three recent years. Canned Soup Company is in the consumer foods industry, a relatively mature industry in the United States.

a. Cash flow from operations each year approximately equals net income plus addbacks for depreciation, deferred taxes, and other. What is the likely explanation for this relation?

b. In the Investing section of Canned's statement of cash flows, what are the indications that the company is in a relatively mature industry?

c. In the Financing section of Canned's statement of cash flows, what are the indications that the company is in a relatively mature industry?

EXHIBIT 15.19

Canned Soup Company
Statement of Cash Flows
(all dollar amounts in millions)
(Problem 15)

	2009	2008	2007
OPERATIONS			
Net Income	$ 274	$ 247	$ 223
Depreciation	171	145	127
Deferred Income Taxes	31	46	29
Other Addbacks	11	34	21
(Increase) in Accounts Receivable	(55)	(40)	(19)
(Increase) Decrease in Inventories	6	(13)	13
(Increase) in Prepayments	(40)	(11)	(7)
Increase in Accounts Payable	72	53	27
Increase (Decrease) in Other Current Liabilities	(1)	2	29
Cash Flow from Operations	$ 469	$ 463	$ 443
INVESTING			
Sale of Property, Plant, and Equipment	$ 41	$ 21	$ 30
Sale of Marketable Securities	319	535	328
Acquisition of Property, Plant, and Equipment	(245)	(250)	(275)
Acquisition of Marketable Securities	(70)	(680)	(472)
Acquisition of Investments in Securities	(472)	—	—
Other Investing Transactions	(48)	(34)	(5)
Cash Flow from Investing	$(475)	$(408)	$(394)
FINANCING			
Increase in Short-Term Borrowing	$ 86	$ 5	—
Increase in Long-Term Borrowing	103	29	$ 220
Issue of Common Stock	—	2	4
Decrease in Short-Term Borrowing	(5)	—	(3)
Decrease in Long-Term Borrowing	(106)	(27)	(168)
Acquisition of Common Stock	(28)	—	—
Dividends	(103)	(92)	(84)
Cash Flow from Financing	$ (53)	$ (83)	$ (31)
Change in Cash	$ (59)	$ (28)	$ 18
Cash, Beginning of Year	145	173	155
Cash, End of Year	$ 86	$ 145	$ 173

16. **Interpreting the statement of cash flows.** Prime Contracting Services provides various services to government agencies under multiyear contracts. In 2006, the services primarily involved transportation of equipment and furniture. Beginning in 2007, the firm began exiting these transportation services businesses and began offering more people-based services (clerical, training). Sales increased at a compounded annual rate of 28.9% during the five-year period. **Exhibit 15.20** presents a statement of cash flows for Prime Contracting Services for 2006 to 2010. Changes in Other Current Liabilities primarily represent salaries.

a. What evidence do you see of the strategic shift from asset-based to people-based services?

b. What are the likely reasons that net income decreased between 2006 and 2008 while cash flow from operations increased during the same period?

c. What are the likely reasons that net income increased between 2008 and 2010 while cash flow from operations was less during 2009 and 2010 than in 2008?

d. How has the risk of Prime Contracting Services changed during the five years?

EXHIBIT 15.20	Prime Contracting Services Statement of Cash Flows (all dollar amounts in millions) (Problem 16)				
	2010	**2009**	**2008**	**2007**	**2006**
OPERATIONS					
Net Income	$ 593,518	$ 412,908	$ 46,799	$ 249,438	$ 261,243
Depreciation	606,633	664,882	826,745	616,335	306,423
Deferred Income Taxes	(154,000)	(110,116)	55,000	179,584	158,966
Loss (Gain) on Disposition of Assets	(35,077)	(117,804)	—	—	20,000
Other	9,100	(19,377)	(51,711)	(7,226)	2,200
(Increase) Decrease in Accounts Receivable	175,408	(864,555)	(263,164)	(647,087)	(1,420,783)
(Increase) Decrease in Other Current Assets	127,548	(9,333)	(40,067)	(25,792)	(38,031)
Increase (Decrease) in Accounts Payable	(166,672)	(272,121)	(32,732)	(177,031)	507,386
Increase (Decrease) in Other Current Liabilities	(416,856)	927,478	422,929	99,417	266,260
Cash Flow from Operations	$ 739,602	$ 611,962	$ 963,799	$ 287,638	$ 63,664
INVESTING					
Fixed Assets Sold	$ 175,075	$ 117,804	—	—	$ 80,000
Employee and Officer Loans	—	—	—	$ 62,894	(16,960)
Fixed Assets Acquired	(48,296)	(19,222)	$ (56,370)	(911,470)	(2,002,912)
Cash Flow from Investing	$ 126,779	$ 98,582	$ (56,370)	$(848,576)	$(1,939,872)
FINANCING					
Net Increase (Decrease) in Notes Payable	$ 325,354	$ 12,650	$(126,932)	$ 275,475	$ 204,817
Borrowings under Equipment Loans	—	—	208,418	793,590	943,589
Borrowings under Capital Leases	—	—	—	—	915,596
Borrowings from Shareholder Loans	—	—	—	117,422	127,500
Repayments under Equipment Loans	(736,793)	(437,660)	(564,585)	(389,268)	(236,229)
Repayments under Capital Leases	—	(304,054)	(296,495)	(268,556)	(124,012)
Repayments under Shareholder Loans	(28,710)	—	(150,000)	—	(63,077)
Cash Flow from Financing	$(440,149)	$(729,064)	$(929,594)	$ 528,663	$ 1,768,184
Change in Cash	$ 426,232	$ (18,520)	$ (22,165)	$ (32,275)	$ (108,024)
Cash, Beginning of Year	5,913	24,433	46,598	78,873	186,897
Cash, End of Year	$ 432,145	$ 5,913	$ 24,433	$ 46,598	$ 78,873

17. **Interpreting the statement of cash flows. Exhibit 15.21** presents a statement of cash flows for Cypress Corporation.

   a. What are the likely reasons that net income increased between 2011 and 2013, but cash flow from operations decreased?

   b. What are the likely reasons for the increased cash flow from operations between 2013 and 2015?

   c. How has the risk of Cypress Corporation changed over the five-year period?

18. **Deriving cash flows from financial statement data; comprehensive review, including other comprehensive income. Exhibit 15.22** presents financial data, including a partial statement of cash flows, for LKR Company for the year. Fill in the numbers in the statement of cash flows. (*Hint*: work from the bottom up.) Then respond to the following questions. Use positive numbers for cash inflows (receipts) and negative numbers for cash outflows (expenditures).

   a. What were the proceeds of sale of the old Buildings and Equipment?

   b. What were the proceeds of sale of the Securities Available for Sale?

   c. What were the purchases during the year of new Securities Available for Sale?

EXHIBIT 15.21

Cypress Corporation
Statement of Cash Flows
(all dollar amounts in thousands)
(Problem 17)

	2015	2014	2013	2012	2011
OPERATING					
Net Income	$ 6,602	$ 6,583	$ 3,716	$ 1,733	$ 1,045
Depreciation and Amortization	643	586	513	490	491
Other Addbacks	299	151	243	25	20
Other Subtractions	(97)	0	0	0	0
Working Capital Provided by Operations	$ 7,447	$ 7,320	$ 4,472	$ 2,248	$ 1,556
(Increase) Decrease in Receivables	4,456	(5,452)	(3,589)	(2,424)	(750)
(Increase) Decrease in Inventories	1,068	1,867	(7,629)	(4,111)	(1,387)
Increase (Decrease) Accts. Pay-Trade	(2,608)	1,496	1,393	2,374	1,228
Increase (Decrease) in Other Current					
Liabilities	(1,508)	1,649	4,737	2,865	473
Cash Flow from Operations	$ 8,855	$ 6,880	$ (616)	$ 952	$ 1,120
INVESTING					
Fixed Assets Acquired (net)	$(1,172)	$(1,426)	$ (749)	$ (849)	$ (347)
Marketable Securities Acquired	(3,306)	0	0	0	0
Other Investment Transactions	39	(64)	81	0	45
Cash Flow from Investing	$(4,439)	$(1,490)	$ (668)	$ (849)	$ (302)
FINANCING					
Increase in Short-Term Borrowing	$ 0	$ 0	$ 2,800	$ 700	$ 0
Increase in Long-Term Borrowing	0	0	0	0	0
Issue of Capital Stock	315	0	0	0	0
Decrease in Short-Term Borrowing	0	(3,500)	0	0	0
Decrease in Long-Term Borrowing	(170)	(170)	(170)	(170)	(170)
Acquisition of Capital Stock	0	0	0	0	(27)
Dividends Paid to Shareholders	(2,243)	(1,427)	(964)	(730)	(614)
Other Financing Transactions	0	0	0	0	0
Cash Flow from Financing	$(2,098)	$(5,097)	$ 1,666	$ (200)	$ (811)
Change in Cash	$ 2,318	$293	$ 382	$ (97)	$ 7
Cash, Beginning of Year	1,540	1,247	865	962	955
Cash, End of Year	$ 3,858	$ 1,540	$ 1,247	$ 865	$ 962

d. During the year, the market value of the Securities Available for Sale changed while LKR held them. By how much did the aggregate market value increase or decrease? Give the amount and whether *increase* or *decrease*.

e. What dividends, if any, did LKR receive from its 40%-owned affiliate?

f. What was the net income, if any, of the 90%-owned subsidiary?

g. What was the amount of expenditure for the year for warranty service, repairs, and replacements?

h. What was the amount of accounts receivable LKR wrote off as uncollectible during the year?

i. What was the total depreciation deduction LKR claimed on its income tax return for the year?

j. What were total cash dividends LKR paid during the year?

k. What was total cash flow for or from *Financing* activities for the year?

l. What was total cash flow for or from *Investing* activities for the year?

m. What was total cash flow for or from *Operations* for the year?

n. What were the total receipts from customers for the year?

o. What were the total expenditures for inventory during the year?

p. What were the total expenditures for income taxes during the year?

q. Did LKR use a LIFO or a FIFO cost-flow assumption for the year?

r. By what amount would LKR's pretax income for the year have changed if LKR had used the other cost-flow assumption? Give the amount and whether *larger* or *smaller*.

s. By the end of the year, what was LKR's total unrealized holding gain on inventory?

t. Refer to the total unrealized holding gain in the preceding question. In which of the following is that gain more likely reflected in the statements for the current year?

    A. Other Comprehensive Income

    B. Accumulated Other Comprehensive Income

    C. Net Income

    D. Retained Earnings

    E. None of the above

EXHIBIT 15.22

LKR Company
Statement of Earnings and Comprehensive Income
(Problem 18)

		For Year
Revenues		$ 1,500,000
Gain on Sale of Securities Available for Sale		3,300
Gain on Sale of Buildings and Equipment		23,000
Equity in Earnings of Affiliate		1,600
Expenses:		
Cost of Goods Sold	$788,000	
Wages and Salaries	280,000	
Depreciation	54,000	
Bad Debt Expense	125,000	
Warranty Expense	34,000	
Interest	12,000	
Income Taxes (Current)	90,400	
Income Taxes (Deferred)	1,600	
Total Expenses		(1,385,000)
Noncontrolling Interest in Subsidiary's Earnings[a]		(1,100)
Earnings		$ 141,800
Other Comprehensive Income		7,000
Comprehensive Income		$ 148,800

Statement of Cash Flows	For Year
Cash Flow from Operations	$ _____ [9]
Investing/Disinvesting:	
(Purchase) of Securities Available for Sale	_____ [8]
Proceeds of Selling	
Sale of Securities Available for Sale	_____ [7]
(Purchase) of Land	_____ [6]
Sale of Old Buildings and Equipment	_____ [5]
(Purchase) of New Buildings and Equipment	_____ [4]
Financing:	
Increase (Decrease) Long-Term Debt	_____ [3]
Increase (Decrease) Common Shares	_____ [2]
Cash Dividends (Paid)	_____ [1]
Net Change in Cash	_____ [0]
Cash, Beginning of Year	52,000
Cash, End of Year	$65,000

[a]IFRS does not allow showing Noncontrolling Interest as an expense and U.S. GAAP does not allow this after June 2009.

EXHIBIT 15.22

**LKR Company
Statement of Earnings and Comprehensive Income
(Problem 18) (Continued)**

Balance Sheet	End of Year 31 December	Start of Year 1 January	Additional Information
Assets			
Cash	$ 65,000	$ 52,000	Asset Sale: Initial Cost of B&E Sold During Year Was: $40,000
Accounts Receivable	197,000	184,000	
Allowance for Uncollectibles	(43,000)	(41,000)	
Advances to Suppliers of Inventory	4,000	5,000	No Purchases or Sales of Shares of Affiliates and Subsidiaries During Year; LKR Owns 40% of Affiliate and 90% of Subsidiary.
Inventory at FIFO Cost	212,000	192,000	
Allowance to Reduce to LIFO Valuation	(58,000)	(50,000)	
Prepaid Income Taxes	—	18,000	
Deferred Income Taxes	9,800	9,000	Cost of Securities Available for Sale Sold During Year Was: $4,000
Investment in Securities Available for Sale	80,000	68,000	
Investment in Affiliate	13,700	13,000	
Land	39,000	28,000	Fair Value on Dates of Sale of Securities Available for Sale Sold During the Year Was: $5,000
Buildings and Equipment (Cost)	858,000	790,000	
Accumulated Depreciation	(504,000)	(460,000)	
Total Assets	$ 873,500	$ 808,000	
Liabilities and Shareholders' Equity			
Accounts Payable for Inventory	$ 141,000	$ 136,000	Income Tax Rate was 40%; All Deferred Tax Assets Result from Warranties and Uncollectible Accounts Causing Temporary Differences
Advances from Customers	6,000	14,000	
Warranty Liability	28,000	28,000	
Interest Payable	8,000	10,000	All Deferred Tax Liabilities Result from Depreciation Causing Temporary Differences
Income Taxes Payable	19,000	—	
Deferred Income Taxes	34,400	32,000	Accumulated Other Comprehensive Income Relates only to Investments in Securities Available for Sale
Mortgage Payable	118,000	120,000	
Minority Interest in Subsidiary	2,100	1,000	
Common Stock	257,000	250,000	
Retained Earnings	236,000	200,000	
Accumulated Other Comprehensive Income	24,000	17,000	
Total Liabilities and Shareholders' Equity	$ 873,500	$ 808,000	

Synthesis of Financial Reporting

1. Review the conceptual framework underlying the authoritative guidance for financial reporting and potential changes in that framework.

2. Review financial reporting standards discussed in previous chapters, including instances where U.S. GAAP and IFRS diverge.

3. Understand proposed changes in financial statement presentation.

Recent changes in the financial reporting environment include the following:

1. The adoption or planned adoption of IFRS, or standards based on IFRS, for financial reporting in over 100 countries.

2. The willingness of the Securities and Exchange Commission in the United States to permit non-U.S. firms that list and trade their securities in the United States to report using IFRS without a reconciliation to U.S. GAAP.

3. The requirement to measure certain assets and liabilities at fair value instead of acquisition cost, and in some cases, to include the changes in fair value in net income instead of other comprehensive income.

4. The codification of U.S. GAAP into a single body of literature.

Change will likely continue. Any attempt to synthesize financial reporting, as discussed in this book, is analogous to describing a moving target. Yet, synthesizing the material covered provides an integrated review. Indicating the issues currently under discussion by standard-setting bodies and the possible direction they will take in addressing those issues provides a sense of future changes.

CONCEPTUAL FRAMEWORK

Both the FASB and the IASB rely on a conceptual framework to guide their standard-setting decisions. The conceptual framework is not a rigorous set of principles from which standard setters can logically deduce appropriate financial reporting standards. Its purpose is to guide standard-setting decisions in order to enhance the quality and consistency of those decisions. **Figure 16.1** summarizes the components of the conceptual framework.

The FASB and the IASB have separately developed their conceptual frameworks, and those frameworks are similar. The two standard-setting bodies are currently working to develop a common conceptual framework for financial reporting. We discuss the direction of those efforts in the following sections. We designate in parentheses the chapters that discuss these topics more fully.

FINANCIAL REPORTING OBJECTIVES (CHAPTER 1)

Financial reporting objectives speak to the purpose of financial reports and the primary users and uses of those reports. The FASB's conceptual framework lists the following as financial reporting objectives.[1] Financial reporting should accomplish the following:

1. Provide information useful for making rational investment and credit decisions.

2. Provide information to help current and potential investors and creditors assess the amount, timing, and uncertainty of future cash flows.

3. Provide information about the economic resources of a firm and the claims on those resources.

4. Provide information about a firm's operating performance during a period.

5. Provide information about how an enterprise obtains and uses cash.

6. Provide information about how management has discharged its stewardship responsibility to owners.

7. Include explanations and interpretations to help users understand the financial information provided.

These financial reporting objectives identify current and potential investors and creditors as the principal users of financial reports and the provision of information to make investment and credit decisions as the principal purpose of financial reports. The remaining objectives describe the need for a balance sheet, an income statement, a statement of cash flows, notes to the financial statements, and management's discussion of information in the financial statements and notes. The financial reporting objectives in the IASB's conceptual framework[2] resemble those of the FASB framework.

The FASB[3] and IASB are working jointly to develop a revised, coordinated set of financial reporting objectives. They envision the primary user groups as present and potential

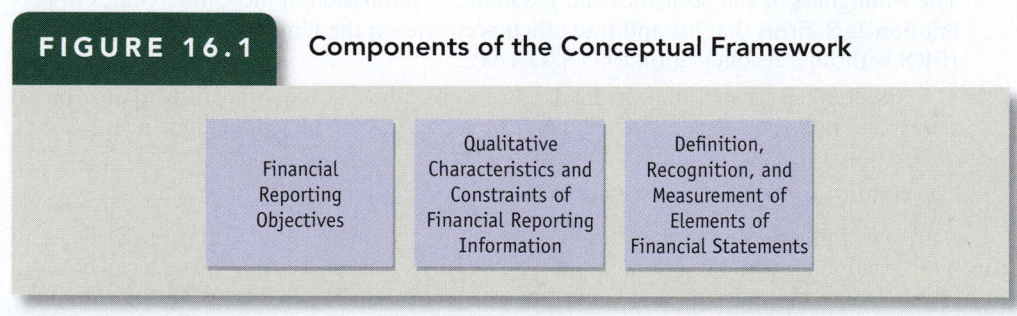

FIGURE 16.1 Components of the Conceptual Framework

Financial Reporting Objectives	Qualitative Characteristics and Constraints of Financial Reporting Information	Definition, Recognition, and Measurement of Elements of Financial Statements

---

[1]Financial Accounting Standards Board, *Statement of Financial Accounting Concepts No. 1*, "Objectives of Financial Reporting by Business Enterprises," 1978.

[2]International Accounting Standards Board, "Framework for the Preparation and Presentation of Financial Statements," 1989, adopted by the IASB in 2001.

[3]Financial Accounting Standards Board, "Conceptual Framework for Financial Reporting: The Objectives of Financial Reporting and Qualitative Characteristics and Constraints of Decision-Useful Financial Reporting Information," 2008.

providers of resources, including equity investors and creditors. The users want information useful for making resource allocation decisions and for making decisions about protecting and enhancing their investments. The proposed reporting objectives would also specify that firms should prepare financial reports from the perspective of the reporting entity (entity perspective), rather than from the perspective of its owners or a particular class of owners (proprietary perspective). Although the reporting objectives of U.S. GAAP and IFRS recognize that the user group is broader than just shareholders, some accounting standards, particularly those related to consolidated financial statements, have historically taken a proprietary perspective instead of an entity perspective.

QUALITATIVE CHARACTERISTICS OF FINANCIAL REPORTING INFORMATION (CHAPTER 1)

The *qualitative characteristics* describe the attributes that enhance the usefulness of financing reporting information. The FASB's conceptual framework sets forth the following qualitative characteristics:[4]

1. **Relevance** refers to information that can make a difference in a resource allocation decision by helping users to form predictions about the outcomes of future events and to confirm or correct prior information or expectations. Receiving information in a timely manner (referred to as *timeliness*) so that it can influence decisions is an aspect of relevance.

2. **Reliability** refers to the faithfulness with which accounting information represents what it purports to represent and the extent to which the information is both verifiable by independent measurers and neutral with respect to the interest of a particular user group.

3. **Comparability** refers to financial reporting that treats similar items the same way and different items differently. **Consistency** refers to financial reporting that treats an item the same way over time.

4. **Materiality** envisions that the nature of the information is relevant and that its effect is large enough to influence a decision.

As standard setters make decisions about financial reporting standards, they consider the **costs and benefits** of those standards. They assess whether the benefits to users of financial reports from a particular financial reporting requirement exceed the costs of providing the information.

The IASB identifies understandability, relevance, reliability, and comparability as the qualitative attributes of accounting information.[5] *Relevance, reliability*, and *comparability* appear as qualitative characteristics in the conceptual frameworks of both standard-setting bodies. *Understandability* refers to the attribute that users of financial reports will perceive the significance of a reported item to their decisions. Such perception involves understanding the economic effects of a firm's actions and the measurement and reporting of those economic effects in the financial reports. Understandability is an implicit aspect of relevance in the qualitative characteristics set forth in the FASB's conceptual framework.

The joint efforts of the FASB and the IASB to set forth qualitative characteristics of financial reporting information have led to the following tentative framework:

Fundamental Qualitative Characteristics

1. Relevance
2. Faithful representation

Enhancing Qualitative Characteristics

1. Comparability
2. Verifiability
3. Timeliness
4. Understandability

---

[4]Financial Accounting Standards Board, *Statement of Financial Accounting Concepts No. 2*, "Qualitative Characteristics of Accounting Information," 1980.

[5]International Accounting Standards Board, "Framework for the Preparation and Presentation of Financial Statements," 1989, adopted by the IASB in 2001.

Pervasive Constraints

1. Materiality
2. Cost

These qualitative characteristics are similar to those in the existing conceptual frameworks of the FASB and the IASB. However, the proposals would distinguish among the fundamental, enhancing, and constraining attributes, providing standard-setters with a framework for making trade-offs in setting particular reporting standards.

DEFINITION, RECOGNITION, AND MEASUREMENT OF ELEMENTS OF FINANCIAL STATEMENTS (CHAPTERS 3 AND 4)

The elements of financial statements are the building blocks for the balance sheet and income statement. The principal elements are as follows:

Balance Sheet

1. Asset
2. Liability
3. Equity

Income Statement

1. Revenue
2. Expense
3. Gains and losses

In addition to discussing these financial statement elements, this section also discusses two important and related concepts: (1) income, specifically comprehensive income, net income (or profit), and other comprehensive income, and (2) accrual accounting. This section summarizes the definitions and the recognition and measurement criteria for financial statement elements in the existing conceptual frameworks of the FASB and the IASB[6] and discusses proposals for changing the elements' definitions and measurement criteria.

Asset The FASB's conceptual framework defines an asset as a probable future economic benefit obtained or controlled by a particular entity as a result of a past transaction or event. The IASB's conceptual framework defines an asset as a resource controlled by an entity as a result of past events and from which a firm expects future economic benefits. Like the definition of an asset, the criteria for asset recognition are similar under the two frameworks:

1. The firm owns or controls the right to use the asset.
2. The right to use the item arises as a result of a past transaction or exchange.
3. The future benefit has a relevant measurement attribute that a firm can quantify with sufficient reliability.

The two conceptual frameworks also discuss measurement attributes, for example, acquisition cost, current replacement cost, and net realizable value.

The definition of an asset and the recognition criteria focus on a past transaction, which provides evidence of an economic sacrifice in the past to acquire the asset, and the probability of measurable future benefits, which involves assessments of the likelihood of the firm receiving future benefits. This definition of an asset excludes expected benefits related to rights under executory contracts, mere exchanges of promises, because authoritative guidance does not view the signing of a contract as evidence of a past transaction. This definition of an asset also excludes contingent assets, because receiving future benefits depends on the outcome of a future event.

---

[6]The definitions of financial statement elements and the related recognition criteria are in Financial Accounting Standards Board, *Statement of Financial Accounting Concepts No. 6*, "Elements of Financial Statements," 1985, and Financial Accounting Standards Board, *Statement of Financial Accounting Concepts No. 5*, "Recognition and Measurement in Financial Statements of Business Enterprises," 1984; International Accounting Standards Board, "Framework for the Preparation and Presentation of Financial Statements," 1989, adopted by the IASB in 2001.

The FASB and the IASB are reconsidering the definition of an asset and the criteria for asset recognition. Their proposed definition emphasizes the *present* existence of an economic resource and de-emphasizes the notions of a *past* exchange and the probability of *future* benefits. Resources would satisfy the definition of an asset if (1) the entity can separate the resources from the entity (by sale, exchange, license, or other disposal), or (2) the resources arise from contractual or other legal rights, suggesting that negotiations between independent parties in establishing the rights permit estimation of fair value, even if the entity cannot exchange the item.

Asset recognition criteria also focus on which entity should recognize an asset. The issue is particularly pertinent as it applies to asset *derecognition*, that is, the removal of an asset from a firm's balance sheet. As discussed in **Chapter 11** and elsewhere in this book, an entity should derecognize (remove from the balance sheet) an asset that it no longer controls. Standard setters have struggled with this concept and have changed the criteria several times over the last 30 years.

Asset recognition criteria also affect the treatment of expenditures that create future benefits, but the firm cannot measure those future benefits with sufficient reliability. Examples include expenditures for creating a brand name and researching new technologies. U.S. GAAP and IFRS differ in the extent to which they require firms to recognize a portion of these expenditures as assets versus treating the expenditures fully as expenses. A related issue is the inconsistent treatment of expenditures incurred internally versus amounts spent to acquire brand names, technologies, and other intangibles in external market transactions.

Liability The FASB's conceptual framework defines a liability as a probable future sacrifice of economic resources arising from present obligations of a particular entity to transfer assets or provide services to other entities in the future as a result of past transactions or events. The IASB's framework defines a liability as a present obligation of an entity arising from past events the settlement of which is expected to result in an outflow of resources embodying economic benefits. The criteria for recognition of a liability are as follows:

1. The obligation represents a present obligation, not a potential future commitment or intent.

2. The obligation exists as a result of a past transaction or exchange, called the *obligating event*.

3. The obligation requires the probable future sacrifice of an economic resource that the firm has little or no discretion to avoid.

4. The obligation has a relevant measurement attribute that the firm can quantify with sufficient reliability.

Firms report many financial liabilities as the present value of the amount payable, except that firms can ignore discounting for liabilities due within one year. Nonfinancial liabilities, those settled by providing goods and services instead of cash, appear at either the amount of cash received (for example, advances from customers) or the expected cost of providing goods and services (for example, warranty liability).

Obligations under executory contracts do not usually appear as liabilities because they do not represent a present obligation. An exception involves leases accounted for as capital, or finance, leases. Firms also do not recognize certain obligations that are uncertain as to amount or timing or both as liabilities, unless those items meet a probability threshold and have a reliable measurement attribute. U.S. GAAP refers to these unrecognized obligations, such as the possible obligation under an unsettled lawsuit, as unrecognized *contingencies*, and IFRS uses the term *contingent liability*.

As previously discussed for assets, the FASB and the IASB are reconsidering the definition of a liability. Their proposed definition focuses on a *present* obligation and de-emphasizes a *past* obligating event and a probable *future* sacrifice of resources. For example, the proposed definition might result in the accounting for all leases as capital leases, the recognition of many executory contracts as liabilities, and the recognition of more obligations with uncertain amount or timing as liabilities.

The FASB and the IASB are reconsidering the role of uncertainty, or probability, in the definition, recognition, and measurement of liabilities. Existing recognition criteria include a probable future sacrifice of resources; one issue involves the minimum probability level to warrant recognition of an uncertain obligation as a liability. U.S. GAAP does not specify a minimum probability level, although the rule-of-thumb in practice is approximately 80%. IFRS specifies that *probable* means more likely than not, implying greater than 50%.

Sometimes the FASB and the IASB view probability of payment as relating to measurement of a liability, not to its definition and recognition. One of the characteristics of a fair value measurement is that the measurement does not embody a minimum probability for recognition. For example, an entity that guarantees the debt of another entity has incurred an unconditional obligation to stand ready to repay the other entity's debt. The probability of having to make a payment does not affect that unconditional obligation. Under current guidance, the *unconditional* obligation is a liability, measured at fair value incorporating both the probability of payment and the possible amounts of payment. The *conditional* obligation, which depends on whether the guaranteed firm is able to repay the debt, does not appear as a liability until it becomes probable.

Equity   Equity, or shareholders' equity for a corporation, is the residual interest of owners in the assets of an entity, after subtracting liabilities. Equity includes assets exchanged by owners in return for an ownership interest and net assets generated by earnings activities in excess of net assets distributed to owners as dividends. Repurchases by a firm of its ownership interests reduce equity. Firms may issue equity interests with different rights, such as one class of common stock with 10 votes per share and another class of common stock with one vote per share.

Hybrid securities have characteristics of both debt and equity. Examples include convertible bonds and some preferred stock issues subject to redemption. **Chapter 14** discusses the accounting for such securities. We also consider the accounting for such securities later in this chapter.

Revenue   The FASB's conceptual framework defines revenues as inflows or other enhancements of assets of an entity or settlements of its liabilities from delivering or producing goods, rendering services, or other activities that constitute the entity's ongoing major or central operations. The IASB's conceptual framework defines income as increases in economic benefits during an accounting period in the form of inflows or enhancements of assets or decreases in liabilities that result in increases in equity, other than those relating to contributions from equity participants. Firms recognize revenue, or income, when they satisfy two conditions:

1. **Completion of the earnings process.** The firm has done all, or nearly all, it has promised to do for the customer.

2. **Receipt of assets from the customer.** The firm has received either cash or some other asset that the firm can convert into cash, for example, by collecting an account receivable.

Firms measure revenue at the amount of cash they expect to collect from customers. If firms expect to receive cash more than one year after the time of recognizing revenue, they measure revenues at the present value of the amount of cash they expect to receive.

Arrangements with multiple deliverables create difficulties in both the timing and measurement of revenues. For example, if a firm sells a product bundled with an obligation to provide additional services over time, should the firm recognize the selling price for the bundled product and services at the time of delivery of the product? Or, should the firm recognize revenue from the sale of the product at the time of delivery and revenue from the services as the firm renders the services? How should the firm measure the portion of the selling price related to the product and the portion related to the services?

Expenses   The FASB's conceptual framework defines expenses as outflows or other using up of assets or incurrences of liabilities from delivering or producing goods, rendering services, or carrying out other activities that constitute the entity's ongoing major or central operations. The IASB's conceptual framework defines expenses as decreases in economic benefits during an accounting period in the form of outflows or depletions of assets or incurrences of liabilities that result in decreases in equity, other than those relating to distributions to equity participants. Firms recognize expenses under the following conditions:

1. The consumption of an asset (or incurrence of a liability) results from a transaction that leads to the recognition of revenue. That is, firms attempt to match expenses with associated revenues.

2. The consumption of an asset (or incurrence of a liability) results from the passage of time and does not lead to the creation of another asset.

Firms measure expenses at the same amount as the asset consumed or the liability incurred.

Gains and Losses Gains (losses) are increases (decreases) in net assets from peripheral or incidental transactions of an entity and from other transactions and events affecting the entity except those that result from revenues (expenses) or investments by (distributions to) owners. Firms usually report gains and losses from sales of assets or settlements of liabilities at a net amount; that is, equal to the difference between the net asset received and the carrying value of the asset sold or between the net asset given and the carrying value of the liability settled. Gains and losses may also arise from the remeasurement of assets and liabilities. Firms *realize* gains and losses when they sell or exchange assets or settle liabilities in market transactions. Firms *recognize* gains and losses when those items enter the measurement of net income or other comprehensive income

COMPREHENSIVE INCOME, NET INCOME, AND OTHER COMPREHENSIVE INCOME

Comprehensive income equals the net amount of revenues, expenses, gains, and losses during an accounting period. Authoritative guidance classifies revenues and expenses arising from a firm's core business as components of net income. Net income also includes gains and losses from sales or exchanges of assets or settlements of liabilities related incidentally or peripherally to the firm's core business. Authoritative guidance classifies gains and losses from the remeasurement of certain assets and liabilities as either net income or other comprehensive income. However, neither the FASB's conceptual framework nor the IASB's conceptual framework contains a conceptual model for classifying items in net income versus in other comprehensive income. Firms reclassify gains and losses initially classified in other comprehensive income into net income when a confirming event subsequently occurs. Firms close amounts in other comprehensive income for a period to Accumulated Other Comprehensive Income at the end of the period. Accumulated Other Comprehensive Income is a shareholders' equity account that acts for other comprehensive income the way retained earnings acts for net income. Comprehensive income for a period equals net income plus other comprehensive income.

Accrual Accounting Accrual accounting measures the effects of transactions and events in the periods when they occur. In contrast, cash-basis accounting recognizes only cash receipts and disbursements. Under accrual accounting, firms recognize revenues when an arrangement satisfies the revenue recognition criteria previously listed, increasing net assets but not necessarily cash at the time of revenue recognition. Firms recognize expenses when an arrangement satisfies one of the two expense recognition criteria previously listed, decreasing net assets but not necessarily cash at the time of expense recognition. Accrual accounting often uses the amount of cash received or paid in some period to measure the *amount* of revenues and expenses recognized during the current period, but the *timing* of revenue and expense recognition does not necessarily coincide with the timing of cash receipts and disbursements. Accrual accounting underlies the measurements of revenues and expenses on the income statement.

Accrual accounting also affects balance sheet carrying amounts. Firms report economic resources with measurable future benefits as assets, even if the resources are not in the form of cash. Firms report obligations arising from economic benefits received in the past as liabilities, even though the firm has not yet paid cash. Shareholders' equity reflects changes in the residual interest of owners from transactions involving capital stock and from earnings activities independent of when cash flows in or out of a firm.

Accrual accounting separates the timing of recognition in the income statement and the balance sheet from the timing of cash flows. Therefore, the need arises for a financial statement that reports the effects of operating, investing, and financing activities on cash flows. This is the purpose of the statement of cash flows, discussed in **Chapters 5** and **15**.

Entity The definitions of financial statement elements, including assets, liabilities, revenues, and expenses, refer to a reporting entity. The concept of a reporting entity pertains to a group of entities pursuing a common business purpose under the control of one of the entities in the group. For example, a single entity may operate through subsidiaries, joint ventures, trusts, partnerships, and other corporations. It may control some or all of these other entities.

The concept of control includes both the power, or capacity, to direct the strategic, operating, investing, and financing activities of another entity, and the ability to benefit from increases in the value of the other entity and to incur losses from decreases in value.

Both U.S. GAAP and IFRS often refer to ownership of a majority of the voting stock of another entity as indicating control, unless evidence indicates that the majority owner cannot exercise control. Firms sometimes operate through entities that lack economically meaningful ownership interests, like a trust, or entities where control arises through contractual rights without ownership of voting stock. Identifying the reporting entity in these cases is more difficult.

FINANCIAL REPORTING STANDARDS

Chapters 7 to **14** discuss authoritative guidance in accounting for particular assets, liabilities, shareholders' equity, revenues, expenses, gains, and losses. This section summarizes the required accounting, noting certain similarities and differences between U.S. GAAP and IFRS. This section also discusses certain unresolved issues currently under study by standard-setting bodies. We indicate in parentheses the chapter that discusses the particular financial reporting standard more fully.

Ideally, financial reporting standards should flow from and be consistent with the financial reporting objectives, qualitative characteristics of accounting information, and elements of financial statements that comprise the FASB's and the IASB's conceptual frameworks. Although these conceptual frameworks guide the development of financial reporting standards, they are not intended as a rigorous set of principles from which standard-setting bodies can (and must) logically deduce acceptable accounting methods. In some cases, standards conflict with the conceptual frameworks. In all cases, standards take precedence over the conceptual frameworks.

REVENUE RECOGNITION (CHAPTER 7)

The discussion of revenue in a previous section of this chapter indicated that firms recognize revenue when they have (1) completed an earnings process or performed most or all of their obligations to customers, usually the delivery of a product or service, and (2) received cash or a receivable capable of sufficiently reliable measurement. In some cases firms apply the revenue recognition criteria to each component of an arrangement with multiple deliverables. Firms that sell products under long-term contracts, such as construction companies, often recognize revenue using the percentage-of-completion method. U.S. GAAP allows the use of the competed contract method when firms cannot reasonably estimate revenues and costs, whereas IFRS requires a variant of the cost-recovery method under these circumstances.

ACCOUNTS RECEIVABLE (CHAPTER 7)

Firms report accounts receivable they expect to collect within one year at the amount of cash the firms expect to receive. This amount may differ from the gross amount receivable from customers because of estimated uncollectible accounts. Both U.S. GAAP and IFRS require firms with significant uncollectible accounts receivable to estimate the amount of uncollectible accounts related to a particular period's sales and recognize that amount as bad debt expense in the same period as the related revenues. Firms typically use a contra account to accounts receivable, such as Allowance for Uncollectibles, to reflect the amount of accounts receivable they do not expect to collect. The entry to recognize estimated uncollectible amounts involves a debit to Bad Debt Expense and a credit to Allowance for Uncollectibles. The write-off of a particular customer's account that becomes uncollectible involves a debit to Allowance for Uncollectibles and a credit to Accounts Receivable. Common terminology refers to this accounting as the *allowance method*.

Firms may also use the allowance method to account for estimated sales discounts, returns, and allowances (**Chapter 7**), as well as for warranties (**Chapter 8**).

INVENTORIES (CHAPTER 8)

Firms initially record inventories at acquisition cost. Acquisition cost for a merchandising firm includes the costs incurred to purchase and transport the inventory prior to sale. Acquisition cost for a manufacturing firm includes the direct material, direct labor, and manufacturing overhead cost to produce the inventory.

If the market values of inventory items decline below acquisition cost prior to sale, firms must reduce their balance sheet carrying values using the lower of cost or market method. U.S. GAAP uses a combination of replacement cost and net realizable values to measure market value. IFRS defines market as net realizable value, the estimated selling price in the ordinary course of business less the estimated costs of completion and the estimated costs to make the sale. Neither U.S. GAAP nor IFRS permits firms to remeasure inventories upward when market value exceeds acquisition cost. However, if the market values of inventories increase during a period, IFRS permits firms to recognize the unrealized gain to the extent that the firm had previously recognized an unrealized loss on those inventory items. U.S. GAAP does not permit recognition of such reversals of previously recognized unrealized losses.

Firms measure the cost of goods sold and the amount of ending inventories for a period either using specific identification or making a cost-flow assumption. U.S. GAAP permits firms to use a first-in, first-out (FIFO), weighted-average, and last-in, first-out (LIFO) cost-flow assumption. IFRS does not permit the use of LIFO.

PROPERTY, PLANT, AND EQUIPMENT (CHAPTER 9)

Firms initially record property, plant, and equipment, sometimes referred to as *fixed assets*, at acquisition cost, the cash paid or the fair value of other consideration given in exchange for the asset. Acquisition cost includes all costs necessary to prepare the asset for its intended use. Firms capitalize into the asset's carrying amount subsequent expenditures that extend the service life or increase the benefits of a fixed asset beyond those initially anticipated. Buildings and equipment have a finite life, so firms must depreciate their acquisition cost less estimated salvage over the expected service life. Firms may use a straight-line method or accelerated depreciation methods. If new information becomes available that indicates that the expected service life or estimated salvage value differs significantly from that initially anticipated, the firm revises its depreciation prospectively.

IFRS permits firms to remeasure property, plant, and equipment upward for increases in fair value under certain conditions. U.S. GAAP does not permit such upward remeasurements. Firms must test property, plant, and equipment for possible asset impairment when conditions indicate that a significant decrease in fair value has occurred. Under U.S. GAAP, firms initially compare the undiscounted cash flows expected from the asset to the asset's carrying value. A fixed asset impairment occurs when the asset's carrying value exceeds the undiscounted cash flows. The amount of the recognized impairment loss is the excess of the carrying value over the fair value of the asset. IFRS does not apply the initial test comparing undiscounted cash flows with the carrying value. Instead, IFRS requires that firms recognize an impairment loss when the carrying value of a fixed asset exceeds its recoverable amount, the higher of (1) the fair value less cost to sell, and (2) value in use (present value of future cash flows from the asset in its current use by the firm).

The financial reporting standards for property, plant, and equipment are similar under U.S. GAAP and IFRS except for upward remeasurements for fair value increases and for recognition and measurement of asset impairment losses. Controversial issues involve (1) the appropriateness of the undiscounted cash flow recoverability test under U.S. GAAP, and (2) the use of recoverable amount instead of fair value under IFRS. Recoverable amount under IFRS differs from fair value under U.S. GAAP in that fair value excludes transaction, or selling, costs and measures value based on how external market participants would use the asset.

INTANGIBLES OTHER THAN GOODWILL (CHAPTER 9)

U.S. GAAP and IFRS require firms to treat some or all expenditures made to *internally* develop brand names, customer lists, new technologies, and other intangibles as expenses in the period of the expenditure. U.S. GAAP treats all such expenditures as expenses of the period (except for certain software development costs). IFRS treats research costs as immediate expenses but treats development costs incurred after a research project reaches the stage of technical feasibility as assets.

In contrast to costs incurred internally to develop intangibles, U.S. GAAP and IFRS require firms to recognize as assets identifiable intangibles acquired in *external* market transactions. The exchange between an independent buyer and seller provides evidence of the existence of expected future benefits, and the exchange price provides evidence of the fair value of those benefits. Identifiable intangibles include patents, trademarks, customer lists, and other economic resources ready for use, as well as in-process technologies with uncertain future benefits.

Identifiable intangible assets have either finite lives or indefinite lives. Firms must amortize intangible assets with finite lives, generally using the straight-line method. Firms do not amortize intangible assets with indefinite lives.

Firms must test intangible assets for impairment. U.S. GAAP applies the same provisions to intangible assets with finite lives as it does to property, plant, and equipment, as previously described. Firms cannot apply the undiscounted cash flow recoverability test to indefinite-lived intangible assets because of the uncertain period of future benefits. Thus, the impairment loss for intangibles with an indefinite life (other than goodwill) equals the excess of the carrying value over the fair value of the intangible. The impairment provisions for intangibles (other than goodwill) under IFRS, whether amortized or not, are the same as for property, plant, and equipment. The impairment loss equals the excess of the carrying value of the intangible assets over their recoverable amount (higher of fair value less cost to sell and value in use to the firm). Firms must test nonamortized intangibles annually for possible impairment under IFRS.

GOODWILL (CHAPTER 9)

In ordinary usage, goodwill refers to various unidentifiable intangible resources of a firm, such as a well-trained labor force or a reputation for quality products or customer service. As previously discussed, firms that incur expenditures internally to develop these intangible resources must treat them as expenses in the period incurred. For accounting purposes, goodwill arises only when a firm acquires another entity in an external market transaction and pays more for that entity than the fair value of the identifiable assets net of identifiable liabilities. Goodwill is the excess of the amount paid for the acquired company over the fair value of identifiable net assets.

Goodwill, because it includes unidentifiable intangible resources, has an indefinite life. Indefinite does not mean infinite, only not knowable. Firms therefore do not amortize goodwill. However, firms must test goodwill annually for impairment. Because a firm cannot separate goodwill from other assets, it tests for impairment of goodwill as part of a reporting unit (U.S. GAAP), or a cash-generating unit (IFRS), which contains the goodwill. The provisions for deciding whether a loss has occurred and then measuring the amount of the loss are complex.

NOTES AND BONDS (CHAPTER 10)

U.S. GAAP and IFRS account for notes and nonconvertible bonds payable similarly. Firms initially record long-term notes and bonds at their issue price, the present value of the future contractual cash flows discounted at the market interest rate for the bonds at the time of issue. The market interest rate at the time of issue is the rate that discounts the contractual cash flows to the initial issue price. If the market interest rate equals the coupon rate for the bonds, the firm will issue the bonds for face value. If the market interest rate exceeds the coupon rate, the firm will issue the bonds for less than face value. If the coupon rate exceeds the market interest rate, the firm will issue the bonds for more than face value.

Firms must amortize the difference between the issue price and the face value as an adjustment to interest expense over the life of the bonds. Amortization uses the effective interest method, in which interest expense each period equals the market interest rate for the bonds at the time of issue times the carrying value of the debt at the beginning of the period. The difference between interest expense and any cash payment increases (in the case of debt initially issued for less than face value) or decreases (in the case of debt initially issued for more than face value) the carrying value of the debt. Firms that repay debt prior to maturity record a gain or loss for the difference between the purchase price and the carrying value of the debt.

U.S. GAAP and IFRS require firms to disclose the fair value of long-term notes and bonds in notes to the financial statements. Fair value is the amount the firm would pay to settle the debt on the date of the balance sheet, the current market price in the case of items that trade in active markets. For other items, firms measure fair value using techniques and assumptions that market participants would use, for example, the present value of the contractual cash flows discounted at a current market interest rate that reflects all the factors that market participants would consider, including the item's credit risk.

Firms can adopt the fair value option for long-term notes and bonds. If so, the balance sheet carrying amounts for these items are the fair value amounts that they disclose in the notes if they did not adopt the fair value option. The offsetting debit or credit for the remeasurement is to an unrealized loss or gain, which under the fair value option the firm includes in net income.

LEASES (CHAPTER 10)

Firms account for leases using either the operating lease method or the capital (finance) lease method. The operating lease method treats leases as executory contracts, with neither the leased asset nor the lease liability recognized on the lessee's balance sheet. The lessor and lessee recognize rent revenue and rent expense respectively as the lessee uses the leased asset over time. The capital, or finance, lease method treats leases equivalent to installment purchases or sales, where the lessee borrows funds from the lessor to purchase the asset and the lessor recognizes profit at the time of sale. The lessee records the leased asset and the lease liability on the balance sheet at the present value of the contractual cash flows at the time of signing the lease. The lessee amortizes the leased asset, similar to recognizing depreciation on buildings and equipment. The lessee recognizes interest expense on the lease liability, similar to recognizing interest expense on long-term notes or bonds. The lessor records the signing of a capital lease the same as if the lessor sold the leased asset for an installment note receivable. The lessor records the lease receivable at the present value of the contractual cash flows, removes the cost of the leased asset from its accounting records, and recognizes income for the difference. Over time, the lessor recognizes interest revenue in amounts paralleling interest expense recognized by the lessee (borrower).

U.S. GAAP and IFRS provide criteria for distinguishing operating leases from capital leases. The criteria attempt to identify the entity, whether lessor or lessee, that enjoys the benefits and incurs the risk of the leased asset. When the lessor enjoys the benefits and bears the risk, the lease is an operating lease. When the lessee enjoys the benefits and bears the risk, the lease is a capital lease. U.S. GAAP provides four criteria, any one of which qualifies a lease as a capital lease. IFRS provides more general criteria for identifying the entity enjoying the rewards and incurring the risk. Firms cannot currently apply the fair value option to capital leases.

The FASB and the IASB have undertaken a joint project involving the lessee's accounting for leases. The accounting for operating leases may change in the future in light of deliberations of standard-setting bodies regarding the definition of an asset and a liability. The emphasis on a present economic benefit for an asset and a present obligation for a liability, as opposed to a past transaction for an asset and past benefits received for a liability, may have the result of treating all leases as capital leases.

RETIREMENT BENEFITS (CHAPTER 11)

U.S. GAAP and IFRS require firms to recognize the cost of retirement benefits (pensions, health care, life insurance) as an expense while employees work, not when they receive payments or other benefits during retirement. Employers often contribute cash to a trust, an entity legally separate from the employer, to fund their retirement obligations. The trust invests the funds received to generate a return. Payments to employees come from both the employer's contributions and investment returns. The accounting records of the trust are separate from the accounting records of the employer, and the amounts on the two sets of books usually differ. Two issues in accounting for defined benefit retirement benefits are as follows:

1. What items in the accounting records of the retirement trust should the employer recognize in its financial statement?

2. How quickly should the employer recognize in its accounting records changes in the performance of the investments held by the trust and the funded status of the retirement obligation of the trust?

U.S. GAAP and IFRS do not permit the employer to prepare consolidated financial statements with the retirement trust. However, the employer must report the net funded status of each defined benefit retirement plan (that is, the fair value of retirement trust assets minus the retirement trust obligation) as either an asset or a liability on its balance sheet. The offsetting credit (for an overfunded plan) or debit (for an underfunded plan) is to Other Comprehensive Income. Notes to the financial statements provide information about investments made by the retirement trust and how trust assets and liabilities changed during a period.

Although an employer must recognize changes in the funded status of a defined benefit retirement plan on its balance sheet each period, U.S. GAAP and IFRS do not require the employer to recognize these changes immediately in net income. Changes in the net funded status of a defined benefit retirement plan because investment performance differs from expectations, or because of changes in actuarial assumptions, or in the retirement benefit formula, initially affect other comprehensive income. Firms then amortize the amounts in Other Comprehensive Income over the expected period of benefit as an adjustment to retirement plan cost. **Chapter 11** describes the calculation of retirement plan cost more fully.

One issue in accounting for the cost of retirement benefits is whether firms should defer and then amortize changes in the funded status of a retirement plan or whether these changes should affect net income immediately. Those favoring the defer-and-amortize approach argue that accounting should reflect the long-term perspective of retirement plans and smooth out the effects on net income of annual deviations related to investment performance, changes in actuarial assumptions, and changes in the benefit formula. Furthermore, they argue that users of the financial statements can obtain information about the funded status of a defined benefit retirement plan by examining the balance sheet and notes to the financial statements. Those favoring immediate recognition argue that recognizing the effect of these changes in net income as they occur provides the financial statement user with more timely information and makes the nature and amount of changes in the funded status in a particular year more obvious than amortizing changes of several years into a single net amortized amount.

INCOME TAXES (CHAPTER 11)

Income before taxes for financial reporting usually differs from taxable income reported to tax authorities. The differences arise because of (1) permanent differences (items that affect income for financial reporting but never affect taxable income, or vice versa), or (2) temporary differences (items that affect income for financial reporting in a different period than for tax reporting). U.S. GAAP and IFRS require firms to measure income tax expense based on income for financial reporting (excluding permanent differences). Income tax authorities impose taxes on taxable income. The difference between income tax expense and income tax payable represents the tax effects of temporary differences: either the firm will receive future benefits (deferred tax assets) or it must pay future taxes (deferred tax liabilities).

The preceding description suggests that deferred tax assets and deferred tax liabilities result from the computation of income tax expense and income tax payable. Thus,

$$\frac{\text{Income Tax}}{\text{Expense}} - \frac{\text{Income Tax}}{\text{Payable}} = \frac{\text{Changes in Deferred Tax Assets}}{\text{and Deferred Tax Liabilities}}$$

U.S. GAAP and IFRS require firms to compute income tax payable and changes in the amounts of deferred tax assets and deferred tax liabilities, and the result is income tax expense. Thus,

$$\frac{\text{Income Tax}}{\text{Payable}} + \frac{\text{Changes in Deferred Tax Assets}}{\text{and Deferred Tax Liabilities}} = \frac{\text{Income Tax}}{\text{Expense}}$$

Deferred tax assets and deferred tax liabilities can change because of temporary differences and because of changes in income tax rates affecting future tax benefits and obligations. The net deferred tax asset reported on a firm's balance sheet will also change with changes in the valuation allowance for deferred tax assets.

Firms measure deferred tax assets and deferred tax liabilities at undiscounted amounts. One issue in accounting for income taxes is whether firms should discount these items to present values. Proponents of discounting point out that firms must measure long-term receivables and long-term liabilities at present value amounts. Consistency suggests that firms also express deferred tax assets and deferred tax liabilities at present values. Opponents argue that it is impractical to estimate the time when temporary differences will reverse and give rise to cash flow effects. Tax laws impose taxes on income before taxes, not on individual revenues and expenses. Whether a firm receives a tax benefit or pays taxes in a particular year for an individual temporary difference (such as depreciation) depends on the net effect of all other taxable revenues and expenses.

Marketable Securities (Chapter 12)

Firms sometimes acquire bonds or capital stock of other entities for their expected returns (through interest, dividends, and price appreciation) without any intent to exert influence or control over the other entity. U.S. GAAP and IFRS presume that the acquisition of any amount of bonds, and the acquisition of less than 20% of the voting stock of another entity implies an inability to exert significant influence or control. Firms account for such securities as passive investments. Firms classify such securities into three categories:

1. Debt securities held to maturity (IFRS uses the term *held-to-maturity investments*).
2. Trading securities (IFRS uses the term *financial assets at fair value through profit or loss*).
3. Securities available for sale (IFRS uses the term *available-for-sale financial assets*).

Securities with an expected holding period of less than one year appear in current assets on the balance sheet, usually labeled Marketable Securities, and those with an expected holding period longer than one year appear in noncurrent assets, usually labeled either Marketable Securities or Investments in Securities.

U.S. GAAP and IFRS prescribe the following accounting for marketable securities:

1. Debt securities held to maturity: amortized acquisition cost, subject to impairment.
2. Trading securities: fair value, with unrealized gains and losses recognized in net income.
3. Securities available for sale: fair value, with unrealized gains and losses recognized in other comprehensive income as fair values change and realized gains and losses, measured as disposal proceeds less amortized acquisition cost, recognized in net income at the time of sale. Net income also includes impairment losses.

Firms can apply the fair value option to marketable securities, in which case firms account for debt securities held to maturity and securities available for sale as if they were trading securities. Firms remeasure these securities to fair value each period and recognize unrealized gains and losses in net income, not other comprehensive income.

Derivative Instruments (Chapter 12)

Firms often acquire derivative instruments to hedge interest rate, exchange rate, commodity price, and other risks. U.S. GAAP and IFRS classify derivatives into three categories:

1. Fair value hedges of a recognized asset or liability or of an unrecognized firm commitment.
2. Cash flow hedges of an existing asset or liability or of a forecasted transaction.
3. Nonhedging derivative.

Firms must designate each derivative as a hedging instrument, or else accounting views the derivative as a nonhedging instrument. Furthermore, firms must designate each hedging instrument as either a fair value hedge or a cash flow hedge. The following summarizes the accounting for each of these three categories of derivatives:

1. Fair value hedges: remeasure both the hedged item and the derivative to fair value each period and recognize any unrealized gains and losses in net income.
2. Cash flow hedges: remeasure the derivative to fair value each period and include the unrealized gain or loss in other comprehensive income to the extent that the derivative instrument is effective in neutralizing risk. When the firm settles the hedged item, transfer the previously unrealized gain or loss from other comprehensive income to net income.
3. Nonhedging derivatives: remeasure the derivative to fair value each period and include the unrealized gain or loss in net income.

Firms can apply the fair value option to derivatives. Under the fair value option, the principal change in accounting for derivatives relates to cash flow hedges. Changes in the fair value of cash flow hedges affect net income as they occur instead of initially affecting other comprehensive income.

INTERCORPORATE INVESTMENTS IN COMMON STOCK (CHAPTER 13)

Firms sometimes invest in the common stock of other entities in order to exert significant influence or control over the other entity. U.S. GAAP and IFRS assume that firms owning between 20% and 50% of the voting stock of another entity can exert significant influence, and firms owning more than 50% can exert control, unless other information indicates the contrary.

A firm that can exert significant influence over another entity accounts for its intercorporate investment using the equity method. The investor recognizes its share of the net income or net loss of the investee, after eliminating any intercompany income items, and increases (in the case of net income) or decreases (in the case of net loss) its investment account in an equal amount. The investor decreases the investment account for dividends received. If the acquisition cost of the investment exceeds the investor's interest in the net assets of the investee at the time of the acquisition, the investor must decide if the excess relates to assets or liabilities of the investee with a limited life. If so, the investor must amortize a portion of the acquisition cost of the investment to reflect the decline in expected benefits. Firms can apply the fair value option to equity method investments under certain conditions.

A firm that controls another entity prepares consolidated financial statements with that entity. The consolidated financial statements reflect the results of the legally separate entities as if they were a single entity. Thus, consolidated financial statements eliminate intercompany balance sheet and income statement accounts and intercompany profit or loss on transactions between the entities. If the parent company does not own 100% of the other entity, the remaining shareholders hold a noncontrolling (formerly, minority) interest. Consolidated balance sheets consolidate all of the assets and liabilities of the controlled entity and then show the claim of noncontrolling shareholders against consolidated net assets as part of shareholders' equity. Likewise, consolidated income statements consolidate all of the revenues and expenses of the controlled entity and then show the portions of the consolidated net income to which the noncontrolling shareholders and the controlling shareholders have a claim.

The usual criterion for preparing consolidated financial statements with another entity is ownership of a majority of the voting stock. A firm might conduct business with or through another entity, which it controls through contractual agreements and ownership of nonequity instruments, not share ownership. In this case, the firm must apply criteria specified in U.S. GAAP and IFRS to determine if the other entity qualifies as a variable interest entity (VIE) under U.S. GAAP or a special purpose entity (SPE) under IFRS. If so, the firm must then assess if it is the primary beneficiary of a VIE under U.S. GAAP or if it controls the SPE under IFRS, in which case it would consolidate the financial statements of the VIE or SPE with its own.

Standard-setting bodies are reconsidering the concept of an accounting entity, including the use of majority equity ownership to gauge control of another entity. The evolving concept of control involves both the capacity to direct the strategic, operating, investing, and financing decisions of another entity and the ability to benefit from value increases and to bear the loss from value decreases of the other entity.

REDEEMABLE PREFERRED SHARES (CHAPTER 14)

The classification of redeemable preferred shares on the balance sheet depends on the conditions for redemption. If only the issuing firm has the option to redeem, then the preferred shares are part of its shareholders' equity. If the issuing firm must redeem the preferred shares (so-called "mandatory redemption"), either at a specified time or upon a specified condition certain to occur, the issuing firm treats the preferred shares as a liability. If the preferred shareholders have the option to require redemption, then the preferred shares appear between liabilities and shareholders' equity under U.S. GAAP and as a liability under IFRS. U.S. authorities are considering adopting the IFRS treatment.

EMPLOYEE STOCK OPTIONS (CHAPTER 14)

Firms compute a fair-value-based measure of employee stock options on the date of the grant using an option-pricing model that incorporates information about the current market price, the exercise price, the expected time between grant and exercise, the expected volatility of the stock, the expected dividends, and the risk-free interest rate. Total compensation cost is the number of options the firm expects to vest times the value per option. Firms amortize this total cost over the requisite service period, which is the expected period of benefit. This period is usually the period between the grant date and the vesting date. Firms do not typically remeasure most types of stock options after the initial grant date.

ISSUE OF SECURITIES WITH WARRANTS ATTACHED OR CONVERSION PRIVILEGES (CHAPTER 14)

Firms sometimes issue bonds with stock warrants attached. They allocate the amount received between the bonds and the warrants based on their respective fair values. When firms issue convertible bonds U.S. GAAP requires firms to allocate the full issue price to the bonds and none to the conversion feature. IFRS, however, requires firms to allocate the issue price between the bonds and the conversion feature. The allocation involves estimating the issue price of bonds with terms similar to those issued but without the conversion feature. The firm allocates this amount to the bonds and the remainder of the issue price to the conversion option.

TREASURY SHARES (CHAPTER 14)

Firms recognize no gain or loss from purchasing their own shares or reissuing previously purchased shares. Differences between the purchase and reissue price are not earnings transactions but affect contributed capital accounts. Firms account for the purchase of treasury shares using either the cost method or the par value method or the constructive retirement method. These methods differ in terms of the shareholders' equity accounts affected, but all result in an equal reduction in total shareholders' equity when firms purchase their own shares.

ACCOUNTING FOR ERRORS AND CHANGES IN ACCOUNTING PRINCIPLES AND CHANGES IN ACCOUNTING ESTIMATES (CHAPTER 14)

Firms account for material errors in previously issued financial statements by retrospectively restating net income of prior periods and adjusting the beginning balance in Retained Earnings of the current period. If practical, firms also account for *voluntary* changes in accounting principles, such as from a LIFO to a FIFO cost-flow assumption for inventories, by retrospectively restating net income of prior periods and adjusting the beginning balance in Retained Earnings of the current period. Firms account for changes in accounting principles *required* by a new reporting standard in accordance with the guidance specified in the standard. Firms account for changes in estimates, such as for depreciable lives, uncollectible accounts, or warranty cost, prospectively, in current and future periods' earnings.

SUMMARY OF FINANCIAL REPORTING STANDARDS

Exhibit 16.1 summarizes certain differences between U.S. GAAP and IFRS. This exhibit also appears on the inside front cover of the book. The FASB and the IASB have agreed to, and issued, a Memorandum of Understanding (MoU) that lays out plans and timetables for improving and converging U.S. GAAP and IFRS to a single set of high-quality standards. The Web sites of the FASB and IASB contain information on the current status of various convergence activities.

In light of the ongoing convergence activities of the FASB and the IASB, one unanswered question relates to the two boards' future roles. Will both the FASB and the IASB continue to provide authoritative guidance in some coordinated structure, or will one of the boards, most likely the FASB, cease to exist? The response to this question depends on several factors:

1. A decision by the U.S. Securities and Exchange Commission to permit or require U.S. registrants to apply IFRS without reconciliation to U.S. GAAP in their reports filed with the SEC.

2. The ability of the IASB to develop and maintain a strong financial base that will permit it to operate independently and to fund the research needed to set worldwide accounting standards.

EXHIBIT 16.1 **Examples of Differences Between U.S. GAAP and IFRS**

Chapter	Reporting Topic	U.S. GAAP	IFRS
7	Revenue recognition	Must have delivered a product or service in return for net assets capable of sufficiently reliable measurement. Over 200 documents provide industry-specific and transaction-specific guidance.	One general standard and a few documents with industry-specific guidance. For long-term contracts, use percentage-of-completion method if amounts are estimable. Otherwise, use cost-recovery method. Completed contract method not permitted.
8	Inventories and cost of goods sold: lower of cost or market	Measurement of market value uses a combination of replacement cost and net realizable values.	Measurement of market value uses net realizable value.
8	Inventories: cost flow	Specific identification, FIFO, weighted-average, and LIFO cost-flow assumptions permitted.	Specific identification, FIFO, and weighted-average cost-flow assumptions permitted. LIFO not permitted.
9	Property, plant, and equipment: revaluations above acquisition cost	Not permitted.	Permitted under certain conditions.
9	Research and development cost	Recognize as an expense in the period incurred.	Recognize research costs as an expense in the period incurred. Capitalize development costs and amortize them over the expected period of benefit.
9	Property, plant, and equipment: impairment loss	If carrying value exceeds undiscounted cash flows value, recognize an impairment loss equal to the excess of carrying value over fair value.	Recognize an impairment loss for the excess of carrying value over recoverable amount. Recoverable amount is larger of the fair value less cost to sell and the value in use. Can subsequently reverse the impairment loss but not above acquisition cost.
9	Intangible assets with finite lives: impairment loss	If undiscounted cash flows exceed carrying value, recognize an impairment loss equal to the excess of carrying value over fair value.	Recognize an impairment loss for the excess of carrying value over recoverable amount. Recoverable amount is larger of the fair value less cost to sell and the value in use. Can subsequently reverse the impairment loss but not above acquisition cost.
9	Intangible assets, other than goodwill, with indefinite lives: impairment loss	Recognize an impairment loss for the excess of carrying value over fair value.	Recognize an impairment loss for the excess of carrying value over recoverable amount. Recoverable amount is the larger of the fair value less cost to sell and the value in use. Test these assets annually for impairment losses and recoveries of impairment losses.

(continued)

3. The willingness of the U.S. government, stock exchanges, accounting firms, business firms, investors, and others to cede control of the standard-setting process and the types of information reported in the financial statements to an entity outside the United States.

Responses to these issues will emerge in the years ahead.

FINANCIAL STATEMENT PRESENTATION PROJECT

The preceding section on financial reporting standards discussed the accounting for certain assets, liabilities, shareholders' equities, revenues, expenses, and other financial statement items. The FASB and the IASB have undertaken a joint project to provide converged and improved guidance for presentation of these items in the financial statements. The objective is to develop guidance for preparing a set of integrated financial statements that classifies activities related to financing (both with owners and nonowners) separately from business activities (which include operating activities and investing activities). This section summarizes the results of deliberations thus far and illustrates the type of presentations suggested by both Boards' preliminary views.

EXHIBIT 16.1   (Continued)

9	Goodwill: impairment loss	Step 1: Compare the carrying value to the fair value of a reporting unit. If the carrying value exceeds the fair value, proceed to Step 2. Step 2: Allocate the fair value of the reporting unit to assets and liabilities based on their fair values and any excess to goodwill. Recognize an impairment loss on the goodwill if the carrying value exceeds the allocated fair value. Step 3: Test goodwill annually for impairment loss or whenever a goodwill impairment loss is probable.	Step 1: Compare the carrying value to the recoverable amount for a cash-generating unit. Step 2: Recognize an impairment loss for any excess of carrying value over recoverable amount of the cash-generating unit. First write down goodwill and then allocate any remaining loss to other assets based on their relative recoverable amounts. Step 3: Test goodwill annually for impairment losses.
11	Contingent obligations (U.S. GAAP) and Provisions (IFRS)	Recognize as liabilities if payment is probable (probability usually exceeds 80%). Measure at low end of range if no one estimate is better than any other.	Recognize as liabilities if payment is more likely than not (probability exceeds 50%). Measure at the best estimate of the amount to settle the obligation.
10, 12	Fair value	Provides a hierarchy of measurement inputs from market prices of identical items to other observable inputs to unobservable (entity-developed) inputs.	No specific measurement guidance.
11	Leases	A lease is a capital lease if it satisfies one of four conditions; otherwise, it is an operating lease.	Judgment required based on several indicators to identify the entity that enjoys the rewards and bears the risk of leasing.
13	Consolidation of joint ventures	Not permitted. Firms must use the equity method.	Firms have option to use proportionate consolidation or the equity method.
13	Variable interest entities (VIE) or special purpose entities (SPE): consolidation policy	Primary beneficiary consolidates a VIE.	Firm controlling a SPE consolidates it.
14	Preferred stock redeemable at the option of the preferred shareholders	Classified between liabilities and shareholders' equity.	Classified as a liability.
14	Convertible bonds	Allocate issue price entirely to bonds and none to conversion option.	Allocate issue price between the bonds and the conversion option.

OVERVIEW OF PROPOSED FINANCIAL STATEMENT PRESENTATION

Figure 16.2 depicts the preliminary views for the format of the financial statements. The proposed reporting format incorporates the following general guidelines:

1. Classifications are consistent across the three financial statements. The proposed requirement to use consistent categories aims to aid users in understanding how events and transactions affect a firm's financial position, cash flows, and earnings. For example, consider the classification of changes in marketable securities during a period:

Marketable Securities, December 31, 2008 (Statement of Financial Position)	$450,000
Purchases of Marketable Securities During 2009 (Cash Outflow in the Statement of Cash Flows)	145,000

Sales During 2009 for $148,000 of Marketable Securities with a Carrying Value
  of $130,000 at a Realized Gain of $18,000 (Cash Inflow in the Statement
  of Cash Flows of $148,000; Realized Gain in Net Income in the Statement
  of Comprehensive Income of $18,000) . . . .
	(130,000)

Remeasurement of Marketable Securities to Fair Value (Unrealized Gain
  in Other Comprehensive Income in the Statement of Comprehensive Income
  of $12,000) . . . .
	12,000

Marketable Securities, December 31, 2009 (Statement of Financial Position)	$477,000

The consistent classification of transactions relating to marketable securities permits the statement user to understand more easily why the amounts in marketable securities

FIGURE 16.2	Proposed Format of Financial Statements

Statement of Financial Position	Statement of Cash Flows	Statement of Comprehensive Income
Business • Operating assets and liabilities • Investing assets and liabilities	**Business** • Operating cash flows • Investing cash flows	**Business** • Operating income and expense • Investment income and expense
Financing • Financing assets • Financing liabilities	**Financing** • Financing asset cash flows • Financing liability cash flows	**Financing** • Financing asset income • Financing liability expense
Income Taxes	**Income Taxes**	**Income Taxes** *(related to business and financing)*
Discontinued Operations	**Discontinued Operations**	**Discontinued Operations, Net of Tax**
Equity	**Equity**	**Other Comprehensive Income, Net of Tax**

Source: Financial Accounting Standards Board, "Financial Statement Presentation Project, Phase B: Summary of Tentative Preliminary Views as of June 30, 2008."

changed during the period and how those changes affected cash flows and comprehensive income. The information needed to perform this analysis appears in the financial reports as currently presented, but the user must search the financial statements and notes to access the information.

2. The proposed format uses five categories, although the Business section includes operating and investing subcategories.

   a. **Business** Assets and liabilities related to a firm's primary business activities to create value, such as producing goods or providing services.

      ■ **Operating** Assets and liabilities related to the central purposes(s) for which an entity is in business; its primary revenue and expense-generating activities. This category likely includes accounts receivable; inventories; prepayments; property, plant, and equipment;[7] accounts payable; advances from customers; and salaries payable.

      ■ **Investing** Assets and liabilities unrelated to a firm's central business purpose and invested to generate a return. This category might include marketable securities and investments in affiliates (see further discussion below).

   b. **Financing** Assets and liabilities related to financing a firm's business activities. The financing classification envisions assets and liabilities that are independent of specific business activities and interchangeable with other sources of financing. For example, accounts payable to suppliers relates specifically to the business purpose of acquiring inventory and would likely appear as an operating item. Proceeds of long-term debt would likely appear as a financing item.

   c. **Income Taxes** Prepaid income taxes, income taxes payable, deferred tax assets, and deferred tax liabilities in the statement of financial position, taxes paid during the period in the statement of cash flows, and income tax expense in the statement of comprehensive income, allocated to continuing operations, discontinued operations, other comprehensive income, and other items charged or credited directly to equity.

   d. **Discontinued Operations** Assets, liabilities, cash flows, and income related to discontinued operations as defined by other reporting standards. The proposed reporting framework eliminates extraordinary items.

---

[7]The proposed classification of operating, investing, and financing activities differs from that currently used to prepare the statement of cash flows.

e. **Equity** The same activities currently classified as shareholders' equity, including issuances and repurchases of common or preferred stock and dividends.

Under the proposed framework, a firm would classify each asset and liability based on its use by that firm. For example, a firm that invests temporarily excess cash from operations in marketable securities to provide liquidity would likely classify marketable securities as an operating asset. On the other hand, a firm might issue long-term bonds every three years to provide financing for various business purposes and invest the cash temporarily in marketable securities. That firm might classify those marketable securities as a financing asset. Issuing debt every three years instead of issuing a smaller amount of debt every year saves transactions costs.

STATEMENT OF FINANCIAL POSITION

Under the proposed reporting format, firms need not present a statement of financial position in which assets equal liabilities plus shareholders' equity. Although this balance sheet equality still holds, firms may find that classification consistency across the three principal financial statements requires a different pattern of presentation. Thus, firms will no longer refer to this financial statement as a *balance sheet*. Firms would still show short-term and long-term subcategories of assets and liabilities. **Exhibit 16.2** presents a statement of financial position for Nordstrom, Inc. using one possible format.

The classification of several items requires additional explanation.

1. **Investment in Asset-Backed Securities:** Nordstrom transfers selected accounts receivable to a trust in return for cash and an interest in the cash flows that the trust will generate when it collects the receivables. Nordstrom includes its interest in Investment in Asset-Backed Securities. Although the transfer of the accounts receivable is a means of financing, the funding relates to an operating asset. Thus, the Investment in Asset-Backed Securities appears as a short-term operating asset.

2. **Land, Buildings, Equipment, Goodwill, and Trade Name:** These accounts relate to Nordstrom's principal business of operating retail stores or to other retail stores acquired and therefore appear as long-term operating assets. Cash flows paid to acquire, or received from disposing of, these assets appear in the Investing section of the statement of cash flows under current reporting practices.

3. **Deferred Property Incentives, net:** This account includes cash advances from developers to build stores in certain locations. The incentives relate to a long-term operating asset, so we classify this item as a long-term operating liability.

4. **Other Long-Term Operating Liabilities:** This account includes underfunded defined benefit retirement plan obligations, so we classify it as an operating liability.

5. **Short-Term Investments:** Nordstrom likely acquired the securities as a temporary investment of excess cash and would classify them as an operating asset. We classify them as an investing asset in order to illustrate the presentation of an investing activity.

6. **Deferred Tax Assets:** Nordstrom discloses its long-term deferred tax assets in notes to the financial statements and includes them in Other Assets on its conventional balance sheet. **Exhibit 16.2** includes these assets in the Income Taxes section.

Exhibit 16.2 shows an equality between net assets and liabilities and shareholders' equity. Under the proposed presentation, firms need not present the statement of financial position to reflect this or any other specific equality. **Exhibit 16.2** also nets short-term operating liabilities against short-term operating assets and long-term operating liabilities against long-term operating assets. This would also not be a required format. The statement of financial position might list short- and long-term operating assets and then subtract short- and long-term operating liabilities.

STATEMENT OF CASH FLOWS

The proposed reporting format for the statement of cash flows separates cash flows into the same categories as those previously discussed for the statement of financial position. The definitions of operating, investing, and financing differ from those in the existing guidance for the statement of cash flows. In addition, the proposed statement of cash flows no longer includes

EXHIBIT 16.2

Nordstrom, Inc.
Statement of Financial Position
Under the Proposed Statement Format
(amounts in thousands)

	February 3, 2007	January 28, 2006
BUSINESS ASSETS AND LIABILITIES		
Short-Term Operating Assets:		
Cash	$ 402,559	$ 462,656
Accounts Receivable, net	684,376	639,558
Investment in Asset-Backed Securities	428,175	561,136
Merchandise Inventories	997,289	955,978
Prepaid Expenses and Other Short-Term Operating Assets	60,474	55,359
Total Short-Term Operating Assets	$ 2,572,873	$ 2,674,687
Short-Term Operating Liabilities:		
Accounts Payable	$ (576,796)	$ (540,019)
Accrued Salaries, Wages, and Retirement Benefits	(339,965)	(285,982)
Other Current Liabilities	(433,487)	(409,076)
Total Short-Term Operating Liabilities	$(1,350,248)	$(1,235,077)
Net Short-Term Operating Assets	$ 1,222,625	$ 1,439,610
Long-Term Operating Assets:		
Land, Buildings, and Equipment, net	$ 1,757,215	$ 1,773,871
Goodwill	51,714	51,714
Acquired Trade Name	84,000	84,000
Other Long-Term Operating Assets	133,827	127,834
Total Long-Term Operating Assets	$ 2,026,756	$ 2,037,419
Long-Term Operating Liabilities:		
Deferred Property Incentives, net	$ (356,062)	$ (364,382)
Other Long-Term Operating Liabilities	(240,200)	(213,198)
Total Long-Term Operating Liabilities	$ (596,262)	$ (577,580)
Net Long-Term Operating Assets	$ 1,430,494	$ 1,459,839
Net Short-Term and Long-Term Operating Assets	$ 2,653,119	$ 2,899,449
Short-Term Investing Assets:		
Short-Term Investments	—	54,000
Net Business Assets and Liabilities	$ 2,653,119	$ 2,953,449
FINANCING ASSETS AND LIABILITIES		
Short-Term Financing Liabilities:		
Current Portion of Long-Term Debt	$ (6,800)	$ (306,618)
Long-Term Financing Liabilities:		
Bonds Payable	(623,652)	(627,776)
Total Financing Liabilities	$ (630,452)	$ (934,394)
INCOME TAXES		
Short-Term Deferred Tax Assets, net	$ 169,320	$ 145,470
Short-Term Income Taxes Payable	(76,095)	(81,617)
Long-Term Deferred Tax Assets, net	52,629	9,773
Total Income Tax Assets, net	$ 145,854	$ 73,626
Net Assets and Liabilities	$ 2,168,521	$ 2,092,681
EQUITY		
Common Stock	$ 826,421	$ 685,934
Unearned Stock Compensation	—	(327)
Retained Earnings	1,350,680	1,404,366
Accumulated Other Comprehensive Income	(8,580)	2,708
Total Shareholders' Equity	$ 2,168,521	$ 2,092,681

cash equivalents as cash, and would require firms to use the direct method of computing cash flow from operations. The direct method shows cash receipts from customers and cash disbursements for operating costs and expenses. The direct method of reporting cash flow from operations parallels the reporting of revenues and expenses in the income statement more closely than showing cash flow from operations using the indirect method.

Exhibit 16.3 shows the statement of cash flows for Nordstrom, Inc. following the proposed format.

Operating cash flows in **Exhibit 16.3** differ from cash flow from operations in the usual statement of cash flows in several respects:

1. Use of the direct method instead of the indirect method of computing cash flow from operations.
2. Classification of cash flows related to purchases and sales of property, plant, and equipment as operating cash flows, not investing cash flows.

EXHIBIT 16.3

Nordstrom, Inc.
Statement of Cash Flows
Under the Proposed Reporting Format
(amounts in thousands)

Fiscal Year:	2006	2005	2004
BUSINESS CASH FLOWS			
Operating Cash Flows:			
Cash Receipts from Customers	$ 8,516,461	$ 7,728,638	$ 7,153,077
Cash Received from Finance Charges	366,509	60,564	22,972
Cash Disbursed for Merchandise and Related Buying and Occupancy Costs	(4,993,064)	(4,551,298)	(4,262,623)
Cash Disbursed for Selling, General, and Administrative Expenses	(2,258,160)	(2,073,867)	(1,972,557)
Cash Received from Sales of Property, Plant, and Equipment	224	107	5,473
Cash Disbursed to Acquire Property, Plant, and Equipment	(264,437)	(271,659)	(246,851)
Cash Disbursed for Other Operating Cash Flows	(8,067)	(8,366)	(2,830)
Total Operating Cash Flows	$ 1,359,466	$ 884,119	$ 696,661
Investing Cash Flows:			
Cash Received for Interest on Investments in Securities	$ 14,654	$ 13,273	$ 7,929
Cash Received from Sales of Investments in Securities	163,550	530,750	3,366,425
Cash Disbursed for Purchases of Investments in Securities	(109,550)	(542,925)	(3,232,250)
Total Investing Cash Flows	$ 68,654	$ 1,098	$ 142,104
Total Business Cash Flows	$ 1,428,120	$ 885,217	$ 838,765
FINANCING CASH FLOWS			
Cash Disbursed for Interest Expense	$ (55,367)	$ (57,187)	$ (88,876)
Cash Disbursed to Repay Long-Term Debt	(307,559)	(101,047)	(205,252)
Other Financing Cash Flows	(50,431)	4,594	(3,432)
Total Financing Cash Flows	$ (413,357)	$ (153,640)	$ (297,560)
INCOME TAX CASH FLOWS			
Cash Disbursed for Income Tax Expense	$ (448,668)	$ (343,891)	$ (253,576)
EQUITY CASH FLOWS			
Cash Receipts from Exercise of Stock Options	$ 89,193	$ 73,023	$ 87,061
Cash Receipts from Employee Stock Purchase Plan	16,300	15,600	12,892
Cash Disbursed for Dividends	(110,158)	(87,196)	(67,240)
Cash Disbursed to Repurchase Common Stock	(621,527)	(287,080)	(300,000)
Total Equity Cash Flows	$ (626,192)	$ (285,653)	$ (267,287)
Net (Decrease) Increase in Cash	$ (60,097)	$ 102,033	$ 20,342
Cash at Beginning of Year	462,656	360,623	340,281
Cash at End of Year	$ 402,559	$ 462,656	$ 360,623

3. Classification of cash inflows from investment income as an investing, not an operating, activity.

4. Classification of cash outflows for interest and other debt service as a financing, not an operating, activity.

5. Classification of cash outflows for income taxes as an income tax, not an operating, activity.

STATEMENT OF COMPREHENSIVE INCOME

The proposed reporting format combines net income with other comprehensive income into a statement of comprehensive income. **Exhibit 16.4** presents the statement of comprehensive income for Nordstrom, Inc. in the proposed reporting format.

The proposed reporting format provides for the disclosure of operating income, the pretax income recognized from using net operating assets. For Nordstrom these net operating assets include accounts receivable; investment in asset-backed securities; inventories; property, plant, and equipment; goodwill; and brand name. Neither U.S. GAAP nor IFRS currently defines operating income, although many firms voluntarily report an amount for operating income.

The proposed format includes both net income and other comprehensive income in a single statement. Although authoritative guidance currently permits this reporting format, most firms include other comprehensive in the statement of changes in shareholders' equity.

ASSESSMENT OF PROPOSED REPORTING FORMAT

The proposed reporting format classifies related accounts consistently across the three financial statements, permitting the user to understand the amounts at the beginning and end of the period and how cash flows and comprehensive income affected the change in the amounts

EXHIBIT 16.4

Nordstrom, Inc.
Statement of Comprehensive Income
Under the Proposed Reporting Format
(amounts in thousands)

Fiscal Year:	2006	2005	2004
BUSINESS INCOME			
Sales Revenue	$ 8,560,698	$ 7,722,860	$ 7,131,388
Income from Finance Charges	238,525	196,354	172,942
Cost of Goods Sold, Including Related Buying and Occupancy Costs	(5,353,949)	(4,888,023)	(4,559,388)
Selling, General, and Administrative Expenses	(2,296,863)	(2,100,666)	(2,020,233)
Operating Income	$ 1,148,411	$ 930,525	$ 724,709
Interest Revenue on Investments in Securities	14,654	13,273	7,929
Total Business Income	$ 1,163,065	$ 943,798	$ 732,638
FINANCING			
Interest Expense	(57,412)	(58,573)	(85,357)
INCOME TAXES			
Income Tax Expense	(427,654)	(333,886)	(253,831)
Net Income	$ 677,999	$ 551,339	$ 393,450
OTHER COMPREHENSIVE INCOME			
Foreign Currency Translation Adjustment	1,309	(1,815)	493
Unrecognized Gain (Loss) on Supplemental Employee Retirement Plan	3,032	(7,742)	(119)
Fair Value Adjustment to Investment in Asset-Backed Securities	(2,805)	2,930	93
Total Other Comprehensive Income	$ 1,536	$ (6,627)	$ 467
Comprehensive Income	$ 679,535	$ 544,712	$ 393,917

during the period. The proposed reporting format does not change the recognition and measurement of assets, liabilities, revenues, expenses, and cash flows, but does affect the arrangement and classification of these items in the principal financial statements. The extent of the proposed changes in arrangement and classification is considerable and will require users to rethink how they read, interpret, and analyze financial reports.

PROBLEM 16.1 for Self-Study

Review of Chapters 1–16. A set of financial statements for Kaplan Corporation follows, including a consolidated income statement for 2009 (**Exhibit 16.5**), a comparative consolidated balance sheet on December 31, 2008 and 2009 (**Exhibit 16.6**), and a consolidated statement of cash flows for 2009 (**Exhibit 16.7**). A series of notes provides additional information on certain items in the financial statements.

Respond to each of the questions beginning on page 787, using information from the financial statements and notes for Kaplan Corporation. We suggest that you study the statements and notes carefully before attempting to respond to the questions.

Note 1: Kaplan Corporation selected the following accounting policies:

- *Basis of consolidation.* Kaplan Corporation consolidates its financial statements with those of Heimann Corporation, an 80%-owned subsidiary acquired on January 2, 2008.

- *Marketable securities.* Kaplan Corporation classifies its marketable securities as available for sale. These securities appear at fair value.

- *Accounts receivable.* Kaplan Corporation uses the allowance method for uncollectible accounts.

- *Inventories.* Kaplan Corporation uses a last-in, first-out (LIFO) cost-flow assumption for inventories and cost of goods sold.

- *Investments.* Kaplan Corporation reports investments of less than 20% of the outstanding common stock of other companies at fair value and applies the equity method for investments of 20% to 50% of the outstanding common stock of unconsolidated affiliates.

(continued)

EXHIBIT 16.5	Kaplan Corporation Consolidated Income Statement For 2009 (all dollar amounts in thousands) (Problem 16.1 for Self-Study)

Revenues and Gains

Sales	$12,000
Equity in Earnings of Unconsolidated Affiliates	300
Dividend Revenue	20
Gain on Sale of Marketable Securities	30
Total Revenues and Gains	$12,350

Expenses and Losses

Cost of Goods Sold	$ 7,200
Selling and Administrative	2,709
Loss on Sale of Equipment	80
Interest (Notes 7 and 8)	561
Total Expenses and Losses	$10,550
Net Income Before Income Taxes	$ 1,800
Income Tax Expense	540
Net Income	$ 1,260

EXHIBIT 16.6

Kaplan Corporation
Consolidated Balance Sheets
December 31, 2008 and 2009
(all dollar amounts in thousands)
(Problem 16.1 for Self-Study)

	December 31, 2009	December 31, 2008
ASSETS		
Current Assets		
Cash	$ 2,919	$ 1,470
Marketable Securities (Note 2)	550	450
Accounts Receivable (net; Note 3)	2,850	2,300
Inventories (Note 4)	3,110	2,590
Prepayments	970	800
Total Current Assets	$10,399	$ 7,610
Investments (Note 5)		
Investment in Maher Corporation (10%)	$ 185	$ 200
Investment in Johnson Corporation (30%)	410	310
Investment in Burton Corporation (40%)	930	800
Total Investments	$ 1,525	$ 1,310
Property, Plant, and Equipment		
Land	$ 500	$ 400
Buildings	940	800
Equipment	3,800	3,300
Total Acquisition Cost	$ 5,240	$ 4,500
Less Accumulated Depreciation	(930)	(1,200)
Net Property, Plant, and Equipment	$ 4,310	$ 3,300
Patent (Note 6)	$ 80	$ 90
Total Assets	$16,314	$12,310
LIABILITIES AND SHAREHOLDERS' EQUITY		
Current Liabilities		
Note Payable (Note 7)	$ 2,000	$ —
Accounts Payable	1,425	1,070
Salaries Payable	900	1,100
Interest Payable	100	0
Income Taxes Payable	375	250
Total Current Liabilities	$ 4,800	$ 2,420
Long-Term Liabilities		
Bonds Payable (Note 8)	$ 6,209	$ 6,209
Deferred Tax Liability	940	820
Total Long-Term Liabilities	$ 7,149	$ 7,029
Shareholders' Equity		
Common Shares $(10 par value)	$ 600	$ 500
Additional Paid-In Capital	1,205	800
Accumulated Other Comprehensive Income:		
Unrealized Holding Loss on Marketable Securities	(70)	(50)
Unrealized Holding Loss on Investments in Securities	(40)	(25)
Retained Earnings	2,690	1,666
Total	$ 4,385	$ 2,891
Less Treasury Shares (at cost)	(20)	(30)
Total Shareholders' Equity	$ 4,365	$ 2,861
Total Liabilities and Shareholders' Equity	$16,314	$12,310

- *Buildings and equipment.* Kaplan Corporation uses the straight-line method of depreciation for financial reporting and uses accelerated depreciation for tax reporting.

- *Patent.* The corporation amortizes patents straight line over a period of 10 years.

- *Interest on long-term debt.* The calculation of interest expense on bonds payable uses the effective interest method.

- *Deferred income taxes.* The corporation provides deferred income taxes for temporary differences between book income and taxable income.

Note 2: Marketable securities appear at fair values that are less than their acquisition cost by $50,000 on December 31, 2008, and by $70,000 on December 31, 2009.

Note 3: Accounts receivable appear net of an allowance for uncollectibles of $200,000 on December 31, 2008, and $250,000 on December 31, 2009. Selling and administrative expenses include bad debt expense of $120,000.

Note 4: Inventories comprise the following:

	December 31, 2009	December 31, 2008
Raw Materials	$ 380,000	$ 330,000
Work-in-Process	530,000	460,000
Finished Goods	2,200,000	1,800,000
Total	$3,110,000	$2,590,000

The current cost of inventories exceeded the amounts computed on a LIFO basis by $420,000 on December 31, 2008, and $730,000 on December 31, 2009.

Note 5: Burton Corporation had net income of $400,000 and paid dividends of $75,000 in 2009.

Note 6: On January 2, 2008, Kaplan Corporation acquired 100% of the outstanding common shares of Heimann Corporation by issuing 20,000 shares of Kaplan Corporation common stock. The fair value of Kaplan Corporation's shares on January 2, 2008, was $40 per share. The fair values of the recorded assets and liabilities of Heimann Corporation equal their carrying values. Kaplan Corporation attributes any difference between the acquisition price and the fair value of the recorded net assets to a patent that Heimann Corporation developed internally by its research and development efforts. Kaplan Corporation amortizes the patent over a period of 10 years from the date of acquisition.

Note 7: Current liabilities include a one-year, 5% note payable due on January 1, 2010.

Note 8: Bonds payable are as follows:

	December 31, 2009	December 31, 2008
4%, $2,000,000 Bonds Due Dec. 31, 2014, with Interest Payable Semiannually	$1,829,390	$1,800,920
10%, $3,000,000 Bonds Due Dec. 31, 2018, with Interest Payable Semiannually	3,379,790	3,407,720
8%, $1,000,000 Bonds Due Dec. 31, 2024, with Interest Payable Semiannually	1,000,000	1,000,000
Total	$6,209,180	$6,208,640

Required

a. Kaplan Corporation sold marketable securities originally costing $180,000 during 2009. Ascertain the price at which it sold these securities.

b. Refer to part a. Compute the cost of marketable securities purchased during 2009.

c. What was the amount of specific customers' accounts that Kaplan Corporation wrote off as uncollectible during 2009?

d. Compute the amount of cash collected from customers during the year.

(continued)

e. Compute the cost of units completed and transferred to the finished goods inventory during 2009.

f. Direct labor and overhead costs incurred in manufacturing during the year totaled $4,500,000. Compute the cost of raw materials purchased during 2009.

g. Assume that the amounts disclosed in Note 4 for the current cost of inventories represent the amounts that would result from using a first-in, first-out (FIFO) cost-

(continued)

EXHIBIT 16.7

Kaplan Corporation
Consolidated Statement of Cash Flows for 2009
(all dollar amounts in thousands)
(Problem 16.1 for Self-Study)

OPERATIONS

Net Income	$ 1,260	
Additions:		
Depreciation	560	
Deferred Taxes	120	
Loss on Sale of Equipment	80	
Excess of Interest Expense over Coupon Payments	28	
Amortization of Patent	10	
Increase in Accounts Payable	355	
Increase in Interest Payable	100	
Increase in Income Taxes Payable	125	
Subtractions:		
Gain on Sale of Marketable Securities	(30)	
Equity in Earnings of Affiliates in Excess of Dividends Received	(180)	
Amortization of Premium on Bonds	(28)	
Increase in Accounts Receivable	(550)	
Increase in Inventories	(520)	
Increase in Prepayments	(170)	
Decrease in Salaries Payable	(200)	
Cash Flow from Operations		$ 960

INVESTING

Sale of Marketable Securities	$ 210	
Sale of Equipment	150	
Investment in Johnson Corporation	(50)	
Purchase of Marketable Securities	(300)	
Acquisition of:		
Land	(100)	
Building	(300)	
Equipment	(1,400)	
Cash Flow from Investing		(1,790)

FINANCING

Increase in Notes Payable	$ 2,000	
Common Stock Issued	500	
Treasury Stock Sold	15	
Dividends	(236)	
Cash Flow from Financing		2,279
Net Change in Cash		$ 1,449
Cash, January 1		1,470
Cash, December 31		$ 2,919

flow assumption. Compute the cost of goods sold if the firm had used FIFO rather than LIFO.

h. Prepare an analysis that explains the causes of the changes in each of the three intercorporate investment accounts.

i. Prepare an analysis that explains the change in each of the following accounts during 2009: Land; Building; Equipment; and Accumulated Depreciation.

j. Give the journal entry that Kaplan Corporation made on January 2, 2008, when it acquired Heimann Corporation.

k. Compute the carrying value of the net assets of Heimann Corporation on January 2, 2008.

l. Kaplan Corporation initially priced the 4% bonds payable to yield 6% compounded semiannually. The firm initially priced the 10% bonds to yield 8% compounded semiannually. Use the appropriate present value tables at the back of the book to show that $1,800,920 and $3,407,720 (see Note 8) are the correct carrying values for these two bond issues on December 31, 2008.

m. Calculate the amount of interest expense and any change in the carrying value of the bond liability for 2009 on each of the three long-term bond issues (see Note 8).

n. Compute the amount of income taxes actually paid during 2009.

o. On July 1, 2009, Kaplan Corporation issued 10,000 shares of its common stock on the open market for $50 cash per share. Prepare an analysis explaining the change during 2009 in each of the following accounts: Common Shares; Additional Paid-in Capital; Retained Earnings; and Treasury Shares.

SOLUTION TO SELF-STUDY PROBLEM

SUGGESTED SOLUTION TO PROBLEM 16.1 FOR SELF-STUDY

(Kaplan Corporation; review of **Chapters 1–16**)

a.

Cost of Marketable Securities Sold	$180,000
Gain on Sale (from Income Statement)	30,000
Selling Price	$210,000

The statement of cash flows shows the $210,000 cash proceeds from the sale as an investing activity. The accountant must subtract the gain on sale of marketable securities from net income in the operations section to avoid overstating the amount of cash inflow from the transaction.

b.

Marketable Securities at Fair Value on December 31, 2008	$ 450,000
Plus Cost of Marketable Securities Purchased	?
Less Cost of Marketable Securities Sold	(180,000)
Less Increase in Unrealized Holding Loss (OCI)	(20,000)
Marketable Securities at Fair Value on December 31, 2009	$ 550,000

The cost of marketable securities purchased during 2009 was $300,000. The statement of cash flows reports these purchases as an investing activity. The recognition of an unrealized holding loss of $20,000 from fair value declines of marketable securities did not reduce net income or use cash. Thus, the accountant need not adjust net income when computing cash flow from operations.

c.

Allowance for Uncollectibles, December 31, 2008	$200,000
Plus Bad Debt Expense During 2009	120,000
Less Specific Customers' Accounts Written Off as Uncollectible During 2009	?
Allowance for Uncollectibles, December 31, 2009	$250,000

Specific customers' accounts written off as uncollectible during 2009 totaled $70,000.

d.

Gross Accounts Receivable, December 31, 2008[a]	$ 2,500,000
Plus Sales During the Year	12,000,000
Less Gross Accounts Receivable, December 31, 2009[b].	(3,100,000)
Cash Sales Plus Accounts Collected or Written Off	$11,400,000
Less Write-Offs	(70,000)
Cash Collected During the Year	$11,330,000

[a]$2,300,000 + $200,000.
[b]$2,850,000 + $250,000.

Kaplan Corporation generated $11,330,000 cash from credit customers during 2009. Net income includes $11,880,000 from credit sales (= sales revenue of $12,000,000 − bad debt expense of $120,000). The accountant subtracts the $550,000 difference (= $11,880,000 − $11,330,000) from net income when computing cash flow from operations. This $550,000 amount equals the increase in accounts receivable (net) during 2009 (= $2,850,000 − $2,300,000).

e.

Finished Goods Inventory, December 31, 2008	$1,800,0000
Plus Cost of Units Completed During the Year	?
Less Cost of Units Sold During the Year	(7,200,000)
Finished Goods Inventory, December 31, 2009	$2,200,0000

The cost of units completed was $7,600,000.

f.

Work-in-Process Inventory, December 31, 2008.	$ 460,000
Plus Cost of Raw Materials Used	?
Plus Direct Labor and Manufacturing Overhead Costs Incurred	4,500,000
Less Cost of Units Completed	(7,600,000)
Work-in-Process Inventory, December 31, 2009.	$ 530,000

The cost of raw materials used during 2009 was $3,170,000.

Raw Materials Inventory, December 31, 2008	$ 330,000
Plus Cost of Raw Materials Purchased	?
Less Cost of Raw Materials Used	(3,170,000)
Raw Materials Inventory, December 31, 2009	$ 380,000

The cost of raw materials purchased was $3,220,000.

g.

	LIFO	Difference	FIFO
Inventory, December 31, 2008	$ 2,590,000	$ 420,000	$ 3,010,000
Purchases Plus Costs Incurred	7,720,000	—	7,720,000
Goods Available for Use or Sale	$10,310,000	$ 420,000	$10,730,000
Less Inventory, December 31, 2009.	3,110,000	730,000	3,840,000
Cost of Goods Sold	$ 7,200,000	$(310,000)	$ 6,890,000

Cost of goods sold under FIFO would have been $6,890,000. Note that cost of goods sold under LIFO of $7,200,000 is less than the cost of purchases plus costs incurred of $7,720,000. The accountant subtracts the difference of $520,000 (= $7,720,000 − $7,200,000), which equals the increase in inventories during 2009 (= $3,110,000 − $2,590,000), when converting net income to cash flow from operations. To compute cash flow from operations, the accountant also adds to net income the increase in accounts payable of $355,000 because Kaplan Corporation did not make cash expenditures for the full amount of the increase in inventories.

h.

Investment in Maher Corporation (fair value method)

Balance, December 31, 2008	$200,000
Plus Additional Investments	0
Less Sale of Investments	0
Less Increase in Unrealized Holding Loss on Investments in Securities	15,000
Balance, December 31, 2009	$185,000

Investment in Johnson Corporation (equity method)

Balance, December 31, 2008	$310,000
Plus Additional Investments	50,0000
Plus Equity in Earnings (total equity in earnings of $300,000 from income statement minus equity in Earnings of Burton Corporation of $160,000)	140,000
Less Sale of Investments	0
Less Dividends Received (plug)	(90,000)
Balance, December 31, 2009	$410,000

Investment in Burton Corporation (equity method)

Balance, December 31, 2008	$800,000
Plus Additional Investments	0
Plus Equity in Earnings (.40 × $400,000)	160,000
Less Sale of Investments	0
Less Dividends Received (.40 × $75,000)	(30,000)
Balance, December 31, 2009	$930,000

Kaplan Corporation recognized a total of $300,000 (= $140,000 + $160,000) equity in earnings, yet received dividends of $120,000 (= $90,000 + $30,000). The statement of cash flows shows a subtraction from net income of $180,000 (= $300,000 − $120,000) for the excess of revenues over dividends from investments when computing cash flow from operations. The statement of cash flows reports the additional investment in Johnson Corporation as an investing activity.

i.

Land

Balance, December 31, 2008	$ 400,000
Plus Acquisitions	100,000
Less Disposals	0
Balance, December 31, 2009	$ 500,000

Building

Balance, December 31, 2008	$ 800,000
Plus Acquisitions	300,000
Less Retirements (plug)	(160,000)
Balance, December 31, 2009	$ 940,000

Equipment

Balance, December 31, 2008	$3,300,000
Plus Acquisitions	1,400,000
Less Disposals (plug)	(900,000)
Balance, December 31, 2009	$3,800,000

Accumulated Depreciation

Balance, December 31, 2008	$1,200,000
Plus Depreciation for 2009	560,000
Less Accumulated Depreciation on Building Retired (plug)	(160,000)
Less Accumulated Depreciation on Equipment Sold (see below)	(670,000)
Balance, December 31, 2009	$ 930,000
Selling Price of Equipment Sold	$ 150,000
Loss on Sale of Equipment	80,000
Carrying Value of Equipment Sold	$ 230,000
Cost of Equipment Sold (from above)	$ 900,000
Less Accumulated Depreciation on Equipment Sold (plug)	(670,000)
Carrying Value of Equipment Sold	$ 230,000

The statement of cash flows shows the acquisitions of land, building, and equipment as investing activities. The cash proceeds from the sale of equipment of $150,000 appear as an investing activity. The statement of cash flows shows an addback to net income of $80,000 for the loss on sale of equipment to avoid understating the amount of cash generated from the sale. Depreciation expense for 2009 of $560,000 appears as an addback to net income because this expense does not use cash.

j.

Investment in Heimann Corporation		800,000
Common Stock (20,000 × $10)		200,000
Additional Paid-In Capital (20,000 × $30)		600,000

k.

Cost of Investment in Heimann Corporation	$ 800,000
Patent, $80,000 + (2 × $10,000 amortization per year)	(100,000)
Carrying Value of Net Assets	$ 700,000

l.

4% Bond Issue

$40,000 × 9.9540	$ 398,160
$2,000,000 × .70138	1,402,760
Total	$1,800,920

10% Bond Issue

$150,000 × 13.59033	$2,038,550
$3,000,000 × .45639	1,369,170
Total	$3,407,720

		Liability, Beginning of the Period	Market Interest Rate	Interest Expense	Amount Payable	Addition to (or Reduction in) Liability	Liability, End of the Period
m.	**4% Bond Issue**						
	January 1, 2009	$1,800,920	0.03	$ 54,028	$ 40,000	$ 14,028	$1,814,948
	July 1, 2009	1,814,948	0.03	54,448	40,000	14,448	1,829,396
	Total			$108,476	$ 80,000	$ 28,476	
	10% Bond Issue						
	January 1, 2009	$3,407,720	0.04	$136,309	$150,000	$(13,691)	$3,394,029
	July 1, 2009	3,394,029	0.04	135,761	150,000	(14,239)	3,379,790
	Total			$272,070	$300,000	$(27,930)	
	8% Bond Issue						
	January 1, 2009	$1,000,000	0.04	$ 40,000	$ 40,000	$ 0	$1,000,000
	July 1, 2009	1,000,000	0.04	40,000	40,000	0	1,000,000
	Total			$ 80,000	$ 80,000	$ 0	

Interest expense on the 4% bonds of $108,476 exceeds the amount payable of $80,000. The statement of cash flows shows an addback to net income for the difference, the amortization of discount on these bonds. Interest expense on the 10% bonds of $272,070 is less than the amount payable of $300,000. The statement of cash flows shows a subtraction from net income for the difference, the amortization of premium on these bonds. The statement of cash flows also shows an addition to net income for the increase in interest payable of $100,000, indicating that cash expenditures for interest were less than the amounts accrued as payable for 2009.

n.

Income Taxes Payable, December 31, 2008	$ 250,000
Plus Current Income Tax Expense for 2009 (see below)	420,000
Less Cash Payment during 2009	?
Income Taxes Payable, December 31, 2009	$ 375,000

(continued)

Total Income Tax Expense	$ 540,000
Less Increase in Deferred Tax Liability	(120,000)
Current Income Tax Expense	$ 420,000

Cash payments for income taxes totaled $295,000 during 2009. The statement of cash flows should show an addback to net income of $120,000 for the portion of income tax expense that does not require a current expenditure (that is, the increase in the Deferred Tax Liability account). The statement of cash flows also shows an addition to net income for the increase in income taxes payable of $125,000, indicating that cash expenditures for income taxes were less than the amount accrued as payable for 2009.

	Common Shares		Additional		
	Number of Shares	Amount	Paid-In Capital	Retained Earnings	Treasury Shares
o. Balance, December 31, 2008 . . .	50,000	$500,000	$ 800,000	$1,666,000	$ 30,000
Common Stock Issued	10,000	100,000	400,000	—	—
Treasury Stock Sold	—	—	5,000		(10,000)
Net Income	—	—	—	1,260,000	—
Dividends (plug)[a]	—	—	—	(236,000)	—
Balance, December 31, 2009 . . .	60,000	$600,000	$1,205,000	$2,690,000	$ 20,000

[a]Or, see statement of cash flows.

The $500,000 proceeds from issuing common stock appear as a financing activity on the statement of cash flows. The $15,000 cash proceeds from reissuing treasury stock (= $10,000 + $5,000) also appears as a financing activity. Note that the excess of the $15,000 reissue price over the $10,000 cost of the treasury stock increases additional paid-in capital, not net income.

EXERCISES AND PROBLEMS

EXERCISES

1. **Identifying accounting principles.** Indicate the accounting principle or method described in each of the following statements. Explain your reasoning.

   a. This inventory cost-flow assumption results in reporting the largest net income during periods of rising acquisition costs and nondecreasing inventory levels.

   b. This method of accounting for uncollectible accounts recognizes the implied income reduction in the period of sale.

   c. This method of accounting for long-term investments in the common stock of other corporations usually requires an adjustment to net income to calculate cash flow from operations under the indirect method in the statement of cash flows.

   d. This method of accounting for long-term leases by the lessee gives rise to a noncurrent liability.

   e. This inventory cost-flow assumption results in approximately the same balance sheet amount as the FIFO cost-flow assumption.

   f. This method of recognizing interest expense on bonds provides a uniform annual rate of interest expense over the life of the bond.

   g. The accounting for this type of hedging instrument designated as a hedge results in a change in other comprehensive income each period.

   h. This method of accounting for intercorporate investments in securities can result in a decrease in the investor's total shareholders' equity without affecting the Retained Earnings account.

i. This method of recognizing income from a long-term contract generally results in the least amount of fluctuation in earnings over several periods.

j. When a firm identifies specific customers' accounts as uncollectible and writes them off, this method of accounting results in no change in working capital.

k. The accounting for this type of hedging instrument designated as a hedge affects net income each period but not other comprehensive income.

l. This method of accounting for long-term leases of equipment by the lessor shows on the income statement an amount for depreciation expense.

m. This inventory cost-flow assumption results in inventory balance sheet amounts closest to current replacement cost.

n. This method of accounting for long-term investments in common stock results in recognizing revenue for dividends received or receivable.

o. This method of depreciation generally results in the largest amounts for depreciable assets on the balance sheet during the first several years of an asset's life.

p. This inventory cost-flow assumption results in reporting the smallest net income during periods of falling acquisition costs.

q. This method of accounting for long-term leases of equipment by the lessee results in showing an amount for rent expense on the income statement.

r. This inventory cost-flow assumption results in inventory balance sheet amounts that may differ significantly from current replacement cost.

s. This method of accounting for long-term leases of equipment by the lessor results in showing revenue at the time of signing a lease.

t. This inventory cost-flow assumption can result in substantial changes in the relation between cost of goods sold and sales if inventory quantities decrease during a period.

2. Identifying accounting principles. Indicate the accounting principle or procedure apparently used to record each of the following independent transactions. Also, describe the transaction or event recorded in each case.

a. Cash X
  Dividend Revenue X

Assets	=	Liabilities	+	Shareholders' Equity	(Class.)
+				+	IncSt → RE

b. Unrealized Holding Loss on Marketable Securities Available for Sale X
  Marketable Securities X

Assets	=	Liabilities	+	Shareholders' Equity	(Class.)
−				−	OCI → AOCI

c. Cash X
  Investment in Affiliated Company X

Assets	=	Liabilities	+	Shareholders' Equity	(Class.)
+					
−					

Dividend declared and received from affiliated company.

d. Bad Debt Expense X
  Allowance for Uncollectibles X

(continued)

Assets	=	Liabilities	+	Shareholders' Equity	(Class.)
−				−	IncSt → RE

e. Rent Expense for Lease X
    Cash X

Assets	=	Liabilities	+	Shareholders' Equity	(Class.)
−				−	IncSt → RE

f. Investment in Affiliated Company X
    Equity in Earnings of Affiliated Company X

Assets	=	Liabilities	+	Shareholders' Equity	(Class.)
+				+	IncSt → RE

g. Allowance for Uncollectibles X
    Accounts Receivable X

Assets	=	Liabilities	+	Shareholders' Equity	(Class.)
+					
−					

h. Loss from Price Decline of Inventories X
    Merchandise Inventories X

Assets	=	Liabilities	+	Shareholders' Equity	(Class.)
−				−	IncSt → RE

i. Liability Under Long-Term Lease X
Interest Expense X
    Cash X

Assets	=	Liabilities	+	Shareholders' Equity	(Class.)
−		−		−	IncSt → RE

j. Treasury Stock X
    Cash X

Assets	=	Liabilities	+	Shareholders' Equity	(Class.)
−				−	ContriCap

k. Interest Rate Swap Contract X
    Gain on Remeasurement of Swap Contract
    (Income Statement) X

Assets	=	Liabilities	+	Shareholders' Equity	(Class.)
+				+	IncSt → RE

EXHIBIT 16.8

Chicago Corporation
Consolidated Statement of Income and Retained
Earnings for 2009
(Problem 3)

Revenues

Sales		$13,920,000
Gain on Sale of Machinery and Equipment		200,000
Equity in Earnings of Affiliates:		
Chicago Finance Corporation	$1,800,000	
Rosenwald Company	125,000	
Hutchinson Company	75,000	2,000,000
Total Revenues		$16,120,000

Expenses

Cost of Goods Sold		$ 5,000,000
Employee Payroll Expense		3,000,000
Depreciation of Plant and Equipment and Amortization of Leased Property Rights		1,000,000
Amortization of Patent		125,000
Bad Debt Expense		120,000
Interest Expense		455,000
General Corporate Expenses		420,000
Income Taxes—Current		1,430,000
Income Taxes—Deferred		170,000
Total Expenses		$11,720,000
Net Income		$ 4,400,000
Less: Dividends on Preferred Shares		(120,000)
Dividends on Common Shares		(2,080,000)
Increase in Retained Earnings		$ 2,200,000
Retained Earnings, December 31, 2008		2,800,000
Retained Earnings, December 31, 2009		$ 5,000,000
Basic Earnings per Common Share (based on 1,600,000 average shares outstanding)		$ 2.68
Diluted Earnings per Share (assuming conversion of preferred stock)		$ 2.20

3. **Comprehensive review problem. Exhibits 16.8** and **16.9** (on pages 796 and 797) present a partial set of financial statements of Chicago Corporation for 2009, including a consolidated statement of income and retained earnings for 2009 and consolidated comparative balance sheets at December 31, 2008 and 2009. Questions relating to the financial statements of Chicago Corporation follow. You should study the financial statements before responding to these questions and problems. Additional information is as follows:

   (1) The only transaction affecting common or preferred shares during 2009 was the sale of treasury stock.

   (2) The bonds payable have a maturity (face) value of $4 million.

REQUIRED

   a. Compute the amount of specific customers' accounts that Chicago Corporation wrote off as uncollectible during 2009, assuming that it made no recoveries during 2009 on accounts written off in years prior to 2009.

   b. Chicago Corporation uses the LIFO cost-flow assumption in computing its cost of goods sold and its beginning and ending merchandise inventory amounts. If it had used a FIFO cost-flow assumption, the beginning inventory would have been $1,800,000 and the ending inventory would have been $1,700,000. Compute the actual gross profit (net sales less cost of goods sold) of Chicago Corporation for 2009 under

EXHIBIT 16.9

Chicago Corporation
Consolidated Balance Sheets
December 31
(Problem 3)

December 31:	2009	2008
ASSETS		
Current Assets		
Cash	$ 100,000	$ 200,000
Certificate of Deposit	225,000	—
Accounts Receivable (net of estimated uncollectibles of $100,000 in 2008 and $160,000 in 2009)	600,000	500,000
Merchandise Inventory	1,800,000	1,500,000
Prepayments	200,000	200,000
Total Current Assets	$ 2,925,000	$ 2,400,000
Investments		
Chicago Finance Corporation (40% owned)	$ 4,000,000	$ 2,200,000
Rosenwald Company (50% owned)	1,025,000	900,000
Hutchinson Company (25% owned)	175,000	100,000
Total Investments	$ 5,200,000	$ 3,200,000
Property, Plant, and Equipment		
Land	$ 500,000	$ 400,000
Building	4,000,000	4,000,000
Machinery and Equipment	8,000,000	7,300,000
Property Rights Acquired Under Lease	1,500,000	1,500,000
Total	$14,000,000	$13,200,000
Less Accumulated Depreciation and Amortization	(4,000,000)	(3,800,000)
Total Property, Plant, and Equipment	$10,000,000	$ 9,400,000
Intangibles (at net carrying value)		
Patent	$ 750,000	$ 875,000
Goodwill	1,125,000	1,125,000
Total Intangibles	$ 1,875,000	$ 2,000,000
Total Assets	$20,000,000	$17,000,000
LIABILITIES AND SHAREHOLDERS' EQUITY		
Current Liabilities		
Accounts Payable	$ 550,000	$ 400,000
Advances from Customers	640,000	660,000
Salaries Payable	300,000	240,000
Income Taxes Payable	430,000	300,000
Rent Received in Advance	50,000	—
Other Current Liabilities	460,000	200,000
Total Current Liabilities	$ 2,430,000	$ 1,800,000
Long-Term Debt		
Bonds Payable	$ 3,648,000	$ 3,600,000
Equipment Mortgage Indebtedness	332,000	1,300,000
Capitalized Lease Obligation	1,020,000	1,100,000
Total Long-Term Debt	$ 5,000,000	$ 6,000,000
Deferred Tax Liability	$ 1,570,000	$ 1,400,000
Shareholders' Equity		
Convertible Preferred Stock	$ 2,000,000	$ 2,000,000
Common Stock	2,000,000	2,000,000
Additional Paid-In Capital	3,000,000	2,400,000
Retained Earnings	5,000,000	2,800,000
Total	$12,000,000	$ 9,200,000
Less Cost of Treasury Shares	(1,000,000)	(1,400,000)
Total Shareholders' Equity	$11,000,000	$ 7,800,000
Total Liabilities and Shareholders' Equity	$20,000,000	$17,000,000

LIFO and the corresponding amount of gross profit if it had used FIFO (ignore income tax effects).

c. Refer to part **b**. Did the quantity and acquisition cost of merchandise inventory increase or decrease between the beginning and the end of 2009? Explain.

d. Chicago Corporation accounts for its three intercorporate investments in unconsolidated affiliates using the equity method. The acquisition cost of these investments equaled both the carrying value and the fair value of the assets and liabilities of the investees at the time of acquisition. How much did each of these three companies declare in dividends during 2009? How can you tell?

e. Refer to part **d**. Give the journal entry (entries) made during 2009 to apply the equity method.

f. Chicago Corporation acquired its only building on January 1, 2008. It estimated the building to have a 40-year useful life and zero salvage value at that time. Calculate the amount of depreciation expense on this building for 2009, assuming that the firm uses the straight-line method.

g. Chicago Corporation sold machinery and equipment costing $1,000,000, with a carrying value of $200,000, for cash during 2009. Give the journal entry to record the disposition.

h. The bonds payable carry 6% annual coupons and require the payment of interest on December 31 of each year. Give the journal entry made on December 31, 2009, to recognize interest expense for 2009, assuming that Chicago Corporation uses the effective interest method.

i. Refer to part **h**. What was the effective or market interest rate on these bonds on the date Chicago Corporation issued them? Explain.

j. The $170,000 deferred portion of income tax expense for 2009 includes $150,000 relating to the use of different depreciation methods for financial and tax reporting. If the income tax rate was 30%, calculate the difference between the depreciation deduction reported on the tax return and the depreciation expense reported on the income statement.

k. Give the journal entry that explains the change in the treasury shares during 2009.

l. If the original acquisition cost of the patent is $1,250,000, and the firm amortizes that cost on a straight-line basis, how long before December 31, 2009, did the firm acquire the patent?

m. Chicago Corporation acquired the stock of Hutchinson Company on December 31, 2008. If it held the same amount of stock during the year, but the amount represented only a 15% ownership of the Hutchinson Company, how would the financial statements have differed? Disregard income tax effects, and assume the market price of the shares exceeds their acquisition cost of $100,000 by $25,000 on December 31, 2009.

n. During 2009, Chicago Corporation paid $170,000 to the lessor of property represented on the balance sheet by "Property Rights Acquired under Lease." Property rights acquired under lease have a 10-year life, and Chicago Corporation amortizes them on a straight-line basis. What was the total expense reported by Chicago Corporation during 2009 from using the leased property?

o. How would the financial statements differ if Chicago Corporation accounted for inventories on the lower-of-cost-or-market basis and if the market value of these inventories had been $1,600,000 at the end of 2009? Disregard income tax effects.

p. Refer to the earnings-per-share amounts in the income statement of Chicago Corporation. How many shares of common stock would the firm issue if holders of the outstanding shares of preferred stock converted them into common stock?

q. Prepare a T-account work sheet for the preparation of a statement of cash flows for Chicago Corporation for 2009. The certificate of deposit is a cash equivalent.

4. **Comprehensive review problem. Exhibit 16.10** (on page 799) presents a consolidated statement of income and retained earnings for 2009, and **Exhibit 16.11** (on pages 800–801) presents a consolidated balance sheet for Tuck Corporation as of December 31, 2008 and 2009. A statement of accounting policies and a set of notes to the financial statements follow these financial statements. After studying these financial statements and notes, respond to each of the following questions and calculation requirements.

EXHIBIT 16.10	Tuck Corporation Consolidated Statement of Income and Retained Earnings for 2009 (Problem 4)

Revenues and Gains

Sales	$4,000,000	
Gain on Sale of Equipment	3,000	
Rental Revenue	240,000	
Dividend Revenue	8,000	
Equity in Earnings of Unconsolidated Affiliates	102,000	
Total Revenues and Gains		$4,353,000

Expenses, Losses, and Deductions

Cost of Goods Sold (including depreciation and amortization)	$2,580,000	
Selling and Administration Expenses (including depreciation and amortization and bad debt expense)	1,102,205	
Warranty Expense	46,800	
Interest Expense	165,995	
Loss on Sale of Marketable Equity Securities	8,000	
Income Tax Expense	150,000	
Total Expenses, Losses, and Deductions		4,053,000
Consolidated Net Income		$ 300,000
Less Dividends Declared		(119,500)
Increase in Retained Earnings for 2009		$ 180,500
Retained Earnings, December 31, 2008		277,000
Retained Earnings, December 31, 2009		$ 457,500

REQUIRED

a. Prepare an analysis that explains the change in the Marketable Equity Securities account during 2009.

b. Calculate the proceeds from sales of marketable equity securities classified as current assets during 2009.

c. Calculate the amount of the bad debt expense for 2009.

d. Calculate the amount of cost of goods sold assuming Tuck Corporation used a FIFO cost-flow assumption.

e. Give the journal entry (entries) to account for the change in the Investment in Thayer Corporation account during 2009.

f. Calculate the amount of income or loss from the Investment in Thayer Corporation during 2009.

g. Give the journal entry (entries) to account for the change in the Investment in Davis Corporation account during 2009.

h. Refer to Note 5. Give the journal entry to record the sale of equipment during 2009.

i. Refer to Note 9. Demonstrate that the $106,036 is the correct amount of the lease-hold asset at the beginning of the lease term.

j. Calculate the amount of cash received during 2009 for rental fees.

k. Calculate the actual cost incurred to service customers' warranties during 2009.

l. Refer to Note 7. Calculate the amount of interest expense on the $1 million, 6% bonds for 2009.

m. Give the journal entry (entries) for the change in the Mortgage Payable accounts during 2009. Be sure to consider the current portion.

n. Verify that the carrying value of the combined current and noncurrent portions of the Capitalized Lease Obligation on December 31, 2008, should be $62,064.

EXHIBIT 16.11

Tuck Corporation
Consolidated Comparative Balance Sheets
(Problem 4)

	December 31, 2009	December 31, 2008
ASSETS		
Current Assets		
Cash	$ 278,000	$ 240,000
Marketable Securities (Note 1)	141,000	125,000
Accounts Receivable—Net (Note 2)	1,509,600	1,431,200
Inventories (Note 3)	1,525,315	1,257,261
Prepayments	32,000	28,000
Total Current Assets	$3,485,915	$3,081,461
Investments (Note 4)		
Investment in Thayer Corporation (15% owned)	$ 87,000	$ 92,000
Investment in Hitchcock Corporation (30% owned)	135,000	120,000
Investment in Davis Corporation (40% owned)	298,000	215,000
Total Investments	$ 520,000	$ 427,000
Property, Plant, and Equipment (Note 5)		
Land	$ 82,000	$ 82,000
Building	843,000	843,000
Equipment	1,848,418	497,818
Leasehold	106,036	106,036
Total Plant Assets at Cost	$2,879,454	$1,528,854
Less Accumulated Depreciation and Amortization	(420,854)	(383,854)
Total Plant Assets—Net	$2,458,600	$1,145,000
Intangibles		
Goodwill—Net	$ 36,000	$ 36,000
Total Assets	$6,500,515	$4,689,461

(*continued*)

o. Prepare an analysis that explains the change in the carrying value of the combined current and noncurrent portions of the Capitalized Lease Obligation during 2009.

p. Give the journal entry to record income tax expense for 2009.

q. Compute the amount of cash payments for income taxes during 2009.

r. The income tax rate is 30%. Assume that during 2009, Tuck Corporation recognized $12,000 of deferred tax expense related to differences in depreciation methods. Calculate the difference between the amount of depreciation recognized for financial reporting purposes and the amount recognized for tax purposes.

s. Give the journal entry made on July 1, 2009, upon conversion of the preferred stock.

t. Give the journal entry (entries) to account for the change in the Treasury Stock account during 2009.

STATEMENT OF ACCOUNTING POLICIES

■ *Basis of consolidation.* Tuck Corporation consolidates its financial statements with those of Harvard Corporation, a 100%-owned subsidiary acquired on January 2, 2007.

■ *Marketable securities.* The firm classifies marketable securities as available for sale and measures them at fair value.

EXHIBIT 16.11 (Continued)

LIABILITIES AND SHAREHOLDERS' EQUITY

Current Liabilities

Note Payable (Note 6)	$ 200,000	$ 100,000
Accounts Payable	723,700	666,100
Rental Fees Received in Advance	58,000	46,000
Estimated Warranty Liability	78,600	75,200
Interest Payable on Notes	2,000	1,500
Dividends Payable	30,000	25,000
Income Taxes Payable—Current	160,000	140,000
Mortgage Payable—Current Portion	37,383	37,383
Capitalized Lease Obligation—Current Portion	10,000	10,000
Total Current Liabilities	$1,299,683	$1,101,183

Noncurrent Liabilities

Bonds Payable (Note 7)	$1,931,143	$1,104,650
Mortgage Payable (Note 8)	243,560	262,564
Capitalized Lease Obligation (Note 9)	46,229	52,064
Deferred Tax Liability	145,000	130,000
Total Noncurrent Liabilities	$2,365,932	$1,549,278
Total Liabilities	$3,665,615	$2,650,461

Shareholders' Equity

Convertible Preferred Stock, $100 par Value (Note 10)	$ 200,000	$ 700,000
Common Stock, $10 par Value (Note 11)	1,650,000	1,000,000
Additional Paid-In Capital—Common	583,600	130,000
Accumulated Other Comprehensive Income:		
Unrealized Holding Loss on Marketable Securities	(21,000)	(25,000)
Unrealized Holding Loss on Investments in Securities	(21,000)	(16,000)
Retained Earnings	457,500	277,000
Total	$2,849,100	$2,066,000
Less Cost of Treasury Stock (Note 12)	(14,200)	(27,000)
Total Shareholders' Equity	$2,834,900	$2,039,000
Total Liabilities and Shareholders' Equity	$6,500,515	$4,689,461

- **Accounts receivable.** The firm accounts for customers' uncollectible accounts using the allowance method.

- **Inventories.** Tuck Corporation uses a last-in, first-out (LIFO) cost-flow assumption for inventories.

- **Investments.** The firm classifies investments of less than 20% of the outstanding common stock of other companies as available for sale and measures them at fair value. It accounts for investments of 20% to 50% of the outstanding common stock of affiliates using the equity method.

- **Building, equipment, and leaseholds.** Tuck Corporation calculates depreciation for financial reporting purposes using the straight-line method and an accelerated method for income tax reporting.

- **Interest expense on long-term debt.** The firm measures interest expense on long-term debt using the effective interest method.

- **Deferred income taxes.** Tuck Corporation provides for deferred income taxes arising from temporary differences between book and taxable income.

NOTES TO THE FINANCIAL STATEMENTS

- *Note 1:* The balance sheet presents marketable equity securities, all classified as avai-label for sale, at fair value, which is less than acquisition cost by $25,000 on December 31, 2008, and $21,000 on December 31, 2009. Tuck Corporation sold marketable equity securities costing $35,000 during 2009. It received no dividends from marketable equity securities during 2009.

- *Note 2:* The balance sheet presents accounts receivable net of an allowance for uncol-lectibles of $128,800 on December 31, 2008, and $210,400 on December 31, 2009. Tuck Corporation wrote off a total of $63,000 of accounts receivable as uncollectible during 2009.

- *Note 3:* The valuation of inventories on a FIFO basis exceeded the amounts on a LIFO basis by $430,000 on December 31, 2008, and by $410,000 on December 31, 2009.

- *Note 4:* Davis Corporation reported net income for 2009 of $217,500 and declared and paid dividends totaling $60,000 during the year. Tuck Corporation invested an addi-tional $20,000 in Davis Corporation during 2009, but its ownership percentage remained at 40%.

- *Note 5:* Tuck Corporation sold equipment with a cost of $23,000 and a carrying value of $4,000 during 2009. This was the only disposition of property, plant, or equipment during the year.

- *Note 6:* Tuck Corporation paid at maturity a 90-day, 9% note with a face amount of $100,000 with interest on January 30, 2009. On December 1, 2009, Tuck Corporation borrowed $200,000 from its local bank, promising to repay the principal plus interest at 12% in six months.

- *Note 7:* Bonds Payable on the balance sheet comprise the following:

	December 31, 2009	December 31, 2008
$1,000,000, 6%, 20-Year Semiannual Coupon Bonds, Due December 31, 2020, Priced at $1,125,510 to Yield 5%, Compounded Semiannually, at the Time of Issue	$1,099,823	$1,104,650
$1,000,000, 8%, 20-Year Semiannual Coupon Bonds, Due December 31, 2027, Priced at $828,409 to Yield 10%, Compounded Semiannually, at the Time of Issue	831,320	—
Total	$1,931,143	$1,104,650

- *Note 8:* Mortgage Payable represents a building mortgage requiring equal installment payments of $40,000 on December 31 of each year. The loan underlying the mortgage bears interest of 7%, compounded annually. The final installment payment is due on December 31, 2009.

- *Note 9:* The Capitalized Lease Obligation represents a 20-year, noncancelable lease on certain equipment. The lease requires annual payments, in advance, of $10,000 on Janu-ary 2 of each year. Tuck Corporation will make the last lease payment on January 2, 2016. Tuck Corporation capitalizes the lease at its borrowing rate (at the inception of the lease) of 8%.

- *Note 10:* Each share of preferred stock is convertible into five shares of common stock. On July 1, 2009, holders of 5,000 shares of preferred stock exercised their conversion options. Tuck Corporation recorded the conversion using carrying values.

- *Note 11:* On October 1, 2009, Tuck Corporation issued 40,000 shares of common stock on the open market for $15 cash per share.

- *Note 12:* Treasury Stock comprises the following:

December 31, 2008: 2,250 Shares at $12 per Share	$27,000
December 31, 2009: 450 Shares at $12 per Share	$ 5,400
550 Shares at $16 per Share	8,800
	$14,200

During 2009, Tuck Corporation sold 1,800 shares of treasury stock and acquired 550 shares.

5. **Recasting financial statements to proposed reporting format.** Refer to the financial statements of Scania in **Exhibit 1.5** (balance sheet) and **Exhibit 1.6** (income statement) and **Exhibit 1.7** (statement of cash flows).

a. Recast the balance sheet on December 31, 2006, and December 31, 2005, into a statement of financial position for Scania using the proposed reporting format of the joint FASB/IASB financial presentation project. Use **Exhibit 16.2** as a guide. Incorporate the following additional information into the preparation of this financial statement.

   (1) Current and noncurrent receivables, except tax assets, relate to Scania's sales of vehicles.

   (2) Short-term investments serve an investing purpose, whereas short-term investments comprising cash and cash equivalents serve an operating purpose. Assume that the amounts Scania classifies as cash and cash equivalents on its balance sheet are entirely cash equivalents for purposes of this problem. Cash and bank balances also serve an operating purpose.

   (3) Investments in associated companies and joint ventures serve an operating purpose.

   (4) Current interest-bearing liabilities directly finance Scania's trade receivables and noncurrent interest-bearing liabilities provide Scania with financing for its broad corporate needs.

   (5) Other current and noncurrent liabilities relate to Scania's operating activities.

b. Recast Scania's income statement into a statement of comprehensive income for the years ended December 31, 2006, 2005, and 2004, using the proposed reporting format of the joint FASB/IASB financial presentation project. Use **Exhibit 16.4** as a guide. Incorporate the following information into the preparation of this financial statement.

   (1) Scania derives interest income of SEK632, SEK679, and SEK346 for 2006, 2005, and 2004 respectively from short-term investments comprising cash and cash equivalents.

   (2) Scania derives other financial income of SEK142, SEK299, and SEK96, and other financial expenses of SEK81, SEK206, and SEK127 for 2006, 2005, and 2004 respectively from short-term investments.

   (3) Interest expenses of SEK863, SEK866, and SEK638 for 2006, 2005, and 2004 respectively relate to noncurrent interest-bearing liabilities.

   (4) Items of other comprehensive income include hedge reserve and accumulated exchange rate differences. The amounts for these items on December 31, 2003, were zero and (SEK150) respectively.

c. Recast Scania's statement of cash flows for the years ended December 31, 2006, 2005, and 2004 using the proposed reporting format of the joint FASB/IASB financial presentation project. Use **Exhibit 16.3** as a guide, although you will likely require additional line items. To calculate cash received from operating revenues, list all operating revenues and then adjust the sum for changes in receivables. To calculate cash disbursed for manufacturing costs, adjust cost of goods sold for changes in inventory and trade payables. To calculate cash disbursed for operating expenses, list all operating expenses and then adjust the sum for noncash expenses and changes in provisions and other liabilities and provisions. You may wish to refer to **Exhibit 15.5** for assistance in computing cash flow from operatins under the direct method. Be sure to use the amounts for changes in balance sheet accounts from Scania's statement of cash flows and not the amounts on its comparative balance sheet. Be sure that the classification of items as operating, investing, financing, taxes, and equity are consistent with the classifications in parts **a** and **b**. Incorporate the following information into the preparation of this statement.

   (1) The statement of cash flows should explain changes in cash and bank balances. Short-term investments comprising cash and cash equivalents are operating items.

   (2) The balance in cash and bank balances on December 31, 2003, was SEK1,243 million, and the balance in short-term investments comprising cash and cash equivalents on December 31, 2003, was SEK420 million.

(3) List the effect of exchange rate changes on cash and cash equivalents as the last item before summing to the net change in cash and bank balances for each year.

6. **Recasting financial statements to proposed reporting format.** Refer to the financial statements of Wal-Mart Stores in **Exhibit 6.2** (income statement), **Exhibit 6.3** (balance sheet), and **Exhibit 6.4** (statement of cash flows). Recast these financial statements using the proposed reporting format of the joint FASB/IASB financial presentation project.

a. Recast Wal-Mart's balance sheet on January 31, 2008, and January 31, 2007, into a statement of financial position using the proposed reporting format of the joint FASB/IASB financial presentation project. Use **Exhibit 16.2** as a guide. Incorporate the following additional information into the preparation of this financial statement.

(1) Other Noncurrent Assets includes deferred tax assets of $2,724 million on January 31, 2008, and $2,937 million on January 31, 2008. The remaining amount in Other Noncurrent Assets represents goodwill from acquisitions of retail stores.

(2) Other Current Liabilities includes accrued income taxes payable of $1,016 million on January 31, 2008, and $706 million on January 31, 2007.

(3) Other Noncurrent Liabilities includes deferred tax liabilities of $3,486 million on January 31, 2008, and $4,035 million on January 31, 2007. The remaining amount of Other Noncurrent Liabilities relates to pension obligations.

(4) Wal-Mart's borrowing provides funds for all of its corporate needs.

b. Recast Wal-Mart's income statement into a statement of comprehensive income for the years ended January 31, 2008, 2007, and 2006 using the proposed reporting format of the joint FASB/IASB financial presentation project. Use **Exhibit 16.4** as a guide. Incorporate the following information into the preparation of this financial statement (amounts in millions).

For the Year Ended January 31:	2008	2007	2006
Interest Paid	$1,622	$1,553	$1,390
Income Taxes Paid	6,299	6,665	5,962
Items of Other Comprehensive Income:			
Foreign Currency Translation Adjustment	1,218	1,584	(1,691)
Pension Liability	138	(15)	51
Derivatives	0	6	(1)
Adjustment on Adoption of *FAS 158*	0	(120)	0

c. Recast Wal-Mart's statement of cash flows using the proposed reporting format of the joint FASB/IASB financial presentation project. Use **Exhibit 16.3** as a guide, although you will likely require additional line items. To calculate cash received from operating customers, begin with sales revenue and then adjust for the changes in receivables. To calculate cash disbursed for merchandise, adjust cost of goods sold for changes in inventory and trade payables. To calculate cash disbursed for selling and administrative expenses, adjust selling and administrative expense for noncash expenses and changes in prepayments and other current liabilities. Also, adjust the preceding amounts for interest and income taxes paid. Be sure to use the amounts for changes in balance sheet accounts from Wal-Mart's statement of cash flows and not the amounts on its comparative balance sheet. Be sure that the classification of items as operating, investing, financing, taxes, and equity are consistent with the classifications in parts **a** and **b**. Incorporate the following information into the preparation of this statement.

(1) Treat Other Investing Transactions on **Exhibit 6.4** as an operating activity under the proposed reporting format.

(2) Treat Other Financing Transactions on **Exhibit 6.4** as a financing activity under the proposed reporting format.

Time Value of Cash Flows

1. Understand why cash flows that occur at different times have different values.

2. Understand the concepts of present value and future value of single amounts of cash flows and a series of cash flows.

3. Apply the concepts of present value and future value of cash flows to typical business transactions.

Firms engage in various transactions that involve receiving or disbursing cash over time. Consider the following examples:

1. General Electric disburses cash to the trustee of its pension fund each year. These cash payments earn interest and other income over time, accumulating amounts in the pension fund sufficient to pay pensions to retired employees in the future. General Electric needs to know how much cash it must contribute to the pension fund each year in order to accumulate sufficient amounts to pay retired employees.

2. eBay considers replacing its existing computer system with a technologically more advanced one, which will permit the firm to process more transactions and do so more quickly, as well as accumulate information on customer purchases. eBay estimates the expected additional cash flows it will receive in the future from the more sophisticated computer system and wonders if acquiring the computer is a worthwhile investment.

3. Walt Disney needs to obtain cash to build a new exhibit at Disney World. It plans to issue $50 million of 6% long-term bonds that pay $3 million (= .06 × $50 million) annually and require repayment of the $50 million in 20 years. Walt Disney desires to know the likely cash it will receive today from issuing these bonds on the market.

These and other business decisions require firms to compare and aggregate cash flows that occur at different points in time. Cash flows that occur at different times are not directly comparable because cash can, and usually does, earn interest. If a firm can invest cash to earn interest of 6% for the next year, then one dollar today is equivalent to $1.06 one year from today. That is, a firm is indifferent between receiving $1.00 today or receiving $1.06 one year from today. This appendix explores concepts and tools for equating cash flows over time. The combination of cash flows and timing of valuations leads to four basic patterns of analysis:

1. Future value of a single amount.
2. Present value of a single amount.
3. Future value of a series of equal amounts.
4. Present value of a series of equal amounts.

The sections that follow explore each of these four patterns.

FUTURE VALUE OF A SINGLE AMOUNT

The following diagram depicts the **future value** of a single amount:

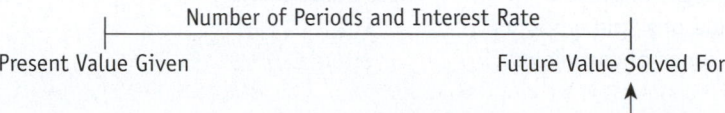

EXAMPLE 1 (FUTURE VALUE OF A SINGLE AMOUNT)

How much will $1,000 deposited today earning 8% grow to in 10 years? A critical assumption underlying calculations involving the time value of cash flows is that interest earned in one period earns interest the next period, a process called **compound interest**. Thus, in this example the initial $1,000 deposit grows to $1,080 (= $1,000 × 1.08) at the end of one year. The $1,080 then grows to $1,166.40 (= $1,080 × 1.08) at the end of the second year, and so on.

Contrast compound interest with **simple interest**, where only the initial investment earns interest. Simple interest does not compound. At simple interest, the $1,000 grows to $1,160.00 [= $1,000 × (1 +(.08 × 2))] at the end of the second year. The formula for simple interest is $F_n = P[1 + (r \times n)]$. From this point on unless we make an explicit contrary statement, we mean compound, not simple, interest.

Three approaches for calculating the time value of cash flows involve the following tools:

1. Formulas
2. Compound interest tables
3. Spreadsheets

Formula   The future value of a single sum equals

$$F_n = P(1 + r)^n,$$

where

$$
\begin{aligned}
F_n &= \text{Future value or accumulated amount} \\
P &= \text{Present value or one-time investment today} \\
r &= \text{Interest rate per period} \\
n &= \text{Number of periods from today}
\end{aligned}
$$

Thus, the future value of $1,000 invested today at 8% per year for 10 years is: $F_n = P(1 + r)^n$ = $1,000 (1 + .08)^{10}$ = $2,158.92. Most calculators have a function for y^x, which permits calculation of $(1 + r)^n$. The result of the calculation, $(1 + r)^n$, is often called the **factor**.

Compound Interest Tables   Compound interest tables for the future value of $1 compute factor values for $(1 + r)^n$ for various combinations of interest rates and numbers of periods. An excerpt of such a table appears in **Exhibit A.1**.

Exhibit A.1 shows that the factor for the future value of $1 for 10 periods at 8% is 2.15892. Multiplying this factor times the $1,000 initial investment yields a future value of $2,158.92 (= $1,000 × 2.15892). **Table 1** at the back of this book provides factors for the future value of $1 for various combinations of interest rates and number of periods.

EXHIBIT A.1	Future Value of $1 at 6% and 8% per Period $F_n = P (1 + r)^n$		

| | | Rate = r | |
Number of Periods = n		6%	8%
1		1.06000	1.08000
2		1.12360	1.16640
3		1.19102	1.25971
10		1.79085	2.15892
20		3.20714	4.66096

Spreadsheet Microsoft's Excel® calculates future values using the following cell formula: =FV(interest rate, number of periods, periodic payment, present value, type). Enter the interest rate as a decimal (enter 8% as .08). For applications involving the future value of a single amount, enter zero for the periodic payment or leave that item blank. This term applies to applications involving the future value of a series of equal amounts, which we discuss later. Enter the present value amount without any commas. Excel is sensitive to the direction of the cash flow. Thus, enter cash outflows with a negative sign and cash inflows with either no sign or a positive sign. **Example 1** asks how much a cash outflow of $1,000 at the beginning of the first year will grow to at the end of 10 periods. Thus, enter −$1,000 for PV. The "type" indicator relates to the timing during the period of periodic payments and also applies only when computing the future value of a series of equal amounts. Leave this factor blank when the application involves the future value of a single amount. Thus, for **Example 1**, the spreadsheet formula is: =FV(.08,10,0,-1000), or =FV(.08,10,,−1000).

   In some settings, such as interest on bank accounts, interest compounds one or more times throughout the year. For example, the bank in **Example 1** might compound interest quarterly. The stated interest rate (8% in **Example 1**) is usually an annual interest rate. The analyst must adjust the interest rate and number of periods to accommodate compounding at an interval shorter than one year. To solve problems that require computation of interest quoted at a nominal rate r per period compounded m times per period for n periods, use the tables for rate r/m and $m \times n$ periods. For example, 8% compounded quarterly for 10 years equals 2% per period (= 8%/4 compounding periods a year) for 40 periods (= 10 years times 4 compounding periods a year). Thus, the $1,000 investment compounded quarterly at 8% for 10 years is: $F_n = P (1 + r)^n = \$1,000 (1 + .02)^{40} = \$1,000 \times 2.20804 = \$2,208.04$. The more frequent the compounding, the larger is the future value. Financial institutions often advertise the **effective annual yield** on savings accounts and certificates of deposit. The effective annual yield exceeds the stated interest rate, as the previous example demonstrates. The formula for the effective annual yield is $(1 + r/m)^m - 1$. The effective annual yield for quarterly compounding of an 8% annual rate is 8.24% [= $(1 + .08/4)^4 - 1$].

EXAMPLE 2 (FUTURE VALUE OF A SINGLE AMOUNT)

Suppose you inherit $10,000 from your Aunt Bessie. You invest this amount in a certificate of deposit that pays 6% compounded quarterly for five years. How much will this certificate grow to at the end of five years? **Table 1** at the end of the book indicates that the factor for the future value of $1 invested for 20 periods (= 4 quarterly compounding periods per year for 5 years) at 1.5% (= 6% annual rate/4 compounding periods per year) is 1.34686. Thus, the future value of $10,000 for 20 periods at 1.5% is $13,468.60 (= $10,000 × 1.34686).

PROBLEM A.1 for Self-Study

Future value of single sums. Compute the future value of $5,000 at the following rates:

a. 6% for 10 years, with interest compounded annually.

b. 6% for 10 years, with interest compounded semiannually.

c. 8% for 33 years, with interest compounded annually.

d. 8% for 33 years, with interest compounded quarterly.

PRESENT VALUE OF A SINGLE AMOUNT

The preceding section discussed the computation of the future value of a single known amount today for n periods at a stated, known interest rate r. P, n, and r are known and you find F_n. The process involves accumulating *forward* in time from P to F_n. This section discusses the computation of the **present value** of a single known future cash flow. That is, F_n is known and you compute P.

The following diagram depicts the present value of a single sum.

Number of Periods and Interest Rate

Present Value Solved For   Future Value Given

The process involves **discounting** the future amount to its present value. The discounting process removes the effect of compound interest from the future amount and leaves a present value amount that excludes the accumulation of interest over time. Common terminology refers to the interest rate as the **discount rate** when used in present value settings.

The formula for the present value of a single sum begins with the formula for the future value of a single sum but solves for P instead of F_n. Thus,

$$F_n = P (1 + r)^n$$

Dividing both sides by $(1 + r)^n$ yields

$$F_n/(1 + r)^n = P$$

or,

$$P = F_n (1 + r)^{-n}$$

The amount $(1 + r)^{-n}$ equals $1/(1 + r)^n$. Thus, the factors for the present value of a single sum equal one divided by the factors for the future value of a single sum. **Exhibit A.2** shows an excerpt from a table for factors for the present value of a single sum. We use the same interest rates and number of periods as in **Exhibit A.1**. **Table 2** at the back of the book presents a table with the factors for the present value of $1 for various combinations of interest rates and numbers of periods.

EXAMPLE 3 (PRESENT VALUE OF A SINGLE AMOUNT)

A firm issues a single-payment note in which it promises to pay $160,000 three years from today in exchange for used equipment. What is the present value of this note if the discount rate appropriate for this note is 6%?

Formula Applying the formula for the present value of a single sum yields a present value of $134,339.09 [= $160,000 × (1.06^{-3})].

Compound Interest Table Exhibit A.2 indicates that the factor for the present value of $1 for three periods at 6% is .83962. The present value of the note is therefore $134,339.20

EXHIBIT A.2	Present Value of $1 at 6% and 8% per Period $P = (1 + r)^{-n}$		
		Rate = r	
Number of Periods = n		6%	8%
1		.94340	.92593
2		.89000	.85734
3		.83962	.79383
10		.55839	.46319
20		.31180	.21455

(= $160,000 × .83962). The slight difference from the amount computed by the previous formula results from the rounding of the present value factor to five decimal places.

Spreadsheet The following is the formula to calculate present values in Excel: =PV (interest rate, number of periods, periodic payment, future value, type). This is the formula to input into Excel: = PV(.06,3,0,−160000), or =PV(.06,3,,−160000). The type variable does not apply to present values of single amounts. The resulting value is $134,339.09.

These calculations suggest that the value today of the used equipment is $134,339.09. The seller of the used equipment should be indifferent between receiving $134,339.09 today or receiving $160,000 three years from today.

EXAMPLE 4 (PRESENT VALUE OF A SINGLE AMOUNT)

Joe Alumnus plans to endow a chaired professorship at his alma mater ten years from today. The university expects to require a payment of $2,000,000 to endow a chair at that time. Joe Alumnus can purchase a single-payment bond (called a *zero coupon bond*, which **Chapter 10** discusses) on the market that has a maturity value in 10 years of $2,000,000. How much would Joe Alumnus have to pay for this bond today if the discount rate is 6% compounded annually? The present value of $2,000,000 discounted at 6% compounded annually for 10 periods is $1,116,780 (=.55839 × $2,000,000).

How much would he have to pay for this bond if the discount rate of 6% compounded semiannually? The present value of $2,000,000 discounted at 3% compounded semiannually for 20 periods is $1,107,360 (= .55368 × $2,000,000). Thus, with semiannual compounding, Joe Alumnus' cost is $9,420 (= $1,116,780 − $1,107,360) smaller than the cash outlay to purchase a bond with annual compounding to fund the chair.

PROBLEM A.2 for Self-Study

> **Present value of single sums.** Compute the present value of $20,000 at the following rates:
>
> **a.** 6% for 5 years, with interest compounded annually.
>
> **b.** 6% for 5 years, with interest compounded monthly.
>
> **c.** 10% for 10 years, with interest compounded semiannually.
>
> **d.** 8% for 13 years, with interest compounded quarterly.

ANNUITIES

Contractual arrangements in business frequently involve periodic cash payments of equal amounts. For example, a firm might lease office space and agree to pay a fixed amount per month for the three-year lease period. A firm might issue a note that promises to pay a fixed amount every six months for a 10-year period. A firm might agree to contribute a fixed amount per month to an employee retirement plan. When cash payments occur in equally spaced intervals and are of equal amount each period, common terminology refers to the stream of payments as an **annuity**. In some settings the question asked involves the *future* value of the annuity, which the next section considers. In other settings the question asked involves the *present* value of the annuity, which a subsequent section discusses.

The contractual arrangement might require that cash payments occur at the *end* of each period, as is typical for debt service payments on bonds. Common terminology refers to such arrangements as an **ordinary annuity**, or **annuity in arrears**. Other contractual arrangements might require payments at the *beginning* of the period, as is common for rental agreements. Common terminology refers to such arrangements as an **annuity due**, or **annuity in advance**. Less commonly, the arrangements might stipulate that the first payment occurs sometime after the end of the first period, referred to as a **deferred annuity**. We consider each type of annuity in the sections that follow.

FUTURE VALUE OF AN ANNUITY

The following diagram depicts the **future value of an ordinary annuity** (annuity in arrears) for a $1 payment per period for three periods at a 6% interest rate.

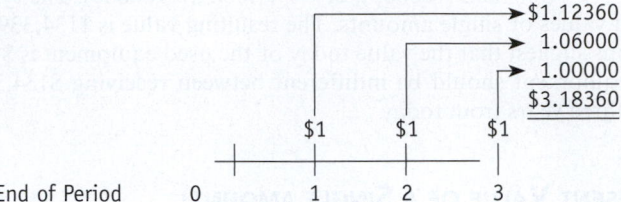

The $1 paid at the end of the first period earns interest for two periods, so it grows to $1.12360 by the end of the third period. The $1 paid at the end of the second period grows to $1.06000 by the end of the third period. The $1 paid at the end of the third period is, of course, worth $1.0000 at the end of the third period. The three factors, 1.0000, 1.06000, and 1.12360, are the factors from **Table 1** for the future value of a single sum for 0, 1, and 2 periods. The factor for the future value of an ordinary annuity (3.18360 in this case) equals the sum of the factors for the future value of a single sum for the number of periods and payments specified. The summing of the factors for individual years to obtain the factor for an annuity is appropriate only because each payment is of equal amount and occurs at equally spaced intervals.

The formula for the future value of an ordinary annuity (FV_A) is as follows:

$$FV_A = \frac{(1 + r)^n - 1}{r}$$

Applying this formula to the example above yields:

$$FV_A = \frac{(1 + r)^n - 1}{r} = \frac{(1 + .06)^3 - 1}{.06} = \frac{1.19102 - 1}{.06} = 3.18360$$

Exhibit A.3 presents an excerpt from a table of factors for the future value of an ordinary annuity. **Table 3** at the back of the book presents a more expanded table.

EXAMPLE 5 (FUTURE VALUE OF AN ORDINARY ANNUITY)

You plan to invest $1,000 at the end of each of the next 10 years in a savings account. The savings account accumulates interest of 8% compounded annually. What will be the balance in the savings account at the end of 10 years?

EXHIBIT A.3

Factors for the Future Value of an Ordinary Annuity at 6% and 8% per Period

Number of Periods (n)	Interest Rate 6%	Interest Rate 8%
1	1.00000	1.00000
2	2.06000	2.08000
3	3.18360	3.24640
5	5.63709	5.86660
10	13.18079	14.48656
20	36.78559	45.76196

$$FV_A = \frac{(1 + r)^n - 1}{r}$$

The time line for this example is as follows:

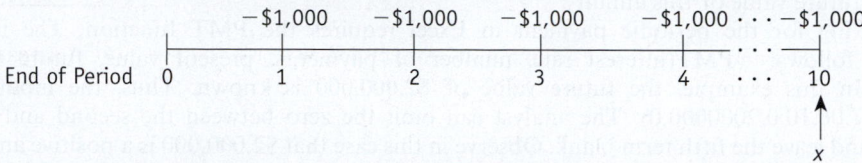

The symbol x denotes the amount you desire to calculate.

We can solve annuity problems in the same ways we solve problems involving single sums: by formula, using compound interest tables, or by using a Microsoft Excel spreadsheet.

Formula Following is the formula for the future value of an ordinary annuity of $1 for 10 periods at 8%:

$$FV_A = \frac{(1 + r)^n - 1}{r} = \frac{(1 + .08)^{10} - 1}{.08} = \frac{2.158925 - 1}{.08} = 14.48656$$

Thus,

Future Value of an Ordinary Annuity	=	Periodic Payment	×	Factor for the Future Value of an Ordinary Annuity
x	=	$1,000	×	14.48656
x	=	$14,487		

Compound Interest Tables Exhibit A.3 indicates that the factor for the future value of an ordinary annuity of 10 payments at 8% is 14.48656, yielding identical results to that computed using the formula.

Spreadsheet The following is the cell formula to solve for the future value of an ordinary annuity of $1,000 at 8% for 10 payments: =FV(.08,10,−1000,0,0). The fourth term is the present value. The fifth term reflects the timing of the payment, which Excel assumes by default is at the end of the period. Thus, in this case the analyst can ignore the last two terms and simply enter the following: =FV(.08,10, −1000). This calculation yields $14,486.56.

EXAMPLE 6 (FUTURE VALUE OF AN ORDINARY ANNUITY; SOLVING FOR PERIODIC PAYMENT)

Refer to **Example 4**, where Joe Alumnus wants to fund a $2,000,000 chaired professorship 10 years from today. Instead of investing a single amount today, he plans to contribute an equal amount at the end of each of the next 10 years in a savings account that pays 6% interest compounded annually. How much must he invest each year to accumulate $2,000,000 at the end of 10 years? In contrast to **Example 5**, this example asks for the amount of the periodic payment instead of the future accumulated value. The problem still involves the future value of an annuity because the interest accumulating process works forward in time. The time line for this example is as follows:

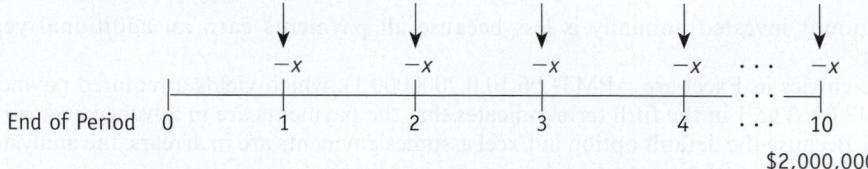

Exhibit A.3 indicates that the future value of $1 for 10 periods at 6% is 13.18079. Thus,

Future Value of an Ordinary Annuity	=	Periodic Payment	×	Factor for the Future Value of an Ordinary Annuity
$2,000,000	=	x	×	13.18079
x	=	$151,735.97		

Note that solving this equation involves *dividing* the future value of $2,000,000 by the factor for the future value of this annuity.

Solving for the periodic payment in Excel requires the PMT function. The inputs are as follows: =PMT(interest rate, number of payments, present value, future value, type). In this example, the future value of $2,000,000 is known. Thus, the inputs are =PMT(.06,10.0,2000000,0). The analyst can omit the zero between the second and third terms and leave the fifth term blank. Observe in this case that $2,000,000 is a positive amount because Joe Alumnus will receive that amount at the end of 10 periods. This approach yields a payment (cash outflow) of $151,735.92. Thus, investing $151,735.92 at the end of each of the next 10 years and leaving in the bank the invested amounts and interest earned will result in $2,000,000 at the end of 10 years.

In some cases the payments occur at the beginning of each period instead of at the end of each period. Such problems involve the future value of an annuity in advance. The following diagram depicts an annuity in advance for three periods at 6% per period:

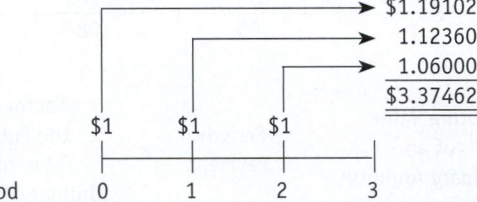

The first payment accumulates interest for three periods, the second payment for two periods, and the third payment for one period. Most tables of factors for the future value of an annuity assume that payments occur at the end of each period. To convert a table of factors for the future value of an ordinary annuity (annuity in arrears) to an annuity in advance, take one more period and subtract 1.00000. For example, **Table 3** at the back of the book indicates that the factor for the future value of an ordinary annuity for four periods at 6% is 4.37462. Subtracting 1.0000 from this value yields the factor of 3.37462, which is the factor for the future value of an annuity in advance for three periods at 6%. The subtraction of 1.0000 recognizes that no payment occurs at the end of the third period.

EXAMPLE 7 (FUTURE VALUE OF AN ANNUITY IN ADVANCE)

Refer to **Example 6**. Assume that Joe Alumnus plans to invest an equal amount at the beginning of each of the next ten years in order to accumulate $2,000,000 at the end of 10 years. How much must he contribute each year? The factor for the future value of an ordinary annuity for 11 periods at 6% is 14.97164. Subtracting 1.0000 from 14.97164 yields 13.97164, the factor for the future value of an annuity in advance for 10 years at 6%. Thus,

Future Value of an Annuity in Advance	=	Periodic Payment	×	Factor for the Future Value of an Annuity in Advance
$2,000,000	=	x	×	13.97164
x	=	$143,147.12		

The amount invested annually is less because all payments earn an additional year of interest.

The entries in Excel are =PMT(.06,10.0,2000000,1), which yields a required payment of $143,147.09. The 1 in the fifth term indicates that the payments are in advance, instead of in arrears. Because the default option in Excel assumes payments are in arrears, the analyst must input the 1 as the fifth term to signal payments in advance.

PROBLEM A.3 for Self-Study

Future value of an annuity. Calculate the requested amount in each of the following scenarios. Today is January 1, 2008.

(continued)

a. Jill Wilson plans to invest $2,500 at the end of each of the next 20 years in her individual retirement account. How much will she have accumulated on December 31, 2027, if she earns 6% each year compounded annually?

b. Refer to part **a**. How much will Jill have accumulated on December 31, 2027, if she invests the $2,500 at the beginning of each of the 20 years instead of at the end of each year?

c. Assume for this part that Jill wants to accumulate $100,000 on December 31, 2027. How much must she invest at the end of each of the next 20 years to accumulate the desired amount if the interest rate is 6% compounded annually?

d. Repeat part **c**, but assume Jill will make the investments at the beginning of each of the next 20 years.

PRESENT VALUE OF AN ANNUITY

The following diagram depicts the **present value of an ordinary annuity** at 6% for three periods.

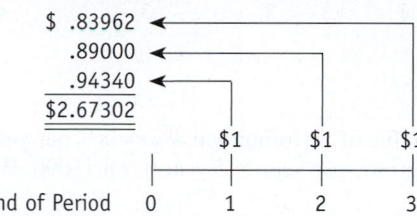

The payment at the end of the first period when discounted back for one period at 6% yields a present value of $.94340. The payment at the end of the second period discounted back two periods at 6% yields a present value of $.89000. The payment at the end of the third period when discounted back three periods yields a present value of $.83962. The factor for the present value of an ordinary annuity for three periods at 6% is the sum of the factors for the three individual years. You can see that any number in **Table 4** is the sum of the numbers in the corresponding cell of **Table 2** plus all the other numbers in that column up to the cell for the first row. Note that, unlike the relation between the factors for the future value of $1 and the present value of $1, the factor for the present value of an annuity is not simply one divided by the factor for the future value of an annuity.

The formula for the present value of an ordinary annuity is as follows:

$$PV_A = \frac{1 - (1 + r)^{-n}}{r}$$

Applying this formula to the preceding example for the present value of an ordinary annuity at 6% for three periods yields the following:

$$PV_A = \frac{1 - (1 + r)^{-n}}{r} = \frac{1 - (1.06)^{-3}}{.06} = \frac{1 - .83962}{.06} = 2.67301$$

This value is slightly more accurate than that computed in the preceding diagram.

Exhibit A.4 shows the factors for the present value of an ordinary annuity at 6% and 8% for various time periods. **Table 4** at the back of the book shows factors for an expanded set of interest rates and numbers of periods.

EXAMPLE 8 (PRESENT VALUE OF AN ORDINARY ANNUITY)

You want to receive $600 every six months, starting six months hence, for the next five years. How much must you invest today if the funds accumulate at the rate of 8% compounded semiannually?

EXHIBIT A.4

Factors for the Present Value of an Ordinary Annuity at 6% and 8% per Period

$$PV_A = \frac{1 - (1 + r)^{-n}}{r}$$

	Interest Rate	
Number of Periods (n)	**6%**	**8%**
1	.94340	.92593
2	1.83339	1.78326
3	2.67301	2.57710
5	4.21236	3.99271
10	7.36009	6.71008
20	11.46992	9.81815

The time line is as follows:

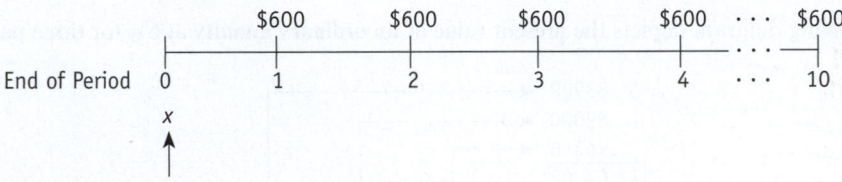

The factor for the present value of an annuity at 4% (= 8% per year/2 semiannual periods per year) for 10 periods (= 2 periods per year × 5 years) is 8.11090. We can compute this factor as well.

$$PV_A = \frac{1 - (1 + r)^{-n}}{r} = \frac{1 - (1.04)^{-10}}{.04} = \frac{1 - .67556}{.04} = 8.11090$$

Thus,

Present Value of an Ordinary Annuity	=	Periodic Payment	×	Factor for the Present Value of an Ordinary Annuity
x	=	$600	×	8.11090
x	=	$4,866.54		

Using Excel, the input formula is: =PV(interest rate, number of periods, periodic payment, future value, type). The inputs for this example are =PV(.04,10,600,0,0). As before, the analyst can omit the fourth and fifth terms when calculating the present value of an ordinary annuity.

EXAMPLE 9 (PRESENT VALUE OF ORDINARY ANNUITY; SOLVING FOR PERIODIC PAYMENT)

(This example also appears as **Example 1** in **Chapter 10**). A company borrows $800,000 from a bank. The interest rate on the loan is 6% compounded semiannually. The company agrees to repay the loan in equal semiannual installments over the next five years, with the first payment to be made six months from now. What is the required semiannual payment?

The time line for this example is as follows:

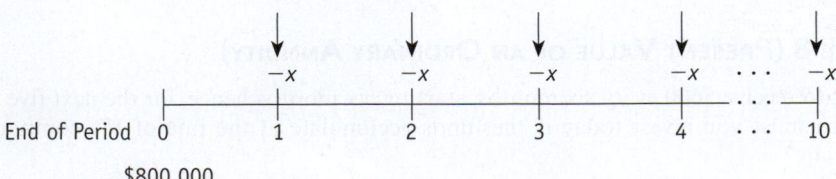

This example solves for the periodic payment that when discounted at 3% (6% per year/2 semiannual periods per year) for 10 periods (= 2 periods per year × 5 years) results in a present value of $800,000. The factor for the present value of an annuity for 10 periods at 3% is 8.53020. Thus,

Present Value of an Ordinary Annuity	=	Periodic Payment	×	Factor for the Present Value of an Ordinary Annuity
$800,000	=	x	×	8.53020
x	=	$\dfrac{\$800,000}{8.53020}$		
x	=	$93,784.41		

The inputs to Excel to solve this problem are: =PMT(.03,10,800000,0,0). Again, the analyst can omit the fourth and fifth terms.

EXAMPLE 10 (PRESENT VALUE OF AN ANNUITY IN ADVANCE)

Some situations involve cash flows that occur at the beginning instead of the end of a period. Leasing arrangements, for example, usually require the lessee to pay the lessor at the beginning of the period. A firm signs a lease requiring it to make lease payments of £19,909 at the beginning of the next three years. The interest rate appropriate to this lease is 8%. What is the present value of the cash flows for this lease?

The time line is as follows:

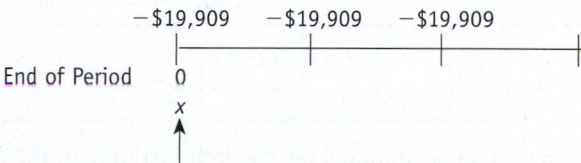

To convert a table of factors for the present value of an ordinary annuity to the factors for the present value of an annuity in advance, take one less period and add 1.0000 to the factor. Thus, we look up the factor for the present value of an annuity for two periods at 8%, which is 1.78326 (see **Exhibit A.4**) and add 1.0000 to obtain the factor of 2.78326. The 1.00000 is for the first payment at time 0 and the 1.78326 is for the present value of the payments at the beginning of the second and third years. Thus,

Present Value of an Annuity in Advance	=	Periodic Payment	×	Factor for the Present Value of an Annuity in Advance
x	=	$19,909	×	2.78326
x	=	$55,412		

The inputs into Excel: =PV(.08,3,−19909,0,1).

EXAMPLE 11 (PRESENT VALUE OF A DEFERRED ANNUITY)

Deferred annuities often occur in retirement planning. In a deferred annuity, the periodic payments do not begin until after at least one period beyond today. For example, assume that you expect to receive an annuity of $50,000 per year beginning on your 66th birthday and continuing to your 85th birthday. You want to know the cost of funding such a deferred annuity on your 45th birthday. Assume an interest rate of 6%.

The time line for this example is as follows:

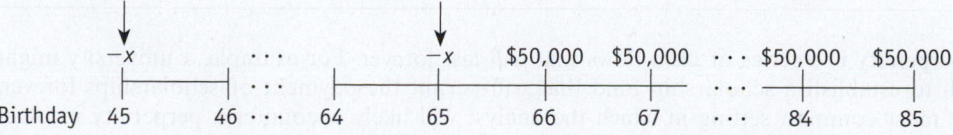

We compute the present value of this annuity in two steps.

1. Compute the present value of the annuity as of the 65th birthday.
2. Compute the present value of the amount in step 1 as of the 45th birthday.

The present value of the annuity as of the 65th birthday involves 20 payments in arrears discounted at 6%. The present value factor for 20 periods and 6% is 11.46992 (see **Exhibit A.4**). Following is the present value of an ordinary annuity of $50,000 per period for 20 periods at 6%:

$$
\begin{array}{ccccc}
\text{Present Value} & & \text{Periodic} & & \text{Factor for} \\
\text{of an} & = & \text{Payment} & \times & \text{the Present} \\
\text{Ordinary Annuity} & & & & \text{Value of an} \\
& & & & \text{Ordinary Annuity} \\
x & = & \$50,000 & \times & 11.46992 \\
x & = & \$573,496 & &
\end{array}
$$

The present value of this single amount on the 45th birthday involves discounting $573,496 back 20 periods at 6%. The factor for the present value of a single sum for 20 periods at 6% is .31180 (see **Exhibit A.2** or **Table 2** at the back of the book). Thus, the present value of the annuity on the 45th birthday is $178,816.05 (= $573,496 × .31180).

Another approach to solving this deferred annuity problem is to subtract the factor for the present value of an ordinary annuity for 20 periods (birthdays 46 to 65) from the factor for the present value of an annuity for 40 periods (birthdays 46 to 85) and multiply the net factor by the $50,000 payments. Thus,

Factor for the Present Value of an Ordinary Annuity for 40 Periods.	15.04630
Factor for the Present Value of an Ordinary Annuity for 20 Periods.	− 11.46992
Difference.	3.57638
Annual Annuity	× 50,000
Present Value of Annuity at Age 45.	$178,819

The difference in present value amounts on the 45th birthday in the preceding calculations results from the rounding of present value factors.

PROBLEM A.4 for Self-Study

Present value of an annuity. Calculate the requested amount in each of the following scenarios.

a. Joan Brown wants to purchase a bond that pays $10,000 at the end of each year for 20 years. If she desires a rate of return of 8%, what is the maximum amount she should be willing to pay for the bond?

b. Paul Rainey purchased an excavator for $150,000, which he plans to rent to construction companies for five years. He wants a rate of return of 12%. Assuming all cash flows occur at the beginning of the year, what is the required annual cash inflow?

c. Diversified Technologies plans to invest $20 million per year for the next three years to develop a new optical scanner. It expects that the new scanner will then generate $15 million annually in cash flows for five years, after which it will become obsolete. Assume that all cash flows occur at the end of each year. If Diversified Technologies requires a rate of return of 12% on its investments, should it develop the scanner?

 # PERPETUITIES

A **perpetuity** is a series of cash flows that will last forever. For example, a university might wish to establish a scholarship fund that will permit the payment of scholarships forever. The most common setting in which the analyst will likely encounter a perpetuity involves the valuation of a firm. Analysts typically project expected cash flows for the next five or ten years and then make some assumptions about the cash flows after the projection period. The analyst assumes that the firm will continue as a going concern; this means that the analyst assumes the firm will continue operating forever. The assumption made about the continuing cash flow usually involves the valuation of a perpetuity.

The formula for the present value of a perpetuity is $1/r$, where r is the discount rate. This formula assumes that the annual cash flow is the same in every year and occurs at the end of each year. If the cash flows occur at the beginning of each year, the formula is $1 + 1/r$. The first term values the first cash flow today, and the $1/r$ values the remaining cash flows to a present value.

EXAMPLE 12 (PRESENT VALUE OF A PERPETUITY)

Western University wishes to establish a scholarship fund that will permit payment of a $5,000 scholarship to 10 students each year forever. The university expects the scholarship fund to earn 6% per year. Compute the required amount to establish the scholarship fund today if the university pays the first scholarship at the end of the first year, one year from now, and subsequent awards at the end of every year forever. The required amount of the scholarship fund is $833,333.33 (= $50,000/.06).

Assume now that the university will pay the first scholarships today and subsequent scholarships at the beginning of each year forever. The required amount to establish the scholarship fund is $883,333.33 [= $50,000 + ($50,000/.06)].

EXAMPLE 13 (PRESENT VALUE OF A GROWING PERPETUITY)

Refer to **Example 12**. Assume that the university wants to increase the amount of the scholarship each year to incorporate expected increases in tuition costs of 4% per year. In this case, the assumption of an equal amount in the formula for the present value of a perpetuity no longer holds. The formula for the present value of a growing perpetuity is $1/(r - g)$, where r is the interest rate and g is the growth rate in cash flows. If the university expects to pay scholarships at the end of the first year and each year thereafter, then the amount needed to establish the scholarship fund is $2,600,000 [= ($50,000 × 1.04) × 1/(.06 - .04)]. If the university expects to award the first scholarship today and subsequent scholarships at the beginning of each year thereafter, then the amount required to establish the scholarship fund today is $2,650,000 (= $50,000 + $2,600,000).

The formula for the present value of a growing perpetuity does not work well when the interest rate and the growth rate are approximately the same. In this case, the value of $r - g$ in the denominator approaches zero, and the present value approaches infinity. The formula also does not work when the growth rate exceeds the discount rate. The value of $r - g$ turns negative and results in a negative net present value. In this latter case, the analyst should reconsider whether a firm can generate growth at a higher rate than its discount rate forever. Perhaps the growth rate assumption is too large or the discount rate is too low.

INTERNAL RATE OF RETURN (IMPLICIT INTEREST RATE)

The examples thus far have solved for a future value or a present value of a single payment or of a series of equally spaced equal-size payments, or the amount of the periodic cash flow of an annuity. In some cases, the unknown variable is the interest rate. The **internal rate of return** for a series of cash flows is the interest rate that discounts all cash flows to a net present value of zero. Common terminology also refers to the internal rate of return as the **implicit interest rate** and, in an investment setting, as the **yield to maturity**.

EXAMPLE 14 (INTERNAL RATE OF RETURN)

Refer to question **c** in **Problem A.4 for Self-Study**. Diversified Technologies expects to pay $20 million per year at the end of each of the next three years to develop an optical scanner and then to receive $15 million per year at the end of the next five years from sales of the scanner.

We wish to know the interest rate that will discount these cash flows to a net present value of zero. Thus, we want to solve for r in the following:

$$0 = \frac{-\$20}{(1+r)^1} + \frac{-\$20}{(1+r)^2} + \frac{-\$20}{(1+r)^3} + \frac{\$15}{(1+r)^4} + \frac{\$15}{(1+r)^5} + \frac{\$15}{(1+r)^6} + \frac{\$15}{(1+r)^7} + \frac{\$15}{(1+r)^8}$$

We could try various interest rates and, by trial and error, find the value of r that results in a zero net present value. This approach, however, is tedious. Microsoft's Excel computes the internal rate of return by inputting: =IRR(specified range of cells of cash flows). The internal rate of return in this example is 5.79%.

EXAMPLE 15 (INTERNAL RATE OF RETURN OF A DEFERRED ANNUITY)

Your 60th birthday is today. With interest rates currently high, you want to purchase a deferred annuity that will begin on your 66th birthday and extend to your 85th birthday. The deferred annuity will pay you $80,000 each year and costs you $422,900 today. Compute the internal rate of return on this deferred annuity.

The time line for this annuity is

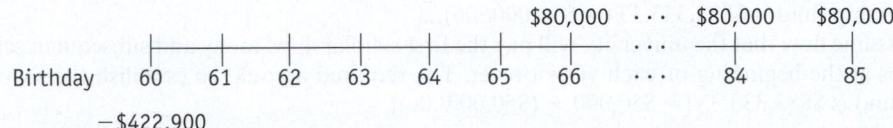

The inputs into the cells of Excel to solve for the internal rate of return are

First Cell: −422900

Second through Sixth Cells: 0

Seventh through Twenty-sixth Cells: 80000

To compute the internal rate of return: =IRR(First Cell:Twenty-sixth Cell), which yields 10.0%.

PROBLEM A.5 for Self-Study

Finding the internal rate of return. Compute the internal rate of return in each of the following cases.

a. You invest $650,000 in a bond that pays you a single amount of $1,000,000 at the end of 10 years.

b. You invest $800,000 in a bond that pays you $75,000 at the end of every six months for 10 years.

c. You invest $100,000 on January 1, 2008 for an annual annuity of $25,000 paid at the end of 2011 to 2017.

SOLUTIONS TO PROBLEMS FOR SELF-STUDY

PROBLEM A.1 FOR SELF-STUDY (FUTURE VALUE OF SINGLE SUMS)

a. $5,000 \times (1 + .06)^{10} = \$5,000 \times 1.79085 = \$8,954.25$. Excel Input: =FV(.06,10,0,−5000).

b. $5,000 \times (1 + .03)^{20} = \$5,000 \times 1.80611 = \$9,030.56$. Excel Input: =FV(.03,20,0,−5000).

c. $5,000 \times (1.08)^{33} = \$5,000 \times 12.67605 = \$63,380.25$. Excel Input: =FV(.08,33,0,−5000).

d. $5,000 \times (1.02)^{132} = \$5,000 \times 13.65283 = \$68,264.15$.
   Excel Input: =FV(.02,132,0,−5000).

PROBLEM A.2 FOR SELF-STUDY (PRESENT VALUE OF SINGLE SUMS)

a. $20,000 \times (1 + .06)^{-5} = \$20,000 \times .74726 = \$14,945.16$.
   Excel Input: =PV(.06,5,0,−20000).

b. $\$20,000 \times (1 + .005)^{-60} = \$20,000 \times .74137 = \$14,827.44$.
Excel Input: $=PV(.005,60,0,-20000)$.

c. $\$20,000 \times (1 + .05)^{-20} = \$20,000 \times .37689 = \$7,537.79$.
Excel Input: $=PV(.05,20,0,-20000)$.

d. $\$20,000 \times (1 + .02)^{-52} = \$20,000 \times .35710 = \$7,142.02$.
Excel Input: $=PV(.02,52,0,-20000)$.

PROBLEM A.3 FOR SELF-STUDY (FUTURE VALUE OF AN ANNUITY)

a. $\$2,500 \times \dfrac{(1 + .06)^{20} - 1}{.06} = \$2,500 \times 36.78559 = \$91,963.98$.
Excel Input: $= FV(.06,20,-2500)$.

b. $\$2,500 \times \left[\dfrac{(1 + .06)^{21} - 1}{.06} - 1\right]$; $x = \$2,500 \times 38.99273 = \$97,481.82$.
Excel Input: $=FV(.06,20,-2500,0,1)$.

c. $\$100,000 = x\left[\dfrac{(1 + .06)^{20} - 1}{.06} - 1\right]$; $x = \$100,000/36.78559 = \$2,718.46$.
Excel Input: $= PMT(.06,20,0,100000)$.

d. $\$100,000 = x\left[\dfrac{(1 + .06)^{21} - 1}{.06} - 1\right]$; $x = \$100,000/38.99273 = \$2,564.58$.
Excel Input: $= PMT(.06,20,0,100000,1)$.

PROBLEM A.4 FOR SELF-STUDY (PRESENT VALUE OF AN ANNUITY)

a. $\$10,000 \times \dfrac{1 - (1 + .08)^{-20}}{.08} = \$10,000 \times 9.81815 = \$98,181.47$.
Excel Input: $=PV(.08,20,10000)$.

b. $\$150,000 = x\left[\dfrac{1 - (1 + .12)^{-4}}{.12} + 1\right]$; $x = \$150,000/4.03735 = \$37,153.09$.
Excel Input: $=PMT(.12,5,-150000,0,1)$.

c. Present Value of Development Cost: $\$20 \times \dfrac{1 - (1 + .12)^{-3}}{.12} = \$20 \times 2.40183$

= $\$48.036$ million.

Present Value of Deferred Annuity: $\$15 \times \dfrac{1 - (1 + .12)^{-5}}{.12} \times \dfrac{1}{(1.12)^3}$

= $\$15 \times 2.56581 = \$38.487$ million.

The net present value is ($\$9,549$ million), which equals $\$38.487 - \$48.036$. The inputs into Excel are as follows:

Present Value of Development Costs: $=PV(.12,3,-20)$

Present Value of Deferred Annuity: $=PV(.12,8,15)$, and then subtract: $=PV(.12,3,15)$.

PROBLEM A.5 FOR SELF-STUD Y (FINDING THE INTERNAL RATE OF RETURN)

a. Excel Inputs: Cell 1: -650000. Cells 2 to 10: 0. Cell 11: 1000000. The internal rate of return is 4.4%.

b. Excel Inputs: Cell 1: -800000. Cells 2 to 21: 75000. The internal rate of return is 6.9%.

c. Excel Input: Cell 1: -100000. Cells 2 to 4: 0. Cells 5 to 11: 25000. The internal rate of return is 8.5%.

KEY TERMS AND CONCEPTS

Future value	Ordinary annuity or annuity in arrears
Compound interest	Annuity due or annuity in advance
Simple interest	Deferred annuity
Factor	Future value of an ordinary annuity
Effective annual yield	Present value of an ordinary annuity
Present value	Perpetuity
Discounting	Internal rate of return
Discount rate	Implicit interest rate
Annuity	Yield to maturity

QUESTIONS, EXERCISES, AND PROBLEMS

QUESTIONS

1. Review the terms and concepts listed above in Key Terms and Concepts.

2. How does interest equate cash flows over time?

3. Distinguish between simple and compound interest.

4. Distinguish between the discounted present value of a stream of future payments and their net present value. If there is no distinction, then so state.

5. Distinguish between an annuity due and an ordinary annuity.

6. Describe the implicit interest rate for a series of cash flows and a procedure for finding it.

7. Does the present value of a given amount to be paid in 10 years increase or decrease if the interest rate increases? Suppose that the amount is due in 5 years? 20 years? Does the present value of an annuity to be paid for 10 years increase or decrease if the discount rate decreases? Suppose that the annuity is for 5 years? 20 years?

8. Rather than pay you $1,000 a month for the next 20 years, the person who injured you in an automobile accident is willing to pay a single amount now to settle your claim for injuries. Would you rather use an interest rate of 6% or 12% in computing the present value of the lump-sum settlement? Comment or explain.

9. The perpetuity with growth formula involves several assumptions. Which one seems least plausible?

EXERCISES

Exercises 10 through 15 involve calculations of present and future value for single payments and for annuities. To make the exercises more realistic, we do not give specific guidance with each individual exercise.

10. Mr. Altgeldt has $5,000 to invest. He wants to know how much it will amount to if he invests it at the following rates:

    a. 6% per year for 21 years

    b. 8% per year for 33 years

11. Mme. Barefield wishes to have $150,000 at the end of 8 years. How much must she invest today to accomplish this purpose if the interest rate is

    a. 6% per year?

    b. 8% per year?

12. Mr. Case plans to set aside $4,000 each year, the first payment to be made on January 1, 2008, and the last on January 1, 2013. How much will he have accumulated by January 1, 2013, if the interest rate is

    a. 6% per year?

    b. 8% per year?

13. Ms. Namura wants to have ¥45 million on her 65th birthday. She asks you to tell her how much she must deposit on each birthday from her 58th to 65th, inclusive, in order to receive this amount. Assume the following interest rates:

  a. 8% per year

  b. 12% per year

14. If Mr. Enmetti invests €90,000 on June 1 of each year from 2008 to 2018 inclusive, how much will he have accumulated on June 1, 2019 (note that one year elapses after the last payment), if the interest rate is

  a. 5% per year?

  b. 10% per year?

15. Ms. Fleming has £145,000 with which she purchases an annuity on February 1, 2008. The annuity consists of six annual receipts, the first to be received on February 1, 2009. How much will she receive in each payment? Assume the following interest rates:

  a. 8% per year

  b. 12% per year

16. In the preceding **Exercises 10** through **15**, you computed a number. To do so, first you must decide on the appropriate factor from the tables, and then you use that factor in the appropriate calculation. Notice that you could omit the last step. You could write an arithmetic expression showing the factor you want to use without actually copying down the number and doing the arithmetic. For example, the notation $T(i, p, r)$ means Table i (1, 2, 3, or 4), row p (periods 1 to 20, 22, 24 . . . , 40, 45, 50, 100), and column r (interest rates from 1/2% up to 20%). Thus, $T(3, 16, 12)$ would be the factor in **Table 3** for 16 periods and an interest rate of 12% per period, which is 42.75328. Using this notation, you can write an expression for any compound interest problem. A clerk or a computer can evaluate the expression.

   You can check that you understand this notation by observing that the following are true statements:

$T(1, 20, 8)$	=	4.66096
$T(2, 12, 5)$	=	0.55684
$T(3, 16, 12)$	=	42.75328
$T(4, 10, 20)$	=	4.19247

   In the following questions, write an expression for the answer using the notation introduced here, but do not attempt to evaluate the expression.

  a. Work the **a** parts of **Exercises 10** through **15**.

  b. How might your instructor use this notation to write examination questions on compound interest without having to supply you with tables?

17. Effective interest rate. State the rate per period and the number of periods in the following:

  a. 12% per year, for 5 years, compounded annually

  b. 12% per year, for 5 years, compounded semiannually

  c. 12% per year, for 5 years, compounded quarterly

  d. 12% per year, for 5 years, compounded monthly

Exercises 18 through 26 involve calculations of present and future value for single payments and for annuities. To make the exercises more realistic, we do not give specific guidance with each individual exercise.

18. Compute the future value of the following:

  a. $100 invested for 5 years at 4% compounded annually

  b. $500 invested for 15 periods at 2% compounded once per period

  c. $200 invested for 8 years at 3% compounded semiannually

  d. $2,500 invested for 14 years at 8% compounded quarterly

  e. $600 invested for 3 years at 12% compounded monthly

19. Compute the present value of the following:

    a. $100 due in 30 years at 4% compounded annually

    b. $250 due in 8 years at 8% compounded quarterly

    c. $1,000 due in 2 years at 12% compounded monthly

20. Compute the amount (future value) of an ordinary annuity (an annuity in arrears) of the following:

    a. 13 rental payments of $100 at 1% per period

    b. 8 rental payments of $850 at 6% per period

    c. 28 rental payments of $400 at 4% per period

21. Mr. Grady agrees to lease a certain property for 10 years, at the following annual rental, payable in advance:

    Years 1 and 2—$1,000 per year
    Years 3 to 6—$2,000 per year
    Years 7 to 10—$2,500 per year

    What single immediate sum will pay all of these rents, discounted at

    a. 6% per year?

    b. 8% per year?

    c. 10% per year?

22. To establish a fund that will provide a scholarship of $3,000 per year indefinitely, with the first award to occur now, how much must a donor deposit if the fund earns

    a. 6% per period?

    b. 8% per period?

23. Consider the scholarship fund in the preceding question. Suppose that the first scholarship award occurs one year from now and the donor wants the scholarship to grow by 2% per year. How much should the donor deposit if the fund earns

    a. 6% per period?

    b. 8% per period?

    Suppose that the first scholarship award occurs five years from now but is to grow at 2% per year after the fifth year, the time of the first $3,000 award. How much should the donor deposit if the fund earns

    c. 6% per year?

    d. 8% per year?

24. An old agreement obliges the state to help a rural county maintain a bridge by paying $60,000 now and every two years thereafter forever. The state wants to discharge its obligation by paying a single sum to the county now for the payment due and all future payments. How much should the state pay the county if the discount rate is

    a. 8% per year?

    b. 12% per year?

25. Find the interest rate implicit in a loan of $100,000 that the borrower discharges with two annual installments of $55,307 each, paid at the end of each of the next two years.

26. A single-payment note promises to pay $140,493 in three years. The issuer exchanges the note for equipment having a fair value of $100,000. The exchange occurs three years before the maturity date on the note. What is the implicit interest rate for the single-payment note?

27. A single-payment note promises $67,280 at maturity. The issuer of the note exchanges it for land with a fair value of $50,000. The exchange occurs two years before the maturity date on the note.

    a. What is the implicit interest rate for this single-payment note?

    b. Using the implicit interest rate, construct an amortization schedule for the note. Show the carrying value of the note at the start of each year, the amount of interest expense for each year, the amount reducing or increasing the carrying value each year, and the carrying value at the end of the year.

28. **Finding implicit interest rates; constructing amortization schedules**. Berman Company purchased a plot of land for possible future development. The land had fair value of $86,000. Berman Company gave a 3-year interest-bearing note. The note had face value of $100,000 and provided for interest at a stated rate of 8%. The note requires payments of $8,000 at the end of each of three years, the last payment coinciding with the maturity of the note's face value of $100,000.

   a. What is the interest rate implicit in the note, accurate to the nearest tenth of 1%?

   b. Construct an amortization schedule for the note for each year. Show the carrying value of the note at the start of the year, interest for the year, payment for the year, amount reducing or increasing the carrying value of the note for each payment, and the carrying value of the note at the end of each year. Use the interest rate found in part **a**. See **Exhibit 10.2** for an example of an amortization schedule.

29. **Find equivalent annual rate offered for purchase discounts**. The terms of sale "2/10, net/30" mean that the buyer can take a discount of 2% from gross invoice price by paying the invoice within 10 days; otherwise, the buyer must pay the full amount within 30 days.

   a. Write an expression for the implicit annual rate of interest being offered by viewing the entire discount as interest for funds received sooner rather than later. (Note that by not taking the discount, the buyer borrows 98% of the gross invoice price for 20 days.)

   b. The tables at the back of the book do not permit the exact evaluation of the expression derived in part **a**. The rate of interest implied is 44.59% per year. Use the tables to convince yourself that this astounding (to some) answer must be close to correct.

PROBLEMS

Problems 30 through 44 involve using future value and present value techniques, including perpetuities, to solve a variety of realistic problems. We give no hints as to the specific calculation with the problems.

30. An oil-drilling company figures that it must spend $30,000 for an initial supply of drill bits and that it must spend $10,000 every month to replace the worn-out bits. What is the present value of the cost of the bits if the company plans to be in business indefinitely and discounts payments at 1% per month?

31. If you promise to leave $35,000 on deposit at the Dime Savings Bank for 4 years, the bank will give you a new large, flat-screen Sony TV today and your $35,000 back at the end of 4 years. How much are you paying today for the TV, in effect, if the bank pays other customers 8% interest compounded quarterly (2% paid 4 times per year)?

32. When Mr. Shafer died, his estate after taxes amounted to $300,000. His will provided that Mrs. Shafer would receive $24,000 per year starting immediately from the principal of the estate and that the balance of the principal would pass to the Shafers' children upon Mrs. Shafer's death. The state law governing this estate provided for a dower option. If Mrs. Shafer elects the dower option, she renounces the will and can have one-third of the estate in cash now. The remainder will then pass immediately to their children. Mrs. Shafer wants to maximize the present value of her bequest. Should she take the annuity or elect the dower option if she will receive 5 payments and discounts payments at

   a. 8% per year?

   b. 12% per year?
   (Note this problem explicitly states that Mrs. Shafer will receive 5 payments. In reality, life expectancy is uncertain. The correct calculation combines a mortality table with the present value tables. Actuaries deal with such calculations.)

33. Mrs. Heileman occasionally drinks beer. (Guess which brand.) She consumes one case in 20 weeks. She can buy beer in disposable cans for $25.20 per case or for $24.00 per case of returnable bottles if she pays a $3.00 refundable deposit at the time of purchase. If her discount rate is 1/2% per week, how much in present value dollars does she save by buying the returnables and thereby losing the use of the $3.00 deposit for 20 weeks?

34. When General Electric Company first introduced the Lucalox ceramic, screw-in light bulb, the bulb cost three and one-half times as much as an ordinary bulb but lasted five

times as long. An ordinary bulb cost $1.00 and lasted about 8 months. If a firm has a discount rate of 12% compounded 3 times a year, how much would it save in present-value dollars by using one Lucalox bulb?

35. Oberweis Dairy switched from delivery trucks with regular gasoline engines to ones with diesel engines. The diesel trucks cost $2,000 more than the ordinary gasoline trucks but costs $600 per year less to operate. Assume that Oberweis saves the operating costs at the end of each month. If Oberweis uses a discount rate of 1% per month, approximately how many months, at a minimum, must the diesel trucks remain in service for the switch to be sensible?

36. **Calculating impairment**. On January 1, 2008, assume that Levi Strauss opened a new textile plant to produce synthetic fabrics. The plant is on leased land; 20 years remain on the nonrenewable lease.

    The cost of the plant was $20 million. Net cash flow to be derived from the project is estimated to be $3,000,000 per year. The company does not normally invest in such projects unless the anticipated yield is at least 12%.

    On December 31, 2008, the company calculates that cash flows from the plant were $2,800,000 for 2008. On the same day, farm experts predict cotton production will be unusually low for the next two years. Levi Strauss estimates the resulting increase in demand for synthetic fabrics will boost cash flows to $3,500,000 for each of the next two years. Subsequent years' estimates remain unchanged at $3,000,000 per year. Ignore tax considerations.

    a. Calculate the present value of the future expected cash flows from the plant when it opened.

    b. What is the present value of the plant on January 1, 2009, immediately after the re-estimation of future cash flows?

    c. On January 2, 2009, the day following the cotton production news release, a competitor announces plans to build a synthetic fabrics plant to open in three years. Levi Strauss keeps its 2009 to 2011 estimates but reduces the estimated annual cash flows for subsequent years to $2,000,000. What is the value of Levi Strauss's plant on January 1, 2009, after the new projections?

    d. On January 2, 2009, an investor contacts Levi Strauss about purchasing a 20% share of the plant. If the investor expects to earn at least a 12% annual return on the investment, what is the maximum amount that the investor should pay? Assume that the investor and Levi Strauss both know all relevant information and use the same estimates of annual cash flows described in part **c**.

37. **Finding implicit interest rates (truth-in-lending laws reduce the type of deception suggested by this problem)**. Friendly Loan Company advertises that it is willing to lend cash for five years at the low rate of 8% per year. A potential borrower discovers that a 5-year, $10,000 loan requires that the borrower pay the 8% interest in advance, with interest deducted from the loan proceeds. The borrower will collect $6,000 [= $10,000 − (5 × 0.08 × $10,000)] in cash and must repay the "$10,000" loan in five annual installments of $2,000, one each at the end of the next 5 years.

    Compute the effective interest rate implied by these loan terms.

38. **Deriving net present value of cash flows for decision to dispose of asset.** Suppose that yesterday Black & Decker Company purchased and installed a made-to-order machine tool for fabricating parts for small appliances. The machine cost $100,000. Today, Square D Company offers a machine tool that will do exactly the same work but costs only $50,000. Assume that the discount rate is 12%, that both machines will last for 5 years, that Black & Decker will depreciate both machines on a straight-line basis with no salvage value for tax purposes, that the income tax rate is and will continue to be 40%, and that Black & Decker earns sufficient income that it can use any loss from disposing of or depreciating the "old" machine to offset other taxable income.

    How much, at a minimum, must the "old" machine fetch on resale at this time to make purchasing the new machine worthwhile?

39. **Computation of present value of cash flows; untaxed acquisition, no change in tax basis of assets.** The balance sheet of Lynch Company shows net assets of $100,000 and shareholders' equity of $100,000. The assets are all depreciable assets with remaining lives of 20 years. The income statement for the year shows revenues of $700,000, depreciation of

$50,000 (= $1,000,000 ÷ 20 years), no other expenses, income taxes of $260,000 (40% of pretax income of $650,000), and net income of $390,000.

Bages Company is considering purchasing all of the stock of Lynch Company. It is willing to pay an amount equal to the present value of the cash flows from operations for the next 20 years discounted at a rate of 10% per year.

The transaction will be a tax-free exchange; that is, after the purchase, the tax basis of the assets of Lynch Company will remain unchanged so that depreciation charges will remain at $50,000 per year and income taxes will remain at $260,000 per year. Revenues will be $700,000 per year for the next 20 years.

a. Compute the annual cash flows produced by Lynch Company.

b. Compute the maximum amount Bages Company should be willing to pay.

40. **Computation of the present value of cash flows; taxable acquisition, changing tax basis of assets.** Refer to the data in the preceding problem. Assume now that the acquisition is taxable, so that the tax basis of the assets acquired changes after the purchase. If the purchase price is $V, then depreciation charges will be $V/20 per year for 20 years. Income taxes will be 40% of pretax income. What is the maximum Bages Company should be willing to pay for Lynch Company?

41. **Valuation of intangibles with perpetuity formulas.** When the American Basketball Association (ABA) merged with the National Basketball Association (NBA), the owners of the ABA St. Louis Spirits agreed to dissolve their team and not enter the NBA. In return, the owners received a promise in perpetuity from the NBA that the NBA would pay to the Spirits' owners an amount each year equal to 40% of the TV revenues that the NBA paid to any one of its regular teams. Currently, the owners receive $4 million per year. The NBA wants to pay a single amount to the owners now and not have to pay more in the future. Of course, the owners prefer to collect more, rather than less, but here they want to know the reasonable minimum that will make them indifferent to the single payment in lieu of receiving the annual payments in perpetuity. Ignore income tax effects.

a. Assume the owners expect the TV revenues to remain constant, so that they can expect $4 million per year in perpetuity and use an interest rate of 8% in their discounting calculations. What minimum price should these owners be willing to accept?

b. Refer to the specifications for the preceding question. If the owners use a smaller interest rate for discounting, will the minimum price they are willing to accept increase, decrease, or remain unchanged?

c. The owners use an 8% discount rate, and they expect TV revenues to increase by 2% per year in perpetuity, with the next collection, due one year from today, being $4.08 (= 1.02 × $4.00) million. What minimum price should the owners be willing to accept?

d. Refer to the specifications in **c**. If the owners use a smaller interest rate for discounting, will the minimum price they are willing to accept increase, decrease, or remain unchanged?

e. Refer to the specifications in **c**. If the owners assume a smaller rate for growth in future receipts from the NBA, will the minimum price they are willing to accept increase, decrease, or remain unchanged?

42. **(Adapted from a problem by S. Zeff.)** Lexie T. Colleton is the chief financial officer of Ragazze, and one of her duties is to give advice on investment projects. Today's date is December 31, 2008. Colleton requires that, to be acceptable, new investments must provide a positive net present value after discounting cash flows at 12% per year.

A proposed investment is the purchase of an automatic gonculator, which involves an initial cash disbursement on December 31, 2008. The useful life of the machine is nine years, through 2017. Colleton expects to be able to sell the machine for cash of $30,000 on December 31, 2017. She expects commercial production to begin on December 31, 2009.

Ragazze will depreciate the machine on a straight-line basis. Ignore income taxes.

During 2009, the break-in year, Ragazze will perform test runs in order to put the machine in proper working order. Colleton expects that the total cash outlay for this purpose will be $20,000, incurred at the end of 2009.

Colleton expects that the cash disbursements for regular maintenance will be $60,000 at the end of each of 2010 through 2013 inclusive, and $100,000 at the end of each of 2014 through 2016 inclusive.

Colleton expects the cash receipts (net of all other operating expenses) from the sale of products that the machine produces to be $130,000 at the end of each year from 2010 through 2017, inclusive.

a. What is the maximum price that Ragazze can pay for the automatic gonculator on December 31, 2008, and still earn a positive net present value of cash flows?

b. Independent of your answer to part **a**, assume the purchase price is $250,000, which Ragazze will pay with an installment note requiring four equal annual installments starting December 31, 2009, and an implicit interest rate of 10% per year. What is the amount of each payment?

43. **(Adapted from a problem by S. Zeff.)** William Marsh, CEO of Gulf Coast Manufacturing, wishes to know which of two strategies he has chosen for acquiring an automobile has lower present value of cost.

Strategy L. Acquire a new Lexus at the beginning of 2008, keep it until the end of 2013, then trade it in on a new car.

Strategy M. Acquire a new Mercedes-Benz at the beginning of 2008, trade it in at the end of 2010 on a second Mercedes-Benz, keep that for another three years, then trade it in on a new car at the end of 2013.

Data pertinent to these choices appear below. Assume that Marsh will receive the trade-in value in cash or as a credit toward the purchase price of a new car. Ignore income taxes and use a discount rate of 10% per year. Gulf Coast Manufacturing depreciates automobiles on a straight-line basis over 8 years for financial reporting, assuming zero salvage value at the end of 8 years.

a. Which strategy has lower present value of costs?

b. What role, if any, do depreciation charges play in the analysis and why?

	Lexus	Mercedes-Benz
Initial Cost at the Start of 2008	$60,000	$ 45,000
Initial Cost at the Start of 2011		48,000
Trade-in Value		
End of 2010		23,000
End of 2013[1]	16,000	24,500
Estimated Annual Cash Operating Costs		
Except Major Servicing	4,000	4,500
Estimated Cash Cost of Major Servicing		
End of 2011	6,500	
End of 2009 and End of 2012		2,500

[1]At this time Lexus is 6 years old; second Mercedes-Benz is 3 years old.

44. **(Wal Mart Stores; perpetuity growth model derivation of results in Chapter 6.)** Refer to the discussion on page 284 in **Chapter 6**. There, in estimating the value of a share of common stock of Wal-Mart Stores, we computed the present value of excess cash flows at the end of fiscal year 2008 (= beginning of fiscal year 2009) to be $269,244 million. This exercise requires you to confirm that computation.

To compute the amount for the years after 2013, note we assume that the excess cash flows are $7,884 million at the end of 2013 and grow at the rate of 10% per year thereafter. That means the cash flows for the end of fiscal year 2014 are $8,672.4 (= 1.10 × $7,884) million. You can use the perpetuity growth model to verify that the present value at the end of 2013 of that growing stream of payments is $433,620 million (= $8,672.4/(.12 − .10). That is, if a payment (in this case $7,884 million), grows at rate g (in this case, 10%) per period forever, the discount rate is r (in this case, 12%) per period, and the first payment occurs at the end of the first period, then the present value of that stream is $433,620 [= $8,672.4/(r − g) = $8,672.4/(0.12 − 0.10)] million. Then, we discount that amount to the end of fiscal 2008 to derive $246,048 million. Analysts describe the $246,048 million valuation in such computations as the terminal value.

(We do not expect that Wal-Mart's excess cash flows could increase forever at 10% per year. After a century or so, such a firm would be larger than the rest of the entire U.S. economy, combined. We use such computations to estimate values. When the discount rate (here 12% per year) exceeds the growth rate (here 10% per year) by a substantial amount (here only 2 percentage points), the present value of payments far in the future, say more than 40 years out, is negligible.)

    a. Reproduce the numbers in Column **(6)** on page 284 using the data from Column **(5)** and the appropriate present value computations.

    b. Re-do the valuation changing the growth rate after 2013 from 10% to 9%.

    c. Re-do the valuation changing the growth rate after 2013 from 10% to 5%.

    d. Comment on the sensitivity of this valuation modeling tool to the effect of assumed growth rates on terminal values.

45. **(Fast Growth Start-Up Company; valuation involving perpetuity growth model assumptions.)** Fast Growth Start-Up Company (FGSUC) has a new successful Internet business. It expects to earn $100 million of after-tax free cash flows this year. The company proposes to go public and the company's internal financial staff suggests to the board of directors that a valuation of $2.5 billion seems reasonable for the company. The investment banking firm's analyst and the financial staff at the company agree that the growth rate in free cash flows will be 25% per year for several years before the growth rate drops back to one more closely resembling the growth rate in the economy as a whole, which all assume to be 4% per year. Assume that the after-tax discount rate suitable for such a new venture is 15% per year.

    How many years of growth in after-tax free cash flow of 25% per year will FGSUC need to earn to justify a market valuation of $2.5 billion? Do not attempt to work this problem without using a spreadsheet program.

Compound Interest
and Annuity Tables

TABLE 1

Future Value of $1

$$F_n = P(1 + r)^n$$

r = interest rate; n = number of periods until valuation; P = $1

Periods = n	½%	1%	1½%	2%	3%	4%	5%	6%	7%	8%	10%	12%	15%	20%	25%
1	1.00500	1.01000	1.01503	1.02000	1.03000	1.04000	1.05000	1.06000	1.07000	1.08000	1.10000	1.12000	1.15000	1.20000	1.25000
2	1.01003	1.02010	1.03023	1.04040	1.06090	1.08160	1.10250	1.12360	1.14490	1.16640	1.21000	1.25440	1.32250	1.44000	1.56250
3	1.01508	1.03030	1.04568	1.06121	1.09273	1.12486	1.15763	1.19102	1.22504	1.25971	1.33100	1.40493	1.52088	1.72800	1.95313
4	1.02015	1.04060	1.06136	1.08243	1.12551	1.16986	1.21551	1.26248	1.31080	1.36049	1.46410	1.57352	1.74901	2.07360	2.44141
5	1.02525	1.05101	1.07728	1.10408	1.15927	1.21665	1.27628	1.33823	1.40255	1.46933	1.61051	1.76234	2.01136	2.48832	3.05176
6	1.03038	1.06152	1.09344	1.12616	1.19405	1.26532	1.34010	1.41852	1.50073	1.58687	1.77156	1.97382	2.31306	2.98598	3.81470
7	1.03553	1.07214	1.10984	1.14869	1.22987	1.31593	1.40710	1.50363	1.60578	1.71382	1.94872	2.21068	2.66002	3.58318	4.76837
8	1.04071	1.08286	1.12649	1.17166	1.26677	1.36857	1.47746	1.59385	1.71819	1.85093	2.14359	2.47596	3.05902	4.29982	5.96046
9	1.04591	1.09369	1.14339	1.19509	1.30477	1.42331	1.55133	1.68948	1.83846	1.99900	2.35795	2.77308	3.51788	5.15978	7.45058
10	1.05114	1.10462	1.16054	1.21899	1.34392	1.48024	1.62889	1.79085	1.96715	2.15892	2.59374	3.10585	4.04556	6.19174	9.31323
11	1.05640	1.11567	1.17795	1.24337	1.38423	1.53945	1.71034	1.89830	2.10485	2.33164	2.85312	3.47855	4.65239	7.43008	11.64153
12	1.06168	1.12683	1.19562	1.26824	1.42576	1.60103	1.79586	2.01220	2.25219	2.51817	3.13843	3.89598	5.35025	8.91610	14.55192
13	1.06699	1.13809	1.21355	1.29361	1.46853	1.66507	1.88565	2.13293	2.40985	2.71962	3.45227	4.36349	6.15279	10.69932	18.18989
14	1.07232	1.14947	1.23176	1.31948	1.51259	1.73168	1.97993	2.26090	2.57853	2.93719	3.79750	4.88711	7.07571	12.83918	22.73737
15	1.07768	1.16097	1.25023	1.34587	1.55797	1.80094	2.07893	2.39656	2.75903	3.17217	4.17725	5.47357	8.13706	15.40702	28.42171
16	1.08307	1.17258	1.26899	1.37279	1.60471	1.87298	2.18287	2.54035	2.95216	3.42594	4.59497	6.13039	9.35762	18.48843	35.52714
17	1.08849	1.18430	1.28802	1.40024	1.65285	1.94790	2.29202	2.69277	3.15882	3.70002	5.05447	6.86604	10.76126	22.18611	44.40892
18	1.09393	1.19615	1.30734	1.42825	1.70243	2.02582	2.40662	2.85434	3.37993	3.99602	5.55992	7.68997	12.37545	26.62333	55.51115
19	1.09940	1.20811	1.32695	1.45681	1.75351	2.10685	2.52695	3.02560	3.61653	4.31570	6.11591	8.61276	14.23177	31.94800	69.38894
20	1.10490	1.22019	1.34686	1.48595	1.80611	2.19112	2.65330	3.20714	3.86968	4.66096	6.72750	9.64629	16.36654	38.33760	86.73617
22	1.11597	1.24472	1.38756	1.54598	1.91610	2.36992	2.92526	3.60354	4.43040	5.43654	8.14027	12.10031	21.64475	55.20614	135.5253
24	1.12716	1.26973	1.42950	1.60844	2.03279	2.56330	3.22510	4.04893	5.07237	6.34118	9.84973	15.17863	28.62518	79.49685	211.7582
26	1.13846	1.29526	1.47271	1.67342	2.15659	2.77247	3.55567	4.54938	5.80735	7.39635	11.91818	19.04007	37.85680	114.4755	330.8722
28	1.14987	1.32129	1.51722	1.74102	2.28793	2.99870	3.92013	5.11169	6.64884	8.62711	14.42099	23.88387	50.06561	164.8447	516.9879
30	1.16140	1.34785	1.56308	1.81136	2.42726	3.24340	4.32194	5.74349	7.61226	10.06266	17.44940	29.95992	66.21177	237.3763	807.7936
32	1.17304	1.37494	1.61032	1.88454	2.57508	3.50806	4.76494	6.45339	8.71527	11.73708	21.11378	37.58173	87.56507	341.8219	1262.177
34	1.18480	1.40258	1.65068	1.96068	2.73191	3.79432	5.25335	7.25103	9.97811	13.69013	25.54767	47.14252	115.80480	492.2235	1972.152
36	1.19668	1.43077	1.70914	2.03989	2.89828	4.10393	5.79182	8.14725	11.42394	15.96817	30.91268	59.13557	153.15185	708.8019	3081.488
38	1.20868	1.45953	1.76080	2.12230	3.07478	4.43881	6.38548	9.15425	13.07927	18.62528	37.40434	74.17966	202.54332	1020.675	4814.825
40	1.22079	1.48886	1.81402	2.20804	3.26204	4.80102	7.03999	10.28572	14.97446	21.72452	45.25926	93.05097	267.86355	1469.772	7523.164
45	1.25162	1.56481	1.95421	2.43785	3.78160	5.84118	8.98501	13.76461	21.00245	31.92045	72.89048	163.9876	538.76927	3657.262	22958.87
50	1.28323	1.64463	2.10524	2.69159	4.38391	7.10668	11.46740	18.42015	29.45703	46.90161	117.3909	289.0022	1083.65744	9100.438	70064.92
100	1.64667	2.70481	4.43205	7.24465	19.21863	50.50495	131.5013	339.3021	867.7163	2199.761	13780.61	83522.27	117×10^4	828×10^5	491×10^7

TABLE 2

Present Value of $1

$$P = F_n(1 + r)^{-n}$$

r = discount rate; n = number of periods until payment; $F_n = \$1$

Periods = n	½%	1%	1½%	2%	3%	4%	5%	6%	7%	8%	10%	12%	15%	20%	25%
1	.99502	.99010	.98522	.98039	.97087	.96154	.95238	.94340	.93458	.92593	.90909	.89286	.86957	.83333	.80000
2	.99007	.98030	.97066	.96117	.94260	.92456	.90703	.89000	.87344	.85734	.82645	.79719	.75614	.69444	.64000
3	.98515	.97059	.95632	.94232	.91514	.88900	.86384	.83962	.81630	.79383	.75131	.71178	.65752	.57870	.51200
4	.98025	.96098	.94218	.92385	.88849	.85480	.82270	.79209	.76290	.73503	.68301	.63552	.57175	.48225	.40960
5	.97537	.95147	.92826	.90573	.86261	.82193	.78353	.74726	.71299	.68058	.62092	.56743	.49718	.40188	.32768
6	.97052	.94205	.91454	.88797	.83748	.79031	.74622	.70496	.66634	.63017	.56447	.50663	.43233	.33490	.26214
7	.96569	.93272	.90103	.87056	.81309	.75992	.71068	.66506	.62275	.58349	.51316	.45235	.37594	.27908	.20972
8	.96089	.92348	.88771	.85349	.78941	.73069	.67684	.62741	.58201	.54027	.46651	.40388	.32690	.23257	.16777
9	.95610	.91434	.87459	.83676	.76642	.70259	.64461	.59190	.54393	.50025	.42410	.36061	.28426	.19381	.13422
10	.95135	.90529	.86167	.82035	.74409	.67556	.61391	.55839	.50835	.46319	.38554	.32197	.24718	.16151	.10737
11	.94661	.89632	.84893	.80426	.72242	.64958	.58468	.52679	.47509	.42888	.35049	.28748	.21494	.13459	.08590
12	.94191	.88745	.83639	.78849	.70138	.62460	.55684	.49697	.44401	.39711	.31863	.25668	.18691	.11216	.06872
13	.93722	.87866	.82403	.77303	.68095	.60057	.53032	.46884	.41496	.36770	.28966	.22917	.16253	.09346	.05498
14	.93256	.86996	.81185	.75788	.66112	.57748	.50507	.44230	.38782	.34046	.26333	.20462	.14133	.07789	.04398
15	.92792	.86135	.79985	.74301	.64186	.55526	.48102	.41727	.36245	.31524	.23939	.18270	.12289	.06491	.03518
16	.92330	.85282	.78803	.72845	.62317	.53391	.45811	.39365	.33873	.29189	.21763	.16312	.10686	.05409	.02815
17	.91871	.84438	.77639	.71416	.60502	.51337	.43630	.37136	.31657	.27027	.19784	.14564	.09293	.04507	.02252
18	.91414	.83602	.76491	.70016	.58739	.49363	.41552	.35034	.29586	.25025	.17986	.13004	.08081	.03756	.01801
19	.90959	.82774	.75361	.68643	.57029	.47464	.39573	.33051	.27661	.23171	.16351	.11611	.07027	.03130	.01441
20	.90506	.81954	.74247	.67297	.55368	.45639	.37689	.31180	.25842	.21455	.14864	.10367	.06110	.02608	.01153
22	.89608	.80340	.72069	.64684	.52189	.42196	.34185	.27751	.22571	.18394	.12285	.08264	.04620	.01811	.00738
24	.88719	.78757	.69954	.62172	.49193	.39012	.31007	.24698	.19715	.15770	.10153	.06588	.03493	.01258	.00472
26	.87838	.77205	.67902	.59758	.46369	.36069	.28124	.21981	.17220	.13520	.08391	.05252	.02642	.00874	.00302
28	.86966	.75684	.65910	.57437	.43708	.33348	.25509	.19563	.15040	.11591	.06934	.04187	.01997	.00607	.00193
30	.86103	.74192	.63976	.55207	.41199	.30832	.23138	.17411	.13137	.09938	.05731	.03338	.01510	.00421	.00124
32	.85248	.72730	.62099	.53063	.38834	.28506	.20987	.15496	.11474	.08520	.04736	.02661	.01142	.00293	.00079
34	.84402	.71297	.60277	.51003	.36604	.26355	.19035	.13791	.10022	.07305	.03914	.02121	.00864	.00203	.00051
36	.83564	.69892	.58509	.49022	.34503	.24367	.17266	.12274	.08754	.06262	.03235	.01691	.00653	.00141	.00032
38	.82735	.68515	.56792	.47119	.32523	.22529	.15661	.10924	.07646	.05369	.02673	.01348	.00494	.00098	.00021
40	.81914	.67165	.55126	.45289	.30656	.20829	.14205	.09722	.06678	.04603	.02209	.01075	.00373	.00068	.00013
45	.79896	.63905	.51171	.41020	.26444	.17120	.11130	.07265	.04761	.03133	.01372	.00610	.00186	.00027	.00004
50	.77929	.60804	.47500	.37153	.22811	.14071	.08720	.05429	.03395	.02132	.00852	.00346	.00092	.00011	.00001
100	.60729	.36971	.22563	.13803	.05203	.01980	.00760	.00295	.00115	.00045	.00007	.00001	.00000	.00000	.00000

TABLE 3

Future Value of an Annuity of $1 in Arrears

$$FV_A = \frac{(1 + r)^n - 1}{r}$$

r = interest rate; n = number of payments

No. of Payments = n	½%	1%	1½%	2%	3%	4%	5%	6%	7%	8%	10%	12%	15%	20%	25%
1	1.00000	1.00000	1.00000	1.00000	1.00000	1.00000	1.00000	1.00000	1.00000	1.00000	1.00000	1.00000	1.00000	1.00000	1.00000
2	2.00500	2.01000	2.01500	2.02000	2.03000	2.04000	2.05000	2.06000	2.07000	2.08000	2.10000	2.12000	2.15000	2.20000	2.25000
3	3.01503	3.03010	3.04523	3.06040	3.09090	3.12160	3.15250	3.18360	3.21490	3.24640	3.31000	3.37440	3.47250	3.64000	3.81250
4	4.03010	4.06040	4.09090	4.12161	4.18363	4.24646	4.31013	4.37462	4.43994	4.50611	4.64100	4.77933	4.99338	5.36800	5.76563
5	5.05025	5.10101	5.15227	5.20404	5.30914	5.41632	5.52563	5.63709	5.75074	5.86660	6.10510	6.35285	6.74238	7.44160	8.20703
6	6.07550	6.15202	6.22955	6.30812	6.46841	6.63298	6.80191	6.97532	7.15329	7.33593	7.71561	8.11519	8.75374	9.92992	11.25879
7	7.10588	7.21354	7.32299	7.43428	7.66246	7.89829	8.14201	8.39384	8.65402	8.92280	9.48717	10.08901	11.06680	12.91590	15.07349
8	8.14141	8.28567	8.43284	8.58297	8.89234	9.21423	9.54911	9.89747	10.25980	10.63663	11.43589	12.29969	13.72682	16.49908	19.84186
9	9.18212	9.36853	9.55933	9.75463	10.15911	10.58280	11.02656	11.49132	11.97799	12.48756	13.57948	14.77566	16.78584	20.79890	25.80232
10	10.22803	10.46221	10.70272	10.94972	11.46388	12.00611	12.57789	13.18079	13.81645	14.48656	15.93742	17.54874	20.30372	25.95868	33.25290
11	11.27917	11.56683	11.86326	12.16872	12.80780	13.48635	14.20679	14.97164	15.78360	16.64549	18.53117	20.65458	24.34928	32.15042	42.56613
12	12.33556	12.68250	13.04121	13.41209	14.19203	15.02581	15.91713	16.86994	17.88845	18.97713	21.38428	24.13313	29.00167	39.58050	54.20766
13	13.39724	13.80933	14.23683	14.68033	15.61779	16.62684	17.71298	18.88214	20.14064	21.49530	24.52271	28.02911	34.35192	48.49660	68.75958
14	14.46423	14.94742	15.45038	15.97394	17.08632	18.29191	19.59863	21.01507	22.55049	24.21492	27.97498	32.39260	40.50471	59.19592	86.94947
15	15.53655	16.09690	16.68214	17.29342	18.59891	20.02359	21.57856	23.27597	25.12902	27.15211	31.77248	37.27971	47.58041	72.03511	109.6868
16	16.61423	17.25786	17.93237	18.63929	20.15688	21.82453	23.65749	25.67253	27.88805	30.32428	35.94973	42.75328	55.71747	87.44213	138.1085
17	17.69730	18.43044	19.20136	20.01207	21.76159	23.69751	25.84037	28.21288	30.84022	33.75023	40.54470	48.88367	65.07509	105.9306	173.6357
18	18.78579	19.61475	20.48938	21.41231	23.41444	25.64541	28.13238	30.90565	33.99903	37.45024	45.59917	55.74971	75.83636	128.1167	218.0446
19	19.87972	20.81090	21.79672	22.84056	25.11687	27.67123	30.53900	33.75999	37.37896	41.44626	51.15909	63.43968	88.21181	154.7400	273.5558
20	20.97912	22.01900	23.12367	24.29737	26.87037	29.77808	33.06595	36.78559	40.99549	45.76196	57.27500	72.05244	102.44358	186.6880	342.9447
22	23.19443	24.47159	25.83758	27.29898	30.53678	34.24797	38.50521	43.39229	49.00574	55.45676	71.40275	92.50258	137.63164	271.0307	538.1011
24	25.43196	26.97346	28.63352	30.42186	34.42647	39.08260	44.50200	50.81558	58.17667	66.76476	88.49733	118.15524	184.16784	392.4842	843.0329
26	27.69191	29.52563	31.51397	33.67091	38.55304	44.31174	51.11345	59.15638	68.67647	79.95442	109.18177	150.33393	245.71197	567.3773	1319.489
28	29.97452	32.12910	34.48148	37.05121	42.93092	49.96758	58.40258	68.52811	80.69769	95.33883	134.20994	190.69889	327.10408	819.2233	2063.952
30	32.28002	34.78489	37.53868	40.56808	47.57542	56.08494	66.43885	79.05819	94.46079	113.28321	164.49402	241.33268	434.74515	1181.881	3227.174
32	34.60862	37.49407	40.68829	44.22703	52.50276	62.70147	75.29883	90.88978	110.21815	134.21354	201.13777	304.84772	577.10046	1704.109	5044.710
34	36.96058	40.25770	43.93309	48.03380	57.73018	69.85791	85.06696	104.18375	128.25876	158.62667	245.47670	384.52098	765.36535	2456.118	7884.609
36	39.33610	43.07688	47.27597	51.99437	63.27594	77.59831	95.83632	119.12087	148.91346	187.10215	299.12681	484.46312	1014.34568	3539.009	12321.95
38	41.73545	45.95272	50.71989	56.11494	69.15945	85.97034	107.70955	135.90421	172.56102	220.31595	364.04343	609.83053	1343.62216	5098.373	19255.30
40	44.15885	48.88637	54.26789	60.40198	75.40126	95.02552	120.79977	154.76197	199.63511	259.05652	442.59256	767.09142	1779.09031	7343.858	30088.66
45	50.32416	56.48107	63.61420	71.89271	92.71986	121.0294	159.7002	212.7435	285.7493	386.5056	718.9048	1358.230	3585.12846	18281.31	91831.50
50	56.64516	64.46318	73.68283	84.57940	112.7969	152.6671	209.3480	290.3359	406.5289	573.7702	1163.909	2400.018	7217.71628	45497.19	280255.7
100	129.33370	170.4814	228.8030	312.2323	607.2877	1237.624	2610.025	5638.368	12381.66	27484.52	137796.1	696010.5	783×10^4	414×10^6	196×10^8

Note: To convert from this table to values of an annuity in advance, determine the annuity in arrears above for one more period and subtract 1.00000.

TABLE 4

Present Value of Annuity of $1 in Arrears

$$P_F = \frac{1 - (1+r)^{-n}}{r} \times \$1.00$$

r = discount rate; n = number of payments

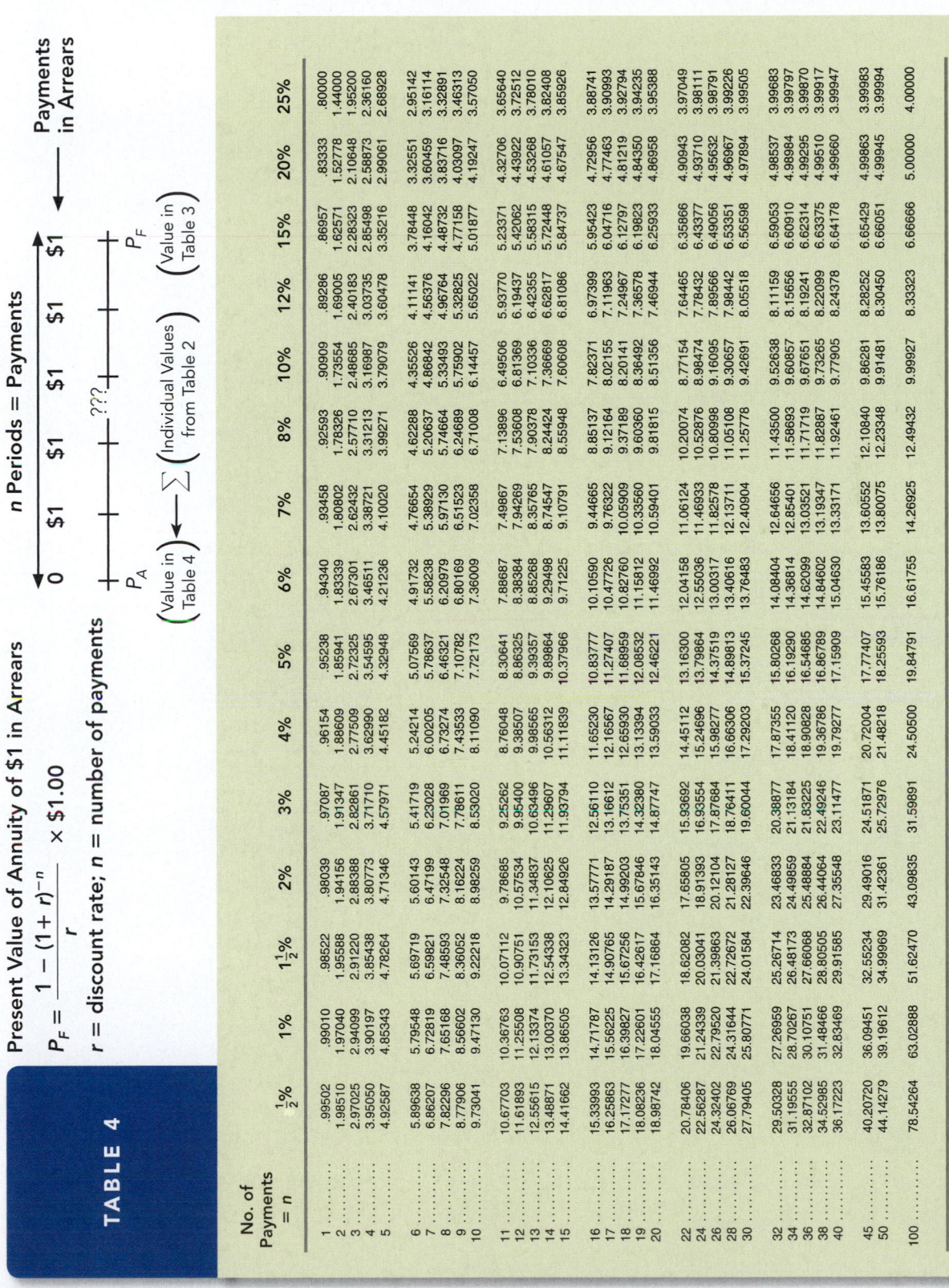

No. of Payments = n	½%	1%	1½%	2%	3%	4%	5%	6%	7%	8%	10%	12%	15%	20%	25%
1	.99502	.99010	.98522	.98039	.97087	.96154	.95238	.94340	.93458	.92593	.90909	.89286	.86957	.83333	.80000
2	1.98510	1.97040	1.95588	1.94156	1.91347	1.88609	1.85941	1.83339	1.80802	1.78326	1.73554	1.69005	1.62571	1.52778	1.44000
3	2.97025	2.94099	2.91220	2.88388	2.82861	2.77509	2.72325	2.67301	2.62432	2.57710	2.48685	2.40183	2.28323	2.10648	1.95200
4	3.95050	3.90197	3.85438	3.80773	3.71710	3.62990	3.54595	3.46511	3.38721	3.31213	3.16987	3.03735	2.85498	2.58873	2.36160
5	4.92587	4.85343	4.78264	4.71346	4.57971	4.45182	4.32948	4.21236	4.10020	3.99271	3.79079	3.60478	3.35216	2.99061	2.68928
6	5.89638	5.79548	5.69719	5.60143	5.41719	5.24214	5.07569	4.91732	4.76654	4.62288	4.35526	4.11141	3.78448	3.32551	2.95142
7	6.86207	6.72819	6.59821	6.47199	6.23028	6.00205	5.78637	5.58238	5.38929	5.20637	4.86842	4.56376	4.16042	3.60459	3.16114
8	7.82296	7.65168	7.48593	7.32548	7.01969	6.73274	6.46321	6.20979	5.97130	5.74664	5.33493	4.96764	4.48732	3.83716	3.32891
9	8.77906	8.56602	8.36052	8.16224	7.78611	7.43533	7.10782	6.80169	6.51523	6.24689	5.75902	5.32825	4.77158	4.03097	3.46313
10	9.73041	9.47130	9.22218	8.98259	8.53020	8.11090	7.72173	7.36009	7.02358	6.71008	6.14457	5.65022	5.01877	4.19247	3.57050
11	10.67703	10.36763	10.07112	9.78685	9.25262	8.76048	8.30641	7.88687	7.49867	7.13896	6.49506	5.93770	5.23371	4.32706	3.65640
12	11.61893	11.25508	10.90751	10.57534	9.95400	9.38507	8.86325	8.38384	7.94269	7.53608	6.81369	6.19437	5.42062	4.43922	3.72512
13	12.55615	12.13374	11.73153	11.34837	10.63496	9.98565	9.39357	8.85268	8.35765	7.90378	7.10336	6.42355	5.58315	4.53268	3.78010
14	13.48871	13.00370	12.54338	12.10625	11.29607	10.56312	9.89864	9.29498	8.74547	8.24424	7.36669	6.62817	5.72448	4.61057	3.82408
15	14.41662	13.86505	13.34323	12.84926	11.93794	11.11839	10.37966	9.71225	9.10791	8.55948	7.60608	6.81086	5.84737	4.67547	3.85926
16	15.33993	14.71787	14.13126	13.57771	12.56110	11.65230	10.83777	10.10590	9.44665	8.85137	7.82371	6.97399	5.95423	4.72956	3.88741
17	16.25863	15.56225	14.90765	14.29187	13.16612	12.16567	11.27407	10.47726	9.76322	9.12164	8.02155	7.11963	6.04716	4.77463	3.90993
18	17.17277	16.39827	15.67256	14.99203	13.75351	12.65930	11.68959	10.82760	10.05900	9.37189	8.20141	7.24967	6.12797	4.81219	3.92794
19	18.08236	17.22601	16.42617	15.67846	14.32380	13.13394	12.08532	11.15812	10.33560	9.60360	8.36492	7.36578	6.19823	4.84350	3.94235
20	18.98742	18.04555	17.16864	16.35143	14.87747	13.59033	12.46221	11.46992	10.59401	9.81815	8.51356	7.46944	6.25933	4.86958	3.95388
22	20.78406	19.66038	18.62082	17.65805	15.93692	14.45112	13.16300	12.04158	11.06124	10.20074	8.77154	7.64465	6.35866	4.90943	3.97049
24	22.56287	21.24339	20.03041	18.91393	16.93554	15.24696	13.79864	12.55036	11.46933	10.52876	8.98474	7.78432	6.43377	4.93710	3.98111
26	24.32402	22.79520	21.39863	20.12104	17.87684	15.98277	14.37519	13.00317	11.82578	10.80998	9.16095	7.89566	6.49066	4.95632	3.98791
28	26.06769	24.31644	22.72672	21.28127	18.76411	16.66306	14.89813	13.40616	12.13711	11.05108	9.30657	7.98442	6.53351	4.96967	3.99226
30	27.79405	25.80771	24.01584	22.39646	19.60044	17.29203	15.37245	13.76483	12.40904	11.25778	9.42691	8.05518	6.56598	4.97894	3.99505
32	29.50328	27.26959	25.26714	23.46833	20.38877	17.87355	15.80268	14.08404	12.64656	11.43500	9.52638	8.11159	6.59053	4.98537	3.99683
34	31.19555	28.70267	26.48173	24.49859	21.13184	18.41120	16.19290	14.36814	12.85401	11.58693	9.60857	8.15666	6.60910	4.98984	3.99797
36	32.87102	30.10751	27.66068	25.48884	21.83225	18.90828	16.54685	14.62099	13.03521	11.71719	9.67651	8.19241	6.62314	4.99295	3.99870
38	34.52985	31.48466	28.80505	26.44064	22.49246	19.36786	16.86789	14.84602	13.19347	11.82887	9.73265	8.22099	6.63375	4.99510	3.99917
40	36.17223	32.83469	29.91585	27.35548	23.11477	19.79277	17.15909	15.04630	13.33171	11.92461	9.77905	8.24378	6.64178	4.99660	3.99947
45	40.20720	36.09451	32.55234	29.49016	24.51871	20.72004	17.77407	15.45583	13.60552	12.10840	9.86281	8.28252	6.65429	4.99863	3.99983
50	44.14279	39.19612	34.99969	31.42361	25.72976	21.48218	18.25593	15.76186	13.80075	12.23348	9.91481	8.30450	6.66051	4.99945	3.99994
100	78.54264	63.02888	51.62470	43.09835	31.59891	24.50500	19.84791	16.61755	14.26925	12.49432	9.99927	8.33323	6.66666	5.00000	4.00000

Note: To convert from this table to values of an annuity in advance, determine the annuity in arrears above for one fewer period and add 1.00000.

GLOSSARY

The definitions of many words and phrases in the glossary use other glossary terms. In a given definition, we *italicize* terms that themselves (or variants thereof) appear elsewhere under their own listings. The cross-references generally take one of two forms:

1. **absorption costing** See *full absorption costing*.
2. **ABC** *Activity-based costing*.

Form (1) refers you to another term for discussion of this bold-faced term. Form (2) tells you that this bold-faced term is synonymous with the *italicized* term, which you can consult for discussion if necessary.

A

AAA *American Accounting Association*.

Abacus A scholarly *journal* containing articles on theoretical aspects of *accounting*, prepared for publication by the Accounting Foundation of the University of Sydney.

abatement A complete or partial cancellation of a levy imposed by a government unit.

ABC *Activity-based costing*.

abnormal spoilage Actual *spoilage* exceeding that expected when *operations* are normally efficient. Usual practice treats this *cost* as an *expense* of the *period* rather than as a *product cost*. Contrast with *normal spoilage*.

aboriginal cost In public utility accounting, the *acquisition cost* of an *asset* incurred by the first *entity* devoting that asset to public use; the cost *basis* for most public utility regulation. If regulators used a different cost basis, then public utilities could *exchange* assets among themselves at ever-increasing *prices* in order to raise the rate base and, then, prices based on them.

absorbed overhead *Overhead costs allocated* to individual products at some *overhead rate*; also called *applied overhead*.

absorption costing See *full absorption costing*.

Abstracts of the EITF See *Emerging Issues Task Force*.

accelerated cost recovery system (ACRS) A form of *accelerated depreciation* that Congress enacted in 1981 and amended in 1986, so that now most writers refer to it as *MACRS*, or *Modified Accelerated Cost Recovery System*. The system provides percentages of the *asset*'s *cost* that a *firm* depreciates each year for *tax* purposes. The percentages derive, roughly, from 150%-*declining-balance depreciation* methods. ACRS ignores *salvage value*. We do not generally use these amounts for *financial accounting*.

accelerated depreciation In calculating *depreciation charges*, any method in which the charges become progressively smaller each *period*. Examples are *double declining-balance depreciation* and *sum-of-the-years'-digits depreciation methods*.

acceptance A written promise to pay; equivalent to a *promissory note*.

account A device for representing the amount (*balance*) for any line (or a part of a line) in the *balance sheet* or *income statement*. Because income statement accounts explain the changes in the balance sheet account *Retained Earnings*, the definition does not require the last three words of the

preceding sentence. An account is any device for accumulating additions and subtractions relating to a single *asset*, *liability*, or *owners' equity* item, including *revenues* and *expenses*.

account analysis method A method of separating *fixed costs* from *variable costs* based on the analyst's judgment of whether the cost is fixed or variable. Based on their names alone, the analyst might classify *direct labor* (*materials*) *costs* as variable and *depreciation* on a *factory* building as fixed. In our experience, this method results in too many fixed costs and not enough variable costs—that is, analysts have insufficient information to judge *management*'s ability to reduce costs that appear to be fixed. Companies with strong unions, where layoffs can be costly, often have near-fixed labor costs. Analysts in Western Europe often treat labor costs as relatively fixed.

account form The form of *balance sheet* in which *assets* appear on the left and *equities* appear on the right. Contrast with *report form*. See *T-account*.

accountability center *Responsibility center*.

accountancy The British word for *accounting*. In the United States, it means the theory and practice of accounting.

accountant's comments Canada: a written communication issued by a *public accountant* at the conclusion of a review engagement. It consists of a description of the work performed and a statement that, under the terms of the engagement, the accountant has not performed an *audit* and consequently expresses no *opinion*. (Compare *auditor's report*; *denial of opinion*.)

accountant's opinion *Auditor's report*.

accountant's report *Auditor's report*.

accounting A system conveying information about a specific *entity*. The information is in financial terms and will appear in accounting statements only if the accountant can measure it with reasonable *precision*. The *AICPA* defines accounting as a service activity whose "function is to provide quantitative information, primarily financial in nature, about economic entities that is intended to be useful in making economic decisions."

accounting adjustments *Prior-period adjustments*, changes in *accounting principles*, and corrections of errors. See *accounting changes*. The *FASB* indicates that it will tend to call these items "accounting adjustments," not "accounting changes," when it requires the reporting of *comprehensive income*. See also *adjusting entry* for another use of this term.

Accounting and Tax Index A publication that indexes, in detail, the accounting literature of the *period*. Published by Dialog ProQuest.

accounting changes As defined by *FASB Statement No. 154* (**Codification Topic 250**), a change in (1) an *accounting principle* (such as a switch from *FIFO* to *LIFO* or from *sum-of-the-years'-digits depreciation* to *straight-line depreciation*), (2) an accounting estimate (such as estimated useful lives or *salvage value* of depreciable *assets* and estimates of *warranty* costs or *uncollectible accounts*), or (3) the reporting *entity*. If practical, the firm should restate *financial statements* retroactively for changes of type (1). The firm should treat changes of type (2) as affecting only the *period* of change and, if necessary, future periods. The firm should disclose reasons for changes of type (3) in statements reporting on *operations* of the period of the change, and it should show the effect of the change on all other periods, for comparative purposes. Correcting an error in previously issued financial statements is not an accounting change. See *all-inclusive (income) concept* and *accounting errors*.

accounting conventions Methods or procedures used in accounting. Writers tend to use this term when the method or procedure has not yet received official authoritative sanction by a pronouncement of a group such as the *APB, EITF, FASB*, and *SEC* for *U.S. GAAP* and the *IASB* for *IFRS*. Contrast with *accounting principles*.

accounting cycle The sequence of accounting procedures starting with *journal entries* for various *transactions* and events and ending with the *financial statements* or, perhaps, the *post-closing trial balance*.

accounting deficiency Canada: a failure to adhere to *generally accepted accounting principles* or to disclose essential information in *financial statements*.

accounting entity See *entity*.

accounting equation *Assets = Equities*; *Assets = Liabilities + Owners' Equity*.

accounting errors Arithmetic errors and misapplications of *accounting principles* in previously published *financial statements*. The *firm* corrects these items retrospectively by adjusting *balance sheet* and *income statements* amounts beginning with the earliest *period* reported. In this regard, the firm treats them like *prior-period adjustments*, but technically *FASB Statement No. 154* (**Codification Topic 250**) does not classify them as prior-period adjustments. See *accounting changes*, and contrast with changes in accounting estimates as described there.

accounting event Any occurrence that is recorded in the *accounting* records.

Accounting Horizons A quarterly *journal* of the *American Accounting Association*.

accounting methods *Accounting principles*; procedures for carrying out accounting principles.

accounting period (convention) The time period between consecutive *balance sheets*; the time period for which the *firm* prepares *financial statements* that measure *flows*, such as the *income statement* and the *statement of cash flows*. See *interim statements*.

accounting policies *Accounting principles* adopted by a specific *entity*.

accounting principles The methods or procedures used in *accounting* for events reported in the *financial statements*. We tend to use this term when the method or procedure has received official authoritative sanction from a pronouncement of a group such as the *APB, EITF, FASB*, or *SEC* for *U.S. GAAP* and the *IASB* for *IFRS*. Contrast with *accounting conventions* and *conceptual framework*.

Accounting Principles Board See *APB*.

accounting procedures See *accounting principles*. However, this term usually refers to the methods for implementing accounting principles.

accounting rate of return *Income* for a *period* divided by *average investment* during the period; based on income, rather than *discounted cash flows*, and hence a poor decision-making aid or tool. See *ratio* and **Exhibit 6.14**.

Accounting Research Bulletin (ARB) The name of the official pronouncements of the former *Committee on Accounting Procedure (CAP)* of the *AICPA*. The committee issued fifty-one bulletins between 1939 and 1959. *ARB No. 43* restated and codified the parts of the first forty-two bulletins not dealing solely with definitions.

Accounting Research Study (ARS) One of a series of studies published by the Director of Accounting Research of the *AICPA* and "designed to provide professional accountants and others interested in the development of accounting with a discussion and documentation of accounting problems." The AICPA published fifteen such studies in the *period* 1961–73.

Accounting Review A journal of the *American Accounting Association*.

Accounting Series Release (ASR) See *SEC*.

accounting standards *Accounting principles*.

Accounting Standards Executive Committee (AcSEC) The senior technical committee of the *AICPA* authorized to speak for the AICPA in the areas of *financial accounting* and reporting as well as *cost accounting*.

accounting system The procedures for collecting and summarizing financial data in a *firm*.

Accounting Terminology Bulletin (ATB) One of four releases of the Committee on Terminology of the *AICPA* issued in the *period* 1953–57.

Accounting Trends and Techniques An annual *AICPA* publication that surveys the reporting practices of 600 large *corporations*. It presents tabulations of specific practices, terminology, and *disclosures* along with illustrations taken from individual *annual reports*. We use it, for example, to see how many *firms* use the *direct method* to report *cash flow from operations*.

accounts payable; trade payables A *liability* representing an amount owed to a *creditor*; usually arising from the purchase of *merchandise* or *materials* and supplies, not necessarily due or past due; normally, a *current liability*.

accounts payable turnover ratio Purchases divided by average *accounts payable*. See *ratio* and **Exhibit 6.14**.

accounts receivable Claims against a *debtor*; usually arising from *sales* or *services* rendered, not necessarily due or past due; normally, a *current asset*. With the word "*gross*," the amount owed to the holder; with the word "*net*," the amount the holder expects to collect, which equals the gross amount less the *allowance for uncollectible accounts*.

accounts receivable turnover ratio *Net sales* on *account* divided by average *accounts receivable*. See *ratio* and **Exhibit 6.14**.

accretion Occurs when a *carrying value* grows over time, such as a *bond* originally issued at a *discount*; the correct technical term is "accretion," not "*amortization*." This term also refers to an increase in economic *worth* through physical change caused by natural growth, usually said of a natural resource such as timber. Contrast with *appreciation*. See *amortization*.

accrual Recognition of an *expense* (or *revenue*) and the related *liability* (or *asset*) resulting from an *accounting event*, frequently from the passage of time but not signaled by an explicit *cash transaction*; for example, the recognition of *interest* expense or revenue (or *wages*, *salaries*, or *rent*) at the end of a *period* even though the *firm* makes no explicit cash transaction at that time. *Cash flow* follows accounting recognition; contrast with *deferral*.

accrual basis of accounting The method of recognizing *revenues* as a *firm* sells *goods* (or delivers them) and as it renders *services*, independent of the time when it receives *cash*. This system *recognizes expenses* in the *period* when it recognizes the related revenue, independent of the time when it pays cash. *SFAC No. 1* says, "Accrual accounting attempts to record the financial effects on an *enterprise* of *transactions* and other events and circumstances that have cash consequences for the enterprise in the periods in which those transactions, events, and circumstances occur rather than only in the periods in which cash is received or paid by the enterprise." Contrast with the *cash basis of accounting*. See *accrual* and *deferral*. We could more correctly call this "accrual/deferral" accounting.

accrue See *accrued*, and contrast with *incur*.

accrued Said of a *revenue* (*expense*) that the *firm* has earned (*recognized*) even though the related *receivable* (*payable*) has a future due date. We prefer not to use this adjective as part of an *account* title. Thus, we prefer to use *Interest Receivable* (*Payable*) as the account title rather than Accrued Interest Receivable (Payable). See *matching convention* and *accrual*. Contrast with *incur*.

accrued depreciation An incorrect term for *accumulated depreciation*. Acquiring an *asset* with *cash*, *capitalizing* it, and then *amortizing* its *cost* over *periods* of use is a process of *deferral* and *allocation*, not of *accrual*.

accrued payable A *payable* usually resulting from the passage of time. For example, *salaries* and *interest accrue* as time passes. See *accrued*.

accrued receivable A *receivable* usually resulting from the passage of time. See *accrued*.

accumulated benefit obligation See *projected benefit obligation* for definition and contrast.

accumulated deficit Negative balance in the *Retained Earnings account*.

accumulated depreciation A preferred title for the *asset contra account* that shows the sum of *depreciation charges* on an asset since the time the *firm* acquired it. Other account titles are *allowance* for depreciation (acceptable term) and *reserve* for depreciation (unacceptable term).

accumulated other comprehensive income *Balance sheet* amount in *owners' equity* showing the total of all *other comprehensive income* amounts from all prior *periods*.

accurate presentation The qualitative accounting *objective* suggesting that information reported in *financial statements* should correspond as precisely as possible with the economic effects underlying *transactions* and events. See *fair presentation* and *full disclosure*.

acid test ratio *Quick ratio*.

acquisition (historical) cost Of an *asset*, the *net invoice price* plus all *expenditures* to place and ready the asset for its intended use. The other expenditures might include legal fees, transportation *charges*, and installation *costs*.

acquisition, or purchase, method Accounting for a *business combination* by recognizing the acquired company's *assets* and *liabilities* at the *price* paid for them (*purchase method*) or their *fair value* (*acquisition method*). Contrast with *pooling-of-interests method*. The *firm* adds the acquired assets and liabilities to the *books* at current fair values rather than *original costs*; the subsequent *amortization expenses* usually exceed those (and reported *income* is smaller than that) for the same business combination accounted for as a pooling of interests. *U.S. GAAP* and *IFRS* now requires that the acquirer use the acquisition method.

ACRS *Accelerated Cost Recovery System*.

AcSEC *Accounting Standards Executive Committee* of the *AICPA*.

activity accounting *Responsibility accounting*.

activity-based costing (ABC) Method of assigning *indirect* costs, including nonmanufacturing *overhead costs*, to *products* and *services*. ABC assumes that almost all overhead costs associate with activities within the *firm* and vary with respect to the *drivers* of those activities. Some practitioners suggest that ABC attempts to find the drivers for all indirect costs; these people note that in the *long run*, all *costs* are *variable*, so *fixed* indirect costs do not occur. This method first assigns costs to activities and then to products based on the products' usage of the activities.

activity-based depreciation *Production method* (*depreciation*).

activity-based management (ABM) Analysis and *management* of activities required to make a *product* or to produce a service. ABM focuses attention to enhance activities that add *value* to the customer and to reduce activities that do not. Its goal is to satisfy customer needs while making smaller demands on costly resources. Some refer to this as "activity management."

activity basis *Costs* are *variable* or *fixed* (*incremental* or *unavoidable*) with respect to some activity, such as production of units (or the undertaking of some new project). Usage calls this activity the "activity basis."

activity center Unit of the organization that performs a set of tasks.

activity variance *Sales volume variance*.

actual cost (basis) *Acquisition* or *historical cost*. Also contrast with *standard cost*.

actual costing (system) Method of *allocating costs* to *products* using actual *direct materials*, actual *direct labor*, and actual *factory overhead*, typically averaged over several units of *output*. Contrast with *normal costing* and *standard costing*.

actuarial An adjective describing computations or analyses that involve both *compound interest* and probabilities, such as the computation of the *present value* of a life-contingent *annuity*. Some writers use the word even for computations involving only one of the two.

ad valorem A method of levying a *tax* or duty on *goods* by using their estimated *value* as the tax base.

additional paid-in capital An alternative acceptable title for the *capital contributed in excess of par* (*or stated*) *value account*.

additional processing cost *Costs* incurred in processing *joint products* after the *split-off point*.

adequate disclosure An auditing standard that, to achieve *fair presentation* of *financial statements*, requires *disclosure* of *material* items. This *auditing standard* does not, however, require publicizing all information detrimental to a company. For example, the company may face a lawsuit, and disclosure might require a *debit* to a *loss account* and a *credit* to an *estimated liability*. But the court might view the making of this entry as an admission of liability, which could adversely affect the outcome of the suit. The *firm* should debit *expense* or loss for the expected loss, as required by *SFAS No. 5* (**Codification Topic 450**), but need not use such accurate account titles that the court can spot an admission of liability.

adjunct account An *account* that accumulates additions to another account. For example, Premium on Bonds Payable is adjunct to the *liability* Bonds Payable; the effective liability is the sum of the two account *balances* at a given date. Contrast with *contra account*.

adjusted acquisition (historical) cost Sometimes said of the *carrying value* of a *plant asset*, that is, *acquisition cost* less *accumulated depreciation*. Also, *cost* adjusted to a *constant-dollar* amount to reflect *general price-level changes*.

adjusted bank balance of cash The *balance* shown on the statement from the bank plus or minus amounts, such as for unrecorded *deposits* or *outstanding checks*, to reconcile the bank's balance with the correct *cash* balance. See *adjusted book balance of cash*.

adjusted basis The *basis* used to compute *gain* or *loss* on the disposition of an *asset* for *tax* purposes. See also *book value* and *carrying value*.

adjusted book balance of cash The *balance* shown in the *firm*'s account for *cash* in bank plus or minus amounts, such as for *notes* collected by the bank or bank service *charges*, to reconcile the account balance with the correct cash balance. See *adjusted bank balance of cash*.

adjusted trial balance *Trial balance* taken after *adjusting entries* but before *closing entries*. Contrast with *pre-* and *post-closing trial balances*. See *unadjusted trial balance* and *post-closing trial balance*. See also *work sheet*.

adjusting entry An entry made at the end of an *accounting period* to record a *transaction* or other *accounting event* that the *firm* has not yet recorded or has improperly recorded during the accounting period; an entry to update the accounts. See *work sheet*.

adjustment An *account* change produced by an *adjusting entry*. Sometimes accountants use the term to refer to the process of restating *financial statement* amounts to *constant dollars* or for a *change in accounting principles*.

administrative costs (expenses) *Costs* (*expenses*) incurred for the *firm* as a whole, in contrast with specific functions such as manufacturing or selling; includes items such as salaries of top executives, general office *rent*, legal fees, and auditing fees.

admission of partner Occurs when a new partner joins a *partnership*. Legally, the old partnership dissolves, and a new one comes into being. In practice, however, the *firm* may keep the old *accounting* records in use, and the accounting entries reflect the manner in which the new partner joined the firm. If the new partner merely purchases the *interest* of another partner, the accounting changes the name for one *capital account*. If the new partner contributes *assets* and *liabilities* to the partnership, then the firm must recognize them. See *bonus method*.

advances from (by) customers A preferred title for the *liability account* representing *receipts* of *cash* in advance of delivering the *goods* or rendering the *service*. After the *firm* delivers the *goods* or services, it will *recognize revenue*. Some refer to this as "*deferred revenue*" or "*deferred income*," terms likely to confuse the unwary because the item is not yet revenue or *income*.

advances to affiliates *Loans* by a parent company to a *subsidiary*; frequently combined with "*investment* in subsidiary" as "investments and advances to subsidiary" and shown as a *noncurrent asset* on the parent's *balance sheet*. The consolidation process eliminates these advances in *consolidated financial statements*.

advances to suppliers A preferred term for the *asset* account representing *disbursements* of *cash* in advance of receiving assets or *services*.

adverse opinion An *auditor's report* stating that the *financial statements* are not fair or are not in accord with *U.S. GAAP*.

affiliated company A company controlling or controlled by another company. Some users of this term mean *significant influence*, not control.

AFS; Available for Sale See *Available for Sale* (*Securities*).

after closing Post-closing; a *trial balance* at the end of the *period*.

after cost A term sometimes used for *estimated expenses*.

AG (Aktiengesellschaft) Germany: the form of a German company whose *shares* can trade on the *stock exchange*.

agency cost The *cost* to the *principal* caused by *agents* pursuing their own interests instead of the principal's interests. Includes both the costs incurred by principals to control agents' actions and the cost to the principals if agents pursue their own interests that are not in the interest of the principals.

agency fund An *account* for *assets* received by governmental units in the *capacity* of trustee or *agent*.

agency theory A branch of economics relating the behavior of *principals* (such as owner nonmanagers or bosses) and that of their *agents* (such as nonowner *managers* or subordinates). The principal assigns responsibility and authority to the agent, but the agent's own *risks* and preferences differ from those of the principal. The principal cannot observe all activities of the agent. Both the principal and the agent must consider the differing risks and preferences in designing incentive contracts.

agent One authorized to transact *business*, including executing contracts, for another.

aging accounts receivable; aging-of-accounts receivable procedure The process of classifying *accounts receivable* by the time elapsed since the claim came into existence for the purpose of estimating the amount of *uncollectible accounts receivable* as of a given date. See *sales contra*, *estimated uncollectibles*, and *allowance for uncollectibles*.

aging schedule A listing of *accounts receivable*, classified by age, used in *aging accounts receivable*.

AICPA (American Institute of Certified Public Accountants) The national organization that represents *CPAs*. See *AcSEC*. It oversees the writing and grading of the Uniform CPA Examination. Each state sets its own requirements for becoming a CPA in that state. See *certified public accountant*. Web Site: www.aicpa.org. While the AICPA once set many auditing and professional standards for *public accountants*, the *PCAOB* now regulates auditing of public companies and the profession.

all-capital earnings rate *Rate of return on assets*.

all-current method *Foreign currency translation* in which all *financial statement* items are translated at the *current exchange rate*. Contrast with *monetary-nonmonetary method*.

all-inclusive (income) concept A concept that does not distinguish between *operating* and *nonoperating revenues* and *expenses*. Thus, the only entries to *retained earnings* are for *net income* and *dividends*. Under this concept, the *income statement* reports all *income*, *gains*, and *losses*; thus, *net income* includes events usually reported as *prior-period adjustments* and as *corrections of errors*. *U.S. GAAP* does not include this concept in its pure form.

allocate, allocation As a verb, to divide or spread a *cost* from one *account* into several accounts, to several *products* or activities, or to several *periods*. As a noun, a spreading of costs to accounts or to products or to periods.

allocation base The systematic method that assigns *joint costs* to *cost objectives*. For example, a *firm* might assign the cost of a truck to *periods* based on miles driven during the period; the allocation base is miles. Or the firm might assign the cost of a *factory* supervisor to a *product* based on *direct labor* hours; the allocation base is direct labor hours.

allocation of income taxes See *deferred income tax*.

allowance A *balance sheet contra account* generally used for *receivables* and depreciable *assets*. See *sales* (or *purchase*) *allowance* for another use of this term.

allowance for funds used during construction In accounting for public utilities, a *revenue* account *credited* for *implicit interest earnings* on *shareholders' equity balances*. One *principle* of public utility regulation and rate setting requires that customers should pay the *full costs* of producing the *services* (e.g., electricity) that they use, nothing more and nothing less. Thus, an electric utility must *capitalize* into an *asset account* the full costs, but no more, of producing a new electric power-generating *plant*. One of the costs of building a new plant is the *interest* cost on *cash* tied up during construction. If *funds* are explicitly borrowed by an ordinary *business*, the *journal entry* for *interest* of $1,000 is typically:

Interest Expense	1,000	
Interest Payable		1,000

Interest expense for the period.

If the firm is constructing a new plant, then another entry would be made, capitalizing interest into the plant-under-construction account:

Construction Work-in-Progress	750	
Interest Expense		750

Capitalize relevant portion of interest relating to construction work in progress into the asset account.

The cost of the *plant asset* increases; when the *firm* uses the plant, it charges *depreciation*. The interest will become an *expense* through the *depreciation* process in the later *periods* of use, not currently as the firm pays for interest. Thus, the firm reports the full cost of the electricity generated during a given period as expense in that period. But suppose, as is common, that the electric utility does not explicitly borrow the funds but uses some of its own funds, including funds raised from equity issues as well as from debt. Even though the firm incurs no explicit interest expense or other explicit expense for *capital*, the funds have an *opportunity cost*. Put another way, the plant under construction will not have lower economic cost just because the firm used its own cash rather than borrowing. The public utility using its own funds, on which it would have to pay $750 of interest if it had explicitly borrowed the funds, will make the following entry:

Construction Work-in-Progress	750	
Allowance for Funds Used During Construction		750

Recognition of interest, an opportunity cost, on own funds used.

The allowance account is a form of revenue, to appear on the *income statement*, and the firm will *close* it to *Retained Earnings*, increasing it. On the *statement of cash flows* it is an *income* or revenue item not producing funds, and so the firm must subtract it from *net income* in deriving *cash provided by operations*. SFAS No. 34 (**Codification Topic 835**) specifically prohibits nonutility companies from capitalizing, into plant under construction, the opportunity cost (interest) on their own funds used. See *allowance method* for the usual context of the word "*allowance*" as a *contra-asset account*.

allowance for uncollectibles (accounts receivable) A *contra account* that shows the estimated *accounts receivable*

amount that the *firm* expects not to collect. When the firm uses such an allowance, the actual write-off of specific accounts receivable (*debit* allowance, *credit* specific customer's account) does not affect *revenue* or *expense* at the time of the *write-off*. The firm reduces revenue when it debits *bad debt expense* (or, our preference, a revenue contra account) and credits the allowance; the firm can base the amount of the credit to the allowance on a percentage of *sales* on *account* for a period of time or compute it from *aging accounts receivable*. This contra account enables the firm to show an estimated receivables amount that it expects to collect without identifying specific uncollectible accounts. See *allowance method*.

allowance method; allowance method for uncollectibles; allowance method for warranties A method of attempting to match all *expenses* of a transaction with their associated *revenues*; usually involves a *debit* to expense and a *credit* to an *estimated liability*, such as for estimated warranty expenditures, or a debit to a revenue (*contra*) account and a credit to an *asset* (contra) account, such as in some firms' accounting for uncollectible accounts. See *allowance for uncollectibles* for further explanation. When the firm uses the *allowance method* for *sales discounts*, the firm records *sales* at *gross invoice prices* (not reduced by the amounts of *discounts* made available). The firm debits an estimate of the amount of discounts to be taken to a revenue contra account and credits an allowance account, shown contra to *accounts receivable*.

American Accounting Association (AAA) An organization primarily for academic accountants but open to all interested in *accounting*. It publishes the *Accounting Review* and several other *journals*.

American Institute of Certified Public Accountants See *AICPA*.

American Stock Exchange (AMEX) (ASE) A *public market* where various corporate *securities* are traded.

AMEX *American Stock Exchange*.

amortization Strictly speaking, the process of liquidating or extinguishing ("bringing to death") a *debt* with a series of payments to the *creditor* (or to a *sinking fund*). From that usage has evolved a related use involving the accounting for the payments themselves: *amortization schedule* for a *mortgage*, which is a table showing the allocation between *interest* and *principal*. The term has also come to mean writing off ("liquidating") the *cost* of an *asset*. In this context it means the general process of *allocating* the *acquisition cost* of an asset either to the *periods* of benefit as an *expense* or to *inventory accounts* as a *product cost*. This is called *depreciation* for *plant assets*, *depletion* for *wasting assets* (natural resources), and "amortization" for *intangibles*. SFAC No. 6 refers to amortization as "the *accounting* process of reducing an amount by periodic payments or write-downs." The expressions "unamortized debt discount or premium" and "to amortize debt discount or premium" relate to *accruals*, not to *deferrals*. The expressions "amortization of long-term assets" and "to amortize long-term assets" refer to deferrals, not accruals. Contrast with *accretion*.

amortization schedule A table that shows, *period* by period, the opening *balance* of an item, such as a *bond payable* (or bond *investment* held as *asset*), the *interest expense* (*revenue*) for the period (= beginning balance multiplied by the historical *interest rate* for this item), the *cash* payment (receipt for asset), and the ending balance (= beginning balance plus interest expense (revenue) less cash paid (received)). Some amortization schedules have other columns of redundant information.

amortized cost A measure required by *SFAS No. 115* (**Codification Topic 320**) for *held-to-maturity securities*. This amount results from applying the method described at *effective interest method*. The *firm* records the *security* at its initial cost and computes the *effective interest rate* for the security. Whenever the firm receives *cash* from the issuer of the security, or whenever the firm reaches the end of one of its own *accounting periods* (that is, reaches the time for its own *adjusting entries*), it takes the following steps. It multiplies the amount currently recorded on the *books* by the effective interest rate (which remains constant over the time the firm holds the security). It *debits* that amount to the *debt* security account and *credits* the amount to Interest Revenue. If the firm receives cash, it debits Cash and credits the debt security account. The firm recomputes the *carrying value* of the debt security as: the carrying value before these entries; plus the increase for the interest revenue; less the decrease for the cash received. The resulting amount is the amortized cost for the end of that period.

analysis of variances See *variance analysis*.

annual report (to shareholders) A *report* prepared once a year for shareholders and other interested parties. It includes a *balance sheet*, an *income statement*, a *statement of cash flows*, a reconciliation of changes in *owners' equity accounts*, a *summary of significant accounting principles*, other explanatory *notes*, the *auditor's report*, and comments from *management* about the year's events. See *10-K* and *financial statements*.

annuitant One who receives an *annuity*.

annuity A series of payments of equal amount, usually made at equally spaced time intervals.

annuity certain An *annuity* payable for a definite number of *periods*. Contrast with *contingent annuity*.

annuity due An *annuity* whose first payment occurs at the start of the first *period*. Contrast with *annuity in arrears*.

annuity in advance An *annuity due*.

annuity in arrears An *ordinary annuity* whose first payment occurs at the end of the first *period*.

annuity method of depreciation See *compound interest depreciation*.

antidilutive Said of a potentially *dilutive security* that will increase *earnings per share* if its holder *exercises* it or converts it into common *stock*. In computing *diluted earnings per share*, the *firm* must assume that holders of antidilutive securities will not exercise their *options* or convert securities into *common shares*. The opposite assumption would lead to increased reported earnings per share in a given period.

APB Accounting Principles Board of the *AICPA*. It set *accounting principles* from 1959 through 1973, issuing 31 *APB Opinions* and 4 *APB Statements*. The *FASB* superseded the APB but retained the APB's *Opinions* and *Statements*, although it has, by now, modified, or repealed, or amended many of them.

APB Opinion The name for the *APB* pronouncements that compose parts of *generally accepted accounting principles*; the APB issued 31 *APB Opinions* from 1962 through 1973.

APB Statement The *APB* issued four *APB Statements* between 1962 and 1970. The *Statements* were approved by at least two-thirds of the *board*, but they state recommendations, not requirements. For example, *Statement No. 3* (1969) suggested the publication of *constant-dollar financial statements* but did not require them.

APBs An abbreviation used for *APB Opinions*.

applied cost A *cost* that a *firm* has *allocated* to a department, product, or activity; not necessarily based on *actual costs* incurred.

applied overhead *Overhead costs charged* to departments, products, or activities. Also called *absorbed overhead*.

appraisal In valuing an *asset* or *liability*, a process that involves expert *opinion* rather than evaluation of explicit market *transactions*.

appraisal costs In *cost accounting*, *costs incurred* to detect individual units of *products* that do not conform to specifications, including end-process sampling and field-testing. Also called "*detection costs*." In other contexts, a term referring to the cost of an *appraisal* of *land*, or equipment, or a building.

appraisal method of depreciation The periodic *depreciation charge* that equals the difference between the beginning-of-period and the end-of-period appraised *values* of the *asset* if that difference is positive. If negative, there is no charge. Not based on *historical cost*, this method is thus not generally accepted.

appreciation An increase in economic *value* caused by rising market prices for an *asset*. Contrast with *accretion*.

appropriated retained earnings See *retained earnings, appropriated*.

appropriation In governmental *accounting*, an *expenditure* authorized for a specified amount, purpose, and time.

appropriation account In governmental *accounting*, an *account* set up to record specific authorizations to spend. The governmental unit *credits* this account with *appropriation* amounts. At the end of the period, the unit *closes* to (*debits*) this account all *expenditures* during the *period* and all *encumbrances* outstanding at the end of the period.

approximate net realizable value method A method of assigning *joint costs* to *joint products* based on *revenues* minus *additional processing costs* of the end products.

ARB *Accounting Research Bulletin*.

arbitrage Strictly speaking, the simultaneous purchase in one market and sale in another of a *security* or commodity in hope of making a *profit* on price differences in the different markets. Often writers use this term loosely when a trader sells an item that is somewhat different from the item purchased; for example, the *sale* of shares of common stock and the simultaneous purchase of a *convertible bond* that is convertible into identical common shares. The trader hopes that the market will soon see that the similarities of the items should make them have equal *market values*. When the market values converge, the trader closes the positions and profits from the original difference in prices, less trading *costs*.

arbitrary Having no causation basis. *Accounting* theorists and practitioners often, properly, say, "Some *cost allocations* are arbitrary." In that sense, the accountant does not mean that the allocations are capricious or haphazard but does mean that theory suggests no unique solution to the allocation problem at hand. Accountants require that arbitrary allocations be systematic, rational, and consistently followed over time.

arm's length A transaction negotiated by unrelated parties, with both acting in their own self-interests; the basis for a *fair value* estimation or computation.

arrears *Cumulative dividends* on *preferred shares* that the *firm* has not yet declared; overdue *debt* payments. See *annuity in arrears* for another context.

ARS *Accounting Research Study*.

articles of incorporation Document filed with state authorities by persons forming a *corporation*. When the state returns the document with a *certificate* of incorporation, the document becomes the corporation's *charter*.

articulate The relation between any *operating* statement (for example, *income statement* or *statement of cash flows*) and comparative *balance sheets*, where the operating statement explains (or reconciles) the change in some major balance sheet category (for example, *retained earnings* or *cash*).

ASE *American Stock Exchange*.

ASR *Accounting Series Release*.

assess To value property for the purpose of property taxation; to levy a *charge* on the owner of property for improvements thereto, such as for sewers or sidewalks. The taxing authority computes the assessment.

assessed valuation For real estate or other property, a dollar amount that a government uses as a *basis* for levying taxes. The amount need not have some relation to *market value*.

asset definition and recognition *SFAC No. 6* defines *assets* as "probable future economic benefits obtained or controlled by a particular *entity* as a result of past transactions. . . . An asset has three essential characteristics: (a) it embodies a probable future benefit that involves a *capacity*, singly or in combination with other assets, to contribute directly or indirectly to future net *cash* inflows, (b) a particular entity can obtain the benefit and control others' access to it, and (c) the transaction or other event giving rise to the entity's right to or control of the benefit has already occurred." A footnote points out that "probable" means that which we can reasonably expect or believe but that is not certain or proved. You may understand condition (c) better if you think of it as requiring that a future benefit cannot be an asset if it arises from an *executory contract*, a mere exchange of promises. Receiving a purchase order from a customer provides a future benefit, but it is an executory contract, so the order cannot be an asset. An asset may be *tangible* or *intangible*, short-term (current) or long-term (noncurrent).

As this book goes to press, the *FASB* and the *IASB* are reconsidering the definition of an asset and the criteria for asset recognition Their proposed asset definition emphasizes the *present* existence of an economic resource and de-emphasizes the notions of a *past* exchange and the probability of *future* benefits. Even though these de-emphasized notions do provide a basis for understanding, the standard setters have judged that using those concepts often does not resolve ambiguity. Resources would be an asset, according to the new definition (1) if the entity can separate the resources from the entity as through sale, exchange, and licensing, which implies a market in which a firm can measure the fair value of the resource, or (2) if they arise from contractual or other legal rights, suggesting that negotiations between independent parties in establishing the rights permit estimation of fair value, even if the firm cannot exchange the item with another. We cannot predict the future development of these tentative definitions and concepts and the changes in reporting that might result.

asset revaluation Under some circumstances, when the *firm* can readily observe *market values*, the *IASB* allows firms to increase the *carrying value* of assets to *fair values*. The matching *credit* is to *other comprehensive income* for *property, plant, and equipment* (*IAS 36*, par. 39 and 40) and to profit and loss for investment property (*IAS 40*, par. 35). The *FASB* allows firms to increase the *carrying value* of financial assets to fair value; with the matching credit to *income*.

asset securitization *Securitization*.

asset turnover *Net sales* divided by *average assets*. See *ratio* and **Exhibit 6.14**.

assignment of accounts receivable Transfer of the legal ownership of an *account receivable* through its *sale*. Contrast with *pledging accounts receivable*, where the receivables serve as *collateral* for a *loan*.

ATB *Accounting Terminology Bulletin*, issued more than fifty years ago by a committee of the organization that preceded the *AICPA*.

at par A *bond* or *preferred shares* issued (or selling) at *face amount*.

attachment The laying claim to the *assets* of a *borrower* (or debtor) by a lender (or *creditor*) when the borrower has failed to pay *debts* on time.

attest An *auditor*'s rendering of an *opinion* that the *financial statements* are fair. Common usage calls this procedure the "attest function" of the *CPA*. See *fair presentation*.

attestor Typically independent *CPA*s, who *audit financial statements* prepared by *management* for the benefit of users. The *FASB* describes *accounting*'s constituency as comprising preparers, attestors, and users.

attribute measured The particular attribute, such as *cost* or *fair value* reported in the *balance sheet*. When making physical measurements, such as of a person, one needs to decide the units with which to measure, such as inches or centimeters or pounds or grams. One chooses the attribute height or weight independently of the measuring unit, English or metric. Conventional accounting has used for many years *historical cost* as the attribute measured and *nominal dollars* as the measuring unit. Standard setters have moved towards using more fair value attributes. Some theorists argue that accounting would better serve readers if it used *constant dollars* as the measuring unit. Some, including us, think accounting should change both the measuring unit and the attribute measured. One can measure the attribute historical cost in nominal dollars or in constant dollars. One can also measure the attribute fair value in nominal dollars or constant dollars. Choosing between the two attributes and the two measuring units implies four different *accounting systems*. Each of these four has its uses.

attribute(s) sampling The use of sampling technique in which the observer selects each item in the sample on the basis of whether it has a particular qualitative characteristic, in order to ascertain the rate of occurrence of this characteristic in the population. See also *estimation sampling*. Compare *variables sampling*. Example of attributes sampling: take a sample population of people, note the fraction that is male (say, 40%), and then infer that the entire population contains 40% males. Example of variables sampling: take a sample population of people, observe the weight of each sample point, compute the mean of those sampled people's weights (say 160 pounds), and then infer that the mean weight of the entire population equals 160 pounds.

audit Systematic inspection of *accounting* records involving analyses, tests, and *confirmations*. See *internal audit*.

audit committee A committee of the *board of directors* of a corporation, usually comprising *outside directors*, who nominate the independent *auditors* and discuss the auditors' work with them. If the auditors believe the shareholders should know about certain matters, the auditors, in principle, first bring these matters to the attention of the audit committee; in practice, the auditors may notify *management* before they notify the audit committee.

Audit Guides See *Industry Audit Guides*.

audit opinion See *opinion*.

audit program The procedures followed by the *auditor* in carrying out the *audit*.

audit trail A reference accompanying an entry, or *post*, to an underlying source record or document. Efficiently checking the accuracy of accounting entries requires an audit trail. See *cross-reference*.

Auditing Research Monograph Publication series of the *AICPA*.

auditing standards Standards promulgated by the *PCAOB* or the *AICPA*, including general standards, standards of field work, and standards of reporting. According to the AICPA, these standards "deal with the measures of the quality of the performance and the objectives to be attained" rather than with specific auditing procedures.

Auditing Standards Board *AICPA operating* committee that promulgates auditing rules for private companies. The *PCAOB* promulgates rules for public companies.

auditor Without a modifying adjective, usually refers to an external auditor—one who checks the accuracy, fairness, and general acceptability of *accounting* records and statements and then *attests* to them. See *internal auditor*.

auditor's opinion *Auditor's report*.

auditor's report The *auditor's* statement of the work done and an *opinion* of the *financial statements*. The auditor usually gives unqualified ("clean") opinions but may qualify them, or the auditor may disclaim an opinion in the report. Often called the "*accountant's report*." See *adverse opinion*.

AudSEC The former Auditing Standards Executive Committee of the *AICPA*, now functioning as the *Auditing Standards Board*.

authorized capital stock The number of *shares* of stock that a *corporation* can issue; specified by the *articles of incorporation*.

available for sale (securities) AFS *Marketable securities* a *firm* holds that are classified as neither *trading securities* nor *held-to-maturity* (*debt*) *securities*. This classification is important in *SFAS No. 115* (**Codification Topic 320**), which requires the owner to carry marketable equity securities on the *balance sheet* at *market value*, not at *cost*. Under *SFAS No. 115* (**Codification Topic 320**), the *income statement* reports *holding gains and losses* on trading securities but not on securities available for sale. The required *accounting credits* (*debits*) holding gains (losses) on securities available for sale to *other comprehensive income*. On sale, the firm reports realized gain or loss as the difference between the selling price and the *original cost*, for securities available for sale, and as the difference between the selling price and the *carrying value* at the beginning of the *period* of sale, for trading securities and for debt securities held to maturity. By their nature, however, the firm will only rarely sell *held-to-maturity* debt securities. *U.S. GAAP* allows firms to elect to use the *fair value option* for SAS, as well as for trading securities and held-to-maturity securities.

average The arithmetic mean of a set of numbers; obtained by summing the items and dividing by the number of items.

average collection period of receivables See *ratio* and **Exhibit 6.14**.

average-cost flow assumption An inventory *flow assumption* in which the *cost* of units equals the *weighted average* cost of the *beginning inventory* and purchases. See *inventory equation*.

average tax rate The rate found by dividing *income tax expense* by *net income* before *taxes*. Contrast with *marginal tax rate* and *statutory tax rate*.

avoidable cost A *cost* that *ceases* if a *firm* discontinues an activity; an *incremental* or *variable cost*. See *programmed cost*.

B

backflush costing A method of *allocating indirect costs* and *overhead*; used by companies that hope to have zero or small *work-in-process inventory* at the end of the period. The method *debits* all *product costs* to *cost of goods sold* (or *finished goods inventory*) during the period. To the extent that work in process actually exists at the end of the period, the method then debits work-in-process and *credits* cost of goods sold (or finished goods inventory). This method is "backflush" in the sense that costing systems ordinarily, but not in this case, allocate first to work-in-process and then forward to cost of goods sold or to finished goods. Here, the process allocates first to cost of goods sold (or finished goods) and then, later if necessary, to work-in-process.

backlog In *financial reporting*, orders for delivery at a future date. In *managerial accounting*, orders for which a *firm* has insufficient *inventory* on hand for current delivery and will fill in a later *period*.

backlog depreciation In *current cost accounting*, a problem arising for the *accumulated depreciation* on *plant assets*. Consider an *asset* costing $10,000 with a 10-year life depreciated with the straight-line method. Assume that a similar asset has a current cost of $10,000 at the end of the first year but $12,000 at the end of the second year. Assume that the firm bases the *depreciation charge* on the *average* current cost during the year, $10,000 for the first year and $11,000 for the second. The depreciation charge for the first year is $1,000 and for the second is $1,100 (= .10 × $11,000), so the accumulated depreciation *account* is $2,100 after two years. Note that at the end of the second year, the firm has used 20% of the asset's future benefits, so the accounting records based on current costs must show a *net carrying value* of $9,600 (= .80 × $12,000), which results only if accumulated depreciation equals $2,400, so that carrying value equals $9,600 (= $12,000 − $2,400). But the sum of the depreciation charges equals only $2,100 (= $1,000 + $1,100). The *journal entry* to increase the accumulated depreciation account requires a *credit* to that account of $300. The backlog depreciation question arises: what account do we *debit*? Some theorists would debit an *income* account, and others would debit a *balance sheet owners' equity* account without reducing current-period earnings. The answer to the question of what to debit interrelates with how the firm records the *holding gains* on the asset. When the firm debits the asset account for $2,000 to increase the recorded amount from $10,000 to $12,000, it records a holding gain of $2,000 with a credit. Many theorists believe that whatever account the firm credits for the holding gain is the same account that the firm should debit for backlog depreciation. This is sometimes called "*catch-up depreciation*."

bad debt An *uncollectible account*; see *bad debt expense* and *sales contra, estimated uncollectibles*.

bad debt expense The name for an *account debited* in both the *allowance method* for *uncollectible accounts* and the *direct write-off method*. Under the allowance method, some prefer to treat the account as a *revenue contra*, not as an *expense*, and give it an account title such as Uncollectible Accounts Adjustment.

bad debt recovery Collection, perhaps partial, of a specific *account receivable* previously written off as uncollectible. If a *firm* uses the *allowance method*, it will usually *credit* the *allowance* account, assuming that it has correctly *assessed* the amount of *bad debts* but has merely misjudged the identity of one of the nonpaying customers. If the firm decides that its charges for bad debts have been too large, it will credit the Bad Debt Expense account. If the firm uses the *direct write-off* method, it will credit a *revenue account*.

bailout period In a *capital budgeting* context, the total time that elapses before accumulated *cash* inflows from a project, including the potential *salvage value* of *assets* at various times, equal or exceed the accumulated cash outflows. Contrast with *payback period*, which assumes completion of the project and uses terminal salvage value. Bailout, in contrast with payback, takes into account, at least to some degree, the *present value* of the *cash flows* after the termination date that the analyst is considering. The potential salvage value at any time includes some estimate of the flows that can occur after that time.

balance As a noun, the opening balance in an *account*, plus the amounts of increases, less the amounts of decreases. (In the absence of a modifying adjective, the term means closing balance, in contrast to opening balance. The closing balance for a period becomes the opening balance for the next period.) As a verb, "balance" means to find the closing value described above or to correct an error in an account, so that its ending balance is correct.

balance sheet Statement of financial position that shows Total *Assets* = Total *Liabilities* + *Owners' Equity*. The *balance sheet* usually classifies Total Assets as (1) *current assets*, (2) *investments*, (3) *property*, *plant*, and *equipment*, or (4) *intangible assets*. The balance sheet accounts composing Total Liabilities usually appear under the headings Current Liabilities and Long-Term Liabilities.

balance sheet account An *account* that can appear on a *balance sheet*; a *permanent account*. Contrast with *temporary account*.

balance sheet equation Assets = *Liabilities* + *Owners' Equity*, or Assets = All Sources of Financing. In some countries: Assets − Liabilities = Owners' Equity.

balanced scorecard A set of performance targets, not all expressed in dollar amounts, for setting an organization's goals for its individual employees or groups or divisions. A community relations employee might, for example, set targets in terms of number of employee hours devoted to local charitable purposes.

balloon Most *mortgage* and *installment loans* require relatively equal periodic payments. Sometimes the loan requires relatively equal periodic payments with a large final payment. Usage calls the large final payment a "balloon" payment and the loan, a "balloon" loan. Although a *coupon bond* meets this definition, usage seldom, if ever, applies this term to *bond* loans.

bank balance The amount of the *balance* in a checking *account* shown on the *bank statement*. Compare with *adjusted bank balance of cash*, and see *bank reconciliation schedule*.

bank prime rate See *prime rate*.

bank reconciliation schedule A *schedule* that explains the difference between the *book balance* of the *cash* in a bank *account* and the bank's statement of that amount; takes into account the amount of items such as *checks* that have not cleared or deposits that have not been recorded by the bank, as well as errors made by the bank or the *firm*.

bank statement A statement sent by the bank to a checking account customer showing deposits, *checks* cleared, and service *charges* for a *period*, usually one month.

bankrupt Occurs when a company's *liabilities* exceed its *assets* and the *firm* or one of its *creditors* has filed a legal petition that the bankruptcy court has accepted under the bankruptcy law. A bankrupt firm is usually, but need not be, *insolvent*.

bankruptcy The state or condition of being *bankrupt*.

bargain purchase Said of a *purchase acquisition* when the *fair value* of the *net assets* acquired exceeds the fair value of all consideration given. Both *U.S.GAAP* and *IFRS* require the acquirer to use the fair valuations for initial *balance sheet* amounts and *recognize* a *gain* in *income* for the period of acquisition for the excess of fair valuations over purchase price.

base stock method A method of *inventory* valuation that assumes that a *firm* must keep on hand at all times a minimum normal, or base, stock of goods for effective *continuity of operations*. The firm *values* this base quantity at *acquisition cost* of the inventory on hand in the earliest period when inventory was on hand. Firms may not use this method, either for financial reporting or for tax reporting, but most theorists consider it to be the forerunner of the *LIFO cost flow assumption*.

basic accounting equation *Accounting equation*.

basic cost-flow equation *Cost-flow equation*.

basic earnings per share (BEPS) *Net income* to *common shareholders*, divided by the weighted *average* number of *common shares outstanding* during the *period*. Required by *SFAS No. 128* (**Codification Topic 260**) and by *IASB*. Formerly called "primary earnings per share."

basis *Acquisition cost*, or some substitute therefore, of an *asset* or *liability* used in computing *gain* or *loss* on disposition or retirement; *attribute measured*. This term appears in both *financial* and *income tax reporting*, but the basis of a given item need not be the same for both purposes.

basis point; bp One one-hundredth ($=1/100$). Terminology usually quotes *interest rates* in percentage terms, such as "5.60%" or "5.67%." The difference between those two interest rates is described as "7 basis points" or seven one-hundredths of one percent. Why this term? Consider "interest rates increased by one percent." Does this mean that 6.00% increased to 7.00% or from 6.00% to 6.06% ($= 1.01 \times 6\%$)? In order to avoid confusion, we say in the first case, interest rates increased by 100 basis points and in the second, by 6 basis points. Financial writers often extend this usage to other contexts involving decimals. For example, if the mean grade point average in the class is 3.25 and a given student scores 3.30, we might say that the student scored "5 basis points" above the class *average*. Some pronounce the abbreviation as "bip."

basket purchase Purchase of a group of *assets* (and *liabilities*) for a single *price*; the acquiring firm must assign *costs* to each item so that it can record the individual items with their separate amounts in the *accounts*.

batch-level activities Work required to ready equipment or people for a production run.

bear One who believes that *security prices* will fall. A "bear market" refers to a time when *stock* prices are generally declining. Contrast with *bull*.

bearer bond See *registered bond* for contrast and definition.

beginning inventory Measurement of *inventory* on hand at the beginning of the *accounting period*; equals *ending inventory* from the preceding period.

behavioral congruence *Goal congruence*.

benchmarking Process of measuring a *firm's* performance, or *products*, or *services* against standards based on best levels of performance achievable or, sometimes, achieved by other firms.

benefit element in stock option On the *exercise* date of a *stock option*, the excess of *market price* of the stock over the *exercise price*. Same as "intrinsic value."

BEPS *Basic earnings per share.*

betterment An *improvement*, usually *capitalized*, not *expensed*.

bid An offer to purchase. The amount of an offer to purchase.

bid-ask spread The range in *prices* between the maximum the buyer of an item is willing to pay and the minimum the seller is willing to accept. Unless the buyer's maximum exceeds the seller's minimum, then the parties will not transact.

big bath A *write-off* of a substantial amount of *costs* previously treated as *assets*; usually occurs when a *corporation* drops a *business* line that earlier required a large *investment* but that proved to be unprofitable. The term is sometimes used to describe a situation in which a corporation takes a large write-off in one period in order to free later periods of gradual write-offs of those amounts. In this sense it frequently occurs when the top *management* of the *firm* changes.

Big 4; Final 4 The four largest U.S. *public accounting partnerships*; in alphabetical order: Deloitte & Touche; Ernst & Young; KPMG Peat Marwick; and PricewaterhouseCoopers. See *Big N*.

Big N The largest U.S. *public accounting partnerships*. When we first prepared this glossary, there were eight such partnerships, referred to as the "Big 8." See *Big 4*. The term "Big N" came into use when various of the Big 8 proposed to merge with each other and the ultimate number of large partnerships was in doubt. Most public policy makers who address the subject think that fewer than four would pose issues of competition and conflicts of interest, so that the number will not likely decline below four in the near future.

bill An *invoice* of *charges* and *terms of sale* for *goods* and *services*; also, a piece of currency.

bill of materials A specification of the quantities of *direct materials* that a *firm* expects to use to produce a given *job* or quantity of *output*.

blocked currency Currency that the holder, by law, cannot withdraw from the issuing country or exchange for the currency of another country.

board *Board of directors.*

board of directors The governing body of a *corporation*; elected by the shareholders.

bond A *certificate* to show evidence of *debt*. The *par value* is the *principal* or face amount of the bond payable at *maturity*. The *coupon rate* is the amount of the yearly payments divided by the principal amount. Until 1982, *coupon bonds* had coupons attached with perforations, that the holder could detach and redeem at stated dates. Increasingly, firms issue not coupon bonds but registered bonds; the firm or its *agent* keeps track of the owners of registered bonds. Normally, bonds call for semiannual payments. Physical coupons enabled some holders to engage in *income tax* evasion, so the *tax* authorities have outlawed physical coupon arrangements. Even though bonds no longer have physical coupons, common terminology continues to refer to "coupon rate" as the amount of the yearly payments divided by the principal amount.

bond conversion The act of exchanging *convertible bonds* for *preferred* or *common shares*.

bond discount From the standpoint of the issuer of a *bond* at the issue date, the excess of the *par value* of a bond over its initial sales *price* and, at later dates, the excess of par over the sum of the following two amounts: initial issue price and the portion of *discount* already *amortized*; from the standpoint of a bondholder, the difference between par value and selling price when the bond sells below par.

bond indenture The contract between an issuer of *bonds* and the bondholders.

bond premium Exactly parallel to *bond discount* except that the issue price (or current selling price) exceeds *par value*.

bond ratings Corporate and *municipal bond* issue ratings, based on the issuer's existing *debt* level, its previous record of payment, the *coupon rate* on the *bonds*, and the safety of the *assets* or *revenues* that are committed to paying off *principal* and *interest*. Moody's Investors Service, Standard & Poor's Corporation, and Fitch publish bond ratings: Moody's top rating is Aaa; both Standard & Poor's and Fitch use AAA for the top.

bond redemption Retirement of *bonds*.

bond refunding To *incur debt*, usually through the issue of new *bonds*, intending to use the proceeds to retire an *outstanding* bond issue.

bond sinking fund See *sinking fund*.

bond table A table showing the current price (as *present values* or percentages of *par*) of a *bond* as a function of the *coupon rate*, current (remaining) term *maturity*, and effective *yield to maturity* (or *effective rate*). In the financial press, a bond table shows for each bond issue, the issuer, coupon, maturity date, *bid price*, and *yield* percentage based on the bid price. Some bond tables include the ask price.

Bonds Payable An *account* title for the *liability* resulting from the obligation arising from a *bond* issue.

bonus Premium over normal *wage* or *salary*, paid usually for meritorious performance.

bonus method One of two methods to recognize an excess, say $10,000, when a *partnership* admits a new partner and when the new partner's *capital account* is to show an amount larger than the amount of *tangible assets* that he or she contributes. First, the old partners may transfer $10,000 from themselves to the new partner. This is the bonus method. Second, the partnership may recognize *goodwill* in the amount of $10,000, with the credit to the new partner's capital account. This is the *goodwill method*. (Notice that the new partner's percentage of total ownership differs under the two methods.) If the new partner's capital account is to show an amount smaller than the tangible assets that he or she contributed, then the old partners will receive *bonus* or goodwill, depending on the method.

book As a verb, to record a transaction; as a noun, usually plural, the *journals* and *ledgers*; as an adjective, see *book value*.

book cost *Book value.*

book inventory An *inventory* amount that results not from physical count but from the amount of *beginning inventory* plus *invoice* amounts of *net* purchases less invoice amounts of *requisitions* or *withdrawals*; implies a *perpetual inventory method*.

book of original entry *Journal.*

book value Formerly, a nontechnical term describing the *balance sheet* amount for an item, such as an *asset* or total *owners' equity*. It often referred to *amortized cost* of a *debt* a *firm* issued or of a *fixed-income security* the firm held as an asset. It also refers to the *historical cost* of a fixed asset, less *accumulated depreciation*. *Accounting standards*, such as *SFAS 115* (**Codification Topic 320**), often require, or allow, the firm to show items at *fair value*. The balance sheet amount of an item can now mean the fair value of that item, such as a marketable security classified as *available for sale.* Thus the "book value" of a marketable security available for sale is also the fair value of the security. Of a firm, it continues to refer to the excess of total assets over total *liabilities; net assets,* or owners' equity. Contrast with *carrying amount.*

book value per share of common stock Common *shareholders' equity* divided by the number of shares of common stock *outstanding.*

bookkeeping The process of analyzing and recording transactions in the *accounting* records.

boot The additional *cash* paid (or received), along with a used item, in a trade-in or *exchange transaction* for another item. See *trade-in.*

borrower See *loan.*

bottleneck An operation in which the work to be performed equals or exceeds the available *capacity,* thus holding up further *operations.*

branch A sales office or other unit of an enterprise physically separated from the home office of the enterprise but not organized as a legally separate *subsidiary.* Writers seldom use this term to refer to manufacturing units.

branch accounting An *accounting procedure* that enables the *firm* to report the financial position and *operations* of each *branch* separately but later combine them for published statements.

brand; brand name See *trademark* and *trademark right.*

breakeven A measure of activity at which *revenues* or other inflows equal some measure of *costs* of other outflows.

breakeven analysis See *breakeven chart.*

breakeven chart Two kinds of breakeven charts appear here. The charts use the following information for one month. Revenue is $30 per unit.

Cost Classification	Variable Cost, Per Unit	Fixed Cost, Per Month
Manufacturing costs:		
Direct material	$ 4	—
Direct labor	9	—
Overhead	4	$3,060
Total manufacturing costs	$17	$3,060
Selling, general, and administrative costs	5	1,740
Total costs	$22	$4,800

The *cost-volume-profit graph* presents the relation between changes in volume to the amount of *profit,* or *income.* Such a graph shows total *revenue* and total *costs* for each volume level, and the user reads profit or *loss* at any volume directly from the chart. The profit-volume graph does not show revenues and costs but more readily indicates profit (or loss) at various *output* levels. Keep in mind two caveats about these graphs:

1. Although the curve depicting *variable cost* and total cost appears as a straight line for its entire length, at low or high levels of output, variable cost will probably differ from $22 per unit. The variable cost figure usually results from studies of *operations* at some broad central area of production, called the *relevant range.* The chart will not usually provide accurate results for low (or high) levels of activity. For this reason, the total cost and the profit-

(a) Cost-Volume-Profit Graph

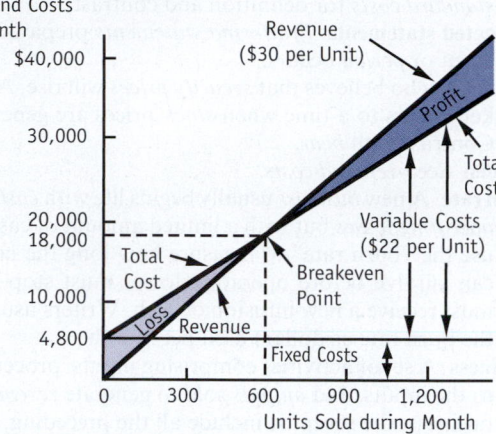

(b) Profit-Volume Graph

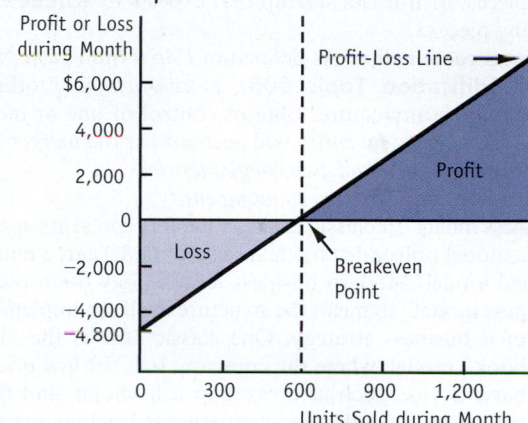

loss curves sometimes appear as dotted lines at lower (or higher) volume levels.

2. This chart, simplistically, assumes a single-product *firm.* For a multiproduct firm, the horizontal axis would have to be stated in dollars rather than in physical units of output. Breakeven charts for multiproduct firms necessarily assume that the firm sells constant proportions of the several products, so that changes in this mixture, as well as in costs or selling prices, invalidate such a chart.

breakeven point The volume of *sales* required so that total *revenues* equals total *costs;* may be expressed in units (*fixed costs + contribution per unit*) or in sales dollars [selling price per unit × (fixed costs + contribution per unit)].

break-even time Time required before the *firm* recovers the amounts it invested in developing a new *product.*

budget A financial plan that a *firm* uses to estimate the results of future *operations;* frequently used to help control future operations. In governmental operations, budgets often become the law. See *standard costs* for further elaboration and contrast.

budgetary accounts In governmental *accounting,* the accounts that reflect estimated *operations* and financial condition, as affected by estimated *revenues, appropriations,* and *encumbrances.* Contrast with *proprietary accounts,* which record the *transactions.*

budgetary control *Management* of governmental (nongovernmental) unit in accordance with an official (approved) *budget* in order to keep total *expenditures* within authorized (planned) limits.

budgeted cost; budgeted fixed cost; budgeted variable cost See *standard costs* for definition and contrast.

budgeted statements *Pro forma statements* prepared before the event or *period* occurs.

bull One who believes that *security prices* will rise. A "bull market" refers to a time when *stock* prices are generally rising. Contrast with *bear*.

burden See *overhead costs*.

burn rate A new *business* usually begins life with *cash*-absorbing *operating losses* but with a limited amount of cash. Analysts use the "burn rate" to measure how long the new business can survive before operating losses must stop or the firm must receive a new infusion of cash. Writers usually express the burn rate as dollars used per month.

business A set of activities comprising inputs, processes applied to the inputs, and *outputs* sold to generate *revenues*. To be a business, the set must include all the preceding, except that a unit can be a business if it can easily acquire the missing pieces, or if it is a startup that expects to acquire the missing pieces.

business combination As defined in *FASB Statement No. 141R* (**Codification Topic 805**), a *transaction* or other event in which an acquirer obtains control of one or more *businesses*. The new *entity* will account for the *merger* with the *acquisition method*. See *conglomerate*.

business entity *Entity*; *accounting entity*.

business model In classic usage, a model represents a structure: a model railroad, a model house, a model car, a mathematical model. Modern business terminology often uses "business model" to mean the structure itself, an implementation of a business strategy. One classic case is the "bait and hook" model, where the company sells for low prices some basic device, such as a razor or cell phone, and then sells the critical non-durable components, such as razor blades and air time minutes, at high prices. More recently, some retailers implement a "bricks and clicks" model, with both physical and on-line stores.

BV (besloten vennootschap) Netherlands: a private *limited-liability* company.

bylaws The rules adopted by the shareholders of a *corporation*; specify the general methods for carrying out the functions of the corporation.

by-product A *joint product* whose *sales value* is so small relative to the sales value of the other joint product(s) that it does not receive normal *accounting* treatment. The *costs* assigned to by-products reduce the costs of the main *product(s)*. Accounting *allocates* by-products a share of joint costs such that the expected *gain* or *loss* at their sale is zero. Thus, by-products appear in the *accounts* at *net realizable value*.

C

C corporation In *tax* terminology, a *corporation* paying its own *income taxes*. Contrast with *S corporation*.

CA *Chartered accountant*.

call (option) An *option* to buy *shares* of a publicly traded *corporation* at a fixed price during a fixed time span. Contrast with *put*.

call premium See *callable bond*.

call price See *callable bond*. The *price* of a *call option*.

callable bond A *bond* for which the issuer reserves the right to pay a specific amount, the *call price*, to retire the obligation at specified times before its *maturity* date. If the issuer agrees to pay more than the *face amount* of the bond when called, the excess of the payment over the face amount is the "*call premium*."

callable preferred shares Refer to the definition of *callable bond* and substitute the word "*shares*" for "*bond*." Also, in the context of *preferred shares*, we'd use the word "issue" not "obligation."

called-up share capital UK: *common stock* at *par value*.

Canadian Institute of Chartered Accountants; CICA The national organization that represents *chartered accountants* in Canada. Web Site: www.cica.ca.

cancelable lease See *lease*.

CAP Committee on Accounting Procedure.

capacity Stated in units of *product*, the amount that a *firm* can produce per unit of time; stated in units of input, such as *direct labor* hours, the amount of input that a firm can use in production per unit of time. A firm uses this measure of *output* or input in *allocating fixed costs* if the amounts producible are normal, rather than maximum, amounts.

capacity cost A *fixed cost* incurred to provide a *firm* with the *capacity* to produce or to sell. Consists of *standby costs* and *enabling costs*. Contrast with *programmed costs*.

capacity variance *Production volume variance*.

capital *Owners' equity* in a *business*; often used, equally correctly, to mean the total *assets* of a business; sometimes used to mean *long-term assets*. Sometimes used to mean *funds* raised or all assets or long-term financing. This word causes confusion in *accounting* and finance. Uninformed users mix up the funds (and their uses) with the sources of the funds. Consider the following *transactions*. A *firm* raises $100 cash by issuing *shares* and uses the $100 to acquire *inventory* and *plant assets*. Did the investor "invest capital" of $100 or did the firm "invest capital" of $100 or both? You will hear "invest capital" used for both sides of that transaction. Now focus on the firm who issued the shares and received the *cash*. Some would say the first transaction, the issue of shares, "raised capital." (If you ask of a person who answers this way, "What is the *capital*, the increase in owners' equity or the increased cash?" you will not get a clear answer, consistent across all such people.) Others would say only the second transaction, spending the cash, raised capital and only then for the plant assets, not the inventory. When a regulator focuses on a bank's capital ratios, it looks to the right-hand side of the *balance sheet*, not to how the firm has invested its funds. Sometimes bank regulators will take the owners' equity total and subtract from that amount the amount of intangible assets, resulting in a total with no clear conception, which they call "tangible capital." See *cost of capital* for further discussion of the confusion between the cost of raising funds and the return to, or *opportunity cost* of, investing funds. The confusion is so prevalent that we tend to avoid using the word, except to mean *shareholders' equity*.

capital asset A term used by the *IRS* to designate the kinds of property that qualify for taxation at a *capital gains* tax rate, which is lower than the tax rate for *ordinary income*. Lower capital gains rates primarily relate to individuals. The IRS designates the following as capital assets: *stocks* and *bonds*, a home owned and occupied by the taxpayer, timber on home property or *investment* property, even if the individual makes *sales* of the timber, household furnishings, a car used for pleasure or commuting, coin or stamp collections, gems and jewelry, and gold, silver, and other metals. The IRS excludes from capital gains taxation, property that the taxpayer acquires to generate *income* as a *business*, such as: *cash*, inventoriable *assets*, *goods* held primarily for sale, most depreciable property, *real estate*, *receivables*, and certain *intangibles*. Sometimes writers use this term imprecisely to describe *plant* and *equipment*, which are clearly not capital assets under the *income tax* definition. Writers often use the term to refer to an *investment* in *securities*.

capital budget Plan of proposed outlays for acquiring long-term *assets* and the means of *financing* the acquisition.

capital budgeting The process of choosing *investment* projects for an enterprise by considering the *present value* of *cash flows* and deciding how to raise the *funds* the investment requires.

capital consumption allowance The term used for *depreciation expense* in national *income accounting* and the reporting of *funds* in the economy.

capital contributed in excess of par (or stated) value A preferred title for the *account* that shows the amount received by the issuer for *capital stock* in excess of *par* (or *stated*) *value*. Often called *additional paid-in capital*.

capital expenditure (outlay) An *expenditure* to acquire long-term *assets*.

capital gain The excess of *proceeds* over *cost*, or other *basis*, from the sale of a *capital asset* as defined by the Internal Revenue Code. If the taxpayer has held the capital asset for a sufficiently long time before sale, then the *gain* is *taxed* at a rate lower than that used for other gains and *ordinary income*.

capital lease (method) A *lease* treated by the *lessee* as both the borrowing of *funds* and the acquisition of an *asset* to be *amortized*. The lessee (tenant) recognizes both the *liability* and the asset on its *balance sheet*. *Expenses* consist of *interest* on the *debt* and *amortization* of the asset. The *lessor* (landlord) treats the lease as the sale of the asset in return for a series of future *cash receipts*. Same as *financing lease* (method) as used by *IFRS*. Contrast with *operating lease*.

capital loss A negative capital gain; see *capital gain*.

capital rationing In a *capital budgeting* context, the imposition of constraints on the amounts of total *capital expenditures* in each *period*.

capital stock The ownership *shares* of a *corporation*. Consists of all classes of *common* and *preferred shares*.

capital stock contract The legal document stating the agreements between the *corporation* and its *shareholders*.

capital structure The composition of a *corporation's equities*; the relative proportions of short-term *debt*, long-term debt, and *owners' equity*.

capital structure leverage ratio See *ratio* and **Exhibit 6.14**.

capital surplus An inferior term for *capital contributed in excess of par (or stated) value*.

capitalization of a corporation A term used by investment analysts to indicate *shareholders' equity* plus *bonds outstanding*.

capitalization of earnings The process of estimating the *fair value* of a *firm* by computing the *net present value* of the predicted *net income* (not *cash flows*) of the firm for the future. If one assumes that the future amounts are constant and persist forever, then one divides the annual amount by the *discount rate*. See *perpetuity*.

capitalization rate An *interest rate* used to convert a series of payments or *receipts* or earnings into a single *present value*.

capitalize To record an *expenditure* that may benefit a future *period* as an *asset* rather than to treat the expenditure as an *expense* of the period of its occurrence. Whether expenditures for advertising or for research and development should be capitalized is controversial, but *SFAS No. 2* (**Codification Topic 730**) forbids capitalizing *R&D* costs. We believe *U.S. GAAP* should allow *firms* to capitalize expenditures when they lead to future benefits and thus meet the criterion to be an asset.

carryback, carryforward, carryover The use of *losses* or *tax credits* in one *period* to reduce *income taxes* payable in other periods. Two common kinds of carrybacks exist: for *net operating* losses and for *capital losses*. They apply against *taxable income*. Different tax jurisdictions have different rules for the length of the carryback and carryforward periods.

carrying cost *Costs* (such as property *taxes* and *insurance*) of holding, or storing, *inventory* from the time of purchase until the time of *sale* or use.

carrying value (amount) The *balance sheet* amount of an item. Can be an *acquisition cost*, an *amortized* acquisition cost, or a *fair value*. Whereas the term is synonymous with *book value* with respect to a single balance sheet item, when one refers the total amount of *owners' equity* of a *firm*, or that amount per *share*, common terminology uses only "book value" or "*book value per share*."

CASB (Cost Accounting Standards Board) A *board* authorized by the U.S. Congress to "promulgate *cost-accounting* standards designed to achieve uniformity and *consistency* in the cost-accounting principles followed by defense contractors and subcontractors under federal contracts." The *principles* the CASB promulgated since 1970 have considerable weight in practice wherever the *FASB* has not established a standard. Congress allowed the CASB to go out of existence in 1980 but reinstated it in 1990. It is a function located within the Office of Federal Procurement Policy, itself a part of the Office of Management and Budget, part of the Executive Office of the President of the United States.

cash Currency and coins, negotiable *checks*, and *balances* in bank accounts. For the *statement of cash flows*, "cash" also includes *cash equivalents*.

cash basis of accounting In contrast to the *accrual basis of accounting*, a system of *accounting* in which a *firm recognizes revenues* when it receives *cash* and recognizes *expenses* as it makes *disbursements*. The firm makes no attempt to *match* revenues and expenses in measuring *income*. See *modified cash basis*.

cash budget A *schedule* of expected *cash receipts* and *disbursements*.

cash change equation For any *period*, the change in *cash* equals the change in *liabilities* plus the change in *owners' equity* minus the change in noncash *assets*.

cash collection basis The *installment method* for recognizing *revenue*. Do not confuse with the *cash basis of accounting*.

cash conversion cycle *Cash cycle*.

cash cycle The period of time during which a firm converts *cash* into *inventories*, inventories into *accounts receivable*, and *receivables* back into cash. Sometimes called *earnings cycle* or *operating cycle*.

cash disbursements journal A specialized *journal* used to record *expenditures* by *cash* and by *check*. If a *check register* is also used, a cash disbursements journal records only expenditures of currency and coins.

cash discount A sales or purchase price reduction allowed for prompt payment.

cash dividend See *dividend*.

cash equivalents According to *SFAS No. 95* (**Codification Topic 230**), "short-term, highly *liquid investments* that are both readily convertible to known amounts of *cash* [and] so near their *maturity* that they present insignificant risk of changes in value because of changes in interest rates. . . . Examples of items commonly considered to be cash equivalents are Treasury bills, *commercial paper*, [and] money market *funds*."

cash equivalent value A term used to describe the amount for which an *asset* could be sold. Sometimes called *fair value*, *market value*, or *fair market price* (*value*).

cash flow *Cash receipts* minus *disbursements* from a given *asset*, or group of assets, for a given *period*. Financial analysts sometimes use this term to mean *net income + depreciation + depletion + amortization*. See also *operating cash flow* and *free cash flow*.

cash flow from financing activities Section of *statement of cash flows* reporting *cash* inflows related to raising *funds* through issues of *securities* and cash outflows related to retiring *securities* and for paying *dividends*.

cash flow from investing activities Section of *statement of cash flows* reporting *cash* outflows related to acquisitions of non-operating *assets*, such as property, plant, equipment, investments, and intellectual property purchased from others, and inflows related to selling these.

cash flow from operations *Receipts* from customers and from *investments*, less *expenditures* for *inventory*, labor, and *services* used in the usual activities of the *firm*, less *interest* expenditures. See *statement of cash flows* and *operations*. Same as *cash provided by operations*.

cash flow from operations to current liabilities ratio See *ratio* and **Exhibit 6.14**.

cash flow from operations to total liabilities ratio See *ratio* and **Exhibit 6.14**.

cash flow hedge A *hedge* of an exposure to variability in the *cash flows* of a recognized *asset* or *liability* or of a forecasted *transaction*, such as expected future foreign *sales*. The cash flows hedged do not themselves appear on the *balance sheet*. The hedging instrument itself is a *marketable security* and appears on the balance sheet at *fair value*. If the *firm* uses hedge *accounting* and the hedging instrument is highly effective, then it will be able to report in *other comprehensive income* the *gains* and *losses*, so these amounts will not appear in periodic *net income* until the firm settles or closes the hedging instrument.

cash flow statement *Statement of cash flows*.

cash generating unit IFRS term for *reporting unit* in *U.S. GAAP*, which is a *segment* or a component of a segment that is a *business* with separate financial information that *management* regularly reviews.

cash provided by operations An important subtotal in the *statement of cash flows*. This amount equals revenues producing *cash* minus *expenses* requiring cash. Often, the amount appears as *net income* plus expenses not requiring cash (such as *depreciation charges*) minus *revenues* not producing cash (such as revenues recognized under the *equity method* of *accounting* for a long-term *investment*). The statement of cash flows maintains the same distinctions between *continuing operations*, *discontinued operations*, and *income* or *loss* from *extraordinary items* as does the *income statement*.

cash receipts journal A specialized *journal* used to record all *receipts* of *cash*.

cash (surrender) value of life insurance An amount equal not to the face value of the policy to be paid in the event of death but to the amount that the owner could *realize* by immediately canceling the policy and returning it to the insurance company for *cash*. A *firm* owning a life insurance policy reports it as an *asset* at an amount equal to this *value*.

cash yield See *yield*.

cashier's check A bank's own *check* drawn on itself and signed by the cashier or other authorized official. It is a direct obligation of the bank. Compare with *certified check*.

catch-up depreciation *Backlog depreciation*.

cause-and-effect analysis An identification of potential causes of defects and taking actions to cure the problem found. To use this analysis, first define the effect and then identify the causes of the problem. The potential causes fall into four categories: human factors, methods and design factors, machine-related factors, and materials or components factors. As *management* identifies the prevailing causes, it develops and implements corrective measures.

CCA *Current cost accounting*; *current value accounting*.

central corporate expenses General *overhead expenses* incurred in running the corporate headquarters and related supporting activities of a *corporation*. *Accounting* treats these expenses as *period expenses*. Contrast with *manufacturing overhead*. *Line of business reporting* must decide how to treat these expenses—whether to *allocate* them to the individual segments and, if so, how to allocate them.

central processing unit (CPU) The computer system component that carries out the arithmetic, logic, and data transfer.

certificate The document that is the physical embodiment of a *bond* or a *share of stock*; a term sometimes used for the *auditor's report*.

certificate of deposit A form of *deposit* in a bank or thrift institution. Federal law constrains the rate of *interest* that banks can pay to their depositors. Current law allows banks to pay a rate higher than the one allowed on a *time deposit* if the depositor promises to leave *funds* on deposit for several months or more. When the bank receives such funds, it issues a certificate of deposit. The depositor can withdraw the funds before *maturity* by paying a penalty.

certified check The *check* of a depositor drawn on a bank. The bank inserts the words "accepted" or "certified" on the face of the check, with the date and a signature of a bank official. The check then becomes an obligation of the bank. Compare with *cashier's check*.

certified financial statement A *financial statement* attested to by an independent *auditor* who is a *CPA* or who hold a similar certification such as *CA*.

certified internal auditor See *CIA*.

certified management accountant *CMA*.

certified public accountant (CPA) An *accountant* who has satisfied the statutory and administrative requirements of his or her jurisdiction to be registered or licensed as a *public accountant*. In addition to passing the Uniform CPA Examination administered by the *AICPA*, the CPA must meet certain educational, experience, and moral requirements that differ from jurisdiction to jurisdiction. The jurisdictions are the 50 states, the District of Columbia, Guam, Puerto Rico, and the Virgin Islands.

CFA Chartered Financial Analyst.

CGA (Certified General Accountant) Canada: an accountant who has satisfied the experience, education, and examination requirements of the Certified General Accountants' Association.

chain discount A series of *discount* percentages. For example, if a chain discount of 10 and 5% is quoted, then the actual, or *invoice*, *price* is the nominal, or list, price times .90 times .95, or 85.5%, of invoice price.

change fund Coins and currency issued to cashiers, delivery drivers, and so on.

change in accounting principle See *accounting changes*.

change in estimates See *accounting changes*.

changes, accounting See *accounting changes*.

changes in financial position See *statement of cash flows*.

channel stuffing Assume a company's ordinary practices record *revenue* when it ships to customers *goods* previously ordered. A company engaging in channel-stuffing will ship goods not yet ordered but record them as *sales*, as though a real customer had ordered them. It might even get permission from the customer to ship, saying it will not *bill* the customer until next *period* and that the customer will get its usual grace period to pay the bill starting from that later date, next period. Often, sales staff eager to boost their own sales *commissions* will send a letter to the customer laying out the agreement: the customer will accept the shipment and if asked, confirm that it ordered the goods, but the seller will not send an invoice until later, and the customer need not pay until later or can return the goods. Such a letter is called a "side letter" and even honest *managements* have a hard time locating these. All a management can do is to be diligent and deal severely with employees found issuing side letters.

Chapter 7; Chapter 11 Provisions of the Bankruptcy Code. Chapter 7 provides for the *liquidation* of the *business*. Chapter 11 provides for its continued *operations*.

charge As a noun, a *debit* to an *account*; as a verb, to *debit*.

charge off To treat as a *loss* or *expense* an amount originally recorded as an *asset*; use of this term implies that the *charge* is not in accord with original expectations.

chart of accounts A systematic list of *account* names and numbers.

charter Document issued by a state government authorizing the creation of a *corporation*.

chartered accountant(s) (CA) The title used in British Commonwealth countries, such as Australia, Canada, India, the United Kingdom, and New Zealand, for an accountant who has satisfied the requirements of the institute of his or her jurisdiction to be qualified to serve as a *public accountant*.

Chartered Financial Analyst (CFA) A person who has passed three examinations, over at least an 18-month period, covering topics in *accounting*, economics, financial economics, portfolio *management*, and *security* analysis. The CFA Institute administers the program. Beyond passing examinations, the person needs to have approved working experience and satisfy standards of professional conduct.

check You know what a check is. The Federal Reserve Board defines a check as "a *draft* or order upon a bank or banking house purporting to be drawn upon a deposit of *funds* for the payment at all events of a certain sum of money to a certain person therein named or to him or his order or to bearer and payable instantly on demand." It must contain the phrase "pay to the order of." The amount shown on the check must be clearly readable, and the check must have the signature of the *drawer*. The drawer need not date the check. In the *accounts*, the drawer usually reduces the *balance* in the *cash* account when it issues the check, not later when the check clears the bank. See *remittance advice*.

check register A *journal* to record *checks* issued.

CIA (Certified Internal Auditor) One who has satisfied certain requirements of the *Institute of Internal Auditors* including experience, ethics, education, and passing examinations.

CICA *Canadian Institute of Chartered Accountants*.

CIF (cost, insurance, and freight) In contracts, a term used along with the name of a given port, such as New Orleans, to indicate that the quoted *price* includes insurance, handling, and freight *charges* up to delivery by the seller at the given port.

circulating capital *Working capital*.

clean opinion See *auditor's report*.

clean surplus concept The notion that all entries to the *retained earnings account* must record *net income* and *dividends*. See *comprehensive income*. Contrast with *current operating performance concept*. This concept, with minor exceptions, now controls *U.S. GAAP*.

clearing account An *account* containing amounts to be transferred to another account(s) before the end of the *accounting period*. Examples are the *income summary* account (whose *balance* transfers to *retained earnings*) and the purchases account (whose balance transfers to *inventory* or to *cost of goods sold*).

close As a verb, to transfer the *balance* of a *temporary* or *contra* or *adjunct account* to the main account to which it relates; for example, to transfer *revenue* and *expense* accounts directly, or through the *income summary* account, to an *owners' equity* account or to transfer *purchase discounts* to purchases.

closed account An *account* with equal *debits* and *credits*, usually as a result of a *closing entry*.

closing entries (process) The entries that accomplish the transfer of *balances* in *temporary accounts* to the related *balance sheet accounts*. See *close*. See *work sheet*.

closing inventory *Ending inventory*.

CMA (Certified Management Accountant) certificate Awarded by the Institute of Certified Management Accountants of the *Institute of Management Accountants* to those who pass a set of examinations and meet certain experience and continuing-education requirements.

CoCoA *Continuously Contemporary Accounting*.

Codification (Project) The *FASB* has issued a compilation of *U.S. GAAP*, including *Statements of Financial Accounting Standards*, *Accounting Principles Board Opinions*, *Accounting Research Bulletins*, *Staff Accounting Bulletins*, *EITF* Consensuses, *FASB Interpretations*, and several other sorts of pronouncements. This compilation, which organizes the material by topic, brings together into one place the various *accounting methods* and procedures that treat that topic. The codification does not include *Statements of Financial Accounting Concepts*, so it omits definitions of such fundamental concepts as *asset* and *revenue*.

coding of accounts The numbering of *accounts*, as for a *chart of accounts*, that is necessary for computerized *accounting*.

coinsurance Common condition of insurance policies that protect against hazards such as fire or water damage. These often specify that the owner of the property may not collect the full amount of insurance for a loss unless the insurance policy covers at least some specified "coinsurance" percentage, usually about 80%, of the *replacement cost* of the property. Coinsurance clauses induce the owner to carry full, or nearly full, coverage.

COLA Cost-of-living adjustment. See *indexation*.

collateral *Assets* pledged by a *borrower* who will surrender those assets if he or she fails to repay a *loan*.

collectible Capable of being converted into *cash*—now if due, later otherwise.

collusion Cooperative effort by employees to commit fraud or another unethical act.

combination See *business combination*.

combined financial statements Financial statements for a group of companies under common control, but for which there is no *parent-subsidiary* relation. Such statements eliminate *intercompany transactions* and *balances*.

comfort letter A letter in which an *auditor* conveys negative assurances as to unaudited *financial statements* in a *prospectus* or *draft* financial statements included in a preliminary prospectus.

commercial paper Short-term *notes* issued by corporate borrowers.

commission Employee remuneration, usually expressed as a percentage, based on an activity rate, such as *sales*.

committed costs *Capacity costs*.

Committee on Accounting Procedure (CAP) Predecessor of the *APB*. The *AICPA*'s *principles*-promulgating body from 1939 through 1959. Its 51 pronouncements are *Accounting Research Bulletins*.

common cost *Cost* resulting from the use of *raw materials*, a facility (for example, *plant* or machines), or a *service* (for example, fire insurance) that benefits several *products* or departments. A *firm* must *allocate* this cost to those products or departments. Common costs result when two or more departments produce multiple products together even though the departments could produce them separately; joint costs occur when two or more departments must produce multiple products together. Many writers use "common costs" and "joint costs" synonymously. See *joint cost*, *indirect costs*, *overhead*, and *sterilized allocation*.

common-dollar accounting *Constant-dollar accounting*.

common monetary measuring unit For U.S. corporations, the dollar. See also *stable monetary unit assumption* and *constant-dollar accounting*.

common shares (stock) *Shares* representing the class of owners who have residual claims on the *assets* and *earnings* of a *corporation* after the *firm* meets all *debt* and *preferred shareholders'* claims.

common-size statement; common-size balance sheet; common-size income statement A *percentage statement* usually based on total *assets* (*balance sheet*) or *net sales* or *revenues* (*income statement*).

common-stock equivalent A *security* whose primary *value* arises from its holder's ability to exchange it for *common shares*; includes *stock options*, *warrants*, and also *convertible bonds* or *convertible preferred stock* whose *effective interest rate* at the time of issue is less than two-thirds the *average* Aa corporate bond *yield*. See *bond ratings*.

company-wide control See *control system*.

comparable The qualitative characteristic of *accounting* information that *firms* record like *transactions* and events similarly.

comparative (financial) statements *Financial statements* showing information for the same company for different times. The *SEC* requires two successive years for *balance sheets* and three for *income* and *cash flow statements*; the *IASB* requires two successive years for all financial statements. Nearly all published financial statements are in this form. Contrast with *historical summary*.

compensating balance The amount required to be left on deposit for a *loan*. When a bank lends *funds* to customers, it often requires that the customers keep on deposit in their checking *accounts* an amount equal to some percentage— say, 20%—of the loan. Such amounts effectively increase the *interest rate*. The *borrower* must disclose the amounts of such *balances* in *notes* to the *financial statements*.

completed contract method Recognizing *revenues* and *expenses* for a *job* or order only when the *firm* finishes it, except that when the firm expects a *loss* on the contract, the firm must *recognize* all revenues and expenses in the *period* when the firm first foresees a loss. *Accountants* generally use this term only for long-term contracts. This method is otherwise equivalent to the *sales basis of revenue recognition*.

completed sale(s) basis; completed sale(s) method See *sales basis of revenue recognition*.

compliance audit Obtaining and evaluating verifiable evidence regarding assertions, actions, and events to ascertain the degree of correspondence between them and established performance criteria.

compliance procedure An *audit* procedure used to gain evidence as to whether the prescribed internal controls are operating effectively.

composite cost of capital See *cost of capital*.

composite depreciation or composite life method *Group depreciation* when the items are of unlike kind. The term also applies when the *firm* depreciates as a whole a single item (for example, a crane, which consists of separate units with differing service lives, such as the chassis, the motor, the lifting mechanism, and so on), rather than treating each of its components separately.

compound entry A *journal entry* with more than one *debit* or more than one *credit* or both. See *trade-in transaction* for an example.

compound interest *Interest* calculated on *principal* plus previously undistributed interest.

compound interest depreciation A method designed to hold the *rate of return* on an *asset* constant. First find the *internal rate of return* on the *cash* inflows and outflows of the asset. The periodic *depreciation charge* equals the *cash flow* for the *period* less the internal rate of return multiplied by the asset's *carrying value* at the beginning of the period. When the cash flows from the asset are constant over time, usage sometimes refers to the method as the *"annuity method"* of *depreciation*.

compounding period The time period, usually a year or a portion of a year, for which a *firm* calculates *interest*. At the end of the *period*, the *borrower* may pay interest to the *lender* or may add the interest (that is, convert it) to the *principal* for the next interest-earning period.

comprehensive budget *Master budget*.

comprehensive income Defined in *SFAC No. 3* as "the change in *equity* (*net assets*) of an *entity* during a *period* from *transactions* and other events and circumstances from nonowner sources. It includes all changes in equity during a period except those resulting from *investments* by owners and distributions to owners." In this definition, "equity" means *owners' equity* or *shareholders' equity*. *SFAS No. 130* **(Codification Topic 220)** requires *firms* to report comprehensive income as part of a *statement* showing *earnings* (primarily from realized transactions), *other comprehensive income* (with additions for all other changes in owners' equity, primarily *holding gains and losses* and *foreign exchange gains and losses*), and comprehensive income plus *accounting adjustments*. The *FASB* encourages the discontinuation of the term *"net income."* The terms "earnings" and "comprehensive income" denote different concepts, with totals different from that of the old "net income." *SFAS No. 130* **(Codification Topic 220)** requires that the firm report comprehensive income in a format having the same prominence as other *financial statements*. We cannot predict which "income total"—earnings or comprehensive income—users of financial statements will focus on.

comptroller Same meaning and pronunciation as *controller*. Modern users, however, tend to use this form for government and *not-for-profit entities* and *controller* for profit-seeking ones.

computer-based accounting systems Most modern record keeping systems operate on computers, not on paper and in books such as physical *ledgers* and *journals*. A data base contains *journal entries*. The data entry discipline requires equal *debits* and *credits*—the system won't let you continue without them. (The data entry discipline will not correct conceptual errors in journal entries, such as *debiting* an *asset account* rather than an *expense* account.) Computer programs—instructions—query this data base and perform arithmetic operations to construct whatever the user requests: a *general journal* or a *general ledger* or a *special-purpose ledger* or a *budget report* comparing *actual* and budgeted expenses for a department or a single *financial statement* or a set of financial statements or *schedule*. A manual record keeping process records transactions in journal entries, *posts* journal entry amounts into *accounts* in a ledger, totals the amounts in accounts to derive account *balances*, and uses the account balances to construct financial statements and other schedules. Even though a computer-based accounting system does not formally undertake these steps, one needs to understand the steps of manual record keeping in order to program the computer in the first place and to understand common business terminology. Students have difficulty understanding the differences between

- temporary and permanent accounts,
- transaction and adjusting entries, and
- pre- and post-closing balances in the Retained Earnings account

even when studying manual record keeping systems. Mastering these distinctions with a computer-based system is more difficult. We recommend you master the record keeping cycle, as presented in this book in **Chapter 2**, before thinking about how computer-based systems work.

conceptual framework A coherent system of interrelated objectives and fundamentals, promulgated by the FASB primarily through its SFAC publications, intended to lead to consistent standards for financial accounting and reporting. The IASB has a similar conceptual framework.

confidence level The measure of probability that the actual characteristics of the population lie within the stated precision of the estimate derived from a sampling process. A sample estimate may be expressed in the following terms: "Based on the sample, we are 95% sure [confidence level] that the true population value is within the range of X to Y [precision]." See *precision*.

confirmation A formal memorandum delivered by the customers or suppliers of a company to its independent *auditor* verifying the amounts shown as *receivable* or *payable*. The auditor originally sends the confirmation document to the customer. If the auditor asks that the customer return the document whether the *balance* is correct or incorrect, usage calls it a "positive confirmation." If the auditor asks that the customer return the document only if it contains an error, usage calls it a "negative confirmation."

conglomerate See *holding company*. This term implies that the owned companies operate in dissimilar lines of *business*. In a conglomerate, the top company often is, itself, an operation company.

conservatism A *reporting* objective that calls for anticipation of all *losses* and *expenses* but defers recognition of *gains* or profits until they are *realized* in *arm's-length transactions*. In the absence of certainty, report events to minimize cumulative *income*. Conservatism does not mean reporting low income in every *accounting period*. Over long-enough time spans, income is cash-in less cash-out. If a (conservative) reporting method shows low income in early periods, it must show higher income in some later period.

consignee See *on consignment*.

consignment See *on consignment*.

consignor See *on consignment*.

consistency Treatment of like *transactions* in the same way in consecutive *periods* so that *financial statements* will be more *comparable* than otherwise; the reporting policy implying that a reporting *entity*, once it adopts specified procedures, should follow them from period to period. See *accounting changes* for the treatment of inconsistencies.

consol A *bond* that never matures; a *perpetuity* in the form of a bond; originally issued by Great Britain after the Napoleonic wars to consolidate *debt* issues of that period. The term arose as an abbreviation for "consolidated *annuities*."

consolidated entity See *consolidated financial statements*.

consolidated (financial) statements; consolidated balance sheet; consolidated income statement; consolidated statement of cash flows Statements issued by legally separate companies under the control of a *parent company* and that show financial statements as they would appear if the companies were one economic *entity*, called the "consolidated entity."

consolidation policy A company's statement of which *entities* it includes in a particular set of *consolidated financial statements*. Sometimes *firms* have a choice as to which to consolidate, but most often in *U.S. GAAP*, the firm has little choice.

consolidation work sheet The paper or software representation thereof, which shows the *firms* being consolidated along with various additions and subtractions to eliminate double counting and inter-company *transactions*.

constant dollar A hypothetical unit of *general purchasing power*, denoted "C\$" by the *FASB*.

constant-dollar accounting Accounting that measures items in *constant dollars*. See *historical cost/constant-dollar accounting* and *current cost/nominal-dollar accounting*. Sometimes called "general price level–adjusted accounting" or "general purchasing-power accounting."

constant-dollar date The time at which the *general purchasing power* of one *constant dollar* exactly equals the general purchasing power of one *nominal dollar*; that is, the date when C\$1 = \$1. When the constant-dollar date is midperiod, the nominal amounts of *revenues* and *expenses* spread evenly throughout the *period* equal their constant-dollar amounts but end-of-period *balance sheet* amounts measured in constant midperiod dollars differ from their nominal-dollar amounts. When the constant-dollar date is at the end of the period, the constant-dollar amounts equal the nominal-dollar amounts on a balance sheet for that date.

constrained share company Canada: a public company whose *charter* specifies that people who are Canadian citizens or who are *corporations* resident in Canada must own a prescribed percentage of the shares.

constructive capitalization Some long-term noncancellable *leases* are *operating leases*. Consider, for example, a ten-year lease on a shopping center store site. An analyst might want to see the effect on the *lessee's financial statements* of treating the *present value* of the contractual commitments as *balance sheet* items, an *asset* for the *leasehold* and a *liability* for the obligations to pay. This term refers to the process of *debiting* the *present value* of the lease commitments to an asset and *crediting* the amount to a *liability*, for analysis.

constructive liability *FASB*'s term for an item recorded as an *accounting liability*, which the firm has no obligation to pay but intends to pay. An example is the liability with related *expense* that *management* establishes for future *cash* payments for severance payments for employees it intends to discharge in a *restructuring*.

constructive receipt An item included in *taxable income* when the taxpayer can control *funds* whether or not it has received cash. For example, *interest* added to *principal* in a savings *account* is constructively received.

Consumer Price Index (CPI) A *price index* computed and issued monthly by the Bureau of Labor Statistics of the U.S. Department of Labor. The index attempts to track the price level of a group of *goods* and *services* purchased by the average consumer. The CPI is used in *constant-dollar accounting*.

contingency A potential *liability*. If a specified event occurs, such as a *firm*'s losing a lawsuit, it would *recognize* a liability. The *notes* disclose the contingency, but so long as it remains contingent, it does not appear in the *balance sheet*. *SFAS No. 5* (**Codification Topic 450**) requires treatment as a contingency until the outcome is "probable" (interpreted to mean 75% to 80% likely to occur) and the amount of payment can be reasonably estimated, perhaps within a range. When the outcome becomes probable (the future event is "likely" to occur) and the firm can reasonably estimate the amount (using the lower end of a range if it can estimate only a range), then the firm recognizes a liability in the accounts, rather than just disclosing it. A *material* contingency may lead to a qualified, "*subject to*" *auditor's opinion*. Firms do not record *gain* contingencies in the *accounts* but merely disclose them in notes.

contingent annuity An *annuity* whose number of payments depends on the outcome of an event whose timing is uncertain at the time the annuity begins; for example, an annuity payable until death of the *annuitant*. Contrast with *annuity certain*.

contingent asset An item that meets some, but not all, the tests to be an *asset* and, hence, is not an asset, but might become one, such as the potential *proceeds* from winning a lawsuit or other lottery.

contingent issue (securities) *Securities* issuable to specific individuals at the occurrence of some event, such as the *firm*'s attaining a specified level of earnings.

contingent liability; contingent obligation; contingent provision *Contingency*. Avoid the term "contingent liability" because it refers to something not (yet) a *liability* on the *balance sheet*. The *IASB* has said it will formally express disapproval of the term "contingent liability." See *provision*.

continuing appropriation A governmental *appropriation* automatically renewed without further legislative action until altered or revoked or expended.

continuing operations See *income from continuing operations*.

continuity of operations The assumption in *accounting* that the *business entity* will continue to operate long enough to carry out its current plans. The *going-concern assumption*.

continuous budget A *budget* that adds a future *period* as the current period ends. This budget, then, always reports on the same number of periods.

continuous compounding *Compound interest* in which the *compounding period* is every instant of time. See *e* for the computation of the equivalent annual or periodic rate.

continuous flow processing Mass production of homogeneous *products* in a continuous flow, such as chemicals or petroleum products. Companies manufacturing with continuous flow processes use *process costing* to account for product costs.

continuous improvement Modern *total quality management* (*TQM*) practitioners believe that the process of seeking quality is never complete. This attitude reflects that assumption, seeking always to improve activities.

continuous inventory method The *perpetual inventory method*.

Continuously Contemporary Accounting (CoCoA) A name coined by the Australian theorist Raymond J. Chambers to indicate a combination of *current value accounting* in which the *measuring unit* is *constant dollars* and the *attribute measured* is *exit value*.

contra account An *account*, such as *accumulated depreciation*, that accumulates subtractions from another account, such as machinery. Contrast with *adjunct account*.

contributed capital Name for the *owners' equity account* that represents amounts paid in, usually in *cash*, by owners; the sum of the *balances* in *capital stock* accounts plus *capital contributed in excess of par* (or *stated*) *value* accounts. Contrast with *donated capital*.

contributed surplus An inferior term for *capital contributed in excess of par value*.

contribution approach *Income statement* preparation method that reports *contribution margin*, by separating *variable costs* from *fixed costs*, in order to emphasize the importance of cost-behavior patterns for purposes of planning and control.

contribution margin *Revenue* from *sales* less all variable *expenses*. Contrast with *gross margin*.

contribution margin ratio *Contribution margin* divided by *net sales*; usually measured from the *price* and *cost* of a single unit; sometimes measured in total for companies with multiple *products*.

contribution per unit *Selling price* less *variable costs* per unit.

contributory Said of a *pension plan* in which employees, as well as employers, make payments to a pension *fund*. Note that the provisions for *vesting* apply only to the employer's payments. Whatever the degree of vesting of the employer's payments, employees typically gets back all their payments, with *interest*, in case of death or other cessation of employment before retirement.

control (controlling) account A summary *account* with totals equal to those of entries and *balances* that appear in individual accounts in a *subsidiary ledger*. Accounts Receivable is a control account backed up with an account for each customer. Do not change the balance in a control account unless you make a corresponding change in one of the subsidiary accounts. A control account in a computerized accounting system is programmed to be the sum of individual accounts that comprise the subsidiary ledger for that control account.

control charts Presentations of warning signals that help *management* distinguish between random or routine variations in quality and variations that it should investigate. The presentations show the results of statistical process-control measures for a sample, batch, or some other unit. These presentations depict variation in a process and its behavior over time. Management specifies an acceptable level of variation and plans to investigate the causes of deviations beyond that level.

control system A device used by top *management* to ensure that lower-level management carries out its plans or to safeguard *assets*. Control designed for a single function within the *firm* is "operational control"; control designed for autonomous segments that generally have responsibility for both *revenues* and *costs* is "*divisional control*"; control designed for activities of the firm as a whole is "*company-wide control*." "Internal control" systems include those designed for safeguarding assets and to ensure that *financial statements* and their components are correct.

controllable cost A *cost* influenced by the way a *firm* carries out operations. For example, marketing executives control advertising costs. These costs can be *fixed* or *variable*. See *programmed costs* and managed costs.

controlled company A company in which an individual or *corporation* holds a majority of the voting *shares*. An owner can sometimes exercise effective control even though it owns less than 50% of the shares.

controller A title for the chief *accountant* of an organization; often spelled *comptroller* when used to identify that person in a government or not-for-profit *entity*.

convergence (process) The intention of the *FASB* and *IASB* to eliminate differences between *U.S. GAAP* and *IFRS*.

conversion The act of exchanging a convertible *security* for another security.

conversion audit An examination of changeover procedures, and new *accounting procedures* and files, that takes place when a significant change in the *accounting system* (e.g., a change from a manual to a computerized system or a change of computers or computer systems) occurs.

conversion cost *Direct labor costs* plus *factory overhead* costs *incurred* in producing a *product*; that is, the cost to convert raw materials to finished products. *Manufacturing cost*.

conversion period *Compounding period*; also, period during which the holder of a *convertible bond* or *convertible preferred stock* can convert it into *common shares*.

convertible bond A *bond* whose owner may convert it into a specified number of *shares* of *capital stock* during the *conversion period*.

convertible preferred shares (stock) *Preferred shares* whose owner may convert them into a specified number of *common shares*.

cookie-jar accounting A name, most prominently used by a chairman of the *SEC*, to indicate the practice of reporting lower *income* in an early *period*, so that *management* at its discretion can report higher income in a later period. Consider, for example, the entry to estimate normal *warranty costs* for *products* sold. The *journal entry debits* an *expense account*, reducing income, and *credits* a *liability* account. In some later period, the *firm* can debit a warranty cost to the liability account, not to an expense account, relieving that later period of the income reduction that an expense would have caused. "Cookie-jar accounting" occurs when the amount debited is larger than necessary, resulting in lower-than-correct income in the current period. In a later period, income can be higher as the debit for warranty costs can be to the liability account, rather than to expense, which would reduce income in that period. See *quality of earnings*. Often, users refer to the excess liability amount, the amount in the cookie jar, later available for income enhancement, as a "reserve." See *reserve* for our warnings about using that word in any context.

cooperative An incorporated organization formed for the benefit of its members (owners), who are either producers or consumers, in order to acquire for them *profits* or savings that otherwise *accrue* to middlemen. Members exercise control on the basis of one vote per member.

coproduct A *product* sharing production facilities with another product. For example, if an apparel manufacturer produces shirts and jeans on the same line, these are coproducts. Distinguish coproducts from *joint products* and *by-products* that, by their very nature, a *firm* must produce together, such as the various grades of wood a lumber factory produces.

copyright Exclusive right granted by the government to an individual author, composer, playwright, or the like for the life of the individual plus 70 years. *Corporations* and anonymous authors get copyrights for varying *periods* set out in the law. The *economic life* of a copyright can be less than the legal life, such as, for example, the copyright of this book.

core deposit intangible A bank borrows *funds* from its customers, called "depositors," who open checking and savings *accounts*. Those depositors can take out their funds at any time, but usually don't. The amount that depositors leave on deposit for long periods of time are called "core deposits." The bank lends those funds to other customers, called "*borrowers*," at *interest rates* larger than the amount it pays the depositors for the funds. (For checking accounts, the rate the bank pays depositors is often zero.) The fact that the depositors can remove their funds at any time, but, on average, leave amounts on deposit relatively permanently means that the bank can lend those funds for relatively long periods of time, usually at higher interest rates, than it can charge for shorter-term *loans*. (See *yield curve*.) The bank's ability to borrow from some customers at a low rate and lend to other customers at a high rate creates wealth for the bank. Bankers and banking analysts call this wealth the "core deposit intangible." It represents an *asset* not *recognized* in the *financial statements* by the bank that created the wealth, although some *SEC* commissioners have expressed the thought that *accounting* should recognize such items as assets. When one bank buys another in a *purchase*, however, it will pay for this asset and will record it as an asset. Usually, the acquiring bank does not use the specific account title "Core Deposit Intangible," but instead uses the account title *Goodwill*.

corner The control of a quantity of *shares*, or a commodity, sufficiently large that the holder can control the *market price*.

corporate bylaws The set of rules and procedures for the *operations* of the *corporation* enacted by its founders or *board of directors*.

corporate charter The document provided by a state, such as Delaware, to a corporate to operate as a *corporation*.

corporation A *legal entity* authorized by a state to operate under the rules of the entity's *charter*.

correcting entry An *adjusting entry* that results in the proper entry for a previously, improperly recorded *transaction*. If one were to reverse the original, incorrect, entry, then record the correct entry, and then reduce the two previous entries to a single one, perhaps with multiple debit and credit parts, one has the correcting entry. Do not confuse with entries that correct *accounting errors*.

correction of errors See *accounting errors*.

cost The sacrifice, measured by the *price* paid or to be paid, to acquire *goods* or *services*. See *acquisition cost* and *replacement cost*. Terminology often uses "cost" when referring to the valuation of a good or service acquired. When writers use the word in this sense, a cost is an *asset*. When the benefits of the acquisition (the goods or services acquired) expire, the cost becomes an *expense* or *loss*. Some writers, however, use "cost" and "expense" as synonyms. Contrast with expense. The word "cost" appears in more than 50 *accounting* terms, each with sometimes subtle distinctions in meaning. See *cost terminology* for elaboration. Clarity requires that the user include with the word "cost" an adjective or phrase to be clear about intended meaning.

cost accounting Classifying, summarizing, recording, reporting, and *allocating* current or predicted *costs*; a subset of *managerial accounting*.

Cost Accounting Standards Board See *CASB*.

cost accumulation Bringing together, usually in a single *account*, all *costs* of a specified activity. Contrast with *cost allocation*.

cost allocation Assigning *costs* to individual *products*, organizational units, or time periods. Contrast with *cost accumulation*.

cost basis *Cost* in contrast to *fair value* or other measurement.

cost-based transfer price A *transfer price* based on *historical costs*.

cost behavior The functional relation between changes in activity and changes in *cost*; for example: *fixed* versus *variable costs*; linear versus *curvilinear cost*.

cost/benefit criterion Some measure of *costs* compared with some measure of benefits for a proposed undertaking. If the costs exceed the benefits, then the analyst judges the undertaking not worthwhile. This criterion will not yield good decisions unless the analyst estimates all costs and benefits flowing from the undertaking.

cost center A unit of activity for which a *firm* accumulates *expenditures* and *expenses*.

cost driver A factor that causes an activity's costs. See *driver* and *activity basis*.

cost driver rate Rate at which the *cost driver* causes *costs*.

cost-effective Among alternatives, the one whose benefit, or payoff, per unit of *cost* is highest; sometimes said of an action whose expected benefits exceed expected costs whether or not other alternatives exist with larger benefit-cost *ratios*.

cost estimation The process of measuring the functional relation between changes in activity levels and changes in *cost*.

cost flow assumption See *flow assumption*.

cost-flow equation Beginning *Balance* + *Transfers* In = Transfers Out + Ending Balance; BB + TI = TO + EB. Equivalent to: BB + TI − TO = EB.

cost flows *Costs* passing through various classifications within an *entity*. See *flow of costs* for a diagram.

cost hierarchy Categorizes *costs* according to whether they are *capacity*, *product*, *customer*, batch, or unit costs.

cost method (for investments) In accounting for an *investment* in the *capital stock* or *bonds* of another company, method in which the *firm* shows the investment at *acquisition cost* and treats only *dividends* declared or *interest receivable* as *revenue*; not allowed by *U.S. GAAP*.

cost method (for treasury stock) The method of showing *treasury stock* in a *contra account* to all other items of *shareholders' equity* in an amount equal to that paid to reacquire the stock.

cost object(ive) Any activity for which *management* desires a separate measurement of *costs*. Examples include departments, *products*, and territories.

cost of capital *Opportunity cost* of *funds* invested in a *business*; the rate of return that rational owners require an asset to earn before they will devote that *asset* to a particular purpose; sometimes measured as the *average* annual rate that a company must pay for its *equities*. In *efficient capital markets*, this *cost* is the *discount rate* that equates the expected *present value* of all future *cash flows* to common shareholders with the market value of common stock at a given time. Analysts often measure the cost of capital by taking a *weighted average* of the *firm's debt* and various *equity securities*. We sometimes call the measurement so derived the "*composite cost of capital*," and some analysts confuse this measurement of the cost of capital with the cost of capital itself. For example, if the equities of a firm include substantial amounts for the *deferred income tax liability*, the composite cost of capital will underestimate the true cost of capital, the required rate of return on a firm's assets, because the deferred income tax liability has no explicit cost.

cost of goods manufactured The sum of all *costs allocated* to *products* completed during a *period*, including *materials*, labor, and *overhead*.

cost of goods purchased *Net* purchase *price* of *goods* acquired plus *costs* of storage and delivery to the place where the owner can productively use the items.

cost of goods sold Inventoriable *costs* that *firms expense* because they sold the units; equals *beginning inventory* plus *cost of goods purchased* or *manufactured* minus *ending inventory*.

cost of goods sold percentage See *ratio* and **Exhibit 6.14**.

cost of sales Generally refers to *cost of goods sold*, occasionally to *selling expenses*.

cost of services rendered *Costs* the *firm incurs* to provide *services*, in contrast to selling *goods*, to its customers.

cost or market, whichever is lower See *lower of cost or market*.

cost percentage One minus the *markup percentage*; *cost* of *goods available for sale* divided by selling *prices* of goods available for sale (when *FIFO* is used); cost of *purchases* divided by selling prices of purchases (when *LIFO* is used). See *markup* for further detail on inclusions in the calculation of cost percentage.

cost-plus transfer pricing *Transfer price* equal to the *cost* of the *product* transferred to another company in an affiliated group, plus a *markup*.

cost pool *Indirect cost pool*; groupings or aggregations of costs, usually for subsequent analysis or *allocation*.

cost principle The *principle* that requires reporting *assets* at *historical* or *acquisition cost*, less accumulated *amortization*. This principle relies on the assumption that *cost* equals *fair value* at the date of acquisition and that subsequent changes are not likely to be significant.

cost recovery method; cost-recovery-first method A method of *revenue* recognition that *credits inventory* as the *firm* receives *cash* collections and continues until the firm has collected cash equal to the sum of all costs. Only after the firm has collected cash equal to costs does it recognize *income*. A firm may not use this method in financial reporting unless the total amount of collections is highly uncertain. It is never allowed for income tax reporting. Contrast with the *installment method*, allowed for both *book* and *tax*, in which the firm credits constant proportions of each cash collection both to cost and to income.

cost sheet Statement that shows all the elements composing the total *cost* of an item.

cost structure For a given set of total *costs*, the percentages of *fixed* and *variable* costs, typically two percentages that add to 100%.

cost terminology The word "*cost*" appears in many accounting terms. The accompanying exhibit classifies some of these

Cost Terminology Distinctions Among Terms Containing the Word "Cost"

Terms (Synonyms Given in Parentheses)			Distinctions and Comments
			1. The following pairs of terms distinguish the basis measured in accounting.
Historical Cost (Acquisition Cost)	v.	Current Cost	A distinction used in financial accounting. Current cost can be used more specifically to mean replacement cost, net realizable value, or present value of cash flows. "Current cost" is often used narrowly to mean replacement cost.
Historical Cost (Actual Cost)	v.	Standard Cost	The distinction between historical and standard costs arises in product costing for inventory valuation. Some systems record actual costs; others record the standard costs.
			2. The following pairs of terms denote various distinctions among historical costs. For each pair of terms, the sum of the two kinds of costs equals total historical cost used in financial reporting.
Variable Cost	v.	Fixed Cost (Constant Cost)	Distinction used in breakeven analysis and in the design of cost accounting systems, particularly for product costing. See (4), below, for a further subdivision of fixed costs and (5), below, for the economic distinction between marginal and average cost closely paralleling this one.
Traceable Cost	v.	Common Cost (Joint Cost)	Distinction arises in allocating manufacturing costs to product. Common costs are allocated to product, but the allocations are more or less arbitrary. The distinction also arises in preparing segment reports and in separating manufacturing from nonmanufacturing costs.
Direct Cost	v.	Indirect Cost	Distinction arises in designing cost accounting systems and in product costing. Direct costs can be traced directly to a cost object (e.g., a product, a responsibility center), whereas indirect costs cannot.
Out-of-Pocket Cost (Outlay Cost; Cash Cost)	v.	Book Cost	Virtually all costs recorded in financial statements require a cash outlay at one time or another. The distinction here separates expenditures to occur in the future from those already made and is used in making decisions. Book costs, such as for depreciation, reduce income without requiring a future outlay of cash. The cash has already been spent. See future cost v. past cost in (5), below.
Incremental Cost (Marginal Cost; Differential Cost)	v.	Unavoidable Cost (Inescapable Cost; Sunk Cost)	Distinction used in making decisions. Incremental costs will be incurred (or saved) if a decision is made to go ahead (or to stop) some activity, but not otherwise. Unavoidable costs will be reported in financial statements whether the decision is made to go ahead or not, because cash has already been spent or committed. Not all unavoidable costs are book costs, such as, for example, a salary that is promised but not yet earned and that will be paid even if a no-go decision is made.
			The economist restricts the term marginal cost to the cost of producing one more unit. Thus the next unit has a marginal cost; the next week's output has an incremental cost. If a firm produces and sells a new product, the related new costs would properly be called incremental, not marginal. If a factory is closed, the costs saved are incremental, not marginal.
Escapable Cost	v.	Inescapable Cost (Unavoidable Cost)	Same distinction as incremental cost v. unavoidable cost, but this pair is used only when the decision maker is considering stopping something—ceasing to produce a product, closing a factory, or the like. See next pair.
Avoidable Cost	v.	Unavoidable Cost	A distinction sometimes used in discussing the merits of variable and absorption costing. Avoidable costs are treated as product costs and unavoidable costs are treated as period expenses under variable costing.
Controllable Cost	v.	Uncontrollable Cost	The distinction here is used in assigning responsibility and in setting bonus or incentive plans. All costs can be affected by someone in the entity; those who design incentive schemes attempt to hold a person responsible for a cost only if that person can influence the amount of the cost.
			3. In each of the following pairs, used in historical cost accounting, the word "cost" appears in one of the terms where "expense" is meant.
Expired Cost	v.	Unexpired Cost	The distinction is between expense and asset.
Product Cost	v.	Period Cost	The terms distinguish product cost from period expense. When a given asset is used, is its cost converted into work-in-process and then finished goods on the balance sheet until the goods are sold, or

(continued on next page)

Terms (Synonyms Given in Parentheses)			Distinctions and Comments

is it an expense shown on this period's income statement? Product costs appear on the income statement as part of cost of goods sold in the period when the goods are sold. Period expenses appear on the income statement with an appropriate caption for the item in the period when the cost is incurred or recognized.

4. The following subdivisions of fixed (historical) costs are used in analyzing operations. The relation between the components of fixed costs is as follows:

$$\underbrace{\text{Semifixed Costs} + \text{``Pure'' Fixed Costs}}_{\text{Fixed Costs}} + \underbrace{\text{Fixed Portions of Semi-variable Costs}}{} = \underbrace{\text{Standby Costs}}_{\text{Capacity Costs}} + \underbrace{\text{Enabling Costs}}_{\text{Programmed Costs}}$$

Capacity Cost (Committed Cost)	v.	Programmed Cost (Managed Cost; Discretionary Cost)	Capacity costs give a firm the capability to produce or to sell. Programmed costs, such as for advertising or research and development, may not be essential, but once a decision to incur them is made, they become fixed costs.
Standby Cost	v.	Enabling Cost	Standby costs will be incurred whether capacity, once acquired, is used or not, such as property taxes and depreciation on a factory. Enabling costs, such as for a security force, can be avoided if the capacity is unused.
Semifixed Cost	v.	Semivariable Cost	A cost that is fixed over a wide range but that can change at various levels is a semifixed cost or "step cost." An example is the cost of rail lines from the factory to the main rail line, where fixed cost depends on whether there are one or two parallel lines but is independent of the number of trains run per day. Semivariable costs combine a strictly fixed component cost plus a variable component. Telephone charges usually have a fixed monthly component plus a charge related to usage.

5. The following pairs of terms distinguish among economic uses or decision-making uses or regulatory uses of cost terms.

Fully Absorbed Cost	v.	Variable Cost (Direct Cost)	Fully absorbed costs refer to costs where fixed costs have been allocated to units or departments as required by generally accepted accounting principles. Variable costs, in contrast, may be more relevant for making decisions, such as setting prices.
Fully Absorbed Cost	v.	Full Cost	In full costing, all costs, manufacturing costs as well as central corporate expenses (including financing expenses), are allocated to products or divisions. In full absorption costing, only manufacturing costs are allocated to products. Only in full costing will revenues, expenses, and income summed over all products or divisions equal corporate revenues, expenses, and income.
Opportunity Cost	v.	Outlay Cost (Out-of-Pocket Cost)	Opportunity cost refers to the economic benefit forgone by using a resource for one purpose instead of for another. The outlay cost of the resource will be recorded in financial records. The distinction arises because a resource is already in the possession of the entity with a recorded historical cost. Its economic value to the firm, opportunity cost, generally differs from the historical cost; it can be either larger or smaller.
Future Cost	v.	Past Cost	Effective decision making analyzes only present and future outlay costs, or out-of-pocket costs. Opportunity costs are relevant for profit maximizing; past costs are used in financial reporting.
Short-Run Cost	v.	Long-Run Cost	Short-run costs vary as output is varied for a given configuration of plant and equipment. Long-run costs can be incurred to change that configuration. This pair of terms is the economic analog of the accounting pair, see (2) above, variable and fixed costs. The analogy is not perfect because some short-run costs are fixed, such as property taxes on the factory, from the point of view of breakeven analysis.
Imputed Cost	v.	Book Cost	In a regulatory setting some costs, for example the cost of owners' equity capital, are calculated and used for various purposes; these are

(continued on next page)

Terms (Synonyms Given in Parentheses)			Distinctions and Comments
			imputed costs. Imputed costs are not recorded in the historical costs accounting records for financial reporting. Book costs are recorded.
Average Cost	v.	Marginal Cost	The economic distinction equivalent to fully absorbed cost of product and variable cost of product. Average cost is total cost divided by number of units. Marginal cost is the cost to produce the next unit (or the last unit).
Differential Cost (Incremental Cost)	v.	Variable Cost	Whether a cost changes or remains fixed depends on the activity basis being considered. Typically, but not invariably, costs are said to be variable or with respect to an activity basis such as changes in production levels. Typically, but not invariably, costs are said to be incremental or not with respect to an activity basis such as the undertaking of some new venture. For example, consider the decision to undertake the production of food processors, rather than food blenders, which the manufacturer has been making. To produce processors requires the acquisition of a new machine tool. The cost of the new machine tool is incremental with respect to a decision to produce food processors instead of food blenders but, once acquired, becomes a fixed cost of producing food processors. If costs of direct labor hours are going to be incurred for the production of food processors or food blenders, whichever is produced (in a scenario when not both are to be produced), such costs are variable with respect to production measured in units but are not incremental with respect to the decision to produce processors rather than blenders. This distinction is often blurred in practice, so a careful understanding of the activity basis being considered is necessary to understand the concepts being used in a particular application.

terms according to the distinctions between the terms in *accounting* usage. Joel Dean was, to our knowledge, the first to attempt such distinctions; we have used some of his ideas here. We discuss some of the terms in more detail under their own listings.

cost-to-cost The *percentage-of-completion method* in which the *firm* estimates the fraction of completion as the *ratio* of *costs incurred* to date divided by the total costs the firm expects to incur for the entire project.

cost-volume-profit analysis A study of the sensitivity of *profits* to changes in units sold (or produced) or *costs* or *prices*, often done with a *cost-volume-profit graph*.

cost-volume-profit graph (chart) A graph that shows the relation between *fixed costs*, *contribution per unit*, *breakeven point*, and *sales*. See *breakeven chart*.

costing The process of calculating the *cost* of activities, *products*, or *services*; the British word for *cost accounting*.

counterparty The term refers to the opposite party in a legal contract. In *accounting* and finance, a frequent usage arises when an *entity* purchases (or sells) a *derivative* financial contract, such as an *option*, *swap*, *forward contract*, and *futures contract*.

coupon That portion of a *bond* document redeemable at a specified date for payments. Its physical form resembles a series of tickets; each coupon has a date, and the holder either deposits it at a bank, just like a check, for collection or mails it to the issuer's *agent* for collection. Coupons have been made illegal in the United States since 1982 because of the possibility of tax fraud.

coupon bond A *bond* that promises periodic payments. See *coupon*.

coupon (interest) rate Of a *bond*, the total dollar amount of *coupons* paid in any one year divided by par value. Contrast with *effective rate*. Better not to use the word "*interest*" in this term. See *interest payment* for discussion of why.

covenant A promise with legal validity. A loan covenant specifies the terms under which the *lender* can force the *borrower* to repay *funds* otherwise not yet due. For example, a *bond* covenant might say that the *principal* of a bond issue falls due on December 31, 2010, unless the firm's *debt-equity ratio* falls below 40%, in which case the amount becomes due immediately.

CPA See *certified public accountant*. The *AICPA* suggests that no periods appear in the abbreviation.

CPI *Consumer price index*.

CPP Current purchasing power; usually used, primarily in the UK, as an adjective modifying the word "*accounting*" to mean the accounting that produces *constant-dollar financial statements*.

Cr. Abbreviation for *credit*, always with initial capital letter. Quiz: what do you suppose Cr. stands for? For the answer, see *Dr*.

creative accounting Selection of *accounting principles* and interpretation of *transactions* or events designed to manipulate, typically to increase but sometimes merely to smooth, reported *income from continuing operations*; one form of *fraudulent financial reporting*. Many attempts at creative accounting involve premature *revenue recognition*.

credit As a noun, an entry on the right-hand side of an *account*; as a verb, to make an entry on the right-hand side of an account; records increases in *liabilities*, *owners' equity*, *revenues*, and *gains*; records decreases in *assets* and *expenses*. See *debit and credit conventions*. This term also refers to the ability or right to buy or borrow in return for a promise to pay later.

credit bureau An organization that gathers and evaluates data on the ability of a person to meet financial obligations and sells this information to its clients.

credit loss The amount of *accounts receivable* that the *firm* finds, or expects to find, *uncollectible*.

credit memorandum A document used by a seller to inform a buyer that the seller is crediting (reducing) the buyer's *account receivable* because of errors, *returns*, or *allowances*; also, the document provided by a bank to a depositor to indicate that the bank is increasing the depositor's *balance* because of some event other than a deposit, such as the collection by the bank of the depositor's *note receivable*.

creditor One who lends. In the UK, *account payable*.

critical accounting judgments All numbers on a *balance sheet*, except the date, require some judgment or estimate. (The previous sentence passes for a joke in *accounting*.) The SEC requires that *management* in its *annual report* to *shareholders* identify the accounting issues whose judgments and estimates have potential for significant effect on *earnings* and *financial position*. Examples include *inventory* valuation, measurement of *goodwill impairment*, accounting for *hedges*, and *revenue recognition*.

critical path method (CPM) A method of *network analysis* in which the analyst estimates normal duration time for each activity within a project. The critical path identifies the shortest completion period possible based on the most time-consuming sequence of activities from the beginning to the end of the network. Compare *PERT*.

critical success factors The important things a company must do to be successful; may vary from one company to another.

cross-reference (index) A number placed beside each *account* in a *journal entry* indicating the *ledger* account to which the record keeper posted the entry and placing in the ledger the page number of the *journal*, or the journal entry number, where the record keeper first recorded the journal entry; used to link the *debit* and *credit* parts of an entry in the ledger accounts back to the original entry in the journal. Nearly every *firm* now uses a computerized accounting system which provides cross-references. See *audit trail*.

cross-section analysis Analysis of *financial statements* of various *firms* for a single period of time; contrast with *time-series analysis*, in which analysts examine statements of a given firm for several periods of time.

Crown corporation Canada and UK: a *corporation* that is ultimately accountable, through a minister of the Crown, to Parliament or a legislature for the conduct of its affairs.

cum div. (dividend) The condition of *shares* whose quoted *market price* includes a declared but unpaid *dividend*. This condition pertains between the declaration date of the dividend and the record date. Compare *ex div. (dividend)*.

cum rights The condition of *securities* whose quoted *market price* includes the right to purchase new securities. Compare *ex rights*.

cumulative dividend (rights) Preferred *stock dividends* that, if not paid, *accrue* as a commitment that the *firm* must pay before it can declare dividends to common shareholders.

cumulative preferred shares *Preferred shares* with *cumulative dividend rights*.

current An adjective referring to something that will require cash inflow or outflow within the company's *operating cycle*, usually one year.

current amount A valuation or *basis* using *fair values* or *market values* as of the *balance sheet* date, in contrast an *historical cost*.

current assets *Cash* and other *assets* that a *firm* expects to turn into cash, sell, or exchange within the normal *operating cycle* of the *firm* or one year, whichever is longer. One year is the usual period for classifying asset *balances* on the *balance sheet*. Current assets include cash, *marketable securities*, *receivables*, *inventory*, and *current prepayments*.

current cost *Cost* stated in terms of current values (of *productive capacity*) rather than in terms of *acquisition cost*. See *net realizable value* and *current selling price*.

current cost accounting The *FASB*'s term for *financial statements* in which the *attribute measured* is *current cost*.

current cost/nominal-dollar accounting *Accounting* based on *current cost* valuations measured in *nominal dollars*. Components of *income* include an *operating margin* and *holding gains and losses*.

current exchange rate The rate at which the holder of one unit of currency can convert it into another at the end of the *accounting period* being reported on or, for *revenues*, *expenses*, *gains*, and *losses*, the date of recognition of the transaction.

current exit value *Exit value*.

current fund In governmental *accounting*, a synonym for *general fund*.

current funds *Cash* and other *assets* readily convertible into cash; in governmental *accounting*, *funds* spent for *operating* purposes during the current *period*; includes *general*, special *revenue*, *debt service*, and *enterprise funds*.

current (gross) margin See *operating margin based on current costs*.

current liability A *debt* or other obligation that a *firm* must discharge within a short time, usually the *earnings cycle* or one year, normally by expending *current assets*.

current market interest rate At a given time, the rate the market charges a *borrower*. Pertinent for *fair value accounting* for *debt*.

current operating performance concept The notion that reported *income* for a *period* ought to reflect only ordinary, normal, and recurring *operations* of that period. A consequence is that *extraordinary* and *nonrecurring* items are entered directly in the *Retained Earnings* account. Contrast with *clean surplus concept*. This concept is no longer acceptable. (See *APB Opinion No. 9* and *No. 30*.)

current ratio Sum of *current assets* divided by sum of *current liabilities*. See *ratio* and **Exhibit 6.14**.

current realizable value *Realizable value*.

current replacement cost Of an *asset*, the amount currently required to acquire an identical asset (in the same condition and with the same service potential) or an asset capable of rendering the same service at a current *fair market price*. If these two amounts differ, use the lower. Contrast with *reproduction cost*.

current selling price The amount for which an *asset* could be sold as of a given time in an *arm's-length transaction* rather than in a forced sale.

current service costs *Service costs* of a *pension plan*.

current value accounting The form of *accounting* in which all *assets* appear at *current replacement cost* (*entry value*) or *current selling price* or *net realizable value* (*exit value*) and all *liabilities* appear at *present value*. Entry and exit values may differ from each other, so theorists have not agreed on the precise meaning of "current value accounting."

current yield Of a *bond*, the annual amount of *coupons* divided by the current *market price* of the bond. Contrast with *yield to maturity*.

currently attainable standard cost *Normal standard cost*.

curvilinear (variable) cost A continuous, but not necessarily linear (straight-line), functional relation between activity levels and *costs*.

customer-level activities Work performed to meet the needs of a specific customer, aggregated over all customers.

customer response time *Period* that elapses from the moment a customer places an order for a *product* or requests *service* to the moment the *firm* delivers the product or service to the customer.

customers' ledger The *ledger* that shows *accounts receivable* of individual customers. It is the *subsidiary ledger* for the *control account Accounts Receivable*.

cutoff rate *Hurdle rate*.

D

data bank An organized file of information, such as a customer name and address file, used in and kept up-to-date by a processing system.

database A comprehensive collection of interrelated information stored together in computerized form to serve several applications.

database management system Generalized *software* programs used to handle physical storage and manipulation of *databases*.

days of average inventory on hand See *ratio* and **Exhibit 6.14**.

days of grace The days allowed by law or contract for payment of a *debt* after its due date.

days receivables outstanding *Accounts receivable turnover ratio* divided into 365.

DCF *Discounted cash flow*.

DDB *Double declining-balance depreciation*.

debenture bond A *bond* not secured with *collateral*.

debit As a noun, an *entry* on the left-hand side of an *account*; as a verb, to make an entry on the left-hand side of an account; records increases in *assets* and *expenses*; records decreases in *liabilities*, *owners' equity*, and *revenues*. See *debit and credit conventions*.

debit and credit conventions The conventional use of the *T-account* form and the rules for *debit* and *credit* in *balance sheet accounts* (see below). The *equality* of the two sides of the *accounting equation* results from recording equal amounts of debits and credits for each *transaction*.

Typical Asset Account

Opening Balance	
Increase	Decrease
+	−
Dr.	Cr.
Ending Balance	

Typical Liability Account

	Opening Balance
Decrease	Increase
−	+
Dr.	Cr.
	Ending Balance

Typical Owners' Equity Account

	Opening Balance
Decrease	Increase
−	+
Dr.	Cr.
	Ending Balance

Revenue and *expense* accounts belong to the owners' equity group. The relation and the rules for debit and credit in these accounts take the following form:

Owners' Equity

Decrease	Increase
−	+
Dr.	Cr.

Expenses		Revenues	
Dr.	Cr.	Dr.	Cr.
+	−	−	+
*			*

*Normal balance before closing.

debit memorandum A document used by a seller to inform a buyer that the seller is *debiting* (increasing) the amount of the buyer's *accounts receivable*. Also, the document provided by a bank to a depositor to indicate that the bank is decreasing the depositor's *balance* because of some event other than payment for a *check*, such as monthly service *charges* or the printing of checks.

debt An amount owed. The general name for *notes*, *bonds*, *mortgages*, and the like that provide evidence of amounts owed and have definite payment dates.

debt capital *Noncurrent liabilities*. See *debt financing*, and contrast with *equity financing*.

debt-equity ratio Long-term *debt* divided by *shareholders' equity*. See *ratio* and **Exhibit 6.14**. Some analysts put long-term debt and total shareholders' equity in the denominator. Sometimes debt includes all *liabilities*.

debt financing *Leverage*. Raising *funds* by issuing *bonds*, *mortgages*, or *notes*. Contrast with *equity financing*.

debt guarantee See *guarantee*.

debt ratio *Debt-equity ratio*.

debt retirement The issuer of *debt* gives *cash* or *shares* or other *assets* to the holder of the obligation and then removes the associated *liability* from the *balance sheet*.

debt securities held to maturity A *debt* issue held by an investor who has both the ability and intent to hold the *security* until it matures. See *security held to maturity* for *accounting procedures*.

debt service fund In governmental *accounting*, a *fund* established to account for payment of *interest* and *principal* on all general-obligation *debt* other than that *payable* from special *assessments*.

debt service payment The payment required by a lending agreement, such as periodic *coupon* payment on a *bond* or *installment* payment on a *loan* or a *lease* payment. It is sometimes called "interest payment," but this term will mislead the unwary. Only rarely will the amount of a debt service payment equal the *interest expense* for the *period* preceding the payment. A debt service payment will always include some amount for interest, but the payment will usually differ from the interest expense.

debt service requirement The amount of *cash* required for payments of *interest*, current maturities of *principal* on *outstanding debt*, and payments to *sinking funds* (corporations) or to the *debt service fund* (governmental).

debtor One who borrows; in the UK, *account receivable*.

decentralized decision making *Management* practice in which a *firm* gives a *manager* of a *business* unit responsibility for that unit's *revenues* and *costs*, and sometimes for *investments*, freeing the manager to make decisions about *prices*, sources of supply, and the like, as though the unit were a separate business that the manager owns. See *responsibility accounting* and *transfer price*.

declaration date Time when the *board of directors* declares a *dividend*.

declining-balance (methods) depreciation The method of calculating the periodic *depreciation charge* by multiplying the *carrying value* at the start of the *period* by a constant percentage. In pure declining-balance depreciation, the constant percentage is $1 - n s/c$, where n is the *depreciable life*, s is *salvage value*, and c is *acquisition cost*. See *double declining-balance depreciation*.

deep discount bonds Said of *bonds* selling much below (exactly how much is not clear) *par value*.

defalcation Embezzlement.

default Failure to pay *interest* or *principal* on a *debt* when due.

defeasance *Transaction* with the economic effect of *debt retirement* that does not retire the debt. When *interest rates* increase, many *firms* find that the *market value* of their outstanding *debt* has dropped substantially below its *carrying value*. In *historical cost accounting* for debt retirements, retiring debt with a *cash* payment less than the carrying value of the debt results in a *gain* (generally, an *extraordinary item*). Many firms would like to retire the *outstanding* debt issues and report the gain. Two factors impede doing so: (1) the gain can be a taxable event generating adverse *income tax* consequences; and (2) the transaction *costs* in retiring all the debt can be large, in part because the firm cannot easily locate all the debt holders or persuade them to sell back their *bonds* to the issuer. The process of "defeasance" serves as the economic equivalent to retiring a debt issue while it saves the issuer from experiencing adverse tax consequences and from actually having to locate and retire the bonds. The process works as follows. The debt-issuing firm turns over to an independent trustee, such as a bank, amounts of cash or low-risk government bonds sufficient to make all debt service payments on the outstanding debt, including bond retirements, in return for the trustee's commitment to make all debt service payments. The debt issuer effectively retires the outstanding debt. It *debits* the *liability account*, *credits* Cash or *Marketable Securities* as appropriate, and credits Extraordinary Gain on Debt Retirement. The trustee can retire debt or make debt service payments, whichever it chooses. For income tax purposes, however, the firm's debt remains outstanding. The firm will have taxable interest *deductions* for its still-outstanding debt and taxable interest *revenue* on the *investments* held by the trustee for debt service. In law, the term "defeasance" means "a rendering null and void." This process renders the outstanding debt economically null and void, without causing a taxable event.

defensive interval A financial *ratio* equal to the number of days of normal *cash expenditures* covered by *quick assets*. It is defined as follows:

$$\frac{\text{Quick Assets}}{\text{(All Expenses Except Amortization and Others Not Using Funds} \div 365)}$$

The denominator of the ratio is the cash expenditure per day. Analysts have found this ratio useful in predicting *bankruptcy*.

deferral The *accounting* process concerned with past *cash receipts* and *payments*; in contrast to *accrual*; recognizing a liability resulting from a current cash receipt (as for magazines to be delivered) or recognizing an *asset* from a current cash payment (as for prepaid *insurance* or a long-term depreciable asset).

deferral method See *flow-through method* (of *accounting* for the *investment credit*) for definition and contrast.

deferred annuity An *annuity* whose first payment occurs sometime after the end of the first *period*.

deferred asset *Deferred charge*.

deferred charge *Expenditure* not recognized as an *expense* of the *period* when made but carried forward as an *asset* to be *written off* in future periods, such as for advance *rent* payments or *insurance* premiums. See *deferral*.

deferred compensation Compensation earned by an employee in the current *period*, but not paid by employer until a later period, sometimes many years later.

deferred cost *Deferred charge*.

deferred credit Sometimes used to indicate *advances from customers*.

deferred debit *Deferred charge*.

deferred expense *Deferred charge*.

deferred gross margin *Unrealized gross margin*.

deferred income *Advances from customers*.

deferred income tax (liability) A *liability* that arises when the pretax *income* shown on the *tax return* is less than what it would have been had the *firm* used the same *accounting principles* and *cost basis* for *assets* and liabilities in tax returns as it used for financial reporting. *SFAS No. 109* (**Codification Topic 740**) requires that the firm *debit income* tax *expense* and *credit* deferred income tax liability with the amount of the taxes delayed by using accounting principles in tax returns different from those used in financial *reports*. See *temporary difference*, *timing difference*, *permanent difference*, and *installment sales*. If, as a result of temporary differences, cumulative taxable income exceeds cumulative reported income before taxes, the deferred income tax account will have a debit *balance*, which the firm will report as a "*deferred tax asset*."

deferred performance obligations The seller has promised the buyer that after the *sale* seller will provide further *goods* or *services* as part of the initial sale. Examples are *warranty repairs*, technical support, and *software* upgrades.

deferred revenue Sometimes used to indicate *advances from customers*.

deferred tax See *deferred income tax*.

deferred tax asset See *deferred income tax*. The taxpayer will not report a deferred tax asset unless it believes that it will have future taxable *income* sufficiently high so that it can offset that income with the *expenses* subject to temporary differences—appearing in the *financial statements* in a *period* before they appear as deductions on the *tax return*. To the extent the taxpayer thinks future income will be insufficient for it to be able to offset taxable income with the items generating the deferred tax asset, it will report the effect of the shortfall in an *account*, contra to the deferred tax asset, called "*deferred tax asset valuation allowance*."

deferred tax asset valuation allowance See *deferred tax asset*.

deficit A *debit balance* in the *Retained Earnings account*; presented on the *balance sheet* in a *contra account* to *shareholders' equity*; sometimes used to mean negative *net income* for a *period*.

defined-benefit (pension) plan A *pension plan* in which the employer promises specific dollar amounts per month to each eligible employee, usually until death of the employee, or at a reduced amount until death of both the employee and the employee's spouse; the amounts usually depend on a formula that takes into account such things as the employee's earnings, years of employment, and age at retirement. The employer adjusts its *cash* contributions and pension *expense* to *actuarial* experience in the eligible employee group and investment performance of the pension *fund*. This is sometimes called a "fixed-benefit" pension plan. Contrast with *money purchase plan* or *defined-contribution plan*.

defined-contribution plan A *money purchase (pension) plan* or other arrangement, based on formula or discretion, in which the employer makes *cash* contributions to eligible individual employee *accounts* under the terms of a written plan document. The employee or trustee of the *funds* in the account manages the funds, and the employee-beneficiary receives at retirement (or at some other agreed time) the amount in the fund. The employer makes no promise about that amount. Profit-sharing pension plans are of this type.

deflation A *period* of declining *general price-level changes*.

Delphi technique Forecasting method in which members of the forecasting group prepare individual *forecasts*, share them anonymously with the rest of the group, and only then compare forecasts and resolve differences.

demand deposit *Funds* in a checking *account* at a bank. See *check*.

demand loan See *term loan* for definition and contrast.

denial of opinion Canada: the statement that an *auditor*, for reasons arising in the *audit*, is unable to express an opinion on whether the *financial statements* provide *fair presentation*.

denominator volume *Capacity* measured in the number of units the *firm* expects to produce this *period*; when divided into *budgeted fixed costs*, results in fixed costs applied per unit of *product*.

department(al) allocation Obtained by first accumulating *costs* in *cost pools* for each department and then, using separate rates, or sets of rates, for each department, *allocating* from each cost pool to *products* produced in that department.

dependent variable See *regression analysis*.

depletion Exhaustion or *amortization* of a *wasting asset* or *natural resource*. Also see *percentage depletion*.

depletion allowance See *percentage depletion*.

deposit intangible See *core deposit intangible*.

deposit, sinking fund Payments made to a *sinking fund*.

deposit method (of revenue recognition) A method of *revenue* recognition that is the same as the *completed sale* or *completed contract method*. In some contexts, such as when the customer has the right to return *goods* for a full refund or in retail *land sales*, the customer must make substantial payments while still having the right to back out of the deal and receive a refund. When the seller cannot predict with reasonable precision the amount of *cash* it will ultimately collect and when it will receive cash, the seller must *credit* Deposits, a *liability account*, rather than *revenue*. (In this

regard, the *accounting* differs from that in the completed contract method, in which the account credited offsets the *Work-in-Process inventory* account.) When the sale becomes complete, the *firm* credits a revenue account and *debits* the Deposits account.

deposits (by customers) A *liability* that the *firm* credits when receiving *cash* (as in a bank, or in a grocery store when the customer pays for soda-pop bottles with cash to be repaid when the customer returns the bottles) and when the firm intends to discharge the *liability* by returning the cash. Contrast with the liability account *Advances from Customers*, which the firm credits on *receipt* of cash, expecting later to discharge the liability by delivering *goods* or *services*. When the firm delivers the goods or services, it credits a *revenue* account.

deposits in transit Deposits made by a *firm* but not yet reflected on the *bank statement*.

depreciable cost That part of the *cost* of an asset, usually *acquisition cost* less *salvage value*, that the *firm* will *charge off* over the life of the asset through the process of *depreciation*.

depreciable life For an *asset*, the time period or units of activity (such as miles driven for a truck) over which the *firm* allocates the *depreciable cost*. For *tax returns*, depreciable life may be shorter than estimated *service life*.

depreciation *Amortization of plant assets*; the process of *allocating* the *cost* of an *asset* to the *periods* of benefit—the *depreciable life*; classified as a *production cost* or a *period expense*, depending on the asset and whether the *firm* uses *full absorption* or *variable costing*. Depreciation methods described in this glossary include the *annuity method*, *appraisal method*, *composite method*, *compound interest method*, *declining-balance method*, *production method*, *replacement method*, *retirement method*, *straight-line method*, *sinking fund method*, and *sum-of-the-years'-digits method*.

depreciation reserve An inferior term for *accumulated depreciation*. See *reserve*. Do not confuse with a replacement *fund*.

derecognize Remove an *asset* or *liability* from the *balance sheet*.

derivative (financial instrument) A *financial instrument*, such as an *option* to purchase a *share* of *stock*, whose value depends on the underlying value of another financial instrument, such as a share of stock, or some variable, such as an *interest rate* or currency; an instrument, such as a *swap*, whose value depends on the value of another *asset* called the "underlying"—for example, the right to receive the difference between the *interest payments* on a fixed-rate five-year *loan* for $1 million and the interest payments on a floating-rate five-year loan for $1 million. To qualify as a derivative under *FASB* rules, *SFAS No. 133* (**Codification Topic 815**), the instrument has one or more *underlyings*, and one or more *notional amounts* or payment *provisions* or both, it either does not require an initial *net investment* or it requires one smaller than would be required for other types of contracts expected to have a similar response to changes in market factors, and its terms permit settlement for *cash* in lieu of physical delivery or the instrument itself trades on an *exchange*. See also *forward contract* and *futures contract*.

Descartes' rule of signs In a *capital budgeting* context, a rule that says a series of *cash flows* will have a nonnegative number of *internal rates of return*. The number equals the number of variations in the sign of the cash flow series or is less than that number by an even integer. Consider the following series of cash flows, the first occurring now and the others at subsequent yearly intervals: $-100, -100, +50, +175,$

−50, +100. The internal rates of return are the numbers for *r* that satisfy the following equation:

$$-100 - \frac{100}{(1+r)} + \frac{50}{(1+r)^2} + \frac{175}{(1+r)^3} - \frac{50}{(1+r)^4} + \frac{100}{(1+r)^5} = 0$$

The series of cash flows has three variations in sign: a change from minus to plus, a change from plus to minus, and a change from minus to plus. The rule says that this series must have either one or three internal rates of return; in fact, it has only one, about 12%. But also see *reinvestment rate*.

detection costs See *appraisal costs*.

detective controls *Internal controls* designed to detect, or maximize the chance of detecting errors and other irregularities.

determination See *determine*.

determine A term often used (in our opinion, overused) by *accountants* and those who describe the *accounting* process. A leading dictionary associates the following meanings with the verb "determine": settle, decide, conclude, ascertain, cause, affect, control, impel, terminate, and decide upon. In addition, accounting writers can mean any one of the following: measure, *allocate*, report, calculate, compute, observe, choose, and legislate. In accounting, there are two distinct sets of meanings: those encompassed by the synonym "cause or legislate" and those encompassed by the synonym "measure." The first set of uses conveys the active notion of causing something to happen, and the second set of uses conveys the more passive notion of observing something that someone else has caused to happen.

An accountant who speaks of *cost* or *income* "determination" generally means measurement or observation, not causation; *management* and economic conditions cause costs and income to be what they are. One who speaks of *accounting principles* "determination" can mean choosing or applying (as in "determining *depreciation charges*" from an allowable set) or causing to be acceptable (as in the *FASB*'s "determining" the accounting for *leases*). In the long run, income is cash-in less cash-out, so management and economic conditions "determine" (cause) income to be what it is. In the short run, reported income is a function of accounting principles chosen and applied, so the accountant "determines" (measures) income. A question such as "Who determines income?" has, therefore, no unambiguous answer. The meaning of "an accountant determining acceptable accounting principles" is also vague. Does the clause mean merely choosing one principle from the set of generally acceptable principles, or does it mean using professional judgment to decide that some of the generally accepted principles are not correct under the current circumstances? We try never to use "determine" unless we mean "cause." Otherwise we use "measure," "report," "calculate," "compute," or whatever specific verb seems appropriate. We suggest that careful writers will always "determine" to use the most specific verb to convey meaning. "Determine" seldom best describes a process in which those who make decisions often differ from those who apply technique. The term *predetermined (factory) overhead rate* contains an appropriate use of the word.

development stage enterprise As defined in *SFAS No. 7* (**Codification Topic 915**), a *firm* whose planned principal *operations* have not commenced or, having commenced, have not generated significant *revenue*. The *financial statements* should identify such *enterprises*, but no special *accounting principles* apply to them.

diagnostic signal See *warning signal* for definition and contrast.

differentiable cost The *cost* increments associated with infinitesimal changes in volume. If a total cost curve is smooth (in mathematical terms, differentiable), then we say that the curve graphing the *derivative* of the total cost curve shows differentiable costs.

differential An adjective used to describe the change (increase or decrease) in a *cost*, *expense*, *investment*, *cash flow*, *revenue*, *profit*, and the like as the *firm* produces or sells one or more additional (or fewer) units or undertakes (or ceases) an activity. This term has virtually the same meaning as *incremental*, but if the item declines, "decremental" better describes the change. Contrast with "marginal," which means the change in cost or other item for a small (one unit or even less) change in number of units produced or sold.

differential analysis Analysis of *differential costs*, *revenues*, *profits*, *investment*, *cash flow*, and the like.

differential cost See *differential*.

differential cost analysis See *relevant cost analysis*.

diluted earnings per share For *common stock*, smallest *earnings per share* figure that one can obtain by computing an *earnings per share* for all possible combinations of assumed *exercise* or *conversion* of *potentially dilutive securities*.

dilution A potential reduction in *earnings per share* or *book value* per *share* by the potential *conversion* of *securities* or by the potential *exercise* of *warrants* or *options*.

dilutive Said of a *security* that will reduce *earnings per share* if it is exchanged for *common shares*.

dip(ping) into LIFO layers See *LIFO inventory layer*.

direct access Access to computer storage where information can be located directly, regardless of its position in the storage file. Compare *sequential access*.

direct cost *Cost* of *direct material* and *direct labor* incurred in producing a *product*. See *prime cost*. In some *accounting* literature, writers use this term to mean the same thing as *variable cost*.

direct costing Another, less-preferred, term for *variable costing*.

direct-financing (capital) lease See *sales-type (capital) lease* for definition and contrast.

direct labor (material) cost *Cost* of labor (*material*) applied and assigned directly to a *product*; contrast with *indirect labor* (*material*).

direct labor variance Difference between actual and *standard direct labor* allowed.

direct method See *statement of cash flows*.

direct posting A method of *bookkeeping* in which the *firm* makes *entries* directly in *ledger accounts*, without using a *journal*.

direct write-off method See *write-off method*.

disbursement Payment by *cash* or by *check*. See *expenditure*.

disclaimer of opinion An *auditor's report* stating that the auditor cannot give an opinion on the *financial statements*. Usually results from *material* restrictions on the scope of the *audit* or from material uncertainties, which the *firm* has been unable to resolve by the time of the audit, about the *accounts*.

disclosure The showing of facts in *financial statements*, *notes* thereto, or the *auditor's report*.

discontinued operations See *income from discontinued operations*.

discount In the context of *compound interest*, *bonds* and *notes*, the difference between *face amount* (or *future value*) and *present value* of a payment; in the context of *sales* and *purchases*, a reduction in *price* granted for prompt payment. See also *chain discount*, *quantity discount*, and *trade discount*.

discount to face value; premium to face value See *discount* and *premium*.

discount factor The reciprocal of one plus the *discount rate*. If the discount rate is 10% per period, the discount factor for three *periods* is $1/(1.10)^3 = (1.10)^{-3} = 0.75131$.

discount rate *Interest rate* used to convert future payments to *present values*.

discounted bailout period In a *capital budgeting* context, the total time that must elapse before discounted *value* of *net* accumulated *cash flows* from a project, including potential *salvage value* at various times of *assets*, equals or exceeds the *present value* of net accumulated cash outflows. Contrast with *discounted payback period*.

discounted (future) cash flow(s) (DCF) Using either the *net present value* or the *internal rate of return* in an analysis to measure the *value* of future expected *cash expenditures* and *receipts* at a common date. In discounted cash flow analysis, choosing the alternative with the largest *internal rate of return* may yield wrong answers given *mutually exclusive projects* with differing amounts of initial *investment* for two of the projects. Consider, to take an unrealistic example, a project involving an initial investment of $1, with an *IRR* of 60%, and another project involving an initial investment of $1 million, with an IRR of 40%. Under most conditions, most *firms* will prefer the second project to the first, but choosing the project with the larger IRR will lead to undertaking the first, not the second. Usage calls this shortcoming of choosing between alternatives based on the magnitude of the internal rate of return, rather than based on the magnitude of the *net present value* of the *cash flows*, the "scale effect."

discounted payback period The shortest amount of time that must elapse before the discounted *present value* of *cash* inflows from a project, excluding potential *salvage value*, equals the discounted present value of the cash outflows.

discounting a note See *note receivable discounted* and *factoring*. See also *discounted cash flow*.

discounts lapsed (lost) The sum of *discounts* offered for prompt payment that the purchaser did not take because the discount *period* expired. See *terms of sale*.

discovery sampling *Acceptance* sampling in which the analyst accepts an entire population if and only if the sample contains no disparities.

discovery value accounting See *reserve recognition accounting*.

discretionary cost center See *engineered cost center* for definition and contrast.

discretionary costs *Programmed costs*.

Discussion Memorandum A neutral discussion of all the issues concerning an *accounting* problem of current concern to the *FASB*. The publication of such a document usually signals that the FASB will consider issuing a new pronouncement on this particular problem. The discussion memorandum brings together *material* about the particular problem to facilitate interaction and comment by those interested in the matter. A public hearing follows before the FASB will issue an *Exposure Draft*.

dishonored note A *promissory note* whose maker does not repay the *loan* at *maturity*, for a *term loan*, or on demand, for a *demand loan*.

disintermediation Moving *funds* from one *interest*-earning *account* to another, typically one promising a higher rate. Federal law regulates the maximum *interest rate* that both banks and savings-and-loan associations can pay for *time deposits*. When free-market *interest rates* exceed the regulated interest ceiling for such time deposits, some depositors withdraw their funds and invest them elsewhere at a higher interest rate. This process is known as "*disintermediation*."

distributable income The portion of conventional *accounting net income* that the *firm* can distribute to owners (usually in the form of *dividends*) without impairing the physical capacity of the firm to continue *operations* at current levels. Pretax *distributable income* is conventional pretax *income* less the excess of *current cost* of *goods* sold and *depreciation charges* based on the *replacement cost* of productive capacity over *cost of goods sold* and *depreciation* on an *acquisition cost basis*. Contrast with *sustainable income*. See *inventory profit*.

distributable surplus Canada and UK: the statutory designation to describe the portion of the *proceeds* of the issue of *shares* without *par value* not *allocated* to share *capital*.

distribution expense *Expense* of selling, advertising, and delivery activities.

dividend A distribution of *assets* generated from *earnings* to owners of a *corporation*. The *firm* may distribute *cash* (*cash dividend*), *stock* (stock dividend), property, or other *securities* (dividend in kind). Dividends, except stock dividends, become a legal *liability* of the corporation when the corporation's board declares them. Hence, the owner of stock ordinarily recognizes *revenue* when the board of the corporation declares the dividend, except for stock dividends. See also *liquidating dividend* and *stock dividend*.

dividend yield *Dividends* declared for the year divided by *market price* of the *stock* as of the time for which the analyst computes the *yield*.

dividends in arrears *Dividends* on *cumulative preferred shares* that the *corporation's board* has not yet declared in accordance with the preferred stock contract. The corporation must usually clear such arrearages before it can declare dividends on *common shares*.

dividends in kind See *dividend*. Sometimes called a "*property dividend*."

division A more or less self-contained *business* that is part of a larger family of business units under common control. A division may be, but need not be, a separate *legal entity*.

divisional control See *control system*.

divisional reporting See *segment reporting*.

division return on investment (ROI) Equals the *division profit* divided by the *investment* in the division.

dollar sign rules In *accounting* statements or *schedules*, place a dollar sign beside the first figure in each column and beside any figure below a horizontal line drawn under the preceding figure. This rule applies for other currency symbols and the percentage sign, as well.

dollar-value LIFO method A form of *LIFO inventory accounting* with inventory quantities (*layers*) measured in dollar, rather than physical, terms. The method adjusts for changing *prices* by using specific *price indexes* appropriate for the kinds of items in the inventory.

donated capital A *shareholders' equity account credited* when the company receives gifts, such as land or buildings, without issuing *shares* or other *owners' equity interest* in return. A city might donate a *plant* site hoping the *firm* will build a *factory* and employ local residents. Do not confuse with *contributed capital*.

double declining-balance depreciation (DDB) *Declining-balance depreciation* in which the constant percentage used to multiply by *carrying value* in computing the *depreciation charge* for the year is $2/n$, where n is the *depreciable life* in *periods*. Omit *salvage value* from the depreciable amount. Thus if the *asset* cost $100 and has a depreciable life of five years, the depreciation in the first year would be $40 = 2/5 \times \$100$, in the second year would be $24 = 2/5 \times (\$100 - \$40)$, and in the third year would be $14.40 = 2/5 \times (\$100 - \$40 - \$24)$. By the fourth year, the remaining undepreciated *cost* could be depreciated under the straight-line method at $10.80 = 1/2 \times (\$100 - \$40 - \$24 - \$14.40)$ per year for *tax* purposes. Note that salvage value does not affect these computations except that the method will depreciate the carrying value to salvage value.

double entry In recording *transactions*, a system that maintains the equality of the *accounting* equation or the *balance sheet*. Each *entry* results in recording equal amounts of *debits* and *credits*.

double taxation Occurs when the taxing authority (U.S. or state) *taxes* corporate *income* as earned (first tax) and then the same taxing authority taxes the after-tax income, distributed to owners as *dividends*, again as personal *income tax* (second tax).

doubtful accounts *Accounts receivable* that the *firm* estimates to be *uncollectible*.

Dr. The abbreviation for *debit*, always with the initial capital letter. *Dr.* is a shortened from of the word "debitor," and *Cr.* comes from the word "creditor." In the early days of double-entry record keeping in the UK, the major *asset* was *accounts receivable*, called creditors, and the major *liability* was accounts payable, called debitors. Thus the *r* in Cr. does not refer to the *r* in *credit* but to the second *r* in creditor.

draft A written order by the first party, called the *drawer*, instructing a second party, called the *drawee* (such as a bank) to pay a third party, called the *payee*. See also *check*, *cashier's check*, *certified check*, *NOW account*, *sight draft*, and *trade acceptance*.

drawee See *draft*.

drawer See *draft*.

drawing account A *temporary account* used in *sole proprietorships* and *partnerships* to record payments to owners or partners during a *period*. At the end of the period, the *firm* *closes* the drawing account by *crediting* it and *debiting* the owner's or partner's share of *income* or, perhaps, his or her *capital account*.

drawings Payments made to a *sole proprietor* or to a *partner* during a period. See *drawing account*.

driver, cost driver A cause of *costs* incurred. Examples include processing orders, issuing an engineering change order, changing the production *schedule*, and stopping production to change machine settings. The notion arises primarily in *product costing*, particularly *activity-based costing*.

drop ship(ment) Occurs when a distributor asks a manufacturer to send an order directly to the customer (ordinarily a manufacturer sends *goods* to a distributor, who sends the goods to its customer). Usage calls the shipment a "drop shipment" and refers to the goods as "drop shipped."

dry-hole accounting See *reserve recognition accounting* for definition and contrast.

dual effects of transactions The proper recording of any *transaction* in *accounting* records results in equal amounts *debited* to various *accounts* as *credited* to various accounts.

dual-transactions assumption (fiction) Occurs when an analyst, in understanding *cash flows*, views *transactions* not involving *cash* as though the *firm* first generated cash and then

used it. For example, the analyst might view the issue of *capital stock* in return for the *asset* land as though the firm issued *stock* for *cash* and then used cash to acquire the land. Other examples of transactions that could involve the dual-transaction assumption are the issue of a *mortgage* in return for a *noncurrent* asset and the issue of stock to bondholders on *conversion* of their *convertible bonds*.

dual transfer prices Occurs when the *transfer price charged* to the buying *division* differs from that *credited* to the selling division. Such *prices* make sense when the selling *division* needs to recover *full costs*, which exceed *market price*, while the buying division wants not to pay more than market price. Seldom seen in practice when the two divisions operate in different *income tax* jurisdictions, as the differences in price lead to arguments with at least one of the taxing authorities. An exception occurs when the minimum selling price required by regulatory authorities in the selling country exceeds the maximum buying price allowed by the regulatory authorities in the purchasing country.

duality The *double entry* record-keeping axiom that every *transaction* must result in equal *debit* and *credit* amounts.

due diligence An investigation of the financial affairs of a company for the purpose of disclosing matters that may influence the terms or conclusion of a potential acquisition.

dumping A foreign *firm*'s selling a *good* or *service* in one country at a *price* below *market price* at home or, in some contexts, below some measure of *cost* (which concept is not clearly defined). The practice is illegal in the United States if it harms (or threatens to harm) a U.S. industry.

E

e The base of natural logarithms; $2.71828\ldots$. If *interest* compounds continuously during a *period* at stated rate of r per *period*, then the effective *interest rate* is equivalent to interest compounded once per period at rate i where $i = e^r - 1$. Tables of e^r are widely available. If 12% annual interest compounds continuously, the effective annual rate is $e^{.12} - 1 = 12.75\%$. The Excel *function* is =exp(number). The formula for the effective annual rate is $r = \exp(.12) - 1 = 12.75\%$. Interest compounded continuously at rate r for d days is $e^{rd/365} - 1$. For example, interest compounded for 92 days at 12% is $e^{.12 \times 92/365} - 1 = 3.07\%$ [=exp(.12*92/365) − 1 = 3.07%].

earn-out For two merging *firms*, an agreement in which the amount paid by the acquiring firm to the acquired firm's shareholders depends on the future *earnings* of the acquired firm or, perhaps, of the *consolidated entity*.

earned surplus A term that writers once used, but no longer use, for *retained earnings*.

earnings A term with no precise meaning but used to mean *income* or sometimes *profit*. The *FASB*, in requiring that *firms* report *comprehensive income*, encouraged firms to use the term "earnings" for the total formerly reported as *net income*. Firms will likely only slowly change from using the term "net income" to the term "earnings."

earnings, retained See *retained earnings*.

earnings cycle The period of time, or the series of *transactions*, during which a given *firm* converts *cash* into *goods* and *services*, then sells goods and services to customers, and finally collects cash from customers. *Cash cycle*.

earnings per (common) share (of common stock) *Net income* to common shareholders (net income minus *preferred dividends*) divided by the *average* number of *common shares* *outstanding*; see also *basic earnings per share* and *diluted earnings per share*. See *ratio* and **Exhibit 6.14**.

earnings per share (of preferred stock) *Net income* divided by the *average* number of *preferred shares outstanding* during the *period*. This *ratio* indicates how well *income* covers (or protects) the preferred *dividends*; it does not indicate a legal share of *earnings*.

earnings statement *Income statement*.

easement The acquired *right* or privilege of one person to use, or have access to, certain property of another. For example, a public utility's right to lay pipes or lines under the property of another and to service those facilities.

EBIT Earnings before *interest and (income) taxes*; acronym used by analysts.

EBITDA Earnings before *interest, (income) taxes, depreciation, and amortization*; acronym used by analysts to focus on a particular measure of *cash flow*; used in valuation. This is not the same as, but is similar in concept to, *cash flow from operations*. Some analysts exclude *nonrecurring* items from this total.

economic consequences The *FASB* says that in setting *accounting principles*, it should take into account the real effects on various participants in the business world. It calls these effects "economic consequences."

economic depreciation Decline in *current cost* (or *fair value*) of an *asset* during a *period*.

economic entity See *entity*.

economic life The time span over which the *firm* expects to receive the benefits of an *asset*. The economic life of a *patent*, *copyright*, or *franchise* may be less than the legal life. *Service life*.

economic order quantity (EOQ) In mathematical *inventory* analysis, the optimal amount of *stock* to order when demand reduces inventory to a level called the "reorder point." If *A* represents the *incremental cost* of placing a single order, *D* represents the total demand for a *period* of time in units, and *H* represents the *incremental* holding cost during the period per unit of inventory, then the economic order quantity is Usage sometimes calls *EOQ* the "optimal lot size."

economic transfer pricing rule Transfer at the *differential outlay cost* to the selling division (typically *variable costs*), plus the *opportunity cost* to the company of making the internal transfers ($0 if the seller has idle capacity, or selling price minus variable costs if the seller is operating at capacity).

economic value added (EVA®) The amount of *earnings* generated above the *cost* of *funds* invested to generate those earnings. To calculate *economic value added*, find the difference between (the *net after-tax operating profit*) and (the product of the *weighted-average cost of capital* multiplied by the *investment* in the economic unit).

ED *Exposure Draft.*

EDGAR Electronic Data, Gathering, Analysis, and Retrieval system; rules and systems adopted by the *SEC* in 1993 to ensure that each of the more than 15,000 public companies electronically submits all the paperwork involved in its filings.

EDP *Electronic data processing.*

effective interest method In computing *interest expense* (or *revenue*), a systematic method that makes the interest expense (revenue) for each *period* divided by the amount of the *net liability* (*asset*) at the beginning of the period equal to the *yield rate* on the liability (asset) at the time of issue (acquisition). Interest for a period is the yield rate (at time of issue) multiplied by the net liability (asset) at the start of the period. The *amortization* of *discount* or *premium* is the *plug* to give equal *debits* and *credits*. (Interest expense is a debit, and the amount of *debt service payment* is a credit.)

effective annual yield See *effective (interest) rate*.

effective (interest) rate Of a *liability* such as a *bond*, the *internal rate of return* or *yield to maturity* at the time of issue. Contrast with *coupon rate*. If the *borrower* issues the bond for a price below *par*, the effective rate is higher than the coupon rate; if it issues the bond for a price greater than par, the effective rate is lower than the coupon rate.

In the context of *compound interest*, the effective rate occurs when the *compounding period* on a *loan* differs from one year, such as a *nominal interest rate* of 12% compounded monthly The effective *interest* is the single rate that one could use at the end of the year to multiply the *principal* at the beginning of the year and give the same amount as results from compounding interest each period during the year. For example, if 12% per year compounds monthly, the effective annual *interest rate* is 12.683%. That is, if you compound $100 each month at 1% per month, the $100 will grow to $112.68 at the end of the year. In general, if the nominal rate of *r*% per year compounds *m* times per year, then the effective rate is $(1 + r/m)^m - 1$.

effective (income) tax rate For a taxpayer, the amount of *income tax expense* (not amount *payable*) divided by *pretax income*.

efficiency variance A term used for the *quantity variance* for *materials* or labor or *variable overhead costs* in a *standard costing system*.

efficient capital market A market in which *security prices* reflect all available information and react nearly instantaneously and in an unbiased fashion to new information.

efficient market hypothesis The finance supposition that *security prices* trade in *efficient capital markets*.

EITF *Emerging Issues Task Force.*

electronic data processing Performing computations and other data-organizing steps in a computer, in contrast to doing these steps by hand or with mechanical calculators.

eligible Under *income tax* legislation, a term that restricts or otherwise alters the meaning of another *tax* or *accounting* term, generally to signify that the related *assets* or *operations* may receive a specified tax treatment.

eliminations In preparing *consolidated statements*, *work sheet entries* made to avoid duplicating the amounts of *assets, liabilities, owners' equity, revenues*, and *expenses* of the consolidated *entity* when the *firm* sums the *accounts* of the *parent* and *subsidiaries*. These entries eliminate any *intercompany profit* in *beginning inventory*, if any.

Emerging Issues Task Force (EITF) A group convened by the *FASB* to deal more rapidly with accounting issues than the FASB's due-process procedures can allow. The task force comprises about 15 members from *public accounting*, industry, and several trade associations. Several FASB *board* members usually attend and participate. The chief *accountant* of the *SEC* has indicated that the SEC will require that published *financial statements* follow guidelines set by a consensus of the *EITF*. The EITF requires that nearly all its members agree on a position before that position receives the label of "consensus." Such positions appear in *Abstracts of the EITF*, published by the FASB and now included in its

Codification. Since 1984, the EITF has become one of the promulgators of *U.S. GAAP*.

employee stock option; ESOs See *stock option*.

Employee Stock Ownership Trust (or Plan) See *ESOT*.

employer, employee payroll taxes See *payroll taxes*.

enabling costs A type of *capacity cost* that a *firm* will stop *incurring* if it shuts down *operations* completely but will incur in full if it carries out operations at any level. Examples include *costs* of a security force or of a quality-control inspector for an assembly line. Contrast with *standby costs*.

encumbrance In governmental *accounting*, an anticipated *expenditure* or *funds* restricted for an anticipated *expenditure*, such as for *outstanding purchase orders*. *Appropriations* less *expenditures* less outstanding *encumbrances* yields unencumbered *balance*.

ending inventory The *cost* of *inventory* on hand at the end of the *accounting period*; often called "*closing inventory*." *Ending inventory* from the end of one *period* becomes the *beginning inventory* for the next period.

endorsee See *endorser*.

endorsement See *draft*. The *payee* signs the *draft* and *transfers* it to a fourth party, such as the *payee*'s bank.

endorser A *note* or *draft payee*, who signs the note after writing "Pay to the order of X," *transfers* the note to person X, and presumably receives some benefit, such as *cash*, in return. Usage refers to person X as the "*endorsee*." The endorsee then has the *rights* of the payee and may in turn become an endorser by endorsing the note to another endorsee.

engineered cost center Responsibility center with sufficiently well-established relations between inputs and outputs that the analyst, given data on inputs, can predict the outputs or, conversely, given the outputs, can estimate the amounts of inputs that the process should have used. Consider the relation between pounds of flour (input) and loaves of bread (output). Contrast *discretionary cost center*, where such relations are so imprecise that analysts have no reliable way to relate inputs to outputs. Consider the relation between advertising the corporate logo or trademark (input) and future revenues (output).

engineering method (of cost estimation) To estimate unit *cost* of *product* from study of the *materials*, labor, and *overhead* components of the *production* process.

enterprise Any *business* organization, usually defining the *accounting entity*.

enterprise fund A *fund* that a governmental unit establishes to account for acquisition, operation, and *maintenance* of governmental *services* that the government intends to be self-supporting from user *charges*, such as for water or airports and some toll roads.

entity A person, *partnership*, *corporation*, or other organization. The *accounting entity* that issues *accounting* statements may not be the same as the *entity* defined by law. For example, a *sole proprietorship* is an accounting entity, but the individual's combined *business* and personal *assets* are the *legal entity* in most jurisdictions. Several affiliated corporations may be separate legal entities but issue *consolidated financial statements* for the group of companies *operating* as a single *economic entity*.

entity theory The *corporation* view that emphasizes the form of the *accounting equation* that says *assets = equities*. Contrast with *proprietorship theory*. The entity theory focuses less on the distinction between *liabilities* and *shareholders' equity* than does the proprietorship theory. The entity theory views

all *equities* as coming to the corporation from outsiders who have claims of differing legal standings.

entry value The *current cost* of acquiring an *asset* or *service* at a *fair market price*. *Replacement cost*.

EOQ *Economic order quantity*.

EPS *Earnings per share*.

EPVI *Excess present value index*.

equalization reserve An inferior title for the *allowance* or *estimated liability account* when the *firm* uses the *allowance method* for such things as *maintenance expenses*. Periodically, the *accountant* will *debit* maintenance expense and *credit* the allowance. As the firm makes *expenditures* for maintenance, it will debit the allowance and credit *cash* or the other *asset* used in maintenance.

equities *Liabilities* plus *owners' equity*. See *equity*.

equity A claim to *assets*; a source of assets. *SFAC No. 3* defines *equity* as "the residual *interest* in the assets of an entity that remains after deducting its *liabilities*." Thus, many knowledgeable people use "equity" to exclude liabilities and count only *owners' equities*. We prefer to use the term to mean all liabilities plus all owners' equity because there is no other single word that serves this useful purpose. We fight a losing battle.

equity financing Raising *funds* by issuing *capital stock*. Contrast with *debt financing*.

equity method In *accounting* for an *investment* in the *stock* of another company, a method that *debits* the proportionate *share* of the *earnings* of the other company to the investment *account* and *credits* that amount to a *revenue* account as earned. When the investor receives *dividends*, it debits *cash* and credits the investment account. An investor who owns sufficient shares of stock of an unconsolidated company to exercise significant control over the actions of that company must use the equity method. It is one of the few instances in which the *firm* recognizes revenue without an increase in *working capital*.

equity ratio *Shareholders' equity* divided by total *assets*. See *ratio*.

equivalent production *Equivalent units*.

equivalent units (of work) The number of units of completed *output* that would require the same *costs* that a *firm* would actually *incur* for the production of completed and partially completed units during a *period*. For example, if at the beginning of a period the firm starts 100 units and by the end of the period has incurred costs for each of these equal to 75% of total costs to complete the units, then the *equivalent units* of work for the period would be 75. This is used primarily in *process costing* calculations to measure in uniform terms the output of a continuous process.

ERISA (Employee Retirement Income Security Act of 1974) The federal law that sets most *pension plan* requirements.

error accounting See *accounting errors*.

escalator clause Inserted in a purchase or rental contract, a clause that permits, under specified conditions, upward adjustments of *price*.

escapable cost *Avoidable cost*.

ESOP (Employee Stock Ownership Plan) See *ESOT*.

ESOT (Employee Stock Ownership Trust) A trust *fund* that is created by a corporate employer and that can provide certain *tax* benefits to the *corporation* while providing for employee *stock* ownership. The corporate employer can contribute up to 25% of its payroll per year to the trust. The corporation may deduct the amount of the contribution from otherwise *taxable income* for federal *income tax* purposes. The trustee of the *assets* must use them for the benefit of employees—for example, to fund death or retirement benefits. The assets of the trust are usually the *common shares*, sometimes nonvoting, of the corporate employer. For an example of the potential *tax shelter*, consider the case of a corporation with $1 million of *debt outstanding*, which it wants to retire, and an annual payroll of $2 million. The corporation sells $1 million of common stock to the ESOT. The ESOT borrows $1 million with the *loan guaranteed* by, and therefore a *contingency* of, the corporation. The corporation uses the $1 million *proceeds* of the stock *issue* to retire its outstanding debt. (The debt of the corporation has been replaced with the debt of the ESOT.) The corporation can contribute $500,000 (= .25 × $2 million payroll) to the ESOT each year and treat the contribution as a deduction for tax purposes. After a little more than two years, the ESOT has received sufficient funds to retire its loan. The corporation has effectively repaid its original $1 million debt with pretax dollars. Assuming an income tax rate of 40%, it has saved $400,000 (= .40 × $1 million) of after-tax dollars *if* the $500,000 expense for the contribution to the ESOT for the pension benefits of employees would have been made, in one form or another, anyway. Observe that the corporation could use the proceeds ($1 million in the example) of the stock issued to the ESOT for any of several different purposes: financing expansion, replacing *plant assets*, or acquiring another company. Basically this same form of pretax-dollar financing through pensions is available with almost any corporate *pension plan*, with one important exception. The trustees of an ordinary pension trust must invest the assets prudently, and if they do not, they are personally liable to the employees. Current judgment about prudent *investment* requires diversification—trustees should invest pension trust assets in a wide variety of investment opportunities. (The trustee may not ordinarily invest more than 10% of a pension trust's assets in the parent's common stock.) Thus the ordinary pension trust cannot, in practice, invest all, or even most, of its assets in the parent corporation's stock. This constraint does not apply to the investments of an ESOT. The trustee may invest all ESOT assets in the parent company's stock. The ESOT also provides a means for closely held corporations to achieve wider ownership of shares without *going public*. The laws enabling ESOTs provide for the independent professional appraisal of shares not traded in public markets and for transactions between the corporation and the ESOT or between the ESOT and the employees to be based on the appraised values of the shares.

estate planning The arrangement of an individual's affairs to facilitate the passage of *assets* to beneficiaries and to minimize *taxes* at death.

estimated expenses *Expenditures* to be made after *revenue* recognition. For example, expenditures for *repairs* under *warranty* are after *cost*. Proper recognition of after cost involves a *debit* to *expense* at the time of the sale and a *credit* to an *estimated liability*. When the *firm* discharges the *liability*, it debits the estimated liability and credits the assets consumed. Sometimes called "*after cost*."

estimated liability The preferred terminology for estimated *costs* the *firm* will *incur* for such uncertain things as *repairs* under *warranty*. An *estimated liability* appears on the *balance sheet*. Contrast with *contingency*.

estimated revenue A term used in governmental *accounting* to designate *revenue* expected to *accrue* during a *period* independent of whether the government will collect it during the period. The governmental unit usually establishes a *budgetary account* at the beginning of the *budget period*.

estimated salvage value Synonymous with *salvage value* of an *asset* before its retirement.

estimates, changes in See *accounting changes*.

estimation sampling The use of sampling technique in which the sampler infers a qualitative (e.g., fraction female) or quantitative (e.g., mean weight) characteristic of the population from the occurrence of that characteristic in the sample drawn. See *attribute(s) sampling*; *variables sampling*.

EURL (entreprise unipersonnelle à responsabilité limitée) France: similar to *SARL* but having only one shareholder.

event certain to occur See *redeemable* (*preferred shares*).

ex div (dividend) Said of *shares* whose *market price* quoted in the market has been reduced by a *dividend* already declared but not yet paid. The *corporation* will send the dividend to the person who owned the share on the *record date*. One who buys the share ex dividend will not receive the dividend although the corporation has not yet paid it.

ex rights The condition of *securities* whose quoted *market price* no longer includes the *right* to purchase new securities, such rights having expired or been retained by the seller. Compare *cum rights*.

except for Qualification in *auditor's report*, usually caused by a change, approved by the *auditor*, from one acceptable *accounting principle* or procedure to another.

excess present value In a *capital budgeting* context, *present value* (of anticipated *cash* inflows minus cash outflows including initial cash outflow for a project. The analyst uses the *cost of capital* as the *discount rate*.

excess present value index *Present value* of future *cash* inflows divided by initial cash *outlay*.

exchange The generic term for a *transaction* (or, more technically, a reciprocal *transfer*) between one *entity* and another; in another context, the name for a market, such as the *New York Stock Exchange*.

exchange gain or loss The phrase used by the *FASB* for *foreign exchange gain or loss*.

exchange rate The *price* of one country's currency in terms of another country's currency. For example, the British pound sterling might be worth U.S.$1.95 at a given time. The exchange rate would be stated as "one pound is worth one dollar and ninety-five cents" or "one dollar is worth £.513" (= £1/$1.95).

excise tax *Tax* on the manufacture, *sale*, or consumption of a commodity.

executory contract A mere *exchange* of promises; an agreement providing for payment by a payor to a *payee* on the performance of an act or *service* by the payee, such as a labor contract. Accounting does not *recognize* benefits arising from *executory contracts* as *assets*, nor does it recognize obligations arising from such contracts as *liabilities*. See *partially executory contract*.

exemption A term used for various amounts subtracted from *gross income* in computing *taxable income*. Usage does not call all such subtractions "exemptions." See *tax deduction*.

exercise Occurs when owners of an *option* or *warrant* purchase the *security* that the option entitles them to purchase.

exercise price See *option*.

exit value The *proceeds* that would be received if *assets* were disposed of (or the amounts the *firm* would have to pay to *transfer* a *liability*) in an *arm's-length transaction*. *Current selling price*; *net realizable value*. Some definitions of fair value in *U.S. GAAP* define *fair value* in terms of *exit value*.

expectancy theory The notion that people act in ways to obtain rewards and prevent penalties.

expected value The mean or arithmetic *average* of a statistical distribution or series of numbers.

expected value of (perfect) information Expected net benefits from an undertaking with (perfect) information minus expected net benefits of the undertaking without (perfect) information.

expendable fund In governmental accounting, a *fund* whose resources, *principal*, and *earnings* the governmental unit may distribute.

expenditure Payment of *cash* for *goods* or *services* received. Payment may occur at the time the purchaser receives the goods or services or at a later time. Virtually synonymous with *disbursement* except that disbursement is a broader term and includes all payments for goods or services. Contrast with *expense*.

expense As a noun, a decrease in *owners' equity* accompanying the decrease in *net assets* caused by selling *goods* or rendering *services* or by the passage of time; a "gone" (net) asset; an *expired cost*. Measure *expense* as the cost of the (net) assets used. Do not confuse with *expenditure* or *disbursement*, which may occur before, when, or after the *firm recognizes* the related expense. Use the word "cost" to refer to an item that still has *service potential* and is an asset. Exceptions sometimes occur, as in "Cost of Goods Sold." Use the word "expense" after the firm has used the asset's service potential. As a verb, "expense" means to designate an expenditure—past, current, or future—as a current expense.

expense account An *account* to accumulate *expenses*; *closed* to *retained earnings* at the end of the *accounting period*; a *temporary owners' equity account*; also used to describe a listing of expenses that an employee submits to the employer for reimbursement.

expense recognition The process of recording an *expense*, to appear in the current *period*'s *income statement*. Often, the timing of expense recognition results from the *matching principle*, which suggests the *firm recognize* the expense in the same period when it recognizes the *revenue* that expenses helped generate.

experience rating A term used in *insurance*, particularly unemployment insurance, to denote changes from ordinary rates to reflect extraordinarily large or small amounts of claims over time by the insured.

expired cost An *expense* or a *loss*.

***Exposure Draft* (*ED*)** A preliminary statement of the *FASB* showing the contents of a pronouncement being considered for enactment by the board.

external failure costs Costs that a *firm incurs* when it detects nonconforming *products* and *services* after delivering them to customers, including *warranty* repairs, product liability, marketing costs to reach consumers, and *sales allowances*.

external reporting Reporting to shareholders and the public, as opposed to *internal reporting* for *management*'s benefit. See *financial accounting*, and contrast with *managerial accounting*.

extraordinary gains (losses) (item) A *material expense* or *revenue* item characterized both by its unusual nature and by its infrequency of occurrence; appears along with its *income tax* effects separately in the *income statement*. A *firm* first *reports* its income after tax. It then reports three items, *net* of tax: Changes in *accounting principles*, extraordinary items, and *income from discontinued operations*. Accountants would probably classify a *loss* from an earthquake as an extraordinary item.

extrinsic rewards Rewards that come from outside the individual, such as rewards from a teacher, a parent, an organization, and a spouse; they include grades, money, praise, and prizes. Contrast with *intrinsic rewards*.

F

face (par) amount (value) The *nominal amount* due at *maturity* from a *bond* or *note* not including the contractual periodic *coupon* payment that may also come due on the same date. Good usage calls the corresponding amount of a stock certificate the *par* or *stated value*, whichever applies. Not all shares have such an amount; such shares are called "no-par."

facility-level activities Work that supports the entire organization. Examples include top *management*, human resources, and *research and development*.

factor For an *interest rate* r, a number of the form $(1 + r)^n$. When n is positive, then the number is a "*future value* factor" or an "accumulation factor." When n is negative, then the number is a "*discount factor*" or "*present value* factor." In another context, as a noun, a firm who buys accounts receivable from their owner; as a verb, the process of *factoring*; to *factor*.

factoring The process of buying *notes* or *accounts receivable* at a *discount* from the holder of the *debt*; from the holder's point of view, the selling of such notes or accounts. When the *transaction* involves a single note, usage calls the process "*discounting a note*."

factory Used synonymously with "manufacturing" as an adjective. See *manufacturing cost*.

factory burden *Manufacturing overhead*.

factory cost *Manufacturing cost*.

factory expense *Manufacturing overhead*. *Expense* is a poor term in this context because the item is a *product cost*.

factory overhead Usually an item of *manufacturing cost* other than *direct labor* or *direct materials*.

fair market price (value) See *fair value*.

fair presentation (fairness) One of the qualitative standards of financial reporting. When the *auditor's report* says that the *financial statements* "present fairly . . . ," the auditor means that the accounting alternatives used by the entity all comply with *U.S. GAAP*. In recent years, however, courts have ruled that conformity with *generally accepted accounting principles* may be insufficient grounds for an *opinion* that the statements are fair.

fair value, fair market price *Price* (*value*) negotiated at *arm's length* between a willing buyer and a willing seller, each acting rationally in his or her own self-interest in an unrestricted market, neither compelled to transact and both have reasonable knowledge of the relevant facts. The accountant may estimate this amount in the absence of a monetary *transaction*. *U.S. GAAP* presents a *hierarchy* of methods for measuring fair value, starting with observation of prices in market transactions. The *FASB* and *SEC* have made clear that accountants need not base fair value measurements of observed prices if the transactions generating those prices were in inactive markets. Accountants sometime measure fair value as the *present value* of expected *cash flows*. In some contexts, fair value differs from *market value* in that the former takes into account the identify, tastes, and utility of the specific parties to the transaction, while market value assumes typical buyers and sellers. In this sense a fair value may exceed a market value if the parties to a transactions attach value to the item than do other market participants. The market value of used silverware might be less than the fair value two siblings are willing to pay for a piece of their grandfather's collection.

fair-value hedge A hedge of an exposure to changes in the *fair value* of a *recognized asset* or *liability* or of an unrecognized *firm commitment*. If the firm uses *hedge accounting*, it will report both the hedged item and the hedging instrument at fair value, with *gains* and *losses* reported in *net income*. If the hedge is effective, the gains and losses on these items will offset each other, although both will appear in net income.

fair value option Investors in *marketable securities* must report *carrying value* at *fair value*, with changes reported in *income* for *trading securities* and in *other comprehensive income* for *securities available for sale*. This option allows the investor to report the carrying value of these items at fair value, with changes in fair value reported in income, not other comprehensive income. Issuers (see *issue*) of *debt* may, but need not, report the carrying value of these items at fair value, with changes in fair value reported in income, not other comprehensive income.

FAS *Statement of Financial Accounting Standards* of the *FASB*.

FASAC *Financial Accounting Standards Advisory Council*.

FASB (Financial Accounting Standards Board) An independent *board* responsible, since 1973, for establishing *U.S. GAAP*: *generally accepted accounting principles*. Its official pronouncements are *Statements of Financial Accounting Concepts* (*SFAC*), *Statements of Financial Accounting Standards* (*SFAS*), and *FASB Interpretations*. See also *Discussion Memorandum* and *Technical Bulletin*. The FASB publishes its *Codification* to bring all its guidance into a single place. Web Site: www.fasb.org.

FASB Interpretation FIN An official *FASB* statement interpreting the meaning of *Accounting Research Bulletins*, *APB Opinions*, and *Statements of Financial Accounting Standards*. *FIN 46*, for example, has curtailed the use of *off-balance-sheet financings*. Part of the FASB *Codification*.

FASB Technical Bulletin See *Technical Bulletin*.

favorable variance An excess of actual *revenues* over expected revenues; an excess of *standard cost* over actual cost.

federal income tax Income tax levied by the U.S. government on individuals and *corporations*.

Federal Insurance Contributions Act See *FICA*.

Federal Unemployment Tax Act See *FUTA*.

feedback The process of informing employees about how their actual performance compares with the expected or desired level of performance, in the hope that the information will reinforce desired behavior and reduce unproductive behavior.

FEI *Financial Executives International*.

FICA (Federal Insurance Contributions Act) The law that sets *Social Security taxes* and benefits.

fiduciary Someone responsible for the custody or administration of property belonging to another; for example, an executor (of an estate), *agent*, receiver (in *bankruptcy*), or trustee (of a trust).

FIFO (first-in, first-out) The *inventory flow assumption* that *firms* use to compute *ending inventory cost* from most recent purchases and *cost of goods sold* from oldest purchases including *beginning inventory*. FIFO describes *cost flow* from the viewpoint of the *income statement*. From the *bal-*

ance sheet perspective, *LISH* (last-in, still-here) describes this same cost flow. Contrast with *LIFO*.

finance As a verb, to supply with *funds* through the *issue* of *stocks*, *bonds*, *notes*, or *mortgages* or through the retention of *earnings*.

financial accounting The accounting for *assets*, *liabilities*, *equities*, *revenues*, *expenses*, and *cash flows* of a *business*; primarily concerned with the historical reporting, to external users, of the *financial position* and *operations* of an *entity* on a regular, periodic basis. Contrast with *managerial accounting*.

Financial Accounting Foundation The independent foundation (committee), governed by a *board* of trustees, that raises *funds* to support the *FASB* and *GASB*.

Financial Accounting Standards Advisory Council (FASAC) A committee of academics, preparers, *attestors*, and users giving advice to the *FASB* on matters of strategy and emerging issues. The council spends much of each meeting learning about current developments in standard-setting from the FASB staff.

Financial Accounting Standards Board *FASB*.

Financial Executives International (FEI) An organization of financial executives, such as chief accountants, *controllers*, and *treasurers*, of large *businesses*. In recent years, the *FEI* has been a critic of the *FASB* because it views many of the FASB requirements as burdensome while not *cost-effective*.

financial asset Cash or the ownership *interest* in a contract, such as an *account receivable*, that gives its owner the right to receive cash or another financial instrument. This definition is recursive. See *financial instrument*.

financial expense An *expense* incurred in raising or managing *funds*.

financial flexibility As defined by *SFAC No. 5*, "the ability of an *entity* to take effective actions to alter amounts and timing of *cash flows* so it can respond to unexpected needs and opportunities."

financial forecast See *financial projection* for definition and contrast.

financial instrument The *FASB* defines this term as follows.: "*Cash*, evidence of an ownership interest in an *entity*, or a contract that both:

[a] imposes on one entity a contractual obligation (1) to deliver cash or another *financial instrument* to a second entity or (2) to exchange financial instruments on potentially unfavorable terms with the second entity, and

[b] conveys to that second entity a contractual *right* (1) to receive cash or another financial instrument from the first entity or (2) to exchange other financial instruments on potentially favorable terms with the first entity."

For some *derivatives* that qualify as financial instruments the obligation can be to deliver a commodity.

financial leverage See *leverage*.

financial liability An obligation to pay a specified amount of *cash* or to give another financial liability. See *financial instrument*.

financial literacy The *NYSE* and the *NASDAQ* have required that companies who list their *shares* with these groups have an *audit* committee comprising at least three independent *board* members who are financially literate. The organizations mention the ability to understand the *financial statements*, but leave the definition of *financial literacy* to the individual boards to define. We think financial literacy in this sense requires the ability to understand the *transactions* requiring *critical accounting judgments* or estimates;

the accounting issues and choices for those judgments; what *management* chose, and why; and what opportunities management's choices provide for *earnings* management. See *critical accounting judgments*.

financial model Model, typically expressed with arithmetic relations, that allows an organization to test the interaction of economic variables in a variety of settings.

financial position (condition) Statement of the *assets* and *equities* of a *firm*; displayed as a *balance sheet*.

financial projection An estimate of *financial position*, results of *operations*, and changes in *cash flows* for one or more future *periods* based on a set of assumptions. If the assumptions do not represent the most likely outcomes, then *GAAS* call the estimate a "projection." If the assumptions represent the most *probable* outcomes, then GAAS call the estimate a "*forecast*." "Most probable" means that *management* has evaluated the assumptions and that they are management's judgment of the most likely set of conditions and most likely outcomes.

financial ratio See *ratio* and **Exhibit 6.14**.

financial reporting objectives Broad objectives that are intended to guide the development of specific *accounting standards*; set out by *FASB SFAC No. 1*.

financial reporting (process) Managers and *governing boards* of reporting *entities* select from *accounting principles* provided by standard setters and regulatory bodies and prepare *financial statements*, which independent external *auditors* attest to, to enable users of financial statements to make informed decisions.

Financial Reporting Release Series of releases, issued by the *SEC* since 1982; replaces the *Accounting Series Release*. See *SEC*.

financial statements The *balance sheet, income statement, statement of retained earnings, statement of cash flows*, statement of changes in *owners' equity* accounts, statement of *comprehensive income*, and *notes* thereto.

financial structure *Capital structure*.

financial vice president Person in charge of the entire accounting and finance *function*; typically one of the three most influential people in the company.

financial year Australia and UK: term for *fiscal year*.

financing (activities) Obtaining resources from (a) owners and providing them with a *return* on and a return of their *investment* and (b) *creditors* and repaying amounts borrowed (or otherwise settling the obligation). See *statement of cash flows*.

financing lease *Capital lease*.

finished goods (inventory account) Manufactured *product* ready for *sale*; a *current asset* (*inventory*) account.

finite life The owner of an *intangible asset* with an *indefinite life* does not *amortize* it, but tests it periodically for *impairment*. If the asset has non-indefinite life and a non-infinite life, it has a "finite life." If an asset does not have a finite life, it has an indefinite life; "indefinite" does not mean "infinite."

firm Informally, any *business entity*. (Strictly speaking, a firm is a *partnership*.)

firm commitment The *FASB*, in *SFAS No. 133* (**Codification Topic 815**), defines this as "an agreement with an unrelated party, binding on both parties and usually legally enforceable," which requires that the *firm* promise to pay a specified amount of a currency and that the firm has sufficient disincentives for nonpayment that the firm will probably make the payment. A firm commitment resembles a *liability*, but it is an *executory contract*, so is not a liability. *SFAS No. 133* (**Codification Topic 815**) allows the firm to *recognize*

certain financial *hedges* in the *balance sheet* if they hedge firm commitments. The FASB first used the term in *SFAS No. 52* (**Codification Topic 830**) but made the term more definite and more important in *SFAS No. 133* (**Codification Topic 815**). This is an early, perhaps the first, step in changing the recognition criteria for *assets* and liabilities to exclude the test that the future benefit (asset) or obligation (liability) not arise from an executory contract.

first-in, first-out See *FIFO*.

fiscal year A *period* of 12 consecutive months chosen by a *business* as the *accounting period* for *annual reports*, not necessarily a *natural business year* or a calendar year.

FISH An acronym, conceived by George H. Sorter, for *first-in, still-here*. FISH is the same *cost flow assumption* as *LIFO*. Many readers of accounting statements find it easier to think about inventory questions in terms of items still on hand. Think of LIFO in connection with *cost of goods sold* but of FISH in connection with *ending inventory*. See *LISH*.

fixed Said of an item that does not vary with volume of activity, at least in the short run.

fixed assets *Plant assets*.

fixed assets turnover (ratio) *Sales* divided by average total *fixed assets*. See *ratio* and **Exhibit 6.14**.

fixed benefit plan A *defined-benefit plan*.

fixed budget A plan that provides for specified amounts of *expenditures* and *receipts* that do not vary with activity levels; sometimes called a "*static budget*." Contrast with *flexible budget*.

fixed charges earned (coverage) ratio *Income* before *interest expense* and *income tax expense* divided by interest expense.

fixed cost; fixed expense An *expenditure* or *expense* that does not vary with volume of activity, at least in the *short run*. See *capacity costs*, which include *enabling costs* and *standby costs*, and *programmed costs* for various subdivisions of fixed costs. See *cost terminology*.

fixed cost price variance (spending variance) The difference between actual and *budgeted fixed costs*.

fixed interval sampling A method of choosing a sample: the analyst selects the first item from the *population* randomly, drawing the remaining sample items at equally spaced intervals.

fixed liability *Long-term* liability.

fixed manufacturing overhead applied The portion of *fixed manufacturing overhead cost allocated* to units produced during a *period*.

fixed overhead variance Difference between actual *fixed manufacturing costs* and fixed manufacturing costs applied to production in a *standard costing system*.

flexible budget *Budget* that projects *receipts* and *expenditures* as a *function* of activity levels. Contrast with *fixed budget*.

flexible budget allowance With respect to *manufacturing overhead*, the total *cost* that a *firm* should have *incurred* at the level of activity actually experienced during the *period*.

float *Checks* whose amounts the bank has *added* to the depositor's bank account but whose amounts the bank has not yet reduced from the *drawer*'s bank account. The number of shares publicly owned and available for trading, or the dollar *value* of a bond issue publicly owned and available for trading.

flow The change in the amount of an item over time. Contrast with *stock*.

flow assumption An assumption used when the *firm* makes a *withdrawal* from *inventory*. The firm must compute the *cost* of the withdrawal by a flow assumption if the firm does

Flow of Costs (and Sales Revenue)

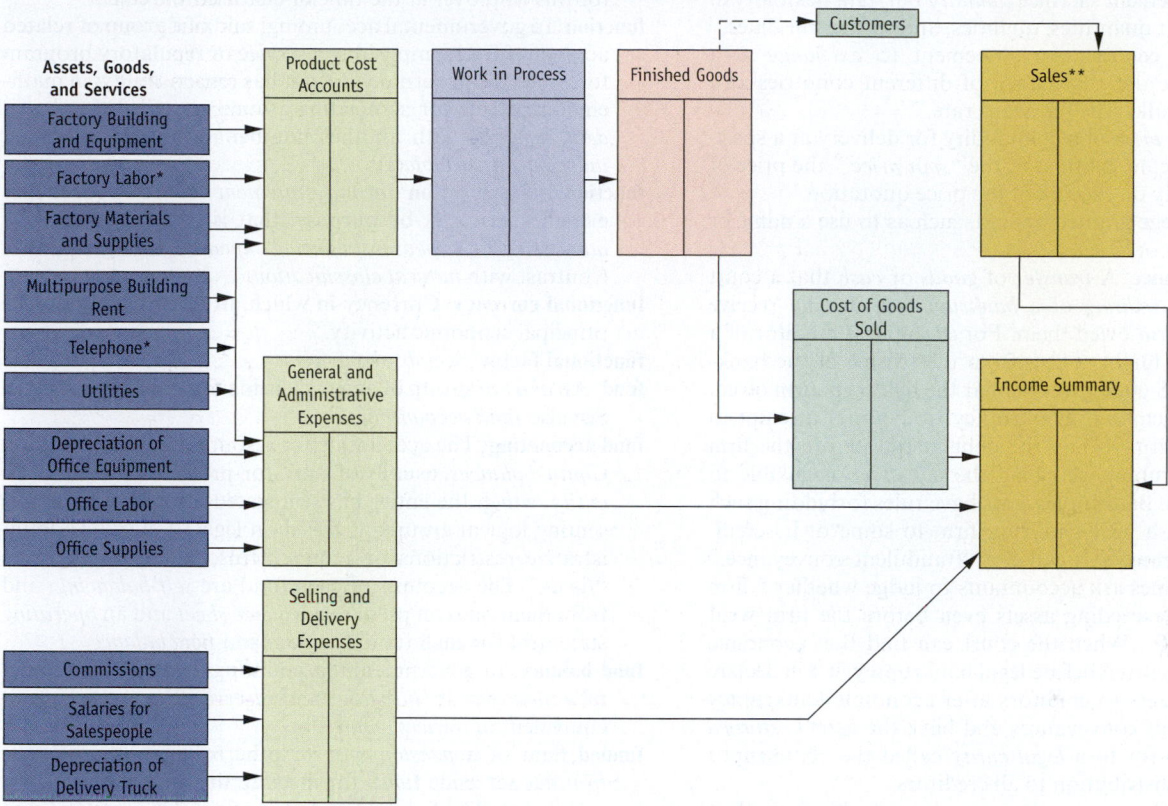

*The credit in the entry to record these items is usually to a payable; for all others, the credit is usually to an asset, or to an asset contra account.

**When the firm records sales to customers, it credits the Sales account. The debit is usually to Cash or Accounts Receivable.

not use the *specific identification method*. The usual flow assumptions are *FIFO*, *LIFO*, and *weighted average*.

flow of costs *Costs* passing through various classifications within an *entity* engaging, at least in part, in manufacturing activities. See the above diagram for a summary of *product* and *period cost flows*. See also *cost flow assumption*.

flow-through method Accounting for the *investment credit* to show all *income statement* benefits of the *credit* in the year of acquisition rather than spreading them over the life of the asset acquired (called the "*deferral method*"). The *APB* preferred the deferral method in *Opinion No. 2* (1962) but accepted the flow-through method in *Opinion No. 4* (1964); both now in **Codification Topic 740**.

FOB *Free on board* some location (for example, FOB shipping point, FOB destination). The *invoice price* includes delivery at seller's *expense* to that location. Title to *goods* usually passes from seller to buyer at the FOB location.

folio A page number or other identifying reference used in *posting* to indicate the source of entry.

footing Adding a column of figures.

footnotes A less-preferred word for the more detailed information than that provided in the *income statement*, *balance sheet*, *statement of retained earnings*, and *statement of cash flows*. These are an integral part of the statements, and the *auditor's report* covers them. Better to call them "notes," because they are not footnotes in the classic sense.

forecast See *financial projection* for definition and contrast.

foreclosure Occurs when a *lender* takes possession of property for his or her own use or *sale* after the *borrower* fails to make a required payment on a *mortgage*. Assume that the lender sells the property but that the *proceeds* of the sale are too small to cover the *outstanding balance* on the *loan* at the time of foreclosure. Under the terms of most mortgages, the lender becomes an unsecured *creditor* of the borrower for the still-unrecovered balance of the loan.

foreign currency For *financial statements* prepared in a given currency, any other currency.

foreign currency translation Reporting in the currency used in *financial statements* the amounts denominated or measured in a different currency.

foreign exchange gain or loss Gain or loss from holding *net* foreign *monetary items* during a *period* when the *exchange rate* changes.

foreign private issuer See *U.S. SEC registrant* for definition and contrast.

forfeited share A *share* to which a subscriber has lost title because of nonpayment of a *call*.

Form 10-K See *10-K*.

Form 10-Q See *10-Q*.

Form 20-F See *20-F*.

forward (commodity) contract An agreement to purchase or sell a specific commodity or *financial instrument* for a specified *price*, the *forward price*, at a specified date. Contrast with *futures contract*. Typically, forward contracts are not traded on organized *exchanges* (unlike futures contract), so the parties to the agreement sacrifice *liquidity* but gain flexibility in setting contract quantities, qualities, and settlement dates.

forward-exchange contract An agreement to *exchange* at a specified future date currencies of different countries at a specified rate called the "forward rate."

forward price The *price* of a commodity for delivery at a specified future date; in contrast to the "*spot price*," the price of that commodity on the day of the price quotation.

franchise A privilege granted or sold, such as to use a name or to sell *products* or *services*.

fraudulent conveyance A *transfer* of *goods* or *cash* that a court finds illegal. *Creditors* of a *bankrupt firm* usually receive less than the firm owed them. For example, a creditor of a bankrupt firm might collect from the trustee of the bankrupt firm only $.60 for every dollar the bankrupt firm owed. Creditors, anticipating bankruptcy, sometimes attempt to persuade the firm to pay the debt in full before the firm declares bankruptcy, reducing the *net assets* available to other creditors. Bankruptcy laws have rules forbidding such transfers from a near-bankrupt firm to some of its creditors. Such a transfer is called a "fraudulent conveyance." Courts sometimes ask accountants to judge whether a firm had *liabilities* exceeding assets even before the firm went into bankruptcy. When the court can find that economic bankruptcy occurred before legal bankruptcy, it will declare transfers of assets to creditors after economic bankruptcy to be fraudulent conveyances and have the assets *returned* to the trustees (or to a *legal entity* called the "bankrupt's estate") for redistribution to all creditors.

fraudulent financial reporting Intentional or reckless conduct that results in materially misleading *financial statements*. See *creative accounting*.

free cash flow This term has no standard meaning. Some *financial statement* analysts use it to mean *cash flow from operations + interest expense + income tax expense*. Others mean the excess of *cash flow from operations* over *cash flow for investing*. Usage varies so much that you should ascertain the meaning intended in context by this phrase.

free on board *FOB*.

freight-in The *cost* of freight or shipping *incurred* in acquiring *inventory*, preferably treated as a part of the cost of inventory; often shown temporarily in an *adjunct account* that the acquirer *closes* at the end of the *period* with other purchase accounts to the inventory account.

freight-out The *cost* of freight or shipping *incurred* in selling *inventory*, treated by the seller as a selling *expense* in the *period* of sale.

full absorption costing The *costing* method that assigns all types of *manufacturing costs* (*direct material, direct labor, fixed* and *variable overhead*) to units produced; required by *U.S. GAAP*; also called "*absorption costing*." Contrast with *variable costing*.

full costing, full costs The total *cost* of producing and selling a unit; often used in *long-term profitability* and pricing decisions. Full cost per unit equals *full absorption cost* per unit plus *marketing, administrative, interest*, and other *central corporate expenses*, per unit. The sum of full costs for all units equals total costs of the *firm*.

full disclosure The reporting policy requiring that all significant or *material* information appear in the *financial statements*. See *fair presentation*.

fully vested Said of a *pension plan* when an employee (or his or her estate) has *rights* to all the benefits granted by an employer's pension plan even if the employee does not work for this employer at the time of death or retirement.

function In governmental accounting, said of a group of related activities for accomplishing a service or regulatory program for which the governmental unit has responsibility; in mathematics, a rule for associating a number, called the *dependent variable*, with another number (or numbers), called *independent variable(s)*.

functional classification *Income statement* reporting form that classifies *expenses* by purpose, that is, *cost of goods sold, administrative expenses, financing expenses*, selling expenses. Contrast with *natural classification*.

functional currency Currency in which an *entity* carries out its principal economic activity.

functional factor See *obsolescence*.

fund An *asset* or group of assets set aside for a specific purpose. See also *fund accounting*.

fund accounting The accounting for resources, obligations, and *capital balances*, usually of a not-for-profit or governmental *entity*, which the entity has segregated into *accounts* representing logical groupings based on legal, donor, or administrative restrictions or requirements. The groupings are "*funds*." The accounts of each fund are *self-balancing*, and from them one can prepare a *balance sheet* and an *operating* statement for each fund. See *fund* and *fund balance*.

fund balance In governmental accounting, the excess of *assets* of a *fund* over its *liabilities* and *reserves*; the not-for-profit equivalent of *owners' equity*.

funded Said of a *pension plan* or other obligation when the *firm* has set aside *funds* for meeting the obligation when it comes due. The federal law for pension plans requires that the firm fund all *normal costs* when it *recognizes* them as *expenses*. In addition, the firm must fund *prior service cost* of pension plans over 30 or over 40 years, depending on the circumstances.

funding Replacing *short-term liabilities* with *long-term debt*.

funds Generally *working capital; current assets* less current *liabilities*; sometimes used to refer to *cash* or to cash and *marketable securities*.

funds provided by operations See *cash provided by operations*.

funds statement An informal name often used for the *statement of cash flows*.

funny money Said of *securities*, such as *convertible preferred stock, convertible bonds, options*, and *warrants*, that have aspects of *common shares* but that did not reduce reported *earnings per share* before the issuance of *APB Opinion No. 9* in 1966; now **Codification Topic 250**.

FUTA (Federal Unemployment Tax Act) Provides for *taxes* to be collected at the federal level, to help subsidize the individual states' administration of their unemployment compensation programs.

future value Value at a specified future date of a sum increased at a specified *interest rate*.

futures contract An agreement to purchase or sell a specific commodity or *financial instrument* for a specified *price*, at a specific future time or during a specified future *period*. Contrast with *forward contract*. When traded on an organized *exchange*, the exchange sets the minimum contract size and expiration date(s). The exchange requires that the holder of the contract settle in *cash* each day the fluctuations in the *value* of the contract. That is, each day, the exchange marks the contract to *market value*, called the "(daily) settlement price." A contract holder who has lost during the day must put up more cash, and a holder who has gained receives cash.

G

GAAP Generally accepted accounting principles; a singular noun. In the UK and elsewhere, this means "generally accepted accounting practices." In this book, we use *U.S. GAAP* for this concept. The international analog is *IFRS*.

GAAS Generally accepted auditing standards; a plural noun. Do not confuse with *GAS*.

gain In *financial accounting* contexts, the increase in *owners' equity* caused by a *transaction* that is not part of a *firm's* typical, day-to-day *operations* and not part of owners' *investment* or *withdrawals*. Accounting distinguishes the meaning of the term "gain" (or *loss*) from that of related terms. First, gains (and losses) generally refer to *nonoperating*, incidental, peripheral, or nonroutine *transactions*: gain on *sale* of *land* in contrast to *gross margin* on sale of *inventory*. Second, gains and losses are *net* concepts, not *gross* concepts: gain or loss results from subtracting some measure of *cost* from the measure of inflow. *Revenues* and *expenses*, on the other hand, are *gross* concepts; their difference is a *net* concept. Gain is nonroutine and net, profit or margin is routine and net; revenue from *continuing operations* is routine and gross; revenue from *discontinued operations* is nonroutine and gross. Loss is net but can be either routine ("loss on sale of inventory") or not ("loss on disposal of segment of business").

In *managerial accounting* and lay contexts, the difference between some measure of revenue or *receipts* or *proceeds* and some measure of costs, such as direct costs or variable costs or fully absorbed costs or full costs (see *cost terminology*). Because the word can have so many different meanings, careful writers should be explicit to designate one.

gain contingency See *contingency*.

GAS *Goods available for sale*. Do not confuse with *GAAS*.

GASB (Governmental Accounting Standards Board) An independent body responsible, since 1984, for establishing *accounting standards* for state and local government units. It is part of the *Financial Accounting Foundation*, parallel to the *FASB*, and currently consists of five members.

GbR (Gesellschaft des bürgerlichen Rechtes) Germany: a *partnership* whose members agree to *share* in specific aspects of their own separate *business* pursuits, such as an office. This partnership has no legal form and is not a separate accounting *entity*.

GDP Implicit Price Deflator (index) A *price index* issued quarterly by the Office of Business Economics of the U.S. Department of Commerce. This index attempts to trace the *price level* of all *goods* and *services* composing the *gross domestic product*. Contrast with *Consumer Price Index*.

gearing UK: *financial leverage*.

gearing adjustment A *revenue* representing part of a *holding gain*. Consider a *firm* that has part of its *assets* financed by *noncurrent liabilities* and that has experienced holding gains on its assets during a *period*. All the increase in wealth caused by the holding gains belongs to the owners; none typically belongs to the *lenders*. Some British accounting authorities believe that published *income statements* should show part of the holding gain in *income* for the period. The part they would report in income is the fraction of the gain equal to the fraction that debt composes of total financing; for example, if debt equals 40% of total *equities* and the holding gain equals $100 for the period, the amount to appear in income for the period would be $40. Usage calls that part the "*gearing adjustment*."

general debt A governmental unit's *debt* legally payable from general *revenues* and backed by the full faith and *credit* of the governmental unit.

general expenses *Operating expenses* other than those specifically identified as *cost of goods sold*, selling, *administrative*, and *research and development*.

general fixed asset (group of accounts) Accounts showing a governmental unit's *long-term assets* that are not accounted for in *enterprise*, trust, or intragovernmental service funds.

general fund A nonprofit *entity's assets* and *liabilities* not specifically earmarked for other purposes; the primary *operating fund* of a governmental unit.

general journal The formal record in which the *firm* records *transactions*, or summaries of similar *transactions*, in *journal entry* form as they occur. Use of the adjective "general" usually implies that the firm also uses various *special journals*, such as a *check register* or *sales journal*.

general ledger The name for the formal *ledger* containing all the *financial statement accounts*. It has equal *debits* and *credits*, as evidenced by the *trial balance*. Some of the accounts in the general ledger may be *control accounts*, supported by details contained in *subsidiary ledgers*.

general partner *Partnership* member who is personally liable for all debts of the partnership; contrast with *limited partner*.

general price index A measure of the aggregate *prices* of a wide range of *goods* and *services* in the economy at one time relative to the prices during a base *period*. See *Consumer Price Index* and *GDP Implicit Price Deflator*. Contrast with *specific price index*.

general price level–adjusted statements See *constant-dollar accounting*

general price-level changes Changes in the aggregate *prices* of a wide range of *goods* and *services* in the economy. These price measurements result from using a *general price index*. Contrast with *specific price changes*.

general purchasing power The command of the dollar over a wide range of *goods* and *services* in the economy. The general purchasing power of the dollar is inversely related to changes in a *general price index*. See *general price index*.

general purchasing-power accounting See *constant-dollar accounting*.

generally accepted accounting principles (GAAP) As previously defined by the *CAP*, *APB*, and now the *FASB*, the conventions, rules, and procedures necessary to define accepted accounting practice at a particular time; includes both broad guidelines and relatively detailed practices and procedures. In the United States the FASB defines *U.S. GAAP* to include accounting pronouncements of the *SEC* and other government agencies as well as a variety of authoritative sources, such as this book. In this book, we use U.S. GAAP for this concept. *SFAS No. 162 (2008)* (**Codification Topic number not yet assigned**) provides a *hierarchy* of GAAP standards, starting with *Statements of Financial Accounting Standards*, and *Interpretations* and ending with textbooks, such as this one. The international analog is *IFRS*.

generally accepted auditing standards (GAAS) The standards, as opposed to particular procedures, formerly promulgated by the *AICPA* (in *Statements on Auditing Standards*), and now promulgated by the *PCAOB*, and that concern "the *auditor's* professional quantities" and "the judgment exercised by him in the performance of his examination and in his *report*." Currently, there are ten such standards: three general ones (concerned with proficiency, *independence*, and degree of care to be exercised), three standards of field work, and four standards of reporting. The first standard of reporting requires that the *auditor's report* state whether the *firm* prepared the *financial statements* in accordance with *generally accepted accounting principles*. Thus the typical auditor's report says that the auditor conducted the examination in accordance with generally accepted auditing standards and that the firm prepared the statements in accordance with generally accepted accounting principles. See *auditor's report*.

geographic segment A single *operation* or a group of operations that are located in a particular geographic area and that generate *revenue*, incur *costs*, and have *assets* used in or associated with generating such revenue.

GIE (groupement d'intérêt économique) France: a *joint venture*, normally used for exports and *research-and-development* pooling.

GmbH (Gesellschaft mit beschränkter Haftung) Germany: a private company with an unlimited number of shareholders. *Transfer* of ownership can take place only with the consent of other shareholders. Contrast with *AG*.

goal congruence The idea that all members of an organization have incentives to perform for a common interest, such as *shareholder* wealth maximization for a *corporation*.

goals contrasted with strategies A goal describes an ending position, while a strategy describes a process of getting from the current position to the goal.

going concern (assumption) For accounting purposes, accountants' assumption that a *business* will remain in operation long enough to carry out all its current plans. This assumption partially justifies the *acquisition cost* basis rather than a *liquidation* or *exit value* basis, of accounting.

going public Said of a *business* when its *shares* become widely traded rather than being closely held by relatively few shareholders; issuing shares to the general investing public.

goods Items of *merchandise*, supplies, *raw materials*, or *finished goods*. Sometimes the meaning of "goods" is extended to include all *tangible* items, as in the phrase "*goods and services*."

goods available for sale (GAS) The sum of *beginning inventory* plus all acquisitions of *merchandise* or *finished goods* during an *accounting period*.

goods-in-process *Work-in-process*.

goodwill The excess of *cost* of an acquired *firm* (or *operating unit*) over the current *fair value* of the separately identifiable *net assets* of the acquired unit. Before the acquiring firm can *recognize goodwill*, it must assign a fair value to all identifiable assets, even those not recorded on the *books* of the acquired unit. For example, assume a firm has developed a *patent* that does not appear on its books because of *SFAS No. 2* (**Codification Topic 730**). If another company acquires the firm, the acquirer will recognize the patent at an amount equal to its estimated fair value. The acquirer will compute the amount of goodwill only after assigning values to all assets it can identify. Informally, the term indicates the value of good customer relations, high employee morale, a well-respected *business* name, and so on, all of which the firm or analyst expects to result in greater-than-normal earning power.

goodwill method A method of accounting for the *admission of a new partner* to a *partnership* when the new partner will receive a portion of *capital* different from the *value* of the *tangible assets* contributed as a fraction of tangible assets of the partnership. See *bonus method* for a description and contrast.

governing board *Board of directors*.

Governmental Accounting Standards Advisory Council A group that consults with the *GASB* on agenda, technical issues, and the assignment of priorities to projects. It comprises more than a dozen members representing various areas of expertise.

Governmental Accounting Standards Board *GASB*.

GPL (general price level) Usually used as an adjective modifying the word "accounting" to mean *constant-dollar accounting*.

GPLA (general price level–adjusted accounting) *Constant-dollar accounting*.

GPP (general purchasing power) Usually used as an adjective modifying the word "accounting" to mean *constant-dollar accounting*.

graded vesting Said of a *pension plan* in which not all employees currently have *fully vested* benefits. By law, the benefits must vest according to one of several formulas as time passes.

grandfather clause An *exemption* in new accounting pronouncements exempting *transactions* that occurred before a given date from the new accounting treatment.

gross Not adjusted or reduced by deductions or subtractions. Contrast with *net*, and see *gain* for a description of how the difference between net and gross affects usage of the terms *revenue*, *gain*, *expense*, and *loss*.

gross domestic product (GDP) The *market value* of all *goods* and *services* produced by *capital* or labor within a country, regardless of who owns the capital or of the nationality of the labor; most widely used measure of production within a country. Contrast with *gross national product* (*GNP*), which measures the market value of all goods and services produced with capital owned by, and labor services supplied by, the residents of that country regardless of where they work or where they own capital. In the United States in recent years, the difference between GDP and GNP equals about two-tenths of 1% of GDP.

gross income In *financial accounting* a nontechnical term meaning the same as *gross margin*. Income tax regulations define this term to mean, approximately, total *revenues*, from which the taxpayer makes various *deductions* to derive *taxable income*.

gross margin *Net sales* minus *cost of goods sold*.

gross margin percent $100 \times (1 - \text{cost of goods sold}/\text{net sales}) = 100 \times (\text{gross margin}/\text{net sales})$.

gross national product (GNP) See *gross domestic product* for definition and contrast.

gross price method (of recording purchase or sales discounts) The *firm* records the purchase (or *sale*) at the *invoice price*, not deducting the amounts of *discounts* available. Later, it uses a *contra account* to purchases (or sales) to record the amounts of discounts taken. Since information on discounts lapsed will not emerge from this system, most firms should prefer the *net price method* of recording *purchase discounts*.

gross profit *Gross margin*.

gross profit method A method of estimating *ending inventory* amounts. First, the firm measures *cost of goods sold* as some fraction of *sales*; then, it uses the *inventory equation* to *value ending inventory*.

gross profit ratio *Gross margin* divided by *net sales*.

gross sales All *sales* at *invoice prices*, not reduced by *discounts*, *allowances*, *returns*, or other adjustments.

group depreciation In calculating *depreciation charges*, a method that combines similar *assets* rather than depreciating them separately. It does not *recognize gain* or *loss* on retirement of items from the group until the *firm* sells or retires the last item in the group. See *composite life method*.

guarantee A promise to answer for payment of *debt* or performance of some obligation if the person liable for the debt or obligation fails to perform. A guarantee is a *contingency* of the *entity* making the promise. Often, writers use the words "guarantee" and "*warranty*" to mean the same thing. In precise usage, however, "guarantee" means some person's promise to perform a contractual obligation such as to pay a sum of *cash*, whereas "warranty" refers to promises about pieces of machinery or other *products*. See *warranty*.

H

half-year convention In *tax accounting* under *ACRS*, and sometimes in *financial accounting*, an assumption that the *firm* acquired *depreciable assets* at midyear of the year of acquisition. When the firm uses this convention, it computes the *depreciation charge* for the year as one-half the charge that it would have used if it had acquired the assets at the beginning of the year.

hardware The physical equipment or devices forming a computer and peripheral equipment.

hash total Used to establish accuracy of data processing; a control that takes the sum of data items not normally added together (e.g., the sum of a list of part numbers) and subsequently compares that sum with a computer-generated total of the same *values*. If the two sums are identical, then the analyst takes some comfort that the two lists are identical.

Hasselback An annual directory of accounting faculty at colleges and universities; gives information about the faculty's training and fields of specialization. James R. Hasselback, of the University of West Florida, has compiled the directory since the 1970s; Prentice-Hall distributes it.

health-care benefits obligation At any time, the *present value* of the nonpension benefits promised by an employer to employees during their retirement years. See *other postemployment benefits*.

hedge To reduce, perhaps cancel altogether, one *risk* the *entity* already bears, by purchasing a *security* or other *financial instrument*. For example, a farmer growing corn runs the risk that corn *prices* may decline before the corn matures and can be brought to market. Such a farmer can arrange to sell the corn now for future delivery, hedging the risk of corn price changes. A *firm* may have a *receivable* denominated in Euros due in six months. It runs the risk that the *exchange rate* between the dollar and the Euro will change and the firm will receive a smaller number of dollars in the future than it would receive from the same number of Euros received today. Such a firm may hedge its exposure to risk of changes in the exchange rate between dollars and Euros in a variety of ways. See *cash-flow hedge* and *fair-value hedge*. Do not confuse with *hedge accounting*.

hedge accounting *Firms* may, but need not, use hedge accounting. If the firm elects hedge accounting and if its hedging instrument is highly effective, it will report *gains* and *losses* on hedging instruments for *cash-flow hedges* in *other comprehensive income*, rather than in *net income*. For *fair-value hedges*, the firm using hedge accounting will report the hedged *asset* or *liability* at fair value; it reports the hedging instrument at fair value in any event.

held-to-maturity securities *Marketable debt securities* that a *firm* expects to, and has the ability to, hold to *maturity*; a classification important in *SFAS No. 115* (**Codification Topic**

320), which generally requires the owner to carry marketable securities on the *balance sheet* at *market value*, not at *cost*. Under *SFAS No. 115* (**Codification Topic 320**), the firm may show held-to-maturity *debt* securities at *amortized cost*. If the firm lacks either the expectation or the intent to hold the debt security to its maturity, then the firm will show that security at market value as a *security available for sale*.

hidden reserve An amount by which a *firm* has understated *owners' equity*, perhaps deliberately. The understatement arises from an undervaluation of *assets* or overvaluation of *liabilities*. By undervaluing assets on this *period's balance sheet*, the firm can overstate *net income* in some future period by disposing of the asset: actual *revenues* less artificially low *cost* of assets sold *yields* artificially high net income. No *account* in the *ledger* has this title.

hierarchy See *generally accepted accounting principles*.

hire-purchase agreement (contract) UK: a *lease* containing a purchase *option*.

historical cost (amount) *Acquisition cost; original cost; a sunk cost*.

historical cost/constant-dollar accounting Accounting based on *historical cost* valuations measured in *constant dollars*. The method restates *nonmonetary items* to reflect changes in the *general purchasing power* of the dollar since the time the *firm* acquired specific *assets* or *incurred* specific *liabilities*. The method recognizes a *gain* or *loss* on *monetary items* as the firm holds them over time *periods* when the general purchasing power of the dollar changes.

historical exchange rate The rate at which one currency converts into another at the date a *transaction* took place. Contrast with *current exchange rate*.

historical market interest rate Implicit interest rate (*internal rate of return*) in the *cash* inflows and outflows at the time of original issue of the *debt* instrument or the time of first acquisition of the *asset* by an *investor*. The *amortized cost method* of accounting for the *financial instrument* uses this rate throughout the accounting for the item.

historical summary A part of the *annual report* that shows items, such as *net income, revenues, expenses, asset*, and *equity* totals, *earnings per share*, and the like, for five or ten *periods* including the current one. Usually not as much detail appears in the *historical summary* as in *comparative statements*, which typically *report* as much detail for the two preceding years as for the current year. Annual reports almost always contain comparative statements but not always a historical summary.

holdback Under the terms of a contract, a portion of the progress payments that the customer need not pay until the contractor has fulfilled the contract or satisfied financial obligations to subcontractors.

holding company A company that confines its activities to owning *stock* in, and supervising *management* of, other companies. A holding company usually owns a controlling interest in—that is, more than 50% of the voting stock of—the companies whose stock it holds. Contrast with *mutual fund*. See *conglomerate*. In British usage, the term refers to any company with controlling interest in another company.

holding gain or loss Difference between end-of-period *price* and beginning-of-period price of an *asset* held during the *period*. The *financial statements* ordinarily do not separately report realized holding gains and losses. *Income* does not usually report unrealized gains at all, except on *trading securities* or other *securities* accounted for with the *fair value option*. See *lower of cost or market*. See *inventory profit* for further refinement, including *gains* on *assets* sold during the period.

holding gain or loss net of inflation Increase or decrease in the *current cost* of an *asset* while it is held; measured in units of *constant dollars*.

horizontal analysis *Time-series analysis*.

horizontal integration An organization's extension of activity in the same general line of *business* or its expansion into supplementary, complementary, or compatible *products*. Compare *vertical integration*.

house account An *account* with a customer who does not pay *sales commissions*. Or, from a sales person's perspective, a customer whose commissions go to another person or to the *firm* itself, the "house."

human resource accounting A term used to describe a variety of proposals that seek to report the importance of human resources—knowledgeable, trained, and loyal employees—in a company's earning process and total *assets*.

hurdle rate *Required rate of return* in a *discounted cash flow* analysis.

hybrid security *Security*, such as a *convertible bond*, containing elements of both *debt* and *owners' equity*.

hypothecation The *pledging* of property, without *transfer* of title or possession, to secure a *loan*.

I

IAA *Interamerican Accounting Association*.

IASB *International Accounting Standards Board*.

ICMA (Institute of Certified Management Accountants) See *CMA* and *Institute of Management Accountants*.

IDEA; Interactive Data Electronic Applications The *SEC's* 2009 replacement for *EDGAR*. Registrants will file SEC-required data in format suitable for storage and retrieval in IDEA. Each data item will have a tag—think bar code. By querying the database by company name and tag, the user can retrieve, in machine readable form, any particular item of data from the database. Users can then do their own *time-series* and *cross-section analysis* without keying any data.

ideal standard costs *Standard costs* set equal to those that a *firm* would *incur* under the best-possible conditions.

IFRS; International Financial Reporting Standard(s) Refers broadly to all the pronouncements of the *IASB* and, with numbers after the letters, to specific reporting standards issued by the IASB.

iGAAP Some writers' acronym for international *accounting standards* and *principles*. We use the term *IFRS*, short for *International Financial Reporting Standards*, for this body of accounting literature.

IIA *Institute of Internal Auditors*.

IMA *Institute of Management Accountants*.

impairment (loss) Reduction in *market value* of an *asset*. When the *firm* has information indicating that its long-lived assets, such as *plant*, identifiable *intangibles*, and *goodwill*, have declined in *market value* or will provide a smaller future benefit that originally anticipated, for items other than goodwill, it tests to see if the decline in value is so drastic that the expected future *cash flows* from the asset have declined below *carrying value*. In *U.S. GAAP*, if then-current carrying value exceeds the sum of expected cash flows, an asset impairment has occurred. At the time the firm judges that an impairment has occurred, the firm writes down the carrying value of the asset to its then-current *fair value*, which

is the market value of the asset or, if the firm cannot *assess* the market value, the expected *net present value* of the future cash flows. Goodwill has a different impairment test. In *IFRS*, the test for impairment compares the *recoverable amount* to the carrying value.

implicit interest Interest not paid or received. See *interest, imputed*. All transactions involving the deferred payment or receipt of *cash* involve interest, whether explicitly stated or not. The implicit interest on a single-payment *note* equals the difference between the amount collected at maturity and the amount lent at the start of the loan. One can compute the implicit *interest rate* per year for loans with a single cash inflow and a single cash outflow from the following equation:

$$\left[\frac{\text{Cash Received at Maturity}}{\text{Cash Lent}}\right]^{(1/t)} - 1$$

where *t* is the term of the loan in years; *t* need not be an integer.

imprest fund *Petty cash fund*.

improvement An *expenditure* to extend the *useful life* of an *asset* or to improve its performance (rate of *output, cost*) over that of the original *asset*; sometimes called *"betterment."* The *firm* capitalizes such expenditures as part of the asset's cost. Contrast with *maintenance* and *repair*.

imputed cost A *cost* that does not appear in accounting records, such as the *interest* that a *firm* could earn on *cash* spent to acquire inventories rather than, say, government *bonds*. Or, consider a firm that owns the buildings it occupies. This firm has an imputed cost for *rent* in an amount equal to what it would have to pay to use similar buildings owned by another or equal to the amount it could collect from someone renting the premises from the firm. *Opportunity cost*.

imputed interest See *interest, imputed*.

in the black (red) Operating at a profit (*loss*).

in-process R&D (IPR&D) When one *firm* acquires another, the acquired firm will often have *research and development* activities under way that, following *U.S. GAAP*, it has *expensed*. The acquiring firm will pay for these activities to the extent they have value and recognize them as *assets*. The acquirer will record the in-process R&D as an asset even if it does not intend to use it, so long as the R&D would have value for an unidentified market participant.

incentive compatible compensation Said of a compensation plan that induces managers to act for the interests of owners while acting also in their own interests. For example, consider that a time of rising prices and increasing inventories when using a *LIFO cost flow assumption* implies paying lower *income taxes* than using *FIFO*. A *bonus* scheme for managers based on accounting *net income* is not incentive-compatible because owners likely benefit more under LIFO, whereas managers benefit more if they report using FIFO. See *LIFO conformity rule* and *goal congruence*.

income Excess of *revenues* and *gains* over *expenses* and *losses* for a period; *net income* or *profit*. The term is sometimes used with an appropriate modifier to refer to the various intermediate amounts shown in a *multiple-step income statement* or to refer to revenues, as in "rental income." See *comprehensive income*.

income accounts *Revenue* and *expense accounts*.

income before taxes On the *income statement*, the difference between all *revenues* and *expenses* except *income tax* expense; *income from continuing operations* before subtractions for income taxes. Some would say all items of revenue, *gains*, expenses, and *losses* except income tax expense. Contrast with *net income*.

income determination See *determine*.

income distribution account *Temporary account* sometimes *debited* when the *firm* declares *dividends*; *closed* to *retained earnings*.

income from continuing operations As defined by *APB Opinion No. 30* (**Codification Topic 225**), all *revenues* less all *expenses* except for the following: results of *operations* (including *income tax* effects) that a *firm* has discontinued or will discontinue; *gains* or *losses*, including income tax effects, on disposal of segments of the *business*; gains or losses, including income tax effects, from *extraordinary items*; and the cumulative effect of *accounting changes*.

income (gains, losses) from discontinued operations *Income*, net of *tax* effects, from parts of the *business* that the *firm* has discontinued during the *period* or will discontinue in the near future. Accountants report such items on separate lines of the *income statement*, after *income from continuing operations* but before *extraordinary items*.

income (revenue) bond See *special revenue debt*.

income smoothing A method of timing *business transactions* or choosing *accounting principles* so that the *firm* reports smaller variations in *income* from year to year than it otherwise would. Although some managements set income smoothing as an objective, no standard-setter does.

income statement The statement of *revenues*, *expenses*, *gains*, and *losses* for the *period*, ending with *net income* for the period. Accountants usually show the *earnings-per-share* amount on the income statement; the *reconciliation* of beginning and ending *balances* of *retained earnings* may also appear in a combined statement of income and retained earnings. See *income from continuing operations*, *income from discontinued operations*, *extraordinary items*, *multiple-step*, and *single-step*.

income summary In problem solving, an *account* that serves as a surrogate for the *income statement*. In using an income summary, *close* all *revenue* accounts to the Income Summary as *credits* and all *expense* accounts as *debits*. The *balance* in the account, after you make all these *closing entries*, represents income or loss for the period. Then, close the income summary balance to *retained earnings*.

income tax An annual tax levied by the federal and other governments on the taxable income of an entity, which often does not equal pretax *net income* for *financial reporting*.

income tax expense Financial reporting amount of *income taxes payable* plus *deferred income taxes* arising from *temporary differences*. In the United States, *firms* often use the word *provision* in the account title. See *provision* for our reasons not to use the word.

income tax allocation See *deferred income tax* (*liability*) and *tax allocation: intra-statement*.

income tax reporting Computation of taxable income, in contrast to financial statement pretax *income*.

income taxes payable The amount the taxpayer pays to taxing authority for *income taxes*. As an *account* title, in capital letters, the *balance sheet liability* for taxes now owed to taxing authorities. In the sense of liability, contrast with *Deferred Income Taxes*.

incremental An adjective used to describe the increase in *cost*, *expense*, *investment*, *cash flow*, *revenue*, *profit*, and the like if the *firm* produces or sells one or more units or if it undertakes an activity. See *differential*.

incremental cost See *incremental*.

incur Said of an obligation of a *firm*, whether or not that obligation is *accrued*. For example, a firm incurs *interest expense* on a *loan* as time passes but accrues that interest only on payment dates or when it makes an *adjusting entry*.

indefinite life See *finite life* for definition and contrast. The concept arises in accounting for *intangibles*; the required accounting does not *amortize assets* with indefinite lives, but subjects them to periodic *impairment* tests. "Indefinite" does not mean "infinite."

indenture See *bond indenture*.

independence The mental attitude required of the *CPA* in performing the *attest* function. It implies that the CPA is impartial and that the members of the *auditing* CPA *firm* own no *stock* in the *corporation* being audited.

independent accountant The *CPA* who performs the *attest* function for a *firm*.

independent variable See *regression analysis*.

indexation An attempt by lawmakers or parties to a contract to cope with the effects of *inflation*. Amounts fixed in law or contracts are "indexed" when these amounts change as a given measure of price changes. For example, a so-called escalator clause (*COLA*—cost of living allowance or adjustment) in a labor contract might provide that hourly wages will be increased as the *Consumer Price Index* increases. Many economists have suggested the indexation of numbers fixed in the *income tax* laws. If, for example, the personal *exemption* is \$2,500 at the start of the period, if prices rise by 10% during the period, and if the personal exemption is indexed, then the personal exemption would automatically rise to \$2,750 (= \$2,500 + .10 × \$2,500) at the end of the period.

indirect cost pool Any grouping of individual *costs* that a *firm* does not identify with a *cost objective*.

indirect costs Production costs not easily associated with the production of specific *goods* and *services*; *overhead costs*. Accountants may *allocate* them on some *arbitrary* basis to specific *products* or departments.

indirect labor (material) cost An *indirect cost* for labor (*material*), such as for supervisors (supplies).

indirect method See *statement of cash flows*.

individual proprietorship *Sole proprietorship*.

Industry Audit Guides A series of *AICPA* publications providing specific accounting and *auditing principles* for specialized situations. Audit guides have been issued covering government contractors, state and local government units, investment companies, finance companies, brokers and dealers in *securities*, and many other subjects.

inescapable cost A *cost* that the *firm* or manager cannot avoid (see *avoidable cost*) because of an action. For example, if management shuts down two operating rooms in a hospital but still must employ security guards in unreduced numbers, the security costs are "inescapable" with respect to the decision to close the operating rooms.

inflation A time of generally rising *prices*. An increase in prices.

inflation accounting Strictly speaking, *constant-dollar accounting*. Some writers incorrectly use the term to mean *current cost accounting*.

information circular Canada: a document, accompanying the notice of a shareholders' meeting, prepared in connection with the solicitation of proxies by or on behalf of the *management* of the *corporation*. It contains information concerning the people making the solicitation, election of directors, appointment of *auditors*, and other matters to be acted on at the meeting.

information system A system, sometimes formal and sometimes informal, for collecting, processing, and communicating data that are useful for the managerial functions of decision making, planning, and control and for financial reporting under the *attest* requirement.

inherent interest rate *Implicit interest* rate.

initial cash flows Cash flows associated with the beginning of an investment project. Often include *asset cost*, freight and installation costs, reduced by *cash proceeds* from disposing of existing assets made redundant or unnecessary by the new project, and adjusted for the *income tax* effect of *gain* (*loss*) on disposal of existing assets.

insolvent Unable to pay *debts* when due; although most insolvent companies have *liabilities* that exceed *assets* in amount, this term applies to a company who is unable to pay even though assets exceed liabilities.

installment Partial payment of a *debt* or partial collection of a *receivable*, usually according to a contract.

installment contracts receivable The name used for *accounts receivable* when the *firm* uses the *installment method* of recognizing *revenue*. Its *contra account, unrealized gross margin*, appears on the *balance sheet* as a subtraction from the amount receivable.

installment sales Sales on *account* when the buyer promises to pay in several separate payments, called *installments*. The seller may, but need not, account for such sales using the *installment method*. If the seller accounts for installment sales with the *sales basis of revenue recognition* for financial reporting but with the installment method for income tax returns, then it will have *deferred income tax* (*liability*).

installment (sales) method Recognizing *revenue* and *expense* (or *gross margin*) from a *sales transaction* in proportion to the fraction of the selling price collected during a period; allowed by the *IRS* for *income tax* reporting but acceptable in *U.S. GAAP* only when the *firm* cannot estimate *cash* collections with reasonable precision. See *realized* (and *unrealized*) *gross margin*.

Institute of Internal Auditors (IIA) The national association of accountants who are engaged in internal *auditing*; administers a comprehensive professional examination. Those who pass the exam qualify to be designated *CIA* (*Certified Internal Auditor*).

Institute of Management Accountants (IMA) Formerly, the National Association of Accountants, NAA; a society open to those engaged in *management accounting*; oversees the *CMA* program.

insurance A contract for reimbursement of specific *losses*; purchased with insurance premiums. "Self-insurance" is not insurance but is merely the uninsured's willingness to assume the risk of *incurring* losses while saving the premium.

intangible asset A nonphysical *right* that gives a *firm* an exclusive or preferred position in the marketplace. Examples are *copyright, patent, trademark, goodwill, organization costs*, computer programs, licenses for any of the preceding, government licenses (e.g., broadcasting or the right to sell liquor), *leases, franchises*, mailing lists, exploration permits, import and export permits, construction permits, and marketing quotas. (Other items, such as advertising *costs*, are intangibles providing future benefits; neither *U.S. GAAP* nor *IFRS* treat them as accounting *assets*.) Accountants often define "intangible" using a "for example" list, as we have just done, because accounting has been unable to devise a definition of "intangible" that will include items such as those listed above but exclude *financial assets*, such as *stock* and *bond* certificates. Accountants classify these items as *tangibles*, even though they give their holders a preferred position in receiving *dividends* and *interest* payments. The *FASB* has defined "intangible" as "assets (not including financial assets) that lack physical substance." In most accounting contexts, the term "intangible assets" excludes *goodwill*, which, although it is intangible, gets its own classification.

Interactive Data Electronic Applications See *IDEA*.

Interamerican Accounting Association (IAA) An organization, headquartered in Miami, devoted to facilitating interaction between accounting practitioners in the Americas.

intercompany (intra-entity) elimination See *eliminations*.

intercompany (intra-entity) profit Profit within an organization. If one *affiliated company* sells to another, and the *goods* remain in the second company's *inventory* at the end of the *period*, then the first company has not yet realized a *profit* by a *sale* to an outsider. The profit is "intercompany profit," and the accountant eliminates it from *net income* when preparing *consolidated income statements* or when the firm uses the *equity method*.

intercompany (intra-entity) transaction *Transaction* between a *parent company* and a *subsidiary* or between subsidiaries in a *consolidated entity*; the accountant must eliminate the effects of such a transaction when preparing *consolidated financial statements*. See *intercompany profit*.

intercorporate investment Occurs when a given *corporation* owns *shares* or *debt* issued by another.

interdepartment monitoring An *internal control* device. The advantage of allocating *service department costs* to *production departments* stems from the incentives that this gives those charged with the *costs* to control the costs incurred in the service department. That process of having one group monitor the performance of another is interdepartment monitoring.

interest The *charge* or *cost* for using *cash*, usually borrowed *funds*. Interest on one's own cash used is an *opportunity cost, imputed interest*. The amount of interest for a *loan* is the total amount paid by a *borrower* to a *lender* less the amount paid by the lender to the borrower. Accounting seeks to *allocate* that interest over the time of the loan so that the interest rate (= interest charge/amount borrowed) stays constant each period. See *interest rate* for discussion of the quoted amount. See *effective interest rate* and *nominal interest rate*.

interest costs during construction A *firm* that self-constructs an *asset*, such as a new factory, will often borrow *funds* to help finance the project. Accounting views the *interest cost* on those borrowings as part of the cost of construction, not a *period expense*. Hence, the firm will *debit* the interest cost, not to *expense*, but to a Construction in Process account. This will increase the cost of the asset and increase subsequent *depreciation charges*. This process delays the recognition of the borrowing costs from immediate interest expense to later depreciation charges, which may themselves be immediate expenses or accumulated in *product cost* accounts (*work-in-process inventory*) until the firm sells the goods manufactured in the facility. A firm *capitalizes* interest costs on self construction even if it does not borrow for the construction, as long as it does have some debt. It will not capitalize any more interest than the amount of interest expense.

interest coverage ratio See *ratio* and **Exhibit 6.14**.

interest, imputed The difference between the *face amount* and the *present value* of a promise. If a *borrower* merely promises to pay a single amount, sometime later than the present, then the face amount the borrower will repay at *maturity* will exceed the present value (computed at a *fair market* interest rate, called the "imputed interest rate") of the promise. See also *imputed cost*.

interest factor One plus the *interest* rate.

interest method See *effective interest method*.

interest payment This entry warns you not to use the term "interest payment" until you understand why most often it incorrectly describes what you're talking about. "Interest" means a *charge* for using *funds*. Almost everyone in *business* refers to periodic payments a *borrower* makes to a *lender* (such as *coupon* payments on a *bond*) as "interest payments." This term causes confusion because, as **Chapter 10** explains, the amount of *interest expense* for a *period* almost never equals the amount of the payments for that same period. The periodic payment will always include some amount to pay interest to the lender, but not necessarily all interest *accrued* since the last payment. If the payment exceeds all accrued interest, then the payment will discharge some of the principal amount. Both payment of interest and payment of principal serve to reduce *debt* (the amount owed), so one all-purpose term suitable for the payment is *debt-service payment*. We urge you not to call these payments, nor to think of them as "interest payments" until you understand why they do not typically equal interest expense. You will never be wrong to call them "debt-service payments."

interest rate A *basis* used for computing the *cost* of borrowing *funds*; usually expressed as a *ratio* between the number of currency units (e.g., dollars) charged for a *period* of time and the number of currency units borrowed for that same period of time. When the writers and speakers do not state a period, they almost always mean a period of one year. See *interest*, *simple interest*, *compound interest*, *effective (interest) rate*, and *nominal interest rate*.

interest rate swap See *swap*.

interfund accounts In governmental accounting, the *accounts* that show *transactions* between *funds*, especially interfund receivables and *payables*.

interim statements Statements issued for *periods* less than the regular, annual *accounting period*. The *SEC* requires most *corporations* to issue interim statements on a quarterly basis. Many other countries require semi-annual reports. In preparing interim reports, a problem arises that the accountant can resolve only by understanding whether interim reports should report on the interim period (1) as a self-contained accounting period or (2) as an integral part of the year so that analysts can make forecasts of annual performance. For example, assume that at the end of the first quarter, a retailer has *dipped into old LIFO layers*, depleting its *inventory*, so that it computes *LIFO cost of goods sold* artificially low and *net income* artificially high, relative to the amounts the *firm* would have computed if it had made the "normal" purchases, equal to or greater than *sales*. The retailer expects to purchase inventory sufficiently large so that when it computes cost of goods sold for the year, there will be no dips into old LIFO layers and *income* will not be artificially high. The first approach will compute the quarterly income from low cost of goods sold using data for the dips that have actually occurred by the end of the quarter. The second approach will compute quarterly income from

cost of goods sold assuming that purchases were equal to "normal" amounts and that the firm did not dip into old LIFO layers. *APB Opinion No. 28* and the SEC require that interim reports be constructed largely to satisfy the second purpose. *IFRS* rules would require the first alternative, but IFRS forbids LIFO, so we would need a different example.

internal audit, internal auditor An *audit* conducted by the *firm*'s own employees, called "internal auditors," to ascertain whether the firm's *internal control* procedures work as planned. A firm can contract with outside accountants to provide internal audit services, so long as the outsiders do not work for the firm that audits the *financial statements* for *GAAS* reporting. Contrast with an external audit conducted by a *CPA*.

internal controls Policies and procedures designed to provide *management* with reasonable assurances that employees behave in a way that enables the *firm* to meet its organizational goals. See *control system*.

internal failure costs Costs incurred when a *firm* detects nonconforming *products* and *services* before delivering them to customers; these include scrap, rework, and retesting.

internal rate of return (IRR) The *discount rate* that equates the *net present value* of a stream of *cash* outflows and inflows to zero.

internal reporting Reporting for *management*'s use in planning and control. Contrast with *external reporting* for *financial statement* users.

Internal Revenue Service (IRS) Agency of the U.S. Treasury Department responsible for administering the Internal Revenue Code and collecting *income* and certain other *taxes*.

International Accounting Standards Board (IASB) An organization that sets international *accounting standards* (Web site: www.iasb.org). Successor to the International Accounting Standards Committee, IASC, which it superseded in 2001. A good site for tracing developments in international accounting is www.iasplus.com, maintained by the worldwide Deloitte *firm*, and recommended by the renowned expert on international accounting, Professor Stephen A. Zeff of Rice University.

International Organization of Securities Commissions *IOSCO*.

interperiod tax allocation See *deferred income tax (liability)*.

interpolation The estimation of an unknown number intermediate between two (or more) known numbers.

Interpretations See *FASB Interpretation*.

intrastatement tax allocation See *tax allocation: intrastatement*.

intrinsic rewards Rewards that come from within the individual, such as the satisfaction from studying hard, providing help to someone in need, or doing a good job. Contrast with *extrinsic rewards*.

intrinsic value of stock option At any time, the excess of the *market price* over the *exercise price* of a *stock option*.

inventoriable costs *Costs incurred* that the *firm* adds to the cost of manufactured *products*; *product costs (assets)* as opposed to *period expenses*.

inventory As a noun, the *balance* in an *asset account*, such as *raw materials*, supplies, *work-in-process*, and *finished goods*; as a verb, to calculate the *cost* of *goods* on hand at a given time or to count items on hand physically. Items held for sale or for production of items produced for sale.

inventory equation *Beginning inventory + net* additions − *withdrawals = ending inventory*. Ordinarily, additions are net purchases, and withdrawals are *cost of goods sold*. Notice that *ending inventory*, appearing on the *balance sheet*, and cost of goods sold, appearing on the *income statement*, must add to a fixed sum. The larger is one; the smaller must be the other. In valuing inventories, the *firm* usually knows beginning inventory and net purchases. Some *inventory methods* (for example, some applications of the *retail inventory method*) measure costs of goods sold and use the equation to find the cost of ending inventory. Most methods measure cost of goods sold (withdrawals) and use the equation to find the ending inventory. In *current cost* (in contrast to *historical cost*) *accounting*, additions (in the equation) include *holding gains*, whether realized or not. Thus the current cost inventory equation is as follows: Beginning Inventory (at Current Cost) + Purchases (where Current Cost is Historical Cost) + Holding Gains (whether Realized or Not) − Ending Inventory (at Current Cost) = Cost of Goods Sold (Current Cost).

inventory holding gains See *inventory profit*.

inventory layer See *LIFO inventory layer*.

inventory method A vague term, best avoided. In order to specify the accounting for *inventory*, one needs to make four choices: a *cost basis* (such as *historical cost* or *lower of cost or market* or *fair value*), an inclusion rule for manufactured inventories (such as *absorption costing* or *direct costing*), a *cost flow assumption* (such as *FIFO* or *LIFO* or *weighted average* or, avoiding an assumption—*specific identification*), and the time for making computations (*periodic inventory*— one per period, or *perpetual inventory*). Imprecise usage often refers to "FIFO basis," "periodic basis," "absorption costing basis," and other combinations. Strictly speaking "inventory basis" refers to the cost basis.

inventory profit A term with several possible meanings. Consider the data in the accompanying illustration. The *firm* uses a *FIFO cost flow assumption* and derives its *historical cost* data. The assumed *current cost* data resemble those that the *FASB* suggested in *SFAS No. 89* (**Codification Topic 255**). The term *income from continuing operations* refers to *revenues* less *expenses* based on current, rather than historical, costs. To that subtotal, add *realized holding gains* to arrive at *realized* (conventional) *income*. To that, add *unrealized holding gains* to arrive at economic income. The term "inventory profit" often refers (for example in some *SEC* releases) to the realized holding gain, $110 in the illustration. The amount of inventory profit will usually be *material* when the firm uses FIFO and when *prices* rise. Other analysts, including us, prefer to use the term "inventory profit" to refer to the total holding gain, $300 (= $110 + $190, both realized and unrealized), but writers use this meaning less often. In *periods* of rising prices and increasing inventories, the realized holding gains under a FIFO cost flow assumption will exceed those under LIFO. In the illustration, for example, assume under LIFO that the historical *cost of goods sold* is $4,800, that historical LIFO cost of *beginning inventory* is $600, and that historical LIFO cost of *ending inventory* is $800. Then income from continuing operations, based on current costs, remains $350 (= $5,200 − $4,850), realized holding gains are $50 (= $4,850 − $4,800), realized income is $400 (= $350 + $50), the unrealized holding gain for the year is $250 [= ($1,550 − $800) − ($1,100 − $600)], and economic income is $650 (= $350 + $50 + $250). The cost flow assumption has only one real effect on this series of calculations: the *split* of the total holding gain into realized and unrealized portions. Thus, economic income does not depend on the cost flow assumption. Holding gains total $300 in the illustration. The choice of cost flow assumption determines the portion reported as realized.

Inventory Profit Illustration

	(Historical) Acquisition Cost Assuming FIFO	Current Cost
ASSUMED DATA		
Inventory, 1/1	$ 900	$1,100
Inventory, 12/31	1,160	1,550
Cost of Goods Sold for the Year	4,740	4,850
Sales for the Year	$5,200	$5,200
INCOME STATEMENT FOR THE YEAR		
Sales	$5,200	$5,200
Cost of Goods Sold	4,740	4,850
(1) Income from Continuing Operations		$ 350
Realized Holding Gains		110[a]
(2) Realized Income = Conventional Net Income (under FIFO)	$ 460	$ 460
Unrealized Holding Gain		190[b]
(3) Economic Income		$ 650

[a]Realized holding gain during a period is current cost of goods sold less historical cost of goods sold; for the year the realized holding gain under FIFO is $110 = $4,850 − $4,740. Some refer to this as "inventory profit."

[b]The total unrealized holding gain at any time is current cost of inventory on hand at that time less historical cost of that inventory. The unrealized holding gain during a period is the unrealized holding gain at the end of the period less the unrealized holding gain prior to this year. The unrealized holding gain at the beginning of the year in this example is: $200 = $1,100 − $900. Unrealized holding gain during the year = ($1,550 − $1,160) − ($1,100 − $900) = $390 − $200 = $190.

inventory turnover (ratio) Number of times the *firm* sells the average *inventory* during a *period*; *cost of goods sold* for a period divided by *average* inventory for the period. See *ratio* and **Exhibit 6.14**.

invested capital *Contributed capital*.

investee A company in which another *entity*, the "investor," owns *stock*.

investing activities Acquiring and selling *securities* or productive *assets* expected to produce *revenue* over several *periods*.

investment An *expenditure* to acquire property or other *assets* in order to produce *revenue*; the asset so acquired; hence a current *expenditure* made in anticipation of future *income*; said of other companies' *securities* held for the *long term* and appearing in a separate section of the *balance sheet*; in this context, contrast with *marketable securities*.

investment in securities See *investment*.

investment center A *responsibility center*, with control over *revenues*, *costs*, and *assets*.

investment credit A reduction in *income tax liability* sometimes granted by the federal government to *firms* that buy new equipment. This item is a *credit* in that the taxpayer deducts it from the *tax* bill, not from pretax income. The tax credit has been a given percentage of the purchase *price* of the *assets* purchased. The government has changed the actual rules and rates over the years. As of 2009, there is no investment credit. See *flow-through method* and *carryforward*.

investment decision The decision whether to undertake an action involving production of *goods* or services; contrast with financing decision.

investment tax credit *Investment credit.*

investment turnover ratio A term that means the same thing as *total assets turnover ratio.*

investments A *balance sheet* heading for *tangible assets* held for *periods* longer than the *operating cycle* and not used in *revenue* production (assets not meeting the definitions of *current assets* or *property, plant, and equipment* or *land* or *goodwill* or other intangibles).

investor See *investee* for definition and contrast.

invoice A document showing the details of a *sale* or purchase *transaction.*

IOSCO (International Organization of Securities Commissions) The name, since 1983, of a confederation of regulators of *securities* and futures markets. Members come from over 80 countries. The IOSCO encourages the *IASB* to eliminate accounting alternatives and to ensure that *accounting standards* are detailed and complete, with *adequate disclosure* requirements, and that *financial statements* are user-friendly.

I.O.U. "I owe you." An informal document acknowledging a debt, setting out the amount of the debt and signed by the debtor.

IRR *Internal rate of return.*

IRS *Internal Revenue Service.*

isoprofit line On a graph showing feasible production possibilities of two *products* that require the use of the same, limited resources, a line showing all feasible production possibility combinations with the same *profit* or, perhaps, *contribution margin.*

issue A *corporation*'s *exchange* of its *stock* (or *bonds*) for *cash* or other *assets.* Terminology says the corporation, the "issuer," "issues," not "sells," that stock (or bonds). Also used in the context of *withdrawing* supplies or *materials* from *inventory* for use in *operations* and of drawing a *check.*

issued shares Those *shares* of *authorized capital stock* that a *corporation* has distributed to the shareholders. See *issue.* Shares of *treasury stock* are legally issued but are not *outstanding* for the purpose of voting, *dividend declarations*, and *earnings-per-share* calculations.

J

JIT See *just-in-time inventory.*

job cost sheet A schedule showing actual or budgeted inputs for an order.

job development credit The name used for the *investment credit* in the 1971 *tax* law, since repealed, on this subject.

job (-order) costing Accumulation of *costs* for a particular identifiable batch of *product*, known as a *job*, as it moves through production.

jobs Customized *products.*

joint cost Cost of simultaneously producing or otherwise acquiring two or more *products*, called *joint products*, that a *firm* must, by the nature of the process, produce or acquire together, such as the cost of beef and hides of cattle or cocoa butter and cocoa powder from cocoa beans. Generally, accounting *allocates* the joint costs of production to the individual products in proportion to their respective *sales* value (or, sometimes and usually not preferred, their respective physical quantities) at the *split-off* point. Such allocations should not affect decision making; that is, good decisions do not depend on any specific allocation or whether the firm

allocated the joint costs at all. Other examples include *central corporate expenses* and *overhead* of a department when it manufactures several products. See *common cost* and *sterilized allocation.*

joint cost allocation See *joint cost.*

joint process A process that converts a common input into several *outputs.*

joint product One of two or more *outputs* with significant *value* that a *firm* must produce or acquire simultaneously. See *by-product* and *joint cost.*

joint venture Two or more *firms* invest in a project or company or *division*, sharing *risks* and rewards of ownership and *management.*

journal The place where the *firm* records *transactions* as they occur; the *book of original entry.* Typically, a computerized database.

journal entry A dated *journal* recording, showing the *accounts* affected, of equal *debits* and *credits*, with an explanation of the *transaction*, if necessary.

Journal of Accountancy A monthly publication of the *AICPA.*

Journal of Accounting and Economics Scholarly journal published by the William E. Simon Graduate School of Business Administration of the University of Rochester.

Journal of Accounting Research Scholarly journal containing articles on theoretical and empirical aspects of accounting; published by the Graduate School of Business of the University of Chicago.

journal voucher A *voucher* documenting (and sometimes authorizing) a *transaction*, leading to an entry in the *journal.*

journalize To make an entry in a *journal.*

judgment(al) sampling A method of choosing a sample in which the analyst subjectively selects items for examination, in contrast to selecting them by statistical methods. Compare *random sampling.*

junk bond A low-rated *bond* that lacks the merit and characteristics of an investment-grade bond. It offers high yields, typically in excess of 15% per year, but also possesses high *risk* of default. Sometimes writers, less pejoratively, call these "high-yield bonds." No clear line separates junk from nonjunk bonds.

just-in-time inventory (production) (JIT) In managing *inventory* for manufacturing, a system in which a *firm* purchases or manufactures each component just before the firm uses it. Contrast with systems in which firms acquire or manufacture many parts in advance of needs. JIT systems have much smaller carrying *costs* for inventory, ideally none, but run higher risks of *incurring stockout* costs. As fuel costs have soared, JIT has become less cost effective.

K

k Two to the tenth power (2^{10} or 1,024). The one-letter abbreviation derives from the first letter of the prefix "kilo-" (which means 1,000 in decimal notation).

Kaizen costing A *management* concept that seeks continuous improvements, likely occurring in small incremental amounts, by refinements of all components of a production process.

KG (Kommanditgesellschaft) Germany: similar to a general *partnership* (*OHG*) except that some of its members may limit their liability. One of the partners must be a *general partner* with unlimited *liability.*

kiting A term with slightly different meanings in banking and auditing contexts. In both, however, it refers to the wrongful practice of taking advantage of the *float*, the time that elapses between the deposit of a *check* in one bank and its collection at another. In the banking context, an individual deposits in Bank A a check written on Bank B. He (or she) then writes checks against the deposit created in Bank A. Several days later, he deposits in Bank B a check written on Bank A, to cover the original check written on Bank B. Still later, he deposits in Bank A a check written on Bank B. The process of covering the deposit in Bank A with a check written on Bank B and vice versa continues until the person can arrange an actual deposit of *cash*. In the auditing context, kiting refers to a form of *window dressing* in which the *firm* makes the amount of the *account* Cash in Bank appear larger than it actually is by depositing in Bank A a check written on Bank B without recording the check written on Bank B in the *check register* until after the close of the *accounting period*.

know-how Technical or *business* information that is of the type defined under *trade secret* but that a *firm* does not maintain as a secret. The rules of accounting for this *asset* are the same as for other *intangibles*.

L

labor efficiency variance Measures labor productivity by multiplying the *standard* labor *price* times the difference between the standard labor hours and the actual labor hours.

labor price (or wage) variance Measures the difference between the actual and *standard* labor prices (*wage* rates).

labor variances The *price* (or *rate*) and *quantity* (or *usage*) variances for *direct labor* inputs in a *standard costing system*.

laid-down cost Canada and UK: the sum of all direct *costs incurred* for procurement of *goods* up to the time of physical receipt, such as *invoice* cost plus customs and excise duties, freight and cartage.

land An *asset* shown at *acquisition cost* plus the *cost* of any nondepreciable *improvements*; in accounting, implies use as a *plant* or office site rather than as a *natural resource*, such as timberland or farmland.

lapping (accounts receivable) The theft, by an employee, of *cash* sent in by a customer to discharge the latter's *payable*. The employee conceals the theft from the first customer by using cash received from a second customer. The employee conceals the theft from the second customer by using cash received from a third customer, and so on. The process continues until the thief returns the funds or can make the theft permanent by creating a fictitious *expense* or receivable write-off or until someone discovers the fraud.

lapse To expire; said of, for example, an *insurance* policy; discounts that the seller makes available for prompt payment and that the purchaser does not take are said to "lapse."

last-in, first-out See *LIFO*.

layer See *LIFO inventory layer*.

lead time The time that elapses between placing an order and receiving the *goods* or *services* ordered.

learning curve A mathematical expression of the phenomenon that *incremental* unit *costs* to produce decrease as managers and labor gain experience from practice.

lease A contract calling for the *lessee* (user) to pay the *lessor* (owner) for the use of an *asset*. A *cancelable lease* allows the lessee to cancel at any time. A noncancelable lease requires payments from the lessee for the life of the lease and usually shares many of the economic characteristics of *debt financing*. Most *long-term* noncancelable leases meet the usual criteria for classifying them as *liabilities*, and *U.S. GAAP*

requires the *firm* to show them as liabilities. *SFAS No. 13* (**Codification Topic 840**) and the *SEC* require disclosure, in notes to the financial statements, of the commitments for long-term noncancelable leases. See *capital lease*, *financing lease*, and *operating lease*.

leasehold The *asset* representing the *right* of the *lessee* to use leased property. See *lease* and *leasehold improvement*.

leasehold improvement An *improvement* to leased property. The *firm* should *amortize* it over the *service life* or the life of the *lease*, whichever is shorter.

least and latest rule Paying the least amount of *taxes* as late as possible within the law to minimize the *present value* of tax payments for a given set of *operations*. Sensible taxpayers will follow this rule. When a taxpayer knows that tax rates will increase later, the taxpayer may reduce the present value of the tax burden by paying lower taxes sooner. Each set of circumstances requires its own computations.

ledger A *book* of *accounts*; book of final entry. See *general ledger* and *subsidiary ledger*. Contrast with *journal*.

legal capital The amount of *contributed capital* that, according to state law, the *firm* must keep permanently in the firm as protection for *creditors*.

legal entity See *entity*.

lender See *loan*.

lessee See *lease*.

lessor See *lease*.

letter stock Privately placed *common shares*; so called because the *SEC* requires the purchaser to sign a letter of intent not to resell the *shares*.

leverage More than proportional result from extra effort or *financing*. Some measure of *output* increases faster than the measure of input. "Operating leverage" refers to the tendency of *net income* to rise at a faster rate than sales in the presence of *fixed costs*. A doubling of *sales*, for example, usually implies a more than doubling of net income. "Financial leverage" (or "capital leverage") refers to an increase in rate of return larger than the increase in explicit financing costs—the increased rate of return on *owners' equity* (See *ratio* and **Exhibit 6.14**) when an *investment* earns a return larger than the after-tax *interest rate* paid for *debt* financing. Because the *interest charges* on debt usually do not change, any *incremental income* benefits owners and none benefits *debtors*. When writers use the term "leverage" without a qualifying adjective, the term usually refers to financial leverage, the use of *long-term* debt in securing *funds* for the *entity*.

leveraged lease A special form of lease involving three parties: a *lender*, a *lessor*, and a *lessee*. The lender, such as a bank or *insurance* company, lends a portion, say 80%, of the *cash* required for acquiring the *asset*. The lessor puts up the remainder, 20%, of the cash required. The lessor acquires the asset with the cash, using the asset as *security* for the *loan*, and leases it to the lessee on a *noncancelable* basis. The lessee makes periodic lease payments to the lessor, who in turn makes payments on the loan to the lender. Typically, the lessor has no obligation for the debt to the lender other than transferring a portion of the receipts from the lessee. If the lessee should *default* on the required lease payments, then the lender can repossess the leased asset. The lessor usually has the right to benefit from the tax deductions for *depreciation* on the asset, for *interest expense* on the loan from the lender, and for any *investment credit*. The lease is leveraged in the sense that the lessor, who takes most of the risks and enjoys most of the rewards of ownership, usually borrows most of the funds needed to acquire the asset. See *leverage*.

liability (definition and recognition) An obligation to pay a definite (or reasonably definite) amount at a definite (or reasonably definite) time in *return* for a past or current benefit (that is, the obligation arises from a *transaction* that is not an *executory contract*); a probable future sacrifice of economic benefits arising from present obligations of a particular *entity* to *transfer assets* or to provide *services* to other entities in the future as a result of past *transactions* or events. *SFAC No. 6* says that "*probable*" refers to that which we can reasonably expect or believe but that is neither certain nor proved. A liability has three essential characteristics: (1) the obligation to transfer *assets* or services has a specified or knowable date, (2) the entity has little or no discretion to avoid the transfer, and (3) the event causing the obligation has already happened, that is, it is not *executory*. Accounting does not recognize many obligations to pay definite amounts at definite times because it views the mutual obligations of the parties as executory, a mere *exchange* of promises.

lien The right of person A to satisfy a claim against person B by holding B's property as *security* or by seizing B's property.

life annuity A *contingent annuity* in which payments cease at the death of a specified person(s), usually the *annuitant(s)*.

LIFO (last-in, first-out) An *inventory flow assumption* in which the *cost of goods sold* equals the *cost* of the most recently acquired units and a *firm* computes the *ending inventory cost* from the costs of the oldest units. In periods of rising *prices* and increasing *inventories*, LIFO leads to higher reported *expenses* and therefore lower reported *income* and lower *balance sheet* inventories than does *FIFO*. *IFRS* does not allow LIFO. Contrast with *FIFO*. See *FISH* and *inventory profit*.

LIFO conformity rule The *IRS* rule requiring that companies that use a *LIFO cost flow assumption* for *income taxes* must also use LIFO in computing *income* reported in *financial statements* and forbidding the disclosure of *pro forma* results from using any other cost flow assumption. The *SEC* requires *firms* using LIFO to disclose *balance sheet inventory* amounts valued at *replacement cost* or *current cost*, which is effectively *FIFO* or *average cost*.

LIFO, dollar-value method See *dollar-value LIFO method*.

LIFO inventory layer A portion of LIFO inventory *cost* on the *balance sheet*. The *ending inventory* in physical quantity will usually exceed the *beginning inventory*. The *LIFO cost flow assumption* assigns to this increase in physical quantities a cost computed from the *prices* of the earliest purchases during the year. The LIFO inventory then consists of *layers*, sometimes called "slices," which typically consist of relatively small amounts of physical quantities from each of the past years when purchases in physical units exceeded sales in units. Each layer carries the prices from near the beginning of the *period* when the *firm* acquired it. The earliest layers will typically (in periods of rising prices) have prices much less than current prices. If inventory quantities should decline in a subsequent period—a "dip into old LIFO layers"—the latest layers enter *cost of goods sold* first.

LIFO liquidation A firm using *LIFO* uses more *inventory* than it acquired during a *period*, hence uses some of the inventory in its *LIFO layers*, the most recent ones first.

LIFO reserve Unrealized holding gain in *ending inventory*; current or *FIFO historical cost* of ending inventory less *LIFO* historical cost. A better term for this concept is "excess of *current cost* over LIFO historical cost." See *reserve*.

limited liability The legal concept that shareholders of *corporations* are not personally liable for *debts* of the company.

limited partner A *partnership* member who is not personally liable for *debts* of the partnership. Every partnership must have at least one *general partner*, who is fully liable.

line-of-business reporting See *segment reporting*.

line of credit An agreement with a bank or set of banks for *short-term* borrowings on demand.

linear programming A mathematical tool for finding *profit*-maximizing (or *cost*-minimizing) combinations of *products* to produce when a *firm* has several products that it can produce but faces linear constraints on the resources available in the production processes or on maximum and minimum production requirements.

liquid Said of a business with a substantial amount (the amount is unspecified) of *working capital*, especially *quick assets*.

liquid assets Cash, current marketable securities, and sometimes, current *receivables*.

liquidating dividend A *dividend* that a *firm* declares in the winding up of a *business* to distribute its *assets* to the shareholders. Usually the recipient treats this as a *return* of *investment*, not as a return on investment or *revenue*.

liquidation Payment of a *debt*; *sale* of *assets* in closing down a *business* or a segment thereof.

liquidation value per share The amount each *share* of *stock* will receive if the *board* dissolves a *corporation*; for *preferred stock* with a *liquidation* preference, a stated amount per share.

liquidity Refers to the availability of *cash*, or near-cash resources, for meeting a *firm*'s obligations.

LISH An acronym, conceived by George H. Sorter, for *last-in, still-here*. LISH is the same *cost flow assumption* as *FIFO*. Many readers of accounting statements find it easier to think about *inventory* questions in terms of items still on hand. Think of FIFO in connection with *cost of goods sold* but of LISH in connection with *ending inventory*. See *FISH*.

list price The published or nominally quoted *price* for *goods*.

list price method See *trade-in transaction*.

loan An arrangement in which the owner of an *asset*, called the *lender*, allows someone else, called the *borrower*, the use of the asset for a *period* of time, which the agreement setting up the loan usually specifies. The borrower promises to return the asset to the lender and, often, to make a payment for the use of the asset. This term is generally used when the asset is *cash* and the payment for its use is *interest*.

LOCOM *Lower of cost or market*.

long-lived (term) asset An asset whose benefits the *firm* expects to receive over several years; a *noncurrent* asset, usually includes *investments*, *plant assets*, and *intangibles*.

long run; long term A term denoting a time or time *periods* in the future. How far in the future depends on context. For some securities traders, "long-term" can mean anything beyond the next hour or two. For most managers, it means the period of time long enough to allow change in total productive capacity. For government policymakers, it can mean anything beyond the next decade or two. For geologists, it can mean millions of years. In contrast to the *short run*. Use a hyphen when the phrase is an adjective, but no hyphen when it is a noun.

long-term (construction) contract accounting The *percentage-of-completion method* of *revenue recognition*; sometimes used to mean the *completed contract method*.

long-term debt ratio *Long-term debt* divided by total *assets*. See *ratio* and **Exhibit 6.14**.

long-term liability (debt) *Noncurrent liability*.

long term See *long run*.

long-term liquidity (solvency) risk The risk that a firm will not have sufficient *cash* to pay its *debts* sometime in the *long run*.

loophole Imprecise term meaning a technicality allowing a taxpayer (or *financial statements*) to circumvent the intent, without violating the letter, of the law (or *U.S. GAAP*).

loss Excess of *cost* over *net proceeds* for a single *transaction*; negative *income* for a *period*; a cost expiration that produced no *revenue*. See *gain* for a discussion of related and contrasting terms and how to distinguish loss from *expense*.

loss contingency See *contingency*.

lower of cost or market (LOCOM) A *basis* for valuation of *inventory* and, formerly in the United States, of *marketable securities*. This basis sets inventory *value* at the lower of *acquisition cost* or *current replacement cost* (market), subject to the following constraints. First, the market value of an item used in the computation cannot exceed its *net realizable value*—an amount equal to selling *price* less reasonable *costs* to complete production and to sell the item. Second, the market value of an item used in the computation cannot be less than the net realizable value minus the normal *profit* ordinarily realized on disposition of completed items of this type. The basis chooses the lower-of-cost-or-market valuation as the lower of acquisition cost or replacement cost (market) subject to the upper and lower bounds on replacement cost established in the first two steps. Thus,

Market Value = Midvalue of (Replacement Cost, Net Realizable Value, Net Realizable Value Less Normal Profit Margin)

Lower of Cost or Market Valuation = Minimum (Acquisition Cost, Market Value)

The accompanying exhibit illustrates the calculation of the lower-of-cost-or-market valuation for four inventory items. Notice that each of the four possible outcomes occurs once in measuring lower of cost or market. Item 1 uses acquisition cost; item 2 uses net realizable value; item 3 uses replacement cost; and item 4 uses net realizable value less normal profit margin.

	Item			
	1	2	3	4
Calculation of Market Value				
(a) Replacement Cost	$92	$96	$92	$96
(b) Net Realizable Value	95	95	95	95
(c) Net Realizable Value Less Normal Profit Margin [= (b) − $9]	86	86	86	86
(d) Market = Midvalue [(a), (b), (c)]	92	95	92	95
Calculation of Lower of Cost or Market				
(e) Acquisition Cost	90	97	96	90
(f) Market [= (d)]	92	95	92	95
(g) Lower of Cost or Market = Minimum [(e), (f)]	90	95	92	90

A taxpayer may not use the lower-of-cost-or-market basis for inventory on tax returns in combination with a *LIFO cost flow assumption*. In the context of inventory, once the firm writes down the *asset*, it establishes a new "origi-

nal cost" basis and ignores subsequent increases in market value in the *accounts*.

The *firm* may apply lower of cost or market to individual items of inventory or to groups (usually called "pools") of items. The smaller the group, the more *conservative* the resulting valuation.

Omit hyphens when you use the term as a noun, but use them when you use the term as an adjectival phrase.

Ltd.; Limited UK: a private limited *corporation*. The name of a private limited company must include the word "Limited" or its abbreviation "Ltd."

lump-sum acquisition Basket purchase.

M

MACRS *Modified Accelerated Cost Recovery System*. See *Accelerated Cost Recovery System*. Since 1986, MACRS has been the *accelerated depreciation* method required for U.S. *income tax* purposes.

maintenance *Expenditures* undertaken to preserve an *asset*'s service potential for its originally intended life. These expenditures are *period expenses* or *product costs*. Contrast with *improvement*, and see *repair*.

majority (active) investments A *firm* owns more than 50% of another firm, giving it majority ownership, typically because it wishes to control some aspects of the other firm's *operations*, giving it an active, not passive, motive.

make money; making money Users of these words can mean any of the following: earn *income*; earn *other comprehensive income*; save *opportunity costs*; earn *revenues*; earn *gross margin*; sell for *cash*; generate *cash flow from operations*; and maybe others, as well, not to mention counterfeiting. You can see that you should avoid these words in clear communications. See *money*.

make-or-buy decision A managerial decision about whether the *firm* should produce a *product* internally or purchase it from others. Proper make-or-buy decisions in the short run result only when a firm considers *incremental costs* in the analysis.

maker (of note) (of check) One who signs a *note* to borrow; one who signs a *check*; in the latter context, synonymous with "*drawer*." See *draft*.

management Executive authority that operates a *business*.

management accounting See *managerial accounting*.

Management Accounting Publication of the *IMA*.

management audit An *audit* conducted to ascertain whether a *firm* or one of its *operating* units properly carries out its objectives, policies, and procedures; generally applies only to activities for which accountants can specify qualitative standards. See *audit* and *internal audit*.

management by exception A principle of *management* in which *managers* focus attention on performance only if it differs significantly from that expected.

management by objective (MBO) A *management* approach designed to focus on the definition and attainment of overall and individual objectives with the participation of all levels of management.

management discussion and analysis See *management's discussion and analysis*.

management information system (MIS) A system designed to provide all levels of *management* with timely and reliable information required for planning, control, and evaluation of performance.

management's discussion and analysis (MD&A) A discussion of *management*'s views of the company's performance;

required by the *SEC* to be included in the *10-K* and in the *annual report* to shareholders. The information typically contains discussion of such items as *liquidity*, results of *operations*, *segments*, and the effects of *inflation*.

managers Business executives with decision making authority, who are *agents* of the *shareholders*, and are responsible for safeguarding and properly using the *firm's* resources.

managerial (management) accounting Reporting designed to enhance the ability of *management* to do its job of decision making, planning, and control. Contrast with *financial accounting*.

mandatorily redeemable preferred share See *redeemable (preferred shares)*.

manufacturing cost Cost of producing *goods*, usually in a factory.

manufacturing expense An imprecise, and generally incorrect, alternative title for *manufacturing overhead*. The term is generally incorrect because these *costs* are usually *product costs*, not *expenses*.

manufacturing firm A *firm* that converts *raw materials* and labor into *finished goods*, or intermediate goods, which can be parts of finished goods assembled by others. A firm that assembles parts into goods nearer to becoming finished goods.

manufacturing overhead General manufacturing *costs* that are not directly associated with identifiable units of product and that the *firm* incurs in providing a capacity to carry on productive activities. Accounting treats *fixed* manufacturing overhead cost as a *product cost* under *full absorption costing* but as an *expense* of the *period* under *variable costing*, which none of the *IRS*, *U.S. GAAP*, and *IFRS* allow.

margin Revenue less specified *expenses*. See *contribution margin*, *gross margin*, and *current margin*.

margin of safety Excess of actual, or budgeted, *sales* over *break-even* sales; usually expressed in dollars but may be expressed in units of *product*.

marginal cost The *incremental cost* or *differential cost* of the last unit added to production or the first unit subtracted from production. See *cost terminology* and *differential* for contrast.

marginal costing *Variable costing*.

marginal revenue The increment in *revenue* from the *sale* of one additional unit of *product*.

marginal tax rate The amount, expressed as a percentage, by which *income taxes* increase when taxable income increases by one dollar. Contrast with *average tax rate*.

markdown See *markup* for definition and contrast.

markdown cancellation See *markup* for definition and contrast.

market-based transfer price A *transfer price* based on external market data rather than internal company data.

market multiple The ratio of the market price of a share of stock to the earnings per share of that security.

market price See *fair value*.

market (interest) rate The rate of *interest* a company must pay to borrow *funds* currently. See *effective rate*.

market value *Fair market value*.

marketable securities; marketable debt securities; marketable equity securities Other companies' *bonds* and *stocks* a company holds that it can readily sell on *stock exchanges* or *over-the-counter* markets and that the company plans to sell as *cash* is needed; classified as *current assets* and as part of "cash" in preparing the *statement of cash flows*. If the *firm* holds these same securities for *long-term* purposes, it will classify them as *noncurrent assets*. *SFAS No. 115* (**Codification Topic 320**) requires that all *marketable equity* and all

debt securities (except those debt securities the holder has the ability and intent to hold to maturity) appear at market value on the *balance sheet*. The firm reports changes in market value in income for *trading securities* but *debits* holding *losses* (or *credits* holding *gains*) directly to *owners' equity* accounts for *securities available for sale* unless the firm has elected the *fair value option*.

marketing costs *Costs* incurred to sell; includes locating customers, persuading them to buy, delivering the *goods* or *services*, and collecting the *sales* proceeds.

mark to market As a verb, to record an item in the *books* at *current fair value*. When used as an adjective, such as mark-to-market accounting, hyphenate the phrase.

markon See *markup* for definition and contrast.

markup The difference between the original selling price of items acquired for *inventory* and the *cost*. Precise usage calls this "markon," although many businesspeople use the term "markup." Because of confusion of this use of "markup" with its precise definition (see below), terminology sometimes uses "original markup." If the originally established retail *price* increases, the precise term for the amount of price increase is "markup," although terminology sometimes uses "additional markup." If a *firm* reduces selling price, terminology uses the terms "markdown" and "markup cancellation." "Markup cancellation" refers to reduction in price following "additional markups" and can, by definition, be no more than the amount of the additional markup; "cancellation of additional markup," although not used, is descriptive. "Markdown" refers to price reductions from the original retail price. A price increase after a markdown is a "markdown cancellation." If *original cost* is $12 and original selling price is $20, then markon (original markup) is $8; if the firm later increases the price to $24, the $4 increase is markup (additional markup); if the firm later lowers the price to $21, the $3 reduction is markup cancellation; if the firm further lowers the price to $17, the $4 reduction comprises $1 markup cancellation and $3 markdown; if the firm later increases the price to $22, the $5 increase comprises $3 of markdown cancellation and $2 of markup (additional markup). Accountants track markup cancellations and markdowns separately because they deduct the former (but not the latter) in computing the selling prices of *goods* available for sale for the denominator of the *cost percentage* used in the conventional *retail inventory method*.

markup cancellation See *markup* for definition and contrast.

markup percentage Markup divided by (acquisition cost plus markup).

master budget A *budget* projecting all *financial statements* and their components.

matching convention The concept of recognizing *cost* expirations (*expenses*) in the same *accounting period* during which the firm recognizes related *revenues*; combining or simultaneously recognizing the revenues and expenses that jointly result from the same *transactions* or other events.

material As an adjective, it means relatively important, capable of influencing a decision (see *materiality*); as a noun, *raw material*.

materiality The concept that accounting should disclose separately only those events that are relatively important (no operable definition yet exists) for the *business* or for understanding its statements. *SFAC No. 2* suggests that accounting information is material if "the judgment of a reasonable person relying on the information would have been changed or influenced by the omission or misstatement." The *SEC*'s *SAB 99* provides the current rule on materiality, based on *SFAC No. 2*.

materials efficiency variance Measures materials waste by multiplying the *standard* materials *price* times the difference between the standard materials quantity used and the actual materials quantity used.

materials price variance Measures the difference between the actual and *standard* materials prices. Measures the effect of *price* differences by multiplying the quantity purchased times the difference between the actual price paid and the standard price.

materials variances *Price* and *quantity variances* for *direct materials* in *standard costing systems*; difference between *actual cost* and standard cost.

matrix A rectangular array of numbers or mathematical symbols.

maturity The date at which an obligation, such as the *principal* of a *bond* or a *note*, becomes due.

maturity value The amount expected to be collected when a *loan* reaches *maturity*. Depending on the context, the amount may be *principal* or principal and *interest*.

MBO *Management by objective*.

MD&A *Management's discussion and analysis* section of the *annual report*.

measuring unit See *attribute measured* for definition and contrast.

merchandise Finished goods bought by a retailer or wholesaler for resale; contrast with finished goods of a manufacturing *business*.

merchandise costs Costs incurred to sell a *product*, such as *commissions* and advertising. Some use this term to refer to the cost of merchandise acquired.

merchandise turnover *Inventory turnover* for merchandise. See *ratio* and **Exhibit 6.14**.

merchandise firm; merchandising business As opposed to a *manufacturing* business or service business, one that purchases (rather than manufactures) *finished goods* for resale.

merger The joining of two or more *businesses* into a single *economic entity*. See *holding company*.

minority active investment *Minority investment* where the *investor* holds sufficient *shares* to be able to exercise significant influence over the other *firm*'s *operating*, or investing, or financial decisions.

minority interest (income statement and balance sheet) See *noncontrolling interest*.

minority investment A holding of less than 50% of the voting *shares* in another corporation; accounted for with the *equity method* when the investor owns sufficient shares that it can exercise "significant influence" and as *marketable securities* otherwise. See *mutual fund*. Generally, a holding of at least 20% but less than 50% of the voting stock in another corporation.

minority passive investment A holding of less than 50% of the voting *shares* in another *corporation* when the investor owns insufficient *shares* to enable it to exercise significant influence.

minutes book A record of all actions authorized at corporate *board of directors* or shareholders' meetings.

MIS *Management information system*.

mix variance One of the *manufacturing variances*. Many *standard cost* systems specify combinations of inputs—for example, labor of a certain skill and materials of a certain quality grade. Sometimes combinations of inputs used differ from those contemplated by the standard. The mix variance attempts to report the cost difference caused by those changes in the combination of inputs. Can be a sales mix variance.

mixed cost A *semifixed* or a semivariable cost.

model See *business model*.

Modified Accelerated Cost Recovery System (MACRS) Name used for the *Accelerated Cost Recovery System*, originally passed by Congress in 1981 and amended by Congress in 1986.

modified cash basis The *cash basis of accounting* with long-term *assets* accounted for using the *accrual basis of accounting*. Most users of the term "cash basis of accounting" actually mean "modified cash basis."

monetary amount See *attribute measured* for the discussion of this concept as a *measuring unit*.

monetary assets and liabilities See *monetary items*.

monetary gain or loss The *firm*'s *gain* or *loss* in *general purchasing power* as a result of its holding *monetary assets* or *liabilities* during a *period* when the *general purchasing power* of the dollar changes; explicitly reported in *constant-dollar accounting*. During periods of *inflation*, holders of *net* monetary assets lose, and holders of net monetary liabilities gain, general purchasing power. During periods of *deflation*, holders of net monetary assets gain, and holders of net monetary liabilities lose, general purchasing power.

monetary items Amounts fixed in terms of currency (such as dollars or Euros) by statute or contract; *cash*, *accounts receivable*, *accounts payable*, and *debt*. The distinction between monetary and *nonmonetary items* is important for *constant-dollar accounting* and for *foreign exchange gain or loss* computations. In the foreign exchange context, *account* amounts denominated in the *firm*'s own currency are not monetary items, whereas amounts denominated in any other currency are monetary.

monetary-nonmonetary method *Foreign currency translation* method that translates all *monetary items* at the *current exchange rate* and translates all *nonmonetary items* at the *historical rate*. Contrast with *all-current method*.

money A word seldom used with precision in accounting, at least in part because economists have not yet agreed on its definition. Economists use the term to refer to both a medium of exchange and a store of value. See *cash* and *monetary items*. Consider a different set of issues concerning the phrase, "*making money*." Lay terminology uses this to mean "earning *income*" whether, as a result, the firm increased its *cash balances* or other *net assets*. The user does not typically mean that the firm has increased cash equal to the amount of net income, although the unaware listeners often think the phrase means this. Given that usage equates "making money" with "earning income," in this sense "money" has a *credit* balance not a *debit* balance. Since cash typically has a debit balance, the phrase "making money" is even more troublesome. Consider the following language from the U.S. statutes on forfeitures required of some who commit illegal acts: ". . . the amount of money acquired through illegal *transactions* . . . ." Does the law mean the cash left over after the lawbreaker has completed the illegal transactions the income earned from the transactions or something else?

Focus on the following four sets of questions and see how much difficulty you have in answering the questions associated with 3 and 4.

1. I took a cab and it cost $10; I spent money. Did the cabbie earn money? If so, how much?

2. I asked Jerry to give me a ride and he did, so I didn't spend $10. Did I earn money? If so, how much?

3. I decided to walk, so I didn't spend $10. Did I earn money? If so, how much?

4. I canceled the trip, so I didn't spend $10. Did I earn money? If so, how much?

Now, you can better appreciate why careful writers avoid using the word.

"Money" sometimes refers to debits and sometimes to credits; "making money" sometimes means earning accounting income and sometimes avoiding a cost, not reported in accounting, so careful writing about accounting avoids the word.

money purchase plan A *pension plan* in which the employer contributes a specified amount of *cash* each year to each employee's *pension fund*; sometimes called a *defined-contribution plan*; contrast with *defined-benefit plan*. The plan does not specify the benefits ultimately received by the employee, since these benefits depend on the rate of *return* on the cash invested. *ERISA* makes money purchase plans relatively more attractive than they had been. Most newly formed companies since the 1980's have used defined contribution plans and, since the late 1990s, many industrial *firms*, where defined-benefit plans were most common, have eliminated their defined-benefit plans.

mortality table Data of life expectancies or *probabilities* of death for persons of specified age and sex.

mortgage A claim given by the *borrower* (mortgagor) to the *lender* (mortgagee) against the borrower's property in *return* for a *loan*.

moving average An *average* computed on observations over time. As a new observation becomes available, analysts drop the oldest one so that they always compute the average for the same number of observations and use only the most recent ones.

moving average method *Weighted-average inventory method.*

multiple element contract The seller makes a single *sale* of a combination of *goods* and *services*, which the seller must disaggregate for *revenue recognition*. For example, consider that Xerox sells a copier, toner, paper, a service contract, and emergency repair services for a single price.

multiple-step Said of an *income statement* that shows various subtotals of *expenses* and *losses* subtracted from *revenues* to show intermediate items such as *operating income*, income of the enterprise (operating income plus *interest* income), income to investors (income of the enterprise less *income taxes*), *net income* to shareholders (income to investors less interest charges), and income retained (net income to shareholders less *dividends*). See *entity theory*.

municipal bond A *bond* issued by a village, town, or city, or an *operating* unit of one of them, such as a library or a hockey arena. *Interest* on such bonds is generally exempt from federal *income taxes* and from some state income taxes. Because bonds issued by state and county governments often have these characteristics, terminology often calls such bonds "municipals" as well. These are also sometimes called "tax-exempts."

mutual fund An *investment* company that *issues* its own stock to the public and uses the *proceeds* to invest in *securities* of other companies. A mutual fund usually owns less than 5% or 10% of the stock of any one company and accounts for its investments using current *market values*. Contrast with *holding company*.

mutually exclusive (investment) projects Competing *investment* projects in which accepting one project eliminates the possibility of undertaking the remaining projects.

mutually unexecuted contract *Executory contract.*

N

NAARS *National Automated Accounting Research System.*

NASDAQ (National Association of Securities Dealers Automated Quotation System) A computerized system to provide brokers and dealers with *price* quotations for securities traded *over the counter* as well as for some *NYSE* securities.

National Association of Accountants (NAA) Former name for the *Institute of Management Accountants* (*IMA*).

National Automated Accounting Research System (NAARS) A computer-based information-retrieval system containing, among other things, the complete text of most public corporate *annual reports* and Forms *10-K*. Users may access the system through the *AICPA*.

natural business year A 12-month *period* chosen as the reporting period so that the end of the period coincides with a low point in activity or inventories. See *ratio* and **Exhibit 6.14** for a discussion of analyses of *financial statements* of companies using a natural business year.

natural classification *Income statement* reporting form that classifies *expenses* by nature of items acquired, that is, *materials*, *wages*, *salaries*, *insurance*, and *taxes*, as well as *depreciation*. Contrast with *functional classification*.

natural resources Timberland, oil and gas wells, ore deposits, and other products of nature that have economic value. Terminology uses the term *depletion* to refer to the process of *amortizing* the cost of natural resources. Natural resources are "nonrenewable" (for example, oil, coal, gas, ore deposits) or "renewable" (timberland, sod fields); terminology often calls the former "wasting *assets*." See also *reserve recognition accounting* and *percentage depletion*.

negative confirmation See *confirmation*.

negative goodwill See *goodwill*. When a *firm* acquires another company, and the *fair value* of the *net assets* acquired exceeds the purchase price, *U.S. GAAP* requires that the acquiring company recognize a gain from a *bargain purchase*.

negotiable Legally capable of being transferred by *endorsement*. Usually said of *checks* and *notes* and sometimes of *stocks* and *bearer bonds*, which U.S. law no longer allow.

negotiated transfer price A *transfer price* set jointly by the buying and the selling divisions.

net Reduced by all relevant deductions.

net assets Total *assets* minus total *liabilities*; equals the amount of *owners' equity*. Often, we find it useful to split the *balance sheet* into two parts: owners' equity and all the rest. The "rest" is total assets less total liabilities. To take an example, consider one definition of *revenue*: the increase in owners' equity accompanying the *net* assets increase caused by selling *goods* or rendering *services*. An alternative, more cumbersome way to say the same thing is: the increase in owners' equity accompanying the assets' increase or the liabilities' decrease, or both, caused by selling goods or rendering services. Consider the definition of *goodwill*: the excess of purchase *price* over the *fair value* of identifiable net assets acquired in a purchase *transaction*. Without the phrase "net assets," the definition might be as follows: the excess of purchase price over the fair value of identifiable assets reduced by the fair value of identifiable liabilities acquired in a purchase transaction.

net bank position From a *firm*'s point of view, *cash* in a specific bank less *loans* payable to that bank.

net book value *Book value. Carrying value.*

net current asset value (per share) *Working capital* divided by the number of *common shares outstanding*. Some analysts think that when a common share trades in the market for an amount less than *net* current *asset* value, the shares are undervalued and investors should purchase them. We find this view naive because it ignores, generally, the efficiency of *capital markets* and, specifically, unrecorded *obligations*, such as for executory contracts and contingencies, not currently reported as *liabilities* in the *balance sheet* under *U.S. GAAP.*

net current assets *Working capital = current assets − current liabilities.*

net income The excess of all *revenues* and *gains* for a *period* over all *expenses* and *losses* of the period. The *FASB* is proposing to discontinue use of this term and substitute *earnings*. See *comprehensive income.*

net loss The excess of all *expenses* and *losses* for a period over all *revenues* and *gains* of the period; negative *net income.*

net markup In the context of *retail inventory methods*, *mark-ups* less markup cancellations; a figure that usually ignores *markdowns* and markdown cancellations.

net of tax method A nonsanctioned method for dealing with the problem of *income tax allocation*. The method subtracts deferred *tax* items from specific *asset* amounts rather than showing them as a deferred *credit* or *liability*.

net of tax reporting Reporting, such as for *income from discontinued operations*, *extraordinary items*, and *prior-period adjustments*, in which the *firm* adjusts the amounts presented in the *financial statements* for all *income tax* effects. For example, if an extraordinary loss amounted to $10,000, and the marginal tax rate was 40%, then the extraordinary item would appear "net of taxes" as a $6,000 loss. Hence, not all a firm's income taxes necessarily appear on one line of the income statement. The reporting *allocates* the total taxes among *income from continuing operations*, *income from discontinued operations*, *extraordinary items*, cumulative effects of *accounting changes*, and *prior-period adjustments*.

net operating profit *Income from continuing operations.*

net present value Discounted or *present value* of all *cash* inflows and outflows of a project or of an *investment* at a given *discount rate.*

net price method (of recording purchase or sales discounts) Method that records a *purchase* (or *sale*) at its *invoice price* less all *discounts* made available, under the assumption that the *firm* will take nearly all discounts offered. The purchaser *debits*, to an *expense* account, discounts lapsed through failure to pay promptly. For purchases, *management* usually prefers to know about the amount of discounts lost because of inefficient *operations*, not the amounts taken, so that most managers prefer the net price method to the *gross price method.*

net realizable (sales) value Current selling price less reasonable *costs* to complete production and to sell the item. Also, a method for *allocating joint costs* in proportion to *realizable values* of the *joint products*. For example, joint products A and B together cost $100; A sells for $60, whereas B sells for $90. Then a firm would allocate to A ($60/$150) × $100 = .40 × $100 = $40 of cost while it would allocate to B ($90/$150) × $100 = $60 of cost. This cost allocation should not, however affect any decision making.

net sales Sales (at gross invoice amount) less *returns*, *allowances*, freight paid for customers, and *discounts* taken.

net settlement Many *derivative* contracts obligate both *counterparties* to do something. (Most exchange traded derivatives only require only one party to do something.) "Net settlement" means that the contract provides that, when the derivative contract settles, one of the counterparties pays the other the *fair value* of the contract. For example, at the *maturity* of the derivative A owes B 9% of $100,000 and B owes A 6% of $110,000. Rather than A writing B a check for $9,000 while B writes A check for $6,600, net settlement allows A to write B a check for $2,400 (= $9,000 − $6,600).

net working capital *Working capital*; the term "*net*" is redundant in accounting. Financial analysts sometimes mean *current assets* when they speak of working capital, so for them the "net" is not redundant.

net worth A misleading term with the same meaning as *owners' equity*. Avoid using this term; accounting valuations at historical cost do not show economic worth.

network analysis A project planning and scheduling method, usually displayed in a diagram, that enables *management* to identify the interrelated sequences that it must accomplish to complete the project.

new product development time The period between a *firm*'s first consideration of a *product* and delivery of it to the customer.

New York Stock Exchange (NYSE) A public market in which those who own seats (a seat is the right to participate) trade various corporate *securities* for themselves and for their customers.

next-in, first-out See *NIFO.*

NIFO (next-in, first-out) A *cost flow assumption*, one not allowed by *U.S. GAAP*. In making decisions, many managers consider *replacement costs* (rather than *historical costs*) and refer to them as NIFO costs.

no par Said of *stock* without a *par value.*

nominal accounts *Temporary accounts*, such as *revenue* and *expense* accounts; contrast with *balance sheet accounts*. The firm *closes* all nominal accounts at the end of each *accounting period* to *retained earnings.*

nominal amount (value) An amount stated in dollars, in contrast to an amount stated in *constant dollars*. Contrast with *real amount (value).*

nominal dollars The measuring unit giving no consideration to differences in the *general purchasing power* of the dollar over time. The face amount of currency or coin, a *bond*, an *invoice*, or a *receivable* is a nominal-dollar amount. When the analyst adjusts that amount for changes in *general purchasing power*, it becomes a *constant-dollar* amount.

nominal interest rate A rate specified on a *debt* instrument; usually differs from the market or *effective rate*; also, a rate of *interest* quoted for a year. If the interest compounds more often than annually, then the *effective interest rate* exceeds the nominal rate.

noncancelable See *lease.*

nonconsolidated subsidiary An *intercorporate investment* in which the parent owns more than 50% of the *shares* of the *subsidiary* but accounts for the investment with the *cost method*. This might happen when the *firm* owns another firm located in a country, such as Venezuela as this book goes to press, where the owner cannot easily remove *cash* and other *assets* from the country.

noncontributory Said of a *pension plan* in which only the employer makes payments to a pension *fund*. Contrast with *contributory.*

noncontrollable cost A cost that a particular *manager* cannot control.

noncontrolling interest A *balance sheet account* on *consolidated statements* showing the *equity* in a less-than-100%-owned *subsidiary* company; equity allocable to those who are not part of the controlling (majority) interest; classified as shareholders' equity on the consolidated *balance sheet*. The *income statement* must subtract the noncontrolling interest in the current *period*'s *income* of the less-than-100%-owned subsidiary to arrive at *net income* for the period. Previous terminology referred to noncontrolling interest as the "*minority interest.*"

noncurrent Of a *liability*, due in more than one year (or more than one *operating cycle*); of an *asset*, the firm will enjoy the future benefit in more than one year (or more than one operating cycle).

nonexpendable fund A governmental fund whose *principal*, and sometimes *earnings*, the *entity* may not spend.

nonfinancial assets See *financial assets* for contrast.

noninterest-bearing note A *note* that does not specify explicit interest. The *face value* of such a note will exceed its *present value* at any time before *maturity* value so long as *interest rates* are positive. *APB Opinion No. 21* (**Codification Topic 835**) requires that firms report the present value, not face value, of long-term noninterest-bearing notes as the *asset* or *liability* amount in financial statements. For this purpose, the firm uses the *historical interest rate*. See *interest, imputed*.

nonmanufacturing costs All *costs* incurred other than those necessary to produce *goods*. Typically, only manufacturing *firms* use this designation.

nonmonetary items All items that are not monetary. See *monetary items*.

nonoperating In the *income statement* context, said of *revenues* and *expenses* arising from *transactions* incidental to the company's main line(s) of *business*; in the *statement of cash flows* context, said of all financing and investing sources or uses of *cash* in contrast to *cash provided by operations*. See *operations*.

nonprofit corporation An incorporated *entity*, such as a hospital, with owners who do not share in the *earnings*. It usually emphasizes providing services rather than maximizing *income*.

nonreciprocal transfer Transfer of *assets* or *services* from an *entity* without receiving something of equal value in return.

nonrecurring Said of an event that is not expected to happen often for a given *firm*. *APB Opinion No. 30* (**Codification Topic 225**) requires firms to disclose separately the effects of such events as part of ordinary items unless the event is also unusual. See *extraordinary* item.

nonregistrant *U.S. SEC registrant* for definition and contrast.

nonvalue-added activity An activity that causes *costs* without increasing a *product*'s or *service*'s *value* to the customer.

normal cost Former name for *service cost* in accounting for pensions and other postemployment benefits.

normal costing Method of charging costs to *products* using actual *direct materials*, actual *direct labor*, and predetermined *factory overhead* rates.

normal costing system *Costing* based on actual material and labor costs but using *predetermined overhead* rates per unit of some *activity* basis (such as *direct labor* hours or machine hours) to apply overhead to production. Management decides the rate to charge to production for overhead at the start of the *period*. At the end of the period the accountant multiplies this rate by the actual number of units of the base activity (such as actual direct labor hours worked or actual machine hours used during the period) to apply overhead to production.

normal spoilage Costs incurred because of ordinary amounts of spoilage. Accounting prorates such costs to units produced as *product costs*. Contrast with *abnormal spoilage*.

normal standard cost, normal standards The *cost* a *firm* expects to incur under reasonably efficient *operating* conditions with adequate provision for an average amount of rework, spoilage, and the like.

normal volume The level of production that will, over a time span, usually one year, satisfy purchasers' demands and provide for reasonable *inventory* levels.

note (payable and receivable) An unconditional written promise by the *maker* (*borrower*) to pay a certain amount on demand or at a certain future time. The borrower has the *payable* and the *lender*, the *receivable*.

note receivable discounted A *note* assigned by the holder to another. The new holder of the note typically pays the old holder an amount less than the *face value* of the note, hence the word "discounted." If the old holder assigns the note to the new holder with recourse, the old holder has a *contingent liability* until the maker of the note pays the *debt*. See *factoring*.

notes The preferred word, not "footnotes," for referring to the detailed information included by management as an integral part of the *financial statements* and covered by the *auditor's report*.

notional amounts A number of currency units, bushels, shares, or other units specified in a *derivative* contract. The notional amount of a derivative typically exceeds *fair value* of a derivative contract; for example, a swap contract on a $100 million borrowing might have a fair value under $1 million.

NOW (negotiable order of withdrawal) account Negotiable order of *withdrawal*. A *savings account* whose owner can draw an order to pay, much like a *check* but technically not a check, and give it to others, who can redeem the order at the savings institution.

number of days sales in inventory (or receivables) Days of average *inventory* on hand (or *average collection period for receivables*). See *ratio* and **Exhibit 6.14**.

NV (naamloze vennootschap) Netherlands: a public limited liability company.

NYSE *New York Stock Exchange*.

OASDI *Old Age, Survivors, and Disability Insurance*.

objective See *reporting objectives* and *objectivity*.

objective function In *linear programming*, the name of the *profit* (or *cost*) criterion the analyst wants to maximize (or minimize).

objectivity Having existence independent of the observer. Formerly, the reporting policy implying that the *firm* will not give formal recognition to an event in *financial statements* until the firm can measure the magnitude of the events with reasonable accuracy and check that amount with independent verification. The *FASB* has said *SFAC No. 2*, par. 158, "Accounting terminology will be improved if verifiability, which reflects what accountants do, replaces objectivity in the accountant's lexicon."

obsolescence An *asset*'s *market value* decrease caused by physical deterioration or by improved alternatives becoming available that will be more *cost-effective*. The decline in market value does not necessarily relate to physical changes in the asset itself. For example, computers become obsolete long before they wear out. The former is said to result from "physical factors," while the latter is said to result from "functional factors." See *partial obsolescence*.

Occupational Safety and Health Act *OSHA*.

off-balance-sheet financing A description often used for an obligation that meets all the tests to be classified a *liability* except that the obligation arises from an *executory contract* and, hence, is not a liability. Consider the following example. Miller Corporation desires to acquire land costing $25 million, on which it will build a shopping center. It could borrow the $25 million from its bank, paying *interest* at 12%, and buy the land outright from the seller. If so, both an *asset* and a liability will appear on the *balance sheet*. Instead, it borrows $5 million and purchases for $5 million from the seller an *option* to buy the land from the seller at any time within the next six years for a price of $20 million. The option costs Miller Corporation $5 million immediately and provides for continuing "option" payments of $2.4 million per year, which precisely equal Miller Corporation's borrowing rate multiplied by the remaining *purchase price* of the land: $2.4 million = .12 × $20 million. Although Miller Corporation need not continue payments and can let the option *lapse* at any time, it also has an obligation to begin developing on the site immediately. Because Miller Corporation has invested a substantial sum in the option, will invest more, and will begin immediately developing the land, Miller Corporation will almost certainly exercise its option before expiration. The seller of the land can take the option contract to the bank and borrow $20 million, paying interest at Miller Corporation's borrowing rate, 12% per year. The continuing option payments from Miller Corporation will be sufficient to enable the seller to make its payments to the bank. *Generally accepted accounting principles* view Miller Corporation as having acquired an option for $5 million rather than having acquired land costing $25 million in return for $25 million of debt. The *firm* will likely be able to structure this *transaction* so that it need not *recognize debt* on the balance sheet until it borrows more funds to exercise the option.

The *FASB* has curtailed the use of such financings with *FIN 46R* (**Codification Topic 810**). See also *variable interest entity*. Accountants would probably classify a *loss* from an earthquake as an extraordinary item.

off-balance-sheet risk A contract that exposes an entity to the possibility of *loss* but that does not appear in the *financial statements*. For example, a *forward-exchange contract* that does not allow for *net settlement* generally does not appear on the *balance sheet* because it is an *executory contract*. The contract may reduce or increase the *entity*'s exposure to *foreign-exchange risk* (the chance of loss due to unfavorable changes in the foreign-exchange rate). It may also expose the entity to credit risk (the chance of loss that occurs when the *counterparty* to the contract cannot fulfill the contract terms).

OHG (Offene Handelsgesellschaft) Germany: a general *partnership*. The partners have unlimited *liability*.

Old Age, Survivors, and Disability Insurance, or OASDI The technical name for *Social Security* under the *Federal Insurance Contributions Act* (*FICA*).

on consignment Said of *goods* delivered by the owner (the *consignor*) to another (the *consignee*) to be sold by the consignee. The arrangement entitles the owner either to the return of the property or to payment of a specified amount. The goods are *assets* of the consignor. Such arrangements provide the consignor with better protection than an outright *sale on account* to the consignee in case the consignee becomes *bankrupt*. In event of *bankruptcy*, the ordinary seller, holding an *account receivable*, has no special claim to the return of the goods, whereas a consignor can reclaim the goods without going through bankruptcy proceedings, from which the consignor might recover only a fraction of the amounts owed to it. Some consignors believe their total proceeds of sale will be greater if they give the goods to the consignee, who later sells the goods and takes a *commission*, rather than have the consignee buy the goods from the consignor and incur *holding costs* until time of eventual sale to a third party.

on (open) account Said of a *purchase* (or *sale*) when the seller expects payment sometime after delivery and the purchaser does not give a *note* evidencing the *debt*. The purchaser has generally signed an agreement sometime in the past promising to pay for such purchases according to an agreed time *schedule*. When the firm sells (purchases) on *open account*, it *debits* (*credits*) Accounts Receivable (*Payable*).

one-line consolidation Said of an *intercorporate investment* accounted for with the *equity method*. With this method, the *income* and *balance sheet* total *assets* and *equities* amounts are identical to those that would appear if the parent consolidated the *investee firm*, even though the *income* from the *investment* appears on a single line of the *income statement* and the *net investment* appears on a single line in the Assets section of the balance sheet.

one-write system A system of *bookkeeping* that produces several records, including original documents, in one *operation* by the use of reproductive paper and equipment that provides for the proper alignment of the documents.

on-time performance The *firm* delivers the *product* or *service* at the time scheduled for delivery.

OPEB *Other post-employment benefits*.

open account Any *account* with a nonzero *debit* or *credit balance*. See *on (open) account*.

operating (asset, liability, revenue, expense) An adjective used to refer to *asset*, *liability*, *revenue*, and *expense* items relating to the company's main line(s) of *business*. See *operations*. Contrast with *financial asset* and peripheral.

operating accounts *Revenue*, *expense*, and *production cost accounts*. Contrast with *balance sheet accounts*.

operating activities For purposes of the *statement of cash flows*, all *transactions* and events that are neither *financing activities* nor *investing activities*. See *operations*.

operating budget A formal *budget* for the *operating cycle* or for a year. Typically, this excludes *investing* and *financing activities*.

operating cash flow *Cash flow from operations*. Financial statement analysts sometimes use this term to mean *cash flow from operations − capital expenditures − dividends*. This usage leads to such ambiguity that the reader should always confirm the definition that the writer uses before drawing inferences from the reported data.

operating cycle *Earnings cycle*.

operating expenses *Expenses* incurred in the course of *ordinary* activities of an *entity*; frequently, a classification including only selling, *general*, and *administrative expenses*, thereby excluding *cost of goods sold*, *interest*, and *income tax* expenses. See *operations*.

operating lease A *lease* accounted for by the *lessee* without showing an *asset* for the lease rights (*leasehold*) or a *liabil-*

ity for the lease payment obligations. The lessee reports only rental payments or *rent* incurred during the *period* as *expenses* of the period. The asset remains on the lessor's *books*, where rental collections appear as *revenues*. Contrast with *capital lease*.

operating leverage Usually said of a *firm* with a large proportion of *fixed costs* in its total costs. Consider a book publisher or a railroad: such a firm has large costs to produce the first unit of *service*; then, the *incremental costs* of producing another book or transporting another freight car are much less than the *average cost*, so the *gross margin* on the sale of the subsequent units is relatively large. Contrast this situation with that, for example, of a grocery store, where the *contribution margin* can be smaller than 5% of the selling price. For firms with equal profitability, however defined, we say that the one with the larger percentage increase in income from a given percentage increase in dollar sales has the larger operating leverage. See *leverage* for contrast of this term with "financial leverage." See *cost terminology* for definitions of terms involving the word "*cost*."

operating margin *Revenues* from *sales* minus *cost of goods sold* and *operating expenses*.

operating margin based on current costs *Operating margin* where *cost of goods sold* is based on *current*, not *historical costs*; a measure of operating efficiency that does not depend on the *cost flow assumption* for *inventory*; sometimes called "current (gross) margin." See *inventory profit* for illustrative computations.

operating profit (loss) *Earnings* (*losses*) before *discontinued items*, *changes in accounting principles*, *extraordinary items*, *financial costs* and *revenues*, and, typically, *income taxes*.

operating segment The *FASB* defines this as a component of a *business*

- that engages in activities from which it can earn *revenues* and incur *expenses*,
- whose *operating* results the chief decision makers of the firm regularly review to consider resource allocation decisions and to make performance assessments,
- and for which discrete, that is separate from other components, financial information is available.

operational control See *control system*.

operational measures of time Indicators of the speed and reliability with which organizations supply *products* and *services* to customer. Companies generally use two operational measures of time: *customer response time* and *on-time performance*.

operations A word not precisely defined in *accounting*. Generally, analysts distinguish *operating activities* (producing and selling *goods* or *services*) from *financing activities* (raising *funds*) and *investing activities*. Acquiring goods *on account* and then paying for them one month later, though generally classified as an operating activity, has the characteristics of a financing activity. Or consider the transaction of selling plant assets for a price in excess of *carrying value*. On the *income statement*, the gain appears as part of income from operations ("*continuing operations*" or "discontinued" operations, depending on the circumstances), but the *statement of cash flows* reports all the funds received as a nonoperating source of *cash*, "disposition of noncurrent assets." In income tax accounting, an "operating loss" results whenever deductions exceed taxable *revenues*.

opinion The *auditor's report* containing an attestation or lack thereof; also, *APB Opinion*.

opinion paragraph Section of *auditor's report*, generally following the *scope paragraph* and giving the auditor's conclusion that the *financial statements* are (rarely, are not) in accordance with *U.S. GAAP* and present fairly the *financial position*, *changes in financial position*, and the results of *operations*. The paragraph also includes the *auditor's opinion* about the adequacy, or not, of the *internal control* processes.

opportunity cost The *present value* of the *income* (or *costs*) that a *firm* could earn (or save) from using an *asset* in its best alternative use to the one under consideration.

opportunity cost of capital *Cost of capital*.

option The legal *right* to buy or sell something during a specified *period* at a specified *price*, called the *exercise* price. If the right exists during a specified time interval, it is known as an "American option." If it exists for only one specific day, it is known as a "European option." Do not confuse employee stock options with *put* and *call* options, traded in various public markets.

ordinary annuity An *annuity in arrears*.

ordinary income For *income tax* purposes, reportable *income* not qualifying as *capital gains*.

organization costs The *costs* incurred in planning and establishing an *entity*; example of an *intangible asset*. The *firm* must treat these costs as *expenses* of the *period*, even though the *expenditures* clearly provide future benefits and meet the test to be assets.

organization goals Broad objectives for an organization established by management.

original cost *Acquisition cost*; in public utility accounting, the acquisition cost of the *entity* first devoting the *asset* to public use. See *aboriginal cost*.

original entry Entry in a *journal*.

OSHA (Occupational Safety and Health Act) The federal law that governs working conditions in commerce and industry.

other comprehensive income (OCI) According to the *FASB*, *comprehensive income* items that are not themselves part of *earnings*. See *comprehensive income*. To define other comprehensive income does not convey its essence. To understand other comprehensive income, you need to understand how it differs from earnings (or *net income*), the concept measured in the *earnings* (*income*) *statement*. The term earnings (or net income) refers to the sum of all components of comprehensive income minus the components of other comprehensive income. OCI includes items, such as unrealized gains and losses on *securities available for sale*, some foreign currency transactions, and *cash flow hedges* that affect a *firm's owners' equity*, but which standard setters decide the firm should report separately from net income.

The FASB allows several formats for disclosing OCI. See the left side of the accompanying exhibit, based on the 2007 earnings statement of the General Electric Company (GE) for one preferred approach, rarely used, that we prepared using GE's financial information. You can see that the format de-emphasizes conventional net income, called "Earnings" in the statement, but leads the eye to the total Comprehensive Income, with subtotals for Net Earnings and OCI. In December 2008, the SEC expressed a preference for the format in the left-hand column, which gives more equal prominence to the components of comprehensive income. Many *managements* want to focus on earnings, that is, conventional net income, and so prefer formats that give less emphasis to OCI, whose components, typically, management can less easily control.

**Comprehensive Income Disclosure Adapted from
General Electric Company [See Notes]
(Dollar amounts in billions)**

ONE-STATEMENT APPROACH (Developed from GE's data)	
Statement of Comprehensive Income	**2007**
Sales of goods and services	$169.7
Gain on sale of securities	3.0
Total revenues	172.7
Cost of goods and services sold	105.8
Other costs and expenses	40.3
Total costs and expenses	146.1
EARNINGS FROM CONTINUING OPERATIONS BEFORE INCOME TAXES	26.6
Income Tax Expense	(4.1)
EARNINGS FROM CONTINUING OPERATIONS	22.5
Earnings (loss) from discontinued operations, net of taxes	(0.3)
NET EARNINGS	22.2
Other Comprehensive Income, Net of Tax:	
Investment securities—net	(1.5)
Currency translation adjustments—net	4.5
Cash flow hedges—net	(0.5)
Benefit plans—net	2.6
OTHER COMPREHENSIVE INCOME	5.1
COMPREHENSIVE INCOME	$27.3

GE's ACTUAL DISCLOSURE (Disguising Both Other and Total Comprehensive Income)	
Statement of Changes in Shareowners' Equity	**2007**
CHANGES IN SHAREOWNERS' EQUITY	
Balance at January 1	$111.5
Dividends and other transactions with shareowners	(23.1)
Changes other than transactions with shareowners	
Investment securities—net	(1.5)
Currency translation adjustments—net	4.5
Cash flow hedges—net	(0.5)
Benefit plans—net	2.6
Total changes other than earnings	5.1
Increases attributable to net earnings	22.2
Total changes other than transactions with shareowners	27.3
Cumulative effect of changes in accounting principles	(0.1)
Balance at December 31	$115.6

Notes:

General Electric calls the top part of this statement the Statement of Earnings

General Electric shows five lines of revenues, condensed here into two, and eight lines of costs/expenses, here condensed into two.

General Electric does not show the blue-shaded portions.

The right side of the accompanying exhibit presents the statement that GE included in its 2007 financial statement—a separate statement of changes in shareholders' equity, which the FASB allows. Neither the caption "other comprehensive income" nor "comprehensive income" appears. GE's total OCI is $5.1 billion and carries the caption "Total changes other than earnings," which is a sub-caption under "Changes other than *transactions* with shareowners," so the full caption implied by this presentation is "Changes other than transactions with shareholders [that are] total changes other than earnings." GE's total comprehensive income is $27.3 billion and carries the caption "Total changes [in shareowners' equity] other than transactions with shareowners." Unless you know what you're looking for, you'd not easily spot it nor comprehend it. If you find a cleverer disguise for OCI and comprehensive income, please let us know.

other post-employment benefits During their working years, employees earn rights, promised by employers, for *pensions*, health care, and other benefits the employees collect after retirement. Accounting for these divides them into pension plans and other post-employment benefits. The accounting rules for these two, although not identical, result from similar principles.

outlay The amount of an *expenditure*.

outlier Said of an observation (or data point) that appears to differ significantly in some regard from other observations (or data points) of supposedly the same phenomenon; in a *regression analysis*, often used to describe an observation that falls far from the fitted regression equation (in two dimensions, line).

out-of-pocket Said of an *expenditure* usually paid for with cash; an *incremental cost*.

out-of-stock cost The estimated decrease in future *profit* as a result of losing customers because a *firm* has insufficient quantities of *inventory* currently on hand to meet customers' demands.

output Physical quantity or monetary measurement of *goods* and *services* produced.

outside director; independent director A corporate *board of directors* member who is not a company officer and does not participate in the *corporation*'s day-to-day *management*.

outstanding Unpaid or uncollected; when said of *stock*, refers to the *shares* issued less *treasury stock*; when said of *checks*, refers to a check issued that did not clear the *drawer*'s bank prior to the *bank statement* date.

over-and-short Title for an *expense account* used to account for small differences between the book balance of *cash* and the sum of actual cash and vouchers or receipts in *petty cash* or *change funds*.

overapplied (overabsorbed) overhead *Costs* applied, or *charged*, to product and exceeding actual *overhead costs* during the *period*; a *credit balance* in an overhead account after overhead is assigned to product.

overdraft A *check* written on a checking account that contains funds less than the amount of the check.

overhead costs Any *cost* not directly associated with the production or sale of identifiable goods and services; sometimes called "*burden*" or "*indirect costs*" and, in the UK, "oncosts"; frequently limited to manufacturing overhead. See *central corporate expenses* and *manufacturing overhead*.

overhead rate Standard, or other predetermined rate, at which a *firm* applies *overhead costs* to *products* or to *services*.

over-the-counter Said of a *security* traded in a negotiated *transaction*, as on *NASDAQ*, rather than in an auctioned one on an organized stock exchange, such as the *New York Stock Exchange*.

owners' equity *Proprietorship*; *assets* minus *liabilities*; *paid-in capital* plus *retained earnings* of a *corporation*; partners' capital accounts in a *partnership*; owner's capital account in a *sole proprietorship*.

P

paid-in capital Sum of *balances* in *capital stock* and *capital contributed in excess of par* (or *stated*) *value* accounts; same as *contributed capital* (minus *donated capital*).

paid-in surplus See *surplus*.

P&L *Profit-and-loss statement*; *income statement*.

paper profit A *gain* not yet realized through a *transaction*; an *unrealized holding gain*.

par See *at par* and *face amount*.

par (nominal or stated) value *Face amount* of a *security*.

par value method In accounting for *treasury stock*, method that *debits* a common stock account with the *par value* of the shares required and *allocates* the remaining debits between the *Additional Paid-in Capital* and *Retained Earnings* accounts. Contrast with *cost method*.

parent (company) Company owning more than 50% of the voting *shares* of another company, called the *subsidiary*.

Pareto chart A graph of a skewed statistical distribution. In many *business* settings, a relatively small percentage of the potential population causes a relatively large percentage of the business activity. For example, some businesses find that the top 20% of the customers buy 80% of the *goods* sold. Or, the top 10% of products account for 60% of the revenues or 70% of the profits. The statistical distribution known as the Pareto distribution has this property of skewness, so a graph of a phenomenon with such skewness has come to be known as a Pareto chart, even if the underlying data do not actually well fit the Pareto distribution. Practitioners of *total quality management* find that in many businesses, a small number of processes account for a large fraction of the quality problems, so they advocate charting potential problems and actual occurrences of problems to identify the relatively small number of sources of trouble. They call such a chart a "Pareto chart."

partial obsolescence One cause of decline in *market value* of an *asset*. As technology improves, the economic value of existing assets declines. In many cases, however, it will not pay a *firm* to replace the existing asset with a new one, even though it would acquire the new type rather than the old if it did make a new acquisition currently. In these cases, the accountant should theoretically recognize a loss from partial obsolescence from the firm's owning an old, out-of-date asset, but *U.S. GAAP* does not permit recognition of partial obsolescence until the sum of future *cash flows* from the asset total less than carrying value; see *impairment*. The firm will carry the old asset at *cost* less *accumulated depreciation* until the firm retires it from service so long as the un-*discounted future cash flows* from the asset exceed its *carrying value*. Thus *management* that uses an asset subject to partial obsolescence reports results inferior to those reported by a similar management that uses a new asset. See *obsolescence*.

partially executory contract *Executory contract* in which one or both parties have done something other than merely promise.

partially funded Said of a *pension plan* in which the *firm* has not funded all earned benefits. See *funded* for funding requirements.

partially vested Said of a *pension plan* in which not all employee benefits have *vested*. See *graded vesting*.

participating dividend *Dividend* paid to preferred shareholders in addition to the minimum preferred dividends when the *preferred shares* contract provides for such sharing in *earnings*. Usually the contract specifies that dividends on *common shares* must reach a specified level before the preferred shares receive the participating dividend.

participating preferred stock *Preferred shares* with rights to *participating dividends*.

participative budgeting Using input from lower- and middle-*management* employees in setting goals.

partner's drawing A payment made to a partner and debited against his or her share of *income* or *capital*. The name of a *temporary account*, closed to the partner's capital account, to record the *debits* when the partner receives such payments.

partnership; partner Contractual arrangement between individuals, called "partners," to share resources and *operations* in a jointly run *business*. See *general* and *limited partner* and *Uniform Partnership Act*.

patent A right granted for up to 20 years by the federal government to exclude others from manufacturing, using, or selling a claimed design, *product*, or plant (e.g., a new breed of rose) or from using a claimed process or method of manufacture; an *asset* if the *firm* acquires it by purchase. If the firm develops it internally, current *U.S. GAAP* requires the firm to *expense* the development *costs* when incurred, but to *capitalize* legal costs and filing fees.

payable Unpaid but not necessarily due or past due.

pay-as-you-go Said of an *income tax* scheme in which the taxpayer makes periodic payments of income taxes during the period when it earns the income to be taxed; in contrast to a scheme in which the taxpayer owes no payments until the end of, or after, the period when it earned the income being taxed (called PAYE—pay-as-you-earn—in the UK). The phrase is sometimes used to describe an *unfunded pension plan*, or retirement benefit plan, in which the *firm* makes payments to *pension plan* beneficiaries from general corporate funds, not from *cash* previously contributed to a fund. Under this method, the firm debits expense as it makes payments, not as it incurs the obligations. This is not acceptable as a method of accounting for pension plans, under *SFAS No. 87* (**Codification Topic 715**), or as a method of *funding*, under *ERISA*. Many firms fund other postemployment benefits, which are primarily retiree health insurance plans, this way.

payback period Amount of time that must elapse before the undiscounted *cash* inflows from a project equal the cash outflows.

payback reciprocal One divided by the *payback period*. This number approximates the *internal rate of return* on a project when the project life exceeds twice the payback period and the cash inflows are identical in every period after the initial period.

PAYE (pay-as-you-earn) See *pay-as-you-go* for contrast.

payee The person or *entity* who receives a *cash* payment or who will receive the stated amount of cash on a *check*. See *draft*.

payout ratio *Common share dividends* declared for a year divided by net *income* to common stock for the year; a term used by financial analysts. Contrast with *dividend yield*.

payroll taxes Taxes levied because the taxpayer pays salaries or wages; for example, *FICA* and unemployment compensation insurance taxes. Typically, the employer pays a portion and withholds part of the employee's wages for the portion paid by the employee.

PCAOB *Public Company Accounting Oversight Board.*

P/E ratio *Price-earnings ratio.*

Pension Benefit Guarantee Corporation (PBGC) A federal *corporation* established under *ERISA* to guarantee basic pension benefits in covered pension plans by administering terminated pension plans, paying benefits to those who have *vested* benefits from those plans, and placing *liens* on corporate *assets* for certain unfunded pension liabilities.

pension fund *Fund*, the *assets* of which the trustee will pay to retired ex-employees, usually as a *life annuity*; generally held by an independent trustee and thus not an *asset* of the employer.

pension plan Details or provisions of employer's contract with employees for paying retirement *annuities* or other benefits. See *funded, vested, service cost, prior service cost, money purchase plan*, and *defined-benefit plan*.

per books An expression used to refer to the *carrying value* of an item at a specific time.

percent Any number, expressed as a decimal, multiplied by 100.

percentage depletion (allowance) Deductible *expense* allowed in some cases by the federal *income tax* regulations; computed as a percentage of gross income from a *natural resource* independent of the unamortized *cost* of the *asset*. Because the amount of the total deductions for tax purposes usually exceeds the cost of the asset subject to *depletion*, many people think the deduction is an unfair tax advantage or *loophole*.

percentage-of-completion method Recognizing *revenues* and *expenses* on a *job*, order, or contract (1) in proportion to the *costs* incurred for the period divided by total costs expected to be incurred for the job, or order, or contract ("cost to cost") or (2) in proportion to engineers' or architects' estimates of the incremental degree of completion of the job, order, or contract during the period. Contrast with *completed contract method*.

percentage statement A statement containing, in addition to (or instead of) dollar amounts, ratios of dollar amounts to some base. In a percentage *income statement*, the base is usually either *net sales* or total *revenues*, and in a percentage *balance sheet*, the base is usually total *assets*. Often referred to as a "common-size(d) financial statement."

period *Accounting period.*

period cost An inferior term for *period expense* (because in most contexts, the word "*cost*" means an *asset* not an expense—a common exception being *cost of goods sold*).

period expense (charge) *Expenditure*, usually based on the passage of time, charged to *operations* of the *accounting period* rather than *capitalized* as an *asset*. Contrast with *product cost*.

periodic cash flows *Cash flows* that occur during the life of an investment project. Often include *receipts* from *sales, expenditures* for *fixed* and *variable production costs*, and savings of *fixed* and *variable* production costs, to name a few. They do not include noncash items, such as *financial accounting depreciation charges* or *allocated* items of *overhead* not requiring *differential* cash expenditures.

periodic inventory In recording *inventory*, a method that uses data on *beginning inventory*, additions to inventories, and *ending inventory* to find the *cost* of withdrawals from inventory. Contrast with *perpetual inventory*.

periodic procedures The process of making *adjusting entries* and *closing entries* and preparing the *financial statements*, usually by use of *trial balances* and *work sheets*.

permanent account An account that appears on the *balance sheet*. Contrast with *temporary account*.

permanent difference Difference between reported income and taxable income that will never reverse and, hence, requires no entry in the *deferred income tax* (*liability*) account; for example, nontaxable state and municipal *bond* interest that will appear on the financial statements. Contrast with *temporary difference*. See *deferred income tax liability*.

permanent file The file of working papers that are prepared by a public accountant and that contain the information required for reference in successive professional engagements for a particular organization, as distinguished from working papers applicable only to a particular engagement.

perpetual annuity *Perpetuity.*

perpetual inventory *Inventory* quantity and dollar amount records that the *firm* changes and makes current with each physical addition to or *withdrawal* from the stock of *goods*; an inventory so recorded. The records will show the physical quantities and, frequently, the dollar valuations that should be on hand at any time. Because the firm explicitly computes *cost of goods sold*, it can use the *inventory equation* to compute an amount for what *ending inventory* should be. It can then compare the computed amount of ending inventory with a physical count of the actual amount, either using cycle counts throughout the year (inventory counts for only one or a few inventory items), or a complete inventory count of ending inventory as a *control* device to measure the amount of *shrinkages*. Contrast with *periodic inventory*.

perpetuity An *annuity* whose payments continue forever. The *present value* of a perpetuity in *arrears* is p/r where p is the periodic payment and r is the *interest rate* per period. If a perpetuity promises $100 each year, in arrears, forever and the interest rate is 8% per year, then the perpetuity has a *value* of $1,250 = $100/.08.

perpetuity growth model See *perpetuity*. A perpetuity whose cash flows grow at the rate g per *period* and thus has *present value* of $1/(r - g)$. Some call this the "Gordon Growth Model" because Myron Gordon wrote about applications of this formula and its variants in the 1950s. John Burr Williams wrote about them in the 1930s.

personal account *Drawing account.*

PERT (Program Evaluation and Review Technique) A method of *network analysis* in which the analyst makes three time estimates for each activity—the optimistic time, the most likely time, and the pessimistic time—and gives an expected completion date for the project within a probability range.

petty cash fund Currency and coins maintained for *expenditures* that the *firm* makes with *cash* on hand.

physical factor See *obsolescence*.

physical units method A method of *allocating* a *joint cost* to the *joint products* based on a physical measure of the joint products; for example, allocating the cost of a cow to sirloin steak and to hamburger, based on the weight of the meat. This method usually provides nonsensical (see *sterilized allocation*) results unless the physical units of the joint products tend to have the same *value*.

physical verification *Verification*, by an *auditor*, performed by actually inspecting items in *inventory*, *plant assets*, and the like, in contrast to merely checking the written records. The auditor may use statistical sampling procedures.

planning and control process General name for the *management* techniques comprising the setting of organizational goals and *strategic plans*, *capital budgeting*, *operations* budgeting, comparison of plans with actual results, performance evaluation and corrective action, and revisions of goals, plans, and budgets.

plant *Plant assets.*

plant asset turnover *Fixed asset turnover.*

plant assets *Assets* used in the revenue-production process. Plant assets include buildings, machinery, equipment, *land*, and *natural resources*. The phrase "*property, plant, and equipment*" (though often appearing on *balance sheets*) is therefore a redundancy. In this context, "plant" used alone means buildings.

plantwide allocation method A method for *allocating overhead costs* to *product*. First, use one *cost pool* for the entire *plant*. Then, allocate all costs from that pool to products using a single overhead *allocation* rate, or one set of rates, for all the products of the plant, independent of the number of departments in the plant.

PLC (public limited company) UK: a publicly held *corporation*. Contrast with *Ltd*.

pledging The *borrower* assigns *assets* as *security* or *collateral* for repayment of a *loan*.

pledging of receivables The process of using expected collections on *accounts receivable* as *collateral* for a *loan*. The borrower remains responsible for collecting the receivable but promises to use the *proceeds* for repaying the *debt*.

plow back To retain *assets* generated by *earnings* for continued *investment* in the *business*.

plug Process for finding an unknown amount. For any *account*, beginning balance + additions − deductions = ending balance; if you know any three of the four items, you can find the fourth with simple arithmetic, called "plugging." In making a *journal entry*, often you know all *debits* and all but one of the *credits* (or vice versa). Because *double-entry* bookkeeping requires equal debits and credits, you can compute the unknown quantity by subtracting the sum of the known credits from the sum of all the debits (or vice versa), also called "plugging." Accountants often call the unknown the "plug." For example, in amortizing a *discount* on *bonds payable* with the *straight-line depreciation* method, *interest expense* is a plug: interest expense = *interest payable* + *discount amortization*. See *trade-in transaction* for an example. The term sometimes has a bad connotation for accountants because plugging can occur in a slightly different context. During the process of preparing a *preclosing trial balance* (or *balance sheet*), often the sum of the debits does not equal the sum of the credits. Because almost all real businesses now use computerized accounting systems, it is impossible not to have debits equal credits. This problem arises more for students than in reality. Rather than find the error, some students are tempted to force *equality* by changing one of the amounts, with a plugged debit or credit to an account such as Other Expenses. No harm results from this procedure if the amount of the error is small compared with asset totals, since spending much time to correct a small error will not be *cost-effective*. Still, most accounting teachers rightly disallow this use of plugging because *exercises* and problems set for students provide enough information not to require it.

point of sale The time, or the location, at which a *sale* occurs. A point of sale system refers to a system located at the point where a sale occurs, although the system also keeps track of the time each sale occurs.

pooling-of-interests method Accounting for a *business combination* by adding together the *carrying value* of the *assets* and *equities* of the combined *firms*; generally leads to a higher reported *net income* for the combined firms than results when the firm accounts for the *business combination* as a purchase because the *market values* of the merged assets generally exceed their carrying values. *U.S. GAAP* does not allow this method, although it previously did, so *financial statements* still reflect the effects of pooling accounting. Called *uniting-of-interests method* by the *IASB*. Contrast with *acquisition method*.

population The entire set of numbers or items from which the analyst samples or performs some other analysis.

positive confirmation See *confirmation*.

post; posting (process) To record entries in an *account* to a *ledger*, usually as *transfers* from a *journal*. Computerized accounting systems do not necessarily do *steps* the way one does them by hand, but one needs to understand the how a record keeping system operated by hand operates in order to understand common terminology heard in accounting contexts.

post-closing trial balance *Trial balance* taken after the accountant has *closed* all *temporary accounts*.

post-statement events Events that have *material* impact and that occur between the end of the *accounting period* and the formal publication of the *financial statements*. Even though the events occur after the end of the period being reported on, the *firm* must disclose such events in *notes* if the auditor is to give a *clean opinion*.

potentially dilutive A *security* that its holder may convert into, or *exchange* for, common *stock* and thereby reduce reported *earnings per share*; *options*, *warrants*, *convertible bonds*, and *convertible preferred stock*.

PPB *Program budgeting*. The second "P" stands for "plan."

practical capacity Maximum level at which a *plant* or department can operate efficiently.

precision The degree of accuracy for an estimate derived from a sampling process, usually expressed as a range of *values* around the estimate. The analyst might express a sample estimate in the following terms: "Based on the sample, we are 95% sure [confidence level] that the true *population value* is within the range of X to Y [*precision*]." See *confidence level*.

preclosing trial balance *Trial balance* taken at the end of the period before *closing entries*; in this sense, an *adjusted trial balance*; sometimes taken before *adjusting entries* and then synonymous with *unadjusted trial balance*.

predatory prices Setting *prices* below some measure of *cost* in an effort to drive out competitors with the hope of recouping *losses* later by charging monopoly prices. Illegal in the United States if the prices set are below long-run *variable costs*.

predetermined (factory) overhead rate Rate used in applying *overhead costs* to *products* or departments developed at the start of a *period*. Compute the rate as estimated overhead cost divided by the estimated number of units of the overhead *allocation base* (or *denominator volume*) activity. See *normal costing*.

preemptive right The privilege of a *shareholder* to maintain a proportionate *share* of ownership by purchasing a proportionate share of any new *stock* issues. Most state *corporation* laws allow corporations to pay shareholders to waive their *preemptive rights* or state that preemptive rights exist only if the *corporation charter* explicitly grants them. In practice, then, preemptive rights are the exception rather than the rule.

preference as to assets The rights of *preferred shareholders* to receive certain payments before common shareholders receive payments in case the *board* dissolves the *corporation*.

preferred shares (stock) *Capital stock* with a claim to *income* or *assets* after *bondholders* but before *common shares*. *Dividends* on preferred shares are *income* distributions, not *expenses*. See *cumulative preferred shares*.

premium For *shares*, the excess of issue (or market) price over *par value*. For *debt*, the excess of *carrying value* over *face value* of the debt instrument. For a different context, see *insurance*.

premium on capital stock Alternative but inferior title for *capital contributed in excess of par* (*or stated*) *value* or *additional paid-in capital*.

prepaid assets *Prepayments*.

prepaid expense An *expenditure* that leads to a *deferred charge* or *prepayment*. Strictly speaking, this is a contradiction in terms because an *expense* is a gone *asset*, and this title refers to past *expenditures*, such as for *rent* or *insurance premiums*, that still have future benefits and thus are *assets*. We try to avoid this term and use "prepayment" instead.

prepaid income An inferior alternative title for *advances from customers*. Do not call an item *revenue* or *income* until the firm earns it by delivering *goods* or rendering *services*.

prepayments *Deferred charges*; *assets* representing *expenditures* for future benefits. *Rent* and *insurance premiums* paid in advance are usually current prepayments.

present value (of future [net] cash flows) Value today (or at some specific date) of an amount or amounts to be paid or received later (or at other, different dates), discounted at some *interest* or *discount rate*; an amount that, if invested today at the specified rate, will grow to the amount to be paid or received in the future.

pretax (income) Said of the number on an income statement (financial reporting) from which is subtracted income tax expense to derive net income or earnings. Do no confuse with *taxable income*, the number on a tax return to which the tax formula is applied to derive taxes payable.

prevention costs *Costs* incurred to prevent defects in the *products* or *services* a *firm* produces, including procurement inspection, processing control (inspection), design, *quality* training, and machine inspection.

price The quantity of one *good* or *service*, usually *cash*, asked in *return* for a unit of another good or service. See *fair value*.

price-earnings (P/E) ratio At a given time, the *market value* of a company's *common share*, per *share*, divided by the *earnings per* common share for the past year. The analyst usually bases the denominator on *income from continuing operations* or on some estimate of the number if the analyst thinks the current figure for that amount does not represent a usual situation—such as when the number is negative or, if positive, close to zero. See *ratio* and **Exhibit 6.14**.

price index A series of numbers, one for each *period*, that purports to represent some *average* of prices for a series of periods, relative to a base period.

price level The number from a *price index* series for a given *period* or date.

price level–adjusted statements *Financial statements* expressed in terms of dollars of uniform *purchasing power*. The statements restate *nonmonetary* items to reflect changes in general *price levels* since the time the *firm* acquired specific

assets and incurred *liabilities*. The statements recognize a *gain* or *loss* on *monetary items* as the firm holds them over time *periods* when the general *price level changes*. Conventional financial statements show *historical costs* or *fair values* and ignore differences in purchasing power in different periods.

price variance In accounting for *standard costs*, an amount equal to (*actual cost* per unit − *standard cost* per unit) times actual quantity.

primary beneficiary *U.S. GAAP* uses this term in describing who should *consolidate a variable interest entity* (*VIE*). This usage is unrelated to *insurance* policies. U.S. GAAP provides no technical definition of this term, but relies on common understanding.

prime cost Sum of *direct materials* plus *direct labor* costs assigned to *product*.

prime rate The *loan* rate charged by commercial banks to their creditworthy customers. Some customers pay even less than the *prime rate* and others, more. The *Federal Reserve Bulletin* is the authoritative source of information about historical prime rates.

principal; principal (face) value An amount on which *interest accrues*, either as *expense* (for the *borrower*) or as *revenue* (for the *lender*); the *face amount* of a *loan*; also, the absent owner (principal) who hires the manager (*agent*) in a "principal-agent" relationship.

principle See *generally accepted accounting principles*.

prior-period adjustment A *debit* or *credit* that is made directly to *retained earnings* (and that does not affect *income* for the *period*) to adjust *earnings* as calculated for prior periods. Such *adjustments* are now rare. Theory suggests that accounting should correct for errors in accounting estimates (such as the *depreciable life* or *salvage value* of an *asset*) by adjusting retained earnings so that statements for future periods will show correct amounts. But *U.S. GAAP* requires that corrections of such estimates flow through current, and perhaps future, *income statements*. See *accounting changes* and *accounting errors*.

prior service cost *Present value* at a given time of a *pension plan*'s *retroactive benefits*. "Unrecognized *prior service cost*" refers to that portion of *prior service cost* not yet *debited* to *expense*. See *funded*. Contrast with *normal cost*.

pro forma income See *pro forma statements*.

pro forma statements Hypothetical statements; *financial statements* as they would appear if some event, such as a *merger* or increased production and *sales*, had occurred or were to occur; sometimes spelled as one word, "proforma." The phrase "*pro forma income*" has come to disrepute, as some companies have published *pro forma income statements* that include their good news as *recurring income*, and omitting the bad news as *nonrecurring income*. They have attempted to focus the *investment* community on their own presentation of this good news, de-emphasizing *U.S. GAAP* net income. The *SEC* and others have attempted to make these *disclosures* less misleading.

probable In many of its definitions, the *FASB* uses the term "probable." See, for example, *asset, firm commitment, liability*. A survey of practicing accountants revealed that the *average* of the probabilities that those surveyed had in mind when they used the term "probable" was 85%. Some accountants think that any event whose outcome is greater than 50% should be called "probable." The FASB uses the phrase "more likely than not" when it means greater than 50%. The *IASB* defines "probable" to mean more likely than not.

proceeds The *funds* received from the disposition of *assets* or from the *issue* of securities.

process costing A method of *cost accounting* based on average costs (total cost divided by the *equivalent units* of work done in a *period*); typically used for assembly lines or for *products* that the *firm* produces in a series of steps that are more continuous than discrete.

product *Goods* or *services* produced.

product cost Any *manufacturing cost* that the *firm* can—or, in some contexts, should—*debit* to an *inventory* account. See *flow of costs*, for example. Contrast with *period expenses*.

product life cycle Time span between initial concept (typically starting with *research and development*) of a *good* or *service* and the time when the *firm* ceases to support customers who have purchased the good or service.

production cost *Manufacturing cost*.

production cost account A *temporary account* for accumulating *manufacturing costs* during a *period*.

production cycle efficiency Measures the efficiency of the production cycle by computing the *ratio* of the time spent processing a unit divided by the *production cycle time*. The higher the percentage, the less the time and costs spent on *nonvalue-added activities*, such as moving and storage.

production cycle time The total time to produce a unit. Includes processing, moving, storing, and inspecting.

production department A department producing salable *goods* or *services*; contrast with *service department*.

production method (depreciation) One form of *straight-line depreciation*. The *firm* assigns to the depreciable *asset* (e.g., a truck) a *depreciable life* measured not in elapsed time but in units of *output* (e.g., miles) or perhaps in units of time of expected use. Then the *depreciation* charge for a period is a portion of *depreciable cost* equal to a fraction computed as the actual output produced during the period divided by the expected total output to be produced over the life of the asset. This method is sometimes called the "units-of-production (or output) method."

production method (revenue recognition) *Percentage-of-completion method* for recognizing *revenue*.

production volume variance Standard fixed *overhead* rate per unit of normal *capacity* (or base activity) times (units of base activity budgeted or planned for a *period* minus actual units of base activity worked or assigned to *product* during the period); often called a "*volume variance*."

productive capacity One *attribute measured* for *assets*. The current cost of *long-term assets* means the cost of reproducing the *productive capacity* (for example, the ability to manufacture one million units a year), not the cost of reproducing the actual physical assets currently used (see *reproduction cost*). *Replacement cost* of productive capacity will be the same as reproduction cost of assets only in the unusual case when no technological *improvement* in production processes has occurred and the relative *prices* of *goods* and *services* used in production have remained approximately the same as when the *firm* acquired the currently used goods and services.

product-level activities Work that supports a particular *product* or service line. Examples include design work, supervision, and advertising that are specific to each type of product or *service*.

profit Excess of *revenues* over *expenses* for a *transaction*; sometimes used synonymously with *net income* for the *period*, especially under *IFRS*.

profit and loss account UK: *retained earnings*.

profit-and-loss sharing ratio The fraction of *net income* or *loss* allocable to a partner in a *partnership*; need not be the same fraction as the partner's *share* of *capital*.

profit-and-loss statement *Income statement*.

profit center A *responsibility center* for which a *firm* accumulates both *revenues* and *expenses*. Contrast with *cost center* and *investment center*.

profit margin; profit margin for ROA ratio; profit margin for ROCE ratio *Sales* minus all *expenses*.

profit margin percentage *Profit margin* divided by *net sales*. See *ratio* and **Exhibit 6.14**.

profit maximization The doctrine that the *firm* should account for a given set of *operations* so as to make reported *net income* as large as possible; contrast with *conservatism*. The concept of profit maximization in accounting differs from the profit-maximizing concept in economics, which states that the firm should manage operations to maximize the *present value* of the firm's wealth, generally by equating *marginal costs* and *marginal revenues*.

profit plan The *income statement* portion of a *master budget*.

profit-sharing plan A *defined-contribution plan* in which the employer contributes amounts based on *net income*.

profit variance analysis Analysis of the causes of the difference between budgeted profit in the *master budget* and the profits earned.

profit-volume analysis (equation) Analysis of effects, on *profits*, caused by changes in volume or *contribution margin* per unit or *fixed costs*. See *breakeven chart*.

profit-volume graph See *breakeven chart*.

profit-volume ratio *Net income* divided by *net sales* in dollars.

profitability A nontechnical term meaning the potential for, or actual earning of, *net income*.

profitability accounting *Responsibility accounting*.

program budgeting (PPB) Specification and analysis of inputs, *outputs*, *costs*, and alternatives that link plans to *budgets*.

programmed cost A *fixed cost* not essential for carrying out *operations*. For example, a *firm* can control costs for *research and development* and advertising designed to generate new business, but once it commits to incur them, they become *fixed costs*. These costs are sometimes called managed costs or *discretionary costs*. Contrast with *capacity costs*.

progressive tax Tax for which the rate increases as the taxed base, such as *income*, increases. Contrast with *regressive tax*.

project financing arrangement As defined by *SFAS No. 47* (**Codification Topic 440**), the *financing* of an investment project in which the lender looks principally to the *cash flows* and *earnings* of the project as the *source of funds* for repayment and to the *assets* of the project as *collateral* for the *loan*. The general *credit* of the project *entity* usually does not affect the terms of the financing either because the borrowing entity is a *corporation* without other assets or because the financing provides that the lender has no direct *recourse* to the entity's owners.

projected benefit obligation The *actuarial present value* at a given date of all pension benefits attributed by a *defined-benefit pension* formula to employee service rendered before that date. The analyst measures the obligation using assumptions as to future compensation levels if the formula incorporates future compensation, as happens, for example, when the plan bases the eventual pension benefit on *wages* of the last several years of employees' work lives. Contrast to *accumulated benefit obligation*, where the analyst measures the obligation using employee compensation levels at the time of the measurement date.

projected financial statement *Pro forma financial statement*.

projection See *financial projection* for definition and contrast.

promissory note An unconditional written promise to pay a specified sum of *cash* on demand or at a specified date.

proof of journal The process of checking the arithmetic accuracy of *journal entries* by testing for the equality of all *debits* and all *credits* since the last previous proof.

property dividend A *dividend in kind*.

property, plant, and equipment See *plant assets*.

proportionate consolidation A presentation of the *financial statements* of any investor-investment relationship, whereby the investor's pro rata *share* of each *asset*, *liability*, *income* item, and *expense* item appears in the *financial statements* of the investor under the various *balance sheet* and *income statement* headings. Allowed by *IFRS* but not by *U.S. GAAP*.

proprietary accounts See *budgetary accounts* for definition and contrast in the context of governmental accounting.

proprietorship *Assets* minus *liabilities* of an *entity*; equals *contributed capital* plus *retained earnings*. See *sole proprietor* for another context.

proprietorship theory The *corporation* view that emphasizes the form of the *accounting equation* that says *assets* − *liabilities* = *owners' equity*; contrast with *entity theory*. The major implication of a choice between these theories deals with the treatment of *subsidiaries*. For example, the proprietorship theory views *noncontrolling interest* as a *liability* with indeterminate term. The proprietorship theory implies using a *single-step income statement*.

prorate To *allocate* in proportion to some base; for example, to allocate *service department* costs in proportion to hours of service used by the benefited department or to allocate manufacturing *variances* to *product* sold and to product added to *ending inventory*.

prorating variances See *prorate*.

prospectus Formal written document describing *securities* a *firm* will issue. See *proxy*.

protest fee Fee charged by banks or other financial agencies when the bank cannot collect items (such as *checks*) presented for collection.

provision Part of an *account* title. Often the *firm* must recognize an *expense* even though it cannot be sure of the exact amount. The entry for the estimated expense, such as for *income taxes* or expected *costs* under *warranty*, is as follows:

Retained Earnings (Expense) (Asset Decrease or Liability Increase) (Estimated)	X
Liability Increase (Estimated)	X

American terminology often uses "provision" in the *expense account* title of the above entry. Thus, Provision for Income Taxes means the estimate of income tax expense. (*IFRS* terminology uses "provision" in the title for the *estimated liability* of the above entry, so that Provision for Income Taxes is a *balance sheet account*.)

proxy Written authorization given by one person to another so that the second person can act for the first, such as to vote *shares* of *stock*; of particular significance to accountants because the *SEC* presumes that *management* distributes financial information along with its proxy solicitations.

public accountant Generally, this term is synonymous with *certified public accountant* or *Chartered Accountant*. Some jurisdictions, however, license individuals who are not CPAs as public accountants.

public accounting That portion of accounting primarily involving the *attest function*, culminating in the *auditor's report*.

Public Company Accounting Oversight Board PCAOB A *board* established by the Sarbanes-Oxley Act of 2002 that regulates the auditing profession and sets standards for audits of public companies. The *SEC* appoints its members and approves its *budget*. The PCAOB directly *invoices publicly traded* companies and their *auditors* to *fund* its *operations*.

publicly traded An adjectival phrase describing *firms* whose *securities* trade in active markets or the securities themselves.

PuPU Acronym for *purchasing power unit*; conceived by John C. Burton, former chief accountant of the *SEC*. Those who think that *constant-dollar accounting* is not particularly useful poke fun at it by calling it "PuPU accounting."

purchase The acquisition of goods and services in exchange for some *asset*. See *purchase method* for the context of acquisition of another company or division.

purchase allowance A reduction in sales *invoice price* usually granted because the purchaser received *goods* not exactly as ordered. The purchaser does not return the goods but agrees to keep them for a price lower than originally agreed upon.

purchase discount A reduction in purchase *invoice price* granted for prompt payment. See *sales discount* and *terms of sale*.

purchase investigation *Due diligence*.

purchase method *Acquisition method*.

purchase order Document issued by a buyer authorizing a seller to deliver *goods*, with the buyer to make payment later.

purchasing power gain or loss *Monetary gain or loss*.

push-down accounting An *accounting method* used in some *purchase transactions*. Assume that Company A purchases substantially all the *common shares* of Company B but that Company B must still issue its own *financial statements*. The question arises, shall Company B change the *basis* for its *assets* and *equities* on its own *books* to the same updated amounts at which they appear on Company A's *consolidated financial statements*? Company B uses "push-down accounting" when it shows the new asset and *equity* bases reflecting Company A's purchase, because the method "pushes down" the new bases from Company A (where *U.S. GAAP* requires them) to Company B (where the new bases would not appear in *historical cost accounting*). Since 1983, the *SEC* has required push-down accounting under many circumstances.

put (option) An option to sell *shares* of a *publicly traded corporation* (or other items) at a fixed *price* during a fixed time span. Contrast with *call*.

Q

qualified report (opinion) *Auditor's report* containing a statement that the auditor was unable to complete a satisfactory examination of all things considered relevant or that the auditor has doubts about the financial impact of some *material* item reported in the *financial statements*. See *except for* and *subject to*.

qualifying special-purpose entity See *special purpose entity*.

quality In modern usage, a *product* or service has quality to the extent it conforms to specifications or provides customers the characteristics promised them.

quality of earnings A phrase with no single, agreed-upon meaning. Some who use the phrase use it with different meanings on different occasions. "Quality of earnings" has an accounting aspect and a *business* cycle aspect.

In its accounting aspect, *managers* have choices in measuring and reporting *earnings*. This discretion can involve any of the following: selecting *accounting principles* or standards when *U.S. GAAP* allows a choice; making estimates in the application of accounting principles; and timing *transactions* to allow recognizing *nonrecurring* items in earnings. In some instances the range of choices has a large impact on reported earnings and in others, small.

(1) Some use the phrase "quality of earnings" to mean the degree to which management can affect reported *income* by its choices of accounting estimates even though the choices recur every *period*. These users judge, for example, *insurance* companies to have low-quality *earnings*. Insurance company management must re-estimate its liabilities for future payments to the insured each period, thereby having an opportunity to report periodic earnings within a wide range.

(2) Others use the phrase to mean the degree to which *management* actually takes advantage of its flexibility. For them, an insurance company that does not vary its methods and estimating techniques, even though it has the opportunity to do so, has high-quality earnings.

(3) Some have in mind the proximity in time between *revenue recognition* and *cash* collection. For them, the smaller the time delay, the higher will be the quality.

(4) Still others use the phrase to mean the degree to which managers who have a choice among the items with large influence on earnings choose the ones that result in income measures that are more likely to recur. For them, the more likely an item of earnings is to recur, the higher will be its quality.

Often these last two groups trade off with each other. Consider a dealer leasing a car on a long-term lease, receiving monthly collections. The dealer who uses sales-type lease accounting scores low on proximity of revenue recognition (all at the time of signing the lease) to cash collection but highlights the nonrepetitive nature of the transaction. The leasing dealer who uses operating lease accounting has perfectly matching revenue recognition and cash collection, but the recurring nature of the revenue gives a misleading picture of a repetitive transaction. The phrase "item of earnings" in (4) is ambiguous. The writer could mean the underlying economic event (which occurs when the lease for the car is signed) or the revenue recognition (which occurs every time the dealer using operating lease accounting receives cash). Hence, you should try to understand what other speakers and writers mean by "quality of earnings" when you interpret what they say and write. Some who refer to "earnings quality" suspect that managers will usually make choices that enhance current earnings and present the firm in the best light, independent of the ability of the firm to generate similar earnings in the future.

In the business cycle aspect, management's action often has no impact on the stability and recurrence of earnings Compare a company that sells consumer products and likely has sales repeating every week with a construction company that builds to order. Companies in noncyclical businesses, such as some public utilities, likely have more stable earnings than ones in cyclical businesses, such as steel. Some use "quality of earnings" to refer to the stability and recurrence of basic revenue-generating activities. Those who use the phrase this way rarely associate earnings quality with accounting issues.

quality of financial position Because of the linkage between the *income statement* with the change in *retained earnings* between the beginning and ending *balance sheet*, the *factors* that imply a high (or low) *quality of earnings* also affect the balance sheet. Users of this phrase have in mind the same accounting issues as they have in mind when they use the phrase "quality of earnings." In the recent past many *firms* held subprime *mortgages* overvalued, in aggregate, by \$1 trillion or more, suggesting a low quality of *financial position*.

quantitative performance measure A measure of *output* based on an objectively observable quantity, such as units produced or *direct costs* incurred, rather than on an unobservable quantity or a quantity observable only nonobjectively, like *quality* of service provided.

quantity discount A reduction in purchase *price* as quantity purchased increases. The Robinson-Patman Act constrains the amount of the *discount*. Do not confuse with *purchase discount*.

quantity variance *Efficiency variance*; in *standard cost* systems, the *standard price* per unit times (standard quantity that should be used minus actual quantity used).

quasi-reorganization A *reorganization* in which no new company emerges or no court has intervened, as would happen in *bankruptcy*. The primary purpose is to rid the *balance sheet* of a *deficit* (negative *retained earnings*) and give the *firm* a "fresh start."

quick assets *Assets* readily convertible into *cash*; includes cash, current *marketable securities* (that is, not held as *investments*), and current *receivables*.

quick ratio Sum of (*cash*, current *marketable securities*, and current *receivables*) divided by *current liabilities*; often called the "*acid test ratio*." The analyst may exclude some nonliquid receivables from the numerator. See *ratio* and **Exhibit 6.14**.

R

R^2 The proportion of the statistical *variance* of a *dependent variable* explained by the equation fit to *independent variable(s)* in a *regression analysis*.

Railroad Accounting Principles Board (RAPB) A *board* brought into existence by the Staggers Rail Act of 1980 to advise the Interstate Commerce Commission on accounting matters affecting railroads. The *RAPB* was the only cost-accounting body authorized by the government during the decade of the 1980s (because Congress ceased *funding* the *CASB* during the 1980s). The RAPB incorporated the pronouncements of the CASB and became the government's authority on cost accounting principles, until the Congress re-instated the CASB. Refer to CASB, above in the Glossary.

R&D See *research and development*.

random number sampling For choosing a sample, a method in which the analyst selects items from the *population* by using a random number table or generator.

random sampling For choosing a sample, a method in which all items in the *population* have an equal chance of being selected. Compare *judgment(al) sampling* and *stratified sampling*.

RAPB *Railroad Accounting Principles Board*.

rate of return on assets; ROA *Return on assets*. See *ratio* and **Exhibit 6.14**.

rate of return on common stock equity; ROCE See *ratio* and **Exhibit 6.14**.

rate of return on shareholders' (owners') equity See *ratio*.

rate of return (on total capital) See *ratio* and *return on assets*.

rate variance *Price variance*, usually for *direct labor costs*.

ratio The number resulting when one number divides another. Analysts generally use ratios to *assess* aspects of profitability, solvency, and liquidity. The commonly used *financial ratios* fall into three categories: (1) those that summarize some aspect of *operations* for a *period*, usually a year, (2) those that summarize some aspect of *financial position* at a given moment—the moment for which a *balance sheet* reports, and (3) those that relate some aspect of operations to some aspect of financial position. **Exhibit 6.14**, in **Chapter 6**, defines many commonly used financial ratios.

For all *ratios* that require an *average balance* during the period, the analyst often derives the average as one half the sum of the beginning and the ending balances. Sophisticated analysts *recognize*, however, that particularly when companies use a *fiscal year* different from the calendar year, this averaging of beginning and ending balances may mislead. Consider, for example, the rate of *return on assets* of Sears, Roebuck & Company, whose *fiscal year* ends on January 31. Sears chooses a January 31 closing date at least in part because *inventories* are at a low level and are therefore easy to count—it has sold the Christmas *merchandise*, and the Easter merchandise has not yet all arrived. Furthermore, by January 31, Sears has collected for most Christmas *sales*, so *receivable* amounts are not unusually large. Thus at January 31, the amount of total assets is lower than at many other times during the year. Consequently, the denominator of the rate of return on assets, total assets, for Sears more likely represents the smallest amount of total assets on hand during the year rather than the average amount. The return on assets rate for Sears and other companies that choose a fiscal year-end to coincide with low points in the inventory cycle is likely to exceed the ratio measured with a more accurate estimate of the average amounts of total assets.

raw material *Goods* purchased for use in manufacturing a *product*.

reacquired stock *Treasury shares*.

real accounts *Balance sheet accounts*, as opposed to *nominal accounts*. See *permanent accounts*.

real amount (value) An amount stated in *constant dollars*. For example, if the *firm* sells an *investment* costing $100 for $130 after a *period* of 10% general *inflation*, the *nominal amount* of *gain* is $30 (= $130 − $100) but the *real amount* of gain is C$20 (= $130 − 1.10 × $100), where "C$" denotes constant dollars of purchasing power on the date of *sale*.

real estate *Land* and its *improvements*, such as landscaping and roads, but not buildings.

real interest rate *Interest rate* reflecting the productivity of *capital*, not including a *premium* for *inflation* anticipated over the life of the *loan*.

realizable value *Fair value* or, sometimes, *net realizable (sales) value*.

realization (convention) The accounting practice of delaying the recognition of *gains* and *losses* from changes in the *market price* of *assets* until the *firm* sells the assets. However, the firm recognizes unrealized losses on *inventory* (or *marketable securities* classified as *trading securities*) prior to sale when the firm uses the *lower-of-cost-or-market* valuation basis for inventory (or the *fair value* basis for marketable securities) or when it recognizes *impairments*.

realize (v. recognize) To convert into *funds*; when applied to a *gain* or *loss*, implies that an *arm's-length transaction* has taken place. Contrast with *recognize*; the firm may recognize a loss (as, for example, on *marketable equity securities*) in the *financial statements* even though it has not yet realized the loss via a *transaction*.

realized gain (or loss) on marketable equity securities An *income statement* account title for the difference between the proceeds of disposition and the *acquisition cost* of *marketable equity securities*.

realized gross margin *Gross margin* in a *transaction* with a *counterparty* outside the firm.

realized holding gain See *inventory profit* for definition and an example.

rearrangement costs *Costs* of reinstalling *assets*, perhaps in a different location. The *firm* should *capitalize* them as part of the assets cost, just as is done with original installation cost. The firm will *expense* these costs if they merely maintain the asset's future benefits at their originally intended level before the relocation.

recapitalization *Reorganization*.

recapture Name for one kind of tax payment. Various *provisions* of the *income tax* rules require a refund by the *taxpayer* (*recapture* by the government) of various tax advantages under certain conditions. For example, the taxpayer must repay tax savings provided by *accelerated depreciation* if the taxpayer prematurely retires the item providing the tax savings.

receipt Acquisition of *cash*. Written acknowledgment that the signer has received a good or service or cash.

receivable Any *collectible*, whether or not it is currently due.

receivable turnover See *ratio* and **Exhibit 6.14**.

reciprocal holdings Company A owns *stock* of Company B, and Company B owns stock of Company A; or Company B owns stock of Company C, which owns stock of Company A.

recognize To enter a *transaction* in the accounts; contrast with *realize*.

reconciliation A calculation that shows how one *balance* or figure derives from another, such as a *reconciliation* of retained earnings or a *bank reconciliation schedule*. See *articulate*.

record date The date at which the *firm* pays *dividends* on payment date to those who own the *stock*.

recourse The *rights* of the *lender* if a *borrower* does not repay as promised. A *recourse loan* gives the lender the right to take any of the borrower's *assets* not exempted from such taking by the contract. See also *note receivable discounted*.

recoverable amount Under *IFRS*, the larger of (1) *fair value* less *cost* to sell, and (2) *value* in use, defined as the *present value of future cash flows* of the *asset* in its current use by the *firm*. Used in measuring the amount of an *impairment loss*.

recovery of unrealized loss on trading securities An *income statement* account title for the *gain* during the current *period* on *trading securities*.

recurring Occurring again; occurring repetitively; in accounting, an adjective often used in describing *revenue* or *earnings*. In some contexts, the term "recurring revenue" is ambiguous. Consider a construction contractor who accounts for a single long-term project with the *installment method*, with revenue recognized at the time of each cash collection from the customer. The recognized revenue is recurring, but the *transaction* leading to the revenue is not. See *quality of earnings*.

redeemable (preferred shares) *Preferred shares* that carry one of three types of *redemption* rights or obligations:

- Redemption right of the issuer: The issuing firm has the right but not the obligation—the option—to redeem the *preferred stock* under certain conditions Same as *callable preferred stock*. *U.S. GAAP* and *IFRS* require the issuer to classify as a component of *shareholders' equity*.

■ Redemption obligation of the issuer at specified time or upon a specified event certain to occur: Often called "*mandatorily redeemable preferred stock.*" This preferred stock has attributes of both long-term debt and shareholders' equity. The specified redemption time is analogous to the maturity date of long-term debt. An example of an event certain to occur that would trigger redemption is the death of the preferred shareholder. U.S. GAAP and IFRS require the issuer to classify as a *liability*.

■ Redemption obligation of the issuer conditional on a specified event not certain to occur: Some preferred shares give the holder the option, but not the obligation, to force the issuer to redeem. The owner of the preferred stock has a *put option*, the right to require the issuing firm to repurchase the shares. Such redemption is an event not certain to occur. U.S. GAAP requires the issuer to classify the security as neither liability nor shareholders' equity, but to show the amounts in between. IFRS requires classification as a liability.

redemption Retirement by the issuer, usually by a purchase or *call*, of *stocks* or *bonds*.

redemption premium *Call premium*.

redemption value The *price* a *corporation* will pay to retire *bonds* or *preferred stock* if it calls them before *maturity*.

refinancing An *adjustment* in the *capital structure* of a *corporation*, involving changes in the nature and amounts of the various classes of *debt* and, in some cases, *capital* as well as other components of *shareholders' equity*. *Asset carrying values* in the accounts remain unchanged.

refunding bond issue Said of a *bond* issue whose *proceeds* the *firm* uses to retire bonds already *outstanding*.

register A collection of consecutive entries, or other information, in chronological order, such as a *check register* or an *insurance register* that lists all *insurance* policies owned.

registered bond A *bond* for which the issuer will pay the *principal* and *interest*, if registered as to interest, to the owner listed on the *books* of the issuer.

registrant See *U.S. SEC registrant*.

registrar An *agent*, usually a bank or trust company, appointed by a *corporation* to keep track of the names of shareholders and distributions to them.

registration statement Required by the Securities Act of 1933, statement of most companies that want to have owners of their securities trade the securities in public markets. The statement discloses financial data and other items of *interest* to potential investors.

regression analysis A method of *cost estimation* based on statistical techniques for fitting a line (or its equivalent in higher mathematical dimensions) to an observed series of data points, usually by minimizing the sum of squared deviations of the observed data from the fitted line. Common usage calls the cost that the analysis explains the "*dependent variable*"; it calls the variable(s) we use to estimate *cost behavior* the "*independent variable*(s)." If we use more than one independent variable, the term for the analysis is "multiple *regression analysis*." See R^2, *standard error*, and *t-value*.

regressive tax *Tax* for which the rate decreases as the taxed base, such as *income*, increases. Contrast with *progressive tax*.

Regulation S-K The *SEC*'s standardization of nonfinancial statement *disclosure* requirements for documents filed with the SEC.

Regulation S-T The *SEC*'s regulations specifying formats for electronic filing and the *EDGAR* system. See *XBRL*.

Regulation S-X The *SEC*'s principal accounting regulation, which specifies the form and content of financial reports to the SEC.

rehabilitation The improving of a used *asset* via an extensive *repair*. Ordinary repairs and *maintenance* restore or maintain expected *service potential* of an asset, and the *firm* treats them as *expenses*. A *rehabilitation* improves the asset beyond its current service potential, enhancing the service potential to a significantly higher level than before the rehabilitation. Once rehabilitated, the asset may be better, but need not be, than it was when new. The firm will *capitalize expenditures* for rehabilitation, like those for *betterments* and *improvements*.

reinvestment rate In a *capital budgeting* context, the rate at which the *firm* invests *cash* inflows from a project occurring before the project's completion. Once the analyst assumes such a rate, no project can ever have multiple *internal rates of return*. See *Descartes' Rule of Signs*.

relative performance evaluation Setting performance targets and, sometimes, compensation in relation to the performance of others, perhaps in different *firms* or *divisions*, who face a similar environment.

relative sales value method See *net realizable (sales) value*.

relevance; relevant According to *SFAC No. 2*, the *financial reporting objective* stating that accounting information is appropriate or helpful for the purposes to be served by that information.

relevant cost *Cost* used by an analyst in making a decision. *Incremental cost; opportunity cost*.

relevant cost analysis Identifies the *costs* (or *revenues*) relevant to the decision to be made. A cost or revenue is relevant only if an amount differs between alternatives. Also called *differential cost analysis*.

relevant range Activity levels over which costs are linear or for which *flexible budget* estimates and *breakeven charts* will remain valid.

reliability According to *SFAC No. 2*, the *financial reporting objective* stating that accounting information "represents what it purports to represent."

remit earnings An expression likely to confuse a reader without a firm understanding of accounting basics. A *firm* generates *net assets* by earning *income* and retains net assets if it does not declare *dividends* in the amount of *net income*. When a firm declares dividends and pays the *cash* (or other net assets), some writers would say the firm "*remits earnings*." We think the student learns better by conceiving earnings as a *credit balance*. When a firm pays dividends it sends net assets, things with *debit* balances, not something with a *credit* balance, to the recipient. When writers say firms "remit earnings," they mean the firms send assets (or net assets) that previous earnings have generated and reduce *retained earnings*.

remittance advice Information on a *check s*tub, or on a document attached to a check by the *drawer*, that tells the *payee* why a payment is being made.

rent A *charge* for use of *land*, buildings, or other *assets*.

reorganization In the *capital structure* of a *corporation*, a major change that leads to changes in the *rights*, *interests*, and implied ownership of the various *security* owners; usually results from a *merger* or an agreement by senior security holders to take action to forestall *bankruptcy*.

repair An *expenditure* to restore an *asset's service potential* after damage or after prolonged use. In the second sense, after prolonged use, the difference between *repairs* and *maintenance* is one of degree and not of kind. A repair is treated as an *expense* of the *period* when incurred. Because the *firm* treats repairs and maintenance similarly in this regard, the distinction is not important. A repair helps to maintain *capacity* at the levels planned when the firm acquired the asset. Contrast with *improvement*.

replacement cost For an *asset*, the *current fair market price* to purchase another, similar asset (with the same future benefit or *service potential*). *Current cost*. See *reproduction cost* and *productive capacity*. See also *distributable income* and *inventory profit*.

replacement cost method of depreciation Method in which the analyst augments the original-cost *depreciation charge* with an amount based on a portion of the difference between the *current replacement cost* of the *asset* and its *original cost*.

replacement system of depreciation See *retirement method of depreciation* for definition and contrast.

report *Financial statement*; *auditor's report*.

report form *Balance sheet* form that typically shows *assets* minus *liabilities* as one total. Then, below that total appears the components of *owners' equity* summing to the same total. Often, the top section shows *current* assets less current liabilities before *noncurrent assets* less noncurrent liabilities. Contrast with *account form*.

reporting objectives (policies) The general purposes for which the *firm* prepares *financial statements*. The *FASB* has discussed these in *SFAC No. 1*.

reporting unit A *segment* or a component of a segment that is a *business* with separate financial information that *management* regularly reviews. Pertinent for *impairment* considerations involving *goodwill*. *IFRS* refers to the same concept as a "*cash generating unit*."

representative item sampling Sampling in which the analyst believes the sample selected is typical of the entire *population* from which it comes. Compare *specific item sampling*.

reproduction cost The *cost* necessary to acquire an *asset* similar in all physical respects to another asset for which the analyst requires a *current value*. See *replacement cost* and *productive capacity* for contrast.

required rate of return (RRR) *Cost of capital*.

requisition A formal written order or request, such as for withdrawal of supplies from the storeroom.

resale value *Exit value*; *net realizable value*.

research and development (R&D) A form of economic activity with special accounting rules. *Firms* engage in research in hopes of discovering new knowledge that will create a new *product*, process, or service or of improving a present product, process, or service. Development translates research findings or other knowledge into a new or improved product, process, or service. *SFAS No. 2* (**Codification Topic 730**) requires that firms expense costs of such activities as incurred on the grounds that the future benefits are too uncertain to *warrant capitalization* as an *asset*. This treatment seems questionable to us because we wonder why firms would continue to undertake *R&D* if there was no expectation of future benefit; if future benefits exist, then R&D *costs* should be assets that appear, like other assets, at *historical cost*. *IFRS* allows *capitalization* of costs once the

projects reach the development stage. *U.S. GAAP* requires *capitalization* of *software* development costs once the projects reach the development stage.

reserve The worst word in accounting because almost everyone not trained in accounting, and some who are, misunderstand it. The common confusion is that "reserves" represent a pool of *cash* or other *assets* available when the *firm* needs them. Wrong. Cash always has a *debit balance*. Reserves always have a *credit* balance. When properly used in accounting, "reserves" refer to an *account* that appropriates *retained earnings* and restricts dividend declarations. Appropriating retained earnings is itself a poor and vanishing practice, so the word should seldom appear in accounting. In addition, "reserve" was used in the past to indicate an asset *contra account* (for example, "reserve for *depreciation*") or an *estimated liability* (for example, "reserve for *warranty costs*"). In any case, reserve accounts have *credit* balances and are not pools of *funds*, as the unwary reader might infer. If a company has set aside a pool of *cash* (or *marketable securities*) to serve some specific purpose such as paying for a new *factory*, then it will call that cash a *fund*. No other word in accounting causes so much misunderstanding by nonexperts as well as by "experts" who should know better. A leading unabridged dictionary defines "*reserve*" as "cash, or assets readily convertible into cash, held aside, as by a *corporation*, bank, state or national government, etc. to meet expected or unexpected demands." This definition is absolutely wrong in accounting. Reserves are not funds. For example, the firm creates a *contingency fund* of $10,000 by depositing cash in a fund and makes the following entry:

Contingency Fund (Asset Increase)	10,000	
Cash (Asset Decrease)		10,000

The following entry may accompany the previous entry, if the firm wants to appropriate retained earnings:

Retained Earnings (Shareholders' Equity Decrease).	10,000	
Reserve for Contingencies (Liability Increase)		10,000

The transaction leading to the first entry has economic significance. The second entry has little economic impact for most firms. The problem with the word "reserve" arises because the firm can make the second entry without the first—a company can create a reserve, that is, appropriate retained earnings, without creating a fund. The problem results, at least in part, from the fact that in common usage, "reserve" means a pool of assets, as in the phrase "oil reserves." The *Internal Revenue Service* does not help in dispelling confusion about the term "reserves." The federal *income tax* return for corporations uses the title "Reserve for Bad Debts" to mean "Allowance for Uncollectible Accounts" and speaks of the "Reserve Method" in referring to the *allowance method* for estimating *revenue* or *income* reductions from estimated *uncollectibles*.

reserve recognition accounting (RRA) One form of *accounting* for *natural resources*. In exploration for natural resources, the problem arises of how to treat the expenditures for exploration, both before the *firm* knows the outcome of the efforts and after it knows the outcome. Suppose that the firm spends $10 million to drill 10 holes ($1 million each) and that nine of them are dry whereas one is a gusher containing oil with a *net realizable value* of $40 million. Dry hole, or *successful efforts*, accounting would *expense* $9 million and *capitalize* $1 million, which the firm will *deplete* as it lifts the oil from the ground. *Full costing* would expense nothing but would capitalize the $10 million of drilling costs that the firm will deplete as it lifts the oil from the single productive well. *Reserve recognition accounting* would capitalize $40 million, which the firm will deplete as it lifts the oil, with a $30 million *credit* to *income* or *contributed capital*. The *balance sheet* shows the *net realizable value* of proven oil and gas reserves. The *income statement* has three sorts of items: (1) current income resulting from production or "lifting profit," which is the *revenue* from *sales* of oil and gas less the *expense* based on the current valuation amount at which these items have appeared on the balance sheet, (2) *profit* or *loss* from exploration efforts in which the current value of new discoveries is revenue and all the exploration cost is expense, and (3) gain or loss on changes in current value during the year, which accountants in other contexts call a *holding gain or loss*.

reset bond A *bond*, typically a *junk bond*, that specifies that periodically the issuer will reset the *coupon rate* so that the bond sells at *par* in the market. *Investment* bankers created this type of instrument to help ensure the purchasers of such bonds of getting a fair *rate of return*, given the riskiness of the issuer. If the issuer gets into financial trouble, its bonds will trade for less than par in the market. The issuer of a reset bond promises to raise the *interest rate* and *preserve* the *value* of the bond. Ironically, the reset feature has often had just the opposite effect. The *default risk* of many issuers of reset bonds has deteriorated so much that the bonds have dropped to less than 50% of par. To raise the value to par, the issuer would have to raise the interest rate to more than 25% per year. That rate is so large that issuers have declared bankruptcy rather than attempt to make the new large *interest payments*; this then reduces the *market value* of the bonds rather than increases them.

residual income In an *external reporting* context, a term that refers to *net income* to *common shares* (= net income less *preferred stock dividends*). In *managerial accounting*, this term refers to the excess of income for a *division* or *segment* of a company over the *product* of the *cost of capital* for the company multiplied by the average amount of capital *invested* in the division during the *period* over which the division earned the *income*.

residual security A *potentially dilutive security*. Options, *warrants*, *convertible bonds*, and *convertible preferred stock*.

residual value At any time, the estimated or actual *net realizable value* (that is, *proceeds* less removal *costs*) of an *asset*, usually a depreciable *plant asset*. In the context of *depreciation accounting*, this term is equivalent to *salvage value* and is preferred to *scrap value* because the *firm* need not scrap the asset. It is sometimes used to mean net *carrying value*. In the context of a *noncancelable* lease, it is the estimated *value* of the leased asset at the end of the lease period. See *lease*.

resources supplied *Expenditures* made for an activity.

resources used *Cost driver* rate times cost driver volume.

responsibility accounting Accounting for a *business* by considering various units as separate entities, or *profit centers* or *revenue centers*, or *cost centers*, or *investment centers*, giving management of each unit responsibility for the unit's *revenues* and *expenses*. See *transfer price*.

responsibility center An organization part or *segment* that top *management* holds accountable for a specified set of activities. Also called "*accountability center*." See *cost center*, *investment center*, *profit center*, and *revenue center*.

restricted assets Governmental resources restricted by legal or contractual requirements for specific purpose.

restricted retained earnings That part of *retained earnings* not legally available for *dividends*. See *retained earnings*, *appropriated*. *Bond indentures* and other *loan* contracts can curtail the legal ability of the *corporation* to declare dividends without formally requiring a *retained earnings appropriation*, but the *firm* must disclose such restrictions.

restructuring (liability, provisions) The *FASB Codification*, quoting *IFRS*, defines this as "a program that is planned and controlled by *management*, and materially changes either the scope of the *business* undertaken by an *entity*, or the manner in which that business is conducted." The *liability* or, in IFRS, the *provision* reports the amounts the business expects to pay as a result of the plan. *U.S. GAAP* and IFRS differ in details as to when the *firm* recognizes a liability (U.S. GAAP) or provision (IFRS); see discussion in **Chapter 8**.

retail inventory method Ascertaining *cost* amounts of *ending inventory* as follows (assuming *FIFO*): cost of *ending inventory* = (selling *price* of *goods available for sale* − sales) × *cost percentage*. The analyst then computes *cost of goods sold* from the *inventory equation*; costs of *beginning inventory*, purchases, and ending inventory are all known. (When the *firm* uses *LIFO*, the method resembles the *dollar-value LIFO method*.) See *markup*.

retail terminology See *markup*.

retained earnings *Net income* over the life of a *corporation* less all *dividends* (including capitalization through *stock dividends*); *owners' equity* less *contributed capital*.

retained earnings, appropriated An *account* set up by *crediting* it and *debiting retained earnings*; used to indicate that a portion of retained earnings is not available for *dividends*. The practice of appropriating retained earnings is misleading unless the *firm* marks all *capital* with its use, which is not practicable, nor sensible, since capital is fungible—all the *equities* jointly *fund* all the *assets*. The use of formal retained earnings appropriations is declining.

retained earnings statement A *reconciliation* of the beginning and the ending *balances* in the *retained earnings account*; required by *generally accepted accounting principles* whenever the *firm* presents *comparative balance sheets* and an *income statement*. This reconciliation can appear in a separate statement, in a combined statement of income and retained earnings, or in the balance sheet.

retirement method of depreciation A method in which the *firm* records no entry for *depreciation expense* until it retires an *asset* from service. Then, it makes an entry *debiting* depreciation expense and *crediting* the asset account for the *cost* of the asset retired. If the retired asset has a *salvage value*, the firm reduces the amount of the debit to depreciation expense by the amount of salvage value with a corresponding debit to cash, *receivables*, or salvaged materials. The "*replacement system of depreciation*" is similar, except that the debit to depreciation expense equals the cost of the new asset less the salvage value, if any, of the old asset. Some public utilities used these methods. For example, if the firm acquired ten telephone poles in Year 1 for $60 each and replaces them in Year 10 for $100 each when the salvage value of the old poles is $5 each, the accounting would be as follows:

Retirement Method

Plant Assets (Asset Increase)	600	
Cash (Asset Decrease)		600
To acquire assets in Year 1.		
Retained Earnings (Depreciation Expense) (Shareholders' Equity Decrease)	550	
Salvage Receivable (Asset Increase)	50	
Plant Assets (Asset Decrease)		600
To record retirement and depreciation in Year 10.		
Plant Assets (Asset Increase)	1,000	
Cash (Asset Decrease)		1,000
To record acquisition of new assets in Year 10.		

Replacement Method

Plant Assets (Asset Increase)	600	
Cash (Asset Decrease)		600
To acquire assets in Year 1.		
Depreciation Expense (Shareholders' Equity Decrease)	950	
Salvage Receivable (Asset Increase)	50	
Cash (Asset Decrease)		1,000
To record depreciation on old asset in amount quantified by net cost of replacement asset in Year 10.		

The retirement method is like *FIFO* in that it records the cost of the first assets as *depreciation* and puts the cost of the second assets on the balance sheet The replacement method is like *LIFO* in that it records the cost of the second assets as depreciation expense and leaves the cost of the first assets on the balance sheet.

retirement plan *Pension plan.*

retroactive benefits In initiating or amending a *defined-benefit pension plan*, benefits that the benefit formula attributes to employee *services* rendered in *periods* prior to the initiation or amendment. See *prior service costs.*

return A *schedule* of information required by governmental bodies, such as the *tax return* required by the *Internal Revenue Service*; also the physical return of *merchandise*. See also *return on assets* and *return on investment*.

return and risk Modern financial economics shows that under most realistic circumstances, if an investor wants to earn a higher rate of *return on investment*, then the investor must bear more *risk*. Conversely, an investor who bears more risk expects to earn a higher return on investment as compensation for that risk bearing.

return on assets (ROA) *Net income* plus after-tax *interest charges* plus *noncontrolling interest* in *income* divided by average total *assets*; perhaps the single most useful *ratio* for *assessing management*'s overall *operating* performance. Most financial economists would subtract average noninterest-bearing *liabilities* from the denominator. Economists realize that when liabilities do not provide for explicit *interest* charges, the *creditor* adjusts the terms of contract, such as setting a higher selling *price* or lower *discount*, to those who do not pay cash immediately. (To take an extreme example,

consider how much higher *salary* a worker who receives a salary once per year, rather than once per month, would demand.) This ratio requires in the numerator the income amount before the *firm accrues* any charges to suppliers of *funds*. We cannot measure the interest charges implicit in the noninterest-bearing liabilities because they cause items such as *cost of goods sold* and salary expense to be somewhat larger, since the interest is implicit. Subtracting their amounts from the denominator adjusts for their implicit cost. Such subtraction assumes that assets financed with noninterest-bearing liabilities have the same *rate of return* as all the other assets.

return on investment (ROI), return on capital *Income* (before distributions to suppliers of *capital*) for a *period*; as a rate, this amount divided by *average* total *assets*. The analyst should add back *interest*, net of tax effects, to *net income* for the numerator. See *ratio.*

revenue The *owners' equity* increase accompanying the *net assets* increase caused by selling *goods* or rendering *services*; in short, a service rendered; *sales* of products, *merchandise*, and *services* and *earnings* from *interest*, *dividends*, *rents*, and the like. Conceptually (in contrast to specific guidance in *accounting standards*) measure *revenue* as the expected *net present value* of the net assets the firm will receive. Do not confuse with *receipt* of *funds*, which may occur before, when, or after revenue is recognized. Contrast with *gain* and *income*. See also *holding gain*. Some writers use the term *gross income* synonymously with *revenue*; avoid such usage.

revenue center Within a *firm*, a *responsibility center* that has control only over *revenues* generated. Contrast with *cost center*. See *profit center* or *investment center*.

revenue expenditure A term sometimes used to mean an *expense*, in contrast to a capital *expenditure* to acquire an *asset* or to discharge a *liability*. Avoid using this term; use *period expense* instead.

revenue recognition Standard setters prescribe when a *firm* can *recognize revenue*. The general criteria require that the firm have delivered a *product* or *service* to the customer, have received *cash* or a *financial asset* capable of reasonably precise measurement, and be able to measure with reasonable *precision* the remaining *costs* (such as for *warranties*, technical services, and software upgrades) to complete the *transaction*.

revenue received in advance An inferior term for *advances from customers*.

reversal (reversing) entry An *entry* in which all *debits* and *credits* are the credits and debits, respectively, of another entry, and in the same amounts. The accountant usually records a reversal entry on the first day of an *accounting period* to reverse a previous *adjusting entry*, usually an *accrual*. The purpose of such entries is to make the bookkeeper's tasks easier. Suppose that the *firm* pays salaries every other Friday, with paychecks compensating employees for the two weeks just ended. Total salaries accrue at the rate of $5,000 per five-day workweek. The bookkeeper is accustomed to making the following entry every other Friday:

(1) Retained Earnings (Salary Expense) (Shareholders' Equity Decrease)	10,000	
Cash (Asset Decrease).		10,000
To record salary expense and salary payments.		

If the firm delivers paychecks to employees on Friday, November 25, then the *adjusting entry* made on November 30 (or perhaps later) to record accrued salaries for November 28, 29, and 30 would be as follows:

(2) Retained Earnings (Salary Expense)
    (Shareholders' Equity Decrease)   3,000

    Salaries Payable (Liability Increase)   3,000

To charge November operations with all salaries earned in November.

The firm would close the Salary Expense account as part of the November 30 closing entries. On the next payday, December 9, the salary entry would be as follows:

(3) Retained Earnings (Salary Expense)
    (Shareholders' Equity Decrease)   7,000

    Salaries Payable (Liability Decrease)   3,000

      Cash (Asset Decrease)   10,000

To record salary payments split between expense for December (seven days) and liability carried over from November.

To make entry **(3)**, the bookkeeper must look back into the records to see how much of the debit is to Salaries Payable accrued from the previous month in order to split the total debits between December expense and the liability carried over from November. Notice that this entry forces the bookkeeper both (a) to refer to balances in old accounts and (b) to make an entry different from the one customarily made, entry **(1)**. The reversing entry, made just after the books have been closed for the second quarter, makes the salary entry for December 9 the same as that made on all other Friday paydays. The reversing entry merely *reverses* the adjusting entry **(2)**:

(4) Salaries Payable (Liability Decrease)   3,000

    Retained Earnings (Salary Expense)
    (Shareholders' Equity Increase)   3,000

To reverse the adjusting entry.

This entry results in a zero balance in the Salaries Payable account and a credit balance in the Salary Expense account If the firm makes entry **(4)** just after it closes the books for November, then the entry on December 9 will be the customary entry **(1)**. Entries **(4)** and **(1)** together have exactly the same effect as entry **(3)**.

    The procedure for using reversal entries is as follows: the firm makes the required adjustment to record an accrual (*payable* or *receivable*) at the end of an *accounting period*; it makes the closing entry as usual; as of the first day of the following period, it makes an entry reversing the adjusting entry; when the firm makes (or receives) a payment, it records the entry as though it had not recorded an adjusting entry at the end of the preceding period. Whether a firm uses reversal entries affects the record-keeping procedures but not the financial statements.

    This term is also used to describe the entry reversing an incorrect entry before recording the correct entry.

reverse stock split A stock split in which the *firm* decreases the number of *shares outstanding*. See *stock split*.

revolving fund A *fund* whose amounts the *firm* continually spends and replenishes; for example, a *petty cash fund*.

revolving loan A *loan* that both the *borrower* and the *lender* expect to renew at *maturity*.

right The privilege to subscribe to new *stock* issues or to purchase stock. Usually, securities called *warrants* contain the rights, and the owner of the warrants may sell them. See also *preemptive right*.

risk A measure of the variability of the *return on investment*. For a given expected amount of *return*, most people prefer less risk to more risk. Therefore, in rational markets, *investments* with more risk usually promise, or investors expect to receive, a higher *rate of return* than investments with lower risk. Most people use "risk" and "*uncertainty*" as synonyms. In technical language, however, these terms have different meanings. We use "risk" when we know the probabilities attached to the various outcomes, such as the probabilities of heads or tails in the flip of a fair coin. "Uncertainty" refers to an event for which we can only estimate the probabilities of the outcomes, such as winning or losing a lawsuit.

risk-adjusted discount rate Rate used in discounting *cash flows* for projects more or less risky than the *firm's average*. In a *capital budgeting* context, a decision analyst compares projects by comparing their net *present values* for a given *interest rate*, usually the *cost of capital*. If the analyst considers a given project's outcome to be much more or much less risky than the normal undertakings of the company, then the analyst will use a larger interest rate (if the project is riskier) or a smaller interest rate (if less risky) in discounting, and the rate used is "risk-adjusted."

risk-free rate An *interest rate* reflecting only the pure interest rate plus an amount to compensate for *inflation* anticipated over the life of a *loan*, excluding a *premium* for the *risk* of *default* by the *borrower*. Financial economists usually measure the *risk-free rate* in the United States from U.S. government securities, such as Treasury bills and *notes*.

risk premium Extra compensation paid to employees or extra *interest* paid to *lenders*, over amounts usually considered normal, in *return* for their undertaking to engage in activities riskier than normal.

ROA *Return on assets*.

ROI *Return on investment*; usually used to refer to a single project and expressed as a *ratio*: *income* divided by average *cost* of *assets* devoted to the project.

royalty Compensation for the use of property, usually a *patent*, copyrighted *material*, or *natural resources*. The amount is often expressed as a percentage of *receipts* from using the property or as an amount per unit produced.

RRA *Reserve recognition accounting*.

RRR *Required rate of return*. See *cost of capital*.

rule of 69 Rule stating that an amount of *cash* invested at $r\%$ per *period* will double in $69/r + .35$ periods. This approximation is accurate to one-tenth of a period for *interest rates* between 1/4 and 100% per period. For example, at 10% per period, the rule says that a given sum will double in $69/10 + .35 = 7.25$ periods. At 10% per period, a given sum actually doubles in 7.27+ periods.

rule of 72 Rule stating that an amount of *cash* invested at $r\%$ per *period* will double in $72/r$ periods. A reasonable approximation for *interest rates* between 4 and 10% but not nearly as accurate as the *rule of 69* for interest rates outside that range. For example, at 10% per period, the rule says that a given sum will double in $72/10 = 7.2$ periods.

An Open Account, Ruled and Balanced
(Steps indicated in parentheses correspond to steps described in "ruling an account.")

	Date 2009	Explanation	Ref.	Debit (1)	Date 2009	Explanation	Ref.	Credit (2)	
	Jan. 2	Balance	✓	100.00					
	Jan. 13		VR	121.37	Sept. 15		J	.42	
	Mar. 20		VR	56.42	Nov. 12		J	413.15	
	June 5		J	1,138.09	Dec. 31	Balance	✓	1,050.59	(3)
	Aug. 18		J	1.21					
	Nov. 20		VR	38.43					
	Dec. 7		VR	8.64					
(4)	2010			1,464.16	2010			1,464.16	(4)
(5)	Jan. 1	Balance	✓	1,050.59					

rule of 78 The rule followed by many *finance* companies for *allocating earnings* on *loans* among the months of a year on the sum-of-the-months'-digits basis when the *borrower* makes equal monthly payments to the *lender*. The sum of the digits from 1 through 12 is 78, so the rule *allocates* 12/78 of the year's earnings to the first month, 11/78 to the second month, and so on. This approximation allocates more of the early payments to *interest* and less to principal than does the correct, compound-interest method. Hence, lenders still use this method even though present-day computers can make the compound-interest computation as easily as they can carry out the approximation. See *sum-of-the-years'-digits depreciation*.

ruling (and balancing) an account The process of summarizing a series of entries in an *account* by computing a new *balance* and drawing double lines to indicate that the new balance summarizes the information above the double lines. An illustration appears below. The steps are as follows: (1) Compute the sum of all *debit* entries including opening debit balance, if any—$1,464.16. (2) Compute the sum of all *credit* entries including opening credit balance, if any—$413.57. (3) If the amount in (1) exceeds the amount in (2), then write the excess as a credit with a checkmark—$1,464.16 − $413.57 = $1,050.59. (4) Add both debit and credit columns, which should both now sum to the same amount, and show that identical total at the foot of both columns. (5) Draw double lines under those numbers and write the excess of debits over credits as the new debit balance with a checkmark. (6) If the amount in (2) exceeds the amount in (1), then write the excess as a debit with a checkmark. (7) Do steps (4) and (5) except that the excess becomes the new credit balance. (8) If the amount in (1) equals the amount in (2), then the balance is zero, and only the totals with the double lines beneath them need appear.

S

S corporation A *corporation* taxed like a *partnership*. Corporation (or partnership) agreements *allocate* the periodic *income* to the individual shareholders (or partners) who report these amounts on their individual *income tax* returns. Contrast with *C corporation*.

SA (société anonyme) France: A *corporation*.

SAB *Staff Accounting Bulletin* of the *SEC*.

safe-harbor lease A form of *tax-transfer lease*.

safety stock Extra items of *inventory* kept on hand to protect against running out.

salary Compensation earned by *managers*, administrators, and professionals, not based on an hourly rate. Contrast with *wage*.

sale A *revenue transaction* in which the *firm* delivers *goods* or *services* to a customer in *return* for *cash* or a contractual obligation to pay.

sale and leaseback A *financing transaction* in which the *firm* sells improved property but takes it back for use on a long-term *lease*. Such *transactions* often have advantageous *income tax* effects but usually have no effect on *financial statement income*.

sales activity variance *Sales volume variance*.

sales allowance A sales *invoice* price reduction that a seller grants to a buyer because the seller delivered *goods* different from, perhaps because of damage, those the buyer ordered. The seller often accumulates amounts of such *adjustments* in a temporary *revenue contra account* having this, or a similar, title. See *sales discount*.

sales basis of revenue recognition Recognition of *revenue* not when a firm produces *goods* or when it receives orders but only when it has completed the *sale* by delivering the goods or *services* and has received *cash* or a claim to cash. Most firms recognize revenue on this basis. Compare with the *percentage-of-completion method* and the *installment method*. This is identical with the *completed contract method*, but the latter term ordinarily applies only to *long-term* construction projects.

sales contra, estimated uncollectibles A title for the contra-revenue account to *recognize* estimated reductions in *income* caused by *accounts receivable* that will not be collected. See *bad debt expense*, *allowance for uncollectibles*, and *allowance method*.

sales discount A *sales invoice price* reduction usually offered for prompt payment. See *terms of sale* and *2/10, n/30*.

sales return The physical *return* of *merchandise*. The seller often accumulates amounts of such returns in a temporary *revenue contra account*.

sales-type (capital) lease A form of *lease*. See *capital lease*. When a manufacturer (or other *firm*) that ordinarily sells *goods* enters a capital lease as *lessor*, the lease is a "sales-type lease." When a financial firm, such as a bank or *insurance* company or leasing company, acquires the *asset* from the manufacturer and then enters a capital lease as lessor, the lease is a "direct-financing-type lease." The manufacturer recognizes its ordinary *profit* (*sales price* less *cost of goods sold*, where sales price is the *present value* of the contractual lease payments plus any down payment) on executing the sales-type capital lease, but the financial firm does not recognize profit on executing a capital lease of the direct-financing type. Instead, it earns interest because the sum of lease payments exceed the cost of the leased asset. Manufacturers who enter a sales-type lease earn both an ordinary profit on the sale and interest.

sales value method *Relative sales value method.* See *net realizable value method.*

sales volume variance Budgeted *contribution margin* per unit times (actual *sales* volume minus planned sales volume).

salvage value Actual or estimated selling *price*, *net* of removal or disposal *costs*, of a used *asset* that the firm expects to sell or otherwise retire. See *residual value.*

SAR *Summary annual report.*

Sarbanes-Oxley Act; SOX The law, passed in 2002 in the wake of the Enron, WorldCom, and other scandals, to stiffen the requirements for corporate governance, including accounting issues. It speaks, among other things, to the regulation of the accounting profession, the standards for *audit committees* of public companies, the certifications *managements* must sign, and standards of internal control that companies must meet.

SARL (*société à responsabilité limitée*) France: a *corporation* with *limited liability* and a life of no more than 99 years; must have at least two and no more than 50 *shareholders.*

SAS *Statement on Auditing Standards* of the *AICPA.*

scale effect See *discounted cash flow.*

scatter diagram A graphic representation of the relation between two or more variables within a *population.*

schedule A supporting set of calculations, with explanations, that show how to derive figures in a *financial statement* or tax return.

scientific method *Effective interest method* of *amortizing bond discount* or *premium.*

scope paragraph A section of the *auditor's report* where the auditor describes the nature of the work undertaken, the procedures performed, and any limitations.

scrap value *Salvage value* assuming the owner intends to junk the item. A *net realizable value. Residual value.*

SEC (Securities and Exchange Commission) An agency authorized by the U.S. Congress to regulate, among other things, the financial reporting practices of most public *corporations.* The SEC has indicated that it will usually allow the *FASB* to set *accounting principles*, but it often requires more *disclosure* than the FASB requires. The SEC states its accounting requirements in its *Accounting Series Releases* (*ASR*—replaced in 1982 by the following two), *Financial Reporting Releases, Accounting and Auditing Enforcement Releases, Staff Accounting Bulletins* (these are, strictly speaking, interpretations by the accounting staff, not rules of the commissioners themselves), and *Regulation S-X and Regulation S-K.* See also *registration statement, 10-K, 10-Q, and 20-F.*

secret reserve *Hidden reserve.*

Securities and Exchange Commission *SEC.*

securitization The bundling of *financial assets* into groups that can become the basis for raising *cash.* For example, a bank might have loaned to hundreds of customers under home *mortgages.* It could bundle a defined set of mortgages and offer for *sale* fractional interests, called "*securities*," in the cash inflows from the pool of mortgages. An example of "financial engineering." This has roughly the same economic effect as using the *assets* as *collateral* for a borrowing, but the *securitization transaction* enables the seller to sell to many investors and the items sold are *marketable securities.*

security Document that indicates ownership, such as a *share* of *stock*, or indebtedness, such as a *bond*, or potential ownership, such as an *option* or *warrant.*

security available for sale According to *SFAS No. 115* (1993) (**Codification Topic 320**), a *debt* or *equity security* that is not a *trading security*, or a debt security that is not a *security held to maturity.* See *available for sale.*

security held to maturity According to *SFAS No. 115* (1993) (**Codification Topic 320**), a *debt security* the holder has both the ability and the intent to hold to *maturity*; valued in the *balance sheet* at amortized acquisition cost: the carrying value of the *security* at the end of each *period* is the carrying value at the beginning of the period multiplied by one plus the historical *yield* on the security (measured as of the time of purchase) less any *cash* the holder receives at the end of this period from the security. The preceding assumes that cash receipts come at the end of a period. If they come before period-end, the computations are more complex.

segment (of a business) As defined by *APB Opinion No. 30* (**Codification Topic 845**), "a component of an *entity* whose activities represent a separate major line of *business* or class of customer. . . . [It may be] a *subsidiary*, a *division*, or a department, . . . provided that its *assets*, results of *operations*, and activities can be clearly distinguished, physically and operationally for financial reporting purposes, from the other assets, results of operations, and activities of the entity." *SFAS No. 131* (**Codification Topic 280**) defines operating segments using the "*management* approach" as components of the *enterprise* engaging in revenue- and expense-generating business activities "whose operating results are regularly reviewed by the enterprise's chief operating decision maker to make decisions about resources . . . and asset performance."

The *IFRS* defines a segment as "a component of an entity that engages in business activities . . . whose operating results are regularly reviewed by the entity's chief operating decision maker to make decisions about resources to be *allocated* to the segment . . . for which discrete financial information is available."

segment reporting Reporting of *sales*, *income*, and *assets* by *segments of a business*, usually classified by nature of *products* sold but sometimes by geographical area where the firm produces or sells *goods* or by type of customers; sometimes called "line of *business* reporting." The accounting for segment income does not *allocate central corporate expenses* to the segments.

self-balancing A set of records with equal *debits* and *credits* such as the *ledger* (but not individual accounts), the *balance sheet*, and a *fund* in nonprofit accounting.

self-check(ing) digit A digit forming part of an *account* or code number, normally the last digit of the number, which is mathematically derived from the other numbers of the code and is used to detect errors in transcribing the code number. For example, assume the last digit of the account number is the remainder after summing the preceding digits and dividing that sum by nine. Suppose the computer encounters the account numbers 7027261-7 and 9445229-7. The program can tell that something has gone wrong with the encoding of the second account number because the sum of the first seven digits is 35, whose remainder on *division* by 9 is 8, not 7. The first account number does not show such an error because the sum of the first seven digits is 25, whose remainder on division by 9 is, indeed, 7. The first account number may be in error, but the second surely is.

self-insurance See *insurance*.

self-sustaining foreign operation A foreign operation both financially and operationally independent of the reporting *enterprise* (owner) so that the owner's exposure to exchange-rate changes results only from the owner's *net investment* in the foreign *entity*.

selling and administrative expenses *Expenses* not specifically identifiable with, or assigned to, production.

semifixed costs *Costs* that increase with activity as a step *function*.

semivariable costs *Costs* that increase strictly linearly with activity but that are positive at zero activity level. *Royalty* fees of 2% of *sales* are variable; royalty fees of $1,000 per year plus 2% of sales are semivariable.

senior securities; senior rights *Bonds* as opposed to *preferred stock*; preferred stock as opposed to *common stock*. The firm must meet the senior *security* claim against *earnings* or *assets* before meeting the claims of less-senior securities.

sensitivity analysis A study of how the outcome of a decision-making process changes as one or more of the assumptions change.

separability criterion An *intangible* can be an *asset* if it meets this criterion, which requires that the *firm* be able to sell or to transfer or to license or to *rent* or to *exchange* it with a *counterparty*.

sequential access Computer-storage access in which the analyst can locate information only by a sequential search of the storage file. Compare *direct access*.

serial bonds An *issue* of *bonds* that mature in part at one date, another part on another date, and so on. The various *maturity* dates usually occur at equally spaced intervals. Contrast with *term bonds*.

service basis of depreciation *Production method*.

service bureau A commercial data-processing center providing service to various customers.

service cost, (current) service cost *Pension plan expenses incurred* during an *accounting period* for employment *services* performed during that *period*. Contrast with *prior service cost*. See *funded*.

service department A department, such as the personnel or computer department, that provides *services* to other departments rather than direct work on a salable *product*. Contrast with *production department*. A *firm* must *allocate costs* of *service departments* to *product costs* under *full absorption costing* if the services benefit manufacturing *operations*.

service department cost allocation A procedure in which firms *allocate* the *costs* of *operating service departments* to other departments.

service life *Period* of expected usefulness of an asset; may differ from *depreciable life* for *income tax* purposes.

service potential The future benefits that cause an item to be classified as an *asset*. Without *service potential*, an item has no future benefits, and accounting will not classify the item as an asset. *SFAC No. 6* suggests that the primary characteristic of service potential is the ability to generate future *net cash* inflows.

services Useful work done by a person, a machine, or an organization. See *goods*.

setup The time or *costs* required to prepare production equipment for doing a *job*.

SFAC *Statement of Financial Accounting Concepts* of the *FASB*.

SFAS; FAS *Statement of Financial Accounting Standards*. See *FASB*.

shadow price An *opportunity cost*. A *linear programming* analysis provides as one of its *outputs* the potential *value* of having available more of the scarce resources that constrain the production process, for example, the value of having more time available on a machine tool critical to the production of two products. Common terminology refers to this value as the "shadow price" or the "dual value" of the scarce resource.

share A unit of *stock* representing ownership in a *corporation*.

share premium UK: *additional paid-in capital* or *capital contributed in excess of par value*.

shareholder One who owns a *share*.

shareholders' equity *Proprietorship* or *owners' equity* of a *corporation*. Because *stock* means *inventory* in Australia, the UK, and Canada, their writers use the term "shareholders' equity" rather than the term "*stockholders' equity*."

short run; short term Contrast with *long run*. *Managers* mean a *period* of time long enough to allow change the level of production or other activity within the constraints of current total *productive capacity*. In a *balance sheet* context, it means *current*, ordinarily due within one year. Use a hyphen when the phrase is an adjective, but no hyphen when it is a noun.

short-term liquidity risk The *risk* that an *entity* will not have enough *cash* in the *short run* to pay its *debts*.

short-term operating budget *Management*'s quantitative action plan for the coming year.

shrinkage An excess of *inventory* shown on the *books* over actual physical quantities on hand; can result from theft or shoplifting as well as from evaporation, excess scrap, or general wear and tear. Some accountants, in an attempt to downplay their own errors, use the term to mean record-keeping mistakes that they later must correct, with some embarrassment, and that result in material changes in reported *income*. One should not use the term "shrinkage" for the correction of mistakes because adequate terminology exists for describing mistakes.

shutdown cost Those *fixed costs* that the *firm* continues to incur after it has ceased production; the costs of closing down a particular production facility.

side letter See *channel stuffing*.

sight draft A demand for payment drawn by Person A to whom Person B owes cash. Person A presents the *draft* to Person B's (the *debtor*'s) bank in expectation that Person B will authorize his or her bank to disburse the *funds*. Sellers often use such *drafts* when selling *goods* to a new customer in a different city. The seller is uncertain whether the buyer will pay the *bill*. The seller sends the bill of lading, or other evidence of ownership of the goods, along with a sight draft to the buyer's bank. Before the warehouse holding the goods can release them to the buyer, the buyer must instruct its bank to honor the sight draft by withdrawing funds from the buyer's account. Once the bank honors the sight draft, it hands to the buyer the bill of lading or other document evidencing ownership, and the goods become the property of the buyer.

significant influence An *investor* has significant influence over an *investee* if it can change the course of *operations* from those the investee would otherwise have undertaken. *U.S. GAAP* contains a rebuttable presumption that an investor has (does not have) significant influence if it does (does not) own 20% or more of the investee's voting *shares*.

simple interest *Interest* calculated on *principal* where interest earned during *periods* before *maturity* of the *loan* does not increase the principal amount earning interest for the subsequent periods and the *lender* cannot *withdraw* the *funds* before maturity. Interest = principal × interest rate × time, where the rate is a rate per period (typically a year) and time is expressed in units of that period. For example, if the *rate* is annual and the time is two months, then in the formula, use 2/12 for *time*. Simple interest is seldom used in economic calculations except for periods of less than one year and then only for computational convenience. Contrast with *compound interest*.

single-entry accounting Accounting that is neither *self-balancing* nor *articulated*. That is, it does not rely on equal *debits* and *credits*. The firm makes no *journal entries* and must *plug* to derive *owners' equity* for the *balance sheet*.

single proprietorship *Sole proprietorship*.

single-step Said of an *income statement* in which *ordinary revenue* and *gain* items appear first, with their total. Then come all ordinary *expenses* and *losses*, with their total. The difference between these two totals, plus the effect of *income from discontinued operations* and *extraordinary items*, appears as *net income*. Contrast with *multiple-step* and see *proprietorship theory*.

sinking fund *Assets* and their *earnings* earmarked for the retirement of *bonds* or other long-term obligations. Earnings of sinking fund *investments* become taxable *income* of the company.

sinking fund method of depreciation Method in which the periodic *charge* is an equal amount each *period* so that the *future value* of the charges, considered as an *annuity*, will accumulate at the end of the *depreciable life* to an amount equal to the *acquisition cost* of the *asset*. The firm does not necessarily, or even usually, accumulate a *fund* of *cash*. Firms rarely use this method.

skeleton account *T-account*.

SMAC (Society of Management Accountants of Canada) The *national association of accountants* whose provincial associations engage in industrial and governmental accounting. The association undertakes research and administers an educational program and comprehensive examinations; those who pass qualify to be designated *CMA (Certified Management Accountants)*, formerly called RIA (Registered Industrial Accountant).

SNC (*société en nom collectif*) France: a *partnership*.

soak-up method The *equity method*.

Social Security taxes *Taxes* levied by the federal government on both employers and employees to provide *funds* to pay retired persons (or their survivors) who are entitled to receive such *payments*, either because they paid *Social Security taxes* themselves or because Congress has declared them *eligible*. Unlike a *pension plan*, the Social Security system does not collect funds and invest them for many years. The tax collections in a given year pay primarily for benefits distributed that year. At any given time the system has a multitrillion-dollar *unfunded* obligation to current workers for their eventual retirement benefits. See *Old Age, Survivors, and Disability Insurance*.

software The programming aids, such as operating systems, programming languages, compilers, application programs,

and report writers that extend the capabilities of and simplify the use of the computer. Compare *hardware*.

sole proprietorship A firm in which all *owners' equity* belongs to one person and that is not incorporated.

solvent Able to meet *debts* when due.

SOP *Statement of Position* (of the *AcSEC* of the *AICPA*).

source of funds Any *transaction* that increases *cash* and *marketable securities* held as *current assets*.

sources and uses statement *Statement of cash flows*.

SOYD *Sum-of-the years'-digits depreciation*.

SOX *Sarbanes-Oxley Act*.

SP (*société en participation*) France: a silent *partnership* in which the managing partner acts for the partnership as an individual in transacting with others who need not know that the person represents a partnership.

special assessment A compulsory levy made by a governmental unit on property to pay the *costs* of a specific *improvement* or *service* presumed not to benefit the general public but only the owners of the property so assessed; accounted for in a special assessment *fund*.

special journal A *journal*, such as a *sales journal* or *cash disbursements journal*, to record *transactions* of a similar nature that occur frequently.

special purpose entity; SPE; QSPE In general, the goal of creating a SPE or *variable interest entity* is for an *investor* to achieve *off-balance-sheet financing*, by constructing a *business* which itself engages in substantial borrowing, for which the investor has economic obligation to repay under some circumstances, but which the investor need not *consolidate*. In *U.S. GAAP*, the name for a business now known as a "*qualifying special-purpose entity (QSPE)*" or a variable interest entity. U.S. GAAP never defined the SPE, but brought it into existence with an *EITF* consensus in 1990. U.S. GAAP (**Codification Topic 860-40**) gives detailed guidance as to when an entity qualifies as a QSPE and becomes exempt from consolidation. *IFRS* defines SPE in terms of control: if the investor has control, then it must consolidate. IFRS gives several indicia of control, but no rules.

special revenue debt A governmental unit's *debt* backed only by *revenues* from specific sources, such as tolls from a bridge.

specific identification method Method for valuing *ending inventory* and *cost of goods sold* by identifying actual units sold and remaining in *inventory* and summing the *actual costs* of those individual units; usually used for items with large unit values, such as precious jewelry, automobiles, and fur coats.

specific item sampling Sampling in which the analyst selects particular items because of their nature, *value*, or method of recording. Compare *representative item sampling*.

specific price changes Changes in the *market prices* of specific *goods* and *services*. Contrast with *general price-level changes*.

specific price index A measure of the *price* of a specific *good* or *service*, or a small group of similar goods or services, at one time relative to the price during a base *period*. Contrast with *general price index*. See *dollar-value LIFO method*.

spending variance In *standard cost systems*, the *rate* or *price variance* for *overhead costs*.

split *Stock split*. Sometimes called "split-up."

split-off point In accumulating and allocating *costs* for *joint products*, the point at which all costs are no longer *joint costs* but at which an analyst can identify costs associated with individual *products* or perhaps with a smaller number of joint products.

spoilage See *abnormal spoilage* and *normal spoilage*.

spot price The *price* of a commodity for delivery on the day of the *price* quotation. See *forward price* for contrast.

spreadsheet Since personal-computer *software* has become widespread, this term has come to refer to any file created by programs such as Microsoft Excel®. Such files have rows and columns, but they need not represent *debits* and *credits*. Moreover, they can have more than two dimensions.

squeeze A term sometimes used for *plug*.

SSARS Statement on Standards for Accounting and Review Services.

stabilized accounting *Constant-dollar accounting.*

stable monetary unit assumption In spite of *inflation*, which appears to be a way of life, the assumption that underlies *historical cost*/nominal-dollar accounting—namely that one can meaningfully add together current dollars and dollars of previous years. The assumption gives no specific recognition to changing *values* of the dollar in the usual *financial statements*. See *constant-dollar accounting*.

Staff Accounting Bulletin An interpretation issued by the staff of the Chief Accountant of the *SEC* "suggesting" how the accountants should apply various *Accounting Series Releases* in practice. The suggestions are part of *U.S. GAAP*.

stakeholder An individual or group, such as employees, suppliers, customers, and *shareholders*, who have an interest in the *corporation*'s activities and outcomes.

standard(s) See *standard cost* for manufacturing context and *GAAP* for another.

standard (cost) Anticipated *cost* of producing a unit of *output*; a predetermined cost to be assigned to *products* produced. Standard cost implies a norm—what costs should be. *Budgeted cost* implies a *forecast*—something likely, but not necessarily, a "should," as implied by a norm. Firms use standard costs as the *benchmark* for gauging good and bad performance. Although a firm may similarly use a *budget*, it need not. A budget may be a planning document, subject to changes whenever plans change, whereas standard costs usually change annually or when *technology* significantly changes or when costs of labor and *materials* significantly change.

standard costing *Costing* based on *standard costs*.

standard costing system *Product costing* using *standard costs* rather than *actual costs*. The firm may use either *full absorption* or *variable costing* principles, although the *IRS*, *FASB*, and *IASB* allow only full absorption costing.

standard error (of regression coefficients) A measure of the *uncertainty* about the magnitude of the estimated parameters of an equation fit with a *regression analysis*.

standard manufacturing overhead *Overhead costs* expected to be incurred per unit of time and per unit produced.

standard price (rate) Unit *price* established for materials or labor used in *standard cost systems*.

standard quantity allowed The direct *material* or direct labor (inputs) quantity that production should have used if it had produced the units of *output* in accordance with preset *standards*.

standby costs A type of *capacity cost*, such as property *taxes*, incurred even if a firm shuts down *operations* completely. Contrast with *enabling costs*.

stated capital Amount of *capital* contributed by *shareholders*; sometimes used to mean *legal capital*.

stated value A term sometimes used for the *face amount of capital stock*, when the *board* has not designated a *par value*.

Where there is *stated value* per *share*, *capital contributed in excess of stated value* may come into being.

statement of affairs A *balance sheet* showing immediate *liquidation* amounts rather than *historical costs*, usually prepared when *insolvency* or *bankruptcy* is imminent. Such a statement specifically does not use the *going-concern assumption*.

statement of cash flows A *schedule* of *cash receipts* and *payments*, classified by *investing*, *financing*, and *operating activities*; required by the *FASB* for all for-profit companies. Companies may report operating activities with either the *direct method* (which shows only receipts and payments of *cash*) or the *indirect method* (which starts with *net income* and shows adjustments for *revenues* not currently producing cash and for *expenses* not currently using cash). "Cash" includes cash equivalents such as Treasury bills, commercial paper, and some *marketable securities* held as *current assets* (not as *investments*). This is sometimes called the "*funds statement*." Before 1987, the FASB required the presentation of a similar statement called the *statement of changes in financial position*, which tended to emphasize *working capital*, not cash.

statement of changes in financial position A *statement*, required by *U.S. GAAP* in the 1970s, that explains the changes in *working capital* (or *cash*) *balances* during a *period* and shows the changes in the working capital (or cash) accounts themselves. The *statement of cash flows* has replaced this statement.

statement of charge and discharge A *financial statement*, showing *net assets* or *income*, drawn up by an executor or administrator, to account for *receipts* and dispositions of *cash* or other *assets* in an estate or trust.

Statement of Financial Accounting Concepts (*SFAC*) One of a series of *FASB* publications in its *conceptual framework* for *financial accounting* and reporting. Such *statements* set forth *objectives* and fundamentals to be the basis for specific *financial accounting* and reporting standards.

Statement of Financial Accounting Standards (*SFAS*, *FAS*) See *FASB*.

statement of financial position *Balance sheet*.

Statement of Position (*SOP*) A recommendation, on an emerging accounting problem, issued by the *AcSEC* of the *AICPA*. The AICPA's Code of Professional Ethics specifically states that *CPAs* need not treat *SOPs* as they do rules from the *FASB*, but a CPA would be wary of departing from the recommendations of an *SOP*.

statement of retained earnings (income) A *statement* that reconciles the beginning-of-*period* and the end-of-period *balances* in the *retained earnings* account. It shows the effects of *earnings*, *dividend declarations*, and *prior-period adjustments*.

statement of significant accounting policies (principles) A summary of the significant *accounting principles* used in compiling an *annual report*; required by *APB Opinion No. 22* (**Codification Topic 235**). This summary may be a separate exhibit or the first *note* to the *financial statements*.

Statement on Auditing Standards (*SAS*) A series addressing specific auditing standards and procedures. *No. 1* (1973) of this series codifies all *statements* on auditing standards previously promulgated by the *AICPA*. Contrast with *auditing standards* and *PCAOB*.

Statement on Standards for Accounting and Review Services (*SSARS*) Pronouncements issued by the *AICPA* on unaudited *financial statements* and unaudited financial information of nonpublic entities.

static budget *Fixed budget*. Budget developed for a set level of the driving variable, such as production or *sales*, which the analyst does not change if the actual level deviates from the level set at the outset of the analysis.

status quo Events or *cost* incurrences that will happen or that a *firm* expects to happen in the absence of taking some contemplated action.

statutory tax rate The *tax* rate specified in the *income tax* law for each type of *income* (for example, *ordinary income*, *capital gain or loss*).

step allocation method *Step-down method*.

step cost *Semifixed cost*.

step-down method In *allocating service department costs*, a method that starts by allocating one service department's costs to *production departments* and to all other service departments. Then the firm allocates a second service department's costs, including costs allocated from the first, to production departments and to all other service departments except the first one. In this fashion, a firm may allocate all service departments costs, including previous allocations, to production departments and to those service departments whose costs it has not yet allocated.

step method *Step-down method*.

step(ped) cost *Semifixed cost*.

sterilized allocation Desirable characteristics of *cost allocation* methods. Optimal decisions result from considering *incremental costs* only. Optimal decisions never require *allocations* of *joint* or *common costs*. A "sterilized allocation" causes the optimal decision choice not to differ from the one that occurs when the accountant does not allocate joint or common costs "sterilized" with respect to that decision. Arthur L. Thomas first used the term in this context. Because *absorption costing* requires that *product costs* absorb all *manufacturing costs* and because some allocations can lead to bad decisions, Thomas (and we) advocate that the analyst choose a sterilized allocation scheme that will not alter the otherwise optimal decision. No single allocation scheme is always sterilized with respect to all decisions. Thus, Thomas (and we) advocate that decisions be made on the basis of incremental costs before any allocations.

stewardship Principle by which *management* is accountable for an *entity*'s resources, for their efficient use, and for protecting them from adverse impact. Some theorists believe that accounting has as a primary goal aiding users of *financial statements* in their assessment of management's performance in *stewardship*.

stock A measure of the amount of something on hand at a specific time. Because of this meaning, careful writers do not use this word to refer to *common* or *preferred shares*. Contrast with *flow*. See *inventory* and *capital stock*.

stock appreciation rights An employer's promise to pay to the employee an amount of *cash* on a certain future date, with the amount of cash being the difference between the *market value* of a specified number of *shares* of *stock* in the employer's company on the given future date and some base *price* set on the date the rights are granted. *Firms* sometimes use this form of compensation because changes in tax laws in recent years have made *stock options* relatively less attractive. *U.S. GAAP* computes compensation based on the difference between the market value of the shares and the base price set at the time of the grant.

stock dividend A so-called *dividend* in which the *firm* distributes additional *shares* of *capital stock* without *cash payments* to existing *shareholders*. It results in a *debit* to *retained earnings* in the amount of the *market value* of the shares issued and a *credit* to *capital stock* accounts. Firms ordinarily use stock dividends to indicate that they have permanently reinvested *earnings* in the business. Contrast with a *stock split*, which requires no entry in the capital stock accounts other than a notation that the *par* or *stated value* per share has changed.

stock option The *right* to purchase or sell a specified number of *shares* of *stock* for a specified *price* at specified times. *Employee stock options* are purchase rights granted by a *corporation* to employees, a form of compensation. Traded stock options are *derivative* securities, rights created and traded by investors, independent of the corporation whose stock is optioned. Contrast with *warrant*.

stock (purchase) right See *right*.

stock split(-up) Increase in the number of *common shares outstanding* resulting from the issuance of additional *shares* to existing *shareholders* without additional *capital* contributions by them. Does not increase the total *value* (or *stated value*) of common shares outstanding because the *board* reduces the *par* (or stated) *value* per share in inverse proportion. A three-for-one stock split reduces par (or stated) value per share to one-third of its former amount. A stock split usually implies a distribution that increases the number of shares outstanding by 20% or more. Compare with *stock dividend*.

stock subscriptions See *subscription* and *subscribed stock*.

stock warrant See *warrant*.

stockholders' equity See *shareholders' equity*.

stockout Occurs when a firm needs a unit of *inventory* to use in production or to sell to a customer but has none available.

stockout costs *Contribution margin* or other measure of *profits* not earned because a seller has run out of *inventory* and cannot fill a customer's order. A firm may incur an extra *cost* because of delay in filling an order.

stores *Raw materials*, parts, and supplies.

straight-debt value An estimate of the *market value* of a *convertible bond* if the bond did not contain a *conversion* privilege.

straight-line (time or use) depreciation (method) Method in which, if the *depreciable life* is n periods, the periodic *depreciation charge* is $1/n$ of the *depreciable cost*; results in equal periodic charges. Accountants sometimes call it "straight-time depreciation."

strategic plan A *statement* of the method for achieving an organization's goals.

stratified sampling In choosing a *sample*, a method in which the investigator first divides the entire *population* into relatively homogeneous subgroups (strata) and then selects random samples from these subgroups.

strike price *Exercise* price of a *stock option*. See *option* for discussion of this and related terms.

street security A *stock certificate* in immediately transferable form, most commonly because the issuing firm has registered it in the name of the broker, who has endorsed it with "*payee*" left blank.

Subchapter S corporation A firm legally organized as a *corporation* but taxed as if it were a *partnership*. Tax terminology calls the corporations paying their own *income taxes* C *corporations*.

subject to In an *auditor's report*, qualifications usually caused by a *material uncertainty* in the valuation of an item, such as future promised *payments* from a foreign government or outcome of pending litigation.

Subordinated (rights) *Debt* (or other *security*) whose claim on *income* or *assets* has lower priority than claims of other debt (or other security).

subscribed stock A *shareholders' equity* account showing the *capital* that the *firm* will receive as soon as the share-purchaser pays the *subscription price*. A subscription is a legal contract, so once the share-purchaser signs it, the firm makes an entry *debiting* an *owners' equity contra account* and *crediting* subscribed stock.

subscription Agreement to buy a *security* or to purchase periodicals, such as magazines.

subsequent events *Poststatement events*.

subsidiary A company in which another company owns more than 50% of the voting *shares*.

subsidiary ledger The *ledger* that contains the detailed accounts whose total appears in a *controlling account* of the *general ledger*.

subsidiary (ledger) accounts The *accounts* in a *subsidiary ledger*.

successful efforts costing In petroleum accounting, the *capitalization* of the drilling *costs* of only those wells that contain gas or oil. See *reserve recognition accounting* for an example.

summary annual report (SAR) Condensed *financial statements* distributed in lieu of the usual *annual report*. Since 1987, the *SEC* has allowed *firms* to include such *statements* in the annual report to *shareholders* as long as the firm includes full, detailed statements in SEC filings and in *proxy materials* sent to shareholders.

summary of significant accounting principles *Statement of significant accounting policies (principles)*.

sum-of-the-years'-digits depreciation method (SYD, SOYD) An *accelerated depreciation* method for an asset with *depreciable life* of *n* years where the *charge* in *period i* ($i = 1, \ldots, n$) is the fraction $(n + 1 - i)/[n(n + 1)/2]$ of the *depreciable cost*. If an asset has a depreciable cost of $15,000 and a five-year depreciable life, for example, the depreciation charges would be $5,000 (= 5/15 × $15,000) in the first year, $4,000 in the second, $3,000 in the third, $2,000 in the fourth, and $1,000 in the fifth. The name derives from the fact that the denominator in the fraction is the sum of the digits 1 through *n*.

sunk cost Past *costs* that current and future decisions cannot affect and, hence, that are irrelevant for decision making aside from *income tax* effects. Contrast with *incremental costs* and *imputed costs*. For example, the *acquisition cost* of machinery is irrelevant to a decision of whether to scrap the machinery. The current *exit value* of the machinery is the *opportunity cost* of continuing to own it, and the cost of, say, the electricity to run the machinery is an incremental cost of its operation. Sunk costs become relevant for decision making when the analysis requires taking income taxes (*gain or loss* on disposal of asset) into account, since the *cash payment* for income taxes depends on the tax basis of the asset. Avoid this term in careful writing because it is ambiguous. Consider, for example, a machine costing $100,000 with current *salvage* value of $20,000. Some (including us) would say that $100,000 (the *gross* amount) is "sunk"; others would say that only $80,000 (the *net* amount) is "sunk."

supplementary statements (schedules) *Statements (schedules)* in addition to the four basic *financial statements* (*balance sheet, income statement, statement of cash flows,* and the *statement of retained earnings*).

surplus A word once used but now considered poor terminology; prefaced by "earned" to mean *retained earnings* and prefaced by "capital" to mean *capital contributed in excess of par (or stated) value*.

surplus reserves *Appropriated retained earnings*. A phrase with nothing to recommend it: of all the words in accounting, *reserve* is the most objectionable, and *surplus* is the second-most objectionable.

suspense account A *temporary account* used to record part of a *transaction* before final analysis of that transaction. For example, if a *business* regularly classifies all *sales* into a dozen or more different categories but wants to deposit the proceeds of *cash* sales every day, it may *credit* a sales suspense account pending detailed classification of all sales into Durable Goods Sales, Women's Clothing Sales, Men's Clothing Sales, Housewares Sales, and so on.

sustainable income The part of *distributable income* (computed from *current cost* data) that the *firm* can expect to earn in the next *accounting period* if it continues *operations* at the same levels as were maintained during the current period. *Income from discontinued operations*, for example, may be distributable but not sustainable.

swap A currency swap is a *financial instrument* in which the holder promises to pay to (or receive from) the *counterparty* the difference between *debt* denominated in one currency (such as U.S. dollars) and the *payments* on debt denominated in another currency (such as German marks). An interest-rate swap typically obligates the party and counterparty to *exchange* the difference between fixed- and floating-rate *interest payments* on otherwise similar *loans*.

S-X See *Regulation S-X*.

SYD *Sum-of-the-years'-digits depreciation*.

T

T-account *Account form* shaped like the letter T with the title above the horizontal line. *Debits* appear on the left of the vertical line, *credits* on the right.

T-account work sheet A group of *T-accounts* used to work problems or to construct a *statement of cash flows*.

take-home pay The amount of a paycheck; earned *wages* or *salary* reduced by deductions for *income taxes*, Social Security *taxes*, contributions to fringe-benefit plans, union dues, and so on. Take-home pay might be as little as half of earned compensation.

take-or-pay contract As defined by *SFAS No. 47* (**Codification Topic 440**), a purchaser-seller agreement that provides for the purchaser to pay specified amounts periodically in *return* for *products* or *services*. The purchaser must make specified minimum *payments* even if it does not take delivery of the contracted products or services.

taking a bath To incur a large *loss*. See *big bath*.

tangible (asset) Having physical form. Accounting has never satisfactorily defined the distinction between *tangible* and *intangible assets*. Typically, accountants define intangibles by giving an exhaustive list, and everything not on the list is defined as tangible. See *intangible asset* for such a list.

target cost *Standard cost*. Sometimes, *target price* less expected *profit margin*.

target price Selling *price* based on customers' *value in* use of a *good* or *service*, constrained by competitors' prices of similar items.

tax A nonpenal, but compulsory, *charge* levied by a government on *income*, consumption, wealth, or other basis, for the benefit of all those governed. The term does not include fines or specific charges for benefits accruing only to those paying the charges, such as licenses, permits, *special assessments*, admission fees, and tolls.

tax allocation: interperiod See *deferred income tax liability*.

tax allocation: intrastatement The showing of income tax effects on *extraordinary items*, *income from discontinued operations*, and *prior-period adjustments*, along with these items, separately from income taxes on other *income*. See *net-of-tax reporting*.

tax avoidance See *tax shelter* and *loophole*.

tax basis of assets and liabilities A concept important for applying *SFAS No. 109* (**Codification Topic 740**) on *deferred income taxes*. Two *assets* will generally have different *carrying values* if the *firm* paid different amounts for them, *amortizes* them on a different *schedule*, or both. Similarly a single asset will generally have a carrying *value* different from what it will have for *tax* purposes if the firm recorded different *acquisition* amounts for the asset for *book* and for tax purposes, amortizes it differently for book and for tax purposes, or both. The difference between financial carrying value and income tax basis becomes important in computing deferred income tax amounts. The adjusted *cost* in the financial records is the "book basis," and the adjusted amount in the tax records is the "tax basis." Differences between book and tax basis can arise for *liabilities* as well as for *assets*.

tax credit A subtraction from *taxes* otherwise *payable*. Contrast with *tax deduction*.

tax deduction A subtraction from *revenues* and *gains* to arrive at taxable *income*. Tax deductions differ technically from tax *exemptions*, but both reduce *gross income* in computing taxable income. Both differ from *tax credits*, which reduce the computed tax itself in computing taxes payable. If the tax rate is the fraction *t* of pretax income, then a tax credit of $1 is *worth* $1/*t* of tax deductions.

tax evasion The fraudulent understatement of taxable *revenues* or overstatement of deductions and *expenses* or both. Contrast with *tax shelter* and *loophole*.

tax-exempts See *municipal bonds*.

tax shelter The legal avoidance of, or reduction in, *income taxes* resulting from a careful reading of the complex income-tax regulations and the subsequent rearrangement of financial affairs to take advantage of the regulations. Often writers use the term pejoratively, but the courts have long held that a taxpayer has no obligation to pay taxes any larger than the legal minimum. If the public concludes that a given tax shelter is "unfair," then Congress can, and has, changed the laws and regulations but courts have ruled some tax shelters illegal without the need for legislative action. The term is sometimes used to refer to the *investment* that permits *tax avoidance*. See *loophole*.

tax shield The amount of an *expense*, such as *depreciation*, that reduces taxable *income* but does not require *working capital*. Sometimes this term includes expenses that reduce taxable income and use working capital. A depreciation deduction (or *R&D expense* in the expanded sense) of $10,000 provides a tax shield of $3,700 when the marginal tax rate is 37%.

taxable income *Income* computed according to *IRS* regulations and subject to *income taxes*. Contrast with income, net income, income before taxes (in the *income statement*), and *comprehensive income* (a *financial reporting* concept). Use the term "pretax income" to refer to income before taxes on the income statement in financial reports.

tax-transfer lease One form of *capital lease*. Congress has in the past provided *business* with an incentive to invest in qualifying *plant and equipment* by granting an *investment credit*, which, though it occurs as a reduction in *income taxes* otherwise *payable*, effectively reduces the purchase *price* of the *assets*. Similarly, Congress continues to grant an incentive to acquire such assets by allowing the *Modified Accelerated Cost Recovery System* (*MACRS*, form of unusually *accelerated depreciation*). Accelerated *depreciation* for tax purposes allows a reduction of taxes paid in the early years of an asset's life, providing the firm with an increased *net present value* of *cash flows*. The *IRS* administers both of these incentives through the income tax laws, rather than paying an outright cash payment. A business with no taxable income in many cases had difficulty reaping the benefits of the investment credit or of accelerated depreciation because Congress had not provided for tax refunds to those who acquire qualifying assets but who have no taxable income. In principle, a company without taxable income could *lease* from another *firm* with taxable income an asset that it would otherwise purchase. The second firm acquires the asset, gets the tax-reduction benefits from the acquisition, and becomes a lessor, leasing the asset (presumably at a lower price reflecting its own costs lowered by the tax reductions) to the unprofitable company. Before 1981, tax laws discouraged such leases. That is, although firms could enter into such leases, they could not legally transfer the tax benefits. Under certain restrictive conditions, the tax law now allows a profitable firm to earn tax credits and take deductions while leasing to the firm without tax liability in such leases. These are sometimes called "*safe-harbor leases*."

Technical Bulletin The *FASB* has authorized its staff to issue bulletins to provide guidance on *financial accounting* and reporting problems. Although the FASB does not formally approve the contents of the bulletins, their contents are part of *U.S. GAAP*.

technology As an *account* classification, typically the sum of a *firm*'s technical *trade secrets* and *know-how*, as distinct from its *patents*, which tend to be in their own account.

temporary account *Account* that does not appear on the *balance sheet*; *revenue* and *expense* accounts, their *adjuncts* and *contras*, *production cost accounts*, *dividend distribution accounts*, and purchases-related accounts (which close to the various *inventories*); sometimes called a "*nominal account*."

temporary difference According to the *SFAS No. 109* (**Codification Topic 740**) definition: "A difference between the *tax* basis of an *asset* or *liability* and its reported amount in the *financial statements* that will result in taxable or deductible amounts in future years." Temporary differences include *timing differences* and differences between *taxable income* and pretax *income* caused by different cost bases for assets. For example, a *plant* asset might have a cost of $10,000 for financial reporting but a basis of $7,000 for income tax purposes. This temporary difference might arise because the firm has used an *accelerated depreciation* method for tax but straight-line for book, or the firm may have purchased the asset in a transaction in which the fair *value* of the asset exceeded its tax basis. Both situations create a temporary difference.

temporary investments *Investments* in *marketable securities* that the owner intends to sell within a short time, usually one year, and hence classifies as *current assets*.

10-K; 10-Q The name of the annual (K) or quarterly (Q) report that the *SEC* requires of nearly all publicly held *corporations*.

term bonds A *bond issue* whose component bonds all mature at the same time. Contrast with *serial bonds*.

terminal cash flows *Cash flows* that occur at the end of an *investment* project. Often include proceeds of *salvage* of equipment and *tax* on *gain (loss)* on disposal. See *terminal value*.

terminal value In *cash flow projections* which persist for many *periods*, the analyst often summarizes the far distant future in a medium distant period. For example, the analyst might give a *cash* inflow for Year 20, which is the *present value* of expected cash flows for all the years after Year 20. That last value is called the "terminal value" and is often derived using the *perpetuity growth model*.

term loan A *loan* with a *maturity* date, as opposed to a *demand loan*, which is due whenever the *lender* requests *payment*. In practice, bankers and *auditors* use this phrase only for loans for a year or more.

term structure A phrase with different meanings in *accounting* and financial economics. In accounting, it refers to the pattern of times that must elapse before *assets* turn into, or produce, *cash* and the pattern of times that must elapse before *liabilities* require cash. In financial economics, the phrase refers to the pattern of *yields* or *interest rates* as a *function* of the time that elapses for *loans* to come due. For example, if six-month loans cost 6% per year and 10-year loans cost 9% per year, this is called a "normal" term structure because the longer-term loan carries a higher rate. If the six-month loan costs 9% per year and the 10-year loan costs 6% per year, the term structure is said to be "inverted." See *yield curve*.

terms of sale The conditions governing payment for a *sale*. For example, the terms *2/10, n(et)/30* mean that if the purchaser makes payment within 10 days of the *invoice* date, it can take a *discount* of 2% from invoice *price*; the purchaser must pay the invoice amount, in any event, within 30 days, or it becomes overdue.

theory of constraints (TOC) Concept of improving *operations* by identifying and reducing *bottlenecks* in process *flows*.

thin capitalization A state of having a high *debt-equity ratio*. Under *income tax* legislation, the term has a special meaning.

throughput contract As defined by *SFAS No. 47* (**Codification Topic 440**), an agreement that is signed by a shipper (processor) and by the owner of a transportation facility (such as an oil or natural gas pipeline or a ship) or a manufacturing facility and that provides for the shipper (processor) to pay specified amounts periodically in return for the transportation (processing) of a *product*. The shipper (processor) must make *cash payments* even if it does not ship (process) the contracted quantities.

throughput contribution Sales dollars minus the sum of all short-run *variable costs*.

tickler file A collection of *vouchers* or other memoranda arranged chronologically to remind the person in charge of certain duties to make *payments* (or to do other tasks) as *scheduled*.

time-adjusted rate of return *Internal rate of return*.

time cost *Period cost*.

time deposit *Cash* in bank earning *interest*. Contrast with *demand deposit*.

time-series analysis See *cross-section analysis* for definition and contrast.

time value element in stock options The longer one can hold an *option* before exercising it or letting it *lapse*, the more valuable the option. In assessing the *fair value* of options, one can try to isolate the two components of *value*: this time value and the *benefit value*, which equals *intrinsic value*.

times-interest (charges) earned Ratio of pretax *income* plus *interest charges* to interest charges. See *ratio* and **Exhibit 6.14**.

timing difference The major type of *temporary difference* between taxable *income* and pretax income reported to *shareholders*; reverses in a subsequent *period* and requires an entry in the *deferred income tax* account; for example, the use of *accelerated depreciation* for *tax returns* and *straight-line depreciation* for financial reporting. Contrast with *permanent difference*.

Toronto Stock Exchange (TSX) A public market where various corporate securities trade.

total assets turnover ratio *Sales* divided by average total *assets*. See *ratio* and **Exhibit 6.14**.

total quality management (TQM) Concept of organizing a company to excel in all its activities in order to increase the *quality* of *products* and *services*.

traceable cost A *cost* that a firm can identify with or assign to a specific *product*. Contrast with a *joint cost*.

trade acceptance A *draft* that a seller presents for signature (*acceptance*) to the buyer at the time it sells *goods*. The draft then becomes the equivalent of a *note receivable* of the seller and a *note payable* of the buyer.

trade credit Occurs when one *business* allows another to buy from it in *return* for a promise to pay later. Contrast with "consumer *credit*," which occurs when a business extends a retail customer the privilege of paying later.

trade discount A *list price discount* offered to all customers of a given type. Contrast with a *discount* offered for prompt payment and with *quantity discount*.

trade-in Acquiring a new *asset* in *exchange* for a used one and perhaps additional cash. See *boot* and *trade-in transaction*.

trade-in transaction The accounting for a *trade-in*; depends on whether the *firm* receives an *asset* "similar" to (and used in the same line of *business* as) the asset traded in and whether the accounting is for *financial statements* or for *income tax* returns. Assume that an old asset cost $5,000, has $3,000 of *accumulated depreciation* (after recording depreciation to the date of the trade-in), and hence has a *carrying value* of $2,000. The old asset appears to have a *market value* of $1,500, according to price quotations in used asset markets. The firm trades in the old asset on a new asset with a *list price* of $10,000. The firm gives up the old asset and $5,500 cash (*boot*) for the new asset. The generic entry for the trade-in transaction is as follows:

New Asset (Asset Increase)	A
Accumulated Depreciation (Old Asset Decrease)	3,000
Retained Earnings (Adjustment on Exchange of Asset) (Shareholders' Equity Change)	B or B
Old Asset (Asset Decrease)	5,000
Cash (Asset Decrease)	5,500

(1) The list price method of accounting for trade-ins rests on the assumption that the list price of the new asset closely approximates its market value The firm records the new asset at its list price (A = $10,000 in the example); B is a *plug* (= $2,500 credit in the example). If B requires a *debit* plug, the Adjustment on Exchange of Asset is a *loss*; if B requires a *credit* plug (as in the example), the adjustment is a *gain*.

(2) Another theoretically sound method of accounting for trade-ins rests on the assumption that the price quotation from used-asset markets gives a market value of the old asset that is a more reliable measure than the market value of the new asset determined by list price This method uses the *fair market price* (*value*) of the old asset, $1,500 in the example, to determine B (= $2,000 carrying value − $1,500 assumed proceeds on disposition = $500 debit or loss). The exchange results in a loss if the carrying value of the old asset exceeds its market value and in a gain if the market value exceeds the carrying value. The firm records the new asset on the books by plugging for A (= $7,000 in the example).

(3) For income tax reporting, the taxpayer must recognize neither gain nor loss on the trade-in. Thus the taxpayer records the new asset for tax purposes by assuming B is zero and plugging for A (= $7,500 in the example). In practice, firms that want to recognize the loss currently will sell the old asset directly, rather than trading it in, and acquire the new asset entirely for cash.

(4) *Generally accepted accounting principles* (*APB Opinion No. 29* (**Codification Topic 845**)) require a variant of these methods. The basic method is (1) or (2), depending on whether the list price of the new asset (1) or the quotation of the old asset's market value (2) provides the more reliable indication of market value. If the basic method requires a debit entry, or loss, for the Adjustment on Exchange of Asset, then the firm records the trade-in as in (1) or (2) and recognizes the full amount of the loss currently. If, however, the basic method requires a credit entry, or gain, for the Adjustment on Exchange of Asset, then the firm recognizes the gain currently if the old asset and the new asset are not "similar." If the assets are similar and the party trading in receives no cash, then it recognizes no gain and the treatment resembles that in (3); that is B = 0, plug for A. If the assets are similar and the firm trading in receives cash—a rare case—then it recognizes a portion of the gain currently. The portion of the gain recognized currently is the fraction cash received/fair value of total consideration received. (When the firm uses the list price method, (1), it assumes that the market value of the old asset is the list price of the new asset plus the amount of cash received by the party trading in.)

A summary of the results of applying *U.S. GAAP* to the example follows.

More Reliable Information as to Fair Market Value	Old Asset Compared with New Asset	
	Similar	Not Similar
New Asset List Price	A = $7,500	A = $10,000
	B = 0	B = 2,500 gain
Old Asset Market Price	A = $7,000	A = $ 7,000
	B = 500 loss	B = 500 loss

trade payables (receivables) *Payables* (*receivables*) arising in the ordinary course of *business transactions*. Most *accounts payable* (*receivable*) are of this kind.

trade secret Technical or *business* information such as formulas, recipes, computer programs, and marketing data not generally known by competitors and maintained by the *firm* as a secret; theoretically capable of having an indefinite, *finite life*. A famous example is the secret process for Coca-Cola® (a *registered trademark* of the company). Compare with *know-how*. The firm will *capitalize* this *intangible asset* only if purchased. If this *intangible* has a finite, expected *useful life*, *U.S. GAAP* requires *amortization* over that estimate of its life. If the *right* has indefinite life, then U.S. GAAP requires no amortization, but annual tests for *impairment*. If the firm develops the intangible internally, the firm will *expense* the *costs* as incurred and show no asset.

trademark A distinctive word or symbol that is affixed to a *product*, its package, or its dispenser and that uniquely identifies the *firm's* products and *services*. See *trademark right*.

trademark right The *right* to exclude competitors in *sales* or advertising from using words or symbols that are so similar to the *firm's* *trademarks* as possibly to confuse consumers. Trademark rights last as long as the firm continues to use the trademarks in question. In the United States, trademark rights arise from use and not from government registration. They therefore have a legal life independent of the life of a registration. Registrations last 20 years, and the holder may renew them as long as the holder uses the trademark. If this *intangible* has a finite, expected *useful life*, *U.S. GAAP* requires *amortization* over that estimate of its life. If the right has *indefinite life*, then U.S. GAAP requires no amortization, but annual tests for *impairment*. Under *SFAS No. 2* (**Codification Topic 730**), the firm must *expense* internally developed trademark rights.

trading on the equity Said of a *firm* engaging in *debt financing*; frequently said of a firm doing so to a degree considered abnormal for a firm of its kind. *Leverage*.

trading securities *Marketable securities* that a *firm* holds and expects to sell within a relatively short time; a classification important in *SFAS No. 115* (**Codification Topic 320**), which requires the owner to carry *marketable equity securities* on the *balance sheet* at *market value*, not at *cost*. Contrast with *available for sale*, securities and *held-to-maturity securities*. Under *SFAS No. 115* (**Codification Topic 320**), the balance sheet reports trading securities at market value on the balance sheet date, and the *income statement* reports *holding gains and losses* on trading securities. When the firm sells the securities, it reports *realized gain* or loss as the difference between the selling *price* and the market value at the last balance sheet date.

tranche A slice or portion. Used in *finance* to refer to securities with different *rights*, usually along a common spectrum. For example one group of investors might be entitled to the first $1 million of *cash flows* from an *asset* and a second group might be entitled to the second $1 million. The groups are referred to as "tranches."

transaction A *transfer* (of more than promises—see *executory contract*) between the accounting *entity* and another party or parties.

transfer Under *SFAC No. 6*, consists of two types: "reciprocal" and "nonreciprocal." In a reciprocal transfer, or "*exchange*," the *entity* both receives and sacrifices. In a *nonreciprocal transfer*, the entity sacrifices but does not receive (examples include gifts, distributions to owners) or receives but does not sacrifice (*investment* by owner in entity). *SFAC No. 6* suggests that the term "internal transfer" is self-contradictory and that writers should use the term "internal event" instead.

transfer agent Usually a bank or trust company designated by a *corporation* to make legal transfers of *stock* (*bonds*) and, perhaps, to pay *dividends* or *debt service payments*.

transfer price A substitute for a *market*, or *arm's-length*, *price* used in *profit*, or *responsibility center*, *accounting* when one segment of the *business* "sells" to another segment. Incentives of *profit center* managers will not coincide with the best interests of the entire business unless a *firm* sets transfer prices properly.

transfer-pricing problem The problem of setting *transfer prices* so that both buyer and seller have *goal congruence* with respect to the parent organization's goals.

translation adjustment The effect of *exchange-rate* changes caused by converting the *value* of a *net investment* denominated in a *foreign currency* to the *entity*'s reporting currency. *SFAS No. 52* (**Codification Topic 830**) requires *firms* to translate their net investment in relatively self-contained foreign operations at the *balance sheet* date. Year-to-year changes in value caused by exchange-rate changes accumulate in an *owners' equity* account, sometimes called the "cumulative translation adjustment."

translation gain (or loss) *Foreign exchange gain (or loss)*.

transportation-in *Freight-in*.

transposition error An error in problem solving resulting from reversing the order of digits in a number, such as recording "32" for "23." If the only errors in a *trial balance* result from one or more transposition errors, then the difference between the sum of the *debits* and the sum of the *credits* will be divisible by nine. Not all such differences result from transposition errors.

treasurer The financial officer responsible for managing *cash* and raising *funds*.

treasury bond A *bond* issued by a *corporation* and then reacquired. Such bonds are treated as retired when reacquired, and an *extraordinary gain or loss* on reacquisition is *recognized*. This term usually refers to a bond issued by the U.S. Treasury Department.

treasury shares *Capital stock* issued and then reacquired by the *corporation*. Such reacquisitions result in a reduction of *shareholders' equity* and usually appear on the *balance sheet* as *contra* to shareholders' equity. Accounting recognizes neither *gain* nor *loss* on *transactions* involving treasury stock. The accounting *debits* (if positive) or *credits* (if negative) any difference between the amounts paid and received for treasury stock transactions to *additional paid-in capital*. See *cost method* and *par value method*.

treatment of changes in periodic depreciation and amortization See *accounting changes*.

treasury stock *Treasury shares*.

trend analysis Investigation of *sales* or other economic trends. Can range from a simple visual extrapolation of points on a graph to a sophisticated computerized time series analysis.

trial balance A two-column listing of *account balances*. The left-hand column shows all accounts with *debit* balances and their total. The right-hand column shows all accounts with *credit* balances and their total. The two totals should be equal. Accountants compute trial balances as a partial check of the arithmetic accuracy of the entries previously made. See *adjusted, preclosing, post-closing, unadjusted trial balance, plug, slide,* and *transposition error*.

troubled debt restructuring As defined in *SFAS No. 15* (**Codification Topic 310 and 470**), a concession (changing of the terms of a *debt*) that is granted by a *creditor* for economic or legal reasons related to the *debtor*'s financial difficulty and that the creditor would not otherwise consider.

true up In accounting, an *adjusting entry* to match an ending *account balance* with physical reality. In *finance*, it some-times refers to a *cash expenditure* to have total expenditures match a number given by some rules or regulations; for example: The employer contributed an extra $12,000 to the *pension fund* at the end of December to true up the amount in the fund to the amount required by year end.

TSX *Toronto Stock Exchange*. Abbreviated "TSE" until 2001.

t-statistic For an estimated *regression* coefficient, the estimated coefficient divided by the *standard error* of the estimate.

turnover The number of times that *assets*, such as *inventory* or *accounts receivable*, are replaced on average during the *period*. Accounts *receivable turnover*, for example, is total *sales* on account for a period divided by the average accounts receivable *balance* for the period. See *ratio* and **Exhibit 6.14**. In the UK, "turnover" means *sales*.

turnover of plant and equipment See *ratio* and **Exhibit 6.14**.

t-value In *regression analysis*, the *ratio* of an estimated regression coefficient divided by its *standard error*.

20-F Form required by the *SEC* for foreign companies issuing or trading their securities in the United States. This form reconciles the foreign accounting amounts resulting from using foreign *accounting principles* to amounts resulting from using *U.S. GAAP*. Since November 2007, foreign company *financial statements* prepared in accordance with *IFRS* no longer require reconciliation to U.S. GAAP.

two T-account method A method for computing either (1) *foreign-exchange gains and losses* or (2) *monetary gains or losses* for *constant-dollar accounting* statements. The left-hand *T-account* shows actual *net balances* of *monetary items*, and the right-hand T-account shows implied (common) dollar amounts.

2/10, n(et)/30 See *terms of sale*.

U

unadjusted trial balance *Trial balance* taken before the accountant makes *adjusting* and *closing* entries at the end of the *period*.

unappropriated retained earnings *Retained earnings* not *appropriated* and therefore against which the *board* can declare *dividends* in the absence of retained earnings restrictions. See *restricted retained earnings*.

unavoidable cost A *cost* that is not an *avoidable cost*.

uncertainty See *risk* for definition and contrast.

uncollectible account; uncollectible amount An *account receivable* that the *debtor* will not pay. If the *firm* uses the preferable *allowance method*, the entry on judging a specific account to be uncollectible *debits* the allowance for uncollectible accounts and *credits* the specific account receivable. See *bad debt expense* and *sales contra, estimated uncollectibles*.

unconsolidated subsidiary A *subsidiary* not consolidated perhaps because it is a foreign country from which the *parent* cannot take *assets*.

uncontrollable cost The opposite of *controllable cost*.

underapplied (underabsorbed) overhead An excess of actual *overhead costs* for a *period* over *costs* applied, or *charged*, to *products* produced during the period; a *debit* balance remaining in an overhead account after the accounting assigns overhead to product. See *overapplied overhead*.

underlying document The record, memorandum, *voucher*, or other signal that is the authority for making an *entry* into a *journal*.

underlyings A *derivative* contract specifies its various payoffs in terms of variables, called "underlyings" such as a common *stock*, or specified *interest rate*, or commodity *price*, or foreign *exchange rate*.

underwriter One who agrees to purchase a *security issue* for a specified *price*, usually for resale to others. Often underwriters join together to buy the entire issue then *allocate* the issue among themselves for subsequent resale.

undistributed earnings *Retained earnings*. Typically, this term refers to that amount retained for a given year.

unearned income (revenue) *Advances from customers*; strictly speaking, a contradiction in terms because the terms "*income*" and "*revenue*" mean earned.

unemployment tax See *FUTA*.

unencumbered appropriation In governmental accounting, portion of an *appropriation* not yet spent or encumbered.

unexpired cost An *asset*.

unfavorable variance In *standard cost* accounting, an excess of expected *revenue* over actual revenue or an excess of *actual cost* over standard cost.

unfunded Not *funded*. An obligation or *liability*, usually for *pension costs*, exists, but no *funds* have been set aside to discharge the obligation or liability.

Uniform Partnership Act A model law, enacted by many states, to govern the relations between partners when the *partnership* agreement fails to specify the agreed-upon treatment.

unissued capital stock *Stock* authorized but not yet issued.

uniting-of-interests method The *IASB*'s term for the *pooling-of-interests method*. No longer allowed.

unit-level activities Work that converts resources into individual *products*. Examples include *direct materials*, *direct labor*, and energy to run the machines.

units-of-production method The *production method of depreciation*.

unlimited liability The legal obligation of *general partners* or the sole proprietor for all *debts* of the *partnership* or *sole proprietorship*.

unqualified opinion See *auditor's report*.

unrealized appreciation An *unrealized holding gain*; frequently used in the context of *marketable securities*.

unrealized gain (loss) on marketable securities An *income statement account* title for the amount of *gain (loss)* during the *current period* on the *portfolio of marketable securities* held as *trading securities*. *SFAS No. 115* (**Codification Topic 320**) requires the *firm* to *recognize*, in the income statement, gains and losses caused by changes in *market values*, even though the firm has not yet *realized* them.

unrealized gross margin (profit) A *contra account* to *installment accounts receivable* used with the *installment method* of *revenue recognition*; shows the amount of *profit* that the *firm* will eventually *realize* when it collects the *receivable*. Some accountants show this account as a *liability*.

unrealized holding gain See *inventory profit* for the definition and an example.

unrecovered cost *Carrying value* of an *asset*.

unsecured borrowing Borrowing without specified *collateral*. See *debenture bond*.

unused capacity The difference between *resources supplied* and *resources used*.

U.S. GAAP *Generally accepted accounting principles*; a singular noun. In this book, we use "U.S. GAAP" for this concept. The international analog is *IFRS*.

U.S. GAAP hierarchy See *generally accepted accounting principles*.

U.S. SEC registrant A *firm* incorporated based in the United States that lists and trades its *securities* in the United States;

a non-U.S. *SEC registrant* (sometimes called "*foreign private issuer*") is a firm incorporated outside the U.S that has filed the necessary documents with the SEC to list and trade its securities in the United States.

usage variance *Efficiency variance*.

use of funds Any *transaction* that reduces *funds* (however "funds" is defined).

useful life *Service life*.

V

valuation account A *contra account* or *adjunct account*. When the *firm* reports *accounts receivable* at expected *collectible* amounts, it will *credit* any expected uncollectible amounts to the *allowance for uncollectibles*, a valuation account. In this way, the firm can show both the *gross receivables* amount and the amount it expects to collect. *SFAC No. 6* says a valuation account is "a separate item that reduces or increases the carrying amount" of an *asset* (or *liability*). The accounts are part of the related assets (or liabilities) and are not assets (or liabilities) in their own right.

valuation allowance A *contra account* for *deferred income tax assets*, reducing its *nominal amount* to the amount the *firm* expects to *realize* because it has future *taxable income* that the *expenses* and *losses* reflected in the deferred tax assets can offset. Deferred income tax assets arise when the *taxpayer* records expenses on the *financial statements* before it can take deductions on its *tax returns*. Examples are for *bad debts* and *warranty costs*. In some future *period*, the firm will be able to deduct the bad debt and warranty costs from its taxable income in those future periods. If the firm has some doubts that it will earn future *income*, which the bad debt and warranty costs can offset, then it will report a reduction in deferred tax assets in the earlier periods.

value *Monetary worth*. This term is usually so vague that you should not use it without a modifying adjective unless most people would agree on the amount. Do not confuse with cost. See *fair market price (value)*, *fair value*, *entry value*, and *exit value*.

value added *Cost* of a *product* or *work-in-process* minus the cost of the *material* purchased for the product or work-in-process.

value-added activity Any activity that increases the usefulness to a customer of a *product* or *service*.

value chain The set of *business functions* that increase the usefulness to the customer of a *product* or *service*; typically including *research and development*, design of products and services, production, marketing, distribution, and customer service.

value engineering An evaluation of the activities in the *value chain* to reduce *costs*.

value variance *Price variance*.

variable annuity An *annuity* whose periodic payments depend on some uncertain outcome, such as *stock market prices*.

variable budget *Flexible budget*.

variable costing In allocating *costs*, a method that assigns only *variable manufacturing costs* to *products* and treats *fixed manufacturing costs* as *period expenses*. Contrast with *full absorption costing*.

variable costs *Costs* that change as activity levels change. Strictly speaking, variable costs are zero when the activity level is zero. See *semivariable costs*. In accounting, this term most often means the sum of *direct costs* and variable *overhead*.

variable interest entity; VIE An *entity* arranged so that one cannot ascertain controlling financial *interest* by analyzing voting interest, because the entity meets either or both of the following conditions:

(1) The entity has insufficient *owners' equity* at *risk*, which means it cannot *finance* its *operations* without additional financial support, such as the promises of another entity.

(2) The entity's owners' equity lacks one or more of the attributes associated with equity: the ability to absorb *losses*, the *right* to receive residual *returns*, and the ability, conveyed by voting rights, to make decisions.

A VIE may, but need not, have a *primary beneficiary*, which absorbs (or receives) a majority of the variability of outcomes of the entity If there is a primary beneficiary, that *business* will consolidate the VIE, regardless of ownership.

variable overhead efficiency variance The difference between the *actual* and *standard cost driver* volume times the standard cost driver rate.

variable overhead price variance The difference between the *actual* and *standard cost driver* rate times the actual cost driver volume.

variable overhead variance Difference between actual and *standard variable overhead costs*.

variable rate debt Debt whose *interest rate* results from the periodic application of a formula, such as "three-month LIBOR [London Interbank Offered Rate] plus 1% [one hundred *basis points*] set on the 8th day of each February, May, August, and November."

variables sampling The use of a sampling technique in which the sampler infers a particular quantitative characteristic of an entire *population* from a sample (e.g., mean amount of accounts receivable). See also *estimation sampling*. See *attribute(s) sampling* for contrast and further examples.

variance Difference between *actual* and *standard costs* or between *budgeted* and actual *expenditures* or, sometimes, *expenses*. The word has completely different meanings in accounting and in statistics, where it means a measure of dispersion of a distribution.

variance analysis *Variance investigation*. This term's meaning differs in statistics.

variance investigation A step in managerial control processes. *Standard costing systems* produce *variance* numbers of various sorts. These numbers seldom exactly equal zero. *Management* must decide when a variance differs sufficiently from zero to study its cause. This term refers both to the decision about when to study the cause and to the study itself.

variation analysis Analysis of the causes of changes in *financial statement* items of *interest* such as *net income* or *gross margin*, or of variances from *budget* or from *standard costs*.

VAT (Value-added tax) A *tax* levied on the *market value* of a *firm's outputs* less the *market value* of its purchased inputs.

vendor A seller; sometimes spelled "vender."

verifiability See *verifiable*.

verifiable A qualitative *objective* of financial reporting specifying that accountants can trace items in *financial statements* back to *underlying documents*—supporting *invoices*, canceled *checks*, and other physical pieces of evidence.

verification The *auditor's* act of reviewing or checking items in *financial statements* by tracing back to *underlying documents*—supporting *invoices*, canceled *checks*, and other *business* documents—or sending out *confirmations* to be returned. Compare with *physical verification*.

vertical analysis Analysis of the *financial statements* of a single *firm* or across several firms for a particular time, as opposed to *horizontal* or *time-series analysis*, in which the analyst compares items over time for a single firm or across firms.

vertical integration The extension of activity by an organization into *business* directly related to the production or distribution of the organization's end *products*. Although a *firm* may sell products to others at various stages, a vertically integrated firm devotes the substantial portion of the *output* at each stage to the production of the next stage or to end products. Compare *horizontal integration*.

vested An employee's *pension plan* benefits that are not contingent on the employee's continuing to work for the employer.

vesting The process of becoming *vested*.

VIE *Variable interest entity*.

visual curve fitting method One crude form of *cost estimation*. Sometimes, when a *firm* needs only rough approximations of the amounts of *fixed* and *variable costs*, *management* need not perform a formal *regression analysis* but can plot the data and draw a line that seems to fit the data. Then it can use the parameters of that line for the rough approximations.

volume variance *Production volume variance*; less often, used to mean *sales volume variance*.

voucher A document that signals recognition of a *liability* and authorizes the *disbursement* of *cash*; sometimes used to refer to the written evidence documenting an *accounting entry*, as in the term *journal voucher*.

voucher system In controlling *cash*, a method that requires someone in the *firm* to authorize each *check* with an approved *voucher*. The firm makes no *disbursements* of currency or coins except from *petty cash funds*.

vouching The *function* performed by an *auditor* to ascertain that underlying data or documents support a *journal entry*.

W

wage Compensation of employees based on time worked or *output* of *product* for manual labor. But see *take-home pay*.

Wages and Salaries Payable A *liability account* title.

warning signal Tool used to identify quality-control problems; only signals a problem. Contrast with *diagnostic signal*, which both signals a problem and suggests its cause.

warrant A *certificate* entitling the owner to buy a specified number of *shares* at a specified time(s) for a specified *price*; differs from a *stock option* only in that the *firm* grants options to employees and issues warrants to the public. Warrants are similar to stock options originated on an *exchange*. See *right*.

warranty A promise by a seller to correct deficiencies in *products* sold. When the seller gives warranties, proper accounting practice *recognizes* an estimate of warranty *expense* and an *estimated liability* at the time of *sale*. See *allowance method*. See *guarantee* for contrast in proper usage.

Warranty Liability (Provision) Account title in *U.S. GAAP* (*IFRS*) for the estimated *cost* to satisfy *warranties*.

wash sale The *sale* and purchase of the same or similar *asset* within a short time period. For *income tax* purposes, the *taxpayer* may not *recognize losses* on a sale of *stock* if the taxpayer purchases equivalent stock within 30 days before or after the date of sale.

waste *Material* that is a residue from manufacturing *operations* and that has no *sale value*. Frequently, this has negative value because a *firm* must incur additional *costs* for disposal.

wasting asset A *natural resource* that diminishes in *value* because of extractions of oil, or ore, or gas, or the removal of timber and, hence, is subject to *amortization*, called *depletion*.

watered stock *Shares* issued for *assets* with *fair market price* (*value*) less than *par* or *stated value*. The *firm* records the assets on the *books* at the *overstated values*. In the law, for shares to be considered watered, the *board of directors* must have acted in bad faith or fraudulently in issuing the shares under these circumstances. The term originated from a former practice of cattle owners who fed cattle ("*stock*") large quantities of salt to make them thirsty. The cattle then drank much water before their owner took them to market. The owners did this to make the cattle appear heavier and more valuable than otherwise.

weighted average An *average* computed by counting each occurrence of each *value*, not merely a single occurrence of each value. For example, if a *firm* purchases one unit for $1 and two units for $2 each, then the simple average of the purchase *prices* is $1.50, but the weighted average price per unit is $5/3 = $1.67. Contrast with *moving average*.

weighted-average cost of capital Measured as the *weighted-average* of the *after-tax cost* of *long-term debt* and the cost of *equity*.

weighted-average inventory method Valuing either *withdrawals* or *ending inventory* at the *weighted-average* purchase *price* of all units on hand at the time of withdrawal or of computation of ending inventory. The *firm* uses the *inventory equation* to calculate the other quantity. If a firm uses the *perpetual inventory method*, accountants often call it the *moving average method*.

where-got, where-gone statement A term allegedly used in the 1920s by W. M. Cole for a statement much like the *statement of cash flows*. Noted accounting historian S. Zeff reports that Cole actually used the term "where-got-gone" statement.

wind up To bring to an end, such as the life of a *corporation*. The *board* winds up the life of a corporation by following the winding-up *provisions* of applicable statutes, by surrendering the *charter*, or by following *bankruptcy* proceedings. See also *liquidation*.

window dressing The attempt to make *financial statements* show *operating* results, or a *financial position*, more favorable than they would otherwise show.

with recourse See *note receivable discounted*.

withdrawals *Assets* distributed to an owner. *Partner's drawings.* See *inventory equation* for another context.

withholding Deductions that are taken from *salaries* or *wages*, usually for *income taxes*, health insurance, and social security and that the employer remits, in the employee's name, to the taxing authority or insurance firm.

without recourse See *note receivable discounted*.

work sheet (program) (1) A computer program designed to combine explanations and calculations. This type of program helps in preparing *financial statements* and *schedules*. (2) A tabular schedule for convenient summary of *adjusting* and *closing entries*. The work sheet usually begins with an *unadjusted trial balance*. Adjusting entries appear in the next two columns, one for *debits* and one for *credits*. The work sheet carries the horizontal sum of each line to the right into either the *income statement* or the *balance sheet* column, as appropriate. The *plug* to equate the income statement column totals is, if a debit, the income or, if a credit, a *loss*

for the *period*. That income will close retained earnings on the balance sheet. The income statement credit columns are the *revenues* for the period, and the debit columns are the expenses (and revenue contras) that appear on the income statement. "Work sheet" also refers to schedules for ascertaining other items that appear on the financial statements and that require *adjustment* or compilation.

working capital *Current assets* minus *current liabilities*; sometimes called "*net working capital*" or "*net current assets*."

working capital ratio See *ratio* and **Exhibit 6.14**.

work(ing) papers The *schedules* and analyses prepared by the *auditor* in carrying out investigations before issuing an *opinion* on *financial statements*.

work-in-process; work-in-progress (inventory account) Partially completed *product*; appears on the *balance sheet* as *inventory*. *SEC Regulation S-X* requires that *firms* report inventory amounts for *raw material*, *work-in-process*, and *finished goods*.

worth *Value*. See *net worth*.

worth-debt ratio Reciprocal of the *debt-equity ratio*. See *ratio* and **Exhibit 6.14**.

write down To *write off*, except that the *firm* does not charge all the *asset*'s *cost* to *expense* or *loss*; generally used for *nonrecurring* items.

write off To *charge* an *asset* to *expense* or *loss*; that is, to *debit* expense (or loss) and *credit* the asset. To *derecognize* a specific *account receivable* that the holder has decided is uncollectible; the debit is to the *Allowance for Uncollectibles* account.

write-off method For treating *uncollectible accounts*, a method that *debits bad debt expense* and *credits accounts receivable* of specific customers as the *firm* identifies specific accounts as uncollectible. The firm cannot use this method when it can estimate uncollectible amounts and they are significant. See *bad debt expense*, *sales contra*, *estimated uncollectibles*, and the *allowance method* for contrast.

write up To increase the recorded *cost* of an *asset* with no corresponding *disbursement* of *funds*; that is, to *debit* asset and *credit revenue* or, perhaps, *owners' equity*; seldom done in the United States because currently accepted *accounting principles* await actual *transactions* before recording asset increases. An exception occurs in accounting for *marketable equity securities*.

writing off See *write off*.

X

XBRL eXtensible Business Reporting Language A specification of information taxonomies and classifications used, and encouraged by the *SEC*, to make information retrieval and analysis easier than otherwise.

Y

yield (rate) *Internal rate of return* of a stream of *cash flows*. *Cash yield* is cash flow divided by carrying *value*. See also *dividend yield*.

yield curve The relation between *interest rates* and the term to *maturity* of *loans*, or the duration (a technical term in financial economics) of *bonds* and *notes*. Ordinarily, longer-term loans have higher interest rates than shorter-term loans. This is called a "normal" yield curve. Sometimes long-term and short-term rates are approximately the same—a "flat" yield curve. Sometimes short-term loans have a higher rate than long-term ones—an "inverted" yield curve. *Term structure* of interest rates.

yield to maturity At a given time, the *internal rate of return* of a series of *cash flows*.

yield variance Measures the input-output relation while holding the standard mix of inputs constant: (*standard price* multiplied by actual amount of input used in the standard mix) − (standard price multiplied by *standard quantity allowed* for the actual *output*). It is the part of the *efficiency variance* not called the *mix variance*.

Z

zero-base(d) budgeting (ZBB) One philosophy for setting budgets. In preparing an ordinary *budget* for the next *period*, a manager starts with the budget for the current period and makes adjustments as seem necessary because of changed conditions for the next period. Since most *managers* like to increase the scope of the activities managed and since most prices increase most of the time, amounts in budgets prepared in the ordinary, incremental way seem to increase

period after period. The authority approving the budget assumes that managers will carry out *operations* in the same way as in the past and that next period's *expenditures* will have to be at least as large as those of the current period. Thus, this authority tends to study only the increments to the current period's budget. In ZBB, the authority questions the process for carrying out a program and the entire budget for the next period. The authority studies every dollar in the budget, not just the dollars incremental to the previous period's amounts. The advocates of ZBB claim that in this way, (1) management will more likely delete programs or *divisions* of marginal benefit to the *business* or governmental unit, rather than continuing with *costs* at least as large as the present ones, and (2) *management* may discover and implement alternative, more *cost-effective* ways of carrying out programs. ZBB implies questioning the existence of programs and the fundamental nature of the way that *firms* carry them out, not merely the amounts used to fund them. Experts appear to divide evenly as to whether the middle word should be "base" or "based."

zero coupon bond A *debt* issue with a single promised *cash flow* on the *maturity* date; a "single-payment *note*."

INDEX

A

Abandonment of assets, 442

Accelerated depreciation method, 429

   See also Declining balance methods of depreciation; Sum-of-the-years'-digits method of depreciation

Account, defined, 44

Accounting changes. *See* Adjustments for accounting changes

Accounting conventions and concepts, 25–6

Accounting cycle. *See* Accounting process for revenues

Accounting equation, 15

Accounting errors. *See* Errors, correction of

Accounting estimates. *See* Estimates

Accounting period convention, 7–8, 26

Accounting principles. *See* Changes in accounting principles; Generally accepted accounting principles

Accounting Principles Board. *See* APB

Accounting process for revenues, expenses and dividends, 61–2

Accounting rate of return. *See* Rate of return on assets

Accounting Research Bulletin. See AICPA. Committee on Accounting Procedure. *Accounting Research Bulletin*

Accounting standard setting, 22–5

   See also Generally accepted accounting principles; International financial reporting standards (IFRS)

Accounts, defined, 45

   See also T-accounts

Accounts payable

   as current liability account, 46, 383–4

   effect on statement of cash flows, 729

   on pro forma balance sheet, 279

   turnover ratio, 268, 273

Accounts receivable

   as asset account, 45

   as investment, 6

   defined, 315

   effect on statement of cash flows, 729–30

   financial statement presentation, 325–6, 770

   gross, defined, 317

   in exchange for cash, 327–8

   net, defined, 317

   on pro forma balance sheet, 278

   turnover ratio, 251, 273

Accrual basis of accounting, 28, 769

Accumulated benefit obligations (ABO), 525

Accumulated deficit, defined, 121, 658n

Accumulated depreciation, as asset account, 46

Accumulated other comprehensive income (AOCI), 47, 159, 690

   on pro forma balance sheet, 280

Ace Hardware, report of errors, 691

Acid test ratio, 266, 273

Acquisition cost

   defined, 110–1

   measurement of, 422–5, 567

   treatment of, 425–31

Acquisition method for business combinations, 625–8

Addback for depreciation, 721–4

Additional paid-in capital, as shareholders' equity account, 47, 120

Adjusting entries, 64–8

Adjustments for accounting changes, 690–2

Administration, as operating activity, 6

Administrative costs, as expenses, 157

Advance sales. *See* Advances from customers

Advances from customers

   as liability account, 47, 330–4

   effect on statement of cash flows, 729

   See also Deferred performance obligations

Advances from tenants, as liability account, 47

Advances to suppliers, as asset account, 45

Advertising expense, on income statement, 58

Affiliated group, defined, 624

Aging-of-accounts-receivable procedure of estimating uncollectible accounts, 319–21

Aggregates, defined, 44

AICPA

   Accounting Standard Executive Committee, Statement of Position 937 (Advertising costs), 127n

   Accounting Trends and Techniques, 395n

   as authority, 23

   Committee on Accounting Procedure, *Accounting Research Bulletin (ARB)* No. 43, 111n, 375n, 675n, 678n

   Committee on Accounting Procedure, *Accounting Research Bulletin (ARB)* No. 45, 337n

   Statement of Position 98-5, 46n

All capital earning rate. *See* Rate of return on assets

Allowance for depreciation account. *See* Accumulated depreciation

Allowance method

   for sales returns, 328–30

Simplified Statement of Cash Flows
(Exhibit 5.16, p. 214)

Operations

Cash Receipts from Customers	(1)
Less: Cash Payments to Suppliers, Employees, and Others	−(2)
Cash Flow from Operations [= (1) − (2)]	S1
Reconciliation of Net Income to Cash Flow from Operations	
Net Income	(3)
Additions to Net Income to Compute Cash Flow from Operations	+(4)
Subtractions from Net Income to Compute Cash Flow from Operations	−(5)
Cash Flow from Operations [= (3) + (4) − (5)]	S1

Investing

Proceeds from Dispositions of "Investing" Assets	+(6)
Cash Used to Acquire "Investing" Assets	−(7)
Cash Flow from Investing [= (6) − (7)]	S2

Financing

Cash Provided by Increases in Debt or Capital Stock	+(8)
Cash Used to Reduce Debt or Capital Stock	−(9)
Cash Used for Dividends	−(10)
Cash Flow from Financing [= (8) − (9) − (10)]	S3
Net Change in Cash [= S1 + S2 + S3]	(11)
Cash, Beginning of the Period	S4
Cash, End of the Period [= (11) + S4]	S5

Comprehensive Income Disclosure

GE does not show the material appearing here shaded blue.

The material shaded blue at the bottom of the column to the left shows the same material as GE gives (below in this column), but here the format is easier to comprehend.

Adapted from General Electric Company [See Notes]
(Dollar amounts in billions)

ONE-STATEMENT APPROACH (Developed from GE's data)

Statement of Comprehensive Income	2007
Sales of goods and services	$169.7
Gain on sale of securities	3.0
Total revenues	172.7
Cost of goods and services sold	105.8
Other costs and expenses	40.3
Total costs and expenses	146.1
EARNINGS FROM CONTINUING OPERATIONS BEFORE INCOME TAXES	26.6
Income Tax Expense	(4.1)
EARNINGS FROM CONTINUING OPERATIONS	22.5
Earnings (loss) from discontinued operations, net of taxes	(0.3)
NET EARNINGS	22.2

Other Comprehensive Income, Net of Tax:	
Investment securities—net	(1.5)
Currency translation adjustments—net	4.5
Cash flow hedges—net	(0.5)
Benefit plans—net	2.6
OTHER COMPREHENSIVE INCOME	5.1
COMPREHENSIVE INCOME	$27.3

GE's ACTUAL DISCLOSURE
(Disguising Both Other and Comprehensive Income)

Statement of Changes in Shareowners' Equity	2007
CHANGES IN SHAREOWNERS' EQUITY	
Balance at January 1	$111.5
Dividends and other transactions with shareowners	(23.1)
Changes other than transactions with shareowners	
Investment securities—net	(1.5)
Currency translation adjustments—net	4.5
Cash flow hedges—net	(0.5)
Benefit plans—net	2.6
Total changes other than earnings	5.1
Increases attributable to net earnings	22.2
Total changes other than transactions with shareowners	27.3
Cumulative effect of changes in accounting principles	(0.1)
Balance at December 31	$115.6

Notes:

General Electric calls the top part of this statement the Statement of Earnings

General Electric shows five lines of revenues, condensed here into two, and eight lines of costs/expenses, here condensed into two.

General Electric does not show the shaded portions.

Notes:

GE calls the top part of this statement the "Statement of Earnings" and shows five lines of revenues, condensed here into two, and eight lines of costs/expenses here condensed into two.

GE does not show the blue-shaded material at the bottom of the column above, but uses the format in the right-hand column.

Notes:

See **Glossary** at Other Comprehensive Income for discussion.

Normal Title	GE's Title
Other Comprehensive Income	Total Changes [in Shareholders' Equity] Other than Earnings
Comprehensive Income	Total Changes [in Shareholders' Equity] Other than Transactions with Owners

How to use this exhibit for learning:

1. Study the presentation on the left, which shows in a single statement, all components of comprehensive income: earnings and other comprehensive income. In December 2008, the SEC expressed a preference for the format on the left, including the portion shaded blue.

2. Note that companies may report components of other comprehensive income in a Statement of Changes of Shareholders' Equity and need not use the title Other Comprehensive Income nor Comprehensive Income in doing so.